CENTRAL ASIA

CENTRAL EURASIA IN CONTEXT SERIES

Douglas Northrop, *Editor*

CENTRAL ASIA
CONTEXTS FOR UNDERSTANDING

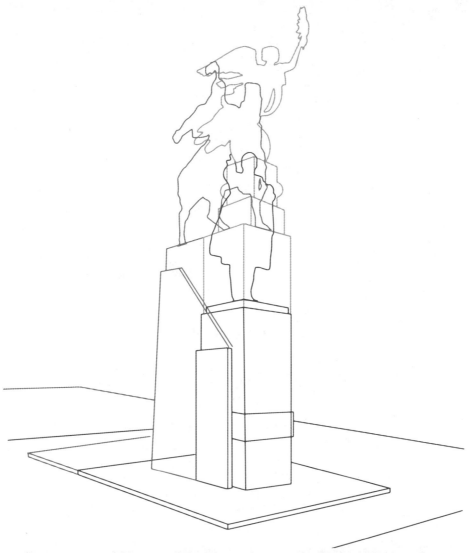

EDITED BY DAVID W. MONTGOMERY

UNIVERSITY *of* PITTSBURGH PRESS

Published by the University of Pittsburgh Press, Pittsburgh, Pa., 15260
Copyright © 2022, University of Pittsburgh Press
All rights reserved
Manufactured in the United States of America
Printed on acid-free paper
10 9 8 7 6 5 4 3 2 1

Cataloging-in-Publication data is available from the Library of Congress

ISBN 13: 978-0-8229-4678-6
ISBN 10: 0-8229-4678-5

Cover art: Digital print adapted from Erbolssyn Meldibekov's *Pedestal*, 2016–17.
Courtesy of the artist.

Cover design: Alex Wolfe

TO OUR FRIENDS

Біздің достарымызға

Биздин достор үчүн

Ба дӯстони мо

Bizin dostlarymyza

Do'stlarimizga

Нашим друзьям

دوستلىرىمىزغا

Dostlarımıza

دوستلرىمىزگه

ما دوستان به

ته ملکرو زموږ

Arkadaşlarımıza

AND TO SARAH, GABRIEL, AND ISABEL

To know an object is here to lead to it through a context which the world supplies.

—WILLIAM JAMES,
The Meaning of Truth

CONTENTS

PART VIII   CONTEXTS OF AESTHETICS

CASES

ABOUT THIS BOOK

Understanding exists in context, yet we bring our own contexts—our organization of social relations, repository of knowledge, and ways of conveying meaning—to interpreting the contexts of other people's lives. This is as one would expect, but it also implicates the limits to understanding others when we do not appreciate the contexts in which they toil. To ameliorate such deficiencies in understanding the region, in this book we offer for consideration a multitude of "contexts" in which Central Asians live, so that anyone interested in the region may more thoughtfully engage with it.

This is not an idle aspiration. In 2005, shortly after the Kyrgyz government was overthrown, I was approached by a reporter from a highly respected US newsmagazine who was visiting Kyrgyzstan for the first time and looking for background to write a story about the salient issues underlying the putsch. For almost two hours, we spoke in detail about the broader environment in which people were living and why many of her early assumptions about causes of conflict were misguided. Later that evening, I introduced her to an anthropologist friend, who was also conducting research in Kyrgyzstan at the time (and also a contributor to this volume), and my friend remarked how informed the journalist seemed. It was not that I was so persuasive in my explanations but, rather, that in being given some context that comes from appreciating nuance about a place, the journalist could tell a more accurate and honest story.

What stayed with me about the encounter with the journalist was that in the space of seven hours—from when I first met her to when we later met up with my colleague—she had been able to present a narrative about events that sounded authoritative. Her presentation of certainty after learning just a little more about the region stood in sharp contrast to my own feeling that, after six years engaging the region, I was only just starting to appreciate the complexity of it and thus could say less with certainty than could the journalist. With complexity comes an awareness that presentations of "certainty" often obfuscate—most often, a single cause is insufficient to explain events. Although there is a general tendency to essentialize a region and want to comment on it authoritatively, we should always be cautious in explanations that are too neat.

In many ways, the authoritative narrative captured by the journalist worked to manage the complexity of the situation, but we must be cautious not to simplify to the point of obscuring the implications of divergent explanations of experience. In this volume we offer not only a multitude of data points for making sense of Central Asia, we also offer a frame for holistically thinking through the nature of experience. Specifically, we aim to show that there is an explanatory tension across the various perspectives in how we make sense of a place and to remind ourselves that ambiguity often plays a constructive role in life and in interpretation. To manage ambiguity—without having to resort to erroneous generalizations—we must have context, and it is context that allows us to tell more accurate and honest stories.

All the contributors to this volume share a conviction about the importance of Central Asia and the value in more deeply understanding the region. But we also recognize that what people know about the region is often guided by simplified generalizations and inaccurate assumptions that are more markers of ignorance than of malice. In this regard, in this book we hope to provide a foundation upon which readers can come to better understand the region across a broad range of experiences. In this respect, why the book came to be is connected to how it came to be.

The recognized need for a broader context-based understanding of the region evolved while I was teaching courses on Central Asia and having students question why anyone would want to live there. While those of us who lived and worked in the region for years knew what made life meaningful for our interlocutors (the majority of whom love their homeland), this is not always reflected in writing concerned with the problems of the region. This was exacerbated by the fact that, in policy terms, scenarios that see a problem in need of a solution predominate.

This problem-centric approach is common, but what scholars working on the region are able to distinguish—that my students (and others) just learning about the region could not—was the contexts in which people were living and in which their problems were situated. This led to a group of Central Asian scholars exploring well-being as an analytical category. A corresponding series of papers was published in *Central Asian Survey* (2013, 32[4]) and *Central Asian Affairs* (2015, 2[1]) in hopes of offering something of a corrective, in order to highlight that understanding problems requires the context of local well-being, which includes notions of joy, contentment, and feelings of security.

Around the same time (March 2014), there emerged an opportunity from the Global Studies Center at the University of Pittsburgh to organize a mini weekend course with Carnegie Mellon University on the theme of "Muslims in a Global Context: Central Asia." Great flexibility was given in how the course was structured, which allowed us to have a dozen Central Asianists lecture on a wide range of topics. The success of the course gave nearly two hundred participants a basic understanding of the region, and it became the frame upon of which this book was built.

Although the focus of the mini course was "Muslims in a Global Context," Islam was only a minor part of the course. The general feeling was that for anyone to understand what it meant to be Muslim in Central Asia, there was a much more foundational context that needed to be learned. Focusing in on any topic in isolation—absent the varying social contexts that act upon it—cannot help but lead to misunderstandings. When we wove together the various topics covered that weekend, we gained a deeper appreciation of the region that deserved being shared.

Expanding from the topics offered in the course, this book evolved to cover thirty-two topics and twenty-four cases, structured in such a way as to add complexity and context to the narratives about Central Asia. This represents the most comprehensive overview of the region as yet to be produced. While modeled after my own approach to teaching about the region (though easily adapted to other approaches to teaching), this should not be seen as merely a text for the classroom. Rather, at its core—and described in detail in the closing chapter on the translation of contexts to policy—is a perspective on how contexts afford understanding to more sensitive and nuanced forms of engagement, be it in policy, development, and so on.

With sixty-five contributors, this volume highlights the research of many leading scholars working on the region. It would be wrong, however, to see the contributors' perspectives as exhaustive. There are many other excellent scholars whose work benefits efforts to understand context, yet is not included because of space and the topical structure that drove the compilation. No doubt, as future publications emerge, there will be opportunity to nuance what is offered here. What we attempt to capture in this book is not only a moment in time (the period covered by the authors) but, more important, a way of looking at context itself. This, I contend, is central to understanding and the foundation from which we must approach the region, and elsewhere.

ABOUT THE NOTES

The aim in this book is to reach a broad readership with diverse needs, and the question of notes presents a unique challenge. Academics have noting conventions that are the guideposts of scholarship yet are often extraneous to more casual readers. The varied textbook markets in which this book is likely to be used have their own conventions, as well, with textbooks in the United States often lacking notes while those in Europe being more likely to contain them. One goal of the project has been to maximize the accessibility of the volume so more people can efficiently learn about the Central Asian region. This issue of accessibility is not only about language and style but also about cost. Thus, to produce the most cost-effective and widely accessible volume possible, standard academic citations are available for most chapters in a separate online notes volume. Readers will be able to get the full meaning of the authors' arguments from the main text; those wishing to see some of the scholarship underlying the text can follow along in the corresponding notes volume. The notes volume is available online at the University of Pittsburgh Press website and can be downloaded and printed free of charge or at cost as a print-on-demand title.

NOTE ON TRANSLITERATION AND SPELLING

Generally, this work uses the standard version of the Library of Congress system for transliterating Russian names and works cited. Exceptions to this rule are personal and geographical names that have accepted English spellings, such as Leo Tolstoy instead of Lev Tolstoi. The spelling issue becomes more complex with Central Asian personal and geographical names, which have changed since the collapse of the Soviet Union and are no longer russified; for example, Andijan instead of Andizhan, Almaty instead of Alma-Ata. The issue is complicated by the more recent trend to transliterate Central Asian personal and geographical names directly from the Central Asian languages and not from the Russian. Thus, Andijan becomes Andijan, and so on. Given the broad time frames this book covers, this becomes even more complicated because transliteration practices have (political) lives of their own wherein one location may have multiple appropriate spellings based on the period discussed, such as Khoqand (based on old Uzbek, Persian script) before the Russians, Kokand (based on Russian) during the Soviet period, and Qo'qon (based on modern Uzbek) after independence. None of this can be easily reconciled but efforts have been made to provide some standardization of transliterated terms by drawing upon the Library of Congress's *Name Authority Files*, the *GeoNames Geographical Database*, *Merriam-Webster's Geographical Dictionary*, *Merriam-Webster's Biographical Dictionary*, and *Merriam-Webster's Collegiate Dictionary* to make some of these distinctions. In most instances, spellings are adopted throughout the book that reflect more conventional usage, such as Andijan and Kokand (with some exceptions to historical period). In other instances, however, where there are cognate terms common to different Central Asian languages that would naturally be transliterated differently, we default to the linguistic context being referenced. This creates some variability, such as when an elder "white beard" is referred to as an *aksakal* in a Kyrgyz-focused chapter, *aqsaqal* in a Kazak-focused chapter, or *oqsoqol* in an Uzbek-focused chapter, and so on. Regardless the transliteration adopted, in all contexts the word's meaning should be clear. The unevenness of efforts to standardize spellings across the book, however, is yet another reminder of the variability across the region we broadly refer to as Central Asia, and the importance of context.

ACKNOWLEDGMENTS

The argument in this book is for contextualization as a reflexive practice, that we should look to the myriad of influences that shape how events unfold in our effort to understand social life. Such is the case for how this book came to be. From the outset, it has been a collective endeavor, and it is important to emphasize this. All books, of course, receive inspiration and nurturing support from many places, and authors incur many debts that can never be fully repaid, but a project this large and encompassing cannot come into existence without drawing upon extensive networks and relationships of support; to many I owe thanks.

Obviously, the many authors who contributed chapters and shared their expertise were essential; they were supportive and generous beyond what can be expected. Their contributions came from personal places, including a belief that it was important to produce a text that would help others learn about a region for which we all care deeply. What makes it personal here is that our affection for the region is intimately tied to countless friendships made over the decades we have worked there. It is only appropriate, therefore, that it be collectively acknowledged, in the various languages in which we work, that this book is "to our friends," in appreciation for the friendships that have made meaningful our time in the region.

Central Asia has changed significantly over three decades of independence, and many of the book's contributors came of age as scholars during this time. It is in such a span of change, marked by friendships with others, that any acknowledgments must be understood. There are far more to thank than space and memory allow—for sometimes, significant influences come in passing moments shared with strangers never to be seen again. I hope this volume serves to recognize a debt of gratitude, unevenly repaid here.

Names and faces that continue to inspire our work underlie these general acknowledgments, and for me, a few deserving recognition include: Jamilia Nurkulova, Rysbai Sarybayev, Volodia and Ludmila Fransov, Sergei and Nina Fransov, Gulnara Aitpaeva, Sasha and Sveta Titov, Alisher Khamidov, Urunsa Egemberdieva, Nazilia Muratova, Abdujabbor Kayumov, Medina Aitieva, Georgy Mamedov, Emil Nasritdinov, Aigoul Abdoubaetova, Elena Molchanova, Rahimjon and Donohon Abdugafurov, Cheng-Un Stephen Lam, Carrie O'Rourke, Susan Hicks, Irina Burns, Madeleine Reeves, Sophie Roche, Saidazim Ake, Junus Karimov, Nookatski Tovarishi, Alper Akin, Mustafa Demir, Serkan Aykan, Mustafa Sahin, Durkadir Arslan, Jangyl Apa, Veronica Dristas, Maja Budovalcev Konitzer, Elaine Linn, Kasia Ploskonka, Michael Lombardo, and Kerry Wiersma. Colleagues

John Heathershaw, Eric McGlinchey, Benjamin Gatling, and Noor Borbieva taught early versions of this book and offered useful feedback. Several contributors read and commented on all or parts of the book and deserve recognition: David Abramson, Laura Adams, Victoria Clement, Adeeb Khalid, Del Schwab, and Tommaso Trevisani. Similarly, Peter Kracht and Douglas Northrop improved the volume through their valuable editorial guidance and overall support of the project from the beginning, while Amy Sherman and Alex Wolfe helped move the volume to print. I am grateful to all for their contributions at various stages, though I accept all responsibilities for any of the book's shortcomings.

All contributing authors have received support—personal as well as institutional—from many places, some of which are indicated in the corresponding chapter in the notes volume. Research support that helped facilitate my work has, at various times, come from the Aigine Cultural Research Center, the International Research and Exchanges Board (IREX), the Center for Russian and East European Studies at the University of Pittsburgh, the Global Studies Center at the University of Pittsburgh, the Center for International Development and Conflict Management at the University of Maryland, and the Office of Naval Research (award number N00014-17-1-3014). Any opinions, findings, or recommendations are those of the authors alone and do not represent the views of any of these or other organizations.

As this book has an interest in the everyday and the contexts in which it is lived, I close by acknowledging the contribution my family made to this work—alongside friends mentioned above. My parents, Dee and Luke Montgomery, have always been generous and constant in their support, even when they wished I was closer to home. Their visit to the region in 2000 not only afforded the opportunity to share with them a place I was learning, it manifested the lengths a parent will go to understand and be part of a child's life. Jennifer, Nathan, Lauren, and Reed Tegtmeyer and Denise, Tim, and Deirdre Ligget are regular reminders of the importance of family, near and far. Lastly, my wife, Sarah, is a daily source of support and inspiration, and it is to her and our children, Gabriel and Isabel (who I hope will grow up appreciating the importance of context), that I express my deepest gratitude. They are the contexts of meaning that frame my days, and animate all that is good within them.

ABBREVIATIONS AND ACRONYMS

AMD	acid mine drainage
ASSR	Autonomous Soviet Socialist Republic
BITs	Bilateral Investment Treaties
BRI	Belt and Road Initiative
BTI	*Bertelsmann Transformation Index*
CIS	Commonwealth of Independent States
CSTO	Collective Security Treaty Organization
EAEU	Eurasian Economic Union
EU	European Union
EurAsEC	Eurasian Economic Community
FCPA	Foreign and Corrupt Practices Act
FDI	foreign direct investment
FSU	Former Soviet Union
GATS	General Agreement on Trade in Services
GIZ	German Development Agency
GLOF	glacial lake outburst flood
GONGOs	Government-Organized Non-Governmental Organizations
GTD	Global Terrorism Database
GWOT	Global War on Terror
ICTs	information and communication technologies
IDPs	internally displaced persons
IFIs	international financial institutions
IMF	International Monetary Fund
IREX	International Research and Exchanges Board
IRPT	Islamic Revival Party of Tajikistan
ISIS	Islamic State of Iraq and Syria (Daesh)
NATO	North Atlantic Treaty Organization
NDN	Northern Distribution Network
NTD	National Territorial Delimitation
ODIHR	Office for Human Rights and Democratic Initiatives
OSCE	Organization for Security and Co-operation in Europe
POPs	persistent organic pollutants
RATS	Regional Anti-Terrorism Structure
RFE/RL	Radio Free Europe/Radio Liberty
SADUM	Spiritual Administration of the Muslims of Central Asia and Kazakhstan
SCO	Shanghai Cooperation Organization
SSR	Soviet Socialist Republic
TsUM	Central Universal Department Store (*Tsentral'nyi Universal'nyi Magazin*)
UNHCR	United Nations High Commissioner for Refugees
USSR	Union of Soviet Socialist Republics
WTO	World Trade Organization

Central Asia in Context

David W. Montgomery

All of life—its constraints and opportunities—is lived in relation to surroundings. It is within a particular environment that relationships unfold and meaning gets formed. That experience is tied to context is, to no small extent, obvious. Nonetheless, in trying to analytically make sense of experience and of that which emerges from the social worlds tied to it, we make moves to simplify, to find the explanatory essence of what leads people to do what they do. This is what David Hume captures in a dictum attributed to him that "explanation is where the mind rests." Most often, however, the answers to questions are neither simple nor short; as Rafik Schami poetically notes in *The Dark Side of Love*, "olive trees and answers both need time." Implicit here is the incompleteness of knowledge and an acceptance that knowing—that having something close to answers—takes effort.

Such constraints—that work is required to understand a people and their place, for example—seem at odds with how knowledge gets generalized and acted upon, shared across media platforms in sound bites that are at times more intriguing than they are accurate. In the case of Central Asia (though I would argue, not only here), gaps in knowledge are filled in by the prejudices and assumptions of one's own experience of the world, wherein one may underappreciate the role of extended family, religion, economic struggle, and so on in meaning-making for the interlocutors in question. There is no reason to assume, of course, that behaviors are irrational if they look different from what is considered "rational" in a different cultural environment; it is simply more likely that we do not know enough to appreciate the context in which the other is making decisions.

It is thus a generalized claim that we need to be cognizant of different visions of the experience of others, to be self-reflective on the limits of what we know about the environment in which others live. This book is a collective reflection on how to understand a place. We accept as its premise that an understanding of any region must be gained through an appreciation of the context in which people live, and that context is multivocal, filled with different dialects—at times, even languages—of experience.

The aim in this book is to facilitate such an understanding by thematically exploring various contexts in which Central Asians encounter, experience, and frame their world. The assumption is that context informs meaning, and although chapter themes are presented as distinct topics, life is not so neat and the events that define it seldom, if ever, emerge in isolation. Rather, events are always only part of the causal explanation of social behavior. Moving from singular explanations to appreciating more complicated, interconnected explanations is an underlying goal of this work.

Contextualizing as an Approach to the Region

As we see across this book, what constitutes "Central Asia," is not as neatly bounded as it seems at first. Generally, we focus on the spaces characterized as the five former Soviet Muslim Central Asian republics: Kazakhstan, Kyrgyzstan, Tajikistan, Turkmenistan, and Uzbekistan. Even here, however, the characterization is uneven, given, for example, the difficulty of conducting research in Turkmenistan. Despite this general focus on the "Five Stans," what could be considered part of Central Asia can be framed more broadly to also encompass—in different contexts with varied rationales—Afghanistan, Azerbaijan, Xinjiang (East Turkestan), Mongolia, Tartarstan, parts of Siberia, and even parts of Iran (Persia). Boundaries are seldom exact; context allows us a sense of the fluidity in meanings—and experience—they can convey.

To complicate the boundaries of Central Asia, some chapters in the volume reach outside the "post-Soviet Central Asian" space. Various political transitions brought about the borders of the contemporary states, but these boundaries also belie a more fluid, differently bounded sense of territory that most of history knew. Thus, in our thinking about any one place, we also need to consider place in relation to what surrounds it and what impacted differentiation across other ways of demarcating boundaries—whether khanate, tribal, Soviet, or independent; whether mountain or valley, rural or urban, language or ethnicity, and so on. Although there is a lot that made the region and the five 'stans seem coherent following the collapse of the Soviet Union, after three decades of independence the various countries have developed characteristics that are unique to their distinct trajectories. Yet, in looking to present relationships, we must also recognize where more underlies what made them than what can be neatly contained on a map.

Thus, our very aim of suggesting Central Asia *in context* forces us to look broadly, to look beyond confined spaces, and to consider relationships that exist within, across, between, in relation to, and in opposition with multiple

DAVID W. MONTGOMERY

experiences. This pushes us to consider not only disciplinary approaches to specific questions but multidisciplinary contributions to addressing problems. Although there are pressures within university departments to reify disciplinarity, area studies such as those we see in Central Asian Studies offer a space where the breadth of connections associated with place can be explored, and where multiple disciplinary approaches offer multiple ways of seeing places. And it is these collaborative, multidisciplinary, and interdisciplinary approaches—fostered in areas such as Central Asian Studies—that can offer us hope in our efforts to address the complex problems that people face.

The contributors to this volume come from diverse backgrounds—anthropology, environmental studies, geography, history, linguistics, literature, musicology, political science, religious studies, sociology—and yet represent the best of collaboration that can emerge in area studies broadly. The end of the Soviet Union created new opportunities for research in the region, and it is during this post-Soviet period that many of the relationships developed between our contributors and their interlocutors in the field. Because of the paucity of literature previously available, people read each other's work, independent of the disciplinary approach, and it is this type of multidisciplinary conversation about the region that is advanced in this volume. With so many authorial voices present, we must recognize that there are at least that many approaches to the region being offered, but the diversity of the region is more poignantly (and pragmatically) represented in the quotidian spaces where people socially navigate their worlds. It is the environment where people navigate across micro, meso, and macro levels of the social world that fluidity of place and diversity of analysis have the most purchase.

Structuring Context

All context is structured, though there is variation in how it is structured. Text is no different, and thus a word on the book's layout is appropriate. It is assumed that people will read the volume in multiple ways, but the overall vision is one where thematic chapters give a topical focus, and case studies complicate those chapters by showing the interconnectedness of life across a multitude of themes. Therein the contributors seek to both focus and expand thinking about the region.

The book is divided into eight parts, each beginning with a short overview followed by four thematic chapters. Each section also contains three case studies, which offer complexity for thinking through the themes and drawing upon not only the themes of the section chapters but other themes across the book. The book begins with a part on general approaches to seeing the region in context, offering perspectives on the region as global, local, place, and story, with each thematic approach demonstrating a particular way of prioritizing and valuing. We see at the offset how the way we frame context impacts the issues viewed as most salient for understanding. Usually introductory texts begin with history, but here we begin with ways of seeing the present, before we shift in the second part to exploring the historical context.

Underlying this progression is the notion that the varied ways of framing contexts will influence perspectives all the way through—and, more important, that history is not an isolated series of events with scant contemporary relevance. On the contrary, in chapters moving from the precolonial era through the colonial, Soviet, and post-Soviet eras, we see the significance of history to any understanding of the contemporary, whether in the differently constructed experience of boundaries or in the nature of how pasts frame the environment of present behavior and the references to which people point for legitimacy. Here, the very frames provided by the themes in the early sections are open to critique, with the corresponding cases providing further context to the nature of contextualization and the role that history continues to play.

The next six parts of the book set forth to overview the Contemporary Context, to include the contexts of living, structure, transformation, work, vision, and aesthetics. Within the Contexts of Living section, chapters on rural, urban, migratory, and diaspora life provide a sense of the varied environments in which people live and the implications of such experiences. In the Contexts of Structure section, the focus of the chapters is on family, social, moral, and gender structures, to show the varied relational forces that shape individual and communal behavior in the region. Likewise, themes that fundamentally shape how people interact with their world through religion, politics, law, and education are the focus of the Contexts of Transformation chapters. Within the Contexts of Work section, authors discuss resources, economics, property, and labor, to give a sense of the material environment in which people live and its implications for work. The Contexts of Vision section has as its focus the idea that there are varied ways of thinking through what society should look like, including media messaging, identities constructed around nations, the natural environment, and development agendas. And lastly, chapters in the Contexts of Aesthetics section explore the role of music, art, literature, and film in Central Asia, showing the active and creative role played in translating experience and imagination that meaningfully and intimately weaves its way into daily life. In all of these parts, the cases touch upon the broader thematic category of the constituent sections in order to facilitate dynamic thinking across the chapters of the book.

The focus at the end of the book is on how contexts are translated and applied. While it is reasonable to assume that the volume will be used in the classroom, this last chapter is intended to give guidance in how people working on and with the region could more thoughtfully engage with the area. The purpose here is to help translate information into practice. In some respects, this reflects the very task of engaging with context: most professional engagements in life require us to apply knowledge to an end that is most efficiently met if the contextual environment is understood—which is to say that, while the book offers direct utility to those who are

DAVID W. MONTGOMERY

professionally engaged with the region, students could also benefit from its pedagogic approach to the importance of contextualized knowledge.

●

Although this is a large volume with thematic diversity, the chapters covered are not an exhaustive taxonomy of everyday decision-making in practice. Rather, there are many other views that could have been included, and a number of very good researchers working on the region whose absence here was constrained by space and availability. The conversations carried out across the book, and the online bibliography on which it rests, point to important contributions beyond what is contained in this volume, and thus it represents a starting rather than an ending point for thinking about the region. Contexts, after all, are open discussions that start somewhere but do not always end in the same place.

The process of putting the book together was uniquely collaborative, reflecting the spirit in which many of the contributors and scholars of the region work. Throughout the process contributors were given the opportunity to offer feedback on each other's work; many did so across the sections in which their contributions were placed, and a number of others reviewed the entire volume. This highlights something quite important about the generosity of the community and how others contribute to both understanding and the experience of sociality itself. In learning about Central Asia in context, we should always be mindful that it is such generosity of sociality that yields meaning to experience and makes any place a reference for home, purpose, and value.

No doubt those using the book will do so in multiple ways, pulling out the various themes and supplementing them with other resources and discussions to fill in the gaps. People will adapt the book to their own teaching and reading styles, picking and choosing in relation to what people are seeking to better understand. Such a selective and nonlinear way of working through the text is itself reflective of how people socially navigate their worlds—in nonlinear ways. But to understand the context of life in Central Asia, the chapters contained herein reveal issues we need to appreciate if we are to have something closer to understanding. Short of experiencing the tastes, sounds, smells, and vistas of the region as our own, this is the minimum of what we can expect needs to be considered.

Mapping Context

Julien Thorez and Emmanuel Giraudet

It is important to appreciate that the cartographic imagination is a way of consolidating data that shape the context for making sense of problems. Since the work of Henri Lefebvre, space has been commonly considered as a social product, a social construction. Space is one of the main objects of geographic studies and has become a significant dimension of social science publications, notably thanks to the "spatial turn." The implication is that maps have become among the main tools used to describe and interpret the spatial organization of environments, people, and places.

There is a wide array of maps, appropriate to format, projection, scale, generalization, semiology, and theme. As representations of localized phenomena and objects, they reveal scientific choices on the nature of the data represented or on the scale of the territories mapped. The maps are also the result of graphic (and aesthetic) biases (e.g., the "semiology of graphics"). One cannot ignore that maps are particularly powerful in disseminating knowledge and visions of the societies and territories represented. Mapping the national territory gives substance to the state. Mapping a phenomenon (ethnic distribution, social inequalities, health system, etc.) can create and legitimize political demands. Because of these instrumental functions, the production and dissemination of maps are subject to political control in many countries and circumstances, especially since maps can "lie."

The corpus of maps contained here offers a vision of contemporary Central Asia that is dependent on constraints related to data, their access, and their quality. Some data are available in one country but impossible to obtain in another. In Turkmenistan, for example, statistical data publication is strictly controlled and limited. Some data can be available at the national level but then not accessible by region or by district. In addition, data quality is uneven. Aware of frequent discussions on the reliability of demographic and economic data (such as population size, population growth, migrations, or economic growth, etc.), we knowingly use data published by the statistics committees of each country, including data from population censuses, when they are available.

In this map collection, we do not aim to present an exhaustive atlas of contemporary Central Asia. No map has been made at the scale of a city or a village. Several issues are missing (decollectivization of agriculture, urban transformations, civil war in Tajikistan, military activities, tourism, trade, education, standard of living, social inequalities, electoral geography, etc.) and others are only partially presented (environment, industry, migration, etc.). Nevertheless, these maps shed light on several major features of contemporary Central Asian societies and spaces. These features include the shaping of the current political map with the emergence, in the twentieth century, of "Nation-States-Territories"; the unequal geographical distribution of the population; the tribal and ethnic diversity with an increase in the share of "Central Asian" populations to the detriment of "Russian-speaking" populations; agricultural systems (on irrigated areas in oases, on deserts, steppes, or mountain pastures, in Virgin Lands); transport networks (air and rail networks, which play a key role in the territorial integration of the region globally); and oil production and export in Kazakhstan.

These maps emerge out of a long history of cartographic production on Central Asia, which was initially characterized by the predominance of Western productions. The first map that mentioned "Central Asia" was published in Paris by the German orientalist Julius Klaproth in 1828. Then, during the tsarist period, colonial geographers and cartographers developed an important cartographic corpus, symbolized by the 1914 publication of the *Atlas of Asiatic Russia*, published by the Resettlement Department of the Land Regulation and Agriculture Administration.

During the Soviet period, map production increased significantly. In every Soviet region, a meticulous cartographic investigation was conducted, but many maps were deliberately distorted in order to not divulge information (false localization, lack of mention, distortion of the territory represented by the use of several scales on the same map, etc.). In addition to numerous topographic and thematic maps whose distribution was strictly reserved for administrative and military use, several atlases were published by Soviet cartographers and geographers, often relying on collaborations between Central Asian and Russian institutions. From the 1960s to the end of the Soviet period, the first national atlases of the Central Asian republics were issued, as well as regional ones (such as the *Atlas of the North Kazakhstan* and the *Atlas of the Kustanay Region*, etc.) and urban ones (such as the *Tashkent: Geographical Atlas*).

Cartographic production on Central Asia has diversified since 1991, corresponding with the widespread dissemination of cartographic studies across many regions of the world. Foreign institutions and international organizations such as the UN Specialized Agencies, the World Bank, and the Asian Development Bank have contributed to the development of maps and atlases by their financial support, technical collaboration, or even publication. Unsurprisingly, young sovereign states ordered new national atlases. Some atlases rely on a scientific approach, whereas most recent atlases are designed for teachers and students, and thus to territorialize a particular vision of the state. Several prestigious atlases have also been issued for a lay but wealthy audience in Kazakhstan. These coffee-table books describe the Kazakh national culture, history, or geography and advance a nationalist narrative.

From a thematic point of view, the corpus of maps on the region has been notably enriched by more recent works, such as Yuri Bregel's remarkable *Historical Atlas of Central Asia*. Published in 2003, Bregel's atlas presents the political and military history of Central Asia from the time of Alexander the Great to the twentieth century through the use of maps and historical texts connected to the maps. In an effort both to expand access to the rich cartographic history of the region and to diffuse cartographical studies on Central Asia, digital libraries and contemporary online platforms such as CartOrient have also come to provide an invaluable service to those trying to think through maps. Across the varied presentations and motives underlying maps, we find utility and an appreciation for what maps can accomplish, all of which is rooted in how maps map context.

MAPS

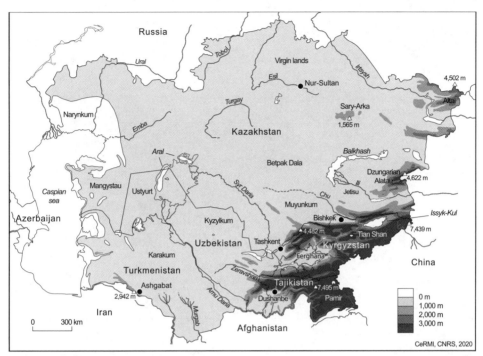

Map 1   Physical map of Central Asia

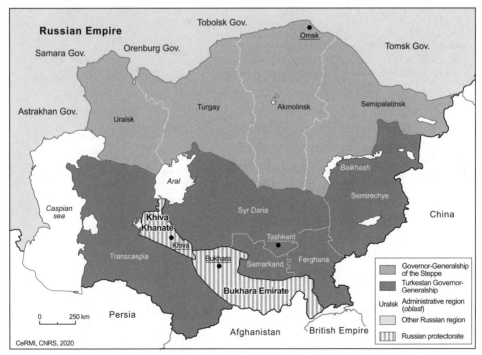

Map 2   Political map of Central Asia in 1900

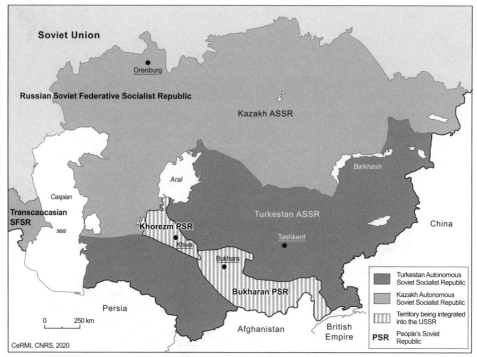

Map 3 Political map of Central Asia in 1923

Map 4 Political map of Central Asia in 1924

JULIEN THOREZ AND EMMANUEL GIRAUDET

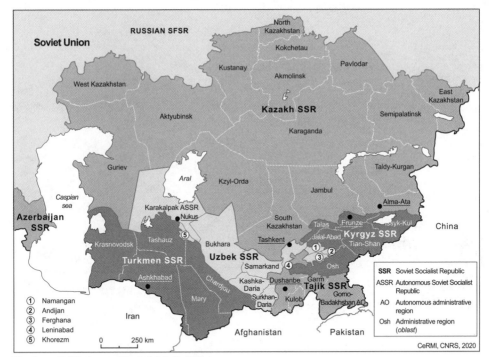

Map 5   Political map of Central Asia in 1953

Map 6   Political map of Central Asia in 2020

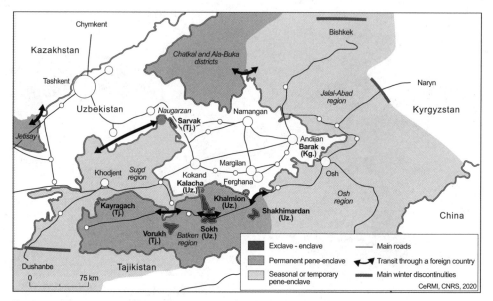

Map 7   Enclaves and pene-enclaves in the Ferghana Valley after independence

Map 8   The relocation of the capital of Kazakhstan (1920-1997)

JULIEN THOREZ AND EMMANUEL GIRAUDET

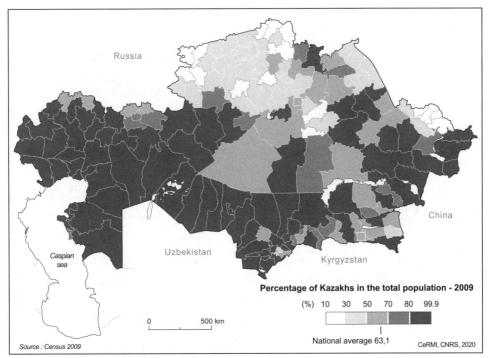

Map 9   Kazakhs in Kazakhstan in 2009 (by district)

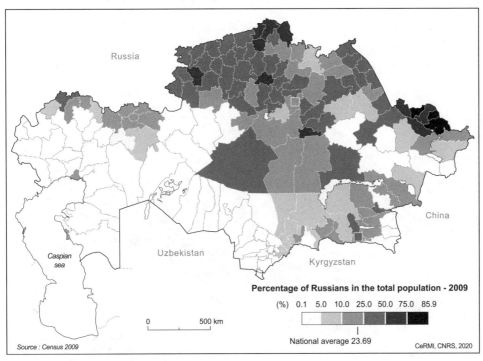

Map 10   Russians in Kazakhstan in 2009 (by district)

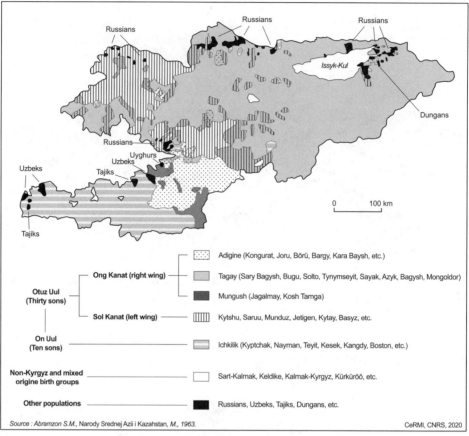

Map 11   **Kyrgyz tribes at the beginning of the twentieth century**

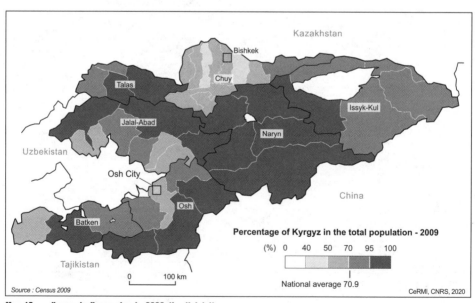

Map 12   **Kyrgyz in Kyrgyzstan in 2009 (by district)**

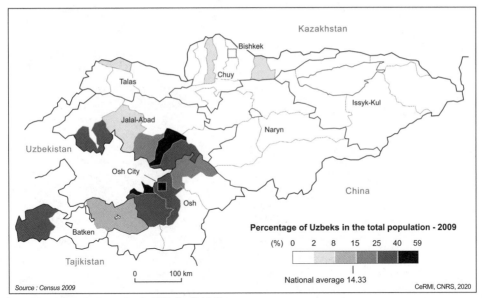

Map 13   Uzbeks in Kyrgyzstan in 2009 (by district)

Percentage of Uzbeks in the total population - 2009

(%)   0   2   8   15   25   40   59

National average 14.33

Source : Census 2009

CeRMI, CNRS, 2020

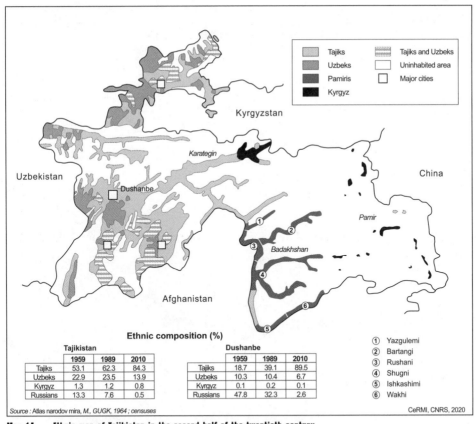

Ethnic composition (%)

Tajikistan

	1959	1989	2010
Tajiks	53.1	62.3	84.3
Uzbeks	22.9	23.5	13.9
Kyrgyz	1.3	1.2	0.8
Russians	13.3	7.6	0.5

Dushanbe

	1959	1989	2010
Tajiks	18.7	39.1	89.5
Uzbeks	10.3	10.4	6.7
Kyrgyz	0.1	0.2	0.1
Russians	47.8	32.3	2.6

① Yazgulemi
② Bartangi
③ Rushani
④ Shugni
⑤ Ishkashimi
⑥ Wakhi

Source : Atlas narodov mira, M., GUGK, 1964 ; censuses

CeRMI, CNRS, 2020

Map 14   Ethnic map of Tajikistan in the second half of the twentieth century

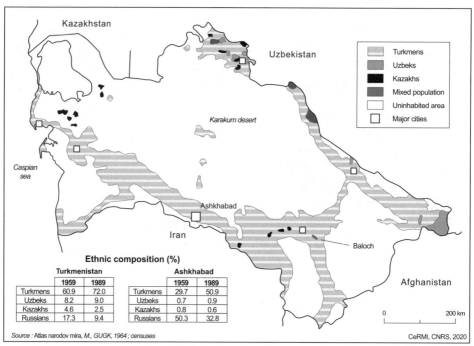

Ethnic composition (%)

Turkmenistan

	1959	1989
Turkmens	60.9	72.0
Uzbeks	8.2	9.0
Kazakhs	4.6	2.5
Russians	17.3	9.4

Ashkhabad

	1959	1989
Turkmens	29.7	50.9
Uzbeks	0.7	0.9
Kazakhs	0.8	0.6
Russians	50.3	32.8

Source : Atlas narodov mira, M., GUGK, 1964 ; censuses

CeRMI, CNRS, 2020

Map 15   Ethnic map of Turkmenistan in the second half of the twentieth century

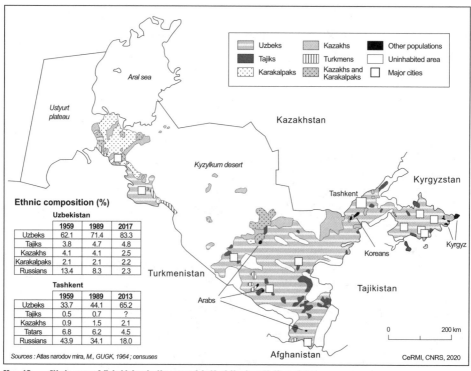

Ethnic composition (%)

Uzbekistan

	1959	1989	2017
Uzbeks	62.1	71.4	83.3
Tajiks	3.8	4.7	4.8
Kazakhs	4.1	4.1	2.5
Karakalpaks	2.1	2.1	2.2
Russians	13.4	8.3	2.3

Tashkent

	1959	1989	2013
Uzbeks	33.7	44.1	65.2
Tajiks	0.5	0.7	?
Kazakhs	0.9	1.5	2.1
Tatars	6.8	6.2	4.5
Russians	43.9	34.1	18.0

Sources : Atlas narodov mira, M., GUGK, 1964 ; censuses

CeRMI, CNRS, 2020

Map 16   Ethnic map of Uzbekistan in the second half of the twentieth century

JULIEN THOREZ AND EMMANUEL GIRAUDET

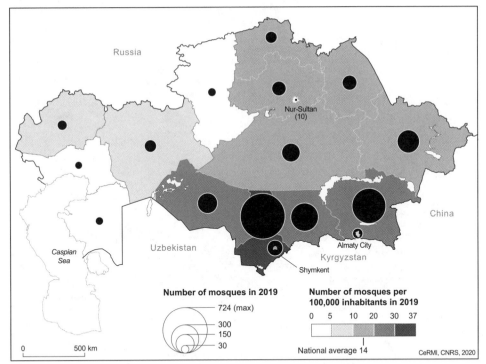

Number of mosques in 2019

724 (max)

300
150
30

Number of mosques per 100,000 inhabitants in 2019

0   5   10   20   30   37

National average 14

CeRMI, CNRS, 2020

Map 17   Mosques in Kazakhstan in 2019 (by region)

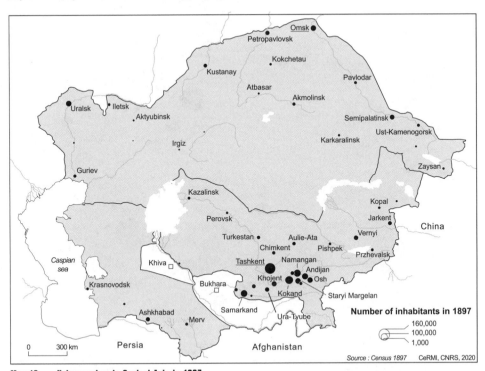

Number of inhabitants in 1897

160,000
100,000
1,000

Source : Census 1897   CeRMI, CNRS, 2020

Map 18   Urban system in Central Asia in 1897

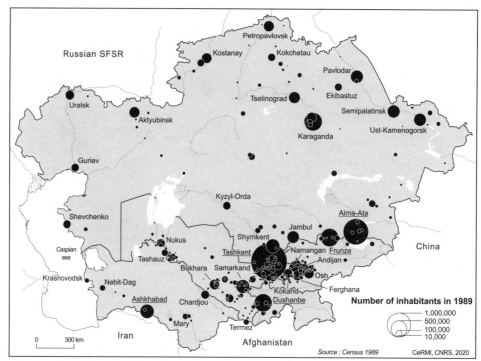

Map 19   Urban system in Central Asia in 1989

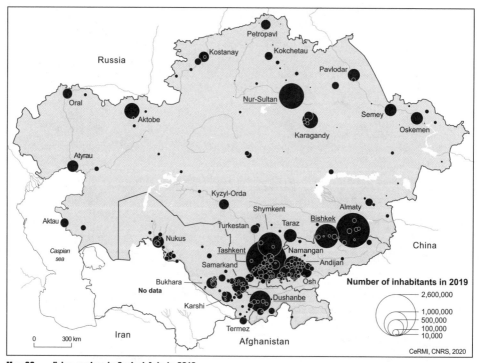

Map 20   Urban system in Central Asia in 2019

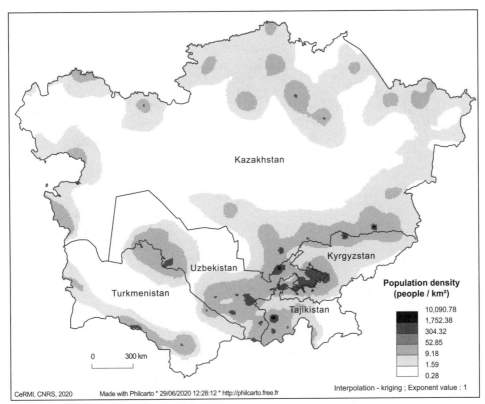

Map 21   Population density in Central Asia in 2020

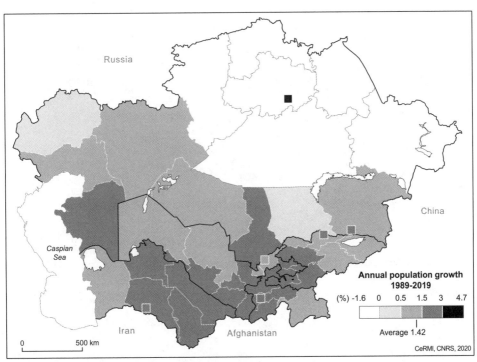

Map 22   Annual population growth rate in Central Asia (1989-2019), by region

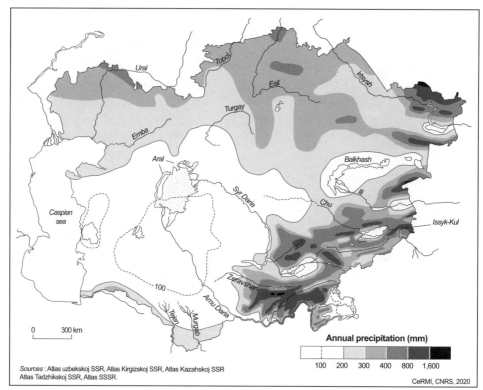

Map 23   Annual average precipitation in Central Asia (mm)

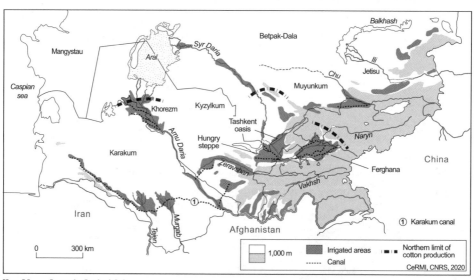

Map 24   Oases in Central Asia

JULIEN THOREZ AND EMMANUEL GIRAUDET

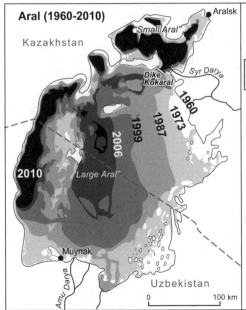

Aral (1960-2010)

Aralsk

"Small Aral"

Kazakhstan

Dike Kokaral

Syr Darya

1960
1973
1987
1999
2006

2010

"Large Aral"

Muynak

Amu Darya

Uzbekistan

0   100 km

Water Consumption in the Aral Sea Basin

	Population (Mio)	Irrigated areas (Mio ha)	Water withdrawal (km³/an)	Inflows (km³/an)
1960	≈ 15	4.5	60	55
2010	≈ 60	8.0	105	10

Source : UNEP

Drying Out and Salinization of the Aral Sea

	Volume (km³)		Area (km²)	Salinity (g/L)
1960	1,093		67,500	10
1977	749		54,800	15
	SA	LA		
1987	22	323	44,700	25
1999	27	168	28,700	45
2009	22	79	9,400	130

SA : "Small Aral,"   LA : "Large Aral"
Source : Gaybullaev B. et al., 2012

CeRMI, CNRS, 2020

Map 25   Aral Sea (1960-2010)

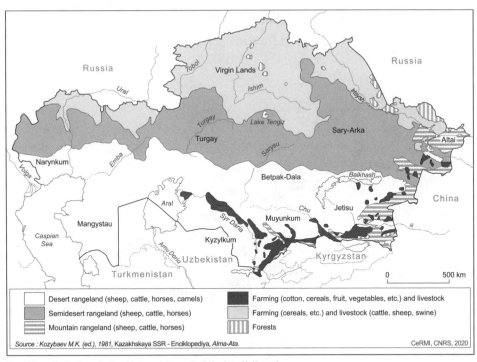

Russia

Tobol
Virgin Lands
Ishim
Ural

Russia

Irtysh

Turgay
Lake Tengiz
Turgay
Sary-Arka
Altai

Narynkum
Emba

Betpak-Dala
Balkhash
China

Volga

Caspian Sea

Mangystau

Aral
Syr Darya
Muyunkum
Chu
Jetisu
Ili

Kyzylkum

Amu Darya
Uzbekistan
Kyrgyzstan

Turkmenistan

0   500 km

☐ Desert rangeland (sheep, cattle, horses, camels)	■ Farming (cotton, cereals, fruit, vegetables, etc.) and livestock
▨ Semidesert rangeland (sheep, cattle, horses)	▨ Farming (cereals, etc.) and livestock (cattle, sheep, swine)
▤ Mountain rangeland (sheep, cattle, horses)	▥ Forests

Source : Kozybaev M.K. (ed.), 1981, Kazakhskaya SSR - Enciklopediya, Alma-Ata.

CeRMI, CNRS, 2020

Map 26   Agriculture in Kazakhstan at the end of the twentieth century

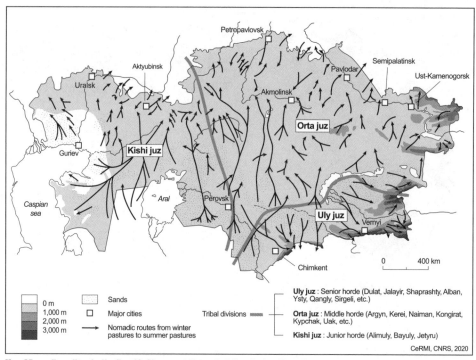

Map 27   **Nomadism in the Kazakh Steppes at the end of the nineteenth century**

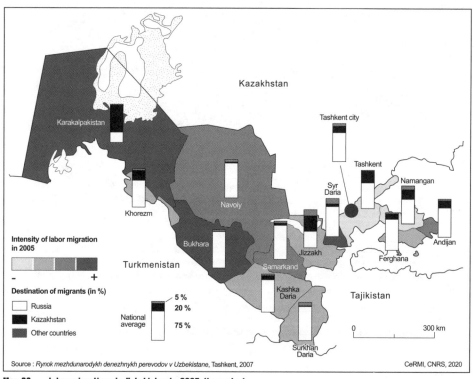

Map 28   **Labor migrations in Uzbekistan in 2005 (by region)**

JULIEN THOREZ AND EMMANUEL GIRAUDET

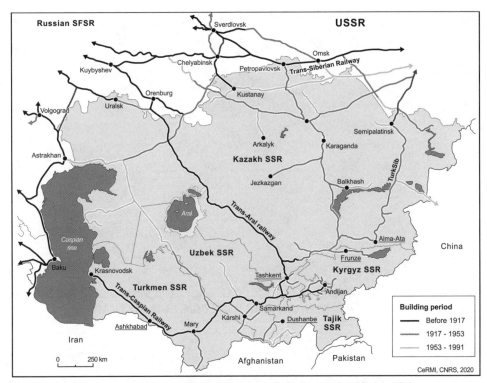

Map 29   The construction of the Central Asian railway network during the tsarist and Soviet periods

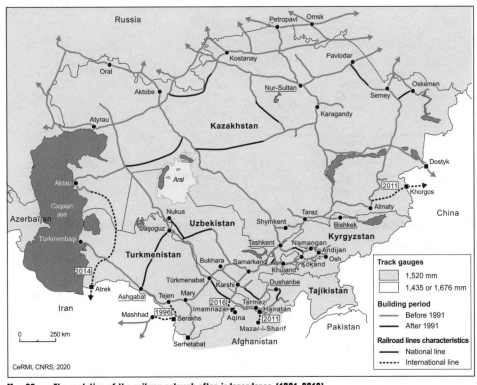

Map 30   The evolution of the railway network after independence (1991-2019)

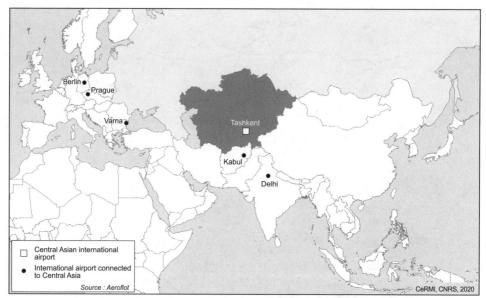

Map 31 International Central Asian air transport network in 1989 (annual and seasonal destinations)

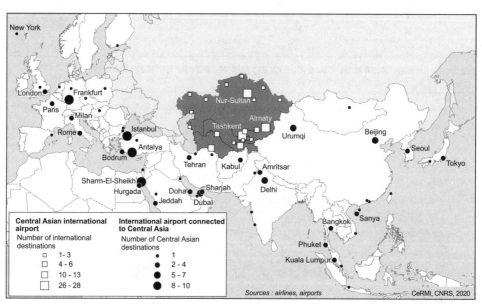

Map 32 International Central Asian air transport network in 2019 (except Former Soviet Union) (annual and seasonal destinations)

JULIEN THOREZ AND EMMANUEL GIRAUDET

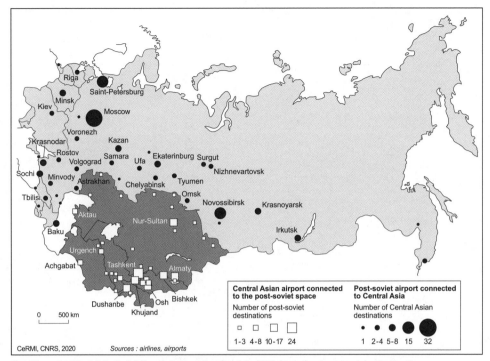

Map 33   Post-Soviet Central Asian air transport network in 2019 (annual and seasonal destinations)

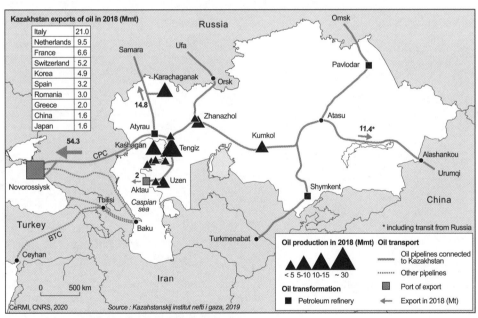

Map 34   Oil in Kazakhstan: production and export in 2018

PART I

CONTEXTUALIZING CENTRAL ASIA

Contexts have beginnings that are not always linear. While we frequently think the answer to understanding lies in a beginning told by history, it is quite often the case that contemporary perspectives make their own sense of history and build with it. In this section we glimpse some of the general ways in which Central Asia is seen: globally, locally, geographically, and narratively. Taken together, these perspectives offer an approach to seeing how context can emerge.

In Alexander Cooley's chapter we see through a global lens where Central Asia is connected to the concerns of great powers and the nature of influence is both dynamic and complex. Morgan Liu, in his chapter, offers a local street-level view, where we think of individual meaning-making in relation to surroundings. Where Cooley gives the macro context of the outside looking in, Liu gives the micro context of the inside looking out. At a practical level these two perspectives are traded back and forth with such frequency that we often overlook the ways in which such dialectics contribute to how we make sense of a place.

While looking both inside and outside is a theme running throughout the book, Alexander Diener and Nick Megoran advance another overarching theme: complicating the boundedness assumed of the region. There is a "Central Asia" that we discuss in geographical and geopolitical terms, but as with all places it is a constructed and more fluid concept than is often assumed. Such fluidity is often explained through story, the focus of Benjamin Gatling's chapter. As Gatling shows, stories provide context to all manner of things, from nation and community to entertainment; in short, stories are the medium through which Central Asians understand life.

Understanding life is, of course, about understanding the context in which it is experienced and lived. Each of the three cases in this section illustrates perspectives put forth in the chapters and sets up frames for understanding later chapters in the book. Marianne Kamp tells the story of the Soviet collectivization process, as experienced from local perspectives, in relation to what were more distant expectations of the leadership in Moscow. Tim Epkenhans explains the emergence of Islam under authoritarianism in Tajikistan, a story drawn from the Soviet period to the present. And Marlène Laruelle tells of Central Asians who migrate to the Russian arctic, where they occupy space that is part global and part local. Together, the cases begin to show the interrelated nature of the various themes in this section. And overall, these chapters move us toward a way of contextualizing Central Asia.

1

Central Asia as Global

Alexander Cooley

Introducing Central Asia to the world has become a minor cottage industry. In the thirty years since independence from the Soviet Union, a plethora of books, articles, and travelogues have periodically sought to reacquaint us with the former republics of Kazakhstan, Kyrgyzstan, Tajikistan, Turkmenistan, and Uzbekistan. A generation ago such introductions seemed appropriate and even urgently needed—the region's character to the outside world had been obscured by its Soviet history, while the absence of tumultuous nationalist mobilizations during the late Soviet era and the region's heavy reliance on Soviet subsidies led some Western analysts to characterize its extrication as an "unwanted" independence.

After a sleepy start, the Central Asian states did manage to adopt all the major features of sovereign statehood. In most cases, late Soviet era republican party bosses took over the reins of power, forged new bureaucracies of political clients, built security services and national militaries, managed a system of economic transition to market economy, and brought state resources and major companies under their control. In their foreign relations, these new heads of state eagerly attended regional and international summits and declared themselves open to partnership with the world. They visited Beijing and Moscow, toured Mecca and Istanbul, and courted New Delhi and Tokyo, attempting to present themselves as partners of interest to the outside world. The notable exception was Tajikistan, which plunged into a brutal civil war pitting an old Soviet elite power structure backed by Russia and Uzbekistan against a coalition of opposition forces that included an Islamic party, liberal democrats, and ethnic Pamiris and Garmis from its outer provinces.

And yet the uncertainty of how, exactly, Central Asia fits into the international system of states, laws, and norms has persisted over a generation. Indeed, key episodes seem only to have ushered in fresh introductions to the region. The US-led war in Afghanistan in response to the attacks of 9/11 was perhaps the most dramatic of these episodes, but so too were two revolutions (2005 and 2010) and an ethnic pogrom (2010) in Kyrgyzstan, the passing of Turkmenistan's self-aggrandizing ruler Saparmurat Niyazov in 2006, Uzbekistan's bloody crackdown on demonstrators in the eastern city of Andijan in May 2005, and even the Ukraine crisis of 2014. Such regional crises have prompted commentators to take stock of Central Asia's possible foreign policy futures and exact global significance.

Perhaps there is a deeper reason that such periodic introductions seem necessary. Central Asia's relationship with the world is often interpreted as being subject to outside pressures and new global trends. It is a region constantly deemed to be in need of more connections to the world, more external attention and engagement, and (the favorite virtue of the outside world) greater regional integration. The frequent use of historical analogies—including imperial competition or flourishing ancient trading routes—often obscure the relevant issues at hand and substitute for informed analysis. As a result, Central Asia perpetually seems on the brink of going global but is never quite worldly enough for the satisfaction or interests of outsiders.

In this chapter I expand on three themes that tend to inform the world's fascination and conceptual terms of engagement with the region—great power competition, isolation and connectivity, and competing identities and values. The purpose is not to fix these relationships definitively or to provide a checklist of Central Asia's global ties but, rather, to show how these themes tend to resurface in contemporary grand strategies and narratives about the region.

The External Great Powers

The first broad theme of Central Asia's place in the world is the interest the region attracts from global "great powers" and their geopolitical rivalry and competition. The so-called Great Game, a term made popular by Rudyard Kipling in his 1901 book *Kim*, refers to the alleged high-stakes competition for influence between imperial Britain and Russia over Afghanistan and its surrounding areas. The term has been recycled since Central Asian independence to refer to the supposed new geopolitical competition among Russia, China, and the United States to influence the region's regimes and to secure access to its natural resources and strategic location.

The narrative of great power competition is notable for two further reasons. First, when dealing with Central Asia, all external governments feel compelled to publicly deny that they in fact harbor any regional geopolitical ambitions. US officials, for example, during the military campaign in neighboring Afghanistan publicly referred to their interest in securing "great gains" as opposed to playing great games. Chinese officials maintain that their investments in regional infrastructure are meant to promote "win-win"

ALEXANDER COOLEY

connectivity, devoid of any geopolitical intentions. Even in denial, the Great Game narrative continues to weave itself through the public diplomacy of the great powers. Second, although the great powers do indeed have some important strategic interests in Central Asia, for the most part these agendas have coexisted and even complemented each other; certainly, there has been some competition, as in any area of the world, but the interactions among the great powers have also involved active cooperation, tacit collusion, and even unabashed mimicry and imitation of one another.

Moscow's Lost and Found Empire

The most engaged and politically consequential external power remains Russia, the former center of imperial control and Soviet rule. Although it is tempting and sometimes instructive to draw parallels between Russia's post-Soviet relationship with Central Asia and other postcolonial relationships, this frame of reference is often vigorously contested within the region. For some, Soviet rule brought repression, economic dependence, the eradication of nomadic communities during Stalin's rule, and environmental catastrophe, but for others it was the source of modernization and universal education, while Central Asian citizens took pride in formative Soviet experiences, such as their service during the Second World War and hosting highly acclaimed Soviet development projects. In any case, Soviet legacies endure decades after the Soviet collapse. Central Asian elites shared similar educational and professional experiences under the Soviet system, bureaucratic norms and procedures were inherited from Soviet practices, the region's security and intelligence services have retained their extensive connections to Moscow, while Russia is still viewed as a place of economic opportunity or at least work. More intangibly, a nostalgia for Soviet rule in Central Asia permeates Central Asian public opinion and is reflected in consistently high favorability ratings toward Russia.

Interestingly, the most significant instruments and institutions employed by Moscow to reengage with the region have been pioneered and developed since 2000. During the 1990s, as Russia struggled with its own economic disruptions and political uncertainty, it withdrew its interest and engagement from the region, which was a painful blow for the Central Asian economies that had to extricate themselves from a complex network of Soviet planning and the subsidies that had supported Central Asian republican budgets. President Vladimir Putin's ascension to the Russian presidency in 1999 marked a turning point, as Moscow once again turned to Central Asia as part of a more robust engagement with its near abroad. Under the mantra of cooperating on counterterrorism and in the wake of its successful second campaign in Chechnya, the Kremlin promoted newly invigorated Russian-led regional economic and security initiatives, introducing the Collective Security Treaty Organization (CSTO), the successor to the Commonwealth of Independent States (CIS) Collective Security Treaty, the Russian-led counterpart to NATO. Moscow renewed a range of bilateral leases that governed a network of Russian military installations across the region, which continued from the Soviet era, and pushed the Central Asian states to purchase Russian-made weaponry, integrate their air defense network, and develop a joint NATO-style CSTO rapid reaction force. Concerns over Russia's security leadership in the region were heightened by the entry of US forces in 2001 to fight the campaign in neighboring Afghanistan, while the Russia-Georgia War in 2008 marked the region in Russia's "sphere of privileged interest" as termed by then president Dmitry Medvedev, though the Central Asian states did not recognize the independence of the breakaway territories of Abkhazia and South Ossetia. The Ukraine crisis of 2014 also sent shock waves throughout the region, as alarmed Central Asian governments feared similar interventions might be launched by Russia over areas such as northern Kazakhstan. In response to the UN General Assembly Resolution of April 2014 affirming Ukraine's sovereignty over recently annexed Crimea, both Kazakhstan and Uzbekistan abstained, and Kyrgyzstan, Tajikistan, and Turkmenistan did not even register a vote on the question.

In the economic realm, Moscow also pushed for new modes of integration. During the 2000s, as the Russian economy started to recover and then accelerated its growth, Russia became the destination for millions of Central Asian migrants looking to find temporary work and send remittances back home. The Eurasian Economic Union (EAEU), which now includes Kazakhstan, Kyrgyzstan, Armenia and Belarus, is the successor to the Customs Union and Eurasian Economic Community (EurAsEC) and was formally established in May 2014. It is modeled on the supranational structure of the European Union, an attempt to institutionalize a rules-based economic body with a common customs and external tariff area, regulatory framework, and commercial dispute settlement mechanism. Taken together the CSTO, EAEU, and other Russian-led regional bodies seek to institutionalize Russia's regional primacy, and the participation of the Central Asian states in these bodies helps to cement Russia's self-image as a great power with a sphere of influence, which is critical to Moscow's foreign policy identity as a great power in a multipolar or polycentric world.

At the same time, one of the biggest sources of solidarity between Moscow and the Central Asian governments is concern about Western-backed attempts to democratize or promote political pluralism in the region. Following the Color Revolutions in the mid-2000s, which swept away regimes that were relatively friendly to the Kremlin in Georgia (2003), Ukraine (2004), and Kyrgyzstan (2005), Moscow strongly supported the Central Asian governments as they cracked down on media, expelled and restricted the activities of NGOs, and stigmatized externally sponsored democracy and human rights initiatives. Most dramatically, Moscow backed the Uzbek government after its hard-line president Islam Karimov cracked down on demonstrators in the eastern city of Andijan in May 2005, killing hundreds, while the West called for an international investigation, leveled economic sanctions, and cut off most security assistance. The fallout of the Arab Spring and the Ukraine crisis has once again heightened concerns among Central Asian elites and the Kremlin who are apprehensive about the threat of externally sponsored street protests. And despite the deep sense of insecurity and economic uncertainty unleashed by the crisis in Ukraine, along with the accompanying Western economic sanctions and Russian counter-sanctions and a plummeting oil price and ruble, the Central Asian publics remain broadly supportive of their ties to Russia, with Moscow considered a stabilizing force in the region.

China Looks Westward

The second great power in the region is China. Like Moscow, Beijing views the region as a zone of critical national interest. However, it does so primarily through the lens of stabilizing its restive Western province of Xinjiang, home of a large Uyghur population and a number of other ethnic minorities. For decades, China has sought to promote the modernization of Xinjiang through large-scale infrastructure investments and development projects, while at the same time adopting a "strike hard" campaign against expressions of autonomy and separatism in the region. Xinjiang borders Kazakhstan, Kyrgyzstan, and Tajikistan, as well as Afghanistan and Pakistan, making any instability in Central Asian countries a matter of critical concern.

At the same time, China considers the economic development of Central Asia to be critical for expanding Xinjiang's economic connections and opportunities. Hence, the financing, subsidies, and investment that Beijing provides to Central Asia is as much a function of its domestic Xinjiang strategy as it is the exercise of a "foreign" economic policy. Since 2000, trade with the region has exploded from one billion US dollars to well over fifty billion dollars a year, while Beijing has invested billions in new infrastructure, including completing the Central Asia–China gas pipeline that links Turkmenistan, Uzbekistan, and Kazakhstan with Xinjiang. China is now also the region's most important developmental assistance provider, having extended eight billion dollars' and ten billion dollars' worth of emergency loans to Turkmenistan and Kazakhstan, respectively, during the financial crisis in 2009 in exchange for shares in energy projects and exports.

In 2013, at Nazarbayev University in Kazakhstan, Premier Xi Jinping publicly announced the launching of the Silk Road Economic Initiative, later referred to as the Belt and Road Initiative (BRI). The BRI—promising hundreds of billions of dollars in infrastructure investments and upgrades to over seventy countries—has been widely hailed as Xi's transformative geopolitical vision, intended to create a China-friendly community of nations by expanding economic partnerships with Chinese companies, the global use of Chinese technological standards, and increasing awareness of China's foreign policy and security priorities among partner countries. Central Asia is located at the heart of the BRI, with Kyrgyzstan, Tajikistan, and Turkmenistan highly dependent on Chinese investment and loans.

China has attempted to institutionalize many of its security interests and strategic objectives by establishing a new regional organization—the Shanghai Cooperation Organization (SCO), comprised of China, Russia, Kazakhstan,

Kyrgyzstan, Tajikistan, and Uzbekistan. The SCO was founded in 2001 as a direct successor to the Shanghai Five Forum, which had successfully negotiated the final border demarcation between China and the Central Asian states. Presenting itself as a "new-style" organization that supports the sovereignty of and noninterference in its members' affairs (the so-called Shanghai Spirit) and that rejects the universalism of Western hegemony in international relations, the SCO has pursued a number of initiatives on the security, economic, and cultural fronts. In terms of security, it has conducted biannual so-called peace missions, which serve as joint exercises involving the Chinese, Russian, and Central Asian militaries. In 2004 the SCO formally established the Regional Anti-Terrorist Structure (RATS) in Tashkent, Uzbekistan, a center for information-sharing among the internal security forces of the member states. The SCO has made less progress on the economic front, as the other states have remained hesitant to use the vehicle to promote the free-trade area initially proposed by Beijing, while Russia blocked a number of attempts by Beijing to establish an SCO regional development bank or emergency lending facility. Although supporting the anti-Western tone and statements made by the SCO, Russia prefers to promote its own economic regional architectures such as the EAEU or the related Eurasian Development Bank. As a result, even as it expanded membership in 2017 to include India and Pakistan, the SCO's public pronouncements about the scope and depth of its cooperation have not been matched by actual achievements, although many of these internal rivalries and disagreements are kept from the public eye.

But even as China's overarching preoccupation with Xinjiang creates the potential for a broad coexistence with Moscow, Beijing continues to expand its security footprint in the region, with or without Russian acquiescence and despite perceptions that there is a broad division of labor in the region, in which Russia provides security and political leadership and China provides investment and economic engagement. A suicide bombing of the Chinese embassy in Kyrgyzstan on August 30, 2016, emphasized to Chinese officials the need for intense security cooperation with Central Asian security services. In 2018 world media reports confirmed that the Chinese government had established a network of extralegal reeducation camps in Xinjiang for the internment of hundreds of thousands of Uyghurs and Central Asian conationals such as Kazakhs, while severely restricting their mobility across the region. And in 2019 Western investigative newspaper stories confirmed that the government of Tajikistan had signed an agreement with Beijing allowing Chinese troops to be stationed near the Wakhan Corridor and even to patrol broad swathes of the Tajik-Afghan border. Despite China's careful public deference to Russia's regional leadership, China's economic and security roles continue to expand.

The Eagle Lands (and then Leaves Again)

The dramatic entry of the United States into Central Asia was a direct consequence of the attacks of 9/11. Prior to the fall of 2001, US interests in

Central Asia were relatively minor, with Washington supporting US energy companies in their investments in Kazakhstan and the US adhering to a policy of strengthening the "sovereignty" and "independence" of the Central Asian states. However, the 9/11 attacks immediately elevated the region as a strategic priority for the ensuing Afghanistan campaign (Operation Enduring Freedom).

Within weeks, US defense officials concluded basing rights agreements with the Uzbek government to open a logistics facility in Karshi-Khanabad (K2) near the Afghan border, and in December 2001 US officials concluded an agreement over the use of the Manas airport, near the Kyrgyz capital of Bishkek, to conduct refueling operations and to stage US personnel moving in and out of Afghanistan. US military aid and security assistance to the Central Asian militaries and security services (especially Uzbekistan) skyrocketed, in part in cooperation on regional counterterrorism and in part to provide a tacit quid pro quo to these countries for granting access rights. In addition to basing rights, the US secured flyover rights from all of the Central Asian states and refueling rights in Turkmenistan and Tajikistan. In 2008, following a spate of attacks on US supply lines in Pakistan, US officials opened up a network of Eurasian-based supply routes—known as the Northern Distribution Network (NDN)—to bring nonlethal supplies from ports in the Baltic states all the way down through Central Asia and Afghanistan. In short, US policy toward Central Asia became more engaged but almost exclusively as an instrumental function of its Afghanistan activities.

The initial US agreements in 2001 to establish bases in Central Asia were supported and facilitated by President Putin. However, by 2003, a broader deterioration in United States–Russia relations altered Moscow's view of the US presence in the region from one of partnership and common interests in the Global War on Terror (GWOT) to that of a geopolitical rival bent on using its new military presence at Moscow's expense. In 2009, in an attempt to pressure the government of Kyrgyz and President Kurmanbek Bakiev (Bakiyev) to close Manas, Moscow entered a bidding war against the United States, with Washington prevailing by offering the Bakiev regime more rent (a jump from seventeen million dollars per year to sixty-three million dollars) and renaming the facility the Manas Transit Center. A few months later, Moscow's "soft-power" and anti-Bakiev media barrage proved critical in toppling the Kyrgyz president, after he cracked down on protestors in April 2010, and ushered in an interim government more publicly aligned with Moscow. In 2013, under some Russian pressure, the Kyrgyz government refused to extend the US lease to Manas beyond July 2014, forcing the US to relocate its basing operations to Romania. Post-Manas, without major operations in Afghanistan, US strategy in Central Asia has sought to emphasize more people-to-people contacts and has even launched a new format for discussing issues of common concern, the C5+1 (the five Central Asian states plus the US), during which US Secretary of State John Kerry met with all the Central Asian leaders at a summit in Tashkent in 2015. But as a result of the decision to draw down from Afghanistan, the overwhelming view in the region is that Central Asia is no longer a foreign policy priority for the United States. Furthermore, the US prioritization of good working relations with the Central Asian regimes, in order to preserve basing and access rights, has seriously eroded the image of the United States in the region as a champion for liberal values such as human rights and democracy. Its commitment to the region came to be viewed less as guided by values and principles and more by how the United States could use the region's assets.

Big Games from Middle Powers

Beyond the "big three" powers, Central Asia has also seen heightened interest from other external suitors. The European Union (EU) has steadily engaged in the region, promoting a number of objectives ranging from security cooperation to promoting regional cooperation, to pushing its so-called values agenda and a number of project-based developmental initiatives. The EU strategy was codified in a strategy paper adopted by Brussels during the German chairmanship in 2007 and then was extended after review. However, European countries such as Germany, France, Poland, and Latvia have also separately pursued their own bilateral security and economic agendas.

Asian powers have been increasing their ties and engagement with the region. Japan, most notably, has reengaged with the region by promoting the multilateral summit format "Central Asia plus Japan," to discuss regional security and economic challenges. Having been a leading provider of official development assistance to Central Asia in 1990, but then having dropped off the geopolitical map in the 2000s, Tokyo has been spurred back by concern over China's regional rise and influence, offering its own infrastructure and connectivity plan that emphasizes quality investments. South Korea also remains heavily involved in large-scale investments in energy and industrial projects in both Kazakhstan and Uzbekistan, as a result of an active Korean population in the region that has helped to forge these social and business links. India has viewed the region as a natural area to signal the country's status as a rising international actor and to promote itself as an important regional player. India had even sought to open its first foreign air base in the Ayni airfield in Tajikistan, but it appears to have fallen into the trap of expecting to have more influence than it actually did. Shortly after Indian-sponsored upgrades to the facility were completed, the Tajik government announced that it would not be extending basing rights to the Indian government. Still, India's activities in the region seems likely to expand. Not only does India want to enhance its role as an important aid provider in neighboring Afghanistan, but its new membership in the SCO offers a platform for institutionalizing many of India's outreach efforts to the Central Asian states. The question of "Central Asia's role in Asia" appears set to become more important, as Asian countries offer an additional source of partnership, investment, and interest in the region, especially in light of perceptions that the West's interests in the region are waning.

Central Asia and the Multivector Foreign Policy Doctrine

This interest in the region among the external powers, along with their perceived competition for influence, has spawned the trademark broad foreign policy doctrine of the Central Asian states—their pursuit of a multivector foreign policy. Multivectorism has two core tenets. First, it refers to engaging with a broad variety of external partners and avoiding being locked into the exclusive sphere of influence of any one regional power; and second, it refers to an active effort by Central Asian policy makers, even the smaller ones, of playing external suitors off one another in an effort to preserve their autonomy and sovereignty of decision making.

The exact contours of this multivectorism have varied from country to country. In Kazakhstan it has involved expanding commercial and investment ties, especially in the lucrative energy sector, with Russia, China, and the West, including the United States and the European Union, even while supporting Eurasian integration initiatives led by Russia, and all while promoting Kazakhstan itself as a key global player. Uzbekistan (more autarkic in its economic orientation until the death of President Karimov in 2016 and a new opening to external investors by his successor, President Shavkat Mirziyoyev) has avoided remaining locked into agreements that undermined its sovereignty and has shifted its security orientation dramatically, from cooperating closely with the United States post-9/11 to joining the Russian-led CSTO in 2006, to then exiting the organization as Tashkent reestablished ties again with NATO countries. Turkmenistan's courting of external companies such as China National Petroleum Company (CNPC) to help it develop its natural gas resources and break its dependency on the Russian state-monopolist Gazprom now makes it beholden to Beijing. Finally, Kyrgyzstan and Tajikistan, the smaller and poorer states, actively managed the interests of Russia, China, and the United States, especially during the military campaign in Afghanistan, by offering security partnership and extracting economic and security assistance from the great powers. Indeed, from 2001 to 2014, Kyrgyzstan was the only country in the world that hosted both US and Russian military bases within a few kilometers of one another, all the time acting as a reexporting hub for Chinese goods destined to other Eurasian states.

But multivectorism will remain only aspirational if the Central Asian states cannot secure significant interest and engagements from multiple outside powers. The withdrawal of the United States from the region and the intensification of Russian and Chinese interest in Central Asia present a challenge to all the region's governments. While they value Russia's political and security support and China's economic engagement, there is also widespread concern that other robust external partnerships are needed to preserve their autonomy of decision making, sovereignty, and leverage over their more powerful neighbors.

1·1   A modernization of the original Soviet rail system, pictured is a high-speed Afrosiyob Talgo train arriving into Samarqand Railway Station, Uzbekistan 2019. Photograph by Kasia Ploskonka.

Globally Isolated or Connected?

The second recurring theme about Central Asia and the world is its supposed isolation from globalizing forces and international centers of political power. This has been an especially dominant theme in how US and Chinese officials approach the region, as both Washington and China have publicly trumpeted regional strategies emphasizing the need to promote the Central Asia's "connectivity" to other parts of the world and the global market. For the United States, this has meant promoting the "New Silk Road" vision, for which the US government has promoted infrastructure and commercial projects that would link Central Asia to Afghanistan and South Asia, such as the Turkmenistan-Afghanistan-Pakistan-India gas pipeline or the Central Asia-South Asia hydroelectric project (CASA-1000). For China, the vision has been even more ambitious, as Premier Xi Jinping in 2013 announced China's intention to build both a New Silk Road Economic Belt and a Maritime Belt, which collectively are now referred to as the Belt and Road Initiative. Ambitiously, China has indicated that it plans on investing tens of billions of US dollars across Eurasia to promote its ties with Europe, the Middle East, and South Asia. Interestingly, Washington and Beijing are very quick to downplay any geopolitical intent in the new connectivity initiatives, while Beijing axiomatically believes, as with Xinjiang, that investments in infrastructure will necessarily bring development and accompanying political stability.

The emphasis on "connectivity" and ending the region's alleged isolation is echoed in previous readings of the regional part of the strategically important Eurasian landmass. Since the writings of British geographer Sir Halford Mackinder (who viewed the control of Eurasia as a potentially key pivot in the world power balance and warned of Russia's power potential should it successfully construct a railway network in the region), the idea that integrating or connecting Eurasia to other parts of the globe will fundamentally transform the regional and global balance of power informs a great deal of outside strategic thinking about the region's importance and its needs. Looking further back historically, authors such as Peter Frankopan have reminded us that Central Asia's location on the Silk Road placed it at the crossroads of the interaction of Eastern and Western conquering powers, global trade, ideas, and religions. In other words, Central Asia's global integration, for many eras, is an indicator of how "globalization" itself has been managed and channeled.

Selective Isolationism

But beyond the geopolitical intent embedded in these latest Silk Road visions, just how accurate is it to accept the characterization of the region as globally isolated? Certainly, in terms of formal regional trade, Central Asia, according to World Bank data, remains one of the least trade-friendly areas of the world, with informal trade barriers, such as delayed customs checks, making waiting times for the processing of import and exports in the 2000s and 2010s nearly triple what they are in Eastern Europe or double the Middle East and North Africa. Central Asia's notorious informal restrictions and trade barriers continue to stunt the region's economic exchange. Foreign direct investment continues to lag, especially outside the energy and mining sectors, while navigating the region's acute governance problems is a deterrent to investors.

On the other hand, the region is far more connected to the global economy in ways not appreciated by many policy makers and commentators. Even as internal trade barriers within the region remain high, Central Asia's trade with the outside world—especially China, Russia, and the European Union—exploded in the 2000s, increasing from one billion to thirty billion dollars with China and from five billion to twenty-five billion dollars with Russia. Although they are members of the Russian-led EAEU, Kyrgyzstan and Kazakhstan, along with Tajikistan, are now also members of the World Trade Organization (WTO)—indeed, since acquiring WTO membership in 1998, Kyrgyzstan has served as a reexport hub for Chinese goods into Eurasia.

Another form of economic connectivity involves the regional movement of labor. From five to six million Central Asian migrants temporarily work abroad—most of them in Russia, but some also in Kazakhstan. Overall, as a percentage of remittances to GDP, Tajikistan is the most remittance-dependent economy in the world (about 50 percent of GDP), and Kyrgyzstan often ranks second (about 30–35 percent). Such linkages tie the economic fortunes of Central Asia to economic conditions in the hosting countries but also create new transnational understandings of identities, family life, and informal employment networks and value chains.

1-2a-b　In the city center one can find a mixture of global and local influences from double-decker sightseeing buses and skyscrapers (*top*) to camel statues and I Heart Astana signs (*bottom*), Nur-Sultan, Kazakhstan 2018. Photograph by Kasia Ploskonka.

Contra popular myths of isolation, Central Asia also finds itself enmeshed in a system of global administrative law and extraterritorial commercial frameworks that have significantly curtailed the sovereign autonomy of these states, even as they have sought more control over economic policy. Particularly important has been the activation of international arbitration clauses included within the Bilateral Investment Treaties (BITs) that the Central Asian states signed during the 1990s. International arbitration proceedings are usually secretive and take place overseas in an internationally recognized court of arbitration such as London or Stockholm; their judgments are enforceable across all countries that have signed the New York Convention (1959), which permits damaged parties to petition for the recovery of assets to cover an arbitration judgment in any of the signatory countries. According to one survey of Central Asian BITs undertaken by Borzu Sabahi and Diyara Ziyaeva, the governments of the region had signed a total of 176 BITs by the beginning of 2013. It is interesting that Uzbekistan, usually viewed as the most self-reliant economy, had signed the most agreements (49), followed by Kazakhstan (42), Tajikistan (32), Kyrgyzstan (29), and Turkmenistan (24). In the Kyrgyz case, following the collapse of Kyrgyz president Kurmanbek Bakiev, Kyrgyz authorities were taken to court nine times around the world in cases involving legal disputes over alleged breaches of contracts and forced nationalizations of mining and financial institutions. Cumulatively, the judgments against Kyrgyzstan have amounted to nearly one billion US dollars, the equivalent of the annual Kyrgyz state budget.

Connections to the Offshore World

Perhaps no other area emphasizes the hidden connectivity than the region's widespread use of shell companies and offshore financial networks to facilitate economic transactions with the outside world and to launder gains from illicit activities and insider elite deals. Although observers often attribute the region's developmental problems to its lack of connectivity, in truth the region is characterized by some of the highest rates of capital flight and transfers in the world, fueled by the nearly unrestricted grand corruption of the ruling elites and their allies who take their proceeds outside of the region and into banking centers such as London, New York, and Switzerland. For example, according to the International Monetary Fund (IMF), capital flight in 2013 in Tajikistan was an astonishing 65 percent of GDP.

Such capital flight and hidden flows could not be accomplished without very significant connections to the anonymous offshore world. In fact, offshore shell companies have been implicated in a number of corruption scandals involving the elite members of each of the Central Asian regimes. These include the use of a network of offshore companies and Swiss bank accounts to structure bribe payments from Western energy companies to senior Kazakh officials in the 1990s (the so-called Kazakhgate scandal); the use of opaque shell companies to mediate the lucrative energy trade between Turkmenistan and its neighbors; the offshoring to the British Virgin Islands of the opaque management structure of Tajikistan's prized state company Tajikistan's Aluminum Company (TALCO); the uncovering of shell companies that channeled corrupt payments from international telecommunications companies to Uzbekistan's elites; and the use of banks in Kyrgyzstan as money-laundering vehicles, with hundreds of correspondent relations with offshore entities. The leak of the so-called Panama Papers, the dump of over eleven million documents detailing the industrial-sized creation of offshore firms by the Panama-registered company Mossack Fonseca, revealed an array of Central Asian clients and holdings. Moreover, research by Jason Sharman and his colleagues in the book *Global Shell Games* found that company service providers in the West—when presented with requests from Central Asian officials with ties to government procurement contracts, an obvious red flag for corruption—were all too likely to sell companies without demanding proper identification documents from these risky prospective clients.

Beyond these international proceedings involving governments and state-operated institutions, a growing number of Central Asian elites have themselves been implicated in global corruption scandals that have been the subjects of extraterritorial investigations and enforcement actions. The most important of these have been the enforcement actions taken by the US Justice Department and Security and Exchange Commission to uphold the Foreign and Corrupt Practices Act (FCPA). These settlements have involved energy company and oil service providers in Kazakhstan, but, between 2016 and 2019, US authorities leveled some of the largest fines ever for FCPA enforcements against the Dutch-registered company Vimpelcom ($795 million), the Swedish-Finnish-based Telia ($965 million), and the Russian-based Mobile TeleSystems (MTS) ($850 million), for bribing Uzbek officials in order to gain access to the Uzbek telecom market. A number of international investigations tied Uzbekistan's Gulnara Karimova, daughter of the former Uzbek president, to these schemes, and her overseas assets and properties have been frozen in the United States, Switzerland, France, and Sweden. These global criminal and anti-bribery investigations, again, reveal complex and dense networks of shell companies, secret bank accounts, brokers, and accountants.

An Arena of Colliding Values and Influences?

The third theme that emerges is that the Central Asian region is a dynamic arena for the projection of different political values, identities, influences, and normative frameworks. Much has been made of the region's now celebrated historical role as a hub of innovation, cultural production, and high civilization during medieval times, while a parade of empires continued to scatter a number of lingering influences and cultural fragments. From this perspective, the seventy years of Soviet rule in the region and the attempt to assimilate the region into the Soviet social and political project could be viewed as an exception to these more general historical trends of cross-pollination and multiple influences. Indeed, once freed from Soviet rule during the 1990s, the region was perceived as new territory by a variety of external religious groups and other cultural organizations. From Saudi-backed Wahhabi movements to the liberal mission of the New York–based Open Society Foundations and other Western NGOs, external actors flocked to the region in order to project their own values, preferred identities, and social agendas, most notably in the education sphere. However, even extensive interactions with global influences, such as studying in Western universities, have not led Central Asian youth to wholly adopt Western norms or the values of globalization; rather, Central Asia's new generations seem quite comfortable to selectively adopt outside elements, referred to by Douglass Blum as hybridization, without being homogenized by their interaction with global processes.

Perhaps the most concerning of these, both to domestic governments and to many global observers, has been the possibility that Islam, long suppressed and controlled under Soviet times, would once again become a potent vehicle for identity claims and political action. At the outset of independence, Western commentators even speculated that Turkey and Iran might become locked in a struggle for regional influence based on their models of "secular" or "religious" Islam, a formulation that revealed gross Western ignorance of the region's challenges and affiliations as well as a simplistic notion of regional foreign policy. Other observers were tempted to couch events such as Tajikistan's civil war or the unrest in the region's Ferghana Valley as evidence of a coming surge in political Islam. Concerns were heightened in the summers of 1999 and 2000, when members of the Islamic Movement of Uzbekistan launched incursions into the Kyrgyz portion of the Ferghana Valley, kidnapping a group of foreign workers and highlighting the porous nature of regional borders. The onset of the US-led "Global War on Terror" in Afghanistan gave further material backing and legitimacy to these governments as they cracked down on political opponents and religious figures under the new antiterrorism mantra. In China, as well, 9/11 served as an opportunity for Beijing to try and connect Uyghur separatists in Xinjiang with external-sponsored movements such as Al-Qaeda. The rise of the Islamic State of Iraq and Syria (ISIS) in 2014 and 2015 triggered alarm across the region that Central Asians who had been recruited by the organization to go and fight in Syria and Iraq might return and carry out attacks against targets in their home countries or in third countries. Although the number of Central Asians joining ISIS appears to be systematically exaggerated by Central Asian governments, the crackdown on ISIS affiliates appears to have further fueled the securitization of the region.

The Evolution of Authoritarianism

The most important political value throughout the region may be widespread authoritarianism. With the exception of Kyrgyzstan, which has thrice seen organized street protests topple three presidents who were perceived as authoritarian and corrupt, strong presidential rule and powerful dynastic families appear to be the norm in most countries. The regimes themselves have different flavors, ranging from the more "soft authoritarianism" of Kazakhstan, which is concerned with global image making and its international reputation, to the more repressive and theatrical rule of Turkmenistan's Gurbanguly Berdimuhamedow (Berdimuhamedov). But authoritarianism has been central to the construction of new national identities, symbols, and public events, setting the parameters of new national mythmaking and cultural production, while autocrats across the region have readily mimicked and emulated each other's illiberal institutions and practices.

Regional fears of the potential of external actors and NGOs to destabilize and even topple these regimes reached a frenzy in the mid-2000s with the onset of the so-called Color Revolutions, which saw long-standing corrupt governments toppled from power for pro-Western rulers in Georgia (2003), Ukraine (2005), and Kyrgyzstan (2005). Following the Andijan crackdown in May 2005, the Uzbek government clamped down on the activities of NGOs and evicted a number of foreign-sponsored organizations that had been operating in the country such as Freedom House and the Open Society Foundations. All of the Central Asian states from 2005 to 2006 passed new laws restricting the activities and registration requirements for NGOs and the media. The backlash continued after the Arab Spring of 2011, as authorities turned their attention to monitoring and restricting social media outlets out of concern that these might mobilize street protests. The 2014 Ukraine crisis concerned Central Asian rulers not only because of Russia's actions but also because Maidan-like street protests and their perceived external backing are viewed as an enduring threat to regime stability. Throughout the decade, Russian and Russian-language media have propagated conspiracy theories regarding the West's interests in destabilizing the region and have emphasized the double standards and hypocrisy of the West's so-called values agenda of promoting democracy and human rights in the region. For example, focus groups interviewed by political scientists Edward Schatz and Renan Levine suggest that this coverage has had a devastating effect on the West's credibility in the region, as Central Asians are now highly skeptical of the United States as a credible champion for democracy and human rights.

Promoting regime security has not only been a domestic priority but has also informed the regional initiatives of the Central Asian regimes. For example, all of the Central Asian regimes strongly backed Russia's attempts to restrict the activities of the Organization for Security and Co-operation in Europe (OSCE) and, after a decade of its highly critical assessments of their elections, to curtail the election-monitoring efforts of the OSCE's Office for Human Rights and Democratic Initiatives (ODIHR). Beginning in 2005 the Central Asian states eagerly welcomed the "alternative election monitors" of regional groups such as the CIS and the SCO, which provided far less critical assessments of their flawed national elections. Central Asian regimes also used new regional legal frameworks provided by the CIS Minsk treaty and the SCO's Anti-Terror Convention to create common blacklists of political opponents, demand the return or rendition of "extremists" without due process, and broadly use these new regional security organizations to shield themselves from international humanitarian and legal obligations such as human rights treaties. In certain instances, such as the killing of Tajik political dissident Umarali Kuvatov in Istanbul in March 2015 or the attempted assassination of Uzbek imam Obid kori Nazarov in Sweden in 2012, the security services of the Central Asian states appear to have sent contracted agents on extraterritorial missions to eliminate exiled political opponents. Political authoritarianism and regime survival, then, provide most of the parameters for the extent to which each Central Asian country actually engages with or accepts these external normative influences.

There is one final twist to this survey of Central Asia's relations with the world and the general trend of the decline of Western influence across the region. Although it is clear that the Central Asian governments have increasingly taken steps to protect their societies from the normative influence of human rights and democracy-promoting NGOs, often by invoking the idea of the cultural specificity of Central Asian societies and political systems, a cursory look at the actual lifestyles and the transnational connections of the Central Asian elites themselves reveals that they actively participate within global networks as high–net worth individuals. Central Asian elites and exiled former elites spend much of their time in Western capitals and cultural centers. They promote their international charities, rub shoulders with Western entertainers and socialites, and litigate their disputes in international arbitration tribunals and court hearings. They have been revealed to have purchased luxury real estate holdings such as the most expensive property in Beverly Hills, the mythical address of Sherlock Holmes in London, and even the Berkshire mansion of Prince Andrew of England. The irony here is instructive—while the Central Asian regimes have increasingly sought to curb foreign, especially Western, support for the NGO sector, media, and political position within the region, the elites themselves have proved eager to accumulate real estate holdings in the West, develop links between their cultural foundations and charities and Western partners, and spend a significant part of their lives outside of the region as self-styled global cosmopolitans.

Central Asia as Global

Central Asia's relations to the world are multifaceted and multilayered. They involve both the high politics of diplomacy and the management of great power relations and unacknowledged transnational connections and ties to the offshore world. Above all, the recurring themes about Central Asia and the global—geopolitical competition, isolation and connectivity, and clashing identities and norms—should give us pause about the usefulness of simple frameworks that purport to assess or define the foreign policies or global interactions of the Central Asian states. Ultimately, how we choose to fix and delimit Central Asia's relations to the global speaks more about our own recurring biases, priorities, and geopolitical agendas than it does about the complexity of the region's global ties.

2

Central Asia as Local

Morgan Y. Liu

We are going local. We are zooming in on everyday Central Asian lives at the small scale of city, village, and neighborhood so as to reveal what people are habitually saying, doing, and thinking. A ground-level view of Central Asia allows us to appreciate what makes the region distinctive. An up-close look at people's lives also gives us leverage to understand larger-scale issues about Central Asian societies, such as what factors promote community cohesion and economic development. Specific features of local places may offer insight on questions like relations between rich and poor, pride in cultural traditions, peaceful coexistence between ethnic groups, and the nature of religious piety. The local, in other words, enables a closer understanding of the entire Central Asian region and how it fits into the globe.

The very idea of local places, however, carries misleading associations. Some think of Central Asian localities as isolated corners of the earth, cut off from global influences. Others see them as bound to old traditions, so that the locals only repeat the past and never innovate. Others regard local places as exotic lands where people are driven by beliefs and motivations that are incomprehensible to outsiders. These are misconceptions. On the other hand, local places in Central Asia are indeed marked by particular cultures and histories that set them apart from many other parts of the globe. In the explorations below, we show that Central Asians have distinct features in their social life but at the same time share deep connections with the rest of the world.

Does Local Mean Isolated?

If any part of the world appears isolated today, it is Central Asia. Distances are vast across expanses of mountain chains, steppe, or desert. The region is not very well connected by international flights even today. It was politically inaccessible to most outsiders until the end of the twentieth century, being under the control of empires and states that restricted access.

The image of Central Asia as a kind of "final frontier" influenced even scholars who are supposed to be knowledgeable about the world. Right before I started graduate school in cultural anthropology, one professor said, "Great, Central Asia is one of the last places you can still do *real* anthropology!" She meant that I could study isolated communities cut off from the modern world, what anthropologists used to be famous for doing. This professor was half joking, but I got the point. In the popular imagination, Central Asia is a poster child for remoteness. My friends even gave me an Indiana Jones hat as a farewell present when I set out to study the region.

But is Central Asia really isolated like that? Let us begin by considering the region when it was ruled by the Soviet Union for seventy-some years. From the viewpoint of Moscow, the center of Soviet power, Central Asia started as a distant and outlying territory. Over the course of the twentieth century, however, that government progressively integrated the region with the rest of the country in administration, economy, transportation, and infrastructure. Soviet efforts modernized Central Asia in material conditions and transformed its social and cultural life—the hearts and minds—of its Central Asian citizens through mass education, radio, television, newspapers, publishers, libraries, theaters, film industries, music and dance conservatories, science academies, and other institutions. The authorities sought to "emancipate" women from what they denounced as backward patriarchal oppression. At one point they literally tore off the veils (*paranjas*) that town-dwelling women wore in public and then promoted women's education, work outside the home, and fuller participation in society.

As a result, Central Asians changed profoundly under Soviet rule. They were educated and became restaurant cooks, bus drivers, teachers, factory workers, mechanized farmers, doctors, technicians, engineers, scientists, athletes, violinists, chess players, and even cosmonauts—in short, increasingly modern and Soviet. The Second World War was a formative experience for Central Asians. The wartime hardships, sacrifices, and casualties gave Central Asians a clear purpose of struggle against the Nazi "fascists" and a proud sense of being a part of the Soviet Union. The Soviet Union's only spaceport, the Baikonur Cosmodrome, is located in Kazakhstan and continues to operate to this day as one of the world's busiest space launch facilities. All of these changes have meant that the trappings, rhythms, and mind-sets of modern life have become routine for Central Asians. These are now people who stream movies on their phones, get stuck in commuter traffic, run small businesses, maintain hydroelectric dams, and follow world events. They are a far cry from the isolated natives of anthropological lore.

But even before the Soviets came, Central Asians were never really isolated. The continent-crossing network of trade routes commonly called the Silk Road provided the commercial and social exchange of goods, people, and ideas that integrated Central Asia in every direction. Historians have recently shown that we cannot properly understand political developments in the region during the seventeenth, eighteenth, and nineteenth centuries without knowing the broader trends in economy, finance, technology, and religion across the Eurasian continent. Before that, traders, pilgrims, artists, and Islamic scholars moved back and forth between Central Asia, India, Persia (Iran), the Ottoman empire (which extended across most of today's Middle East), and beyond, forming an integrated region.

Today, the region is more connected than ever. Central Asians watch TV news from Russia; see movies from Hollywood, Bollywood (India), and Hong Kong; buy consumer goods from China, Korea, Turkey, and Iran; and change local currencies into US dollars and Euros. More and more Central Asians relocate for jobs in Russia, Korea, the Persian Gulf, western Europe, and North America. The wealthy regularly travel abroad, where they shop, buy property, and stash their money in offshore accounts. The privileged send their children for education in the elite universities of the United States and the rest of the world. Foreign aid and development workers, businesspeople, diplomats, and missionaries live throughout the region. Tourists from Europe, the United States, and Japan come to experience the nature, mountaineering, hunting, and culture. Multinational oil and mining companies work in resource-rich areas in Kazakhstan, Turkmenistan, Uzbekistan, and Kyrgyzstan. Connections such as these are shaping the multilayered character of Central Asian localities.

In Central Asia, "local" does not mean isolated but *connected* in many specific ways to the world. This insight from looking at the local can illuminate a big picture problem like the future economic development in the region. If Central Asian businesses and governments are to leverage the history of connection for the benefit of the region's people, how should they now participate in global flows of capital, commodities, labor, and ideas? Can the region move beyond offering primarily natural resources (oil, gas, minerals) and low skill labor (migrant workers) to the world market? Could it even contribute intellectual labor (software, artistic production, fashion), as some Central Asians at home and abroad are beginning to do? Tracing how the region's connections develop in the coming years is an important story to follow.

Does Local Mean Homogenous?

I tell my students that every place on planet Earth is fascinating, but Central Asia is special. There is a rhapsodic richness to a region that has sat for centuries at a nexus of Turkic, Persian, Arab, Indian, Chinese, Mongolian, Russian, and other cultural influences. Not every land has this combination of sheer continental reach, "civilizational" diversity, and time depth. This confluence has meant that localities have a distinct mix of experiences that has allowed them to forge their own societies and cultures. Far from being homogenous, then, Central Asia is made up of multiple cultural layers. Let's take a quick tour of how Central Asian localities are diverse. The focus is on ethnicity, which turns out to have a specifically Central Asian meaning and history different from those in other places.

We best begin with a basic historical distinction for the region: *nomadic* and *sedentary*. Nomadic people lived off their large herds of livestock, primarily sheep, goats, and horses. Because Central Asia generally has low rainfall and sparse seasonal pastures, nomads had to keep moving across the landscape over the year to keep their animals fed. They lived in portable structures such as the famous yurt, leading for millennia a lifestyle adapted to the environment. Sedentary people, on the other hand, were settled folk, living in permanent houses and towns with water and arable land. They relied on farming, craft, and trade for their sustenance. Nomadic and sedentary people were mutually dependent through trade in milk, meat, and wool from one side and grain, vegetables, wood, and tools from the other. When Soviet rule came in the early twentieth century, the government forced the nomads to settle (a violent, traumatic episode) in order to reorganize production and modernize society. Today, there are few pure nomads who have no permanent dwelling. Rather, there are herders, who work and live with their flocks on the mountains during the warm months of the year but still have fixed addresses in town. Being a nomad has become a job—and a part-time job at that.

The nomadic-sedentary distinction still matters in how Central Asians make distinctions among themselves today, even though few live in a truly nomadic lifestyle anymore. This is in part due to the celebration of traditional culture and ethnic histories that began during the Soviet period and really took off after independence. Each of the Central Asian republics, the "-stans," has publicly promoted the achievements of the dominant national group, which includes particularities of its nomadic or sedentary history.

And so, this past matters to everyday life in local places. Central Asians, like people anywhere else, maintain stereotypes about each other. The descendants of nomads are often seen as adaptable, flexible, and friendly, on one hand, but moody, fickle, and undependable, on the other. Both the positive and negative sides of these stereotypes assume a connection between present-day mentality and the nomadic past. As the thinking goes, just as nomads had to be adaptable to the environment (weather, season, pastures, water), so they have a flexible mind-set today. The yurt was literally open to the sky at the top, enabling the nomads' constant connection to their surroundings. The claim is that a herder's environmental responsiveness cultivated a kind of mental elasticity. Some Central Asians have even taken this idea further to claim that former nomads are more open to new ideologies since the Soviet collapse, like democracy, capitalism, and Christianity. It is true that Kyrgyzstan and Kazakhstan, republics run by ex-nomads, have tended to exhibit more political diversity, democratic process (though problematically), free markets, and a relatively vibrant evangelical church scene, compared with the region's other republics. However, one must not accept at face value claims about national character or mentalities but, rather, examine the actual social and political processes leading to these trends.

On the other side, descendants of historically sedentary populations are often seen as cultured, refined, conservative, on the one hand, and inflexible, guarded, and devious, on the other. Both sides of these stereotypes assume a connection between current mentality and sedentary past. They are seen to be the inheritors of the refined Central Asian cultures of art, architecture, poetry, music, Islamic scholarship, and handicraft, and this is supposed to carry over to even their cuisine and table manners. At the same time, as the thinking goes, just as settled folk lived for generations in houses and neighborhoods whose layouts are inward-facing (the interior courtyard), they are suspicious of outsiders and change. Some Central Asians point out that the republics run by these historically sedentary peoples have the most authoritarian governments, the most state-managed economies, and the strongest adherence to Islam. Again, one must avoid simple appeals to an alleged "conservative mentality" but, instead, look to dynamic processes of decisions made within structures of power and ideology.

Perhaps you have noticed that I have not mentioned familiar names like Uzbek, Kazakh, Tajik, Turkmen, Kyrgyz, Uyghur, Tatar, and many others. Are not those ethnic labels the primary way people distinguish themselves? So why avoid them so far in this discussion about social distinctions? This was a deliberate move, and one that few others take. I believe starting with the nomadic-sedentary distinction allows us to understand diversity in Central Asia more accurately and deeply. Let me explain.

It is true that Central Asians and outside observers alike talk about the region's society in terms of ethnic groups. When they describe a particular town, for example, one of the first things they mention is something like: "the people there are mostly Kazakhs, but with some Uyghurs and Russians living there too." Certainly, in cases where violent conflict has occurred, people focus on the problems between, for example, Uzbeks and Kyrgyz in the troubled city of Osh. Both outsiders and locals consider ethnicity as fundamental to social life. They tend to assume that the peoples of Central Asia naturally fall into ethnic categories, and those categories are the primary consequential factor driving their lives. These assumptions are misleading.

The intent of the discussion above about nomads and town dwellers is to show that Central Asians were not always "naturally" divided into the ethnic groups that are taken for granted today. In fact, the way that Central Asians today understand what it means to be Tajik, or Karakalpak, or a Meskhetian Turk has been in existence for less than a hundred years. I am talking about the *idea* of ethnicity, not the people themselves. The indigenous populations of Central Asia, of course, have lived there for centuries. But the terms by which they understand themselves and others have changed dramatically because of Soviet rule. Let me take a step back for a moment.

Do not think of ethnicity as a natural attribute of being human. One is not Swedish or Chinese in the same sense as being red-haired or of blood type A. An ethnic group is not a biological category but a social one. A social idea is subject to consensus and change. Ethnicity is a socially defined idea about belonging. It is a concept that tells people with whom they should identify and whom they should exclude. The funny thing is that if you look in different parts of the world, and at different times, people use different kinds of criteria to judge who belongs with whom. Often the criteria concern physical appearance (and only what is observable on the outside, never things like ear wax type or genetic markers), or language, or religion, or traditions, or territory. Those criteria are grounded not in anything permanent in the human condition but, rather, in the particularities of a population's circumstances and history. Think about ethnicity as a particular package of ideas about belonging, and that package can vary from place to place and from time to time.

Ethnicity under the Soviet Union came to mean a specific package of concepts, so that it took on a meaning that differed from elsewhere outside of the former Soviet sphere. The Soviet ethnic package came from the ways in which the government conceptualized ethnic difference, formulated its policies surrounding it, and made it part of everyday life in the Soviet Union. It meant that each ethnic group had to have a shared history, language, territory, customs, and mentality. However, there was often no single group that neatly shared all of these characteristics, because the linguistic and cultural varieties had no standard forms and varied across the land in complicated, overlapping ways. Moreover, the people throughout Central Asian history did not see themselves as constituting ethnic groups in this sense but, rather, distinguished between themselves in other ways. The Soviet government essentially made Central Asians fit into the ethnic categories that they determined were there, in part by promoting the development of ethnic cultures through state institutions of culture, education, and media. Each group came to understand themselves and each other through the Uzbek film industry, or Tajik music schools, or academies of Kazakh literature, or Turkmen newspapers, or textbooks that taught all Soviet citizens *the* Ukrainian traditional dress, *the* national food of Lithuania, *the* Kyrgyz epic poem. After seven decades of living under Soviet definitions of ethnicity, Central Asians have thoroughly internalized these understandings of themselves. With the Soviet collapse in 1991, the independent Central Asian states have promoted and further elaborated conceptions of ethnic distinction as a means to legitimate their power. And today, outsiders and natives alike take for granted these ethnic categories in making sense of the politics and culture of the region.

Ethnicity very much matters today in Central Asia. But it is important to realize that it represents not an eternal distinction between people but instead a specific package of understandings about belonging that is rather recent, not much more than one hundred years old. Keeping that in mind will allow us to evaluate claims of "ethnic identity," land, or heritage more objectively.

Reconnecting to the earlier discussion, the descendants of nomads became the Kazakhs, Kyrgyz, Turkmen, and others. Descendants of historic sedentary populations became the Uzbeks, Tajiks, Uyghurs, and others. The story is more complicated, of course—Uzbeks, for example, have a hybrid history, and distinctions between speakers of Turkic and Persian languages were complex across the centuries—but this is the broad outline. The ethnic labels of today did exist before, but they were not understood according to the modern package of concepts. A man in the nineteenth century might have assented to the designation "Kazakh," but his family name and tribal affiliation would have been more important to him, and "Kazakh" would not have been the overarching primary way he located himself in the world, the way his descendants do today. He certainly did not think of being Kazakh as meaning he participated in definite, standard forms of dress, food, art, history, language, customs, and so on. Likewise, a town dweller identified herself primarily according to her city and neighborhood—not as, say, "Tajik." And so, ethnicity in Central Asia was based on old distinctions that were recast and packaged into standardized content under Soviet rule.

There are other ways in which Central Asian localities are diverse. One important distinguishing factor today is knowledge of the Russian language. Everyone had to learn Russian during the Soviet period (though actual Central Asian competencies varied then). Since independence, Russian skills have generally declined, and more Central Asians are speaking their native languages. There are still some Central Asians in major cities who primarily speak Russian, and there is demand to know Russian among the many Central Asian labor migrants in Russia. The so-called Russian-speaking populations—Russians, Ukrainians, Koreans, and Germans—remain mostly in the cities. The latter two groups have dwelt in Central Asia since the Second World War, when Stalin, fearing possible loyalties to enemy states, deported ethnic Germans from the western Soviet Union and Koreans from the east. There are also some Chinese Muslims, called Dungans, living in Central Asian cities and a few villages who also speak Russian in their daily lives. Their families came from western China over a hundred years ago. Sometimes Dungans are frustrated today, when Kazakhs or Kyrgyz speak to them in their Central Asian languages (Dungans resemble the former nomads in facial features), and they can only reply in Russian. Koreans can also face the same social disapproval.

One reason that knowledge of Russian is declining among the Central Asians is that more of them are learning English or Chinese, or other so-called world languages such as German, Japanese, and Arabic. Some of the educated young generation are seeking connection with the wider world for education and jobs outside the region. Wealthier families travel widely and have cosmopolitan worldviews. Social and economic class, indeed, is another aspect of diversity increasingly found in Central Asian local places. In some ways, the powerful and monied classes that emerged since independence have interests that cross-cut ethnicity. For them, being Kazakh or Uzbek is not as important as being prosperous and mobile. Other ways in which Central Asians distinguish among themselves—such as rural-urban, religious-secular, or "authoritarian-democratic"—are taken up elsewhere in this volume.

In Central Asia, the term "local" means not homogenous but widely diverse. Our discussion, in particular, presented an unconventional account of ethnicity that cautions against regarding ethnic labels as natural and eternal distinctions, even though most in the region see themselves in those terms. This lesson on Central Asian ethnicity, coming from a focus on the local, has broad implications. If one's ethnic identification is a product of history and circumstance, then ethnic sentiments could change in the right circumstances toward more inclusive ways of belonging. Such a shift could work toward addressing the unproductive recent history of interethnic conflict and nationalist ideologies that marginalize minorities. Moving the notions of belonging away from culturally defined heritage and toward civically defined citizenship, for example, is a difficult task. Still, Central Asia's long history of diverse coexistence presents optimism for its future.

Does Local Mean Exotic?

Central Asia has long seen a convergence of different influences that produce a rich layering of cultures. Outsiders who enjoy the many fine documentaries on the region, from travel shows to food programs to Silk Road histories, may be tempted to regard Central Asia as an exotic landscape. My hope, however, is that any public fascination about the region would serve as an invitation to venture beyond a touristic view toward a closer knowing of its people. Scholars avoid treating any place as exotic. It is a matter of treating locals as full human beings. When we regard a group as exotic, we are in some sense denying that they are fundamentally people like us. Sometimes it means we regard them according to flat stereotypes rather than as complicated persons who think for themselves in negotiating the multiple influences in their lives. Sometimes it means we see them effectively as robots, whose thoughts and actions are determined by strict customs or religion. Central Asians, however, have needs, aspirations, and ideals like anyone else. They have the capacity for choice and innovation, even as they are shaped by their culture and society, like anyone else. As best we can, we want to observe, understand, and appreciate their local lives without effectively putting them on exhibit. Our task is to recognize both their cultural distinctiveness and their basic humanity at the same time. If we try to do that, what can we learn?

A striking feature of Central Asian life is the character of the face-to-face communities. Honestly, this is what I enjoy the most about spending time in the region. When I talk to people there, I often get questions about what life is like in America. How much does a teacher make? How much is a loaf of bread or a car? Do I live in my own house? How high is the tallest building in the United States? They see a lot of American life, or a representation of it, in the Hollywood movies that air on local television. They aspire to material living standards that they witness in Western countries. But I tell them, in all sincerity, that they possess a treasure that Western societies tend to lack: the quality of their local community. There is a closeness, a commitment, and a supportiveness in their daily collective life that one does not generally find in Western contexts, especially in the cities (with exceptions in certain immigrant districts). The strongest bonds of solidarity are found in Central Asia's rural villages and some urban neighborhoods.

There is a certain kind of neighborhood called a *mahalla*. A mahalla is a residential quarter of usually narrow streets and sometimes hand-made one-story houses with internal courtyards (see figure 2-1). Central Asian town dwellers have lived in mahallas for centuries, and today many of their descendants (Uzbeks, Tajiks, Uyghurs, and other modern ethnic groups) are found there. These people generally say they prefer living in this kind of neighborhood than in the urban districts of multistory apartment buildings found in every Central Asian city and first built by Soviet town planning. The reason? A house in a mahalla offers more space and more flexible use of space than in a modern apartment. You can comfortably accommodate a multigenerational family in one of them. In the interior courtyard of each house (the house rooms surround the courtyard in the middle), a family can plant crops, raise animals, fix cars, prepare meals, eat together, take care of children, do homework, entertain guests, and even host weddings. There is another reason mahallas are preferred: there is close communal intimacy compared with the more alienating apartment life.

Living in a mahalla neighborhood means being both known and informally monitored. These are places where to a large extent everyone knows what everyone else is doing. Part of my own work has shown that the reason social life is so close in mahalla neighborhoods is because of their material qualities and spatial organization. The layouts of streets and houses have visual and even sound characteristics that promote a sense of intimacy and mutual involvement. Away from the grand boulevards of Soviet institutions and squares, the local streets do not feel "public" at all, because so much daily work and social activity of the neighborhood spill out from the houses and take place there. In the warmer months of the year, the neighborhood is alive with activity. After school the kids play freely until dark. Groups of old men sit on street corners for hours, chatting and greeting passers-by. Young men gather in their own spots. Young women appear for moments outside their homes, carrying buckets of water from the street faucets. Most houses do not have indoor plumbing, and some have narrow canals running through their courtyards, where women do their laundry and wash the dishes when there is seasonal water flow from the mountains. There are few flush toilets, incidentally, but latrines that are essentially deep holes in the ground in a shed or separate room on the courtyard.

2-1   Courtyard of a house in an Uzbek-majority mahalla, Osh, Kyrgyzstan, 2011. Photograph by Morgan Y. Liu.

Street life is what makes any neighborhood vibrant. The urban activist Jane Jacobs famously observed that successful, desirable city neighborhoods anywhere are where people see each other constantly and interact regularly. Because many mahalla residents spend much of their time working and socializing on local streets, they remain involved in each other's lives. It is hard to keep a secret in a mahalla. Everyone knows about who just got married, had a baby, graduated, got a job, left for Russia to work, got divorced, or died. I spent much time exploring many mahallas in the city of Osh, Kyrgyzstan. An outsider like me walking down a street is quickly noticed. After getting to know one or two residents, I would later return to the neighborhood and meet people for the first time who already knew everything about me. Once I went to visit one man, and the kids playing outside told me he was not home. So, I went to visit someone else nearby, and when I came out again, the kids told me the first man was now home and waiting for me. Word travels fast in this kind of face-to-face communities.

Mutual knowledge goes with mutual help. Neighbors are expected to provide assistance to each other at any time, whether borrowing things or putting in labor to help fix a roof or build a latrine. In this sense, living in a mahalla means one is always involved in a "thick" community of strong and extensive ties. This aspect makes mahalla life appealing to its residents. But tight community has its detrimental aspects too. There is little privacy and lots of gossip. Mutual knowledge can become oppressive monitoring and policing of social expectations. Mutual involvement can become interference and conflict. There is no "freedom of conscience" or "freedom of assembly" in the mahalla. One cannot just decide to go against group norms or lead an alternative lifestyle without great communal shaming and opprobrium, whether to remain a single woman, have an affair, get divorced, live as a handicapped person, practice as a sexual minority, or convert to Christianity. Those who do not fit in usually move out to the more anonymous apartment block complexes, to the capital, or abroad. A mahalla can be both nurturing and cruel. For better and for worse, this kind of community forms one of the distinctive features of Central Asian local places.

The close and durable nature of community was also evident when I spent time hanging out at regular social gatherings in mahallas during the 1990s and 2000s. These gatherings have a different flavor and organization than Western parties. Called across the region by various names like *gap* (talk), *ziyofat* (feast), or *olturash* (sitting), they involve groups of people who, as the names imply, sit around eating and chatting (see figure 2-2). But the gatherings involve a definite stable membership of from ten to sixteen people of the same gender and age. They meet every week, biweekly, or monthly, and each time they rotate houses where it takes place, so that every member gets to host in turn. Hosts seem to spare no expense for the food, which the young women of the host household spend at least the entire day preparing. The guests sit on floor cushions around low tables laden with round flat breads (called *nan*), fruits, jams, raisins, nuts, candies, dry yogurt balls, soda, and tea. Courses of cooked food come in waves: soups, a rice and lamb dish called *ash* or *plov* (related to the word *pilaf*), and other meat dishes. All this fare is also served for weddings.

Food is another reason I love Central Asia. I tell my Central Asian friends that their fresh fruits beat my American supermarket produce hands down. When they are in season, fruits—mostly locally grown—are naturally ripe and full of flavor, especially the apricots, pears, pomegranates, and the persimmons that melt in your mouth. Of course, the peak season for each fruit is relatively short, which is why each household needs to preserve its own fruits and vegetables by canning to get through the entire year. Unlike on a modern Western table, where jams and pickles merely add variety, here they are a matter of survival throughout the year.

I did not mention alcohol, so important for entertaining in many other parts of the world. Central Asian Muslims know they are required to abstain from it completely. Still, many do drink, some to the point of alcoholism, especially people in the older generation who were raised in the Soviet Union. The practice of drinking is blamed on the Russians, who brought vodka into the region as the obligatory social lubricant. After the independence of the Central Asian countries, there has been an Islamic "revival" where more and more Central Asians have become observant and knowledgeable in their faith. One clear marker of piety is avoiding alcohol, and so regular social gatherings and weddings have increasingly become Islamic in this way, a trend that picked up in the 2000s. Wedding speeches of congratulations and well-wishing are still performed as per Soviet custom, but toasts are not.

The regular gatherings in mahallas allow the building of close, durable relationships to a degree that goes beyond many other human communities

2-2   Food and talk around the *dastorkon*, the floor cloth to set a meal, among Kyrgyz colleagues. Jalalabad,
       Kyrgyzstan, 2011. Photograph by Morgan Y. Liu.

in the modern world. The depth of their friendship hit home when I was
attending a weekly elder men's group. One time, they were celebrating the
sixtieth birthday of a member. Just watching them bantering, I heard all sorts
of inside jokes and references to some stupid thing someone did years back,
which the group will never let him forget. I then realized that these men grew
up together in that neighborhood and have been meeting together regularly in
this manner for decades. Being intimately, regularly, and persistently involved
with the same fifteen or so guys for sixty years—in an age of mobility and
change, not too many people today can claim to have friends like that.

     This kind of situation may not continue in the same way. One import-
ant change to Central Asian neighborhood life comes from a dominant
population trend since the mid-2000s in the poorer republics of Tajikistan,
Kyrgyzstan, and Uzbekistan. Many able-bodied men and women from
there have been working abroad in Russia and other wealthier countries
for economic reasons, although this trend has gone down with the fall of oil
prices and economic sanctions against Russia after 2014 and the COVID-19
pandemic crisis of 2020. Still, city streets became noticeably emptier than
before the labor migration surge, which affects the activity and cohesion of
neighborhoods. Just about every household has at least a few members away
for months at a time, working and sending money home, and many social
gatherings described above have stopped meeting. There is more anonymity
in the large cities of the region and in multistory apartment complexes than
the intimate connections described above. People tend not to know each

other well at all in the ever-growing new districts of cities like Tashkent in Uzbekistan, Almaty and Nur-Sultan in Kazakhstan, Bishkek in Kyrgyzstan, and Dushanbe in Tajikistan. Still, the neighborhoods described here continue to characterize much of urban life in the region, even as change is afoot.

In Central Asia, "local" means not so much exotic as distinctive in character, including in its face-to-face communities. A high degree of mutual interdependence and obligation characterizes social life there, and this quality has broad potential. Economic changes in recent decades have generally meant that a few rich are getting richer and the many poor are getting poorer. The thick social matrix, with everyone being closely involved with each other's lives, serves to keep communities together when growing inequalities are pulling them apart. Central Asian societies are not exotic curiosities but resources to enable resilience to change.

Does Local Mean Traditional?

Local places outside of major cities in Central Asia may appear largely untouched by the modern world. It is true that cars, buses, tractors, paved streets, buildings, and cell phones are now everywhere, but one may be tempted to regard these elements as only a thin layer over a deeply traditional society in values and outlook. There are the traditional-looking clothes—some older men in robes, some women in colorful silk dresses, other women covered in modest Islamic garb. Many men wear distinctive ethnic hats, such as the four-cornered *dopi* or tall white *kalpak*, or the religious ones don the white Islamic skullcaps. People are hauling bales of cotton on foot, or carrying vegetables on horse-drawn carts, or driving sheep through the streets. The old houses in the neighborhoods with dirt winding streets like the mahallas exude the patina of age, with their hand-made mud walls and improvised look. The bazaars are full of activity all day, with sellers sitting with their wares in rows on the ground or in stalls. These outdoor markets are arranged by section: vegetables and fruit, dried fruits and nuts, eggs, meat, milk, bread, household items, metal tools, electronics, carpets, books, money changing, and so on. There are stores within buildings, but much of the buying and selling in many cities happens at the bazaars. Central Asian bazaars and horse-drawn carts may give an outsider the impression that the local places are primarily ruled by tradition.

But are they? This question goes to the heart of a debate about what Soviet rule actually accomplished in Central Asian societies. Did the experience of being under the Soviet government for seven decades change Central Asians only superficially or did it transform them deeply? If you believe the first view, then you see all the modern trappings as simply a veneer on top of a basically conservative and tradition-bound people. Most Soviet officials took this view—they were frustrated that, despite their best efforts to educate and modernize their Central Asian subjects, the locals still stubbornly kept their social habits such as living with the values of face-to-face communities, or patriarchy, or Islam. If you take the second view, then you focus on the fundamental ways in which life changed under the Soviets, including how Central Asians now think about the world and see themselves. I lean more toward the second view of profound transformation. Even with their observance of tradition, Central Asians are a thoroughly modern people, more modern than many of them realize about themselves. Let me explain.

There is no denying that many Central Asians today take their ethnic and religious traditions seriously, and that their social life reveals enduring patterns such as the character of face-to-face communities described above. True, they use things with old histories (types of dress, tools, decoration, food, etc.) and follow practices with long precedents (weddings, festivals, arts, religion, social relations, etc.). But being "traditional" involves more than what you wear, sing, or do. It also involves how you think, how you look at the world. One key observation of anthropologists working across the world is that modern ways of thinking and understanding infuse every person on this planet today. The fancy word for this is "epistemology," which concerns the mental categories and reasoning patterns by which humans comprehend the world. Most observed "traditions" have been shown to be modifications and reinterpretations of historical practices that, it must be added, were always changing in the past as well. Few traditions are performed today exactly as they used to be. More important, those traditions mean different things today than before. Even when people appear to behave traditionally, they do so in a modern way.

Consider Islam. Since independence in 1991, there has been a veritable surge of Islamic observance among many Central Asians, after public Islamic practice and knowledge had been largely suppressed under Soviet rule. Most Central Asian Muslims knew little about their faith when the Soviet Union collapsed, and great interest in Islam hit the Central Asian republics with their independence. Large numbers of people started to observe the requirements of their faith publicly, such as praying five times a day, attending mosque, fasting during the month of Ramadan, abstaining from alcohol and pork, learning Arabic, and going on the pilgrimage to Mecca. Hundreds of mosques were built, Islamic literature proliferated in the bazaars, mullahs preached on television, religious study groups formed in neighborhoods, women increasingly dressed modestly with head coverings, men grew out their beards, seminaries opened to train clerics, missionaries from Islamic countries came to educate their fellow Muslims, and quite a few Central Asians left for those countries (especially Turkey, Saudi Arabia, Egypt, Pakistan, and Malaysia) to study Islam.

Central Asians and outside observers alike have called this an "Islamic revival," seeing this activity as evidence that a once suppressed Islam has returned. However, that characterization is oversimplified and misleading. First, there is no single version of Islam in Central Asia that can be reinstated. Islamic practices and understandings varied across Central Asia before the Soviets came, particularly between nomads and town folk. Second, some

Islamic beliefs and practices today in Central Asia are new to the region. They reflect interpretations from other Muslim countries and global Islamist movements whose missionaries and religious education are influencing the post-Soviet generation of Central Asians. Some of those interpretations explicitly reject age-old local practices that many Central Asians consider integral to their Islamic heritage, but others absolutely forbid certain practices, such as visiting saint shrines and holy places. There is ongoing dispute among sincere Central Asian Muslims about what true Islam entails, just as there is among Muslims worldwide. The kinds of Islam being taught from other countries are modern interpretations of the faith, because Muslims have reframed Islam as they study it through the lenses of modern education and mass media. Islam means different things to Muslims today than it did before the twentieth century.

Islamic activity today in Central Asia also differs from former times because the entire context of society is different. Before the Soviet era, Islamic institutions pervaded everyday life. Islamic frameworks informed or determined how education, law, commerce, and government ran, what schoolboys studied, how marriage was contracted, how business deals were sealed, how property was inherited, how murder was punished, how charities dispersed funds, and so on. Instead, religion pervaded life and did not sit as a separate domain of life. Soviet rule did away with this entire institutional matrix and replaced it with its own. Soviet laws now governed marriage, inheritance, and criminality. Soviet institutions—schools, ministries, bureaucracies—now oversaw Central Asian education, health, economy, and culture. The very meaning of religion changed. Religion ceased to relate broadly to life but became a narrow cultural domain, although such a view was resisted by those with Islamic education both during and after the Soviet era. Many Central Asians came to see Islam as one part of their cultural heritage rather than as an active institution organizing life.

Central Asian Islam thus changed, because the way it fits into society has been utterly altered, even with the so-called Islamic revival. Although some Muslim activists want to undo the Soviet legacy and Islamicize society's institutions and public behavior more comprehensively, their efforts reflect modern visions of the original Islamic community. Islam represents a notable example of the region's traditional "revivals," but parallel arguments could be made in other domains of Central Asian life after the Soviet Union. Those "restored traditions" include innovations as much as faithful adherence to how Central Asian life was organized in an earlier time.

In Central Asia today, "local" does not mean "traditional," in the sense of merely restoring or following the past. Rather, "local" means proud traditions perceived to be ancient but interpreted through modern needs and conditions. The broader lesson here is that Central Asian societies can draw both strength and wisdom from religious piety and cultural heritage, while adapting to novel circumstances in the world.

Lessons from the Local

What did we learn from focusing on local places? By looking at the "ground level" of Central Asian societies, we glimpsed some of the distinctive features of people's actual lives, dispelling flat stereotypes about the region. We find that Central Asia is connected to the world in surprising ways and is ethnically diverse, distinct in community life, and "traditional" in a modern way. There are also lessons that the local scale can offer for the region's larger-scale issues. We can ponder the advantageous terms of Central Asia's participation in the global economy today, in light of its long history of global connection. We can imagine alternative understandings of belonging based on inclusive civic citizenship rather than on exclusive cultural features, in light of the contingent and recent nature of Central Asian ethnicity. We can contemplate the resilience of Central Asians to disruptive change in light of the close mutual interdependence of its face-to-face communities. We can think about the cohesion of the region's societies amid divisive disputes, in light of Central Asians working out traditional practices and religious piety under modern circumstances. What have we learned from going local? We can know the places and the people as both distinct yet familiar.

3

Central Asia as Place

Alexander C. Diener and Nick Megoran

What do we mean by "Central Asia"?
In the final months of the Soviet Union, a friend of ours from the region who was working in the Soviet diplomatic services visited the United States for the first time. His abiding memory of that trip was a map. Not an unusual map, but a standard world map as frequently displayed on the walls of schools, homes, and offices in the United States. "I always thought Tashkent was closer to Moscow, but on this map, I could see it was closer to Delhi!" he remarked, unsettled at the startling vision presented to him in this familiar-yet-alien document. What he meant was that the maps he was used to seeing emphasized, through a variety of cartographic conventions, the identification of Central Asia with Russia and the rest of the USSR—even though Tashkent is some seven hundred miles closer to the Indian capital than the Russian one.

Our friend's puzzlement forms the basic questions of this chapter: Where exactly *is* Central Asia in the world? What do we mean by invoking the regional designation "Central Asia"? This regional toponym and its alternatives embody very different political and historical visions. We thus consider "Central Asia" not as a self-evident natural region but as a "geographical imaginary." We define geographical imaginaries as spatial orderings of the world, which may frequently be taken for granted.

Our friend's sense of cartographic vertigo is understandable. How is Central Asia to be imagined? As "post-Soviet" or as part of the "Greater Middle East"? "Inner Asian" or "Eurasian"? "Middle Asia" or "Central Eurasian"? Does it encompass "the Caucasus," Eastern Turkestan (Xinjiang), Afghanistan, and Mongolia? Central Asia achieved independence as the moniker "Third World" was going out of fashion, but it has somehow never made it into the geographically problematic label of the "Global South." So, in many ways, it defies simple classification, falling at the edges of atlas pages and (at least until the 2000s) regional studies conferences alike.

It would be a mistake to conclude that Central Asia is difficult to label because of its geography. Large regions that dominate current global maps are not permanent geographical facts but problematic categories for the study of varied geographic and cultural processes. It is not that Central Asia is a problem because we cannot easily identify which region it is in; rather, it is that Central Asia provides an exemplary study of why the very concept of regions itself is problematic.

But we would go further. Geography argues not merely that our geographical imaginaries reveal our assumptions about the world but that they inform political choices, including external relationships and types of intervention. How we think about the world has material consequences. As the very premise of this book demonstrates we probably cannot avoid using geographical imaginaries, we cannot afford to use them uncritically.

We have structured this chapter around six imaginaries of the place about which this book is written: continental, trade route, subjugator, imperial, class, and geostrategic. For each one of these we sketch out the *nature* and *implications* of seeing Central Asia in that particular way.

Continental Imaginary

Is Central Asia *Asian*? And if so, what sort of "Asian" is it?

Those might sound like redundant questions for a book on Central Asia, but the "Asianness" of Central Asia is far from clear. Referred to as Transoxiana by the Greeks and as Maverannahr by the Persians/Arabs, the area under consideration in this book was thus defined in terms of fluvial plains, of physical geography. The term "Inner Asia" emphasizes its connectedness with and similarity to China and Tibet. "Eurasia" stresses the region's commonalities with Russia and post-socialist states in Europe. This concept found its most advanced formulation in the Russian doctrine of "Eurasianism," linking our region to Russia and Siberia as heir of a unique civilizational destiny that is neither properly Asian nor European. In contrast, "Central Eurasia" divests the region of most of Eurasia's European space, adding Afghanistan and Iran. The "Greater Middle East" goes further, cleaving the region from Russia and viewing it as part of a cultural entity that encompasses the Middle East, North Africa, and part of South Asia. Each geographical imaginary has academic and political premises and implications. Clearly, the "Asianness" of Central Asia is contested—it means different things to different people.

As its moniker implies, Central Asia occupies a unique position between the currently prominent geographic imaginaries of Europe, South Asia, Southwest Asia, and East Asia. The Ural Mountains are often cited as the geographic boundary between the broadly defined concepts of Europe and

Asia, but such a demarcation can be regarded as rather arbitrary from both physical and human geographical perspectives. First, from a physical and biogeographical view, similar regimes of both flora and fauna can be found on both sides of the Urals. There is no such faunal dividing line as exists between Southeast Asia and Australia (the Wallace Line). Also, landforms are similar and climate type remains generally consistent in a latitudinal vector. Second, from a human geographic perspective similar linguistic and religious groups can be found on both sides of the Urals. Islam, Eastern Orthodox Christianity, Buddhism, and various indigenous faiths span the Urals. Languages of the Turkic, Altaic, and Slavic families are also found throughout the region. Historical political geographies such as the Abbasid Caliphate, the Turkic khanate, various Persian empires, and the Mongol empire gave no credence to a regional distinction marked by the Urals. Even today, the political boundaries of Russia extend from Central Europe (Kaliningrad) to Lavrentiya on the Bering Sea and thereby engulf the continental divide within one state. This brief consideration of the geographic region currently known as Central Asia would suggest that it has for millennia constituted a place of meeting and exchange between varieties of people.

The limitations involved in regarding Central Asia as "Asian" are demonstrated by the existence of Eurasianism, a fusion of political thought and philosophy that emerged among early twentieth-century Russian thinkers and has enjoyed a revival in Russia and Kazakhstan since 1991. The nineteenth-century geopolitical and sociocultural orientation of Russia was a hot topic among tsarist elites. One camp included the Westernizers (*Zapadniki*), who advocated Russia's mimicking western Europe's embrace of technology and liberal government. Another camp included the Slavophiles and their interpretation of contiguity to Asia as affording Russia a unique role among world powers. This group contended that the tsarist regime had cultivated a more viable perspective on governance and national ideology than that of the West. At its core, this ideal held that Russia was neither European nor Asian. Positing the empire to be a unique cultural-geographic entity unto itself, the works of Pan Slavic scholars such as N.Ia. Danilevskii and V.I Lamanskii defined Russian territory as extending naturally into Siberia but not into the Far East or Central Asia. This argument was based on cultural and physiographic evidence that sought the unity of all Slavic peoples. Central Asia and the Russian Far East were considered colonial possessions akin to those of other European powers of the time.

Seeking to pave a new way for humankind, the Pan-Slavs and later Eurasianists viewed the territories brought into the Russian empire as a fertile field for cultivating a society that would deviate from the political and cultural trajectories of Europe. Due to space constraints, in this chapter we can offer only a basic characterization of the multifaceted and at times contradictory geo-philosophies and political movements within the broad category of "Eurasianism." It is, nevertheless, fair to suggest that the Eurasianist movement is of particular significance to contemporary conceptions

ALEXANDER C. DIENER AND NICK MEGORAN

of Central Asia as a geographic imaginary, in that neo-Eurasianist discourses appear to be influencing Moscow's foreign policy, and varied forms of Eurasianism have emerged in different Central Asian states.

Advancing what might be called a geo-philosophy (or geosophy), classical Eurasianists regarded western European and Asian culture and civilizational ideals to be problematic. They rejected the bifurcation of Russia into European and Asian parts. Instead, "Eurasia" or "Russia-Eurasia" became the new geographic referent and was supported with physiographic, biogeographic, and historical-ethnographic data. The Eurasianist approach was more geographically expansive than the Pan Slavic imaginary and included both Russia and Central Asia in the cultural sphere influenced by Genghis Khan. The product of the classical Eurasianist discourse was a reimagined Russia that to greater and lesser degrees integrated and celebrated its geo-historical, geopolitical, geo-cultural, geo-ethnographical, and even geo-economic expanse. In the post-Soviet period, Kazakhstan obscures more than it reveals of (neo)Eurasianist ideas, a vision that has found political incarnation in the Eurasian Economic Union, set up by Russia and Kazakhstan in 2014 as an alternative to the European Union. The meaning of "Asia" here has specific philosophical and historical coordinates, and it frames a very particular type of political formation.

Labeling our region as Central *Asia* raises a series of questions about what its "Asianness" means. The continental geographical imaginary of Central Asia as "Asian" is clearly problematic. This arises not because "Central Asia" occupies an anomalous position but because "Asia" itself is not a stable category. As Martin Lewis and Karen Wigen argue in their germinal text *The Myth of Continents*, the division of the world into seven "continents" is far from natural or obvious. It is, they argue, a "metageography" that "obscures more than it reveals." However, as the next example shows, not all geographical imaginaries of our region have been "Asian."

The Trade Route Imaginary

As of October 2021, a Google search for the term "Silk Road" provides over four hundred million hits. These relate to all things Central Asian, from tourist packages to intercontinental infrastructural building programs. They also include references to less desirable goods, from a US mail–based drugs smuggling network to a plethora of travelogues purporting to discover this apparently "lost" region. For good or ill, Central Asia has become popularly identified as a place of intercontinental caravan trade: "the Silk Road." But this popular geographical imaginary is a relatively new one, coined only in the nineteenth century by the German geographer Ferdinand von Richtofen. How useful is it?

With the powerful civilizational centers at Central Asia's eastern and western margins becoming increasingly mutually aware of one another over the course of time, the region between them was imagined more as space than

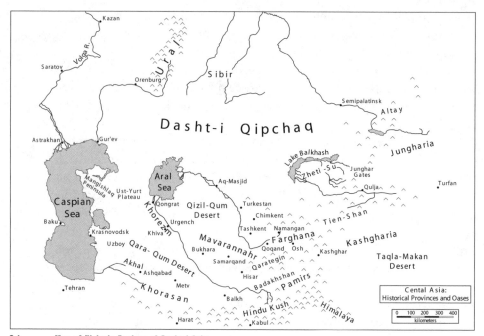

3-1   Map of Historic Regions of Central Asia.

place by the recorders of history. For Europeans and Chinese, Central Asia was somewhere to go through to get to the places beyond; it was the setting for the "Silk Road." Too often lost or subjugated in this metaphorical geographic reference were the people and places through which the Silk Road was routed.

The Silk Road cannot simply be treated as a network of transportation routes. It was a concept of interaction that illustrates the ways in which commodities, identity groups, religions, and even music and art traveled throughout Eurasia for thousands of years. The Silk Road was a connecting concept over the "West" and "East" divide, providing an ongoing exchange of human experience in which the indigenous peoples of Central Asia played a central role. The city-states, steppe regions, river valleys, and mountain passes through which caravans, armies, raiding parties, musicians, artists, explorers, and missionaries traveled were the homes to a great many groups that made an array of contributions to world history (see figure 3-1). The caravans whose movement they either facilitated or impeded carried both the good (e.g., poetry, carpets, spherical geometry, quadratic equations, astronomy, geology, medicine, chemistry, music, social science, philosophy, and theology, etc.) and the bad (e.g., Bubonic plague, murderous raids, slavery, destruction of material culture, etc.) of their own making as well as that of Asia and Europe to and from the Mediterranean, Persian, Indian, and Chinese capitals and coasts.

Possession of natural resources and control of the transit routes between great coastal empires brought wealth and power to the Samanids, Safavids, Yuezhi-Kushans, Khorezamshahs, and other sedentary empires of Central Eurasia. This drew the ire of the Greeks, Chinese, and Romans, who

ALEXANDER C. DIENER AND NICK MEGORAN

each attempted to gain control of the transcontinental trade routes. These conflicts suggest the region came to constitute a place of contestation and competition wherein internal powers operated at times in opposition to and at other times in conjunction with external powers in pursuit of autonomy. This characterization remains applicable even today.

Rome's tentative claim on lands within the western reaches of Eurasia drew the attention of rising powers of the steppe. Starting in 350 CE, Hunic horsemen began testing the Roman empire's defenses and eventually, in conjunction with other peoples such as the Vandals and the Goths, toppled it in 476 CE. Some two hundred years later, Islam expanded into the Persian realm, setting the stage for a clash with China in Central Asia. In 751, combined forces of Arabs, Persians, and converted or allied Turkic peoples confronted China's army and its allied Turkic tribes at the Battle of Talas. A reversal of loyalty by the Karluk tribe tipped the victory toward the Arab/Persian forces, and China was forced to retreat across the Tien Shan Mountains. This geographic feature would thereafter constitute the westernmost boundary of China's empire. Although imperially demarcative, this "clash of civilizations" failed to stymie the linkages between peoples through Central Asia.

Although few people actually traveled the full extent of the trans-Eurasian routes, the interactions facilitated by the Silk Road profoundly impacted European, Chinese, Indian, and Persian history. These interactions also shaped the political, economic, and cultural trajectories of the varied peoples between. The single group most associated with this expanse of territory is the Mongols. But their effect on Central Asia's rising civilization may not be altogether fairly assessed in historical sources generally penned by the conquered. That the Mongols personified the very pastoral nomads against which most sedentary civilizations defined themselves also tended to vilify them in many historical writings. Herein, the rather subjective distinction between "civilized" and "barbaric" comes to the fore, as does the value of sedentary versus nomadic spatialities (i.e., agricultural, pastoral).

Having forged a mounted army from the disparate nomadic tribes of what is now the Mongolian Steppe at the start of the thirteenth century, Ghengis Khan came to establish the largest contiguous land empire in human history. Spanning most of the Eurasian landmass, the Mongol conquests redeposited vast numbers of Turkic peoples from China's northern frontiers into the very heart of Central Asia. One portion of this army ultimately laid claim to the vast territories of the Islamic Caliphate at the southern-center of Eurasia, while another branch of the Mongol legion established the Yuan Dynasty (1271) in China and put the Mongols on the doorstep of Southeast Asia. Yet another prong of the Mongols' westward advance known as the Golden Horde drove toward Europe, ultimately engulfing the divided principalities of the Kievan-Rus. With no polity or military in medieval Europe capable of meeting the full force of the Mongols, a clear turning point of history took form. In the end, a defeat at the hands of the Teutonic Knights, the death of the Great Khan (1227), and the subsequent contest of succession compelled the Mongols to withdraw from their most westward positions in eastern Europe in 1241. The largely Turkic (commonly referred to as Tatar) components of the army subsequently settled on the frontier of *Rus* territory and in Central Asia and established what came to be known as "the Mongol yoke." It is this political juncture between Asia's nomads and Europe that casts a pall over the relationship in general. It is worth noting that, at various times, emissaries of the Vatican were sent to recruit the Mongols to aid in conquest of the "Holy Land." The long-standing legend of a "lost" royal Christian dynasty in the East descended from an emperor and patriarch known as Prester John—along with Marco Polo's journeys of 1269–1293 and his subsequent book—reflects a more positive view of the Mongol Khans.

All of this is perhaps a far cry from the rather romantic popular ideas of the Silk Road. How useful is this imaginary? Although it may lack analytical depth, it is nonetheless useful as a geographical imaginary suggesting patterns of communications among communities in Eurasia.

The Subjugator Imaginary

Modern Western and Russian geographical imaginaries have often seen Central Asia as a site of imperial or colonial exploration, a pawn on what the former US presidential national security advisor Zbigniew Brzezinski termed "the grand chessboard." It is worth considering that, in contrast, an important strand of Russian historiography has seen the region as a subjugator. In particular, this has been the imaginary of the "Mongol Yoke."

Central Asia, as a geographic imaginary, is profoundly impacted by its association with the Mongols. Without question the Mongols altered certain patterns of extant power and cultural growth at the time of the conquest. But rather than ending trans-Eurasian trade, a "coin of the realm" ideal emerged during the Mongol era that both enabled a commonwealth to function and facilitated movement within the empire. Much of Russian history is nevertheless written in denigration of the Mongols as bloodthirsty barbarians and in celebration of Ivan III's (the Grand Duchy of Moscow) rallying of the *Rus* peoples in 1480 to reject their vassal status and assert sovereignty over the northern reaches of western Eurasia. A more positive light was not shone on the subject until classical Eurasianists recast the Mongol influence on Russia as positive in opposition to Westernizing elements of the nineteenth-century tsarist state.

Ivan IV's conquest of the Kazan Tatars nevertheless marked the outset of Russia's influence over Central Asia. While the Russian state claimed authority over the waning Tatar Khanates' lands, caravan trade continued along Central Asia's overland routes. Only nineteen years separated the rise of the modern Russia and Vasco de Gama's circumnavigation of the Cape of Good Hope (1497). Seeking to avoid the inflationary middlemen entrenched within overland transit between Europe and Asia, western Europeans invested in large oceangoing vessels with the capacity to transport goods

ALEXANDER C. DIENER AND NICK MEGORAN

directly from the "Far East" to the ports of Europe. Although not marking an absolute termination of various forms of overland trade between Europe and Asia, the establishment of a direct sea route set in motion a process by which the center of the Eurasian landmass diminished in economic and political significance.

The Western European powers' colonizing of the Western Hemisphere as well as African and Asian coastal territories expanded their wealth and established their presence in regions coveted by Russia. India proved particularly vexing for tsarist elites who longed for warm-water seaports and an opportunity to equalize their civilizational standing with their cousins to the west. This turned Russia's attention to the vast contiguous territory to its south and east and concomitantly created a tsarist Central Asian geographic imaginary.

Although Russian/Soviet sovereignty was withdrawn from the region in 1991, "Central Asia" remains within Russia's perceived sphere of influence. Put simply, the Kremlin regards the historical and cultural ties to work in conjunction with the legacy of Russian/Soviet investment in infrastructure and development to require Central Asian states' ascension to Russian leadership. This has not proved out in a variety of circumstances. Central Asia's independent states have embraced their sovereignty and established relationships with a variety of global powers. The tsarist and Soviet histories of sovereignty over the region, nonetheless, continue to shape international relations, economics, mobilities, language, and a variety of sociocultural processes.

The Imperial Imaginary

In 1894 Leo Tolstoy wrote *The Kingdom of God Is Within You*, based on a saying of Jesus from the Gospel of Luke. In it he set out a vision of Christian pacifism as an alternative to imperial violence. One of the most influential works in the history of the peace movement, this book later inspired Gandhi, the US civil rights movement, and countless others. The text pitted imperialism in direct opposition to the humanity of Christ's teachings. Tolstoy railed against Russian imperialism in Central Asia, conquered by Russian General Mikhail Skobelev. "Why do good men and even women," he lamented, "quite unconnected with military matters, go into raptures over the various exploits of Skobelev and other generals, and vie with one another in glorifying them?" In sharp contrast, in 1881 Fyodor Dostoevsky mused that the subjugation of Central Asia would allow the flowering of the Russian people: "In Europe, we were Asiatics, whereas in Asia we, too, are Europeans. Our civilizing mission in Asia will bribe our spirit and drive us thither." Both great novelists used the geographical imaginary of "Central Asia" to reflect on contemporary Russia, one to indict imperial violence, the other to incite it.

Russia, like other contemporary expanding colonial European states, possessed a variety of rationalizations for conquest. Some motives were moralistic, involving refrains of the "White Man's Burden" and evangelical dogmas of Christianity, whereas others were more pragmatic, such as

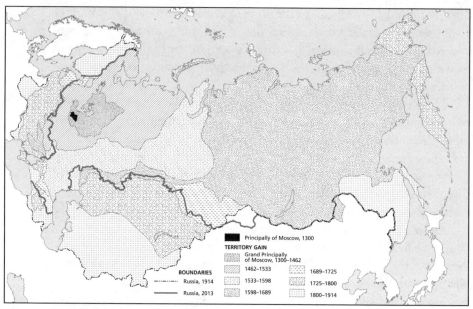

3-2   Map of Russian Empire.

the state's desire for warm-water ports and resources that drove the tsarist armies to conquer contiguous territories. Gathering the disparate *Rus* under the banner of Ivan III (the Great) and Ivan IV (the Terrible) and extending imperial territories under Peter I (the Great), Anna of Russia, Catherine II (the Great), Alexander I, Nicholas I, and Alexander II and III, the tsar came to rule an empire from the Pacific to the Arctic, Black, and Baltic Seas (figure 3-2).

Enacting a geographical imaginary of Central Asia as empty space awaiting the orderings of a civilized colonizer, Russia took it upon itself to map and rename the region. To this point in history the Eurasian landmass was cartographically portrayed not so differently than were unexplored oceans. European maps of Central Eurasia were often sparse in detail, with rumors of monsters and topographic wonders widespread. This reimagined expanse of territory consequentially became the subject of not only "scientific discovery" but also military conquest. Attaching meaning (scientific and political) to the region, measuring it, and assigning boundaries to it transformed it into a specific place (as opposed to a space of traversal as in the Silk Road imaginary) for not only Russia but also much of the world. This process was not, however, unilateral. Rather, a series of conflicting geographic imaginaries of the region were advanced within and outside the Russian state.

From a purely geostrategic perspective, however, the Russian advance into Central Asia was about acquiring lands for Russian settlers. This had the added benefit of securing the frontier from which many past invasions/raids had launched. Access to Indian and Iranian warm-water ports was hoped to ultimately enhance Russia's economic and geopolitical standing. The British Raj responded to Russian ambitions with a "forward policy" that stationed British forces across the Hindu Kush and Karakoram mountain ranges. The result was the late nineteenth and early twentieth centuries' "Great Game." Known to Russians as the Tournament of Shadows (*Turniry Teney*), this symbolizes Central Asia as a place of contestation.

This was perhaps most famously captured by the British geographer Halford Mackinder's depiction of the region as core to the "heartland" or "pivot of world history." If control of this region was crucial to the outcome of global power competition, then this demanded an aggressive British foreign policy to contain a potential German or Russian challenge to imperial hegemony. Mackinder devoted both his intellectual life and his career as a public servant to the cause of empire. This was an imaginary that was itself an incitement to imperial violence.

European aspirations and machinations for political and economic dominion over the center of the Eurasian landmass subsided with the signing of the Anglo-Russian Convention of 1907 and Afghanistan's establishment as a buffer between the Raj and Russia. The First World War saw an alliance between the tsar and the British Crown (1914–1917), but the rise of Communism and the chaos of the Russian Revolution revived the Great Game and turned our region into the focus of a new, class-based geographical imaginary.

The Class Imaginary

The Bolshevik takeover of Central Asia and its incorporation into the USSR produced a very different, class-based geographical imaginary. This was premised on a twofold move of both diagnosing the problem of "economic and cultural backwardness" in the region and proscribing the remedy of socialism as its cure. Central Asia thus became, for the Soviets, a place of experiment where the advance to socialism could progress straight from feudalism, leapfrogging the stage of capitalism as identified in classical Marxist theory.

These apparently abstract ideological ambitions were pursued through novel concrete political geographical structures. Between 1924 and 1927, the USSR implemented a policy of National Territorial Delimitation (NTD), reordering tsarist Central Asia into the Kazakh, Kyrgyz, Tajik, Turkmen, and Uzbek Autonomous Soviet Socialist Republics (ASSRs) and Soviet Socialist Republics (SSRs). New capital cities were designated, and boundaries were drawn; dialects were codified as languages for which new scripts were provided; and new histories of these republics were written, providing teleological justification for their existence. NTD paradoxically combined a nonnational federal superstructure (the USSR) composed of ethnically defined constituent republics (Uzbek, Kyrgyz, Georgian, and so on), which in turn often had substate ethnically defined autonomous regions nested within them.

The Soviet Union was bullish about its success, with officials claiming that "the national question" in Central Asia had been "solved." Not only that, but during the Cold War, Central Asia was held up as an example of socialist development for the Third World. Indeed, by the early 1980s

Central Asian republics were sending hundreds of development specialists around the world to assist pro-Soviet lower income countries.

Although Central Asia had undoubtedly been transformed by the Soviet Union, these changes were not as thorough as scholars and party elites claimed. Some Western scholars of Central Asia regarded the region more as "the failed transformation." This school of scholarship found in latent Turkic national pride a "firmest and surest refuge" against Soviet attempts to remake the region. Moreover, an "Islamic threat to the Soviet state" was regarded by some Western analysts as immanent. These bold claims proved overblown, the product of a vehemently anti-Soviet geographical imaginary. Nonetheless, even some Soviet scholars decried what they saw as the failure of the Soviet system to properly overcome class-based vestiges of feudal societies.

In the end, the challenge to the Soviet Union came not from Central Asia but from the European Soviet republics. By constituting Central Asia in national terms, the Soviet Union prepared the way for its own demise, as it fell apart into independent states precisely along the lines of the republics originally constituted to keep it together. In 1991, while parts of Central Asia remained under the control of great powers (such as Tatarstan under Russia or East Turkestan under China), the Central Asian republics became independent states. This birth of new countries on the borders of China and of Russia itself gave rise to the final geographical imaginary to consider: Central Asia as a site of geostrategic competition.

The Geostrategic Imaginary for a New Great Game in Landlockedstan?

In 2016 one of the authors of this chapter (Megoran) gave a seminar at a university in Washington, DC. In the talk he explored the detailed history of a single village on the Kyrgyzstan-Uzbekistan border, using ethnographic evidence to narrate stories of political change in the two republics and the role of outside actors in that change. At the end of the seminar, an analyst in the "D.C. policy community," asked, "Yes, but what can you tell me about the situation of Russia and China in Central Asia?" He meant, who was going to "win" a perceived struggle for political influence. The specificities of the village as a unique place and what that village says for our broader understanding of the region were of no interest to him whatsoever, as they could not be mapped onto his two-dimensional geographical imaginary of Central Asia as site of geostrategic competition.

This imaginary was not new. The Russian imperial imaginary saw Central Asia as a site of colonial self-realization, whereas Britain saw its relevance primarily as a way to protect the British south Asian empire. There are, however, two strikingly new dimensions of this geographical imaginary: the multiplicity of "players" and the perceived problem of "landlockedness."

First, because of the diversity of scenarios possible in this new Great Game, the post-1991 geostrategic imaginary of Central Asia is different from that of the Britain-versus-Russia imperial imaginary. Articles in the 1990s speculated about new and old players in this game, such as Russia, China, Turkey, Iran, Saudi Arabia, the United States, the European Union, and India, being augmented by competing ideological visions of democracy, authoritarianism, pan-Turkism, and radical Islam. More nuanced contributions to this literature stressed that this new Great Game was played by "local rules" but persisted in imagining Central Asia primarily as a "great power context."

In the 2000s, this imaginary was redrawn with reference to the so-called War on Terror. After 2001, a rather security-centric Washingtonian analysis of Central Asia emerged. This sees the region not only as a place of great power competition but also as a "key theatre in the war on terror" or part of a "non-integrating gap" that includes most of Africa, the Middle East, South America, and Pakistan/Afghanistan, but not Russia or Europe. For advocates of this perspective, globalization is threatened by Central Asia's disconnectedness from it. The late US defense secretary Donald Rumsfeld identified threats to US interests from a "broad arc of instability that stretches from the Middle East to Northeast Asia." In this geopolitical imagination, the region's significance derives from its being on the "front line" with Afghanistan—and even part of the same region.

This geographical imaginary has important policy implications. Following the establishment of US military bases in Kyrgyzstan and Uzbekistan in 2001 to facilitate the invasion of Afghanistan, the US State Department moved responsibility for Central Asia from the Department of European and Eurasian Affairs to a new South and Central Asia section. Similarly, the US Defense Department ascribed Central Asia to Central Command, whereas most of the rest of the former Soviet Union was ascribed to Europe Command. The geographical imagining of Central Asia with South Asia rather than Europe meant that US foreign aid became focused less on democratization and more on state-building and antiterrorism operations.

Second, the idea of landlockedness has proved remarkably significant in structuring geographical imaginaries of post-Soviet Central Asia. One of the authors of this chapter (Megoran) was formerly book review editor of the discipline's leading scholarly journal, *Central Asian Survey*. He was once sent for consideration an otherwise splendid volume entitled *Port Cities of Europe and Asia*. For a region that can reasonably be described as the most landlocked region in the world, he found this lack of attention to detail amusing at the time. But in their apparently willful disregard of the geography of our region, the publishers inadvertently posed an important question: does the landlockedness of Central Asia really matter?

After all, one might argue that the Pamir Mountains are no closer to the oceans than they were at the time of Timur, but this is to miss the point. The idea that lack of access to the sea is problematic is itself a product of a peculiarly modern globalized geographical imaginary. This imaginary has geostrategic significance in that external "players" in this new Great Game have fallen over themselves to offer Central Asian states

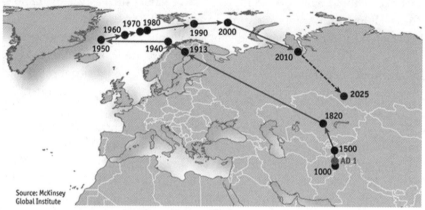

■ **Evolution of the earth's economic centre of gravity**
AD 1 to 2025

Source: McKinsey
Global Institute

3-3   Map of Shifting Global Economic Center of Gravity.

competing visions of connectivity to overcome the apparent disadvantage of landlockedness.

Consider the advent of new corridors of connection through transportation and communication infrastructure that constitute the core of "globalization." Many of these projects are premised on increasing "connectivity" across Afro-Eurasia. Different external actors' motives for funding these projects vary profoundly. China's Belt and Road Initiative posits a rather non-territorial mercantilist approach to Central Asia that seeks to avoid entanglements in security, governance, and development that are extraneous to Beijing's desire for capacity offloading and acquiring access to highly prized natural resources, as well as the secondary goal of bringing political influence to bear if needed. By contrast, Russia maintains a Cold War–like territorial sphere of influence imaginary of Central Asia in which Moscow retains both economic and cultural/political primacy. The West (US/EU) weighs in with its own geopolitical interests, which include enhancing autonomy among the Central Asian states, promoting development in Afghanistan (at least until August 2021), and compelling liberal governance alongside neoliberal economics. These forms of governance and economics are intended to bend to Western values by nevertheless avoiding Iran, curtailing drug trafficking, promoting democracy, and impeding the spread of Islamic radicalism. In combination, these great power imaginaries could portend Central Asia's reclaiming its role as place of connection. The degree to which these strategies are compatible with each other and with the state ideologies of the Central Asian states will determine if the region becomes a place of contestation. For some, the growing focus on connectivity across Central Asia heralds an eastward shift in the global economic center of gravity (see figure 3-3).

Facilitating overland linkages across Eurasia has compelled a variety of efforts to ameliorate and even recast the notion of "landlockeness." While ocean-going transit gained greater standing with the advent of modern container ships, canals (e.g., Suez, Panama), expanded ports, arctic routes, refrigeration, and maritime law enforcement, the end of the Cold War and the economic growth

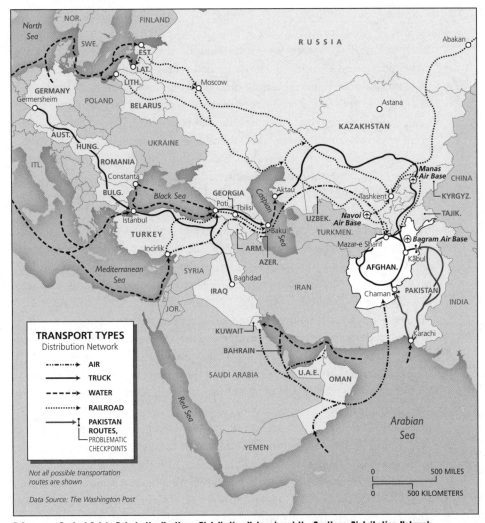

3-4   Central Asia's Role in the Northern Distribution Network and the Southern Distribution Network.

of China, India, and Russia (at least prior to the latter's recent sanction-driven downturn) presaged a possible rebooting of Eurasian overland trade. The hinge of new linkages is therefore the landlocked place of Central Asia.

In contrast to a detractive dependence on neighboring states for transit of goods and resources to and from global markets, Central Asian leaders have recently found themselves courted by great powers to become a key node in a neoliberal globalized network (see figure 3-4). The 2001 Millennium Development Goals and the 2003 Almaty Programme of Action integrate a wide range of actors (landlocked developing states, transit states, donors, private sector, international and regional organizations) emphasizing five priority areas relating to the removal of barriers between landlocked states and the sea. These include (1) fundamental transit policy issues, (2) infrastructure development and maintenance, (3) international trade and trade facilitation, (4) provision of development assistance and technical support from the international community, and (5) implementation and review. In the period since the Almaty Programme's launch, development levels of landlocked states have improved. Better roads, enhanced railways, larger ports, and cheaper fuel have opened vectors of transit that previously were unavailable, but establishing neoliberal regional institutions that would unencumber transit for landlocked states is far from a fait accompli. Moreover, the degree to which such developments can be achieved equitably and in an environmentally responsible manner remains a significant question.

In fact, envisioning Central Asia as a single, unified, unproblematically integrated, and politically coordinated place has proved to be one of the biggest challenges in policy making and analysis pertaining to the region. Efforts to foment and sustain effective regional organizations in Central Asia have proved limited in success. Russia's efforts to lead the region followed the ineffective Commonwealth of Independent States Customs Union (1996) and Central Asian Economic Cooperation Organization (1998) with the Eurasian Economic Community (2000). Free-riderism, rent seeking, and beggar-thy-neighbor policies of various member states limited the success of each of these efforts. Such failure inspired a rising presence of China and the West in Central Asia and ultimately catalyzed Russia's launch of a new "Customs Union" in 2010. Designed to create a common economic space between the states of Russia, Belarus, and Kazakhstan, the union afforded Ukraine observer status prior to the turmoil of 2014, integrated the Kyrgyz Republic in 2015, and has plans to pull in Tajikistan in the coming years. Renamed the Eurasian Economic Union (EAEU) in 2015, it is advertised as coordinating a system of common duties and customs procedures so as to enable the flow of trade, investment, and labor between member states. But the degree to which it can work alongside the Chinese-led Shanghai Cooperation Organization (SCO) and the expansion of WTO status among actors in the region (Kyrgyzstan, Russia, Tajikistan, Kazakhstan) remains an open question.

It is self-evident to many analysts that Central Asia should be seen as the site of a new Great Game in what we might call Landlockedstan. But the idea that this region is a key site of geopolitical contest is as much a contingent geographical imaginary as is the idea that it is landlocked. These are not merely "ideas." They influence policy decisions of the utmost importance, from multi-billion-dollar infrastructural spending projects over decades to the conduct of new forms of war.

Ideas with Legs

> The geography of the world is not a product of nature but a product of histories of struggle between competing authorities over the power to organize, occupy, and administer space.

> —GEARÓID Ó TUATHAIL

After Megoran presented some of the ideas in this chapter at Chatham House, the UK's leading independent foreign policy forum, the head of a major European government's aid department approached him "Thank you," she said. "We have been trying to decide which section to put Central Asia in, and your talk has helped me reach a decision." As each department of her ministry has different budgets and priorities, this will have identifiable effects in what happens in parts of Central Asia. Ideas have legs—they walk out of the pages of books like this one and get up to all sorts of mischief.

But, even here we are talking about "Central Asia" as though we all knew what it meant. We argue, rather, that there is no such thing as "Central Asia." Regions, like continents, are geographical imaginaries, not grounded in a coherent or self-evident physical or human geography but, rather, being spatial orderings of the world. They help us reduce the complexity of social life over time to neat blocks of space. Even apparently "objective" ways of dividing up and describing the region—such as those based on fluvial systems or apparent distance from oceans—are themselves oversimplifications that are products of the age in which they were generated.

These geographical imaginaries are not neutral. The choice of label we use tells a story about what sort of place we think the region is. Who do Central Asian societies and peoples have more in common with? Who do they differ from? How are they located, both in world history and world geography? What types of places are they, populated by what types of people, and characterized by what types of social processes? The same regional label may have significantly different connotations when used by different people at different times and in different places.

The geographical imaginary of "Central Asia" or its alternatives may be useful for organizing academic labor and knowledge production—conferences, academic journals, research centers, and the like. It is a category used in this book to corral the labor of over sixty academics across certain parts of the earth's surface. But this imaginary has other material effects in the world. It helps policy makers decide how foreign relations and departments and military commands are to be organized and how their large budgets are to be spent. It informs the production of documentary films, movies, and novels, which in turn reinforces popular geopolitical visions. It frames the possibilities of thought for individuals who make crucial choices.

So does this mean we should dispense with the language of regions? Not necessarily. At least in the present we may not be able to think without such regional geographical imaginaries. We are not in fact arguing that we should; if we did, we would immediately be guilty of hypocrisy, because in this chapter we have been unable to stand outside the use of "Central Asia" as a regional geographical imaginary.

We are not arguing that we should eschew using the label "Central Asia" or its various cognates. Rather, we are saying that we should remember it is not a given, uncontested, unproblematic label, and when we do use it we should critically reflect on its implications. That is the purpose of a broad-ranging book such as this.

4

Central Asia as Story

Benjamin Gatling

Ever comes the scent of the Muliyon stream,
Ever comes the memory of our kind friends.

—**Rudaki**

Every child in Tajikistan learns this poem by heart. An oil painting of its author—Rudaki (858–941 CE), arms outstretched, the poem painted in Persian-script below—hangs imposingly in the entrance to Dushanbe's Rudaki Institute of Language and Literature. Rudaki is the first poet to write in an idiom that is still intelligible to a mass readership across the Persian-speaking world (Iran, Afghanistan, Tajikistan, and surrounding areas), and his importance to Persian literature is without debate, his place akin to Shakespeare's in English or Dante's in Italian. Still, the first time I saw the painting I remember thinking that its geographic reference seemed incongruent, most obviously because the Muliyon does not flow through Tajikistan but, rather, through Bukhara (first under the administration of the Uzbek SSR and later of independent Uzbekistan), which, since 1924 has been cut off from the territory of soon-to-be Tajikistan. The painting's Persian script, too, seemed slightly off. Rudaki's poetry abounds in bookstalls around the city, but in Cyrillic. Analogies do not always carry over across distinct cultural contexts, but it might be as if someone had copied early seventeenth-century cursive penmanship in a printing of *Hamlet*.

When I offhandedly asked a senior colleague who had taught at the institute since the 1960s about the painting, he fondly reminisced about lectures concerning Rudaki that he had heard from famous Soviet-era Orientalists Iosef Braginskii (d. 1989) and Abdulghani Mirzoev (d. 1976), among others. The scholar's personal memories melded into a conversation about Rudaki's nationalist importance: how Rudaki—the originator of key genres of Persian poetry still written until the present, he argued—significantly hailed from within the territory of contemporary Tajikistan, in Panjrud,

4-1   Rudaki Park, Dushanbe, Tajikistan, 2008. Photograph by Benjamin Gatling.

near the northern town of Panjakent. A fedora on his head, the white-haired
literary scholar even skeptically narrated a legend about Rudaki's blinding
at the hands of the emir, how the poet was expelled from the Samanid court
only to live his last days in impoverished ignominy, a fact memorialized
in the widely screened Soviet-era film *Sud'ba poeta* (The fate of the poet)
(1959). The poem, too, the scholar said, was especially fitting to grace the en-
tranceway of the premier academic institution devoted to the study of Tajik
language and literature because it wistfully evokes memories of Bukhara, the
center of Central Asian literary production until the early twentieth century.
Its national chauvinism, Samanid provenance, and aspirational longing for
greater Tajikistan—what Tajik historians refer to as *Tojikzamin*—all echo
themes that are common in public discourse.

The relevance of stories about Rudaki does not just come from how they
capture literary history (a useful endeavor for sure) but, rather, from how the
poem links to multiple events across time and space: personal narratives about
listening to Soviet-era, Marxist-Leninist literary lectures; my ethnographic vignette about visiting the institute and talking with a senior colleague;
and Central Asian history and legend. One domain of life carries over and
interprets, explains, and amplifies the next; memory, history, art, cultural
creativity, fiction, truth, the global, and personal experience converge. The
relationships between these suggest some of the power of stories. The ubiquity
of stories often obscures the fundamental ways that stories, like the ones

about Rudaki, ultimately are what allow individuals to make meaning out of their experiences of life, as they did for my colleague at the institute.

In this chapter, I offer *story* as an entry point into life in Central Asia. I discuss some examples of stories that are shared in the region, many of them not unlike the ones introduced above, and more important, the social work of these narratives: how Central Asians make meaning from experience. Here, I foreground four broad, non–mutually exclusive, functions of stories in Central Asia: stories as a tool for elites to project national ideology and for individuals to contest it; stories as performances of self, indexing the hopes, concerns, fears, presuppositions, and values of many Central Asians; stories as entertainment and exercises in virtuosity; and stories as mediating relationships, enabling individuals to make sense of their worlds.

Story as National Culture

The stories that are the most glaring to outside observers unaccustomed to everyday life in the republics of Central Asia are often framed objectively as history or, more pejoratively, as mere nationalist mythmaking. These include stories told by the governing elites that historians, at each republic's academy of sciences, dutifully relate so as to match the sloganeering of state propaganda. The first thing one might note when strolling down the street of any Central Asian capital are the seeming omnipresence of these stories, though not always in compact form. For example, the new architecture of central Dushanbe evokes disparate historical and narrative strands. Relief columns recall Achaemenid Persia. Intricate tile work conjures Samanid Central Asia, with a statue dedicated to the founder of the dynasty, Ismoil Somoni, in the place of greatest prominence. The statue almost stands as an object waiting for its story to be told, its didacticism difficult to dismiss. In Kazakhstan, elites marshal disparate narratives to assert continuities with Mongol history; in Uzbekistan, elites narrate the history of Emir Temur, known to European history as Tamarlane.

Sometimes, authorities even mobilize nationalist narratives into mass spectacle or turn them into popular entertainments, as in the case of the Kazakh television serials memorializing the fight against the Jungar hordes. Heritage sites materialize narratives, as at the imposing Timurid-era structures of Samarqand's Registan in Uzbekistan, which objectify stories about Emir Temur's prowess. In the same vein, I recall visiting a small village shrine several hours' drive from Dushanbe, which villagers held as a *qadamgoh*, the stepping place of a grandchild of Imam Hussein, himself a grandchild of the prophet Muhammad. A caretaker told a legend about a dream that in centuries past alerted villagers to the site's sacred significance, and how the site and its story substantiated Tajikistan's early foundational history as a Muslim nation.

The *Manas* epic cycle—and not just because of its length of more than five hundred thousand lines—dwarfs other examples of story and nation in

Central Asia. How many narratives, oral or written, have lent their titles to the name of a country's primary international airport as with Bishkek's Manas International? A comparable Les Miserables International Airport in Paris or Moby Dick International in Washington would seem absurd to some, for instance. In Kyrgyzstan, *Manas* stands at the center of the state constructions of identity. Multi-episodic, with alternating passages of prose and poetry, the story follows the battles and feasting of its eponymously named hero, and in subsequent cycles his descendants. Tellers—traditionally called *jomukchu* but now much more often by the Soviet-era neologism *manaschi*—learn the work's standard story lines, episodes, and motifs in master/apprentice relationships during which they hone their art and ability to compose ever-more-lengthy plots from the *Manas* epic world simultaneously in the space of performance. Although the epic's history is speculative (the earliest written versions date back only to the nineteenth century, and other extant records only date its earliest oral performance to the fifteenth century), The Kyrgyz state celebrated the work's one-thousand-year-jubilee in 1995 and sponsored its 2013 inscription on UNESCO's list of humanity's intangible cultural heritage. The face of the most famous twentieth-century *Manas* storyteller, Sayaqbay Qaralaev (1894–1971), has even graced Kyrgyz currency.

The degree to which *Manas* exists as a living, dynamic tradition remains a matter of some dispute. The patronage of the state and its valorization of the story as exemplary of Kyrgyz national character mean that the work is predominantly told at state banquets and other official occasions. Now domesticated into a vehicle for national cultural heritage, it has become elite literature, its primary purpose to provide historical roots to the nation rather than as entertainment in yurts as in previous centuries. Critics bemoan this change from living story into identity emblem as presaging the end of traditional manaschi apprenticeships, which have allowed performers to cultivate those repertoires of hundreds of thousands of lines. Yet still, the stories have held their resiliency because *Manas* plots have moved to other venues such as print, film, and the stage, precisely because many Kyrgyz see them as authentic forms of national culture.

For Central Asian states, stories (particularly those codified into emblems of national culture, like *Manas*, and other epic or narrative cycles with less international acclaim such as the Uzbek *Alpomish*, Tajik *Gurgali*, or even Karalkalpak *Edige*) instantiate national identity and work as instruments of state power precisely because of their status as authoritative forms of national culture in the imaginations of many Central Asian citizens. Soviet-era nationality policies left an indelible imprint on cultural production across the republics of the former Soviet Union. Communist Party cadres, supported by ethnographers and other scholars, worked to buttress the national identities of each constituent union republic through literature, art, music, costume, and folklore. Not that these things did not exist before, but Soviet nationality policies codified them into neat taxonomies, and perhaps most important, cultural forms—of which local narratives, folktales, historical legends, and epic were a part—became the product of one discrete nationality rather than shared across national boundaries. For example, in the Tajik Soviet Socialist Republic (Tajik SSR), scholars catalogued what they saw as the canonical genres of uniquely Tajik oral expression: proverbs (*zarbumasal*), maxims (*maqol*), riddles (*chiston*), folk poetry (*bayt, dubayti, robai*), folksongs, and stories (*afsona, qissa, rivoyat, naql, latifa*). Officially recognized minorities such as the Yaghnobis or Pamiris in the Tajik SSR had their own distinct catalogues of related genres. This is not to say that there are not discrete forms evident across the region, but stories do not exist in isolation. They are related to stories that are told in other places and in other times, sharing motifs, themes, and characters. The Socialist-era folklorization of national culture lives on, and many stories still circulate within nationalist frames—yet now, just as often explicitly anti-Soviet or at least in tacit support of independent governments and the authenticity of national cultures rather than as constituent parts of the Socialist-era project of the friendship of nations.

Just because narratives and other forms of expressive culture get wielded as potent tools of state power does not mean that Central Asians do not also marshal nationalist narratives for sociopolitical critique. In particular, poetry as the expressive form that Central Asians most often use to share their experience of their world offers a compelling vehicle for contestation. For example, Kazakh poets often recite *aitys*, or improvised poetry, accompanied by music, and this often takes place in the context of a verbal duel of wit and metaphor between two poets, sometimes in front of a television audience. Each poet competes against the other to better represent the Kazakh people. Significantly, poets frequently use aitys as barbed, open criticisms of authoritarian power in Kazakhstan. Precisely because aitys are authoritative vehicles of authentic national culture, the critique they deliver transcends the strictures on open political expression in autocratic Kazakhstan. In the authoritarian space of Central Asia, story can be a place for riposte, used to subvert state themes, or a place for Central Asians to take agency over disempowering circumstances and give voice to their experiences or simply to perform self and community.

Story as Community and Self

I had a middle-aged neighbor in Tajikistan who somehow always managed to turn our conversations back to a discussion of his late Soviet-era military service: seeing the Ukraine, drilling in Belarus. I later learned that the man's father until his recent death had told similar stories about the Great Patriotic War, as the Second World War is known in Central Asia, but coupled with tales about the privation his family had experienced on the home front in a village in the south of the Uzbek SSR not far from the Tajik border. Nationalist stories may be the most visually prominent and the most echoed in state media, but one is most likely to hear stories like my neighbor's in everyday conversation.

Indeed, a significant proportion of conversation is narrative, most often stories of personal experience. Personal narratives—stories told in the first person, as true, and absent traditional plots and motifs—are not always as predictable as the ones recounted in the *Manas* epic or glossed in a televised performance of aitys. Yet their content is also more than idiosyncratic, because such tellings communicate more-than-personal meanings, connecting storytelling situations to the wider contexts of their tellers' lives. Personal stories, too, operate not so much as commentaries on the pasts that their plots recount but as evaluations of the present. It is not insignificant that the same themes as were engaged by my veteran neighbor and his father carry over into the political sphere. For example, Tajikistan's president, Emomali Rahmon, likes to remind Tajiks about the events of the civil war: its indiscriminate violence, electricity rationing, and privation.

Sherali, a man I came to know well in Tursunzoda, Tajikistan, had spent a number of his early adulthood years in Krasnodar in southern Russia working on construction sites and farms, similar experiences in Russia as he shared with millions of other Central Asian migrants. Sherali talked about Russia in conflicting ways, as many migrants do. He admired Russia's geopolitical prowess and the gleaming shops and avenues he had seen in Moscow. Now unemployed and back in Tajikistan, he enjoyed watching Russian satellite television channels, the main activity that filled his days during the time I knew him. However, Sherali was bitter at the racism he had encountered in Russia and at the ways he and others had been treated by a succession of indifferent bosses in Russia's south. Sherali told me stories about Russian girlfriends and classmates he knew who still lived across Eurasia and with whom he stayed in touch via social media. He liked to tell about one cramped train journey he took from Dushanbe to Moscow, when he passed most of the trip standing.

"Did you hear about the guy in the village who died in Russia several years back?" he asked me one day. I had not. I did know, however, that upward of one thousand Tajiks died each year in Russia, many as the result of tragic workplace accidents. The man's family did not have enough money to repatriate his remains. "The Russians buried him," Sherali said. Several years later, the man's family secured the necessary funds and had the body exhumed and returned to Tajikistan. When they opened the grave, they saw that the body hadn't decomposed at all. Miraculously, it was as if the man had died the day before, so the family could rebury him according to Muslim tradition in Sherali's village. "It was like no ant, worm could get to it," Sherali said.

Ravshan, a bodybuilder by vocation, relished talking about what had predicated his increased piety of late. He saw his personal stories as part of his Muslim duty of *da'vat* (inviting someone to the faith), something he often directed at me. Several years previously he had lived in Russia with four other migrants. One night, an acquaintance arrived carrying a metal bar and ready to fight. The man felt his honor had been slighted by one of Ravshan's roommates at the market earlier in the day. In the melee, Ravshan suffered an errant blow to his face and immediately lost sight in his right eye. Ravshan redoubled his strength-building efforts. He vowed he would not be caught in a situation like that again. Back home in Tajikistan, not long after his thirty-fourth birthday, a white-bearded relative asked him what benefit being like Arnold Schwarzenegger would provide on the Day of Judgment. He told me that the comment disquieted him. As a result he began attending Friday prayers and eventually became a close disciple of a Sufi *pir*, who lived not far from his home.

Ravshan told me how he is not concerned anymore with threats of violence, but his new worry revolves around what his neighbors think of his newfound devotion. Recently, he had raised the ire of a local *imom* when Ravshan expressed how he wanted to be God's dog, an idea he had learned from the *pir*. Ravshan quoted a line of poetry, "If you want to be the *axis mundi*, become a dog on Gilani's doorstep, because the dog in Gilani's court has the dignity of lions." Ravshan followed with a story about the mystic Ahmadi Jomi who, tradition relates, had a lion that served as his protector and traveling companion. Ravshan told about how whenever Jomi reached a caravan stop, Jomi sought out rich benefactors to provide for the lion's sustenance. One time Jomi came to the home of the well-known saint Abdulqadori Gilani and asked some of the saint's disciples to feed the lion. Now, there was a small dog that lived at the lodge to whom Gilani had given the strength of a hundred lions, Ravshan said. Gilani's dog killed Jomi's lion. "Whose dog is this?" Jomi wanted to know. When he learned that it belonged to Gilani, Jomi took out his pen and wrote the poem. "Everyone is like a dog next to God's saints," Ravshan said.

For both Sherali and Ravshan, the personal easily melded into the transcendent, the local into the global. Sherali's experiences as a migrant in Russia provided grounding for a local legend about a body's miraculous reburial. The circumstances surrounding Ravshan's increased personal piety mapped neatly onto Muslim legendary history. Personal narratives became the venue for asserting those connections and the more-than-personal vitality of each man's individual experiences. Story allowed the men to put forward a notion of self and to express agency over potentially disempowering circumstances such as migration and religious marginalization.

These sorts of narratives do not exist in a vacuum, neatly performed on a stage in front of an audience but, rather, interspersed with other speech, sometimes even in ritualized ways. Uyghur groups both in Kazakhstan and in Xinjiang have maintained a tradition of events called *mashrap*, which are formalized predominantly male gatherings for sociality, ethical instruction, and the performance of verbal art. At times lubricated by vodka and group meals, lessons in personal piety accompany stories from Muslim history or joking anecdotes. Most dramatically, participants sometimes even participate in performative punishments for behavior contrary to the community norms, which the gatherings support. Such gatherings in Uyghur mahallas across southeastern Kyrgyzstan and into Xinjiang contribute to a unified Uyghur worldview among individuals with diverse experiences. Participants consciously attempt to revive traditions that they believe their male ancestors practiced for centuries, though the forms may have been different. Mashrap offer a venue for resisting marginalization and, as such, have drawn the ire and active suppression of the security forces on the Chinese side of the border. Authorities fear the political potentialities of such gatherings and the notions of Uyghur communal identity that they help constitute.

Analogous groups also exist in Tajikistan and Uzbekistan, some called *gashtak*, yet most often without any conscious pious inflection and never accompanied by the communal, ritualized punishment for which Uyghur mashrap are best known. Gashtak are voluntary groups that meet for a season, with a set membership of men with shared affinities, perhaps tied to a village or kinship group, occupation, social standing, or common experience such as *hajis*, individuals who have completed the pilgrimage to Mecca. Gashtak, too, include toasting, music, and stories such as histories, legends, and personal narratives. In gashtak, as well as in mashrap and my conversations with Sherali and Ravshan, story becomes foundational for sociality, as a performance of both self and community. Sometimes, though, stories are not about jockeying for power or asserting voice—in either nationalist or individual venues—but instead exist primarily as entertainment and displays of artistic virtuosity.

Story as Entertainment

Storytelling, like any skill, can be done well or poorly. Beyond the manaschi of the *Manas* tradition, Central Asia has numerous professional and amateur storytellers (in Uzbekistan and some parts of Tajikistan called *bakhshi*), who perform at *tuis*, weddings, circumcisions, and other special occasions, regaling guests with standards from oral tradition. Sometimes accompanied instrumentally (usually by different kinds of lute [*dambira, tor*] or tambourine [*doira*]), storytellers recite both prose and poetry extemporaneously from memory or with the use of written memory aids. Repertoires and performance styles vary dramatically across the region. For example, there are extreme differences between bakhshi in Khorezm in Uzbekistan's northwest and bakhshi of Surkhandarya and the south, from religious content intended to facilitate healing to humorous folktales, all with their own distinct melodies or prosodies.

The Tajik folklorist Tagmurod Yorzoda analogously demonstrated to me some of the diversity of narrative material found in the Folklore Archive of the Tajikistan's Academy of Sciences and collected from professional storytellers in the Tajik SSR and later independent Tajikistan. Content included heroic epic, such as episodes from the Persian *Shahnameh*, and numerous *dastan*, narrative romances with themes spanning the comedic to the borderline erotic, including racy tales of sexual escapades, cuckolded husbands, foolish monarchs, and more. Accomplished amateur storytellers in Tajikistan tell magic tales, drawing on a large repertory of communally well-known stories such as "The Yellow Cow," a variant of "Cinderella," in which an evil stepmother causes her stepdaughter immense suffering until the girl can be saved, and "The Story of Ahmadi Davlat," a tale in which a dog and a cat work together to return a magical knife to its owner. Many Tajiks do not encounter these stories as oral tradition but, rather, in print. Soviet-era folktale collections are still widely available. Many storytellers I heard also told narratives they had read in published classics from Middle Eastern literature, like the *Arabian Nights*, animal fables adapted from the *Kalila and Dimna*, or in chapbook editions containing stories about the exploits of popular heroes—in Tajikistan, men such as Hatami Tay or Luqmoni Hakim.

Taken together, oral epics, narrative romances, magic tales, and folktales are commonly referred to as *durugh* (literally, lies and falsehoods), which emphasizes their primary value as entertainment and popular diversions. However, even story genres offered as entertaining diversions for guests at weddings can still be tools of state power. Take, for example, the 1996 folktale theme of Uzbekistan's widely attended and broadcast Navruz productions. Performers that year adapted stories and legends about the origins of the New Year's dish, *sumalak*, and depicted a folktale battle between the forces of darkness and light with resonances from Zoroastrian tradition. Both story sets succeeded because most Uzbek citizens likely saw their forms as properly nationalist, of justifiably ancient provenance, and like aitys before then, as authentic emblems of national culture. Thus, entertaining folktales, too, can be wielded as appropriate venues to inculcate national pedagogy. Even as displays of virtuosity and means for entertainment, stories are not merely epiphenomenal or tangential to Central Asian life experience.

The accomplished amateur Tajik storyteller Davlat Khalav recounts how teachers in his Soviet-era village schools sought to mitigate villagers' beliefs in the supernatural worlds of oral tradition, as if already naming them *durugh* did not immediately diminish them as sites for real belief. Teachers claimed the stories' fantastic plots and their protagonists—fairies (*pari*), demons (*dev*), and other beings who lived on the mythical "other side" of the Mount Qaf—were not real, and villagers should not trade in their stories. However, as Khalav presciently noted: "No one can [live] without fantasy."

Khalav's point is well taken. His stories, though not true in the sense of courtroom veracity, still communicated something deeply held; they carried serious meanings and served vital social functions. Davlat seemed to suggest that his stories operated as a kind of vernacular theory making. They were not exactly analytical statements about the nature of wider Tajik reality, but instead, they suggested schemas one might emulate or strategies one might adopt for dealing with the exigencies of everyday life. They may be fictions, or in a literal sense *durugh*, but not because the events they related did not happen in real, chronological time. Their fictional qualities come from the creative possibilities they provide for tellers and listeners to make sense of their worlds. That is another function of stories, those told both as lies and as truth. Beyond entertainment, stories like the ones Khalav told or that bakhshi in Uzbekistan narrated in song provide a place for people to attempt to make sense of the world around them.

Story as Meaning Making

By virtue of their linear structure, stories necessarily instantiate sequences of cause and effect, ordering life's chaotic ambiguity and filling in the gaps that remain. This becomes most clear with rumors, legends, and their more elaborated iterations as conspiracy theories. All three narrative forms proliferate in environments in which individuals have little critical ability to assess the quality of information circulating around them or to parse the intricate realities they encounter in their everyday lives. This is something by no means limited to post-Soviet Central Asia, yet a feature that Central Asia's authoritarian governments unintentionally foster. Rumors fill the void, adhering to preexisting schemas about the way the world works, and provide their tellers with a way to explain the chaos that exists around them, to give it order and coherence.

During one of my extended stays in Tajikistan, an acquaintance asked about my ongoing research concerning Muslim life in the republic. She told me she wanted to make sure I understood the political gravity of the present situation. She followed by describing how new converts to Salafism in Tajikistan receive four thousand US dollars, a handsome sum considering the annual per capita income in 2010 was not much more than five hundred dollars. To boot, she talked about how recruiters pay an additional two thousand dollars' bonus for each referral. She asked rhetorically: "Why else would they risk it?" The woman was not sure exactly who these recruiters were. I asked. They visited mosques, she thought. She did not know where they got their money. I wanted to know that too. Probably Saudi Arabia, she said.

"Who told you? Do you know someone who was paid?"

"Everyone knows," she said with seeming finality.

The woman's rumor about Salafi recruiters was a narrative waiting to be told, an event ready to be fleshed out with pertinent plot details through story. The story's truthfulness was attested by the degree to which the story conformed to the way the woman knew the world to work: Islamists are, above all, foreigners, seeking to lure unsuspecting Tajiks. The only way she could make sense of the seeming recklessness of adhering to an alleged foreign ideology that engendered penalties both immediate and harsh, that cut one off from wider networks of social solidarity, and that received daily condemnation from authorities on state media was ample financial reward. The rumor reflected what she likely felt were the asymmetries of reward and punishment or perhaps her bafflement at the increasing piety she saw around her and the dangers she recognized in subscribing to a foreign religious ideology.

When fully narrativized, such rumors (in Uzbekistan, *mish mish*) take forms similar to the copious body of stories that circulated about Gulnara Karimova, the pop singer, aspirational fashion icon, erstwhile diplomat, and jet-setting daughter of and oft-rumored successor to the now deceased Uzbek president Islam Karimov. Karimova's glamorous exploits garnered her little popular support in her home country, particularly after news surfaced in 2013 of her involvement in bribe schemes and money-laundering scandals in Europe, which had purportedly given Karimova total assets worth more than 1.5 billion US dollars—or at least so Uzbek officials claimed in 2017. In February 2014, Karimova disappeared from public view, said to be under house arrest in Tashkent for her crimes. Early on Karimova had media access, and her complaints surfaced about the conditions of her imprisonment. Later, communication fizzled out. In the absence of reliable information, stories filled the void, which provided shape and coherence to the ambiguity surrounding the circumstances of her mysterious imprisonment. Among the most prominent story was one that told how Uzbek security services had entered Karimova's home, not long after her father's death and poisoned her, burying her on November 5 in an unmarked grave in Tashkent's Minor cemetery. Storytellers believed this explained her absence from her father's funeral and the reappearance of discredited Twitter accounts in her name, which had reposted old photos as supposed pictures of her in captivity. To counter the swirling legends, in the summer of 2017 Uzbek officials confirmed that Karimova had been tried, convicted, and had been living under house arrest for her crimes since 2015—and, to boot, was still under investigation for further alleged instances of corruption.

Narrative scholars call these stories contemporary legends to differentiate them from their historical parallels. To be sure, historical legends also constitute an effective resource for meaning making in Central Asia, Sherali's story about Jomi's lion being a prime example. Similar tales about monarchs or saints like Bahouddin Naqshband, or even figures from prophetic history such as Sulayman (Solomon), loom large in the imaginations of many Central Asians. Sometimes, a historical legend's saliency derives from the way it makes sense of place, as with the legends that circulate at Solomon Mountain in Osh or at Ahmed Yasawi's mausoleum in Turkestan. Other times, legends situate individuals in time, allowing Central Asians to make sense of history and of their place within it. I have written previously about contemporary Tajiks telling stories about pious Muslim ancestors and Bukharan emirs, but the work of Kyrgyz and Kazakh *aqyns* could work here as well.

Like stories about the emirs, contemporary legends frequently involve the machinations of politics, as is also the case with Karimova's story. It could be the unexplained death of a Tajik civil-war-era commander in the Pamir Mountains or a candidate's byzantine jockeying for position in a crowded Kyrgyz presidential field. Sometimes, legends evolve into conspiracy theories—stories that become a totalizing discourse connecting disparate and unordered facts with their explanations. Even the ruling elite is not immune to such theorizations via *mish mish* and other innuendo, sometimes narrativized in story or sometimes merely gestured at. Recent political life is replete with examples, such as when Rahmon attributed instability in Rasht to "outside agitators." Or when Hoji Akbar Turajonzoda—one of the most important religious figures in Tajikistan, former vice prime minister of the country, and stalwart government critic—invoked the "fact" that

BENJAMIN GATLING

Freemasonry stands as the obstacle to good governance in the region. He has variously argued that Freemasons have been the masterminds behind political violence in Tajikistan, supporters of foreign Islamist political organizations, and prime instigators of Rahmon's ill-conceived religious policies. In the question-and-answer section on the family's former popular website, a supplicant once asked about the lawfulness of drinking Coca-Cola, incidentally a product bottled in Tajikistan by a Turkish consortium with ties to the governing regime. Hoji Akbar responded that Coca-Cola is controlled by a global Jewish cabal and had thus been outlawed in Saudi Arabia.

Many such rumors, legends, and conspiracy theories have worldwide distribution. I have heard neighbors warn of malevolent taxi drivers, telling legends similar to organ-snatching stories documented across Africa, South Asia, Europe, and North America. I have listened to Sufis in Tajikistan tell anodyne conspiracy theories, such as alleging that moon landings were faked, because God would not allow mankind to leave the atmosphere. While Central Asians likely narrate rumors, legends, and conspiracy stories no more or less than others around the world, what is expressly unique in the Central Asian context, perhaps, are the specific themes engaged. For example, the political scientist John Heathershaw has catalogued three overarching themes that are present in many conspiracy theories in Tajikistan: patriarchal power, the hegemonic role of Russia, and the workings of a regional Islamist conspiracy. The last is a theme not so different from my acquaintance's rumor about Salafis, and they both work to make sense of the world by narrating it in story.

Narrating Life in Central Asia

In 2010 a friend—Nasrullah, then an instructor at the Islamic University in Dushanbe and government bureaucrat within the Ministry of Education—told me a story from the life of the Prophet Muhammad, concerning Muhammad's visits to the Kaaba and the questions Muhammad received from a prominent Meccan merchant that presaged God's revelation of Sura 80, 'Abasa. Nasrullah immediately followed with a line of poetry from the Persian poet Sa'adi, which amplified and explained the themes from the story he had just told. He ended with a legend about an early twentieth-century Sufi *pir*, which explained the suffering the pir had experienced at the hands of the Bolsheviks in the 1920s. Nasrullah also told me about his own interactions with the pir's son as a child during the 1960s and 1970s. He talked about how he had lived in Russia and had hoped to apply to graduate programs in religion in Europe and North America. His teenage son now studied in an after-school Chinese language program, he told me. One story drew on and amplified the other: prophetic history, poetry, legend, and personal narrative.

Stories like Nasrullah's offer a complementary angle whereby one can read the themes of previous chapters in this book, since stories provide bridges between and across those seemingly disparate domains of global, local, and place. Nasrullah engaged the global, in this case referencing his life's intersections with great powers—living in Russia, studying Chinese—and Central Asia's connections to global Islamic history. Nasrullah's local belied any notion of Central Asia's isolation, homogeneity, or exoticism. Nasrullah embodied this synthesis. A product of the Soviet educational system (his job even created because of it), Nasrullah told stories that emphasized Tajikness as Persianate, as well as the importance of local community. The pir, villagers, and his family lived in webs of communal intimacy. Nasrullah offered a complex picture of where Central Asia is "located." His stories drew together the Middle East, Eurasia, and greater Asia with disparate geographic, temporal, and geopolitical imaginaries.

Many of the examples I have drawn upon have been skewed toward Tajikistan and the Islamic, not so much because both are somehow representative of the region writ large but because they are what I know best. However, I have tried to demonstrate that it is not difficult to identify analogues in Uzbekistan, Kyrgyzstan, and Kazakhstan, and with no religious inflection. Story—something so foundational to everyday speech and human interaction—offers a vital lens whereby to explore the wide breadth of complex ways in which Central Asians experience and shape their worlds.

CASE I-A

Ordinary Soviet Life through Collectivization

Marianne Kamp

e may think of farming as a way of life that is slow to change, but in Uzbekistan and across the whole Soviet Union, agricultural collectivization remade farming and the lives of rural people in four years (1929–1933) by ending private ownership of land and driving farmers to consolidate small plots into large fields. In global terms, farming entered a phase of modernization in the 1920s, when combustion engine tractors became affordable and made planting very large fields not only possible but efficient. Stalin imposed collectivization of agriculture across the Soviet Union in 1929 in order to institute state control over both producers and their products. But collectivization was also driven by dreams of efficient, mechanized farming. Tractorization transformed American farm production in the 1920s, and among Texas cotton growers it led to consolidation by large owners, who eventually replaced tenant farmers and sharecroppers with wage labor. American tractorization inspired Soviet agricultural economists, and the USSR rapidly expanded its imports of American-made tractors.

In the 1920s Soviet economic planners laid out a path for autarky in cotton, ending imports from abroad and insisting that Soviet textile mills rely on Soviet raw materials. For decades Central Asia had been producing the dominant share of raw cotton for Russian factories, and with collectivization, the majority of Uzbekistan's newly formed collective farms were tasked with producing cotton. In local terms, this meant that families that previously had made their own decisions about how much cotton to plant were pressured to join *kolkhoz*es (collective farms), to use new state-owned tractors for plowing, and to increase cotton production for a cotton price set by the state.

In this chapter two elderly collective farm members—Zulayho, who was born in 1916, and Boltaboy, born in 1914—remember their lives before collectivization and the early days of their collective farms in Uzbekistan's Xorazm (Khwarazm) province. Interviewed in 2003, more than a decade after Uzbekistan became independent, both of them told of lives that diverged from those of previous generations, with new access to education and infrastructure, under Communist economic plans that emphasized producing cotton. Zulayho's family, struggling to make a living on marginal lands, welcomed the opportunity to join the kolkhoz, but Boltaboy, who did not appreciate having to do the kinds of labor

I-A-1   Komil Kalonov (*left*) interviews Boltaboy K (*right*) in Khiva, as part of a research project on collectivization in Uzbekistan, 2003. Photograph courtesy of the Oral Histories project.

previously done by his father's farmworkers, turned toward the Communist Party for an opportunity to leave the kolkhoz.

In 1929 the Soviet Communist Party decided that farmers and herders should jointly own their farmed lands or their herds and should produce crops or livestock by working together in brigades. The Soviet government gave each kolkhoz a production plan and determined the prices a kolkhoz would earn for its wheat, cotton, or cattle. The Party declared that *kulaks* (wealthy farmers) had exploited rural laborers and promised that, on the kolkhoz, all would be equal. Kolkhoz members were encouraged to seize lands from kulaks, who were arrested, tried, and exiled or executed. Activists for collectivization told the rural poor that the kolkhoz would improve their lives, replacing draft animals with tractors. In Soviet Ukraine and Kazakhstan, collectivization led to mass starvation in the early 1930s. In Uzbekistan, the results did

not lead to such widespread risk to life, though many thousands of kulak families were exiled to Ukraine and to the North Caucasus. Exile, in Stalin's view, would remove the politically unreliable kulaks from their communities, reducing the threat they posed to collectivization. Uzbek kulaks were instructed to expand cotton production in their places of exile, a fate that could have befallen Boltaboy and his family (see figure I-A-1).

Ordinary Lives under Stalinism

Boltaboy's father worked as a rural administrator under the government of the Khanate of Khiva, until that region, now known as Xorazm province, became part of Soviet Uzbekistan in 1924. He owned a shop, two hectares (4.9 acres) of land, and had three wives. Sharecroppers (tenant farmers who farmed those lands in exchange for half of the crop) raised melons and alfalfa for him. Boltaboy's father died before collectivization began, and "because he died when I was young, he was not dekulakized. If he had lived, they would have taken this land and sent him away." Boltaboy's mother also passed away, and his father's third wife, whom he called Auntie, raised him. "We had an oil press in our house, a guest room, a farm laborer, a barn for livestock, cows and calves." Boltaboy's family had been wealthy; in collectivization, the land and livestock they inherited was joined to the kolkhoz and the sharecroppers became kolkhoz members.

Zulayho was born in a Xorazm province village that had very little water, to a father who had one wife and three daughters. Her father drove an oxcart and planted wheat and cotton on his own land. He hired some day laborers for harvest, but he was not wealthy. "We had a waterwheel. . . . The horse or camel was always turning it . . . to water the fields, and that was our drinking water. We went with our father to turn the waterwheel. . . . Then the kolkhoz started, they took our livestock, our cow, everything." Those who were not well-off were forced to turn farm fields and draft animals over to the newly formed kolkhoz when they joined.

Boltaboy's father was well educated, and Boltaboy studied in an "old-style" school for boys with a traditional Islamic curriculum. In 1930, when Boltaboy was sixteen years old, the collective farm formed, and he was appointed as the *tabelchi* (record keeper), writing down how much daily labor each kolkhoz member performed so that they would be paid accordingly. In the early 1930s the job of tabelchi often went to a young boy who was literate and numerate. Many tabelchis moved into leadership roles when they grew up. Boltaboy's kolkhoz "used children's labor when they needed to. For example, I was an orphan, and I worked digging irrigation channels. When I couldn't stand slogging in the mud, I went away to study."

Zulayho was perhaps fifteen years old when the kolkhoz opened a new-style school, where "boys and girls sat together at tables." Although this was a new opportunity, she did not remember how long she attended school, and education did not shape her working life on the kolkhoz. Before collectivization, she helped her father with the camel-driven waterwheel, and she continued that work as a kolkhoz member. In the mid-1930s, an infrastructure project transformed her village's prospects: "A canal brought water from the river to us. . . . Many people from my household worked on the canal; everyone from the kolkhoz was taken there. Every kolkhoz designated people for it; we were digging it for ourselves. I was about seventeen or eighteen years old and I worked carrying a hand-caddy. . . . Then they brought in these iron machines and they could dig it." Water from the canal allowed the kolkhoz to plant more cotton, the crop that the Soviet government demanded, and some rice. "Back then [before the canal] we did not have much rice here, didn't really know what it was." Rice is essential to plov, a dish that Uzbeks view as the pinnacle of good eating; Zulayho's comment reflected the ways that investing in the canal improved local diets, even though increasing cotton production was the purpose of this investment.

Collectivization-related famine struck the Soviet Union in the early 1930s. The state's aggressive coercive approach to grain and cattle requisitioning left Kazakh herders and grain growers from Ukraine and other areas to starve. Uzbekistan, where kolkhozes concentrated on raising cotton and relied on imports of grain, also was threatened by starvation in 1933. Zulayho noted that her father "had it a bit better, and we were not hungry," because the kolkhoz paid him in wheat for working as a driver. Although Boltaboy lived on a more prosperous kolkhoz than Zulayho, he and his auntie "would get up early and go pick leaves, cook them, chop them up, add flour and make it into bread." He noted, "Earlier, Uzbeks did not know what a potato was," but in this time of hardship they started planting tomatoes and potatoes in their garden plots. In the early 1930s the USSR opened so-called gold stores, where Soviet citizens could exchange their gold coins and jewelry for coveted goods. Boltaboy remembered that during the famine, "a lot of people went to sell gold and buy flour."

Zulayho's collective farm gained a canal and expanded its productivity, but the Second World War added to her challenges. Her husband was drafted into the Red Army and was killed. Of the several babies she bore, only one boy survived, and she raised him as a single parent. "All the working age men were gone from here. We had old women and children, and we did the work ourselves." Zulayho and other kolkhoz women planted cotton, using camel power to drive their seeders. When her kolkhoz finally obtained tractors, "people were happy that it would plow the fields." Tractors came to Boltaboy's village earlier, as soon as the collective farm organized in 1930. A "Machine and Tractor Station" (MTS) would contract with the kolkhoz to plow and plant, and the kolkhoz paid the MTS in harvested cotton or money.

Social changes that made a meaningful difference in the lives of Uzbeks trickled unevenly into rural communities. As a teenager Boltaboy taught in short-term "end illiteracy" courses for rural adults, in villages that organized state-funded schools in response to Soviet laws requiring universal public education. In Zulayho's village, a traditional midwife provided the only medical assistance until doctors arrived after the Second World War. Both Zulayho and Boltaboy recalled that, when they were young, women covered their faces and bodies with veiling robes (*paranji*). Zulayho's mother had worn a paranji, but "everyone uncovered and threw it into the fire . . . I never wore it." Boltaboy said that, in his region, "women were forced to remove the paranji, around 1925," but that he continued to see women wearing the paranji when he worked in Uzbekistan's Fergana Valley in the 1930s: "Religion was strong there."

In 1932 Boltaboy's literacy earned him admission to a Communist Party school, where he was trained as a propagandist for collectivization; then he went on to a technical school to study math and became a teacher. He worked in provinces of Uzbekistan that were distant from his native Xorazm. Unlike most men of his generation in Uzbekistan, Boltaboy was not drafted into the army in the Second World War, perhaps because there was a critical shortage of teachers. He eventually returned to Xorazm, using the opportunities provided by Party membership and his profession to establish a comfortable life. By comparison, Zulayho stayed on her kolkhoz and continued to perform heavy farm labor throughout her working years. In the late 1930s her husband built her a house that she regarded as much better than "my father's house," which "did not have windows" and was very small. A war widow who never remarried, Zulayho used some of her kolkhoz earnings, which increased significantly in the 1950s, to pay for her son's special art lessons, and by doing so, she was able to protect him from demands that he pick cotton. "If the child was forced to pick cotton, he would be ruined . . . but he also did heavy labor." She said: "He walked all the way to Urgench" for art lessons, and then he studied in Tashkent, ultimately becoming a successful artist whose works graced Zulayho's house.

Stalinism, Rural Modernization, and Individual Memory

Although one might expect those who lived through Stalin's rule to focus on the political oppression that pervaded Soviet life, they instead related accounts of slow modernization and of the ways that an entirely new form of farm organization, the kolkhoz, became the foundation for a stable and gradually improving life. Elderly Uzbeks who remembered how their own lands were collectivized told their own life stories in ways that reflected a sense of either injustice or pride in accomplishment. Many of the people whom our project interviewed noted that some from their communities suffered harsh fates under Soviet Stalinism: Zulayho and Boltaboy recalled the men from their villages who were charged as "kulaks" and were arrested, exiled, or executed. Other interviewees recounted stories about religious oppression: the communists closed village mosques and arrested mullahs. They told of people who died in the 1933 famine. Their lives were shaped not only by the Soviet Union's policies in Central Asia but also by global events: they remembered the names of husbands and brothers who lost their lives in military service during the Second World War. Between the 1930s and the 1960s collective farms were consolidated into ever larger entities. By the 1980s each kolkhoz had thousands of members, a complex management system, and significant investments in tractors and other machinery. Soviet forms of agricultural modernization in cotton-producing areas followed some of the trends in global industrialized agriculture, such as emphasizing mechanization.

Many of the processes that shaped life in Uzbekistan, such as the cotton-growing kolkhoz, were not global but, rather, were specific to the Soviet Union. After 1953, when Joseph Stalin died, kolkhoz members no longer needed to fear such threats as "dekulakization," and rural life stabilized. The state continued to control agriculture through the kolkhoz, and unlike what happened in the West, kolkhoz members stayed on their farms, and mechanization of some aspects of farming did not lead to rural depopulation. Those whom we interviewed, like Zulayho and Boltaboy, were young when the Soviet Union initiated efforts toward collectivization of agriculture, industrialization, and cultural transformation. They belonged to a generation that was able to benefit from the opportunities offered by Communism's shake-up of economy and society, if they survived all of its risks and threats. Boltaboy, who became a math teacher and Communist Party member, and Zulayho, a single mother who earned a decent living for herself and her son through labor on the kolkhoz, offer us not the dramatic voices of collectivization's victims or its dissenters but, rather, mundane accounts from Uzbekistan's version of ordinary Soviet life.

CASE I-B

Regulation and Appropriation of Islam in Authoritarian Political Contexts

Tim Epkenhans

Since the early 2000s Tajikistan's authoritarian government under President Emomali Rahmon (in power since 1992) has forcefully reshaped the public Islamic religious field by appropriating Islam and by imposing restrictive regulations on its organization. The way Islam is organized, perceived, and practiced in Tajik society has always been a contentious political and societal issue since the authoritarian Soviet modernization project sought to transform the Central Asian societies. Following Marxist ideological parameters, Soviet authorities considered religion as part of the superstructure concealing the "real" class structures and, therefore, as the main obstacle for the enforcement of Soviet rule and the creation of a communist society. Islam was considered a particularly restive religion, defying Soviet modernization. However, the actual matter of contention was related not only to the alleged "traditionalism" or "backwardness" of Muslim communities (as Orientalist discourses repeatedly insinuated) but also to the social and political relevance of Islamic practice and thought alongside the autonomy of Muslim religious institutions. In short, Islam—with its emphasis on social justice and moral-

ity conveyed by independent institutions embedded in the local Central Asia history—constituted a strong obstacle to the implementation of Soviet rule.

Eventually, the Stalinist Great Terror destroyed the Islamic religious field in Central Asia. Religious authorities were persecuted, arrested, and often executed, and religious institutions were banned. The traditional setting in which Islamic authority and normativity in religious practice were taught, negotiated, and eventually experienced disappeared in the late 1920s. Despite the Stalinist terror, many Muslims retained their religious practice and belief in Central Asia; they did this clandestinely and often without the authoritative guidance by Islamic scholars (the *ulama*, lit. "scholars" of the Islamic sciences). Religious practice and belief became less regulated and often synonymous with local tradition (which was perceived as "authentic"). The resilience of religious belief and practice in Central Asia and elsewhere in the Soviet Union caused a major policy shift in the 1940s. Since then, Moscow decided to appropriate and regulate Islam (as well as other religions) with formal religious institutions and an "official" concept of Islamic normativity. The Spiritual Board of Muslims in Central Asia (abbreviated with its Russian acronym SADUM), chaired by a senior religious figure, re-established a small network of Muslim religious institutions such as mosques and schools and appointed a small group of loyal Soviet ulama. In close cooperation with Soviet academia and political cadres, SADUM facilitated the emergence of a distinct analytical and instrumentalist framework to categorize "Islam" and "Muslims" in the USSR. In short, the institutionalization reduced the complexity of Islam and made the religion legible for the state.

The Soviet authorities determined a dichotomy between an essentialist, scriptural, normative, "pure" Islam as represented by the SADUM and an essentialist, "traditional," or "popular" Islam as practiced outside the SADUM (and ultimately outside the socialist society as such). Unsurprisingly, the scriptural-normative Islam was presented as apolitical, supporting the Soviet transformation as well as its social and political hierarchies, and the unregulated "popular" Islam was branded as cosmopolitan, foreign, extremist, and generally alien to Central Asian Muslims. In the later Soviet Union, however, the population increasingly perceived the Soviet modernization project as socially, politically, and morally failed. Since the 1980s (after the revolution in Iran and the Soviet invasion of Afghanistan), the "popular" variations of Islam gradually emerged as markers for cultural and spiritual authenticity enriched with conservative religious morality as an alternative to the Soviet system (which was, in addition, increasingly considered as colonial by perestroika and glasnost debates).

Islamic activism—initially clandestinely—proliferated in the final years of the Soviet Union and in Soviet Tajikistan, where the early Islamic Revival Party of Tajikistan (IRPT, Hizbi nahzati Islomii Tojikiston) challenged the Communist *nomenklatura*. The Soviet state and SADUM eventually lost their monopoly on the interpretation of Islam, and public debates on the meaning of Islam in Tajik society contributed to the aggressive political polarization. During the tumultuous years between perestroika and independence, a reformist religious scholar was elected head of the Tajik branch of SADUM (known as *qoziyot*) and transformed the institution—albeit only for a few months—to an important independent political actor in Tajikistan. However, the enormous challenge of the Soviet Union's disintegration, compounded by the rise of organized crime networks, severe inner-elite conflicts (including a postcolonial interpretation of the Soviet legacy), and a catastrophic economic collapse finally triggered the outbreak of the devastating civil war in 1992.

Although Islamic fundamentalism or extremism as such was not causative for the outbreak of violence in 1992, the reference to Islam became an important strategy to categorize and rationalize the civil war as a "secular-religious" conflict enriched with nationalism and perceptions of particular ethnic-regionalist identities. Likewise, the international community and the parties to the conflict referred in the general peace accord of 1997 (which formally ended the civil war) to the particular religious-secular nature of the conflict. The general peace accord stipulated the official registration of an Islamic party, the IRPT, in Tajikistan, and for about a decade after 1997 the peace accord established a unique political arrangement in Central Asia by conceding political rights to a conservative but moderate Islamic party.

I-B-1   Men going to Jumma prayers, Dushanbe, Tajikistan, 2008. Photograph by David W. Montgomery.

But it was not only the registration of an Islamic party that was a remarkable development after the peace accord. Simultaneously, the religious field experienced a decade of relative independence and consolidation. Although the Tajik government belligerently insisted on the (albeit vaguely defined) secular character of Tajikistan's statehood, it did not have the capacity at the time to impose stricter regulations on the ulama and their institutions (mosques and schools). The reduced state intervention facilitated the proliferation of independent ulama, who contributed to the renegotiation of what Islamic normativity could mean in post-Soviet and post-conflict Tajikistan. The majority of ulama promoted a regional variation of the Sunni-Hanafi tradition, which accentuated a conservative morality and the moderation of religious practice. The ulama's conservativism in regard to morals and values intuitively responded to the major social and economic transformations of Tajik society since the early 2000s—namely, labor migration and the absence of working-age men in rural Tajikistan.

Although the ulama perpetuated the patriarchic hierarchies in Tajik society in their religious guidance, the so-called commanding right (*amri ma'ruf*), they acknowledged the increasing social and economic responsibilities of women by adjusting their religious guidance to the needs and expectations of women. In regard to religious practice, the ulama demanded the "return" to a moderate variation of the Sunni-Hanafi tradition, which the ulama described as "authentic" Tajik, or Central Asian, weaving Sunni-Hanafi Islam into the narratives of Tajik nationalism. The combination of authentic morality embedded in a Tajik tradition and tangible life-world guidance proved extremely successful. The public observance of religious practice and the adoption of an Islamic habitus (dress code, diet, language) significantly increased, particularly among a younger generation of Tajiks.

Since the ulama did not question the secular character of Tajikistan's statehood and distanced themselves from the IRPT and ubiquitous debates on Islamism, Tajik authorities initially did not

TIM EPKENHANS

realize the intrinsic political and social relevance of the ulama's teaching. However, in the late 2000s, the government gradually realized that its projection of a secular Tajik nationalism—that is, the "Aryan" ethnogenesis of the Tajiks and their early statehood during the Somonid dynasty in the tenth century CE—had no societal relevance or meaning for large parts of the population. More worrying for the authoritarian regime, it had lost the ability to control and manipulate the religious field and therefore the ownership (or legibility) of what Islam could mean in Tajik society.

In 2008–2009 the government fundamentally realigned its religious policy. First, President Rahmon integrated Islam into the narrative of Tajik nationalism with the celebration of the year 2009 as the "Year of Imomi A'zam"—that is, Abu Hanifa, the founder of the Hanafi law school in Sunni Islam. Second, the Tajik rubber-stamp parliament adopted a range of laws imposing stiff regulations on religious associations, directly intervening in the internal affairs of a given religion to the point of the substantive evaluation of its alleged merits or dangers. Third, the government intervened with an iron fist in the religious field by restructuring the quasi-official religious administration, the so-called Islamic Center (*Markazi Islomi*) and successor of the Soviet SADUM. After independence and during the civil war, the Rahmon administration dismantled the Tajik SADUM (the *qoziyot*) since the institution played a prominent role in the political mobilization against the Communist *nomenklatura* during perestroika, glasnost, and independence when Islam resurfaced as a relevant public political and societal issue. The relative weakness of the Islamic Center facilitated the rise of independent ulama throughout the 1990s and 2000s.

With the realignment of its religious policy, the government also strengthened the Islamic Center and reestablished its regulatory authority in the religious field. The government appointed Saidmukarram Abdulqodirzoda, an aggressively interventionist religious scholar who determinedly marginalized independent ulama and imposed a narrow, statist, and Salafi version of the Sunni Hanafi tradition. Thus, the Islamic Center—as a quasi-government institution—reduced the enormous complexity of how Islam had been negotiated in post-Soviet Tajikistan and silenced any dissident voice, both from "reformist" and conservative ulama. By imposing this narrow concept of Islamic normativity, the Islamic Center made Islam again legible for the government and therefore easier to categorize, control, and appropriate by immediate social practice and intervention. The government either reintegrated obedient ulama in its administration of Islam (by, for instance, implementing the formal attestation of their knowledge, by imposing a uniform dress code, and by dictating a mandatory list of sermon topics) or it oppressed any form of dissent or deviation. Furthermore, the regime has integrated this narrow variation of Islam in its larger authoritarian legitimation narrative: President Rahmon is presented not only as the one who reestablished peace and Tajik statehood but also as the one who allowed Tajik Muslims to return to their "authentic" tolerant Sunni-Hanafi tradition.

The dynamics of control and appropriation of religion are by no means a unique feature of Tajikistan. One can observe similar trends in other authoritarian contexts not only in neighboring Central Asia (Uzbekistan or Kazakhstan) but likewise in Egypt, Turkey, or Pakistan. The authoritarian manipulation of the religious field too often underestimates the complexity—including the social, political, and cultural relevance—of religion (here Islam) in its myriad variations. Despite the apparent desire of control, regulation, and order, the potential for failure is immense. As for Tajikistan, neither the incapacitated civil society nor the suppressed independent ulama are able to counterbalance the authoritarian state by offering a more inclusive or sophisticated understanding of the Islamic tradition, acknowledging its complexity and dynamics. Therefore, resistance to this policy has the potential to endanger the very stability the government (and often the international community) conjures in Central Asia.

TIM EPKENHANS

Migration from the Deep South to the Far North as Central Asian "Glocalism"

Marlène Laruelle

ew Russian cities call forth as many clichés as Norilsk. Along with Vorkuta and Kolyma, it carries within it the memory of the horrors of the Gulag, which reigned over the city and its metallurgical company for two decades. Its memory is still felt today. The most polluted city in Russia, Norilsk embodies the excesses of an "industrializing" ideology professing that it was possible to dominate nature, which led to ecological dramas similar to the one further to the south in the Aral Sea. Norilsk illustrates the gigantism of the Soviet regime, which was intent on creating, ex nihilo, a city of several hundreds of thousands of inhabitants above the polar circle at a latitude of 69° N. The city developed in isolation, symbolized by its status as a closed city for foreigners. Since the fall of the Soviet Union, one-third of the population has deserted. Among the decrepit buildings of the city's streets, devoid of vegetation, small kiosks sell an abundance of fruits and vegetables. The sellers come from Tajikistan and Uzbekistan.

Like other resource-rich Arctic cities, Norilsk attracts workers from as far away as Ukraine and Azerbaijan, as well as from the North Caucasus (principally Dagestan) and Central Asia. Reliable statistical data on migrants are difficult to get. But between the 2002 and 2010 censuses, the number of Russian citizens who gave Kyrgyz as their ethnicity rose by 281 percent in the Tyumen region, 243 percent in the Khanty-Mansi district, 317 percent in the Yamal-Nenets district, and 207 percent in the Krasnoyarsk region. The number of Russian citizens listing Tajik nationality follows a similar pattern: it rose 179 percent in the Tyumen region, 173 percent in the Khanty-Mansi district, 254 percent in the Yamal-Nenets district, and 176 percent in Krasnoyarsk Krai. Perhaps these figures are in and of themselves unrepresentative, since the scale is only for several thousand people, but they reflect the tip of an iceberg, as only a small portion of Central Asian migrants ever obtain a Russian passport.

The Azerbaijani pioneers to Norilsk settled in the 1980s and today own the majority of the city's restaurants, cafes, and nightclubs; the second Azerbaijani generation dominate the markets and supermarket chains—along with the Central Asians, in particular the sellers of fruits and vegetables, which are brought in from the south. The Kazakhs occupy a more specific niche: the metallurgical company Norilsk Nickel has invited several hundreds of graduates from Kazakhstani technical institutes to fill in for the lack of qualified personnel. Other migrants who originally had no diploma have succeeded in climbing the ladders of the company. This is the case with some Tajiks, who were the first Central Asian migrants to come to Russia when escaping the civil war that ravaged their country between 1992 and 1997. Over the next decade, many succeeded in acquiring the skills necessary to hold an engineering position in one of the Norilsk Nickel mines or plants.

These migrants have altered the city's urban space. They contribute to creating ethnic districts or at least to giving "ethnic" color to the neighborhoods where they live compactly, developing their own social networks, and opening cafes, restaurants, and new places of worship. Most of these migrants live in the former dwellings of the Komsomols (*gostinnaia*); they have only individual rooms and are exposed to the chemical winds filled with smells from the mining factories of the old town. Migrants also modify the city's social and cultural hierarchies. The definition of who is a newcomer and who is a *korennoe* (local) is shifting dramatically. The old pattern whereby urban Russians are contrasted with indigenous peoples has been transformed, with the former claiming a privileged status of being "local" and the latter increasingly in competition with labor migrants for accessing the urban job market and its services.

Norilsk is a city unlike any other for Central Asian migrants. The city's migrants are surprised by the extremity of the climate and the city's geographical isolation from the rest of Russia. But they also quickly incorporate Norilsk Nickel's symbolic and physical domination over the city. For these migrants, to join the company is the peak of a professional career, as it includes good material conditions and job security as well as the social prestige of being among the "elected."

They internalize the local narrative about the "people of the North" (*Severiane*), said to be hardworking, welcoming, and abstemious, and they celebrate the myth of Norilsk as the last frontier. Further, they remark upon the smooth functioning of the local service economy: even if they often work in sectors remote from their initial qualifications, the profitability of having a *business* in Norilsk heightens the feeling of personal success during migration.

Like the previous generations of Komsomols, who came to develop the metallurgical company, Central Asian migrants share the feeling of having succeeded. Abufarrukh, a native of Khudjand, states: "Here you have a sense of security, you earn more than elsewhere in Russia, even if in recent times the situation is far more difficult, and you do not have any problems with the locals." His colleague Safo adds: "Life is hard especially in winter, but it is hard for everyone, and only those who are courageous and do not fear work can survive here." Through their own professional and individual pathways as migrants who left the southern regions of Eurasia to "realize" themselves in the Far North, these migrants renew the myth of the pioneer inherited from the Soviet regime, adapting it to the post-Soviet conditions of the market economy and freedom of movement.

What do these migrants working in Russia's Far North tell us about contemporary Central Asia? They tell us the extent to which Central Asia is simultaneously local, regional, and global. Central Asia is local because migrants, as everywhere in the world, try to maintain what they consider their way of life, and especially their social networks, which function as a critical safety net to help them when facing unexpected situations. Another important element of their "localism" is the strong will to maintain traditional relationships between genders. As Abdulloh baldly put it, Russian women are great girlfriends but not good wives, as they are considered sexually "freer" than Central Asian women. Central Asia is regional, because these migration flows are profoundly rooted in Soviet and post-Soviet frameworks: each region or village has its own pattern and network of migration in a specific Russian city.

And Central Asia is global, because migrants are connecting more and more with the broader world. The Uzbeks selling fruit and vegetables and the Kyrgyz cooking *shashiks* in Dudinka (the port city on the Yenisei River near Norilsk) work closely with the Chinese traders of clothes and shoes and the Azerbaijanis who run the main supermarket on the central square. They have exchanges over their working conditions and their respective situations at home. Tajik and Uzbek workers in Norilsk play to great effect on their different layers of identity: not only are they from a Central Asian country, but they are "post-Soviet Muslims" (their networks are often closely interlinked with those of Azerbaijani and Tatars and Bashkirs), they are based in Russia and often want to stay there, get the citizenship, and integrate into the Russian social fabric, and they are also just "migrants," who share a similar situation with all migrants around the world.

For Central Asian migrants, Islam often plays a role of glocalism. Each migrant reproduces in Norilsk his or her own relationship to Islam. Some see in Islam only a collection of traditional rituals, others see an identity by which to distinguish themselves from the "Russians," and others see it as a religious practice or a narrative of social justice. But Islam also allows for the creation of a new community, one for all migrants of Muslim background. This new identity layer is embodied by the Norilsk mosque,

the most northern mosque in the world. The building, built by an Azerbaijani businessman at the end of the 1990s, is run by an imam from Tatarstan and is frequented by North Caucasians and Central Asians, thus creating a pan-Muslim feeling of belonging.

The fact that Russia is the main host country of Central Asian migrants is in many ways a key element of its soft power over the region and is obviously a plus in the great power competition efforts to influence Central Asia. Migrants indeed represent a unique "conveyer belt" for Russia's narratives and worldviews to spread into Central Asia. Moreover, migrants constitute one of the main drivers of Central Asia's new connectivity. They globalize the region even more than the railway and road projects sponsored by the international community. The difficulties involved in integrating the knowledge and experience that migrants acquire in Russia into the state of Central Asian affairs by this same international community—and especially by international financial institutions—demonstrate the need to comprehend connectivity not as an issue of infrastructure but, rather, as one of human capital.

Last but not least, Central Asian migrants working in Norilsk display a complex "mental atlas" structured by multiple geographical scales and imaginaries. This mental atlas is not based on the realities of physical geography but on the feeling of proximity, grounded in their everyday experiences and social networks. In this mental geography, the village or region of origin forms the central point around which space is organized. The national capital city is often nonexistent in this geography, as is the rest of Central Asia. Other key places of reference are in Russia. Almost all migrants have a specific relationship to Moscow and its region, where fruit and vegetables are transited wholesale, before dispatch to the Arctic cities. Many migrants also refer to some other provincial cities, often in southern Siberia, such as Krasnoyarsk, where they may have spent some years before moving to Norilsk and where they may still have family or a business. Practicing Muslim migrants in Norilsk display a specific geographical representation of the city, insofar as they know which small groceries shops sell halal meat.

Living in an Arctic environment, they have to deal with polar nights and therefore base the calendar of daily Islamic prayers on the more southern city of Krasnoyarsk. They feel attached to Ufa, because the Norilsk mosque is under the Ufa Spiritual Board umbrella, not the Moscow-based Council of Muftis. All these geographical imaginaries that are present in migrants' everyday life embody the multiple scales and meanings of Central Asia.

DISCUSSION QUESTIONS

PART I: CONTEXTUALIZING CENTRAL ASIA

1. Central Asia as Global

1. What criteria should we use to assess whether Central Asia is "connected" to the world? Can "connectivity" ever be a neutral concept, or is it always tied to an outside actor's agenda?

2. Why is the metaphor of the Great Game so popular for explaining the international relations of Central Asia? What is lost when we adopt this formulation?

2. Central Asia as Local

3. What do you find interesting about Central Asia? Why are you reading this book or taking this course? Do you expect Central Asians to be radically different from you in beliefs and motivations? Or do you see them as basically human in the way you are, even if customs may differ?

4. Does it make sense to you to think of ethnicity as a "package" of understandings about belonging? Do you think of your own ethnicity (or race, for that matter) as something predetermined and unchanging? Or do you have some choice in what your ethnicity is or means? Do communities and societies have the power to alter what it means to belong to any particular ethnic group?

3. Central Asia as Place

5. How would you define the geographical limits of Central Asia as a world region? Is the way we define Central Asia as place important?

6. How does imagining Central Asia as a distinct region affect geopolitical thinking?

4. Central Asia as Story

7. What contextual factors shape the stories Central Asians tell?

8. How do the stories that Central Asians tell compare to similar expressions that circulate in your own cultural context?

Case I-A: Ordinary Soviet Life through Collectivization

9. Based on these two stories, where did you see examples of coercion transforming ordinary life, and where did you see examples of new opportunities made possible by collectivization?

10. In what ways might these accounts be different if they had been recorded in the 1930s, when Boltaboy and Zulayho were young, rather than when they were octogenarians looking back over their whole lives?

Case I-B: Regulation and Appropriation of Islam in Authoritarian Political Contexts

11. How do you assess the control and appropriation of religion by an authoritarian state in the light of Article 18 of the Universal Declaration of Human Rights (right to freedom of thought, conscience, and religion)?

12. Discuss the potential long-term impact of authoritarian regulation on religious associations and religious thought in Tajikistan and Central Asia.

Case I-C: Migration from the Deep South to the Far North as Central Asian "Glocalism"

13. How would you compare Central Asian migrants' "glocalization" in Russia to other migrants' transnationalism in the country where you live?

14. In what aspects are migrants representative of the fact that Central Asia is both a periphery and a center?

FURTHER READING

1. Central Asia as Global

Adamson, Fiona B. "Global Liberalism Versus Political Islam: Competing Ideological Frameworks in International Politics." *International Studies Review* 7, no. 4 (2005): 547–69.

Clarke, Michael E. *Xinjiang and China's Rise in Central Asia, 1949–2009: A History*. New York: Routledge, 2011.

Cooley, Alexander. *Great Games, Local Rules: The New Great Power Contest in Central Asia*. New York: Oxford University Press, 2012.

Cooley, Alexander, and John Heathershaw. *Dictators without Borders: Power and Money in Central Asia*. New Haven, CT: Yale University Press, 2017.

Frankopan, Peter. *The Silk Roads: A New History of the World*. London: Bloomsbury, 2015.

Kalinovsky, Artemy M. *Laboratory of Socialist Development: Cold War Politics and Decolonization in Soviet Tajikistan*. Ithaca, NY: Cornell University Press, 2018.

Laruelle, Marlène, ed. *The Nazarbayev Generation: Youth in Kazakhstan*. Lanham, MD: Lexington, 2019.

Laruelle, Marlène, and Sébastien Peyrouse. *The Chinese Question in Central Asia: Domestic Order, Social Change, and the Chinese Factor*. New York: Columbia University Press, 2012.

Mackinder, Halford John. "The Geographical Pivot of History." London: Royal Geographical Society, 1904.

Olcott, Martha Brill. *Central Asia's Second Chance*. New York: Brookings Institution Press, 2010.

Omelicheva, Mariya. *Counterterrorism Policies in Central Asia*. London: Routledge, 2010.

Owen, Catherine, Shairbek Juraev, David Lewis, Nick Megoran, and John Heathershaw, eds. *Interrogating Illiberal Peace in Eurasia: Critical Perspectives on Peace and Conflict*. Lanham, MD: Rowman & Littlefield, 2018.

Spector, Regine A. *Order at the Bazaar: Power and Trade in Central Asia*. Ithaca, NY: Cornell University Press, 2017.

2. Central Asia as Local

Liu, Morgan Y. "Central Asia in the Post–Cold War World." *Annual Review of Anthropology* 40 (2011): 115–31.

Liu, Morgan Y. *Under Solomon's Throne: Uzbek Visions of Renewal in Osh*. Pittsburgh: University of Pittsburgh Press, 2012.

Tyrnauer, Matt. *Citizen Jane: Battle for the City*. Videodisc (93 min.). New York: MPI Media Group, Altimeter Films, 2017.

3. Central Asia as Place

Allison, Roy. "Virtual Regionalism, Regional Structures and Regime Security." *Central Asian Survey* 27, no. 2 (2008): 185–202.

Amineh, M. Parvizi, ed. *The Greater Middle East in Global Politics: Social Science Perspectives on the Changing Geography of the World Politics*. Leiden: Brill, 2007.

Bregel, Yuri. *An Historical Atlas of Central Asia*. Leiden: Brill, 2003.

Cooley, Alexander. *Great Games, Local Rules: The New Great Power Contest in Central Asia*. Oxford: Oxford University Press, 2012.

Hauner, Milan. *What Is Asia to Us? Russia's Asian Heartland Yesterday and Today*. London: Unwin Hyman, 1990.

Heathershaw, John, and Nick Megoran. "Contesting Danger: A New Agenda for Policy and Scholarship on Central Asia." *International Affairs* 87, no. 3 (2011): 589–612.

Lewis, Martin, and Kären Wigen. *The Myth of Continents: A Critique of Metageography*. Berkeley: University of California Press, 1997.

Myers, Karl E., and Shareen Blair Brysac. *Tournament of Shadows: The Great Game and the Race for Empire in Central Asia*. Washington, DC: Counterpoint, 1999.

Schoeberlein, John. "Setting the Stakes of a New Society." *Central Eurasian Studies Review* 1, no. 1 (2002): 4–8.

4. Central Asia as Story

Dubuisson, Eva-Marie. "Confrontation in and through the Nation in Kazakh *Aitys* Poetry." *Journal of Linguistic Anthropology* 20, no. 1 (2010): 101–15.

Heathershaw, John. "Of National Fathers and Russian Elder Brothers: Conspiracy Theories and Political Ideas in Post-Soviet Central Asia." *Russian Review* 71, no. 4 (2012): 610–29.

Levin, Theodore. *The Hundred Thousand Fools of God: Musical Travels in Central Asia (And Queens, New York)*. Bloomington: Indiana University Press, 1996.

Mills, Margaret, and Ravshan Rahmoni. *Conversations with Davlat Khalav: Oral Narratives from Tajikistan*. Moscow: Humanitary, 2000.

Reichl, Karl. Oral Epics into the Twenty-First Century: The Case of the Kyrgyz Epic Manas. *Journal of American Folklore* 129, no. 513 (2016): 327–44.

Case I-A: Ordinary Soviet Life through Collectivization

Cameron, Sarah. "The Kazakh Famine of 1930–33: Current Research and New Directions." *East/West: Journal of Ukrainian Studies* 3, no. 2 (2016): 117–32.

Ewing, Thomas. "Ethnicity at School: Educating the 'Non-Russian' Children of the Soviet Union, 1928–1939." *History of Education*. 35, no. 4–5 (2006): 499–519.

Kamp, Marianne. *The New Woman in Uzbekistan: Islam, Modernity, and Unveiling under Communism*. Seattle: University of Washington Press, 2006.

Kamp, Marianne, and Russell Zanca. "Recollections of Collectivization in Uzbekistan: Stalinism and Local Activism." *Central Asian Survey* 36, no. 1 (2017): 55–72.

Osokina, Elena. "Torgsin: Gold for Industrialization." *Cahiers du monde Russe* 47, no. 4 (2006): 715–48.

Case I-B: Regulation and Appropriation of Islam in Authoritarian Political Contexts

Khalid, Adeeb. *Islam after Communism: Religion and Politics in Central Asia*. Berkeley: University of California Press, 2007.

Khalid, Adeeb. *Central Asia: A New History from the Imperial Conquests to the Present*. Princeton, NJ: Princeton University Press, 2021.

Louw, Maria Elisabeth. *Everyday Islam in Post-Soviet Central Asia*. London: Routledge, 2007.

Mandaville, Peter. *Islam and Politics*. New York: Routledge, 2014.

McBrien, Julie. *From Belonging to Belief: Modern Secularisms and the Construction of Religion in Kyrgyzstan*. Pittsburgh: University of Pittsburgh Press, 2017.

Rasanayagam, Johan. *Islam in Post-Soviet Uzbekistan: The Morality of Experience*. Cambridge: Cambridge University Press, 2011.

Case I-C: Migration from the Deep South to the Far North as Central Asian "Glocalism"

Laruelle, Marlene, and Sophie Hofmann. "Polar Islam: Muslim Communities in Russia's Arctic Cities." *Problems of Post-Communism* 67, no. 4–5 (2020): 327–37.

Reeves, Madeleine. "Economies of Favour and Indifference in Moscow's Temporary Housing Market." In *Economies of Favour after Socialism*, edited by David Henig and Nicolette Makovicky, 73–95. Oxford: Oxford University Press, 2017.

Roche, Sophie. "Illegal Migrants and Pious Muslims: The Paradox of Bazaar Workers from Tajikistan." In *Tajikistan on the Move: Statebuilding and Societal Transformations*, edited by Marlène Laruelle, 247–78. Lanham, MD: Lexington Books, 2018.

Urinboyev, Rustamjon. "Establishing an 'Uzbek Mahalla' via Smartphones and Social Media: Everyday Transnational Lives of Uzbek Labor Migrants in Russia." In *Constructing the Uzbek State: Narratives of Post-Soviet Years*, edited by Marlène Laruelle, 119–48. Lanham, MD: Lexington Books, 2018.

Urinboyev, Rustamjon. "Migration, Transnationalism, and Social Change in Central Asia: Everyday Transnational Lives of Uzbek Migrants in Russia." In *Eurasia on the Move: Interdisciplinary Approaches to a Dynamic Migration Region*, edited by Marlène Laruelle and Caress Schenk, 27–41. Washington, DC: George Washington University, Central Asia Program, 2018.

PART II

CONTEXTS OF HISTORY

All pasts have histories, and those that get carried forward become part of the landscape in which the contemporary sits. But it is also more than just scenery; place and past hold meaning. Despite the arc of history being narrated as linear, what people do with history is quite often more complicated, interpreted with bits of information cobbled together by texts, stories retold, and imaginations seeking to understand the cloth from which people's lives were (are) made, to understand what took place before that made what is now seem natural.

Events come to hold meaning beyond the historical environment in which they occur(red)—where past and present tense can get blurred—and this section begins to give us the substance with which to see the critical role of history vis-à-vis how we understand context. The past, of course, starts somewhere, and where it starts—in the retelling and situating of its relevance—matters to the ends for which it is used. The ancient and medieval periods, of course, were the foundations upon which subsequent periods rest. Yet as Scott Levi situates within his chapter, it is in the sixteenth to nineteenth centuries that the historical foundation of early modern Central Asia develops a frame still recognizable today. We see a place of transformation, where the main currents of the near past lead into colonial engagement with Russian and the subsequent periods of Soviet rule and eventual independence of the Central Asian states. This marks the emergence of what eventually develops into the contemporary nation-states, but perhaps most importantly, the context out of which social order continues to evolve.

Such transformations in how Central Asians conceptualize their political and social selves come most dramatically in the colonial and Soviet periods. Alexander Morrison's chapter tells how the region was impacted by the expansion of the Russian empire and how it was a "colonial" experience: it came about through conquest; administrative structures were imposed; economic opportunities largely sought to benefit Russia more than Central Asia; yet also the relationship evolved into one understood by Russians—and not necessarily Central Asians—as having a civilizing mission. The transformations during this time were gradual compared to the transformations of the Soviet period, which were both more radical and traumatic.

As Ali İğmen describes, following the 1917 Bolshevik Revolution,

Central Asians were transformed from Russian imperial subjects to Soviet citizens. This came, however, within a context of standardizing—through ascription—the "culture" of Soviet citizens, as well as enacting a vision for "emancipating" people from their pasts. New social structures were imposed, which, as David Lewis shows in his chapter, became the backdrop out of which contemporary Central Asia emerged as post-Soviet and independent. Overviewing the first quarter century of independence, we see that the new states accepted the legitimacy of the titular claims of their Soviet-defined territorial boundaries and drew upon Soviet experiences in governing. Yet in time, through different decisions made by leaders acting in varied contexts, each country began to distinguish itself in independence.

As we see in the cases, there are problems framing the past within broader conceptual epochs like precolonial, colonial, Soviet, and post-Soviet, because, as with all things, the boundaries marking time are often described post hoc and people live across historical change. David Brophy tells the story of Vali Bay, a nineteenth-century entrepreneur whose reach expanded across parts of Kazakhstan and Xinjiang, China, before both were known by their current national boundaries. Adeeb Kalid writes of how Islam was managed during the late Soviet period, and we recognize the antecedent to how independent Central Asian states approach religion. And in the case offered by Botakoz Kassymbekova, we see how—in the case of female emancipation in a Soviet mining town—implementing some of the policies of the Soviet system was uneven due to existing gender structures.

Much of what is contained in this section is in the background of today. But moving forward, it becomes clear that we need history to appreciate the framings people use to provide context to experience and interpretation. These become the threads from which the contemporary fabric is woven.

5

Precolonial Central Asia

Scott C. Levi

I n considering the scope of Central Asia's long and remarkable history, the period from the sixteenth through nineteenth centuries remains poorly investigated. There are several reasons why this is the case. The most obvious of these is the absence of any great nomadic imperial powers such as the Scythians or Xiongnu of the ancient period, or the medieval *Türk* Qaghanate, the Mongols, or even Timur to draw scholarly attention. One can also point to the difficulties associated with working with the original manuscripts and other sources. Only a very small proportion of these are available in translation, or in any published formats, and so researchers must master multiple languages and travel great distances to conduct their work in reading rooms of manuscript libraries across Europe and Asia. Yet another reason stems from the long-standing, though now discredited, theory that European commercial activities in the Indian Ocean brought about the collapse of the overland "Silk Road" caravan trade, casting Central Asia into several centuries of unremarkable isolation and rendering the region and its peoples unworthy of serious consideration until the onset of the Russian colonial period. Whatever the reasons, the results have been a marked imbalance in the historiography that has led many of those scholars whose work focuses on the modern period to disregard the earlier history and place a disproportionately large amount of agency in the hands of the Russian imperial and Soviet states.

Looking backward past the post-Soviet independence era and seven decades of Soviet rule, and even farther beyond another layer of Russian imperial history, one can identify numerous ways in which the legacy of Central Asia's long history at the heart of the Eurasian landmass continues to shape peoples' lives in the region. This is visible in the region's ethnic demographics, which is reflected in Soviet-era border drawing and nationalities policies but in fact is largely a product of successive waves of nomadic migrations and settlement within the region that stretch back into antiquity. It is also apparent in terms of religion, as Sunni Muslim practices eclipsed other confessions, including Zoroastrianism, Buddhism, Nestorian Christianity, and more. One must look back to the medieval era to understand the reasons why Muslim mystics, or Sufis, were drawn to the Central Asian frontier and how the Central Asian Sufi orders came to occupy such an important social position in the region. Even in contemporary times, one does not have to look far to find traces of the imprint that influential mystical orders have left on Islamic practices within the region and beyond.

That said, in recent years, scholars working both within Central Asia and beyond it have made a number of important advancements in the early modern history of the region. The collective results include reaching a deeper understanding of the complexities of Central Asian societies in the era preceding Russian colonization, as well as a greater appreciation for the importance of questioning assumptions embedded within the region's historiography. These scholars have achieved new insights into the ways in which Central Asians remained connected with historical developments unfolding beyond the region, and the ways that Central Asians were influenced by, and influenced, those developments. This work also demonstrates that many of the historical processes often attributed to the Russian imperial or early Soviet periods have deeper historical roots. It is with that thought in mind that the essay below presents a short survey of the main currents of Central Asian history in the centuries leading up to the Russian colonial era.

The Timurids and Their Legacy

Timur (1336–1405, also Tamerlane) was a Turkic Muslim noble born into the Barlas tribe in the city of Shahrisabz, a short distance south of his later capital of Samarqand. Timur came of age at a time when Central Asia's Turkic nobility were struggling for power and authority, partly against their Chaghatai-Mongol overlords, though primarily against each other. In 1370, Timur emerged as the most successful of these Turkic amirs, defeating his rivals, casting off the Chaghataid khans, and eventually establishing his own dynastic rule in their place.

Timur is renowned for having given rise to Central Asia's last great imperial power. Drawing on the region's vast resources of nomadic manpower, he ran campaigns deep into the territory of the Golden Horde in modern Russia; southward into India, where he infamously sacked Delhi in 1398; and as far to the west as Anatolia, where in 1402 he defeated the Ottoman Sultan Bayezid I (r. 1389–1402) at the Battle of Ankara. After each campaign, his armies returned to Samarqand rich with loot and captives, many of whom were skilled laborers whom he put to work building the imperial architecture

5-1   The Registan, Samarqand, Uzbekistan, 2000. Photograph by David W. Montgomery.

for which his capital is famous. But for many of the peoples he conquered, his campaigns resulted in little more than death and destruction. Timur was considerably more talented at conquering regions than in establishing lasting control over them. Recurrent rebellions provoked repeated invasions and additional devastation. While some maps and contemporary descriptions portray Timur's empire as truly grand in size and power—and his armies certainly did venture far afield—in reality he held a firm grasp over only the sedentary portions of Central Asia and much of Afghanistan and Iran.

In 1405, while in the process of launching a campaign against Ming forces in China, Timur grew sick and died. His body was returned to Samarqand and interred in the tomb known today as the Gur-i Amir, and his sons and grandsons struggled against one another to claim the right to succeed him. By the time Timur's son Shah Rukh established himself as the rightful Timurid heir in 1409, any territorial claims that the Timurids may have had beyond their core region of Central Asia, Afghanistan, and Iran had slipped away. Before long, western Iran would follow.

For two centuries, steppe tradition had dictated that male descendants of Genghis (Chinggis) Khan (d. 1227) enjoyed an unquestionable right to rule. That is not to say that all of them were rulers, of course, but rather that in order to become a ruler one had to be able trace one's male ancestry to Genghis Khan himself. Timur rose to power despite this tradition, primarily through military might and forced submission. But for his heirs, the fifteenth century unfolded as a period of consolidation rather than conquest, and without Timur's monopoly on coercive power his successors found it necessary to develop new mechanisms to establish a compelling claim to political legitimacy. The strategy that Shah Rukh devised included efforts to project an image of dynastic power and imperial grandeur, working to maintain a secure and peaceful environment, fostering the support of the Turkic tribal nobility and their considerable manpower, and earning the consent of the Muslim religious elite through the strategic promotion of Islamic institutions, culture, and the arts.

Historians have come to refer to this era as the Timurid Renaissance. It began during the long reign of Shah Rukh (r. 1409–47) and was, one might argue, perfected under Sultan Husayn Baiqara (r. 1469–1506), whose court in Herat was adorned with such celebrated artists and luminaries as the poet Jami (d. 1492), the painter Bihzad (d. 1535), and, of course, the poet and statesman Alisher Navai (d. 1501). This Timurid model of governance would have a lasting legacy across much of the Islamic world. Within Central Asia itself, it was also in this period that the Sufi orders, spearheaded by the austere Naqshbandi sheikh Khoja Ahrar (1404–90), emerged as important landholding entities and first began to exercise considerable influence in the political arena as well. The Ahraris paved the way, and other influential Sufi orders followed.

Zahir al-Din Muhammad Babur (1483–1530) proved to be the most accomplished of the later Timurid rulers in Central Asia. He was born in the city of Andijan, in the Ferghana Valley, and he was the final Timurid to rule from the ancestral capital of Samarqand, before the Chinggisid ruler Muhammad Shibani Khan (1451–1510) and his Uzbek followers forced him from his homeland. Babur is most famously celebrated as the founder of the Mughal Empire in India (1526–1707/1857), a state that would, under his grandson Akbar (r. 1556–1605), become one of the greatest imperial powers in the early modern world. The Timurid legacy shaped Mughal administrative policies in India as well. Over the sixteenth and seventeenth centuries, Mughal territory grew to cover nearly the entire Indian subcontinent, its population totaled some one hundred million people, and foreign merchants pumped silver into the Mughal economy. Among East India Company employees, the word *Mogul* itself became synonymous with opulent wealth.

To the west, as the Shibanid Uzbek brought Timurid rule in Central Asia to an end, a new dynasty, the Safavids, rose to replace the more localized tribal forces that had asserted leadership over Iran. In terms of population and wealth, Safavid Iran (1501–1736) was less grand than its Mughal and Ottoman neighbors. Elevating Shi'a Islam to the level of the state religion—as it is today—the Safavids established a uniquely religious basis for their political legitimacy that stood in opposition to their Sunni Muslim neighbors. Despite frequent conflict, they managed to protect their western frontier against Ottoman incursions, and they maintained a tenuous eastern frontier with the Mughals and Uzbeks through diplomacy punctuated by occasional hostilities. Even with European maritime interests becoming ever more present in the Indian Ocean, the Safavids leveraged the presence of Armenians, Indians, and other merchant communities in their realm, and they drew considerable benefit from their position on overland routes connecting India with the Mediterranean Sea.

Nevertheless, Safavid control began to weaken noticeably toward the end of the seventeenth century. In 1722, the Ghilzai Afghan invasion and occupation of Isfahan, the Safavid capital at the time, effectively brought the state to an end. The Turkmen commander in the Safavid army, Nadir Tahmasp Quli Khan, managed to force the Afghans from Iran a few years later, but in 1736 he deposed Shah Abbas III (r. 1732–36) and assumed regal authority for himself. He ruled as Nadir Shah until his brutality and despotism prompted his own military commanders to fear for their own lives and, in 1747, conspire to have him assassinated.

The Bukharan Khanate

To the north, as the fifteenth century drew to a close, Muhammad Shibani Khan led between two hundred thousand and four hundred thousand Uzbek followers southward into the sedentary stretches of Central Asia, displacing Babur and conquering the Timurid capital of Samarqand. This was the last of many large-scale nomadic migrations from the steppe into Central Asia that had begun with Indo-European nomads in antiquity, who were followed in the medieval era by multiple waves of Turks. This most famously included the Oghuz (or Ghuzz, a linguistic term) Turkic Seljuks, the ancestors of the titular populations of Turkmenistan, Azerbaijan, and Turkey. It also included several Turkic groups that were repositioned to Central Asia during the Mongol era. These "Uzbeks" were Qipchaq (as opposed to Oghuz) Turkic Muslims who had emerged from the Qipchaq Khanate, commonly known as the Golden Horde, and who belonged to a number of tribes that had several decades earlier followed Shibani Khan's grandfather, Abu'l Khayr Khan (1412–68), to the southernmost stretches of the steppe. There, they took up a position as the immediate neighbors to, and occasional collaborators with, the Timurid rulers in Samarqand.

Not everyone under Abu'l Khayr Khan's leadership considered this to be an agreeable move. The Kazakhs (Qazaqs) represent those Qipchaq Turks who found fault in following Abu'l Khayr Khan's leadership. Rather than move southward toward the sedentary zone, they elected to split from the Uzbeks and remained in the north under the joint Chinggisid leadership of Kiray and Janibek. From the mid-fifteenth century well into the seventeenth century, the Kazakhs represented a powerful force in steppe politics, although the degree to which there was ever a unified Kazakh Khanate is an ongoing question. By the early eighteenth century, the Kazakhs constituted three separate political powers, commonly referred to in Western literature as Hordes: the Junior Horde (Kishi Zhüz), Middle Horde (Orta Zhüz), and Senior Horde (Uly, or Ulu Zhüz). These were by no means the only significant steppe powers at the time. The Kazakhs experienced recurrent conflict with their expansionist neighbors to the east, the non-Chinggisid Qalmaq, or western Oirot Mongols commonly known as the Jungar (Zungar, Dzungar), as well as the Khoqand Khanate to the south (discussed below). Over the course of the eighteenth and nineteenth centuries, owing primarily to advances in gunpowder weapons technology, the Kazakhs would gradually come under Russian domination.

The Uzbek migration into sedentary Central Asia ended the Timurid interregnum and ushered in another two and a half centuries of Chinggisid (i.e., descendants of Genghis Khan) rule in the region. There were a number of ways in which the Shibanids sought to distinguish their reign from that of their predecessors. To reference one example, Samarqand was reduced in importance and replaced by Bukhara as the seat of the senior member of the ruling dynasty. This individual exerted the most political influence, but only as the greatest among equals. As was the case among the Chinggisid Mongols, authority was shared among the ruling family with multiple leadership figures each effectively serving as principal ruler over their own territory, or appanage. In the early modern era, two distinct Chinggisid dynasties ruled what has become commonly referred to as the Bukharan Khanate. Beginning with Muhammad Shibani Khan, the Shibanids (or Abu'l Khayrids) ruled from 1500 to 1599, when their lineage was supplanted by the Toqay-Timurids (also known as the Janids or Astrakhanids), whose rule continued in earnest to 1747. This rival Chinggisid dynasty had its origins in the Astrakhan Khanate, a successor state of the Golden Horde that had as its capital the city of Astrakhan, located at the mouth of the Volga River on the northern shores of the Caspian Sea.

Under the Russian Tsar Ivan IV (r. 1547–84), Muscovy extended its control down the Volga and conquered the Khanates of Kazan in 1552 and Astrakhan in 1556. In the wake of the Russian victory, some members of the Toqay-Timurid ruling family fled for Bukhara, where, during a period of dynastic crisis, they managed to replace the Shibanids. Throughout this period, the Bukharan khans exerted some efforts to increase centralized authority, most notably during the reign of the Shibanid ruler 'Abdallah Khan II (r. 1583–98). But 'Abdallah Khan's reign was exceptional, and, in general, there was little difference between the governmental structures of these two dynasties. Bukharan leadership remained a corporate affair among the royal family, relying heavily on the Uzbek tribal nobility for their loyalty and support. At times, Toqay-Timurid governance over the Bukharan Khanate was so decentralized and the Turkic tribal leadership so strong that it is difficult to justify characterizing it as a singular state, much less an empire. Order was managed by maintaining a balance of patronage and pressure; the Bukharan khans retained the Uzbek nobility's loyalty only so long as they could provide incentives or, failing that, force them into submission.

From the late seventeenth century to the middle of the eighteenth century, the Bukharan Khanate progressively weakened and then collapsed. The causal factors behind that collapse have remained a topic of some debate. Moving beyond the notion that the region fell into isolation and decline as a result of the end of the so-called Silk Road trade, one might instead point to developments in gunpowder weapons technologies, a spike in demand for silver in China, and perhaps several other factors that have more to do

5-2   Locals outside of Kalon Mosque in Bukhara, Uzbekistan, 2019. Photograph by Kasia Ploskonka.

with the deleterious effects of global integration than isolation. During this period, the Bukharan Khanate suffered a worsening fiscal crisis, a growing crisis in legitimacy, and multiple Kazakh invasions southward into Bukharan territory in the early eighteenth century. The most devastating of these was in 1723, as a Jungar invasion of Kazakh pastures propelled the so-called Kazakh Barefooted Flight southward into Bukharan territory, where they destroyed crops, placed the capital under siege, and then left.

In response to this growing crisis, the Uzbek tribes that formed the backbone of the Bukharan military turned away from their weakened and ineffective leadership. Desperation drove the final Toqay-Timurid ruler of Bukhara, Abu'l Fayz Khan (r. 1711–47), to impose a series of military reforms in an effort to assert greater centralized control over the Uzbek amirs. His efforts at reform failed and in effect worsened the situation by further antagonizing the Uzbeks. Then, in 1737 and again in 1740, Nadir Shah's forces invaded the region and the decisive Persian victories sealed the fate of the Bukharan Khanate. Nadir Shah appointed Muhammad Hakim Ataliq, leader of the Uzbek Manghit tribe, to serve in a supervisory role at the court of the defeated Bukharan khan. He then returned to Persia with Muhammad Hakim's son, Muhammad Rahim, in his company. When the father died in 1743, Nadir Shah dispatched Muhammad Rahim back to Bukhara to take his place and restore order. In the wake of Nadir Shah's assassination in 1747, Muhammad Rahim killed Abu'l Fayz Khan and usurped authority for himself. This event marks the transition from the Bukharan Khanate to the Bukharan Amirate (or Emirate), as the Manghit tribal leadership generally claimed to rule as amirs, as Timur himself had done several centuries earlier, and not khans.

As Toqay-Timurid control teetered in Bukhara, even more dramatic changes were taking shape farther to the east. Since the Manchurian Qing dynasty (1644–1911) overthrew the Ming (1368–1644) in the middle of the seventeenth century, the Qing had struggled to achieve peace and stability on its western frontier. Efforts to subjugate the Jungar Mongols proved ineffective, and peace treaties were short-lived. The Qing forces were formidable in strength and armed with technologically current artillery, but the Jungar forces exhibited a determined independence, exceptional agility on the battlefield, and (for a nomadic power) a surprising willingness to incorporate gunpowder weapons into their own arsenal. For the Qing, this rendered the Jungar a serious threat that time and again undermined Qing interests in the region. Their relatively advanced military abilities also equipped the Jungar with a decisive advantage over their Kazakh neighbors to the west.

Determined to bring an end to the Jungar threat and stabilize his western frontier, the Qing dynasty's Qianlong emperor (r. 1735–96) began plans to launch a massive campaign into Jungar territories. The Qianlong emperor poured resources into strengthening his military and developing supply lines that extended thousands of miles. In 1756, tens of thousands of Qing troops began to make their way into Jungar territories. The emperor ordered his generals to show no mercy as they extinguished the Jungar state.

In an effort to make certain that the Jungar had no foothold from which they could launch a recovery, the Qing generals continued their campaigns southward into Altishahr. For eight decades, the Buddhist Jungars had governed this sparsely populated oasis zone through the mediation of the Muslim Afaqi, or Aqtaghliq ("White Mountain") Khojas, a Naqshbandi Sufi dynasty that the great Jungar ruler Galdan Khan (1644–97) had installed at the behest of the Dalai Lama himself. By 1758, the Qing forces had defeated the Khojas and secured Beijing's authority over all of modern Xinjiang—a vast new Qing territory that included the pastoral nomadic zone occupied by the Buddhist Jungar Mongols in the north and the sedentary oases that were home to Muslim Turks in Altishahr in the south, known today as the Uyghur. The Qing had conquered farther to the west than any ruling Chinese dynasty had achieved since the Tang dynasty lost the Battle of Talas in 751, a full millennium earlier.

The Uzbek Tribal Dynasties

As the Qing forged crucial alliances with local nobles and developed other techniques to consolidate their control over Xinjiang, other Central Asian peoples farther to the west charted a different course out of the political crisis of the first half of the eighteenth century. The events and processes of the eighteenth and nineteenth centuries reshaped many of Central Asia's social, religious, political, and environmental structures and institutions. In Bukhara, the Manghit dismissed their Chinggisid puppets in 1785 and ruled on their own as the amirs of Bukhara until 1920. Other Uzbek tribal powers were less reluctant to adopt the erstwhile Mongolian title of khan. The Uzbek

Qongrat tribe established the Khanate of Khiva in the Khwarezmian oasis to the north of Bukhara, and the Uzbek Ming established the Khanate of Khoqand in the Ferghana Valley, to the east. These Uzbek tribal dynasties devised new techniques to support their claims to legitimacy, and they remained major political forces in the region right up to the Russian colonial era. In recent work, there has also developed a greater appreciation for the unique and contrasting features of Central Asia's regional and local histories, including Khoqand, Bukhara, and Khiva, of course, but also smaller polities.

Khoqand

According to virtually all of the official histories of Khoqand (the Khoqand chronicles), the rise of the Khanate of Khoqand can be traced back to 1709. Although state structures would not be in place for several decades and the earliest accounts themselves were penned roughly a century after the fact, the narrative records attribute the rise of the family that would rule Khoqand until 1876 to a noble of the Uzbek Ming tribe named Shah Rukh. According to these accounts, Shah Rukh engineered the Uzbeks' victory over a group of politically ambitious Naqshbandi Khojas centered in the small city of Chadak, in the western stretches of the Ferghana Valley. The Valley was sparsely populated and mostly wilderness at the time. In subsequent years, the "Shahrukhid" rulers would establish critical alliances with neighboring tribal powers, extend their control throughout the Valley, and defend their realm from multiple external threats, including the Jungars. In 1740, Shah Rukh's son 'Abd al-Karim Biy founded the city of Khoqand to serve as the capital for his fledgling state.

The Qing conquest of neighboring Kashgar in 1758 was arguably the single greatest factor contributing to Khoqand's rise from a minor local power to a major expansionist khanate. Rather than prompting rebellion and instability, the Qing sought to pacify the population of their new acquisition by encouraging collaboration among local nobles, an objective that involved pumping wealth into Xinjiang, encouraging the development of the region's agricultural and commercial economies, and encouraging Chinese merchant groups to extend their networks westward into Xinjiang. Upon learning of the Qing victory, the Shahrukhid ruler Irdana Biy (r. 1751–52, 1753–69) successfully established an official relationship with the Qing and dispatched multiple official embassies to Beijing. He used this relationship to bolster his claim to legitimacy in the Ferghana Valley and also to secure commercial privileges in Qing markets for his own subjects, the so-called Andijani merchants of Khoqand. For nearly a century, revenue from this official relationship streamed into Khoqand and made it possible for the Shahrukhid rulers to secure loyalty through patronage systems, strengthen their military, and create new and expand existing irrigation networks that made it possible to settle the multiple waves of migrants that made their way into the Valley and brought about an increase in agricultural revenues in the process.

5-3   The Palace of Khudayar Khan, Khoqand, Uzbekistan, 2005. Photograph by David W. Montgomery.

By the end of the eighteenth century, the Shahrukhid rulers had effectively asserted their authority across the Ferghana Valley. Narbuta Biy (r. 1770–99) had overseen a long period of stability, during which he maintained close relations with Beijing, established useful alliances with local tribal and religious elite, and oversaw the excavation of the first large-scale irrigation networks in the Valley. Narbuta's son and successor 'Alim favored more aggressive reforms. Widely known as 'Alim Zalim, or 'Alim the Tyrant, 'Alim began his reign by purging Khoqand of a substantial portion of his father's administration, killing many and forcing many more to flee. He then transformed Khoqand's military to make it a stronger and more dependable fighting force. His military was comprised of traditional Turkic cavalry as well as the Ghalcha corps, a standing artillery force of vehemently loyal and well-trained mountain Tajiks armed with technologically current gunpowder weapons. 'Alim was also perhaps the first ruler of Khoqand to set aside Mongolian traditions that had persisted in the region since the time of Genghis Khan himself (d. 1227) and assume the title of khan for himself.

Under 'Alim Khan's leadership, Khoqand entered a period of rapid expansion. In 1808, Khoqandi forces conquered Tashkent from its Kazakh leadership and soon thereafter took the cities of the southern steppe. Over the next three decades, 'Alim Khan's successors (his brother 'Umar orchestrated a coup in 1811) ran campaigns deep into the Pamirs of modern Tajikistan and far into Kazakh territory—making Khoqand the first sedentary power in Central Asia to control vast portions of the steppe since Timur, four centuries earlier. In less than four decades, the Shahrukhids increased their territory by a factor of thirty, asserting Khoqandi control over caravan routes leading northward to Russian commercial outposts on the Irtysh River and eastward to Qing markets in Xinjiang. By 1840, Khoqand's population is estimated to have reached five million, three million in the sedentary zone and another two million nomadic subjects.

'Umar Khan (r. 1811–22) benefited from his brother's unbridled ambitions, but he set aside 'Alim Khan's tyrannical tendencies. 'Umar Khan is most famous for applying a decidedly urbane and sophisticated method to establish the legitimacy of his rule. He endeavored to govern through multiple constituencies and build support among the religious elite, but a central component of his method was to project the image of a court culture that recalled the now-mythological grandeur of the Sultan Husayn Baiqara's Timurid court in fifteenth-century Herat. 'Umar Khan looked to other ways to use the Timurid legacy to bolster his legitimacy as well. This included, most notably, the propagation of the Altun Beshik legend, which was deliberately crafted in order to link the Shahrukhid lineage to none other than Zahir al-Din Muhammad Babur (1483–1530), who was, again, the final Timurid prince to rule in Central Asia and first Mughal emperor of north India, and who was himself born in the city of Andijan, in the Ferghana Valley.

Khoqand's territorial expansion continued even throughout the troubled reign of 'Umar Khan's son and (reputedly debaucherous) successor Muhammad 'Ali, or Madali Khan (r. 1822–42), as he was commonly called. But toward the end of his reign, several factors converged to reverse the khanate's fortunes. Concerned with Khoqand's rapid territorial expansion, the Bukharan ruler, Amir Nasrallah (discussed below), exploited widespread dissatisfaction with Madali Khan's reign to launch several campaigns against Khoqand. Finally, in 1842, Bukharan armies entered the Valley, occupied the city of Khoqand, and then captured and executed Madali Khan, his mother, and other members of the royal family. However, within a matter of weeks, Shahrukhid forces had rallied to remove the Bukhara-appointed *hakim* (governor) and recover control over the Valley.

This was followed by two events that had even more deleterious effects on the stability of Khoqand, both of which occurred in 1853. First, after nearly a century of the Qing providing silver subsidies to Turkic Muslim nobles in Altishahr in exchange for their loyalty, the Taiping Rebellion and other problems in China caused a fiscal crisis that forced the Qing to bring the subsidies to an end. The political environment in Altishahr quickly deteriorated, Khoqandi merchants lost access to Chinese markets, and Khoqand's treasury suffered. Second, and even more disruptive, was the 1853 Russian conquest of the Khoqandi fortress at Aq Masjid, on the lower stretches of the Syr Darya River. Over the next eleven years, Russian forces advanced to Chimkent at the southernmost limits of the steppe. Then, in 1865, General M. G. Cherniaev led his Russian troops to victory over Tashkent, the gateway to the steppe and Khoqand's most valuable territorial possession.

Even in the wake of Cherniaev's conquest of Tashkent, Khudayar Khan worked to establish a viable commercial relationship with his new Russian neighbors in the hope that doing so might return some prosperity to his realm and secure Khoqand's autonomy. He also sought to ease financial pressures by ordering the excavation of yet another large-scale irrigation project, the Ulugh Nahr, that drew water from the Syr Darya west of Andijan. In total, Khoqand's irrigation programs had converted an estimated 2,300 square miles of wilderness, an amount of land equal to roughly 27 percent of the Ferghana Valley, into productive farmland. Crops included grains and the fruits for which the region is rightly famous, as well as cotton as a cash crop for export to Russian markets. While the process by which Central Asian agriculture transformed into a cotton monoculture is often attributed to Russian imperial or Soviet initiatives, this example highlights the importance of looking deeper into precolonial historical processes.

But quite unlike the Qing conquest of Altishahr a century earlier, the Russians staked out a significantly more aggressive colonial presence in the region, and for the rulers of Khoqand it proved to be terminally destabilizing. Russian interference in regional politics provoked multiple rebellious movements within Khoqand with little in common other than an anti-Russian platform, and even Khudayar Khan's most determined efforts to calm them proved insufficient. In 1875, with anti-Russian forces threatening to take over Khoqand, Governor General Konstantin von Kaufman (1818–82) ordered Major-General Mikhail Skobelev (1843–82) to invade the Ferghana Valley and put down this final rebellion. On February 2, 1876, Tsar Alexander II (r. 1855–81) officially extinguished the Khanate of Khoqand and incorporated its remaining territory into the Russian empire.

Bukhara

Within the region itself, Khoqand's greatest rival was the Bukharan Amirate, the successor to the Bukharan Khanate. The Bukharan Amirate did not enjoy the dramatic territorial expansion of Khoqand, but it matched Khoqand in military strength and was by no means isolated from events and processes external to the region. During the eighteenth century, while Khoqandi merchants were extending their interests eastward into Qing territories, Bukharans exploited their own long-standing commercial linkages with neighboring economies. This was especially true for the north, where the markets became more important from the seventeenth century as Russian commercial interests extended their reach deeper into the region. Undermining arguments pertaining to Central Asia's presumed relative isolation: even as the Bukharan Khanate fell into political crisis during the first half of the eighteenth century, Bukharan merchants extended their networks in Siberia even farther.

Dismissing the practice of maintaining Chinggisid puppets, the Bukharan ruler Shah Murad (r. 1785–99) took the title of amir (commander) and emphasized religion over Chinggisid birth right as the cornerstone for the Manghit claim to legitimacy. Shah Murad's son and successor, Amir Haydar (1799–1826), even took the caliphal title of *amir al-mu'minīn*, or Commander of the Faithful, to emphasize his lofty political stature and the seriousness with which he made it his duty to "permit what is good and forbid what is evil," and generally to provide a just environment in which his Muslim subjects could live their lives. Not to be outdone, Amir Haydar's contemporary in neighboring Khoqand, 'Umar Khan, took for himself the title of *amīr al-muslimīn*, or Commander of the Muslims. The early Bukharan amirs also undertook efforts to strengthen the state through monetary reforms, the restoration of certain public monuments, and the revitalization of pious foundations.

In 1826, Amir Haydar's death set in motion a battle for succession among three of his sons. Nasrallah (r. 1826–60) emerged victorious and he worked over the course of his long reign to consolidate and strengthen his centralized authority. Amir Nasrallah began by purging nobility and other powerful individuals who had supported his brothers, or whom he otherwise suspected of questionable loyalty. In some ways echoing 'Alim Khan's earlier reign in Khoqand, this earned Amir Nasrallah the nickname of *amir-i qassāb*, or the Butcher. But where 'Alim Khan's brutal methods for enforcing his reforms led to his untimely death, Nasrallah's reforms were more successful. The military reforms he implemented in the mid-1830s included developing a more capable standing army that included an elite infantry force known as the *sarbāz* ("those risking the head"), equipping the *sarbāz* with technologically current artillery, and training them to use those weapons effectively.

Amir Nasrallah is also renowned as the Bukharan ruler responsible for imprisoning the British officers, Colonel Charles Stoddart and Captain Arthur Conolly, who had come to appeal for his friendship, patience, and support during the First Anglo-Afghan War (1839–42). In the wake of the British defeat in 1842, Nasrallah ordered both Stoddart and Conolly to be executed. Though it has attracted considerable attention in the popular imagination, the Anglo-Russian colonial cold war often memorialized as the "Great Game" had very little influence on the actual trajectory of Central Asian history. It did, however, help to shape British perspectives of Amir Nasrallah as a religious zealot and paranoid despot, and of Bukharan culture and society as benighted and regressive.

Bukharan losses piled up in the wake of the Russian conquest of Tashkent in 1865. The cities of Jizzakh, Urateppe, and Khojand were among the first to fall to Russian forces, and Samarqand followed in 1868. Securing the boundaries of the new Guberniya of Turkestan, General Kaufman forced a commercial treaty on Amir Muzaffar al-Din (r. 1860–86), Amir Nasrallah's son and successor, that equipped Russian merchants with unfettered access to Bukharan markets. In essence, Kaufman had reduced the Bukharan Amirate to a de facto Russian protectorate.

Khiva

At the beginning of the thirteenth century, the Central Asian region of Khwarazm (Khorezm) was home to an extensive and rapidly expanding empire ruled by a dynastic family known as the Khwarazmshah. Khwarazm itself was a lush green oasis on the southern shores of the Aral Sea, an agricultural island surrounded by arid steppe and desert and fed by the waters of the Amu Darya River. Already by the 1210s, the Khwarazmshahs had extended their control from the city that is today known as Old, or "Kone," Urgench (or Gurganj) in modern Turkmenistan southward into Afghanistan and Iran. Khwarazm was poised to become the heart of the greatest Muslim power in the world at the time. The Khwarazmshah's decision to provoke Genghis Khan by confiscating the goods of a Mongol caravan and then executing the ambassadors that Genghis Khan had sent to demand compensation brought an end to that possibility.

Several centuries later, in 1516, as the Shibanids and their Uzbek followers were consolidating their authority in Bukhara, a separate Chinggisid dynasty established their rule in Khwarazm (Khorezm). These were the Arabshahids, also known as the Yadigarid Shibanids, as they emanated from a separate branch of the Shibanid lineage. In Khwarazm, they ruled first from Kone Urgench. But in 1576, silting caused the Amu Darya to shift course to the east, making large-scale inhabitation of Kone Urgench impractical. After several decades of trying to overcome nature, in 1619 Arab Muhammad Khan (r. 1603–23) elected to move his capital eastward to Khiva. It is for this reason that the Chinggisid state in Khwarezm has become known as the Khanate of Khiva.

Khiva was the smallest of the three states in Central Asia's sedentary zone, and it was distinguished by the relative ethnic uniformity of the population. The population of the Bukharan Amirate was predominantly comprised of two groups: Sarts, or settled farmers, whether Tajik or Turk, who occupied the oasis zones; and the sizeable number of nomadic Uzbek tribesmen who occupied the nonarable wasteland between oases. The population of Khoqand was a thorough mix of Sarts (both Tajik and Turk) as well as Uzbeks and Kyrgyz. But the process of Turkicization in Khiva was substantially more advanced, leaving few Tajiks among the Uzbek, Turkmen, Kazakhs, and Karakalpak populations. Some have argued that Khiva was also distinctive in terms of its relative isolation from foreign influences.

Like the Manghit in Bukhara and the Ming in Khoqand, in the period leading up to Russian colonial expansion into the region the Khivans also cast off Chinggisid rule in favor of an Uzbek tribal dynasty. In the wake of his occupation of Bukhara and Khiva in 1740, Nadir Shah placed Manghit nobles as his representatives in both realms. The Manghit usurped supreme authority in Bukhara after Nadir Shah's death in 1747. But in Khwarezm, after several decades of conflict, it was the leadership of the Qongrat tribe who emerged to displace both the Chinggisid and the Manghit. In 1804, the Qongrat leader Eltuzer established an autonomous dynasty independent of the Chinggisids. He perished soon after, but his brother and successor, Muhammad Rahim, enjoyed a considerably longer and more prosperous reign (1806–26).

Muhammad Rahim led his Khivan forces to finally subjugate the determinedly resistant Uzbek nomadic groups in the region, which improved security for long-distance traders as well as Khivan agricultural settlements.

5-4   Entrance to the Kunya Ark Palace within Itchan Kala, Khiva, Uzbekistan, 2019. Photograph by Kasia Ploskonka.

Khivan khans also fostered a close relationship with the neighboring Turkmen tribesmen, large numbers of whom served in the Khivan military. This Khivan-Turkmen alliance enabled the Qongrat to assert their authority within the region, to protect the region from Bukhara and other periodically hostile neighbors, and to run raids into those same regions as well. For their part, it was during this period that Turkmen grew infamous for running raids into the poorly defended settlements in nearby Iran, capturing many thousands of Shi'a Muslim Persians and selling them into slavery across both sedentary and nomadic Central Asia.

Within the Khivan state itself, the Qongrat administration diverted resources into expanding irrigation networks in the Khwarezmian oasis in order to increase the amount of arable land. Echoing the policies of the Ming in the Ferghana Valley, the Khivan khans leveraged their ability to provide or deny access to those resources as a way to exert control over certain elements of their population. In Khiva, this proved to be an effective means to settle problematic Turkmen tribes, for example, while simultaneously enhancing the tax revenues for the small state. Issues pertaining to the Khivan commercial economy and Khwarezm's economic linkages with other, more distant regions in the eighteenth and nineteenth centuries stand in need of further investigation.

The states that the "tribal dynasties" of the Uzbek Ming, Manghit, and Qongrat gave rise to in Khoqand, Bukhara, and Khiva developed their own historical trajectories and they exhibit a number of distinctive features that merit careful attention. But ultimately, it was the Russian colonial expansion into the region that brought each of them to an end. In the case of the Khivan Khanate, the process began in earnest with the Russian establishment of an outpost at Krasnovodsk, on the eastern shores of the Caspian Sea, just one year after the 1868 Russian victory over Bukhara and annexation of Samarqand. Five years later, in the scorching summer heat of 1873, Russian troops marched on Khiva from Tashkent, Orenburg, and Mangishlaq. The Russians took the capital on June 10, and two months later, the defeated Khivan ruler Muhammad Rahim II (r. 1864–1910) ceded authority over all international matters to General Kaufman and accepted his state's new position as a Russian protectorate.

Precolonial Central Asia

The history of modern Central Asia is built upon a deep foundation. This is evidenced in the complex demographic makeup of the region, the defining features of which took shape over centuries—even millennia—as successive waves of nomadic migrations and other forces brought a layering of diverse peoples. It is also evidenced in the religious history of the region, with Islam supplanting other faiths as it took root and spread in its own distinctive forms. Sufi mystics played a critical role in this medieval process, and their legacy remains prominent even in contemporary times.

The brief discussion here has outlined only a few of the many ways in which historical processes rooted in the early modern era also continue to shape modern Central Asian society. The ecological transformation of the Ferghana Valley from largely wilderness into a more densely populated, cash crop–producing region represents one example. Far from being a product of Soviet or even Russian imperial policies, this transformation began to take shape already in the middle of the eighteenth century, and it was well underway when the Russians first entered the Valley in the 1870s. After dismissing their Chinggisid overlords, the increasing importance that the Manghit placed on religion and religious institutions in supporting their claims to legitimacy as the amirs of Bukhara is another example. Bukhara's role as an important center of Islamic civilization famously goes back to the Middle Ages. But if one is to understand the religious history of the region in the twentieth century, one must consider the changing context of the eighteenth and nineteenth centuries as well. The close relationship that the Khivans maintained with the Turkmen and their strategic use of irrigation (like Khoqand) to settle problematic subjects in the Khwarezmian oasis while expanding their agricultural tax base is a third example. Considered as a whole, early modern water politics in Central Asia provide insight into the deeper history of the water crisis that culminated during the twentieth century with the disappearance of the Aral Sea. But in all of these cases, the ways in which history unfolded during the Russian and Soviet periods appear not as a series of events that a foreign power forced upon a static and isolated region but as a continuation of a long-standing historical process, the origins of which are fully Central Asian.

SCOTT C. LEVI

6

Colonial Central Asia

Alexander Morrison

Central Asia and the Russian Empire

The very title of this chapter asserts a view of the relationship between Central Asia and Russia that is not universally shared. "Russia did not have colonies" is a common refrain, not just in Russophone but in some English-language historiography. The reasons cited vary, from the lack of a clear sea barrier to the absence of any clear political distinction between metropole and colony in Russia, claims that Russian rule brought economic and civilizing benefits, assertions that racial distinctions were unimportant in Russia, or even that Russians are incapable of being racist. The roots of these objections are to be found almost exclusively in the Soviet period—while Tsarist officials often claimed that their colonialism was more humane and civilized than that of Russia's European rivals, Britain and France, they were perfectly comfortable with using the language of colonialism. Russia was a member of the International Colonial Institute, and Russian authors and officials routinely described Central Asia as a colony, with open recognition that it bore a family resemblance to the colonies of the British and French in Asia and Africa. In the Soviet period, however, *colonialism* became an exclusively pejorative term: it was what the USSR's enemies, the bourgeois powers, did in *their* colonies, a matrix of economic exploitation and cultural subordination that had nothing in common with Soviet practices. The USSR did not have colonies—its people were all citizens, and the inhabitants of its more "backward" regions (for such notions of backwardness and civilization certainly did cross the revolutionary divide) were no longer colonial subjects but part of a radical new nation-building experiment. From the 1920s, when Soviet policies of "nativization" (*kore-nizatsiya*) were at their most radical, until the mid-1940s, Soviet historians did indeed denounce Tsarist rule in Central Asia as "colonial." After 1951, as the idea of the Russians as the "elder brother" of the peoples of the USSR was consolidated, the "friendship of peoples" narrative was projected back beyond 1917, Russian rule came to be characterized as "absolute good" for Central Asian peoples, and Russian colonialism largely disappeared from the Soviet lexicon.

This chapter takes a different approach; it assumes that Russian rule in Central Asia before 1917 was "colonial" in the commonly understood sense of the term—namely, that it was a territory acquired by force, against the desires of its indigenous inhabitants; that there was a hierarchy of political rights, in which Central Asians were placed below Europeans; that Russia claimed to have a "civilizing mission" in Central Asia, and that this was used as a justification for this inequality of both people and territory; that rhetorically, at least, it was viewed as a region that could and should be exploited for the benefit of the Russian metropole. Racial divisions between colonizer and colonized were less stark in Russian Central Asia than in most other colonial contexts, but the religious divide—between Christian and Muslim—played a similar role of demarcation, as did firmly entrenched beliefs in the superiority of European civilization, to which most Russians in Central Asia assumed they belonged. Russian views of the region were frequently Orientalist, in the sense popularized by Edward Said—that is, they saw in Central Asia a negative reflection of themselves, backward where Russia was advanced, feminine where Russia was masculine, passive where Russia was active, fanatical where Russia was rational. These stereotypes were never absolute or consistent, but they did form the dominant Russian discourses about Central Asia and its inhabitants, and served to justify their rule over them.

Conquest

Central Asia's largely unequal political and economic relationship with the Russian Empire can be dated long before any of it was claimed as Russian sovereign territory. Deciding exactly when the conquest of Central Asia began is complicated by the lack of any clear definition of where and what it is. Sometimes it is limited to the sedentary regions of southern Central Asia (*Sredniaia Aziia*, or "Middle Asia" in Russian), sometimes it also includes the Kazakh Steppe, and sometimes it is expanded to include the Volga-Ural region, the Caspian Steppes, Mongolia, and Jungharia. While tsarist historians often traced the Russian conquest back to the fall of Muslim Kazan to the forces of Ivan IV ("The Terrible") in 1552, for the purposes of this chapter we will assume that "Central Asia" corresponds roughly to the five post-Soviet republics of Central Asia, or what was known as the Turkestan governor-generalship and the Steppe Region in the tsarist period. Taking this as our territory, we can say that the conquest and colonization of Central

Asia by Russia began with a gradual shift of military advantage away from steppe nomadic peoples toward the sedentary states that surrounded them, notably Muscovite Russia and Qing China, in the course of the seventeenth century. In 1755, the Qianlong emperor's forces defeated the Junghar confederacy; this was the last significant attempt at state-building by a nomadic power in Central Asia, and its demise signaled a permanent shift in the balance of power from nomadic to sedentary. Even so, we should still think of the extension of Russian control over the steppe in the subsequent century as a long process, not a single event. It was complicated by the fact that the main nomadic inhabitants of the steppe, the Kazakhs, were divided into three hordes (*zhuz*) with decentralized networks of power and political authority. Soviet historians invariably wrote that the Kazakhs voluntarily "united" with Russia in 1731, dating this from the supposed "submission" of Abu'l-Khayr Khan of the Junior Horde to the Empress Anna that year. However, even assuming that the Junior Horde can stand for all Kazakhs (which of course it cannot) and that Abu'l-Khayr spoke for all his people (which he did not, as the only contemporary account of the negotiations, by the Russian ambassador Kutlu-Muhammad Tevkelev clearly shows), Abu'l-Khayr did not understand the agreement he had signed as a permanent cession of sovereignty, but rather as a temporary alliance or marriage of convenience, designed to boost his own authority and provide protection from the Bashkirs and the Qalmyqs, also nominally Russian subjects. By 1743, angered by the holding of his son as an *amanat*, or hostage, in the newly founded fortress town of Orenburg, he was in full rebellion against Russia. While 1731 marks the point at which Russian rulers began *claiming* the Kazakhs as Russian subjects, it did not signal any real control over either the people or the territory where they grazed their animals. Ablai Khan of the Middle Horde was able to maintain fairly stable diplomatic relations with both Qing China and the Russian empire until his death, and correspondence between Kazakh Sultans and the Qing continued into the 1820s. Not until the 1790s, with the creation of the Orenburg frontier commission and the abolition of the position of khan, did the Kazakhs of the Junior Horde come under anything resembling Russian administration, and not until 1822, with the introduction of Mikhail Speranskii's *Regulations for the Siberian Kirgiz*, did the Russians attempt to build fortresses, levy taxation, and administer justice in the territories of the Middle Horde in the northern part of the steppe. From this point onward, they would have to fight to gain control of both territory and people in Central Asia—it was a conquest (*zavoevanie*), not a "uniting" (*prisoedinenie*).

In 1839, Count V. A. Perovskii, the governor-general of Orenburg, launched a five-thousand-man expedition to conquer the "insolent" Khanate of Khiva, south of the Aral Sea. While the expedition ended in disaster, as all ten thousand of its camels and a quarter of its men died of winter cold, it marked a new chapter of Russian conquest. Anxious to reverse this humiliation, and the corresponding loss of prestige that the Russians feared,

Perovskii's successor, V. A. Obruchev, received authorization to build fortresses and station garrisons far deeper in the steppe, at Irgiz and Turgai in 1845, and at Raim, on the Aral Sea, in 1847. Obruchev was also responding to the challenge posed by the Kazakh Sultan Kenesary, a grandson of Ablai Khan of the Middle Horde, who simultaneously sought recognition from Russia of his right to rule as khan and raided Kazakhs whom the Russians thought of as their subjects. His movement is usually described as a "rebellion," but it is perhaps more appropriate to see it as a last, doomed attempt to create a steppe-based polity that could negotiate with neighboring sedentary powers on equal terms. Kenesary's death at the hands of the Kyrgyz in 1847 did not signal the end of resistance to Russian expansion in the steppe. The Khanate of Khoqand (Kokand), which had extended its rule over much of the Syr-Darya Valley and Semirechie in the first half of the nineteenth century, was in many ways a more formidable opponent. Perovskii would erase the memory of his earlier failure by capturing the Khoqandi fortress of Aq Masjid (renamed Perovsk, now Kyzylorda) in 1853, allowing the creation of a new, though highly problematic, Russian frontier line on the Syr-Darya. In 1854, at the end of a simultaneous advance southward from Semipalatinsk and Ayaguz along the Chinese frontier, Russian forces crossed the Ili river and established a new fortress in the Almaty depression, which they christened "Fort Vernoe" ("Faithful"). For the next ten years they halted, as the Crimean War and its aftermath distracted the leadership in St. Petersburg, and the Ministries of Finance and War wrangled over where the new Russian frontier should run—the main point of contention being whether to include the great commercial city of Tashkent. When it resumed, in 1864, the Khoqandi fortifications at Pishpek, Toqmaq, Aulie-Ata, Turkestan, and Chimkent all fell in swift succession, and for the first time the whole of the Kazakh Steppe and its inhabitants had been brought within the frontiers of the Russian empire, while Khoqand had suffered a series of shattering defeats from which it would never fully recover.

Tashkent fell to the forces of General M. G. Cherniaev the following year. As we have seen, this did not mark the beginning of the Russian conquest of Central Asia, nor was it something entirely unexpected and accidental, as is widely supposed. Cherniaev's personal ambition certainly played a role in accelerating the Russian advance, but the minister of war, D. A. Miliutin, had been lobbying for Tashkent's annexation as the anchor point of a new fortified frontier since 1862. Instead, the significance of Tashkent's fall was that it marked Russia's advance into a new environmental, economic, and cultural zone—that of the sedentary societies of Central Asia, based on riverine irrigated agriculture. In particular, Russian interests now came into direct conflict with those of Bukhara, whose amir had taken advantage of Khoqand's misfortunes to annex territory at the mouth of the Ferghana Valley, and who now had designs on Tashkent. Operating for the first time in a region where their troops could live off the land, freed from the constraints imposed by the need to round up and pay for thousands of camels to carry their supplies, with their superiors at least six weeks' journey away in Orenburg and Omsk, it was at this point that the Russian "men on the spot"—Cherniaev, D. M. Romanovskii, and N. A. Kryzhanovskii—really did launch themselves on a path of unauthorized conquest. First Khujand and then Jizzakh fell to their forces, while the Bukharans were routed at the Battle of Irjar. The appointment of the first governor-general of the newly created province of Turkestan, K. P. von Kaufman (see figure 6-1), did nothing to slow the pace of annexations. Trusted by Miliutin in St. Petersburg, Kaufman exploited his connections to obtain retrospective authorization for the capture of Samarkand (Samarqand) in 1868 (provoked by minor border disputes with Bukhara) and permission in advance for the complex, costly, but successful campaign against remote Khiva in 1873. Both khanates became Russian protectorates, with considerable internal autonomy, on the model of the princely states of British India, and their territories were only absorbed into the new Uzbek Soviet Republic in 1924. In 1875, a rebellion broke out in the Ferghana Valley against the Khan of Khoqand, Khudoyar. His legitimacy eroded by repeated defeats at the hands of the Russians, he had sought to rebuild his authority through heavy taxation to fund a modernized army, but his rule ended with his flight to Russian territory. After a "pacification" campaign of extreme brutality led by General M. D. Skobelev and an initial attempt to maintain Khoqand as a protectorate, von Kaufman received permission to annex it as the new province of Ferghana—one that would rapidly become the richest in the whole of Russian Turkestan. With the suppression of the Khoqand Khanate, the Russians also inherited its vague claims to sovereignty over the Pamir plateau and Badakhshan, although these would only be annexed, by mutual agreement with Britain, in 1895.

The last major Russian military campaigns in Central Asia were fought in Transcaspia (modern Turkmenistan). The Russians had established a fortress on the Caspian coast at Krasnovodsk in 1869, and from this bridgehead in the 1870s they gradually extended their authority over the Turkmen of the coastal areas and the Kazakhs of the Adai tribe on the Mangishlaq peninsula. In 1879, General N. A. Lomakin led an unsuccessful assault on the fortress of Denghil-Tepe, where most of the Akhal-Teke Turkmen tribe had taken refuge. In 1881, to wipe out the memory of this reverse, Skobelev attacked the Akhal-Teke once again, storming their fortress of Gök-Tepe and slaughtering fourteen thousand men, women, and children. It was his bloody victory that would prompt Fyodor Dostoevsky to pen his triumphalist essay "What is Asia to Us?," celebrating Russia's future civilizing destiny in Asia. This campaign was also notable for the construction of the first railway in Central Asia, from Uzun-Ada on the Caspian Sea to Qizil-Arvat. Once the Turkmen had been pacified, it was quickly extended to Ashgabat and Merv, and then across the Amu-Darya to Bukhara and Samarkand, which it reached in 1888. Though originally constructed for military purposes, it would soon take on considerable commercial significance.

The seemingly relentless Russian advance, which added 1.5 million square miles of territory to the empire in the space of sixty years, has

attracted different explanations, most of them wrong. The British firmly believed that it was directed at their possessions in India, either for the purpose of invasion or to allow the Russian empire to apply pressure to their frontiers in Central Asia in order to extract concessions in European diplomacy, the so-called Great Game. As British sources and interpretations have tended to dominate the historiography of the Russian conquest, so has this interpretation, but in fact the British figured relatively rarely in Russian calculations and correspondence, certainly by comparison with Central Asian rulers and peoples. Soviet historians, and many Western historians who relied on them, assumed the motivation must have been economic, taking their cue from Lenin's idiosyncratic interpretation of the British anti-imperialist J. A. Hobson's arguments about the origins of the Boer War. In particular, they anachronistically projected the obsession of later Soviet planners with transforming southern Central Asia into a vast cotton plantation back into the middle of the nineteenth century, adding a conspiratorial cabal of Moscow textile mill owners for good measure; once again, there is little or no contemporary evidence for the importance of cotton, either as raw material import or textile export, in debates among Russian officials as to the desirability of advancing further into Central Asia. Finally we come to the most plausible explanation—that of the "man on the spot," out of control. This was perhaps a factor in the mid-1860s, after the fall of Tashkent, and certainly the original initiative for most Russian advances can be found on the frontier, as officers and governors wrote back to St. Petersburg urging annexations; however, in almost all cases they still needed approval, and ultimately this came from the tsar himself. The steppe and desert campaigns that marked all Russian advances up to the 1860s, and the Khivan and Transcaspian expeditions thereafter, required large budgets for supplies and camels to carry them, which could not be obtained without St. Petersburg's say-so.

We are left, then, with a multitude of local factors—environmental, political, and personal—and perhaps one overarching explanation, which was the consuming need for prestige, and fear of losing it, of the Russian empire and its representatives in Central Asia. Time and again a reverse—the failed Khivan expedition of 1839, Cherniaev's first, failed assault on Tashkent in 1864, or the repulse of Lomakin's attack on Denghil-Tepe in 1879—would become the justification for a subsequent attack. The Russians conquered Central Asia because they feared they would appear weak if they did not.

Administration

The administrative structures the Russians created in Central Asia can be charted through a series of statutes from the early nineteenth to the early twentieth century. These all shared certain features, notably a clear division between a higher administration that wielded executive power and was staffed by Europeans, and a "native" (*tuzemnyi*) administration at the lower level, which devolved certain responsibilities in the name of "local self-government" (*mestnoe samoupravlenie*). The first iteration of this principle, so characteristic of nineteenth-century colonial regimes, can be seen in Mikhail Speranskii's *Regulations on Siberian Kirgiz* of 1822, which established a series of inner and outer *okrug*s beyond the existing fortified frontier line, administered by a Russian official together with Kazakh sultans, who, in principle at least, had to be of Chinggisid descent. At this stage, the Russians were still seeking to make use of existing structures of legitimacy and authority among their Central Asian subjects, something also reflected in the creation of the Bukei or Inner Horde on the steppes east of Astrakhan in 1803 and the granting of a khanal title to its rulers. However, the 1822 statute also abolished the title of khan of the Middle Horde, and that of the Junior Horde would follow in 1824. This pointed the way to the future: the system of loose, indirect rule through Chinggisid sultans was substantially revised under the Steppe Statute of 1867, which marked the steppe's full incorporation into the empire and the "internalization" of what had been a frontier region. It was divided into four regular provinces (*oblast*s)—Ural'sk, Turgai, Akmolinsk, and Semipalatinsk, with a structure of districts (*uezd*s) and cantons (*volost*s) that outwardly, at least, conformed to that in European Russia. The smallest unit of administration was the aul, or nomadic settlement, although by their nature these did not always have fixed locations. The year 1867 also saw the first temporary Turkestan statute, under which the new provinces of Semirechie and Syr-Darya were administered as the new Turkestan governor-generalship, administered from Tashkent. This included the southern part of the Kazakh Steppe, mountainous areas inhabited mainly by Kyrgyz, and the settled population of the Syr-Darya Valley. As Russian territory in the sedentary regions of Central Asia expanded through conquest, Samarkand and Ferghana also became provinces of Turkestan. Semirechie became part of the steppe governor-generalship from 1883 to 1898, before returning to Turkestan, while Transcaspia was administered under its own statute from 1890 to 1899, before also becoming part of the Turkestan governor-generalship. In 1886, a new Turkestan statute replaced the temporary statute of 1867, and this was further revised in 1900. The year 1891 saw a new statute for the steppe, article 120 of which contained a notorious clause allowing the state to expropriate land deemed surplus to the requirements of the nomadic population (*izlishki*) so that it could be used to resettle peasants from European Russia.

The administrative system created by these statutes was known as *voenno-narodnoe upravlenie*, or "military-popular government," a term that reflected both Turkestan and the steppe's subordination to the Ministry of War and a division between the upper military layer of administration and the lower "native" level. The key figure in the administrative hierarchy in both Turkestan and the steppe was the district commandant (*uezdnyi nachal'nik*). This position was reserved for military officers seconded from their regiments (many had never seen active service), attracted by higher rates of pay and more assured promotion if they transferred to administrative duties. Until 1886, they also acted as the local military commanders, and according to one contemporary source, even in the early twentieth century their duties, which ranged from supervising the collection of agricultural taxes to chairing the local sanitary board, would have been performed by at least twelve different officials in a district in European Russia. Like most colonies, Central Asia was underadministered: in 1898, Samarkand province, with a population of 860,000, had just eleven Russian administrative officials. This threadbare administrative structure reflected the general exclusion of the region from the nascent civic and representative structures of the empire. The *zemstva*, or provincial elected assemblies created as part of the Great Reforms in 1864, which provided a measure of representative government and many essential services in agriculture, education, and public health in European Russia, were never extended to the steppe or Turkestan: when this was recommended by Senator Count Konstantin Pahlen's commission of inspection in 1910, it was rejected on the grounds that the Russian population of the region was too small. Thus, the local district commandants continued to wield enormous executive power on paper, but this was constrained by a lack of financial and human resources, as well as a lack of local knowledge (most did not manage to learn Turkic or Persian).

In practice, a great deal of authority had to be devolved to local officials—the *volostnoi upravitel'* (canton administrator), the *aqsaqal* or *aul'naya starshina* (village elder), the *qazi* or *bii* (judge), and the *mirab* and *ariq-aqsaqal* (irrigation officials). Apart from the last, these were all elected locally to three-year terms by so-called *pyatidesyatniki* or *ellikbosh*, electors representing fifty households each, mostly drawn from the wealthier social strata. Probably the most crucial areas of devolution were tax collection, water management, and justice. The Russian administration defined a fixed amount of tax that each agricultural or pastoral community (*sel'skoe obshchestvo*—usually this was not a single settlement but a group of villages or auls that had been bundled together for tax purposes) was supposed to pay on their harvest or livestock each year, but not how the tax burden was distributed *within* each community. This remained in the hands of the local aqsaqal and those who had elected him. The distribution of water from irrigation canals (*ariqs*) between communities and households was also too complex and rooted in local forms of knowledge to be fully legible to Russian officials, who left this in the hands of locally elected mirabs and appointed ariq-aqsaqals. While the Russians did establish military courts and, after 1886, magistrates' courts (*mirovoi sud'ia*) administering Russian law, the administration of most civil and criminal justice was also devolved to the "native administration," in the form of qazis (for the settled population) and biis (for the Kyrgyz and Kazakh population) administering what the Russians called *shariat* or Islamic law in the first instance and *'adat* or customary law in the second. In reality, the distinction between them was a colonial construct—Kazakh and Kyrgyz 'adat carried a heavy admixture of Islamic law, while Central Asian *shari'a* had many local, customary characteristics. Something else they had in common was that the Russians found both systems difficult to understand; this caused considerable disquiet, as they were suspected of being in contradiction with the general laws of the empire and also of fostering the continued separation and "alienness" of the Central Asian population. While the qazis and biis were officially renamed "People's Judges" (*narodnyi sud'ia*) after the 1886 statute, and there were half-hearted attempts both to reduce the role of shari'a and to codify it, these had little effect. On the other hand, there is considerable evidence that Russian colonial rule did produce significant, if unintended, changes in Central Asian law, from an increasing willingness to appeal against the judgments of qazis and biis in Russian courts to changes in notarial practice and a marked decline in the role and status of the *mufti* as a source of Islamic authority. Other religious structures in Central Asia were left largely intact. Von Kaufman initiated a policy of what he called *ignorirovanie* of Islam, which in practice meant noninterference. The state would cease to offer direct patronage to Islam, but all Christian proselytization was banned, *waqf* endowments were preserved, and mosques, madrasas, and other religious institutions continued to function with only minimal official oversight. While this policy sometimes came under strain, notably in 1898 when an attack on the Russian garrison in Andijan by a Sufi spiritual leader and his followers led to calls for a more active anti-Islamic policy, in its essentials it was preserved until the revolution. Islam would continue to be the main marker of difference between the Russians and those whom they ruled.

The effects of this double administrative separation—of Central Asia from Russia proper and of the higher, Russian levels of administration from the lower, "native" ones—remain poorly understood. Falling into a legal category defined literally as "those of a different birth" (*inorodtsy*), Central Asians were clearly not citizens of the empire, but some would argue that nobody was, as there was no such thing as Russian citizenship, or even that this amounted to a privilege, as Central Asians were exempt from military service. Others (myself included) would say that the civic structures that emerged out of the "Great Reforms"—notably local elected assemblies (*zemstva*) and an independent judiciary, together with the introduction of a Duma franchise after 1906—did amount to a gradual extension of recognizable rights of citizenship to the population of European Russia, and that Central Asians were consistently excluded from these. Certainly, Central Asian intellectuals viewed their inferior status in these terms and by the early twentieth century were using the language of citizenship to demand equal rights, while on the Russian side the argument that Central Asians had insufficient levels of *grazhdanstvennost'* (which can be translated as "citizen-like qualities" or "civic values") was used to justify denying them.

The social and political role of the "native administration," and its relations with the Russian hierarchy above it, are still less well understood. Russian officials almost invariably considered their "native" subordinates to be incorrigibly corrupt and wrung their hands over their abuses of power, and the party politics and factionalism that accompanied elections, referring to the native administration as a "living wall" that cut the local population off from the benefits of Russian civilization. The archives are also overflowing with petitions complaining about bribery, corruption, and violence, with the aim of rigging elections, redistributing tax burdens or water flows, and delivering unjust verdicts in order to reward friends and punish enemies, or simply for personal enrichment. While these might seem to corroborate the fears of Russian officials, they need to be interpreted carefully—firstly, because blaming administrative failings on corrupt native subordinates is one of the oldest tricks in the colonial book; secondly, because petitioners needed to use whatever language was necessary to attract official attention and support; and finally, because, as James Scott has suggested, what is perceived as corruption by colonial officials can sometimes be a subtle form of peasant resistance to authority and reflects local political divisions. The widespread violence directed against native officials during the 1916 revolt is one indication that resentment of their role as privileged and corrupt intermediaries was genuine, although in other cases they actually took leadership of the rebels. It seems probable that, as in other colonial contexts, for most Central Asians the immediate face of the state was not the European administrator but the native subordinate to whom he paid his taxes or from whom he received justice. This devolution of power, and the fact that most of these positions were elected, had important social consequences that we still do not fully understand but may have included the emergence of new elites and the fostering of factional politics within Central Asian society.

Rural and Urban Colonization

The northern Kazakh steppes had been a destination for Russian settlers since the late seventeenth century: this was the origin of the two oldest Cossack hosts, the Yaiq (later Ural) and Siberian Cossacks, which were joined by the Orenburg Cossacks in the late eighteenth century. While traditionally Cossack communities had been hybrid societies, born out of the intermingling of escaped Slavic serfs with the Turkic nomads of the steppe, and they had often had a troubled relationship with the Russian state (seen most obviously in the Pugachev Rebellion of 1771, which was led by the Ural Cossacks), by the early nineteenth century they were firmly under state control and increasingly viewed as a spearhead of Russian, Orthodox colonization. As the steppe was conquered and subdued, Russian settlement grew. The Russian population in southern Central Asia was initially very small, and it was a highly militarized community with a strong gender imbalance. The one exception was the province of Semirechie, where a new Cossack host of fourteen thousand was established in 1867, but otherwise Russian rural settlement remained confined to small villages along the post roads through the steppe. Initially, at least, it was in urban areas that the Russian presence had the greatest impact. As with the cantonments of British India and the *Nouvelles Villes* of French North Africa, the Russians stigmatized the existing urban areas of Central Asia as disorganized, dirty, and disease-ridden, and instead constructed new, self-consciously European settlements. Sometimes these took the form of a new European quarter alongside the "native" city, as in Tashkent and Samarkand, where the regular, radial design of the new boulevards was explicitly contrasted with the winding alleyways of what now became the old city. Elsewhere, the Russians constructed entirely new garrison towns, as in New Marghelan (later Skobelev) in the Ferghana Valley and Termez on the Amu-Darya in the Bukharan Emirate. Perhaps the most ambitious "new town" was Vernyi in Semirechie, laid out by the French architect Paul Gourdet in 1889 on a strict grid pattern that still forms the basis of the city plan of modern Almaty. Ashgabat was built on the site of an earlier settlement but was a mushroom town that sprang up almost overnight with the arrival of the Transcaspian Railway in 1885, though the majority of its population were Persian and Armenian immigrants rather than Russians. These new European towns and quarters had certain common features: regular street patterns, with a program of planting along them that would eventually yield the long avenues of shade-giving plane, poplar and oak trees that are still the glory of so many Central Asian cities; a military club, which was the main center of social life for a society dominated by the military and its hierarchies; an Orthodox church, which in larger towns would be joined by Lutheran and Catholic counterparts; low, whitewashed bungalows as accommodation and offices for administrative and military officials; a barracks, usually within purpose-built fortifications; and a brewery or distillery, the best known of which was probably the Filatov distillery in Samarkand, founded in the 1870s (and still producing cognac to this day). Larger settlements would have more varied social amenities, such as theaters, hotels, or Ashgabat's bicycling club. From the outset, these new urban centers were intended to be islands of un-contaminated "Europeanness," a shining example of civilization and planning to the backward Muslim civilization around them, but as in other European colonies it proved impossible to police these boundaries effectively. Wealthy Muslims soon began to move into the European quarters of Samarkand and Tashkent, and to settle in Vernyi, while a poor and unruly European under-class also emerged, spilling over into the "native" quarters and bazaar areas. With the coming of the railways in the 1880s and 1890s, they were joined by a nascent industrial working class who would go on to play an important role in the 1917 revolutions, but who also shared a "settler colonial" mentality. Relations between lower-class Europeans and Muslims in urban areas were often very poor, with anxieties over disease and cultural contamination spill-ing over into open violence during the Tashkent cholera riots of 1892.

Many of the urban "poor whites" who caused so much anxiety to co-lonial elites in Tashkent were failed peasant settlers, a group that became increasingly visible in Turkestan and the steppe from the 1890s onward. In 1889, peasant settlement in "Asiatic Russia" (Siberia, Central Asia, and the Far East) was legalized, and from 1896 a dedicated "Resettlement Ad-ministration" (*Pereselencheskoe Upravlenie*) was charged with facilitating the movement of peasants from land-hungry areas of European Russia (principally the Central Agricultural Region around Moscow and parts of the Black Earth regions of Russia and Ukraine) to the supposedly empty lands "beyond the Urals." This was supposed to simultaneously reduce political and economic tensions in the empire's heartland, and strengthen control over its borderlands by settling them with Slavic peasants. By the early 1900s, it had become a central plank of the policy of agricultural modernization championed by Prime Minister P. A. Stolypin and was also increasingly seen as the key means of Russifying stubbornly unassimilable areas such as Turkestan.

Initially, most settlers in Central Asia were bound for the northern steppe, where more than six hundred thousand had settled by 1908 and in some regions already outnumbered the Kazakh population. From 1903, when the *Pereselencheskoe Upravlenie* established an office in Semirechie, and above all from 1906, with the opening of the Orenburg-Tashkent railway, the number of settlers bound for southern Central Asia rapidly increased, with highly disruptive consequences for this much more densely populated region. With the exception of the newly irrigated "Hungry Steppe" and a few settlements created in Ferghana on the site of villages destroyed as a punitive measure after the Andijan Uprising, there remained very few peasant settlers in the irrigated regions of Turkestan. Instead, northern Syr-Darya province (the Chimkent and Aulie-Ata Districts) and Semirechie were the most favored destinations. While the latter province was apparently large and sparsely populated, the areas suitable for settled agriculture—the immediate neighborhood of Vernyi, the Chuy Valley, and the Issyk Kul region—were relatively limited and already quite densely settled with Kazakhs and Kyrgyz who had abandoned pastoralism for sedentary agriculture. The Resettlement Administration's policy of expelling "natives" from land that they had brought under cultivation in favor of incomers from European Russia, which it justified in terms of economic rationality and the supposed availability of "surplus land," was the clearest possible expression of the inferior, colonized status of Central Asia's indigenous population—and its effects were explosive. There was no shortage of voices pointing out the dangers: local military administrators generally resented the additional problems posed by settlers and the fact that they were usually exempted from taxes. Count Pahlen, who led a commission of inspection to Turkestan in 1908, roundly condemned the Resettlement Administration for "sowing the seed of national strife in an alien region" and alleged that its officials were both incompetent and deeply corrupt. The strongest criticism of all came from Kazakh intellectuals, who were bitterly opposed to the expropriation of what they considered to be their people's land, not just for the economic hardship it created but because it was a clear expression of their unequal and inferior status within the empire. These voices were not acknowledged: the peasant colonization of Asiatic Russia was an issue on which conservative and liberal currents of opinion in late Tsarist Russia were aligned, the former for nationalist, the latter for "progressive," technocratic reasons. In the years leading up to the First World War, it had the unqualified support of the powerful minister of agriculture, A. V. Krivoshein, who envisaged a "New Turkestan," flooded with a million Russian settlers growing cotton on newly irrigated land. While this was a pipe dream, the ethnic conflict provoked by attempts to realize this vision was all too real, and it erupted into open violence in the summer of 1916 with the Central Asian revolt.

The Economy of Pastoralism, Agriculture and Irrigation, and Trade

The economy of Central Asia under Russian colonial rule remains the least researched and the least understood aspect of its history. Patterns of agrarian change (in what remained an overwhelmingly agrarian society), terms of trade with European Russia, living standards, industrialization, and other forms of economic development—all of these remain virtually untouched in modern scholarship, leading to a continued reliance on often misleading Soviet-era publications. Above all, the economic history of Central Asia under tsarist rule has remained dominated by the topic of cotton, to the exclusion of almost everything else. This is based on a host of misconceptions and unjustified assumptions: that the Russians conquered Central Asia largely for economic reasons, in order to turn it into a giant cotton plantation in which case it is difficult to explain the thirty years that elapsed between the conquest of irrigated regions and the widespread cultivation of commercial American varieties of cotton, which began only in the late 1890s; that there was already a "cotton monoculture" in Central Asia before 1917, this might have been true for the Ferghana Valley, where 70 percent of irrigated land was under cotton by 1915, but not of anywhere else; that the Russians extended artificial irrigation in Central Asia in order to grow more cotton when in fact hardly any new canals were completed before 1917, and the few that had been were dedicated mainly to peasant colonization; that the cotton "boom" of the late 1890s and early 1900s, which saw a vast expansion in production, was part of an inherently exploitative and unequal economic relationship, from which "bourgeois" textile producers in Moscow profited when in fact Turkestan cotton was more expensive than that produced in the United States, and was only rendered competitive through a combination of high import tariffs and tax breaks. Whoever was profiting from the boom, it was not the Moscow factory owners, who simply ended up paying more for their raw materials.

The real origins of the cotton boom were more accidental, and its consequences possibly more benign, than any of these scenarios envisages. Although von Kaufman had distributed the seeds of commercially viable strains of American cotton in the mid-1870s, the short-lived production boom this provoked soon fizzled out. It was only in the late 1890s that a set of tax breaks on cotton cultivation aimed at benefiting Russian settlers had the unintended consequence of stimulating thousands of small peasant farmers into turning over all or part of their plots from grain to cotton: it was their collective agency, in other words, that allowed cotton in Turkestan to take off, not some grand plan worked out by the Russian imperial state. At the same time, the extension of the Transcaspian Railway from Samarkand through the Ferghana Valley to Andijan drastically reduced the transportation costs of export to European Russia. This, combined with the favorable tax regime and a high tariff on imported cotton, made its cultivation extremely profitable and generated considerable wealth *within* Turkestan—if not for the peasant cultivators

6-2　"Workshop for Extracting Cotton-Seed Oil, Murghab Estate," Prokudin-Gorskii Collection, c. 1905-1915 (Library of Congress).

themselves (though possibly even for them), then certainly for a new class of middlemen who advanced them loans and seeds and built cotton-cleaning and pressing factories (see figure 6-2). Many of these entrepreneurs were Bukharan Jews, who played a prominent but as yet underresearched role in the economy of prerevolutionary Turkestan, owning three of its largest firms.

Changes in other sectors of the agrarian economy also seem to have been substantial, though once again there is no accurate quantitative research on the topic. Anecdotally, there seems to have been an expansion of rice cultivation in the areas closest to cities (a sign of more general prosperity, as this was an extremely thirsty crop and its consumption in *pilav* a luxury): in Samarkand District, 24 percent of cultivated land was under rice by 1908, and in Tashkent District an astonishing 48 percent. The irrigated area expanded substantially, from ca. 300,000 to 600,000 hectares in Samarkand province alone, on one estimation. This had very little to do with initiatives by the colonial state to build more canals: the only substantial schemes completed before 1917 were the Romanov canal through the "Hungry Steppe" between Jizzakh and Tashkent, which irrigated ca. 45,000 hectares, and the rebuilding of an earlier dam on the Murghab in Transcaspia, which irrigated a small imperial demesne. Instead, it was the gradual extension of existing irrigation networks and the bringing of previously marginal land under cultivation that accounted for this expansion. Cultivation of grain on rain-fed (*Bogara* or *Lalmi*) land also expanded substantially, both in the "core" areas of Turkestan and also in northern Syr-Darya province and Semirechie. Here it was partly owing to Russian peasant settlement but also to the settlement of previously nomadic Kazakhs and Kyrgyz, of Dungans and Uyghurs from China, and of "Sarts" from elsewhere in Turkestan. While Russian colonization created substantial pressure on the nomadic and seminomadic pastoral economy, it also created new markets for meat. Even before the Russian conquest, livestock had been the main export from Central Asia to Russia by value, and the completion of the Orenburg-Tashkent railway in 1906 allowed Central Asian meat to reach markets in European Russia much more easily, while at the same time the growth of population in Southern Central Asia, and in particular of the city of Tashkent, created new local markets.

Any conclusions on the performance of the Central Asian economy under Russian colonial rule remain highly speculative. In the absence of complete series of wages and prices, for instance, it is impossible to be definitive about whether living standards for the bulk of the population were rising or falling. However, there is evidence—notably the increase in land under cultivation and the large flows of inward migration to Turkestan from Kashgaria, Afghanistan, and Iran—to suggest that the economy of the region was booming until 1915, while the income levels and degrees of marketization in cotton-growing regions such as Ferghana may even have been higher than in much of European Russia, an inversion of what is usually thought of as the normal colonial economic relationship. Large-scale industrialization remained limited to cotton-cleaning factories, flour and oil mills, breweries and distilleries, and employed very few people, although as in India it seems that traditional textile and other handicrafts may have been much more resilient than previously thought. However, there does not seem to have been any systematic policy of "underdeveloping" Central Asia for the benefit of capitalists in the Russian metropole, as Soviet historians often alleged, and as has frequently been argued for British India, while because of the persistent Russian fear of revolt levels of taxation remained low until the outbreak of the First World War. There are tentative indications that Russian colonial rule may have stimulated economic growth and brought about a rise in living standards in some parts of Central Asia before 1914.

A Colonial Society?

Did anything resembling a "colonial society" emerge in Russian Central Asia before the revolution? This question is considerably harder to answer than those relating to state policies and administration, on which this chapter has focused, for which archival sources are much more eloquent than on anything relating to social history. This is also an area where sources in Central Asian languages become much more important, though many of those that explore social issues are later memoirs and novels written in the Soviet period, expressing an ideologically inflected, elite point of view. As we have seen, the structures of Russian colonial rule did not really penetrate deeply into Central Asian society, and Russian official knowledge of how it functioned was in many ways quite limited. Social interaction between Russians and Central Asians, while not as restricted by racial concerns as in some other European colonies, nevertheless seem to have been largely limited to official contexts, while intermarriage remained almost unknown until the later Soviet period. Central Asia was in no sense assimilated to Russia before 1917—indeed, its stubborn separateness and continued alienness were a source of despair to officials who supported the frequently invoked goals of *sblizhenie* (rapprochement) and *sliyanie* (merging). The puzzling refusal of Central Asians to abandon Islam, learn Russian, and embrace Christianity and Russian culture was often explained in terms of their "fanaticism," and by the early twentieth century many observers had concluded that only mass settlement by Slavic peasants could truly Russify the region.

At the same time, Russian rule had important effects on Central Asian society that are still not fully understood: some of these were a product of improved communications, notably the railway, the telegraph, and the printing press. These innovations were introduced by the Russians for their own purposes, but as in other colonies they had many unintended consequences, allowing the creation of new "imagined communities" among the local population through the use of print media and facilitating movement and connections between Central Asians and other Muslim communities not only in Russia but in India, Iran, Afghanistan, and the Ottoman Empire. While the intellectual ferment visible among literate elites in Central Asia in the early twentieth century did not arise exclusively out of the encounter with Russian colonial rule and was not necessarily unprecedented in its content, the *media* through which these ideas were being transferred and discussed were frequently new. The relaxation of censorship after the 1905 Revolution in Russia saw an explosion of mostly rather short-lived newspapers, some produced by the Kazakh intelligentsia in the steppe region (*Ai-Qap*, published in Troitsk, and *Qazaq*, published in Orenburg) and a larger number by Turkestani intellectuals in Tashkent, Samarkand, Kokand, and Bukhara (the best known being perhaps *Ayina*, published by Mahmud Khwaja Behbudi in Samarkand). It would be a mistake to see these self-styled and often rather humorless and priggish reformers of religion and society as the only significant intellectual force in Central Asia (though that was certainly how they presented themselves); in many ways, they were an unrepresentative minority, but they were a minority whose ideas were most clearly influenced by the encounter with Russian colonial rule, and who would go on to wield significant power in the early Soviet period.

As we have seen, economic change stimulated in part by Russian policies must have had a considerable effect on everyday life even in remote rural areas where officialdom would rarely have penetrated. The structure of local elections to most positions in what the Russians called the "native" administration seems to have generated significant social conflict and competition, another instance of the unexpected and unintended ways in which colonial rule influenced Central Asian societies. However, the best evidence for the shallow roots of Russian rule in colonial Central Asia, and the failure to make most Central Asians feel that they were truly citizens of the empire, is the way in which it unraveled under the stresses of the First World War. Central Asia was remote from the horrors of the front with Germany, yet it was here, not in Petrograd, that the compact between society and the tsarist state first broke down. Turkestan and the steppe initially felt the impact of war as a series of requisitions of livestock and other materiel, then through rapid inflation in food and fuel prices, which meant that real wages had fallen by at least 25 percent by 1916. A steady stream of refugees from devastated regions in the western borderlands of the empire also undermined imperial prestige, and was not offset by the simultaneous arrival of thousands of Austro-Hungarian prisoners of war in the region. However, it was the attempt to recruit Central Asian Muslims into labor battalions that triggered outright rebellion in the summer of 1916, beginning in the settled regions of Khujand and Jizzakh, then spreading to the main centers of peasant settlement in Pishpek and Przhevalsk, and to the northern steppe region of Turgai. While the poor timing, preparation, and communication of the conscription order played a part, the fundamental issue at stake was that Central Asians were being asked to perform their civic duty toward the empire when, as colonial subjects, they had never been citizens. This would change under the USSR, but the end of colonial rule would also bring far more radical and traumatic interventions by the state in Central Asian society than the Tsarist regime had ever contemplated.

7

Soviet Central Asia

Ali İğmen

> It was 1934, the year of starvation. Kazakhs were suffering a lot at this time. Maldybaev came to me and asked "Can you gather all your children? We are in a hurry; we will give them a concert and leave."
>
> **—SABIRA KÜMÜSHALIEVA**

During one of my interviews with her, Sabira Kümüshalieva, a legendary Kyrgyz actress (1917–2007), lamented the loss of that kind of urgency and camaraderie among the peoples of the Soviet Union. In 1934, Abdylas Maldybaev (1906–1978), an actor, tenor, and composer, was only a twenty-eight-year-old actor whose theater troupe was visiting the school where Kümüshalieva was a seventeen-year-old substitute teacher. She remembered that Maldybaev and his fellow actors went from town to town to give free concerts and put on small plays to cheer up people who were in desperate conditions during "the starvation." She was referring to the catastrophe that enveloped the rural Soviet landscape during the collectivization of farms and farm animals. It is estimated 1.5 million or more Kazakhs starved between 1928 and 1934, during several periods of famine. The Soviet state initiated various policies against Kazakhs that resulted in these famines. They, like Kygyz nomads, were to be sedentarized while grain acquisition and collectivization of animals took place in the steppe. Many in the early 1930s refused to turn in their livestock to the emerging collective farms, and slaughtered them in protest; this resulted in wholesale starvation. Kümüshalieva's recounting of that particular day reflected the sentiments of a significant number of elderly Kyrgyz who reported an era of cooperation in the face of adversity.

It was this kind of rhetoric that the Soviet authorities longed and called for in "the friendship of peoples" slogan. By the end of the 1930s, the nationalities of the Soviet Union were to demonstrate the old colonial "prison of nationalities" turned into a place where every citizen found only friendship among other nationalities. Although scholars continue to consider whether the

Soviet Union shed its imperial past, abandoned its Russian-dominated nature, or became a society of diasporas, by the end of the Soviet era, in Central Asia every republic took pride in repeating slogans such as "the friendship of peoples," declaring their republic a home to more than a hundred nationalities.

For most of the Central Asians, the Soviet Union was established violently, despite the gradually developing language of friendship and optimism over two decades following the Bolshevik Revolution. Violent beginnings affected ordinary lives, as the Kyrgyz story shows. Even Kümüshalieva, who was a genuine believer of the Soviet project, began our interview with a remark that she was a granddaughter and a daughter of a *bai* (the Turkic word for a wealthy livestock owner or a community leader) or *kulak* (the Russian word for any peasant who hired a laborer), and her saviors and heroes came in the form of actors and directors of all nationalities. Soviet culture in Central Asia burgeoned as a modernist project while indigenous ways of knowing were being transformed into something new. By the end of the Soviet era, it became difficult to distinguish a Central Asian practice from a Soviet one.

Sovietness first was represented as Russian in Central Asia. During the first decades of the Soviet era, being a Soviet authority in Central Asia first meant that the person was from Russia or various western parts of the Union of Soviet Socialist Republics (USSR). Beginning with the actual implementation of the policy of *korenizatsiia* (meaning indigenization, launched in 1921 by the Tenth Congress of the Communist Party of the Soviet Union, approved in 1923 at the Twelfth Party Congress, suspended in 1934, and reinstated after the Second World War), Soviet-educated indigenous cadres began to take significant administrative positions. Korenizatsiia came to a halt officially during the Great Purges of the mid-to-late 1930s when the leadership from the Kremlin cleansed the indigenous elites who were seen as too powerful and dangerous. Despite these often brutal and at times fatal removals, many of the surviving local and regional leaders remained in administrative positions. By the end of the Soviet era, the political culture of the administrators at all levels had very little to do with ethnicity or nationality.

This merging of political culture did not mean, however, that individual Central Asians lost their pre-Soviet identification with their local, regional, and national cultures. As in Kümüshalieva's case, most Central Asians learned to construct a blend of modern Soviet and Central Asian everyday ways of knowing and living. A case in point was the linguistic change. Although it varied from republic to republic, town to town, village to village, and even neighborhood to neighborhood, many Central Asians began to speak Russian as the practical language of public exchange. Even if they spoke their own languages and dialects at home, they became comfortable speaking Russian in the market, at school, in the factory, or in other public spaces. The language policy sanctioned a preferred dialect as an official language for each titular nationality, often with the expertise of indigenous elites. The selection of the official languages was not necessarily arbitrary, but also not without the biases of the officials involved. Just as certain ethnic and regional groups became the official titular nationalities at the expense of many others, so did the official languages. With compulsory elementary school education and single official language policy, as well as the Russian language as the lingua franca of the whole USSR, homogenization of each republic was the ultimate goal of this nationalities policy. Kümüshalieva, for example, pointed out that her family had Kypchak origins. The Kypchak ethnicity was one of the many indigenous identities that were absorbed into various titular nationalities.

There were several particular periods and influential events that constructed Soviet ways of being in Central Asia. The creation of the Soviet republics that were carved out of the imperial Russian territories in the region was the obvious first development, a process that reached its conclusion by the end of the 1920s. The industrialization era of the late 1920s and the collectivization in the early 1930s came next. The purging of the leaders by the end of the 1930s left its mark on Soviet life. The attack on nomadism by way of sedentarization and *hujum*, unveiling policies, compounded the introduction of anti-traditional ways. In addition to these overarching policies, the everyday lives of the Central Asians incorporated Soviet practices in every public space, beginning with schools and ending with retirement.

From Imperial Subjects to Soviet Citizens

If we consider Sabira Kümüshalieva's life as a case study, we see the trajectory of a Soviet life. Obviously, Kümüshalieva was an extraordinary individual, but her early life was anything but unusual. Like her, many children in the first decade of the Soviet era were born into an era of hardships after the First World War. The Ürkün period, as the Kyrgyz and Kazakh call it, began in 1916 with an uprising against the authorities even before the establishment of the Bolshevik era. Kümüshalieva's own family with Kypchak origins was well-off and included Madaminbek (Muhammad Aminbek Ahmadbek-ugli, 1892–1920), the revolutionary leader who initiated a rebellion in Margilan, in present-day Uzbekistan, in 1918 against the Bolsheviks. This era resulted in tragic consequences for all involved, including indigenous populations and the settlers from other parts of the Russian empire. The local populations resented the increasing numbers of non–Central Asian settlers, the imperial authorities, the conscription of the men into the imperial army, and the injustices suffered under landowning wealthy men. Many Central Asian families escaped to China to avoid clashes with the more powerful state and its supporters.

To place this uprising in a larger historical context, however, one needs to remember that the Russian imperial interest and consequent conquest into the Kazakh Steppe and Turkestan dated back to the first military expedition under Peter the Great in 1715. Some argue that the engagement with the Turkic people became a defining military characteristic for both the Russians and the Turkic people as early as the fourteenth century with the negotiations and struggles between the Russians and the Golden Horde for power and territory. The descendant and successor khanates of the Chingizid and Timurid

7-1   Sabira Kümüshalieva in her home, Bishkek, Kyrgyzstan, 2002. Photograph by Ali İğmen.

lineage, Islamized between the thirteenth and seventeenth centuries, fell one by one to the relentlessly expanding Russian empire. Once under Mongol and later Islamized Tatar and Turkic rule, Russian leaders (Ivan III in 1480) defeated the remaining khanates beginning north with Kazan (1552), Astrakhan (1556), the Kazakh Hordes (1822, 1824, and 1848), and Crimea (1783), and continuing with southern Central Asia, Bukhara (1868), Khiva (1873), Kokand (1876), Teke Turkmens (1881), and the cities of Tashkent (1865) and Samarkand (Samarqand) (1868). By 1884, with the occupation of the Merv oasis, the Russian conquest of the Kazakh Steppe and Central Asia was complete.

The Central Asians did not readily or easily become subjugated to Russian power. The Kazakhs revolted intermittently between the 1820s and 1840s, culminating into a more cohesive resistance under Kenesary Kasymov (1802–47) during 1837–38 and again in 1846–47. One must also keep in mind that in the east in Chinese territories, the Turkic and Muslim populations had resisted Chinese occupation and rule since the Chinese conquest of the Tarim Basin in 1759, which they named Xinjiang in 1768 and decisively occupied as a Chinese province in 1884. The various Muslim populations of China—which included Uygurs, Kazakhs, Kyrgyz, and non-Turkic populations such as the Hui—continuously resisted and revolted against Chinese rule, most famously under Yaqub Beg (c. 1820–77) of Altishahr.

The Russian-Chinese competition for power in Central Asia continued into the revolutionary eras (1905 in Russia and 1911 in China). The Central Asians too continued to resist with uprisings, most notably in Ferghana (1885), Andijan (1898), and finally during the Ürkün (1916). The Russian imperial administration, in the meantime, managed to connect the Russian heartland to Merv (by completing the Trans-Caspian Railway in 1885) and to Samarkand in 1888. By 1906, the Orenburg-Tashkent Railway linked Russia to Turkestan, aiding the mass immigration of Russian and Ukrainian settlers into the Kazakh Steppe and gradually into the rest of Central Asia.

The Central Asian intellectuals, on the other hand, did not sit idly but organized as Young Bukharans (1909) and the Kazakh Alash Orda (1912), leading their populations to recognize the revolutionary trends and initiate reforms in their societies.

The February Revolution in Russia in 1917 brought about the Tashkent Committee of the Provisional Government. In addition, the Tashkent Soviet of Workers' and Peasants' Deputies emerged as one of the first organizations that led to the Bolshevik Revolution in Central Asia. After the February Revolution, the Bolshevik Party supported the right to self-determination and independence of every nation within Russia. The Muslim populations of Russia held several congresses, which took place in Orenburg, Tashkent, and Moscow, to determine their future until the Bolsheviks seized power in Moscow. Consequently, the Tashkent Soviet established its domination over any other committees in Central Asia, but within a month the Bolshevik-backed Council of People's Commissars asserted its leadership in Tashkent.

Between November of 1917 and the start of 1920, Central Asian leaders attempted to stop the Bolshevik-led administrators and the Red Army from dominating Kazakhstan and Turkestan, both of which vied for autonomy, if not independence. As the Central Asian leaders failed to halt the Russians and their backers, the uprisings known as the Basmachi Revolt erupted in 1918, just as the civil war began in Russia between the Bolsheviks and their various enemies, including the White Army. Basmachi leaders, known to the local populations as *kurbashi*, led revolts as a defense against outside invasions, often without a clearly defined or unified ethnic, national, or religious ideology. The revolts continued in several phases in the 1920s, continuing into the early 1930s. When the USSR emerged at the end of 1922, the Turkestan and Kirghiz (misnamed for Kazakh) Autonomous Soviet Socialist Republic (ASSR) became part of the new union. In the early 1920s, People's Soviet Republics (PSR) also emerged after, for example, the Emirate of Bukhara and the Khanate of Khorezm accepted protectorate status and became the Bukharan PSR and the Khorezm PSR. They were soon thereafter replaced by newly created Soviet Socialist Republics (SSRs), such as the Turkmen and Uzbek SSRs. Gradually, by the mid-1930s, the Tajiks (1929), Kazakhs (1936), and Kyrgyz (1936) were granted their own SSRs. This top-down policy of national delimitation was a radical reenvisioning of Central Asian communities. During this fifteen-year-long process, local party cadres gradually became the participants, and occasionally the leaders, of this sweeping transformation.

Once a possibility, most legitimate political organizing among Muslim populations melted into thin air by the end of 1920s. The slow and painful abolition of the Kazakh Alash-Orda in 1927 was a symbolic end to what began with the Jadid movement, Muslim intellectuals who believed in reform toward a modern educational system within the Russian Empire as early as the 1860s. Furthermore, as a reversal of the early Bolshevik promise, in 1927 the Soviet administration began an anti-Islamic campaign, which included *hujum* and abolishment of Islamic courts and charitable endowments (*waqfs*). The distancing of the culture and people from Islam did not only come from Soviet policy, however. The Latin script's official replacement of Arabic came as a proposal in the Baku Turkology Congress in 1926. Arabic script represented conservatism and backward traditions not only in the eyes of modernizing intellectuals, such as many who attended the Turkology Congress in Baku, but among the Bolshevik leaders who wanted to erect a boundary between Islam and modernity. The other modernizing Turkic state in postimperial Turkey initiated similar drastic changes under Mustafa Kemal Atatürk during the same era.

The Goals and Consequences of Soviet Modernization

The sweeping industrialization of Soviet agriculture and economy in favor of large-scale farming and heavy industry began to affect Central Asians after 1928. In addition to the late Tsarist era Trans-Caspian and Orenburg-Tashkent Railways (1879–1906), the construction of the Turksib (Turkestan-Siberian) Railroad in 1930 began to bring technology, goods, and people to these far-flung regions of the Soviet Union. Coupled with turning the Fergana Valley and other suitable lands in Central Asia into cotton fields, many farmers became workers on large collective farms and in factories. The industrialization of the region developed mostly around cotton, wool, silk, and other textile-related fields. These natural fibers constituted the main materials for the textiles and carpets produced in the region. Outdated production techniques and equipment desperately needed improvement. The expansion of the railroads made it possible to modernize production and transportation of these industries. Mining of minerals, such as copper, lead, sulfur, and zinc, had been part of the industry since the mid-1800s. Coal, iron, and oil fields gained importance during the Soviet era, but most of the industrial outcome had a direct connection to agricultural production and animal husbandry, such as leather tanneries.

The collectivization of the farmlands and livestock began in earnest from 1928 to 1933. Uzbekistan practically turned into one large cotton field with irrigation canals beginning to divert the waters of the Aral Sea in the 1940s. In the 1960s, under Joseph Stalin's successor Nikita Khrushchev, the thirsty cotton fields guzzled up the waters of the Aral Sea, once the world's fourth largest saline lake (68,000 sq. km.; 26,300 sq. mi.) that was surrounded by small fishing villages with an estimated thirty-four species of fish. This turned out to be one of the worst environmental disasters of the USSR, if not the world, symbolizing the misguided collaboration of agriculturalists and politicians. The Aral Sea tragedy, however, was only one of several environmental disasters. The lack of interest in protecting the environment in favor of economic and social progress by way of industrialization and modernized agriculture polluted everything—the soil, water, air, and people's health, minds, and emotions. Repeated nuclear testing in Semipalatinsk bombarded both the environment and the people with extreme levels of radiation. Approximately two million people in this region received a regular dose of radiation for forty years, until 1991, when the Soviet authorities deemed it environmentally uninhabitable.

The environmental damage, carried out for the sake of modernization, went hand in hand with the modernizing educational policies to create a new Soviet citizen, the *Homo Sovieticus*. The victims of misguided policies had many parallels in Soviet Central Asia. In regard to educational and cultural policies, another change took place when the Soviet administration replaced the Latin alphabet with Cyrillic in all of Central Asia in 1939 and 1940. Just as the Arabic alphabet symbolized religion and tradition to be purged, the Latin alphabet represented connections to Turkey or Western Europe. The replacement of the Latin script with Cyrillic, however, was the least worrisome for Central Asian educators and intellectuals. The Great Purges of 1937 and 1938 wiped out many of the first Bolshevik leaders in Central Asia. These leaders included regional elites such as the most prominent Uzbek educator and reformist Abdulrauf Fitrat, politicians Faizullah Khojaev and Akmal Ikramov, Kazakh poet and educator Akhmet Baitursynov, writer and environmentalist Alikhan Bukeikhanov, politician Turar Ryskulov, poet and writer Saken Seifullin, multitalented engineer and ethnographer Mukhamedzan Tynyshpaev, poet and writer Ilyas Zhansugurov, Kyrgyz politician Törökul Aitmatov, linguist and activist Kasym Tynystanov, politician Jusup Abdrakhmanov, and others. This is merely a short list of prominent early Bolshevik leaders who served the Soviet regime until the state accused them of being "enemies of the people" and led them to their executions.

One particularly cruel case is the ALZhIR prison camp in Akmolinsk (Akmola in Kazakh language), Kazakhstan. ALZhIR was designed as a forced labor camp for "wives of traitors to the Motherland," and imprisoned the female relatives and children (younger than age three) of Soviet intellectuals who were sent to the Gulags (Soviet Forced Labor Camps operating between 1919 and 1960, the last of which closed in Perm in 1987). In other words, this case appears to be especially cruel because these women and children were considered guilty by association, and when they were sent to the camp, they were told they were going to visit their imprisoned male relatives. Most of these 7,000 (at its highest population) women were wives, mothers, sisters, and daughters of well-known writers, poets, artists, actors, directors, and other people of the arts. Some of the women were in the arts themselves between 1938 and 1953, representing sixty-two recognized ethnicities and nationalities. ALZhIR closed its doors after Stalin's death. Russian women constituted the majority with 4,390 prisoners, followed by 855 Jews, 740 Ukrainians, and several other groups such as Germans, Poles, Byelorussians, Georgians, and Latvians totaling more than 100 prisoners. The most heartbreaking reality was that more than one thousand women gave birth to children as a result of rape by guards. ALZhIR was only one of many Gulags that imprisoned more than eighteen million people. KarLag, another massive penal colony in Karaganda, Kazakhstan, was twice the size of Belgium and operated between 1930 and 1959.

Central Asia became a dumping ground for deported nationalities mostly from the Caucasus and the eastern regions of the USSR. Although an unknown number of Cossacks were deported out of Turkestan to the Ukrainian SSR and northern Russian SSR in the early 1920s to halt the "colonization" of Turkestan, beginning in the 1930s "dekulakization" drove more than two million kulaks (lit. "fist," the Soviet definition of those who were seen as tight-fisted land- and property-owning capitalists) from Russia and Ukraine to Kazakh and Kyrgyz ASSR as well as the northern territories, the Ural region, Siberia, and Northern Caucasus. This estimated number included the people who were hauled out during the collectivization era until 1936. At least a quarter of a million Kazakhs who refused to collectivize were forced out to China, Mongolia, Iran, Afghanistan, and Turkey in 1933. In the 1930s, especially during the Great Purges, more than two million Chinese, Germans, Kurds, Harbin Russians, Ingrian Finns, Persian Jews, Poles, and a particularly large number of Koreans, estimated at 172,000, were sent to various locations in Central Asia. Kazakhstan and Uzbekistan received the largest portion of the deportees. The alleged crimes were often a mystery to the deported populations, necessitating such a brutal overhaul of their lives, and resulted in irreversible displacement. Moreover, in the 1940s, more than a quarter of a million Poles; almost a million Germans, Romanians, and Kalmyks; and more than three million Soviet and foreign citizens of many nationalities—from the Caucasus, such as Armenians, Balkars, Chechens, Greeks, Ingush, Kabardins, Karachais, Laz, and Meskhetian Turks—were put on trains and dumped in Central Asia because they were seen as traitors during the Second World War. In 1942, nearly 200,000 Crimean Tatars became the target of suspicion and were deported to the Uzbek SSR and other republics, and many were never allowed to return home. Finally, as late as 1951 and 1952, almost one hundred thousand kulaks (e.g., people from the Baltic states as well as the Byelorussian, Moldavian, and Ukrainian SSRs) and others seen as a nationalist threat to the Soviet system (e.g., the Basmachis from Tajikistan) were sent to Kazakhstan and Siberia. In the eyes of Soviet officials, those who were deported from the Caucasus and Western territories of the USSR during the Second World War could be traitors and collaborators of the Nazis; without much, or in many cases any, evidence, whole families disappeared and villages were left empty.

Making Soviets Citizens "Cultured"

This was the ethnic landscape that ironically justified ubiquitous Soviet slogans such as "brotherhood of nationalities" and "republic of one hundred nationalities," which were meant to comfort disheartened newcomers and "host" nations. Although each republic had its own Congress of Soviets, the people of each republic, ethnically indigenous or not, were to be governed officially from the top offices in the Kremlin by the legislative branches of the Congress of Soviets (1922–36) and the Supreme Soviet (1936–89), the executive branch of the Premier and the Council (1922–91), and the judicial branch of the Supreme Court. The procurator-general was appointed to supervise most of the ministries and committees. The ultimate decision maker was the party itself in Moscow while the National Congress of Soviets followed the orders of the party. The language of all the judicial proceedings was to be conducted in the native language of each SSR, ASSR, and smaller unit. Each republic had its own procurator-general, who reported to the highest office of the procurator in Moscow. The most significant office, however, the Communist Party of the Soviet Union (CPSU), was seen as the "the leading and guiding force of Soviet society," which placed handpicked administrators, popularly known as *nomenklatura*, in the most influential positions in every field of the government. The administrators of the institutions of education and culture established—but never without the party's approval—what it meant to be a literate and "cultured" Soviet individual.

The People's Commissariat for Education began to introduce Marxism and Leninism everywhere, including in Central Asia, as early as 1918. Although the Russian Civil War, which followed the Bolshevik Revolution, and the era following WWI known as War Communism (1918–1921) disrupted the widespread establishment of the new socialist system of education, the policy of *likbez* (liquidation of illiteracy) began to be implemented in 1919. During War Communism, everything was to be rationed—food, goods, and education alike—to provide the Red Army with food, uniforms, and weapons against the Whites (anti-communist forces) and other enemies, but propaganda was essential in order to continue the transformation of the Soviet society into a modern competitor in the world.

Education was the main component of the transformation that included centralization of all industries, agriculture, and social structures. New socialist schools and literacy institutes established universal compulsory education for Soviet children and likbez education for adults. Most of the Soviet republics established Pioneers (youth organizations for children between the ages of ten and fifteen, officially called the Vladimir Lenin All-Union Pioneer Organization) and Komsomol (for youth up to age twenty-eight, officially called the All-Union Leninist Young Communist League), whose members were sent in large numbers to local villages in Central Asia and elsewhere to begin spreading Marxist-Leninist ideology and anti-religious activity. During the 1920s, indigenous languages were to be developed in addition to Russian as a common language of communication among hundreds of linguistic groups. The Soviet administrators and teachers were required to fight "Great Russian chauvinism," in Lenin's words, which was seen as a colonial remnant, by helping legitimate official indigenous languages in Central Asia. Several dominant dialects in each republic became official national languages. By the beginning of the 1930s, each republic established its own national schools, attempting to introduce the official language of instruction, but at the end of the 1930s the Russian language became a required subject.

In the 1920s, the Houses of Culture, Clubs, Lenin's Corners, Red Yurts, Red Chaikhanas (teahouses), and other organizations began to supplement adult education, aiding activities such as "Literates, teach one illiterate!" or societies such as "Down with Illiteracy Society." Theater, too, became an essential institution to introduce Soviet culture and ideology but also Western ways of education and entertainment, which went hand in hand. Mobile literacy centers went to Kazakh *auls* and Kyrgyz *ails* (villages, rural settlements, or tribal family units) alike to follow the nomadic herders to educate and indoctrinate. Soviet leaders understood that without literacy neither industry nor agriculture could be developed. Furthermore, to make the consolidation of the Soviet State there needed to be a universal and standardized education policy and system. The Five-Year Plans, beginning in 1932, initiated and organized the education policies as well as other social and cultural initiatives. The Soviet censuses claimed that by the end of the 1930s, literacy rates reached an average of 76 percent (in Central Asia, there was a high of 84 percent in Kazakhstan and a low of 63 percent in Tajikistan).

The centralist and pluralist policies of *sliianie* (a hopeful idea of melding people together under a single Soviet identity without national consciousness) of the 1930s both supported the development of national languages and weakened them with linguistic Russification of the technical knowledge and vocabulary in Central Asia. Gradually, in the second half of the Soviet era, most urbanized and educated people ended up code-switching between Russian and their own languages without effort. The more urbanized and educated the person, the more fluent and comfortable that person was with Russian. Most Central Asian intellectuals and those who occupied high positions in the government (mostly men) did not see this as an attack on their indigenous culture but simply as a channel of communication among multiple nationalities that made up the population of Central Asia. During and after the Second World War, the desperate need for scientific technical knowledge compelled the Soviet government to establish the Academy of Sciences in Central Asia, beginning with the Uzbek SSR in 1943 and completing the project with the Kyrgyz SSR in 1954.

From the academy emerged an unexpected benefit for some Central Asian Republics during the Second World War, however. The Kyrgyz SSR, for example, became home to important Soviet research institutes—such as the Institutes of Evolutionary Morphology, Genetics, Biochemistry, and Physiology—when they needed to be evacuated from Russia and sheltered from potential Nazi attacks or invasion. These academies became a source of pride in each republic, indicating that they could also produce scientists and philologists who studied and conducted research in other republics, and their peoples also learned to be well-rounded, well-traveled Soviet citizens. During the Stalin era, the academies experienced centralization, censorship, and lack of academic freedom in favor of politically appropriate behavior. Even in the most unexpected fields, such as physics, the relationship between academics and politics became the target of the system that operated under such restrictions, with the primary goal of competing with the more scientifically advanced Western Europe and the United States.

In order to show the world that the USSR was keeping up with, if not

7-2   The House of Culture in Maily Sai Workers Town in Jalal Abad Oblast, Kyrgyzstan, 1959. Photograph by Mashentzev.

superior to, the West, the Soviet state acknowledged that the arts were as crucial as science and technology. In Central Asia, theaters, music conservatories, philharmonics, opera and ballet schools, and grand buildings began operating as early as the 1930s in some capital cities of the republics. The Soviets needed to have a "high culture" to move the agricultural and nomadic societies toward modern socialist cultural forms, which meant teaching them how to appreciate, practice, and teach Western performing arts, including theater, cinema, opera, and ballet. The most significant Soviet objective, however, was the creation of national expressions of culture, favoring the titular nationalities of each republic. This meant that each nationality would engender and nurture what it and its administrators saw as indigenous: creating Kazakh operas, Uzbek plays, Kyrgyz ballets, and so on as a way to represent their nationalities. Much like the scientific community, many musicians, composers, and other members of the artistic community moved to Central Asia during the Second World War–era evacuations from the western USSR. These highly educated and highly regarded professionals trained the first and second generation of indigenous members of the arts. Sabira Kümüshalieva pointed out in her interview that Kyrgyz actors learned to be actors thanks to many Russian, Jewish, and other professional theater directors and instructors.

Such a centrally directed cultural policy also encouraged the *rastvet* (blooming) of high culture and cultural exchanges between all Soviet republics, thereby enforcing the standardization of cultural forms, which many Western critics deemed as kitsch. Soviet administrators who constructed and implemented policy ensured the *sblizhenie* (drawing together) of individual ethnic expressions of cultural forms. By the 1940s, most capital cities contained a complex of grand buildings that featured opera and ballet houses, philharmonic halls, theaters, and museums of various kinds. At the beginning of this process, Slavic and other non–Central Asian art professionals trained the young indigenous talent to apply Western artistic forms to local, ethnic, and national expressions. By the mid-1930s and early 1940s, composers wrote Kazakh operas such as *Kyz Zhibek* (1934) and *Abai* (1944), Uzbek opera *Layli va Mejnun* (1940), and Kyrgyz opera *Ai Chürek* (1939), as well as Kazakh ballet *Köktem* (1940), Uzbek ballet *Shahida* (1939), and Kyrgyz ballet *Cholpon* (1944), among others in Turkmenistan and Tajikistan in later years.

Theater administrators and professionals acted as the best representatives of the fusion of entertainment and education. The Kyrgyz SSR provides many examples of this fusion. Kümüshalieva and two other actresses and an opera singer represent four Soviet overachievers who were collectively known as the "Four Daughters of Tököldösh." Like Sabira Kümüshalieva (1917–2007), two young girls from Tököldösh—Baken Kydykeeva (1923–93) and Darkul Kuiukova (1917–97)—ended up on the Soviet stage and screen via Kyrgyz theater and film between the 1930s and the end of the Soviet era in Kyrgyzstan. The opera singer Saira Kiyizbaeva (1917–88), although from the same *ail*, took a different path to achieve success in her singing career and in her later years represented the Kyrgyz SSR as an educator in the Supreme Soviet. The three actresses solidified how Kyrgyz women, and people in general, were to be portrayed and represented on stage and in film, in such renown plays and films based on Chingiz Aitmatov's *Mother Earth*, *The White Ship*, *The First Teacher*, and many others. No matter what paths their careers took, these four women waded through the murky waters of the continuously changing political and cultural landscape of the USSR. Their lives and careers demonstrate the ways in which many Central Asian women survived. In some cases, they even thrived despite the hardship their families endured during breakneck industrialization in the form of canal, dam, and factory building; collectivization in the form of creating a monoculture around cotton production; various purges; and the Second World War.

These four women's stories show that they not only had to convince their families that they had to leave their *ail* to receive art training—which allowed them to move into the world of Soviet theater, cinema, and opera—but as women on stage they also had to endure negative societal pressures because such presentations of women were counter to traditional cultural norms. But the state was on their side. First, the Soviet educational and cultural policies forced the most conservative families to send their daughters to school. Second, the ideology of *Proletkul't* (proletarian culture) and the ideal of achieving *kul'turnost* (culturedness) for every Soviet citizen required Kyrgyz intellectuals to introduce theater as one of the artistic expressions based on class that would allow them to reach high culture. Third, being civilized and being Soviet meant that Western forms of culture, such as theater (and later cinema), had to be practiced in Central Asia for it to be an established part of the USSR.

The Central Asian Association of Proletarian Writers and the Kyrgyz Association of Writers turned to Socialist Realism after 1933. The First All-Union Congress of Soviet Writers defined the artistic expression of Socialist Realism as an ideological approach to show political and social ideals of socialism. This new step meant that every artist needed to become a member of the Union of Soviet Writers and Artists. As writers, artists, and other professionals of the arts, they were required to make their work accessible (*dostupnoi*), representing the people (*narodnost'*) and, most significantly, the party (*partiinost'*). The main slogan that delivered such a tall order was "Socialist in content, national in form." Kyrgyz playwrights and directors created plays to stage for these actresses and their fellow actors that were down-to-earth, folksy, and less technical in artistic expression. Yet, they were all expected to "raise the culture" of the people. These four Kyrgyz women found a way to honor their nomadic societies on stage and later in film by showing that a seemingly simple way of living did not imply backwardness or unsophistication.

Emancipation of Women

Gender in the Soviet cultural landscape mattered, however. Like most Soviet women, these four remarkable women were limited by the opportunities presented to them because of their gender. Even Saira Kiyizbaeva, who was a deputy of the Supreme Soviet, never headed managerial positions in the highest administrations of the arts. As the leading female leaders of the Bolshevik era, women carried out much of the hard work as administrators or educators, a handful of them being recognized as leaders in practice. They rarely broke the proverbial glass ceiling. Yet, the complexity of gender and state relations is exposed in the lives and careers of these four women, as well as other less notable women who were both subjects and participants of anti-religious unveiling, as well as other female-oriented activities. Many women officially reported that they were the liberated Soviet citizens who fought patriarchy and religiously sanctioned misogyny. In a personal story from another republic, Bazaraim Khasenova (1909–2003), the first Kazakh female Komsomol member, met with Nadezhda Krupskaia (Lenin's spouse) in 1935 and 1936 to examine the remaining and persistent hurdles for women in Central Asia, such as *kalym* (*kalyng* in Kyrgyz language, meaning bride price), child marriage, polygamy, and other practices that victimized women. Khasenova's long political career demonstrated that Central Asian women could be role models for young girls. The message was that a girl need not be a shepherdess or a housewife for the rest of her life in Central Asia.

In a glaring irony and a major policy shift, the Soviet administration banned abortions in 1936, made divorce more restrictive, and began to reward mothers who gave birth to multiple children. In a significant reversal, the marriage law, which since 1926 had been quite liberal on issues such as abortion, turned out to be considered problematic if not flat-out "evil" in regard to abortion. The declining birth rates after the war needed to be reversed. As a result, like many Soviet women, Central Asian mothers had "a great and honorable duty" to produce future Soviet generations. They were told by the Party that giving birth was no longer a private affair but a social and patriarchal responsibility. The state promised more midwife and nursing facilities, maternity homes, childcare facilities, communal kitchens, and other services to make working mothers' lives easier. In 1944, the state established the honorary title "Mother Heroine" for women who gave birth and raised ten or more children. The women with more than five living children were also given the "Order of Maternal Glory" and the "Maternity Medal." The benefits for almost half a million women all over the USSR included a retirement pension, and they received food and other supplies while being exempt from utility charges. Many Central Asian women earned these accolades, but they received mixed messages about learning to be a working woman while being rewarded for producing more than five children. As a particularly gruesome case in point, the incidents of self-immolation among Uzbek and Tajik women multiplied because many were crushed under the daily obligations of housework and cotton picking. Despite the 1950, 1952, and 1955 fatwas (religious rulings) against self-immolation by SADUM (the Spiritual Administration of the Muslims of Central Asia), the state could not halt this cruel practice.

Altogether, the Central Asian way of life—whether it was nomadic, semi-nomadic, or religiously guided—was to be reformed. The Soviet state targeted Islam, or the complex set of traditions and rituals seen as Muslim practices. One way to regulate these diverse practices, and control the influence of the ulema (the religious leaders), came with the establishment of four muftiyyats in 1943. Stalin allowed some freedoms to the Muslim populations that Orthodox Christians did not have the luxury to experience. The practitioners of Islam did not follow a unified path; some followed Sufi traditions such as the Naqshbandi order, often practicing Islam in their private spheres without attending the mosque; others, such as many populations with nomadic origins, did not follow some of the basic tenets of Islam closely. Muslim spirituality did not disappear despite the atheist efforts of the officials, such as the "Unions of the Godless," perhaps because the local and regional solidarity groups protected the highly private and elusive practices of male circumcision, gender segregation, and funeral rituals. The modern Soviet lifestyle did not necessarily prevent many, such as Kümüshalieva and her family, from considering themselves Muslim. There was no clear boundary between Islam or Kyrgyzness for her, for both were an intertwined way of being and a way of knowing. Oral histories indicate that she was not unique in this understanding.

Life after Stalin

During the Second World War, Stalin gave some relief to religious institutions, including allowing Muslim leadership to offer their followers spiritual guidance. It was during the Khrushchev years, between 1958 and 1964, when Islam became a target and most mosques in Central Asia were closed. After Joseph Stalin's death in 1953, Soviet life in Central Asia changed quite drastically under Nikita Khrushchev's rule. The most significant change under Khrushchev emerged with his "Secret Speech" at the Twentieth Party Congress in 1956, in which he denounced Stalin's failings both as a person and a leader and condemned his purges. The prisoners of the Gulags and other incarcerated populations began, in 1953, to be granted amnesty. Upward of four million prisoners returned home in a five-year period. They returned to towns where they were not always welcomed because of years of propaganda against them. Many had been alienated from their families and hometowns. Scapegoating had been the norm beginning at an early age by the elevation of boys such as Pavlik Morozov, who gave away his father for being anti-government. Therefore, Khrushchev's de-Stalinization did not always bring relief to Soviet families and society overnight. Many intellectuals hoped and waited for greater change under the new regime, only to be disappointed by repeated smaller purges and censorship. In the 1950s, a number of factors—the revival of Leninist ideals, educational reforms, anti-religious activities, and campaigns against "hooliganism" to instill morality, such as anti-homosexual rhetoric making a connection between prisoners and homosexuality—led to difficulties of released prisoners being reintegrated. The anxieties of the Cold War also changed the political and cultural landscape once again. For Central Asians, the promise of the cultivation of the "virgin lands" of the Kazakh Steppe brought both hope and anxiety. Along with promises in agricultural development, the government began to initiate industrial modernization and large housing projects. On the whole, the political elites who survived the Stalin era in Central Asia became more powerful under the Khrushchev government.

Political elites had strong clan ties despite the condemnation of clan politics (tribal, ethnic, and local alliances) under Stalin. There seemed to be strong support and guidance from the Kremlin for industrial development in Central Asia in the 1960s. Many people who were part of the Central Asian party apparatus mimicked the patterns of the elite in Moscow but managed to protect their own clan members in the process. Tashkent, the capital of Uzbekistan, began to solidify its regional leadership position under Khrushchev in the 1960s to be continued until the end of the Brezhnev era, even possibly until the fall of the USSR. The main reason for this was the strength of Communist Party leaders in regard to communicating with Moscow. Nuritdin Akramovich Mukhitdinov (first secretary of the Communist Party of Uzbekistan between 1955 and 1957) and Dinmukhamed Akhmetuly Kunaev (first secretary of the Communist Party of Kazakhstan between 1964 and 1986) were the first two Central Asian members of the Politburo of the Communist Party, while Sharof Rashidovich Rashidov of Uzbekistan (first secretary of the Communist Party of Uzbekistan between 1959 and 1983) was a candidate, all of whom were close allies of Leonid Brezhnev.

National interests overrode clan alliances, however, when it came to borders and land. Land transfers took place between the republics with the aim of settling long-brewing disputes after the demarcation (drawing the borders of the Central Asian Republics between 1925 and 1945). For example, the transfer of 70,000 hectares, including the northern part of Sokh, from the Kyrgyz SSR to Uzbek SSR in 1955 was later disputed by

Kyrgyz politicians. This and several other transfers stirred up quite a bit of resentment and anger among the politicians and people of the Ferghana Valley, but the central government invoked the old slogan "friendship of peoples," reminding the people that the borders between the republic would eventually disappear to construct a single socialist union. To achieve such union among the nationalities, the state devised a system to parade individual Soviet workers and farmers as models of success for their fellow citizens.

Stakhanovite ideology and methods devised during the Stalin years continued to propel both industrial workers and collective farmers to accomplish the states' quotas. Named after Aleksei Grigorievich Stakhanov during the second five-year plan in 1935, the party established a socialist competition movement. Stakhanov had mined 102 tons of coal in less than six hours. This competitive pattern became the norm to goad the workers and kolkhoz farmers to overachieve their quotas to be recognized as heroes. One such stakhanovite, Zuurakan Kainazarova (1902–1982), a Kyrgyz sugar beet grower in Kyrgyzstan, broke a record and received the title "Hero of Socialist Labor" twice in the 1940s and 1950s, which opened her path toward becoming a deputy of the Communist Party of the USSR. Kainazarova and many other Soviet heroes upheld the ideal of earning the respect of the whole nation with the promise of improving their lives through various titles and medals. Their successes appeared in newspapers. Many received apartments in the center of their capital cities and were able to shop in stores that were off-limits to ordinary citizens.

The personal and collective rewards were significant for fulfilling the quotas. Many "enthusiasts" flocked to construction projects such as hydroelectric plants and fertilizer factories to improve cotton production. This could only be done by engaging "shock workers" to work long hours, building industry and products. There were newspaper and radio stories about all-female silk workers surpassing the quotas for silk garments in the Uzbek SSR. The shortage of skilled workers required Russians and Ukrainians to relocate to Central Asia to earn higher salaries. Among these workers and local laborers, the "inventors and innovators" movement stirred enthusiasm and innovation to build upon the factories that were relocated in the Ferghana Valley during the Second World War. These successful workers and farmers were able to rest in sanatoriums and health spas on idyllic mountain lakes and at resorts such as Issyk Kol, Arslanbob, and Sary Chelek in the Kyrgyz mountains. The lives of Central Asians improved quite a bit; nevertheless, chronic problems such as overspecialization in the industry and agriculture, and lack of proper medical care for these overachieving populations were also produced.

Between the end of Stalin's brutal yet formative years in 1953 and the end of the USSR in 1991, the often naively enthusiastic policies of Nikita Khrushchev (in office 1953–64) and the monotonous, if not stagnant, policies of Leonid Brezhnev (in office 1964–82) dominated the political landscape until Mikhail Gorbachev ascended the Kremlin in 1990. Central Asian populations did not necessarily allow the Soviet political policies to replace their indigenous structures. Many of the local and regional leaders

ALI İĞMEN

who survived the purges—both smaller purges beginning in 1933 and in the 1940s after the Great Purge of 1936–38—took on new titles, such as kolkhoz managers. In other words, the solidarity groups hung on to their alliances, whether they were conceived of as clans, tribes, mahallas, or other local, regional, or nomadic structures.

The titular nationalities in each republic constructed national intelligentsia who led the Communist Party and other political, social, and cultural institutions. The very idea of reforming the traditional ways failed for the most part because most of the apparatchiks continued to operate within their solidarity groups, favoring their own to work with and succeed them. Yet, non–Central Asian intelligentsia still dominated many positions of power in the military, industry, higher education, and cultural institutions such as theaters. Kümüshalieva and her fellow theater and cinema professionals always had Russian and other non–Central Asian instructors, administrators, and mentors. Each republic was required to accommodate Russian and other European nationalities in education, as well as in other social and cultural spheres. A case in point: there needed to be Russian-language cohorts and classes in all universities in addition to the national cohorts. Similarly, most major cities with theaters had a Russian-language theater in addition to the national one. Kümüshalieva, for example, played Tolgonai of Chinghiz Aitmatov's *Mother Earth* in the Kyrgyz National Theater while acting as Madame Butterfly in the National Theater of the Kyrgyz SSR, the grander and more prestigious of the two. On the other hand, Saira Kiyizbaeva, the opera singer of the four daughters of Tököldösh, sang and taught classes in Russian in the National Opera and Ballet of the Kyrgyz SSR.

Despite the official Soviet policy against tribalism and nationalism, Central Asian political elites found various ways to maintain their allegiances within the familial networks and solidarity groups. At the very top levels, five Central Asian leaders remained in power as the first secretaries of their respective Communist Parties during the Brezhnev years: Dinmukhamed A. Kunaev of Kazakhstan (1964–86), Turdakun U. Usubaliev of Kyrgyzstan (1961–85), Jabbor R. Rasulov of Tajikistan (1961–82), Muhammetnazar G. Gapurov of Turkmenistan (1969–85), and Sharof R. Rashidov of Uzbekistan (1959–83). As these men comfortably aged in their offices for twenty years or longer, they perpetuated a system that abided by newly established rituals that were national in form and Soviet in content. They and their subordinates led their respective titular nationalities, who were given a national language, an anthem, a flag, an academy of sciences, an opera and ballet, and a theater, among many other institutions that solidified their Soviet Central Asian identities. The four daughters of Tököldösh, all urbanized (former rural) folks, benefited from both the national form and the Soviet content, improving their lives and allowing them to feed their families. They, however, lived in crowded Soviet-style high-rises that were often in need of repairs. They worked in theaters and film studios that were falling apart. They were confronted with alcoholism and other modern ailments. Yet, they lived in cities with tree-lined boulevards without worrying about utility bills or unemployment. They were well versed in the literatures of the world and familiar with the high culture of most societies, such as the classical music of Europe. When the end came in 1991, in the eyes of outsiders they looked like they were stuck in earlier decades in fashions, technology, industry, infrastructure, and other spheres. Yet, these women and their colleagues and relatives reported that they were proud of what they had created as Soviet people, and that they had not abandoned who they were as Central Asians.

8

Post-Soviet Central Asia

David G. Lewis

ollowing the dissolution of the Soviet Union at the end of 1991, five new states in Central Asia faced the unexpected challenge of establishing national governments and developing diplomatic relations with the outside world. These new states faced deep-seated domestic political, social, and economic problems but were also forced to find their place in a rapidly changing international order. The post-Soviet history of Central Asian states is dominated by these two themes: (1) the search for external legitimacy in an international system dominated by a resurgent United States and by liberal ideals of democracy and human rights, and (2) attempts to manage relations domestically between newly formed state authorities and rapidly changing societies. In both areas, Central Asia's states had a mixed track record, embracing different variants of authoritarianism to manage internal problems but largely avoiding the mass conflict and state collapse that some in the early 1990s predicted as their fate.

Although independence came quickly to Central Asia, it is easy to overemphasize the reluctance of Central Asian elites to embrace this opportunity. In the March 1991 referendum, Central Asians had voted overwhelmingly for a renewed Union, but it would be wrong to assume that Central Asian elites were content with the Soviet status quo. The 1980s had been a traumatic period of purges and russification for much of Central Asia. Yuri Andropov's anti-corruption campaign—continued for several years by Mikhail Gorbachev—had replaced local Communist Party leaders with pro-Moscow officials who had little local social support. Between 1984 and 1988, nearly sixty thousand Central Asian officials were dismissed in Moscow's purges. Moreover, the Soviet experience had consolidated the borders of these new republics in the public consciousness; a republican-level bureaucracy and security apparatus was already in place; and the titular nations in each republic had developed a largely coherent national historical narrative that would underpin national identity projects in each state. Nevertheless, when Central Asian republics did declare independence in 1991, it was a profound political, economic, and social shock to societies and elites who had never seriously considered that the Soviet system might collapse. Nevertheless, following the failure of the August 1991 coup attempt in Moscow, one by one Central Asian states declared independence. Kyrgyzstan was first on August 31, followed by Uzbekistan (September 1), Tajikistan (September 9), Turkmenistan (October 27), and—rather belatedly—Kazakhstan (December 16).

Politics and Civil War

In three states, incumbent Communist Party leaders retained control during the transition to independence. Saparmurat Niyazov in Turkmenistan, Nursultan Nazarbayev in Kazakhstan, and Islam Karimov in Uzbekistan all rapidly shed any pretense of adherence to Marxist-Leninist ideology. Instead, they presented themselves as national state builders, intent on maintaining order, building independent states, and pursuing economic stabilization. Local police and KGB agencies—quickly rebadged as national bodies—soon adjusted to the new reality. With the help of the security services, Uzbek, Turkmen, and Kazakh leaders managed to consolidate their power and broker intra-elite deals that avoided wider civil conflict, albeit at the cost of any semblance of democracy.

The process was still contested. In Uzbekistan, Islam Karimov, the first secretary of the Communist Party, only since 1989, had become president of the Uzbek SSR through a vote in the Supreme Soviet (legislature) in 1990. After Uzbekistan declared independence, Karimov was elected as the country's first president at a poll in December 1991, running as the candidate of the People's Democratic Party of Uzbekistan, effectively the renamed Communist Party. Karimov won with 87 percent of the vote in a poll marred by fraud; Karimov's main opponent, the avant-garde poet and dissident Mohammed Solih, fled the country, as did other opposition members. Members of Solih's *Erk* (Liberty) Party were singled out for subsequent repression. Abdurahim Polat, the leader of the largest opposition movement, *Birlik*, was attacked and forced into exile. Karimov avoided direct elections throughout the 1990s, instead having his term in office extended through a 1995 referendum, before again facing national polls in 2000, 2007, and 2015.

In Turkmenistan, Saparmurat Niyazov, who had been Communist Party first secretary since 1985, was even more averse to facing the voters. He won a presidential poll in 1992 with 99.5 percent of the vote, but there were no other candidates. Potential challengers, such as Avdy Kuliev, the first Turkmen foreign minister, were forced into exile. In 1994, Niyazov extended his period in office until 2002 in a referendum, winning 99.9 percent of the

DAVID G. LEWIS

votes. For the rest of his life, he never again held a presidential election. Instead, in December 1999, the Turkmen parliament declared Niyazov president for life. Elections to Turkmenistan's legislature did take place in 1994, 1999, and 2004, but they always had the same result: the country's only legal party, the Democratic Party of Turkmenistan, won all the seats.

Kazakhstan had a much more active opposition, a lively media, and some genuinely pluralistic politics in the 1990s, but its presidential elections were never competitive. Communist Party leader Nursultan Nazarbayev was appointed as the first President of Kazakhstan in April 1990 by the Supreme Soviet. In the first ever presidential election on December 1, 1991, Nazarbayev won an uncontested poll, gaining 99 percent of the votes. President Nazarbayev quickly consolidated both formal and informal powers, and used a referendum in 1995 to extend his rule, only facing reelection in 1999.

It was the smallest Central Asian Republic, Kyrgyzstan, that went furthest with democratic experiments. The incumbent first secretary of the Communist Party, Absamat Masaliyev, who had been in office since November 1985, failed to win an election in the Supreme Soviet, and in October 1990 deputies instead voted for the liberal Askar Akaev, a physicist and the president of the Kyrgyz Academy of Sciences. He won an uncontested poll in October 1991 with 95 percent of the vote, but subsequent polls in 1995 and 2000 became highly contested affairs, marked by frequent malpractice and the exclusion of serious opponents before polls opened. A chaotic parliament—later dubbed by its members the "legendary parliament"—gave Akaev a bumpy ride, prompting increasing crackdowns on the opposition and a consolidation of power around the presidential family.

In Tajikistan, elites were more sharply divided by regional affiliation and ideological stance than in any other Central Asian state. Splits in the ruling elite—and opposition to the traditional domination of the northern region of Leninabad (renamed Khujand after 1991)—broke out into protests in Dushanbe in February 1990. Further demonstrations in August 1991 forced Kakhar Makhamov, the Communist Party head, to resign after he apparently supported the Moscow coup attempt. He was replaced by Rakhmon Nabiev, who had been ousted in 1985 amid corruption allegations. On November 24, 1991, Nabiev won presidential elections, with some 57 percent of the vote, against the Pamiri filmmaker Davlat Khudonazarov, who was supported by a new opposition coalition of the Islamic Revival Party of Tajikistan (IRPT), democratic nationalists, and regional leaders from Gorno-Badakhshan and Gharm Districts. The election did little to address the fundamental divides inside Tajikistan, and by the spring of 1992 there were frequent outbreaks of unrest across the country. After months of demonstrations and protests in Dushanbe, in May 1992 a Government of National Reconciliation was formed, including opposition members, and opposition fighters forced the resignation of Nabiev as president in September 1992. But by late 1992, the country had descended into full-scale civil war.

Regional leaders, mainly from the southern region of Kulob, had set up militias, loosely aligned as the People's Front of Tajikistan, led by criminal authority Sangak Safarov, and backed by Uzbekistan. Against them were the forces of the United Tajik Opposition (UTO), comprising the Democratic Party of Tajikistan, the IRPT, the People's Movement Rastokhez, and the Lali Badakhshan Society, representing the people of Gorno-Badakhshan. This opposition grouping was a heterogenous array, increasingly led by Islamist forces, but with its main roots among discontented regional elites in the eastern districts of the country, notably those from the northeast ("Gharmis") and Gorno-Badakhshan ("Pamiris"). By late 1992, at least fifteen thousand civilians had been killed in the fighting, and hundreds of thousands had fled the country, as the Popular Front advanced on the capital, Dushanbe. A meeting of the Supreme Soviet in November 1992 in Khujand resulted in the appointment of Emomali Rakhmonov (he later derussified his name as Rahmon) as president. In December, Popular Front forces seized Dushanbe and proceeded to pursue a brutal campaign against Gharmi and Pamiri communities and against other suspected opposition supporters. Many opposition supporters went into exile in Afghanistan.

Fighting continued in the eastern districts of the country for several years, but the opposition could never overcome its internal differences or the military strength of the Dushanbe-based government. In 1994, the UN launched peace talks, and three years later the two sides agreed on a compromise peace deal, in which the opposition laid down its arms in exchange for positions in a coalition government. The war had cost at least fifty thousand lives and displaced as many as eight hundred thousand people. The spirit of compromise of the peace agreements did not last. In reality, the peace agreement disguised a military and political victory for President Rahmon, who went on to consolidate power and gradually remove his erstwhile opponents one by one.

Energy and Authoritarianism, Kazakhstan and Turkmenistan

Across the region, post-Soviet economies suffered from the disruption caused by the end of the Soviet central planning system—and with it the generous subsidies from Moscow—and subsequent hyperinflation. As states scrambled to establish national currencies and central banks, economic output declined sharply; in Kyrgyzstan, GDP declined by 45 percent between 1991 and 1995, and Tajikistan's war-affected economy contracted by almost one-third in 1992 alone. Uzbekistan's official figures were suspect but indicated a less traumatic transition, although its reluctance to reform agriculture also perpetuated some of the worst rural poverty in the region. In Kazakhstan, the economy also contracted sharply, and only regained its 1989 level of output in the early 2000s, but the new political leaders were also quickly coming to terms with the realities of international business and finance. Western oil companies had long before viewed the Caspian Sea as a potential area for exploration, and an initial deal had been reached by Gorbachev in

8-1 Public city space and an internet game club, Almaty, Kazakhstan, 2013. Photograph by Morgan Y. Liu.

1990 with the US company Chevron. In 1993, Chevron agreed on a $20 billion joint venture in the post-Soviet energy sector in the Tengiz oil field, near the remote town of Atyrau in the far west of Kazakhstan.

Foreign investment in the energy sector appeared to offer the possibility of prosperity for the Kazakh economy. Yet Western investment in the country was soon accompanied by rumors of grand corruption and bribery associated with oil deals. US prosecutors traced multimillion-dollar bribes and illicit payments passed to senior Kazakh officials, including President Nazarbayev and Nurlan Balgimbayev, the prime minister and later a leading official in the oil industry in the 1990s. The sudden access to vast riches had a major impact on Kazakh elites; not only did it produce hugely luxurious lifestyles for a tiny minority, but it also connected them to the opportunities of the global financial system. Kazakh officials and businesspeople began to appear in Zurich, London, and Geneva, seeking confidential bank accounts and high-end property.

Turkmenistan also enjoyed vast energy reserves: its reserves of natural gas were second only to Russia in the region. Initially, it only had one export pipeline and was reliant on Russia to buy its gas. Attempts to attract Western investment, as Kazakhstan had done so effectively, were stymied by the highly personalized, corrupt dictatorship that emerged under Saparmurat Niyazov, who later styled himself as "Turkmenbashi," the leader of the Turkmen. Income from gas sales was channeled into Niyazov's vast personality cult and a plethora of new buildings in Ashgabat, including a huge revolving gold statue of the president. In 2001, Niyazov published a

8-2 Female dancers performing in traditional dress at the Khan Shatyr Mall in Nur-Sultan, Kazakhstan, 2018. Photograph by Kasia Ploskonka.

book of folksy philosophy, the *Ruhnama*, which became required reading for students in an increasingly ideological education system. The system was brutally repressive and became even more so after a failed coup in 2002, launched by a former foreign minister turned dissident, Boris Shikhmuradov. The authorities arrested Shikhmuradov and dozens of his associates, many of whom disappeared in Turkmenistan's brutal prison system. Niyazov's increasingly bizarre behavior disguised the brutality of the regime, its discrimination against ethnic minorities, and its ideological nationalism.

In 2005, Niyazov launched a new wave of arrests among government officials, including the leading official in the oil sector, Yolly Gurbanmuradov (who reportedly died in prison in December 2015). As the repressions continued, Niyazov suddenly died of heart failure on December 21, 2006. There were rumors that he had been murdered by elites nervous about further purges, although there was no evidence to back up these claims. In the murky and ruthless palace politics that followed, Gurbanguly Berdimuhamedow, the deputy chairman of the council of ministers and health minister, seized power with the support of Akmurat Rejepov, the head of the presidential guard. Hopes that Berdimuhamedow would take Turkmenistan in a more positive direction were short-lived. He held early elections in February 2007, winning 89 percent of the votes, but quickly consolidated authoritarian power. He arrested and imprisoned his erstwhile ally Rejepov in 2007, and rapidly developed a cult of personality almost as widespread as that of his predecessor. Rejepov died in prison in 2017, one of more than one hundred people, mostly former officials—considered to have been "disappeared" in Turkmenistan's prisons—sentenced to long prison terms without any contact with the outside world.

The Turkmen regime was protected from any international pressure to address these human rights abuses because of its huge gas resources and a new export deal struck with China. A 1,800-kilometer pipeline was built from Turkmenistan, across Uzbekistan and Kazakhstan, to China in 2009. As Turkmenistan's gas exports to China increased, two more lines came on track, and China also invested in other sectors of the economy. Although the regime prided itself on its official policy of neutrality in international affairs, in reality it had become almost a client state of China. Plans to diversify its exports—through a trans-Caspian route or the long-awaited Turkmenistan-Afghanistan-Pakistan-India (TAPI) pipeline—failed to overcome the obstacles of regional geopolitics and the difficult business environment inside Turkmenistan.

Uzbekistan, Islam, and Authoritarianism

While Kazakhstan opened to the global economy, Uzbekistan resisted external recommendations to pursue rapid economic reform. The government avoided any large-scale privatization program and reintroduced exchange controls in 1996, in response to a balance of payments crisis. The Uzbek authorities claimed that this so-called Uzbek economic model limited the post-Soviet economic collapse: by 1999, according to official figures, Uzbekistan had recovered to 95 percent of its 1991 GDP level. Over two decades, however, the model became dysfunctional, curtailing cross-border trade and investment while offering prime rent-seeking opportunities to a well-connected elite. Although inequality was less overt compared with Kazakhstan, which had pursued more rapid privatization, in Uzbekistan the central role of cotton in the economy and the resistance to any agricultural reform ensured that the predominantly rural population experienced some of the highest levels of poverty in the region.

By 1993–94, virtually all secular political opposition in Uzbekistan had been either co-opted, exiled, or repressed. Militant Islamist groups, however, posed a serious challenge to the regime, and the struggle with both genuine and invented "terrorist" threats would dominate Uzbek security policy for the next decade. Islamist groups had become publicly active in the late 1980s, particularly in the eastern Fergana Valley region of the country. In December 1991, during a meeting in the town of Namangan, Karimov was confronted by Juma Namangani, head of an Islamist group, Adolat. The group had effectively taken control of the town and was advocating the establishment of an Islamic state. In March 1992, the Uzbek authorities began a crackdown on Islamist groups, including Adolat, who were driven out of Uzbekistan to Tajikistan, where they joined the Islamist opposition in the civil war and renamed themselves the Islamic Movement of Uzbekistan (IMU).

In February 1999, a series of car bombs exploded in Tashkent. The

8-3   Located at the eastern entrance of Itchan Kala, women prepare meat-filled samsa in the tandoor in Khiva, Uzbekistan, 2019. Photograph by Kasia Ploskonka.

government blamed the IMU, although there were multiple other theories about who was behind the bombs. The government responded with a campaign of repression against Muslims suspected of belonging to nonorthodox groups, with thousands rounded up and jailed. The IMU then launched a series of cross-border raids from their base in northern Tajikistan to southern Kyrgyzstan in 1999–2001, sparking fears of a wider regional conflict. Eventually, the IMU fled to Afghanistan, where they became allies of the Taliban, lingering into the 2010s but largely divorced from their origins in Uzbekistan. Rumors of IMU revivals in Central Asia have recurred regularly since the 2000s; further, occasional attacks in Uzbekistan were attributed to little-known groups such as the Islamic Jihad Union. There was little popular support for violent jihadism, but there was a groundswell of interest in other radical Islamist groups such as Hizb ut-Tahrir, thousands of whose members ended up in the notorious Uzbek prison system.

Uzbekistan had sought a closer relationship with the West during the 1990s. President Karimov met President Bill Clinton in Washington in 1996. However, it was the US intervention in Afghanistan in 2001 that provided an opportunity for Uzbekistan to leverage its geographical position to its advantage. Within weeks of the 9/11 terrorist attacks, Uzbekistan found itself on the front line of a global military campaign. By early 2002, Uzbekistan was host to a US military base at Karshi-Khanabad. The new security relationship with the United States was accompanied by economic and political support; President Karimov was awarded with an official visit to Washington in March 2002. The US and Uzbekistan signed a far-reaching strategic partnership, offering US financial and political support in exchange for the Uzbek government launching economic and political reforms.

At first, there were a few liberalizing measures to allow some human rights activists and nongovernmental organizations (NGOs) to function. But these faltering reforms did not assuage critics of the government, who highlighted the lack of any political freedoms and the systematic use of torture in Uzbekistan's prisons. The government was also reluctant to embark on reforms of the sclerotic economy. Far from opening the economy, the government began to clamp down more on cross-border trade and small business. The relationship with the West became increasingly fraught after a meeting of the European Bank for Reconstruction and Development in 2003, when President Karimov was confronted by Western officials and activists over claims that torture was systemic in Uzbekistan. The failure to improve the human rights situation finally led to the suspension of US aid in 2004. The so-called Color Revolutions in Georgia (2003) and Ukraine (2004) further fueled government suspicions of international engagement, and the authorities began to restrict international NGOs and other organizations working in the country, expelling the Open Society Foundations and restricting visas and registrations for many others.

Despite government repression, small public demonstrations were quite common in Uzbekistan in 2004–05, typically protesting new government trading regulations or a growing crisis in gas and electricity supplies. Protests in Andijan in May 2005 over the arrest of a group of twenty-three local businesspeople initially received little attention. The businesspeople had set up something akin to a business cooperative in the city, but operating along religious lines; they were subsequently accused of adhering to an Islamic group called Akromiya. When the businesspeople were arrested, thousands of their supporters held silent vigils in the streets leading to the courthouse where the trial was taking place. On May 12, ahead of the expected court verdict, armed men stormed the local prison and freed the businessmen, before seizing control of a local administrative building on the city's central Babur Square and taking officials hostage. Thousands of people crowded into the square to hear anti-government speeches, but later in the day government troops attacked the gunmen and the protestors, killing hundreds of people, the vast majority of whom were unarmed. International NGOs and the Organization for Security and Co-operation in Europe (OSCE) issued reports accusing Uzbek troops of killing hundreds of unarmed demonstrators; Amnesty International described the events as "a mass killing of civilians." Hundreds of people fled to neighboring Kyrgyzstan to seek refuge. A wave of government repressions followed the violence in Andijan, ending any hopes of political liberalization under Karimov or improved relations with the West.

The Andijan violence was the starkest illustration of the Uzbek state's failure to effectively manage relations with its own society, but it also had a major impact on Uzbekistan's relations with the outside world. From the very beginning, President Karimov blamed the Andijan violence on unidentified "external forces." Government spokesmen hinted at Western support for Islamist groups in plotting the Andijan violence, drawing parallels with Russian theories of "color revolutions," which viewed anti-government protests in former Soviet states as inspired and funded by the West. The US State Department sharply criticized the killings, and in October 2005 the EU imposed limited sanctions on Uzbekistan. The US Department of Defense did not join the condemnation, however, citing a continued partnership in the Global War on Terror. Former defense secretary Donald Rumsfeld argued that the US criticism of Karimov over Andijan was "one of the most unfortunate, if unnoticed, foreign policy mistakes of our administration." Despite this support from the Pentagon, Uzbekistan ordered the United States to leave its base at Karshi forthwith, thus abruptly ending the hopes of a US-Uzbek partnership in the region. Instead, Uzbekistan turned to Russia and China for diplomatic support.

Kyrgyzstan's Revolutions

In post–Soviet Central Asian history, the year 2005 marked a watershed. Alongside events in Uzbekistan, neighboring Kyrgyzstan was also engulfed in chaos, when presidential elections sparked off mass protests, ultimately leading to the downfall of President Askar Akaev. For many observers, the events in Kyrgyzstan in April 2005 were unexpected: Akaev remained the most pro-Western figure in the region and was widely seen as the most liberal leader in Central Asia. Yet his rule had been marked by increasing discontent and growing opposition. At parliamentary elections in 2000, a popular opposition leader, Feliks Kulov, was disbarred from running and subsequently jailed on charges of corruption. Akaev won presidential elections in October 2000 easily, but the poll was marred by widespread malpractice. The consolidation of economic power around the president disrupted a fragile equilibrium among business elites; southern elites, in particular, felt marginalized by Akaev and his northern backers. Akaev—from a Russian-speaking background, and with a Soviet upbringing—struggled to connect with ordinary, rural Kyrgyz, who saw little benefit from his ambitious reform programs and lofty visions.

Early signs of growing popular and elite discontent with Akaev were evident in 2002, when Azimbek Beknazarov, a parliamentary deputy from the southern Aksy region, was arrested after he led a campaign against Kyrgyz territorial concessions to China in a border dispute. Protests at his arrest led to a confrontation with police, who shot and killed five unarmed protestors. The killings sparked a wave of protests that paralyzed the country over the summer of 2002. Although the government finally prevailed, the regime's weakness was apparent. Gradually, elite support for Akaev began to ebb; former prime minister Kurmanbek Bakiev joined the opposition, alongside

8-4   The texture of material objects in a rural home, Jalalabat Province, Kyrgyzstan, 2011. Photograph by
       Morgan Y. Liu.

more liberal figures such as former foreign minister Roza Otunbaeva. Ahead of parliamentary elections due in February 2005, the government reformed the political system, reducing the number of seats available in the legislature. Family members and close allies of Akaev packed the candidate lists. Inevitably, many powerful figures seemed likely to be excluded from the new parliament. Despite evidence of multiple-voting and ballot stuffing, there were many upsets in the first round of voting on February 14, 2005. Even the president's daughter, Bermet Akaeva, failed to win a seat in the first round and was forced into a second round of voting.

Candidates who lost in the first round accused the authorities of malpractice and began anti-government protests. A second round of voting did little to resolve these disputes. Instead, protestors seized administrative buildings in the southern cities of Jalalabad and Osh. The government was slowly losing control. The opposition began converging on the capital, Bishkek, which had hitherto been quiet. On March 24, a mass demonstration in Bishkek quickly descended into riots, during which protestors broke into the presidential administration and—to almost everybody's surprise—seized power. Akaev fled into exile in Russia.

Western journalists dubbed these events the "Tulip Revolution" (although nobody in Kyrgyzstan used the term), and it was often viewed from outside the country as a democratic breakthrough in the region. In reality, although students and NGOs had been involved in the demonstrations, there was also organized mobilization of supporters by powerful regional leaders who had little interest in democratic ideals. New presidential elections were held in July 2005, won easily by opposition leader Kurmanbek Bakiev, with 89 percent of the vote. However, Bakiev's conversion to democratic politics was shallow: in truth, he was an unimaginative bureaucrat, with no vision either for the economy or for a more liberal political regime. Indeed, postrevolutionary politics under Bakiev became more corrupt and criminalized than under the ousted Akaev, and eventually became significantly more repressive.

The apparent ease of Bakiev's victory in the presidential election disguised deep-seated intra-elite disputes. Many of these were over business and resources, including illegal business such as the trade in heroin from Afghanistan. The new Kyrgyz parliament was notable primarily for the proportion of its deputies involved in organized crime; during 2005–06, a series of assassinations and standoffs between crime groups highlighted the close linkages between crime and politics. In politics, Bakiev's attempts to consolidate power by appointing his own officials—predominantly originating from the south—irritated many northerners, who coalesced around the prime minister Feliks Kulov. Bakiev responded by ousting Kulov as prime minster, while continuing to consolidate power both in politics and in business. The president's son, Maxim Bakiev, was appointed to head a new Central Agency for Development, Investment, and Innovation in October 2009, which attempted to consolidate control over foreign aid and investment. Bakiev's brothers played key roles in managing the security forces and the regions.

Together, the presidential family was intent on rebuilding a "single pyramid" of patronage networks, leaving little room for other business and political elites.

For a while, it seemed Bakiev might succeed. He co-opted many opposition politicians and easily won presidential elections in 2009, gaining 76 percent of votes cast, amid reports of widespread malpractice at the polls. Despite this apparent success, the government increasingly reverted to repression against political opponents, including the murder of Medet Sadyrkulov, the chief of the presidential administration, in March 2009, and that of a journalist, Gennady Pavlyuk, later the same year in Almaty. There was little criticism from Western states. The United States had persuaded Bakiev to keep open the Manas airbase; lucrative fuel supply and base rental agreements and a tacit agreement to remain silent on human rights cases appeared to have been part of this murky deal. In early 2010, Bakiev further increased repression against opponents, closing media outlets and harassing NGOs. The government also introduced price rises on utilities and telecoms; the beneficiaries were energy and telecom companies recently privatized in favor of businesspeople close to the regime. This mix of repression and corruption began to spark protests around the country, particularly in northern regions. In early April in the northern province of Talas, protestors took control of the regional governor's office and declared the establishment of a "People's Government." Within days, the protests had spread to the capital, but—unlike in 2005—there were armed clashes between government forces and protestors, most of whom were unarmed. At least eighty people were reported dead as crowds stormed the "White House"—the main government building in central Bishkek. President Bakiev fled the country on April 15 to Belarus, and an interim government took power.

The fall of Bakiev left behind a power vacuum, in which many of the unresolved social tensions in the country resurfaced. Relations between ethnic Kyrgyz and a sizeable Uzbek minority in the south of the country had often been tense; in June 1990, some three hundred people had been killed in interethnic rioting. Two decades later, in June 2010, with the political elite focused on forming a functioning interim government in the capital, interethnic riots broke out in Osh and Jalalabad in the south. During several days of riots and pogroms, characterized by extreme brutality, almost five hundred people were killed, and more than two thousand houses and businesses destroyed, a majority belong to ethnic Uzbeks. More than one hundred thousand residents fled Kyrgyzstan and temporarily sought refuge in neighboring Uzbekistan. Local and international analysts accused local authority figures and in some cases the state security forces of being complicit in the violence.

Despite the violence, the government went ahead with a constitutional referendum in June, which reduced the powers of the presidency, and approved a mixed parliamentary-presidential system of government. Acting president Roza Otunbaeva remained in office until presidential elections were held in December 2011, easily won by Social Democratic Party leader Almazbek

Atambaev, with some 63 percent of the votes cast. The Atambaev presidency had a mixed record. It achieved little in terms of economic development and was accused of growing numbers of politicized prosecutions against opponents.

President Atambaev did fulfill his promise to leave office after one term in 2017, setting the stage for what became a genuinely competitive presidential election in October 2017. Sooronbay Jeenbekov, a former prime minister and a close ally of Atambaev, won the election with 54 percent of votes cast against another former prime minister and businessman, Omurbek Babanov (33 percent). Although the poll passed off peacefully, after the election Babanov left the country, fleeing spurious charges of inciting ethic unrest. Jeenbekov soon turned on his patron Atambaev in an ugly stand-off that resulted in Atambaev being sentenced to eleven years in prison in June 2020 on charges of illegally releasing a Chechen criminal in 2013.

Under Jeenbekov's administration, there was still a good deal of political competition among regional elites—evident at highly contested parliamentary elections in October 2020. In a further twist of Kyrgyzstan's circular policies, Jeenbekov and his allies repeated the same mistakes of his predecessors, resorting to vote-buying to exclude opposition candidates from the new parliament. Protests about the conduct of the election soon degenerated into clashes, with protestors seizing control of central government institutions and opposition figures vying to form a new government. On October 15, Jeenbekov resigned as president. Opposition leader Sadyr Japarov, who had been serving a prison sentence for an alleged kidnapping until his release by protestors during the unrest, replaced Jeenbekov as acting president. Japarov easily won a presidential election on January 10, 2021, with some 79 percent of votes cast. He also pushed through constitutional changes to strengthen the role of the presidency in a referendum in April 2021. The outcome deepened Kyrgyzstan's long-standing governance crisis and further weakened its fragile democratic tradition and institutions.

Consolidating Power in Kazakhstan, Turkmenistan, and Tajikistan

The Kazakh authorities liked to point to the upheavals in Kyrgyzstan as a warning of the chaos and violence that would accompany rapid democratization. The Kazakh government used its high budget revenues from oil and gas sales to boost social spending and to invest in infrastructure. As GDP per capita advanced from a low of just US$3,740 in 1995 to some US$10,570 in 2016, a new Kazakh middle class—concentrated in Almaty and Astana (renamed Nur-Sultan in 2019)—experienced rapidly growing real incomes. However, society was still marked by significant inequalities; the western, oil-producing regions, in particular, complained that financial benefits accrued largely to the central government and to a small group of oligarchs close to the presidential family. Growing economic prosperity helped reduce

DAVID G. LEWIS

support for opposition parties, but the regime also sought increased political control and reduced the political space for pluralistic politics.

Ahead of presidential elections scheduled for January 1999, the government barred the former prime minister Akezhan Kazhegeldin from running, and he left the country to avoid prosecution. President Nazarbayev was easily reelected, winning 81 percent of the votes; Serikbolsyn Abdildin, of the Communist Party of Kazakhstan, was runner-up with 11.9 percent. Although multiparty elections to the two chambers of parliament in September and October 1999 were designed to bolster Kazakhstan's democratic credentials, in reality, opposition parties and activists faced harassment, surveillance, and politically motivated prosecutions, and the elections consolidated presidential control over a compliant parliament. After the 1999 elections, there was no longer any pretense at genuine political pluralism, and the political space for any unsanctioned political activity began to close. No serious opposition candidates were allowed to contest subsequent presidential elections: Nazarbayev won 91 percent of votes in 2005, 96 percent in 2011, and 98 percent in 2015.

Parliamentary elections were also increasingly uncompetitive. In 2007, the new ruling party, Nur Otan, won all ninety-eight elected seats in the new Mazhilis. The negative international reaction to this one-party legislature prompted the authorities to allow two other pro-Nazarbayev parties into parliament at the 2012 elections, but still leaving Nur Otan with eighty-three seats. The situation remained virtually unchanged after parliamentary elections in March 2016, and parliament in any case played no significant role in the policy-making process.

Alongside complete control of the political system, the presidential family and its close allies increasingly controlled (directly or indirectly) all strategic businesses in Kazakhstan, not only in extractive industries (oil, gas, uranium, and other mining enterprises) but also in the media sector, and, after 2009, in banking and financial services. Political activity shifted away from the public sphere to internal infighting and business disputes among oligarchs. One group of business leaders had attempted to enter the formal political process in 2001, forming the Democratic Choice of Kazakhstan Party (DCK), but they were quickly closed down; two of their leaders, Mukhtar Ablyazov and Galymzhan Zhakiyanov, were arrested and imprisoned. Other challengers also faced prosecutions on corruption charges, or died in suspicious circumstances. In November 2005, Zamanbek Nurkadilov, a former mayor of Almaty and minister of emergencies, who had publicly criticized President Nazarbayev, was found dead. Officially, his death was declared a suicide, but opposition activists claimed he had been murdered. In February 2006, Altynbek Sarsenbayev, a former government minister and ambassador who joined the opposition in 2003, was murdered.

One of the most unpopular of Kazakhstan's oligarchs, Rakhat Aliyev, was married to Dariga Nazarbayeva, the president's eldest daughter; between them they had developed a significant media and business empire. Aliyev fell out of favor after an internal conflict with President Nazarbayev in 2007. An investigation was launched into Aliyev's alleged involvement in the kidnapping and killing of two of his former employees at one of his companies, Nurbank, and Aliyev was quickly dismissed from his position as ambassador to the OSCE. He was divorced from his wife and found his economic assets confiscated or redistributed. The Kazakh authorities pursued Aliyev's extradition from Europe, but in February 2015 he was found dead in a cell in Vienna, having apparently committed suicide.

The Kazakh authorities pursued political exiles abroad with obsessive zeal, but none more so than opposition politician and banker Mukhtar Ablyazov. After a short imprisonment for his involvement with the DCK political party, Ablyazov was permitted to resume his business career, and built up Kazakhstan's largest bank, BTA. But in early 2009 he fled to the United Kingdom, leaving behind a failing bank, in which the Kazakh authorities claimed to have uncovered a multibillion-dollar fraud. The Kazakh authorities pursued Ablyazov and his associates in multiple jurisdictions abroad, winning civil proceedings in the UK courts, where Ablyazov received a prison sentence for contempt of court. Ablyazov fled to France, where he was subsequently arrested and almost deported to Russia. At the last minute, his extradition was blocked by the French authorities on the suspicion that the process against him was political. Many of his associates were also refused extradition on the same grounds.

The pursuit of Ablyazov intensified after claims that he was involved in Kazakhstan's worst outbreak of violence since independence. In the remote western town of Zhanaozen, in December 2011, a long series of peaceful protests by oil workers broke down into attacks on government buildings. The police responded by firing live ammunition at unarmed protestors— including some who were recorded fleeing from the police—killing at least fourteen people and injuring many more. In response, the government prosecuted five police officers, who received sentences of up to seven years in prison in May 2012. At least two of those officers were released on parole within two years. Many more security officials who were involved in the violence appear to have avoided prosecution. The protests were the culmination of many months of strikes and peaceful protests by oil workers, demanding better wages and improved conditions. Many strikers lost their jobs, and others reportedly faced harassment, threats, and arrests.

The Kazakh authorities claimed that Ablyazov had funded and organized the protests, together with Vladimir Kozlov, leader of the unregistered Alga Party and a supporter of Ablyazov. Kozlov received a seven-and-a-half-year prison sentence, on charges including "public incitement of social discord and hatred" and "violent seizure of power." The US State Department argued that "most observers found the evidence against him unconvincing." Despite the violence in Zhanaozen and the increasingly repressive political system, Kazakhstan's strategic position, its apparent stability, and its vast energy resources ensured that it remained a partner of choice for Russia, China, and the West.

Turkmenistan also had the potential to be one of the most prosperous economies in the region by exploiting its extensive energy reserves, but instead it squandered its resources through high-level corruption and economic mismanagement. After Niyazov's death in 2006, there was hope that some of the worst excesses of Niyazov—his brutality, his destruction of the education system, and his cult of personality—would be curbed under his successor, Gurbanguly Berdimuhamedow, but the defining features of the personalized dictatorship continued largely unchanged. Formal constraints on executive power were almost nonexistent: the prosecutor's office dominated the judicial process; the legislature played no role in developing legislation; and the government was little more than a branch of the presidential administration. The Ministry of National Security, the successor to the KGB, had almost unlimited powers. Members of Berdimuhamedow's family and close associates from his home in Western Ahal province dominated appointments, and there were also reports that regional officials were building up their own patronage networks.

There were some formal changes to the political system. In 2012, a Law on Political Parties was adopted, allowing for a multiparty system to be established. Two artificial, pro-government parties, the Party of Industrialists and Entrepreneurs (PIE) and the Agrarian Party, were established alongside the Democratic Party of Turkmenistan (DPT). The 2012 presidential election was the first in which there were multiple candidates, although the seven individuals who participated were handpicked loyalists, and Berdimuhamedow won 97.1 percent of the votes. "Multiparty" elections were held in December 2013 to parliament, with 283 candidates contesting 125 seats. Among the new deputies, 47 were DPT members, 14 were from PIE, and the remainder were from trade unions and government-controlled civic groups. Despite the changes in electoral processes, parliament remained powerless, with all political influence centralized in the presidential administration. The only articulated opposition to the regime came from opposition activists in exile publishing critical commentary online. In 2016, only 14.5 percent of the population were on the internet, and the long-term effects of Niyazov's attacks on the education system and the intelligentsia were also felt: according to one account, 80 percent of the country's scientists had emigrated, the education system was in sharp decline, and hundreds of libraries were closed.

The end of the civil war in Tajikistan introduced some formal pluralism in the political system, reflecting a compromise between government and opposition, achieved through co-optation of warlords by providing them with formal positions and informal rent-seeking opportunities. After 1997, Rahmon and his allies gradually picked off powerful warlords one by one, not only former opposition commanders but also erstwhile allies from the Popular Front. The most powerful was General Ghaffor Mirzoyev, head of the Presidential Guard and president of Tajikistan's Olympic Committee, who was arrested in August 2004 and sentenced to life imprisonment on an array of charges, including drug trafficking and murder. In May 2008, another powerful figure from Kulob, Sukhrob Langariev, was arrested after a gun battle with police. Many of these figures were also alleged to be involved in the lucrative trade in Afghan heroin; their arrest did not reduce the volumes crossing the border, but by removing "independent" criminal groups, the central authorities effectively achieved a monopolization of the trade by groups linked closely to the state.

As the regime shifted attention from criminal groups in the south to move against informal networks in the east, it faced much more significant challenges, since these groups often had much deeper roots in local societies. Government forces engaged in armed clashes against rebel groups in the Rasht District on several occasions during 2009–11, characterizing them as terrorist groups; most had some connection to civil war–period Islamist groups and were under the control of former opposition commanders such as Mirzo Ziyoyev, a former UTO leader and minister of emergency situations in the compromise postconflict government. In 2009, government troops were involved in serious fighting against local militias, under the guise of an anti-narcotics drive, "Operation Poppy." In September 2010, amid further fighting, dozens of security personnel were killed in an ambush. In January 2011, the security forces killed a local informal leader, Alovuddin Davlatov (known as Ali Bedaki), and in April 2011 shot dead Mullo Abdullo, a militant Islamist. The clampdown in the Rasht Valley was another step in the government's consolidation of power across its territory and its suppression of Islamist networks, although clashes were probably also driven by a struggle for control of resources—including cross-border smuggling and local businesses.

The next region to be targeted was the Gorno-Badakhshan Autonomous Oblast, where residents were concerned by any encroachment by central government on their limited autonomy. Local criminal leaders were widely believed to be involved in the narcotics trade and other smuggling networks across the Afghan-Tajik and Tajik-Chinese borders, but they also enjoyed some local support, reflected in reports of anti-government protests. In 2012, fighting broke out between government forces and the supporters of local civil war–era commanders; more than fifty people—including unarmed civilians—were killed. There were further clashes and protests reported in 2014.

Alongside this consolidation of control over the regions, the government also became increasingly repressive toward other forms of political opposition. Rahmon consolidated power over the political system and business in his immediate family and close allies. In 2013, Zaid Saidov, a major businessman and former interior minister, was arrested after he announced the creation of a new political party, "New Tajikistan," and sentenced to twenty-six years in prison on charges widely seen as politically motivated. In January 2017, Mahmadsaid Ubaidulloev, for a long time viewed as the second most powerful figure in the political system, was replaced as mayor of Dushanbe after nearly twenty years in the post by Rahmon's son, Rustam Emomali. Tajik politics increasingly resembled a family business, with other relatives, such as the president's brother-in-law, Hasan Asadullozoda, wielding influence in the business world. Rustam Emomali appeared to have been designated as Rahmon's chosen successor, although President Rahmon won reelection for another seven-year term in October 2020.

Despite the government's repressive crackdown, Tajikistan still faced opposition from radical groups. In 2015, Colonel Gulmurod Halimov, the commander of the Interior Ministry's special forces, announced that he had joined the Islamic State group in Syria; he was later appointed "minister of war" in ISIS's government, but killed in an airstrike in 2017. Halimov was one of hundreds of Tajiks who joined ISIS in Syria, sparking fears that ISIS-linked groups would also appear inside Tajikistan. The government responded in August by banning the IRPT, which had remained a legal party since the 1997 peace accord. Later in the same month, General Abdukhalim Nazarzoda, deputy defense minister, was involved in armed clashes near Dushanbe, which government officials claimed was an attempted coup. Nazarzoda denied that he had been involved in a coup and accused the government of attempting to arrest former opposition leaders. He fled Dushanbe to the Romit Gorge some 150 kilometers outside the capital but was tracked down by government forces and killed. The details of the alleged coup were very unclear, but the authorities convicted more than 170 people for alleged involvement, and in September they declared the IRPT an extremist, terrorist organization.

Islamic State recruitment mostly occurred outside Central Asia, among diasporas formed by millions of migrants who responded to social and economic crisis at home by migrating to find work abroad, primarily in Russia. Labor migrants primarily came from Tajikistan, Uzbekistan, and Kyrgyzstan and filled many manual jobs in Russia's cities. These new migratory patterns had significant economic and social consequences, reducing pressure on governments to improve their economic success at home while offering an escape route for young people seeking work. Remittances from Russia to Tajikistan and Kyrgyzstan came to form a large proportion of real incomes for many families. According to the International Monetary Fund, the level of remittances to Tajikistan rose fivefold from 2004 to 2008, reaching $2.7 billion (more than 46 percent of GDP) in 2008. As the Russian economy slowed, the level of remittances to Uzbekistan and Tajikistan declined, but in 2016 migrants in Russia still sent $1.9 billion home to Tajikistan and $1.7 billion to Kyrgyzstan.

Economic development at home was partly limited by the lack of regional cooperation and extensive trade barriers that existed among Central Asian states. A difficult business environment also dissuaded many external investors, outside the energy sector. The best hope for external investment and more trade was through growing ties with China. In 2013, during a visit to Astana (now Nur-Sultan), President Xi Jinping announced the Belt and Road Initiative, an investment and connectivity program, which viewed Central Asia as the main gateway from Western China to Europe. China promised significant new investments in logistics and infrastructure, but progress was slowed by the difficult business environment of Central Asia, and by popular suspicions of Chinese expansion into the region. Although Russia and China developed close relations, particularly after 2014, Russia also championed a new regional customs union, the Eurasian Economic Union, which appeared to be partly designed to retain Russian influence in the region but only included Kazakhstan and Kyrgyzstan as members. All regional initiatives were stymied by Uzbekistan's autarkic economic policy and its consistent refusal to engage in any cross-border cooperation initiatives. Since the early 2000s, Uzbekistan's relations with neighboring Kyrgyzstan and Tajikistan had slowly worsened, with many borders being almost closed or becoming very difficult to cross for local residents. Any prospects for more effective regional cooperation depended on a change in political leadership in Tashkent.

Leadership Succession and Political Change

Analysts had often argued that political succession would be a major challenge to Central Asian stability. Yet, in Turkmenistan, Uzbekistan, and Kazakhstan, the process was managed with minimal political upheaval. In August 2016, President Islam Karimov died after more than twenty-five years as Uzbek leader, and the long-awaited succession process began. Although some tipped Rustam Azimov, the finance minister, as a possible successor, it was Shavkat Mirziyoyev, the long-standing Uzbek prime minister, who was confirmed by parliament as acting president on September 8. He easily won elections on December 4, 2016, in a poll that the OSCE described as "devoid of genuine competition." Mirziyoyev won with a reported 89 percent of the vote but faced no genuine challengers. Mirziyoyev quickly began installing his own allies in key posts, appointing Abdulla Aripov as prime minister in December 2016, and dismissing many regional governors and security officials. In January 2018, it was announced that powerful National Security Service (SNB) chief Rustam Inoyatov had also resigned, and Mirziyoyev initiated a far-reaching purge of the security services, which he admitted had been involved in unfair detentions, prosecutions, and torture. President Mirziyoyev actively sought more regional cooperation, easing border restrictions with Kyrgyzstan and Tajikistan, and initiated a reform of the restrictive exchange rate regime and other Karimov-era economic policies to encourage foreign investment. Some political prisoners were also released, but there was no indication that Mirziyoyev would be prepared to contemplate more extensive democratic reforms to the political system.

Kazakhstan followed a different model of succession. President Nazarbayev unexpectedly stepped down on March 19, 2019, to allow a successor to take over. Nazarbayev retained considerable powers as chairman of the Security Council but installed Kassym-Jomart Tokayev, a diplomat, as the acting president. Tokayev was confirmed in office by an election in June, at which he won 71 percent of votes. Tokayev committed to following

Nazarbayev's domestic and foreign policies, but there were still signs of intra-elite disputes behind the scenes. On May 2, 2020, Nazarbayev's daughter Dariga Nazarbayeva lost her position as chair of the Senate. Tokayaev's reputation was as a government technocrat, not a visionary politician, and he appeared to struggle to connect with a new, more activist younger generation. His promise to focus on social and economic improvements faced a first major test during the coronavirus pandemic in 2020, when the government was challenged both by a national public health crisis and also by a serious downturn in the economy.

Central Asia's Post-Soviet History

On the surface, Central Asia's post-Soviet history appears to be a story of remarkable continuity, marked by limited political change. Until the death of Karimov in 2016, Kazakhstan and Uzbekistan had been ruled by the same leader since the late 1980s. In Tajikistan, which experienced the trauma of civil war in the early 1990s, President Rahmon had ruled the country for more than a quarter of a century by 2020, when he was reelected for a further term in office. Turkmenistan's change of leadership in 2006 did not have a substantial impact on the nature of the political system, nor did it improve the everyday lives of most Turkmen. Kyrgyzstan appeared to be an outlier, with a more open political system in which mass protests three times caused major political change at the top. But Kyrgyz politics was more cyclical than progressive, with each revolution revealing more of the persistent problems of governance that made far-reaching change so difficult.

Behind this veil of apparent political stability, however, Central Asia's post-Soviet history was characterized by far-reaching social change and economic turmoil, often polarized understandings of personal and group identities, and the dominance of authoritarian political systems that relied on frequent use of state coercion and violence. While Central Asia's post-Soviet history is often characterized as remarkably peaceful, compared with other postcolonial historical transitions, the nature of this "peace" is highly contested, imbued as it has been with extensive trauma, displacement, and violence. Popular understandings of legitimacy in Central Asian states often diverged from liberal, democratic ideals, but even in terms of more localized understandings of justice and good governance, governments in the region often struggled to achieve a sustainable social contract with the societies that they sought to govern. While Western ideas of democratization and liberal values in Central Asia often failed to gain traction with elites and with the wider population, the Eurasian authoritarian alternative was far from a panacea to resolve Central Asia's deep-seated political, social, and economic problems.

CASE II-A

The Rise of Vali Bay, an Entrepreneur between Two Empires

David Brophy

One of the most eye-catching constructions of the colonial period in Central Asia is a grandiose mosque that stands in the town of Zharkent, in southeastern Kazakhstan. A classically Central Asian portal, with a tiled archway lined with Quranic inscriptions and dedications, shields it from the dusty streets. Step inside, however, and the visitor is confronted by an unmistakably Chinese-style prayer hall, said to have been modeled on the main mosque in Ghulja (Yining), lying to the east in Xinjiang, or Eastern Turkistan. The hall's interior, meanwhile, with two rows of columns and a mezzanine, bears a curious resemblance to a Christian church—something that Russian orientalist V. V. Bartold first remarked upon after a visit there in the 1890s.

The stylistic mishmash of the Zharkent mosque is a fitting reflection of the various migrations and empire-building enterprises that have shaped this region and its people. Lying east from Almaty along the Ili River, Zharkent was originally founded as a Qing garrison town, and until the mid-nineteenth century it was known by its Manchu name of Samar. Burnt to the ground in a Muslim rebellion that swept through northwest China in the 1860s, Zharkent eventually was revived in the 1880s, though no longer as an outpost of the Qing empire but at the center of a tract of land ceded to Russia by the 1881 Treaty of Saint Petersburg. Alongside Kazakhs and Cossacks, its population grew with an influx of migrant Chinese-speaking Dungans, as well as Taranchis (today's Uyghurs), who found refuge there from Qing reprisals. Among them was the mosque's patron, the local entrepreneur Vali Bay, or Vali Akhun Yoldashev (d. 1916). His life provides a window into the clash of empires along the Russia-China frontier.

From Cart Dealer to Grain Baron

In the 1860s, rumors of an impending massacre of Muslims in the Qing Empire traveled up the Gansu corridor and into Xinjiang, sparking a series of uprisings. Xinjiang at the time was a patchwork of jurisdictions, not the single administrative entity that it is today. The top-ranking official in the region was the Ili military governor (*Yili jiangjun*), with his seat in the strategically significant Ili Valley. Rebellion here initially stirred among the Chinese-speaking Dungans, who were more responsive to events in the interior, but they were soon joined by local Taranchis in a joint venture to topple the Qing military elite who had dominated them since the 1750s. An independent Taranchi sultanate was

II-A-1   The Vali Bay mosque in Zharkent, 1911. The man in the dark coat in the foreground is most likely Vali Bay himself. M. Philips Price Collection. Royal Geographical Society rgsF039/0169.

briefly established, soon to give way to Russian occupation. Watching on from a line of forts across the Kazakh Steppe, Russia seized on the instability in the frontier zone to invade the Ili Valley in 1871, commencing a decade of colonial rule that would have dramatic consequences for its inhabitants.

Vali Bay is first mentioned in the local historian Mulla Bilal's verse chronicle of the Taranchi sultanate, *Holy War in China* (*Ghazat dar mulk-i Chin*). These passing mentions inform us that Vali Bay was a Kashgari (i.e., a migrant from the south of Xinjiang). Throughout the Qing period, Kashgaris had drifted north seeking out commercial opportunities in the Ili region, where the local Taranchi (a word meaning "peasant") population was mostly tied to state-run Muslim agricultural colonies (Huitun). Judging from Mulla Bilal's work, Vali Bay had inserted himself into one such niche as a cart dealer (*arbakäsh*), an oc-

cupation with a critical role to play in sustaining the flow of commerce.

With a fleet of carts at his disposal, men such as Vali Bay were well positioned to profit from the growth of trade with Russia in this period. Long carried on surreptitiously, trade with Russia had been formalized in the north of Xinjiang by the 1851 Treaty of Ghulja. When Russia took possession of the Ili Valley, these opportunities only multiplied. Soon, Vali Bay would find himself occupying an advantageous position in a commercial chain linking ambitious Siberian investors, local agriculturalists, and the Qing military.

Russia's merchantry was not a major influence driving the empire's expansion into Central Asia, but it kept a close eye on its progress. In 1875, sensing an opportunity to prize open a back door into China, Russia's Ministry of Foreign Affairs joined with Siberian entrepreneurs to sponsor a reconnaissance mission into the Chinese interior. The Sosnovskii mission, as it was known, was for the most part a disappointment, but on its way back to Russia via the Gansu Corridor, they struck better luck at the encampment of Zuo Zongtang, the Qing general who was then awaiting the Guangxu emperor's approval to continue his counterinsurgency campaign into Xinjiang. Facing the perennial challenge of long supply lines in China's remote northwest, Zuo gladly entered into a contract with Sosnovskii to obtain grain supplies from Russia.

Chief among the merchants hoping to profit from this deal was one Ivan Fedorovich Kamenskii. Originally from Tomsk, Kamenskii soon shifted his base of operations to Russian-held Ghulja, where he went into partnership with Vali Bay. For a few years in the late 1870s, this was a highly lucrative trade. According to one account, Kamenskii was

II-A-2   A street scene of Ghulja from Vali Bay's day. Royal Society for Asian Affairs (RSAA/SC/ SCH/1/18/2).

buying grain on the local market at (in Russian terms) 15 kopeks a pud and selling it to the Qing army stationed down the highway at an extortionate 8 silver rubles, netting a 6,000 percent profit.

The Ghulja grain bonanza was not destined to last, however. Debate was now raging among the tsarist military and foreign policy elite whether to make good on a previous commitment to hand the Ili Valley back to the Qing, or retain its rich agricultural land and prepare to defend it militarily. Anxious at the advance of the Qing army, and at the dwindling supply of grain in Ghulja, Russian officials instituted a ban on its export, leaving Kamenskii high and dry. With Qing officials pressing for missed deliveries, Kamenskii eventually went bankrupt.

In the end, the Russian empire's top brass decided to restore Ili to the Qing, but the initial treaty, that of Livadia in 1879, was so favorable to Russia that the Qing court refused to ratify it, and negotiations continued for a further two years before the revised Treaty of

Saint Petersburg was signed in 1881. Kamenskii's dealings became something of a sticking point in these talks, and an inquiry into the grain trade also implicated Vali Bay. Yet he, unlike the Russian Kamenskii, was a figure still worth cultivating. The Treaty of Saint Petersburg offered the Ili Valley's local Muslims a choice—to migrate into Russian territory as subjects of the tsar, or to stay and await their fate in a restored Qing Xinjiang. More than just a source of supplies and intelligence, Vali Bay's influence locally meant that he had an important role to play in negotiating this transition in Russia's favor.

For their part, the Qing were equally aware of the need to find local allies. According to Vali Bay, the newly appointed Ili military governor offered to make him the Muslim governor (*hakim beg*) of Ili, a post that had been held by an aristocratic family from Turfan since the eighteenth century. Yet Vali Bay decided that his interests lay elsewhere. He had bought up large tracts of land in the territory that the Qing was now ceding to Russia, and he could just as well fill his growing portfolio of contracts with the Qing military from Russian soil. To this day, Chinese historians accuse the Russians of forcing the majority of the Taranchis to migrate, but at the time many Russian officials credited the mass migration to Vali Bay's lobbying efforts. The entrepreneur canceled debts owed to him and provided transport for the exodus, making him the key intermediary in the emergence of a new community of Russian-subject Taranchis in the tsarist province (oblast) of Semirechye.

Semirechye's Harun al-Rashid

While supervised by a thin stratum of Russian officialdom, Vali Bay's wealth and influence rendered Zharkent and its surrounding cantons (uezdy) more or less his own fiefdom. A list of Zharkent electors drawn up in 1899 records Vali Bay's personal fortune at forty thousand rubles, a sum greater than the combined wealth of the next eleven men on the list. With much of the population sharecropping on his private land, Vali Bay simply paid the region's tax obligations himself and maintained a cohort of agricultural officials at his own expense. He continued to avail himself of new commercial opportunities, introducing American cotton into the Ili Valley, exploring coal deposits, and purchasing the first steamship to ply the Ili River, a convenient means of shipping his grain to the threshing mill that he ran on the outskirts of Ghulja. In honor of the Russian general who had led the occupation of Ili, the boat was christened the "Kolpakovskii."

Vali Bay's riches translated easily into political clout, with his entrepreneurial spirit earning him admirers among Russian officialdom. On Count Konstantin Konstantinovich Palen's inspection tour of the Turkestan governor-generalship in 1908, Vali Bay feasted the aristocrat in fine oriental style. He similarly impressed the agronomist Petr Petrovich Rumiantsev during the latter's survey of Semirechye agriculture in 1910. Vali Bay was one of few local Muslims admitted to Russia's mercantile estate (soslovie), as well as the privileged category of "honored citizen" (pochetnyi grazhdan), and in 1896 he represented the "natives" of Semirechye at the coronation of Tsar Nicholas II. Surviving photographs typically show his rich Central Asian garb weighted with rows of medallions. These included not only Russian awards but honors presented to him by Qing envoy Li Hongzhang in Saint Petersburg and by the amir of Bukhara. Through a Salar Muslim from China who had visited Istanbul while on pilgrimage to Mecca, he also came into possession of a prized hair of the Prophet Muhammad's beard, a symbol of the Ottoman sultan's favor.

Naturally, the Taranchis of Semirechye looked to men like Vali Bay to play the role of cultural patron. It was in response to a local petition in 1887 that he directed some of his enormous largesse to the construction of a new mosque and madrasa in Zharkent. In appointing an imam, he drew on the Tatar intellectual networks that now stretched across the Kazakh Steppe to recruit a man by the name of Abd al-Rahman Muhammadi (d. 1909). A native of Kazan, Muhammadi was acquainted with pedagogical trends in the reformist madrasas of central Russia, and introduced to Semirechye a version of the "New Method" of primary instruction, known as the usul-i jadid, from where the term Jadidist derives.

Muhammadi's learning lent prestige to his illiterate patron, but the Tatar's links to Russian Muslim society would eventually bring the two men into conflict. Vali Bay's preeminent position depended on his ability to isolate the Taranchis of Semirechye from the stirrings of reform that were taking hold among the empire's Muslim population in the early twentieth century. In the wake of the 1905 revolution, Muhammadi incurred his patron's wrath by trying to establish a reading room in Zharkent and link the community with initiatives such as the Vernyi Muslim Society. At the same time, self-styled Taranchi progressives known as the "short-shirts" began publishing critiques of Vali Bay's despotism in the fledgling Muslim press. With Russian officials on his side, Vali Bay fought back against these challenges to his authority and did his best to limit the participation of the Taranchis in the emerging empire-wide Muslim public sphere. When word came that Semirechye was to be represented in Russia's new state duma, Vali Bay orchestrated a public meeting in Zharkent to preempt any elections and have himself proclaimed the representative of the Taranchis.

•

Reaching old age, and imagining his enemies to be circling, Vali Bay felt he had political debts to call in. In a letter in 1914, he reminded the governor-general of Semirechye that he had long "strived to stamp out any harmful occurrence of evil sentiment among the people, for the sake of Russia's happiness and well-being, and for the pleasure of His Imperial Majesty." When he died in 1916, the *Semirechye Provincial News* mourned the loss of the man "who had created his enormous wealth out of literally nothing," likening him to Harun al-Rashid, the Abbasid caliph whose name conjures images of a cultural florescence. His

eulogist felt that Vali Bay "embodied in himself (*olitsetvoril soboiu*) the entire Taranchi and part of the Dungan population of the province." Through his industry and loyalty, he had "won for himself a place in the pages of the history of Semirechye and neighboring Chinese territory."

It was a stirring send-off, but there was little time to mourn. Semirechye was about to descend into a storm of rebellion and revolution, which would wipe out colonial intermediaries such as Vali Bay, who had seized on the opportunities created by Russia's imperial expansion to aggrandize themselves. Naturally, Vali Bay's role as a land-owning capitalist earned him a highly negative image during the Soviet period. His grand congregational mosque fell into disuse, and his premises in Ghulja became the base for the Soviet Union's first state trading venture in Xinjiang.

The fall of the Soviet Union has not yet seen Vali Bay's mosque resume its original function, but locals have sought to polish his tarnished reputation. His life now stands at the head of a volume of biographies of prominent Uyghurs of Kazakhstan, for example, and a documentary film portrays him as a patron saint of the Zharkent District. First announced by Xi Jinping in a speech in Kazakhstan in 2013, China's vision of a "Silk Road Economic Belt" now envisages Vali Bay's domains once again buzzing with the hum of trans-Eurasian commerce. Unfortunately for the locals, this present-day exercise in empire building looks unlikely to offer the same room for Uyghur middlemen that the meeting of tsarist and Qing empires once provided.

CASE II-B

The Management of Islam in the Late Soviet Period

Adeeb Khalid

One of the more peculiar features of contemporary Central Asia is the existence of national bodies, generally called "spiritual administrations of Muslims," that regulate the practice of Islam in each state. These represent a remarkable element of both historical continuity and change that ties today's Central Asia to its imperial and Soviet pasts.

The spiritual administrations all descend from SADUM, the Spiritual Administration of the Muslims of Central Asia and Kazakhstan, which was established by the Soviet state in the middle of the Second World War in 1943. Its establishment marked a shift in the Stalinist state's policies toward Islam (and religion in general), which had been characterized by harsh repression for the previous decade and a half. The Soviet regime, on both ideological and practical grounds, sought to extirpate religion from society. It launched its first campaigns against the Russian Orthodox Church right upon seizing power in 1917, but anti-religious activity was muted in Central Asia because of the general weakness of Soviet rule there. It was only in 1927 that party authorities felt confident enough of their power to attack Islam and Islamic institutions in Central Asia. Over the next decade, mosques and shrines were closed (and in many cases destroyed or put to other uses), Islamic education dismantled, and Islamic courts abolished. The press and public space were dominated by virulent attacks on Islam and its carriers. The ulama were persecuted—many were arrested, some executed, and others exiled, while still others fell silent. Soviet public space was de-Islamized. Then came the war.

The state wanted all hands on deck for the war effort and curtailed its persecution of religion. For their part, Central Asian ulama, despite their persecution over the previous decade and a half, threw their energies into the war effort. They mobilized support at a time of low morale and gathered donations for the front. Most importantly, they provided religious sanction for conscription into the Red Army. The regime appreciated these efforts but also sought to manage them. To this end, it decided to create SADUM as an entity that would provide an umbrella for the activities of the ulama but also make them visible to the state and allow them to be monitored. On June 10, 1943, the Politburo issued a decree to "allow the organization of a Spiritual Administration for the Muslims of Central Asia and Kazakhstan." A group of ulama in Tashkent was then tasked with petitioning the state to al-

II-B-1   The fifteenth-century Bibi-Khanim mosque in Samarkand (Samarqand), 2013. The mosque has been lavishly restored by the Uzbek state after independence and turned into a major monument of national heritage. Islam and Islamic monuments did not enjoy such prominence during the later Soviet period. Photograph by Natalie Koch.

low the convocation of a conference of ulama from across Central Asia with the goal of establishing such an organization. The lead in this was taken by the octogenarian Naqshbandi sheikh Ishan Babakhan ibn Abdulmajid Khan of Tashkent. Babakhan was a scholar of some prominence who had suffered along with all other ulama in the 1930s. His house had been confiscated, and he had been in and out of prison in the late 1930s. Yet, he was eager to help in the war effort. He was summoned to Moscow, where he evidently met with Stalin in person, who offered him tea and asked him about the mood of the Muslim population. Babakhan returned to Tashkent to organize the conference of ulama, which then formally established SADUM.

SADUM was to be the Central Asian counterpart to the Central Spiritual Administration of Muslims based in Ufa, with jurisdiction over the Muslim populations of European Russia and Siberia. That organization traced its history to the Orenburg Spiritual Assembly, which had been created by Catherine II in 1788 as a way of assimilating the population of the Volga-Urals region into the Russian imperial state and extending its control onto the Kazakh Steppe. The Orenburg Spiritual Assembly was responsible for appointing and licensing imams and madrasa teachers in the Tatar lands and for overseeing the operation of mosques. Historically, religious authority in Islam has inhered in the learning and piety of its carriers rather than in hierarchical institutions. The Spiritual Assembly was the first attempt by a state to impose such an institution. The first mufti had to struggle to have his authority acknowledged by the ulama. Gradually, however, the Spiritual Assembly became an integral part of the religious landscape of the Volga-Urals region and beyond. Similar bodies were set up in Crimea in 1831 and Transcaucasia in 1872, but not in Turkestan. K. P. von Kaufman, the first governor-general of the region, saw Islam as the main source of the "fanaticism" of the local population and thus an impediment to the establishment of

Russian rule. He also believed that if Islam were denied any official recognition and left to its own devices, it would "decay" and the local population would leave its fanaticism behind. He therefore deployed a policy of disregard (*ignorirovanie*) toward Islam and its elites, which entailed, among other things, a refusal to establish a spiritual assembly in Turkestan or to allow the Orenburg Assembly to extend its jurisdiction into the new territory.

In any case, it seems unlikely that the rather fragile Russian power would have been able to coax the ulama of the newly conquered territory into such a bureaucratic arrangement. The ulama of Turkestan remained autonomous of the state and retained their existing patterns of religious authority. But modernist reformers in the Russian Empire had come to see a spiritual assembly as a desirable locus of reform. This position was unique in the Muslim world at the time, although over the course of the twentieth century, many Muslim states, most notably the Turkish Republic, were to establish similar institutions. Mahmudxo'ja Behbudiy, a leading Jadid figure, thought that a spiritual administration was necessary for carrying out the kinds of religious reform he hoped to implement. In 1917, the establishment of *mahkama-yi shar'iya* (shariat administrations) became part of the reformist agenda. In the early years of Soviet rule, several such administrations existed in different cities of Turkestan, although the hope of a region-wide umbrella organization was never fulfilled. These shariat administrations were among the casualties of the antireligious campaign that began in 1927. Now, in 1943, the state itself seemed to have fulfilled the reformist goal of creating a centralized religious institution in Central Asia. Indeed, SADUM was unique among

Soviet institutions in having a jurisdiction that spanned several republics. The Jadids were all gone by 1943, however, and SADUM was established by ulama who possessed conventional religious authority.

SADUM, like the Tsarist-era Orenburg Spiritual Assembly, was half church and half directorate of religious affairs. It managed all the functioning mosques, appointed their personnel, organized prayers for the two major holidays of the Islamic year, and took care of a few remaining shrines. Presently, the Soviet government allowed SADUM to organize the hajj (the annual pilgrimage to Mecca) for a small contingent of Muslims and to reopen the Mir-i Arab madrasa in Bukhara as a legal venue for Islamic theological education. SADUM also acquired a small publishing program, centered around a magazine called *Muslims of the Soviet East*, whose content was directed at an international audience and published in English, French, and Arabic. In 1971, SADUM was allowed to open the Imam al-Bukhari Islamic Institute in Tashkent as a postgraduate adjunct to the Mir-i Arab madrasa. The number of students remained small (the Mir-i Arab madrasa had an enrollment of eighty-six in 1982, while the Imam al-Bukhari institute had thirty-four enrollees). The choice to attend a religious institution was fraught with difficulties. Matriculating students attracted the attention of the KGB, which no doubt vetted them. Nevertheless, competition for places was intense, and SADUM was able to ensure the continuation of higher religious learning in Soviet conditions. Even more precious, given Soviet conditions, was the opportunity to maintain contact with Muslims outside the Soviet Union. SADUM was able to arrange for a small (carefully handpicked) delegation to the annual pilgrimage to Mecca every year, and in the 1960s it began sending students to study at religious institutions in Muslim countries friendly to the USSR, such as Egypt, Syria, and Libya.

SADUM was answerable to the Council for the Affairs of Religious Cults (which became the Council for Religious Affairs in 1965) of the Soviet government. The regime hoped that by allowing limited religious activity under bureaucratic oversight, it could prevent it from going completely underground, and at the same time remain able to monitor and control it. The relationship was therefore complex. Officials of the Council made sure that SADUM's activity stayed within bounds, but they also acted as watchdogs of legality: they intervened on behalf of SADUM with government and party authorities when SADUM or its constituents were subject to high-handed actions from local or central authorities. In return, SADUM was expected to help with the government's foreign policy agenda, especially in the Muslim world. SADUM was supposed to prove Soviet claims about freedom of religion in the country and about Muslims' active participation in Soviet society. SADUM's ulama traveled the world on goodwill missions and hosted visitors from abroad. They were prominent also in Soviet efforts to court movements for independence in the colonial world, and later they played a role in Soviet campaigns for "international peace and friendship."

SADUM's founders were bona fide ulama who had survived the horrors of the 1930s. Its leadership stayed in the family of Eshon Babakhan until 1989. The ulama participated in the work of SADUM in the hope of preserving some semblance of a tradition of Islamic learning and perhaps of asserting some influence on local society. One of the first actions of SADUM was to establish an office to issue fatwas (legal opinions)

on questions sent in by people from throughout its domain. Although Eshon Babakhan was a Naqshbandi shaykh in the conventional Central Asian mold, his successors acquired an affinity for modernist and rigorist currents of Islam that bore some relation to the Jadids but were also in conversation with contemporary developments in the Arab world. On questions of ritual, a number SADUM fatwas often contradicted the consensus of the Central Asian Hanafi tradition. SADUM also issued fatwas at the request of the Soviet state. These fatwas represented some of the most radical stances of the organization. For instance, SADUM decreed honest work to be an Islamic virtue, the fulfillment of which required Muslims to avoid absenteeism and drunkenness (both of which were perennial problems for the state). Other fatwas went further, declaring the fast of Ramadan not to be obligatory for those involved in physical labor, or that the sacrifice of livestock for the Feast of Sacrifice (*Qurban hayit*), the celebratory breaking of the fast during Ramadan (*iftar*), and the collection of alms for the poor was no longer obligatory in Soviet conditions. Yet other fatwas condemned as "un-Islamic" such customs as visits to shrines, seeking intercession from the dead, the wearing of the *paranji*, the activities of Sufi masters, and excessive expense at *to'ys* (feasts celebrating life cycle events). This opposition to tradition put SADUM's ulama in a precarious position, since they appeared as critics of traditions that could be defended on both "religious" and "national" grounds. They remained liable to marginalization in society on both those grounds.

This is an important point to keep in mind in evaluating the significance of SADUM. There is a temptation to see in the institution an official recognition of the place of Islam in Soviet society and to exaggerate its influence in everyday life. SADUM remained a minor Soviet institution with no direct access to the top political leadership. Its fatwas had no legal basis in terms of Soviet law. The state asked for them as a form of extra insurance, as it were; its legislation was not contingent upon their issuance. At the same time, a great deal of Islamic practice went on beyond SADUM's purview. Equally importantly, we need to remember that the religious landscape of Soviet Central Asia was unusual. The destruction of the 1930s was never undone. There was no wave of reconstruction or reopening of mosques, and the number of officially registered mosques (that SADUM controlled) was very small. Islamic education was limited to the two institutions that SADUM ran (and the tiny number of their graduates who went abroad for higher study), and religious publishing was virtually nonexistent. The state, meanwhile, remained committed to a struggle with religion. The public space was resolutely secular. Levels of observance among Central Asian Muslims were very low in the Soviet period. This is a point that is often lost from sight in the recent historiographical mania for rediscovering Soviet Islam.

However, the model SADUM provided for the state's relationship to religion had become paradigmatic. The winds of change that began to blow during the era of perestroika changed much, but not the assumption that Islam was to be housed in a spiritual administration. SADUM itself experienced perestroika. In February 1989, ordinary Muslims staged a mass demonstration in Tashkent in which they accused SADUM's leadership of corruption and dereliction of duty. As a result, Shamsuddin Babakhanov, Eshon Babakhan's grandson and the head of SADUM, retired, and SADUM's leadership passed out of the family. The following year, the ulama from Kazakhstan seceded from SADUM's jurisdiction and established their own republic-level spiritual directorate. This began the process of the "nationalization" of SADUM, which was completed by the fall of the Soviet Union in 1991. SADUM ceased to exist and was replaced by analogous institutions in each new state. The Soviet-era institution, itself patterned on a Tsarist model, provides the paradigm today for state-Islam relations throughout Central Asia.

CASE II-C

Gendered Aspects of Soviet Industrialization in Ak Tyuz

Botakoz Kassymbekova

Female emancipation is often regarded as a symbol of Soviet advancement in Central Asia, while urbanization and industrialization are often understood as key, neutral processes that enabled it. Yet, a closer look into how industrialization took place in the Soviet Union—and Central Asia—provides some clues on why and how conservative family values persisted in the postwar (the Second World War) Soviet project. Taking an example of two female biographies—a Russian professional from Moscow and a local Kyrgyz manual worker—in the Kyrgyz mining town of Ak Tyuz, I show how individual stories were shaped by a larger Soviet centralized system formed for the distribution of privileges, resources, and power. I suggest that ethnic and spatial hierarchies of the Soviet economy were partially sustained by conservative gender structures, rendering those structures nearly invisible in individual and public memories of the Soviet past.

A Divided World of Soviet Industrialization

Ina and Begaim (names are changed) spent most of their lives in Ak Tyuz, a small Soviet mining town in northern Kyrgyzstan. Although the two women came from different career and cultural backgrounds, Ak Tyuz's mine brought them together. Ina was from Moscow, a graduate of a Moscow university and fluent in several European languages that she utilized working in postwar Berlin as a translator. In the 1950s, when she was in her early twenties, Ina's husband was sent to work in Ak Tyuz as a technical specialist, and she followed him. In Ak Tyuz, people with university training were in high demand, and she quickly received a top position working in a local school. Although she was reluctant to leave Moscow for Kyrgyzstan, she became an enthusiastic teacher who was highly respected in Ak Tyuz, even decades after the Soviet Union's collapse.

Begaim, on the other hand, grew up in Ak Tyuz as the daughter of a single female manual laborer and studied in the Kazakh Soviet Socialist Republic to become a teacher. Her mother came to work in Ak Tyuz when she fled an abusive family. The mine provided the mother a financial basis for independence, albeit at a high cost to her health. Begaim, too, became a manual laborer, despite her pedagogical training.

Ina and Begaim stayed in Ak Tyuz after the Soviet Union's disintegration. Their biographies can help us understand how industrialization contributed to their life trajectory as women and how women contributed to the trajectory of industrialization.

Ina's and Begaim's biographies are part of the general history of Central Asia as a "backup" for wartime production. Central Asia figured as an agricultural region in the earlier Soviet economic planning, but the Second World War introduced important corrections into the initial economic spatial arrangement, moving heavy industry from European parts of the Soviet Union to Central Asia. In Kyrgyzstan, more than a couple dozen plants were built, most of which were military related and formed the basis for mining and heavy industry. Six out of twenty-two towns in Kyrgyzstan and fourteen out of twenty-nine urban-type communities were formed in areas of mineral mining. About two hundred thousand people lived in industrial communities during the 1980s in Kyrgyzstan, but many more worked in industries in earlier periods. The Ak Tyuz settlement was organized around a polymetallic mine, founded in 1938 and launched in 1941. Its mission was to "win the war" and "help the fatherland," but after the Second World War it grew by the 1960s to be home to five thousand inhabitants from all over the Soviet Union. After the Soviet Union's breakup, the settlement's population decreased radically, turning it into a ghost town, a ruin of a past Soviet "civilization." The settlement is both typical and atypical as a symbol of the Soviet past. On the one hand, as a mining site for war production, Ak Tyuz was a closed settlement. Since movement in and out of the settlement was controlled by the police, it was not a regular Soviet Central Asian settlement. On the other hand, if compared to other industrial production sites specializing in strategic industrial production, Ak Tyuz was ultimately a Soviet place. It was built, managed, and policed by Soviet engineers and officials; local party officials, who came from outside of Kyrgyz SSR, directed its social life.

Ina's and Begaim's biographies differ starkly, but the circulation of people from different parts of the Soviet Union was typical for towns like Ak Tyuz. In this new place, individuals and groups of different ethnic and social backgrounds from all over the Soviet Union came (or were sent) to work together. Yet, differences and hierarchies were impossible to conceal. It was inscribed into Ak Tyuz's spatial arrangement and language. The lower part of the settlement was called Shanghai because it was a zone with barracks for poor manual workers and "special settlers," such as purged Chechen and Ingush prisoners, who constituted a major labor force in the settlement's early years. This is where the mine, the factory, and workers' kitchen were located. Bombay, on the other hand, was located on a hill where the "privileged" (by Soviet standards) and, in the words of one of its residents, "white" people lived. Although earlier years in Ak Tyuz were arduous for all residents, its privileged status as a military mining site can be recognized in the postwar period, especially in the 1960s and 1970s. According to Soviet regulations, such strategic settlements were maintained at the expense of mining enterprises, which were managed, sponsored, and directed by Moscow, not local republics or districts. This meant that salaries were often higher than in other towns or villages, and there was better access to many goods, such as foodstuff and clothing, and services, such as sanatorium trips. For skilled workers especially, Ak Tyuz was a place to earn good money. The division between Shanghai and Bombay was made along ethnic lines: Shanghai was a multiethnic place; Bombay was comprised mainly of European skilled workers. Soviet symbols such as a statue of Vladimir Lenin, an eternal fire to commemorate Soviet soldiers who fell in the Second World War, a culture club, and the administration were at the center of the division. It is not surprising that Ina lived in Bombay, while Begaim resided in Shanghai.

Family Values and the Soviet Administration

Ak Tyuz residents had to negotiate differences and hierarchies in their common "home." Soviet ideology of development and emancipation provided a basis. Soviet Europeans believed that they came to develop Kyrgyzstan—this is how residents still remember the process—while Kyrgyz and others were supposedly developed by them. Ina remembered being an exemplar educator, organizing study trips to Russia, while Begaim was able to graduate from college, the first in her family. Both considered the Soviet state as progressive and positive for their careers, even if on different sides of the development scheme.

Yet, while Ina's and Begaim's lives differed—Ina's apartment in Bombay had a sewage system, for instance, while Begaim's barrack did not have running water—their personal lives were detrimental to their communal status and professional opportunities. Both women's choices about their private lives played a key role in their careers in Soviet Ak Tyuz. While both acted as "emancipated" women according to the early Soviet principles, both had to pay a high price for their private choices.

During her studies, Begaim fell in love with a Kyrgyz man. The man's family did not want to accept Begaim due to her family's low social status (brought about by her being the child of a single mother working in manual labor). After graduating from college, the man married Begaim without his parents'

approval. Begaim moved in with her husband's family in another settlement not far from Ak Tyuz. However, soon after giving birth to a daughter in the early 1970s, she fled the family due to recurring insults by her in-laws, and she later divorced her husband. In Ak Tyuz, she worked as a manual laborer at a factory. Although she was trained to become a teacher, she was informally advised by the town's administration to change her profession and work at the factory. As a divorcée, she was not a good example for pupils. And because of this, it was explained to her that there were no vacant positions for her at the school. Begaim was ashamed of her status and never tried to find another school job outside of Ak Tyuz.

Ina's exemplary career as an educator also broke apart due to personal circumstances in the early 1970s. She lost her job and party affiliation, became a manual laborer, and, worst or all, had to move from Bombay to Shanghai. The reason for Ina's downfall was her affair with a married man, another "European" Bombay professional, with whom she fell in love. She wanted to divorce her husband and start a new family. However, in a comrade's court she was stripped of her position and communal status. Ina, according to her colleagues, was not acting as a good Soviet citizen and woman. She was accused of ruining a family and was purged from the local party cell. Although divorces and family ruptures were widespread in Ak Tyuz, Ina represented the local Communist leadership and was expected to lead an exemplary personal and public life. While Ina's and Begaim's stories differ, they both suffered stigma from their private choices and the consequences they brought.

But how are we to understand the Soviet transformation from revolu-

II-C-1   View of "Shanghai," Ak Tyuz, Kyrgyzstan. 2004. Photograph by Botakoz Kassymbekova.

tionary promises of a free woman who could decide for herself to maintaining conservative family values? Historians have long argued that Stalinist and post-Stalinist policies fostered societal traditionalization and the adoption of middle-class conservative family values. It has been argued that family values were a sort of compromise with the Stalinist regime that depended on middle-class professionals, who were the driving force of Soviet industrialization. Middle-class women were also interested in tightening up family values, not loosening them, because women could hardly survive, or at least organize a decent household and raise children, without a husband. This process similarly took place in Soviet Central Asia. While the Second World War fostered the region's industrialization and urbanization, it also nurtured and strengthened traditional family values that became central to Soviet official ideology. A good worker was a good communist only when also a good spouse. Industrialization and private life were intrinsically interconnected. Con-scious family ruptures such as those of Begaim and Ina were not accepted and could not only preclude one's aspired career but also one's communal status and approval. Family values were Soviet values of skilled, privileged workers, such as from Ak Tyuz's Bombay. They did not correspond to the realities of Shanghai residents, who reported on family ruptures and the stigmas of broken families and shame.

Family, Ethnicity, and the "Good" Soviet Past

Despite unfulfilled career dreams and communal exclusion during the Soviet period, Ina and Begaim do not blame the Soviet past for their personal problems. On the contrary, they carefully search for moments of pride in their biographies. This is not unusual as people typically try to invest meaning into their biographies. Moreover, they want to be seen as decent individuals who made something of themselves. It is not the Soviet structures that they discuss in their biographies but themselves in those wider circumstances of the past.

Their current status is also crucial for the memory work. Begaim finally became a teacher in the 1990s, when the Soviet European population and those who could afford it largely abandoned the place, moving to Russia and other "historical homelands." As a teacher and respected member of the Ak Tyuz community at last, Begaim slowly and carefully reflected on her earlier years in the Soviet Union, when she was a manual laborer from Shanghai. She did it from a current position of intelligentsia in post-Soviet Bombay, the social move enabled by the disintegration of the Soviet Union: "I do not remember that we lived well. I lived in one room, no toilet, no water. We had a salary. Every holiday, five times a year, we ate chocolate. We did not eat meat or butter every day. I was trying to compare our previous clothing. We bought clothes only if our old [clothes] were torn. Food—sometimes okay, sometimes we had nothing. I would not say we lived well, neither that we live well today." Ina, on the other hand, was one of the last few Soviet Europeans to stay in Ak Tyuz. She remembered the Soviet past as enabling and powerful. Although she did not move out of Shanghai after the Soviet collapse and was continuously financially supported by the Ak Tyuz (previously Shanghai) population, it is her past career that earned her respect. Just as Begaim during Soviet times had to accept a low-skilled job due to her personal story, Ina, too, had to pay for her personal life choices. Although Begaim and Ina came from distinct backgrounds and were assigned different statuses in Ak Tyuz, both had the same experience of what it meant to follow independent personal choices that did not correspond to contemporary state ideology. The men with whom they had been, of course, did not suffer such repercussions.

While historians have described the traditionalizing of Soviet family values and its connection to industrialization and urbanization, what has been missed from these debates is the function of family values for obscuring vast, unequal Soviet geography and hierarchy of various groups. A full and "functioning" family in the industrializing Soviet Union was not a "natural" category. Divorces, ruptures, and family dysfunctionality were widespread in the harshness of the Second World War and postwar context. Yet, family became a social and political category, and ultimately was construed as natural because it functioned as a space for communicating and distributing power, status, and material wealth. Once perceived as natural and as a Communist moral priority, issues of gender and workers' rights could be sidelined. Privileging "normal and good" families rendered divisions between women and men, as well as between Europeans and non-Europeans, less perceptible.

Soviet industrialization failed to foster female emancipation in Central Asia and other parts of the Soviet Union. Some women indeed left their families to obtain new opportunities in industrial locations, often becoming true believers in Communism. However, while industrial sites used the labor and loyalty of such women, they and their children often found out that personal liberty did not correspond to larger ideological norms. A good Soviet family was still important to most women, and men. On the most materialistic level, it was extremely difficult for a single mother to afford a good living and education for her children. On another level, single women and fatherless children experienced stigma in their communities and at work. While the Soviet state provided various opportunities for social mobility for various kinds of groups—at last Ak Tyuz was a refuge for various stigmatized individuals—it was also a self-perception of being unworthy or deficient that shaped the life path of many members of broken families. There were exceptions; becoming a widow or fatherless because of war, for example, was acceptable. More and more, however, a nuclear Soviet family was needed to succeed in Soviet society. A family, then (or absence thereof), was a space for discrimination, but it was also a space for claiming power. Ak Tyuz's social and spatial division into Shanghai and Bombay had to be explained, legitimized, and processed by its residents. Insights into some biographies are illuminating in that regard. It seems that people did learn to accept differences and hierarchies. In that process, family values played a significant role.

DISCUSSION QUESTIONS

PART II: CONTEXTS OF HISTORY

5. Precolonial Central Asia

1. In what ways did technological developments and other factors external to the region shape Central Asian historical developments in the precolonial period?

2. In what ways does Central Asia's precolonial history continue to shape politics and society in the region today?

6. Colonial Central Asia

3. How and why did the Russian Empire conquer Central Asia?

4. What made Russian rule in Central Asia "colonial"?

7. Soviet Central Asia

5. "The friendship of peoples" was an important slogan that reflected the goal of the Soviet state in Central Asia. Is this policy significant in constructing Soviet identity in Central Asia? In addition to this particular policy, what other policies made Central Asian societies Soviet?

6. How does Sabira Kümüshalieva's story represent the creation of a Soviet citizen in Central Asia?

8. Post-Soviet Central Asia

7. How can we best explain the similarities and differences in historical trajectories among the five Central Asian states after 1991?

8. How important a role was played by the Soviet legacy in the post-Soviet political and social history of Central Asia?

Case II-A: The Rise of Vali Bay, an Entrepreneur between Two Empires

9. What was the role of trade and commerce in expanding and consolidating imperial rule in Central Asia?

10. How has competition between rival empires shaped the lives of people in Central Asia?

Case II-B: The Management of Islam in the Late Soviet Period

11. SADUM was modeled on the Tsarist-era Orenburg Muslim Spiritual Assembly. It was succeeded by five different "national" religious administrations. What are the elements of continuity among all these organizations? And how was SADUM differently positioned from both its predecessor and its successors?

Think about how the relationship of the state to Islam has shifted in the years since the Orenburg Assembly was founded in 1788.

12. The leadership of SADUM was in the hands of classically trained ulama. They worked in difficult conditions, acting between the Soviet state and their own society. What drove them? What political realities did they face? What were the limits and the possibilities for their action?

Case II-C: Gendered Aspects of Soviet Industrialization in Ak Tyuz

13. What were the limitations of female emancipation in the Soviet Union? For what reasons did local party cells judge its members by their behavior in the private/family realm? What was the relationship between family values and Soviet industrialization?

14. Can personal memories of the Soviet past be considered as accurate historical sources? What are the differences in using memories as opposed to life histories/biographies?

FURTHER READING

5. Precolonial Central Asia

Bregel, Yuri. *An Historical Atlas of Central Asia*. Leiden: Brill, 2003.

Di Cosmo, Nicola, Allen Frank, and Peter Golden, eds. *The Cambridge History of Inner Asia: The Chinggisid Age*. Cambridge: Cambridge University Press, 2009.

Levi, Scott C. *The Bukharan Crisis: A Connected History of Eighteenth-Century Central Asia*. Pittsburgh: University of Pittsburgh Press, 2020.

Levi, Scott C., and Ron Sela, eds. *Islamic Central Asia: An Anthology of Historical Sources*. Bloomington: Indiana University Press, 2010.

Millward, James. *Eurasian Crossroads: A History of Xinjiang*. New York, Columbia University Press, 2007.

6. Colonial Central Asia

Abashin, Sergei. "The 'Fierce Fight' at Oshoba: A Microhistory of the Conquest of the Khoqand Khanate." *Central Asian Survey* 33, no. 2 (2014): 215–31.

Afinogenov, Gregory. "Languages of Hegemony on the Eighteenth-Century Kazakh Steppe." *International History Review* 41, no. 5 (2018): 1020–38.

Chokobaeva, Aminat, Cloé Drieu, and Alexander Morrison, eds. *The Central Asian Revolt of 1916: A Collapsing Empire in the Age of War and Revolution*. Manchester: Manchester University Press, 2020.

Khalid, Adeeb. *The Politics of Muslim Cultural Reform. Jadidism in Central Asia*. Berkeley: University of California Press, 1998.

Keller, Shoshana. *Russia and Central Asia: Coexistence, Conquest and Convergence*. Toronto: University of Toronto Press, 2019.

Martin, Virginia. *Law and Custom in the Steppe: The Kazakhs of the Middle Horde and Russian Colonialism in the Nineteenth Century*. Richmond, Surrey, UK: Curzon, 2001.

Morrison, Alexander. *The Russian Conquest of Central Asia: A Study in Imperial Expansion, 1814–1914*. Cambridge: Cambridge University Press, 2020.

Morrison, Alexander. *Russian Rule in Samarkand, 1868–1910. A Comparison with British India*. Oxford: Oxford University Press, 2008.

Morrison, Alexander. "'Sowing the Seed of National Strife in this Alien Region.' The Pahlen Report and Pereselenie in Turkestan, 1908–1910." *Acta Slavica Iaponica* 31 (2012): 1–29.

Penati, Beatrice. "The Cotton Boom and the Land Tax in Russian Turkestan (1880s–1915)." *Kritika* 14, no. 4 (2013): 741–74.

Sahadeo, Jeff. *Russian Colonial Society in Tashkent, 1865–1923*. Bloomington: Indiana University Press, 2007.

Sartori, Paolo, ed. *Explorations in the Social History of Modern Central Asia (19th–Early 20th Century)*. Leiden: Brill, 2013.

Sartori, Paolo. *Visions of Justice: Sharīʿa and Cultural Change in Russian Central Asia*. Leiden: Brill, 2016.

Schimmelpenninck van der Oye, David. *Russian Orientalism: Asia in the Russian Mind from Peter the Great to the Emigration*. New Haven, CT: Yale University Press, 2010.

Tillett, Lowell. *The Great Friendship: Soviet Historians on the Non-Russian Nationalities*. Chapel Hill: University of North Carolina Press, 1969.

Uyama, Tomohiko. "The Geography of Civilizations: A Spatial Analysis of the Kazakh Intelligentsia's Activities, from the Mid-Nineteenth to the Early Twentieth Century." In *Regions—A Prism to View the Slavic-Eurasian World: Towards a Discipline of "Regionology"*, ed. Kimitaka Matsuzato, 70–99. Sapporo: Slavic Research Center, Hokkaido University, 2000.

7. Soviet Central Asia

Cameron, Sarah. *The Hungry Steppe: Famine, Violence, and the Making of Soviet Kazakhstan*. Ithaca, NY: Cornell University Press, 2018.

Dadabaev, Timur. *Identity and Memory in Post-Soviet Central Asia: Uzbekistan's Soviet Past*. New York: Routledge, 2016.

Edgar, Adrienne Lynn. *Tribal Nation: The Making of Soviet Turkmenistan*. Princeton, NJ: Princeton University Press, 2004.

İğmen, Ali. *Speaking Soviet with an Accent: Culture and Power in Kyrgyzstan*. Pittsburgh: University of Pittsburgh Press, 2012.

Kalinovsky, Artemy M. *Laboratory of Socialist Development: Cold War Politics and Decolonization in Soviet Tajikistan*. Ithaca, NY: Cornell University Press, 2018.

Kamp, Marianne. *The New Woman in Uzbekistan: Islam, Modernity, and Unveiling under Communism*. Seattle: University of Washington Press, 2006.

Kassymbekova, Botakoz. *Despite Cultures: Early Soviet Rule in Tajikistan*. Pittsburgh: University of Pittsburgh Press, 2016.

Khalid, Adeeb. *Central Asia: A New History from the Imperial Conquests to the Present*. Princeton, NJ: Princeton University Press, 2021.

Khalid, Adeeb. *Making Uzbekistan: Nation, Empire, and Revolution in the Early USSR*. Ithaca, NY: Cornell University Press, 2015.

Northrop, Douglas. *Veiled Empire: Gender and Power in Stalinist Central Asia*. Ithaca, NY: Cornell University Press, 2004.

Peterson, Maya K. *Pipe Dreams: Water and Empire in Central Asia's Aral Sea Basin*. Cambridge: Cambridge University Press, 2019.

Sahadeo, Jeff. *Russian Colonial Society in Tashkent, 1865–1923*. Bloomington: Indiana University Press, 2007.

Shayakhmetov, Mukhamet. *The Silent Steppe: The Memoir of a Kazakh Nomad under Stalin*. Translated by Jan Butler. New York: Rookery, 2006.

Stronski, Paul. *Tashkent: Forging a Soviet City, 1930–1966*. Pittsburgh: University of Pittsburgh Press, 2010.

Tasar, Eren. *Soviet and Muslim: The Institutionalization of Islam in Central Asia, 1943–1991*. New York: Oxford University Press, 2017.

Yilmaz, Harun. *National Identities in Soviet Historiography: The Rise of Nations under Stalin*. New York: Routledge, 2015.

8. Post-Soviet Central Asia

Cooley, Alexander. *Great Games, Local Rules: The New Great Power Contest in Central Asia*. Oxford: Oxford University Press, 2014.

Cooley, Alexander, and John Heathershaw. *Dictators without Borders: Power and Money in Central Asia*. New Haven, CT: Yale University Press, 2017.

Cummings, Sally. *Understanding Central Asia: Politics and Contested Transformations*. London: Routledge, 2012.

Lewis, David. *The Temptations of Tyranny in Central Asia*. London: Hurst, 2008.

McGlinchey, Eric. *Chaos, Violence, Dynasty: Politics and Islam in Central Asia*. Pittsburgh: Pittsburgh University Press, 2011.

Megoran, Nick. *Nationalism in Central Asia: A Biography of the Uzbekistan-Kyrgyzstan Boundary*. Pittsburgh: University of Pittsburgh Press, 2017.

Pomfret, Richard. *The Central Asian Economies in the Twenty-First Century: Paving a New Silk Road*. Princeton, NJ: Princeton University Press, 2020.

Case II-A: The Rise of Vali Bay, an Entrepreneur between Two Empires

Brophy, David. *Uyghur Nation: Reform and Revolution on the Russia-China Frontier*. Cambridge, MA: Harvard University Press, 2016.

Hsu, Immanuel C. Y. *The Ili Crisis: A Study of Sino-Russian Diplomacy, 1871–1881*. Oxford: Oxford University Press, 1965.

Kim, Hodong. *Holy War in China: The Muslim Rebellion and State in Chinese Central Asia, 1864–1877*. Stanford, CA: Stanford University Press, 2004.

Roberts, Sean R. "Uyghur Neighborhoods and Nationalisms in the Former Sino-Soviet Borderland: An Historical Ethnography of a Stateless Nation on the Margins of Modernity." PhD diss., University of Southern California, 2003.

Shi, Yue. "The Seven Rivers: Empire and Economy in the Russo-Qing Central Asian Frontier, 1860s–1910s," PhD diss., Georgetown University, 2018.

Case II-B: The Management of Islam in the Late Soviet Period

Babakhan, Ziyauddin Khan Ibn Ishan. *Islam and the Muslims in the Land of Soviets*. Translated by Richard Dixon. Moscow: Progress, 1980.

Khalid, Adeeb. *Central Asia: A New History from the Imperial Conquests to the Present*. Princeton, NJ: Princeton University Press, 2021.

Khalid, Adeeb. *Islam after Communism: Religion and Politics in Central Asia*. Berkeley: University of California Press, 2007.

Case II-C: Gendered Aspects of Soviet Industrialization in Ak Tyuz

Bertaux, Daniel, Paul Thompson, and Anna Rotkirch, eds. *On Living through Soviet Russia*. London: Routledge, 2004.

Dunham, Vera. *In Stalin's Time: Middleclass Values in Soviet Fiction*. Durham, NC: Duke University Press, 1990.

Filtzer, Donald. *Soviet Workers and Late Stalinism: Labour and the Restoration of the Stalinist System after World War II*. Cambridge: Cambridge University Press, 2002.

Goldman, Wendy Z. *Women at the Gates: Gender and Industry in Stalin's Russia*. Cambridge: Cambridge University Press, 2002.

Kamp, Marianne. *The New Woman in Uzbekistan: Islam, Modernity, and Unveiling under Communism*. Seattle: University of Washington Press, 2006.

Northrop, Douglas. *Veiled Empire: Gender and Power in Stalinist Central Asia*, Ithaca, NY: Cornell University Press, 2004.

PART III

CONTEXTS OF LIVING

Where we spend our days influences how we make sense of the possibilities around us. The environment in which experience is interpreted shapes our understandings of success, progress, opportunity, longing, hope, despair, and so on, as well as the very context in which our relationships evolve. It is, after all, the environment in which people live that serves as the setting for self-forming dramas to unfold. In this section we begin to see how the nature of experience in rural and urban areas and various imaginations of home shape how people make sense of their own lives.

The majority of Central Asians live in—and imagine a connection to—rural areas. As we see in Tommaso Trevisani's chapter, rural life is not only a space where relationships play out with everyone knowing everyone, but here also there sits an idealized conception of traditional space where people know each other, take care of each other, and persist in relation to ways of life that are consistent with ancestral ways. It is a space both moral and meaningful, filled with hard work, and fraught with contingencies. The idealization of rural life stands in contrast to the actual experience of rural life, which is reliant on the varied (un)predictability of agriculture, impacted by collectivizing and decollectivizing policies, and at times complicated by the struggle involved in accessing resources that are more readily available in urban areas.

Natalie Koch in her chapter gives a sense of urban life with its conveniences and conceptualizing of planned space across different scales of distance. In speaking about capital cities, we see how housing and a way of life increasingly removed from agricultural work and oriented toward consumerism impact the very nature of lived experience. We also see how the place where someone lives might shape the futures that are imagined.

But futures, of course, are not stationary. In both Madeleine Reeves's and Medina Aitieva's chapters we come to appreciate what life is like when lived at a distance from one's place of origin. Reeves focuses on migratory life, where people go abroad, leaving their home villages and cities with the hope of getting ahead, of providing for those back home, and of improving their own future lives back home. Some go for seasonal work, others for longer periods, but there is always a sense of being both connected and disconnected from the place called "home." We see, for example, how migration comes to be part of life, how networks are used, and how racism plays into belonging.

Not all migrants return, of course. Some find themselves becoming ever more embedded within the contingencies of where they first migrated for work. In Aitieva's chapter on diaspora life, we are given a story of migrants in Yakutia, Russia, which resembles the story of diaspora communities elsewhere: reminiscing about home, trying to find ways to remain connected, and wondering how their children will identify.

Through the various cases we see how the contexts of living are unique, and how life is improvised in ways that draw across experiences of rural and urban, mobile and static. Till Mostowlasnksy shows how mobility and rural modernity along the Pamir Highway in Tajikistan, where roads and transportation play a distinct role in connecting people to other parts of the world, makes marginality less marginal. Sebastian Peyrouse shows how narratives of what life should be like can become the place where propaganda plays out—as in the case of Turkmenistan, where a leader's vision impacts the environment in which people live. And the case described by Emil Nasritdinov, Aigoul Abduoubaetova, and Gulnara Iskandarova draws attention to the context of inequality, especially through the lens of education. The focus is on the rising disparity of private education in Kyrgyzstan's capital, while the challenges of uneven educational opportunity affect the country more broadly and impact the movement of populations, whether rural to urban or labor migrations further abroad.

Generalizing about the context of living always leads to simplifications, dramatizations, and in some instances, romanticizing as to what life is like somewhere else—or should be at the place called home. All life is played out somewhere. And as we begin to appreciate here, that somewhere matters.

9

Rural Life

Tommaso Trevisani

ost people in Central Asia still live in rural areas, and often those who do not were born and raised in a village or agricultural small town. Connections to the rural world are strong even among those who long ago left their native village for the city, because they either still rely on the village or feel themselves belonging to it. Those who have newly migrated from rural to urban areas to some degree keep "thinking" rural, as they carry village habits and networks to their new urban homes. Long-established urbanites lament the ruralization of their cities or look condescendingly on people with a rural background for their "uncultured" manners, yet at the same time they might hold rural virtues and values in high esteem. Rural life—real and imagined—is a contentious field. The contradiction runs between an idealized, morally and ideologically heightened conception of rural life and, rooted in narratives of rural decline, a devalued and stigmatized view that sees the rural as the vile uncouth "other." These opposing views relate also to growing real-life contradictions in the countryside, since the gap is widening between a minority of agricultural entrepreneurs with access to knowledge, land, and markets and a majority of rural people who depend on farming for subsistence.

The idealized conception of rural life is nurtured from traditional rural legacies, is prominent in nationalist discourses, and has followers in both city and countryside. It can be propagated by governments and theorized by intellectuals, but it is also "believed" and practiced by ordinary villagers. People value village sociality, hospitality, and feasting, be it at a neighbor's wedding or at the celebrations for the Central Asian New Year, Nowruz, in the concert hall of the former kolkhoz. There is a sense of strong attachment to one's own birthplace, to where one's ancestors are buried, to the sacred landscape of mazars and other holy places. People take pride in rural life and conceive it as a desirable ideal. They cherish rural life as a context that is believed to be conducive to a moral and meaningful existence. They associate it with harmonious kin and neighborly relationships and pleasurable experiences connected to food consumption and conviviality. Living and working in an intimate and familiar space, joining community rituals, the feeling of social embeddedness and mutual care, shared memories, all together create a "thick texture" that can make rural lives rich and fulfilling despite hardship and poverty. The wealth of rural life is in this web of immaterial relations. Places that might appear grim and dilapidated to outsiders' eyes might have strong emotional connotations when seen from an insider's perspective.

Taken in this idealistic-traditional vein, rural life appears to be timeless. People relate their own life in the countryside to their ancestors' interactions with agriculture and the environment. Indeed, despite the ups and downs of history, looking after cattle and *ariks* (Uzbek: small-scale irrigation canals) has not changed much over time. This also holds true for many other routines of everyday life. Peoples still exploit available resources for farming, livestock breeding, fishing, hunting, and they use or reuse manifold freely available products taken from their surrounding environment (clay and weeds for construction, cow dung for heating or cooking, herbs for medical purposes, etc.). An ideology of self-reliance and industriousness informs these attitudes from the past, which present-day economic needs and constraints have greatly revalued.

In Central Asia's traditional rural societies the rift runs between the sedentary, densely populated, and socially conservative "hydraulic" societies of Turco-Iranian descent (in the arid south, where Islam arrived first, water entitlements matter more than landownership, and irrigation-based agriculture makes cooperation a necessity) and the pastoral-nomadic transhumant ways of living of the Turco-Mongolic peoples of the steppe (with its huge spaces and scattered populations, tribal organization, and less pronounced gender segregation). These two different "souls" of rural Central Asia retain distinctiveness until today. In the traditional Central Asian oases, wheat, rice, barley, millet, sorghum, beans, melons, poppy, hemp, tobacco, and cotton were among the most commonly grown crops; later on, during the Soviet period, the importance of wheat, fodder, and industrial crops (cotton especially) grew tremendously. Fruits and vegetables were grown in the walled orchards of the cities and on rural small plots. Mulberry trees were planted along irrigation canals and used for sericulture. Homegrown poplar and elm trees were valued as timber. In the plains, arid in the summer but verdant after the snow melt, pastoral nomads bred horses, camels, cows, goats, and sheep. Over a yearly cycle the routes of transhumance led the herds back and forth from south to north on the plains, and from the valleys to the uphill mountain pastures. These two faces of traditional rural Central Asia were associated with distinctive climates, economies, beliefs, modes of living, and political organization, yet they were not clear-cut separated worlds; they had constant interaction that allowed for variation, gradualism, and overlap.

Peasants and pastoralists were also warriors, traders, craftspeople, builders of their sedentary or nomadic dwellings, repositories of knowledge, and transmitters of their cultural heritage (as preachers, teachers, bards, healers, etc.).

This past wealth and diversity are present in contemporary idealizations of rural life. Today's difficult conditions convey a different image of the countryside, however. Rural Central Asians still have not recovered from the economic and social decline that came with the end of Soviet agriculture. Still today, as since the collapse of the Soviet system, the key issues at stake in these rural societies pertain to the living conditions of the rural households. In Uzbekistan and Turkmenistan, peasants' freedoms and access to agricultural land are the contentious issue between rural people and states that still own all land and impose production quotas. Kazakhstan and Kyrgyzstan have adopted more liberal reforms, but the small farms of ordinary rural households failed to become profitable, and the collapse of rural institutions and markets have crushed rural peoples' hopes of development. As a result, we see that, although land reforms in the last decades have reshaped agriculture all over Central Asia, they have failed to bolster the livelihoods of ordinary peasants. Instead, rural poverty, marginalization, rising inequalities, lack of jobs for those left behind without land, and labor exploitation for those who work the land all characterize the rural condition.

This dire picture of rural life is in sharp contrast with the idealized one. It is rooted in a culture of poverty that has become widespread after the collapse of the Soviet Union and underpins the fact that rural inhabitants have become sort of second-rate citizens. The contradiction between real and imagined rural life is particularly striking in government policies, since on the one hand, they tend to ideologically anchor their national development projects in the rural world, but on the other, they are putting enormous strain on rural livelihoods by prioritizing urban over rural development. Despite the variations and differences, this is a remarkably similar trend across all Central Asian republics.

Soviet Legacies

The Soviet Union left a lasting imprint on Central Asia's countryside by turning traditional farming and herding into large-scale industrial agriculture. Peasants and pastoralists were transformed into "modern" Soviet agricultural wageworkers. Traditional rural societies and the environment were deeply unsettled. New rules, production norms, payment systems, and work statutes were introduced. New institutions and infrastructure reshaped the rural landscape. Oasis and steppe societies came closer together by sharing the common experience of living and working in kolkhozes and sovkhozes. As everywhere else in the Soviet Union, all Central Asian land was either held collectively or by the state. The collectively owned and the state-owned large agricultural enterprises (kolkhozes and sovkhozes, respectively) were the principal agents of modernization in the countryside and later on also a source of its mounting problems. Pervasive waste, mismanagement, and corruption increasingly undermined the achievements of Soviet modernization. At the end of the Soviet period, the economic breakdown of the agricultural collectives triggered social problems that were amplified by severe environmental degradation. Perhaps the most tragic and consequential legacy of Soviet agriculture has been the dramatic shrinking and near drying out of the Aral Sea.

The process of remaking the countryside and its peoples was carried out over a long period. With the "attack" (*hujum* in Uzbek) campaign of the late 1920s, traditional rural lifestyles, "superstition," rituals, and the patriarchal extended family came under sustained attack. The nomadic lifestyles of the steppes came to an end through a forced sedentarization campaign, which decimated the nomadic population through starvation. Oasis cultures were unraveled by confiscating and collectivizing the lands and assets. The Soviet state waged war against the landed classes and religious authorities, closed down rural mosques, and forcefully "liberated" women from their patriarchal and religious "oppression." Fierce local resistance against these policies was opposed militarily. After the Second World War, the Soviet modernization program of the countryside gained speed: it managed to introduce industrial agriculture and to establish a new and distinctively Soviet rural lifestyle. The reorganization of scattered rural settlements into rural townships or "agro-towns" (*agrogorod* in Russian) with better supply and recreational, educational, and health facilities contributed to the diffusion of the Soviet rural lifestyle. Irrigation canals dug in ancient times were enlarged and integrated into more complex, large-scale irrigation schemes. The pasture lands of the steppe were ploughed and turned into wheat fields, fallow lands were shrunk, and the overall share of land used for agriculture grew by about five times between 1913 and 1980.

Central Asian villages acquired a uniform and recognizable Soviet (out) look. In the kolkhozes, peasants (either by force or voluntarily) gave up their scattered housings made of clay and mud bricks to live in compact settlements with gas and electricity supply. Soviet villages and agro-towns shared characteristically uniform settlement patterns transposing features of Soviet urban planning to the countryside. In every rural settlement there would be Soviet styled prefab houses, palaces of culture, concert halls, libraries, medical facilities, schools and kindergartens, socialist monuments, small factories, urban green space, paved streets, all in proportion to the settlement size. Inside the rural homes, modern consumer goods made their appearance, coexisting with (and sometimes replacing) traditional ways of furnishing houses. Living and working in kolkhozes and sovkhozes conferred a new layer of commonality upon previously variegated rural people.

Central Asia came to occupy the role of a predominantly rural, peripheral, and socially conservative part of the Soviet Union. Demographic growth and unemployment had higher rates than elsewhere, and rural families were larger than average. This development was a result of the region's particular form of economic integration. Cotton especially was deemed important for the Soviet textile industry and played a crucial role. To some degree the Soviet policies were reechoing the policies of the tsarist colonial period, as they achieved only a half-accomplished modernization by relegating the region to the peripheral role of a provider of natural resources and of agricultural goods for the industrial "core" of the Soviet Union. On the other hand, repressive and "extractive" policies centered on the imposition of intensive monocultures, mostly cotton, were effectively counterbalanced by economic transfers and social policies. Central Asia's integration into the Soviet Union brought substantial social advancements, rights, and opportunities, especially to rural people and to women.

Soviet rural life offered unprecedented opportunities for education, health care, technology, social mobility, and travel. Although the Soviet moving and mixing of peoples was more visible in the cities, the countryside was not completely immune to it. Large agricultural development projects such as the Virgin Lands campaign and the enlargement of the Hungry Steppe irrigation schemes were accompanied by the resettlement of peoples of Slavic, Korean, and European backgrounds into areas formerly inhabited only by peoples from Central Asia. Their presence added complexity to rural societies by mixing up Muslim segmentary patriarchal and patrilocal communities with new, culturally diverse populations, bringing their own knowledge, languages, and attitudes into the countryside. In the Soviet Army, rural Central Asians achieved fluency in Russian, became acquainted with foreign countries and with comrades from all over the Soviet Union, and sometimes (contradicting customs requiring marriages to be arranged by parents) came back to their villages with a nonlocal spouse.

In the new Soviet world of agriculture shaped by tractors, pumps, chemical fertilizers, and new irrigation and drainage canals made of concrete, land plots were either very large, when used to grow the state-mandated crops, or very small (and more productive), when allocated to the families of the kolkhozes to grow their own vegetables and keep their own livestock. This dualism was also reflected in the perceived antagonism between Soviet modernity and the resilience of "traditionalism" in the modernizing countryside. Traditional mores—marriage preferences, rituals, popular Islam—persisted in the private sphere outside the officialdom of Soviet life thanks to the connivance of kolkhoz authorities, who were caught in a double allegiance both toward their communities and toward the Soviet state. In a tacit division of roles, the extended rural families (and the women's world, in particular) became the carrier of old and seemingly immutable ways of life, beliefs, and wisdom, while the kolkhoz world, with its new technologies and ways of doing agriculture, offered opportunities for skilled employment and for "male" careers within one's native village (female tractor drivers, much celebrated in Soviet media, were few and often made only a transitory appearance). The "modern," or Soviet, countryside coexisted (and sometimes clashed) with the resilience of the "old" one. The kolkhoz partly failed in its alleged mission to overcome the traditional social rules and obligations permeating rural communities; the kolhoz itself became successfully "inhabited" by rural society, meaning that traditional loyalties and obligations based on kin, religion, and neighborly relations became influential in determining the inner workings of the collective farms.

On the political side, Soviet modernization raised and educated native elites who held positions up to the top of their republic-level agricultural hierarchies. Their role was ambiguous, as on the one hand they strongly identified with the socialist state, but on the other, their involvement in a pervasive corruption system effectively undermined Soviet officialdom, as emerged in the disclosing of the "cotton scandal" in the mid-1980s. At the collapse of the Soviet Union, together with the problems caused by the abrupt end of Soviet central planning, hyperinflation, and political insecurity, these elites inherited unrestricted command. When, in the early post-Soviet years, international organizations such as the International Monetary Fund and the World Bank pushed for governments to introduce liberal market reforms, in Central Asia their calls for reform were received without enthusiasm. The newly independent ruling elites had strong reservations about private ownership of land. Besides their interest in maintaining the status quo of power relations and ownership, many of them had been Soviet cadres closely involved in agriculture and were attached to the idea of landownership as the sole prerogative of the state.

Many rural inhabitants who had been educated within the Soviet system also shared the elites' conservative attitudes toward land reforms, since they had grown to profit from their affiliation to collective structures in the past. Memories of pre-collective ownership arrangements being weak or nil, people still associated the kolkhoz with the impressive agricultural and demographic expansion that had occurred after the Second World War period. To many rural inhabitants, these circumstances reinforce the idea of the kolkhoz as agriculture's unquestioned and "natural" arrangement and explain resistance to the idea of its dismantling.

Land Politics and Rural Inequality

Despite post-Soviet nostalgia for the past, at the beginning of the 1990s all Central Asian countries had to reconsider the role of agriculture in their national economies. Unlike during the Khrushchev and Brezhnev periods, when the rural sector thrived thanks to subsidies and budgetary transfers, agriculture rapidly had to become, wherever possible, the net donor for urban-based modernization- and nation-building policies of the newly independent states. Central Asia's large rural population, which used to rely on cheap supplies from Soviet Russia, now increasingly had to depend on its own agricultural produce. The Central Asian states reacted differently to these problems and introduced a diversity of land reforms. Reform courses differed according to the particular conditions of the newly separated countries. Continuity with Soviet agriculture was particularly strong in cotton countries such as Uzbekistan, where agriculture still plays a key role in the national economy. Initially, with the exception of Kyrgyzstan, all states were reluctant to introduce full land-ownership and, instead, privileged granting long-term land leases to farmers. Average farm sizes differ greatly among different areas of the same country as well as between the Central Asian countries more generally. In Kazakhstan, for instance, the wheat-growing north is characterized by very large farms, whereas farm sizes in the irrigated agriculture in the south on average are very small. However, in general terms, in all Central Asian countries structural continuity with Soviet agriculture remains strong.

Despite this, the modalities of access to and usage of land and water, and the availability of tractors, inputs, retail facilities, and access to markets and credit have changed considerably throughout the region. Rather than revolving around formal landownership rights, the agrarian reforms have concerned the "individualization" of agriculture. In the move away from the collective and large-scale character of Soviet agriculture, production responsibilities have been redefined and reassigned in various forms to individuals or families. Everywhere in Central Asia, farmers and governments have been experimenting with new land and water codes. Water-pricing systems and water-user associations have been introduced in order to limit water waste. In this process, rural Central Asia became a recipient of international development policies and donor-funded programs, but the new developmental-technocratic styles and discourses collided with the local ways of doing agriculture and often did not yield expected outcomes.

From the local perspective, a more urgent concern than the introduction of private landed property has been the reforming of collective farms and the privatization of their assets. The collective farms held crucial facilities such as tractors and irrigation services, which are indispensable for agriculture and difficult to split in the privatization process without totally upsetting cultivation schemes and established patterns. For these reasons, Central Asia's southern "cotton belt" countries—Uzbekistan, Turkmenistan, and Tajikistan—were more hesitant to break up the large collective farms than Kazakhstan and Kyrgyzstan, where grain crops and livestock raising prevail. Dependency relations were preserved by staging "window-dressing" reforms, and farmers were kept compliant to centrally mandated agricultural production quotas through indirect levers.

In one way or another, privatization occurred in all Central Asian republics. Everywhere this has resulted in a strong increase in social inequality. Following a general post-socialist trend, privatization usually privileged the former kolkhoz chiefs, those with key administrative positions in the bureaucracy, and the wealthy. Very often it occurred in a context of arbitrary state power and lack of legal certainty, so it has failed everywhere to enhance the condition of ordinary peasants. Privatization thereby created a divide between reform "winners" and "losers." People with powerful connections to the local government (*akimat* in Kyrgyz and Kazakh, *hokimiyat* in Uzbek, *hukumat* in Tajik) got the best shares of the lands, the largest farms, and the best leasing conditions. Regardless of regional differences, everywhere newly

9-1   Village street, Ferghana Valley, Uzbekistan, 1997. Photograph by Georg Elwert.

established large farms needed to have "bureaucratic capital" in order to be viable—that is, connections and knowledge over the complex, newly defined bureaucratic processes that were gradually substituting Soviet regulations, which ordinary farmers often lack. For this reason, in local perceptions, the introduction of capitalism in the countryside is often equated to an "unfair" redistribution of risks and opportunities among small and large entrepreneurs. In irrigated areas, rural demographic growth and increased dependency on agriculture trigger a growing "land hunger," but the "appetite" for land is strongly predetermined by surrounding factors over which ordinary farmers often lack control. Leasing contracts can easily turn land into a liability when agricultural services are too expensive or unavailable or when legal restrictions go against the farmers' interests. This, for instance, happened in Uzbekistan's Khorezm region when farm collectives were being dismantled. While the best farmland ended up in the hands of the usual suspects, many families were pushed by district authorities into farming because of a lack of applicants for the worst plots, and these families eventually went bankrupt.

The decay of the collectives, which had already started during the last Soviet years, coincides with the appearance of new tensions within rural communities. These tensions revolve around the traditional social obligations once fulfilled by kolkhoz elites and the new "egoistic" opportunities opened up by the market. Land reform "winners" do not have the same type of patronal commitment that rural communities could legitimately expect from their kolkhoz managers. Also, newly successful agricultural

9-2   Children carrying water, Ferghana Valley, Uzbekistan, 1997. Photograph by Georg Elwert.

entrepreneurs often do not live anymore in the villages in which their crops grow. Increasingly, as these successful entrepreneurs come to resemble absentee landlords, the old moral economy of the kolkhoz is fading.

Everywhere decollectivization has split rural society into a minority of farmers holding new land titles and a majority of rural laborers with insufficient access to land and with worsened working conditions. Social tensions and resentment on behalf of the excluded are aggravated by the issue of child labor in the cotton fields, which is particularly acute in Uzbekistan and has caused international concern and diplomatic strain between Western countries and Central Asian cotton-growing countries. But also, in less oppressive Kazakhstan and Kyrgyzstan, obstacles (more economic and less political) hamper the development of small farms, as farmers' opportunities are restrained by the lack of capital, low investments, and the difficulty of accessing markets of scale. In Kyrgyzstan, rural areas' problems are connected with the severe poverty of the mountain regions, where small farmers find it difficult to reach essential infrastructure, and by the country's chronic political instability. In Kazakhstan the government has recently started subsidizing agriculture thanks to its oil revenues. But its priority has been the modernization of large farms, while the interests of small family-based peasant holdings—those that matter most to the rural people—are disregarded.

This is not to say that government intervention in rural districts has been limited to the support of large enterprises and agricultural infrastructure. Although much still remains to be done to fill the gap in living standards between cities and the countryside, much has been done in recent years to recover the infrastructural loss of the Soviet Union. The reestablishment of a reliable supply of drinking water, electricity, and gas and the renewal of schools, hospitals, and streets all have had a positive impact on the quality of rural life and livelihoods. However beneficial these interventions (more tangible in Kazakhstan and Uzbekistan and, rather, a result of NGO initiatives in Tajikistan and Kyrgyzstan), they remain a drop in the ocean and do not address the structural problems of rural poverty and unemployment. As a result, all Central Asian countries face similar problems: the productivity of agriculture lags behind by international comparison (and Soviet records) and is not living up to its potential. Oppressive policies, a political framework that discourages private initiative, agricultural stakeholders unreceptive to technological change, the lack of capital and investment, and the resistance to foreign investment in land out of fear of losing control over the agricultural sector are among the factors behind these developments.

Rural Livelihoods

In the initial post-socialist period, all Central Asian republics witnessed a declining agricultural infrastructure, deteriorating capital stock, a great loss of livestock, and dwindling harvest outputs. As a result, in the 1990s rural communities were confronted with severe poverty all over Central Asia. The prevailing image of the rural condition was bleak, with the rising cost of living, severely curtailed social benefits and services, and rural people's lives everywhere becoming more precarious. As a consequence of budget shortages, collective farms were no longer able to pay salaries. Sharecropping emerged as the substitute form of retribution in a context of a severe cash shortage. Unemployment became widespread, and for most people salaries ceased to be the most important source of income. Instead, the role of agriculture in securing one's livelihood became more important, exposing people to the risk of a harvest failure and to malnutrition. Livestock, for instance, once raised in large collective farms, was now being raised almost exclusively by families. The living conditions in rural communities had significantly worsened in a process of "re-agrarianization" and "demonetization." Together with the unmaking of Soviet rural education and health services, social welfare, and salaried jobs, it is the woman's position—in the domestic space, at the workplace, and in the agricultural fields—that has worsened compared to the Soviet past. In the post-kolkhoz agriculture, peasants formerly attached to state-led enterprises conceived for large-scale agroindustry as salaried workers now found themselves caught in a process of "agricultural involution," which forced them toward small-scale agriculture, subsistence economy, and into livelihood struggles for everyday survival. As a consequence, old ways of provisioning, building houses, and growing crops became again "fashionable" and the capacity to rely on family labor and to mobilize family networks became a prerequisite

9-3   Farmer in a village near Namangan, Uzbekistan, 1997. Photograph by Georg Elwert.

for agriculture. In such a context of economic reorientation, social networks and the ritual economy of gift exchanges often became crucial for securing livelihoods. At the same time, the growing poverty made it more difficult for many to maintain such ties of help and reciprocity.

For rural inhabitants, the most pressing problem remains the scarcity of jobs in the countryside. Newly established large farms increasingly shy away from employing labor. For instance, in the cotton-growing district of Makhtaral (Southern Kazakhstan), according to the chair of a large agricultural enterprise: "100 hectares of land used to be operated by twenty workers during the Soviet period. Now it is just five, the remaining had to go." Here and elsewhere, farmers tend to minimize the number of workers in order to increase their profits. Here, unlike Uzbekistan, farmers now prefer to harvest their cotton mechanically, claiming that it is cheaper and more reliable than relying on cotton pickers. Investments in farm equipment and tractors, subsidized by the government, will further reduce the need for agricultural laborers. Among the rural population there is an awareness that, in the future, the land will be operated by a few specialized large farms, and small farms and agricultural jobs will diminish further.

By necessity, small farmers must diversify their income sources and livelihood strategies. Livestock plays an important role for rural families, but small farms' agricultural plots and livestock do not make them self-sufficient. Agricultural earnings of small farms are too low to guarantee a family's sustenance. People integrate agricultural profits with other sources of income or rent and rely on the mutual support of relatives. Where land is of good quality and irrigated, farm sizes have been growing over the independence period (becoming large farms in the hands of few), and rural people often end up not having enough farmland, somehow reechoing the Soviet divide between household mini-farms and large-scale industrial farms. Ordinary peasants therefore either engage in labor migration, work as drivers, or are employed for low salaries in the village schools, nurseries, medical points, police stations, or in other public service jobs. They sell some self-produced goods in bazaars in the nearby provincial towns or run small village shops. For many small farmers, the hope and expectation are that the government will be able to provide them with industrial jobs, someday. In the meantime, pensions and remittances sustain much of villagers' expenditures and integrate modest agricultural family budgets.

In various parts of Central Asia, the combination of the scarcity of rural jobs, the lack of farmland and of non-transparent and nonformal land markets pushes rural families into informal rental arrangements with agricultural land. In Southern Kazakhstan, for instance, the informal subletting of agricultural land occurs among small farmers, and the deal is for a season, usually involving high-value cash crops that will be sold on local markets or abroad. The land provider is a smallholder who has a long-term lease from the state. He either has no money to grow the crop or is away or unable. The land tiller pays the land tax in the owner's name, a fee to the leaseholder, arranges for the inputs, grows the crop, and owns the harvest. Variations of this general trend include sharecropping and subletting. Subletting land is a widespread type of informal agricultural entrepreneurship and regards small-scale farming. It allows tillers to find additional land to work and represents an important opportunity for income in the absence of other jobs. In other regions (in Khorezm, for instance), informal farm sponsoring can also regard large-scale farming and can imply relations of hierarchy and dependency among contractors. Informal forms of land subrenting and sharecropping practices are diffuse throughout the region and are often illegal. Informal land markets encourage a short-term profit-oriented thinking that undermines the interest of states (i.e., taxation) and that often also harms the environment, depletes the quality of the land, and undermines land fertility in the long term. When the unintended collateral of such rural coping strategies appears to be increased soil depletion, rural livelihoods are negatively affected, and often those who depend the most on good harvests to sustain their livelihood are those who are affected the worst.

Soviet irrigation plans turned desert lands into agricultural lands on a grand scale. But this plan created the problem of secondary soil salinization and the deterioration of agricultural soils. After initial hesitation, a drainage infrastructure had to be set up by the Soviet state in response to the threat of soil salinization. Mastering secondary soil salinization required embarking in high costs and coordination efforts that were not always met easily. With the breakdown of the Soviet system, these efforts, knowledge, and infrastructure deteriorated; and thirty years after the end of the USSR, drainage infrastructure reestablishment is still incomplete, formerly irrigated lands are now abandoned, irrigation water is more scarce, and the progressive deterioration of agricultural soils is creating mounting problems for peasants and agricultural enterprises alike.

In the post-Soviet agricultural sector, the environmental burden is unequally distributed among agricultural producers. Often small producers are more exposed to water scarcity, soil deterioration, and secondary soil salinization than are the large farms. This adds to their vulnerability, since soil degradation poses a growing threat to their profits, harvests, and livelihoods. Recent social and economic restructuring has been unbalanced, favoring the elites but also incentivizing economic behavior that does not foster sustainable land or water use.

Beyond the Village

Labor migration started to appear and to change rural life in all Central Asian countries from the early 2000s. By now it has assumed massive dimensions in rural areas all over the region. The main factors pushing migration include the lack of farmland or its deterioration, the lack of rural jobs, and the unattractive rural wages that can hardly keep men of working age in their villages. Rural workers (men more than women) from Tajikistan, Uzbekistan, Kazakhstan, and Kyrgyzstan leave their villages to engage in seasonal labor migration, mostly as unskilled workers in agriculture and construction jobs in urban areas and further abroad, often Russia. Economies that used to be dependent on agriculture now have become dependent on migrants' remittances. Women, children, and elderly people are left behind and engage in agricultural work. But connections between migrants and their villages are only temporarily suspended. Migrants do not lose touch with what they see as their place of belonging, and they come back for a wedding or a circumcision, to take part in village festivities, or to help out when agricultural labor is most needed. Migration remittances fund a rural consumerism and have a vitalizing effect on the economy of rural provinces. Wedding feasts, cars, and houses are all the obvious expenditures of those who come back. Although living standards can differ greatly across Central Asia, flat-screen TVs, kitchen utensils, cell phones, and laptops are everywhere. Credit shops and pawnshops have reached the provinces, and a lot of the rural bazaar economy is probably funded by debt.

The connection to one's village might be idealized or only materialize over a short period of the year, but it remains crucial also when abroad. In times of mass migration the village becomes a place of retreat where one can get provisioning, moral support, and shelter when work in the cities is demeaning or makes one sick, or where one can rest between seasonal labor trips. The home village is the place where housing is available, spacious, and free. One's natal village is the bottom line where one can always return. Migrant parents might leave their children with their grandparents when unable to accommodate them with their work in the expensive city. The old and the young evaluate rural life differently, as the first might see it as desirable and the second might want to escape it. Both find shelter in not fully commodified relations, a decelerated zone where houses and familiar people offer some basic respite and security.

As the perspective of engaging in farm work has lost its attraction among many rural inhabitants, agricultural knowledge is not fully transmitted across generations and gets lost, a growing share of rural people are increasingly alienated from agriculture, and rural societies transit into an identity crisis. This crisis is more tangible where it coincides with severe environmental degradation or when it becomes impossible to live from agriculture. Having lost Soviet and pre-Soviet knowledge about how to farm, many people consider themselves neither fully farmers nor (skilled) workers. They feel they are in-between or, rather, as if they are "nothing": unskilled temporary labor migrants, recipients of pensions and subsidies, and agricultural bricoleurs. The idealizations of the village notwithstanding, the current rural generations of people are facing deteriorating conditions and lamenting a lack of development. They often hope their children will grow up elsewhere. Increasingly, rural people see their children's future in the cities.

Governments put only halfhearted efforts into easing rural hardship. They try to make village life appear more appealing by funding a modicum of infrastructure projects. Nevertheless, especially for the young generation, there is little appeal in rural life, as the rural inhabitants feel left behind in terms of social inclusion and economic development. Villagers, nevertheless, are important for the governments as "human material" in manifold ways: as labor migrants they support the economy, and as the "reserve army of labor" they cheapen the cost of work. Rural people are also a demographic resource and an engine for the country. They are presented as containers and propagators of national cultural values. The military and the security forces find most of their recruits in the villages. Although in the urban context, the term "rural" can be a curse word, it also has a "high" connotation, as a purer, nationally more authentic way of life, and thus some normative power in the nationalist discourse. Paradoxically, despite out-migration, despite environmental degradation, despite being left behind and feeling as "residuals" in the national development trajectory, people still discover a strong appeal and identity in rural life. A proverb that has variations in all Central Asian languages speaks to this: "the land where you have been born calls you back."

Seeing Rural Life in Context

Given the great variety of forms, backgrounds, and conditions, generalizing about rural life in Central Asia is an arduous task, and this account of twenty-first-century trends in Central Asian rural societies must necessarily be partial. I chose to focus on the contradiction between lived and imagined rurality—that is, on the tension between reality and idealized features of rural life and its multiple usages, as a way to counteract a recurring urban bias that tends to diminish the rural world's importance for contemporary transformation processes in Central Asian societies. In its idealized notion, rural life can powerfully confer meaning, longing, and legitimacy. Understood in such a way, village sociality, industriousness, and morality are resources with an aura that shines beyond the countryside. Governments try to anchor their legitimacy in implicit modes of rural living, and they also benefit from rural lives in other direct and indirect ways. On a closer look, while rural life lags behind urban standards, it is not as backward as is commonly imagined or presented. Yet rural societies are certainly more disadvantaged, and people are pushed into labor migration for lack of alternatives. Over the first post-Soviet period, agriculture had a strategic, central role in sustaining economic viability of the newly independent countries. The exploitation of rural wealth and resources were determinant in this process. Nowadays, as the centrality of agriculture for national development is dwindling and giving way to a more urban-based development, the countryside contributes to the national development by conveying its surplus labor and its "cultural resources." The countryside has remained a socially problematic area cut off from urban progress, but it is also a home base for migrants; a reservoir for political legitimation, cultural authenticity, and national identity; a pool of cheap unskilled workers; and a demographic engine for Central Asia's vigorously urbanizing nation-states.

Looking back at over three decades of post-socialist agrarian reforms in Central Asia, we can say that, everywhere, state interests prevailed over the interests of rural communities. Land reform agendas gave priority to administrative and productive exigencies while missing social development objectives. In some countries, where the maintenance of a state order system and centralized inputs and retail hampers the development of private initiative, farmers can end up engaging in agriculture more out of fear of administrative sanctions than for economic incentives. In other countries, a chaotic liberalization has created an island of reform winners in a sea of losers. Common to all countries is the rising inequality and the unresolved problems of rural poverty and stagnation. In Central Asia overall, much has changed in terms of laws and policies, but very little has changed for the peasant condition. During the 1990s the impoverishment of rural masses, the shortage of agricultural land, and the growing social inequality conferred on Central Asia's countryside the image of a problem area associated with instability and potential conflicts. After the turn of the century, this situation has not changed fundamentally because the underlying problems remain unresolved. Across Central Asia the rural world shaped by Soviet kolkhoz and sovkhoz legacies nowadays is more exposed to growing environmental threat at a time when rural people are more dependent on the environment to sustain livelihoods.

10

Urban Life

Natalie Koch

Walking long distances in Central Asia's major cities can be a rewarding experience, but most of the time you will end up with dirty shoes. Frequently, there are no sidewalks, and pedestrians have to walk either in the road itself or in the roadside dreck. Air and noise pollution can be severe, and in some places like Nur-Sultan (Astana until 2019), harsh steppe winds can be cutting in the winter and cover one with dust in the summer. As one recent arrival in Nur-Sultan told me, "That's what I hate about this city—you walk outside and immediately you are dirty. You have to change your clothes all the time, and you cannot even wear nice shoes!" Most cities in Central Asia still lack a metro system—although Tashkent's opened in 1977, and after twenty-three years of construction, Almaty opened a short first line in 2011. Many do have extensive public bus and *marshrutka* networks, but as nearly any urbanite will point out, these vehicles are often dirty, poorly maintained, and unpredictable. The Soviet-era tram lines are nearly extinct in most cities, and the few that remain are the source of endless frightful encounters with daredevil drivers who commandeer their tracks as "suicide lanes" to be used in either direction. Traveling by bicycle can require equally dangerous leanings. But perhaps the biggest challenge of all for any would-be pedestrian, cyclist, or bus rider is the negative social stigma often attached to any means of transportation other than a personal car, which is largely preferred by increasingly affluent residents across the region.

Many people do not immediately think of transportation as a significant issue in approaching "urban life." Usually other things such as housing, neighborhoods, crime, and green space are the first to come to mind. But transportation networks have always been the foundation of urbanism, defining the shape and extent of any city and its residents' choices about where to live and work and how to structure their days. Soviet urban planners were keenly aware of this and designed their cities and transportation infrastructures around communist ideals. This meant, first of all, limiting the population size of cities to ensure that all residents had equal access to municipal services—enforced through the *propiska* system of residential registration. It also meant planning worker housing within close proximity of major factories, often separated from the factories only by a green belt or other shaded paths, so that workers could simply walk to work in a clean environment rather than spending long hours commuting in cramped and unhealthy spaces. Last, institutionalizing these values during the USSR period meant heavy investment in mass transport combined with actively discouraging personal car ownership, which was seen as symbolizing (if not actively promoting) individualism. Not only were cities designed around mass transit rather than cars, but cars were extremely difficult to obtain during Soviet times. Soviet domestic automobile production only began in the 1970s and even then, wait periods for ordinary citizens lasted upward of ten years.

Although these urban design principles are today seeing something of a revival among "sustainable urbanism" promoters in many Western countries, when the Soviet Union disintegrated in 1991 they were quickly abandoned in much of Central Asia. Urbanites with means wanted to live in new and larger homes and in elite neighborhoods rather than close to a factory or other polluting industrial site. They wanted their own cars. And with the lifting or loosening of certain propiska-style residency restrictions, combined with the collapse of many collective farms in Central Asia's countryside, rural migrants flooded into the cities. At both ends of the spectrum, from the already urban nouveau riche to the poor new arrivals, their new aspirations and consumption patterns brought immediate impacts for urban life in Central Asia. Cities grew outward and upward. New prestige districts and makeshift shantytowns at the edges of cities meant more and longer commuting for both the elite and the poor. Tram lines fell into disrepair and other modes of moving about the city became subordinated to the car; city streets became clogged with traffic to an extent never seen before in the region. And with all the new cars on the roads, the air became harder to breathe.

Of course, not all cities in Central Asia have witnessed these transformations since independence to the same extent and in the same manner. While Soviet central planning aimed to unify the urban experience across the vast reaches of the country's territory, the five Central Asian republics have all plotted different trajectories with respect to how their governments and citizens understand the role of cities, both practically and symbolically. Equally, internal differences such as north/south divides mean that urban life can vary dramatically within each of the countries and their constituent regions. To add yet another layer of complexity to this story of spatial diversity, new and exaggerated social divides across the region mean that individuals of different social classes and backgrounds experience urban life in starkly different ways even within the same city. In short, understanding urban life in Central Asia today is an exercise in geography.

Overall, we can understand this geography and the nature of recent changes in urban life through considering the shifting ways in which people "code" the urban landscape, its built forms, and local residents. These codes have many forms, but the most pervasive in the region, and perhaps globally, is the modern/backward binary. It is important to note that drawing the border between these two categorizes can never be correct or incorrect. Rather, any "modern" or "backward" designation is a thoroughly subjective way of interpreting people, things, ideas, and so on. So, rather than seeing "modernity" as a fixed category, scholars have shown that the divide is always in flux, contested, and subjective. The act of labeling something or someone modern or not is an act that will vary based on an individual's personal affinities, life experiences, and personal resources. As a result, the modern/backward divide can be extremely politically charged.

Claims to modernity are also manifested materially—built into the design of new consumer spaces and environments, architectural designs, and methods of policing how certain individuals use and move through urban space. In examining how people and planners navigate this divide, we see that each country, city, and citizen has a different way of relating to the Soviet past and the post-Soviet present. This is important because all of Central Asia's cities continue to be defined, to some extent, by their Soviet inheritance. Even outright rejection of the Soviet past—as in efforts to demolish old *khrushchevki* housing blocks to make way for new high-rise apartment complexes, for example, or transferring the country's capital to a new city (as in Nur-Sultan)—are ways of negotiating this history and narrating new identities in the era of independence. Although my own research focus is on Kazakhstan and Turkmenistan, in this chapter I aim to illustrate how these identity claims work by examining the contrasting ways in which people and their governments have come to relate to this Soviet past. The geography of urbanism in Central Asia thus begins with the multiple scaled spaces where citizens craft their everyday lives.

Monumental Urbanism

In 1913 Lenin claimed that cities are the "centers of economic, political, and intellectual or spiritual life of a people and constitute the chief promoters of progress." Through Soviet times, cities were thus seen as having a special role in "civilizing" the social and territorial peripheries of the USSR. On the eve of the Bolshevik revolution, the Central Asian territories were comparatively recently incorporated into Russian imperial control, and state power remained quite tenuous (to understate the matter). But this region was also characterized by extremely low levels of urbanization. Except in the region of Fergana Valley, where people had long been sedentary, most of the republic's territories were sparsely populated and largely inhabited by nomadic groups.

City building in Central Asia therefore assumed an especially potent role in the Soviet discourses about modernizing these "backward" territories.

Each of the five Soviet republics in Central Asia had its own capital: Almaty in Kazakhstan, Ashgabat in Turkmenistan, Bishkek in Kyrgyzstan, Dushanbe in Tajikistan, and Tashkent in Uzbekistan. As republican capitals, these cities received more planning attention and adornment than other urban hubs in the region. Tashkent, in particular, received even more attention than the others. As the capital of the Uzbek SSR, Central Asia's most populous republic, the city was treated as a symbol of the state's ability to "civilize" the entire region. But Tashkent also seemed to be iconic of an older urban form that the Soviets wished to erase. Planners fixated on the city's "backward" or "primitive" form of organic development, with "disorderly" winding streets and cramped, "unhealthy" dwellings. In short, Tashkent lacked the modernist order of gridded streets and monumental buildings that Soviet developers considered to be the signs of progress. At every opportunity they were afforded, leaders across Central Asia tried to obliterate this old urban morphology. And occasionally they were helped along by devastating earthquakes such as those in Ashgabat in 1948 and Tashkent in 1966, which allowed them to transform the cities significantly.

When the Soviet Union broke up in 1991, the capital of each of the five Central Asian republics became the capital of the new country. All around the world, capital cities are accorded a special symbolic role as the seat of government, and leaders often try to shape the city's outward appearance to reflect national values. For example, as the capital of the USSR, Moscow was seen as a "propagandistic shopwindow" to advertise the country's communist ideology. After 1991 Central Asian states were no longer advertising communism, but state and urban planners retained the idea that the capital city should be a "shopwindow" to display their country's new ideological orientation and geopolitical alignment. As capitals of sovereign states, these cities became not only the apex of their countries' urban hierarchies but their symbolic centers. Not all the countries had the resources to reshape their capitals around their new nationalist ideologies, but the two resource-rich states of Kazakhstan and Turkmenistan certainly do, and their capitals have undergone massive transformations in the era of independence. In the case of Kazakhstan, the capital was moved to an entirely different city.

In 1997 Nur-Sultan replaced Almaty as the capital of Kazakhstan. At the time of the move, the new capital was known as Akmola. Between 1998 and 2019 the town was called Astana, and in 2019 the name was changed again to Nur-Sultan, after the country's first president, Nursultan Nazarbayev, who frequently referred to Nur-Sultan as the "face of the country" (*litso strany*) or its "business card" (*visitnaya kartochka*). The government's development scheme there is one of the most vivid examples of how planners inscribe identity narratives in the built environment. In addition to being moved closer to the center of Kazakhstan, the capital city has been a focal point of ubiquitous nationalist propaganda—proclaiming Nur-Sultan and Kazakhstan more generally as the

10-1   Nur-Sultan's Left Bank skyline, 2011. Photograph by Natalie Koch.

"geopolitical center" or the "heart" of Eurasia. The new government center, in the city's Left Bank area, is defined by monumental architecture and a potpourri of styles, colors, and shapes that the government refers to as an eclectic "Eurasian" style (see figure 10-1). Although built on the site of a Soviet-era town (Tselinograd), Nur-Sultan is portrayed as marking a clean break from the Soviet past and as representing all that is modern and forward-looking about the independent state of Kazakhstan. Pushing the city ever further into the surrounding steppe, new iconic buildings have been developed to craft the city's skyline as a colorful pastiche and to symbolize the state's ability to "domesticate" the best of global standards. For example, the government's much acclaimed Khan Shatyr shopping mall was designed by the world-renowned architect Norman Foster and symbolizes Kazakhstan's new consumerist orientation. Established in 2010, Nur-Sultan's Nazarbayev University also symbolizes the government's effort to promote elite education locally. It largely serves as a monument to Nazarbayev's vision of shaping the country around a "knowledge economy" in the future. As icons, these individual structures and the image of Nur-Sultan as a whole is perhaps more symbolic than "real," in that the values and wealth they represent are not widely available to the vast majority of citizens. This notwithstanding, many people in Kazakhstan look positively on the city's development as a source of renewed pride in their homeland and as a symbol of hope for a better future to come.

In Ashgabat, monumental urban planning has taken a rather different form than in Nur-Sultan. President Nazarbayev openly criticized Soviet architecture for its uniformity, but Turkmenistan's first president, Saparmurat Niyazov (aka Turkmenbashi) desired precisely this. Specifically, he wanted Ashgabat's buildings all to be clad in white marble, standardizing them around this image of opulence and lending the city a truly dramatic feel. Perhaps the most dramatic element of the city, however, is the degree of abandonment contrasting with the scope of the development—nearly everywhere in the city's newest quarters, it is devoid of the "chaos" of pedestrianized movement. Like Nur-Sultan, enormous distances between major buildings and broad multi-lane avenues mark Ashgabat as a car-oriented city, where

10-2   Chuy Avenue in Bishkek. Photography by Natalie Koch.

pedestrians are not welcome. Of course, there are large areas that do not conform with the monumental image that is usually projected of both cities. Having some of the liveliness of the "unplanned" city, these spaces are coded not as part of the new or "modern" Nur-Sultan and Ashgabat but, rather, as the "old," "unofficial," or "Soviet-era" parts of the city. But these are the spaces that most ordinary citizens inhabit in their day-to-day life. The monumental landscapes of Nur-Sultan and Ashgabat are largely reserved for the political elites. And yet, by defining the shining new spaces and structures as icons of the "modern" Kazakhstan or Turkmenistan, political elites use the very language of modernity to destigmatize the practice of exclusion and to transform elite desires into popular desires.

The other capitals of Central Asia have also undergone significant changes in the independence era. However, as capitals of countries that do not have access to as much resource wealth and the various international patronage networks this opens up, Bishkek, Dushanbe, and Tashkent have not been reconfigured so completely nor in such a monumental fashion. Much of these cities' built environment retains their Soviet character, as shown in the arcades along Chuy Avenue, a major east–west artery in Bishkek (see figure 10-2). Pedestrian spaces have not been overtaken by monumental new boulevards as in Nur-Sultan and Ashgabat, but the sidewalks even in the very heart of the city can be in complete disrepair. Dushanbe also retains much of its Soviet flavor, though government officials have been pushing with mounting force to implement a master plan to "reinvent" the capital. In 2015, for example, authorities announced plans to destroy a number of major Soviet-era structures, including the city's Rokhat teahouse, two theaters, the former presidential administration, the mayor's office, and the parliament building. The resulting public outcry has largely focused on government corruption and dubious construction company ties, but it also relates to broader identity narratives concerning respect for the Soviet past. An anti-demolition petition, for example, calls on officials to preserve the buildings that "symbolize the Motherland" and that were "built with love by our ancestors." So, although Central Asia's cities have retained many Soviet-era architectural landmarks, housing complexes, and other infrastructures, broader efforts to de-Sovietize symbolic landscapes remain a contentious issue across the region.

Symbolic Sites and Community Spaces

Most of Central Asia's cities witnessed rapid changes in their symbolic landscapes, which were "re-coded" in the independence era. This has involved the renaming of streets and squares and the removal or reconfiguring of many Soviet-era monuments. "Lenin Street" became something like "Independence Street," and Lenin statues were replaced with Kazakh, Kyrgyz, Tajik, Turkmen, or Uzbek national heroes. Pervasive as this de-Sovietization of the urban landscape was, it did not happen everywhere or to the same extent. The changes have been slower in some places and faster in others. In some cases, these symbols remain because local opposition to their removal is too strong—as for one iconic Pushkin statue in Nur-Sultan (see figure 10-3), which the government tried to remove, but outspoken popular criticism led to his return, albeit in a less central part of the city.

In other cases, Soviet public art or monuments have remained because they reflect deep-seated values that went unchanged with the collapse of the USSR. For instance, all over the region, Second World War memorials still dot the urban landscape, as people's patriotic reverence for veterans has largely persisted. Sometimes the message of Soviet symbolic landscapes still aligns with the independent states' identity narratives, as in parts of Kazakhstan where elaborate mosaics with the theme of "friendship of the peoples" sometimes remain on the edges of large city blocks (figure 10-4). Soviet-era mosaics have been removed from public surfaces elsewhere in the country, but the message of interethnic harmony and tolerance is one that Kazakhstan's official rhetoric emphasizes, particularly in the northern parts of the country where there are higher concentrations of ethnic Russians. Concerned about alienating the Russian and other minority populations in the independence era, political elites in Kazakhstan have largely retained Soviet-era symbols that promoted the notion of "friendship of the peoples."

Elsewhere in Central Asia, where the states' demographic composition is much less diverse than in Kazakhstan, this has been less of a concern. But even in Ashgabat, for example, the government has kept its Lenin statue—according to my government guide because it was the first statue of

10-3 The Pushkin statue in Nur-Sultan, with large Soviet-era apartment blocks in the background, 2011. Photography by Natalie Koch.

Lenin outside of Russia, built in 1927 (figure 10-5). In this case, Turkmenistan's leaders' penchant for superlatives triumphed over their otherwise wide-reaching de-Sovietization campaigns. Turkmenistan's cities, like those of neighboring republics, not only have seen the widespread removal of Soviet icons since 1991 but are increasingly populated with monuments to local heroes. This has taken a somewhat exceptional form in Turkmenistan, though, because President Niyazov, who headed the government until his

10-4 A Soviet-era mosaic on the side of an apartment block in Petropavl, Kazakhstan, 2009. Photograph by Natalie Koch.

sudden death in 2006, also had a penchant for gold statues of himself (figure 10-6). Elsewhere, urban leaders have focused more on commissioning statues of historical figures, such as pre-Soviet khans, *bai*s, and cultural icons. For example, in 2004, a towering statue of the famous Kyrgyz strongman and wrestler Kojomkol (1889–1955) was erected outside of Bishkek's Soviet-era sports palace (figure 10-7).

  Spaces for sports and exercise have long been important aspects of urban life in Central Asia, promoted by Soviet planners as a way to strengthen the bodies and minds of the masses. Sports palaces (*Dvoretz Sporta* or *Sports Sarai*) were a staple of Soviet cities and were typically located in or near parks. Green spaces themselves were similarly seen by Soviet planners as playing a central role in strengthening citizens both physically and spiritually and as a way to overcome the unhealthy aspects of urban life. Green space was considered an important aesthetic element of the city. Especially under Stalin, who was known for his appreciation of attractive cities, Soviet urban planners aimed to beautify Central Asia's cities by "greening" them. From Tashkent to Almaty to Ashgabat, planners supervised the development of extensive new urban parks and encouraged citizens to plant trees in their neighborhoods and all over their cities. Soviet citizens came to view green spaces as bastions of healthfulness and moral order in the city. This attitude remains today, even if contemporary urban planners have overseen the disappearance of much of their greenery to widen roads or develop new lands. Nonetheless, many of

10-5   Built in 1927, the Lenin monument in central Ashgabat was the first Lenin statue outside of Russia, 2014. Photograph by Natalie Koch.

10-6   A gold Niyazov statue in central Ashgabat, 2014. Photograph by Natalie Koch.

the region's sporting facilities and green spaces do remain, albeit adapted and reconfigured as contemporary purposes dictate—as in the case of a Soviet-era park in Ashgabat with refurbished tennis courts, or the park with the newest games and snacks made available to young families and youth gathered on a summer evening in Aral, Kazakhstan.

Religious sites are also important symbolic sites and community spaces that have been reconfigured in the post-Soviet era, and again, this has taken contrasting forms in Central Asia's many cities. Broadly speaking, though, many new places of worship have been constructed across the whole region, such as the Mashkhur Jusup in Pavlodar, completed in 2001 (figure 10-8). In the 1990s and into the early 2000s, foreign governments from Turkey to Qatar poured funds into Central Asia to develop new mosques. The trend has tapered off significantly in recent years, as regional governments have become increasingly suspicious of religious groups, especially those with foreign ties. Some political leaders have preferred to revamp their existing religious structures, especially those with the greatest historical significance such as Samarqand's fifteenth-century Bibi-Khanym Mosque, Bukhara's sixteenth-century Kalân Mosque in Uzbekistan, and the stunning Russian Zenkov Cathedral completed in 1907 in Almaty. Functioning more as tourist destinations than as central sites of religious life, these buildings nonetheless allow government officials to promote the image of religious tolerance. In smaller towns and cities, however, places of worship have increasing significance in urban life, even if actual respect for religious practice is patchy across the region.

10-8   Opened in 2001, the Mashkhur Jusup Mosque in Pavlodar is one of the largest mosques in Kazakhstan, 2011. Photograph by Natalie Koch.

Consumer Spaces

In addition to the changing symbolic landscapes since 1991, Central Asia's cities have undergone major transformations as the countries have reconfigured their economies around the principles of capitalism. For many people, one of the most welcomed aspects of this transition was the sudden availability of foreign-made consumer goods. Although the 1990s were marred by severe economic depression, regional markets were slowly liberalized. Ranging from cars to cheap housewares to electronics, imported goods increasingly became affordable for ordinary urban residents. And by the early 2000s "modern" shopping malls began to open in the largest cities—the Dordoi Plaza in Bishkek, for example, and Kazakhstan's Mega malls (figure 10-9). Especially in the more affluent cities, these upscale commercial centers have become quite popular. Featuring extremely clean, modern-looking interiors and strict security patrols, they offer high-end clothing and luxury stores, food courts and more formal restaurants, movie theaters, and other family-oriented entertainment. These pleasures are out of reach for many of the visitors, but it is nonetheless common for people to simply buy a drink and sit socializing with friends in the climate-controlled malls. Doing so in these comfortable mall spaces can be an important way for locals, young people in particular, to position themselves as "modern" urbanites.

From the mall's clean and ultramodern setting, aspiring middle-class

10-9   Mega Mall in Nur-Sultan, Kazakhstan, 2011. Photography by Natalie Koch.

visitors often come to look even more disdainfully on the "outmoded" retail centers, such as TsUM (*Tsentral'nyi Universal'nyi Magazin*, the Central Universal Department Store). These Soviet-era complexes populated most cities during the Soviet Union era but have slowly been disappearing across much of Central Asia. Their basic model still prevails in most provincial towns and cities, and in some places like Dushanbe, TsUM remains an urban icon. But for increasingly affluent Central Asians, TsUM-style centers seem like a relic of the past, frequently coded as insufficiently urbane and dominated by rural people with a "village mind-set" (*sel'skii mentalitet*). Social hierarchies in Central Asia have long operated through this urban/rural divide, but reconfiguring the region's economies around capitalism has also reconfigured the urban spaces where people code and interpret the significance of this divide. As in other capitalist countries around the world, this often works through the subtle but calculated use of shame. Consumer spaces are organized through a dense web of unofficial codes that lend certain places an aura of exclusivity—for example, at restaurants, clubs, cafés, or malls—such that lower-income individuals feel highly uncomfortable and shameful and simply avoid being in such a place. In Central Asia's cities, these codes of personal conduct and the administration of shame have increasingly been rearranged to match the norms of a neoliberal consumerist economy.

This social stereotyping comes into clear focus at Nur-Sultan's Khan Shatyr mall, which opened to great fanfare for President Nazarbayev's seventieth birthday in 2010. The government consistently described this four-hundred-million-dollar project as being "for the people." Taking this

10-10   A bazaar in Kyzylorda, Kazakhstan, 2015. Photograph by Natalie Koch.

deceit to heart, many rural tourists can be seen making the pilgrimage to their capital's newest attraction. They do not do much more than walk around and take pictures, as everything in the consumerist paradise is far beyond their means. More troubling, perhaps, than being financially excluded is that, once inside, the village visitors encounter the disdain of Nur-Sultan's established middle- and upper-class urbanite shoppers who see them as out of place. Although rural visitors often seem unaware or simply do not care about the contemptuous stares, the consumer-oriented experience at the Khan Shatyr brings Kazakhstan's new inequalities sharply into focus. But if the villagers experience revulsion at the social inequalities that the Khan Shatyr represents, urbanites reject their outlook as symptomatic of their "village mind-set" and lack of "modernity"—never as an example of their higher morality or egalitarian principles. The visitors are simply expected to adjust their norms to match the country's new political economy. In short, in these new consumerist spaces, rural visitors are often negatively stigmatized as being "backward" or "old-fashioned," rather than as having any legitimate grievance about Kazakhstan's newly capitalist orientations. So deep is this stigma that it effectively forecloses any discussions about alternate, perhaps more equal, social and spatial practices.

The urban/rural and modern/backward divide is also visible in how people purchase their groceries. The new shopping malls of Central Asia have large international grocery stores, such as the Turkish chains Ramstore (Kazakhstan) and Beta-Stores (Kyrgyzstan). Although originally catering primarily to foreigners and local elite, these stores are increasingly frequented by Central Asia's growing middle class. However, the vast majority of people still do the bulk of their shopping at local markets or bazaars (figure 10-10). In many cities, urban planners have tried to crack down on bazaars by removing them entirely or by imposing impossibly taxing new regulations. Some bazaars, however, are unlikely to be eliminated in the near future as they are true cultural icons, such as the Green Bazaar in Almaty, the Chorsu Bazaar in Tashkent, and the region's largest, Bishkek's Dordoi Bazaar. In addition to these, a range of smaller weekly markets can be found throughout the region's cities, and street vending is common in various urban neighborhoods. But as Central Asia's urban residents become more affluent, they are beginning to shift their shopping habits and thus a significant element of their urban sociality to more regulated, Western-style commercial spaces—in the process, stigmatizing bazaars as a relic of the past or something reserved for poor rural migrants.

Urban Housing

Paralleling the shift toward increasing socioeconomic differentiation in Central Asia's consumer spaces, urban housing patterns have also been characterized by growing inequalities in the postcommunist period. Cities have seen an influx of rural migrants since the 1990s because of the economic restructuring in the countryside combined with loosened state residency restrictions. People who had never lived in cities before came to see urban life as the way of the future—or at least as offering a glimmer of hope for a more prosperous future. Often not able to afford housing in the established neighborhoods of their destination cities, rural migrants started to build small makeshift dwellings at the urban periphery. These informal settlements, like those in many other parts of the world, tend to lack access to basic services such as sewers, water, and electricity. In the most extreme cases, these communities are located in areas that pose serious health hazards to the residents, such as the Altyn Kazyk settlement located near a waste dump on the outskirts of Bishkek, which housed close to one thousand rural migrants. Slated for removal in 2009, the cluster of small clay houses would be covered in a haze from smoldering waste, and some of the homes were even built on top of human graves.

Although not all informal settlements are as tenuous as the Altyn Kazyk case, in their relative poverty and lack of services many are not too different from some of Central Asia's poorest villages. Of course, elites and urban planners have overwhelmingly considered these communities as threatening the image of the city, marring its modern image with pockets of "backward" village life. They have consequently undertaken extensive efforts to demolish informal housing settlements. For example, numerous such communities have been destroyed in and around Nur-Sultan, Almaty, Bishkek, Dushanbe, and Ashgabat since the mid-2000s. Protests against these actions and insufficient compensation have been widespread, though the nondemocratic nature of urban politics across the region means that planners typically proceed regardless. In the Pervomaisk neighborhood on Ashgabat's outskirts, for instance, dozens of homes were bulldozed in early

2013, after the government gave residents only two weeks' notice to vacate and little or no financial compensation.

In their efforts to eliminate informal housing, state and urban planners have relied heavily on the language of modernity to justify their efforts to "clean up" or "modernize" their cities and housing infrastructures. This attitude has also defined official approaches to more established micro-districts and housing blocks that were characteristic of Soviet planning. This is exemplified in the way that Kazakhstan's president Nursultan Nazarbayev has spoken about the areas of Nur-Sultan that were part of the original Tselinograd settlement, which have slowly but systematically been targeted for removal:

> But on the eve of our move from Almaty, Astana was a typical provincial town. There were a lot of old, decrepit buildings, which were spoiling the look of the new capital. We had to demolish them. . . . They did not match the look of Kazakhstan's new capital at all. As to my views on Soviet architecture, I will say that each epoch leaves its creations. Some of them live forever, others do not pass the test of time [and] quickly become morally outdated and wear out physically.

Nazarbayev's description of Soviet-era homes as "old," "decrepit," and "morally outdated" and his concern that they "spoil the look of the new capital" clearly illustrate how significant urban aesthetics are to state planners. From their vantage point, "outdated" buildings are little more than architectural objects—not places that people live in and love, make their own, and in many cases call home, because they lack any better alternative. Of course, this is not a story that is unique to Central Asia, but the power of a city's master plan and all the other accoutrements of urban planning is their ability to depersonalize these spaces and treat them as problems to be "solved."

Urban planning dictates are not completely arbitrary, however. Wealthier citizens in Central Asia's cities are increasingly demanding modern, high-rise apartment buildings, which are slowly replacing older (and newer) low-rise developments (figure 10-11). This trend is especially strong in the city centers but starts to taper off as one moves outward toward the edges of the city. At the other end of the spectrum from the peripheral shantytowns, upper-class citizens have also appropriated state and private land to build large villa-style homes on city outskirts. In Almaty, for example, I lived with a family in an elite gated community at the city's southern edge, where it starts to climb to the foothills of the Tien Shan Mountains. Residents here enjoy cooler temperatures and dramatically cleaner air than in the city center. In addition to the expense of owning a home in this area, which is off-limits to the vast majority, one must also own a car. There is no bus service. And even then, my hosts explained to me, it had long been necessary to own an SUV with off-road capacity in order to access these homes. For many years, the major access street, Baganashyl (off Al'-Farabi), was not paved. However, this changed when President Nazarbayev started frequenting the tennis

10-11 A new apartment complex being constructed net to older, low-rise housing in Nur-Sultan, 2011. Photograph by Natalie Koch.

courts off Baganashyl, at which point his complaints led to its immediate paving. This small but representative example shows that urban planning and infrastructure priorities in Central Asia are often set by a handful of political elites, working to actualize their desire for modern conveniences and beautiful urban landscapes unblighted by the signs of inequality upon which their own privilege depends.

Seeing Urban Life

In Central Asia's more affluent cities, such as those in Kazakhstan and other countries' capitals, urban life has been increasingly oriented toward consumerism, made possible by the newly capitalist orientations of the states' post-Soviet trajectories. But just because the governments have chosen to liberalize their economies and plan their cities around new market ideals so as to project an image of their countries as "modern" or at least "modernizing," this does not mean that people automatically absorb these values. Among the younger generations and urbanites more generally, we do see an increasing valorization of consumerism and the strengthening of a new moral economy that naturalizes the inequalities brought by Central Asia's transition to market capitalism.

Operating through the language of "modernity," urban planners and residents aspire to domesticate the many pleasures and comforts they associate with urbanism in the world's richest urban centers—with models ranging from more established Western cities to the iconic images of high-rise living and consumerist paradises in contemporary Dubai. As people of the region come to travel more and see the diverse array of urban forms that are open to them, many are seduced by the glimmering images of capitalist urban development. Increasingly marking the older Soviet landscapes as outdated has meant distancing "modern" urban life from that Soviet past and its infrastructures. For any individual, this can take on completely different forms ranging from simply owning a car, on one hand, to shopping in a new Turkish grocery store or supporting the government's decision to remove a Lenin statue.

Not all citizens have been so eager to accept this new moral economy, of course. But more than their rural compatriots, city dwellers have been able to access the benefits of the transition. Although socioeconomic inequalities are part and parcel of any city in the region, the stark contrast between rural and urban life means that, for many, simply living in a city is a marker of status and indeed "modernity." From this perspective, the geography of urban life in Central Asia cannot be understood as the mere product of "top-down" planning from nondemocratic state-based elites. Rather, the built form of the region's cities and the infinite number of interactions and possibilities they channel involve an oscillation between top-down and bottom-up dynamics, between identity narratives about what is "modern" or "backward," and between political understandings of the Soviet past and the post-Soviet present and future.

In crafting their everyday lives in Central Asia's cities, ordinary citizens are always navigating between their own material desires and the material conditions with which they are working. These desires and conditions are often shaped by elite-dominated processes, like monumental urban planning or the demolition of "outdated" city buildings. But the quotidian practices and desires of ordinary citizens always have the power to overflow elite intentions—potentially laying the ground for more substantial change in how these cities are built and inhabited. Sometimes this may look like street protests against government corruption, other times it may look like the simple desire to keep one's shoes clean and demanding a proper sidewalk to one's home.

11

Migratory Life

Madeleine Reeves

For millions of men and women across Central Asia, seasonal or long-term migration abroad in search of work has become part of everyday life. This migration has transformed the demographic profile of towns and villages in Central Asia, just as it has shaped the hopes and fortunes of millions of families who send sons or daughters to work for months and often several years at a time, "in town" (*shaarda*). In Kyrgyzstan, the focus of this chapter, migration has fueled a remittance-driven building boom in the two largest cities, Bishkek and Osh. It has led to innovations in building styles in villages and small towns, as returned migrant workers innovate with methods of construction learned in Russia. Thirty years after the collapse of the Soviet Union and a sharp decline in the size of the country's Russian-speaking population, migration has also led to renewed desires among parents in rural Kyrgyzstan for their children to learn Russian so they will be able to seek seasonal work in the former Soviet center.

It is not just the countries of out-migration that have been shaped by these shifts. In downtown Moscow and St. Petersburg, home to hundreds of thousands of migrant workers from Central Asia, you can find upscale restaurants and back-alley cafes selling Uzbek *plov* (fried meat and rice) and *shashlik* (kebabs) to match any that you might find in Khujand or Bukhara. You can find "Kyrgyz discos" with stars entertaining dancers with Bishkek rap music that switches between Kyrgyz, Russian, and English beats. You can see advertisements in Uzbek announcing cheap transnational calling cards. You can find "Tajik" prayer-rooms and "Kyrgyz" dormitories. And if you look carefully in sites of arrival, such as Moscow's Kazan' railway station, you can see hawkers looking out for newly arrived migrants from Central Asia, offering affordable accommodation and informal leads to obtain the work permits and residence registrations needed for a successful season's labor in Russia.

As in many other parts of the world where significant sectors of the labor market have become dominated by cheap, expendable, and socially visible migrant labor, this migration is raced, classed, and gendered, shot through with histories of empire, of asymmetrical dependencies within the USSR, and more recently, of radically unequal insertion into the global economy. In contemporary Moscow you can find middle-class Muscovites in elite neighborhoods debating the qualities of Filipino and Kyrgyz maids. You can find small ads for temporary housing specifying that only those of "Slavic appearance" (Russian: *slavianskaia vneshnost'*) need apply. You can overhear casual conversation in which "hiring a Tajik" (Russian: *naniat' Tadzhika*) has become a pejorative euphemism for temporary labor hired by word of mouth and paid off the books. And you can find graffiti sprayed on the walls of apartment blocks decrying as "foreign agents" the legal advice clinics that have been founded in apartment basements to defend migrants' rights.

Migrant life is navigated in this environment of administrative vulnerability, banal racism, and existential uncertainty, in which social status and differential capacity for physically demanding work get read onto and from the body. Many migrant workers are employed in conditions in which their labor is undocumented and untaxed, and/or their living accommodation unregistered. They may be working with borrowed documents and with or without a written contract. In some cases, the subcontracting of labor means it is unclear whether one is "documented" or not, "legal" or not, legible to state authorities or not. These are powerful—and for some migrant workers, determining—realities of migrant life. "Who, *who* would work here if not out of necessity?" Diana, one of my co-tenants in a Kyrgyz migrant apartment asked rhetorically in 2010 after a twelve-hour night shift in a confectionary factory, nursing her feet after hours spent packing cakes in a giant walk-in fridge. By the end of her shift, she and her fellow employees were so tired they would take turns lying under the metal work tables, wrapped in coats even when it was 25 degrees Celsius (77 Fahrenheit) outside. "It's just like in your country, where the migrants do the jobs no-one else wants," Diana commented, probing me on whether in England it was really true that it was Russians who ended up with the "shitty jobs the English didn't want."

"Our Others"

The experience of labor migrants from Central Asia, as I was often reminded by my informants, had much in common with other trajectories of seasonal work: from Mexico to the United States, from North Africa to Spain, from Bangladesh to Dubai—a destination that some of my interlocutors looked to hopefully as offering a potentially more lucrative avenue for those fluent in English and with money to invest in a long-haul flight. But although migration trajectories parallel those of other sites that are marginalized within global hierarchies of wealth accumulation, histories of empire and of Soviet membership also make for ambivalent attachments and senses of belonging. To most Russians old enough to remember the Soviet Union, Central Asia is perceived as part of the "near abroad," and Central Asian migrant workers are seen as very different kinds of others—"*our* others" (*svoi chuzie*)—when compared with migrant workers from Vietnam, China, or the Philippines. In contemporary Moscow, alongside explicit articulations of "essential" difference and calls by politicians to introduce a visa regime with the states of Central Asia, you can also find migrants and their employers invoking the Soviet "friendship of peoples" (*druzhba narodov*) and perhaps even enjoying a birthday party together. You can find elderly women in rural Uzbekistan praying for the health of President Putin because he "keeps our family alive." And you can find young men across Central Asia who stick Russian flags to their car dashboards and passionately support Spartak Moskva as "our" (*nasha*) football team. This is the complexity of migratory life between Central Asia and urban Russia: a life characterized simultaneously by othering and disdain, closeness and connection, the situated expansion and contraction of the circle of *svoi*, one's own.

In this chapter I proceed from a recognition that the challenge of understanding migrant life lies in attending to the complexity of this particular social and historical formation, by exploring the meanings of migration for those who navigate this historically constituted, transnational social field. Taking "migratory life" as my core empirical focus, I foreground migration as *part of life*, as embedded in *ways of life*, and as a means of realizing a fully *meaningful and moral life*. What is it, I ask, that migration enables but which working closer to home does not? What is it about the kind of labor that is undertaken in Russia—and the kinds of accumulation it enables—that accords it this value for migrant workers, even as it is often acknowledged to be physically draining, socially demanding, and of uncertain economic benefit?

Drawing on ethnographic research between 2009 and 2015 in Kyrgyzstan and Moscow and situating my analysis in conversation with literature on labor and personhood in contemporary Central Asia, I argue that, although migration is often borne of acute economic necessity or even desperation, economic rationality alone does not exhaust the meanings of migration for those on the move. "Economics" in the abstract does not explain why some countries rather than others and some cities rather than others become the destinations of choice for young people from particular areas. A presumption of economic rationality likewise does little to illuminate how this seemingly most "economic" decision is shot through with a host of other concerns and is embedded within practices of making, acting upon, or reasoning about, having a meaningful life—practices to identify an auspicious time for departure, for instance, or to decide which one of three brothers should leave and which should stay to look after the land.

Perhaps more important, this presumption of economic rationality tells us little about how individual migrants reflect upon and reason about what makes for "good" work in Russia, work that is at once economically efficacious, personally rewarding, and morally satisfying. Here I want to take as my ethnographic starting point a claim I heard repeatedly during my fieldwork: that in Russia you can *really work* (Kyrgyz: *Rossiiada chyn ele ishtese bolot*). I want to take seriously the ways that this work is locally valued, both as a means of enabling future projects to be realized and as a way of affirming one's identity as someone who can provide and nurture others, literally "through the sweat of one's brow" (Batken dialect: *peshina teri menen*). In rural Batken, I suggest, and perhaps especially in those regions marked by a strong tradition of mining and extractive industries, work in Russia allows for the articulation of a distinctive and gendered relationship between physically demanding labor, economic compensation, and moral reward: one that resonates with a much older, socialist ethic of the value of physical labor. This is despite the obvious irony that much of the work in which migrants are engaged in Russia—contingent, unregulated, without the protections of contract, and without compensation in case of injury and death—is the very opposite of the institutionally protected, socially recognized, highly regulated state-oriented labor that characterized the Soviet system.

To illustrate this argument, in this chapter I pan in and out between close ethnographic detail and broader comparative analysis, foregrounding the migration experience of a single couple from Batken town, whom I call Kairat and Albina. I focus on this couple, not to suggest that they are "representative" of some broader sample but, rather, to give a detailed insight into the way in which practical strategies for getting by and reasoning about what constitutes meaningful honest work are woven together. I also deliberately foreground a "successful" couple: one whose persistence and strategizing have allowed them to regularize their status and become "big tenants" within the community. I do so to counter the tendency in narratives of labor migration in Russia to focus excessively on either the migrant as a law-evading, risky subject (the migrant worker as "illegal alien" or *nelegal* in Russian officialese) or the migrant as a victim of exploitation and abuse. In so doing, I seek to contribute to a literature that has foregrounded the agency and ethical reasoning of migrant workers as they navigate a complex social and legal terrain. I proceed by situating these reflections on labor, value, and migrant agency in theoretical terms.

The Value of Work

It is often noted in literature on formerly socialist societies that state socialism accorded distinctive moral valence to labor undertaken for the collective good. In a worker state, labor was not simply a means to an end, the vehicle for achieving individual goals. It was intrinsic to the definition of moral personhood and the basis upon which entitlements were accorded. In her study of the socialist "dreamworld," Susan Buck-Morss shows how Soviet ideology, shaped by Marx's labor theory of value, conceived of industrialization as both a transformative and a redemptive process. In a richly empirical study of how this dreamworld was realized in the vast mining complex of Magnitigorsk, Stephen Kotkin shows how wage labor became the means through which one could access a range of other benefits, from housing to child care to pension payments. It also meant that no one had the right not to work: to work simply was the mark of a "normal," ethical life.

In rural Central Asia, heavy industry was less extensive than in other parts of the Soviet Union, and by the time of its economic dismantling during perestroika, individual garden plots provided a critical supplement to formal wage labor. But even stockbreeding and cotton production was, formally at least, organized along "industrial" lines. Modernization was seen to hinge not simply upon the import of industrial technologies and the creation of "villages of urban type" but upon turning peasants and pastoral nomads into wage earners. As Jeanne Féaux de la Croix has noted in a subtle analysis of the moral meanings of work in rural Kyrgyzstan, wage labor undertaken for the state was at once a source of political membership and an act of personal transformation. It defined not just one's relationship with "the state" but with friends, neighbors, and classmates. As important, the memory of the Soviet system of provision was critical in shaping expectations about the relationship between the state, labor, and moral personhood—even for that growing proportion of the population who have no living memory of the Soviet past.

For my informants in rural Kyrgyzstan, like Féaux de la Croix's informants who thought of themselves as "not working" even as they looked after their flocks for fifteen-hour days to keep their family fed and clothed, paid wage labor was properly understood to be something that the state should provide: this was part of the basic social contract between a state and its citizenry. In a mining region of northeastern Estonia, Eeva Kesküla similarly found that, rather than being seen as "polluting" or dangerous, wages earned from mining were seen as honorable earnings that were used to feed the family. By the same token, my informants in rural Batken expected the state properly to provide wages and pensions at a rate high enough to keep body and soul together. An inadequate pension—particularly a small pension for past industrial labor that was recognized to have been particularly demanding, unpleasant, or full of risk—was not just an inconvenience. It was experienced as an insult: a retrospective devaluing of one's sacrifice for the collective good and a betrayal that a past promised benefit had failed to be realized.

This recognition of wage labor as a central pillar of the late Soviet social contract has significant implications today. Although in the mid-2010s Batken appears as an archetypically "rural" region, in which the vast majority of people make their livings from the land and the raising of livestock, for most of the last century the countryside was entwined in dense networks of

MADELEINE REEVES

interdependence with a series of small, "international" mining towns and so-called villages of urban type. Several of these towns and villages were associated with a particular commodity: mercury in Khaidarkan, antimony in Kadamjai, natural gas in the Bürgündü massif, and coal in Sülüktü and Kyzyl-Kiya. In Kyzyl-Kiya today, at the eastern end of Batken Oblast, the town newspaper is still called *Za Ugol'* (For Coal), and mining still shapes the identity of the town, even as production rates have declined precipitously since the collapse of the Soviet Union. In the villages of Ak-Sai and Ak-Tatyr, where I conducted research in Batken, many families had also lived for and from coal. Older residents to these so-called planned villages had relocated in the 1970s and 1980s from Shorab, a once-thriving mining set-tlement—recently downgraded from town to village because of the scale of out-migration—that had previously enjoyed special provisioning (so-called Moscow provisioning or *moskovskoe obespechenie*) and been celebrated as having the deepest mineshaft in Tajikistan. Many of my informants recalled traveling to Shorab as children, to visit the shops full of goods that were unavailable anywhere else in the area, to walk through the delicatessen, to attend the park and the house of culture.

Batken today, for all its peripherality, is a setting where life is remem-bered as having been intrinsically linked—through kinship, transport net-works, and trade—with an industrial Soviet modernity, with wage labor and the variety of benefits (*nadbavki*) that came from working underground in heavy industry. It is significant in this context that the imperative to migrate in contemporary Batken was often framed less in terms of individual or family need ("our family needs more money") or even collective pressure ("everyone around here is leaving for Russia") than in terms of a response to a categorical state failure to provide opportunities for work ("there is no work here now"). My innocent question as to why a family member had chosen to migrate was often followed by an impassioned commentary on the failure of the state to provide adequately paid work. Likewise, the apprecia-tion—indeed, sometimes the warm affection—ascribed to the leadership of Russia by my informants in Batken frequently took the form of an acknowl-edgment that Russia "*even* provided us [non-citizens] with work"—often with a comparative remark that this was more than the Kyrgyzstan state had succeeded in doing.

This context, I suggest, gives particular poignancy to the fact of going abroad to find "good, honest work." Writing of rural Poland, another scene of considerable contemporary out-migration, Frances Pine notes that migra-tion is an ambivalent locus of collective hope since it contradicts an older socialist ethic that valued the modernizing potential of labor undertaken "in its proper place—in the socialist nation state." In contemporary Poland, Pine argues, migration undermines the value of work in a double sense: first, because migrants often work in conditions and socioeconomic contexts that are undervalued, both in the host country and at home, and second, because labor migration replaces an ethic in which labor is intrinsically valued with a means-ends calculus where labor is only valued to the extent that it brings material reward, taking the moral or social value out of work.

In the case of rural Batken, I suggest, the picture is more ambiguous. For although the reasons for and the results of labor migration can certainly become objects of moral commentary (especially as migration impacts upon family life, gendered expectations of decorum and respect, or the capacity to act as a fully generous, moral being), I never encountered the attitude that migration took the moral value out of work. Indeed, if anything, it was the opposite. In Batken, labor was felt to put the moral value into migration. It was precisely by showing that one could tolerate a fall in status or a drop in prestige, that one could endure long working hours and unsociable shifts, that one could tolerate work that "Europeans" would find impossible, that one could ignore the normalized racism of a boss who called one "stumps" (Russian: *churki*) or "black" (Russian: *chernyi*) that one demonstrated what it was to be both *yimanduu* (moral) and *küchtüü* (strong). Above all, it was by generating "honest, earned money" for the benefit of one's parents or children through physically or emotionally demanding work that one demonstrated what it was to be a responsible, agentive, adult member of one's family and community. I illustrate this argument by introducing Kairat and Albina in more detail.

Introducing Kairat and Albina

Kairat and Albina were in their mid-thirties, and had been working in Moscow for five years by the time I came to meet them in 2010. Unusually for migrant couples from Kyrgyzstan, among whom the husband typically travels to Russia before "inviting" his wife, Albina had been the first of the two to leave for Moscow, living initially with her husband's relatives, before Kairat followed with their four-year-old daughter. As for many migrant couples, the immediate factor precipitating their departure was the need to pay off debts. Kairat's brother had died in a car accident, leaving his family with large and unplanned expenses. Although both Kairat and Albina worked in Batken in professional jobs (she in the hospital as a medical doctor, and he in the regional branch of the tax office), their state salaries would be insufficient to meet the significant costs of a fitting funeral, in which dozens, sometimes hundreds, of visitors would need to be fed as they paid their respects. Indeed, as they and other state employees often pointed out, one of the frustrations of a civil service (*budzhetnyi*) job in Kyrgyzstan was that the salary was laughably low—low enough to normalize and render socially unremarkable the taking of informal payments and low enough to undermine the care or commitment with which one undertook one's work. In 2005, with debts mounting and a young family to care for, the couple joined several of their respective classmates who had already left "for town." The costs of the funeral were simply the immediate precipitating factor in this sequence of events; migration among their classmates was already "in the air." Albina left shortly after the funeral; Kairat a month later.

Both husband and wife experienced a dramatic drop in status upon their arrival in Moscow. Albina initially found work as a live-in maid for a wealthy Jewish family; Kairat as a cleaner for the French car firm Citroen, taking over a job that had previously been held by his brother. In Albina's case, the live-in arrangement was convenient while she sought to regularize her status: during the months she worked as a housemaid, she barely needed to leave her employer's apartment, and she didn't need a work permit. "That's why a lot of Kyrgyz look to work as housemaids when they first get here. You don't need a permit. But the pay is low, and you can't go outside." Albina worked this way for six months before finding an opportunity through acquaintances to join a private medical clinic. She quickly became established as a well-regarded and competent clinician.

For Kairat, the drop in status was more galling. Sitting with Albina shortly after she returned from work for the day, one May evening in 2010, Kairat recalled those early months with emotion: "I really struggled to start with. In Batken I went about like a normal person [*ya normal'no khodil tam*], I worked with tenders, I was in the tax [inspectorate]. And the first day [in Citroen] they give me a mop. . . . The first day I had to wear the special clothes they give you, I had tears in my eyes, as though everyone there was looking at me. I vowed that I wouldn't stay there longer than a week." Kairat did remain, however, determined to pay off the debts he had accumulated for his brother's funeral, and to show that he could stick it out. After three months he was fired along with several other colleagues in an impromptu round of restructuring. He was then formally reinstated, first working in the Citroen showroom warehouse and then with responsibility for mounting demonstration kits. After his boss moved from Citroen to Nike, Kairat moved too—without, he stressed, having any necessary papers at that time. "All of it was through acquaintances [Russian: *cherez znakomykh*]! They took me without a *propiska* [a residence permit], without anything!"

Kairat recounted this trajectory with some pride. He was one of the few workers that his boss took with him as he moved from Citroen to Nike. Kairat was also the last but one to be made redundant when the Nike warehouse in which he was working was relocated. A month and a half later he found a job, which he still held at the time I came to know him, working in the store-room of a central Moscow shoe store. He found this position, too, through an acquaintance: a former workmate of his (*naparnik*) from Batken whom Kairat referred to as his *zemliak* or fellow countryman, who recommended Kairat for his job upon his own return to Kyrgyzstan. Recalling these shifts in employment, Kairat stressed the importance both of "connections" and of proving oneself to be trustworthy. "If you are a good worker, people will notice you. If you have a good director and he knows you, you even don't need to worry [about being documented]. Seriously, they took me with no work permit, no [Russian] citizenship. Literally you can get by without any documents [*voobsche dokument ne nado*] if they trust you, they'll leave you the keys, the money, everything. The most important thing is to gain their trust."

Money and More

Albina, too, had been in almost permanent employment since her first arrival in Moscow. As a qualified doctor and a fluent Russian speaker, she was quickly able to establish herself as a gynecologist and obstetrician in a private medical clinic. By the time we first met she had developed a large pool of private patients who often passed on her details through word of mouth. As I became a temporary tenant in the apartment they rented, our regular evening conversations were frequently interrupted by calls to her mobile phone from Kyrgyz women approaching her for medical consultations in Kyrgyz.

For Kairat and Albina, the opportunity to earn incomparably better salaries than in Kyrgyzstan was their primary motivation in seeking and retaining work in Russia. When I first met them in 2010 they were in the process of building a house in Batken town, so they could live separately from Kairat's parents. By 2014, four successful seasons later, they were in the midst of decorating a recently purchased "modular" apartment in a newly built apartment block in the Kyrgyzstan capital, Bishkek. In a good month in 2010, if they were both earning a steady salary, they could jointly earn as much as forty thousand rubles—around thirteen hundred dollars at the time. Their relatively secure position by that time, in possession of Russian passports and renting a Moscow apartment that they could sublet to friends and relatives, also positioned them well to become so-called big tenants— that is, migrant workers who acted as facilitators and brokers in the migrant community by mediating access to work, helping with obtaining documents, and acting as a hub for the lending and borrowing of documents. As Kairat joked, this ability to "work the system"—whereby multiple people might be working multiple jobs using the same borrowed document—was contingent upon the inability of Muscovites to distinguish the variety of facial features and skin tones that characterize the Kyrgyz-identifying population. "To Russians we all look alike!" he commented sarcastically. "To them we are all identically black [Russian: *odno i to zhe chernyi*]."

The capacity to earn much more than they could in Batken was clearly an important—indeed primary—reason for looking for work in Russia. "We are slowly realizing our dreams, bit by bit," Kairat commented on another occasion. Every job was discussed, first and foremost, in terms of what one could earn from it, and whether it provided opportunities for informal "side-earnings" (*levye deng'i*). A job might compensate for being unprestigious if it had lucrative benefits—as, for instance, was the case if one worked as a caretaker (*dvornik*) in a residential apartment block, which provided opportunities for regular earnings from carrying bags, transporting furniture, or storing packages. A position was particularly valued if it came with access to a basement or a storage space. Many such *dvorniki*, for instance, turned basements into fully functioning mini-dormitories, complete with rigged up showers and pirated internet access, from which they could derive a rent that significantly exceeded their formal earnings. Such positions were typically passed on "hand-to-hand" (*po ruku*) to a friend or a relative and were even "sold" from an existing worker to a prospective future holder of the position.

In this respect, the "means-ends" rationality discussed by Pine for Polish migrants was true in the case of my Kyrgyz interlocutors too. But in contrast to Pine's findings, such reasoning did not exhaust the meanings or value of work in Russia for my interlocutors. During my conversations with Kairat and Albina, for instance, it was precisely the more-than-economic value that each of them attached to their labor in Russia that kept resurfacing in the course of other topics. For Albina, that value was in having patients who, as she put it, "cared for their health," who listened to the prescriptions she gave them and followed her instructions:

> In Russia [female patients] will definitely come for a check-up once a year just as a prophylactic. And in Kyrgyzstan, people always leave things until the last minute, when they have already turned into problems. They don't even want to pay for an ultrasound. They'll say, "Can I just take this one medicine, as I can't afford the rest." This is really the case in Batken. I'll work there all the same in the future, but it scares me, because I have already got used to being here. Here I can take all the analyses I need. I can send women to get other diagnoses if I need to.

The value that Albina derived from her work came from the respect and recognition afforded by her patients as well as from the sense that there was a system (in which her own clinic was inserted) that was reliable and effective. One of the recurrent complaints I heard from medical personnel in Batken was this lack of *systemnost'* (systematicality), the sense that medical officers could make decisions based on reliable diagnostics.

For Kairat, who was still working in employment that he felt under-valued his knowledge and former status, the value lay somewhere slightly different: in the capacity to work honestly, without the need to "give or take" (bribes), and to be able to become a *master*—a term usually reserved for a skilled specialist—in whatever activity to which he put his hand. Later in the conversation from which I quoted earlier, Kairat returned to the question of work, after a long detour discussing the house that they were building in Batken. Work in Russia was not, he insisted, just about the means-ends rationality of earning good money. Instead, it was the sense that one earned *properly*, through stretching oneself to one's limit, physically and psychologically. Switching between Kyrgyz and Russian, Kairat (with frequently indignant interjections here from Albina), elaborated:

Kairat: Really, it's about being able to work with a clean spirit [*chisto ot dushi*], through the sweat of one's brow [*peshina teri menen*], with a good con-science [*na sovest'*], you know? It's like . . . honest, earned money. We really *work*. And sometimes . . . look, in one day, she [Albina] might see five patients, just five!

Albina:	Well, it varies. . . .
Kairat:	OK, well, at a maximum, you've never had more than twenty, right?
Albina:	No, twenty would be too many.
Kairat:	Let's say fifteen. And she's tired from that. And, in a day, I might serve up to one thousand [pairs of shoes]! On average, five hundred women come in during the day, and at a minimum they are going to try on two pairs of shoes. There are some who just come in to pass the time, they've got nothing better to do. They're bored, so they come in. All the more so as we are on [a major tourist street]. So, that's one thousand pairs that I have to find and get for them. There's no computer there, it's an old building, and I'm in the basement for twelve hours at a stretch, and those one thousand pairs of shoes—there might be one over there and the other over there. They try them on. They don't like them—it goes back into the store, so I'm putting one thousand pairs back too. And some people just take the mickey [*izdivayutsia*]. They come in and they order fifteen pairs, they've just got nothing better to do. Fifteen, twenty pairs. I've already got an ulcer from it!

I asked whether Kairat found a way to relax from the pressure of his work. The ensuing, playful exchange between Kairat and Albina gives a good sense of how one's ability to be "strong" comes to be morally valued in such settings:

Kairat:	Of course! I'm two days at work, two days at home. And she's [Albina] got a six-day week. When I'm on my day off I'll call my friends, acquaintances. She tells me off! We meet up, drink beer, put the world to rights! That lightens things a bit. Because otherwise, by the second day, by the afternoon, your nerves can't hold out.
Albina:	You see, men really are the weaker sex [*muzhchiny-slabyi pol*]! That's already 100 percent [evident].
Kairat:	Ha! By the tenth patient, if she's doing an ultrasound, her eyes are already closing. [Kairat mimics, teasingly.] She just said, she's got maximum fifteen patients in a day. And I've got five hundred [clients]. There's a difference, right?! . . . There are also these numbers [to get the right pair of shoes]: sixteen digits, they read them to you through the walkie-talkie: "Kairat, take an order!" They tell you the name of the firm. [Imitating, at great speed] "Germany. Tamaris. 1-slash-1-22, 13, 14, 582-slash-24. Color: pink. Size: 37." You've got to remember all that shit. And as you go, looking for it, you already find that you've forgotten the numbers. And if you ask them to repeat it a second time, they get annoyed. They're also in a hurry. And if you ask a third time, they'll complain to the supervisor.
Madeleine:	It sounds stressful.
Kairat:	Stress! She knows! When I first started, I was in a real state. My heart was like this, my beard [indicates grey hairs]. . . . I was running around like crazy. "Kairat, take an order!" I would stand there like this! You forget how hard it was at the start. You haven't got time to write the order down.

Albina: They made fun of him too. They'd read out the number really fast on purpose; to catch him out.

Kairat: But I got used to it. I started to work [*ishtep kettim*].

Albina: He started to work. Now he's figured the whole thing out.

Kairat: Now I have the walkie-talkie on one ear and my mobile phone on the other, like this! [Kairat demonstrates, swaggering.] But still, I need to change work, I've got an ulcer, my hair is turning grey!

Albina: We're getting old!

Several things are notable about this exchange. Kairat recognizes that the labor in which he is employed is demanding and structurally precarious. He was acutely conscious that he was paid less for the same work than someone who was of Russian ethnicity and who, unlike him, was thus not seen as a "migrant." He was also aware that his work was making him stressed and giving him an ulcer. In this sense his account has much in common with critical accounts of post-Fordist labor that have drawn attention to the demeaning and destructive aspects of "just-in-time" or "flexible" capitalism.

But there was also something else going on here, signaled by the intriguing comment, echoed by Albina, that after some time he "started to work" (Kyrgyz: *ishtep kettim*). Kairat is using here one of the two Kyrgyz terms for work (the other being *jumush*). Depending on context, *ishtep kettim* can mean, quite neutrally, that one has "started to work"; but *ish* also has a much wider spectrum of meanings (roughly equivalent to the Russian *delo*), which can mean business, or affairs, or ways of getting along. The assertion, *ishtep kettim* thus signals something more than just "starting to work"—especially since Kairat had already been working for the shoe store for some time by that stage. It suggests something more akin to "I started making it" or "I figured things out": "working," here, in its encompassing sense of finding a way in which to make the situation of his hurried demanding labor work for him. This allowed him to tolerate the initial teasing and testing by the female employees on the shop floor who dictated the orders to him—the result, he noted at another time, of being seen to speak Russian "with an accent." It also allowed him to see in his ability to handle these demands a manifestation of his gendered capacity for hard work—a claim playfully punctured by his wife's reminder that, unlike her, he only worked for two days before having a "weekend." Within a few months he had come not just to survive the frenetic pace of this shoe store basement on a busy shopping street but to thrive on the adrenaline and the pressure: his ability to juggle the job and the demands of acting as a node—a "fixer" or broker within the migrant economy—captured by his simultaneous handling of the mobile phone on one ear and the walkie-talkie on the other.

Equally significant is the comment Kairat made to preface this whole account: that the satisfaction of work in Russia comes from being able to work with a clean spirit and a clean conscience, through the "sweat of one's brow." Kairat may be alluding here to the ability to earn money without having to resort to the kind of informal payments or sidekicks that are routinized within the tax inspectorate in Kyrgyzstan. But his comment also suggests that it is as much the physically demanding nature of the work itself—the fact that it keeps you on your toes, keeps you having to remember a string of numbers—that is part of the satisfaction. Like many of my interlocutors, Kairat insisted that the work that he now managed to do, literally with one hand, would be impossible for most Russians. It would exhaust them, it would wear them down, they would not stick it out—and certainly not for a measly pay of eighteen thousand rubles per month (about six hundred dollars at the time of our conversation). Indeed, on another occasion he remarked how he had commented in exasperation to a prospective employer during an interview: "Do you want a hardworking Kyrgyz or a heavy-drinking Muscovite?"

This gets me to the final aspect of their working lives in Moscow that I wish to consider here. Kairat and Albina were both "making it work" in an environment in which racism toward visible minorities from Central Asia and the Caucasus was both widespread and routine. Indeed, in one of the medical clinics where she worked Albina was told she should change the name on her name badge, from a Kyrgyz to a Russian-sounding name, and that she should present herself as ethnically Korean (using skin-whitening cream and heavy makeup accordingly), so as "not to deter the clients." At the time, the couple were in the process of formally changing the way that their daughter's surname was registered on her passport (giving her the conventional Russian ending "–ova" instead of the Kyrgyz traditional format, which began with the father's name) so as to make it more easily comprehensible to her teachers and classmates in the school where she was registered.

This racism persisted despite the fact that, formally at least, they enjoyed the same employment rights as Russian citizens. Like many well-established migrants from Kyrgyzstan who, at the time of my research, were able to benefit from a so-called simplified procedure for obtaining Russian citizenship, Kairat and Albina had obtained Russian passports the preceding year. This was a pragmatic move for them in the short term rather than a gesture of intentions toward remaining permanently in Moscow: with a Russian passport, you enjoyed better labor protections, were able to access a wider range of employment, and were not subject to humiliating and potentially costly checks by the federal migration authorities. Ultimately, a Russian passport protected the bearer from deportation: on a vernacular scale of degrees of "documentedness," this was the most secure. With a Russian passport, I was told, one could walk with one's head high in the street rather than constantly keeping an eye out for the police. This was a case of "strategic citizenship," but a strategy of the marginalized rather than that of a globe-hopping elite. I often found my interlocutors debating the merits and demerits of owning a Russian passport. Obtaining one entailed a significant outlay of time and money, and on more than one occasion I saw a husband "present" his wife with a Russian passport as a birthday gift. Moreover, while the "simplified procedure" theoretically eased the process for Kyrgyzstani migrant workers, in practice amassing the package of documents that was needed to demonstrate one's permanent residence (*vid na zhitel'stvo*) in Russia required good contacts and social savvy.

In many cases, moreover, although possession of a passport provided access to an assortment of jobs specifying only Russian citizens would be eligible, the Russian passport in itself did not guarantee equality of pay or conditions. As the following exchange between Kairat and Albina demonstrates, irrespective of citizenship, the perception was nonetheless that it was excessive migrant demand for jobs that was deflating wages:

Kairat: Now in pretty much any organization, where they are hiring cheap laborers, you'll find Kyrgyz working there. It's keeping the prices low. I'm also doing that kind of work! Have you heard of [the name of a shoe store]? They've got fifty or fifty-five shops just in Moscow. It's the biggest [shoe store in the city]. And we receive pennies [*kopeiki*], pennies.

Madeleine: Even if you have [Russian] citizenship?

Kairat: It doesn't make a difference! Anyway, [ethnic] Russians [*russkie*] aren't going to work there.

Albina: It's difficult work, the pay is low, the work is heavy. And if a Russian were to work there, a Muscovite, even *any* Russian, they would ask for a minimum from thirty to thirty-five thousand [rubles], and we work for eighteen thousand.

Madeleine: But, the fact that you've received a [Russian] passport . . . doesn't that mean that you should have equal rights and pay, irrespective of nationality [*natsional'nost'*]? Shouldn't it make a difference?

Albina: Slavic appearance! [*slavianskaia vneshnost'*!]

Kairat [correcting Albina]: No. In this work that we're doing, Russians won't work there! They just won't come. Look, I'll tell you. If you think, there are fifty shops. In forty of those, it's Kyrgyz. Our people are working there. Kyrgyz. But for [the employer] it's more profitable to pay us eighteen thousand than to pay their own Russians thirty thousand or thirty-five thousand. And here too, if it's good [better paid] work, it doesn't matter if I have Russian citizenship or not. I might be a Muscovite, but all the same I'm "Kyrgyz by nationality" [*Kyrgyz po natsional'nosti*] and they're not going to take me.

Albina: Spot on!

Madeleine: Even with a Russian passport?

Kairat: Even if I've got a registration for the *Kremlin*!

This exchange reveals an illuminating moment of reflection by Kairat and Albina about the reasons why Kyrgyz people would be paid less than Russians for the same kind of work. Albina initially presented an argument in terms of categorical discrimination: *Slavianskaia vneshnost'*—literally, "Slavic appearance." The form of her interjection is striking here: the term, which has gained currency in job adverts and accommodation announcements, obviated the need for further explanation: looking Slavic, she suggested, was its own justification for better pay. Yet Kairat rejected this explanation, or at least he suggested that there was a political economy to this de facto stratification of the labor market: the kind of work in which he was engaged was the kind of work that Russians simply would not take. Conversely, the world of better-paid employment that he would like to access was closed to him. Even having a registration in the Kremlin—that is, in the center of political power and the heart of claims to political membership—would be insufficient to trump the categorical discrimination that hinged on ethno-national difference.

Migratory Life beyond Accommodation and Resistance

These comments highlight the powerful structural constraints within which Kyrgyz migrant workers negotiate the Russian labor market. As a growing literature has highlighted, this is an environment in which ethnically marked discrimination is routinized, within the labor market and in access to housing. Indeed Russian sociologist Nikolay Zakharov has suggested that, in the last twenty years, racialization has come to constitute one of Russia's most pressing social problems. As in other global arenas, moreover, racialized discrimination is legitimated through discourses and practices that identify the "illegal immigrant" as a source of danger and of threat. These were constraints that my informants were acutely aware of and about which they had developed sophisticated and often impassioned critiques.

What I have sought to demonstrate in this chapter, however, is the need to look beyond these structural factors in understanding the complexity of migratory life. This is so in a double sense. First, while migrant workers such as Kairat and Albina are certainly subject to racial logics (the kind that oblige Albina to present herself to her patients as "Olga Tsoi," a Russian of Korean heritage), they are not mere pawns of these structural forces. The couple navigate these racial hierarchies, mock them, challenge them, even subvert them, lending their passports to relatives in the knowledge that to Russians "we all look alike." They have also challenged these forces in more modest ways, by developing an expansive set of social relationships with neighbors and local policemen, which has enabled them to feel that Moscow—albeit temporarily—is their home. The most important thing in navigating migrant life, Albina insisted, was to win over your neighbors. On another occasion, as we prepared the food for an upcoming birthday party for one of their tenants, the couple explained:

> Albina: To begin with, ours hated us. [They would say] "Blacks! Again they've descended on us [*chernye! opiat' ponaekhali, koroche*]." But then gradually you make relations, they get used to you. Now we've got great relations. . . .
>
> Kairat: Now I drink with my neighbors: beer, vodka, cognac! Now I stay out

until midnight with them, they don't [even] let Muscovites in, but they let me in. [My neighbor's] wife makes me coffee; we listen to music.

Albina: And when our landlord comes we make *plov, manty.* To start with she said, "Oh, I only eat yoghurt at lunchtime," but we gave them some to take home. And then, the next time, they stayed and ate. In our building there are these four apartments. We cook together sometimes. The *babulya* [affectionate: old lady] comes out sometimes and says, "Why does your food also smell so oily?" And other times she says, "How tasty it smells!" You just can't predict.

What we see, in short, is a pride in their own ability to transform hostility or suspicion into respect and even friendship, through the sharing of greetings, of food and alcohol. In Kairat and Albina's case this capacity to make relations is facilitated—as they both readily recognize—by their outgoing personalities, their knowledge of Russian, and their recognition that sometimes a neighbor, like the unpredictable babulya, might just be in a bad mood.

This points, in turn, to the second way in which their experience complicates reductive readings of migrant life in Moscow. Kairat and Albina both readily acknowledge the long hours, physical hardships, and emotional demands of holding a life together in Moscow: as employees, as tenants, as de facto landlords to those to whom they sublet mattress space, as parents, and as children who are expected to send regular remittances home. In this respect, we might expect the couple to view their labor in purely instrumental terms as a means to an end; or indeed, to find, as Pine did, that migration "takes the moral value out of work." In the case of migrant labor between Batken and Moscow, I have suggested, it is rather the opposite. It is precisely in the capacity to earn "clean, honest money," to send it home, to be seen to be building and materializing a future for one's children, and to survive and thrive on life "in town" that one realizes one's moral agency: one's capacity to act on, and in the world.

12

Diaspora Life

Medina Aitieva

On a deceptively sunny spring afternoon Jamal, a thirty-three-year-old Kyrgyz migrant woman, met me at a bus stop near Yakutsk's Stolichnyi market, frequented mainly by Kyrgyzstani and Chinese vendors. Dressed in a fur-insulated coat with a warm scarf over her head, she appeared to have adjusted well to life in the coldest city on Earth. Sporting tight jeans and bulky boots, untouched by the omnipresent muddy puddles formed from melting permafrost, Jamal passed easily as a local. Out of her heavy plastic bag stuck a carton of juice and a loaf of bread for our dinner at her residence in the outskirts of Yakutsk. This remote Siberian port city of over three hundred thousand inhabitants on the western bank of Russia's Lena River can stun foreigners with its reliable public transport and provision of central heating to schools and offices, where winter temperatures average −35°C (−31°F).

A new "old PAZik" bus, the workhorse of Russian urban and rural transportation, arrived quickly, puffing exhaust into the heavily polluted air. We were lucky to find seats for the hour-long ride. "My first impression of Yakutsk was one of shock," Jamal lamented. "It is Russia, I thought, but why was it so underdeveloped?! There were no trees, no greenery. Nothing grows here, and everything is imported and so expensive . . . but humans apparently get used to anything!" In a bus full of bulky outerwear, smells of perfume and gasoline, and a cacophony of sounds, I looked around to locate, unsuccessfully, other migrants. I was reminded once again of what I heard so often from Kyrgyzstani migrants: "[In Yakutsk you] breathe easily, compared to Moscow, just like at home." In many ways it felt as if you blinked you could wake up back in Kyrgyzstan.

After a few quick exchanges in Kyrgyz at the bus stop, Jama (her preferred Russified nickname) insisted we switch to Russian. With common Turkic roots, the Yakut language was reminiscent of Kyrgyz, but noticeably different from Russian. Sudden breaks in conversation or code switching between languages were intentional when we were in the vicinity of other locals, trying not to stand out. There was a weird sense of comfort, confirmed to me by one Kyrgyz migrant's observation that because the "*Yalar* [physically] look like us," it was easier to blend in. The code word *Yalar* in Kyrgyz was used among the Kyrgyz in public to disguise references to Yakuts. The sense of security clashed with the desire to stay undetectable, almost invisible, to locals, captured in a saying I heard repeatedly: here you mind your own business, keep your head down, and stay "quieter than water, lower than grass." By 2012, four years of working and living in Russia's Republic of Sakha (also known as Yakutia during the Soviet days) had changed Jama: "I don't want to be known as Kyrgyz here. I want to wash my hair, dress well like a townie [*shaarlyk*] . . . and speak Russian." Some of her friends created nicknames—becoming Kolia, Olesia, easier on the ear, and less discernible. Adjustment to place encompasses a wide range of practices, some of which are new expressions of identity resulting from the migration process.

A muddy bus window presented urban contrasts—a new high-rise building standing beside a Soviet-era concrete bloc housing complex, both built on permafrost, visibly clashing styles in any post-Soviet space. Because of the continuous negative temperatures, the region's subsoil is permanently frozen, and thus buildings must be erected on stilts to prevent any warming and melting under them. Electricity lines, pipes, and other utilities run aboveground and become part of the urban landscape. One cannot avoid noticing the sinking appearance of the traditional wooden log houses, *ChBshki*, which survived urban modernization plans because of community preservation efforts. Walking long distances in winter months is fraught with the imminent likelihood of frostbite. One-third of the people in Sakha inhabit its capital, Yakutsk, where economic and educational opportunities continue to attract rural youth. For the largest sub-entity in the world, Sakha's population density is among the lowest in Russia. Such harsh living conditions, however, have not deterred foreign labor migrants, now comprising nearly 10–20 percent of the population in Yakutsk. During the Soviet industrialization period in 1970s, Yakutia's cities were built near ore-mining deposits of diamonds, gold, and coal by migrant labor, enticed into the region from the wider Soviet Union with the promise of higher "northern territory" pensions, which few aspired to even then.

During our ride Jama conveyed her irritation at receiving repeated single-ring calls on her phone, dubbed *maiak* (literally, a beacon light), signaling that she was expected to return a call. The muted vibrations were international calls from in-laws in a mountainous village in Kyrgyzstan. On her daily journeys on public transport, Jama tried to pass as a local and feared being discovered as a foreigner, so she refrained from answering her phone. To some, her constant precautions might seem unnecessary, but a deeper look into the everyday lives of migrants and immigrants—legal or "illegal"—reveals how their sense of fitting in is governed by Russia's ever fortifying migration regime.

Despite the formal visa-free open border regime between Russia and Kyrgyzstan, being documented in Russia is a complicated practice. Madeleine Reeves in her work demonstrates in great detail how impossible it is for Moscow migrants to remain entirely formal and argues how migrant futures are "always potentially revocable," which generates a sense of "cultivated subordination." Daily migrant lives are full of circumstances when someone with allegedly legally acquired documents might be revealed as "illegal" during public interventions by law enforcement officers. Russia's documentary regime—characterized by its weak rule of law, rampant corruption, inefficient institutions, and increasing mistrust expressed toward specific ethnic groups—normalizes xenophobia and *migrantophobia*. Russia, receiving the second-largest number of labor migrants in the world, is also regarded as a state with a large shadow economy, a weak civil society, and a poor record of human rights.

The legal mechanisms that regulate foreign workers' status in Russia are contradictory. The *propiska* (residence registration) system is an administrative restriction designed to manage migration flows from rural to urban areas. It requires that both citizens' and foreign workers' registrations on paper match their actual residence, which in practice is not diligently followed by many Russian internal migrants themselves. Yet, it is people of "non-Slavic appearance" and predominantly Central Asian migrants who are regularly stopped and searched on the streets, on construction sites, in markets and "ethnic" cafes, in small businesses, and in disco clubs, fined and detained, and often taken advantage of because of these vulnerabilities. This kind of racial profiling and the overwhelmingly negative images of Central Asian migrants are reinforced through the Russian media, which constantly paint them as "criminals," "illegals," "blacks," and "diseased," among other terms, which irreversibly promote phobia among the Russians and add to the migrants' daily insecurities.

The Russian economy is highly dependent on foreign labor, especially because of its increasingly shrinking labor force caused by low fertility and the aging population, despite President Vladimir Putin's pronatalist policies of "maternity capital" encouraging second and third childbirth by providing a family safety net. This policy has attracted some Central Asian migrants to naturalize and start families in Russia because of comparatively promising state support. Nonetheless, the 2000s became an era of reprioritization for Russia's primary migration institution. The Federal Migration Service was disbanded in 2016, and migration management was transferred to a law enforcement agency under the Ministry of Internal Affairs. This move was akin to a downgrade and demonstrated a conceptual and symbolic shift in Russian migration policies. By 2020, the Russian government forecasted that its population growth would be contingent on immigration. Yet, the anti-migration rhetoric only intensified—exemplified by regularized raids of migrant localities in search of *nelegaly* (illegals), routinely fining or detaining them throughout the federal districts, which contributes considerably to the state budget and police pockets, and delivers to the electorate the image of the country fighting "illegal" migration.

In 2012, on multiple occasions I observed, through the windows of a beauty salon run by Kyrgyz-Russian nationals, how police raids caused panic and havoc in Yakutsk. The Stolichnyi market entrance was usually surrounded by informal taxicabs operated mainly by Kyrgyz, Tajik, and Uzbek migrants. In a matter of minutes, the market emptied; the unlucky taxi drivers, including Chinese vendors, salespersons, or anyone looking "foreign" enough were deliberately stopped, asked for their documents, rounded up, loaded into police minivans, and driven away. Once the police departed, the market resumed. This panic was also met with nonchalance by the salon's migrant hairdressers, some of whom would admit they had forgotten their documents or lightheartedly recall how they were caught in the last roundup: "You need to walk straight, with certainty, you have got to be *tyng* [dexterous]." Another Kyrgyz female hairdresser started working before her documents were ready and was detained: "It was awful. There were nearly thirty of us in a cell. We all ate together. I got out in two days. I brought back food to those still in the cell. One woman was deported months later, because nobody came to pay a bribe for her, but the rest got out." Migrants mostly feared the arbitrariness of police officers' decisions. Although they dreaded being detained, migrants were more afraid of losing the documents they were expected to carry on them. The monetary and emotional costs of renewing documents and the fear of losing their documents, being deported, or becoming homeless were more frightful in their eyes than being detained; then, at least, kin, friends, community members, or diaspora representative could bring the required documents and secure their release.

On Terms and Concepts

As an old concept, "diaspora" has evolved from references to the dispersion of specific ethnic groups (i.e., Armenian, Jewish) to all forms of migrations and any dispersal of national or religious groups living outside an imagined homeland. The term gained popularity not just in academia but because of its wide use by media, politicians, diaspora groups, and migrants themselves, further stretching its meaning and inflating the concept. In contemporary usage, "new diaspora" refers to embodying characteristics as transnational ties with both country of origin and host country or refers to any migrant group that materially contributes to its country of origin. Without proposing comprehensive definitions, I follow the Wittgensteinian spirit of gathering meanings from their uses. Most definitions include three core elements constituting diaspora—dispersion or division across state borders, orientation to a (real or imagined) homeland, and boundary maintenance through a conscious resistance to assimilation. However, it should be noted that there is a gap between Western social science scholastic terms such as "migrant," "migration," "diaspora," and their translatability and practicality in daily experiences and usages in other languages by the migrants themselves.

The "diaspora life" here refers to the cross-border or transnational processes and practices where migrants maintain enduring ties with family members and relatives "back home" over time and across space. Today, in Yakutsk, you can meet *vyhodtsy* (natives) from Soviet Central Asia who lived there at the time of the Soviet Union's collapse and stayed there, having created interethnic families. You can meet Kyrgyzstanis who experience themselves as migrants and immigrants equally, having naturalized as Russian citizens but still retaining Kyrgyz passports, envisioning their future lives back in Kyrgyzstan with their entire families, or with the nostalgia and commitment to spend their pension years in *tuulgan jer* (place of birth). And you can meet "seasonal" migrants arriving, in their minds temporarily, to work hard during the year but with plans of spending New Year's Eve back home, earning just enough money working on short-term projects and avoiding the harshest of the seasons. Regardless of their intentions, they inevitably circulate back the following season or prolong their stay for another year or more, unable to earn enough or unable to give up the opportunities presented. Throughout the chapter, I use the general term "migrant" to denote both migrants and immigrants, as they similarly experience ambivalent feelings and emotions. Although they may have different legal practices, they may share daily uncertainties about their sense of belonging. We may look at migrants arriving in Russia to find temporary work and immigrants coming to seek permanent residence and acquire citizenship. However, immigrants may see their future back in their country of origin or in a third country, and migrants may change their primary intent of working and living temporarily and grow roots. In the end, in Russia both these groups are largely seen and feel as being treated as migrants, foreigners, and outsiders.

Ethnographic examples are based on my participant observation of the daily lives of transnational families from multi-sited fieldwork in Kyrgyzstan and Russia (and my continued engagements with interlocutors since then) to demonstrate some central aspects of transnational features of the everyday lives of Kyrgyzstani migrants in Russia's Republic of Sakha. By spotlighting the individual, the family, and wider community levels of transnational ties of migrants, I attend to the following questions: How do migrants negotiate their belonging in cross-border migrations conditioned by temporalities? What does it mean for someone born in the USSR to unexpectedly become an out-of-towner (*priezzhiy*), a foreigner, an immigrant, an "ex" (*byvshiy*), a black (*chernyi*), a compatriot (*sootechestvennik*), an expatriate compatriot (*zemliak*), or a diaspora member in contemporary Russia? How does it feel to leave one's natal village in mountainous post-Soviet Kyrgyzstan and *go back* to the country where one once served in the army or received a higher education and self-identified as a Soviet citizen? How do Russians see Kyrgyz diaspora, and how is Kyrgyz diaspora organized in Russia? How is Russia—the country receiving the second-largest number of labor migrants in the world—struggling to adapt its migration policies, regulations, and laws to respond to changing political and economic experiments? And how is it failing to effectively implement migration policies in a country of 144 million people across eleven time zones?

During the first two decades after the Soviet Union's collapse, nearly 12 million immigrants (equivalent to 9 percent of Russia's population) permanently relocated to Russia, most of them from the former Soviet republics, and another 11 million foreign nationals circulated in migration, also primarily nationals of former Soviet countries. In Russian political rhetoric, Central Asian migrants are portrayed as a problem. Even one of Russia's popular opposition leaders, the national democrat Alexey Navalny, has campaigned by petitioning for compulsory visa relations with the Commonwealth of Independent States (CIS). Putin's plan was to assert regional dominance by creating the Eurasian Economic Union (EAEU). Such debates constantly weigh Russia's dependence on migration and the importance of policies versus the dangers of migration's legalization.

In Kyrgyzstan, despite sending one-fifth of its population abroad and receiving the equivalent of one-third of its GDP in remittances, migrants are largely seen as those who have abandoned their families, leaving their children and aging parents behind, neglecting an entire generation of proper parental supervision. According to UNICEF, nearly 12 percent of children live without one of their parents in Kyrgyzstan because of labor migration. For parents in transnational families, remittances sent home are their central goal. Even though women and men, mothers and fathers migrated to Russia with the same hope of "getting on their feet," the realities are structured and gendered. The migrant women were more vulnerable, although they were more reliable remitters to their children (family of procreation) and to their parents (family of origin).

Filmed cases of vigilantism by self-proclaimed "Kyrgyz patriot-men" allegedly defending the Kyrgyz *genofond* (gene pool) caused havoc in the 2000s when migrant women were abused for dating non-Kyrgyz men while living in Russia. Contrary to Central Asian neighbors, significantly more women migrated from Kyrgyzstan, which resulted in attempts by Kyrgyz policy makers to limit young women's options for migration. The social problems of sexual abuse of women were poignantly portrayed in Sergey Dvortsevoy's film *Ayka* (2018), which depicts a Kyrgyz migrant's grim fate, her unwanted pregnancy, and her fleeing a hospital without her newborn in order to pay off her debts to her countrymen.

Ethnic neighborhoods have not developed in Russia as they have in many Western societies. Instead, migrants in Russia can be traced through the businesses that provide various niche services. In Yakutsk one can dine in "ethnic cafes" or fast food cafes run by immigrants and buy fruits and vegetables from an Uzbek or Kyrgyz seller running a convenience shop nearby. One can book a seat, or send a package, in a minivan taking passengers to Kyrgyzstan on a weekly basis. One can be in a public transport vehicle driven mainly by Kyrgyzstani drivers, since nationals of constituent EAEU member states can drive in Russia with foreign licenses. Then there are spaces that are not immediately recognizable as operated by migrants, such as beauty salons and cleaning companies for offices and businesses. A couple of Kyrgyzstani migrants drove me around the city proudly exclaiming how they "built" the city: dozens of metal rails and doors of businesses and malls, city fences around parks and playgrounds, private house gates, and more.

Kyrgyzstani migrants' services today are mostly geared toward the local population; however, migrants often seek services provided by compatriots through diaspora groups on WhatsApp and Telegram. For example, in Moscow, migrants preferred "Kyrgyz clinics," opened by naturalized Kyrgyz-Russian medical specialists who were committed to serving the diaspora. Similarly, mosques serve as safe spaces for migrant entrepreneurship, where migrants can tap into practicing Muslim networks to sell halal products. In Yakutsk, Kyrgyz migrants preferred getting haircuts and shopping from Kyrgyz-speaking entrepreneurs. Mobile users joined WhatsApp groups to solicit advice on registration regulations, to find rooms for rent, to search for short-term jobs, to order cabs with Kyrgyz drivers, to inquire about lost and found IDs, to advertise businesses, and especially to collect funds for ill or deceased compatriots, among other tasks. These information and communication technologies (ICTs) offer quick, practical solutions and provide some comfort for migrants first getting situated in a new social milieu, which at times intensifies a sense of belonging to an imaginary diaspora, by sharing music videos, memes, or offering opportunities to join causes in support of compatriots in need. While the ICTs have powerful ways of enabling migrants to stay informed and to connect with home, there is little political engagement and mobilization within the diaspora on investment in the homeland.

Examining the complexities of everyday Kyrgyzstani transnational family lives in Russia and what constitutes diaspora life benefits from an emphasis on the enduring transnational ties that migrants maintain with their family, kin, and community members left behind. I explore the ways in which migrants' personal and family orientations can be contentious, emotionally charged, and exposed to uncertainties. I emphasize how the increased monetization of transnational family relationships is pushing families to nuclearize, raising questions about belonging and enduring family commitments. Recognizing that the Kyrgyz nation-state is barely thirty years old, I argue that being and becoming diaspora is a process best understood across a longue durée. What is it about migrant life of the Kyrgyz in Yakutsk and the wider Sakha that the Kyrgyz diaspora constitutes for the majority of migrants in Sakha? I offer a look into migrants' transnational community lives, exploring how they utilize the resources available to them so as to maintain a sense of community with other Kyrgyzstanis and how they avoid maintaining ties at the same time. Russia's constantly changing migration regime makes migrants inherently vulnerable and potentially rupturing and prevents the willing migrant communities from integrating into the local culture and way of life.

Living Lives in Limbo with Different Levels of Commitment

Jama switched back to Kyrgyz when we got off the bus in a wealthy Yakutsk neighborhood with multistory houses—many built by migrant labor, with fortress-like fences, concentrated greenery, and endlessly barking dogs. She returned a call from her sister-in-law in a northeastern village of Kyrgyzstan: "So, did you find the medicine?!" Having dropped all pleasantries Jama, in a matter of seconds, bounced to life "back home" where her husband paid his kin monthly to raise the cattle purchased by their remittances over the past six years. She expressed disbelief and visible frustration at her lack of options to solve a dilemma while being physically far away. One of their cows—their only remittance investment in livestock—had fallen ill with *sharp* (murrain), an infectious disease that affects sheep and cattle. According to custom, Kyrgyz herders are expected to immediately notify the owners of their ill-fated cattle and, in unsolved cases, send the owner the meat and carcass of the slaughtered cattle.

We passed two chatting local women, in silence. When she hung up, Jama implied she did not believe the cow was actually sick. Rather, she insinuated her in-laws might be lying to extort additional remittances. She recalled that she and her husband recently saw their livestock while visiting home. Yet, Jama did not articulate her doubts directly to her in-laws. She was visibly irritated, pointing out to me their lack of control in managing their personal investments from afar. Although mobile technologies can shorten physical distances and help resolve problems as they arise, they also plant suspicion in transnational family relations, increasing the emotional burden both on migrants who feel they are being cheated by kin over the management of remittance investments earned through hard work where every ruble counts and on family and relatives who navigate the challenging balance of helping out and getting paid by kin.

In most Kyrgyzstani migrants' own accounts, Russia was considered a place where life is centered mostly around reaching goals "back home" through often "soul-wrenching labor," working all but one day per week, with insufficient rest, and with minimal integration into the receiving society. The mixed feelings of nostalgia for their homeland among established immigrants and seasonal migrants and the burden of kin-keeping demonstrate the challenges in diaspora life—migrants often find they fully belong neither "here" nor "there." Even those migrants who naturalized for the practical purposes of easing employment and residence registration procedures retained enduring ties to their homeland rooted in strong, continuously sustained individual and family commitments.

Jama and her husband, Bakyt, married and migrated together in 2008, using Bakyt's kin ties to follow their dream of quickly earning money "to get on [their] feet." In this respect, they were not unusual. Their initial dreams were to find seasonal work abroad that would allow them to make a living by investing in livestock, followed by building their own house. Having grown up tending large flocks of cattle and varying pastures in different seasons in rural Kyrgyzstan (skills he learned from his professional herder father), Bakyt was determined to maintain the family tradition and quickly disappearing expertise as rural youth were increasingly drawn to city life. Livestock investments were expensive and full of uncertainties: weather conditions affected harvest size and prices for hay. Bakyt's brother's family had his own household to take care of, and his family also planned out how their wages from herding would pay for their own house construction materials. In contrast, Jama sought to diversify their investments by buying land and future house materials—or a container in Dordoi, Central Asia's largest market in Bishkek—for future business opportunities. "The land does not eat grass!" was her retort in many arguments with her husband, who was not ready to accept their investment failures.

The couple regularly envisioned that they would return home and reunite with their elementary-school-aged daughter, who lived with them one academic year in Yakutsk. But Jama then made arrangements with her sister's family to take care of their daughter: "She improved her Russian here quickly . . . but children need good food and vitamins . . . it isn't Moscow here!" Then her real fears followed: "Here they become different . . . how they dress, spend money on makeup, their character changes. Local girls don't respect adults." Many migrant parents shared this sentiment with me, what Paolo Boccagni explained as "a sense of moral duty" not to lose one's own values and national identity. They visited Kyrgyzstan for one or two months every two or three years during the severe Russian winter. When in Kyrgyzstan, they visited kith and kin, paid respect to the deceased, and organized and paid for important family celebrations, all social relations that have to be put on hold while they were away. Having contributed to the culturally relevant local economies of feasting and gift giving, before their savings were depleted, they returned to Russia to start all over, torn between attending to emerging family projects and the unending financial needs to support their personal goals.

This married couple were thrifty, spending money only on things they considered absolutely essential. Bakyt was a handyman for hire with years of experience in Kyrgyzstan's apartment renovation and construction business, which was in demand in expanding Yakutsk. He accepted his employer's offer to "*dacha*-sit" for all but the summer months when the landlord's family vacationed there, during which period they rented a room in an apartment with another Kyrgyz family. They paid his employer half the market rent; in return, they looked after the residence, and Bakyt performed renovation projects around the property in his "spare" time. His responsible attitude, loyalty, and dedication to work opened additional untaxed side job opportunities (*shabashka*) through his landlord's network of upper-middle-class Yakuts needing workers for minor or major upgrades. Most Kyrgyzstani migrants were aware of being praised and valued by local employers for these qualities, and they were often compared to some locals who proved less reliable, skipping work, being unwilling to work extra hours, or not willing to agree to do arduous labor. Living off the stable salary Jama earned as a cook in a local cafe, the pair saved and remitted Bakyt's earnings to his kin, which depended on the short-term jobs he could find.

By 2014 their landlord offered to move them to the Verkhoiansnkiy region of rural Sakha, over an hour by air from Yakutsk. They accepted the offer, deciding to explore new horizons in spite of the even more severe living conditions characterized by remoteness and further isolation, where the village's surroundings melted from March through September and dissolved the winter roads made of frozen lakes. In a village of five thousand inhabitants, Jama quickly learned the ropes, working as a salesperson in a shop making forty thousand rubles a month ($1,130 in 2014, down to $600 by 2019), while Bakyt continued irregular construction side jobs earning from thirty thousand to eighty thousand rubles ($850–2,250). Although dull, village life allowed them to save even more. They co-resided in one room of a three-room apartment with eight other migrants, all working for the same Yakut entrepreneur. Their rent was free except for utilities, their registration was "clean," and since their work was within walking distance, there were no additional expenses:

> Life here is boring. We work during the day, then [we] come home, eat, and go to our rooms and rest and sleep. Some days we watch television. If there is something to talk about, we might have a longer evening chatting, but all of us get tired and we all have families to chat with and we just want to rest. It's freezing out there. We don't leave buildings longer than for half an hour. Time goes by fast, Monday to Saturday. On Sunday we have *bania* [bathhouse] and television; that's it. The Internet is cheaper at night. We pretty much all sit talking to friends and families on WhatsApp. It feels as if we are sitting and talking in the same room. . . . I talk to my friends in the village back in Kyrgyzstan. Nothing has changed, they are living the same lives, raising cattle in cold winters, [eating] the same food, [driving] the same car, and no real work. In Bishkek, most friends are earning money as taxi drivers. Yes, you can find a job, but it doesn't pay the same. . . . But we all wait impatiently for the fall to go back home.

In the move from Kyrgyzstan's village to rural Sakha, the weather adjustments were feasible with local *dublienka*, *unty*, and *ushanka*, all fur-based coat, shoes, and hat. Socially, Bakyt and Jama lived under the radar, engaging with co-tenants only on Sundays and consciously maintaining friendly but distant relations with the locals. In the eleven years of their residence in Sakha, the couple made a meaningful relationship only with Bakyt's employer. "We don't have ties with the [Kyrgyz] diaspora here [outside Yakutsk]. *They* are in the [Yakutsk] city," was his quick response, suggesting that the diaspora is where the diaspora representative was, but also discounting himself and co-tenants as being part of the diaspora. This secluded life meant distancing themselves from other villagers "to stay out of trouble" and not to succumb to "bad" influences such as abusing vodka consumption. New friendships, usually solidified over a meal with drinks, were rendered less likely: "I couldn't eat with them. They eat raw fish. Liver is eaten raw with blood! We boil our meat for hours!"

More than culinary differences, it was the idea that personal relations are maintained for the sake of longevity, which their temporal sense of belonging rendered unlikely. Also, maintenance of relations implied reciprocal hosting, which the migrants I knew shied away from, because they were reluctant to reveal their shabby and limited living conditions. The couple connected with other co-tenants and occasionally shared meals, reproducing the sense of homeland with accompanying smells, tastes, and ways of being Central Asian.

Like a virus, Russian labor legislation changed constantly, never allowing those who relied on it or those who enforced it to adapt to it. In 2015, when Kyrgyzstan joined the EAEU, this significantly eased its migrants' ability to navigate Russia's public spaces. The EAEU also eliminated the need to keep up with a multitude of paperwork in order to stay legal, paperwork that included a work patent, passing a test on Russian language, history, and law, buying health insurance, and passing medical tests (except for migrants from Kazakhstan, also an EAEU member). All of this was so costly some opted to remain undocumented. Kyrgyzstani migrants now needed only to keep their propiska in order within ninety days of their arrival, along with their work contract, health insurance, and proof of point of entry. Getting a residence registration was not difficult—except it was often fake. Very few landlords were willing to personally register migrants in their rented property, a mere bureaucratic challenge. The owners feared the propensity for the property to turn into a "rubber apartment" where additional unregistered tenants would move in without their knowledge. Migrants thus became trapped in Russia's shadow economy, which was governed by corrupt and selective law enforcement, pushing migrants to rely on intermediaries, utilizing adaptive strategies while navigating daily uncertainties.

Despite the promising changes, in 2019, eleven years after their first arrival in Yakutsk, Bakyt and Jama still considered their migration to be temporary. Their dream house stood tall and roofed in Bishkek's outskirts. Their daughter, now a freshman in college, inhabited one of the rooms and waited for her parents to revamp it fully. Despite the couple's rural investments, they wanted to live in the capital (Bishkek), which has become a common trend for returning migrants. Rural connections, however, remain essential to new urban Kyrgyzstanis, as culturally they continue to depend on livestock, farming, and large family and kin gatherings. Their initial expectation of quick gains was met with unstable employment, multiple returns, and slow savings. Returning home prematurely is seen as shameful, a failure in one's migration.

After his long-aspired return in Kyrgyzstan, Bakyt inquired over WhatsApp of my and his friends' networks in Sweden, Canada, or the United States where, he was learning, workers were paid better and "life was more pleasant." By early 2020, neither of them wanted to go back to Sakha, blaming the cold and considering it a finished chapter. Although it is hard to predict the couple's chances of circling back to Yakutsk or other parts of

Russia as migrants again, these chances are rather high as the two of them have to sustain their new livelihood. The couple's dreams of building their own house, getting back on their feet, educating their daughter, although accomplished with a certain degree of success, gave birth to new ideals and new horizons. Empowered by migration and because of this experience, they questioned their attachment to their tuulgan jer. Modern life, increasingly characterized by global interconnectedness, weakens attachments to one's homeland as a specific location to return to, but it remains an important site of belonging and identification in the times of increasing mobility.

A Day in a Migrant's Life, Navigating Yakutsk

Anara, a forty-year-old married mother of two teenagers, migrated alone to Yakutsk in 2010. She considered herself lucky to have received Russian citizenship "when it was easier." Her new passport eased her propiska and was a daily source of self-esteem, but Anara did not identify herself as a *rossianka* (Russian citizen). Anara carried full responsibility for her family of four, the burden entirely on her shoulders ever since her marriage, as her husband never earned a Kyrgyz *som* because of his recurring "drinking habits." With origins in rural Kyrgyzstan, Anara moved in with her in-laws after being kidnapped for marriage; there she raised her two children, earning money working in a rural post office. Her small salary was aided by raising cattle and seasonal farming of staple vegetables. Eventually she was encouraged by her older sister's success and left Kyrgyzstan for the first time with the goal of providing for her children's education. In her absence, her adolescent children took care of themselves and their father. In Yakutsk, Anara used her sister's established networks to rent an apartment room from a single Russian *babushka* (grandmother), who registered her without difficulty. Her first job started at eight in the morning at the Stolichnyi market, where she was hired for her outgoing personality as a vendor selling fabric and clothes. Always elegantly dressed, ten hours later, she entered a beauty salon. Because she lived close by, Anara chose to work extra hours tidying up the salon after the work day and handwashing the myriad towels used by hairdressers in a bathroom shared with an illegally run gambling room.

Anara timed her migration around her children's last years of high school, so she could pay their university tuitions and related expenses. She was prepared to work in Russia as long as her health allowed, because she considered it her parental responsibility to educate them. Despite her success, she regularly faced gossip back in her village community for having left behind her unemployed and troubled husband. She was picked on in conversations with kin on the cell phone. She downplayed her unhappy marriage of twenty years as her push factor for out-migration. Not only did she support her family, sending money "for all their needs," but she fully paid off debts accrued from her daughter's prior hospitalization. Her energy stretched borders as she oversaw, via cell phone, the entire construction of their new house in their backyard in Bishkek.

Anara had a relaxing twenty-minute walk home every day, a citizen's privilege. This was the only time she allowed herself not to think about her problems. On the way home, she shopped at a convenience store in her neighborhood. She kept pleasantries short with her chatty landlord, ate a quick dinner in their shared kitchen, cleaned the dishes, packed leftovers for the next day's lunch, and could not wait to close her bedroom door and lie down to sleep. This could have been the end of her largely routinized day, except Anara prioritized staying connected with family and wider kin. Every day, she dialed her children just to hear their voices. She talked to family members to stay on top of the family news by asking about social gatherings of kin and making sure her family reciprocated gift giving to ensure her family "did not fall out of family and kinship ties." When she picked up the phone, she fully immersed herself in her family's life back in Kyrgyzstan. Distance seemed irrelevant as she enabled acts such as the purchasing of construction materials, negotiated which extracurricular courses her children should take, and advised which clothes they should buy. She admitted she would not have come to Russia if her children were younger. When her oldest son expressed interest in joining her in Russia and working instead of starting studies in the university, Anara strongly opposed the idea: "Children get used to money and would not study. I see it happen here a lot. That is what I do not want to happen to my children. I want them to study, be educated. . . . I tell them, *I came here for the two of you!*"

Migration has a way of putting relationships on hold; for Anara, however, not maintaining relationships with kin back home was inconceivable:

> We are in good relations with kin on both sides equally. My husband has ten siblings, and so do I. We have *raja* [payments among kin] for *jakshylyk* [happy celebrations] and *jamandyk* [commemorations], so we maintain many relationships. . . . [In my absence], my children and husband take turns attending various kin events—weddings, birthdays, *tois* [celebrations of rites of passage], and so on. It is important to keep relations with kin active, because that money [we gave to kin] will be reciprocated when we need support, when our children marry, when they have children. That is the winning side of Kyrgyz culture. So, I stay in touch with our kin as if I have never left [Kyrgyzstan].

Her extraordinary efforts in cross-border kin-keeping, however, demonstrate a strategic use of relations for future family needs, entrusting resources in the present in the hopes of future returns, reinforcing cultural practices of mutual indebtedness. This form of relating to her relatives strengthened her sense of relatedness, rooted in cultural values, and solidified her current and future kin relations. She seemed to have planned her future with kin, but she was clueless about her current status with two passports: "I don't know . . . *Ubagynda köröbüzda!* [We will see when the time comes!] You see, when I went home last time, after a short while, I just wanted to come back here. Not because I didn't miss my children and my home, but because here you get used to working and earning money for a purpose."

In the city outskirts lives Ulan, a forty-three-year-old welder who wakes up at seven in the morning to be at work by eight after a light breakfast of bread with a cold cut of *kolbasa* (sausage) and black tea with sugar. "We walk to work. It's about half an hour. We live in the outskirts, there are no police here checking documents." When we met in 2012, Ulan carried a stack of his documents with him every day, but by 2016 when Kyrgyzstan joined the EAEU he had relaxed. "Nobody is registered where they live!" Ulan laughed at me when I asked him about his propiska: "I know my address [on the registration card] by heart. I show my papers when stopped [by police]. I say my address. And they just let you go . . . as long as you have all your documents on you." By half past seven in the evening, the men returned together with the empty jars they bring lunches in and cleaned up while one of them cooked dinner according to an agreed-upon "duty calendar." They ate together in a common kitchen around nine, often in silence. By 2016 most migrants had switched to smartphones, realizing that with Internet access they could call home for free. Now evenings were spent staring at smartphones, scrolling through WhatsApp group posts, liking Facebook and Instagram posts, and watching YouTube videos, until interrupted by ring tones. The *dezhurnyi* (cook on duty) evenly distributed leftovers in the glass jars, stacked them in the fridge, then tidied up the dishes, and they all used the outhouse privy before they went to bed by eleven to avoid leaving the house in brutal cold nights. On their only day off, a combination of men might work a shabashka, but one would stay behind to heat up the bathhouse.

Between 2012 and 2020 Ulan returned to Yakutsk twice, each time for a short period. In May 2020, over WhatsApp video, he revealed how technologies influenced their lives:

Medina: What can you tell me about the diaspora?
Ulan: Ah, yes, there is [diaspora]. Some Kyrgyz collect [money]. For *jaman-jakshy* [the good and the bad]. Sometimes they go to cafes together.
Medina: And you?
Ulan: Ah, no! *Shart jok* ([I am] not in a position [to do so].) We are migrants here. I don't join them. If you join [the group], you have to spend money.
Medina: How so?
Ulan: They have WhatsApp groups. If you join their group, *katyshysh kerek* ([you] have to maintain [relations] with them). They have such conditions. So we [his co-tenants] don't go anywhere. See, if you join one group, you have to spend money. You go here and there. Diaspora also tends to divide, according to where they are from: Chuy, Naryn, Osh, or [Issyk] Kul. They join groups based on where they are [originally] from [in Kyrgyzstan].
Medina: What about your neighbors? Who do you talk to?
Ulan: We don't talk to neighbors. They don't do that.

Medina: What do you mean?

Ulan: I think they don't like talking to us. We are friendly. We say *zdrasti* (a casual hello) and nod and that's it. No, we don't know each other. *They* [the local neighbors] even don't know each other!

The everyday lives of migrants shed light on the material contexts in which transnational families are sustained, with the affordability of ICTs having transformed how transmigrants organize their days. The routinization of migrant lifestyle, the monotonous grind, and the discipline it requires to keep pushing on is the local social order they have to abide by to be successful both here in Russia and there in Kyrgyzstan. Working without a day off, Anara rarely joined her girlfriends in the diaspora to go out for dinner in cafés, a common marker of socialization within the migrant community. But birthdays were exceptions. She shared feelings of guilt for attending a relatively expensive concert by a group of well-known Kyrgyz singers touring Russia for their Kyrgyz-speaking compatriots. While able to justify the conditions of hard work she endured, Anara's separation from her children was a daily source of guilt and pain that she hid well. Such ambiguous feelings were common. She ensured me that she still exerted control over them, because they conversed daily, and she felt she "even helped them decide what to wear, what courses to sign up for." Yet she would intentionally and consciously avoid talking about her own predicaments "not to worry them," but also, I was told, "they wouldn't understand!" The information flow from Russia to Kyrgyzstan within transnational families was more scarce than in the opposite direction.

In colloquial Kyrgyz, *köröbüzda* is a state of being that connotes a "living in the present" amid the uncertainty of the future. For Anara and Ulan, every day was Groundhog Day, but more complex in Russia, in their minds, than in the village. Many in the diaspora compared their lives in Russia, seen as more rigid yet more meaningful, orderly, and with a higher sense of self-worth, to memories "at home," where they could wake up when they wanted, take countless tea breaks, and use connections to get things done. After several trips "home" to Kyrgyzstan, Anara and Ulan still returned to "home" in Yakutsk. In Russia, they dreamed of Issyk Kul lake vacations, of drinking *kumys* (fermented mare's milk) in summer pastures, and of the mountains and clean air. But once in Kyrgyzstan, they hurried about with their fast-paced lives, making independent decisions and putting off kin-keeping activities. Yet they also felt isolated and excluded from, or at least not fully included in, Russian society. Inevitably, their original migratory goals transformed as they adapted to new needs, making it much harder for them, like other transmigrants, to commit to an exit date from Russia.

Transnational Communities or Being Diaspora

Exploring the putrid halls of the Stolichnyi market, one hears Mandarin, Kyrgyz, and Russian spoken. When I met Fatima, a thirty-five-year-old divorced mother of three school-aged children, she worked as a *pomogaika* (helper, in Chinese Russian parlance) for a Chinese vendor, Sung (also known as Sonia in the market), selling apparel. In Sakha and Russia's Far East, the Chinese topped the number of labor migrants with visas. Most Chinese entrepreneurs hired Central Asian migrants fluent in Russian as sales assistants. In addition, Fatima quickly picked up some basic Chinese, as she was also proficient in Dungan language because of her Kyrgyz-Dungan heritage. When Fatima's mother's friend Klara offered to help them, in 2010 Fatima arrived in Yakutsk from Kyrgyzstan to work as Klara's shop assistant for one year, receiving five hundred rubles a day plus the air ticket Klara paid for. Sonia liked Fatima's hardworking qualities and offered to pay her six hundred rubles a day for the same job. Struggling with the dilemma of feeling indebted to Klara but wanting to earn more, Fatima eventually chose to work for Sonia, which forever strained her relations with Klara and her family. This was especially painful as they worked in the same market, and Klara turned it into a drama, often harassing and insulting her, which Fatima could only ignore.

At home Fatima had left an abusive relationship, and when her ex-husband remarried and refused to pay alimony, Fatima was desperate, but her mother was willing to take care of her grandchildren, and that was a big push for her to migrate. After working at the market, Fatima took a trolley to a funeral home where she mopped the floors and cleaned the offices during the week. Working every day let her forget all the life drama, but she was left without time for recharging. She quickly found co-tenants in the market and co-resided with four girls in one room of a four-room apartment, paying roughly two thousand rubles a month (seventy dollars, in 2012). Two girls worked night shifts, which required her to vacate the bed by their return every morning.

Standing in front of her booth, hailing clients to come in and check out merchandise, Fatima daily observed the market life and had a large repertoire of stories about its subjects. Out of all her experiences, she was most disturbed by the lack of solidarity and unity among the Kyrgyz vendors at the market. In one example, she recounted how, when a brawl arose between Kyrgyz and Chinese merchants, other Chinese sellers would immediately respond to back up their compatriot. She clearly cared less if the reason was just, but it was the principle of camaraderie between the compatriots abroad: "You know, I would try to understand if he was a northerner, you know how we have those divisions, but they all were southerners, and even that should not be a divider, the Kyrgyz abroad should help each other out. I was mad!" Such incidents led her to conclude that the Chinese were "unified," but the Kyrgyz boys who stood by—"dressed well, with phones in hand"—and did not get involved thus demonstrated publicly the lack of unity within the Kyrgyz community.

Migrants' self-image can be boosted through public displays of camaraderie. In a public space like the Stolichnyi, the personal rationale to stay out of trouble largely outweighed the sense of communal belonging and the public display of ethnic, national, and diasporic relatedness. Raided by police on a regular basis, migrants prioritized their own safety in the market, being afraid of ending up behind bars. Fatima's numerous accounts exemplified quite the opposite picture from the Yakut perception of the Kyrgyz diaspora as a close-knit, unified community of people who will help out their compatriots in difficult circumstances. Even the imagined community of a diaspora comes with expectations of ethnic and regional support.

Death, and sometimes illness, in the Kyrgyz diaspora, however, generated thoughtful solidarity among the compatriots. When a Kyrgyzstani citizen dies in Sakha, the diaspora leaders reach out to the entire community for donations related to "cargo 200" expenses—a repatriation of the remains of the deceased by air. This solidarity is usually not just ethnically based but also can be religious based, on the Muslim religious belief that the body should be buried expeditiously and in one's native land. Talant, a thirty-nine-year-old naturalized small-business owner, was often approached by the diaspora leaders to contribute to such efforts, and also to assist in reaching out to the community members to collect cash donations. As a businessman with ten years of residence in Yakutsk, he was an important node in the social network of Kyrgyzstanis and knew where to go to collect cash donations. At such times, he dropped everything and reached out and, as he described, help was also conditional:

> Many times, I was asked to help to collect money when someone died. That is when I learned who our people are. We are much worse [egotistical] than Uzbeks and Tajiks. Even when giving fifty rubles, some would ask, "Where was [the deceased] from?" I would ask them why it mattered, but some did not like giving money if they were not from the same region [of Kyrgyzstan as them]. Or they would fret, "Will you stop asking us for money?" or "I'm tired of giving money to those I don't know!" Very few people give money without a comment.

Talant shared his frustration of how regional divisions were further reproduced across borders in Russia after the 2010 ethnic violence between the Kyrgyz and Uzbeks in Osh in southern Kyrgyzstan. He emphasized that, although he hired two Uzbek-Kyrgyzstanis in his business whose families also moved to Russia after the Osh events, it was rare for the Kyrgyz and Uzbeks to maintain real friendships beyond on-the-surface cordial exchanges. Talant's reflections valuably illuminate how ethnic conflicts, repeated revolutions, and economic and political instability back home can negatively affect and transform migrants' conception of homeland and the decision to return. Moreover, the divisions in regional affiliations among the Kyrgyz, similar to Fatima's story, and the persistence of region-based identity among migrants contribute to weaker overall ethnic solidarity among the diaspora community.

Before moving to Yakutsk, Talant worked in Moscow, then moved to Novosibirsk where his business did not materialize. Throughout the years he felt obliged to help his six siblings living in Kyrgyzstan. When he moved to Yakutsk, he started a family and asked his kin "to leave him alone" for five years until he "got on his feet." This decision caused rifts with kin who talked of him as having become stingy, forgotten his roots, and become Russified (*obrusel*). In his words, Talant equated it to being strong, resilient, and self-confident: "If you are not *tyng*, you don't accomplish much here. You fail." When his parents died, his "youngest son" status no longer obliged him to go back to Kyrgyzstan to take care of them, an expectation and obligation in Kyrgyz culture. His personal drive for achievements in Yakutsk made it easier for him to grow roots in Russia where he accepted himself as an immigrant.

Nonetheless, Talant and his wife, Elina, maintained strong ties with their siblings and other friendships back home. They prioritized their children's ability to speak Kyrgyz, hiring Kyrgyz-speaking nannies to practice their mother tongue. An organized nanny hiring scheme from Kyrgyzstan among established immigrants in Yakutsk was becoming popular by 2012. The couple were determined to send their two children, both Russian citizens, to study English and pursue higher education in Kyrgyzstan, because they believed that educational opportunities in Kyrgyzstan were far better than in Sakha. As newly naturalized Russians, they did not, however, aspire for their children to study in Moscow or other parts of Russia. They ensured that their children kept in touch with their wider kith and kin and maintained their Kyrgyz roots by spending summers in Kyrgyzstan. Another way they promoted pride in Kyrgyz identity was by supporting their daughter's efforts to organize a Kyrgyz ethnic dance group at school. Dressed in Kyrgyz national outfits, purchased and packaged through community networks from Bishkek to Yakutsk, the group performed in their school and beyond, representing the Kyrgyz diaspora during yearly cultural events organized by the Yakutsk city administration and facilitated by diaspora organizations and funds. As Michel Bruneau has noted, transnational communities are based on "mobility know-how," when transmigrants seek citizenship in the host society, but at the same time they retain the original citizenship, forming a "double affiliation." They bring with them the enduring hierarchies and structures of regionalism, ethnicism, and ideas about family values that are further reproduced across borders.

Keeping Feet in Both Worlds

Transnational family lives have become a norm in Kyrgyzstan, characterized by a gradual nuclearization of Kyrgyz family relations because of overstretched commitments and growing economic inequalities. In conversation over cups of tea in 2011 in rural Kyrgyzstan, Mira, a fifty-six-year-old grandmother, explained how her three sons and two daughters-in-law migrated to Yakutsk, where they lived together as one family in order to support each other and to enable greater savings. Migrant individual and familial aspirations intermingle in transnational experiences, especially when migrants' lives are defined by temporal and spatial distance:

> Mira: Family? Well, for the Kyrgyz, family is when you have children. The head of the house is at home [laughs]. You have children,

grandchildren, so all of them together would be considered your family.

Medina: Who constitutes your family?

Mira: In our family . . . everyone! Our children are part of our family. They did not separate from our family. They are just working abroad, but they are considered our family. We have not yet separated them as households. They are building their houses right now here [Kyrgyzstan], but they are just working there [Russia]. However, when we give them five duvets, five bowls [speaking figuratively], and then we can say that we have separated them, but now they are still in our family.

Mira intentionally kept her "big family" together. She encouraged, and at times instructed, her sons and daughters-in-law to reside together as one family, "to support each other when far away, eating from one pot, like a family." Mira's married children and daughters-in-law were expected to commit to their family's connectedness, because Mira exercised immense authority over her children's personal lives. The response of her eldest daughter-in-law, Aidai, to why they did not move out on their own as a married couple demonstrates her subordination as well as a recognition of the importance of having harmonious relations when abroad:

Aidai: When I moved here to Yakutsk, I was told by my mother-in-law that we all had to live together. She said we should live in one place.

Medina: What did she mean?

Aidai: [laughs] If we lived in Kyrgyzstan now, we would have been separated, right? We [married brothers' families] would have lived on our own. Well, [her brother-in-law and his wife], at some point, wanted to separate.

Medina: Why didn't they?

Aidai: You see, they still think that if they live on their own, they could control their money, but the truth is they would not be able to accumulate money the way we have done so far. We had a conflict because of that.

Medina: Why were they convinced that that was better for them?

Aidai: *Apam* [my mother-in-law] feared that we would lose *yntymak* [unity, solidarity, harmony], so she kept us together.

Medina: When are you going to live on your own?

Aidai: [laughs] Hopefully, in a few years . . . after [the family's youngest son's] house is built, then we will work on [the family's second son's] house. One day we will all separate.

Bilim, the family's second daughter-in-law, was becoming concerned about the protracted nature of their migration and wondered when, if ever, they would begin their own (nuclear) lives. When Aidai became pregnant, she gave birth in Russia but traveled with her infant back to Kyrgyzstan where

Mira agreed to raise her two-month-old grandchild despite Aidai's reluctance to part with her first child and go back to Russia for work.

From the start, these family members conceived of their migration as temporary. However, nine years later, Aidai's first son, a Russian citizen, still lived with his grandparents in Kyrgyzstan while his parents continued earning in Russia to support endless family projects in Kyrgyzstan. After paying off the family debts, which pushed them to migrate initially, the transmigrants continued to pool their earnings to rebuild their parental home in their village of birth, a new barn to raise cattle, and then to build their individual houses in Bishkek. In addition, their remittances paid for the daily livelihoods of those family members remaining behind but also paid for numerous celebrations of family members' rites of passage and improved their consumption capacity of household items. Bilim asserted her will to live with her husband in Russia, although Mira sought her assistance around the house back in the village. Before long, Bilim's two children were born in Yakutsk. This is when Bilim felt pressured to bring her toddlers back to Kyrgyzstan and leave them in their grandmother's care so that she could work to contribute financially. The eldest son, both daughters-in-law, and the grandchildren all became Russian citizens, but Mira's two youngest sons did not. Bilim and her husband's marriage was officiated by a mullah, so they did not have formal marriage papers. The family members applied for child support, treating Bilim as a single mother, deceiving the system in order to accrue more savings. The men also worked side jobs in the evenings and on Sundays. All of their earnings were collected into one family pot, which allowed them to raise significant funds to finance multiple family projects. Family members cooked and ate together at home. They rarely spent money on entertainment and socializing. Individually, their opinions on how to live their lives differed, but as a unified family living under one roof, they acted as one and slowly built their future lives back in Kyrgyzstan. This transnational family life demonstrates how migrants can live with minimal integration with the host community even ten years after their arrival.

Building houses or buying flats back home were not the only projects through which this transnational family actively materialized their proxy presence in Kyrgyzstan. They paid for the daily food, utilities, livestock and haystacks, barn renovations, coal for heating, canning for the winter season, clothes for everyone, tuition fees, house renovations, new household items, children's toys, doctor visits and the purchase of medicine, and not least, *raja* for life-cycle events, celebrations, and funerals. In this way, migration reconfigured family structures and family members' roles and responsibilities. The migrant children sent money home, and the non-migrant family members oversaw their projects. The parental house, started in 2011, was fully completed by 2014, when the youngest son returned for good, fulfilling his cultural expectations to marry and care for their aging parents. Divided, they nonetheless maintained strong ties across borders—though stretched, and sometimes overstretched—and the ideational value of family as a site of compelling commitments and gender- and generationally marked hierarchies remained strong.

By 2015 the children had divided their resources into simultaneous investments in Yakutsk, in their village of birth (in Naryn region), and in Bishkek. The Russian citizen son bought land, and the family built a family house and a business in Yakutsk. Over the years they invited numerous villagers to migrate seasonally for work and helped them to get on their feet. Interestingly, their new physical investments in Russia eased their registration struggles as homeowners and seriously boosted the family business interests in Russia, even further stretching the distribution of family funds. In Bishkek the parents took out a bank loan to buy a newly built apartment in the new construction boom enabled by migrant remittances. The parents visited Yakutsk multiple times helping with grandchildren care. When asked seven years later, this transnational family still believed their future was back in Kyrgyzstan and continued with creative ways to sustain the idea of "familyhood" amid dispersal. The perpetual temporariness of this transnational family's life shows they were not uprooted from their country, but they maintain the endless needs of its members in both countries, requiring each family member to adjust personal and family needs in both milieus simultaneously.

Inherent Vulnerabilities

On March 18, 2019, Russian news media announced an ongoing criminal investigation against three Kyrgyz migrants in Yakutsk. The night before, a twenty-three-year-old Kyrgyz migrant had raped a thirty-seven-year-old Yakut woman. The woman escaped and filed charges immediately; the perpetrator and two conspirers were detained. Information of the assault spread rapidly via social networks such as WhatsApp. The same evening, some two hundred Yakutsk residents gathered at a city square for a spontaneous rally, where city leaders attempted to calm them down and invited them to a meeting at a local stadium the following evening. Nonetheless, that night, angry mobs attacked small businesses run by Kyrgyz migrants, as well as those of other Central Asians. The acts of violence were filmed and posted openly on social media, where they were widely shared and were ultimately picked up by social media users and numerous WhatsApp diaspora groups. In these videos, a group of Yakut men harass people whom they suspect of being migrants, asking them for their names, jobs, documents, registration, and citizenship. In two videos the attackers ransacked the merchants' produce, throwing fruits and vegetables at the migrants. In another case, a man shoots an automatic rifle into the air, threatening migrants outside their business. Some well-wishers tell migrant shop vendors, fast food chain workers, and café workers to close down and stay at home for a while, and others tell them to leave the country forever. In one astonishing example, when the vendor shows his Russian passport and tells his harasser that he is a Russian citizen, the harasser expresses disbelief and questions the validity of the vendor's identification, recommending that the Russian citizen business owner of Central Asian descent leave his country.

The following day Sakha's leadership joined at the stadium to respond to an angry mob of nearly six thousand city and neighboring village dwellers chanting in Yakut language "Yakutia for Yakuts!" From videos posted on YouTube it was clear the leadership tried to calm the crowd, emphasizing that "crime has no nationality," but some leaders' speeches appeared just to fuel the anti-migrant sentiments. The leader of the Republic of Sakha, Aisen Nikolaev, stressed: "A guest insulting the host in his house is no longer a guest, but an enemy." The mayor of Yakutsk, Sardana Aksentieva, followed: "We are in our homeland, in our city. We are the masters of our land and we need to make sure that everyone understands that." They also promised to "hunt down the illegal migrants and deport them" and blamed local entrepreneurs for supporting illegal migration. Later, the leaders allegedly claimed they stopped the mob from attacking the only mosque located in the city center—built by Russian Muslims, it was increasingly associated with Central Asian migrants. When news spread that the mob beat a Kyrgyz bus driver, over eighty Central Asian drivers did not come to work the following few days. Many fast food chains and vegetable shops with Central Asian workers decided to stay closed. Local media published and shared official statistics that, in 2018, four out of nearly three hundred sexual offense cases in Sakha were committed by foreigners. Law enforcement agencies detained local vigilantes, charging them with administrative offenses, and took control of the situation.

When videos and information about the riots spread quickly through the numerous WhatsApp groups that I followed, most users felt panic and hysteria over what to do next—whether to wait out the uncertainty or to return immediately to Kyrgyzstan. Many migrants expressed their fears of retribution against Central Asian migrants. During the next few days, Yakutsk felt the effects of migrant labor on the city's life: most vegetable shops and kiosks closed, half the city's public buses did not run, affordable hot food stands and cafes serving lunches remained shuttered. With the reports of mob vigilantism, WhatsApp users warned compatriots to stay at home and avoid public spaces, including going to work. Kyrgyzstani and Russian state representatives arrived in Yakutsk within two days to discuss terms for a thorough investigation, leaving all three jailed migrants in Russia. Kyrgyz diaspora representatives and the Kyrgyz government officials offered apologies and asked forgiveness on behalf of the Kyrgyz people. Unexpectedly, on March 20, 2019, in the runup to President Putin's first state visit to Kyrgyzstan, Russia's State Migration Service announced an amnesty for the Kyrgyzstani migrants, allowing those in violation of their legal status in Russia to freely leave and reenter the country until April 22, 2019, repeating a similar amnesty granted in the fall of 2018.

The March 2019 anti-migrant protest in Yakutsk was not the first of its kind in Russia; similar responses and xenophobic sentiments took place in Karelia in 2006 and in western Biriulievo, in the periphery of Moscow, in 2013, both involving interethnic tensions between the local population and migrant workers. Marlène Laruelle has analyzed how ethnic violence in Biriulievo played a role in remaking Russia's national identity, where religious, sexual, and ethnic minorities "are explicitly excluded from the national community, which is implicitly defined by affiliation with Orthodoxy, moral values symbolized by heterosexuality, and Russian ethno-cultural identity." The Biriulievo events also show the complexities of xenophobia and racism, when "non-Slavic" Russians were regarded as "foreigners," within Russia, by the Russians. Such events demonstrate that it is hard for migrants to stay invisible in times of uncertainty.

Russian human rights activist Svetlana Ganushkina argued that the state created the fear of illegal migration, but "any" Russian citizen will tell you that their life would be adversely affected without migrants—who are their nannies, guards, street cleaners, handymen, and so on. There is a paradox between individual daily experiences and the migrant-dependence of Russians versus their general attitudes toward Central Asian migration as shaped by the government policies and state media. Migrants' dreams and prospects can be shattered overnight, revealing inherent vulnerabilities in their lives. A place conceived by most Central Asians as easy to breathe also felt suffocating, bringing to the surface deeply held phobia. The anti-migrant sentiments throughout Russia's numerous republics have had the tendency to intensify unless Russian government reforms and implements formal migrant integration policies. What is happening in Russia thus far is the opposite: the policing and tightening of control over immigrants, pushing them into a shadow economy, and increasing xenophobic attitudes toward them, leaving migrants to rely on their own informal infrastructures and survival mechanisms.

Alternative Ways of Being Diaspora

Little has changed since Vanessa Ruget and Burul Usmanalieva, in one of the first attempts to study Kyrgyz diaspora in post-Soviet Russia, described the Kyrgyz diaspora in Russia in 2011 as "disengaged" and "largely unorganized." While Kazakhstan, Turkey, the United States, Europe, and South Korea are new popular destinations, Russia remains the primary migration landing point. In Sakha, as in other parts of Russia, a few diasporic organizations formed. The improved and more affordable ICTs made the difference. Using WhatsApp and Telegram as a medium for sharing practical information about registration procedures and changes, finding affordable accommodation, looking for jobs, advertising businesses such as taxi services, sharing lost-and-found documents, and searching for Kyrgyz medics, among many other uses, the Kyrgyz transmigrants inhabit the virtual space and find solace in the virtual diasporic community when unaware or unwilling of trying the formal means. Some immigrants who have learned the ropes of the constantly changing immigration procedures and laws have often served as intermediaries feeding the illegal documentation and legalization schemes that result from Russia's shadow economy. Newly arrived migrants often seek services from "established" compatriots whose business can knowingly cheat the system, therein making their compatriots vulnerable.

This picture is complicated by an interplay of inclusion and belonging. In my experience, such virtual memberships were not always inclusive. In 2018–2019, a self-proclaimed diaspora *Yntymak* group in Yakutsk actively posted and shared information about various aspects of diaspora life in Yakutsk. Its charismatic leader dynamically propagated unity (*yntymak*) among the Kyrgyz, calling the community members to engage in charity, to lead a healthy lifestyle, and to attend Friday mosque prayers. He organized and represented Kyrgyzstanis in numerous cross-cultural festivities. This diaspora leader also imposed his personal views and values—normalizing and banning particular lifestyles and acting as a moral figure. After the March 2019 criminal case, one video circulated where a group of diaspora moralists "raided" nightclubs in search of Kyrgyz youth drinking alcohol to engage with them in "moral talks," allegedly to improve local impressions of the Kyrgyz in Sakha. Word spread quickly and such performative acts divided the migrant community. Genuine or naive, such public displays of nationalism and protection of a particular vision of being Kyrgyz abroad by imposing a diasporic code of conduct is telling of the unity of "the diaspora."

However, this leader eventually left the group, allegedly in order to create a new diaspora fund based on paid membership for his support services. Many migrants who remained in the WhatsApp group experienced a void and confusion, quickly realizing that online and mobile groups often rely on the leadership and organizational skills of a few and can be accessed by those with connections. Diaspora lives are created and are constantly transformed based on transmigrants' agency. Rustam Urinboyev poignantly shed light on the Uzbek transmigrants' agency to cope with their daily struggles in Russia who also create virtual groups based on regions of origin. Such informal arrangements prove especially powerful in smaller communities where migrants cannot easily approach few existing formal institutions, such as civil society institutions and nongovernmental organizations that function primarily in Russia's cities, but which have also been affected by Russia's "foreign agent" laws, and whose reach and resources remain limited. Diasporic organizations could benefit from institutional and financial resources to be treated as equal partners in attending to the needs of the growing transmational community.

●

Thirty years ago, few Kyrgyz were willing to uproot from the Soviet Central Asia to Russia; today, one may meet Kyrgyz transmigrants across Russia, periodically growing and subsiding in numbers. Since Kyrgyzstan has no dual citizenship agreement with Russia, does not invest in its migrants, and does not denounce its emigrants, Emil Nasritdinov and Ruslan Rahimov in their study of transmigrants in Kazan categorize Kyrgyzstan as a weak state interested migration. For this post-Soviet country of six million, with one-fifth of its population living outside the country, transnationalism is an accepted reality that benefits the state through significant remittance inflows that minimizes the pressure of unemployment. In 2020, the COVID-19 global pandemic allowed us to observe reactions and mobilization from various Kyrgyz transnational communities from different parts of Russia, but also from the United States, Turkey, and some European states when they sent financial resources or medical staff and technologies to assist with recovery efforts. The value of the concept of diaspora, as Michel Bruneau suggests, is like "sedimentation" that shows over a longer period of time. While diasporas are constructed over time, the Kyrgyz diasporas can be seen as in the making.

It should be clear, however, that the concept of "diaspora" is best approached from its user perspective, especially because the Kyrgyzstani transmigrants I studied over the past decade reluctantly referred to themselves as part of the diaspora. When Fatima spoke of the brawls between the Kyrgyz and the Chinese vendors at Stolichnyi, she spoke of the lack of *yntymak* (unity) and solidarity among the Kyrgyz vendors and the sense of regionalism without making specific references to the diaspora as such. In 2020, during my WhatsApp engagement with migrants in Yakutsk, several migrants brushed off their relationship with the Kyrgyz diaspora, despite recognition of "there are so many of us here":

> Medina: Tell me about how the Kyrgyz diaspora are doing in Yakutsk?
> Ulan: Oh, I don't deal with them. I don't have any problems.

On the other hand, on numerous occasions I witnessed Yakuts referring to "the Kyrgyz diaspora" as an entity; in their eyes it was unified and supportive of its members. During one of Bilim's monthly child-care claims in Yakutsk in 2012, an officer noticed that Bilim had made some mistakes in her application. Instead of receiving monetary support, Bilim now had a negative balance, which she had to pay back to the Russian government. Teary Bilim was reprimanded: "Go collect money from your diaspora! I'm sure a few thousand [rubles] in a few hours is not a big deal for you all!" The idea of "the diaspora" should also be understood in the context of users and addressees. A Russian citizen, Bilim was treated as an other, not as a full-fledged Russian citizen.

Diaspora as identity or practice can be claimed or prescribed by others. Such instances of racism and ethnicism were omnipresent in the halls of Russian state bureaucracies, on the streets, construction sites, and public service spaces. Most migrants ignored the treatment, avoided direct conflict and confrontations, but exerted agency maneuvering through loopholes and responding with private silent victories. Bilim eventually received her claim in full, and she celebrated how she had outsmarted the system. These contrasts sustain diasporas: the disconnect between exclusion as a citizen and the search for belonging.

In the daily lives of migrants there is both a presence and an absence of the state. The transnational lives portrayed in this chapter shed light on rather strong ties of the Kyrgyz transmigrants in Sakha to their homeland. These attitudes are also reinforced by the non-migrants' increasing dependency on remittances. It does not seem these ties will diminish in the near future, despite events like those in March 2019 but, rather, they will boost transnational ties in a number of ways. First, Kyrgyzstan's current economic development suggests it will continue to depend on the remittances of its nationals or expatriates. Thus, the Kyrgyzstani government made concerted efforts to strengthen bilateral ties with Russia by joining the EAEU and by expanding current economic, political, social, and military relations after Putin's 2019 state visit. Second, Russia's demography is still in crisis and has not resolved its dependency on external labor. Sakha's small entrepreneurs see a loyal and hardworking labor force in the face of the Central Asian migrants, evidenced by local entrepreneurs' continued preference for foreign as opposed to local workers. Russian private entrepreneurs find ways to save on labor costs and to abuse migrant labor rights. Although the Russian state continues to tighten illegal migration and corruption, this process has only made scapegoats out of the migrants. Finally, global anti-immigrant movements as well as the migrant phobia produced by Russian media and politics over the 2010s have utilized the language of exclusion and victimization.

Referred to as *chernye* (blacks) in Russian parlance, the Central Asian migrants daily experience discrimination, racism, and xenophobia, which are not welcoming signs to become "real" Russians even if they wished. The work skills, life experiences, and the economic support they accumulate in Russia boost migrants' self-image and worth in the eyes of the family and kin networks back home. This sense of value and respect remains, regardless of how tough and challenging migrant lives in Russia may be. This is another reason that migrants will continue to maintain strong ties with their sending communities, rely on the informal social safety nets, while accepting injustices and exploitation. In one of the BBC Russia series on Uzbek migrants in the Far East, depicting lives of ordinary men and women living and working in Russia's villages, a man in his seventies who has been living in this Russian village for over a decade shares his position: "If tomorrow Putin says, 'Go home!' to all the migrants, I will go back to Uzbekistan; that's why I kept my house there."

What the future holds for the vyhodtsy from Kyrgyzstan in Russia remains to be seen. When asked about future life plans for an Radio Free Europe/Radio Liberty story about Kyrgyz migration to Russia, three sisters' responses as a naturalized family in central Russia vividly demonstrated the fluidity, multi-locality, and ambiguity of the concepts of home and homeland. The oldest spoke of her attachment to Russia as a country that raised her and where she sees her future. The middle sister similarly liked living in Russia, but her husband romanticized moving back to Kyrygzstan, which she was open to considering. The youngest sister, however, expressed more of a cosmopolitan belonging and saw her future neither in Kyrgyzstan nor in Russia, but in a third country with more opportunities. While the sisters' outlook on the future may still change, their present self-image as "foreigners here, but as Russians in Kyrgyzstan" revealed a shift toward hybrid identities among the second generation.

CASE III-A

Mobility and the Rural Modern along Tajikistan's Pamir Highway

Till Mostowlansky

The contemporary traveler crossing from southern Kyrgyzstan into Tajikistan's Pamir Mountains can see various relics of history along the road: border posts in different stages of development; graves and pilgrimage sites; semi-abandoned settlements; decaying truck stops inhabited by shepherd families; solitary Soviet statues; and—after the crossroads to China—improved road stretches, trade terminals, lines of trucks, and roadhouses advertising in Chinese. Each of these relics is an integral part of the contemporary social fabric of the region. At the same time, each also tells its own story about people's past and present mobility, the legacy of Soviet projects of modernization, contemporary political, economic, and social transformations, and the significance of transnational connections.

The Pamir Highway (*Pamirskii trakt*), part of the M41 in the regional network of roads, was constructed in the 1930s in the course of Soviet efforts to integrate the border region with China and Afghanistan into the larger framework of the Soviet Union. Leading from the city of Osh in the Ferghana Valley (in today's territory of Kyrgyzstan) through the high altitude plains of the Pamir Mountains to Khorog at the

Tajikistan-Afghanistan border, the Pamir Highway is subject to constant erosion. The manifold obstacles to construct the Pamir Highway in thin air and under extreme climatic and geological circumstances make this road a masterpiece of engineering that stands on a par with the highest roads around the world.

When Soviet engineers constructed the highway and paved the road through the Pamirs, they not only transformed the physical landscape. By carving out a distinct Soviet border zone with Afghanistan and China, the Gorno-Badakhshan Autonomous Region, they also altered social and economic ties. Starting in the 1930s, an influx of workers from the surrounding valleys as well as from various parts of the Soviet Union continuously increased the population along the highway. Retrospective Soviet depictions of road construction in the Pamirs tend to proudly emphasize the "international" aspect of the endeavor by mentioning that the first four men who drove their cars on the highway were German, Kyrgyz, Ukrainian, and Uzbek. New settlements were built to serve the road, and the villages in its reach were "modernized" through infrastructure, education, and health care. At the same time, in the 1940s, trade routes and kin relations to

Afghanistan and China were cut off as the Soviets militarized the borders.

Initially, the construction of the road and a socialist society along it were less triumphant than popular Soviet accounts would have us believe. At least the 1930s and 1940s were marked by hardship as an effect of rerouting people's economic and social connections. The region's dependency on the Pamir Highway as its centrally controlled life artery rendered it vulnerable to supply shortages in the course of snowfall and landslides. Throughout this period people sought to escape the establishment of Soviet rule by crossing into Afghanistan, China, and beyond. The positive, nostalgic image of Soviet presence that people along the Pamir Highway often reflect nowadays is linked to a later historical stage starting from the 1960s. For about the last twenty-five years of the Soviet period, we can think of the region as embedded within "Moscow provisioning" (*Moskovskoe obespechenie*), a colloquial umbrella term used to designate access to higher-quality consumer goods, educational opportunities, higher salaries and pensions, and privileged mobility within the Soviet Union. In this regard, places of strategic importance, deriving from the example of the "closed atomic city" (*zakrytye goroda*), not only were well resourced materially but also provided a cultural and aesthetic connection to Moscow as the center.

Against this backdrop, people's self-representations along the highway are often crafted in reference to this "modern past," which has provided many of them with the ability to navigate through the urban spaces of the Soviet Union as familiar territory. The breakup of the Soviet Union in 1991 should also not be seen as a point of rupture between Soviet and post-Soviet. With the beginning of the Tajik civil war in 1992, last-ing up to 1997, many people along the Pamir Highway certainly became impoverished as "Moscow provisioning" and its seemingly never-ending movement of goods vanished. Yet both the presence of the Russian military in high numbers and the influx of humanitarian aid led to prolonged forms of provisioning and an "international" social environment, which lasted until around 2002 when the Russian Army left the region.

Only two years after the Russians left Gorno-Badakhshan, the Tajik and Chinese governments declared open a newly constructed road link between the town of Murghab on the Pamir Highway and the Tajikistan-China border. The short stretch of paved road now connects the former Soviet highway with the extensive Chinese road network and other transnational highways such as the Karakoram Highway linking China and Pakistan. Tajikistan's hybrid of former Soviet and new Chinese road stretches have also begun to feature prominently in China's Belt and Road Initiative (*yi dai yi lu*), which invokes the image of contemporary overland connections between China and Central Asia as reviving the ancient Silk Road. However, even though the Tajik government promoted the new road as a promise of prosperity (see figures III-A-1a, b), a highly regulated and centralized business environment allows few people along the Pamir Highway to participate in and profit from trade with China. Similarly, and counterintuitively, the official opening of the borders with China and Afghanistan did not mean that lost family ties could simply be revived. On the one hand, seventy years of separation have led to the emergence of distinct local identities and have fostered linguistic and cultural differences. On the other hand, the Chinese visa regime and the volatile security situation

III-A-1a, b   A state-funded billboard (with close-up, opposite page) depicting the Pamir Highway and celebrating Tajik Independence Day, Unity Day, and Gorno-Badakhshan's ninetieth anniversary. Murghab, 2015. Photograph by Till Mostowlansky.

in Afghanistan have prevented people along the Pamir Highway from crossing the borders. With a strong sense of distinction as "modern" citizens in a region of unrest, they have thus rather oriented toward the urban centers of Central Asia and Russia in their personal and professional mobility. In the following, I illustrate such movement—and the habitus that it fosters—using two examples from my ethnography.

Parisian Desires and a Heroine Mother

It was a bitingly cold evening when Zhengishbek, his son-in-law, and I drove to their winter pasture (*kyshtak*) on the Chinese border in March 2010. They had to catch and slaughter a yak whose meat they had promised to a wedding party in the Ghunt Valley. After hours of hard work in an icy wind, we entered Zhengishbek's yurt and sat down next to the warming stove. Over dinner Zhengishbek, now in his seventies, felt like sharing the most radiant

stories from the time when he was still young (*jash*). Much to the dislike of his wife, he told us about his studies, travels, and women.

Zhengishbek was born in the Ferghana Valley in the 1940s, and his family moved to the town of Murghab on the highway when he was ten. He was a good student, and after his graduation from high school in Murghab he won a scholarship to study in Dushanbe. Later, he graduated with a PhD from a university in Tashkent and eventually returned to Murghab to work in a research lab. Despite his return to the Pamirs, he continued to travel to conferences and took up fellowships in different parts of the Soviet Union. He told me that he took his family to Tashkent. "But sometimes," he then said, "I traveled all by myself—to Kiev, to Ashgabat, and to Moscow. I had many nights out with drinks and once, at a conference, I met a French girl [*frantsuzhenka*] who almost took me with her." According to Zhengishbek, he had met the French

girl at a conference in Moscow. She was from Paris, and they developed a romantic relationship in the course of the weeklong stay in the Soviet capital, meeting secretly in restaurants and parks. He became attached to her to such an extent that he thought about following her back to France. While telling me about this episode, Zhengishbek remained vague about the reasons for his return to Murghab and for abandoning a plan that would not have been realistic given Soviet restrictions for traveling abroad. He then wagged his head, pointed to his wife who had turned her back toward us, pretending that she did not hear his stories, and said: "It's not important now. But when you came from Gorno-Badakhshan in the Soviet Union you could go anywhere, even to Paris, and you would know what to do and how to behave."

Baktygül is about the same age as Zhengishbek and was born in Murghab. She used to be employed as a teacher and a child-care worker in the Soviet Union. After her retirement she became a well-known herbal healer in my neighborhood in Murghab who treated people for vari-

ous diseases. When I met her for the first time in 2009 she introduced herself as a pedagogue (*pedagog*), healer (*emchi*), and heroine mother (*mat'-geroinia*). This self-representation reflects Baktygül's nuanced positioning in the world. Over the years, she emphasized that she thought of herself as a modern (*sovremennyi*) person who was influenced by Soviet ethics (*Sovietskaia etika*), locally rooted in Murghab and in the framework of Kyrgyz customs (*salt*), yet mobile and following the network of her children and grandchildren between Murghab, Osh, Khorog, and Dushanbe. The title of the heroine mother—awarded to women with ten or more children in the Soviet Union—not only granted her prestige and benefits such as free utilities, a better pension scheme, and other supplies. The large number of children and grandchildren, many of whom moved to places all over former Soviet Union, have also provided her with the opportunity to remain highly mobile well into her old age. Although she does not feel strong enough anymore to travel to Moscow where her daughter works as a hospital nurse, Baktygül still takes the occasional trip to Osh or to Dushanbe where one of her grandsons runs a business. When she travels to Dushanbe, Baktygül once told me, it now feels like going to a wild (*dikii*) and chaotic place that has materially and morally decayed since the Soviet Union vanished. In contrast, Moscow, even though now out of reach for her because of her troubled health, has always been close to her heart as a modern place of opportunity.

Matching Lifestyles and Embodied Modernity

Zhengishbek's and Baktygül's takes on mobility and their connections to centers beyond Gorno-Badakhshan are informed by their socialization along the Pamir Highway during a time of increasing provisioning and privilege. However, such views are not limited to their generation alone, and younger people in the region express similar opinions even if they have hardly any memories of the Soviet Union. For instance, Alikhon, now in his late twenties, grew up along the Pamir Highway and spent many years as a labor migrant in Moscow. While talking to me he never denied the difficulties and struggles he went through as part of the illicit Central Asian labor force in Russia. Yet whenever we met in 2010 and 2011, Alikhon also emphasized that things went comparatively smoothly for him in Moscow, given that he had grown up in Gorno-Badakhshan, went to a Russian

school, had fair hair and a "European face" (*Evropeiskoe litso*), and had been taught a Russian lifestyle (*obraz zhizni*). He tended to juxtapose his own and his friends' experiences with those of "rural" (*kishlachnye*) people from the western parts of Tajikistan. He and his friends from Gorno-Badakhshan often managed to blend in, were more adaptable, spoke "proper" Russian, and knew when to do what, but "those Tajiks" (*eti Tadzhiki*) from the west could easily be distinguished from Russians, were loud, and knew hardly any Russian.

On the one hand, we can conceive of this "modern habitus" along the Pamir Highway as a relic of Soviet history. On the other hand, we also need to understand that such contemporary claims for modernity constitute a social practice that is alive and embedded in the present. In this regard, the rural modern in Gorno-Badakhshan is intricately linked to the transformation of power relations in Tajikistan, in the course of which the region's inhabitants, proudly mobile and educated in the Soviet Union, have been relocated to the economic, political, and cultural margins of the state. The perpetuation of a modern identity along the Pamir Highway, transmitted in families and in select sites of public discourse, inverts this marginality into its positive aspect and stresses distinction from the rest of the country as a resource to connect to the world.

From Potemkin Village to Real Life in Turkmenistan

Sebastien Peyrouse

In July 2016 the Turkmen president Gurbanguly Berdimuhamedow (Berdimuhamedov) inaugurated a new modern urban-type village, Berkarar Zaman. The village was designed for six hundred families and located in the district (*etrap*) of Garabekewul, far from the country's few urban centers. This event took place in a festive atmosphere, with dancers, children, traditionally decorated houses, happy fruit merchants selling in markets overflowing with goods, and horsemen on slender Akhalteke horses. After the president left, the village returned to its previous state: an uninhabited shell in the middle of nowhere. Some days later, the sign indicating the town's name was even taken down.

Berkarar Zaman is one example of propaganda among many, a Potemkin village designed to symbolize the Turkmen miracle that had arrived, in the town as in the countryside. With its immense gas potentials, as the world's fifth-largest supplier of natural gas, the country sees itself as the new Kuwait of Central Asia, led by its Protector (*Arkadag*), Gurbanguly Berdimuhamedow, the great orchestrator of a prosperous life for the entire population, in the era of the so-called Great Renaissance, or the Era of Supreme Happiness and the

Stable State. But the everyday reality of life is drab. The values and wealth of all these symbols are available to only a tiny minority of citizens, illustrating a deep gap between propaganda and the social and economic difficulties that confront the majority of the population, which is at the mercy of an authoritarian and repressive state, a cult of personality, and virtually nonexistent public services.

The Prevalence of Presidents' Megalomania in Everyday Life

Very soon after independence, the architecture and the landscape of Turkmenistan was altered with pharaonic projects of which the cost cut deep into the state budget and mortgaged the country's development. The capital city, in particular, was seen to be the embodiment of late president Saparmurat Niyazov's megalomania. The corruption related to real estate, whether in the context of big construction projects or smaller buildings, was a source of huge gains. Deliberately allowing Soviet Ashgabat to deteriorate, Niyazov commissioned the construction of a number of monuments and luxurious palaces surrounded by huge lawns that were watered continuously while water consumption was limited for ordinary citizens. Many other buildings, often

III-B-1   Monumental buildings along a broad avenue in Ashgabat, 2014. Photograph by Natalie Koch.

decorated in gold and marble but empty of visitors or clients and very costly to maintain, shaped the new face of the capital.

Since 2007, Berdimuhamedow has been as symbolically invested in new building projects as his predecessor, especially in Ashgabat (see figure III-B-1). In addition to the administrative buildings, tens of residential buildings have sprung up in the capital. A marble façade is obligatory, even for civil buildings. Built to order for different ministries, these buildings are supposed to be sold to the employees of these same ministries at preferential prices; they remain largely uninhabited, however, as they are unaffordable for most of the population. This large-scale reshaping of the city has had major consequences for its inhabitants. The Turkmen regime regularly requisitioned sites for these presidential projects. The properties of hundreds of families in the center and suburbs of Ashgabat were expropriated in the days following a decision to raze their homes and build new buildings or parks. The necessity of demolishing people's homes was typically explained as a question of aesthetics or land use. Despite official pronouncements guaranteeing compensation for any expropriated property, the govern-

ment uses many arguments to deny the planned compensatory measures, which rarely correspond to the actual value of the destroyed houses. The value of the land is not taken into account in the compensation process. Many of those expelled are given small apartments in remote areas in return for their houses with land near the city center.

The wind of the "Great Renaissance" also blows in the countryside, which has not escaped the presidential megalomania. Both presidents launched several white elephant projects. In 2000 Niyazov ordered the construction of the "Lake of Golden Century" (Lake Turkmen), in the middle of the Karakum Desert, undertaken in part by prisoners employed as cheap labor. This project adds to the already severe water scarcity in the Amu Darya Valley and, further downstream, in the Aral Sea by diverting a portion of one of its tributaries. Before his death Niyazov launched a project to establish a tourist site at Avaza, which has been further developed by Berdimuhamedow. Located at the east side of the Caspian Sea, twelve kilometers from Turkmenbashi city, this site does not correspond to commercial logic, however: in the summer months the sea there is cold while the climate is hot; the country requires visas that are difficult to obtain; and the site is polluted and thus ecologically unfavorable to tourism activity, given its proximity to oil complexes and an offshore extraction platform. Foreign firms, called to invest in the region, resisted and only became involved under duress when their contracts were at stake. The majority of construction was initiated by the government itself, which obliged each ministry and large state corporation to have its own hotel or sanatorium so that it could send its personnel there.

The reality of such projects, of course, is different from the grandiosity of their presentation. The markets presented for the inauguration of Berkarar Zaman, overflowing with fruits, vegetables, and basic daily items, were intended to show off the local produce and the prosperity of the rural areas. Turkmenistan remains a predominantly rural state. However, agriculture, which employs nearly 50 percent of the population, produces only 13 percent of national GDP. The country faces agrarian overpopulation in arable areas, which represent less than 5 percent of the land area (about 1.9 million hectares) according to World Bank data; the remaining 95 percent is mainly desert or uninhabited. Pressure on the land is increasing since birth rates remain high, especially in rural areas. Moreover, a process of ruralization affected Turkmenistan in the 1980s and 1990s: given the difficulties of urban life in the absence of industrial jobs, many have preferred returning to the land, resettling in native villages, and working on individual plots—all of which has compounded the problem of the lack of arable land.

Social Services and Standards of Living versus Propaganda

The dire picture of real urban and rural life contrasts sharply with the idealized one. The day following Niyazov's death in December 2006, the new president announced reforms that were hailed by the international community as a way to reduce the most negative effects of his predecessor's policies, in particular in the education and health sectors. After Niyazov reduced the mandatory educational curriculum from eleven to nine years, in February 2007 Berdimuhamedow issued a decree reintroducing a period of ten years of mandatory education, and with a new decree in 2012 he extended it to twelve years. New schools have been opened in the country, some fitted with modern equipment. The inauguration of these schools took place with great pomp, but the said reforms were highly cosmetic and did little to conceal the ongoing deterioration of the education system.

A growing number of schools, particularly outside the capital, have classes only in the morning or the afternoon. Many teachers demand bribes to compensate for their poor wages, work simultaneously in other sectors, or hold more than one school position concurrently, exacerbating the disorganization of the system. Most of the country's schools have not been refurbished since independence, apart from a few cosmetic works undertaken during summer vacations using funds collected from teachers and the parents of pupils. The schools also lack enough qualified staff to teach physics and chemistry, among other subjects. Turkmen schools still have a general dearth of textbooks, with some dating from the Soviet era. The computer equipment that the schools have supposedly received appears to be rather superfluous in villages: teachers have not received any training nor has there been any upkeep planned. The personality cult of Niyazov—where pupils and students were systematically obliged to perform on a daily basis, in particular with the

III-B-2   A roadside store in Dashoguz, 2000. Photograph by David W. Montgomery.

compulsory learning of the official book, the *Ruhnama*—was followed by the cult of Berdimuhamedow. Pupils must now study "the policy of the Renaissance Era," in which they are taught about the new summits the country has attained and the justness of presidential decisions.

In a country headed by a former dentist, health has been fully integrated into its nation building. After Niyazov closed many hospitals outside the capital in 2005, the new president committed himself to putting the health system back on its feet. He announced preparations that would see increased preventative medical care and immunization, the reopening of rural clinics, the construction of new hospitals, and he allowed the resumption of contact between domestic and foreign medical experts who had been removed under Niyazov. The country now has several hospital clinics that are equipped with cutting-edge technology.

The launched reforms are criticized for being confined to specific domains, such as cancer or eye surgery in the capital, while urgent reforms in other sectors remain largely forgotten or delayed, or even censored, such as the fight against AIDS, tuberculosis, and other infectious diseases. In Ashgabat, despite the opening of a transplant center, no operation of that kind has been undertaken because of the lack of competent staff. Today Turkmenistan continues to operate based on an infrastructure inherited from Soviet times and has failed to reinvest in it. The number of trained personnel is far too low and the system is suffering because the period of medical training was reduced to two years, again something imposed by Niyazov. The World Health Organization ranks Turkmenistan 168th out of 200 countries based on the number of doctors per capita: thirty-six per ten thousand inhabitants in 1991, a number that had dropped to twenty-two by 2014. Furthermore, although there were ninety midwives per ten thousand people at the end of the Soviet Union, there were only forty-four in 2014. From 2010, despite his so-called political opening, Berdimuhamedow systematically hindered foreign medical cooperation, forcing the few international health organizations still present, such as Doctors without Borders, to leave the country. Since the end of the 2000s no reliable statistics are available on the state of health in the country.

Despite a GDP per capita of seven thousand US dollars in 2018 (the second highest in the region), food security is not guaranteed. Flour shortages have provoked serious social tensions in several regions such as in Lebap and Dashoguz (see figure III-B-2). Problems with the procurement of bread have been reported in some cities since 2009 and some basic foodstuffs have been rationed since 2014.

Given the deteriorating economic situation at the beginning of the 2000s, the number of people living below the poverty line increased to 58 percent in 2003 and then went back down to 30 percent at the end of the decade. Although the unemployment rate is at around 9 percent, unofficial assessments estimate that the real figure is much higher, around 50 percent. The average wage stagnates at less than fifty dollars a month at black market rates. Indicative of a crisis that affects the whole of society, except for the statistically small ruling class, there are few differences in living standards between people of different social classes as differentiated, for example, by education. Those in the public service sector (administration, education, and medicine) who were considered privileged under the Soviet regime have, since independence, experienced a severe decline in living standards with the virtual disappearance of their advantages and with recurrent delays in receiving salaries.

Real Life in Turkmenistan

Great hopes were aroused that, with Berdimuhamedow's arrival in power, the situation would improve. The so-called Great Renaissance was supposed to engage spectacular all-embracing reforms to strengthen and expand the economic power of the country, increase the standard of living of the Turkmen people, and develop all areas of life in society and the state without exception. In spite of some positive changes after Niyazov's death, living standards have far from met expectations. Despite its economic wealth (17.5 trillion cubic meters in gas reserves), Turkmenistan continues to languish—in 108th place—in the Human Development Index released in 2019.

The gas bounty that was supposed to trickle down to the benefit of all people in the country has served mainly to enrich the elites and to finance pharaonic projects. One can observe a deterioration of social welfare since the beginning of the new century. Shortages of subsidized products occur more and more frequently, the price of natural gas and petroleum-based derivatives has skyrocketed, yet pensions are regularly reduced. Since global hydrocarbon prices plummeted in 2014, Turkmenistan has been facing its most serious crisis in thirty years—worsening further, among other things, the social welfare system. The general social situation remains tense, with a total absence of public liberty, serious violations of religious rights, mostly unacknowledged massive unemployment, poverty among the youth, the elderly, and rural populations, loss of confidence among the middle classes whose educational and professional opportunities have been reduced, increasing corruption within state organs, and difficulties in ensuring food security. Today, many Turkmen citizens nostalgically look back to the Brezhnev years as a "golden age" during which food and health care in the country were a given.

Finally, the main long-term problem of Turkmenistan and its population probably remains the lack of human capital, which has been destroyed in the last two decades and will require time to be restored. Niyazov and Berdimuhamedow deliberately broke with the Soviet legacy, including elements that proved valuable to other independent successor states such as very high literacy and a guaranteed minimum of health care for all. Over the course of thirty years, they sacrificed an entire generation and mortgaged the future of the country. In 2020, between one and two million Turkmenistanis—out of a total population of between five and six million—had left the country, discouraged by the social hardship, political authoritarianism, and the lack of economic prospects. Turkmenistan will be unable to cast itself as a Central Asian "emirate" unless it bets on its human capital. An "emirate future" implies a literate population, one that is educated in foreign languages, that has contacts abroad and is able to respond to an international presence, a population that is trained in technological professions in order to better control the country's strategic choices, and one that is competitive in the context of a service, knowledge-based economy. Real life in Turkmenistan is not yet that.

CASE III-C

Private Education, Inequality, and the Growing Social Divide in Bishkek

Emil Nasritdinov, Aigoul Abdoubaetova, and Gulnora Iskandarova

Aizhan and Erkin were born into the Soviet system in the 1970s: Aizhan in the village and Erkin in the city. As kids they felt they were the luckiest kids on the planet to be born and to live in the best country in the world—the USSR—at the time of its highest modernization efforts. The Communist government cared for them: it gave them nice kindergartens, schools, and universities. Not only was it free to study but the kindergarten and schools provided free food; universities provided free housing and a stipend to live on. Aizhan and Erkin brought secondhand clothes and stationary items to send to the poor kids in Angola, and they felt bad for African American kids in the United States who were homeless and could not afford to go to school.

Later, they learned that the Soviet system was also authoritarian, oppressive, and stagnant, and that in some regions of Central Asia it brought the destruction of entire lifestyles and the deaths of millions of people. Yet, when they look at all that the Soviet system of education, health, and infrastructure left to them, they feel appreciative of the Soviet period. The Soviets exploited resources, suppressed freedoms, and arrested and killed millions during Stalin's purges, but they also built cities, roads, schools, hospitals, theaters, and lots of housing. Growing up with all this development taking place—and unaware of the purges—was inspiring for Aizhan and Erkin. There was a strong sense of equality and almost unlimited opportunity, and late Soviet society was in many ways very egalitarian.

Three decades since the Soviet Union collapsed and Kyrgyzstan became an independent country, things have changed. In this case we reflect on some of the changes and try to refrain from nostalgia about Soviet life and pessimism about contemporary life. Yet, the sentiments described above are important for us to appreciate where we stand and how the position and experience of our two main characters affect the way they see present-day educational opportunities for children in Kyrgyzstan.

Aizhan and Erkin have two children, a fourteen-year-old son and an eight-year-old daughter. Naturally, they are concerned with the education and opportunities their children will have. When Aizhan and Erkin's son was three, they took him to a kindergarten in their Bishkek neighborhood. Their son did not like it and he cried every other morning they took him there. The kindergarten

III-C-1a, b Some private schools use the name recognition of elite world universities to convey prestige and therein justify higher costs. Here, the Oxford International School advertises student success in an international math competition (*above*) and the Cambridge United World International School (*opposite page*) highlights advanced placement (AP) offerings on the building's façade, Bishkek, Kyrgyzstan, 2020. Photographs by Aigoul Abdoubaetova.

was for children of mixed ages and the class included over forty boys and girls. At one point he had a female teacher who used to beat children for no apparent reason. He used to get sick quite often when he was there. So by the time he was six and ready to advance to primary school, Aizhan and Erkin were very much disillusioned about the child care and education provided by the state and, after looking through their budget, decided to send him to a private school. There was one not far from where they lived that was more or less affordable: they paid approximately $200 a month, which is nearly the same as an average salary in Kyrgyzstan ($215 in 2018) and that included all-day care (from eight to five) and three meals. The school has its own security guards, and most teachers are nice to the kids. When their daughter was three, they enrolled her in kinder-

garten in the same school. It was very convenient for them considering that both of them were working full-time: they took the kids there in the morning on the way to work and picked them up in the evening on the way home.

If they can afford it this is what many parents opt for these days. The number of private schools and kindergartens has been growing steadily, especially since 2015; between 1995–2017, the number of private schools increased six times, from 19 to 114. The range of options varies significantly. Aizhan and Erkin's children go to one of the less expensive schools, which provides an average-quality education but compensates through all-day care, security, and a small class size. They pay approximately twenty-five hundred dollars a year per child, so five thousand dollars for two, which is quite a strain on their budget. Yet, their school

EMIL NASRITDINOV, AIGOUL ABDOUBAETOVA, AND GULNORA ISKANDAROVA

is not the most expensive by far: if we group all private schools into three categories by the cost of education, it is in the one-third-less-expensive category with tuition around two or three thousand dollars, known for convenience and security rather than quality of teaching. The secondmost expensive category of private schools has a tuition range of from five to seven thousand dollars; many of these are Turkish Lyceums. They provide fairly good-quality education, and their primary language of teaching is either Russian or Kyrgyz. Their graduates mostly aim to enter the more prestigious local universities. As for the most expensive category, there are four private schools in the city that charge between ten thousand and twenty-five thousand dollars a year. All subjects in these four schools are taught in English. Most students do not even bother studying for local standard graduation tests because they are not interested in applying to local colleges. Many experts and interviewed parents see these schools as preparing students for "export," to apply to colleges in the

West—that is, in Europe, the United States, and Canada.

In addition to private schools, there are now many private educational centers in the city that offer language courses and courses on specific school subjects. Many parents opt for this more flexible and less expensive option: they take children to public schools and they send them to these private educational centers after classes. These four categories of primary and secondary education constitute the landscape of private educational choices. Almost all private schools boast better infrastructure, new buildings, new furniture, computers, interactive boards, and so on. They also provide security, all-day care, and small-size classes.

Growing demand in response to both services and lower satisfaction in public schools is met with an increase in the number of private schools. Yet if one considers that the average salary in Bishkek in 2018 was only $263, this growing demand for schools with tuition rates ranging from $2,500 to $25,000 tells you something important—it tells a story of growing inequality. Of those who can afford to send their children to private schools, we can distinguish several categories representing the new social hierarchy. On the very top are representatives of the so-called Kyrgyz elite: top-level state officials, Parliament deputies, and very wealthy businessmen—some of whom built their capital through hard work and entrepreneurial talents and others who did it through various kinds of corruption schemes, appropriation of state property, and criminal engagement. They are the ones who can afford the most expensive schools or who force such schools to accept their children for free. These are followed by the category of "new Kyrgyz"—businessmen who made their fortunes themselves, for example, by working in the Dordoi Bazaar. They are the new Kyrgyz bourgeoisie who are trying to establish their own position in Bishkek's urban society and sending kids to private schools is one such status-making strategy. A third category includes professionals such as Aizhan and Erkin who work for international organizations, have decent stable salaries, and thus can afford the cost of lower-end private schools.

Taken together, these three groups represent the wealthy minority. The poor majority of the city population—those living on an average salary of $263 per month—send their children to regular public schools. The situation in public schools is deteriorating. Because of shortages in the state budget, very few new schools have been built since the breakup of the Soviet Union, though the city has grown steadily since independence, largely because of high rates of internal migration. As a result there is an acute shortage of schools; students study in two or even three shifts; the number of students in class can reach fifty and more; and in some cases, three or four boys and girls must share one table intended for two. Since most of these schools were built in Soviet times, some sixty or seventy years ago, their physical condition is steadily deteriorating. They receive only 20,000 som ($285) a year for renovation purposes. Most public schools are forced to collect money from parents for such purposes. Public schools also suffer from a shortage of qualified teachers since the average teacher's salary is $180 per month—two-thirds of the average monthly salary in the capital. Those who decide to teach anyway have heavy teaching loads. It is no wonder that a child who sits with fifty other kids in one room and takes classes from an overburdened, underpaid, and demotivated teacher learns very little.

On the top of all that, public schools have been suffering from the problems of school racketeering and violence: older students and teenagers from the street regularly extort money from younger kids and beat them up if the latter do not comply. The school administration can do very little about it, because they lack the resources to secure the school premises and provide safe passage home for children. The overall image of public primary and secondary education in Bishkek is extremely grim, particularly in the *novostroikas*, the peripheral squatter settlements populated by internal migrants. The only exception to such pessimistic descriptions is a very few special public schools—gymnasiums and lyceums—that have a special experimental status and receive additional funding from the Ministry of Education. They are known for their students' high results in the standardized graduation tests and victories in various kinds of knowledge-based competitions between schools. However, these few schools are also overcrowded, harder to get accepted into, and harder to stay in because of heavy study loads and high expectations on academic performance: underperforming students get expelled.

Bishkek's story is not unique. In most parts of the world, educational opportunities are differentiated: kids from rich families tend to frequent private schools while kids from poor families can only attend overcrowded public schools. What makes the Bishkek case interesting is its Soviet legacy. Only thirty years ago, all children in the city would have had similar opportunities provided by the socialist state. At that time, education was largely meritocratic: young people's personal skills, intellect, talent, and hard work played a much more important role in their academic and career success than they do now. Today, a talented and motivated kid from a poor family cannot compete with someone whose parents can afford private school and tutors. The state is too poor or too negligent to take proper care of public schools. The neoliberal market is steadily taking over, and increasingly, education is being treated as a business that offers the most services to those with the most resources.

This is seen not only in secondary education but in higher education too. For example, the American University of Central Asia (AUCA) used to be seen as the agent of local change. Up until the late 2000s, the annual tuition was only one thousand dollars and, with up to a 50 percent discount based on need, even low-income families were able to pay for their children. The university used to get very bright and highly motivated students, and AUCA was a great platform from which many began their careers. However, beginning in the early 2010s, the cost of tuition has increased sevenfold; it is now nearly seven thousand dollars and, even with a discount, parents of many talented children simply cannot afford it. The university now boasts a brand-new fancy building designed by a famous American architect. The building has more amenities, but on the whole the university has become less a place of knowledge and opportunity and more a place for breeding the elite—those who can afford the higher tuition. Such students are more likely to see themselves as customers, and they are not as motivated in their studies and extracurricular pursuits because their future is financially more secure because of their parents' status.

It is no wonder that upon graduation, children from private and public schools and colleges are going to have different career paths. For the private-school students, globalization opens a world of new opportunities to travel, study, and work abroad or to have lucrative places among the growing Kyrgyz business and political elites. For the public-school students, globalization at best offers a labor migration path to Russia, where most work in manual labor jobs and live as second-class citizens in the xenophobic Russian society. As in many other contexts around the world, inequalities in education reinforce wider social inequalities.

One cannot help but notice the evidence of wider social inequality in Bishkek. It is common to see people digging through trash at waste-collecting points. They look for paper, plastic, and bottles that can be exchanged for petty cash for recycling. Any large supermarket usually has one or two beggars asking for change outside the main entrance, and sadly most of them are elderly pensioners. From a window at the new AUCA building, one can see a small self-made shelter with homeless people warming themselves by a fire. Similar scenes of urban poverty abound. Poverty has become a common feature of urban life in the capital, but beyond being common it has become normalized. People are no longer shocked, having become so accustomed to the poverty that they do not notice it anymore. There was a lot of poverty on the streets in the 1990s, but then everyone was poor, struggling to survive. Today, poverty contrasts sharply with a new luxurious lifestyle for a few elite: premium-style apartments with penthouses and swimming pools, fancy restaurants, trendy cars, and expensive private schools. It is when looking at this contrast that Aizhan and Erkin become nostalgic about the Soviet past, when neither the wealth nor the poverty was as obvious as it is today and when the opportunities were real for everyone.

For many people, their more secure financial status is the result of decades of hard work, at the bazaar, in Russia, and in international organizations. However, there is also an understanding that many became rich by engaging in various kinds of corrupt practices; 94 percent of young people surveyed perceive the state as corrupt and name corruption as the number one problem in the country. Corruption gives poverty an additional dimension of injustice, and thus the experience of poverty becomes particularly bitter. It is no wonder that Kyrgyzstan has already had multiple revolutions. Corruption also kills the hope for improvement. International donors aimed to help create opportunities for young people, but the underlying neoliberal bias means many get left out. Unfortunately, as we see from the example of AUCA, even international institutions prefer to serve the wealthy, which reinforces social division and creates new social hierarchies.

This is when people become nostalgic about Soviet egalitarianism and depressed about the expansion of neoliberal capitalism. An AUCA student once questioned in class: "Poverty? Do we have any?" She lives in a different Bishkek than most, traveling in an expensive car from an elite residential area to a prestigious private university, where she drinks expensive two-dollar cappuccinos, unaware of—or pretending and preferring not to notice—the dire conditions in which other urbanites live. One reason for this is that Soviet and Kyrgyz egalitarian traditions make people ashamed of their poor condition and many urban poor (aside from the homeless who are easily noticeable) prefer to hide their status. Yet, the difference—inequality and disparity of opportunities, especially in education—exists, and the divide is growing, along with the unresolved tension, pessimism, and bitterness.

DISCUSSION QUESTIONS

PART III: CONTEXTS OF LIVING

9. Rural Life

1. How have rural livelihoods been changing on the collective farms since the end of the Soviet Union?

2. In which way did post-Soviet reform policies alter agricultural production and reshape rural communities in Central Asian countries?

10. Urban Life

3. How do ideas of "modernity" and "backwardness" shape decisions about urban life and built environments in Central Asia? How does this compare with your home country?

4. Urban residents in Central Asia experience their cities in very different ways, depending on their relative wealth, ethnic identity, religious affiliation, age, gender, legal status, and so on. Is Central Asia different from other parts of the world in terms of the scope and type of these diverse urban experiences? Why or why not?

11. Migratory Life

5. What is the significance of the Soviet past for the ways in which Kyrgyzstani migrant workers articulate the value of physically demanding labor in contemporary Russia?

6. Why is being documented insufficient to protect Central Asian migrant workers from racial discrimination in contemporary Russia?

12. Diaspora Life

7. What constitutes diaspora? How are diaspora identities formed, by whom, and for what purposes? How do migrants perceive their belonging in a country that they once were citizens of?

8. How do migrants integrate into society in the context of constantly changing migration policies? What does it mean to call home a place where one lives temporarily? Can temporary migration be eternally temporary?

Case III-A: Mobility and the Rural Modern along Tajikistan's Pamir Highway

9. In the Soviet Union, mobility played an essential part in fostering modern identities and lifestyles. Discuss the types of movement involved in this process as well as the restrictions that the state put in place to manage them.

10. Migration and diaspora are part and parcel of everyday life along the Pamir Highway, as many families have moved there from elsewhere. Discuss how different forms of diaspora—along the Pamir Highway and in labor migration abroad—might relate to each other.

Case III-B: From Potemkin Village to Real Life in Turkmenistan

11. In whichever way President Berdimuhamedow eventually leaves office (whether as a result of death, a coup, voluntary retirement, etc.), the case of post-Niyazov Turkmenistan shows that a change of president does not necessarily entail real change in political practices. Moreover, it reveals how difficult it can be for a dictatorial regime to "soften" or liberalize domestic policies when the same circle of elites remain in place. What could post-Berdimuhamedow Turkmenistan be like, and what could drive change in the Turkmen political system?

12. For more than thirty years, both Presidents Niyazov and Berdimuhamedow have weakened Turkmenistani social capital, particularly the education and health systems, thus undermining the future of the country. What could be the engines to reconstruct and stimulate the country's social capital—for example, fundamental reforms, migration, or foreign assistance?

Case III-C: Private Education, Inequality, and the Growing Social Divide in Bishkek

13. How does private education in Kyrgyzstan result from and contribute to growing social inequalities in the country?

14. How does the Soviet legacy of egalitarian education reinforce the feeling of injustice with regard to the growing socioeconomic divide between public and private schools?

FURTHER READING

9. Rural Life

Dudoignon, Stéphane, and Christian Noack, eds. *Allah's Kolkhozes: Migration, De-Stalinisation, Privatisation, and the New Muslim Congregations in the Soviet Realm (1950s–2000s)*. Berlin: Klaus Schwarz, 2014.

Féaux de la Croix, Jeanne. *Iconic Places in Central Asia: The Moral Geography of Dams, Pastures and Holy Sites*. Bielefeld: Transcript, 2016.

Hofman, Irna. *Cotton, Control, and Continuity in Disguise: The Political Economy of Agrarian Transformation in Lowland Tajikistan*. Enschede: Ipskamp, 2019.

Kandiyoti, Deniz, ed. *The Cotton Sector in Central Asia: Economic Policy and Development Challenges*. London: School of Oriental and African Studies, 2007.

Kandiyoti, Deniz. "The Cry for Land: Agrarian Reform, Gender and Land Rights in Uzbekistan." *Journal of Agrarian Change* 3, no. 1–2 (2003): 225–56.

Khan, Azirur Rahman, and Dharam Ghai. *Collective Agriculture and Rural Development in Soviet Central Asia*. London: Palgrave Macmillan, 1979.

Poliakov, Sergei. *Everyday Islam: Religion and Tradition in Rural Central Asia.* New York: M.E. Sharpe, 1992.

Roy, Olivier. *The New Central Asia: The Creation of Nations.* London: I. B. Tauris, 2000.

Trevisani, Tommaso. *Land and Power in Khorezm: Farmers, Communities, and the State in Uzbekistan's Decollectivisation.* Berlin: LIT, 2011.

Zanca, Russell. *Life in a Muslim Uzbek Village: Cotton Farming after Communism.* Belmont, CA: Wadsworth, 2011.

10. Urban Life

Darieva, Tsypylma, Wolfgang Kaschuba, and Melanie Krebs. *Urban Spaces after Socialism: Ethnographies of Public Places in Eurasian Cities.* Frankfurt am Main: Campus, 2011.

Koch, Natalie. *The Geopolitics of Spectacle: Space, Synecdoche, and the New Capitals of Asia.* Ithaca, NY: Cornell University Press, 2018.

Laszczkowski, Mateusz. *"City of the Future": Built Space, Modernity, and Change in Astana.* New York: Berghahn, 2016.

Siegelbaum, Lewis. *Cars for Comrades: The Life of the Soviet Automobile.* Ithaca, NY: Cornell University Press, 2008.

Stronski, Paul. *Tashkent: Forging a Soviet City, 1930–1966.* Pittsburgh: University of Pittsburgh Press, 2010.

11. Migratory Life

Féaux de la Croix, Jeanne. "After the Worker State: Competing and Converging Frames of Valuing Labor in Rural Kyrgyzstan." *Laboratorium: Russian Journal of Social Research* 6, no. 2 (2014): 77–99.

Kubal, Agnieszka. "Spiral Effect of the Law: Migrants' Experiences of the State Law in Russia—A Comparative Perspective." *International Journal of Law in Context* 12, no. 4 (2016): 453–68.

Maksutova, Aikokul. *Children of Post-Soviet Transnationalism: Integration Potential of Labour Migrants from Central Asia in Russia.* Berlin: LIT Verlag, 2019.

Nikiforova, Elena, and Olga Brednikova. "On Labor Migration to Russia: Central Asian Migrants and Migrant Families in the Matrix of Russia's Bordering Policies." *Political Geography* 66 (2018): 142–50.

Pine, Frances. "Migration as Hope: Time, Space and Imagining the Future." *Current Anthropology* 55, suppl. 9 (2014): S95–S104.

Reeves, Madeleine. "Black Work, Green Money: Remittances, Ritual and Domestic Economies in Southern Kyrgyzstan." *Slavic Review* 71, no. 1 (2012): 108–34.

Reeves, Madeleine. "Clean Fake: Authenticating Documents and Persons in Migrant Moscow." *American Ethnologist* 40, no. 3 (2013): 508–24.

Sahadeo, Jeff. *Voices from the Soviet Edge: Southern Migrants in Leningrad and Moscow.* Ithaca, NY: Cornell University Press, 2019.

Schenk, Caress. *Why Control Immigration? Strategic Uses of Migration Management in Russia.* Toronto: University of Toronto Press, 2018.

Urinboyev, Rustamjon, and Abel Polese. "Informality Currencies: A Tale of Misha, his Brigada and Informal Practices among Uzbek Labour Migrants in Russia." *Journal of Contemporary Central and Eastern Europe* 24, no. 3 (2016): 191–206.

12. Diaspora Life

Abashin, Sergei. "Migration Policies in Russia: Laws and Debates." In *Migrant Workers in Russia: Global Challenges of the Shadow Economy in Societal Transformation*, edited by A.-L. Heusala and K. Aitamurto, 16–34. New York: Routledge, 2017.

Aitieva, Medina. "Reconstituting Transnational Families: An Ethnography of Family Practices between Kyrgyzstan and Russia." PhD diss., University of Manchester, 2015.

Argounova-Low, Tatiana. "Close Relatives and Outsiders: Village People in the City of Yakutsk, Siberia." *Arctic Anthropology* 44, no. 1 (2007): 51–61.

Kashnitsky, Daniel, and Ekaterina Demintseva. "'Kyrgyz Clinics' in Moscow: Medical Centers for Central Asian Migrants." *Medical Anthropology* 37, no. 5 (2018): 401–11.

Kuznetsova, Irina, and John Round. "Postcolonial Migrations in Russia: The Racism, Informality and Discrimination Nexus." *International Journal of Sociology and Social Policy* 39, no. 1–2 (2018): 52–67.

Laruelle, Marlène. "Anti-Migrant Riots in Russia: The Mobilizing Potential of Xenophobia." *Russian Analytical Digest* 141 (2013): 2–4.

Maksutova, Aikokul. *Children of Post-Soviet Transnationalism: Integration Potential of Labour Migrants from Central Asia in Russia.* Berlin: LIT Verlag, 2019.

McBrien, Julie. "Leaving for Work, Leaving in Fear." *Anthropology Today.* 27, no. 4 (2011): 3–4.

Nikolko, Milana, and David Carment, eds. *Post-Soviet Migration and Diasporas: From Global Perspectives to Everyday Practices.* New York: Palgrave Macmillan, 2017.

Reeves, Madeleine. "Living from the Nerves: Deportability, Indeterminacy, and the 'Feel of Law' in Migrant Moscow." *Social Analysis* 59, no. 4 (2015): 119–36.

Roche, Sophie. "Illegal Migrants and Pious Muslims: The Paradox of Bazaar Workers from Tajikistan." In *Tajikistan on the Move: Statebuilding and Societal Transformations*, edited by Marlène Laruelle, 247–78. Lanham, MD: Lexington Books, 2018.

Round, John, and Irina Kuznetsova. "Necropolitics and the Migrant as a Political Subject of Disgust: The Precarious Everyday of Russia's Labour Migrants." *Critical Sociology* 42, no. 7–8 (2016): 1017–34.

Ruget, Vanessa, and Burul Usmanalieva. "Can Smartphones Empower Labour Migrants? The Case of Kyrgyzstani Migrants in Russia." *Central Asian Survey* 38, no. 2 (2019): 165–80.

Ruget, Vanessa, and Burul Usmanalieva. "Social and Political Transnationalism among Central Asian Migrants and Return Migrants: A Case Study of Kyrgyzstan." *Problems of Post-Communism* 58, no. 6 (2011): 48–60.

Schenk, Caress. *Why Control Immigration? Strategic Uses of Migration Management in Russia.* Toronto: University of Toronto Press, 2018.

Siegert, Jens. "Natives, Foreigners and Native Foreigners—The Difficult Task of Coexistence in Russia." *Russian Analytical Digest* 141 (2013): 5–7.

Urinboyev, Rustam. "Migration, Transnationalism, and Social Change in Central Asia: Everyday Transnational Lives of Uzbek Migrants in Russia." In *Eurasia on the Move: Interdisciplinary Approaches to a Dynamic Migration Region*, edited by Marlène Laruelle and Caress Schenk, 27–41. Washington, DC: George Washington University, Central Asia Program, 2018.

Vinokurova, Dekabrina. "Migration in the Cities of Sakha Republic (Yakutia): Temporal-Social Aspects." *Anthropology and Archeology of Eurasia* 56, no. 3–4 (2017): 256–74.

Case III-A: Mobility and the Rural Modern along Tajikistan's Pamir Highway

Bliss, Frank. *Social and Economic Change in the Pamirs (Gorno-Badakhshan, Tajikistan)*. Translated by Nicola Pacult and Sonia Guss, with Tim Sharp. London: Routledge, 2006.

Kreutzmann, Hermann. *Pamirian Crossroads: Kirghiz and Wakhi in High Asia*. Wiesbaden: Harrassowitz, 2015.

Mostowlansky, Till. *Azan on the Moon: Entangling Modernity along Tajikistan's Pamir Highway*. Pittsburgh: University of Pittsburgh Press, 2017.

Reeves, Madeleine. *Border Work: Spatial Lives of the State in Rural Central Asia*. Ithaca, NY: Cornell University Press, 2014.

Case III-B: From Potemkin Village to Real Life in Turkmenistan

Anceschi, Luca. *Turkmenistan's Foreign Policy: Positive Neutrality and the Consolidation of the Turkmen Regime*. London: Routledge, 2008.

Bohr, Annette. "Turkmenistan: Power, Politics and Petro-Authoritarianism." Research paper, Chatham House, London, March 2016.

Clement, Victoria. *Learning to Become Turkmen: Literacy, Language, and Power, 1914–2014*. Pittsburgh: University of Pittsburgh Press, 2018.

Peyrouse, Sebastien. *Turkmenistan: Strategies of Power, Dilemmas of Development*. Armonk, NY: M. E. Sharpe, 2011.

Polese, Abel, and Slavomir Horák. "A Tale of Two Presidents: Personality Cult and Symbolic Nation-building in Turkmenistan." *Nationalities Papers* 43, no. 3 (2015): 457–78.

Case III-C: Private Education, Inequality, and the Growing Social Divide in Bishkek

Abdoubaetova, Aigoul. "Secondary Schools and Inequality: Navigating the Fragmented Landscape of Educational Choices in Bishkek, Kyrgyzstan." *Central Asian Affairs* 7, no. 1 (2020): 80–110.

Koinzer, Thomas, Rita Nikolai, and Florian Waldow, eds. *Private Schools and School Choice in Compulsory Education: Global Change and National Challenge*. Wiesbaden: Springer, 2017.

Ramas, Rubén Ruiz. "Parental Informal Payments in Kyrgyzstani Schools: Analyzing the Strongest and the Weakest Link." *Journal of Eurasian Studies* 7, no. 2 (2016): 205–19.

Shamatov, Duishon. "The Impact of Standardized Testing on University Entrance Issues in Kyrgyzstan." *European Education* 44, no. 1 (2012): 71–92.

PART IV

CONTEXTS OF STRUCTURE

While it often goes unnoticed, the social environment in which people interact has a structure that both guides interactions and gets reinforced through them. We grow into a particular social order that becomes a natural, taken-for-granted part of our everyday life. Such structures form the foundations for norms and community itself, with understandings of well-being often found rooted within them. Though often the structures of social interactions guide us—with a sense of fluidity and constancy that permeates sociality—they can be two sides of the same coin: at times liberating and at others oppressive.

Looking at the way structures begin to emerge in social life, Cynthia Werner introduces the notion of family as a fundamental organizing unit of social and economic life. As would be expected, different family structures have their own set of implications, which we can see in how relatives get categorized, households are composed, and cooperation unfolds. Life-cycle rituals run across generations, but as family life changes, so, too, does the way it shapes roles and behavior.

In his chapter, Edward Schatz moves to social structure more broadly, showing how the underlying influences of social relationships have a somewhat coherent influence on behavior. He uses family, Islam, morality, and the state as frames for seeing social structure play out, and he shows how structures both evolve and are broadly carried across time: the Soviets produced social forms that carried over to independence; ethnicity matters in different contexts; and the imagination of place across the local to global spectrum impacts perceptions of which structures connect people.

But as Maria Louw shows in her chapter, underlying social relations is a moral structure that guides behavior, felt most acutely when ethics and morals break down, or where norms are overstepped both knowingly and unknowingly. Ethics, of course, are not merely prereflective and repetitious, but unfold in response to understandings of the "good life," and they help us manage the challenge ambiguity poses to knowing how to act. We see this across multiple categories—family, age, gender, religion—and it is in this context that the rightness of interactions gets weighed.

One of the more obvious ways people are organized and placed into roles is through gender. In her chapter, Svetlana Peshkova shows how gender comes to life in Central Asia and the various ways it gets constructed. Going further, she explains how even something seemingly self-evident and binary is not consistent over time and can have both political and behavioral implications. In short, structures can become fraught with tension, and universal claims are not always universally shared.

In the cases, we see the instantiation of structure in social life. Julie McBrien talks about the (expected) relationships between mothers- and daughters-in-law in Kyrgyzstan; Johan Rasanayagam looks at the mahalla community structures in Uzbekistan; and Eva-Marie Dubuisson shows how ancestors in Kazakhstan continue to be active participants in influencing social behavior and norms. What emerges from the section chapters is a sense of how sociality is influenced in diverse yet broadly coherent ways, demonstrative of how social life is not random but has an underlying structure that helps to explain behavior and the setting in which experience unfolds.

13

Family Structure

Cynthia Werner

All human societies have a notion of family, a fundamental social and economic unit of a society. In English, there is some ambiguity to the concept of a *family*. The term is used interchangeably to refer to one's close relatives, or to the relatives with whom one lives. Anthropologists distinguish between the former, *family*, and the latter, *household*. A family consists of people who are closely related by blood and marriage, and who typically provide each other with companionship, emotional support, and economic assistance. While some family members may live together, other family members live in different households. A household refers to a group of people who live together, whether or not they are related by blood or marriage. Families and households are key social locations where children are taught culturally informed norms and beliefs.

In this chapter, I use ethnographic examples from my fieldwork in Kazakhstan to illustrate some defining features of Central Asian family structure and dynamics. In so doing, I address the following questions: How do Central Asians define and categorize family members? How are Central Asian family members organized into households? What does it mean to be a member of a Central Asian family? What are the responsibilities and expectations of family members? How do responsibilities and expectations vary depending on age and gender? How are Central Asian cultures reproduced at the family level? How are rural families changing in response to modernization, globalization, and urbanization?

Although raised in an American family, I was informally adopted as a young adult by a Kazakh family in the early 1990s. Members of this large, extended family span across multiple households in various villages, towns,

13-1a   Family in At-Bashi Rayon, Naryn Oblast, Kyrgyzstan, 2000. Photograph by David W. Montgomery.

13-1b   Family in Kochkor Rayon, Naryn Oblast, Kyrgyzstan, 2004. Photograph by David W. Montgomery.

13-1c   Family in Kara-Kulja Rayon, Osh Oblast, Kyrgyzstan, 2005. Photograph by David W. Montgomery.

13-1d   Family in Ysyk-Ata Rayon, Chuy Oblast, Kyrgyzstan, 2012. Photograph by David W. Montgomery.

and cities in the southern part of Kazakhstan. I was an active member of the family for approximately two years (1993–95) while conducting ethnographic fieldwork for my dissertation on Kazakh households and social networks. My living arrangements were somewhat fluid: my primary residence was in a rural household in Southern Kazakhstan Oblast, but I was a welcome family member in multiple related households, including the urban household where I was first adopted as a daughter. For the past two decades, I have continued to maintain my ties to this family by returning for multiple summer visits, staying in touch via email, and occasionally hosting family members in the United States. These experiences with a specific Kazakh family have provided me with insights for understanding family structure in Central Asia. Although some generalizations can be made for the region as a whole, the examples and terms used in this chapter are specific to Kazakh family life in rural, southern Kazakhstan. In an effort to provide some comparison with other Central Asian groups, I conclude this chapter with some observations based on recent scholarly literature on Central Asian families.

Categories of Relatives

My first introduction to this Kazakh family came when I arrived as a guest in a prosperous household in the city of Shymkent. Surrounded by a high wall, which guaranteed privacy, the family compound consisted of a car garage, a sauna-like bathhouse, a long row of storage rooms and living areas, a separate house with six large rooms and a kitchen, outdoor platforms for eating and sleeping in the summertime, a sheep pen, a chicken coop, and a large garden with a variety of fruits and vegetables. At that time, the household consisted of a middle-aged married couple, two of their three adult sons, one younger son, one daughter-in-law, and three grandchildren. This is a fairly typical household configuration in Central Asia, where households are often comprised of multiple generations. As they welcomed me as a daughter, I was told that the family was affiliated with the *Kyrgyzaly* clan (*ru*) of the *Konghyrat* tribe. To be more accurate, this designation applied to all of the men in the household, and the male and female children who descended from those men. This same clan affiliation was extended to me as a "fictional" family member. Among Kazakhs (and other Central Asian ethnic groups with subethnic tribal and clan identities), tribal and clan identities are patrilineal (i.e., passed down from father to child). From an early age, young children learn the name of their lineage and the names of their seven progenitors on their paternal side (*zheti ata*). Marriages tend to be exogamous at the level of the clan. This cultural norm for exogamy prohibits marriages between couples who are less than seven generations apart on the father's side. The easiest way to adhere to this norm is to marry outside of the clan. The women who had married into the family (my Kazakh mother and sister-in-law) therefore belonged to other clans.

These key principles (patrilineal descent and clan-based exogamy) provide the basis for understanding the Kazakh kinship system. All Kazakhs have one primary group of relatives, known in Kazakh as "relatives" (*tuysqandar*). This group is mostly composed of individuals who are blood relatives on the father's side. This word combines two key words: *tuu* ("to be born") and *qan* ("blood"). When Kazakhs (and other Central Asians) speak of their family, they are generally speaking about people who fit into this category (i.e., paternal kinsmen). This is a different conception of family than Western family systems, where one's "blood relatives" are more bilateral in nature, with relatives on the mother's side being structurally equal to relatives on the father's side.

Among Kazakhs, a person may also develop close ties to their mother's relatives, but these individuals are affiliated with a different clan and thus considered to be a separate category of relative known as *nagashylar* or *nagashy tuysqandary* (my mother's relatives). This might be roughly equivalent to how a Westerner might regard their own sibling's son or daughter as more closely related than their spouse's sibling's son or daughter. In English, however, both would be referred to with the same kinship term (i.e., nephew or niece).

Central Asians also distinguish two different categories of "in-laws," or relatives through marriage. In the Kazakh language, the first category (*qaiyndar*) refers to one's spouse's relatives. Due to the principle of exogamy, a person's qaiyndar will be affiliated with the spouse's patrilineal clan.

There is a second category of in-laws (*qudalar*) that is used in reference to in-laws resulting from the marriage of one's children (or other close relatives). When marriages are formed, the marriage is cementing ties between two family groups, and the concept of qudalar is used to refer to this category of individuals. Central Asians place a strong value on their relationships with qudalar. Among Kazakhs, this is expressed in the following proverb commonly displayed at wedding feasts: "A husband is for a hundred years; an in-law is for a thousand years." The bond between in-laws is based on mutual respect and friendship, and in-laws are always regarded as honored guests in a household.

Household Composition in a Patrilineal Society

While conducting a household survey for my dissertation, I learned that household membership in Central Asia can be very fluid. I gathered data from approximately two hundred households in a village. The survey included a section where I asked participants to tell me the age, gender, and occupation of each resident. I quickly discovered that many younger people are often affiliated with multiple households. For example, I lived in a rural household in the district center that, at first glance, looked like a nuclear family household: Akbolat, the household head, lived in the home together with his wife, Nuriya, their college-aged daughter, Aigul, and their two teenaged sons, Doskhan and Samat. Over time, it became clear that household composition changed regularly, in part because children and young adults (both married and unmarried) frequently live with their relatives for weeks, months, or even years. In addition to these five permanent household members, there were eight temporary residents (other than myself) who lived in Akbolat's house for varying lengths of time. All of the temporary residents were relatives as opposed to guests, and thus (with the exception of two infants) they were expected to help with household chores. They each had different reasons for staying in this household. Serik, one of Akbolat's many nephews, lived in the house for several years in order to train with the local wrestling team (an opportunity that was not available in his smaller home village). When he got married, his wife, Asel, also joined the household and was treated as a daughter-in-law (*kelin*). Then there was Murat, another nephew, who lived with the family during his last year of high school. This living situation helped Murat's widowed mother provide more for her younger children and helped his uncle take care of his livestock. A third nephew, Aidos, together with his wife and child, lived with Akbolat's family for several weeks while searching for employment in the district center. During this period of time, his wife helped out with the housework.

In addition to being fluid, household composition also varies from one household to the next. I gathered archival data on household composition for one Kazakh village in what is now known as Turkistan province (previously known as South Kazakhstan province and Shymkent Oblast), covering the years 1972 to 1990. In 1990, approximately 45.7 percent of households could be described as a standard nuclear family household, comprised of a married couple and their children. Although this was the most common configuration of a household, 44.6 percent of households could be considered to be an extended family household, broadly defined as a household comprised of related individuals spanning at least three generations. The sample also included a small number of "single-parent households" (5.9 percent) and a smaller number of "two generation, joint-family households" (1.6 percent) consisting of two married brothers, along with their wives and children. One pattern is consistent across all of these household types: all household members are either affiliated with the household head's patrilineal group (i.e., clan), or they are women who have married into the clan.

The Life Cycle of the Household

During Soviet rule, the transition from large patriarchal family household to a small nuclear family household was considered an inevitable part of the transition to a more modern society. Soviet era scholars stressed that the "large patriarchal family households" (i.e., extended family households) were on the decline in the Soviet period. According to Karmysheva, the "undivided," or multiple-generation household, was assumed to be a contemporary "survival" of the extended family. I used the archival records mentioned earlier to compare household composition over four-year intervals. The results suggest that differences in household type at any given time have more to do with temporary and cyclical differences than with a broad pattern of social change. In other words, any given household is likely to change from one type of household to another during the course of its individual members' lifetimes.

The following example of one particular household over time illustrates this point. In 1972, the household (consisting of a married couple, along with two sons and two daughters) transitioned from a nuclear family household to a more "traditional" household when the eldest son got married and continued to live in his parent's household along with his new wife. By 1976, the household had become a classic example of an extended family household. The eldest son and his wife had two children of their own. By 1980, the eldest son and his wife had formed their own separate household. The parent household remained a classic traditional household, however, because the second son married a woman who joined the household, and this couple gave birth to their first child. Four years later, the second son and his wife established their own household, and the parent household reverted to a small nuclear family household with just one child at home. The remaining daughter was only living in the house on a temporary basis when she was not attending college in Shymkent. In the meantime, the eldest daughter got married and left the household. Finally, in 1990, the matriarch died, and the household head moved into the youngest son's household. This was in line with a common custom throughout Central Asia that the youngest son in a family takes care of the parents when they become elderly.

As the aforementioned example demonstrates, household composition typically changes shortly after children reach the age of adulthood and get married. Most daughters are affiliated with their father's household until the age of marriage. After marriage, they always move to a different household, either with their husband alone or with their husband and his family. Among Kazakhs, sons typically have a longer relationship with their father's household. They may remain in the household after marriage up until the time that they are formally separated from the household by "receiving an inheritance" (*enshi beru*). The inheritance might include funds toward a new home. The Kazakh word for inheritance (*enshi*) implies a parental sanction to live separately and suggests that there is a tangible boundary between the two households. When a couple is granted the enshi depends on a combination of factors, including the number of married sons living in the household, the household resources, the availability of resources to establish a home for the young couple, and the young couple's ability to support themselves. Typically, there are no more than two married sons living with the parents. I did encounter one household, however, that had four daughters-in-law "in hand." The cultural ideal is for at least one married son to live with the parents, preferably the youngest son. Many rural families still follow this practice of ultimogeniture, where the youngest son remains with his parents after marriage and takes care of them in their old age. These sons do not receive the *enshi* until their father dies or steps down as household head.

Inter-Household Cooperation

In addition to having fluid membership, Central Asian households have "fuzzy boundaries." In other words, it cannot be assumed that the household, defined in terms of residency, is necessarily the basic socioeconomic unit of cooperation for production, distribution, consumption, and reproduction. Central Asian cultures are patrilocal, meaning that there is a tendency for newly married couples to live near or with the groom's parents. In practice, this means that the ties between related households are often so close that these basic socioeconomic activities take place in cooperation with other related households. Whether they live close to each other, parents may cooperate with sons living in separate households, and brothers living in different households might cooperate with one another.

With several key activities, the boundaries between households can be ambiguous. The concept of household production refers to any goods and services that members of a family produce for their own use, including income from jobs outside the home. Among rural Kazakhs, related households often cooperate on activities related to household production. For example, the men and women living in one household might regularly help the men and women in another household with herding, milking, and butchering of livestock. Further, adult sons living in separate households might regularly contribute part of their income to their parents' household, or vice versa, the parents may allocate a part of their income to their children.

Parenting, or the social reproduction of children, is another activity that does not always correspond with household boundaries. According to one Kazakh custom, a couple's first child (whether a boy or a girl) should be presented as a "gift" to the father's parents. In addition to being a strong statement of filial respect, this custom of informal child fostering corresponds to a cultural preference for having children present in every household. Actual practice usually depends on whether the younger couple is willing to "give up" their child and whether the paternal grandparents are willing to take on the added responsibility. Children who are raised by their grandparents are aware of their biological parents' identity, but they are expected to address their own parents as "sister" (*apzhe*) and "brother" (*aghai*). Typically, they retain strong ties with their biological parents and often switch households when they get a little older or when one or both grandparents die. One seventeen-year-old girl, for example, was raised primarily by her grandparents, although she frequently spent time with her parents who lived in a nearby village. When she was thirteen, her cherished grandmother died and she went to live with her birth parents and younger siblings. She had a difficult time adjusting to the new situation because she was no longer the youngest, indulged child (*erke*). Instead, she was expected to be more responsible and to set a good example for her younger brother and sister.

Some key domestic activities, however, do correspond well to household boundaries. This includes the consumption of daily meals and the hosting of visitors. This point was best illustrated by a pair of related households who happened to share an unusual duplex-style house. While the typical Kazakh home has a single door, this unique house had two entrances leading to two nearly identical interiors, each consisting of a winter kitchen and several other rooms. The house once belonged to Baidabek, a patriarch who had two wives. Although the Soviet state made polygamy illegal in the late 1920s, Baidabek managed to marry two women by only registering one as his official wife. He built the house to accommodate his family's special situation. When he was alive, the two wives maintained two separate households on their side of the house. For decades, the two households cooperated in many ways yet maintained two distinct "hearths." When I first encountered the family, only one of the two wives was still alive and the house was still occupied by two separate households, headed by two of Baidabek's grown sons. There were twelve individuals in one half of the house and nine individuals in the other half. Although the two households shared a common courtyard, garage, and summer kitchen, they continued to maintain separate gardens and separate livestock pens. They also prepared and consumed meals separately. Thus, on a daily basis, the production, preparation, and consumption of food tend to reflect and reinforce household boundaries that were otherwise blurred.

Social networking is another activity that clearly illustrates the boundaries between households. In rural Kazakhstan, social networks entail a web of social relationships based on one or more of the following criteria: kin relations, tribal affiliations, marriage alliances, geographical proximity, shared schooling, shared workplace, and friendship. Kazakhs maintain these networks by granting personal favors, presenting gifts, hosting dinner parties and feasts, and supplying voluntary labor. Although individual household members may perform some of these activities, their actions benefit the entire household. In other words, Kazakhs consider the balance of favors and gifts between households, not individuals. For example, if a female guest presents a gift to the groom's mother at a wedding feast, it is understood that the gift is an exchange from one household to another household. Gifts exchanged between households symbolize the existence of a social relationship between these households. In most cases, the giving household and the receiving household have already exchanged gifts on other occasions. The current gift simply demonstrates that the giving household seeks to continue the relationship. Through a constant exchange of gifts, favors, and hospitality, households remain in a state of mutual indebtedness with other households, thus providing a form of social security.

The aforementioned information is based on fieldwork in a rural region of southern Kazakhstan, and this concept of "mutual indebtedness" is based on relations between households of relatively similar socioeconomic status. A number of studies conducted in Kyrgyzstan shed further light on the complexities of social networks and the reciprocal exchange of goods, gifts, and services between households of differing socioeconomic levels. As one study of poverty indicates, households that were able to maintain reciprocal exchanges with other households fared better than others during the early post-Soviet years (i.e., the 1990s). The corollary is that poor households could not afford to keep up with social obligations as the costs of participation increased, and the shrinking of their social networks compounded the challenges of poverty. On the other side of the social spectrum, some successful entrepreneurs have used their wealth from business ventures to develop strong patronage networks and increase their political influence. Other entrepreneurial households have opted instead to reinvest business profits at the expense of sharing a portion of their resources with kin. While the former are lauded for their generosity, the latter are judged for not meeting local expectations of morality.

Responsibilities and Expectations of Family Members

Household composition and gender play a large role in determining the household division of labor. In rural Kazakhstan, women's responsibilities reflect more "traditional" gender roles. On a daily basis, women's household chores include a number of daily tasks: caring for children, preparing meals, serving tea to visitors, cleaning the house, washing clothes, arranging the daily bedding, milking cows and horses, working in the household garden, and assisting men with the care of domestic livestock. Many women also bake their own bread, prepare a variety of dairy products, and sew clothes for their family.

Men also perform several household tasks. They take care of the domestic livestock, help out with the garden work, and assist with childcare. Compared to women, however, men have more leisure time at home.

From the age of five or six years, girls and boys are socialized to help with the daily housework. Initially, young girls learn to serve tea, clear tables, and keep an eye on sleeping infants. As they grow older, they learn to clean the house, wash clothes, prepare meals, milk cows, and work in the gardens. Young boys are taught to care for the livestock and work in the gardens. Among children, the boundaries between "female" and "male" household chores are flexible. With the exception of preparing food and washing clothes, boys are known to help out with household chores, especially in households that have a shortage of female labor. The expectations for boys' help, however, is lower than that for girls' help.

Eventually, as children start to get married, child labor is supplemented by the help of one or more daughter-in-law. The addition of a daughter-in-law (kelin) reduces the workload for the mother-in-law. Under the mother-in-law's supervision and direction, the daughter-in-law is likely to be responsible for cleaning clothes, cleaning the house, serving meals, and washing dishes. The mother-in-law is likely to take care of younger children, including grandchildren, and cook meals.

With hospitality as one of the central elements of Kazakh culture, households frequently host dinner parties to socialize with friends, and they occasionally sponsor large feasts to celebrate life cycle events, including birth, male circumcision, and marriage.

Life Cycle Rituals

One prominent feature of Central Asian family life is the ubiquitous presence of large feasts, or parties, to celebrate life cycle events, including the birth of a child (*besik toi*), the circumcision of young boys (*sundet toi*), and the marriage of young adults (*uilenu toi*). In all Central Asian cultures, the general word for these events is *toi*, which is best translated as "feast." If a household has resources to do so, they may also organize a party to celebrate significant birthdays, wedding anniversaries, and the construction of a new home. Sometimes, a household will have a party to celebrate multiple events, such as the circumcision of a son and a grandfather's sixtieth birthday.

The cradle feast (besik toi) is the only feast that is exclusively for women. This smaller feast is always held after a couple's first child has been born. Invited guests present the mother with gifts for the child, and a series of rituals are conducted to guarantee the health and happiness of the baby. These rituals involve the blessing and purification of the cradle (*besik*) that the baby will use.

The other types of toi are much larger in scale and involve the family's entire network of relatives and friends. Food features prominently at these events. Three to five hot dishes are served, in addition to a wide variety of breads, appetizers, sweets, and drinks. During these parties, which last for several hours, guests are entertained with music and dancing. In addition, the master of ceremonies invites guests to come up to the front to give a toast in honor of the occasion.

The size of the event may vary depending on the size of the family network, family resources, and the type of event. The largest feasts are for weddings and circumcision celebrations. In urban areas, these parties are now being celebrated in large banquet halls (*toikhana*) that emerged after independence and can seat up to one thousand guests. In rural areas, these parties are often still held at home in an outdoor clearing near the house. The feast grounds are decorated, and long tables are set up. Generally, the guest tables are lined up perpendicularly to the far side where the guests of honor sit and the near side where the announcer's table and the musician's stand are situated. If the event is a wedding, the guests of honor are the bride and groom, and their wedding party. If the event is for another occasion, the head table is often reserved for the most influential guests, such as local government leaders and respected relatives.

There is a competitive nature to feasting and gift-giving. Wealthy households try to impress their guests by serving high-quality food, hiring professional musicians, and providing expensive gifts. In comparison, poorer households struggle to find the means to pay for feast gifts and to host their own feasts. They are able to save money by inviting fewer guests, providing less expensive appetizer dishes, serving main dishes with less meat, and serving homemade alcohol. As mentioned earlier, some households have scaled back their participation in the ritual economy due to limited resources.

Each toi demands a great deal of financial resources for food, alcohol,

13-2a   A bride having her photograph taken near the Kalon Minaret in Bukhara, Uzbekistan, 2019. Photograph by Kasia Ploskonka.

13-2b   Newly married couple on their way to their wedding reception in Khujand, Tajikistan, 2005. Photograph by David W. Montgomery.

musical entertainment, and decorations. A family's reputation is evaluated by the quality of the toi. In rural areas, many families still rely on their closest kin to help prepare and serve the food. In urban areas, families tend to spend more money on these events by contracting services through a reception venue, known locally as a *toikhana*. The construction of lavish new toikhana coincided with the beginning of the post-Soviet era, when conspicuous consumption gained new levels of social acceptance. When household members attend a feast, they are expected to bring a gift to the hosting household. Despite the expense of hosting a large event, some households are able to recoup their losses through this gift exchange. This is especially true when the household head is a powerful patron within the community.

The concept of a toi, and the value placed on hospitality, is something that is shared by the primary ethnic groups of Central Asia. The family members hosting a toi are simultaneously celebrating a major life cycle event and demonstrating their ability to conform to social norms of hospitality. At the same time, guests attending a toi are affirming their relationships with the host family by participating in the event and providing gifts. Beneath the surface, there is one important thing at stake for host and guest households alike—the reputation of each household. Shame is a powerful motivational force throughout Central Asia, such that a family's honor is based largely on the absence of "shame" (*uyat* in Kazakh). The phrase *uyat bolady!* ("It will be shameful!") is frequently used as a warning and admonition of any action that is likely to dishonor an individual or family. For example, the phrase is often used as a way to regulate and control women's behavior, dress, and mobility. Family honor, however, does not rest solely on the behavior of women. Honor also comes into play during feasting events. On the one hand, the host household's reputation is evaluated on the overall quality of the toi. The introduction of videography ensures that a wider audience will have an opportunity to view (and critique) each event. On the other hand, guest households are judged on the quality of the gifts they present to the host household. If cultural expectations are upheld, then the household is able to maintain its honorable status within the community. In this way, acts of generosity are culturally sanctioned as morally appropriate behavior. This helps explain why a large proportion of the income earned from transnational labor migrants and the illegal hashish trade is used to cover expenses for these ritual events. It also helps explain why families invest so much time and energy into feasts, even when it is not economically feasible to do so. As Tommaso Trevisani notes in the case of Uzbekistan, there is a "divide between those who keep up and those who do not perform to local standards for a decent toi."

Central Asian states, in the past and the present, have long recognized the social and economic challenges that families experience with feasting. Soviet officials, for example, were critical of the "irrational" expenses on ritual life. In the post-Soviet period, several Central Asian states have introduced measures to regulate toi with limited success. Beginning in 2018, the government of Uzbekistan has been critical of "wasteful" wedding expenses, and has charged local neighborhood committees (mahalla) with the task of enforcing limits on the number of guests and the duration of celebrations. Further, in 2015, Uzbekistan introduced a policy that prevents restaurants and banquet halls in rural areas from hosting wedding receptions during the cotton season. Tajikistan has imposed similar regulations on life cycle rituals. Beginning in 2007, the government of Tajikistan has placed limits on the duration, size, and cost of family feasts. In 2017, the state introduced further restrictions to curtail costs spent on family events, including circumcision feasts, wedding festivities, and funerals.

Contemporary Changes to Central Asian Families

Family life in Central Asia has changed continuously over the past century in response to a variety of modern influences. Beginning in the late 1920s, the Soviet state introduced new policies that were intended to destroy "traditional" and "patriarchal" family practices that fell under the broad category of "crimes of custom." Specifically, the state outlawed child betrothals, bride-wealth payments, and polygamy. The state also made it easier for women to seek a divorce. These laws were reinforced by new ideals that placed more emphasis on modern lifestyles, modern education, and gender equality.

These policies and ideals did transform family life during Soviet rule, though the extent to which family life changed under Soviet rule continues to be the subject of scholarly debate.

In the postindependence era, Central Asian families have continued to change in response to new circumstances, including the opening up of borders with the outside world and the creation of new national borders within Central Asia. To begin, Central Asia is now more globally connected to the geographic spaces that fell outside of the Soviet sphere. In this new era of globalization, consumer goods, television serials, and religious missionaries have all simultaneously crossed borders that were previously closed, and have become part of the new landscape. The rapid influx of new consumer goods (especially from China, Turkey, Iran, and Europe) has brought new patterns of consumption for Central Asian families, and new modern conveniences for those families that can afford them. Television serials from Latin America, the Middle East, China, Europe, and North America have generated debate and discussion about competing models for organizing family life. Similarly, both Christian and Muslim missionaries have introduced different religious ideals that impact family life and marriage practices.

The process of globalization has also had notable impacts on household economies. During the Soviet years, the majority of citizens received regular wages as employees of the state. After the fall of the Soviet Union, each newly independent Central Asian country took its own path toward economic reform and development of its national resources. The entire region has witnessed (to varying degrees) inflation for consumer goods, a decline in state jobs, an increase in social inequality, and an increase in rural-urban migration. Some families have also been impacted by transnational labor migration, as some family members travel temporarily to another country in search of greater income. In Kyrgyzstan, Tajikistan, and Uzbekistan, it is often young men who are migrating for work, leaving behind women, children, and the elderly. Migrants send remittances that help pay for consumer goods, wedding expenses, and gifts.

Post-Soviet economic changes have also led to a revival of official and unofficial polygamy—an unexpected modern change in family composition. Throughout the region, legislators have debated the legality of polygamy on grounds of both women's rights and religion. And, in practice, there has been a resurgence of polygamy. As one scholar notes, polygamy can be a coping strategy for certain categories of women, such as divorced and widowed women. The impact, however, is structural.

In short, contemporary Central Asian families are becoming increasingly diverse in the post-Soviet period. There are increasing social divides between the wealthy and the poor, the rural and the urban. In addition, many families are changing in response to new religious ideas as well as media images of life beyond Central Asia.

14

Social Structure

Edward Schatz

Those interested in freedom of choice avoid talk of "social structure." After all, it sounds like something that constrains the individual, preventing her from enjoying the full scope for agency that liberal theory posits. Yet, to understand how individuals—in Central Asia as elsewhere—navigate the complexities of everyday life, we must have some way to characterize the environments in which they make their choices. Starting with static metaphors and then shifting to more fluid ones, I use this chapter to give analytic shape to the complex social terrain on which Central Asians find themselves. And as with most ways into understanding the social world, our interlocutors give us a beginning.

Bakhyt

I first met Bakhyt one unusually hot summer evening in the 1990s, which I spent with Bakhyt's mother discussing North America over green tea in their modest, three-room family apartment in Bishkek, Kyrgyzstan. Since the apartment was at the edge of town and public transportation was virtually nonexistent in the evenings, Bakhyt's mother fixed me a bed for the night. For her part, Bakhyt—a young mother and university instructor—barely participated in the conversation.

When I awoke the next morning, Bakhyt was still sprawled out asleep with her three children on piles of cushy blankets on the apartment floor. Her father had slept in the family home 20 kilometers outside of town, and her mother woke Bakhyt to plan the day. Bakhyt half listened to her mother's instructions before falling back asleep. Waking with a start a short while later, she quickly prepared tea for her family, made several hurried phone calls on their Soviet-era landline, packed up the kids, and was gone in less than half an hour.

Over the years of visiting Central Asia, Bakhyt shared her perspectives with me, to the extent that her busy life allowed it. I was a "safe" interlocutor for her, since I shared none of her professional or personal networks but spoke good Russian. She also seemed to enjoy reflecting on, and sometimes griping about, the society she saw around her. Benefiting from hindsight, and at the risk of radical simplification, I would suggest that in Bakhyt's life three major considerations loomed large.

Family was foremost. More or less a single mother, she demonstrated a profound dedication to her children and exhibited patience with fluid family demands beyond what I had ever before witnessed. That first night's sleeping arrangement was not an ad hoc one; that was where and how the children tended to sleep when they were in the city. On weekends, they would retreat to the family home outside of town, where broader extended kin would often come and go as they pleased. In the city, however, this fluid life was structured by the matriarch, Bakhyt's mother, who would supply ample instructions about her expectations and monitor the comings and goings of her children (and grandchildren) by maintaining sole possession of the keys to the apartment.

For Bakhyt, education was a major preoccupation. She spoke Kyrgyz with her children but was frustrated with the quality of public education in the Kyrgyz language. For her, Soviet rule had brought modern life, and while she recognized the value of her ethnic traditions, she saw a tension between an embrace of ethnic traditions and the demands of modernity. Her father was a "Soviet man," she said, a characterization that he did not dispute; to Bakhyt this meant putting a premium on science and learning. Unfortunately, Kyrgyzstan in the 1990s saw the dramatic erosion of educational standards—from elementary school to postsecondary education—and Bakhyt described a system riddled with inefficiency, run by incompetent bureaucrats, and based on bribes. Although she had a good position teaching law, she complained that the Soviet collapse had deprived Kyrgyzstan of effective teaching material. This would not be remedied until the mid-2000s, when she and her colleagues became globally connected and could avail themselves of myriad online resources.

Bakhyt possessed a strong moral compass—one centered on compassion, family, loyalty, fairness, and hard work. In the 1990s, she considered herself "more Soviet than Muslim," but by the 2000s she described herself as a Muslim who was too busy to practice. She expressed hope that, once the kids were grown, she might explore the faith more actively, although I interpreted her sly smile as an indication that she thought this an unlikely outcome.

Bakhyt's example brings to the fore key dimensions of social structure in Central Asia: Islam, morality, Soviet legacies, ethnicity, and global connections. She was not "typical." As Clifford Geertz reminds us, it is wrongheaded to believe that any single example is "typical" of a broader set of instances. All we can hope is that "small facts speak to large issues" (i.e., that Bakhyt's example helps orient our analytic gaze).

Central Asian Social Structure

To characterize the social landscape of Central Asia is no less than to posit what makes someone a Central Asian, rather than a South American or a Southeast Asian or a Pacific Islander. Following Émile Durkheim, we might ask, What are the "social facts" (i.e., the "way[s] of acting, fixed or not, capable of exercising on the individual an external constraint") that constitute this region as Central Asia and its population as Central Asian? Each of these social facts is contested, prone to change, and experienced to varying degrees by concrete individuals; nonetheless, any effort to come to terms with how Central Asia is *lived* must attempt some moderately broad generalizations. We need some way to *think into* Central Asia, lest it remain impossibly opaque.

Let me propose that all Central Asians experience, by degree and in various ways, the following. First, they reside on territory historically and traditionally associated with Islam. Any Central Asian must grapple with questions of Islamic identity. Second, given the uneven and particular ways in which Soviet modernity was experienced in the region, Central Asians have a peculiar relationship with questions of morality. Third, given the profound imprint of the Soviet period on most of the region, Central Asians typically have to contend with what it means to be Soviet or post-Soviet. Fourth, Central Asians normally encounter strong discourses about ethnic traditions and ethnic community belonging. They must grapple with how these strong discourses relate to their sense of self. Finally, while Central Asia may seem to be a geographically remote region that is largely marginal to the major flows of global culture, trade, and politics, Central Asians increasingly have to locate themselves in a global sense.

Islam and Islamic Identity

This is not the place to recount the history of Islam's arrival in and spread across the region, let alone its syncretic development with indigenous cultural and religious practices. The key point about Central Asia in the 2010s and beyond is that discourses of and about Islam were inescapable. That they were inescapable does not mean that these discourses were mono-vocal or monolithic. Nor does it mean that any given individual necessarily accepted at face value any particular discourse about Islam. But it does mean that Islam was a central, normal reference point for individuals.

To illustrate what I have in mind, consider two people I came to know. The first is Rustam, whom I first met in the mid-2000s. Rustam was the owner of a medium-sized business in the Ferghana region of Uzbekistan. Rustam loved football (soccer), NASCAR racing, and discussing politics. By

14-1a   Public prayers during Eid, Bishkek, 2004. Photograph by David W. Montgomery.

his own admission only moderately religious, he did attend mosque fairly regularly and considered his being Muslim to be a fact of his birth. To him, it was impossible to be Uzbek and not be a Muslim. One night, as he clicked through the channels on his satellite TV while smoking cigarettes, he paused on a show in which Christian Evangelicals were discussing morality. He explained to me how *good* it was that Christians were delivering to Uzbeks the message of morality, given that Uzbekistan had—due to rapid marketization and its accompanying social dislocation—fallen into a state of immorality. When asked about his smoking, he replied that God made people imperfect. Their task was to strive for self-improvement, which in turn would make them better Muslims and more acceptable in God's eyes.

Consider also Guldana, who taught at a university in Almaty, Kazakhstan. Although deeply secular ("Soviet," she insisted), she was no stranger to the religious. It was a part of everyday life that she, by dint of her family connections and upbringing, had to navigate. She needed to attend key rite-of-passage celebrations, which typically were laced through with the language of Islam (even if in fact they had much to do with pre-Islamic practices). She needed to avoid drinking alcohol in certain social settings (even though she usually did not abstain). She was deeply wary of the rise of visibly religious dress and practices (which she took as a worrying sign of unwelcome change), but she accepted that this was a natural development in her society with which she needed to come to terms. Dedicated to raising her child in a secular way, she nonetheless felt the social pull of various Islamic discourses.

14-1b   Men stopping by the side of the road for afternoon prayers, outside of Talas, Kyrgyzstan, 2006. Photograph by David W. Montgomery.

Islam is not a monolith, and Islamic practices are at least as varied as the religious practices of other world religions. Moreover, the pressure to conform to the interpretations of one or another discourse about Islam also varies. In the Ferghana Valley region, the push was much stronger than in the larger, more culturally variegated metropolises of Kazakhstan. Nonetheless, each and every individual born into a Central Asian context had to make sense of their relationship to Islam, even if that sense-making in some cases involved a strong rejection of the faith. As David Montgomery puts it about one interlocutor from Kyrgyzstan: "He was not merely born Muslim and Kyrgyz so much as he became Muslim and Kyrgyz, becoming one of the many possible variations of what that might mean." Johan Rasanayagam echoes the sentiment, describing the "riot of exploration" about religious practice and identity in Uzbekistan that lies behind the "subdued, even fearful atmosphere [that] surrounds religious practice." Islam in any of its various guises does not predetermine forms of identification and belonging, but it does provide a key reference point for constructing one's sense of self.

Put differently, although both Rustam and Guldana have relatively weak connections to Islam per se, they are still shaped by myriad social facts that emanate from Islam's strong presence in the region. This presence shapes even secular spaces and even a-religious individuals in a sociological sense, even if not in a theological one. Indeed, given the wide array of interpretations of Islam at play in Central Asia and the equally diverse, plentiful, and decentralized interpreters of the faith, Islam does not have a single effect but rather diffuse, indirect effects across society on questions of morality.

Morality, the State, and Family

Morality is of course shaped by, though not reducible to, organized religious tradition. Consider Sarah Kendzior's description of *ma'naviyat* (morality), in which she writes: "In Uzbekistan, *ma'naviyat* has come to describe less a relationship with the divine than an essential, almost material moral quality that is innate in every Uzbek yet dependent upon the state for its cultivation." Kendzior shows that the question of how to be a good Muslim Uzbek plays itself out in high politics, with the state proposing one interpretation of ma'naviyat and the opposition in exile offering alternatives. For her part, Maria Louw demonstrates that Muslims in Kyrgyzstan use religion not so much to aspire to an ideal-type of morality but rather as a compass to help navigate the vagaries of everyday life in search of a "golden mean" that lies between extremes of various sorts.

While the Uzbekistani and Kyrgyzstani versions each have their distinctiveness, and while the specifics vary widely from individual to individual, there is no question that morality and community are generally more closely linked in Central Asia than they tend to be in liberal contexts. In liberal societies, we often view morality as a highly personal matter lodged at the level of individuals, and we jealously guard individuals' right to make these highly personal determinations. Central Asia reminds us of an alternative, wherein morality is often lodged at the level of the community. Any given individual may or may not adhere to community norms (and the moral judgments they entail), but Central Asians typically swim in waters thick with moral considerations defined by community standards.

One of the distinguishing features of Central Asians' experience with morality comes from the Soviet period. In the style of modernity that the Soviet era brought, the state was the propagator of modern forms of morality, the guarantor of its success, and the bulwark against dangerous alternatives. This legacy of vesting an explicitly moral role in the state has not disappeared. What this means in practice is significant: while in liberal contexts the state is generally seen as the guarantor of a *negative* liberty that protects space for individuals to construct their own sense of right and wrong, Soviet rule created states that play a more *positive* role in propagating correct ways to think into moral questions.

Thus, the Central Asian state has a history of wading into moral territory. Consider the "unveiling" of women (*hujum*) in the late 1920s in Central Asia. We should *not* read this policy as a state-led drive to protect women's rights (i.e., to ensure that women enjoyed negative freedoms from both the state and from oppressive patriarchies); rather, it should be read as a *positive* state-led drive to propagate the gender equality that Leninist ideology required (i.e., to create—by force, if necessary—the kind of moral society dictated by the emerging political order). Echoes of such state policies designed to *create* a morally correct order can be seen in a "Guidebook to Recommended Outfits in Tajikistan," a 367-page government publication that "outlines acceptable garment colors, shapes, lengths, and materials." Even though the specifically socialist moral project that accompanied Soviet ideology—the intention to remake Central Asian populations as socialist subjects—ultimately failed, essential ways of creating public policy remained decades later.

If questions of morality link up to the state, it is also true that they link up to family, extended family, and kinship groups more robustly than to which we are accustomed. Discourses about familial obligations are legion throughout Central Asia, a stark contrast with what we normally see in North America. If as a Canadian citizen, I had a cousin who worked in a Canadian government office with which I had business, my cousin and I both would do everything possible to avoid even the *impression* of a conflict of interest. I certainly would not accept a position in my cousin's government office (and she certainly would not hire me) unless my cousin were to recuse herself from the hiring process. In Central Asia, the moral logic can be quite different. If I, as a government official, had a family member who needed my assistance, it would be strange (and perhaps considered culturally inappropriate) for me to avoid using my station to be of assistance to her. What kind of ethical human being would not help his kin in a time of need? It is not that one perspective is an ethical one and the other unethical; it is rather that different moral codes structure different ways of being ethical.

I have described the pull of kin and the importance of kin-related discourses elsewhere, suggesting that such ties emerged from the Soviet period as strong and socially salient in part because the state-led economy of shortage made ties of loyalty useful. It is important not to reduce everything to kinship relations, as if they determine everything that a Central Asian thinks and does, but it remains true that social contexts thick with kinship ties exercise a strong pull on Central Asians. We need to characterize such contexts if we are to be aware of the "water" in which Central Asians "swim."

How does the pull of morality and family stand up against major societal changes? After all, given the myriad of processes we sometimes gloss as "globalization," should we not expect concomitant changes in the social structure that Central Asians navigate? Let me briefly introduce two major ones that have indeed made a difference: marketization and migration.

Since the collapse of the Soviet, centrally planned economy, the region's states have—to varying degrees—been exposed to global market forces. The ideal-typical free market is starkly at odds with the logic of community morality and obligations to kin. After all, in the stylized version we read about in textbooks, individuals make rational calculations about their best interest, transacting with other rational actors who are likewise pursuing profit. Textbooks tell us that a certain magic results: from such individually self-interested behaviors that undercut traditional values, public goods arise, and everyone benefits.

And there is no question that marketization indeed changed Central Asia in the 1990s. Consumer goods previously unknown to the region flooded Central Asian markets, bringing exposure to cultural values quite different from what the average Kazakh or Tajik had experienced in the Soviet period. To the extent that the region's governments no longer provided cradle-to-grave welfare assistance and shifted responsibility for gainful employment to citizens themselves, many Central Asians were compelled to make difficult decisions about keeping households financially viable versus fulfilling obligations to extended kin networks. The contours of moral considerations had shifted.

Yet most Central Asians continued to take seriously their moral obligation to kin, even under post-Soviet, increasingly marketized conditions. This should surprise us only if we exaggerate the differences between market situations and nonmarket ones. Whereas the textbook market involves individuals disembedded from social situations, markets in the real world involve complex communities and elaborately networked individuals. Better than asking, "Did Central Asian forms of morality withstand market pressures?" we should ask, "How did Central Asian forms of morality shift with marketization?" Experiences vary widely. In some cases, individuals weave together a commitment to ethnic traditions and the morality they entail with an ability to earn a living in marketized conditions. In other cases, individuals facing material hardship sometimes still described themselves as living well. One of Montgomery's interlocutors related, "Life is difficult. There are no jobs for which I trained, and everything is expensive. But I have friends and family. And we live!"

Likewise, migration changed Central Asia. Specifically, large parts of the region witnessed massive labor out-migration (principally to Russia and principally for work). Given the small populations of Kyrgyzstan and Tajikistan, they in particular were deeply affected, with entire rural communities devoid of able-bodied men. Such male migration strained the social fabric, with obligation to kin sometimes withstanding the great distances and significant absences of men and fathers, and other times giving way to other forms of sociability. The very experience of migrating for work (seasonal or otherwise) introduces Central Asian men to values different from those they might experience within Central Asia itself. The upshot is that migration challenges existing notions of right and wrong. Yet, as with marketization, the real question is less "How could Central Asian morality withstand the onslaught brought on by migration?" and more "How did Central Asian morality shift with mobile populations?"

Though they intertwine in complex ways with new pressures that arise with marketization and migration, it is hard to escape the conclusion that moral questions, linked to community and family and often propagated by the region's states, continue to be among the central issues that Central Asians face as they navigate everyday life.

The Soviet

In 2016, the region's states celebrated twenty-five years of independence. While a quarter century since the Soviet collapse was a significant span of time, the Soviet period continued to loom large in Central Asian societies, for at least four reasons. First, unlike some major cases of decolonization, in the Soviet case the former imperial power remained on the same vast landmass as the former colonial subjects. Soviet power as such disappeared, but Russia remained the neighbor of Kazakhstan and continued to have a military presence in Tajikistan. Moreover, ethnic Russians remained in Central Asia in large numbers, despite a significant post-Soviet out-migration, often abjuring the notion that they were colonial settlers. Third, despite the rise of Central Asian indigenous commercial culture, Russian music, film, and literature remained a large part of how Central Asians engaged their world. Finally, it is worth recalling that Central Asia, compared to its counterparts in other parts of the USSR, had minimal history of independent statehood before the Soviet era. As a result, much of what it means to be modern in Central Asia has a particularly Soviet imprint.

But how powerful and how long-lasting are Soviet legacies? As Mark Beissinger and Stephen Kotkin show, establishing that (and how) legacies matter is no mean feat, analytically speaking. Indeed, although their work covers state socialism in general and not Central Asia in particular, it echoes what Diana Ibañez-Tirado finds in the context of Tajikistan, quoting Zamira from the city of Kulob: "How can I be post-Soviet if I was never Soviet? Perhaps my parents are post-Soviets. Wait! No! My parents were not Soviet, were they? In any case my father is ex-Soviet, but my mother never worked, but instead she was always sitting at home. Is that what you mean by Soviet? Working for the Russians? Then my father is ex-Soviet, not post-Soviet; and my mother was never Soviet. I don't know! You confuse me! I didn't see any of this. How can I know?" Zamira's honest befuddlement betrays an important fact: Soviet categories (and the notion of a fundamental rupture between Soviet and post-Soviet periods) did not resonate with some ordinary Tajiks after more than a quarter century from the Soviet collapse.

Yet, if we move from the identity categories that people invoke to the behaviors that people exhibit, it is hard to dispense with "Soviet" as a principle influencing forms of sociability. Indeed, much of what we see in Central Asia today is of Soviet origins—from the physical infrastructure of most cities, to the forms of public education that the region's citizens enjoy, to the priority given to informal (rather than formal) ways of resolving social, political, and economic problems. Soviet modernity left a deep imprint on Central Asia, and many of those Central Asians who suffer socioeconomically look back to the Soviet era with nostalgia, pointing to its achievements. Although the state-led ideology associated with "Soviet" has been left behind, the social forms it produced are widely accepted as the natural order of things.

Ethnicity

Among the most significant Soviet legacies was an ethnofederal administrative structure, which was based on the premise that each major administrative unit of the USSR represented the natural homeland for a given titular group. The domestic passports that Soviet citizens carried bore their ethnic belonging, which concretized their connection to the ethnofederal unit bearing their name. Thus, it was taken as unproblematic that Kazakhstan was for Kazakhs, Uzbekistan for Uzbeks, and so on, notwithstanding large nontitular populations who resided in each Soviet republic.

With the Soviet collapse, the highest-order administrative units (i.e., the fifteen titular republics) became independent states, solidifying ethnicity as the cornerstone of these new polities. Nontitular residents in the Central Asian cases were typically granted formal citizenship, but informal norms privileged the titular ethnic community and indeed the post-Soviet Central Asian regimes reified ethnic categories by emphasizing them in their writing of official histories, in the creation of new textbooks, in the erecting of new monuments, and in the establishment of official holidays and other symbolic accouterments of statehood. The post-Soviet period did precious little to undermine the principle that people were part of ethnically defined communities that were mutually exclusive and of paramount social and political importance.

In a sense, there was nothing unusual about this. After all, one way (though not the only way) to interpret the principle of "national self-determination" built into the international system of states is in a cultural sense. That is, if a nation is understood to be rooted in historical and cultural commonality (e.g., Anthony Smith's "ethnies"), then the international system itself reifies ethnic belonging. Be that as it may, it was certainly regarded both within Central Asia and by outsiders interacting with Central Asia as a normal principle of social organization.

Central Asians, like other human beings, are more complicated, flexible, and confounding than the categories often invoked to describe them. Thus, it is hard not to sympathize with Rogers Brubaker and Frederick Cooper, who call upon analysts to "avoid unintentionally *reproducing* or *reinforcing* such reification by uncritically adopting categories of practice as categories of analysis." In other words, just because Central Asians sometimes use ethnic categories, we should not necessarily take ethnic categories as analytically productive. Based on his research in the Ferghana Valley, Nick Megoran is likewise correct to reject "the conception of 'ethnicity' as an enduring essence adhering to an individual that awaits uncovering by experts wielding questionnaires or interview schemata."

Yet, without ethnic categories, it is hard to make sense of key aspects of Central Asia's social structure. Without them, we would be unable to explain why in June 2010 people calling themselves Kyrgyz felt threatened by people calling themselves Uzbeks, resulting in three days of intercommunal violence and at least four hundred deaths (disproportionately Uzbeks). We would be unable to appreciate why the early post-Soviet period witnessed a steady out-migration of nontitular Russians, who claimed to feel displaced by ethnic discourses propagated by states seeking to speak on behalf of titular groups. We can and should be open to the potential for ethnic categories to weaken in intensity or shift in meaning, but for the medium term, at least, ethnicity will remain among the most important defining elements of the Central Asian experience.

The Global

All of these important elements that structure Central Asian society—from Islam to moral considerations to Soviet legacies to ethnicity—increasingly come into contact with globalizing trends. I emphasize that these trends are plural; globalization is experienced in various ways by various actors along various dimensions.

Central Asia is less remote and less isolated than outsiders typically assume. Consider global capitalism. Kyrgyzstan was the first post-Soviet state to enter the World Trade Organization (in 1998), opening it up to the worldwide trade of goods and services. Kazakhstan in the 1990s entered into vibrant, large-scale contacts, especially in the extractive industries with foreign multinational firms. Even impoverished and illiberal Tajikistan, with its limited economic opportunities, has seen its regime deeply ensconced in global networks of contestation. In a macro sense, as Alexander Cooley and John Heathershaw effectively demonstrate, much of the direction that each of these states takes is a function of how transnational political economic networks play themselves out.

If elites in geographically distant Central Asia are more global in orientation than we sometimes assume, it is also true that broader swathes of Central Asian publics find themselves navigating social life with distinctly global influences. When citizens of Kazakhstan study abroad in the West via the *bolashaq* program and return to Kazakhstan for work, they must come to terms both with the sensibilities newly acquired abroad and how those map onto domestic Kazakhstani realities. When Central Asians encounter religious literature that provides instruction on how to be a good, practicing Muslim, both the content of the literature and the mechanism of its dissemination are possible only with a Central Asia that is connected to the broader "Muslim world" via global capitalist and religious networks.

The processes by which Central Asians grapple with ethnic identities are little different; they too play themselves out both within Central Asia and beyond its borders. This is especially true where authoritarian rule has squeezed out space for domestic contestation and deliberation about what ethnic belonging entails. Thus, from the early 1990s, much of the vibrant debate about Turkmen ethnic history has taken place among exiles physically outside of Turkmenistan, with the potential to reinform what happens inside Turkmenistan itself. Likewise, online debates among ethnic Tajiks about Persian heritage take place in transnational communities that transcend physical space. Thus, even social processes that might seem inherently anti-global (by virtue of dealing with discrete cultural communities based in particular territories) in fact play themselves out globally.

Central Asians are increasingly online, ranging from an estimated 55.8 percent of Kazakhstani citizens to a low of 15 percent of Turkmenistani citizens in 2016. The numbers rise each year, so the potential for exposure to information flows with a provenance beyond the borders of a given state rises as well. Naturally, the world is not "flat," in Thomas Friedman's misleading metaphor; people simply do not have equal access to information or to the opportunities that information affords. A Tajikistani citizen, for example, may on occasion encounter blocked websites and social media. Moreover, even assuming unfettered access, Central Asians, like everyone else, are more likely to seek out materials in languages they understand and from sources they trust. Thus, Central Asians do indeed have greater access to material produced outside the region, which in their case means a greater penetration of media from the Russian Federation. If intensifying internet connectivity has brought anything to Central Asians, it has brought Central Asia back into the orbit of Russian cultural influences.

Central Asians are also increasingly mobile. As noted earlier, the clearest expression of this mobility is labor migration, largely to Russia. About one million Tajikistani citizens found themselves working in Russia in 2015, and Tajikistan on a per capita basis is the most remittance-dependent country in the world. As scholars have documented, this brings different forms of sociability, compelling Tajik families in remote mountain villages to confront transnational religious networks and novel religious practices, as well as social norms quite different from what their upbringing might have exposed them to. Since Russia has long been the conduit for European cultural influences to arrive in Central Asia, this labor mobility in fact echoes prior trends.

How Central Asians locate themselves vis-à-vis the global, and how global forms of connectivity and sociability alter what it means to be a Central Asian, is highly variable. Central Asia, despite its remote location in the European and North American imagination, has always been a crossroads. Today's Central Asians must explicitly grapple with challenging questions of selfhood and community in the face of expanding regional and global connections.

Changing Patterns of the Social

We should be faithful to the social categories that Central Asians in their everyday lives routinely reify. Thus, it is important to consider how Central Asians grapple with religion, morality, historical legacies, ethnicity, and global connections. Nonetheless, a fuller account of Central Asian society should put these categories in motion. In this final section, I consider additional (and more fluid) considerations about Central Asian society. My contention is that Central Asians, like other human beings, can be profitably described in terms of the behaviors they exhibit as much as by the qualities they possess.

Face-to-Face Exchange

When social scientists and others in the West think of exchange, we often equate it with anonymous interactions among consumers, producers, and facilitators whom we assume to be basically interchangeable. Given the complexity and ubiquity of our market economic transactions, and given the enormous scale on which such transactions occur, it is ironic that we sometimes fail to see that we are in fact involved in exchange. Indeed, our labor has become so deeply specialized that we can be ignorant of the labor provided by others. Moreover, we instrumentalize our exchanges to such a degree that we often assume that their social purpose is simply to satisfy material needs.

Since the Soviet collapse, Central Asia has been introduced to market conditions, even if those market conditions approximate "free market" ones only by degree. Turkmenistan, for example, has highly controlled forms of exchange domestically, but even its fairly closed economy is not immune to the logics of broader global markets. Central Asians do what other global citizens do: they buy, they sell, they trade, they save, they borrow, and so on.

Nonetheless, Central Asians are strikingly likely to be involved in face-to-face exchange. Because face-to-face encounters are normal, Central Asians typically accord social importance to exchange; they have a clear view of how it happens in their everyday lives. Consider Banu, who in 2005 directed a nongovernmental organization in Dushanbe, Tajikistan, and assisted me in arranging some key interviews. Although she worked in a nonprofit, and although it was arguably part of her job to assist people like me, she clearly expected that our transactions would not flow only in one direction. After I had conducted my interviews, she asked me if I could assist her with applications to work or study in the West. That much I was happy to do, but her questions slowly gave way to a request: that I secure her admission to a program at my university. She was dumbfounded by my insistence that I could not (and would not attempt to) influence the admissions process. (From her perspective, I must not be a very important person at my university if I could not be of assistance!) She evidently assumed that because we had a relationship based on face-to-face interactions, it could transcend the limitations imposed by other norms, institutions, processes, and personnel.

Banu's example is far from isolated; informal exchange is an enormous part of life in the post-Soviet space. It is normal for Central Asians to assume that informality penetrates virtually every domain. The sociologist Alena Ledeneva has documented for Russia what occurs broadly in Central Asia as well: the connections (*blat*) forged and reiterated via exchange are an important source of social status and influence. They are a normal and often principal part of social interaction.

Unless you understand the centrality of informal exchange, some aspects of life in Central Asia seem inscrutable. I have conducted a number of academic sessions in the region wherein we have difficulty translating the terms *not-for-profit* or *nonprofit* into Russian. After all, if the employees of nonprofits enjoy salaries significantly higher than the Central Asian average, and if their position allows them to make myriad connections that may produce opportunities for mutual assistance, then in what sense are these entities not producing "profit" for those involved? That the term has a specific legal connotation is of little consolation. Indeed, most Central Asians do not believe such legal designations to be grounded in state regulations that have been developed and executed in fair fashion.

With Central Asian exchange, we therefore end up in a strange place wherein *both* the instrumental dimension (as "profit" is always among the things that are generated) *and* the moral obligation are visible to ordinary people. One can of course have a purely instrumental transaction. An oil company might seek the best work at the best price as it evaluates possible subcontractors. A shopper visiting a local market outside of their home district might make a purchase as an anonymous individual, fairly interchangeable with other shoppers. She will be quoted the market price, which may be higher than that for "regulars." Likewise, many of the upwardly mobile members of the middle class in Kazakhstan have developed different social norms based on the acquisition of material goods with little regard for the social relations involved therein. Yet, while Central Asia is a region in motion, most forms of exchange continue to exhibit elements of both instrumentality and moral obligation.

Playing Roles and the Logics of Appropriateness

How can we link the above considerations? The more time I spend in Central Asia, the more useful I find it to consider the social roles that people play. A role implies a particular way of behaving in particular situations according to a script—in this case, a script established by prevailing norms. So, in Western societies, someone playing the role of "physician" does so in ways that are heavily influenced, though not entirely determined, by customary notions of how someone bearing that moniker ought to behave. Social norms thus hinge on a common sense of appropriateness.

Let us start from the top. One common way to analyze the political elite in Central Asia is to assume that they pursue material self-interest and self-preservation. To be sure, there is no shortage of wealth-seeking, power-hungry behavior exhibited by Central Asia's ruling classes. Yet, without considering what constitutes appropriate behavior, it is analytically impossible to appreciate what "self" and "interest" really mean in any given context. As Michael Schatzberg expertly demonstrates for cases across sub-Saharan Africa, the "horizons of the thinkable" are crucial to delineate if one is to appreciate what can and what simply cannot occur in politics. That is, how political leaders think of self and interest is a function of what is considered normatively appropriate.

Let me make this concrete. Why in 2010 did Kazakhstan, a state with vast energy and mineral wealth, embark on an ambitious program to develop its "green energy" sectors? After all, an authoritarian regime with access to untold wealth and concentrated political power has no particular need to develop an alternative sector, especially one with a slim chance of becoming economically viable. As I have explored elsewhere, the decision emerged in a global normative environment in which a state desiring to demonstrate that it had "arrived" on the global stage as a major power was *normatively expected to develop* a vibrant green energy sector. Going green (at least on a rhetorical level) was Kazakhstan's way to trumpet its achievements globally. Clearly, that it was appropriate for an advanced industrial economy to "go green" does not dictate that all advanced industrial economies will follow suit, and it certainly does not guarantee that the green push will succeed, but the logic of appropriateness does have the power to shape behavior.

If role-playing and behaving appropriately according to expectations can matter for the Central Asian elite, it is even more central in the lives of ordinary people. These are complex societies with a wide range of roles and notions of appropriateness, but one feature that distinguishes Central Asia is an emphasis often placed on social honor. One might bring honor to a religious or cultural tradition. One might bring honor to one's parents, extended family, or the social inheritance of a particular kin group. One might bring honor to a profession, to an ideological principle, or to an aesthetic. Naturally, not everyone succeeds in bringing honor and not everyone shares these motivations. Yet, it strikes me as fair to say that Central Asian behavior is more often characterized by a striving to honor than by the pursuit of individual self-interest.

What does this mean in practice? When Banu asked me to help her gain admission to my Canadian university, she was—as multiple conversations with her eventually made clear—motivated by a desire to make good on her felt obligation to extended family and broader kin who always prized a topflight education. As she explained it, because opportunities for a worthy education

EDWARD SCHATZ

were limited in her native Tajikistan, she had to seek them abroad. Of course, self-interest is never absent in considerations such as those made by Banu, but it would be challenging to appreciate the motivations for her behavior without a clear view of the premium she placed on bringing honor to her kin tradition.

Social Structure in Central Asia

Central Asia, like elsewhere, is a socially complex place, and individual Central Asians make decisions based on highly distinctive considerations. Yet this is not a "free-for-all." Social structure matters, and so Central Asians must contend with (1) what it means to be a Muslim, (2) what it means to be moral, (3) what it means to be Soviet or post-Soviet, (4) what it means to belong to an ethnic group, and (5) how to locate oneself in a global sense. Moreover, they do so on a terrain typically thick with face-to-face forms of exchange and often paramount considerations of social honor and obligation to others.

Let us return to Bakhyt, whom I introduced at the chapter's outset. In 2018, her three children had grown up. They had all received a good education, and those who had conducted their studies in the Russian language seemed to have better career prospects. The eldest was married with a young child and lived in Bishkek with her devout husband; she chose to wear a hijab. The middle child had just started work as a family physician in Bishkek. The youngest was completing a BA at a university in Turkey. Bakhyt was chair of her university department, and she could now afford to attend one or two international scholarly conferences per year. She was deeply frustrated with the Higher Attestation Committee—the state body charged with overseeing academic degree programs—which she described as riddled with corruption and run by incompetents. She believed that the principle that "money decides everything" had nearly destroyed a great Soviet legacy by undermining the value of a good education.

Bakhyt's parents needed regular care, so Bakhyt spent significant time shuttling them to and from medical appointments. The family had sold the apartment in the city and moved full time to their family home, which by this time had been partially absorbed as a "suburb" by expanding construction. Bakhyt still did not have time for organized religion but was happy that her children were exposed to Islamic norms; in her view, this exposure countered the excesses of consumer culture. At the same time, she worried about interpretations of Islam that were "foreign" to Kyrgyzstan; she found them rigid and against progress.

Central Asia in 2018 boasted a population of roughly seventy million people. Bakhyt was just one person among them, living a particular life and making highly individual decisions. Yet, the broad social facts she faced were widely shared across the region. Central Asians are of course not prisoners of these considerations. The social terrain inevitably will shift, in part because individuals like Bakhyt, Banu, Rustam, and Guldana reshape, challenge, and redefine what these social structures mean.

15

Moral Structure

Maria Louw

An Ironic Cinderella

On a summer's day in 2000, my friend and field assistant, Nargiza, and I were invited to participate in an *Osh Bibiyo* in a house on the outskirts of Bukhara by the *oymullo* (female mullah) who led the ritual. Osh Bibiyo is a ritual held by and for women in honor of the female saint Bibi Seshanba, who is regarded as a protector of home and family life, and of women in particular. Nargiza was probably just as excited as I was: in her family, it was only married women who held and attended Osh Bibiyo rituals, and although she had heard of the ritual, as a young unmarried woman it was the first time she had taken part in one. We watched and listened attentively as the oymullo led us and the other attendees—in this case, around eighty women from the whole mahalla (neighborhood)—through the stages of the ritual, including prayers, Qur'an recitation, special ceremonial meals, and the recounting of the story about Bibi Seshanba, a story that explains the importance of the Osh Bibiyo: a Cinderella-like story in which Bibi Seshanba helps an orphan girl escape an abusive stepmother and marry a prince.

Some of the participants seemed to take the ceremony quite lightly, chatting, laughing, and eating during the prayers. However, after a couple of hours, when it was time for each of the women present to ask the oymullo for a particular prayer, the atmosphere changed markedly, becoming very solemn and intense: some women burst into tears; others were just very concentrated on their prayers. The fact that Bibi Seshanba is considered patron of the home and family life was reflected in the wishes that were brought forward in the course of the ceremony: wishes to be blessed with a child; about one's children succeeding at school; about getting money for a new home; and for peace and good health in the family. In the ritual space of the Osh Bibiyo, it seemed, these women felt relatively free to air problems and feelings that haunted them, to share experiences that were private and often shameful: a burden of childlessness, a husband who drank or was violent, or a child who had problems at school. As they attentively listened to each other's prayers and rounded them off in a shared *omin* (amen), these private and shameful experiences were transformed into public meanings; they were granted recognition by the larger community of mahalla women. Then at some point the women sitting around me signaled that it was my turn to ask the oymullo to say a prayer. I became somewhat perplexed and asked Nargiza what to say. Nargiza cautiously took the matter in her own hands and told the oymullo to say a prayer for my work to turn out well. The oymullo then, in the name of Bibi Seshanba, asked Allah that I would write a good dissertation, and that I would find a nice husband and be blessed with children. Neither Nargiza nor I had articulated these last two wishes, but the oymullo found it obvious that I, a twenty-eight-year-old unmarried woman, would have them. Apparently, it was also obvious to the other women, who nodded and gave me a smile while they joined the omin, the confirmation of the prayer.

I discussed the episode with Nargiza on our way home. "These women are very old-fashioned," she said in an indignant tone. "They believe that girls should marry and have children at sixteen or seventeen." With determination in her voice, she continued, "I will never marry." Nargiza, who was in her early twenties, often expressed pity for her girlfriends from school, most of whom had married and now led their lives at the mercy of their mother-in-law, occupying the lowest rung in their new families and spending all their time cooking, cleaning, sewing, looking after children, and feeling burdened with expectations that they would bear lots of children. Talk about Cinderella: when her mother made her stay home to clean, wash, or cook on the weekend, Nargiza would dress up in an old dress, take on an ironic air of a patiently suffering heroine, and refer to herself as *Zolushka*, the Russian equivalent of Cinderella, whom a prince one day would come and rescue from her misery. Nargiza's imaginary prince, however, was not of the kind who would free her from all responsibility outside the domestic sphere but a "modern" one, as she termed it; a smart person who she could talk with, and who would allow her to pursue her career. She, however, was not too optimistic—"90 percent of all Uzbek men want their wife to stay at home," she said—and had resigned herself to the thought that marriage was probably incompatible with the future picture she preferred to draw of herself as a busy and successful modern businesswoman rushing from airport to airport with a cell phone in her hand.

This picture was not altogether unrealistic, as she in fact did have a relatively well-paid job with good career opportunities. Her family, especially her mother, Umida, wavered between being proud of her and supportive of her priorities, including a job that also provided the family with their most important source of income, and being ashamed because neighbors, friends, and colleagues continuously made them feel like they had to justify the anomalous fact that Nargiza had still not married. Once in a while, Umida reproached her, saying that no one would ever come and propose to her, as she could neither sew nor cook, and any marriage proposal party that might show up would find their apartment too dirty and quickly run away. And so Nargiza was again made to stay home doing housework during the weekend, transforming into an ironic Zolushka.

When Umida came back from work, we asked for her opinion about the meaning of the Osh Bibiyo. She said that the Osh Bibiyo was about creating peace at home. When I asked her what she meant by "peace" more specifically, she reflected for a short while and then said that it did not have to be at home, that it could also be at my office; there could be problems with colleagues, there could be disagreement, gossip, and things like that. In this respect, the Osh Bibiyo could indeed help a "woman like you," as she said, directed toward me. Nargiza approved of that interpretation, and together we spent most of the evening discussing the women with whom we had attended the Osh Bibiyo; the worldview in which their ideas about womanhood was grounded; and what kinds of life prospects such a worldview offered a young woman like Nargiza.

Ordinary Ethics and Moral Breakdowns

With this story, taken from my fieldwork in Bukhara, Uzbekistan, in 1998–2000, I do not merely wish to tell a story about the tension between prevalent gender norms expressed and performed in an important women's ritual in Bukhara and the self-image and ambitions of a young Uzbek woman. I also wish, more generally, to bring us into the sphere of morality: norms, values, and criteria for judgment that are perceived as bringing communities together—"moral structures," if you will—as well as the efforts of people to improve themselves; to model themselves after moral values and exemplars of various sorts, sometimes in ways that conflict with dominant norms and values; and to the challenges people face in their everyday lives where they may move between different moral worlds with competing moral claims, and where it may quite often be difficult to discern what constitutes the most appropriate action and what kind of self one ought to become.

What one person sees as essential communal moral values may be experienced as oppressive by others. In his work on the Uzbek community in Osh in southern Kyrgyzstan, Morgan Liu has demonstrated how the mahalla has become an idiom by which residents think about and try to live out moral community. Although many complain that social relations in the mahalla today lack the sense of respect for elders, concern for the communal good, propriety of behavior among women, honesty, and industriousness compared to what they understand mahalla life to have been like before Soviet rule, it is still seen as an Uzbek cultural reservoir and a site for the formation of good persons, or what is locally most often referred to as *tarbiya*—a term that refers to upbringing, training, and discipline, and that has moral and religious connotations. Seeing the mahalla as the space of communal harmony, stewardship, and tarbiya, however, is predominantly, though by no means exclusively, an elderly male view. For those who experience themselves as marginal to dominant ideas about proper moral conduct in the mahalla—divorcées, Christian converts, or Russian-educated Uzbeks, for example—it rather tends to be seen as a space of monitoring, accountability, and control.

Nargiza and her family wavered between praising the mahalla in which they lived, for the social support it offered, and complaining about the social pressure it put on them and their conduct, the way their actions and life choices were perpetually judged and questioned by others who seemed aware of every little detail of how Nargiza and her family lead their lives.

Morality, or ethics (which I do not distinguish here), is to a large extent *ordinary*, in the sense that it is part of everyday life and intrinsic to everyday language and action. It is present, for example, in the commonsense ways we distinguish among various kinds of actors and characters, kinds of acts and manners of acting. As such, it is very often relatively unspoken, grounded in tacit agreement rather than rule. The Osh Bibiyo is a ritual that, as such, made exemplary representations of values socially available and explicit, and was also replete with the performance of unspoken norms, values, and criteria for evaluation—not in the sense of simple rule-following but, rather, good situational judgment in the form of a careful and skilled balancing among various claims to attention, desires, and interests: for example, in the polite ways the women addressed one another, paying careful attention to differences in age and status (in local languages, respect for people older than oneself is expressed in everyday forms of address); in the attention that was paid to whose teacup was empty and needed refilling; in the ways those who served tea made sure to fill them neither too much nor too little. These seemingly small and insignificant acts and utterances, which to a large extent go unnoticed, nonetheless play important roles in the fabric of community and the way acts are perceived among participants.

Ethics is also ordinary in the sense that routine activities that, at first glance, appear repetitive and prereflective at a closer look may stand out as deeply significant episodes in unfolding narratives of moral striving. That is, they may be seen as part of conscious commitments to realize particular versions of the good life. The emotions and moods that accompany everyday life, furthermore, may be morally laden. The attitude of irony that often accompanied Nargiza's sweeping the floor of her family's apartment, for example, could be seen as a moral mood that was significant in her ongoing attempts to realize a good life as she envisioned it—a version of the good life that was not unproblematic but one that demanded the continuous negotiation and reconciliation of conflicting norms and values: notably, of being a good daughter modeling her life after the example of the successful businesswoman. Nargiza did not subscribe to the idea that being good at household chores was essential to being a good woman but engaged in them in order to help her mother, keep peace at home, and sustain the family's reputation in the mahalla. Such an ironic attitude, one could argue, helped her maintain her self-image and hopes for another kind of life.

If morality does indeed often go relatively unnoticed, moral values and concerns become more conspicuous in situations such as those Jarrett Zigon has characterized as instances of "moral breakdown." Making a distinction between the unreflective moral dispositions of everyday life and conscious ethical tactics performed in ethical moments of moral breakdown, Zigon argues that such breakdowns take place when the unreflective being-in-the-world is disturbed and norms can no longer be unproblematically followed, provoking people to stand back from their normal, ongoing mode of living and to reflect and make conscious ethical choices. For Nargiza, one might argue, the clash between the moral self she wanted to become and the gender ideals expressed in the Osh Bibiyo prompted her to stand back and reflect on Uzbek gender norms and their (possible) impact on her own life, further involving both her mom and me in her reflections.

In the remaining part of this chapter, I deal with all these modalities of the moral, touching on some of the subjects generating the most intense moral debate and contestation in contemporary Central Asia: gender, generation, religion, and economy—revealing both widespread moral norms, their history, and the ways they are practiced, contested, and reinterpreted in present-day Central Asia. I touch upon moral breakdowns, which have prompted people to stand back from, make explicit, or rethink existing norms and values, but also some of the more subtle acts of judgment characteristic of everyday moral life.

A Moral Vacuum?

People do not always subscribe to coherent ethical systems but often develop virtues and reflect on moral issues in a much more ad hoc way by relating to moral exemplars, who personify particular ideals. One of the moral exemplars that Nargiza found most inspiring—an image or ideal type picked up from TV series and from meetings with colleagues in Tashkent—was the modern businesswoman, traveling, leading a busy life, dressed up in a suit, making good money. Although she was proud of her daughter and her promising career, Nargiza's mom was skeptical. To her, having come of age during the Soviet period, there was hardly anything exemplary about businesspeople in suits. Quite on the contrary, they represented the moral degeneration of a post-Soviet society in which the pursuit of money, power, and material things played an increasingly dominant role in people's lives, making them compromise a more "traditional" moral concern for others.

The breaking up of the Soviet Union was indeed experienced by many as a large-scale moral breakdown that prompted reflections on a number of fundamental questions, such as the relationship between state and citizen; the question of what central values were to fill out what many perceived as a "moral vacuum" left in society by the demise of communism; the question of the moral status of democracy and market economy; the question of what place religion (in particular Islam) was to take up in society and in people's lives. In short, the moral debating revolved around how to build up good states and communities, how to live a good life, and what a good life, a good person, a good state, and a good community actually was. New ideals and moral exemplars were introduced, some connected with cosmopolitanism and global capitalism, others with the revival of "ancient" local traditions.

The years following the independence of the Central Asian states saw widespread attempts by the state to "revive" allegedly ancient moral values, filling the perceived "moral vacuum." Kyrgyzstan under Askar Akaev, for example, created *aksakal* (elder) courts, tasked with adjudicating according to Kyrgyz moral norms and traditions. In Uzbekistan, former president Islam Karimov published a ceaseless number of books, essays, and speeches on *ma'naviyat*, a moral and spiritual quality that he saw as both intrinsic to Uzbek identity and dependent on the state for its protection and cultivation. In Turkmenistan, Saparmurat Niyazov, who ruled the country until his death in 2006 and promoted a spiritual creed centered on himself, published the *Ruhnama* (Book of the Soul) to give moral and spiritual guidance to the Turkmen and made it mandatory reading for schoolchildren and university students. All sorts of moral exemplars—among the more noticeable being Amir Timur (Tamerlane), the conqueror and founder of the Timurid empire in Uzbekistan, and Manas, hero of the eponymously named epic in Kyrgyzstan—were furthermore promoted by governments as sources of moral inspiration for the population. But also on the local—individual, family, and community—level, there were multiple reflections on, and experimentation with, what a good person, a good life, and a good society implied.

Market Economy and Moral Economy

Economic development, in particular, has been the subject of intense discussion and moral problematization, raising important questions about the principles and values that govern, or should govern, economic activities. The new opportunities for wealth and consumption that accompanied market reforms and the conspicuous consumption by a new wealthy class of business and political elites has been the subject of much fascination, and for many, in particular young people like Nargiza, a source of hope for a better life. However, one finds much more ambiguous, and sometimes hostile, attitudes toward market economy among many who see it as subversive to the social and moral order. This partially has to do with the fact that during the Soviet period, trade was condemned as *spekulatsiya* (profiteering), and was seen as an unproductive form of generating wealth, but, perhaps more importantly, it has to do with the hardship experienced by many in the aftermath of economic reforms.

As Jon P. Mitchell has argued, perceptions of social and economic change often lead to a kind of moralizing against excess that establishes a boundary within which people are censured to remain but that in turn creates a proliferation of images of transgression and the consequences of transgression. Such images of transgression are present all over Central Asia, where the struggle to find new strategies for survival—amid the growing gaps between the rich and the poor, the shrinking of welfare provisions, the increasing monetization of social relations, and the "hidden charges" that meet people everywhere—is the subject of intense discussion and, sometimes, moral condemnation. This is particularly the case among the older and middle-aged generations, many of whom compare what they remember as a relatively well-functioning Soviet medical and educational system with the present systems, where, to many, it seems impossible to pass an exam (at least with a high grade) or receive proper medical attention without offering money or presents to teachers, and where the medical personnel's care for the common good has been replaced by a more narrow-minded attention to one's own well-being and the well-being of one's close relatives. Balihar Sanghera, Aibek Ilyasov, and Elmira Satybaldieva have described how economic reforms have indeed resulted in changing moralities among public sector employees in Kyrgyzstan: how they have come to value economic rewards at the expense of their ethical commitments and professional goals; how doctors and nurses are increasingly interpreting market ideology in ways that place the responsibility of care not on them but on patients, their clients; and how the reception of bribes is seen among morally acceptable survival strategies, which help professionals provide for their families despite insufficient salaries.

Other people, or the same people in different circumstances, may, however, question the moral righteousness of an ever-present pressure to share one's income and resources with extended family and the wider community, complaining how it reflects (Soviet) disrespect for individual property and sponging off the hard-earned money of others. And many, indeed, make great efforts to strike a golden mean between, on the one hand, the effort to make a good living for oneself and one's family and, on the other hand, a concern with communal and, sometimes, transcendental values. During my work among followers of the Naqshbandiyya Sufi order in Bukhara, Uzbekistan, in 1998–2000, for example, I was struck by the ambiguous attitudes they expressed toward recent market economic reforms: On the one hand, they often emphasized how important it was, in present-day society, to tame the *nafs* (desire, ego, or base instincts) through prayers and other techniques, as an uncontrolled nafs seemed to control people's lives and make them obsessed with money, power, and commodities. On the other hand, they expressed the view that the best way to serve God was through hard work, and that the Naqshbandiyya order was the perfect way to practice Islam in a capitalist society, as it was a Sufi order that emphasized the value of hard work and of not wasting one's time. Many were involved in business, and some worked at Bukhara's bazaars—places they found morally dubious because there people tended to cheat each other, to lie, to trade in goods that were *haram* (forbidden, according to Islam), and there greed and materialism ruled. They would, so they told, practice the inner *dhikr*, recollection of God, while they worked, trying to make themselves immune from the temptations of the market. They strove, in other words, to tame capitalism, to cleanse it of its evil aspects.

15-1   Prayers in the courtyard of the Memorial Complex of Khoja Bakhouddin Naqshbandi, founder of the Sufi order, in Bukhara, Uzbekistan, 2019. Photograph by Kasia Ploskonka.

Ambiguous moral attitudes toward people's strategies for making a living in a challenging economic environment have indeed been documented by several researchers. Gulzat Botoeva, for example, demonstrated how, in a village in Kyrgyzstan where the monetization of gift-giving during social celebrations has put constant pressure on families to find cash in a semisubsistence agricultural economy, hashish has gained an increasing importance as a cash crop that helps to maintain social security networks among local residents. If hashish was rather unambiguously morally condemned during the Soviet period, it now enjoys a much more ambiguous status, as an important means for tackling poverty and maintaining community, yet also still somehow "tainted" or dangerous. Making too much hashish and relying only on hashish money as the main means of income is thus perceived as potentially dangerous.

Also labor migration has been an area characterized by moral problematization, by renewed discussions about, and experiments with, what a good life or a good community is. In large parts of rural Central Asia, remittances from migrant labor in Russia have come to constitute a basic source of livelihood. Offering new opportunities in a situation where most sources of employment have been curtailed, and being essential for the maintenance of families and development of community infrastructure, migration has also drastically changed family and community structures in many villages, provoking people to stand back from their normal, ongoing mode of living and reflect on community, intergenerational, and gender norms and values. In Sokh in eastern Uzbekistan, Madeleine Reeves has argued, protracted male absence due to migration is having considerable transformative effects on family relations and the organization of labor, just as it is becoming a touchstone among the women left behind debating the parameters of their own modernity. While the departure of a husband may, in some cases, lead to increased opportunities for autonomy and employment outside the home, the collective regulation of

15-2   Local children playing in a village near Kaindy Lake in Saty, Kazakhstan, 2018. Photograph by Kasia Ploskonka.

female honor (*nomus*) can mean that wives "left behind" often enjoy fewer opportunities for domestic mobility, rather than more.

Family Structure, Gender, and Age

Family structure, and in particular gender and intergenerational relations, has indeed been another subject of intense moral problematization in post-Soviet Central Asia.

For a long time, the relations between the sexes have been considered a key to the achievement of an ideal order of society in Central Asia, just as these same relations between the sexes have been considered a key to understanding why the social order is in fact not ideal. The Bolsheviks regarded the women of Central Asia as victims of patriarchal and religious repression. In Marxist terms, women constituted a "surrogate proletariat," a large, latent group of potential allies that could be mobilized in the class battle. To free them from repression, the Soviet state launched campaigns against Islam and the institutions of *purdah* (the seclusion of women), child marriage, bride price, bride abduction, and veiling. Like elsewhere in the Soviet Union, a number of measures were taken that encouraged women to leave home, join the labor force, and pursue professional careers. The creation of child day care institutions notably facilitated women in moving into the workforce.

During the Glasnost period in the late 1980s, certain local elites began to call for a return to "traditional" or "natural" gender roles—that is, for women to leave the workforce and stay home—and linked social problems with the process of women's emancipation. A search for a more authentic national identity, furthermore, meant the promotion of patriarchal norms in the public and political spheres and in religion. These norms have not been uncontested, but they have resonance among large parts of the population.

Let us return to the Osh Bibiyo ritual and the Cinderella-like myth at the heart of the ritual. Similar myths have been documented worldwide and widely discussed by feminist scholars who note the gender stereotypes articulated in them. The heroine of the story is depicted as helpless, passive, silently suffering, and submissive. She does not take matters into her own hands but is entirely dependent on the agency of outside forces—magical forces and the actions of a man drawn by her beauty—to save her from misery and injustice, and to help her become someone—to help her become a married woman.

During my fieldwork in Bukhara in 2000, I was initially tempted to interpret the Osh Bibiyo as a ritual that encouraged women to imitate a passive and submissive kind of agency that was instrumental in associating them with the domestic, further defining women's self-esteem as inextricably bound up with the social status of wife and mother. Osh Bibiyo represented the art of securing a stable home base for a happy family life. But as the example of Nargiza and her mother shows, and as it became increasingly clear to me after discussing the ritual with other Bukhara women, this interpretation would be a gross oversimplification. Although there are indeed strong normative discourses in Central Asia today that link womanhood unambiguously with the domestic sphere and status of wife and mother—just as there are strong normative discourses that link men's identity with the role as the family's breadwinner—women across the region are contesting these discourses. The Osh Bibiyo ritual and the myth that accompanies it remains open to their experiences and interpretations as well. To Nargiza and her mother, the home and family life that Bibi Seshanba was patron of, and within which the heroine of the Osh Bibiyo myth unfolded her agency, had no fixed and literal meaning. Rather, "home" was more like a metaphor that *also* could convey the more general meaning of a base, or a field, for female agency to unfold within. And, as it increasingly dawned on me after speaking with more women about the ritual, they were not alone in this interpretation. During the 1990s, in order for their families to maintain what was considered a decent living standard, many women in Central Asia had to take jobs in sectors that could be considered as compromising to their respectability, most notably as shuttle traders and market traders. As Mohira Suyarkulova has noted, many women adopted strategies, such as traveling with female companions or male relatives, that would allow them to maintain their income while remaining "good wives" in the eyes of their neighbors. And some joined forces with saints such as Bibi Seshanba, as did Gulnora, another Bukharan acquaintance of mine who was educated as a teacher but who had started engaging in business, buying furs and selling them in Russia, a few years after Uzbekistan's independence and had now become a relatively successful businesswoman. She attributed her success to the help of God, who, she said, provided her with a sense of which people were trustworthy and which were to be avoided, and whose saints had several times appeared in her dreams, giving her warnings and advice. The first time I met Gulnora was on the occasion of an Osh Bibiyo arranged by her in order, among other things, to express her gratitude to Bibi Seshanba for a warning sent in her dreams, a warning that saved her from economic ruin. Considering that Bibi Seshanba is primarily seen as protector of the home and family life, I found it interesting that Gulnora connected her with her business. When I expressed to her my wonder, Gulnora told me that formerly it might have been the case that women only worked at home, but nowadays things were different. Now people needed more money, and many women had to work in order for their families to live a decent life.

Similar to gender, age and intergenerational relations have been a notable subject of moral problematization in post-Soviet Central Asia. Showing care and respect for elders is considered of central moral importance and indeed a distinguishing feature of local tradition and culture. Respect for elders is expressed in many ordinary and subtle practices, such as the order of seating, as was the case with the Osh Bibiyo, where the older women were granted a seat at the most honorable spot, next to the oymullo and opposite the entrance door. However, rules are not written in stone. As Judith Beyer has demonstrated, focusing on aging in Kyrgyzstan, working toward becoming an elder requires more than just being of a certain age. As they come of age, elders gradually learn to comply with and perform "elder-ness" in the expected ways—most notably through the performance of high moral integrity and authority—and only if they successfully do so are they recognized as elders, deserving the authority, rights, and privileges that elders enjoy. And sometimes other differences in status may overrule age differences. When Nargiza and I arrived to the Osh Bibiyo, there was, as I often experienced it on occasions like this, some (discreet) discussion about where we were to sit: on the one hand, we were both unmarried women, and as such we enjoyed a low rank and ought to be seated not in the central room but in one of the adjacent ones. On the other hand, I was a *mehmon*, guest, from abroad, who had been invited by the oymullo to join the ceremony, and as such I had to be treated with great respect and hospitality. In the end, Nargiza and I were seated relatively close to the oymullo but not without (discreet) disapproval from some of the women present.

If the general idea is that older people should be treated with care and respect, there is also much discussion of a perceived decline in family cohesion and respect for senior citizens. The work experience and education of people older than, say, the age of forty-five is also often denigrated as "Soviet" and therefore no longer relevant. As Jeanne Féaux de la Croix has demonstrated, age hierarchies and ideologies come into conflict with the personal desires and aims of younger people, in particular in the context of professional workplaces such as nongovernmental organizations.

Similarly, competing ideas about Islam, to some extent, has appeared as a clash between different generations, causing situations where young people sometimes feel they have to choose between honoring their religion and paying due respect to their parents and grandparents. Manja Stephan has described how in Dushanbe, the capital of Tajikistan, private religious lessons for boys and girls are considerably popular. The secular educational system being insufficient in the eyes of many, numerous Muslim families fall back on religious authorities and institutions when it comes to the upbringing of their offspring. Parents generally prefer to entrust their children to traditional local religious authorities who acquired their religious knowledge during the Soviet era, as these figures represent an extension of parental authority and create continuity and a sense of homogeneity between instruction at school and upbringing at home. In contrast, many adolescent Muslims are more interested in lessons given by younger religious teachers, who have a formal religious education; are more versed in Arabic, foreign languages, and in recent Islamic literature; and are sometimes educated abroad. These younger teachers usually stand for a more scripturally oriented interpretation of Islam, which challenges the traditional understanding dominant among older generations. Criticizing the older generations' ideas about Islam, however, or just going against them in practice (e.g., by choosing to wear the hijab—a practice seen by many as "foreign" or "Arab" and incompatible with local tradition), might be seen as greatly disrespectful toward their authority. And many young practicing Muslims have to strike a difficult balance between behaving according to the rule of Islam as they are taught by religious authorities and behaving according to the standards of acceptable behavior characteristic of society as such, and in particular their senior family members' understanding of Muslimness, being good Muslims, but also being good children and grandchildren.

Religion

This brings me to the last subject of intense moral problematization I wish to take up in this chapter: religion. When the Soviet Union dissolved, there was a sense among large parts of the population in the region that the seventy years of Soviet rule had made them forget what it means to be Muslim, and, correspondingly, there was widespread hope that people would soon be able to recover that lost knowledge, regaining a core part of who they were. But people equally feared that social and economic instability—and the perceived moral vacuum—could make a fertile soil for religious extremism, destructive to local moral sensibilities. Many have stories to tell about people, mostly youngsters, who, being vulnerable and easy prey for extremists, end up turning their backs on their families, communities, and ancestral traditions in their fanatical pursuit of a religious identity—sometimes stories about people they know but more often people they have merely heard of. Most, however, emphasize the importance of moderation in religious practice. Like the previously mentioned Naqshbandis who strove to balance religious piousness with this-worldly industriousness, or the youngsters who endeavored to balance their practice of Islam with the expression of respect toward the older generations, a general feature of the kind of Islam many of Central Asia's Muslims strive for is one that expresses, embodies, and enables a balanced existence: a balance, or golden mean in the Aristotelian sense, notably, between well-being in this world and in the afterlife, and a balance between adherence to abstract dogmas and respect for local moralities.

People's engagement in Islam (or other religions) may indeed often be seen as driven by moral concerns. In his book *Islam in Post-Soviet Uzbekistan: The Morality of Experience*, Johan Rasanayagam demonstrated how people in Uzbekistan do not only deliberate over the nature of what it means to be Muslim, but they are also continually living out a developing moral self as well as notions of moral community. He develops the argument that moral reasoning is not just confined to cognitive reflection upon objective values or a conscious striving to develop a virtuous self. It is inherent within experience itself, in an embodied, ongoing engagement in a social and material world that itself has a transcendent quality. One important moral source through which individuals come to an understanding of what it means to be Muslim, for example, is the very sociality of interacting with others. Participating within networks of obligation and reciprocity by organizing the marriages and settlement of children, holding and attending life cycle rituals, and contributing to communal projects such as building a road or a mosque is central to many people's understanding of Muslimness. This becomes all the more significant in a context like Uzbekistan, where open and free debate is stifled.

For many women in Bukhara, the Osh Bibiyo ritual indeed stood as a central moral source in Rasanayagam's understanding. Most of them saw the ritual and the attendance of it as foundational to their Muslim identity and much more important than, say, the daily prayers or the fast in Ramadan, creating a close link between the understanding of Islam and of local communal norms. But an understanding of Islam—and of local communal norms—as already pointed out, was more open and dynamic than it first appeared.

Moral Structure and Moral Practice

The story about Nargiza, her mom, me, and the Osh Bibiyo brings up a range of topics that are the object of moral problematization in contemporary Central Asia and illustrates the relationship between moral structure and moral practice: how dominant communal norms and values do indeed influence people's lives but also how norms are negotiated and more flexible than they may seem at first sight; how moral "structures" are perpetually negotiated and problematized; and how leading a moral life is not merely a matter of living up to communal norms but often involves dealing with dilemmas, paradoxes, and the balancing of conflicting concerns. Struggling to be a good person, for Nargiza, for example, involved carefully balancing local norms for how a young woman, daughter, and Muslim should act, and what her priorities in life should be. Nargiza found inspiration in the moral exemplar she found most compelling—the modern and independent businesswoman and pursuing a career that, if dubious in the eyes of her neighbors, made her family able to live a decent life. But such negotiation has not been without moral wrestling. Being immanent to social life as such, morality is a dimension of social life in all its aspects, and in all its spheres, as we see in reflecting on experience and its contextual richness.

16

Gender Structure

Svetlana Peshkova

Why Gender

Gender, a key organizing principle of social life in any society, is directly linked to politics and economy. In Central Asia, the last two centuries exemplify how changes in political regimes and economic practices informed transformations of local gender structure. In the late nineteenth century, Russia's Imperial legal reforms, which accompanied criticism of the local religious leadership for sanctioning women's oppression through polygyny (having multiple wives) and seclusion, solidified Russia's rule over the region as a benevolent civilizer in charge of the Central Asian economy. The twentieth century's access to secular education and professional and political possibilities for local women, which came together with the Communist Party's criticism of local gender roles, helped to consolidate the party's rule in the region and paved the way for subsequent economic reforms. Soviet social duties assigned by the party to both women and men ensured women's rights to wage labor and were vital to satisfying growing needs of the Soviet economy. In the twenty-first century, by presenting themselves as "protective patriarchs," local post-Soviet ruling regimes' retraditionalizing of Central Asian societies—a selective revival and preference for customs and understandings of gender roles that reinforce patriarchal institutions—played a central role in the reformulation of national identities. This, in turn, justified further entrenching patronage politics in these post-Soviet states and informed concomitant economic corruption and growing class differentiation.

While the twentieth century's research on gender in the region often focused on women, in the twenty-first century, scholars of Central Asian studies significantly expanded their research foci, including local masculinities, femininities, and gender variance. This wealth of information about gender and sexuality in Central Asia needs to be systematized and integrated. This is no easy task: it is difficult to generalize about gender in a region as diverse and vast as former-Soviet Central Asia, populated by various peoples speaking different languages, professing several religious and/or secular affiliations, and transitioning among economic class divisions depending on the current political context in each one of the five sovereign countries (Kazakhstan, Kyrgyzstan, Tajikistan, Turkmenistan, and Uzbekistan). Central Asia's geographic location and geological complexity also necessitate a variety of lifeways, including agriculture and pastoralism, and hence lead to different sociocultural practices informed by peoples' ecological adaptation. Therefore, the reader should proceed with caution, realizing that the regional gender structure described in the following paragraphs is unable to fully capture local diversity.

In this chapter, I offer an approximation of how to begin thinking about gender structure in twenty-first-century Central Asia. I first define the concept of gender and then demonstrate its sociocultural construction and highlight gender structure's significance in Central Asian social history. The majority of local people do not use the term "gender" (hard "g" and rolling "r" in Russian *gender*) to describe their daily lives. Yet, I still argue that thinking *with* gender, as an analytical category, illuminates Central Asia's sociohistorical context. A closer look at regional gender structure shows that daily life in and social history of the region is more complex than often assumed, described, and theorized.

Gender

The analytical concept of gender originated and matured in American and European academic and activist circles starting in the 1960s. As such, gender refers to a sociocultural process that diminishes similarity and emphasizes differences among humans and, by extension, nonhumans. By differentiating among individuals in a society, of whether and how one is female, male, or any other culturally acceptable gender category, gender structure becomes a means of maintaining social order and control. Such differentiation is imbedded in and informs social institutions and daily life, to the extent that it appears to be natural, commonsensical, and commonplace. Although the concept of gender is not indigenous to Central Asia and may not be widely embraced by local populations, scholars, or governments, thinking with gender becomes a useful lens on local sociocultural, political, and economic diversity. In contemporary Central Asia, both sociocultural expectations and daily practices affirm existing dichotomous views of differences between women and men. From serving in the military to cleaning the house, or from wearing a dress to being circumcised—gender structure informs and affects everyone's daily life. This structure is also contested on a regular basis by those who do not fit into its dichotomous iteration.

Although it is unclear to what extent exactly human biology is related to gender, it is often assumed that genetic predispositions *and* sociocultural experiences determine human attributes. Differences in one's chromosomal makeup result in differences in biological characteristics expressed physiolog-ically and hormonally. These differences, referred to in Russian as "*polovie razlitchiya*," a concept similar to "biological sex" in English, lead to behavioral and attitudinal differences and traits that are assigned to and learned by human individuals, and, as a result, inform a different(ial) treatment of members in any given human society. Even though these differences might be genetically scripted, they emerge from society and culture rather than biology, since even the process of selection among criteria for assigning sex to a human being reflects sociocultural beliefs of what makes one male or female. If biological sex can be understood as an analytical category that refers primarily to our reproductive potential, then gender can be thought of as a social understanding of biological sex.

Anne Fausto-Sterling, for example, argues that "labeling someone as a man or a woman is a social decision. We may use scientific knowledge to help us make the decision, but only our beliefs about gender—not science—can define our sex. Furthermore, our beliefs about gender affect what kinds of knowledge science produces about sex in the first place." Thus, gender is an analytical category referring *not* to something that we are born with or possess but to what we do on a daily basis.

One is not just assigned gender roles but has to perform them on a daily basis. Doing gender includes enacting a set of different(ial) standards and behavioral expectations vis-à-vis other human beings by performing one's gender through garments, hairstyles, language, bodily practices (e.g., growing or shaving hair), and social occupations and activities, such as jobs and sports. For example, in Uzbekistan women are more likely to work as kindergarten teachers and nurses in schools, and as cooks and cleaners at local hospitals. In most cases, Central Asians put a strong emphasis on reinforcing gender dichotomy—"this is how Eastern (or Asian, Tajik, Uzbek, Kyrgyz, Kazakh, and/or Turkmen) men are" and "this is how Eastern (or Asian, Tajik, Uzbek, Kyrgyz, Kazakh, and/or Turkmen) women are." This dichotomy erases both similarities between males and females and differences in personal experiences, understandings, and enactments of gender among them. Despite the implication of a homogeneity of experience within a gender category, there is great experiential and existential variation in whether and how one is male or female in Central Asia. This variation helps to configure a far more complex gender structure than often assumed by pointing out the importance of generational hierarchy, regional variation, class differences, and the degree of one's religiosity.

Becoming Gendered and Entering Gender Structure

Humans learn how to become and act as gendered members of a society through a process of enculturation, by interacting with, learning from, and experiencing their human and nonhuman environment; we watch, listen, reflect on, and repeat what others do. This process continues throughout an individual's life and includes, but is not limited to, the context of one's immediate family, mass media, oral traditions, educational institutions, and personal networks. Childhood experiences directly contribute to learning about gendered behaviors. While learning from both parents, children's gendered practices are often patterned on those of the same gendered parent. In Central Asia, a girl-child would learn how to imitate her mother and other female relatives, including dress code, gait, bodily practices, and gendered activities such as caring for children, serving food, sewing, cooking daily meals, sweeping the courtyard, taking care of livestock, washing clothes and dishes, and tending to a garden or domestic plants. These practices are pertinent to running a household and child-rearing, an important part of gendered social expectations of the majority of females in Central Asia. The girl-child's future is often imagined as "a daughter-in-law," who under the supervision of the mother-in-law is expected to love and care for her husband, his parents, and relatives; prepare food; clean the house; and have an agreeable disposition, virtuous morality, and modest behavior. Frequently, only after becoming a mother, a female is expected to reassert some behavioral autonomy and independent decision making. A boy-child may follow his father to the livestock pastures or to a Friday prayer at a local mosque (often attended by men only), accompany his father to male-only social activities (where, based on the child's age, he may not be permitted to join in), or visit his father's workshop to learn a trade, which he is expected to master to financially provide for his future family. The boy-child may also be observing his father's (verbal or physical) disciplining of other family members or acquiescing to and respecting decisions of the elderly relatives. These are some of the places and experiences that ensure a transmission of gendered knowledge, including ideas about how to be a proper and virtuous male or female, and safeguard gender dichotomy in Central Asia.

These examples of enculturation offered show that sociocultural expectations and degree of personal power and control differ not only between males and females but also among females and males. For example, in Central Asia, a mother-in-law is often in charge of her daughter(s)-in-law; a mother controls a premenarche girl, while a father controls his son and is himself controlled by elderly male and female relatives. In every gender structure, therefore, there is a variation of and power relations among femininities (how one is female) and masculinities (how one is male). In Central Asia, there is a scaled hierarchy among such femininities as premenarche girls, menstruating young women, mothers of a girl/girls, mothers of a boy/boys, and postmenopausal women. The same goes for hierarchies and power relations among such masculinities as precircumcised boys, circumcised young men, husbands/fathers, and grandfathers/elderly.

Sexuality and Gender Order

Any discussion of gender structure would be incomplete without considering the concept of human sexuality. In Central Asia, sociocultural expectations and behavioral norms for heterosexual pairing and care for the resulting children make sexuality an important component of the gender structure. Sexual orientation describes one's sexual preferences, desires, and activities, which could be enacted or felt toward an individual of the opposite sex/gender (heterosexual), between individuals of the same sex/gender (homosexual), toward an individual of the opposite and the same sex/gender (bisexual), or one can have no sexual desires, or feel an attraction but not act on it sexually (asexual). Some societies define gender categories by sexual preference (e.g., "male" and "female" in the United States), others by preference in behavior, occupation, and dress, or a combination of these three. For example, in India this combination underlines a tripartite gender structure that includes "male," "female," and "*kinnar* or *kothi* or *hijra*," a third gender referring to humans who are neither male nor female but are conceptualized as sacred beings/consorts who have special social roles. They often dress like local women, perform at religious ceremonies, claim a power to bless or curse others, and can act as sex workers. Germany's tripartite gender structure reflects human biological and physiological characteristics: "male," "female," and "other," that latter referring to the intersex individuals. Intersex individuals do not fit into the female/male dichotomy, because their physiological bodies differ in some way from what a majority in a particular sociohistorical context might consider to be a male or female body standard.

In any gender structure, one becomes a male or female or another socially acceptable gender category through styled repetitions of practices that are thought to be appropriate for this gender category. This process of becoming is aimed not just at performance of one's gender but also at inculcating practices, sensibilities, and desires associated with acceptable gender identities. Although it is unclear to what extent exactly human biology is related to gender—and males and females differ empirically between and among them on a scale (e.g., height, weight, and voice pitch)—Central Asians support the existing gender dichotomy, explaining it by references to biology, tradition, or religion. In other words, the dichotomous "males" and "females" gender structure in Central Asia reflects individual sexual preferences, as well as physiological and ontological differences; the latter refers to a belief that men and women are created (by a creator) as different species and exist to be sexually paired. This gender structure, in turn, informs the prevalent social organization of gender relations—"gender order"—in the region. This order comes with a binary logic (as in "men" vs. "women") behind it and dominant discourses on how to feel and act as a gendered being, including behaviors, practices, sexuality, and morality. Current gender order in Central Asia was shaped by Russian Imperial/colonial and Soviet state-centered efforts to remake the existing (at the time) social structure in the region. The gender order in precolonial Central Asia, referred to as Turkestan in colonial writings, was markedly different as it reflected a different gender structure; its vestiges are visible in the colonial military reports, travelogues, and ethnographies.

In addition to ontological and physiological characteristics, and sexual preferences, Central Asian precolonial gender structure also reflected such categories as occupation/artistic ability, age and beauty standards. Based on the materials from nineteenth-century Turkestan's Ferghana Valley, populated mainly by settled communities, a precolonial gender structure was nondichotomous and included "males," "females" and "*bachcha*," or young feminine male performers. It is important to note that gender structure among the nomadic and seminomadic populations of Central Asia (e.g., Turkmen, Kyrgyz, and Kazakhs) might have been different from the settled communities. Marina Nalivkina and Vladimir Nalivkin's colonial ethnographic research among some of Turkestan's settled communities demonstrates that the bachcha—young feminine male performers often well skilled in the art of seduction—were accomplished entertainers of older men at parties in private homes, at *choy-xona* (*chai khana*, tea houses), and at public celebrations. Some bachcha had sexual relations with their patrons. Often described as tender, gentle, beautiful, seductive, and sensual, these young feminine males received wide admiration from both local women and men for their aesthetic qualities and dancing and singing skills.

Nalivkina and Nalivkin argued that by the end of the nineteenth century, growing female sex work facilitated by the Russian colonial administration replaced local bachcha, while other scholars and travelers observe and demonstrate a growing moral disdain expressed by the colonizers who limited this gender category to "fallen men," reducing a complex gender identity of the bachcha to their sexuality only. Despite this moral judgment, bachcha's performances continued well into the first decade of the twentieth century. These examples demonstrate that the bachcha's social position, their complex gender identity, and their social reception by the larger local community differed significantly from their depictions and treatment as amoral and pathological by the late colonial, early Communist (Bolshevik), and then Soviet administrations and governments. Therefore, the bachcha exemplify gender identities erased through the efforts to "civilize" and change local social structure by the Russian Imperial and Soviet regimes. This erased gender identity also demonstrates that gender orders are dynamic; they change over time. The cultural labor of changing Central Asian societies during the twentieth century led to further transformations of gender order and gender structure in the region.

Change and Continuity in Gender Order

The precolonial gender structure informed gender orders in the region: the prevalent social organization of gender relations reflected dominant discourses on how to feel and be a gendered being, including behaviors, practices, sexuality, and morality. For instance, in many local communities, this structure led to strict gender segregation: as ontologically different—as different beings created by God—men and women led often homosocial (socializing with the same gender identity) lives outside of the privacy of one's home. Homosocial entertainment and frequent visitations with family and friends were some of the favorite pastimes among women and men.

Sensuality, beauty, and beautiful manners, including generosity and kind etiquette, were desirable attributes of all genders.

In the nineteenth century, while describing sedentary Muslim communities in the region, Nalivkina and Nalivkin observed that the relations between women and men were expected to be based on the principle of exchange and guided by a religious law (or *Sharia*, an interpretation of normative Islamic principles collected in various written sources, including the Qur'an). They noted that at the time, many local wives felt entitled to receive financial support from their husbands and in return would remain faithful and studious housemakers and caretakers; they were not afraid to scold their husbands if their husbands failed to live up to expectations. Only in extremely poor families, or as widows, women earned their living working outside the house. Additionally, prior to the colonialists' arrival, rich families kept male and female slaves. (Slavery, as an institution, further complicated local gender structure in precolonial Central Asia.) In settled communities, socializing between young female and male children was not restricted, and their dress code did not mark their gender till about the age of eight. Then, such socializing decreased, and females often entered a gradual seclusion starting at the age of twelve, when they took on a veil.

Seclusion practices varied from region to region, often reflecting a family's financial state and subsistence strategies. By the age of twelve, females' activities focused mainly on learning how to run a household and rear children, although parenting was expected to be shared by all members of the family, males and females alike. Males of that age often joined the world of trade, craft, and other "manly" activities performed by fathers and male relatives, or became bachcha. For both males and females, marriages were arranged by the parents of the bride and groom, while remarriage and child-marriage were not unusual. Nalivkina and Nalivkin reported that polygyny was rarely practiced among sedentary and nomadic and seminomadic peoples in the region for various reasons, but often it was only the well-off males who could afford to have more than one wife in colonial Turkestan. These researchers concluded that women's rights and their social positions in the region were much better than those of European women.

The precolonial gender order was nonbinary and reflected religious sensibilities and communities' standards of reciprocity, respect, and exchange, not equality, and nonheterosexual companionship; it was hierarchical but less centralized and dogmatic than the subsequent ones. Yet, by the 1910s, as a result of Russia's colonialism, Central Asian gender order became progressively state centered, whereby the state became the main arbiter of social organization of gender relations in the region. The Imperial authorities outlawed such practices as polygyny and child-marriage and increasingly scorned local gender diversity (at least in the settled communities). Since the Russian empire was a religious one, it reaffirmed ontological differences—in God's creation, males and females were different beings—between women and men as fundamental to Central Asian gender structure.

By the end of the colonial rule, Russia's criticism of the existing gender order was mainly aimed at undermining the status of local ruling elites. Because of the region's economic and political viability to the colonial authorities, it was important to establish the colonial regime's legitimacy vis-à-vis the existing—labeled as uncivilized, corrupt, and ignorant—governing structures, including local religious leadership. The colonial period has also reinforced existing social, generational, and gendered hierarchies, while colonial criticism of local customs has achieved the initial racializing of native populations as different but also culturally and religious inferior to Russians, who were predominantly Slavs and Russian Orthodox Christians. This criticism also informed local reformers' (*jadids'*) ideas about modernizing their society and changing women's social status, including heterosexual companionship, as well as their damning responses to local gender varience.

These effects of Russian colonialism on local gender structure were not as critical as the ones that were to follow in the second decade of the twentieth century. When reading against an occasional orientalist judgment, Eugene Schuyler's late nineteenth-century travelogue provides a glance into continued complexity of local colonial gender identities, particularly a variety of masculinities and their dynamic relations, such as transformation from a "boy" to "bacha [*sic*]" to "young man" to "bearded man" to "man." At the brink of the twenty-first century, while analyzing photographs and archival materials, V. A. Prischepova shows the variety of early colonial masculinities by distinguishing among bachchas as "*chuvon* (guy)" and "*besaqol* (beardless guy)," possibly reflecting one's age. This scholar observes that this tradition, highly admired among locals, all but disappeared by the late 1920s.

The transformation of Central Asian gender order continued with the Soviet state codifying gender relations along the lines of dichotomous, markedly nonreligious, gender structure. Since Russia's colonial dichotomous gender structure was adopted wholesale by the Communist organizers, their contempt for local gender diversity led to elimination of the *bachcha*'s gender identity altogether. The colonial criticism of gender segregation, as an index of the natives' unenlightened uneducated behavior, grew exponentially loud in the Communist organizers' speeches calling for liberating local women from their dependence on their families and husbands. This call to increase heterosocializing (socializing with the opposite gender), deemed completely inappropriate by many settled Central Asian communities, served one purpose: to encourage women to join wage labor necessary for the Soviet state building. These calls, educational and cultural campaigns, and legal injunctions that followed did not make women independent agents but reallocated their dependence from the immediate family to the (Soviet) state. By rewarding their reproductive labor with maternity leaves and free childcare, the Soviet state rendered women "more amendable to the state's control"; they, as main caretakers, could extend this control to their offspring and spouses.

The focus on transforming gender order in Central Asia to change social structure ideologically delinked women's (economic) dependence from (male members of) their families; such gendered configuration, in turn, solidified a model of parental and spousal responsibilities that undermined fatherhood, glorified motherhood (e.g., financial assistance, preferential custody, maternity leave), and distanced fathers from parental responsibilities toward children and sharing household chores with their wives. This strategic placement of gender at the center of Central Asia's social transformation further politicized gender roles and women's rights but did little to challenge male primacy associated with in-family and societal leadership. These changes in gender order facilitated an eventual transformation of Central Asia—achieved through juristic means, strategic political activism, violence, and public education—into five Soviet Socialist Republics. Each republic had its titular nation and native leadership and was directly controlled by the central Communist government in Moscow.

Changes in Central Asian gender order led to changes in gender structure by gradually limiting the criteria for differentiating between humans to only *two* genders based on sexual preference and physiological, reflecting biological, differences. The Soviet project of modernizing Central Asia also violently limited the power of religious leadership. Soviet secularism eliminated ontological differences as one of the most important criteria in the precolonial gender structure. In the late 1920s, the party's famous unveiling campaign, public education, and vocational training facilitated women's entrance into a public now expected to be secular. As a result of the Communist organizers' disdain toward bourgeois values, art, and lifestyle, religious sensibilities, and standards of local beauty, such pre-Soviet criteria for gender differentiation as beauty and artistic ability were discarded as well. Soviet state building also did not have space for the old bourgeois pastime activities. Same-sex practices were pathologized and criminalized, and Central Asian bachcha's events and practices were banned. Sensuality and beautiful manners, including emotion and tenderness, formerly desirable attributes of all genders, came to be indexed as feminine. Physiological, reflecting biological, differences and sexual preferences were left as the only criteria for gender differentiation in the Soviet state. Yet, even if the Soviet law banned same-sex practices de jure, a diversity of sexual relations existed de facto. Additionally, the Soviet reforms further racialized gender identities, whereby European or Slavic appearance and linguistic competence in Russian increased one's symbolic and economic capital and social status. These reforms also politicized women's rights as markers of national and societal development. An uneasy relationship between Soviet ideals and rhetoric and national traditions and characteristics, some of which were valorized (e.g., "Eastern women" who were domestic, hardworking, exotic, and modest) and others criticized (e.g., local Islamic practices), never challenged gendered and generational hierarchy, while adding education, class, and ethnicity as other categories of unequal social differentiation.

Russian and local Communist Party organizers' scorn toward Central Asian patriarchy should not be confused with liberal equality: women and men were supposed to be equal only in participating in wage labor and political activism, both necessary for the Soviet (socialist) sociopolitical and economic transformation. In daily life, gender discourses on "strong men" and "support-ive women" were still paramount. Meanwhile, the Soviet universal education and ideological and rhetorical emphasis on equality among men and women that could be achieved through their participation in wage labor and political activism has provided Central Asians with competing models of femininity and masculinity. Some Central Asian women eventually could occupy positions of power in their respective Soviet Socialist Republics, such as scientists, writers, performers, and administrators; some became Communist Party leaders on local levels. A housewife, career woman, mother hero, or a community leader exemplifies some of the acceptable and respected feminine gender models in Soviet Central Asia. And yet, even if/when women (could) have achieved their professional career plans, their families had always come first. As a result, in the early 1990s, at the time of the Soviet Union's disintegration, Central Asian societies' views of women's rights and social change were not inimical to male dominance and included the view of marriage as companionship; the acceptance of an individual right to refuse polygynous marriage and file for divorce (but only in extreme cases), since family values were still paramount; glorified motherhood and education; and a level of individual independence and equality, if it did not clash with social gendered hierarchy.

In contemporary Central Asia, as a continuing legacy of the Soviet Union, the existing gender order is nation-state-centered and reflects a di-chotomous gender structure. Motherhood is glorified and same-sex practices are still criminalized and medicalized in Uzbekistan and Turkmenistan (as of 2021). Biological reproduction remains (minimally) rewarded by the states in the form of "mother's capital" and paid leave for pregnant females from work for a period of gestation, delivery, and a postnatal childcare; the amount of money and paid time off varies from country to country. These strategies also ensure that child and family day-to-day care and child-rear-ing remain mainly mothers' responsibilities, while fathers' participation in parenthood is often reduced to economic provisioning and their role as disciplinarians. Therefore, while the current gender order is as dynamic as the previous ones, it continues to exhibit some continuities with them.

Seeing Gender Structure

The gender order in current Central Asian states is enmeshed with changing political regimes, precarious economies, and national struggles for cultural authenticity. The links among gender, religion, culture, individual emotions and feelings, and the human and nonhuman environment are complex. Each coun-try has its own case of retraditionalizing—of selective revival and preference for customs and understandings of gender roles that reinforce social institutions—a defining feature of local post-Soviet nationalisms. The Central Asian states and their respective governments' nationalist projects and political legitimacy are built heavily on religious ideologies and a selective use of pre-Soviet cul-tural heritage. In search for an authentic nationhood, each state appealed to religious discourses and national heroes, like Amir Timur in Uzbekistan or Manas in Kyrgyzstan, or to ancestral traditions. Hence, Islam became an important component of national identities and a source of competing discourses on gender and power. A growing importance of religious sensibilities, often explained as traditional, brought back a focus on ontological differences as one criterion of distinguishing gender among humans. Such differences between females and males came with related discourses on equally important but radically different for each gender duties and rights, mapping well on the existing gender models emphasizing females' supportive roles and males' inter-family and financial leadership. A focus on such differences rolled back some females' ability to pursue certain career aspirations, unless these fell within religiously sanctioned areas, such as religious education, childcare, elderly care, and health care. At the same time, financial needs fostered by the not-quite-capitalist but certainly not-just-Socialist economy required female wage labor and the changing family roles as acceptable and expected models of a family.

The existing gender structure in Central Asia bears vestiges from its historical predecessors in that it differentiates among humans on an ontological basis, just like a pre-Soviet gender structure did, and is based on their biological (expressed physiologically) characteristics, just like the Soviet one was. In both Soviet and contemporary Central Asian gender orders, the normative femininity centers on motherhood as the pinnacle of female humanhood. In the former order, motherhood was also a duty to the state, not only to the family. For example, Sophie Roche demonstrates how in the current gender order, motherhood is (also) simultaneously a Muslim woman's religious duty and her cultural responsibility to birth and raise a "healthy nation." By increasing a purchase of motherhood as the dominant model, the current gender order undermines previously established feminine gender models, such as women politicians, soldiers, workers, and sportswomen.

Both Soviet and contemporary Central Asian gender orders assume the normative masculinity to reflect a male's duty to provide for the family. In the former order, financial provisioning was a duty to the state as an example of active participation in social transformation through wage labor, whereas in the current one, it is also a duty of a proper Muslim male and a traditional responsibility toward one's family and the nation. In the contemporary gender order, normative masculinity, and not the state (as in the Soviet gender order), is tasked with physical and symbolic protection of the family. Further, since any gender order comes with dominant discourses on how to feel and be a gendered being and a system of morality, the appeal to religious sensibilities increased the importance of privacy, honor, shame, purity, chastity, and respectability; these potent cultural values infuse the models for normative femininity and masculinity. In turn, these morally charged dominant gender models erase gender variance, overshadow a diversity of existing femininities and masculinities, and obscure relations and hierarchies among them, complicated by one's ethnicity, class, access to education, mobility, religiosity, ability, migration, or geographic location.

After the Soviet Union's disintegration, Central Asian countries joined the global neoliberal market economy, and the gendered expectations outlined in the previous paragraphs became increasingly difficult to fulfill. The economic reforms left many local men jobless and necessitated and enabled women's participation in the formal and informal labor market, including employment in the service economy overseers. Local cultural expectations in relation to gender roles in a family combined masculinity, being a financial provider, and the main decision maker in and protector of the household. In the reality of a precarious economy, these expectations became a cultural paradox and made many male heads of local families feel like failures. Even though a male head of the family could find financially stable employment outside the country, he might have been unable to effectively lead the family's decision making or protect the family on a daily basis; he would have to delegate this duty to his extended family or to his wife. On the other hand, if he succeeded in enforcing his decisions on the members of his family but has failed to find meaningful employment within his country, he has failed in his main duty—to financially provide for the family. As a result, his authority, as a protective patriarch, would eventually deteriorate. Some Central Asian families continue to successfully resolve this paradox, but not others.

To negotiate dominant gender discourses and expectations and complex socioeconomic contexts, local people can employ a performative aspect of behavior, which allows Central Asians to potentially conceal their inability of living up to the gendered expectations and traits and behave *as if* succeeding and, as a result, reproduce the illusion of a dichotomous gender structure and stable gender order and the state. Colette Harris exemplifies how individuals' performance of the *as if* helps some Central Asian men remain dominant and powerful, while feeling like failures, and allows some local women to display important cultural values of submission and compliance, even if they de facto assume the role of the decision maker, provider, and protector of the family. Yet, such performative strategies also demonstrate ideological and existential dissonance in the existing gender order. What worked in the pre-Soviet socioeconomic context, including an emphasis on ontological differences between males and females and their concomitant different(ial) duties and rights, did not work as well in the post-Soviet context, which combined a rapidly growing consumerism, economic competition and precarity, increased individual mobility, access to digital information and/or heavy-handed techniques of social control by the state (e.g., Turkmenistan and Uzbekistan).

Discussion of the current gender order will be incomplete without including local sexual diversity. In the region, sexuality is a sensitive and highly politicized subject, particularly after the introduction of local anti-LGBTQ bills that built on Russia's so-called Gay Propaganda Law of 2013 (the Russian Federal Law for the Purpose of Protecting Children from Information Advocating for a Denial of Traditional Family Values). There is also a lack of sex education, which was, in the early Soviet period, outsourced to the state and hence, mainly, nonexistent. Research on partners' sexuality and sexual satisfaction continues to be rare. This lack of information and education can lead to a lack of sexual satisfaction. For example, Harris shows high levels of sexual dissatisfaction among some local people in post-Soviet Tajikistan.

The current gender order, reflecting a dichotomous gender structure differentiating among humans based on sexual preference and physiological and ontological differences, has no provisional space for those whose bodies, desires, and sexual practices do not fit in or differ in some way from what the majority of Central Asians consider to be a male or female body standard and appropriate (read here as heterosexual) desires. Since the current gender order in the region is nation-state-centered, each state, just like the Soviet Union, provides legislative support of heterosexual unions only; nonheterosexual desires and practices are imagined to threaten this order, the institution of family, and individual honor. Strategic performance, again, becomes a coping mechanism for those individuals who do not fit in the existing dichotomous gender structure. Some choose to perform *as if* they are heterosexual through concealment, or by trying to "pass as" heterosexual, by avoiding those practices that can be read as homosexual. Such performance allows one to avoid or prevent stigmatization, shaming by the family, and physical violence by others or by law enforcement agents. One outcome of such performances, however, also reinforces the existing dichotomous gender order. First, performing *as if* ensures an ongoing reproduction of dominant femininity as limited to motherhood paired with guardianship of faith, tradition, minors, and of home while muting other models of femininity and leading to a shrinking space for women's political participation. The second outcome is a rapidly increasing criminalization of and violence against "nontraditional" sexual partnerships and individuals claiming different from normative (heterosexual) gender identities. The third outcome of such performances is a valorization and reproduction of dominant masculinity of a "strong-man," a protector of women, family, and national values. This performative reification of the dichotomous gender structure informs a growing violence against those individuals whose gender identity or behaviors are thought to jeopardize national values. At the same time, a lack of such performances can lead to interpersonal violence and potentially a loss of an individual's life in the context where dichotomous gender structures prevail.

In contemporary Central Asia, the gender order is contested. Personal views and attitudes toward existing gender roles are informed by class, religion, age, location, education, ability, and access to digital information and other similar resources. Growing transnational interconnectivity through various digital technologies, travel, and migration in/outside the region offers a variety of opportunities for interacting with, learning from, and sharing information with other transnational actors and creating goods and images allow young people everywhere to use *glocal*—global and local as mutually informative dynamics—identity discourses to forge their own views on, and sometimes criticism of, the existing social order, including gender relations. From Bollywood films to Eminem, from Islamic preaching to Hollywood, from martial arts to Russian youth culture, the flows of information, especially about gender relations, are not adopted wholesale but negotiated considering familial pressures and obligations, values of moral behavior, specific geographic and historical contexts, and individual and familial pragmatic considerations. The transformations of gender structure that result from such exchanges are not unidirectional. For example, in the late 1980s and early 1990s, in Kazakhstan, a public space for nonheterosexual gender identities did not exist, while in the late 1990s, Almaty, the country's largest city, had a couple of clubs attended by mainly gay men and some local lesbians—by those who were and are in *tema* ("*v teme*" in Russian, meaning "theme" and "in the theme"). Tema has many derivatives that are used as a code word referring to the people who are "in the know"—to those with an insider's knowledge about LGBTQ people's daily lives and practices. Yet, by the second decade of the twenty-first century, there was not a single club left, signaling a growing conservatism of the Kazakh's society.

●

It is important to highlight the most salient feature of the existing gender structure in the region, which is the diversity of individual strategies of challenging the existing gender order. Everyone's unique existential context, current political regimes, and economic structures define the constraints within which local people find potentialities to have meaningful and livable lives. As a result, some local activists produce alternative discourses of empathy and support to those who transgress prevailing models for gendered behavior. Some local artists aim to challenge existing nationalist ideologies by exposing gender struggles that are indigenous and relevant to the Central Asian context of the twenty-first century. Remaining in the region, local LGBTQ activists (some have immigrated) continue to politically organize the struggle for becoming full-sexed citizens who confront, sometimes directly but more often indirectly, the status quo of their contemporary gender order. Some local women continue to seek employment inside and outside their country of origin, while others desire to be free from wage labor. And while some local men prefer (and can afford) to spend the majority of their free time socializing with their male friends, others dedicate themselves to childcare and house chores and coed political and social activism. There is no perfect analytical template that fits all when it comes to gender structure in Central Asia, just like no single template can capture political and economic developments in the respective countries. Still, I propose that we consider thinking with gender not as a requirement but as an option. Such an approach can offer thicker descriptions and analyses of local complex and complicated lives by shedding light on many blind spots screened out by a lack of such focus.

SVETLANA PESHKOVA

On Mothers- and Daughters-in-law

Julie McBrien

The daughter-in-law (*kelin*) is a pitied figure in Kyrgyzstan. She bears the burden not only of her affinal household's labor but also the brunt of her mother-in-law's correction, criticism, anger, and sometimes abuse. This position garners her the sympathy of many in and outside of Kyrgyzstan. Mothers-in-law (*kaiene*), though respected, are also frequently depicted as domineering, heavy-handed, unreasonable, and sometimes outright cruel. There are many stories to bolster these claims and certainly kelins are structurally on the weaker side of an important kinship and labor relationship with their mothers-in-law. Yet the day-to-day relationship is much more complicated, and mothers-in-laws are also constrained by the moral evaluations, affective relationships, and material conditions the relationship entails.

In this case study, I present the story of one mother-in-law/daughter-in-law relationship to look at, in part, the things that drive a mother-in-law's relationship to the new young woman in her home. Though usually reduced to figures of dominance, mothers-in-law also face pressure to conform and are often constrained by expectation and need. I also discuss the story to complicate the typical picture of the passive kelin. Though certainly in a position of weakness, there are ways a kelin, under the right conditions, can maneuver and make space for herself. Finally, I describe this story to illustrate how structures of gender, age, and kinship are experienced, where they, in part, get their force, and how they are sometimes contested.

Aigul, twenty-five, was at her mother's home with her baby when I spoke to her in 2009. She was living there, or *temporarily* living there, depending on who was telling the story. The problem was that by most standards Aigul should have already returned home, to her mother-in-law's house. It is common for a young woman in Kyrgyzstan to stay with her natal family after the birth of a child. Eventually, however, usually after forty days, she returns home, which is often at her parents-in-law's. But Aigul had not followed the pattern; she was still with her own mother. And so the first time I met Aigul and her baby, it was there. Aigul was delighted to receive me and proudly presented her child. At that point, we had known each other for eleven years, and she was excited to share this new part of her life.

Aigul was the wife of Kadyr, Jamila's eldest son; their daughter was Jamila's first grandchild. Jamila was an old friend of mine. She was unhappy and somewhat ashamed that I had not met her grandchild, her *first* grandchild, in her home. Her husband, Temir, had taken me to see Aigul and the baby; Jamila had not joined us. She refused to visit her kelin there. I had known Jamila as long as I had known Aigul, and Jamila, too, could not wait for me to meet the child. But, according to her, this should have happened in her own home. She should have been there, carrying the child over in her cradle (*beshik*), coddling and cooing over her as she presented the little one to me. That this did not happen was a source of pain and discomfort for Jamila. She was angry with Aigul and confused as to why she was staying away. What was wrong with her kelin? What was wrong with her? She often asked herself.

There are some words in Kyrgyz that are impossible to translate, and that most foreigners, whether they know the language or not, seem to learn. One of those is kelin. Kelin has a customary translation. Most people render it as "daughter-in-law," and that usually gives enough of a sense about kelins for communication in English. But much of what the Kyrgyz word *kelin* covers escapes what *daughter-in-law* refers to in English. Kelin is derived from the verb "keloo," meaning "to enter, come, or arrive." A kelin is one who enters or comes into a family. When a young woman marries and "comes into" the family, she and her husband often reside with her in-laws. They may be given one or more rooms in the home and in some cases may have their own house on the family's land. A kelin physically enters the family through co-residence with her in-laws.

The term kelin also denotes a relationship not only between a bride and her husband's parents but also between the bride and the kin of the family into which she has married. A kelin is not merely daughter-in-law to her parents-in-law; she is called "kelin" by everyone older than her in husband's family. She is the family's kelin. An older sister-in-law might speak of "our kelin" and a neighbor might ask about the kelin of the neighbor's family. The young woman has "come into" the family. This is one of the ways that kelin differs from the English "daughter-in-law." The term covers a wider relationship.

A kelin enters a family in a specific role, one of relative weakness, what many would describe as powerlessness. She is young, she is a woman, and she is an outsider. Along three different axes of power—age, gender, and kin—she occupies the disadvantaged position. There are also numerous expectations of household work placed on her, both in the home of her in-laws and also the homes of their wider kin. So when one hears the word kelin in Kyrgyz, one also thinks of more than just an affinal relationship. What most often comes to mind is a labor relationship. How that relation is evaluated, however, often depends on one's position.

Jamila and Aigul first became interlocutors in my research in 2009, though I had known both of them since 1998. They lived in a small town in southern Kyrgyzstan. Both had postsecondary degrees, and both (had) worked outside of the home. Jamila was keenly aware of the burdens of a kelin and the stereotypes surrounding mothers-in-law. She saw herself as socially progressive and portrayed herself as having given her daughter-in-law freedom to pursue her own interests. Jamila had a busy career and was happy for her daughter-in-law to have the same. She did not demand much around the house, and she and her husband had worked hard to build a new two-story house on their property where Aigul and Kadyr could live, at least until there were financial means for them to move out on their own completely. Aigul and Kadyr had their own space and freedom, Jamila would point out to me. Most kelins wanted this but often did not receive it. Most kelins were swimming in work. They did the laundry, washed the dishes, cooked the meals, and several times a day they laid out and rearranged the *tushooks* (large mats of fabric or wool) for sitting and sleeping. They watched children, changed cloth diapers, swept the house and the front courtyard, and attended to guests who might arrive. They tended to small household livestock, milked cows, and watered household garden plots.

Jamila expected very little of this from Aigul, yet in return she felt she got nothing. Worse than this, she was being deprived of her first grandchild. This made the situation with Aigul more confounding for Jamila. She had given Aigul all she could and yet Aigul was disrespectful, not fulfilling the most basic relational duties. And there had been problems before this, she said. Aigul did not help out much around the house. Jamila wondered if Aigul's absence was the first step toward a separation between her son and daughter-in-law. Jamila worried that Aigul would never return. She worried that Aigul and Kadyr would divorce.

Jamila's husband shared many of Aigul's views and worries, but he did wonder if Jamila was perhaps too soft, too permissive with Aigul. Had she been tougher from the beginning, would Aigul have behaved differently? he wondered. Jamila berated herself a bit, especially when her husband seemed to locate some of the responsibility for Aigul's shortcomings on her. It had brought about shame, she said. Jamila was also hurt. Why had her kindness,

openness, and, from her perspective, lenient and open-minded treatment not resulted in a mutual relationship of care and respect? Why was Aigul not doing the very few things Jamila asked of her? Given so much freedom, why did Aigul fail to perform the most basic duties of kelin? Jamila worried about the neighbors, especially the women her age. What must they think? she would say to me. They would gossip about her kelin, how disrespectful she was, how insolent. They would wonder what was wrong with Aigul and, ultimately, what was wrong with Jamila.

Aigul, too, was unhappy. The match with Kadyr had not been her first choice, but her family and his supported it. Though she and Kadyr had been married a few years, she missed her mother and sisters. She saw them regularly but preferred to live with them. She found it difficult to adapt her ways to those of Jamila's. She realized that everyone—her friends, women in her family's social and kin circles, even me—thought that Jamila must be a wonderful mother-in-law. But she said it just was not so. "She still tells me what to do," she said.

As an outsider to the family, the kelins are also expected to need instruction about how to do all of these tasks *properly* (i.e., according to the desires and expectations of the mother-in-law). If, by chance, a kelin has married the youngest son, she will likely be in the role of kelin until her mother-in-law passes away, at which time her husband will inherit the house and she the role of female head of household/housekeeper. This was not Aigul's position. She had married the oldest son. And though Jamila had freed Aigul from a large portion of the expected duties of a daughter-in-law, this was not enough for Aigul. She wanted out of them all.

By 2015, when I returned to conduct research on marriage, Aigul and Kadyr had moved to Osh. Kadyr had found stable work there, and Jamila and her husband were building them a large house in a nearby suburb. Kadyr and Temir had finished the basement first, and the family had moved in with their two daughters. Work on the ground and first floor would take some time, but it was shaping up to be a beautiful home. But Aigul was rarely in Osh. She and her children were to be found most often at her mother's home, in the same town as her parents-in-law. Aigul had never returned to work at the hospital but found herself involved in her mother and sisters' lucrative clothes manufacturing business. She had gotten her driver's license and a car.

Jamila had given up hope that Aigul would ever be the daughter-in-law for which she had hoped. When I inquired after Aigul, Kadyr, and their kids, Jamila would share the latest details of her grandchildren's growth and development and readily filled me in about Kadyr's budding career. About Aigul, however, she would often say "I do not know." "I do not know where she is right now." "I do not know why she does not tell me when she is in town." "I do not know why she does not come to stay or visit more often when she is here." When Aigul came up in conversation, Jamila's reaction was more often marked by irritation than its former sadness. There was also an air of resignation and defeat. Jamila was still wondering what she had done wrong. Although she did not speak much of what the neighbors might say, Jamila told me to be careful not to mention to our common acquaintances that Aigul largely lived at home with her mother. Jamila hinted that if asked, I should say Aigul was in Osh.

Aigul, for her part, said she had accepted her life in the intervening six years. She no longer thought of leaving her husband. She defended her frequent, extended visits to her mother's home with reference to her mother's rapidly declining health, her skills as a former nurse, and the need to care for her mother. Her sisters were off running the business, her father had passed away long ago, and there was no son and therefore no kelin to care for her mother or the household. It fell to her. Plus, she said she wanted to cherish the little time she had left with her mother. She was mostly happy, she said. Aigul did complain, however, that everything in the new home in Osh had been decided on without her, that her mother-in-law had had all the say. Despite this, she had found a degree of happiness with Kadyr and their children, when they were left alone, that is. She said she had stopped caring what Jamila thought of her.

For Jamila, on the other hand, the relationship remained painful and frustrating. Jamila wished she could see her grandchildren more often. By then her daughter had had two children as well, and they often came to stay with Jamila for weeks at a time. She wanted the same with Kadyr and Aigul's children. As she aged and her health worsened, she began to especially miss the help she should have received from Aigul. But she had stopped trying to get it, though she had not stopped complaining about it to those closest to her. She hoped only that no one would find out; that would be shameful, she said. Comments had been made. When she threw a party or when guests came to visit, they would ask Jamila where her kelin was and why she was not receiving the help she should. Jamila usually remained silent.

Household labor and its proper execution are the responsibility of the daughter-in-law. But, the propriety and performance of the daughter-in-law,

JULIE MCBRIEN

including how she executes household tasks, is the mother-in-law's; her kin, friends, colleagues, and neighbors evaluate the mother-in-law based on it. Mothers-in-law are in a position of power over their daughters-in-law; they have the authority to control much of the younger woman's life. Yet this is not authority disconnected from responsibility, affect, and necessity. Mothers-in-law often need the young women's assistance, especially as they age, to keep up a household not only for those residing in it but for the guests who frequently come calling. They are connected to their daughters-in-law in an affective relationship, established in part through the birth of grandchildren but also through the dutiful performance of expected household labor. Mothers-in-law are socially responsible for, and often evaluated on the basis of, the behavior of their daughters-in-law. It is through these complex affective and material relations, and the moral evaluation of them, that the mother-in-law/daughter-in-law relationship is established—and sometimes, broken.

CASE IV-B

Mahalla as State and Community

Johan Rasanayagam

This case study is an account of the leader of a mahalla in the city of Samarkand (Samarqand), Uzbekistan, who I met during field research in 2003 and 2004. The mahalla is a neighborhood institution that has roots in forms of social organization that predate the Soviet era, that the postindependence government formalized as an organ of local self-government, instituted in all residential areas of the country. Within its discursive production of an ideology of national independence, the regime of former president Islam Karimov presented the mahalla as a repository of Uzbek spiritual values and as an authentic local model for governance. An idealized ethos of the mahalla, of mutual cooperation and respect under the leadership of elders known as *oqsoqols*, has been used to legitimate authoritarian rule. While formally independent with a locally elected leadership, the mahalla is routinely coopted by national and local government organs as an extension of their surveillance and control of the population, and as a tool for exercising their own executive authority. Here, I explore the different qualities of community and state structure, the intersection of these in the work of this mahalla committee chairman, and the flexibility and contingency of the notion of structure itself.

Abdulmajid-aka, a lecturer in mathematics at the University of Samarkand and the director of a secondary school, was in his fifties when I met him. A few months before we first met, he had been elected as chairman of his mahalla committee. He told me that his mahalla had been founded around the 1930s. It was located a little outside the historic center of Samarkand, but it was not one of the more "modern" districts made up of Soviet-built apartment blocks. On a chilly February day, I attended a commemoration taking place on the fortieth day after the death of one of his mahalla residents. Men from the mahalla and male relatives and friends of the deceased sat at long tables in Abdulmajid-aka's courtyard and were given a meal while one of the mahalla residents recited Qur'anic verses. The women gathered separately in a neighboring house, where hired mourners cried and wailed for the deceased and the guests had a meal seated indoors, again accompanied by Qur'an recitation.

Abdulmajid-aka recounted how he had organized this event and the funeral itself. When this resident died, Abdulmajid-aka's assistant on the mahalla committee came to inform him at the university where he was working. They had to move quickly to organize the burial before sunset that day so as not to leave the body in the house until the following day. They were conscious of the need to avoid the obligation on the family, if this happened, to slaughter a sheep and invite guests to a meal, as the deceased would be considered a "guest" remaining in the house until buried. In the material difficulties in which many people find themselves, that would be an unwelcome and unexpected expense. He immediately dropped everything at the university and returned to the mahalla. He and his assistant went to the mosque to summon the gravedigger and found the specialist who washes the body. In Samarkand, Abdulmajid-aka said, this task is performed by a distinct lineage group, although in other parts of Uzbekistan relatives might do it. The *paikal*, the person who informs mahalla residents of communal events, went door to door to inform people of the funeral, and Abdulmajid-aka arranged for the imam of the local mosque to read the funeral prayers at the gravesite. He also decided how much the family would pay the imam and handled the payment himself, as well as payment to the mullahs who are present to recite the Qur'an during the three days following the death, when men come to pay their respects (women organize their own participation themselves). Abdulmajid-aka said that he decides this amount depending on the wealth of the household and also the status of the reciter, where, for example, the head imam for Samarkand city, who is based at the mosque located nearest to this mahalla, would be given more than the regular reciter in the mahalla, who is proficient but who has no formal Islamic education or official religious position. Abdulmajid-aka also advised the family on what sort of food to serve on this fortieth day commemoration, advising them to keep to a modest offering. In doing so, he referred to a presidential decree that called for limited expenditure on life

cycle rituals like weddings and funerals, and also to a government-produced guide for mahalla committees that gives guidance on the conduct of such events. His aim was to avoid the family incurring an excessive financial burden while at the same time doing things properly. Mahalla committees often have a Festival (*to'i*) Commission that coordinates major events of households to avoid conflicts.

Abdulmajid-aka's involvement in this funeral is illustrative of how the mahalla might be thought of in terms of "social structure." In the village in the Fergana Valley near the city of Andijan, where I also conducted research, social relations were to an even greater extent manifested through the mahalla. The mahalla oqsoqol would normally advise households on how to conduct collective events like wedding or circumcision feasts, advising on how many guests to invite and how much food to prepare. Commonly owned equipment for this, like large cooking cauldrons, crockery, and tables, were kept in the mahalla mosque, and the mahalla cook is employed for these occasions. Other collective events or enterprises were also conducted on the basis of the mahalla, such as a *mavlud*, a ritual to commemorate the Prophet Muhammad's life, that women in the mahalla I resided in attended and took turns hosting. But the mahalla does not always act as a social institution in this way. In another mahalla in Samarkand, where I lived for a few months, the mahalla committee was much less involved in the social life of its residents, relevant mainly for obtaining certain official documents. In a district of apartment blocks in Andijan, where I also lived, most people were not even aware there was a mahalla committee. A journalist whose family resided in the mahalla neighboring Abdulmajid-aka's was ambivalent about the institution. He felt that the government used the mahalla

IV-B-1   A mahalla in early spring in the Ferghana Valley portion of Uzbekistan, 2001. Photograph by David W. Montgomery.

to monitor and police residents. When he himself got married, he organized the celebrations himself outside the mahalla and without its involvement, but he also had a separate event in his parents' household with the involvement of the mahalla leadership in order to maintain good relations with his neighbors. So while the actuality of the mahalla varied from place to place, the ideal of the mahalla was one that resonated generally and was drawn upon in state discourse.

Abdulmajid-aka was a particularly active mahalla committee chairman in seeking inventive solutions for the material difficulties of his residents. During the period of my research, the city government issued executive instructions to mahalla committee chairmen to fulfil a number of their targets, such as collecting scrap metal or unpaid payments for exemption from full military service. These are extrajudicial directives, as mahallas are not formally included in the structures of local government in a way that puts them directly under the executive authority of city government officials to this extent. One of these directives was for each mahalla committee to appoint a person to collect unpaid electricity and

gas utility bills, with each mahalla being given target amounts of money to be paid into the official banks. This operated alongside a scheme initiated by city government to pay this person a small salary for this work.

Prior to the directive, Abdulmajid-aka had attempted to revive on a local scale a national initiative introduced four years previously that had enabled mahalla committees to keep 10 percent of the unpaid bills they collected from their residents if they managed to collect 100 percent of the money owed. Six percent of this sum had to be used to help poorer households pay their bills, and 4 percent would be controlled by the mahalla committee itself. However, this scheme had fallen by the wayside as mahalla committees failed to reach their targets and the money failed to be returned to them from the utilities companies. When he was elected as chairman, Abdulmajid-aka approached the state electricity company, offering to collect the unpaid bills if they would enter into a similar arrangement with his mahalla, but was not able to convince them to do this.

When the new scheme was initiated by the city government, Abdulmajid-aka made a deal with the local branch of the post office. His residents needed an incentive to pay the bills, so he guaranteed that all the money from the unpaid bills would be paid into this particular post office branch, so long as 80 percent of this money was used to pay the unpaid pensions of his own residents. Although people were due their pensions, the banks did not have the money to pay them. As Abdulmajid-aka explained his scheme, the post office would benefit by being able to fulfill its own state plans and his residents would be able to pay the utilities bills. The scheme worked for two months, but when the city government failed to pay the salary for the mahalla-appointed collector, Abdulmajid-aka stopped his work and the system collapsed. A representative of the city gas company then visited Abdulmajid-aka and told him that each mahalla had to collect 200,000 sum (about US$130 at the time). Abdulmajid-aka felt that if the collector's salary was not paid, then he could not force his residents to pay either. He acknowledged that it was his duty to aid the local government, so he advised his residents to pay but he could not force them. Abdulmajid-aka said that residents told him they could pay when they got their own salaries or pensions.

In a final effort, Abdulmajid-aka directly approached the heads of the local electricity, gas, and water companies, asking them each to pay one-third of the unpaid salary themselves. The electricity chief agreed to pay himself, and accompanied the collector on his rounds, collecting the money from households. Unfortunately for the residents, this money did not go to the post office, so their pensions were not paid. But at least, Abdulmajid-aka said, the collector got his salary for that month. When the electricity chief later attempted to collect the money directly without the mahalla

collector, residents refused to pay. He complained to Abdulmajid-aka, saying that residents told him that the mahalla chairman had instructed them to pay only the mahalla-appointed collector. Abdulmajid-aka wrote out a document for the electricity company representative saying that residents were allowed to pay the company directly. If he did not do this, Abdulmajid-aka said, they would accuse him of being a revolutionary.

What conclusions or insights can we draw from this account about how to think about the "state" or "community" in terms of structure? One might be that the boundary between "state" and "civil society" or "community" is not as clear as we may think. Abdulmajid-aka's mahalla and the mahallas in the village near Andijan might be viewed as nonstate social institutions that manifest, in differing ways, community norms and practices of sociality, obligation, and reciprocity. At the same time, the national government has attempted to coopt the ideal of the mahalla to legitimate authoritarian, top-down rule, and has transformed the mahalla into an officially and legally constituted body. Moreover, both national and local government attempt to extend the reach of the state by coopting the social relations of the mahalla to further their own projects in ways that bring into question the existence of clear boundaries or coherent structures. Abdulmajid-aka and other mahalla committee chairmen have to negotiate this complicated, often dangerous, and blurred boundary. Their own position as community leader is founded on relations of mutual support and reciprocity within the mahalla, but the demands put on them by state authorities might bring them into conflict with these. Abdulmajid-aka is conscious of his duty to the nation and cooperates with state authorities, but he also seeks the best interests and welfare of his mahalla residents.

CASE IV-C

Aitys, Ancestors, and the "Little Sister"

Eva-Marie Dubuisson

Epic narrative, improvisation, humorous wordplay: from Eastern Turkey to Western China and Mongolia, and all across Eurasia, many different cultures take great pride in their poetic heritage. Oral traditions are passed down from one generation to the next through word, song, and apprenticeship, and survive for centuries across various nomadic or semisettled communities. These poems carry the stories and lessons of generations past and reflect a shared ancestry. Oral traditions are *alive* in the sense that they move and grow, as well as acquire relevance in new contexts and times. One example among Kazakhs is the tradition of aitys, where two poets meet in a verbal duel to talk about social and political events, as well as history and culture, but also to joke with their audiences, and even make fun of each other! If a poet's words are rich and clever, and he or she is beloved by their audience, that poet will "win" the duel. Aitys is a form of entertainment that takes place anywhere from village gatherings to national performance halls. In this case study, I analyze one aitys performed in Kazakhstan's largest city, before a live audience of hundreds (and also televised), where the stately poet Dauletkerei Kæpoly met a new younger poet, the feisty Sara Toqtamysova.

There are several metaphoric and performative frames commonly evoked by aitys poets, all of which will fall into place within the first few turns of song. In the example I present here, kinship and ancestry are reframed in dialogue as a central theme and as a framing device of the aitys: poets speak from within that frame to each other and to their audience, in order to respond to and help resolve modern-day dilemmas. The first to sing in this performance was Dauletkerei, who opens in this way:

Бабамыз батыр туған асыл қандай
Айтыспен тон шымылдық ашылғандай
Ақындарың ақ жарма өлең айтып
Æулие бабасына бас ұрғандай.
Сара қыз мен кеп тұрмын қапталдаса
Абыройын өлеңнің асырғандай
Қарындасы кеп қалса қапталыма
Кезім жоқ құтыңызды қашырандай
Ағайын, көресіндер екпінімді
Ертістей ернеуімнен тасыңандай
Тобыңызға деп қалдым тæубе деумен
Жолымызға ақ жусан шашылғандай
Жүіткіп өте шығайық енді Сара
Қоландар бір біріне қасынғандай.

Our grandfather was born a warrior—
what a heritage!
It is as if with aitys a curtain has opened,
poets sing pure songs that are difficult and
    true,
as though they bow their heads to a Holy
    ancestor.
Sara girl I've come to stand side by side
    with you—

in this way the song's prestige has been
  boosted.
If my little sister came to stay close (to my
  side)
I have no chance to escape from your
  richness.
Clansmen, you will see my fervor!
Like the river Irtysh, from my banks [I am]
  overflowing,
I came to your group and wish [you]
  blessings,
as though white artemisia had fallen across
  our path.
So let us race away then Sara,
like wild deer play with one other.

In order to perform effectively
together, poets must understand what
relationships and contexts are offered by
their opponents, in order to answer each
other and collude toward a complete
and culturally comprehensible frame of
interaction. In his opening lines here,
Dauletkerei offers several frames that
Sara should recognize and ideally accept
when it comes her turn to answer. For
example, he posits a fictive kinship relationship by using the terms "little sister"
(karandas), addressed to Sara, and "older brother" (agha), addressed to her and
to all his figurative kin in some imagined audience both past and present
(agha can mean older brother, cousin,
or uncle, depending on the context, and
is used frequently as a respectful term
of address among nonintimates as well).
This older brother has come to "stand
beside" his sister, meaning to protect
her, and together they elevate aitys, the
(humorous and playful) poetry sung in
honor of their whole Kazakh "family."

In addition to praising his own
energy and fervor, Dauletkerei invokes
an ancestral frame in two ways: first,
in his recognition of "our" grandfather.
Famous cultural figures are typically
considered a shared or generalized
Kazakh ancestor; thus, the term "our"
here invokes "us," Dauletkerei and Sara,
as well as "us," everyone hearing this

performance. In other words, not only is
Dauletkerei suggesting a shared ancestry between himself and his opponent
but also between the two of them and
all their audience members—those in
the theater for the live performance,
or those watching a televised version.
In aitys the frame of performance is
an inclusive and telescopic one, where
performers and audiences are ideally
recognizing and creating a cultural ideal
and a shared truth or worldview together. In this form of verbal performativity,
certain words or phrases not only reference a person or group but also function
to put into place contexts or "possible
worlds" of interaction. In a few turns
of song, Dauletkerei is able to suggest
shared contexts of family and social or
genealogical relatedness.

Dauletkerei also metaphorically
refers to the practice of singing aitys
poetry itself as a bowing at an ancestor's
burial site, which is considered holy; in
this way, he invokes the Inner Asian
spiritual traditions of ancestor reverence
and associated visitations to shrines and
other sacred sites. The image of shrines
and prayer may evoke the sacred geography of the steppe for audiences, as well
as the histories of those who have passed
over that land before. Both poets are
from the north—Dauletkerei's relatives
live in Nur-Sultan, the capital city of
Kazakhstan, and Sara is from Semei, a
place with its own famous lineage of poets such as Abai Qunanbayev—and the
invocation of the river Irtysh is a way of
locating them in a "Kazakh" geography.
Beyond being a metaphor for bounding
water and his own exuberance, the river Irtysh runs south across Kazakhstan
from Altai, sometimes seen as a spiritual
homeland in different versions of mythic
and national history, and invokes the
"wild nature" of the steppe, highly romanticized in such imaginaries.

Thus, Dauletkerei offers frames of family, ancestry, spirituality, steppe, and an inclusive "we" for his opponent and audience, and now Sara should pick up on these cues to respond and to establish or fix these frames in her first turn of song. The poets' personalities become important in these negotiations: in this case, both are established and well-known public performers, and they also know each other personally. However, their pairing on stage is a bit unpredictable. While Dauletkerei was nearly thirty and might have been described as more of a classical or traditional poet with a proud and formal style, at the time of this performance Sara was just eighteen years old, a relative newcomer to national performances, and she capitalized on the strength of her position as a brave and beautiful young girl before supportive audiences in her costume, stage presence, and song. While Dauletkerei was more serious, Sara was also very funny; humorous turns of phrase (often delivered with a knowing smile) were her trademark—received well by a wide range of audience members, who very much value wordplay and innuendo in Kazakh oral culture. In this case, she answered:

Ғауһар көз жырдан моншақ тағынайын
Аузыма дуа дарыт, ай Құдайым
Алғаусыз ақ ниеті біздің елде
Жақсының ары, жаманның жаны уайым
Даулеткерей ағаммен тускендіктен
Тобында тарланбоздай танылайын
Ел жұртты жерұйыққа жетелеген
Айналдым æруағынан Абылайын.
Қабаньай, Бөгенбай, мен Наурызбайлар
Райымбек, Қарасай мен Ағыбайым
Тындаудан халқым менің шаршамасын
Жырлаудан мен қалайша жалығайын
Сæт сағатта сіздермен сұхбаттасып
Алдында ағымнан бір жарылайын
Осы айтыста [inaud.] бойдан
Æз халқым, қуат алсын æн арайдан.

From brilliant songs, let me wear beads,
Let charm come to my mouth, O my God.
Our people have clean-hearted intentions,

we are concerned with a good person's
     honor, a bad person's soul.
With my older brother Dauletkerei we've
     been drawn together,
let me become known as a fast horse in
     your group.
The people have been led to heaven.
I esteem my ancestors Ablai [Khan],
Kabanbai, Bogenbai, and the ones like
     Nauruzbai,
Raiymbek, Karasai, and Aghybai [Batyrs].
Let my people not tire of listening,
how could I get bored singing songs?
It is fortune to have this conversation at the
     right time with [all of] you,
From [the side of] my older brother, let me
     burst forth.
At this aitys from the height of [inaud.],
my wise people, may you take strength
     from the song's dawn.

In her response, Sara accomplishes many things; perhaps most importantly, she repeats and thus accepts the parameters of kinship suggested by her opponent, and calls him older brother. She names and praises her ancestors—khans and warriors (Kaz: *batyr*) of the past—placing her song in a mythic frame, and she affirms the poets' relationship to the audience(s), extending her frames of reference. However, she also distinguishes herself, hoping that in her performance she will be able to "burst forth" from the safe place beside her brother, to be recognized in her own right, with his support. She vows to sing something meaningful for her people.

Sara actually introduces *herself* as a topic of conversation in her very first lines, asking that she wear the beads of "brilliant songs" like jewelry, and in asking for "charm" in her words, she prepares the audience for such a tone. While this phrase is likely part of a planned opening, it also functions as a response to Dauletkerei's flattery: "I have no chance to escape from your richness" (above). Sara also adds one important element to the topics and possible interlocutors in this poetic conversation: her God, whom she addresses directly and asks for intercession and help. In doing so, she is identifying before her audience as a Kazakh Muslim. Like most poets, Sara identifies both personally and professionally as a believer, and thus the spiritual realm of this aitys is extended to the diverse cultural Islam of the country and region. It is also linked to the importance of an ancestral worldview, which is quite common in Kazakhstan's cultural and newly national contexts. These opening frames of talk establish the position and collaboration of poets not only to each other but also within an expanding series of many social relationships—they speak not only for themselves but for others living within similar circumstances. This proves to be critical for Sara, who now has the support of her "older brother" and seeks his advice, as she sings about the experience of what it means to be a young woman.

In the aitys from which these openings are excerpted, the pair of poets talks about the idea that young Sara will be married one day, and what role her "older brother" Dauletkerei will play at the wedding. While their song is mostly lighthearted, Sara also brings up her own worries regarding future marriage, and she does so in an interesting way relevant to a more broadly known cultural lore: by telling the story of another famous poet named Sara in Kazakh history. Sara Tastanbek was a young *aqyn* (poet) most well known for an infamous performance with the older bard Birjan. The performance was supposed to have taken place in the late nineteenth century, and was first published in print in 1898. It was popularized both during and after the Soviet period, and is known generally as "the Aitys of Birjan sal (bard) and Sara qyz (girl)." At that time, the competition between a young

woman and an established, venerated poet like Birjan was of great interest. In that aitys, Sara bemoaned her fate, an arranged and unwanted marriage to an unattractive partner (the original version does not name his flaws specifically, which may be of his physical person or of his character). That performance has come to stand in cultural and popular memory as a key moment where the status and concerns of women were explicitly discussed in a public forum, and where Birjan supported Sara in also singing about these topics and agreeing with her perspective. Sara successfully rose to the challenge of competing with an established poet and has been subsequently considered a brave female Kazakh heroine; she is now firmly rooted in the historical tradition of aitys itself.

In the contemporary aitys, modern Sara described for her own audience the life, times, and bad marriage arrangement of the historical Sara, who she refers to as "our mother" (*bizdiñ anemiz*), encouraging her audience to think of this heroine as their own maternal kin. Modern Sara vows that she herself will not befall such a fate, and in so doing metaphorically allows her audiences to imagine the possible dangers and contradictions of marriage today. Sara describes herself and her own wishes and desires, given the leverage of her poetic ancestor with the same name. But of course Sara is also ostensibly describing the worries and experiences of many young Kazakh women who have reached the age of possible marriage. As a "little sister," she is asking for the sympathy and advice of her "older brother" Dauletkerei. She does so in front of God and the ancestors, as well as in front of the audience whom she has identified and praised as "wise" (above). She is asking her listeners to care about her feelings as a young woman, and to see things from her point of view. For young women, marriage means contemplating leaving their natal family—parents, siblings, and other relatives with whom they are generally most close—and moving ritually toward their husband's family as a daughter-in-law (kelin), a subordinate status that traditionally confers a great deal of responsibility and humility.

Marriages in Kazakhstan take many forms, and traditional arrangements do not always apply in a variety of urban or transnational contexts. However, the "duty" of women in marriage, and the desire to enter willingly into such an arrangement, remains a cultural metaphor with which many people could identify, or have actually lived through themselves in some aspect. Sara accomplishes her goal to sing something meaningful, as her opening frame was accepted and in fact dominated the rest of the performance, after Dauletkerei responds as her older brother, to show his support:

Атың Сара болғанмен, затың ақын,
Сара апаңның тағдыр бермесе екен.
Ағаң болып тағы да тілек айтам,
Сенің бағың әрдайым өрлесе екен.
Қазақтың сен сияқты әр қызының,
[inaud] шырығы әркашан сөнбесе екен.

Your forebear poet with the name Sara,
may your grandmother not give you her fate.
As your brother I give you my wish again,
May your happiness ever increase.
All Kazakh girls are like you—
may your [inaud.] peace never be extinguished.

In this way, the poets Sara and their relationship to marriage and family became part of the shared truth of the poets and their audience in performance on that day. Past and present are poetically blended and embodied in the story of young women as part of "the Kazakh family." This seemingly simple example is actually emblematic of one major process of the subtle power of neo-historicization in national contexts across Central and Inner Asia today: naming and claiming the experiences of generalized ancestors to living "kin." That conflation of genealogy, geography, and time means that the present (and national) Kazakh(stani) experience can be performatively likened to the Kazakhs and Khanates of centuries past, in order to create a discursive frame for the discussion and possible resolution of problems in the present—in this case, the politics of youth and gender.

Like most young women, Sara has to negotiate her life choices within the structures of family, society, and morality. Her marriage will be a major moment in her life, where all these norms will come into play, and where her decisions, desires, and obligations will affect not only her own relatives but also her future in-laws; there is a great deal of pressure, as her attitude and behavior will affect the reputation of an entire extended family. But the ideal of a romantic love, and the freedom to shine, to be happy, are a part of epic stories dating centuries back, one told again and again, supported by generations of family and kin. In asking her opponent and audience to listen to these stories once more, Sara reminds them to take into account not only her own uncertainties or perspective but that of all the young women of "the people." Sara is performing as a wide-ranging representative of *everybody's* "little sister" (or daughter or granddaughter), who should ideally be loved and supported. She is fortunate that in this performance, her older brother moves immediately to do just that, and to wish for her happiness.

DISCUSSION QUESTIONS

PART IV: CONTEXTS OF STRUCTURE

13. Family Structure

1. Why is the local kinship system relevant for understanding everyday life among Central Asian families?

2. What have been the key drivers of change for Central Asian families after the fall of socialism?

14. Social Structure

3. What are some of the choices that ordinary Central Asians make as they navigate their own social lives? What are the forces that shape their choices?

4. How do the forces that shape social life in Central Asia change over time? What have been the drivers of major transformations?

15. Moral Structure

5. How does morality emerge from everyday events, and what influences its construction?

6. In what ways do differences in moral structure and practice play out?

16. Gender Structure

7. What are some of the differences and similarities between gendered lives and histories in (former-Soviet post-Socialist) Central Asia and any other geopolitical destination in the world, including yours?

8. Is gender a useful tool with which to think about Central Asian diversity and social history? Is it an appropriate lens on human diversity and social history at your destination?

Case IV-A: On Mothers- and Daughters-in-Law

9. In what ways do Jamila and Aigul's relationship follow the "rules" (structures) for relationships between mothers- and daughters-in-law? How do each of them contest these norms?

10. If Jamila is socially progressive, why does she expect Aigul to adhere to some of the typical duties of a daughter-in-law, which are rather restrictive of young women? Why might it be difficult for Jamila to completely let go of this relationship? What would she loose?

Case IV-B: Mahalla as State and Community

11. How should we think about the notion of structure: Is this best thought about as a set of rules that guide behavior? Are structures performative, meaning that they are produced, contested, and negotiated though the everyday activities of people? Is there another way to think about the notion of structure?

12. How do the different kinds of structure described in this section play out in this case study?

Case IV-C: Aitys, Ancestors, and the "Little Sister"

13. In your own country and cultural context, do people who are not related ever call each other by kinship terms like "brother" and "sister"? Do they ever refer to their ancestors, or invoke them in current conversations? If so, in what way and why (or why not)?

14. Do the notions of family, gender, and morality described here feel familiar or different from your previous understandings? Why do you think that is?

FURTHER READING

13. Family Structure

Beyer, Judith. *The Force of Custom: Law and the Ordering of Everyday Life in Kyrgyzstan*. Pittsburgh: University of Pittsburgh Press, 2016.
Dautcher, Jay. *Down a Narrow Road: Identity and Masculinity in a Uyghur Community in Xinjiang China*. Cambridge, MA: Harvard University Press, 2009.
Harris, Colette. *Control and Subversion: Gender Relations in Tajikistan*. London: Pluto, 2004.
Ismailbekova, Aksana. *Blood Ties and the Native Son: Poetics of Patronage in Kyrgyzstan*. Bloomington: Indiana University Press, 2017.
Liu, Morgan. *Under Solomon's Throne: Uzbek Visions of Renewal in Osh*. Pittsburgh: University of Pittsburgh Press, 2012.
Roche, Sophie. *Domesticating Youth: Youth Bulges and their Socio-political Implications in Tajikistan*. New York: Berghahn Books, 2014.
Roche, Sophie, ed. *The Family in Central Asia: New Perspectives*. Berlin: Klaus Schwarz, 2017.
Sahadeo, Jeff, and Russell Zanca, eds. *Everyday Life in Central Asia: Past and Present*. Bloomington: Indiana University Press, 2007.
Trevisani, Tomasso. "Modern Weddings in Uzbekistan: Ritual Change from 'Above' and 'Below.'" *Central Asian Survey* 35, no. 1 (2015): 61–75.

14. Social Structure

Beyer, Judith. *The Force of Custom: Law and the Ordering of Everyday Life in Kyrgyzstan*. Pittsburgh: University of Pittsburgh Press, 2016.
Jones, Pauline, ed. *Islam, Society, and Politics in Central Asia*. Pittsburgh: University of Pittsburgh Press, 2017.
Kassymbekova, Botakoz. *Despite Cultures: Early Soviet Rule in Tajikistan*. Pittsburgh: University of Pittsburgh Press, 2016.

Khalid, Adeeb. *Making Uzbekistan: Nation, Empire, and Revolution in the Early USSR*. Ithaca, NY: Cornell University Press, 2015.

McBrien, Julie. *From Belonging to Belief: Modern Secularisms and the Construction of Religion in Kyrgyzstan*. Pittsburgh: University of Pittsburgh Press, 2017.

Montgomery, David W. *Practicing Islam: Knowledge, Experience, and Social Navigation in Kyrgyzstan*. Pittsburgh: University of Pittsburgh Press, 2016.

Rasanayagam, Johan. *Islam in Post-Soviet Uzbekistan: The Morality of Experience*. Cambridge: Cambridge University Press, 2010.

15. Moral Structure

Beyer, Judith. *The Force of Custom. Law and the Ordering of Everyday Life in Kyrgyzstan*. Pittsburgh: University of Pittsburgh Press, 2016.

Edwards, David B. *Heroes of the Age: Moral Fault Lines on the Afghan Frontier*. Berkeley: University of California Press, 1996.

Féaux de la Croix, Jeanne. *Iconic Places in Central Asia: The Moral Geography of Dams, Pastures and Holy Sites*. Bielefeld: Transcript, 2016.

Liu, Morgan. *Under Solomon's Throne. Uzbek Visions of Renewal in Osh*. Pittsburgh: University of Pittsburgh Press, 2012.

Louw, Maria. "Even Honey May Become Bitter When There Is Too Much of It: Islam and the Struggle for a Balanced Existence in Post-Soviet Kyrgyzstan." *Central Asian Survey* 32, no. 4 (2013): 514–26.

Louw, Maria. "Haunting as Moral Engine: Ethical Striving and Moral Aporias among Sufis in Uzbekistan." In *Moral Engines: Exploring the Moral Drives in Human Life*, edited by Cheryl Mattingly, Maria Louw, Rasmus Dyring, and Thomas Schwartz Wentzer, 83–99. New York: Berghahn Books, 2018.

McBrien, Julie. *From Belonging to Belief: Modern Secularisms and the Construction of Religion in Kyrgyzstan*. Pittsburgh: University of Pittsburgh Press, 2017.

Montgomery, David W. *Practicing Islam: Knowledge, Experience, and Social Navigation in Kyrgyzstan*. Pittsburgh: University of Pittsburgh Press, 2016.

Pelkmans, Mathijs. *Fragile Conviction: Changing Ideological Landscapes in Urban Kyrgyzstan*. Ithaca, NY: Cornell University Press, 2017.

Rasanayagam, Johan. *Islam in Post-Soviet Uzbekistan: The Morality of Experience*. Cambridge: Cambridge University Press, 2011.

Sanghera, Balihar, Aibek Ilyasov, and Elmira Satybaldieva. "Understanding the Moral Economy of Post-Soviet Societies: An Investigation into Moral Sentiments and Material Interests in Kyrgyzstan." *International Social Science Journal* 58, no. 190 (2006): 715–27.

Stephan, Manja. "Education, Youth and Islam: The Growing Popularity of Private Religious Lessons in Dushanbe, Tajikistan." *Central Asian Survey* 29, no. 4 (2010): 469–83.

Tursunova, Zulfiya. *Women's Lives and Livelihoods in Post-Soviet Uzbekistan: Ceremonies of Empowerment and Peacebuilding*. Lanham, MD: Lexington Books, 2014.

16. Gender Structure

Ashwin, Sarah, ed. *Gender, State, and Society on Soviet and Post-Soviet Russia*. London: Routledge, 2000.

Buelow, Samuel. "The Paradox of the Kyrgyz Crossdressers: Ethno-nationalism and Gender Identity in Central Asia." PhD diss., Indiana University, 2017.

Harris, Colette. *Control and Subversion: Gender Relations in Tajikistan*. London: Pluto, 2004.

Harris, Colette. "State Business: Gender, Sex and Marriage in Tajikistan." *Central Asian Survey* 30, no. 1 (2011): 97–111.

Hoare, Joanna Pares. Doing Gender Activism in a Donor-Organized Framework: Constraints and Opportunities in Kyrgyzstan. *Nationalities Papers* 44, no. 2 (2016): 281–98.

Ismailbekova, Aksana. "Migration and Patrilineal Descent: The Role of Women in Kyrgyzstan." *Central Asian Survey* 33, no. 3 (2014): 375–89.

Kamp, Marianne R. *The New Woman in Uzbekistan: Islam, Modernity, and Unveiling under Communism*. Seattle: University of Washington Press, 2006.

Kandiyoti, Deniz. "The Politics of Gender and the Soviet Paradox: Neither Colonized, Nor Modern?" *Central Asian Survey* 26, no. 4 (2007): 601–23.

Khalid, Adeeb. *The Politics of Muslim Cultural Reform: Jadidism in Central Asia*. Berkeley: University of California Press, 1998.

Kudaibergenova, Diana T. "Between the State and the Artist: Representations of Femininity and Masculinity in the Formation of Ideas of the Nation in Central Asia." *Nationalities Papers* 44, no. 2 (2016): 225–46.

Peshkova, Svetlana. *Women, Islam, and Identity: Public Life in Private Spaces in Uzbekistan*. Syracuse, NY: Syracuse University Press, 2014.

Prischepova, V. A. "A View from the Outside: Urda, Jalab, Bachcha (By the Mae Ras Photograph Collections of 1870–1920)." *Manuscripta Orientalia* 12, no. 1 (2006): 43–68.

Roche, Sophie. "A Sound Family for a Healthy Nation: Motherhood in Tajik National Politics and Society." *Nationalities Papers* 44, no. 2 (2016): 207–24.

Schuyler, Eugene. *Turkistan: Notes of a Journey in Russian Turkistan, Khokand, Bukhara, and Kuldja*. 2 vols. Vol. 1. New York (NY): Scribner, Armstrong & Co., 1877.

Suyarkulova, Mohira. "Becoming an Activist Scholar: Towards More Politically Engaged and Socially Accountable Research Practices in Central Asian Studies." *CESS Blog*, December 12, 2019. http://thecessblog.com/2019/12/becoming-an-activist-scholar-towards-more-politically-engaged-and-socially-accountable-research-practices-in-central-asian-studies-by-mohira-suyarkulova-american-university-of-central-asia/.

Wilkinson, Cai, and Anna Kirey. "What's in a Name? The Personal and Political Meanings of 'LGBT' for Non-heterosexual and Transgender Youth in Kyrgyzstan." *Central Asian Survey* 29, no. 4 (2010): 485–99.

Case IV-A: On Mothers- and Daughters-in-Law

Cleuziou, Juliette, and Lucia Direnberger. "Gender and Nation in Post-Soviet Central Asia: From National Narratives to Women's Practices." *Nationalities Papers* 44, no. 2 (2016): 195–206.

Cleuziou, Juliette, and Julie McBrien. "Marriage Quandaries in Central Asia." *Oriente Moderno* 100, no. 2 (2021): 121–46.

Ibañez Tirado, D. "Intimacy and Touch: Closeness, Separation and Family Life in Kulob, Southern Tajikistan." *Ethnography* 19, no. 1 (2018): 105–23.

Isabaeva, Eliza. "Leaving to Enable Others to Remain: Remittances and New Moral Economies of Migration in Southern Kyrgyzstan." *Central Asian Survey* 30, no. 3–4 (2011): 541–54.

Ismailbekova, Aksana. "Constructing the Authority of Women through Custom: Bulak Village, Kyrgyzstan." *Nationalities Papers* 44, no. 2 (2016): 266–80.

Ismailbekova, Aksana. "Migration and Patrilineal Descent: The Role of Women in Kyrgyzstan." *Central Asian Survey* 33, no. 3 (2014): 375–89.

Roche, Sophie, ed. *The Family in Central Asia: New Perspectives*. Berlin: Klaus Schwarz, 2017.

Roche, Sophie. "A Sound Family for a Healthy Nation: Motherhood in Tajik National Politics and Society." *Nationalities Papers* 44, no. 2 (2016): 207–24.

Suyarkulova, Mohira.. Fashioning the Nation: Gender and Politics of Dress in Contemporary Kyrgyzstan. *Nationalities Papers* 44, no. 2 (2016): 247–65.

Case IV-B: *Mahalla* as State and Community

Dadabaev, Timur. "Community Life, Memory and a Changing Nature of Mahalla Identity in Uzbekistan." *Journal of Eurasian Studies*. 4, no. 2 (2013): 181–96.

Liu, Morgan Y. *Under Solomon's Throne: Uzbek Visions of Renewal in Osh*. Pittsburgh, University of Pittsburgh Press, 2012.

Massicard, Elise, and Trevisani, Tommaso. "The Uzbek Mahalla: Between State and Society." In *Central Asia: Aspects of Transition*, edited by Tom Everett-Heath, 205–18. London: Routledge, 2003.

Rasanayagam, Johan. "Morality, Self and Power: The Idea of the Mahalla in Uzbekistan." In *The Anthropology of Moralities*, edited by Monica Heintz, 102–17. New York: Berghahn Books, 2009.

Case IV-C: *Aitys*, Ancestors, and the "Little Sister"

Dubuisson, Eva-Marie. "Confrontation in and through the Nation in Kazakh *Aitys* Poetry." *Journal of Linguistic Anthropology* 20, no. 1 (2010): 101–15.

Kudaibergenova, Diana T. "Project Kelin: Marriage, Women, and Re-traditionalization in Post-Soviet Kazakhstan." In *Women of Asia: Globalization, Development, and Social Change*, edited by Mehrangiz Najafizadeh and Linda L. Lindsey, 379–90. London: Routledge, 2018.

Privratsky, Bruce. *Muslim Turkistan: Kazak Religion and Collective Memory*. Abington: Routledge, 2001.

Salimjan, Guldana. "Debating Gender and Kazakhness: Memory and Voice in Poetic Duel Aytis between China and Kazakhstan." *Central Asian Survey* 36, no. 2 (2017): 263–80.

PART V

There are some things that fundamentally shape experience, interpretation, and practice. What these are and what gets valued most vary between individuals and populations, but the most moving and the most influential of experiences—the ones that make us not only do but also be and become—are formative to who we are and transformative in nature. In this section, we turn to four different approaches to transforming behavior: religion, politics, law, and education. There are other ways in which social life can be foundationally shaped, but in almost every—if not every—iteration of social engagement, some underlying aspect of religion, politics, law, and education can be found.

In his chapter David Montgomery shows how religion is used in different ways to navigate socially across time and place, offering people a sense of purpose that connects pasts and that guides in the present toward an aspired future. Yet such visions are neither neutral nor without historical variation. Contrary to claims of the purity and historical consistency of practice, religion exists in diverse environments and gets influenced by the possibilities and restrictions in which it is being lived out. Some of the context of religion is political, some individual, some collective, but religion is always relational and fundamental in framing ways of seeing—and interacting in—the world.

The legacy of politics and how it shapes behavior is inherent to religion but carries with it a pervasive position on the parameters of social space—seen, at least in the modern period, to include and extend beyond religion. In his chapter John Heathershaw explores politics and the character of the state more broadly. He focuses on how people engage with politics and asks why so many Central Asians seemingly do not want to be bothered by it. Whether it is the liberal transition, or questions of stateness and nation, or market and civil society played out in a largely authoritarian environment, much of the explanation comes from the experience of ordinary citizens. Yet despite their disengagement with politics, people are nonetheless shaped by decisions made by ruling elites.

Law is one way that elites shape the environment in which both religion and politics play out, and in her chapter Judith Beyer offers a nuanced narrative of law and its legacy. She shows how laws become tools of technocrats, and how historically there has been plurality and complexity in engaging through the legal framework. She draws attention to customs and customary law, the significance of locality to the enactment of law, and the varied discursive practices people employ to spread or circumvent law.

In her chapter Martha Merrill turns attention to education and how it shapes thought and frames the foundation of understanding and interacting with others. A country's educational system provides a baseline of shared understanding, yet throughout the region we see people learning in an environment of shortage. All countries see their educational system as a way of transforming populations, and Merrill focuses on the challenges of education reform, especially in higher education, and how the process plays out unevenly. The unevenness, of course, effectively instantiates disparity in access to education's transformative potential.

The case studies draw upon the themes of the section, showing both the overlaps between transformative experiences and how transformation is more broadly enacted. Wendell Schwab looks at the emotional transformation brought about through religion, and how Islam affects mood in Kazakhstan, with diverse Islamic media outlets seeking to enhance positive moods around Islamic practice, emphasizing fun, celebration, and nostalgic association. Mathijs Pelkmans tells the story of the World Nomad Games—dedicated to the ethnic sports of the region, that were founded and first held in Kyrgyzstan in 2014—where we see the transformation of activities characterized as traditions onto the international stage through sport. And in her case, Jennifer Wistrand focuses on Azerbaijan and other former Soviet states to explore what it means to "belong" and to witness that sense of belonging transformed through displacement and political change.

Underlying all the chapters is a question of what shapes individual and collective lives and transforms communities. At their most basic level, religion, politics, law, and education shape the conditions for imagining, feeling, and ultimately belonging. Therein they contribute significantly to all that animates life.

17

Religion

David W. Montgomery

To discuss religion is to speak of relationships that quite often seem to be in contradiction. Religion is intimate and personal, yet it is also public and shared. It is unique and universal, and it frames all sorts of behaviors with varying degrees of consistency and coherence. Compartmentalized and totalizing, it is both general and specific, meaning different things to different people at different times, all encompassed under the same umbrella term. As such, the very use of the term requires context, for it is only within context that we see how religion makes sense, and for whom. Understanding the sociological aspects of religious practice is not the same as appreciating the affective implications of religiosity. This applies not only to how one thinks and feels about religion—if one is supportive, indifferent, or antagonistic—but also to how one understands the challenges, threats, opportunities, and possibilities foretold within a religious tradition. Efforts to stay "neutral" are always fraught, because religion holds many things—universal and unique—all at the same time.

Even at the surface we see this. Central Asia is predominately Muslim, but not exclusively. Non-Muslims have different framings, different contexts, and very different experiences, and there is much diversity even among the predominately Muslim population. Going further, we see this in how people describe their relationships to religion. Below, we see three Kyrgyz describing themselves as Muslim but in very different ways, indicating how they interpret their surroundings differently. Gulnaz speaks of being faithful to a long tradition of ancestors who engaged the workings of the spirit world before Islam arrived in the region and who were—reflecting back on the nature of their devotion—themselves Muslims. For Gulnaz, ancestral spirits are everywhere; they should be tended to respectfully, and they inform her practice of Islam. She speaks of being Muslim "in tradition," claiming that the ancestors and the traditions they kept still guide her.

Maxim does not consider himself religious, but nonetheless self-characterizes himself as Muslim; not a "good" Muslim (by which he means observant and practicing) but Muslim all the same. He grew up during the Soviet Union and attributes his secular understanding of religion to that period. He views Islam as the unifying cultural tradition of Central Asians, but as an organizing principle Islam seldom plays a role in his way of thinking about the world. He sees himself as a Muslim secularist; culturally Muslim, but not practicing. For him, the state should not be involved in religion except to protect the population from being too influenced by religion—that is, to restrict religion from public overreach. For Maxim, the state has a securitized role regarding religion, a responsibility to protect people from "the wrong type of Muslims, being radicalized," or from religion becoming so dominant that people are forced to go to the mosque.

Nurbek, on the other hand, has a more inclusive view of religion. He talks about his life as being guided by Islam and his desire to bring others to Islam. In the late 2000s he became more interested in religious practice, fashioning himself as a Muslim striving to be a better Muslim. The impetus was a combination of studying abroad and spending time with others who were themselves searching for more moral lives. As others began to observe him as a "practicing" Muslim, he felt further compelled to devote more time to studying and practicing Islam, which contributes to others seeing him as an "expert" on religion.

Gulnaz, Maxim, and Nurbek all have views on religion that they freely share, but it is not uncommon for others to point first to Nurbek as the "authority" on Islam. Certainly, their engagement with Islam differs, and their vision shapes their position on the broader role that religion plays (or should play) in society. How they come to hold these positions is rooted in how they come to understand the present in relation to the past they have inherited and the future to which they aspire. These understandings emerge from how religion is learned, lived, navigated, and ultimately contextualized.

Religious Pasts, Presents, and Futures

Religion moves across time in fungible ways. Histories matter, but not always in the same way. Thus, the history here is focused less on a detailed chronological account of religions unfolding across the space that has come to be recognized as Central Asia, but more along the lines of broad trends that come back to be referenced. For example, petroglyphs, some of which date back to the second millennium BCE, are one of the earliest indications of religious practice, with some etchings suggesting ritual practices situated within the natural world (see figure 17-1). For most people today, these constitute little more than primitive art, a cultural treasure but with no

DAVID W. MONTGOMERY

17-1   Petroglyphs from the Bronze Age on display in front of the eleventh-century Burana Tower, a large minaret, in Kyrgyzstan, 2006. Photograph by David W. Montgomery.

contemporary religious relevance. Gulnaz, however, connects them back to the spirituality of the early ancestors who, for her, are active participants in her cosmology. It is not the historical record that guides her but, rather, stories built upon stories handed down by generations on the significance of the stones. And a bit anachronistically (though neither ironically nor unaware of it), Gulnaz views the pre-Islamic ancestors as Muslim, like herself, because the ancestors "submitted" to Allah—even before Allah was given the name.

The move Gulnaz makes is to situate her practice of ancestral veneration at sacred sites—streams, caves, trees, tombs, and so on—scattered across the region as an extension of practice that is compatible with the dominant Islamic milieu in which Central Asians generally situate themselves. Hers is an interpretation of Islam as a natural extension of the religious practices of ancestors and represents an active spiritual presence in the surrounding world. But the religious environment in which the ancestors lived was influenced by a multitude of religious traditions and outside pressures. It was, as elsewhere, a place of dynamic exchange of ideas and practices with people finding meaning through a diversity of religious and moral framings.

Religion is not entirely a local manifestation. It is also influenced by interactions with long-distance traders, missionaries, and ascetics, among others, moving across the region carrying goods and ideas. Polytheism gave way to other forms of diversity, with ideas drawn from Zoroastrianism, Buddhism, Judaism, Christianity, and Manichaeism (see figure 17-2). Islam emerged on the scene in the seventh century. How the traditions interacted

17-2   Built in the fourth century BC, the Zoastrian fortress Gyaur-Qala, "The Fortress of Infidels," lies west of Nukus, Uzbekistan, 2019. Photograph by Kasia Ploskonka.

and how they impacted each other and the people of the region all varied, but contemporary markers of some of these pre-Islamic traditions are scant. Zoroastrianism, one of the world's oldest surviving religions, has few material reminders of its prevalence despite its influence on other traditions—in concepts such as messianism, heaven and hell, judgment after death, and free will. It has left a mark in uncertain ways. For example, Nowruz is a holiday with roots in Zoroastrianism that celebrates the arrival of spring on the vernal equinox. It is celebrated in much of the region, yet its significance is ambiguous: for some like Gulnaz, it is traditional and religious; for Maxim, it is a celebration of spring without any clear religious meaning; and for Nurbek, it is a tradition of the region, which he sees as *shirk* (idolatry). Similarly, signs of Buddhism can be seen in ruined temples and monastic complexes in Old Termez, Uzbekistan, and in Kurgan Teppa, Tajikistan, with artifacts resting in museums, but few Buddhists remain in contemporary Central Asia. Manichaeism—which was influenced by Zoroastrianism, Buddhism, and Gnostic Christianity—is even less visible.

The extent to which we see the presence and influence of some of these earlier traditions today can be hard to attribute clearly. Conceptually, however, this is part of the point; people reference religious pasts in ways that often undervalue the dynamic environment in which those very traditions evolved. Manicheans and Nestorian Christians, for example, moved into the region as pressures of persecution in the west pushed them eastward. Eventually, they were overcome by the dominance of Islam, but what emerged was not entirely uniform or without traces of influence from what had come before. Likewise,

    DAVID W. MONTGOMERY

the once thriving Jewish community in Bukhara dispersed in the years following the collapse of the Soviet Union, and today the community has only a fraction of its prior influence, with fewer active reminders of the presence that once was (see figure 17-3).

It is thus that different interpretations of the religious past overlay the religious present and the justifications of "proper" religious practice. It is not uncommon, for example, for Uzbek and Kyrgyz Muslims to get stereotyped differently, with Uzbeks being colloquially labeled as "more" Muslim than Kyrgyz. What this generally references is an assumption of particular practices indexing religiosity, as the more sedentary practices of those in the "valley" areas, where mosques and physical structures are more spatially fixed, are seen as more legitimate than the semi-nomadic practices of those in the "mountain" areas, where sacred sites may be encountered with seasonal variation. This is similarly played out in comparisons of the perceived Muslim correctness of Nurbek and Gulnaz, without appreciating syncretic and interpretative variation that can be legitimized across practices.

17-3   A synagogue in Bukhara, home to a once thriving Jewish community in Uzbekistan, 2000. Photograph by David W. Montgomery.

Like other traditions, Islam spread unevenly, being taken up by more sedentary populations in centers like Bukhara and Samarqand earlier than among the semi-nomadic populations. The battle of Talas in 751 CE marked a turning point for Islam's foothold in the region, but it was not uncommon for conversions to occur multiple times among some communities, indicating a certain amount of flux in people's religious engagement. By the ninth century, Bukhara had become the Islamic world's intellectual center, and the hadiths—the sayings and acts done by Muhammad and his companions, used to understand the context of the Qur'an and to guide moral behavior—that were compiled at that time by Muhammad ibn Ismail al-Bukhari were so influential that today they can be found in almost every mosque worldwide. But as Islam spread, it did so into a place filled with competing religious traditions and varied opportunities for differences to emerge. In some more mountainous areas, for example, Islam was slower to take hold (not doing so until the eighteenth century) with some tenets such as washing before prayer being more sporadically followed, in part because of the nomadic environment. But there were different forms of competition, and what played out was marked by diversity and a back-and-forth of integrating, excluding, and reformulating. The process of Islamization could only have been uneven—influenced and influencing the practices already present.

Generally, the story of Islamic expansion in the early years was one of inclusion and openness. Conversion is relatively easy, requiring the recitation of the *shahada* (the profession of faith that "there is no god but Allah, and Muhammad is his messenger"), and certainly there was a mixing of existing practices with new understandings brought by outside interactions. This can be seen most clearly in the Sufi traditions that took hold in the region, where mystical understandings of Islam could be connected to the diverse environment of existing practices. Sufi *pirs* (spiritual guides) did this by showing compatibility of new framings of social morality and spiritual questing. The religious field was dynamic, and as some shed earlier religious framings for Muslim framings, some of the past remained to shape the present.

The Islamization of the population involved norms being imposed on the population (with varying degrees of persuasion) and a later, nativized assimilation of practice and thought. As Islam became internalized within community, pre-Islamic practice was reframed within an Islamic context. The Sufi orders played an active role in these transitions, and the legacy of the Naqshbandi tariqa (which grew out of Bukhara) and the Yassawi tariqa (centered in Turkestan) both played a role in the transformation. Sufism, the mystical branch of Islam, was influential in part because it allowed people to reframe existing beliefs within a more personal and intimate relationship with Allah. And although the openness of Sufism made sense to many, others approached Islam in more legalistic ways.

It is worth noting that, within Islam, there are distinct yet not necessarily exclusionary frames with which it can be approached, the Sufi mystical tradition being one. Another is oriented around approaches to jurisprudence, which is how Islam gets most frequently characterized. Within Islam, normative foundations for how life should be lived draw upon the revelations of the Qur'an and the traditions (sunnah) of the Prophet Muhammad. It is these sunnah that al-Bukhari authoritatively recorded in the hadiths, which give a sense of the foundational significance of the region to contemporary Islam. The process of *fiqh* (jurisprudence)—which combines the Qur'an, sunnah, fatwa (rulings), and ulema (jurists)—creates the moral framework in which life is to be lived, yet it is also an interpretive legal process that results in variations, as seen in the various schools of jurisprudence (madhab) and their approach to fiqh. Most Muslims in Central Asia are characterized as Hanafi Sunnis, and this indexes a particular approach to fiqh, though there is a population of Ismaili Shi'ia in the Badakhshan region of Tajikistan. The point here is that the madhabs become yet another way in which the past is brought into the present in helping to frame knowledge, understanding, and difference.

Transforming Religion

Despite the influence of the madhabs and claims that their foundations were immutably set in the tenth century, religion generally, and Islam specifically, is always being transformed in response to the contemporary environment in which it is being applied. Even when it claims immutability, there are aspects of transformation—or at least an aspiration for transformation—in religious engagement. The past is not static but instead grounding and responsive to the needs that people face. In the late nineteenth century, for example, the Jadids, a Muslim modernist reform movement in Central Asia, sought to transform how people thought about being Muslim and to reinvigorate tradition through modernist educational reforms that were seen as necessary for success in the contemporary world. The Jadids saw nationalism as central to their reform efforts, which allowed them to join with the Bolsheviks in the 1917 revolution, but they were not Marxist, which eventually led the Bolsheviks to redirect the Jadid reform efforts by establishing support for an assemblage of locals ideologically committed to socialism over religious practice.

The history of any region is one that involves periods of religious change, and during the time of the Soviet Union the religious environment in which people lived changed both structurally and dramatically. Religion became more constrained, and although one could still be religious there were consequences; professional advancement was limited, for example. It was harder to enforce restrictions against religion as one moved further from administrative centers, and there were instances of people maintaining religious practices and religious lives, but being religious brought attention that could be complicating. During the Second World War, restrictions against religious practice were loosened, as Stalin needed support for the war effort and Islam still mattered in Central Asia, but increasingly, the space in which religion could be practiced became traditionalized and privatized, with life-cycle rituals becoming contextualized as tradition and their religious context being absent from public discussion. This marked a significant change in religion, a move from religion as ubiquitous (which is not to say that everyone was equally religious, but that religion was not needed as a conscious category because religious practices did not need to be kept out of public view) to religion needing to be individual and private.

It was thus that the secularization of Central Asia was facilitated by two significant structural reforms. One was the creation of the Spiritual Administration of the Muslims of Central Asia and Kazakhstan (SADUM), which established a hierarchical structure in Islam over which the state could appoint religious leaders and control the content of what was taught. The significance here is that Islam traditionally is not doctrinally hierarchical; there is no authoritative leader speaking for all Muslims, and the imam of any mosque comes to lead under credentials deemed locally sufficient. With SADUM, the state institutionalized a role in controlling Islamic behavior—both in the teaching of content and in the regulation of practice. And it is out of this that perhaps the most lasting impact of the Soviet Union on Islam emerged. It came to control education and the frame through which people could learn about religion.

Generations lived through these reforms, and it is out of this environment—a dynamic multireligious past, a center of Islamic learning, and a time of religious control and suppression—that the collapse of the Soviet Union led to new opportunities for engaging religion. The new post-Soviet states advanced a Muslim identity as one way of differentiating from the Soviet past and reconnecting to a (reconstructed) pre-Soviet Islamic heritage. The leaders of the new states were all well established within the Communist Party, and all, with the exception of the Kyrgyz president Askar Akaev, were the leaders of the new titular states prior to independence, so one could not expect a transition overnight. Despite their rhetorical openness to religion and the new countries' culturally Islamic pasts, the leaders had grown up and assumed power within the Soviet system where religion was marginalized and treated with suspicion.

Ultimately, what most leaders of the new states had in mind was a secular form of religion, private and cultural. Uzbek president Islam Karimov, for example, invested in the Bakhautdin Naqshband Mausoleum complex outside of Bukhara, promoting the cultural significance of the country's Sufi past, which in the figure of Naqshband has had global influence. Highlighting a Sufi past—which is largely focused on a personal relationship with Allah and thus internalized and seemingly nonthreatening to the state—made more sense than bringing up more political reform-oriented references like the Jadids, who sought to transform and modernize education prior to the Russian Revolution. What we saw post-independence and continue to see three decades later is people struggling with what it means to be Muslim in secular terms, where the secularized frame set by the Soviets becomes the dominant forum through which terms of Muslim-ness are negotiated.

Thus, in contemporary Central Asia we find a dynamic religious environment where people have been engaging with histories, reworking them along lines of new understandings, and planning paths that shape the social environment in ways that are at times contested. Remnants of the earlier traditions are largely that: remnants. Islam remains the most prevalent of the confessional traditions, though Russian Orthodoxy maintains a presence in the larger cities where ethnic Russian populations remain (see figure 17-4). In many ways, this division between Islam and Russian Orthodoxy is accepted as a reflection of historical precedence; the Slavic population belonging to the Orthodox world and the Central Asian population to the Islamic. This generally accepted parsing out of who belongs to which confessional tradition most clearly plays out in response to missionary activity by some Protestant Christian groups, where Muslims and Orthodox Christians express opposition to these "new" groups trying to convert people away from the traditions to which they might historically be associated.

17-4   The Ascension Cathedral, also known as Zenkov Cathedral, a Russian Orthodox cathedral completed in 1907, considered the second tallest wooden building in the world, Almaty, Kazakhstan, 2005. Photograph by Natalie Koch.

While the Orthodox Christian population has declined with the post-Soviet emigration of ethnic Russians, and there has been missionary activity among some Protestant Christian groups and others, the most significant changes have been among Muslims in Central Asia, working out what it means to be Muslim in a place with a proud Islamic heritage darkened by seventy years (for most, a lifetime) of Soviet efforts to make religion less relevant. Following independence and the opening of opportunities to learn about and practice religion, there has been a variety of responses to how people have negotiated their religious worlds in relation to the histories out of which they have grown and the possibilities seen before them.

Living Religion Differently

Quite often religion is referenced in broad terms by expectations of what it should look like, associated with doctrine and generalized behavior. Such generalized characterizations lead us to expect a certain uniformity of acts and beliefs. A demographic picture of religion in Central Asia offers a view that can be both useful and misleading (see figure 17-5). As shown below, we make sense of data based on generalizations: those who identify as Muslims fast during Ramadan, do not drink, eat halal, go to Juma prayers, are guided morally by the Qur'an and hadiths, and so on. Those identified as Christians go to church, pray, read the Bible, take communion, believe in the redemptive message of Jesus, and so on. Applying such expectations across time, Muslims today represent a continuation of the Islamic past that will not differ significantly in the Islamic future. The assumption is that one Muslim is categorically similar to another. But there is great variation, not only at levels of fiqh and mystical openness but in how people respond to the environment and the opportunities out of which they grow.

The point here is not to disparage demographic data (which are often quite useful to orient us to what a place might look like, in broad strokes) but, rather, to highlight that in the dynamic environment in which people live, religion is often obscured by simplified assumptions made out of context. The religious lives of Gulnaz, Maxim, and Nurbek were only briefly sketched above yet nonetheless convey a note on diversity as to how Islam is understood and experienced. Also, in the face of limited information, we fill in the gaps from our own perspectives of what religion means to others. But understanding another is a complicated and messy affair that pulls out the tension in which religion is lived in relation to the social and political environment in which people live.

It is important to note that religion is lived throughout a lifetime, played out in quotidian spaces across an array of social interactions—some moments seem transformative, though most are simply mundane. Gulnaz, Maxim, and Nurbek all get captured in data as Muslim and yet contest how each other's practices—or views about being "Muslim"—can be counted equally. In each case, the others' views are inconsistent with their own understandings of what religion should look like. While the experiences and understanding of each person are real and unique to that person, the extent to which they represent archetypes of diverse claims to being Muslim—in this case, in Kyrgyzstan—helps us appreciate the underlying multiplicity of meanings always present in religion.

As noted, in her understanding of Islam and of its application in her life, Gulnaz carries forward a view of being actively connected to the past vis-à-vis her surroundings and understandings of knowledge passed down by her ancestors. She learned from her mother, who had learned about the sacred places of the ancestors from her father. Gulnaz had three siblings, but she was the one with "the gift" of being able to connect to the traditions of the past. She reads portions of the Qur'an in Kyrgyz and knows bits of prayers in Arabic but mostly orients her religious practice around sacred sites (mazars)—particular streams, trees, rock formations, tombs—where rituals she learned from her mother, grandfather, and other regional spiritual leaders are conducted for purposes of healing and "making the world aright."

For Gulnaz, the ancestors are active participants in her life, guiding her

DAVID W. MONTGOMERY

Figure 17-5   Demographics of Religion by Country

	Year	Population	Muslim	Christian	Unaffiliated	Other
Kazakhstan	2010	16,030,000	70.4%	24.7%	4.2%	0.7%
(predicted)	2050	21,189,092	77.4%	18.4%	2.8%	1.4%
Kyrgyzstan	2010	5,330,000	88.0%	11.4%	0.4%	0.2%
(predicted)	2050	7,045,406	92.4%	7%	0.4%	0.2%
Tajikistan	2010	6,880,000	96.7%	1.6%	1.5%	0.2%
(predicted)	2050	10,656,993	96.1%	2.1%	1.5%	0.3%
Turkmenistan	2010	5,040,000	93.0%	6.4%	0.6%	<0.1%
(predicted)	2050	7,806,867	92.9%	6.5%	0.5%	0.1%
Uzbekistan	2010	27,440,000	96.7%	2.3%	0.8%	0.2%
(predicted)	2050	40,854,421	97.8%	1.5%	0.6%	0.1%

Source: Based on 2010 data from Pew-Templeton Global Religious Futures Project, at http://global religiousfutures.org. Population numbers for 2050 are based on trends of annual population growth rate between 2000 and 2010 at (respectively) Kazakhstan 0.7%; Kyrgyzstan 0.7%; Tajikistan 1.1%; Turkmenistan 1.1%; and Uzbekistan 1.0%. The CIA World Factbook gives similar distributions but notes that, in Kazakhstan, Tajikistan, and Uzbekistan, the Christian population is predominately Russian (Eastern) Orthodox, and in Kyrgyzstan, Orthodox Christians comprise almost half of the Christian population. Most Muslims in the region are Sunni, though in Tajikistan, around 3% of the population is noted as Shia (though not identified as Ismaili Shi'a, which would be most.) See https://www.cia.gov/library/publications/resources/the-world-factbook/fields/401.html#KZ/.

interactions with the world. This is not an idle position—that is, it is not merely a quaint observation but, rather, one that shows the ancestors playing an active role in the way she interacts with the world. The ancestors also allow her to help heal those who come to her with physical, spiritual, and emotional problems; through this, she assumes a position of spiritual authority in her community. Not all accept her authority as (properly) Islamic, however.

Maxim, on the other hand, does not see himself as religiously knowledgeable. This does not overly concern him either. He is familiar with Kyrgyz traditions, but traditions for him are not living dynamic influencers of his behavior as they are for Gulnaz. He characterizes himself as a modern critical thinker, respectful of the past but aiming to make a future guided by reason and progress. (Gulnaz does not see herself as the opposite of these qualities, quite the contrary, but she sees these things through a different lens.) Maxim is ambivalent about his thoughts on Allah—skeptical but not entirely dismissive—and avoids trying to reconcile otherworldly possibilities with the demands of daily life. Religion may be a thing for others, it is just not for him. And when he describes himself as "culturally Muslim," it is with a meaning that is devoid of any contemporary implications for religious practice.

There is some ambiguity—and at times contradiction—in what being "culturally Muslim" means to Maxim. He accepts that many traditions of Central Asian culture were foundationally shaped by Islam. He describes this by pointing to al-Bukhari (who compiled the hadiths), the Registan in Uzbekistan (which was a historic madrassa), and Solomon's Mountain in Kyrgyzstan (which also had a pre-Islamic heritage) as coming out of an Islamic epoch. He conceives of such an epoch as being directly related to a time where everyone saw what they were doing as part of being Muslim. His generalization here simplifies the complexity of social life at the time and the diverse environment in which people actually lived. But it allows him to reference an understanding of culture as being intimately connected with Islam at every level, yet at the same time distinct from his modern understanding of religion as separate from the active parts of life. So, although he identifies as Muslim, he does not identify as religious and does not want any other's religious beliefs to impact his.

Nurbek, on the other hand, became more committed to Islam in the years following independence. In the waning years of the Soviet Union, when he was in grade school, he, like Maxim, was culturally Muslim—though he never thought in any serious way about what that meant. In encounters at university, he observed others exploring what the Islamic past meant in a particular context and how Islamic practice (as characterized by some foreign missionaries he encountered) differed from what he recognized locally. After some "hooligan years," as he characterized the more mischievous time of his youth, he became more concerned with being a better person. He began going to the local mosque with a classmate and after a few months started to devote time to studying and to (in his view) "properly" practicing Islam.

He distinguishes himself from people like Gulnaz and Maxim who, he claims, are misguided in their relationship with (practicing) Islam. He acknowledges Gulnaz's practices as being consistent with some Kyrgyz traditions, but he believes what she does is incorrect and quite possibly idolatry (shirk), drawing parallels to the practices that Muhammad tried to remove from the Kaaba. And he points out that his practice is consistent with the traditions of the prophet, as practiced by learned Muslims the world over. And he sees in Maxim (a product of the Soviet past and capitalist present) someone he could have become had he not sought moral betterment within religious practice. Increasingly Nurbek spends time with his friends at the mosque and talks more authoritatively about Islam and the role it should play in overcoming the inadequacies of society.

The Political Becoming of Religion

Nurbek's views about the transformative nature of Islam are extensive and conservative, yet he is very clear in his condemnation of Muslims who use violence to change society. His position on Islam is political nonetheless, in the sense of envisioning religion's role vis-à-vis society, and is at odds with that of Gulnaz or Maxim. He believes his vision of Islam should be advanced and that if it was, people would have better lives. He is vague on what this would mean, other than that more people would study, go to mosque, and be like him. It is not that he advocates for a theocratic state, but he complains about corruption, the vast wealth acquired by a few who do not help others in need, and the inadequacies of the state in providing services.

But here there is a distinction to draw, where religion stakes claim on what society—and social order more broadly—should look like. These are arguments about education, law, morality, economics, and so on, largely played out through contested political agendas on what public and private social space should entail. There are multiple ways in which religion influences people's lives including ways of dealing with loss, struggle, grief, joy, purpose, and so on, and we see this in the practices observed by Nurbek and Gulnaz. Maxim, while not observant, is influenced by the acts of those who are and as such aims to protect himself, maintaining a separation of religion from public space. There is a distinction between these influences at an everyday level and how religion gets used in contexts that become political. And discussions of public space are ultimately political.

After the Soviet Union collapsed, there was a sense that a religious revival was taking place in Central Asia and that this revival held potential to fundamentally reshape society within a religious (specifically, Islamic) context. There were, for example, new opportunities for people to talk about, practice, and operationalize religion in ways that seemed different from before. In some instances, this seemed to advance the goals of the state in forming a collective identity that legitimated its very existence—out of the Soviet republics emerged (secular) Muslim states. Though, if we look back at how earlier generations engaged religion and then at how they do today, it is more consistent to see the religious space as transformed rather than revived. Gulnaz, Maxim, and Nurbek's positions on religion evolved into where they are today—which is a sociological process navigated across generations—but they did not grow without reference to what was before.

The Soviet restrictions on religious education and the establishment of SADUM were two reforms that framed the environment out of which the newly independent states evolved. It was a secular model that accepted religion as not having an active role in affairs of the state. The implicit argument was that it was tolerable for people to be religious so long as this did not interfere with their obligations to the state. In other words, religion should be separate from the business of the state; private, with any public engagement being managed (controlled) by state authorities. Much of this is consistent with how Maxim wants religion to be regulated by the state, but it is worth seeing that these discussions of religion are political in ways and ends that are different from what Gulnaz and Nurbek think about religion.

We see this state-level engagement with politics and religion across the region. In Uzbekistan, Karimov's support of Sufism made sense because it drew attention to the country's contribution to global Islam and supported an iteration of practice that was more internal and less challenging to the state. In Kazakhstan, President Nursultan Nazarbayev initiated the Congress of Leaders of World and Traditional Religions, meeting every three years in the Palace of Peace and Reconciliation, to facilitate a dialogue on religion's role in countering terrorism and extremism through a narrative of unity in religious coexistence. In Turkmenistan, President Saparmurat Niyazov instantiated his own vision of "spiritual guidance" for the nation in his book the *Ruhnama*, published in two volumes, that was required reading in schools and present in mosques throughout the country. In 2015 in Tajikistan, the Islamic Revival Party—which fought with the United Tajik Opposition during the civil war and in the late 1990s was the second-largest political party in the country—was banned as a terrorist organization but more, it seems, for being an opposition party than for being a religious group. Similarly in Kyrgyzstan, state authorities at times treat religious pluralism as a threat, restricting groups that do not align with officially sanctioned forms of religion, and consider one of the state's roles to be regulating the public engagement of religion in so far as how it might challenge state authority.

Underlying how states engage religion is a concern with the political instability that might be caused by people who identify as religious if their (political) views come to clash with the hegemonic political authorities. The problem of radicalization is one such framing of this tension, but it is also complicated. To be sure, there are Central Asians who join Islamist movements with the view of bringing about a more prominent presence of Islam in the state, but such individuals do not represent widespread support for an Islamist overtaking of government. Rather, more radical ideas that clash with the state authority are better understood in response to corruption and state predation than theology. Throughout the region (and especially in Uzbekistan and Tajikistan), "Islamic radical" has been used as a label to crack down on potential threats, implying that religious ideology is explanatory of oppositional motives—that is, that "radical" Muslims oppose the state. Many who oppose state leadership, however, do so for reasons that can be quite separate from religion, especially in a region overwhelmingly characterized as Muslim.

Living a religious life is "radical" in the sense of orienting one's behaviors differently, but it need not be political. Within a political context, characterizing someone as radical often implies behavioral deviance (which may or may not be true), but it also quite frequently leads to understanding an individual or theology as flawed. It does not necessarily offer conceptual insights into the broader context in which one is radicalized or how reasons for protest may have little to do with religion. In other words, the foundations of opposition to governments are overlooked in order to facilitate the crackdown on behavior that would be allowed by more open governments.

In the Central Asian context, the vast majority of Muslims accept a secular state wherein religion is privatized—some because this is the environment that emerged out of the Soviet Union and some because being religious holds more value if it is an action of choice. Nonetheless, we do see concerns of public and thus political space playing out around how people should live: questions of education (public or private, religious or secular), legal systems (sharia law, Western law, traditional law), clothing

DAVID W. MONTGOMERY

(headscarves for women and skullcaps for men), and coupling (religious marriages or state marriages, number of wives), to name a few. Within these debates, we see a referencing of pasts in relation to the aspirations for future orders made within moral claims. In this sense there is a battle over public space that cannot be managed merely by privatizing religion because visions of "how the world should be" are religious and secular in varying degrees, relative to those making the claims.

It becomes relevant to delineate two aspects of the political in regard to religion. This is not only a matter for the state, which is concerned about counter-hegemonic claims of rightness and public order that might undermine it; it is also a matter both personal and moral, around which people situate themselves relative to others. For Gulnaz, Maxim, and Nurbek, Islamic radicalism is far from their concerns and their experience, despite its receiving a good deal of media attention. But where their kids go to school, the nature of law, what they can wear, and whom they can marry, these are all open debates. These negotiations are themselves political, made in relation to neighbors and the public writ large, with religion playing a varied part in the decision-making process.

Socially Navigating Religious Life in Central Asia

It is important to keep in mind that most people look to religion as a moral guide to life, as something that is not merely restraining but liberating, purposeful, and at times fun. Fundamentally, religion is not static but dynamic, varying by experience across gender, generation, class, and other markers of differentiation. How people use religion to respond and adapt to their environment is not always consistent or coherent but a socially navigated process of striving and finding ways forward among the possibilities that are available (and imagined). It is important to keep in mind that the past, which has set forth the parameters in which social possibility is ordered, is used creatively, pragmatically, and at times idiosyncratically. And here we return to the conceptual frames with which we began: tradition, culture, and practice.

Gulnaz ties her religious understanding to a tradition that begins with ancestors. She references back to what she learned from her mother, in private, under the restrictive context of the Soviet Union, which co-opted tradition to nationalist ends yet saw ancestor-oriented practices as unmodern folk traditions needing to be reformed through education and restriction. Gulnaz avoids political discussions and is cautious around strangers, having had the experience of being looked down upon by those who do not agree with her religious views and healing practices. But people in her village come to her with their personal and health issues, seeking guidance in life-cycle rituals and in the ways ancestral wisdom continues to shape the present.

Maxim is secular, living in a culturally Islamic milieu. He looks at tradition and the reverence toward ancestors as quaintly rooted in more rural and antiquated ways of thought. He does not appreciate the reverence and sacrality as Gulnaz does, who finds spiritual and religious signs of ancestors and Islam in her surroundings. And he is suspicious of the motives of those who publicly advocate for religion. He supports the government's aggressive position toward cracking down on (religious) extremism, seeing the outward changes of dress and debates of piety and modesty as moving backward from modernization. In talking about his concerns regarding religion, he notes largely how it would be restrictive, antiprogressive, and less pragmatic in business.

Nurbek sees life as an environment of moral striving through religious practice. His commitment and obligation toward others are rooted not only in his local mosque community but more broadly in a growing community of Muslim practitioners who advocate Islam as a guide for behavior (see figure 17-6). His vision is one hoping to influence Maxim and Gulnaz, making them more Muslim like him. They, however, are happy not to be bound by the constraints of Nurbek's community.

How people arrive at an orientation toward religion is narrated differently to different people at different times. Gulnaz has two origin stories she tells, both revolving around a dream or vision she had as a child and her strong sense of calling. Maxim says he has never been religious, that considering Islam as an active part of life was something for others. His father was a mid-level figure in the local Communist Party who had studied in Moscow and never made time to consider religion. It was sufficiently unrelated to Maxim's experience that it only made sense for it not to influence his life. And Nurbek situates his relationship toward Islam as a moral coming-of-age tale: he was in dire straits, and then he became better.

This is in no way to discount their stories, only to highlight that there are multiple reasons underlying their worldviews, which hold implications for how public space is imagined. The political for all of them plays out differently. Nurbek believes there should be a strong component of Islam taught in schools. He sends his children to the local public school because that is what he can afford, but he sees it as less useful than the madrassa classes he sends them to outside of the public school. What they learn at the madrassa, he feels, will give them the moral foundation the state schools do not provide. He also sees a growing role for sharia in managing disputes independent of the state; he insists on modest Islamic dress for his wife and children. His expectation for his children is less oriented toward economics and more toward marrying "good" Muslims and raising a family practicing and morally guided by Islam.

In contrast, Maxim sends his children to an expensive Western-style private school. Gulnaz sends hers to a public school because she cannot afford the private schools and would never consider sending them to a madrassa. Maxim sees only the laws of the state as those that matter; Gulnaz puts much weight in the laws of custom and tradition. Maxim wears slacks and a blazer; Gulnaz wears dresses that are conservative and functional, with a headscarf (*jooluk*) worn in a traditional style, as opposed to the hijab of Nurbek's wife, to indicate marriage status. Gulnaz imagines her children

DAVID W. MONTGOMERY

17-6 After three years of construction, the Hazrat Sultan Mosque was finished in 2012 and is now the largest mosque in Central Asia, Nur-Sultan, Kazakhstan, 2018. Photograph by Kasia Ploskonka.

marrying Kyrgyz who are observant of tradition, which she views as being Muslim though not in the way Nurbek does. And Maxim say he hopes his children will not marry a religious person; most likely for him, they would marry a secular Kyrgyz from the same economic class with a shared sense of "culturalness" about religion.

Each frame prioritizes a different orientation toward time and object of emphasis. Gulnaz speaks about tradition, orienting toward the past and emphasizing history and family. Maxim sees a secular frame, prioritizing the present, concerning himself with the politics and culture around him. Nurbek's is a story of striving to be a better Muslim, of looking toward the future and emphasizing the cosmological implications of Islam. These conceptual framings are not exact, as each individual moves across them with a certain degree of fluidity. In thinking through the role of religion in people's lives, we see stories of variation where claims are made about priorities and about public and private space. "Religion" as a conceptualizing term must be seen as broad, in relation to the person being engaged. It has a life toward political ends, but it plays out differently at different levels—macro, meso, and micro. Seeing this is useful to considering the varied ways in which people make sense of their lives in relation to past meanings, contemporary challenges, and future aspirations. Religion can frame morality through different understandings of tradition while at the same time be categorized as cultural to different explanatory ends. To understand what religion means separately to Gulnaz, Maxim, and Nurbek is to see this.

18

Politics

John Heathershaw

One of the defining features of our age is the long-coming but now undeniable disenchantment with the political. In *Why We Hate Politics*, the British political scientist Colin Hay argues that elite practices of neoliberalism with their "tightly delimited political sphere" and globalization's discourse of "the increasingly anachronistic nature of political intervention" have generated public disdain for politics in general and liberal democracy in particular. Given that politics, with its concern for the construction and realization of the public good, was the erstwhile solution to the recurrent wars of kings and the untrammeled capital of merchants, the pervasive sense of hating politics should cause alarm in all places suffering from this malaise. Apropos, Central Asians, it increasingly seems, also hate politics. The question we face is what particular form and content the region's own disenchantment takes.

In addressing this question, we may distinguish between issues of the demand for and the supply of politics. Political disenchantment is most obvious in demand-side factors including but not limited to the following markers of antipolitics: nostalgia for the Soviet Union; apparently widespread belief in conspiracy theories; the retreat from political participation by embattled ethnic minorities; the prevalence of patriarchy and paternalism in public life; and the cultural and political effects of the mass out-migration of laborers. However, these evident processes are in part responses to supply-side factors including but not limited to the rise of authoritarian kleptocracy as a mode of political economy, enhanced by the use of offshore finance; the spectacular framing of public life as national and uniform, sometimes supported by the "cultural diplomacy" of foreign embassies; the supplanting of the Soviet-era welfare state with a post-Soviet triumph of neoliberalism, often encouraged by international institutions; the closure of space for civil society and political opposition both at home and, with international assistance, abroad. By such means, Central Asians have come to (or been made to) hate politics.

This antipolitics, in both its demand-side and supply-side forms, is itself a form of politics and in this context is entirely to be expected. The widely used moniker *politika* (Russian) is a more limited conception than the "politics" of the English language and the Western world and is often deployed with the meaning of raison d'état. *Politika*, as used in Central Asia, includes both the making of public policy and the (often hidden) elite competition over control of the polis, but not generally the struggle over ideas of the public good and between emergent social forces that is present in the more expansive definitions found in established democracies.

Uzbekistan's delisting of political science from university syllabi in 2015 and its retitling of the one remaining course on the subject to "The Theory and Practice of Building a Democratic Society in Uzbekistan" speak to this official denigration and closure of the political. The Tajik government, which has seen the most dramatic slide from "soft" to "hard" authoritarianism in recent years, routinely associates political opposition with civil war. Most important, neither policy itself nor elite competition for the right to make it has achieved much discernible public good for Central Asians in the years since independent states emerged in 1991. The basic achievement of order and the provision of a greater variety of consumer goods to an elite recomposed from the "uncivil society" of the Soviet era are hardly causes for fanfare.

In this chapter we embark on an exploration of political transformation from the starting point of the felt politics of citizens and consider the rationale for our question of political transformation, before going on to examine demand- and supply-side factors via the data of ratings agencies and the fieldwork of Central Asian Studies. Why do Central Asians hate politics? This is a valid contextual question there as it is in Western democracies. To portray Central Asia's general political stasis as rooted in a lack of demand for politics—as is often claimed by political elites who portray citizens as apathetic "sheep" in need of a shepherd and a rod—is to neglect spatial, economic, and discursive shifts in the supply-side of politics. Sources of antipolitics are both local and global, whereby failures of national and local governance are exacerbated by transnational processes (or "connectivities") that are sometimes portrayed as part of the solution. In such circumstances, it is not clear why Central Asians should bother with politics at all.

What Is Political Transformation in Central Asia?

To assess why the 1989/1991 moment of political change dissipated into a profound sense of disillusionment—that is, to ask why Central Asians hate politics—is to evaluate both the local and the global contexts of this change. The Soviet legacy, Central Asian factionalism, and the relative paucity of mass mobilization in the region during perestroika all matter. So too does the fact that the moment of independence occurred in the late twentieth century alongside the apparent triumph of neoliberalism and globalization. Indeed, so complete was this triumph in the 1990s that neoliberalism and globalization provided the terms of analysis as well as the categories of practice. During this decade, the transformation of the political sphere in the post-Soviet states was understood in terms of the transition from state socialism to a global and neoliberal market economy and democracy without regional specificities. These states were part of a so-called third wave of democratization. In Clause Offe and Pierre Adler's formulation, in the context of central and eastern Europe, this transition was threefold: from single-party authoritarianism to multiparty politics, from a planned economy to a free-market capitalism, and from a state-controlled social sphere to a civil society that was simultaneously free from political interference but acting to hold the rulers to account.

This threefold transition (which we shall consider below in order to assess the transformation) looks broad but is in fact narrow, as its practitioners assumed that the collective good being sought actually exists a priori. This is hardly the case in any country, as states and nations are continually being constructed. However, in Central Asia, where the modern republics emerged under the Soviet Union, a deeper and wider process of state transformation was palpable to those who paid attention to what was actually taking place in the political sphere. "Liberalization" was superseded by at least three other processes. First, Central Asia suffered conflict among elites, including armed conflict, over basic political order and was, in some places, thereby subject to processes of peace-building and conflict management. Second, the region saw state-building, the creation and construction of state sovereignty. Third, Central Asia was transformed by struggles of nationalism—battles over the identity of the human community governed by the state.

These processes are often explored exclusively within the borders of the region's states, but to neglect the global context introduced above is to occlude a great deal of the reality of politics in Central Asia. Across different scales of politics Central Asia is increasingly globalized and subject to neoliberal governance. What seems like "top-down" national governance of extractive industries is a blending of public adherence to a global and neoliberal discourse of transparency with the no less global or neoliberal private practices of kleptocracy. What appears as "bottom-up" social mobilization in the name of the state is better understood as what Madeleine Reeves calls the *ashar* state (denoting the practice of collective labor, known as *ashar*), where potential participants may be absent as labor migrants. Rather than a single national community, we see multiple diasporic populations, stretched by labor migration and wrought by interregional divisions, remaking their own nations in popular culture. Much of state formation extends beyond the state's territories to its offshore spaces, migrant diaspora, and exile communities. The relevant actors range from Chinese investment funds to international financial institutions, from Western public relations firms to Russian security agents. These are states forged in globalization.

The six processes introduced above—three pertaining to liberal transition (the achievement of the public good) and three to state formation (the institutionalization of the public itself)—will be assessed in terms of the wider setting of globalization. In each process, we look at both quantitative indices of performance and field-based studies of political transformation. We start with the neoliberal form that creates disenchantment with "the world order": the global ranking index. The Bertelsmann Transformation Index (BTI), with data from 2005–2017, is deployed critically as a practical and analytical tool of neoliberal globalization particularly with regards to its indices of stateness (1), political participation (2), democratic stability (4), and organization of the market and competition (7). Each index is a composite of several questions where experts judge the country case according to standard criteria, against global measures taken from international organizations, and according to their own knowledge of events in the country. This standardization of concepts, data, and methods—with the recruitment of an "expert" cadre (of whom this author is one) to oversee this process—is typical of global and neoliberal public policies. These data are thereby emic to the supply-side degradation of the political that is drawn to our attention in this chapter.

Rankings and ratings agencies have rapidly gained global preeminence as the standard-bearers for state building, development, democracy, and human rights, despite precious little progress on many of these indicators. However, as Central Asian government officials have become increasingly savvy and adept at navigating global power networks, so they have sought to manipulate the production of knowledge about them in international affairs. For example, Kazakhstan and Kyrgyzstan have, at various times, appeared in the middle ranges on neoliberal and global transition metrics despite their suffering from consolidated authoritarianism and political instability, respectively. The watched are watching the watchers and taking measures accordingly. Assessing political transformation is an unavoidably interpretative exercise where we must stand back from our data and consider the very conceptual, evidential, and normative bases of our claims about the region. Qualitative field studies undertaken by area specialists are used to explore and critique the neoliberal and global standards against which Central Asia's political transformation is measured.

Order/Conflict

Compared to all other regions of states that became independent as a result of twentieth-century decolonization, the five republics of Central Asia have seen relatively little warfare and political violence. In particular, the five republics are in contrast to their neighbor Afghanistan and the post-Soviet Caucasus, both of which have suffered significantly from armed conflict and terrorism. International armed conflict has been limited to a handful of border skirmishes, and since the civil war in Tajikistan in 1992–1997 political violence has been restricted to regional rebellions and bloody purges of

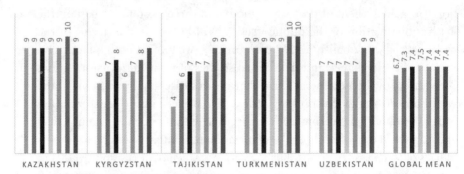

18-1   Monopoly on the Use of Force, 2005-2017.

former insiders, which have quickly been contained. Even terrorism (despite repeated and dire warnings of rising Islamic radicalization) has remained tiny in volume compared to that in other regions—and overwhelmingly external. According to the University of Maryland's Global Terrorism Database (GTD), ninety-two persons died in fifty-seven confirmed or "unambiguous" incidents of terrorism in Central Asia in the period 2001–2016. This corresponds to less than 0.07 percent of recorded incidents in a region with around 1 percent of the world's population. The apparent increase in the number of terrorist acts committed outside the region by Central Asian, particularly Uzbek, migrants in the period since 2014 is not clearly related to conditions within the region. The BTI metric on the monopoly of legitimate violence in its biennial survey (see figure 18-1) lags behind the data we have regarding the relative lack of war, terrorism, and crisis in Central Asia. However, by 2015, all five republics exceeded the global mean. There was significant and consistent improvement for Tajikistan but an inconsistent performance from Kyrgyzstan because of the outbreak of ethnic violence in the south in June 2010, which led to around five hundred deaths and a significant flow of refugees.

Although monopoly on the use force is considered a good, Central Asians experience the dark side of this concentration of coercive power. Field studies have shown how direct violence in Central Asia is more likely to be perpetrated by the state than by rebel groups or terrorists. Much of the violence in the Tajik civil war was undertaken by militias aligned to the state. The peace-building process that followed was characterized by the replacement of widespread physical violence with widespread structural violence, softened by international aid but perhaps encouraged by international disregard. In Andijan (2005), the Uzbek state response to disorder appears to have killed many more than the disorder itself. In southern Kyrgyzstan (2010), much of the violence was committed by gangs of Kyrgyz youths, but they gained assistance from many police and officials. In the eastern Tajikistani regions of Rasht and Gorno-Badakhshan, violence over the period 2008–2015 was prompted by turf wars within the state rather than a rebellion against the state. A key task of Central Asian governments is to occlude the social reality of violence, where the state is often the perpetrator, via the political representation of violence, where the state is the defender. State security discourses routinely legitimize everyday violence against political opponents and unsanctioned religious movements by branding them as "terrorists." These discourses become part of the reality of international security in that they legitimize a policy of counterterrorism through which they receive training and funding from foreign governments.

However, to say that the state has a monopoly on violence, legitimate and illegitimate, is not to say that this violence is directed by the central government. Jesse Driscoll has identified a bottom-up process whereby militias in Tajikistan in the 1990s became the state that emerged out of the civil war, rather than being controlled and co-opted by a preexisting leviathan. In southern Kyrgyzstan, neither Bishkek nor international agencies were in any position to end the violence, and it was the mayoralty of Osh under Melis Myrzakmatov that imposed an authoritarian and nationalist order of conflict management. However, it was interethnic ties between local elites—both state officials and non-state actors—that prevented violence from occurring in some areas and brought it to an end in others. Where violence did occur, there are numerous accounts of Kyrgyz sheltering their Uzbek neighbors and vice-versa.

In sum, violence is integral to both order and conflict in Central Asia. This violence is both physical, in the few cases where local and national regimes of power have broken down locally or nationally and had to be reconsolidated, and structural, where order enriches and empowers the regime of power over and above the general population. Armed conflict is relatively limited in Central Asia, but the use of direct and indirect violence to maintain order is not. There is surely little more disenchanting in political life than violence and the persistent threat of force.

Stateness

The monopoly of legitimate violence is constitutive of and consistent with a high degree of state sovereignty in Central Asia. No external great power, pan-Turkic regional confederation, Islamist insurgency, or irredentist movement has come close to questioning this sovereignty. Tajikistan, aid-dependent and subject to multiple foreign interventions, was labeled a Russian-Uzbek protectorate in the 1990s. However, even here, the trappings of sovereignty were gradually acquired following the peace treaty of 1997 and culminated in Tajikistan's government taking control of its southern border for the first time in 2005–2006. Kyrgyzstan suffered later crises of statehood with repeated political instability, increasing violence, and ethnic conflict during the first decade or so of this millennium but has not actually faced the "separatism" of which its dwindling Uzbek minority has often been accused by the titular Kyrgyz elite. Turkmenistan fetishized its sovereignty to the point of declaring an official doctrine of "permanent neutrality," refusing full membership for regional organizations and "leading to autarky and further political isolation." Uzbekistan's commitment to its ideology of

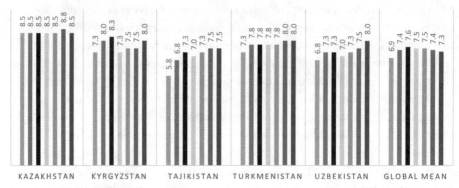

KAZAKHSTAN   KYRGYZSTAN   TAJIKISTAN   TURKMENISTAN   UZBEKISTAN   GLOBAL MEAN

18-2   Stateness, 2005–2017.

national independence under President Islam Karimov (1991–2016), made it averse to pooling sovereignty with Russia and its neighbors. Before Kazakhstan's (and later Kyrgyzstan's) negotiation of and accession to the Common Customs Union of the Eurasian Economic Union, no Central Asian state had pooled or compromised their international political and legal sovereignty—that is, their independence in international affairs and law.

It should therefore be of little surprise that all Central Asian states score highly on the overall stateness metric of the BTI (see figure 18-2), a composite that includes monopoly on the use of force, state identity, the lack of interference of religious dogma, and basic administrative capacity. By 2015, all five former Soviet republics had attained a level of stateness above the global mean, with significant improvements by Tajikistan and Uzbekistan reported over the period from 2005. Kazakhstan and Turkmenistan record consistently high levels of stateness (8.75 and 8 respectively in 2015). And Central Asia as a whole is assessed as consistent with its post-Soviet region. The region is well above the mean recorded by BTI and far in excess of many postcolonial states in Africa, the Middle East, and Asia, despite the fact that these attained independence decades before the former Soviet republics.

Qualitative field studies agree that Central Asian stateness is pervasive and durable in and even beyond the region. Two generations of edited collections have demonstrated the evident strengths found in apparent weaknesses. Although there is variation here, there is also a general strength across all the states, evident from the standpoint of almost all disciplines of the humanities and social sciences. Critics in the field of international relations demure that their foreign policies are, at most, reactive to geopolitical shifts and therefore determined by great power politics. Domestic law may be produced via the substantive emulation of Russia or the formal mimicry of Western models, which were implanted via donor-funded projects in the halcyon days of transition in the 1990s and early 2000s. Central Asian states may be formally independent, but in practice they follow the lead of their Russian security backers or, increasingly, their Chinese creditors. A clutch of regional powers also seek to insert themselves into this non-hegemonic environment. Even Turkmenistan's "neutral" foreign policy has shifted from dependence on exports of gas to Russia to dependence on exports to China. However, it has become increasingly clear that Central Asian states serve as gatekeepers to outside investors and foreign allies, accruing regime power accordingly. The geopolitical, far from making Central Asian states pawns in a "great game," has enabled their acquisition of sovereignty. These states are even manifest in extraterritorial spaces. The articulation of sovereignty through offshore financial vehicles and transnational mechanisms of security governance—especially via the Commonwealth of Independent States (CIS)—has enabled regime enrichment and the control of external opponents and thereby exacerbated disdain for the political.

Nationhood

The Soviet nationalities policy of creating republics of titular ethnic groups with institutionalized minority roles and spaces continues to affect nationalism today. These are nationalizing independent states of a familiar kind via "a process of reappropriation" whereby the Soviet national form has triumphed over its socialist content. But this legacy has been inconsistent. On the one hand, post-Soviet nationalism, though often framed as the invocation of a glorious pre-Soviet past, is heavily reliant on the categories and tropes of the communist period—a lexicon of which post-Soviet elites have taken ownership. It is via a very Soviet model of Tajikness, for example, that the Rahmon government seeks to reclaim the Tajikness of the past. On the other hand, ruptures from the past are visible in the out-migration of ethnic minorities (especially Russians), the retreat from public life by some who remain (such as ethnic Uzbeks in Kyrgyzstan and Tajikistan), and the decline and reversal of a Soviet-era multinational discourse (of "common home") and institutions (e.g., state education in minority languages). The Soviet autonomous regions of Karakalpakstan (Uzbekistan) and Gorno-Badakhshan (Tajikistan) have struggled, given the absence of direct funding from Moscow that was provided to counteract their geographical remoteness. This said, these autonomies have not been formally ended, and most important, borders have not been redrawn either formally or informally as they have in the frozen conflicts that beset the Caucasus, Moldova, and now Ukraine. "State identity," which BTI uses to denote the inclusive or exclusive character of nationalism, is assessed to be around the global mean for all Central Asian states in the period 2005–2015.

However, these general data risk obscuring the political production of nationalism in post-Soviet Central Asia and this nationalism's intrusion into everyday life since the 1990s. For example, Amanda Wooden has deployed the concept of "naturalistic nationalism" to explain Kyrgyzstan's elite's symbolic and practical use of hydropower and water resources in competition with the elites of neighboring states across shared riparian zones. Nick Megoran similarly offers arguments grounded in politics to explain how nationalism and factionalist struggles over the nation generated conflict, violence, and numerous human fatalities in the Ferghana Valley borderlands in the years after the Uzbek government chose to close and militarize its borders in 1999. Megoran notes: "'Border disputes,' formed vehicles for rival political factions to frame their geopolitical visions of Central Asia, and to assert control over national space through a variety of textual, cartographic, security, and governmental strategies." Nationalism of this ethnic and exclusive kind is often assumed by Western liberals—particularly Europeans, who have their own violent history in the backs of their minds—to lead inexorably to more widespread armed conflict. That this has not happened, despite the rise of ethnonationalism, is less puzzling when one recognizes that Central Asia's political transformation has been driven more by the logic of national authoritarian consolidation, empowering and enriching a regime of power, than national expansion or international rivalry.

Democracy/Autocracy

Since a brief period of post-Soviet optimism on the part of outside observers who viewed the region through the prism of transition, it has become banal to observe that authoritarian retrenchment has taken hold in Central Asia. In BTI question 4 (figure 18-3), all Central Asian states, with the stark exception of Kyrgyzstan, are assessed as falling far below the global mean for the stability of democratic institutions. Even in Bishkek, a period of authoritarian control took place from 2005 to 2010 under the presidency of Kurmanbek Bakiev. All states in the region are patronal presidential regimes; an autonomous parliament and, to a lesser extent, independent courts exist only in Kyrgyzstan. This consolidation of autocracy has economic and cultural explanations. In economic terms, centralized control of resources is key to the establishment and maintenance of an authoritarian regime where contestation over "lootable resources" (licit commodities and illicit goods) make certain states, provinces of states, and cross-border regions more unstable. A "coordination game" over the centralized control of resources ensues with uncertain outcomes and the attendant risks of elite defection that strategies of repression seek to deter. In cultural terms, the almost complete absence of a liberal tradition and the presence of a male-dominated social order have nurtured patriarchy in politics, although spaces of female authority are visible at the margins. Symbolic politics and the spectacular form are stage-managed in a resolutely hierarchical and masculinist fashion. Morgan Liu argues controversially, with reference to the concept of *tarbiya* (paternal discipline), that this cultural context is a fundamental obstacle to democracy.

Some Central Asian states have relatively consistent patronal politics. Kazakhstan, Uzbekistan, and Turkmenistan have remained solidly authoritarian since independence—with the latter two remaining extraordinarily stable despite managing presidential transition following the deaths of their first leaders, Islam Karimov (in 2015, succeeded by Shavkat Mirziyoyev) and Saparmurat Niyazov (in 2006, succeeded by Gurbanguly Berdimuhamedow) respectively. We know very little about how such transfers occur despite the

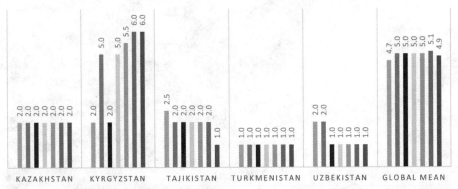

18-3   Stability of Democratic Institutions, 2005-2017.

lack of adherence to formal constitutional processes of succession; in both cases it seems that informal and secret bartering between elites was successful at creating uniformity around a single candidate in a manner that evokes the late Soviet transitions to Brezhnev and his successors. We know a little more about the legitimation to the formation and resilience of authoritarian systems. Although a nebulous concept, beset by endogeneity problems, legitimacy is visible in the political life of Central Asian autocracies. Nursultan Nazarbayev of Kazakhstan served as head of state into his eighties and was almost universally hailed as the master of the country's politics. In such regimes, elections are spectacles and facades. They perform a semblance of democracy to a foreign audience (see figure 18-4) and provide demonstrate-effects of total control for a domestic audience of citizens and, most important, potential rivals. The curse of hydrocarbons, particularly in Kazakhstan and Turkmenistan, has apparently strengthened authoritarian rule, even in Nur-Sultan where privatization and foreign investment required leaders to relinquish some control.

Kyrgyzstan and Tajikistan both depart somewhat from this norm. In Kyrgyzstan, democracy has been accompanied with a level of political instability (see figure 18-5), which makes it the pariah of this authoritarian region: persistent protests since the Soviet era, two "revolutions" that removed presidents in 2005 and 2010, and two constitutions (1993 and 2010), which have been amended on five separate occasions (1996, 2003, 2006, 2007, 2017). Kyrgyzstan has had five presidents and is the only Central Asian republic to have been headed by a woman—albeit the unelected Rosa Otunbaeva who served as interim president (2010–2011). In October 2017, Sooronbay Jeenbekov succeeded Almazbek Atambaev as president with 53 percent of the vote in a competitive election marred by irregularities. The election was a landmark in Central Asian history as the first democratic transfer of power from one elected president to another. In October 2020, however, Jeenbekov was forced from power following disputed elections and anti-corruption protests. The convicted criminal Sadyr Japarov was subsequently elected president in January 2021. Scott Radnitz has explained this competitiveness and instability in terms of "subversive clientelism," whereby clients are able to break away from the

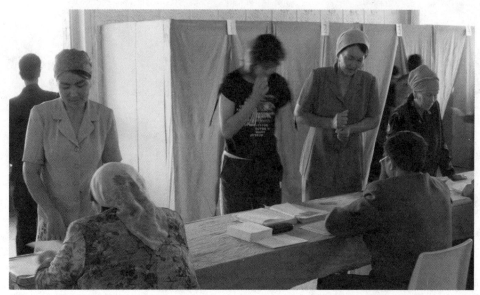

18-4   Ballot stations for the legislative elections in Kyzylorda, Kazakhstan, 2004. Photography by David W. Montgomery.

regime in power and establish new patronal pyramids. The precondition of this instability was the openness of the Kyrgyz economy and the relative lack of "lootable resources," whereby it was possible for a rival to become relatively wealthy and remain independent of the regime. This popular demand for politics makes Kyrgyzstan the exceptional state of Central Asia.

The Market

Central Asia's postulated transformation toward market capitalism shows a similarly sketchy record. All of these states may be considered "investment markets" whereby an employment post in the system—such as a tax inspector or border guard—affords rent-seeking opportunities and is therefore purchased via both patronage and loyalty. But the states' record on creating the conditions for private investment are much weaker (see figure 18-6). Tajikistan, Turkmenistan, and Uzbekistan remain far below the global mean; Kyrgyzstan and Kazakhstan, meanwhile, have exceeded it. This is not to say that the former states are wholly detached from the global market and the latter two states are connected. Rather, it is the terms of their connection that are at stake. In Tajikistan, Turkmenistan, and Uzbekistan, only actors who have formal sovereign power or who are formally tied to the ruling clique are able to shift capital around, be the recipients of foreign direct investment, and set up new and successful businesses. In Kyrgyzstan and Kazakhstan, in contrast, it remains possible for those outside the small circle of the ruling elite to do these things, and therefore the market is somewhat competitive. It appears to be early choices to liberalize that, although generating severe hardships and inequalities, have created these two more open economies.

There are several caveats that must be placed on this Kazakh-Kyrgyz

18-5   Protestors following the parliamentary election, Bishkek, Kyrgyzstan, 2005. Photograph by David W. Montgomery.

story of the emergence of partially open market capitalism, particularly from the perspective of political-economic transformation. First, when businesses reach a certain level, informal incorporation within the patronal system is necessary, as much in Kyrgyzstan and Kazakhstan as in the other states. Even in the dynamic environment of the bazaar, order is generated by informal institutions and authority figures who are, in turn, linked to senior patrons. Second, capital flight appears to be a factor in most states, not just Kazakhstan and Kyrgyzstan. Figures are hard to come by, but one NGO estimates that Kazakhstan's total unaccounted capital flows from 1991–2011 are over 109 billion US dollars, and even a "laggard reformer" such as Tajikistan in 2011 experienced an estimated capital flight of over 60 percent of its GDP, according to the IMF. Third, and consequent to the above, all these states are to some degree globalized, particularly in terms of their vulnerability to instability in the global financial system. There is mounting evidence that sovereign elites from all five republics have access to offshore accounts and launder their monies and reputations overseas. Turkmenistan keeps offshore presidential slush funds just as much as Tajikistan creates "state-owned" shell companies for parking the profits of its industry in the British Virgin Islands.

Therefore, despite Kyrgyzstan's and Kazakhstan's above-average global reputations for open markets, neither they nor their more closed neighbors have substantively achieved anything close to the idealized market economy imagined in the policy frameworks of the international financial institutions. Central Asian polities are "crony capitalist states" or (less charitably, but perhaps more accurately) kleptocracies—that is, regimes of rule by thieves. These political economies require secrecy with regard to their thefts and publicity with regard to their national brands. This is why the laundering of monies and reputations go hand in hand. It is why the former first daughter of Uzbekistan,

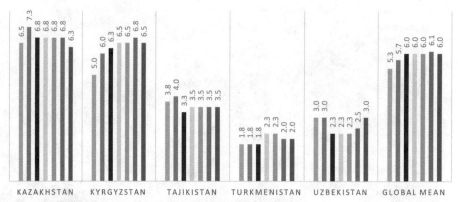

■ 2005 ■ 2007 ■ 2009 ■ 2011 ■ 2013 ■ 2015 ■ 2017

KAZAKHSTAN   KYRGYZSTAN   TAJIKISTAN   TURKMENISTAN   UZBEKISTAN   GLOBAL MEAN

18-6   Organizations of the Market and Competition, 2005–2017.

Gulnara Karimova, was busy promoting her charitable foundation overseas at the same time as receiving payments from the Swedish-Finnish company Teliasonera. It is also the reason that by far the largest foreign investor to Kazakhstan is recorded as the Netherlands—which works as an offshore jurisdiction by virtue of allowing anonymous company registration and low corporate tax rates—and the Nur-Sultan government is increasingly active in promoting its brand overseas. The fact that there are political-economic variations within and between states should not blind us to the bigger picture of consistency: the emergence since 1991 of lesser and greater kleptocracies facilitated by financial globalization and the region's adoption of neoliberal practices. These states exercise control rather than being exercised by politics.

Civil Society

The final feature of the political transformation of Central Asia to be considered here is the question of the emergence of civil society, as understood in liberal terms as institutions occupying the space between family and the state that hold government to account. "Political participation," which includes measures of the activity of civil society and political opposition, serves as a reasonable proxy for the health of civil society (figure 18-7). Unsurprisingly, and in parallel with findings on democracy, Kyrgyzstan is the single outlier. The four other Central Asian states all feature far below the global mean. At the same time, Kyrgyzstan's uneven trajectory reflects the authoritarian moves of the late Askar Akaev and Bakiev periods prior to the revolutions of 2005 and 2010, respectively. The roles of political opposition and, to a lesser degree, civil society in both these uprisings in Kyrgyzstan suggest a relationship between an autonomous civil society and political instability, as feared in the worries of post-Soviet elites about the "colored revolutions." Moreover, we must also recognize that civil society organizations in Kyrgyzstan, far from being guaranteed by government, have been intermittently threatened by new laws requiring re-registration and that place limits on their activities.

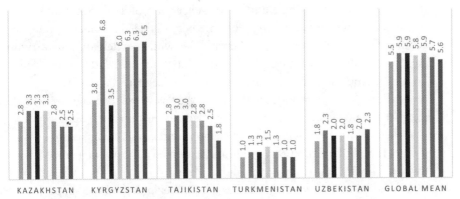

These problems are, however, much more serious in the rest of the region, where civil society has been vigorously repressed. Independent organizations and networks are rare and increasingly under pressure. In their place a state-sanctioned type of Government-Organized Nongovernmental Organizations (GONGOs) has been deployed across the region, most notably in Uzbekistan. In Tajikistan, increased pressure on the media and NGOs through inspections by the security services and the revision of the NGO law in 2015 to target organizations in receipt of international funding have had a chilling effect. International donors who had been behind the dramatic increase in the number of NGOs across Central Asia adapted to this pushback from regimes and criticism within the region by shifting toward, in the words of a policy report, "collaboration and engagement with traditional practices and institutions." Yet this nod to "tradition" is effectively an acknowledgment that "civil society," in the NGO form constructed by neoliberal donors in the 1990s and early 2000s, has been eviscerated from the political sphere. Although "geological layers" of civil society are still found in areas of gender, ecology, and anticapitalism inter alia, political parties, pressure groups, and other politically active civil society organizations have gradually been wound down, deregistered, and/or relocated to either continue their work from a position of exile, or they simply cease to exist.

Politics in Central Asia

Central Asia has undergone a political transformation to independent states while maintaining the political units (the republics) and many of the actor groups (the elites) of the Soviet period. According to neoliberal standards as evaluated in the BTI, Central Asian states score high on stateness, order, and nationhood but score low on democracy, civil society, and the market. In other words, they are high on the supply side of political order and low on the demand for political participation. Almost all Central Asian states (with the single and partial exception of Kyrgyzstan, about whose politics we know the most) remain authoritarian states by any reasonable definition of what this means. With the single and partial exception of Turkmenistan (about whose politics we know so little), they are better labeled neoliberal and global authoritarians that dominate their polities while participating to varying degrees as fully sovereign members of the global political and business clubs. To understand the political transformation of Central Asia today, we must probe the region's emerging global elites as they use their sovereign credentials to govern at home and make friends (and sometimes enemies) abroad.

The region's story, while having its own contextual flavors, is not unique. It is not that the construction of state and nation on a (post-)Soviet model have thwarted liberal transition of the global standard but that the integration of their polities into the global system has allowed regimes grounded in particular families or factions to aggrandize their power over their competitors. Local factional struggles explain some of the dynamics but are insufficient to explain how these Central Asian actors have been able to pursue the very global spoils of power: to park and hide their rents offshore, establish bolt-holes in world cities from Geneva to Los Angeles, track down rivals overseas through INTERPOL, and gain legitimacy for their campaigns against opponents in terms of the pervasive international discourse of counterterrorism. In each of these areas, it is globalization and its neoliberal discourse and practices that have both enabled the entrenchment of authoritarian regimes and provided limited space for the exposure of and resistance to these international activities.

To return to our opening question, the balance of evidence suggests that Central Asians hate politics largely because of supply-side factors that have both local and global aspects—that is, they hate politics because of structural violence, suffocating stateness, exclusive nationalism, consolidated autocracy, gated markets, and managed "civil society" that has its own forms and intensities in Central Asia, but which are by no means unique. Their lack of political opportunity and the precarious livelihoods and migration regimes to which they are subject are in stark contrast to the opportunism of elite families and their cronies who occupy a world of excess consumption and international mobility. The political transformation of Central Asia has entailed the embrace of some aspects of neoliberalism and globalization that benefit this small elite, often facilitated by external actors, alongside a rejection of the wider adoption of democracy, the market, and a liberal society. This combination of the concentration of political power in the hands of a few and their deployment of this power across multiple scales at home and abroad is a defining feature of Central Asia's transition. It is a transition from a world with clear ideological and geopolitical distinctions between East and West to a managed neoliberal globalization where these distinctions have broken down in various ways and without a clear sense of what, if anything, will replace them. As Central Asian disenchantment with politics has both local and global contexts, so too must the recovery of the political in the region be both an "indigenous" and an international praxis. Both norms of paternalism and technologies of neoliberalism must be resisted for Central Asians to become reenchanted by politics.

19

Law

Judith Beyer

My starting point is a stringent critique of the state of legal reforms in Central Asia by Akbar Rasulov, an Uzbek legal scholar at the University of Glasgow. In his article, which appeared in the journal *Law and Critique* in 2014, he gets even with the legacy of twenty-five years of "controlled transition." As a Central Asian scholar with a Western law degree, Rasulov is part of a new generation of academic experts from Central Asia who have attentively observed the arrival and entrenchment of foreign specialists in Central Asia after the breakdown of the Soviet Union. These specialists were to provide economic, political, and legal expertise in their efforts to guide the countries' transformation toward market reform, democracy, and rule of law. "Who were all these experts? Where did they all get their ideas about Central Asia?" he asks.

Rasulov splits the historical—and in his eyes, ultimately failed—encounter between Central Asian governments and Western policy reform entrepreneurs into three stages. The first stage, "The Age of Enthusiasm," lasted until the mid 1990s and was characterized by "the spirit of unbridled hopefulness, mutual trust, and can-do optimism." The second stage, "The Age of Skepticism," was already characterized by "a rapid increase in the general level of scepticism" and "a steadily growing exasperation on the part of the respective international institutions and their Western donors." The third stage, "The Age of Resentment," is framed by "thinly disguised mutual antipathy" between local politicians and Western reform agents.

Although critique of the opportunistic and oftentimes naive assumptions and efforts of outside experts has been voiced repeatedly, including by some of the involved foreign experts themselves, Rasulov's contribution is particularly important since the voices of Central Asian (legal) specialists have been strikingly absent from the whole debate about the effects and outcomes of the "transition" in the new post-Soviet states. Drawing on ideas of the legal philosopher Duncan Kennedy, Rasulov argues that post-Soviet legal reform initiatives should be understood as part of a more general globalization of transnational modes of "legal consciousness," which has "flattened out all traditional differences that used to separate discrete national legal systems at the level of their operative organisation processes." Rasulov combines this critique with an ideological argument (for which he refers to the work of Marxist scholar Nicos Poulantzas) and claims that what "feeds" the diffusion of the contemporary legal consciousness is its essential imperialistic character. Kennedy holds that globalization has led to the erosion of national legal differences, whereas Poulantzas argues that in times of late stage capitalism, national sentiments have entered through the back door as law takes on an exploitive and increasingly ideological character.

Rasulov ties this finding to "the spread of the distinctly US American (as opposed to, say, German or English) model of the organisation of the market of legal services and public interest lawyership on the whole; the establishment of direct presence by US firms and NGOs in foreign legal systems as well as the subsumption of local partner firms and NGOs in US-dominated alliances; the transfer of previously US-based top-level partners into new foreign subsidiaries as well as the promotion of local staff to partnership on the strength of their previous experience in the US legal system (e.g. through graduate level education)." I will not engage with Rasulov's particular critique of the US influence here but, rather, contextualize his argument on "the globalisation of the contemporary legal consciousness" by putting it into a historical context and by adding an anthropological perspective. Rasulov has consulted a wide range of academic literature on the "transition" in post-Soviet states to frame his critique, but he understands the local context in Western legal terms and is stuck (perhaps by his own choosing) in that context. Moreover, anthropological contributions are strikingly absent from his analysis. It is here, in the wealth of ethnographic details and anthropological theorizing that we find the voices of ordinary people who complicate the picture of both the globalizing force of law and the dominance of one particular actor.

Legal Engineering

Legal engineering is an openly technocratic and subversive ideological approach to law. The technocratic aim is to help the country "catch up" to the global legal sphere and profession through legislative reform. Once enacted (so goes the assumption), law will have the capacity not only to make life better, similar to life imagined elsewhere—that is, the "West." Very often, the motivation is an economic one: intensifying foreign investment lies in the interest of Western countries and global institutions, and Central Asian governments are equally keen to reform their legal system in order to open

JUDITH BEYER

avenues of economic cooperation on the global market. Ideologically, legal engineering comes wrapped in the expectation of being able to initiate and guide wider social change in a national context not only different from one's own but imagined as lagging behind in terms of development. Foreign governments and international organization thus gain and retain influence, through legislative reform elsewhere. Law becomes a tool with which to steer the national affairs of other states and through which to forge an entry point into a foreign market and society.

Overall, legal engineering in Central Asia has been a successful endeavor, as it created law on the books that are up-to-date with international standards. Many Central Asian laws are comparable to laws in Western countries, precisely because they were adapted from other national contexts or came into being with the financial support and the technical advice of Western experts. But a principal openness toward Western law does not give the respective state a head start toward democracy, as is often implied. Examples of this can be seen throughout the region. Between 2002 and 2012, the German Federal Ministry of Economic Cooperation and Development donated twenty-one million Euro to support the development of a new administrative procedural code in Kazakhstan and Tajikistan, to reform the civil procedural code as well as administrative procedural law in Kyrgyzstan, and to support family law reform in Uzbekistan.

Turkmenistan's civil code came into being under the guidance of the German Development Agency (Gesellschaft für Internationale Zusammenarbeit, GIZ) and draws on the German civil code (Bürgerliches Gesetzbuch, BGB). By far the most authoritarian and secluded country in Central Asia, with a human rights record that is "disastrous" according to Human Rights Watch, Turkmenistan has a highly developed civil code modeled after a European nation-state. Turkmenistan also expressed particular interest in commercial law reform, and the collaboration helped to modernize the country's law to bring it in accordance with international conventions. The economic motivation behind legal reform becomes evident when, for example, the new rule of law initiative of GIZ is justified: "The programme's main objective is to support Turkmenistan in reform of the legal and judicial sectors. The programme thus seeks to help achieve greater legal certainty. Legal certainty encourages sustainable economic development and increases the willingness of national and international entrepreneurs to invest in the country. A further objective is to strengthen peoples' faith in the legal system and its institutions." The main purpose of legal certainty, it seems, is first of all to encourage economic cooperation, and strengthening citizens' faith in law is only a "further objective." On the one hand, foreign experts have argued that "the destruction of the local legal landscape [would] be one of the most difficult parts of the Soviet heritage, which released the independent states into a lawless space, despite the inauguration of national constitutions." "Overcoming the specific Soviet legal culture" was regarded as the precondition for the transformation of law. On the other hand, European experts strategically postulated a connection between Soviet law and the civil law tradition when arguing against their An-glo-American colleagues who sought to establish common law in the newly independent states. As a result, the manner in which law has been brought to Central Asia after the breakup of the Soviet Union and the overall change it was expected to generate were quite similar to how law entered Central Asia during tsarist and Soviet times—namely, as a technocratic instrument of governance and as an ideological tool.

Legal History

The imperial encounter with Central Asia from the eighteenth century on-ward was envisioned as revolutionary from the start. The tsarist empire intended a common judicial policy for a region that was not only vast but also very diverse in terms of its legal setup. Although some non-sedentary groups were not under effective state control until the nineteenth century, their sedentary neighbors in Bukhara, Khiva, and Khokand had formed elaborate khanates already in the early eighteenth century, which initially accommodated pastoralists as well, before subsequently bringing them un-der khanate control or forcing them to move further north.

At all stages annexations, allegiances, and the creation of vassal-states were mediated by law. Various plural legal orders existed side by side and were invoked according to the context and the people involved. The plurality and complexity of legal orders and how people navigated through and argued with them posed a great challenge to the Russian invaders, one that they never really mastered. Their approach toward Central Asian law had been initially to work through the co-optation of "traditional leaders" via indirect rule, but this eventually led to the corruption of these new "heads" and their increasing alienation from the local population. As a rule, the non-sedentary groups tended to rely on customary law, whereas sedentary groups more often ap-plied Islamic law (sharia). Historical research has also shown that, among the Kazakh in the Emirate of Bukhara, Islamic law was well-known. In general, customary and Islamic law were intertwined in many areas and could not be separated as easily as the Russians had imagined. The Kazakh also possessed written legal codes from the seventeenth century onward, but there were no written records available for the neighboring area, which is now Kyrgyzstan. In these cases, "customary law" first had to be written down and codified by colonial officers and ethnographers. Once codified, it could then be ranked lower than the newly introduced state laws and new legal institutions. In 1927 all customary law was officially abolished. But what the new authorities had gotten rid of was a legal product that they had largely created themselves. It bore little resemblance to the intricate legal realities on the ground.

Writing on British colonial politics in Southeast Asian Burma (today Myanmar), public servant John Furnivall reflected on the irony of colonial state making in the British empire: "Leviathan may be omnipresent and all powerful, but he does not, like your neighbor, live next door, or like your conscience, nearer still. That is the explanation of the paradox that Leviathan is least efficient where he is most effective; he cannot maintain law and order so well as a society that maintains order without law." Like colonial officers in the Russian empire, Furnivall greatly underestimated the force of customary law, particularly its capacity to guise itself in the form of "custom." Whereas the enforcement of state law is dependent on maintaining people at a distance, the force of customary law lies precisely in its capacity of being inextricable from everyday life. Just like people's adherence to sharia, customary law defies regulation and codification.

It is for this reason that people managed to retain a sense of legal autonomy even in times of "revolutionary legalism," which according to Gregory Massell became one out of three basic Soviet strategies of initiating social change in Central Asia. By severely restricting—and in 1927 finally abolishing—all traditional legal institutions and replacing them with a uniform court structure and new laws, the communists aimed at the transformation of the patriarchal family, in particular, that was considered to be the heart of backward tradition. The Soviets also had to strictly control religious activities and practices such as Islamic marriages (*nikah*), inheritance, and pious endowment (*waqf*) throughout Central Asia. Massell shows how targeting the family, and particularly women and youth, was an attempt to transform the entire "way of life" that was deemed incompatible with modern communist ideas. In general, the Soviets established equal rights for women as a way to overcome what they considered "backward" social and cultural practices such as arranged marriages or the payment of bride price. But forced emancipation led to an unintended consequence: "sudden and massive female mobilization tended to lead to widespread and intense alienation from the Soviet system and its works, accompanied by cleavages running along primarily sexual and ethnic lines." Botakoz Kassymbekova has shown how much the Soviet regime relied on individuals to realize their revolutionary politics: "These new communists were entitled to rule in their regions, often above and despite law as long as they pledged loyalty to the Party and implemented top-down agricultural and industrial campaigns. They could punish, civilize, and educate: they had relative liberty to experiment and implement their versions of socialist justice."

Just as in the contemporary legal reform initiatives of the thirty years since independence, so the legal reforms in the Soviet era were directed from outside Central Asia and led by experts who knew very little of the region, particularly people's everyday lives. The area of constitutional reforms is different, however, as constitutions are at the heart of the newly built nation-states. It has been through constitutional reform that the very states have come into being.

Constitutional Reforms

Central Asia came under effective control of the Soviet Union via constitutional reform initiated by Stalin in the mid-1930s when he declared the previous constitution of 1923 not suitable for the new stage of social development. The

Central Asian republics had until then still enjoyed a high degree of autonomy; but with judicial and administrative centralization on the way, Moscow aimed at more than just changing the legal landscape. The plan was to create a new "popular culture" of "new Soviet men and women." Karen Petrone analyses how constitutional referenda, constitutional holidays, and other events related to the new foundational document were designed to substitute for religious rituals, although in the end they tended to blend law and religion.

After independence in the 1990s, all republics began drafting national constitutions. Much of the literature emphasizes the "weaknesses" of the Central Asian states and their "failed" democracies, but it is important to note that in most cases power has been grabbed in accordance with the constitution. Kyrgyzstan's Tulip Revolution in 2005 and the coup d'état in 2010 are the exceptions. All republics designed constitutions that initially favored a strong presidential system. At the later stages, amendments were made and new versions put in practice via nationwide referenda that allowed for parliamentary systems or better checks and balances among the powers. Although the instruments used to bring these reforms into being were democratic (public discussion in the media, nationwide referenda, or elections), manipulation at all stages of this process was imminent.

By now, Kyrgyzstan has a history of constitutional amendments, most of them directly linked to political upheaval. I have written elsewhere that amending the country's constitution via a nationwide referendum has been the standard way to react by new governmental powers after both the Tulip Revolution in 2005 and the overthrow of the Bakiev regime in 2010. Thus, constitutional referenda in Kyrgyzstan should be understood as a faith-based mode of conflict resolution that aims at bringing citizens together in community after violence and upheaval. In addition, the constitution had been amended already in 2003 under the first president (Askar Akaev) after a case of a serious breach in human rights occurred. Changing the constitution and putting it out for a referendum has been a way to eradicate the old nomenclatura—the former version of the text became associated with the former power (in the cases of 2005 and 2010). Also, constitutional reforms have become a way to make up for significant failures of the current power. Internationally, Kyrgyzstan soon developed the notorious reputation of a country that does not honor its own foundational document.

In 2010 the interim president, Roza Otunbaeva, released a decree (*ukaz*) titled "Concerning the Implementation of the Constitution" in which article 4 formulates a moratorium on further constitutional referenda (as now regulated in article 114 of the constitution) until September 1, 2020. Despite this precautious decree, the subsequent president of Kyrgyzstan, Almazbek Atambaev, began to concentrate on constitutional reforms in light of the upcoming presidential elections in October 2017 when former prime minister, Sooronbay Jeenbekov, was elected president. In September 2016, parliament approved his initiative to put constitutional amendments to a nationwide referendum scheduled in December 2016. This move was fueling speculation at the time that Kyrgyzstan was following the path of Uzbekistan, where the constitution was amended in 2014 in order to transfer presidential powers to the position of the prime minister, so that former president Islam Karimov could regulate his own succession. The parallels were obvious, especially given Jeenbekov being elected. In 2021, however, the country again voted in a referendum for the adoption of a new constitution that reestablished a presidential system of governance. Since the new president of Kyrgyzstan, Sadyr Japarov, came to power in what can only be labeled another coup d'état, he began to set up more authoritarian measures. As his predecessors, he justified these by drawing on the rhetoric of "custom and 'tradition." In Kazakhstan and Turkmenistan, constitutional referenda gave the current presidents their office for life.

Throughout Central Asia, constitutional referenda usually have very high turnouts that are above the 90 percent scale. From an outsider's perspective, however, Central Asian constitutional reforms have become almost indifferentiable. When on September 14, 2016, Turkmenistan adopted a new constitution, the daily Russian newspaper *Moskovskii Komsomolets* reported instead that Tajikistan had rewritten its constitution.

Law of the Rulers

From a social science perspective, what is of interest (often more than the actual law itself) are the discursive practices that actors employ to disseminate law or use it as a means of circumvention. Pushing for social and cultural change, for economic performance, and for political control continues to be the prime interest of many Central Asian lawmakers nowadays, which is, according to Massell, the definition of "revolutionary legalism." Immanuel Wallerstein has reminded us that, originally, the etymological sense of revolution referred to a circular movement back to its point of origin rather than to unilineal progress. And, so Wallerstein writes, "as we know, again in the Marxist tradition (but not only), the alternative to 'revolution' is 'reform.'"

In post-independence Central Asia, however, neither legal revolutionism nor legal reform holds the key to real reforms. On an international scale, according to Rasulov, "the formal act of treaty ratification is treated as a de facto stand-in for the actual reforms themselves." Nationally, new state laws continue to be passed shortsightedly and always in connection with major political events and shifts in power. Tajikistan's 1994 Law on Religion, for example, was drafted during the civil war as a measure of control of oppositional forces. When in the late 1990s environmental activists in Turkmenistan became too active for the government to tolerate, the introduction of the Law on Public Associations in 2004 "resulted in the virtual destruction of civil society."

There are also examples where activists managed to hold their governments accountable when their national legal initiatives contravened the international treaties they had signed. NGO activists brought Kazakhstan before the Compliance Committee for noncompliance on the Aarhus Convention on "Access to Information, Public Participation in Decision Making and Access to Justice in Environmental Matters," which Kazakhstan ratified in 2000. Nonetheless, Erika Weinthal and Kate Watters speak of "dependent activism" as the legal strategies and the actual planning of such actions are often directed from outside as well. In fact, it had been the transnationalization of environmental activism itself that severed the ties that had been established between local NGOs and the titular elites during the late Soviet Union when the two groups bonded to enforce a nationalist agenda vis-à-vis Moscow.

Finally, the law of the rulers is nowhere more visible than in the continuing practice of all Central Asian presidents to issue decrees. Through these, they can circumvent parliamentarian intervention. And through these, they display more authoritarian tendencies.

I have so far argued that law has been wielded predominantly as an instrument of governance and as an ideological tool, bearing resemblance to tsarist and Soviet times, but another similarity lies in the way the local population of Central Asia has engaged with law both then and now, as law often continues to be brought to them "from outside" and "from above." We will be able to understand the multiple and plural legal landscapes that are so characteristic of Central Asia better not only if we investigate the contemporary situation in light of historical events but also if we keep sight of people's capacity to turn instruments of power into weapons of the weak or to defy the very instrumentalization of their everyday lives through law in the first place.

Customizations of Law—Then and Now

"In the year 1933 a shepherd on a mountaintop in southern Tajikistan spotted in the dust what appeared to be the lid of a pot. It covered the mouth of a large pottery vessel that had been buried one and a half millenniums earlier by the ruler of Panjikent, named Dewashtich, who was fleeing before the approaching Arab cavalry. The pot on Mount Mug contained not gold and silver but scores of official records written on parchment. Carefully sealed with waxes and resins, it had preserved its contents down to that day in 1933." Through this accidental discovery, we have come to know about Central Asians' laws on dispute regulation way before the Arab conquest in the early eighth century. S. Frederick Starr argues that once the Arab conquerors arrived, it was in the area of law that they "had no choice but to adopt many Central Asian approaches, especially in such critical areas as irrigation, for which neither the Quran nor the Arabs' nomadic experience offered guidance." The local population apparently also managed to retain their pre-Muslim (in this case Zoroastrian) principles in the areas of marriage and divorce. Although the Arabs ultimately succeeded in establishing Islamic law throughout the region (albeit to varying degrees), already in the fourteenth century we encounter an early creative reinterpretation of Arab supremacy by means of what I have called customization. When the famous traveler Ibn Batuta reached the city of Khorezm in contemporary Uzbekistan, he witnessed what he called a "praiseworthy custom":

> Each of the mu'azzins in their mosques goes round the houses of those persons neighbouring his mosque, giving them notice of the approaching hour of prayer. Any person who absents himself from the communal prayers is beaten by the imam [who leads the prayers] in the presence of the congregation, and in every mosque there is a whip hung up for this purpose. He is also fined five dinars, which go towards the expenses of upkeep of the mosque, or of supplying food to the poor and the destitute. *They say that this custom has been an uninterrupted tradition amongst them from ancient times.*

It is much more likely that the practice had its origin in the early times of the Arab conquest, but the locals reclassified it as "theirs," thereby denying that their customs had been forcibly changed.

I have investigated the phenomenon of customization in the context of rural Kyrgyzstan and identified it as a general way of ordering the world by gradually incorporating the results and effects of social change, subsuming them under the umbrella concept of "custom." In doing so, people not only articulate togetherness vis-à-vis outsiders but are able to present historic developments not as alien but as something they themselves make happen. They continued to cultivate this technique throughout tsarist and Soviet times as well: during the tsarist era, when the Russians began the restructuration at village levels by incorporating the traditional hereditary leaders (*biis*) into their new administrative and legal structure via elections, candidates began to manipulate the electoral process. The newly elected biis, on the other hand, began taxing villagers twice as much (usually in the form of cattle) as they were supposed to, in order to generate income for themselves. Adrienne Edgar describes for Turkmenistan how the council of elders was turned into a popular court (*narodnyi sud*) and the *aksakal* (now called *starshina*) responsible for collecting taxes. The historian Virginia Martin emphasizes that people became skeptical at first and then disillusioned with fellow villagers who took up positions within the Russian administrative system. In cases of dispute, the conflicting parties increasingly turned instead to those village elders whom the Russians had not incorporated into their system. When in 1993 the first president of Kyrgyzstan, AskarAkaev, invented the aksakal courts (*aksakaldar sotu*) and made the institution legally manifest by writing it into the country's constitution and later even gave them their own law, he argued that these courts had existed since ancient times. In neighboring Uzbekistan and Kazakhstan, similar developments took place. In Turkmenistan, a council of elders became established as a consultative body to the president.

All Central Asian governments thus tap into the repertoire of "custom" and "customary law" in order to lend their governance practices credibility. Elders, on the other hand, are inclined to participate in these events as this allows them to perform their authority publicly, thus giving them a chance to prove themselves worthy of being an aksakal. In this scenario, it is not useful to divide actors into those who rule and create law and norms to fit

19-1   Aksakals in Kyrgyzstan, 1999. Photograph by David W. Montgomery.

their political (and economic) motivations and those who follow or resist and subvert. Rather, all kinds of actors are engaged in the co-production of a plural legal landscape that is complex and inherently contradictory. Without a doubt, Russian colonialism had a tremendous impact on how Central Asians came to understand law. However, they learned how to navigate the new legal system and also used it strategically against Islamic institutions or customary legislation. Moreover, they were well equipped to petition rulings against them in colonial courts. Paolo Sartori has shown that the archives of the colonial polities are filled with appeals filed by locals.

From an emic perspective, it is important to emphasize that, if necessary, law can be rendered "ours" through a process of reinterpretation and adaptation in order to make it understandable, to "make it count" in a local context. The important thing to remember is that the local context, and how it is understood, has undergone tremendous changes as well. It is the category of "custom" itself that proves most flexible and allows people to order elements of cultural, social, legal, and economic change in a familiar idiom. Even among Kyrgyz labor migrants in Moscow, for example, a council of elders (*aksakaldar kenesh*) has been formed in recent years to deal with local disputes or to act as the migrants' representative body. Rather than looking at this institution as an "invented tradition," it is more fruitful to investigate the practical ways in which tradition is put to use, by whom, and for what ends. Often, the elites' projects of traditionalization and those of ordinary actors speak to and rely on each other.

To give another example from rural Kyrgyzstan: in 2014, Kyrgyzstan's Council of Defense, an institution headed by the former president Almazbek

19-2   A village mahalla committee in Tajikistan, 2008. Photograph by David W. Montgomery.

Atambaev, released a document entitled "Decision of the Council of Defense on the State Policy in the Religious Sphere." This document was later turned into a decree and thus attained the full force of law. The twenty articles take stock of the role played by religion in the country. The document starts out with referencing domestic "terrorist attacks," "inter-religious clashes," and the increasing threat of "Islamic fundamentalism." These "contradictions in the Muslim community lead to a loosening of the traditional Hanafi Sunni Islam," the authors state, and they conclude that, to prevent a further "weakening of traditional Islam," "it is proposed . . . to appoint only those imams and kazis who know and follow the Hanafi school which is customary [*salttuu*] for Kyrgyz Muslims, and to not allow the establishment of foreign behavior, dress, and appearance."

I heard about this new law through the local imam of the village in which I have been doing fieldwork since 2005. He said that Atambaev had written a "fatwa" according to which people should practice *salttuu shariat* (customary Islamic law). I had not encountered this neologism during the previous years of my fieldwork and learned from the imam that it implied the harmonization of custom (*salt*) with the sharia. What this meant in detail, however, was interpreted very differently by the imam, the village population, and politicians in the capital. People handle new laws according to their understanding. For the imam, a legal document was a fatwa. His intent lay in aligning custom with sharia. For other villagers, however, any law coming from the state was not "theirs" but, rather, "made in Bishkek." In order for a law to become valid for them, they needed to adapt and reinterpret it so that it fit their local circumstances. Without actual law enforcement agencies present in the countryside, rumors of law often continue to be much stronger than state law itself. There is, thus, another kind of "legal consciousness" that we encounter alongside the globalized legal norms that Rasulov detected and made responsible for flattening out traditional differences in legal systems. This other kind of "legal consciousness" creates difference as it renders non-customary law both understandable and locally practicable.

Bishkek, Not Bremen

In his take on legal reforms in Central Asia, Rasulov rightly criticizes foreign experts who state that Central Asia is "lagging behind" in terms of legal reform. This trend continues also in the current literature, even when authors are sympathetic toward the region. Although it may be correct that the judiciary and legal education systems are corrupt throughout the region, that there is a lack of local legal experts, and that judges are often dependent on the president's administration, it is interesting that scholars tend to emphasize these negative examples without mentioning how, especially in the legal profession, there have always been local experts who have risked their careers—and lost them—by speaking truth to power. The problem does not lie in a lack of skilled experts. In both rural and urban areas in Kyrgyzstan, I have met highly qualified and motivated lawyers who enjoyed and were proud of their profession and who went to considerable lengths for their clients. The judges were more distanced and more reluctant to talk to me, with the exception of elderly female judges who openly addressed the lack of true independence and the pressure they faced from politicians. Many lawyers and judges in addition to their regular jobs also teach at local universities. Others engage in legal reform initiatives. But many also have had to leave their countries as a direct result of their engagement.

Rasulov seems to regard himself as a member of the "progressive elites of the periphery" as described by Kennedy. But his periphery is no longer Central Asia; it is already Western. The United Kingdom is where he now lives and works and from where he has voiced his critique. Like him, many Central Asian scholars who have the capacity to thoroughly expose both the Soviet and the post-Soviet modes of legal engineering and to suggest alternative approaches have ended up in "Western peripheries" instead. In contrast to those in the United States and Europe, Central Asian legal experts are not sent abroad to strengthen ties with their own governments but to weaken their ties with the population and any oppositional forces. The capital of Kyrgyzstan is not Bremen—as was once jokingly stated in an interview with a German legal expert who pointed to the fact that for many years new laws came out of the GIZ office located at the local university in Germany. Although critique such as Rasulov's is both timely and important, it ultimately will need to come from the center of political power itself—that is, from the region.

20

Education

Martha C. Merrill

I n 2003 Burul graduated from the same regional university in Kyrgyzstan
where she now—fifteen years later—teaches English grammar and phonet-
ics to first-year students. She taught sixth- and seventh-grade students in a
school in her hometown before she was "invited" to come back to the university. When asked what changes had taken place since she was a student, she
answered that students now express their opinions more freely. When asked if
that was a good or a bad thing, she responded: "Bad in family; at class—good."

Burul's ambivalence about the changes in her society and university life
is not unusual. Thirty years after independence, Kyrgyzstan is still making
choices about its future, choices largely guided by people with different
educational experiences from the pedagogies they are called upon to use
in preparing students for the future. Kyrgyzstan, for example, is actively
implementing Bologna Process reforms, which were designed and agreed
to in Europe; this means bachelor's and master's degrees, with graduation
dependent on the completion of credit hours. In contrast, Burul graduated
with a five-year *diplom*, in a system based on contact hours. She would have
been in class for thirty-five hours a week or more, listening to a revered
teacher, whose opinions she learned to emulate. Exams were oral and meant
repeating what she had been taught. Now, she is expected to assign independent work to students and to give written tests, in which students express
their own opinions, although she never did such work herself as a student.

Like many of her colleagues, Burul was "invited" to her current position
by a former professor; the position was not announced publicly and no application process was involved. Although she is teaching in an environment
different from the one in which she was educated, her university has few

resources to assist her in learning new teaching techniques or even in understanding the goals of the reforms. Asked who helps her, she named external sources: a Peace Corps Volunteer on a two-year placement at her university, the mini-library of English-language and American studies materials set up by the US Embassy, and YouTube videos. Although new degrees and credit hours have been mandated, regional universities have few resources for faculty development, library materials, or updated computer labs.

The Context of Educational Reform

Kyrgyzstan is a small country, with six and a half million people, 17 percent of them between the ages of fifteen and twenty-four. It is a poor country, with a GDP per capita of thirty-seven hundred dollars and 32 percent of its population living beneath the poverty level. Russia, Kazakhstan, and Turkey—countries to which Kyrgyzstan is bound historically and economically—are members of the Bologna Process, so it makes sense for Kyrgyzstan to synchronize its higher education system with theirs. But how does a nation go about switching from a contact-hour system, progress toward a degree measured by the number of hours you are in contact with a professor, to a credit-hour system based on demonstrating certain learning outcomes or competencies? On what basis do professors get paid when they are in contact with students for fewer hours than before and students are doing independent work? How do professors learn to assign independent work that helps students learn and how do they assess such work? Infrequently, universities themselves offer training seminars for faculty; the Ministry of Education almost never designs material or workshops to help professors, particularly those at rural universities, to understand the new systems. Thus, instructors like Burul are forced to turn to young bachelor's-educated US (Peace Corps) volunteers and the Internet in order to figure out how to teach in this new educational environment. Or more modestly, as an instructor at another regional university told me, "We're not doing the Bologna Process. We're doing a rehearsal for the Bologna Process."

Kyrgyzstan is not alone in finding the implementation of educational reforms to be a challenge. As a senior faculty member in Dushanbe, Tajikistan, characterized the process: "We are lost somewhere between the Soviet systems and structures and the new system toward which we are aiming. We are living neither in a command nor in a market economy. At present, we are in the middle of nowhere and continue to remain in a prolonged transition."

The Bologna Process

When Burul was asked what she knew about the Bologna Process, she dutifully recited: "A European reform process. The aim is to improve education. About 45 countries participate in it. Kyrgyzstan is preparing to enter it. 1999 was the first meeting in Bologna. The countries meet and decide." She learned this from "The Internet, and other teachers." The process now has forty-nine members, and although any country can adopt Bologna Process reforms, only European countries can join—meaning Kazakhstan is the only Central Asian country that can join, because of "a small portion west of the Ural (Zhayyq) River in easternmost Europe."

So why would Kyrgyzstan—or Kazakhstan, for that matter—want to join what Burul rightly described as "a European reform process"? Elsewhere I offer twelve reasons that higher education in independent Kyrgyzstan is internationally connected:

> Kyrgyzstan cannot isolate itself from the demands, priorities, and pressures of international actors. . . . Three of these reasons are beyond Kyrgyzstan's control: its geographic location, its history and heritages, and the small size of its population. Six are factors over which it has limited control. These include the languages in which academic materials are produced; the fact that the country's poverty means that it often must accept donor-funded reforms (and thus donor priorities); the realities of labour migration and "brain circulation"; the existence of international rankings and the globalization of quality assessment standards; the fact that its membership in the WTO requires it to participate in the General Agreement on Trade in Services (GATS); and the rapid development of the "world-class university" movement. Three are factors which Kyrgyzstan could do something about if it wished to assert priorities different from those of international actors, or, alternatively, if it decided that greater integration with selected international systems was to its advantage. These three are degree structures, the level of Ministry of Education control over many aspects of higher education, and corruption.

Two of these factors—history and heritages and labor migration—link Kyrgyzstan to Russia, Kazakhstan, and Turkey, all of which are in the Bologna Process, as are seven other former Soviet countries: Armenia, Azerbaijan, Belarus, Estonia, Georgia, Latvia, and Lithuania. Soviet-era degrees—the diplom, *kandidat nauk*, and *doktor nauk*—are offered in fewer and fewer places. If Kyrgyzstan, given its small size and inability to offer every discipline at an advanced level, wishes to encourage both student and faculty mobility, it needs to offer degree structures that coordinate with those of its neighbors.

The Practical Problems of Educational Transitions

Changes in higher education structures affect not only professors but also students (figure 20-1). In Kyrgyzstan, as well as in Kazakhstan, Tajikistan, and Uzbekistan, national tests are used in higher education admissions. The highest-scoring students study free of charge in what are called "budget" places (funded from the state budget). Other students are admitted by signing contracts for places for which they pay tuition ("contract" students). A document reportedly produced in Russian some years ago claimed that, because contract students are paying for their education, they cannot be dismissed from their institutions and therefore cannot be failed. Although

20-1   University students following a class lecture in Osh, Kyrgyzstan, 2005. Photograph by David W. Montgomery.

no one has ever been able to produce a copy of this document, a number of professors in Kyrgyzstan have mentioned it and believe that they cannot fail students who have paid for their education. Again, given the lack of official materials and trainings, particularly in the Kyrgyz language, whatever can be found on the Internet becomes a quoted source, and apocryphal statements become understood as law.

The shift from Soviet-era degrees (diplom, kandidat nauk, and doktor nauk) to bachelor's and master's degrees, while facilitating international mobility, has created some unforeseen problems. This is common in educational policy transfer—the movement of educational policies from the place they originated to a new location that has different resources, conditions, and traditions. For example, the first degree in the Soviet era, the diplom, took five years to complete. The newly implemented bachelor's degree in Kyrgyzstan is four years in length (as it is in Russia, Kazakhstan, and Turkey), and most master's degrees are two. The length of time it takes to achieve the degrees raises several problems.

First, although in the United States a bachelor's degree usually takes four years of full-time study, in the United Kingdom and elsewhere in Europe, a three-year first degree is the norm. (Many Europeans have had what in the United States would be known as "general education" in secondary school and are admitted directly into their disciplines when they enter the university.) The Bologna Declaration wording, setting up what was originally a "two-tier" (bachelor's and master's) system among member states, said the first degree should last "a minimum of three years," not that three years was the norm. Since one of the goals of the Bologna Process was to facilitate labor mobility within the European Union, the first degree was designed specifically to prepare students for employment. This was in contrast to Germany and some other nations where the first degree at a university took six years to complete

MARTHA C. MERRILL

(those at universities of applied sciences usually took four and a half) and many students left without a degree. However, again, given the lack of official information in Kyrgyzstan, several professors told me and my colleagues, "We're not really doing the Bologna Process. I know, because I looked it up on the Internet, and in Europe, a Bachelor's degree is three years." The lack of official training and documents—or at least, lack of access to and knowledge of what does exist—undercuts confidence in the Ministry of Education and other authorities, as it seems to professors at universities outside the capital that those authorities do not understand the system they are implementing.

Second, although some disciplinary exceptions were permitted when the shift from diplom to bachelor's was made in 2012 (engineering programs, music conservatories, and a few others were allowed to retain longer degrees), all other programs had to squeeze what had been five years of instruction into four years, and to add independent work by students as well. Every professor in the natural sciences I have spoken to thinks that the Bologna Process leads to a weaker educational system than the Soviet-era structures. Some even believe that the Bologna Process is a Western plot to undermine the educational system of the former Soviet Union, in which math and sciences were strong. A chemistry professor interviewed in June 2018 stated, "I think that the Western countries wanted to destroy the strong Soviet system and brought the Bologna Process as a strategy." Such "discourses of nostalgia" can be found among professors in Kazakhstan as well.

It is not only in the sciences, however, that faculty struggle with how to put five years of content into a four-year degree. Interviews with faculty in political science, diplomacy, pedagogy, and languages in Bishkek in 2015 and 2016 showed faculty struggling with mandates from the Ministry of Education, new course titles, and revised numbers of hours of instruction. Interestingly, however, most of the faculty did not make distinctions between the changes in their professional lives and working conditions that were because of compliance with Bologna Process standards and those that originated locally, because of an order from the Ministry of Education or the decision of a rector. The options for contesting a change would be different depending upon its source, but to most faculty all the changes were simply "reforms" to be accepted and coped with.

One of the other shifts inherent in the Bologna Process is the idea of teaching toward the achievement of learning outcomes and designing courses and assignments around the achievement of those outcomes, rather than focusing on "instruction" and a teacher-centered model. Professors like Burul, whose own education consisted of a teacher-centered contact-hour ("seat time") model, have never had any instruction in how to design learning outcomes and teach toward achievement. Moreover, when a US Fulbright Fellow offered a week of training to faculty from regional universities on how to write learning outcomes and how to design course assignments, with a follow-up evaluation of the initial workshop at the end of the semester, she discovered that most of the participants were unable to implement what they had been taught. This was because the criteria used to evaluate their performance at their home universities was based on an instruction model, and a "learning outcomes" focus was not compatible with how others were teaching. Thus, what Askat Dukenbaev and I found was that:

> The primary problem with the EU's Strategy is that it is not a strategy, but a series of unrelated programmes that are not joined into a coherent framework for addressing the needs of the Central Asian nations, nor for achieving the EU's own objectives. . . . The projects implemented thus seem to have benefits for individual people and institutions, but do little to address the broader issues such as centrally controlled curricular and assessment standards, the need for new structures for continuous rather than ad hoc faculty development, the issue of faculty salaries, the problem of academic integrity and corruption, etc.

In addition to the lack of training in how to teach in the new models and the problems of squeezing five years of content into four years, a third problem with the implementation of the bachelor's and master's degree system is that, in Soviet times, anything less than the five-year diplom was legally classified as "incomplete higher education." Although in Kyrgyzstan the Ministry of Education regulations now say a four-year bachelor's is the first degree, many parents and employers consider it inadequate preparation for students' future professions. For example, Janara Baitugolova, then the head of the International-al Relations Office at Naryn State University, reported that when the changes in degrees were implemented, teachers and principals throughout the Naryn Oblast considered the bachelor's degree inadequate preparation for teachers.

Thus, not only was the new system implemented in Kyrgyzstan with little support for the faculty who would have to carry it out; it also was put into effect without any kind of a public relations campaign to convince employers, parents, and the general public of its validity. Similarly, the credit-hour provision of the reforms and the emphasis on student independent work, both of which result in less time in class, have been equated by some local commentators with *zaouchnaya rabota*, or external, part-time study, which, in Soviet times, was considered of lower quality than full-time attendance, as students had less time in contact with faculty. In fact, when the American University in Central Asia (figure 20-2) implemented a credit-hour system in 1999, parents complained bitterly about the lowering of quality, as credit hours meant fewer hours in class with faculty. Because the university raised tuition at the same time, one parent reportedly said, "That's just like you American capitalists! You cut the number of hours and raise prices at the same time!"

Since a four-year degree is considered invalid by many, students often continue for the master's degree. However, because many master's degrees are two years in length, students following this option are in school for six years rather than the previous five. As the notion of "contracts" has come into effect, most students are paying for six years of education and are staying out of the job market a year longer than before. A number of the faculty, speaking from

20-2   Relocated to a new campus in 2015, the old campus of the American University of Central Asia used the former buildings of the Central Committee of the Communist Party of the Kirghiz SSR, Bishkek, 2006. Photograph by David W. Montgomery.

the perspective of parents, complain about the additional expense. Moreover, as some families are becoming more religious and thinking more traditionally about gender roles, some parents are concerned about keeping daughters in school past the traditional marriageable age. One of Alan DeYoung's informants, "Sabrina," describes the situation in Khujand, Tajikistan:

> You see, in Soviet times, parents were not in a hurry for getting their girls married. They gave them the chance to study for four years or five years [to age twenty-two or twenty-three]. When they finished, then they could go and then get married. But, just little by little, the social level changed. . . . It now appears that if a girl does not get married before about twenty, then it means she is not a good girl. No families will come and want to marry their son to her. And that's why parents increasingly try to get their girl married [earlier]. And unfortunately, a lot of girls marry in order to get their [husbands on time].

Another problem concerns independent work by students. A teacher like Burul, who has only a five-year diplom, has not done research nor written a thesis, as would be required for a kandidat nauk. Although she undoubtedly wrote a *diplomnaya rabota* (diploma paper) for her degree, she likely was given a list of possible topics, and her sources probably were limited to those in the library of her regional university. She was not taught in a system that used learning outcomes and certainly was not taught how to create assignments to help students achieve learning outcomes or design their own research.

Moreover, since many professors note that they are paid for specific tasks (and assessing students' independent work often is not one of them), neither professors nor students take independent work very seriously. Also, as noted above, because the Soviet system was a contact-hour system and quality was associated with the amount of time one had "in contact" with an esteemed professor, in the minds of many parents and employers independent work still is connected with external work (zaouchnaya rabota)—the independent study done by adult workers on collective farms and in factories, those who could come to the university only periodically for instruction. To those parents and employers, independent work means not having access to professors and not having a quality education. Students—unless they attended elite or private secondary schools—have no prior experience with working independently. The combination of professors' lack of experience in assigning meaningful independent work, the fact that their assigned workload does not include assessing such work, and the fact that students both lack experience with independent assignments and have Internet-connected mobile phones means that plagiarized papers copied from the Internet are a common problem.

Other Nations, Other Choices

Other Central Asian nations have made other choices about education in the independence era—but "choices" are influenced by contexts and constraints. Kazakhstan has an ambitious agenda of university reform, including the Bolashak Program, a government-funded program to send Kazakhstanis abroad for education and training; the construction of twenty elite trilingual schools focusing on the sciences for gifted children; the creation of Nazarbayev University (figure 20-3), a "world-class" English-medium university in the capital, Nur-Sultan, with many foreign faculty and administrators and partners worldwide such as Cambridge University, the University of Wisconsin, and the University of Pennsylvania; a new independent, non-state-accreditation agency; and a process of devolving Soviet-era centralized Ministry of Education functions to universities. This program of educational reform and internationalization, however, is part of Kazakhstan's larger strategy of entering the ranks of the thirty most developed nations in the world by 2050, a goal that demands a population with a high level of education. The strategy itself is possible because Kazakhstan has wealth from oil and gas, which permits the funding of such ambitions and, as noted, territory in Europe, which allows it to join the Bologna Process and to benefit from the infrastructure, connections, and support of organizations and processes within Bologna. One such organization is the European Quality Assurance Register. Its member agencies can perform institutional and program evaluations outside their home countries. Such external evaluations help to validate the quality of Kazakhstan's higher education institutions.

Uzbekistan, while also basing educational reform decisions in part on instrumental criteria—the contribution of education to labor force needs—made

20-3   Nazarbayev University in Nur-Sultan, Kazakhstan, 2015. Photograph by Natalie Koch.

different decisions. The Uzbek president Shavkat Mirziyoyev has placed great emphasis on preschool education, citing it as being essential to a child's development, even creating a new Ministry of Preschool Education in 2017. Kobil Ruziev and Umar Burkhanov note that authorities in Uzbekistan until recently focused on developing specialized secondary education rather than higher education. Quoting their own earlier work: "The implicit argument behind the government's choice was that, given the relatively unsophisticated state of the national economy which relied largely on commodity production, services and small-scale manufacturing, the economy would be best served by the expansion and modernisation of the vocational education sector." Uzbekistan's development strategy for 2017–2021 also puts surprisingly little emphasis on higher education. It seems that the government has taken an "import" solution to dealing with Uzbekistan's need to expand higher education enrollments (only 15 percent of the relevant age group in 1991) and to deal with the "mismatch" between needed new skills and faculty preparation in the needed specialties. Although early on in the independence years the government of Uzbekistan funded a much smaller version of Kazakhstan's Bolashak Program, selecting and sending talented youth abroad to the United States, the United Kingdom, Germany, and Japan, the government later decided that inviting universities abroad to set up branch campuses in Tashkent was more cost effective and, likely, permitted the government more control over the students and curricula involved. By January 2020, twenty-one international branch campuses were operating in Uzbekistan. The majority of those institutions are Russian, but they also include five South Korean universities, two from India, and one each from the United Kingdom, the United States, Singapore, Latvia, and Italy.

Tajikistan and Turkmenistan are less open to influences from abroad and maintain tight central government control over education. The Ministry of Education in Tajikistan admits as much, and other stakeholders, as evident in the Open Society Institute report excerpted below, are apprehensive about the situation:

> *The National Strategy for Educational Development of Tajikistan* (Ministry of Education, 2005, 2012) acknowledges that "today the system of public management of education is a legacy of a highly centralized and planned system of the former Soviet Union and to a considerable extent remains unreformed. . . . The dominant position in education belongs to the Government and participation of non-governmental and private sector is minimal" (p. 11). International agencies are also concerned that the country has "a centralized" and "non-participatory governance structure" which is "one of the main obstacles to effective educational change" that "policy key stakeholders, including NGOs, teachers, parents and students are rarely involved, and they have only very limited influence on key decisions at the national level."

In addition, Tajikistan continues to suffer from the aftereffects of its 1992–1997 civil war, which destroyed much of the educational infrastructure. Funding issues (including low salaries for faculty) and tight government regulation (including control of the languages used in instruction) mean that a "mismatch" exists between what graduates are prepared to do and what the economy needs. The issues here are systemic. The lack of contemporary books, access to electronic scholarly material, and a continued reliance on material published during the Soviet era are among the factors contributing to the skills mismatch among the graduates. Employers stated that the shortage of academic literature was exacerbated by a law on language, which necessitates the use of Tajik as the medium of instruction. Those from engineering and health sectors claim that books in Tajik language do not exist in these fields; therefore, for teaching purposes, lecturers are forced to translate material from Russian textbooks into Tajik. Students thus are forced to rely largely upon lecture notes, which are based upon a translated interpretation by their lecturer, and with no formal process to ensure validity and accuracy of translation. To compound these challenges, less than 30 percent of faculty members working in Tajik universities have suitable terminal degrees to teach. And because of the paucity of funding for universities, many teachers must find additional work or other sources of income to get by.

The situation is no better in Turkmenistan where government control, in the form of one-person rule, has had even more deleterious effects. As I noted elsewhere, higher education was decimated under Turkmenistan's first president, Saparmurat Niyazov:

> Niyazov cut the number of years of elementary and secondary school from 10 to 9, thus ensuring that no locally educated students were prepared for higher

education outside of Turkmenistan. Given that students had to spend hours memorizing the *Ruhnama*, Niyazov's eccentric vision of the Turkmen past and Turkmen virtues, and that they were regularly taken out of school for weeks and even months at a time to help with the cotton harvest, less than 9 years formed the actual time spent on academic subjects. University studies were reduced from 5 to 2 years, followed by 2 years of practical work required before the degree was awarded. Recognition of degrees earned abroad was rescinded, meaning that holders of such degrees could not work in their fields in Turkmenistan. The Academy of Sciences and other research institutes, the sites of graduate education, were closed. Thus, the only people available to become university faculty had attained just 11 years of education, much of which was dogmatism.

Turkmenistan's second president, Gurbanguly Berdimuhamedow, has reversed some of the structural changes instituted by Niyazov, but government control remains absolute over higher education as well as over other sectors of society and the economy. Naz Nazar reported in RFE/RL that Turkmen students studying in Turkey, and likely those studying in other countries, are under constant surveillance: "The system is simple, if laborious. The education attaché at the embassy requests a complete list of all Turkmen students from Turkish universities, as well as the courses they are enrolled in. This information is entered into Excel files—some of which have been obtained by *openDemocracy*—along with the students' date of birth, passport number and permanent address in Turkmenistan." The data are then passed on to informers, themselves Turkmen students who are lured into collaborating with the government in exchange for financial aid. According to the documents, there is one designated informer per university dormitory who is assigned a list of students to spy on. Informers work independently and do not know the identity of other informers. They fill in their own entries in the Excel files, which are then sent to the embassy and on to Ashgabat, in a constant back-and-forth of information.

Structurally, however, Berdimuhamedow has reversed many of Niyazov's reductions in the number of years of education. As Victoria Clement and Zumrad Kataeva note, "the school system was restructured from 9 to 10 years, higher educational institutions to 5 years, and medical and some art institutes to 6 years. He also raised the salaries of those in the education sector while decreasing the number of hours worked, reducing class sizes and increasing access to computers. On 30 March 2007, he instructed that the salaries of Turkmenistan's teachers increase by 40 percent." Perhaps Berdimuhamedow's most important initiative in education was his March 1, 2013, extension of secondary schooling to twelve years. This initiative has had ramifications for higher education as well, since it has meant that there are a greater number of students graduating with credentials that will allow them to pursue higher education both domestically and abroad.

Presidential decrees established the English-language based International University for Humanities and Development and the Japanese-language based Oguzkhan University of Engineering Technologies in 2014 and 2016, respectively. It would be a mistake, however, to see the existence of two new, small universities, with combined enrollments under one thousand, as indicative of either internationalization or liberalization of higher education. Both universities lacked faculty with qualifications to teach in a number of fields, were unable to create international partnerships, were required to make students available for public events on short notice, and often had their requests for reforms stymied by Ministry of Education officials.

The Struggle of School and the Challenge of Reform

Educational reforms present their own challenges, but certainly they are not the only challenges students face. In the early years of independence, I visited Kanykei, the sister of a friend, in Kadji Sai, a town on the southern edge of Lake Issyk Kul in Kyrgyzstan. In Soviet times Kadji Sai had been home to a bustling factory and also a branch of the Gulag, or Soviet prison system. This branch was at a uranium mine where the prisoners worked, apparently without protection from cancer-causing radioactivity. A European colleague later took me to see the remnants of the mine and the graveyard nearby. Gravestones in Central Asia often have pictures of the deceased on them, and the graves at Kadji Sai presented, almost uniformly, pictures of young Slavic men. The mine was closed, although it was still an open pit, accessible to anyone who hiked up the hill. The factory had closed as well, putting Kanykei's husband and several of the other men in her extended family out of work.

Kanykei was a Russian teacher at the local school. At the time of my visit, she was on maternity leave, home with her youngest child and his two siblings. She told me that she did not collect her monthly maternity leave benefits, because the bus fare to and from the office where she needed to pick up the benefits cost more than the monthly benefit itself.

We went together to see the school where she worked, a building badly in need of repair. Next door was another building, missing some windows and with a partially caved-in roof. Kanykei said that the second building was used only on sunny days. Puzzled, I asked if it had electricity, and she explained that neither building had working electricity. In the second building, teachers had to wait for sunny days because of the holes in the floor; they wanted to be sure that the children could see the holes and not fall in.

My visit to Kadji Sai took place in the late 1990s, but as interviews in 2018 with teachers in the country attest, the problems presented then still remain: salaries are too small to live on, buildings are in drastic need of repair, schools are lacking not only computers and Internet access but sometimes basic utilities such as electricity and, in some cases, heat in the winter. A language teacher at one of the most elite public schools in the capital complained that she teaches twenty-eight hours a week with twenty-five students in a class, with not enough textbooks for all and no projectors or other technology. She also said that some classes in the sciences were taught by engineers who lost their jobs when factories closed rather than by trained teachers. Another language teacher, at another elite school in the capital, said she taught from thirty to thirty-six hours a week, also with overcrowded classes. A science teacher at a rural school said, "We do not have enough textbooks. For example, in physics, I and my students use the textbooks published in 1979, 1980; even those textbooks are not enough for all our students." She added that classrooms were designed for fifteen students but regularly held twenty-five and that the temperature in the building in the winter sometimes fell to twelve or fifteen degrees below zero (Celsius). By contrast, a teacher at a private school in the capital teaches only from fifteen to seventeen hours a week, has a mentor, and is able to attend professional development workshops.

A list of the problems of schools in Kyrgyzstan includes:

- teacher shortages, particularly in math and science;
- teachers whose salaries are so low that they work in the markets or on family farms in order to survive, and thus have little time or inclination to focus on innovations or even, in some cases, lesson preparation;
- teachers trained in teacher-centered knowledge-transmission techniques, not in learner-centered methods or in preparing pupils to apply knowledge and to ask questions;
- outdated textbooks and an insufficient number of textbooks for all pupils, particularly in local languages;
- control of textbook authoring and selection by scholars in the Kyrgyz Academy of Education and selection of authors who often have limited current experience in schools;
- the loading of the curriculum with new subjects, such as national history, without dropping others;
- rural/urban inequities and public/private school inequities;
- dependence on donors who fund projects of their own interest that are not integrated into existing structures nor provided with mechanisms of sustainability;
- a drastic decline in the provision of kindergartens and kindergarten attendance;
- corruption;
- lack of stability in the population (in- and out-migration as families seek work), so teachers do not know the pupils or their families;
- the absence of social organizations for children;
- out-of-school children; and
- the schools' lack of control over their own budgets and dependence on local authorities for funding.

To understand the emergence of these problems, one needs to keep in mind that funding for education in Soviet times came from the central government. After the collapse of the Soviet Union, ministries of education could not afford to pay anything more than salaries. Building repairs, professional development for teachers, new textbooks, and even utilities were neglected. The results of that fiscal crisis are apparent now in Kyrgyzstan and elsewhere. As DeYoung points out, most Ministry of Education staff were trained to administer and monitor programs, not to design curricula or propose innovations. Thus, even if they wanted to engage in broad-based school restructuring, they would not have the knowledge or experience to do so. As donors have their own priorities and seldom take a comprehensive and contextualized look at educational issues, they are unlikely to rectify this problem.

Moreover, unlike the situation in higher education, elementary and secondary education does not have an external model like the Bologna Process that can be adapted to or modified for local conditions. Elementary and secondary education is much more focused on "fitness for purpose" in the local context. Kyrgyzstan's participation in the Programme for International Student Assessment—which measures the reading, science, and math performance of fifteen-year-olds—was a wake-up call about the quality of its elementary and secondary education. The country took part in 2006 and 2009 and in both cases came in last place, out of more than fifty countries participating. However, the wake-up call provided no plan of what to do next. The Bologna Process, controversial as it is for Kyrgyzstan's context, at least provides a plan: implement bachelor's and master's degrees, switch from contact hours to credit hours, assign independent work to students, create learning outcomes, and design a system of independent accreditation to replace state attestation. At the school level, neither a plan for comprehensive reform nor the funding to carry it out exists.

The fact that there is neither a comprehensive plan for reform nor sufficient resources to implement reforms reflects both the persistence of the problems listed above and the multiple priorities of a nation where 32 percent of the people live in poverty. The central control exerted by the Ministry of Education means that professors have no flexibility in meeting student needs. As Madeleine Reeves points out, children from village schools in rural Batken in no way have the same preparation as the graduates of elite secondary schools in the capital where the focus is on science and math or languages. Yet the Ministry of Education prescribes the same university curriculum for all students in a particular specialization. Thus, the professor at Batken State University may be put in the untenable situation of either teaching what the Ministry of Education plan says, when students do not have the background needed to understand the subject at that level, or alternatively, teaching what the students need but having to call it what the Ministry of Education says should be taught—for example, teaching algebra when the plan calls for calculus. As Reeves notes, the issue is not the lack of integrity of specific individuals but, rather, the lack of integration of the educational system that creates a situation in which faculty in some instances cannot meet student needs and Ministry of Education requirements simultaneously.

Students and their families, in response to such structural issues, may find individual solutions: payment for admissions, payment for grades, payment for degrees, and plagiarized papers and theses. The issue is not, as it is sometimes simplistically portrayed, that students are lazy or that faculty are underpaid. Rather, corruption is pervasive throughout the societies; it is found in the legal system, in government, in the construction industry, in health care, in business contracts—everywhere. Moreover, as was the case in Burul being "invited" back to the university from which she graduated, relationships and connections play a large role in employment decisions. Submitting an application and demonstrating your competence to someone you have never met before is just not the usual way that people find work. Thus being "tested" on whether one has actually acquired the knowledge corresponding to the courses taken is rare. Some employers have started to complain about the low quality of graduates who seemingly have not acquired even the most rudimentary competencies necessary for work in the field corresponding to their degree. It is in this context that the importance of education (and reform) becomes more acute.

Educating between Periods

Educational reform is always difficult because of inconsistencies in the learning experience—where teachers draw upon pedagogies they never experienced as students. While primary and secondary education has lacked a standardizing agenda akin to that of the Bologna Process for higher education, the issue facing educators and students remains tied to what was learned in school. Burul graduated from the university in 2003, meaning she was born in the Soviet Union in the early 1980s. She was around ten when the Soviet Union collapsed, and Kyrgyzstan became independent in 1991. Since she finished secondary school in the late 1990s, the majority of her teachers received all of their education and training in the Soviet era, with Soviet pedagogical methods.

Now Burul is teaching students who were not born when the Soviet Union existed, but who are living in a country governed by people whose formative education and experience come from Soviet times. Directives about new degrees, new systems of evaluation, and new requirements are coming from the Ministry of Education, but there has been little training or support for implementing these new methods. Thus, Burul is left with what she can find on the Internet, the advice of a young Peace Corps Volunteer, and her colleagues' impressions of what they are expected to do. Moreover, if she was asked what Kyrgyzstan would be like when her own four small children are ready to enter the university, she likely would say she does not know. The future always seems uncertain, which poses a challenge for how she is supposed to educate students for it. Burul's approach has been to take one day at a time, daydream about her classmates who moved away to Russia and the United States, see if she can find a new activity on YouTube for her students, and do the best she can.

CASE V-A

Mood and Islam in Kazakhstan

Wendell Schwab

This is a story about how a young man feels when he listens to Sufi chants on his cell phone in twenty-first-century Almaty. It is also the story of how a young girl felt when she muttered "Thanks be to God" to please a pious old man on the way home from school in a Soviet village. It is a story about the different religious moods that Asel, a sixty-year-old Kazakh woman from Turkistan Oblast, and Temirbek, her thirty-year-old son raised in Almaty, experienced as children and young adults.

My focus on moods is meant to evoke a sense that Islam changes even when rituals stay the same. A mood is something that surrounds us and influences our behavior. There are moods in classrooms and in restaurants and on the street. People are influenced by these moods. A home football loss on Saturday changes the feeling of campus and affects classes on Monday, for example. Talking about moods is a way to highlight the change in Central Asians' religious lives from the Soviet to the post-Soviet era. I will focus on the mood surrounding the practice of frying bread and asking for the blessings of God and ancestors. My argument is twofold. First, Soviet antireligious policies did not eliminate Islam in Kazakhstan. Instead, they produced a nostalgic and melancholic Islamic mood.

Second, the diversity of Islamic media in post-Soviet Kazakhstan has expanded the repertoire of moods surrounding Islam in Kazakhstan. There is a mood of possibility surrounding Islamic practice in post-Soviet Kazakhstan: frying bread can be fun, serious, celebratory, or nostalgic.

•

The story of Shukir Ata, literally "Grandfather Thanks," was one of Asel's favorite ways to explain Islam during the Soviet era. Shukir Ata received his nickname from the children of the village because he gave candy to the children with one condition: the children had to say "Thanks be to God" (*Allahqa shukir*) in front of him before they ate the candy. Everyone in the village thought Shukir Ata was somewhat crazy. His nickname was meant as a joke, and most people knew that whatever their own personal beliefs they were expected to mock Shukir Ata's overt religiosity in public. They were in the Soviet Union, after all. However, after a few years, villagers realized that Shukir Ata was one of the few men in the village teaching children to remember God and His presence in the world. They began to accept Shukir Ata's presence in public, although they knew he could not be praised except in private. Asel painted a vivid picture of

V-A-1   Commissioned in 1389 by Timur, the Khoja Ahmet Yasawi Mausoleum is a popular destination for many Kazakhs in Turkestan, a city near Asel's village, Kazakhstan, 2018. Photograph by Kasia Ploskonka.

Shukir Ata: a white-bearded man in a classic Kazakh robe on a dusty street, greeting children coming home from a Soviet school on a collective cotton farm in the desert. People realized the extent of Shukir Ata's holiness when he died. Villagers discovered that he had been 110 years old. They thought he had been blessed with longevity for keeping Islam alive in the village.

In Asel's village, aside from Shukir Ata, Islam was largely absent from public spaces and in the public sphere. There was no mosque. There were no Islamic books. Newspapers, movies, and radio programs denounced Islam as a bunch of silly superstitions. The local graveyard was the most overt public Islamic space. Kazakhs in Asel's village took part in this atheist public sphere. High school students would repeat atheist slogans to fit in with their classmates. Village officials would make anti-Islamic speeches when oblast bureaucrats visited. Factory workers would not fast during Ramadan because of pressure from their supervisors. People mocked

the crazy old Muslim in the village who gave out candy to kids.

Asel's experience is comparable to other Soviet experiences. Official discourse in the Soviet era was hyper-normalized. Russians quoted Brezhnev in official meetings, for example, not because they thought Brezhnev was right but in order to participate in conversations about public matters. What was quoted was less important than the relationships forged through conversations after the repetition of near obligatory official language. Quoting Brezhnev could be almost meaningless, but not quite: repetition made Brezhnev's presence and Soviet power seem inevitable. In Asel's village, anti-Islamic slogans, believed by some and not by others, were repeated as a matter of course, and a secular and atheist public sphere seemed inevitable. Islam seemed to belong to the past, even when it was practiced in the present. The mood surrounding Islam was nostalgic.

Privately, people could continue many Islamic practices. To return to

MOOD AND ISLAM IN KAZAKHSTAN   421

V-A-2   A local worker carrying tires in the Khoja Ahmet Yasawi Mausoleum complex, Kazakhstan, 2018. Photograph by Kasia Ploskonka.

Shukir Ata: after he died, Asel's family would occasionally fry bread on Thursday nights and distribute the bread to neighbors. They would ask God to reward Shukir Ata for his good deeds and for inspiring them to be kind to their neighbors. In return, Asel's family expected the blessings of God and Shukir Ata. In Asel's post-Soviet recounting of this ritual, she was nostalgic for her Soviet childhood, for what she saw as a simpler, happier, more moral time. The mood she set was serious. She did not mention joking with her family while frying bread or relate amusing anecdotes, as she often did when discussing other aspects of her childhood. Rather, she spoke of her relatives telling stories about pre-Soviet ancestors' exemplary religious lives. Frying bread for Shukir Ata was a solemn affair, meant to remember her ancestors and a man who kept Islam alive when others could not. It was a ritual that felt warm and loving, but not fun. For Asel and other villagers in the Brezhnev era, Shukir Ata went from a public joke to a private saint, from a silly man to an ancestor whose memory must be taken seriously.

These domestic rituals were an important continuation of pre-Soviet religiosity. Islam was altered—not destroyed—by Soviet governance. In Asel's village, the conditions of Soviet culture produced the possibility of different practices for different people: retirees giving out candy on the street, mothers asking for God's blessings while cooking at home, children remembering deceased holy men, and atheist communist party members denouncing Islam as a relic of a feudal past. Soviet culture also precluded certain possibilities, such as reading Islamic books, going to the mosque, and publicly debating moral, economic, or political issues using Islamic concepts or vocabulary. And the Soviet experience created new moods for old practices such as frying bread and asking for the blessings of ancestors. This world—privately observant and nostalgic, publicly atheist and progressive—was the world in which Asel learned to feel Islam.

•

On the other hand, Temirbek grew up in the 1990s and the first decade of the 2000s. The 1990s were a difficult economic time for many Kazakhs, including Temirbek's father, who lost his job and turned to drinking during the day. Asel divorced Temirbek's father and supported Temirbek by teaching French at several colleges in Almaty, where she had moved in the late 1980s to attend a foreign language institute. His mother had grown up on an economically stable cotton farm in the 1960s and 1970s,

but Temirbek experienced the economic deprivation of the post-Soviet recession in Almaty while living in a high-rise apartment building. Later, the boom years of economic growth in the 2000s created a sense of economic possibility for Temirbek's generation in Almaty.

The reemergence of Islam in the public sphere in Kazakhstan shifted the moods surrounding Islamic practice. Temirbek's experience with Islam includes engaging with a good deal of Islamic media. Occasionally, when he feels a need for edification, he watches Talim TV (formerly Asyl Arna), an Islamic television channel in Kazakhstan that shows programs such as *Quran Oqyp Uireneiik* (Let's learn the Qur'an) and *Paighmbar Qasietteri* (Characteristics of the Prophet); Talim TV also has a popular presence on social media showing what an Islamic middle-class lifestyle looks like. Temirbek's ring tone is an excerpt of a song by the musical group Yasawi, who take their name from a medieval Islamic saint and perform a cappella songs about Islam and Kazakh life. Yasawi's music videos show romanticized visions of the Kazakh past, like men leading camels on their way to a shrine or a Sufi praying alone in the dun-colored desert.

These media products expand the repertoire of Islamic moods that Temirbek experiences. Talim TV shows him a pious middle-class lifestyle. He sees the possibility of growing a beard, praying five times a day, buying halal meat, and marrying a woman who will stay at home to raise his children. He can imagine the economic security that Talim TV shows as a reward for the pious. He can also imagine life as a miracle-working mystic wearing white robes and chanting all day when he listens to the musical group Yasawi. Temirbek does not currently try to live his life in these ways, but he talked about them as possibilities. It is these media presentations of different lifestyles that make the overall mood surrounding Temirbek's experiences of Islam one of possibility. Where Asel could imagine preserving private rituals from an Islamic past in a Soviet future, Temirbek can imagine his mother's past, or a stereotypically middle-class life as a pious Muslim, or a life as a mystic.

Some of the moods Temirbek has experienced are similar to those of Asel's childhood. For example, the mood surrounding frying bread in Asel and Temirbek's apartment is often nostalgic. One Friday afternoon, while they were frying bread with me, Asel described her childhood as a simple pastoral life: Kazakhs lived among their extended family, had the basic economic essentials, and happily muddled through the Soviet system. This was a nostalgic moment for both Asel and Temirbek. The core of the ritual remained the same as well. Asel and Temirbek dedicated the aroma of the bread and the reward for distributing the bread to others to Shukir Ata and asked for his and God's blessings. However, the mood when Temirbek fried bread with his mother could also be fun and celebratory. On a different Friday, they thanked Shukir Ata for his work in preserving Islam, but then they joked about Soviet party members who aspired to be post-Soviet Hajjis. They made fun of rich businessmen who took "Islamic" second wives who were in fact mistresses. They laughed about aggressive young men who made fools of themselves by loudly mispronouncing Arabic prayers. They talked about going on the Hajj but then considered spending that money on a beach trip to Turkey instead. Asel and Temirbek were not concentrating on keeping Islam alive or connecting to the past. The conversation around frying bread was far-reaching, and Islam was normalized enough to celebrate Islamic pilgrimage, or joke about the seemingly false piety of others, or make plans for a beach trip. The mood was full of possibilities.

•

I do not want to portray the Soviet era as grim and humorless. People had warm relations with friends, loved their families, and made jokes about an old man handing out candy in the streets. However, Asel and her family did not joke while frying bread for Shukir Ata in the Soviet era. That was serious business. This changed in the post-Soviet era. Asel went from regretting Shukir Ata's mocking nickname and solemnly frying bread for him in the Soviet era to making jokes about men and their second wives while frying bread for the same man. The bread remained the same, but the mood had changed.

Spectacular Politics at the World Nomad Games

Mathijs Pelkmans

In early September 2016 a seemingly never-ending, slow-moving traffic jam wound its way up the narrow road toward the Kyrchyn mountain pastures. Two days later, a temporary yurt city had emerged on what was one of the main sites of the second World Nomad Games. One section was cordoned off, featuring grand and expensively decorated yurts for hosting important guests. Upstream there were seven clusters of yurts representing the different regions of Kyrgyzstan; another field had yurts from each municipality of the Issyk Kul region. Across the stream were a hundred or so "commercial" yurts and other tent-like constructions, operating as hotels, restaurants, shops, and one as a mosque. From early morning the air was abuzz with activity: people trading homemade produce and cheap imports, serving food, and attending to guests (figure V-B-1).

The positive buzz converged into intense excitement during the opening festivities. The audience vied for the best places: young men climbed on top of their horses, small children were lifted onto people's shoulders, respected guests were given coveted seats, while many more were standing (figures V-B-2, 3). All eyes focused on the center stage where horse riders performed daring acrobatics while galloping full speed and dramatized versions of traditional games—such as one in which the men chased after the women in pursuit of a kiss, until roles were reversed and the women chased and whipped the men. The main event consisted of the enactment of a historical battle in which a khan mobilized his people to ultimately drive off and humiliate the foreign invader. A narrator, speaking in Kyrgyz, filled in the gaps between the acting, skillfully guiding the audience through the plot. A foreign journalist relayed the amazement that was felt by many in the audience, when he wrote on the CBS Sports website: "Dragging a man by a rope from the back of a horse seems pretty normal in this scenario. Women shooting bows . . . upside down . . . with their feet. These games just can't get any better."

Dinara, a Kyrgyz woman from Bishkek who had previously mocked the Games as just another wasteful government initiative, told me after the spectacle had ended: "It was like, I felt this pride, thinking, wow—this is where I come from!" The enactment of a historical battle on the mountain pastures, attended by hundreds of compatriots, allowed for an intense identification with the idea of the Kyrgyz nation and its history. Tumar, who attended the spectacle in-between her

V-B-1   One of the handicraft exhibitions at the World Nomad Games in Kyrchyn, Kyrgyzstan, 2016. Photograph by Mathijs Pelkmans.

V-B-2   The opening ceremony of the World Nomad Games in Kyrchyn, Kyrgyzstan, 2016. Photograph by Mathijs Pelkmans.

work as a cook in one of the commercial yurts, gave a shorter but equally strong assessment, saying, "I'm simply speechless!" There was some confusion about the name of the khan and the specifics of the historical battle, which neither Dinara nor Tumar had ever heard of before, but this did not dampen their excitement.

For many Kyrgyz, the 2016 World Nomad Games were a celebration of the people, not just the elites, and contribut-ed to a shared sense of identification and recognition. Stretched across six days, the Games hosted numerous "cultural" per-formances and activities, alongside twen-ty different sport competitions ranging from eagle hunting, archery, wrestling, and board games to horse racing and *kok boru*, a version of polo. More than one thousand contestants from forty countries participated, with significant represen-tations from most of the former Soviet

V-B-3 Young men and their horses during the opening ceremony of the World Nomad Games in Kyrchyn, Kyrgyzstan, 2016. Photograph by Mathijs Pelkmans.

Republics, but also from China, Afghanistan, Hungary, Turkey, Oman, and the United Arab Emirates, among others. In contrast to the more modest first World Nomad Games of 2014, this time the government went all out and invested millions of dollars to erect a massive hippodrome on the shores of Lake Issyk Kul, upgraded roads, and produced spectacular opening and closing ceremonies.

As these initial descriptions also suggest, even if only implicitly, the World Nomad Games were riddled with tensions. Although presented as novel and innovative, the Games also appealed to deep historical roots. Although the Games aimed to celebrate indigenous culture, doing so on an international scale required making compromises, and although the government used the World Nomad Games to project a grand vision of cultural heritage and modern accomplishment, these projections constantly risked slipping into the grotesque. In her book *The Spectacular State*, Laura Adams asks the important question of how citizens of small and peripheral countries "understand their nation's greatness." To

conceive of such greatness, it appears we all need to have *our thing*, a need that has intensified as global interconnectedness has deepened. The issue is not straightforward. Claims to historical authenticity that make the "thing" *ours* and outward projections that make the thing a *thing* are fraught with tension. This was evident at the World Nomad Games. Although the Games were a powerful mechanism by which Kyrgyzstan was able to gain visibility in the world, uncertainty remained about what was being seen by foreign audiences. The claims to tradition as well as the outward projection of uniqueness reveal contradictions that are illustrative of how spectacular politics work in the contemporary world.

Transformations Entail Historical Imaginations and Legacies

Speaking during the main opening ceremony in the newly built hippodrome in Cholpon Ata, then-president Almaz Atambaev announced that, in the context of globalization, "unique cultures and peoples risk disappearing." He warned that we forget history at our own peril and emphasized the values of nomadic ways of life in an age of environmental destruction. What is so important about the World Nomad Games, he emphasized, is that because of them "the entire world is now learning about the history of nomads."

References to history and cultural uniqueness reverberated throughout the Games. They certainly dominated the main opening ceremony. Placed on center stage was a *manaschi* (narrator of the *Manas* epic), whose rhythmic narration of the tribulations of the Kyrgyz nation through history was accompanied by traditional music and dance and made visible to the audience on huge screens. As captured by journalist Shaun Walker, the event "featured hundreds of whirling nomad women, stunt horsemen galloping across the arena with their clothes on fire, and graphics on a vast screen telling the story of the Kyrgyz nation, which has a long and storied history as a rugged nomadic tribe." For the benefit of his international audience, Walker added that these nomadic tribes were "conquered by Tsarist Russia and then absorbed into the Soviet Union." But tellingly, this more recent history never made it into the narration, the performances, or the visuals of the opening ceremony.

As in much revisionist post-socialist historiography, the Soviet period was largely bracketed off, squashed between the glorious nomadic past and the current revival of tradition. This revisionist historical narrative, in combination with many of the cultural activities, provided a powerful way of imagining an uninterrupted nomadic tradition and authentic Kyrgyz culture. Or, as the official promotional video declared dramatically with posh English accent narration and stunning visuals: "We are all nomads. Our life is like the flight of an arrow. Throughout centuries, and across continents, we have carried our culture, traditions, and games. Feel the legacy of our ancestors, and experience the spirit of freedom. World Nomad Games, The Kyrgyz Republic."

The evacuation of Soviet history is interesting because, in spite of all the novelty, some aspects of the Games suggest a continuation of Soviet cultural politics. Central among these is the preoccupation with organizing grand spectacles as a way to demonstrate the accomplishments of government. Moreover, the organization of festivals as legitimate expressions of Kyrgyz culture can be traced back to the organization of Olympiads in the 1930s, which served to promote the cultural distinctiveness in socialist appropriate ways, contributing thereby to the formation of the modern Kyrgyz nation. And although the elements of nomadic culture that were highlighted during the World Nomad Games predated the Soviet period, several of them had become popularized through Soviet cultural politics. This is even true of the celebrated *Manas* epic, which played an important part in the culture of some of the Kyrgyz tribes before the twentieth century but only started to be promoted as a symbol of Kyrgyzness in the late Soviet period, and increasingly so in the 1990s.

Apart from reflecting Soviet legacy, the tensions also point to the contradiction of celebrating tradition on a large scale. A small but significant tension in the wrestling competitions can serve as illustration. Under the rubric of "traditional wrestling," there were five different competitions, named Goresh, Gyulesh, Kurosh, Kuresh, and Aba Kurosh, which had the respective additions of Turkmen, Azerbaijani, Kyrgyz, Kazakh, and Turkish. The differences between these forms of wrestling tended to confuse the wrestlers and sometimes annoyed them. This was particularly clear when the arbitrator of Azerbaijani Gyulesh repeatedly intervened when wrestlers forgot or declined to do the ritual dance (involving rhythmic jumps and other body movements) preceding the actual fight. The awkwardness of the non-Azerbaijani competitors, especially the Russian ones, was palpable, when they reluctantly complied and uncomfortably danced toward their opponents.

Sticking to local particularities such as was evident in Azerbaijani Gyulesh led to annoyance among those who did not identify with those particularities or who dismissed their relevance. The thing is that celebrating tradition on a grand scale requires such celebrations to be cast in recognized forms. This process is so common that some of the transformations may go unnoticed. For example, it would be problematic to assume that all nomadic groups identify with any particular nation-state. During the opening ceremony, however, all participating men and women walked behind the flag of their designated country. This, it appeared, was an accepted and necessary ingredient to be seen as a worthy inter-*national* event. Flows and forms are integrally related. Different mediums impose different conditions on the form of social messages, allowing them to circulate across social space, and becoming co-constitutive of those messages.

Circulation between Recognition and Ridicule

A key concern in Kyrgyz media as well as among the public attending the events was how the Games were seen by foreigners. In light of this, it was reassuring when on the last day of the Games a headline in the national newspaper *Megapolis* stated, "Two Billion People Came to Know about the Nomad Games," and the article went on to say that not only was two billion a conservative estimate but "99 % of those who saw the Games were overwhelmingly impressed and astonished by what they saw." Meanwhile, the newspaper *Slovo Kyrgyzstana* stated that with the World Nomad Games the country had crossed the Rubicon to become an acknowledged member of the international community. Hyperbole or not, the Games definitely attracted international attention, and much of it was indeed positive. In their commentary, West European and North American visitors focused particularly on the spontaneous or improvisatory organization, as well as on the authentically exotic quality of the events. But these qualities contained a possible negative, as was captured when a local journalist used the depiction "wild Olympics," or when an organizer announced "that Genghis Khan would have loved it."

The implicit tension between respect and ridicule reverberated particularly strongly in relation to the biggest event of the Games. At the start of the kok boru finals between Kyrgyzstan and Kazakhstan, all five thousand plus seats of the hippodrome were occupied. Eyes oscillated between the screens on the gallery and the drama unfolding on the field. A jumble of horses and men tussling for possession of the dead goat in their midst; one of the Kyrgyz players sped off with the goat; his teammates hindered the Kazakh players but still they got close; nevertheless, the Kyrgyz player reached the artificial water well and dumped the goat into it. The audience erupted into an overwhelming roar, followed by chanting "Kyrgyzstan!! Kyrgyzstan!!" The roars of victory grew even louder with 2–0 and 3–0, but they lost some of their edge after. With a final score of 15–3, Kyrgyzstan won the closing event and the most important competition of the World Nomad Games.

The elation and intense pride made for a fitting end to the Games, bringing it back to a celebration of the Kyrgyz by the Kyrgyz. But this also indicated limitations. Not just because outgunning one's nearest competitor 15–3 signals that kok boru has limited international purchase (though it certainly has appeal across Central Asia) but also because promoting the game in a global context carried other risks. Indeed, how to "translate" kok boru? A sanitized translation might depict it as "a game in which two teams of five horsemen compete to throw a heavy object into the opponent's goal," but this would leave out key aspects. The official booklet explained: "Literally meaning 'gray wolf,' the game today requires teams to throw a dead sheep or goat into their opponent's well on the playing field." When images and stories of kok boru circulated through (social) media outlets, the tension between respect and ridicule was palpable. The *Guardian* tried to strike a balance by respectfully discussing it as a "violent Central Asian form of polo in which two teams battle for control of a decapitated goat carcass," but on Twitter it was the "goat carcass" aspect that drew most attention, in addition to invocations of Genghis Khan. As a typical tweet had it: "If Genghiz khan would be alive today, he would be a kok-boru captain."

Celebration of tradition easily slips into ridicule. Although visitors and reporters were respectful of the Games, they selected those phrases, images, and ideas that resonated with their audiences—with the reports becoming increasingly stereotypical and exotic as they circulated. All this speaks to the fraught politics of recognition in an intimately connected yet deeply uneven world. Being seen or noticed does not necessarily mean being recognized and respected.

Spectacular Politics

The World Nomad Games were a spectacular political success. Atambaev established himself as a father of the nation, standing above everyday politics, espousing the values of the nation, while also casting Kyrgyzstan in a positive "modern" light. Commentators who had been skeptical of the organizational and financial aspects changed their minds or kept silent in the immediate aftermath of the Games. The president was praised, the sportsmen were lauded, and ordinary people basked in the glory of their nation. But this sense of recognition was fragile, reflecting the various tensions that constituted the World Nomad Games. Presented as novel and innovative, the Games claimed legitimacy by appealing to deep historical roots. Aiming to celebrate authentic culture and doing this on an international scale required making compromises. And while the Games projected a grand vision of cultural heritage and modern accomplishment, these projections risked slipping into the grotesque.

Such tensions should not be seen as undercutting the World Nomad Games, because in fact they energized them. Claims to tradition, celebrations of culture, and assertions of modern accomplishment are always open to contestation, particularly when projected onto a global audience. The significance of an event depends on how such projections "resonate" with different audiences—that is, how they engage affective and epistemic sensory registers and how they are enlisted in political projects. It is through such processes of circulation that meaning and significance are established, whether in moments of collective effervescence, in edited media distributions, or in ordinary conversations. The World Nomad Games provided a telling prism on spectacular politics and the paradoxes of recognition in the twenty-first century. And while the images circulated, ideas of the Kyrgyz nation, of nomadic lifestyle, and of what it means to be part of a global world were formed as well as transformed.

Displacement and Belonging in Eurasia

Jennifer S. Wistrand

All of the former Soviet states have created new national narratives since the collapse of the Soviet Union in 1991. These new national narratives have assumed heightened importance in Azerbaijan, Turkmenistan, Uzbekistan, Kazakhstan, Kyrgyzstan, and Tajikistan since neither proto-territorial integrity nor a proto-national identity existed in the pre-Soviet period in the same way as it did in other parts of the former Soviet Union. For example, Armenia and Georgia, which share the Transcaucasia region with Azerbaijan, can date shared written languages and religions, or proto-national identities, to the fourth century.

All of the former Soviet states are also home to displaced peoples who were moved into or out of various regions by the Soviet leaders in Moscow. In Central Asia, the most well-known displaced peoples were the "punished peoples," the more than two million Karachais, Balkars, Ingush, Chechens, Kalmyks, Crimean Tatars, Meskhetian Turks, Volga Germans, and Koreans whom Stalin forcibly relocated from their homes to Central Asia in the years prior to and during the Second World War. In addition to the "punished peoples," however, there were many other peoples whom the Soviet leaders relocated to, or within, Central Asia in order to support the

Soviet state's industrializing goals. For example, political scientist Olivier Ferrando notes that, "as early as the 1920s, the Soviet regime developed a policy of population transfers in order to distribute the existing labour force among different economic sectors. In Central Asia, several hundreds of thousands of people were displaced—voluntarily or forcibly—between 1925 and 1970 and contributed to the transformation of arid steppes into fertile cotton fields."

Although the actions that precipitated these and other displacements of peoples to, and within, Central Asia are different from those that precipitated the displacement of Azerbaijanis within Azerbaijan (see below), the leaders of Azerbaijan, Turkmenistan, Uzbekistan, Kazakhstan, Kyrgyzstan, and Tajikistan share a similar concern regarding their states' present-day displaced peoples: the risk they believe these peoples pose to their states' territorial integrity and national unity and the subsequent attention they believe they need to devote to managing how the displaced "belong." In other words, do state leaders believe these peoples can and should be treated as "regular Azerbaijanis" or "regular Turkmenistanis" or "regular Uzbekistanis," or do they believe they need to be treated as something else in the name of territorial integrity and national unity? For example, geographer Alexander Diener has examined how the leaders of Kazakhstan—which is home to more than one hundred different ethnic groups, including the descendants of the ethnic Germans and ethnic Koreans who were not allowed to repatriate following Stalin's death in 1953—have struggled to develop a Kazakhstani national identity that, from the perspective of the citizens who belong to minority groups, uniformly embraces all Kazakhstanis' ethnic (or clan or linguistic or religious) identities.

Most of Azerbaijan's internally displaced persons (IDPs) are a result of the late 1980s and early 1990s conflict between Azerbaijan and Armenia over Azerbaijan's region of Nagorno-Karabakh. IDPs are similar to refugees in that they may have fled their homes for one or several of the same reasons. Unlike refugees, however, IDPs are displaced within rather than outside of their country of origin. Thus, IDPs are generally citizens of the country in which they are displaced. Most of Azerbaijan's IDPs are citizens of Azerbaijan. From the perspective of the government of Azerbaijan, however, failing to distinguish Azerbaijan's IDPs from "regular Azerbaijanis" is tantamount to accepting Azerbaijan's fractured territorial integrity. In other words, in contrast to the government of Kazakhstan's efforts to promote a broad Kazakhstani national identity for the sake of national unity, the government of Azerbaijan is, for all intents and purposes, promoting national disunity—"regular Azerbaijanis" versus "IDPs"—in an effort to regain Nagorno-Karabakh. Said differently, what we see through the conflict over Nagorno-Karabakh is how Azerbaijan's politics, laws, and education system are employed to promote a post-conflict national narrative that limits the ability of Azerbaijan's IDPs to "belong" to

Azerbaijan. The ways in which former Soviet Azerbaijan and Central Asia have attempted to manage displaced peoples' feelings of belonging to the state represents a broader challenge to states across the region.

•

According to the UN High Commissioner for Refugees (UNHCR), which has been working in Azerbaijan since 1992, as of October 2019 Azerbaijan had 651,458 IDPs. With a total population of around ten million, this means that 6–7 percent of the population is living in a state of protracted displacement and, in some cases, has been doing so for at least twenty-five years. Most of Azerbaijan's IDPs are from the late 1980s and early 1990s conflict between Azerbaijan and Armenia over Azerbaijan's region of Nagorno-Karabakh. A comprehensive account of the conflict is beyond the scope of this case study and would be very difficult to present, as Azerbaijanis' and Armenians' respective understandings of the events leading up to the conflict, let alone the conflict itself, are so different from one another they read like two different histories rather than two versions of the same history. Anthropologist Nora Dudwick suggests that Azerbaijanis generally see the conflict in ahistorical terms, originating in the early stages of the formation of the Soviet Union when Nagorno-Karabakh was included as a part of Azerbaijan. They perceive the Armenians as the "aggressors" who are trying to take their land. In contrast, Dudwick contends that the Armenians generally see the conflict in historical terms. Losing Nagorno-Karabakh to the Azerbaijanis in the early 1920s was but one of a series of losses to the "Turks" over the past several centuries. Consequently, they believe they are the "victims." Dudwick summarizes: "On the Armenian side, we have a language of 'victimization,' 'massacres,' and 'self-defense' alternating with 'liberation' and the 'struggle for survival.' On the Azerbaijani side, we hear about 'expansionism,' 'aggression,' and 'occupation.'" Psychologist Rauf Garagozov has suggested that nothing short of "progressive narrative transformation" will enable reconciliation between Azerbaijanis and Armenians.

Differences aside, a brief summary of the recent past provides useful context, since Azerbaijan's IDPs' initial transformation from "regular Azerbaijanis" to "IDPs" dates to this period. In August 1987, more than seventy-five thousand Armenians in Nagorno-Karabakh and Armenia signed a petition requesting unification of Nagorno-Karabakh with Armenia and sent it to Moscow. Six months later, because of increasing tensions, hundreds of Azerbaijanis left Armenia for Azerbaijan, claiming they no longer felt welcome there. On February 20, 1988, Nagorno-Karabakh voted to break away from Azerbaijan and join with Armenia. One week later, in response to heightened tensions in the disputed territory and elsewhere in Armenia and Azerbaijan, anti-Armenian violence erupted in Sumgayit, an industrial city thirty minutes' travel north of Baku. A number of the Azerbaijanis who had recently come from Armenia had been sent to Sumgayit by the government of Azerbaijan. In the violence, at least twenty-six Armenians were killed, and the majority of the remaining fourteen thousand Armenians in the city left Azerbaijan for Armenia. This prompted a mass departure of Armenians from Azerbaijan, and of Azerbaijanis from Armenia, for their respective titular republics.

Occasional demonstrations and clashes between Azerbaijanis and Armenians continued until the official dissolution of the Soviet Union in December 1991, when the two populations' grievances with one another escalated into an armed conflict that continued until the declaration of a ceasefire in May 1994. The fighting between Azerbaijan and Armenia is estimated to have claimed up to twenty-five thousand lives and to have wounded at least fifty thousand people on both sides. To this day, Armenia controls Nagorno-Karabakh and parts or all of seven neighboring regions. Azerbaijan's IDPs are spread throughout the country, though the greater share live in Baku and Sumgayit or near the buffer zone.

•

The loss of Nagorno-Karabakh and neighboring regions has been psychologically devastating to Azerbaijanis. As a consequence, the government and the schools have employed a variety of means to make sure future generations do not forget what previous generations suffered. At the same time, these measures serve to reinforce the post-conflict national narrative that Nagorno-Karabakh will again be a part of Azerbaijan and that Azerbaijan's IDPs will again live there.

In the mid-2000s the government erected flat-screen television-like billboards throughout downtown Baku. In addition to cycling through advertisements for high-end hotels and clothing stores, the names of Azerbaijani towns and regions and the dates on which the Armenians captured them ran continuously along the bottom of the screens. This information was also printed on the inside cover of every student's "daily journal" (gündəlik). The daily journal is a small thin notebook that students must bring to each class and, at the end of the period, present to their teacher for a grade. As its name suggests, it is something the students carry with them and use every day. The inside cover of the notebook—which, theoretically, students see between six and eight times per day and five or six days per week—was titled: "Blood Memory" (*Qan Yaddaşı*). Below the title were listed three important days: "January 20, Day of National Mourning" (*20 Yanvar, Ümumxalq Hüzn Günü*), "February 26, Day of the Khojali Tragedy" (*26 Fevral, Xocalı Faciəsi Günü*), and "March 31, Day of the [Remembrance of the] Genocide of Azerbaijanis" (*31 Mart, Azərbaycanlıların Soyqırımı Günü*). Below the three important days were listed the names of Azerbaijani towns and regions and the dates on which the Armenians captured them: Khojali (*Xocalı*) 26.02.1992, Shusha (*Şuşa*) 08.05.1992, Lachin (*Laçın*) 18.05.1992, Khojavand (*Xocavənd*) 02.10.1992, Kalbajar (*Kəlbəcər*) 02.04.1993, Aghdara (*Ağdərə*) 17.06.1993, Aghdam (*Ağdam*) 23.07.1993, Jabrayil (*Cəbrayıl*) 23.08.1993, Fizuli (*Füzuli*) 23.08.1993, Gubadli (*Qubadlı*) 31.08.1993, Zangilan (*Zəngilan*) 29.10.1993. Finally, at the bottom of the page the students read "[towns or regions] having been occupied by the Armenian aggressors" (*Erməni təcavüzkarları tərəfindən işğal edilib*).

Additionally, at least one of the Azerbaijani language television channels repeatedly ran a series of statements about the conflict, first in Azerbaijani, then in English. Among others, these included "Azerbaijan is located between the thirty-ninth and forty-second parallels; Azerbaijan has been at war with Armenia for over fifteen years; Armenia continues to occupy 20 percent of Azerbaijan's land; more than one million Azerbaijani citizens have been displaced from their homes and become refugees [*sic*] in their own country; the international community continues to ignore this injustice." Azerbaijan's IDPs are often called "refugees" (*qaçqınlar* in Azerbaijani and *беженцы* in Russian). There is an Azerbaijani word for "internally displaced persons" (*məcburi*

köçkünləri) used by those who work for the State Committee for Refugees and Internally Displaced Persons (Azərbaycan Respublikası Qaçqınların Və Məcburi Köçkünlərin İşləri Üzrə Dövlət Komitəsi). The reason most Azerbaijanis, including many of Azerbaijan's IDPs, use the word "refugee" to describe an IDP is no different from the reason most people use the words interchangeably: they are not very familiar with the distinctions between the two, and the word "refugee" is more recognizable and easily understood.

Another way the government and the schools have succeeded in making sure that future generations do not forget what previous generations suffered and, by extension, the post-conflict national narrative about Nagorno-Karabakh is by maintaining separate schools for IDPs. During the armed phase of the conflict, IDPs fled to different parts of the country. Many IDPs from Aghdam congregated on the outskirts of Baku, while many IDPs from Kalbajar assembled in and around Ganja, a large city near the buffer zone. One of the first steps taken in the aftermath of the conflict, and one of the many steps still being taken today to ensure the continuity of IDP communities, was the establishment of IDP schools. Initially, most IDP schools shared space with non-IDP schools, and the two schools operated in shifts. Over time, however, many IDP schools have been given their own buildings or parts thereof. IDP schools follow the same curricula as non-IDP schools. IDP students are not required to attend IDP schools, and non-IDP students may attend IDP schools if they like. For example, it is not uncommon for IDP and non-IDP students in more rural areas to attend the same school. The point is that, as opposed to being phased out over time, IDP schools continue to exist—indeed, to expand—even though IDP students

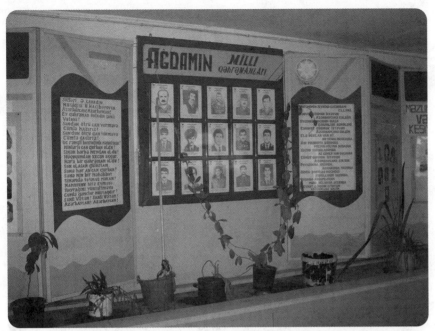

V-C-1   The atrium of an IDP school in Baku for students from Aghdam, honoring some of those who lost
their lives in the conflict over Nagorno-Karabakh, 2008. Photograph by Jennifer S. Wistrand.

are now second-generation IDPs. IDP schools, like IDPs themselves, are intended to be visible reminders of the loss of Nagorno-Karabakh, and IDP students who attend IDP schools are taught that they belong to Nagorno-Karabakh, or the adjacent region from which they were displaced, before belonging—if at all—to the part of Azerbaijan in which they are actually living, such as Baku or Ganja (figure V-C-1).

For example, one Saturday morning after I had observed an IDP school's eleventh-grade civics class discussion of "morality" (*mənəviyyat*), I observed the same school's ninth-grade civics class discussion of a variety of loosely related topics. While the teacher was transitioning from the second to the third topic of discussion, the boy with whom I was sharing a table (who had lost interest in the class around the time it began) asked me if I wanted to know where everyone in the room was from. Confused, I told the boy it was my understanding that most of the school's

administrators, teachers, and students lived in the nearby Soviet-era dormitories. In addition to attending separate schools, many IDPs also live in separate housing. The boy nodded his head and said "Yes" and then said, "But that is not where we are *from*." He then went around the room and told me where everyone was from, which was either Aghdam or Fizuli.

If these ninth-grade students started school at age six, the age most Azerbaijanis begin school, then it is possible they were born in Aghdam or Fizuli. However, it is also possible they were born in Baku, or somewhere else between Nagorno-Karabakh and the capital. And even if they were born in Aghdam or Fizuli, they would have been infants when they left the regions, which means they could not realistically have personal memories of their natal region. Regardless, it seemed to be very important to this boy, and to a significant number of the other IDP students at this IDP school with whom I spoke, to say where

V-C-2   The "last bell" (graduation ceremony) at a non-IDP school in Baku, 2007. Photograph by Jennifer S. Wistrand.

they were *really from*, which was never the outskirts of Baku. While the flat-screen television-like billboards and the daily journal and the ongoing television statements have probably helped to keep the memory of the conflict alive in both young IDPs' and non-IDPs' minds, an unintended outcome of the maintenance of the IDP label and of separate housing and schools for IDPs has been the development of a stigma associated with being an IDP (figure V-C-2).

To illustrate, less than two months after I had started regularly attending a tenth-grade civics class at a regular (non-IDP) school in central Baku, I observed a lesson devoted entirely to the topic of "refugees." First, the teacher presented some basic information about the conflict between Azerbaijan and Armenia over Nagorno-Karabakh that had resulted in a large number of refugees. Then the teacher gave each of the sixteen students one of three different colored dots and told them to form groups according to

the color of their dots. After the students had moved their tables to form three groups, the teacher read a "fictional" story about a group of people who had been caught between two countries that were at war with one another. She then gave each group a sheet of paper that provided additional information about one of the three different types of people presented in the story. One group was supposed to read about the "refugees," another group about an "asylum-seeking agency," and a third group about an "outside observer." Ultimately, the three groups were supposed to decide what to do with the refugees.

The teacher gave the students between ten and fifteen minutes to talk among themselves. Then she told the students who had read about the "refugees" and an "asylum-seeking agency" to go to the front of the classroom and role-play the situation. One of the boys who was supposed to role-play a refugee hunched over, thrust out one of his arms, and tottered around asking his classmates to give him money. One of the girls who was supposed to role-play a refugee wrapped her scarf around her head, bundled her coat like a baby, and rocked back-and-forth while begging for money. The students laughed uncontrollably. The teacher, who was visibly appalled and angered by the demonstration, told everyone to return to their seats immediately. For the last five minutes of the class period, she lectured the students on the seriousness of the topic of refugees. Among other things, she said that Azerbaijan, which has historically welcomed refugees, currently has an unprecedented number of them: Chechens from Russia and Azerbaijanis from northwestern Iran as well as Azerbaijanis from Nagorno-Karabakh. By this point, few of the students were paying attention to the lesson, and when the bell eventually sounded, most of the students jumped up to leave. Although this behavior was outside the norm even for these students, what was not outside the norm was a perception—more prevalent among younger non-IDPs, and more prevalent among those who lived in the capital—that IDPs were poor and dependent on the state. IDPs, especially younger IDPs, were very aware of this perception.

Azerbaijanis and Armenians collectively suffered a tremendous loss of life and near economic collapse as a result of the conflict over Nagorno-Karabakh. For the Azerbaijanis who also lost land and dignity, however, the psychological toll of the conflict has been far greater. Azerbaijan's politics, laws, and education system have done a great deal to make sure the memory of the conflict lives on in people's day-to-day lives. At the same time, however, some of the measures

taken in pursuit of this goal, such as the maintenance of the IDP label, IDP housing, and IDP schools, have had the unintended consequence of isolating IDPs and, in some cases, stigmatizing them.

To return to the discussion of Kazakhstani national identity, Kazakhstan needs to make sure that its national identity is sufficiently inclusive of its ethnic German and ethnic Korean populations, as well as its other minority populations, so that they do not develop an allegiance to a homeland other than Kazakhstan. Such a reality could lead to large-scale out-migration with serious economic consequences, or unwanted foreign meddling, or in the case of Kazakhstan's ethnic Russian population a call for unification with Russia. Following the same logic, Azerbaijan propagates a post-conflict national narrative in which "regular Azerbaijanis" are distinguished from "IDPs" and both "regular Azerbaijanis" and "IDPs" associate "IDPs" first and foremost with Nagorno-Karabakh so that "IDPs" can serve as a visible reminder of the loss of Nagorno-Karabakh to "all Azerbaijanis" as well as, the government of Azerbaijan hopes, the outside world that might help them regain the region.

Former Soviet Azerbaijan and Central Asia share more than related Turkic languages and Islam. They also share a practice of actively managing their present-day displaced peoples' feelings of belonging to the state in the name of the state's territorial integrity and national unity. A not inconsequential challenge that many if not most states will at some point confront is how to create a national narrative that is both acceptable to the state's minority groups and consistent with the state's vision of who belongs.

DISCUSSION QUESTIONS

PART V: CONTEXTS OF TRANSFORMATION

17. Religion

1.   How should we understand religious diversity and religious change? In what ways do different scales—micro, meso, and macro—of analysis impact this?

2.   What can be generalized about the social navigation of religion and what is unique to the Central Asian context?

18. Politics

3.   The author compares supply-side and demand-side explanations for disenchantment with politics. Which do you think are more important in explaining politics in Central Asia?

4.   Why has political transition in Central Asia produced authoritarian order? Are local or global factors more important to explain transition?

19. Law

5.   In what ways have ideas of economic and legal "development" in the region been predicated on the same impetus?

6.   What does the idea of legal customization entail?

20. Education

7.   If education is preparation for the future, then how should education change when a society itself undergoes dramatic change? Think about not only the curriculum but also the preparation of teachers, the culture of the classroom (who can speak, and when, what can be challenged, whether grading emphasizes evidence of having read the assignments or original thought, what should be in the library and what other kinds of resources should be available, etc.), what kinds of people have access to various levels of education, who pays for education, and what, fundamentally, the purposes of education are.

8.   In the four contexts discussed in this section of the book (Religion, Politics, Law, and Education), authority is often held and decisions are often made by an older generation whose formative experiences were in a different society from the ones in Central Asia now. What problems might this create? What kinds of solutions are possible? How might the older generation learn about some of the new social realities that they did not themselves experience?

Case V-A: Mood and Islam in Kazakhstan

9. What examples of a shift in mood from the Soviet to post-Soviet eras can you find in the other chapters of this section?

10. People live in Soviet apartment buildings and study Soviet books, but something makes these feel different thirty years after the dissolution of the Soviet Union. What creates these different moods?

Case V-B: Spectacular Politics in the World Nomad Games

11. How can the revival of tradition be squared with intensifying globalization?

12. In a globalizing world, does the celebration of culture unavoidably imply its commodification?

Case V-C: Displacement and Belonging in Eurasia

13. What is the difference between citizenship and belonging?

14. How and why have Azerbaijan's IDPs struggled to belong to Azerbaijan?

FURTHER READING

17. Religion

Balci, Bayram. *Islam in Central Asia and the Caucasus since the Fall of the Soviet Union*. London: Hurst, 2018.

Foltz, Richard. *Religions of the Silk Road: Premodern Patterns of Globalization*. 2nd ed. New York: Palgrave Macmillan, 2010.

Gatling, Benjamin.. *Expressions of Sufi Culture in Tajikistan*. Madison: University of Wisconsin, 2018.

Jones, Pauline, ed. *Islam, Society, and Politics in Central Asia*. Pittsburgh: University of Pittsburgh Press, 2017.

Khalid, Adeeb. *Islam after Communism: Religion and Politics in Central Asia*. Berkeley: University of California Press, 2007.

Levi, Scott C., and Ron Sela, eds. *Islamic Central Asia: An Anthology of Historical Sources*. Bloomington: Indiana University Press, 2010.

Louw, Maria Elisabeth. *Everyday Islam in Post-Soviet Central Asia*. London: Routledge, 2007.

McBrien, Julie. *From Belonging to Belief: Modern Secularisms and the Construction of Religion in Kyrgyzstan*. Pittsburgh: University of Pittsburgh Press, 2017.

Montgomery, David W. *Practicing Islam: Knowledge, Experience, and Social Navigation in Kyrgyzstan*. Pittsburgh: University of Pittsburgh Press, 2016.

Pelkmans, Mathijs. *Fragile Conviction: Changing Ideological Landscapes in Urban Kyrgyzstan*. Ithaca, NY: Cornell University Press, 2017.

Peshkova, Svetlana. *Women, Islam, and Identity: Public Life in Private Spaces in Uzbekistan*. Syracuse: Syracuse University Press, 2014.

Pickett, James. *Polymaths of Islam: Power and Networks of Knowledge in Central Asia*. Ithaca, NY: Cornell University Press, 2020.

Privratsky, Bruce G. *Muslim Turkistan: Kazak Religion and Collective Memory.* Richmond, Surrey, UK: Curzon, 2001.

Rasanayagam, Johan. *Islam in Post-Soviet Uzbekistan: The Morality of Experience.* Cambridge: Cambridge University Press, 2011.

18. Politics

Cooley, Alexander C., and John Heathershaw. *Dictators without Borders: Power and Money in Central Asia.* New Haven, CT: Yale University Press, 2017.

Dadabaev, Timur. "How Does Transition Work in Central Asia? Coping with Ideological, Economic and Value System Changes in Uzbekistan." *Central Asian Survey* 26, no. 3 (2007): 407–28.

Driscoll, Jesse. *Warlords and Coalition Politics in Post-Soviet States.* Cambridge: Cambridge University Press, 2015.

Hay, Colin. *Why We Hate Politics.* London: Polity, 2008.

Heathershaw, John, and Edward Schatz, eds. *Paradox of Power: Logics of State Weakness in Eurasia.* Pittsburgh: Pittsburgh University Press, 2017.

Ismailbekova, Aksana. *Blood Ties and the Native Son: Poetics of Patronage in Kyrgyzstan.* Bloomington: Indiana University Press, 2017.

Liu, Morgan. "Post-Soviet Paternalism and Personhood: Why Culture Matters to Democratization in Central Asia." In *Prospects for Democracy in Central Asia*, edited by Birgit Schlyter, 225–38. Istanbul: Swedish Research Institute in Istanbul, 2005.

Megoran, Nick. *Nationalism in Central Asia: A Biography of the Uzbekistan-Kyrgyzstan Boundary.* Pittsburgh: Pittsburgh University Press, 2017.

Offe, Claus, and Pierre Adler. "Capitalism by Democratic Design? Democratic Theory Facing the Triple Transition in East Central Europe." *Social Research* 58, no. 4 (1991): 865–92.

Radnitz, Scott. *Weapons of the Wealthy: Predatory Regimes and Elite-Led Protests in Central Asia.* Ithaca, NY: Cornell University Press, 2010.

Reeves, Madeleine. "The Ashar-State: Communal Commitment and State Elicitation in Rural Kyrgyzstan." In *Paradox of Power: The Logics of State Weakness in Eurasia*, edited by John Heathershaw and Edward Schatz, 216–31. Pittsburgh: University of Pittsburgh Press, 2017.

Spector, Regine. *Order at the Bazaar: Power and Trade in Central Asia.* Ithaca, NY: Cornell University Press, 2017.

19. Law

Beyer, Judith. "Constitutional Faith: Law and Hope in Revolutionary Kyrgyzstan." *Ethnos* 30, no. 3 (2015): 320–45.

Beyer, Judith. "Customizations of Law: Courts of Elders (Aksakal Courts) in Rural and Urban Kyrgyzstan." *PoLAR* 38, no. 1 (2015): 53–71.

Beyer, Judith. *The Force of Custom: Law and the Ordering of Everyday Life in Kyrgyzstan.* Pittsburgh: University of Pittsburgh Press, 2016.

Epkenhans, Tim. "Regulating Religion in Post-Soviet Central Asia: Some Remarks on Religious Association Law and 'Official' Islamic Institutions in Tajikistan." *Security and Human Rights* 20, no. 1 (2009): 94–99.

Furnivall, John S. "The Fashioning of Leviathan: The Beginnings of British Rule in Burma." *Burma Research Society Journal* 29, no. 1 (1939): 1–137.

Levi, Scott C., and Ron Sela, eds. *Islamic Central Asia: An Anthology of Historical Sources.* Bloomington: Indiana University Press, 2010.

Martin, Virginia. *Law and Custom in the Steppe: The Kazakhs of the Middle Horde and Russian Colonialism in the Nineteenth Century.* London: Routledge, 2001.

Massell, Gregory J. "Family Law and Social Mobilization in Soviet Central Asia: Some Comparisons with Communist China." *Canadian Slavonic Papers / Revue Canadienne des Slavistes* 17, no. 2/3 (1975): 374–403.

Rasulov, Akbar. "Central Asia and the Globalisation of the Contemporary Legal Consciousness." *Law and Critique* 25, no. 2 (2014): 163–85.

Sartori, Paolo. *Visions of Justice: Shariʻa and Cultural Change in Russian Central Asia.* Leiden: Brill, 2016.

Starr, S. Frederick. *Lost Enlightenment: Central Asia's Golden Age.* Princeton, NJ: Princeton University Press, 2013.

20. Education

DeYoung, Alan. J., Madeleine Reeves, and Galina K. Valyayeva. *Surviving the Transition? Case Studies of Schools and Schooling in the Kyrgyz Republic since Independence.* Charlotte, NC: Information Age, 2006.

Huisman, Jeroen, Anna Smolentseva, and Isak Froumin, eds. *25 Years of Transformations of Higher Education Systems in Post-Soviet Countries: Reform and Continuity.* New York: Palgrave Macmillan, 2018.

Merrill, Martha C. "Kasha and Quality in Kyrgyzstan: Donors, Diversity, and Dis-integration in Higher Education." *European Education* 43, no. 4 (2011): 5–25.

Silova, Iveta, and Sarfaroz Niyozov, eds. *Globalization on the Margins: Education and Post-Socialist Transformations in Central Asia.* 2nd ed. Charlotte, NC: Information Age, 2020.

Silova, Iveta, and Gita Steiner-Khamsi. "Introduction: Unwrapping the Post-Socialist Education Reform Package." In *How NGOs React: Globalization and Education Reform in the Caucasus, Central Asia, and Mongolia,* edited by Iveta Silova and Gita Steiner-Khamsi, 1–42. Bloomfield, CT: Kumarian Press, 2008.

Case V-A: Mood and Islam in Kazakhstan

Ahmed, Sara. "Not in the Mood." *New Formations: A Journal of Culture/Theory/Politics* 82 (2014): 13–28.

Privratsky, Bruce G. *Muslim Turkistan: Kazak Religion and Collective Memory.* Richmond, Surrey, UK: Curzon, 2001.

Schwab, Wendell. "Traditions and Texts: How Two Young Women Learned to Interpret the Qur'an and Hadiths in Kazakhstan." *Contemporary Islam* 6, no. 2 (2012): 173–97.

Schwab, Wendell. "Visual Culture and Islam in Kazakhstan: The Case of Asyl Arna's Social Media." *Central Asian Affairs* 3, no. 4 (2016): 301–29.

Yurchak, Alexei. *Everything Was Forever, Until It Was No More: The Last Soviet Generation.* Princeton, NJ: Princeton University Press, 2005.

Case V-B: Spectacular Politics in the World Nomad Games

Adams, Laura. *The Spectacular State: Culture and National Identity in Uzbekistan.* Durham, NC: Duke University Press, 2010.

Heide, Nienke van der. *Spirited Performance: The Manas Epic and Society in Kyrgyzstan.* PhD diss., Tilburg University, 2008.

İğmen, Ali. *Speaking Soviet with an Accent: Culture and Power in Kyrgyzstan.* Pittsburgh: University of Pittsburgh Press, 2012.

Pelkmans, Mathijs. *Fragile Conviction: Changing Ideological Landscapes in Urban Kyrgyzstan*. Ithaca, NY: Cornell University Press, 2017.

Case V-C: Displacement and Belonging in Eurasia

Broers, Laurence. "The Nagorny Karabakh Conflict: Defaulting to War." Research paper, Chatham House, Royal Institute of International Affairs, Russia and Eurasia Programme, 2016.

De Waal, Thomas. *Black Garden: Armenia and Azerbaijan through Peace and War*. New York: New York University Press, 2003.

Diener, Alexander. "Homeland as Social Construct: Territorialization among Kazakhstan's Germans and Koreans." *Nationalities Papers* 34, no. 2 (2006): 201–35.

Dudwick, Nora. "The Cultural Construction of Political Violence in Armenia and Azerbaijan." *Problems of Post-Communism* 42, no. 4 (1995): 18–23.

Ferrando, Olivier. "Soviet Population Transfers and Interethnic Relations in Tajikistan: Assessing the Concept of Ethnicity." *Central Asian Survey* 30, no. 1 (2011): 39–52.

Garagozov, Rauf. "Narratives in Conflict: A Perspective." *Dynamics of Asymmetric Conflict* 5, no. 2 (2012): 101–6.

Ro'i, Yaacov. "The Transformation of Historiography on the 'Punished Peoples.'" *History and Memory* 21, no. 2 (2009): 150–76.

Rowland, Richard. "National and Regional Population Trends in Azerbaijan." *Eurasian Geography and Economics* 45, no. 4 (2004): 285–315.

PART VI

CONTEXTS OF WORK

In thinking through the context of work, of how people direct their efforts toward the accomplishment or production of something, we often begin with ideas around labor. But as the chapters in this section show, resources, economics, and property all are central to livelihoods and the means by which ends are met.

Jeanne Féaux de la Croix and David Gullette begin the discussion by offering a frame for thinking through resources, of how natural resources have been utilized throughout the region as well as how they have been purposed to varied ends. Resources were central to Soviet efforts to energize the region, facilitating the increase of labor productivity. But whether the use of water for irrigation or the production of energy, or mining and mineral extraction, the exploitation of resources has consequences that are unevenly distributed.

Elmira Satybaldieva and Balihar Sanghera's chapter situates the experience of inequality within the story of economics. While Soviet-planned economic development influenced the nature of work, the post-Soviet neoliberalization of the economy led to extraction-based growth through foreign investment and debt-led growth through foreign loans. Capital, like natural resources, remains an opportunity for corruption and thus a space for exploitation, which we see in Eric McGlinchey's chapter on property. How property was understood and managed changed over time—from being state owned during the Soviet period to the privatization of property at the time of independence—and while property is often at the mercy of elite corruption, occasionally there are opportunities for procedural resistance.

Labor of course drives much of the discussion around work. In his chapter, Russell Zanca writes about the nature of labor and what working was like before and after the Soviet transformation of it. We see the connection of labor to education and the emergence of women as workers and contributors to public production in new ways. With independence, labor is transformed yet again, with authoritarian influence on labor being shaped by geopolitics and notions of development.

As we see in the cases, there is a good deal that influences what work looks like and the opportunities one is afforded. Victoria Clement talks about language and literacy in Turkmenistan, and we see the often overlooked way that language shapes and transforms the possibilities for collectively engaging in one's surroundings. Sophie Roche looks at the growing population of young people and the struggle to find work that leads many to migrate. Through her Tajik interlocutors, we see the impact of privatized land on farming and the strategies of family risk management that migrants employ. And in his case, Olivier Ferrando takes a broader view of national and regional cooperation by looking at Eurasian integration. Focusing on customs unions and the Eurasian Economic Union, we get a sense of how events outside the region—such as the Ukrainian crisis in 2015—impact the response of states within the region and the prospects for work that those in the region seek.

21

Resources

Jeanne Féaux de la Croix and David Gullette

aps are powerful tools: they can invite exploration, occupation, and development plans of all kinds. Maps are of course also the result of exploration, and sometimes occupation. In the map below (figure 21–1), Central Asia is scattered unevenly with small, decorative symbols. Lots of little boxes indicating the presence of oil and gas litter western Kazakhstan, while the mountains of Kyrgyzstan are beset with shapes of all kinds, showing a wide variety of minerals. Turkmenistan, meanwhile, shows a judiciously spaced sprinkling of gas reserves—and very little else. Of course, there are dozens of other ways a region could be described in a map (e.g., by highlighting river basins, the presence of different ethnic groups, or transport networks). In this chapter, we explore the effect of this map and the associated "resource thinking." In discussing natural resources, we also explore how and why something comes to be valued as a "resource" in the first place, and what effect "resource thinking" can have on people and their environment. What are the most important natural resources in Central Asia and how has the balance of this assessment changed over the past century? We provide an in-depth discussion of fresh water and electricity, two resources that are closely related in the region but do not feature at all on the map. Examining their role and co-development reveals all sorts of implications for economic, social, and political changes in Central Asia. In addition, a short outlook on subsoil minerals, such as gold, shows how the mining sector intersects with social development and environmental concerns.

The perception of some regions is dominated by the idea of particular resources, such as oil in the Arab peninsula or diamonds in the Democratic Republic of Congo. Central Asia has lived through many resource booms and

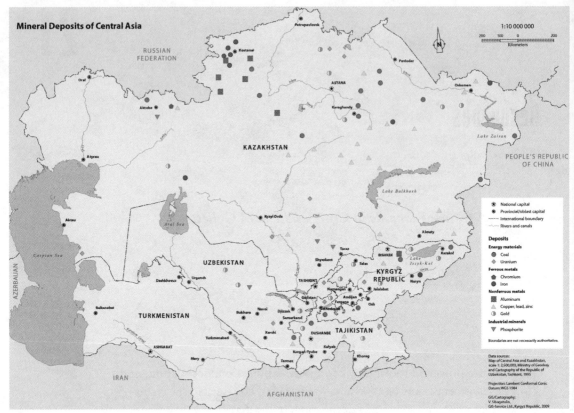

Mineral Deposits of Central Asia

Deposits

Energy materials
- Coal
- Uranium

Ferrous metals
- Chromium
- Iron

Nonferrous metals
- Aluminum
- Copper, lead, zinc
- Gold

Industrial minerals
- Phosphorite

Boundaries are not necessarily authoritative.

Data sources:
Map of Central Asia and Kazakhstan,
scale 1:2,500,000, Ministry of Geodesy
and Cartography of the Republic of
Uzbekistan, Tashkent, 1995

Projection: Lambert Conformal Conic
Datum: WGS 1984

GIS/Cartography:
V. Sibagatulin,
GIS-Service Ltd., Kyrgyz Republic, 2009

- National capital
- Provincial/oblast capital
- International boundary
- Rivers and canals

21-1   Mineral Deposits of Central Asia, 2010. Map courtesy of the Asian Development Bank.

busts, such as the late nineteenth-century European fashion for coats of Kar-akul sheepskins, which had a huge impact on local markets until the Russian revolution, or the boom and bust of fishing on the Aral Sea in the mid-twenti-eth century. Central Asia has long been dominated by an economy focused on exporting natural resources, particularly since the decline of Soviet industries that did, to some degree, locate their further processing within the region.

Today, Kazakhstan, Turkmenistan, and Uzbekistan draw wealth primarily from exporting gas and oil. And all five post-Soviet Central Asian states have significant mining operations, such as gold, coal, and uranium. Harnessing the rivers pouring from the mountain ranges has added hydropower to the port-folio for Kyrgyzstan and Tajikistan, as well as a vastly expanded agricultural sector in the lowlands, with fruit, vegetables, and wheat. Cotton-growing plan-tations still dominate a large sector of Uzbekistan's agriculture in particular.

How Does "Resource Thinking" Work?

The hopes and fears related to the discovery of natural wealth by explorers such as P. P. Semenov (1858) or I. V. Mushketov (1886) on scientific missions has long been part of the story of political struggles over territory. This was true in the days of the British and tsarist empires, as it is in the days of oil boom and bust. But natural resources are not just "there," waiting to be found. For example, rare earth metals were not particularly desirable until the spread of mobile phones. Meanwhile, obsidian is no longer as great a global treasure as in the days of early *Homo sapiens*, who used it to produce the best-quality tools and weapons. In other words, the value of metals or crops not only fluctuates on the stock market but also according to the "job" people foresee for different kinds of things. This comes close to the Oxford English Dictionary definition of a resource as the "source" of something valuable, an asset or reserve. Natural things are not automatically a resource: they have to be appropriated by humans in some way, introduced into a chain of use and exchange. In other words, anything can potentially become a resource—if it is viewed as a resource, treated as a resource, and transformed in some way by people. This means that a natural resource is always imagined as a sort of storage space of value for the future, one that people have every right to acquire and manipulate. It should be noted that this is not the only possible, or even always predominant, way of perceiving and treating the environment: not everyone assumes that humans have the right to simply grab what they see and like. There are many alternative ways of seeing and treating the world, and very few humans think in these terms all the time. The vocabulary to describe a valuable asset as a "resource" seems to be colonizing other domains, as in "human resources." Worldwide we are witnessing multiple, long-term negative consequences for humans and nonhumans based on the transformation of living beings, substance, skills, and people into "resources."

Resource thinking is always about the future ("What could we do with this?"); even rumor or prediction of the existence of a resource such as oil can dramatically affect the economy of regions and countries, as they "gear up" for an oil boom and extraction that may never happen. The inverse dynamic is of course also likely: people may expect a resource crunch or exhaustion and thus position themselves to limit their economic exposure. Looking at the countries of the Middle East in particular, the "resource curse" theory suggests that if a country generates a lot of wealth through a single resource such as oil, this allows a small elite to benefit disproportionality, and other economic sectors are left underdeveloped. This dynamic, in turn, may fuel corruption and stimulate autocratic rather than democratic tendencies. In truth, who has a right to benefit from natural resources such as forests, fish, or coal is always a matter of negotiation, with many different ideas of entitlement at play. For example, should provinces with big hydro-power dams get cheaper electricity rates? How much should oil workers themselves benefit from the treasures they unearth? And who bears the cost of environmental degradation, the displacement of residents to kick-start an industry, or of accidents? Both resource wealth and dearth may precipitate conflict: this is because such conflicts are mainly about the *distribution* of resources, and as such reflect already existing social and political struggles.

A Short History of Identifying and Utilizing Natural Resources from Central Asia

Central Asia has been subjected to an incredible range of reform attempts, from nationalizing resources and integrating them in central Soviet planning, to establishing new resources such as hydropower, which gave mountainous regions like the Kyrgyz or Tajik Soviet Socialist Republics completely new roles. In their conquest of the area, the last tsars were particularly interested in the region as a source of arable land to settle newly freed Russian serfs, as well as seeing Central Asia as an arena of prestigious territorial expansion. Russian surveyors reported the vast steppes and deserts—that we now think of as "Kazakh" or "Turkmen" and part of a once intricate economy of mobile pastoralists—as "empty" and devoid of worth. It was assumed that land would only generate income and become beautiful if it was put under the plough to produce wheat and cotton, in particular. When powerful newcomers assess natural resources and their current management, this often results in a moralizing discourse about how industrious, lazy, or ignorant the local population is. Creating new ways of extracting and trading resources thus often entails claims that not only wealth is brought to the region but also that this is a "civilizing" mission. As in other colonial contexts such as North America, the right of Russian rule was partly legitimated by the claim that they would properly develop the region—that is, to generate wealth from a natural environment "underused," or even "misused," by the local population. The long-term experience, and sophisticated indigenous knowledge of how to manage pastures and irrigated agricultural land, for example, went largely unappreciated. In these terms, Central Asian environments have long been used by conquering powers to intensify resource extraction and redistribute property rights.

This is not to claim that indigenous people are necessarily perfect "managers" of land or biodiversity. Nor is it to ignore that the transhumant pastoralists, farmers, and merchants of Central Asia were not already under pressure from tax demands or population pressure to extract wealth, perhaps unsustainably. Certain Russian observers and travelers did investigate and value these practices, but this perspective did not gain the upper hand in deciding how to manage the region's resources.

The aforementioned example of "empty," "barren," or even "virgin" land already suggests that whether something is recognized as valuable is a question of social practices, economy, and politics. For example, what kind of expectations does an observer, a locally experienced producer, or new user bring to the idea of what "good" (rich) land looks like? And what does "good" natural resource management look like? How do these ideas relate to different economic systems, such as a Soviet five-year plan versus private ownership of a mine? Generating wealth through resources always involves creating new infrastructures, social, economic, and political developments, and the need to draw on other resources. Because they never stand alone, it can be helpful

JEANNE FÉAUX DE LA CROIX AND DAVID GULLETTE

to think about "resource complexes"—that is, specific combinations of these elements. For example, in order to grow and sell cotton in Central Asia, huge volumes of water are channeled from the region's rivers, and fertilizers, pesticides, tractors, and trucks are acquired. Significant human labor is organized to plant and harvest crops, or to care for the irrigation networks. In addition, organizations have to be created to export and deal in raw cotton on the global textile markets. Thus, we see how interconnected relations develop the view of a resource and how it is shaped to a particular end.

Water as Plant and Lightbulb Fuel

From the argument above, it follows that water for drinking and feeding crops like cotton, or the use of water to create electricity, are equally part of such a resource complex. Valuing water for these ends and putting it to use in these specific ways stems from a particular development history. This history includes fashions such as jeans, profiting from the spread of cotton from India through the British Empire, alongside ideas that a modern household should be hooked up to an electricity grid, rather than feeding off solar panels.

In comparison with wide swathes of the Middle East, Central Asia does not rank very high in water stress indexes, which, for example, measure accessible water reserves per citizen. However, since rainfall is sparse, water has always been distributed mainly through the large rivers that flow from the Pamir and Tian Shan massifs, releasing melting snowfall and glacier runoff, especially in the spring. This means that flooding can easily occur, even in a relatively arid region. Because water has always been distributed unevenly across the area, and fluctuates according to the season, established nomadic societies of the steppes, highlands, and deserts regulated the movements of animals and people in relation to known sources—rivers and lakes—and seasonal grazing was dependent on rain and snowfall.

As in Syria or West Africa, rights to drinking water were a common good, though the ability to pass through other groups' territories—and thus use the local water sources—could be bound to tribute or equally costly gestures of goodwill and alliances. Since the Bronze Age, in settled areas of Central Asia, extensive irrigation networks were developed, sometimes piecemeal by generations of farming communities, and sometimes by edict of a central authority. Along rivers, the fluctuating climate could also mean that large swamps and shallow lakes could act as water reservoirs and amphibious biotopes. As in other areas of the world that were put under the plow, Central Asia lost vast swathes of these wetlands and has, with the increased control of water by canals, paradoxically become more prone to unplanned and catastrophic flooding.

Today, the Amu Darya and Syr Darya river basins account for 90 percent of Central Asia's river water, of which 75 percent is tapped for irrigated agriculture. This arterial canal system was vastly extended by Soviet planners, who were concerned with making the USSR independent of US cotton imports and turned the system into one of the most complex networks in the world. Many large dams were built in the postwar period to further harness water as a resource, including Tajikistan's Nurek dam, which at 300 meters long held the record of the highest dam wall in the world.

'In the Soviet era, neighboring republics integrated their water and energy infrastructure, and agreed annual shares in river flow. Since independence, these agreements have disintegrated, as Kyrgyzstan and Tajikistan started to release more water in the winter months to meet their electricity needs. This in turn causes winter flooding and restricts water in spring and summer for irrigation in Uzbekistan and Kazakhstan. As a consequence, Uzbekistan long protested new dam infrastructures upstream in Kyrgyzstan and Tajikistan. Competing uses of the river between hydroelectric dams and irrigation systems have been a cause of the most protracted regional disputes as well as environmental damage. The most extreme example of the consequences of redirecting water flows is the catastrophic shrinking of the Aral Sea, which has lost more than 90 percent of its volume since the mid-twentieth century. A once thriving Soviet fishing industry and several shore towns collapsed in the course of this desertification, with dramatic pictures of rusting hulls on a now polluted desert seabed that even made it into a Pink Floyd video. However, 10 percent of the Aral Sea has recovered quickly due the completion of the Kok-Aral Dam in 2005, funded by the World Bank and Kazakhstan. There is a significant drawback though: this dam replenishes only the northern part, reducing inflow to the rest of the sea's original expanse. Since glacier melt combined with population growth in the region is likely to place increasing human demands on Central Asian rivers, these conflicts of interest will probably intensify. If not conflict, the general risk potential, in a highly seismic region, is still a significant concern in the region. For example, in 2020 the new Sardoba Dam reservoir in Uzbekistan burst its banks during a storm and flooded thousands of homes in downriver Kazakhstan.

Because this "resource complex" is so central, and yet so intractable, transboundary water issues have been under extensive scrutiny by a variety of governmental and international agencies since the 1990s, producing a host of policy-oriented research. The water question in Central Asia is mainly treated as a management issue, recommending the establishment of formal institutions such as the International Fund for Saving the Aral Sea, water user associations, and integrated water management approaches. There has also been a strong effort to establish regional institutions and cooperative agreements on sharing these rivers, but with few positive results. These initiatives have a strong tendency to see rivers, glaciers, and lakes in the abstract as volume, "pure" water resources, as it were.

If we contextualize "resource thinking" in a way that sees natural elements as passive things that can be isolated, appropriated, and "extracted" from their context for the purpose of profit, then that is what rivers become: essentially, nothing more than "drainage ditches" or water storage tanks. Yet large bodies of water, such as the Aral Sea or the Ili River, continue to be much more to the people living along their banks than simply a neutral amount of water to be

JEANNE FÉAUX DE LA CROIX AND DAVID GULLETTE

transformed into goods such as electricity or wheat. For example, Lake Issyk Kul is the most famous among Central Asia's many holy lakes, and sacred springs are common pilgrimage destinations for their healing properties.

In India, Rohan D'Souza describes that groundwater mining, regular canal irrigation, and large dams are not sustainable for water management. This has led people to realize that treating resources as engineering projects or bureaucratic objects to be regulated is deeply misguided. Ecologists and activists highlight how water systems are diverse arrangements of life for people and animals.

This example illustrates that "resource-thinking" is not a neutral activity but shaped, on the one hand, by certain ideas about the natural world and human relationship to it, including rights and responsibilities. On the other hand, it is also shaped by certain economic systems, such as integration in a planned socialist economy or global market system. In this sense, describing Central Asia's resources, whether through the historical narrative above, through maps, or through other means, is by no means an "innocent" exercise. Rather, it is a way of viewing the world that opens up certain possibilities of engagement with water, such as building and managing big dams, and closes off other ways of interacting, such as allowing natural floods to fertilize fields. So, in accordance with the very policy-oriented (one could also say bureau-cratically informed, or top-down) view of water "resources," Central Asian rivers in particular have in the past decades been treated as the main artery of a river basin, rather than entities with a history and human relations attached, or as a biotope in its own right. Thinking entirely in terms of allocating wa-ter quantities also marginalizes unsolved questions about water quality or biotopes: who pays the cost of sapping water from rivers, as in the case of the shrinking Aral Sea; mining glaciers, as at Kumtor gold mine in Kyrgyzstan; or pollution flowing along the Ili River from Chinese factories to Kazakhstan? The transition from the way water was used and owned in the Soviet period to the transboundary conflicts developing between independent republics demon-strates that different ways of scaling and boundary making around water have an enormous impact on how people, institutions such as governments, factories using river water, or urban residents needing drinking water, may access it.

How to "Energize" Central Asia

Apart from functioning as a "drink" for crops and citizens, water in the region has also acquired new value through the development of extensive hydropower facilities. Up to 90 percent of Kyrgyzstan's electricity is generated by the Naryn River cascade of hydroelectric plants, reshaping the landscape of an entire region. Tajikistan is similarly dependent on hydropower along the Vakhsh River, where the large Nurek Dam is being overtaken by the even taller Rogun Dam. In this section, we explain the development of energy re-sources in Central Asia, and their coevolution with the control of fresh water.

Vladimir Lenin's 1920 catchphrase—"Communism equals Soviet power plus the electrification of the whole country"—was the start of an ambitious plan of development through electricity. By 1990, around 95 percent of the total population in each of the Central Asian republics had access to electricity. Small electricity plants in parts of Central Asia were later succeeded by small-scale hydropower and thermoelectric power stations in the 1930s to provide electricity for the agricultural sector. Planning from the 1950s and 1960s saw the construction of large-scale hydropower stations in the region. Many of the hydropower plants that were built after independence have in fact been based on Soviet designs from the 1980s. What developed during the Soviet era was in essence a moral economy that developed between the state and its citizens. In the Soviet Union, some resources, such as import goods, were in scarce supply, with access often facilitated through informal networks. But in the later Soviet period, energy was widely experienced as abundant, guaranteed, and heavily subsidized by the state.

Since the end of the Soviet Union, the amount of energy that can be extracted, processed, and generated has made Central Asia a place of interest for large companies. For example, significant oil reserves in Kazakhstan and large gas reserves in Turkmenistan have attracted interest from neighboring countries. Hydroelectric resources in Kyrgyzstan and Tajikistan are being explored as export potential to South Asia. The strategic location of these republics between Europe, China, and the Far East has led to discussions of the geopolitical significance of the republics and the influence of bigger regional powers and markets on them. The interests of various governments in the region, and especially its energy resources, have led some to compare this period to the "Great Game," when the British and Russian empires competed for influence in the region.

These developments, however, have costs. In post-Soviet republics, heavily subsidized utilities, such as electricity, were enjoyed by many. Engineering achievements, particularly in dam construction, enabled many places to become electrified and to receive other basic utilities. The breakup of the Soviet Union created a challenge in maintaining water and energy infrastructures and distributing them adequately.

Energy Economies, Fair and Square?

While there were difficulties with energy during the Soviet era, most citizens now view it as a better system than the one that replaced it. Privatization, poor management, and rampant corruption are eroding relations with the state energy provider and fomenting popular discontent. The "fair price" that was established in the Soviet era, and continued in many republics after independence, is giving way to market forces and increasing prices that are accompanied by neither investment in infrastructure nor improvements in service.

Large-scale hydropower installations enable Kyrgyzstan to generate electricity for domestic and export use. Though the rhythm and priorities of generating electricity have changed (see above), investments into maintaining the existing infrastructure have not improved general access or the quality of electricity provided. Apart from a few square kilometers in the center of the capital, Bishkek, blackouts are a normal part of life. Poor infrastructure maintenance and poor management of water resources still cause significant anger toward the government. In 2010, this frustration was one element that led to the ouster of then president Kurmanbek Bakiev. The introduction of a poorly developed energy tariff policy and dogged allegations of corruption in the president's family circle sparked demonstrations in April 2010. People objected to the increased rates, which were beyond their ability to pay. In a country where one-third live in poverty, an increase in basic utilities was a significant concern. Moreover, people refused to pay more for electricity when the dilapidated infrastructure frequently resulted in power outages. Bakiev's intransigence and poor management came to be seen as disloyalty to the population and as "shameful" (shame being a particularly powerful social force in Kyrgyzstan). This was combined with people's shock when government troops killed eighty-four protestors. Bakiev's attempts to regain power in the aftermath caused further destabilization, and eventually he sought asylum abroad. In the wake of this tragedy, the government has been cautious not to repeat mistakes with the tariff policy. This caution has of course not solved the problem of electricity supply. Instead, the development focus has been on upgrading existing dams, and partial success in building more hydropower facilities, such as the Kambar-Ata-2 site. These are meant to address both energy security issues and create additional export potential.

The control over such resources has enabled other regimes to stay in power, often at the expense of democratic governance and respecting basic freedoms. Fueled by oil wealth, Kazakhstan built the new capital of Nur-Sultan in the harsh northern steppe environment. Though policies on distributing oil wealth have shifted somewhat, the extravagance of the city's architecture still stands in stark contrast to the underdevelopment of other parts of the country and lower quality of life. People's frustration with a lack of development, coupled with ongoing government support to foreign companies, came to a head in the town of Zhanaozen in December 2011, when Kazakh oil company workers demonstrated for better working rights. Sixteen people were killed as riot police moved in to break up the protest. Protests also broke out in May 2016 over new legislation proposing to expand land sales to private investors. Police made mass arrests of people demonstrating their concerns about the reforms that could make it easier for foreign nationals to acquire land resources in the country. Taken together, we see how the uneven distribution of natural resources and their control can cause conflict in situations of both wealth and dearth.

In other cases, the relationship between the state and the energy consumer has been interrupted by intermediaries that profit from utility charges. In Azerbaijan, for example, gas meter readers have become the chief intermediary that determines costs and whether a person has a connection. The state-run company has lost some of its power and has been replaced by intermediaries that impose their own, potentially corrupt practices. The state that once led and subsidized access to the energy infrastructure is undermined by minor officials, a move that erodes people's trust in the government. In some contexts, the lack of access to energy can also be interpreted as a form of wider discrimination. In Afghanistan, Hazaras in Bamyan see this "exclusion" as a calculated attempt by the majority Pashtuns to further isolate them. In such a situation, the absence of basic utilities creates shared experiences of exclusion.

Consumers' relations with the state and the provision of energy are important aspects of everyday life in Central Asia and other former Soviet countries. But the changed economic and political constellations that affect energy resources have not always changed consumers' expectations about what may constitute as "fair" or "expected" accessibility. These discrepancies become particularly obvious where feelings of entitlement to energy intersect with other changes, such as ethnic and political power struggles or the privatization of energy services. As we have seen, these complex grievances can become a real flashpoint of discontent.

Mining Minerals, Destroying or Harvesting Natural Resources?

The extraction of minerals in Central Asia creates potential economic advantages: employment, taxes, and wider wealth. Public discussion of different kinds of local impact are weighed against each other in a contested narrative of rights and benefits. Local populations often feel the immediate impact of the exploitation of mineral resources, and there are continual health and safety concerns. For example, locals often engage in artisanal gold mining or dig in abandoned coal mines as a source of income and for their own heating needs. But local miners often do not wear protective equipment in these unmaintained pits. Even if mining sites are not located close to communities, pollution at the mine site may still affect people: chemicals used at the mine site can enter local waterways and soils. Although reliable data is hard to come by, this is likely the case with numerous industrial sites along Central Asian rivers, such as the Tajikistan Aluminum Company (TALCO), on the Amu Darya River. A number of radioactive tailing sites that were created in Kyrgyzstan during the Soviet era threaten the Ferghana Valley, a densely populated fertile area where the borders of Kyrgyzstan, Tajikistan, and Uzbekistan wind around each other. Reports indicate that large portions of the population could be at risk if the content of these dumps slide into rivers, during an earthquake, for example.

Environmental challenges surrounding Kumtor, the largest gold mine in the region, are an example of a strategic resource that is under significant scrutiny, particularly since a cyanide spill in 1997 and evidence of damage to the glacier on which the mine operates. Environmental concerns have also been politically exploited during a prolonged campaign to renegotiate the agreement with the Canadian owners, or encourage law makers to nationalize the mine. Although Kumtor is a significant economic resource for Kyrgyzstan, the contestation with people's concerns for their health and environment has not abated.

Regulation on extractive industries has developed significantly, but there are still gaps that create further ambiguity over the future of mining operations, such as environmental protection legislation, including glaciers. In Kyrgyzstan, for example, one of the biggest issues is to agree on a social package or compensation by the local company to the locally affected communities. Yet, the specifics of what this compensation should be or the value of the compensation is not discussed in legislation. This creates disputes on the expected returns of the mineral resources. These local-level issues, conflicts, and forms of activism are an important part of understanding the positive and negative aspects of subsoil resource extraction and how it affects social and political life.

Mineral resources thus contain as much potential for contention as they do value. However, the anticipation of returns and hope of limiting negative impacts to people and the environment often enables mining projects to go forward. The expected financial returns influence the market and legislation to develop infrastructure around mining activities, as well as an arena for shady deals over licensing between investors and government actors. However, these changes bring with them other questions, open up space for contestation, and reveal new visions for communities and the country. The concept of a resource immediately becomes an ambiguous space of future trajectories imagined as good or bad.

A Region of Milk and Honey, or Starved of Rain and Investment?

We see resources, particularly water and energy, as interlinked resource complexes that cannot be understood without comprehending their co-development in the Soviet period and the social experiences people have through and with them today. People's view of natural elements as valuable, and how they are then exploited, is closely related to the kind of society and economy to which they are accustomed or for which they strive. For example, there is currently a lot of attention to the large-scale melting of glaciers because of anxieties around climate change; thus, gold mining on glaciers comes to look even more damaging. The very existence of glaciers secures the potential of rivers to produce hydropower and to feed huge swathes of intensive agriculture.

In the Central Asian resource complex, glaciers have thus come to be viewed as essential resources, that humans have limited power to protect or enrich, at a local scale. Global projections of climate change and discussion of a dwindling freshwater reserve amid an exponentially growing population have, in turn, fed concerns about "water wars" in the region. Worldwide, so far there have in fact only been very isolated incidences of military conflicts in which water scarcity was the primary cause. However, there are indeed conflicts between different groups, particularly between neighboring villages in the Ferghana Valley, about access to drinking and irrigation water.

We saw in the case of Haraza opinions in Afghanistan how resource dearth can be interpreted in different ways, including a political intent to "starve people out." This connection also shows that the water and hydropower resource complex is linked to other important resources (e.g., agricultural land) and other forms of power (e.g., the ability to influence economic decisions). Thus, resources such as cotton cannot be produced on a large scale in Central Asia without also building an extensive irrigation system, settling people to work the cotton in rural areas, and an international textile market. Hydropower in turn could not be produced and distributed without international (or, in the case of the Soviet period, inter-republican) agreements about the use of rivers and investment, infrastructures such as roads, and bringing large numbers of specialist dam builders to the region. We could have written this chapter entirely about potatoes, apricots, tomatoes, and mixed herds of sheep, goats, cows, and horses, but the arguments we make are equally applicable to such resources. If apricots and goats appear less prominently in a country's GDP than gold, gas, and cotton, they remain essential subsistence and small-scale production resources to a huge number of people in Central Asia.

Looking at the natural environment mainly in terms of a bunch of raw materials that can be appropriated is a very particular view, lived out in its most radical form by modern colonizing empires and contemporary global capitalism. Disputes over rights to controlling resources often include the idea that current or previous resource users did not exploit them "properly." For example, tsarist officials argued that "nomads" or farming "sarts" were inefficient or even immoral in their management of land resources. In the twenty-first century, we find similar claims made by demonstrators toward the Kyrgyzstani government: it was resentment of Bakiev's inability or unwillingness to supply electricity that was a major spark leading to his overthrow. These kinds of arguments about efficiency and fairness are invoked both by present governments and development organizations: such claims should be scrutinized carefully. Finally, looking at Central Asia mainly as a region that can offer natural resources puts it in the position of a "peripheral" region in Wallerstein's world systems theory—that is, a region where raw materials are extracted by low-skilled, low-paid laborers and then processed and consumed elsewhere in the world (e.g., raw cotton made into jeans and T-shirts).

In fact, the "human resources" of Central Asia by the end of the Soviet era were well educated and skilled, a "resource" that is in continuous decline in terms of education. Central Asia's "human resources" feature increasingly in the labor they perform as migrants for countries like Russia, Kazakhstan, and Korea. Further, Central Asia's geopolitical position can be viewed as a "resource" in itself—for example, as a transport hub between Europe, the Middle East, India, and China. In other words, the map we introduced this chapter with could be drawn very differently, if one prioritized other kinds of "natural" resources.

JEANNE FÉAUX DE LA CROIX AND DAVID GULLETTE

22

Economics

Elmira Satybaldieva and Balihar Sanghera

The post-Soviet economic development has been predominantly explained through a transition paradigm, where countries are assessed to what extent authoritarian and centralized economies have been liberalized and privatized toward a market economy. Its underlying normative assertion is that economic growth and development are achieved through market mechanisms, and poor economic performance and stagnation are outcomes of a lack of political will for reforms, weak governance structures, cultural conditions, and residues of the Soviet legacy. In this chapter, we examine the economic development trajectory of Central Asian countries and argue that the "economic transition" paradigm is flawed because it fails to discern the complexity of neoliberalism-led capitalism. In particular, there is little scrutiny of "free market" reforms, indebtedness, socioeconomic inequality, corruption, and ecological damage in the region. We investigate how Western-led international financial institutions have pursued two neoliberal strategies of extraction-based and debt-led growth in Central Asia, and their negative impact on society. We also briefly discuss the emergence of two alternative economic imaginaries that can rival the US neoliberal hegemony in the region.

The Soviet Economic Development

The five Central Asian countries had no history of independent nation building. The economic structure the nations inherited by the early 1990s was an outcome of the Soviet economic system that was based on state ownership of means of production, collective farming, and central planning. Prior to the 1950s, the majority of Central Asian republics were predominantly agricultural. Specialization in cotton production was one of the main economic sectors in the Uzbek, Tajik, and Turkmen Soviet Socialist Republics (SSRs), and remained so until the disintegration of the USSR. Initially, the Kirghiz and Kazakh SSRs were pastoral economies, but in the late 1950s the "Virgin Lands" program led the Kazakh SSR to become a major grain producer.

During the Soviet period, Central Asia underwent industrialization. Many economic activities (e.g., hydropower and mineral fertilizers) developed as a consequence of cotton production in the region. The Second World War led to the development of heavy industries in the region. The Kazakh and Kirghiz SSRs were more industrialized than their neighbors, because they were part of the military industrial complex.

From the late 1960s to the late 1980s, the growth of manufacturing enterprises varied in Central Asia. For instance, in 1985 the Kirghiz SSR had thirty-four manufacturing enterprises that supplied eighty countries with seventy-one types of commodities, including pumps, household and automobile electric lamps, cotton fabrics, silk and wool, knitted articles, engineering goods, and antimony and nonferrous metallurgy products. In 1990, the industrial sector in the Kirghiz SSR employed more than 30 percent of the labor force and accounted for 34 percent of the gross domestic product (GDP). In the Uzbek SSR, 40 percent of the workers were employed in agriculture and about 16 percent worked in industry. The agricultural and industrial outputs were linked to the all-Union market and were closely linked with enterprises in other Soviet republics.

Despite the Soviet Union's flaws in economic development strategies (e.g., forced collectivization and monotowns during the Stalinist period), economic resources were often valued for their productive capacity, collective property rights functioned to serve society, industrial enterprises had social obligations, and the state prohibited idle and speculative economic activities. State socialist societies achieved high levels of human development, providing education, health, housing, and employment for all citizens.

But a fundamental contradiction of the Soviet economy was between the system of production and the system of surplus appropriation. The centralized control and allocation of the surplus product meant that individual enterprises had an interest to minimize the surplus that they produced. Like capitalism, state socialism was a system within which the practice of individual rationality produced socially irrational consequences. In addition, the Soviet industrial complex was skewed toward the production of armaments, so that there was a shortage of consumer goods. Soviet enterprises also failed to keep up in advanced technologies and often used informal social networks to overcome the problem of a lack of quality and quantity of products.

During the late 1980s, the Soviet Union implemented market reforms ("perestroika") to help tackle the contradictions. Individual enterprises were given material incentives to increase production and make suppliers more responsive to consumers' needs. But in the end, it was political change, rather than economic failures, that marked the end of the Soviet system.

ELMIRA SATYBALDIEVA AND BALIHAR SANGHERA

Neoliberalizing Central Asia

In the late 1970s, neoliberalism emerged as an economic imaginary to tackle the crisis of Atlantic Fordism in Western economies, and it gained global hegemony by the late 1980s. The Central Asian states did not want the dissolution of the Soviet Union and were unprepared to manage its negative economic repercussions and problems. Western-led international financial institutions, such as the International Monetary Fund (IMF) and the World Bank, promoted neoliberalism as a policy agenda (sometimes also referred to as the Washington Consensus) to address economic problems facing the region. Central Asian states were thus left to choose between economic isolationism or market-driven reforms.

Neoliberalism aimed to extend market values beyond the economic sphere to other areas, thereby becoming a model for society. Neoliberal interventions were political in nature, designed to remove all barriers for the new mode of capital accumulation. It justified and legitimized new economic practices based on highly abstract moral values, such as choice, individualism, autonomy, and freedom. Actually existing markets, however, were shaped by structural and social inequalities.

Neoliberal capitalism has two critical features. First is the ability of economic actors to extract income from existing assets without engaging in anything new in the production sphere, or the real economy. In a reversal of the classical ideal of a "free market" (a market free from land rent, monopoly rent, and interest), neoliberalism seeks to free markets from state control and regulation. This allows the propertied class to receive rent based on the ownership and control of existing scarce assets rather than on their contribution to the provision of new goods and services. Individuals who extract income based on existing assets are called "rentiers." This form of capitalism legitimizes extraction-based and debt-led strategies of capital accumulation.

Second is the construction and consolidation of a "debtfare state," which orients economic and social policy toward the attraction and retention of foreign capital flows, as well as the individualization and commodification of welfare. The debtfare state regulates and normalizes people's dependence on credit to meet basic needs, such as economic survival, housing, and education. Debtfarism involves a set of institutional and ideological practices, such as the deregulation of the financial sector and the rhetoric of financial inclusion and democracy. It legitimizes market-led poverty alleviation strategies, such as loans to poor rural households to start up microenterprises.

In the 1990s, the IMF and the World Bank offered substantial loans to Central Asian countries for monetary stabilization and economic development on the condition that governments implemented neoliberal policies and opened their economies to foreign trade and capital. This meant price and trade liberalization, small- and large-scale privatization, the creation of private property laws and an independent judiciary system, and the transformation of a welfare state into a debtfare state through deregulation and austerity. Loans (read: debt) from international financial institutions were not merely a sum of money; they were an institutionalization of a particular socioeconomic relation between lenders and borrowers. The loan conditionality allowed international financial institutions to take advantage of the relative weakness of Central Asian states and impose their rules of the game. International financial institutions also framed their neoliberal intervention as a pathway to democratization and modernization, thereby asserting a problematic link between the market and democracy.

Central Asian countries differed in their degrees of exposure to market reforms. Kyrgyzstan and Kazakhstan introduced and implemented much of the neoliberal policy agenda. Since 2010, the index of privatization has remained high for both Kyrgyzstan (4) and Kazakhstan (3.67), and the private sector share of GDP constitutes 75 percent and 80 percent, respectively. Tajikistan is characterized as a "hybrid case," with a high privatization score of 3.44 and the private sector share of GDP reaching 55 percent. Although Uzbekistan and Turkmenistan are viewed as "bad reformers" for pursuing state-led development, they have embraced some aspects of neoliberalism, such as attracting foreign direct investment (FDI). Recently, the World Bank ranked Uzbekistan as one of its top ten reformers in the world, though the country is yet to restructure and privatize its large and complex state enterprises.

Extraction-Based Growth through Foreign Investment

The neoliberal program of enhancing the extractive sector, shrinking the manufacturing sector, and reducing spending on welfare and infrastructure first occurred in Latin America and Africa in the 1970s and 1980s. Since independence in Central Asia, natural resources and finance have attracted a considerable share of FDI at the expense of manufacturing and agriculture, despite the latter accounting for a large proportion of employment. The economic transition in the post-Soviet space can be characterized as a shift from a Soviet state-led "productionist" economy to a neoliberalized rentier capitalism, or a transition from "wealth creation" to "rent extraction."

After the collapse of the Soviet Union, a substantial drop in manufacturing and agricultural production occurred in Central Asia. In Kyrgyzstan between 1990 and 2010, the industrial sector fell by 75 percent, agriculture and commercial services dropped by 30–40 percent, and public services more than halved. Kazakhstan's share of agriculture of GDP fell from 34 percent in 1990 to 4 percent in 2014. The lack of funding in the energy sector in both Kyrgyzstan and Tajikistan left the sector in critical condition, resulting in disrupted energy supplies. In contrast, Uzbekistan's cautious approach to market reforms resulted in a less severe recession than its neighbors, as well as the preservation of some of its manufacturing sector.

The Central Asian states have managed economic growth by promoting an open-door policy for transnational capital and supporting foreign ownership of natural resources. Extraction-based economic growth in Central Asia took off between 1998 and 2008 due to a significant increase in international prices for fossil fuels, gold, and other minerals. A large share of FDI was in the natural resource sector, and it was oriented toward extraction, processing, and transportation of hydrocarbons and metals. Resource-rich countries attracted most of the inward foreign investment in Central Asia and achieved economic growth buoyed by oil and gas exports.

FDI inflows have been uneven in Central Asia. Kazakhstan's substantial energy and mineral resources elevated it to the top twenty economies in the world for receiving FDI. Kazakhstan received more than US$120 billion, with the United States and China being the two largest investors. Over twenty-five years, China provided US$30 billion in loans and equity investments to Kazakhstan. By 2016, China had 30 percent control of all oil extraction in Kazakhstan. As a consequence of high dependency on fossil fuels for income, Kazakhstan's annual GDP closely tracked the average price of crude oil from 1991 to 2015.

Turkmenistan, whose gas reserves are among the largest in the world, agreed to a "debt for delivery" policy with China, where Turkmenistan repaid substantial loans through gas deliveries. Turkmenistan exports gas primarily to China and, to a lesser extent, to Iran and Russia. Turkmenistan does not publish information on hydrocarbon revenues and the national budget, making it difficult to estimate the share of FDI and its impact on the economy. Gas is the most significant source of revenue, however, and China is the only country allowed to extract onshore gas reserves.

Uzbekistan ranks third in Central Asia in terms of FDI. For the past two decades, Uzbekistan has relied on exporting oil, gas, cotton, and gold for growth. Uzbekistan's cautious approach to market reforms did not affect US firms doing business in the country. US companies were able to secure finance through the US Export-Import Bank, which alleviated most of the commercial risk. The United States is the second largest joint venture partner for investment in Uzbekistan, behind the United Kingdom. Recent economic reforms have resulted in more investment coming from Russia, China, and South Korea, most of which has been channeled into oil and gas.

Kyrgyzstan's extractive industry largely centers on gold production at the Canadian-owned Kumtor gold mine, which has the largest gold deposits in Central Asia. In 2016, it accounted for 8 percent of GDP and 23.4 percent of the aggregate industrial output. Despite being the most liberalized country in the region, FDI in Kyrgyzstan has been low, half of which has gone into the Kumtor gold mine.

The economic strategy of extracting resources has proven to be economically and environmentally unsustainable in the long term. For resource-rich countries, extraction-based growth can produce the "Dutch disease." (The "Dutch disease" is a phrase in economics used to describe a situation when foreign investment into the natural resource sector can have a negative impact on the economy, because foreign investment causes the domestic currency to appreciate, so damaging the manufacturing sector.) The production of sophisticated manufactured products and services is not a significant part of Central Asian economies. Resource-rich countries have not achieved the expected benefits from inward foreign investment. FDIs have had a limited impact on technology, knowledge transfer, and employment creation outside of the extractive industry. For instance, Kazakhstan has become dependent on hydrocarbons, relying on export of fossil fuels for growth. But other sectors of its economy have failed to develop, lacking economic diversification.

Moreover, the economic strategy to extract fossil fuels and minerals has meant that Central Asia contributes to global warming and ecological damage. The natural resource sector also has a poor record for local environmental pollution. In seeking to increase shareholder value, foreign corporations have pursued short-term profits and have little regard for local communities or the planet.

Western companies have been among the major beneficiaries of neoliberal reforms, acquiring and controlling lucrative assets, including natural resources. The United States is one of the leading sources of foreign capital in Kazakhstan, with around US$24 billion from 2005 to 2016, about 12 percent of the total foreign direct investment. The majority of investment is in the oil and gas sector. US corporations were among the first foreign investors to establish ownership and control in the sector. In 1993, two US oil corporations, Chevron and ExxonMobil, established a 75 percent stake in Tengizchevroil, a leading Kazakhstani oil company.

Foreign investors have exploited host countries' desperate need for capital. Kazakhstan and Kyrgyzstan have signed some bad deals with them. Compared with some other resource-rich countries, the Kazakhstani government does not get a high share of oil profit, around 20 percent of oil profit, whereas the Norwegian government gets 80 percent. In Kyrgyzstan, the 2009 agreement on Kumtor ownership signed the rights to the Canadian corporation Centerra Gold, with the Kyrgyzstani government obtaining a 33 percent share in the corporation. Foreign investors have achieved high average return rates for FDI—between 2006 and 2012, the rates were 25 percent in Kazakhstan and 12.2 percent in Kyrgyzstan.

Debt-led Growth through Foreign Loans

International financial institutions created and developed the banking and microfinance sectors in Central Asia so that businesses and households could have access to credit (read: debt). Foreign and domestic lenders have obtained profit through interest rate, so making money from money rather than production. The banking and microfinance sectors aimed to stimulate entrepreneurial activity, increase household consumption, and develop the private sector in Central Asia. More specifically, microfinance institutions have been framed as tools for poverty alleviation, women's empowerment, and rural development.

Central Asian states have engaged in debtfarism by deregulating the financial sector. The Washington Consensus on banking and finance in developing and transitioning economies supported the separation of commercial banks from the central bank, the abolition of internal convertibility of money, the liberalization of interest rates, the restructuring and privatization of state banks, and the entry of new private banks regulated by minimum capital and licensing requirements. As a result, most Central Asian countries liberalized banking and microfinance legislation.

Banks and microfinance institutions claim to lend to new enterprises and existing businesses. The enterprise culture trumpets the values of a neoliberal moral economy: personal responsibility, making money, competition, and individual creativity. It helps to legitimize and promote capitalism in developing countries by closing off alternative economic arrangements. Poor groups are taught to see loans as their best chance of obtaining a better life, as well as a way to become an entrepreneur. By advocating self-help, poor groups are discouraged from relying on state resources and collective capabilities (e.g., the welfare state, trade unions, and social movements), which were historically important for reducing poverty in the West. Debtfarism relieves the pressure to redistribute income and wealth, as poor groups are left to escape poverty through their own individual creativity.

Commercial banks and microfinance institutions in Central Asia have been integrated into the global circuit of capital. In the 1990s and 2000s, Kazakhstan's and Kyrgyzstan's lending institutions borrowed heavily from US and other Western financial institutions to fund the expansion of credit, largely concentrated in petty production, retail trading, real estate, and consumption. Kazakhstan's banks actively borrowed from abroad through syndicated loans, securitization, and issuance of bonded debt. By 2007, Kazakhstani banks amassed external debt of US$46 billion (44 percent of GDP). The share of foreign currency lending (especially in US dollars) in the total bank credit was: 43 percent in 1998, 71 percent in 2001, 52 percent in 2004, and 42.5 percent in 2010. The bulk of the mortgage loans were US-dollar denominated, partly reflecting the appeal of lower interest rates of US dollar–denominated loans compared to those denominated in Kazakhstani tenge. In 2004, net external liabilities constituted more than 35 percent of the total assets of commercial banks, compared to 5 percent in 2000. In the 2000s, Kazakhstan's banking sector was the second fastest-growing sector in the economy after the oil industry.

The 2007–08 financial crisis exposed Kazakhstani commercial banks' vulnerability to Western credit, resulting in huge losses and instability in the banking sector. The Kazakhstani state spent around US$18 billion in bailing out several banks and ensuring liquidity and stability in the sector. The banking crisis undermined the government's budgetary position and diverted resources from productive investment into debt payment.

During 2002–07, Kyrgyzstan's banking sector expanded strongly, with average annual asset growth of 22 percent and loan growth of 57 percent, or 40 percent in real terms. The total banking assets increased from 7.9 billion soms in 2002 to 178 billion soms in 2015. Kyrgyzstan's microfinance sector was fueled by the availability of cheap credit from Western financial institutions and cross-border lending, especially from Kazakhstani banks. Global and regional financiers benefitted from lax regulation on interest rates and debt collection, enabling them to achieve high returns on equity. In Kyrgyzstan, the average interest rate on microfinance loans was about 34 percent in 2014, of which 6.3 percent was microfinance institutions' profit margin.

Vulnerable and needy members of society have struggled to make repayments, especially at high interest rates. In 2015, a survey of microcredit clients revealed that 56 percent of respondents in Kyrgyzstan and 41 percent in Tajikistan were not even aware of the annual interest rates on their loans. Furthermore, microfinance institutions employed predatory lending techniques, including lax vetting procedures and aggressive tactics, to increase their coverage and to offer larger loans to poor families. These tactics, as well as social shaming to extract payments, led many poor families to overborrow and some individuals to commit suicide.

The neoliberal debt-cum-growth model has produced profits for the few financial elites, and misery and insecurity for the many. Banks' and microfinance institutions' profits are based on interest (or usury), which in the past was criticized for being parasitic, unproductive, and unjust. Rural communities have accused microfinance institutions of "control fraud."

The exploitative and restrictive terms and conditions on which petty entrepreneurs could borrow meant that it was unlikely that they would use loans for innovative ventures. Instead loans often enabled unemployed individuals to join the ranks of a burgeoning class of petty producers and traders, who operated on very small margins in highly competitive markets. Banks and microfinance institutions have not created a culture of enterprise but rather a Hobbesian social world, pitting individuals against each other, largely eroding their sense of social solidarity and collective action.

Furthermore, on a global scale, loans to developing and transitioning countries have produced a net flow from poor countries to rich. In 2005, an estimated US$40.4 billion of aid to the very poorest countries yielded US$43.2 billion in debt service. The debt-led economic development is a form of accumulation by dispossession that enriches Western financial institutions and local financial elites. It has generated profits (or, rather, "unearned income") for lenders, and has indebted large segments of the population in Central Asia, exposing them to the exploitative and unjust practices of the global banking system.

Negative Effects of Neoliberal Capitalism

Legal and Illegal Corruption

Neoliberal ideology asserts that a turn to markets would eliminate corruption and inefficiency and would create opportunities for growth and pluralist politics. But those promises have not been realized in Central Asia. Instead, privatization and deregulation produced a wealthy political class, which captured key assets and reproduced itself through "neoliberal clientelism." It is claimed that corruption and fraud are a feature of the Global South, because low- and middle-income countries have not adequately implemented market reforms, possess weak governance structures, or have not become fully liberalized. This myth of failed liberalization is widespread and persistent. But it obscures how financial deregulation, tax havens, financial centers, and corporate lawyers and accountants in the Global North have facilitated public corruption and looting in the Global South by transferring money to off- and on-shore accounts.

More importantly, legal forms of corruption and fraud are deeply implicated in neoliberal capitalist economic relationships. The propertied class captured the state and the judiciary to promote their interests at the expense of the propertyless. The elites own and control scarce assets (e.g., natural resources, finance, and prime real estate) that others need or want, thereby extracting rent from the latter. Politicians and judges have shaped and sanctioned laws and property rights to favor the interests of the powerful propertied class. The privatization of natural monopolies, the legalization of usury, the legitimization of rent and other forms of unearned income, and the sanctity of private property rights and contracts were all examples of legal corruption. Moreover, state institutions have decriminalized financial fraud by weakening oversight and regulation.

In Central Asia, political regimes have engaged in both legal and illegal forms of rent extraction. Kyrgyzstan's first two presidential families of Akaev (1991–2005) and Bakiev (2005–10) were notorious for privatizing and controlling the country's prime rent-yielding assets, such as utility companies, gold mines, supermarkets, resort hotels, and the international airport. Maxim Bakiev, the eldest son of former president Kurmanbek Bakiev, exercised the most blatant illegal rent-seeking power, culminating in the control and looting of the country's development fund. In Kazakhstan, former president Nursultan Nazarbayev's immediate family members and close associates have been the key beneficiaries of market reforms and legalized corruption. His son-in-law, Timur Kulibayev, whose business empire includes Almex, which has a 35 percent share of the country's banking sector, is the third richest person in Kazakhstan. Kulibayev also manages large parts of the hydrocarbon industry and the country's National Wealth Fund, Samryk-Kazyna. In Tajikistan, President Emomali Rahmon's family members and close associates own and control Tadaz, an aluminum smelter; commercial banks; and the cotton sector, enabling them to extract economic rent.

Global capital has helped to sustain the Central Asian elites. Global financial markets have been willing to invest in the region as long as the economic rewards remain high and secure. Foreign investment and loans have reinforced the power of the countries' oligarchs (or, rather, "plutocrats") in a context where there are no autonomous mechanisms to impose regulation.

The system of deregulation, tax avoidance, legal globalization, and offshore havens, advanced by successive British and American governments, have facilitated both legal and illegal forms of corruption on a grand scale.

Global financial instruments (e.g., holding companies) have been used to secretly embezzle public coffers. An elaborate accounting system helped to conceal Maxim Bakiev's involvement in siphoning off money from Kyrgyzstan's development fund into secret bank accounts in the United Kingdom, Belize, and New Zealand. In Uzbekistan, former president Islam Karimov's daughter, Gulnara Karimova, was charged with embezzlement of US$1.5 billion to offshore accounts. The leaked Panama Papers in May 2016 revealed that in Kazakhstan President Nazarbayev's grandson, Nurali Aliyev; the defense minister, Beibit Atamkulov; and the chairman of the KazMunayGas energy giant, Sauat Mynbayev, had substantial offshore accounts.

Social Inequality and Discontent

International financial institutions and Central Asian governments have underestimated the social and economic costs of neoliberal reforms. Since independence, Central Asia's poverty rates have been high and social inequalities have increased. The poverty rate in Kyrgyzstan and Tajikistan is between 35 and 50 percent. For instance, by 2006 a typical Kyrgyzstani rural schoolteacher's purchasing power of basic goods had declined by 85 percent in comparison to the 1985 level. Kyrgyzstan's Gini coefficient of income inequality had doubled, fluctuating between 0.41 and 0.45 from 1996 to 2009, reflecting the unequal distribution of income. In Kazakhstan, the poverty rate is 36 percent. In Kazakhstan's oil-producing regions, at least 40 percent of the population are poor, and the state-owned KazMunayGas and international corporations did not improve the local population's living standards. The average real income in oil-producing regions of Aktobe and Kyzyl Orda remains below the national average.

Neoliberal economic strategies have also widened the urban-rural divide in Central Asia. The rural economy accounts for a significant share of the population and employment, but it receives little foreign or state investment. The current World Bank data shows that about 47 percent of Kazakhstan's population live in rural areas, and agriculture accounts for 18 percent of total employment. In Kyrgyzstan, the rural population is about 64 percent, and agriculture accounts for 14 percent of GDP and 28 percent of total employment. Despite this, there has been little support for agriculture. In Kazakhstan, FDI in agriculture fluctuates between 0.5 and 2 percent. Kyrgyzstan's government allocates only about 2 percent of its funds to support agriculture. A recent survey conducted in Kyrgyzstan shows that more than 60 percent of farmers had experienced a crop failure in the preceding five years. Kyrgyzstan's agricultural production faces problems of fluctuating market prices, soil erosion, dilapidated irrigation systems, underdeveloped food processing, and weak certification and marketing institutions.

Lack of investment and economic opportunities in the rural economy has contributed to rural depopulation. In Kazakhstan's and Kyrgyzstan's major cities, internal migrants constitute 20 to 30 percent of the urban population. Many face problems of inadequate accommodation, social exclusion, precarious employment, and lack of access to public goods, because they do not have residence permits, or *propiska*. Many rural migrants in Kyrgyzstan and Tajikistan have left to work in Russia and Kazakhstan. The share of remittances to GDP was about 27 percent in Tajikistan and 30 percent in Kyrgyzstan in 2016. Migrant remittances in Tajikistan and Kyrgyzstan are more important than export revenue and FDI. But labor migration can lead to a myriad of socioeconomic problems in rural areas, including strained kinship ties, a low tax base, and poor infrastructure.

Not surprisingly, neoliberal growth strategies, public corruption, and social inequality have contributed to social and political discontent. In Kyrgyzstan, public corruption and poverty resulted in mass protests in 2005 and 2010, ousting incumbent presidents. In addition, Kyrgyzstan's gold miners and local communities rallied against a foreign gold mining company in 2010, 2012, and 2014, demanding better wages, stricter environmental regulation, and a greater share of profits for local investment. In 2011, Kazakhstan's oil workers in Zhanaozen protested about their working and living conditions. The government responded with indiscriminate shooting and imprisonment of protesters. Western countries often ignore governments' suppression of protests in order to protect commercial interests.

Alternative Visions of Economic Development

Although the neoliberal economic framework is dominant in Central Asia, two alternative economic imaginaries have emerged in response to neoliberal contradictions and crises. First, the Eurasian Economic Union (EAEU) was established by Russia, Belarus, and Kazakhstan in 2015, and later Armenia and Kyrgyzstan joined the economic union. It introduces the free movement of goods, capital, labor, and services, and provides for common policies in macroeconomic and industrial spheres. Second, in 2013 President Xi Jinping of China proposed the Belt and Road Initiative (BRI) to create a trade and infrastructure network connecting Asia with Europe and Africa along ancient trade routes, such as the land and maritime Silk Road.

The Eurasian Economic Union

The EAEU can be seen as a response to the US-led neoliberal policy agenda, which envisages global and deterritorialized flows of capital and trade in Central Asia. The EAEU prioritizes deep economic integration over open flows of capital and trade, productive investment in member countries over rent-seeking activities, and regional currencies over the hegemonic US dollar. A successful integration of Eurasian states would also challenge the US regional hegemony.

Deep integration (e.g., an economic union) can offer greater positive benefits than shallow integration (e.g., bilateral trade treaties), which only aims to increase competition through elimination of state interventions and the reduction of market segmentation. In an attempt to deepen integration, the EAEU has pursued several measures, similar to those of the European Union. It allows for the free movement of labor and services, not just trade and capital. The EAEU also makes efforts to reduce nontariff barriers and improve trade facilitation (e.g., common rules on sanitary and phytosanitary standards), thereby reducing the transaction costs of trade and creating trade.

Deep integration also involves members' cooperation over productive investment. Production cooperation is partly a legacy of the Soviet Union, particularly in defense and space industries. In 2006, Russia and Kazakhstan established the Eurasian Development Bank to support regional integration through large-scale productive investment. Russia and Kazakhstan have developed cooperative projects in several sectors, including nuclear power, automobile manufacturing, chemical manufacturing, and mechanical engineering. By the end of 2013, there were more than ten thousand joint ventures between EAEU countries.

Russia gave soft loans, subsidies, and guarantees to secure poorer member countries' commitment to deep integration and to address uneven development within the EAEU. In 2015, Russia gave loans totaling US$500 million to establish the Russian-Kyrgyz Development Fund. The fund's goals include the development and modernization of Kyrgyzstan's export-orientated industries, so that the country could transition to the economic union without experiencing adverse social, economic, and political problems. It has allocated more than half of the fund, mostly for production, particularly in areas of agribusiness, construction, metallurgy, and textile. A total of 781 projects were financed. The attempt to reorient Kyrgyzstan's economy to production helped to develop Kyrgyzstan's clothing industry, which is estimated to account for 5–15 percent of GDP, employing between 150,000–300,000 workers (of which 70–85 percent are women), or 12 percent of the country's labor force. It also issued loans to small and medium-sized enterprises for productive investment, capping interest rates well below market rates. In focusing on production, the fund aimed to minimize Kyrgyzstan's distributive activities, which largely involved reexporting goods from China.

To deepen economic integration, Russia, Kazakhstan, and Belarus envision a new common currency, possibly by 2025. This would ensure greater monetary control and stability and would insulate member countries from disruptive global economic crisis. It would also counter the hegemony of the US dollar and its seigniorage. Russia and China have criticized the international monetary system for sustaining the US economy and military. The hegemonic US dollar has allowed the United States to have a unique and privileged position of running very high government budget and trade account deficits without having to undertake structural adjustment and austerity cuts to tackle its excessive military and consumer spending—measures that are imposed on other countries.

The Belt and Road Initiative

China's BRI seeks to address its crisis of overaccumulation of capital and excess surplus capacity. The BRI aims to invest US$40 billion for infrastructure projects to develop trade routes from China to Europe. Central Asia has been integrated into the BRI's economic imaginary. Kazakhstan has aligned parts of its national development strategy, Nurly Zhol, to the BRI and provided US$9 billion to fund transport infrastructure projects between 2015 and 2019. In 2016, China and Kazakhstan also agreed to establish joint industrial projects worth US$26 billion. Furthermore, China agreed to invest US$1.9 billion to develop Kazakhstan's agricultural industry.

China has invested in the textile industry in Tajikistan and Uzbekistan, contributing to the production of clothing rather than exporting raw cotton. China has also financed the construction of new power plants and high-voltage lines in Kazakhstan, Kyrgyzstan, and Tajikistan. In 2009, China's Tebian Electric Apparatus invested US$750 million on the construction of a 325-kilometer transmission line and a power plant in Dushanbe. In 2014, China spent about US$386 million on the renovation of a power plant in Bishkek and a further US$390 million in 2015 on the construction of a new power line to connect the north and south of the country.

The growing economic presence of Russia and China undermines the US hegemony in the region. This impels the United States to disrupt and contest the emerging alternative projects of the EAEU and BRI that threaten the neoliberal "free market" system. In 2018, President Donald Trump's administration released a new National Defense Strategy, which declared Russia and China as "revisionist powers" and a national security threat to the United States. This marks a fundamental shift in US foreign policy, moving away from nearly two decades of the US War on Terror. The new US strategy toward Central Asia, launched in February 2020, outlines its strategic national security and economic interests in the region. The United States sees itself in a zero-sum game with Russia and China.

Economics in Central Asia

What emerged since the collapse of the Soviet Union is a neoliberal political economy based on rent extraction rather than wealth creation. As agents of neoliberalism, Western-led international financial institutions have helped to create and promote rent-seeking behavior in Central Asian economies. As these economies are integrated into the global flows of capital and trade, they are prone to economic crises and problems arising in the United States and the Global North, such as the 2007–08 financial crisis. National and international elites have successfully transformed the character and function of property, from being valued for its social benefits to income-yielding assets irrespective of its social use. Rentierism and debtfarism have emerged as two key features of the Central Asian transition from the Soviet planned economy to a "free-market" system.

The neoliberalization of Central Asia has involved foreign investors and national elites extracting rent based on their ownership and control of scarce assets, such as oil, gas, minerals, precious metals, credit money, and real estate. The development of productive sectors, such as manufacturing and agriculture, has been secondary to rentier activities. The resource-rich countries, like Kazakhstan and Turkmenistan, generated substantial sums of revenues and dollar reserves during periods of high oil and gas prices in the 2000s, fueling a property and credit boom. The fall in oil and gas prices after the 2007–08 financial crisis exposed Kazakhstan's economic weaknesses and lack of diversification, leading to monetary instability and budgetary problems. The crisis also revealed the extent of corporate and household over-indebtedness and nonperforming loans in Central Asia. Kazakhstan was forced to bail out some of its major banks.

Neoliberal capitalism in Central Asia has spawned two emerging alternative economic projects in the region. The EAEU and the BRI have propelled Central Asia from the periphery to the center in geopolitics. Central Asia offers gainful opportunities for the global powers to own and control scarce assets, export goods and services to an emerging middle-class consumer market, and develop transport infrastructure and trade routes to other economic regions, especially Europe and the Middle East. In seeking to imagine and regulate Central Asia, the global powers also compete to shape the world economy and the international order. It remains to be seen how the global economic rivalry will unfold in Central Asia, how the Central Asian states will navigate and bargain with the global powers, and whether the alternative economic imaginaries will benefit the wider population. What is certain is that the region will witness increasing tension and conflicts over the different economic visions and strategies in the coming decades.

23

Property

Eric McGlinchey

entral Asian economies are portrayed as different from most other economies in the world. Transparency International (TI) consistently ranks Central Asian countries at the bottom of its "corruption perceptions index." Kazakhstan, the least corrupt of the Central Asian states, nevertheless ranks in the bottom third (122 of 180) of TI's global corruption rankings. Only twelve other countries, TI instructs, are more corrupt than Turkmenistan. And Kyrgyzstan, Uzbekistan, and Tajikistan fare little better, taking the 135, 157, and 161 spots on the TI scale. The United Kingdom's Department for International Trade labels the business environment in Turkmenistan "challenging." And the US government's Country Commercial Guide for Uzbekistan instructs, perhaps with a wink and a nod: "When meeting with senior government officials, avoid giving gifts such as pencils, pens, lighters (unless they are expensive ones), poor quality wine or vodka, paper notebooks, or other items of this nature."

Central Asians are corrupt—this is the prevailing narrative among Western governments and international organizations. I do not dispute this narrative. Central Asians, though, are no more corrupt than their international counterparts. It is not unusual to see individuals in all environments maximizing self-interest within the confines of existing institutions. Where institutions are weak, individuals often, though not always, act in ways that undermine the public good. Here in the United States, we value free and fair elections as a public good. The nature of US electoral institutions, however, are such that money privileges some actors over others. The Democratic and Republican campaigns for the 2016 presidential elections spent, combined, more than one billion dollars. The nonpartisan Center for Responsive Politics estimates that the "average winning Senate candidate had spent $10.4 million" in the 2016 elections. Seats in the US House of Representatives are a comparative bargain, with winning candidates spending a mere $1.3 million.

A central contention of this essay is that Central Asians are not, either as a result of culture or history, intrinsically different from you or me. What is different—at times—are the institutions that individuals in Central Asia encounter in their everyday lives. In this chapter, I explore these institutions through the lens of three different actors: (1) Kyrgyz villagers and farmers who saw their livelihood threatened when a Canadian-operated gold mine spilled cyanide into a local river; (2) an entrepreneurial husband and wife in Bishkek who suddenly found their ownership of a modest office building being contested in the Kyrgyz courts; (3) and a group of Kazakh industrialists fighting, through international financial institutions, to maintain their control over a half-billion-dollar investment in Uzbek cement factories.

All of these individuals are navigating the intersection of new and old institutions. Private property—be it the ownership of land, real estate, or formerly state-run factories—is a new institution with, at best, shaky foundations in Central Asia. The foundations of private property are insecure for multiple reasons. Prior to 1991, private property largely did not exist in Central Asia or, for that matter, across the entire former Soviet Union. General Secretary Mikhail Gorbachev's perestroika reforms of the mid-1980s did encourage tentative steps toward private property: entrepreneurs were allowed to open small shops; farmers were able to lease land; and households could sell produce from the plots of their countryside dachas. De jure ownership of property—ownership of a home, land, real estate, or a factory—was something that only emerged in the post-Soviet period. As I demonstrate in this chapter, the inchoate state institutions ostensibly designed to enable de jure property ownership often failed aspiring farmers, real estate developers, and industrialists.

Exploring how these actors encountered and navigated these inchoate state institutions, I suggest, can help us make better sense of current and future challenges to Central Asian property rights. Two of the actors whom I study—the Kyrgyz villagers and the Bishkek couple—have achieved some degree of property guarantees. The third group of actors, the Kazakh investors, are engaged in ongoing international litigation over their Uzbek factories. What all three of these cases tell us, however, is that even in states where rule of law is weak, individuals have agency and can work through formal and informal institutions to achieve some modicum of property security.

Predation and Protection in the Post-Soviet Context

Central Asia's three decades of experience with post-Soviet property rights regimes are characterized by three interweaving processes: (1) bank runs in which weak or nonexistent rule of law allows political elites to grab lucrative assets, (2) local mobilization in which individuals and communities organize to provide the property protections central states do not or will not, and (3) global arbitration in which property owners turn to international institutions in an effort to reassert ownership over contested properties. These processes are ongoing and property rights remain tenuous throughout Central Asia. That property rights remain tenuous, critically however, is not the result of something innate to the Central Asian "condition" or Central Asian "nature" but rather is the result of the region's still-weak institutional environment. All is not dire, however, in the realm of property rights. Although state institutions are weak, individual actors are strong. If Central Asia is a case study in the ills of weak property rights regimes, it is no less a case study in the strengths of local agency. I consider these countervailing tendencies and their implications for property rights broadly before turning to the three case studies.

Predation

The post-Soviet environment is typically portrayed as approaching a Hobbesian state of nature. Here rule of law is weak. Because there is no effective Leviathan to police society, individuals pursue self-interest regardless of the cost to the broader community. Indeed, in some respects the post-Soviet environment is worse than the state of nature. Rather than a total absence of state institutions as befits the state of nature, here we have Soviet era institutional residues that privilege some actors while punishing others.

Steven Solnick in *Stealing the State* describes how these institutional residues led to a bank run in which political elites, empowered by their Soviet-era authority, wantonly stole state assets. These elites, Solnick explains, reasoned they were likely to lose out in the course of political and economic transition and thus "rushed to claim their assets before the bureaucratic doors shut for good." For many officials, though, the doors never shut. Newly wealthy and still in positions of power, these elites put the break on reform. As Joel Hellman's aptly titled "Winners Take All" study explains: "Actors who enjoyed extraordinary gains from the distortions of a partially reformed economy have fought to preserve those gains by maintaining the imbalances of partial reforms over time . . . Winners from an earlier stage of reform have incentives to block further advances in reform that would correct the very distortions on which their initial gains were based." In short, the legacies Soviet-era institutions allowed Soviet-era elites, and now the sons and daughters of Soviet-era elites, to steal and extort. As Stephen Kotkin observed, to this day these elites are "at their desks, using their positions—connections, licensing power, affixing of seals—for private gain."

Protection

There is no denying the vast predation that characterizes post-Soviet Central Asian property rights. The three case studies that follow illustrate this predation in extensive detail. Critically, however, what the case studies also illustrate are responses—often effective responses—to state predation. Local actors are not without agency in their confrontations with elites who seek to steal or diminish community assets. Mancur Olson has described how, in environments where property rights are weak, "stationary bandits"—that is, mafia organizations—offer individuals protections in return for paying a "predictable tax." In Russia, those intimately familiar with violence during the Soviet period—former military and sportsmen from state-sponsored martial arts groups—banded together in competing gangs to provide small businesses protection guarantees in return for a cut of profits.

The role of criminal groups in property protection, though it has received extensive attention in the post-Soviet literature, likely is not the dominant mode through which individuals defend their assets. Property owners—as the villagers, real estate developers, and large-scale foreign investors I examine here suggest—have considerable agency to combat state predation. This agency and the concomitant ability to mobilize against predation has roots in multiple sources—shared norms, an individual's bureaucratic expertise and interpersonal networks, and an ability to tap into international law so as to combat the shortcomings of domestic property rights regimes. What all these cases demonstrate is that Central Asians are not destined to forever be victims of thieving political elites. Property protections are coming to Central Asia, and they are coming by way of everyday local challenges to autocratic predation.

Barskoon Village

An apt illustration of these everyday challenges is the case of the Barskoon villagers and how they took on Cameco Corporation, the international mining conglomerate whose operations at the Kumtor mine constitute the single largest infusion of resources to the Kyrgyz state. Kyrgyzstan, in contrast to oil-rich Kazakhstan, has few readily extractable natural resources. One resource Kyrgyzstan does have, however, is gold.

Kyrgyzstan's gold industry demonstrates how, in some cases, the bank runs Solnick describes can be literal. In 1992, the Akaev government spirited 1.6 tons of Kyrgyz gold to Zurich, Switzerland. Then president Askar Akaev received, in return for the gold, a $13.8 million line of credit. Akaev used the credit to pay for a new fleet of Volvos, updated weapons for his personal guard, and administrative expenses, including a $2 million fee to the Zurich-based consultant who arranged the gold-for-credit deal. Pressed on the transaction in a Kyrgyz parliamentary inquiry in late 1993, Akaev conceded that $4 million of the credit had "went missing."

Boris Birshtein, the Zurich-based fixer who arranged Akaev's nearly $14 million line of credit, also brokered the deal that gave Canadian mining company Cameco Corporation extraction rights to Kyrgyzstan's Kumtor gold mine. Cameco's production agreements with the Kyrgyz government have netted state elites many millions of dollars. The story of Kyrgyz gold, importantly, is not only about political elites' self-enrichment through the theft of state assets; it also is about the degradation of land and property for many Kyrgyz who live downstream from gold mines. In May 1998, a driver with Cameco Corporation failed to navigate a mountain turn and crashed his truck into the Barskoon river. Two tons of sodium cyanide spilled into the river and traveled downstream to the village of Barskoon and to Lake Issyk Kul, Kyrgyzstan's largest tourist attraction.

The Kumtor gold mine facilities, operated by Cameco Corporation, are perched on a glacier at 14,000 feet, an industrial eyesore in Kyrgyzstan's otherwise pristine high-altitude mountains. The eyesore is lucrative for the Kyrgyz government, however. In 1998, at the time of the cyanide spill, the Canadian-operated mine produced 20 tons of gold and contributed 15 percent to the Kyrgyz gross national product.

The villagers of Barskoon see little of this money. They depend on agriculture and tourism, and the May cyanide spill adversely affected both. Although it is unclear if the spill actually damaged the environment or if the cyanide caused human injuries, the psychological toll of the spill was profound. Kumtor officials delayed for hours before contacting officials in Barskoon. Moreover, Kumtor's insular operations meant that, in the hours, days, and months immediately following the spill, the Kyrgyz population was deeply suspicious of the Canadian company's assertion that no harm would come from the diluted cyanide. Hugh Pope, who covered the cyanide spill for the *Wall Street Journal*, aptly describes Cameco's public relations conundrum: the miners, "high up in the clouds and glaciers, had isolated themselves from the local communities by the lake. So they had few local relationships to build on."

Villagers panicked. Thirteen women in the village chose to have abortions rather than risk delivering what they feared were their now severely damaged babies. Agriculture and tourism suffered throughout the entire Lake Issyk Kul region. Media reports in both the Kyrgyz and Russian press (Issyk Kul is a popular summer destination for Russians as well as many other tourists from the former Soviet Union), likening the spill to Hiroshima, made 1998 a lost season for the lake region's tourism entrepreneurs and farmers.

There was a silver lining, though, to the Kumtor gold fiasco: the 1998 accident sparked two decades of sustained social mobilization in which villagers not only in Barskoon, but also in other cities and towns close to gold mines elsewhere in the country, have successfully lobbied for financial compensation as well as tightened environmental policy regulations so as to offset and preclude future damages to local property. In Barskoon, a group of activists lead by Erkingul Imankodjoeva created the nongovernmental organization (NGO) Karek—which means "it is necessary"—to transform local communities' relations with Kumtor. Seeing state inaction and even complicity in partnering with foreign companies to exploit Kyrgyzstan's gold resources, Karek worked to transform the way companies like Cameco interacted with local communities. Amanda Wooden, who has studied Karek and public activism around Kyrgyz mining more broadly, documents how Karek pressed for "company investments in the community, access to jobs at the mine, ecological monitoring, funds for eventual reclamation, safety measures, and, at times, closure of the mine."

Karek has achieved a notable degree of success. As Wooden notes, the NGO, after nearly a decade of work, secured "$3 million in 2005 to be distributed to residents of five villages near the spill, mostly for harvest damages." Karek is one of several examples where local residents mobilize to build institutions and establish some degree of property protections in the absence of state institutions of rule of law. Regine Spector similarly demonstrates how local communities—here "traders, owners, and officials" at Bishkek's Dordoi and Osh bazaars—"interacted in an often fluid and crisis-ridden context to define and establish what they believed to be appropriate relationships, rules, norms, rights, and responsibilities." Central to the order Spector finds in Kyrgyzstan's bazaars is individual agency and norms. Just as Imankodjoeva and Karek were able to mobilize the Barksoon villagers around norms of environmental justice, key individuals—"elders"—in the bazaars were able to mobilize merchants around shared norms: "Traders and owners sought to create respectful and honorable social relationships, including norms of not cheating customers or getting into arguments, and they turned to mediation and negotiation to address problems before they became bigger conflicts." Individual agency, the ability to create order in the absence of rule of law, is pervasive in post-Soviet Central Asia. Spector points to how bazaar elders—former trade unionists as well as village aksakals—instill order in Kyrgyzstan's markets. David Montgomery has documented how "mothers and village elders" encourage men, returning from migrant labor jobs abroad, to give up their "vices, including gambling and spending money on alcohol, drugs, and prostitutes." And Alisher Khamidov, Nick Megoran, and John Heathershaw illustrate how "a communal feast of plov (rice and mutton) in one of Aravan's districts, an event that brought together Kyrgyz and Uzbek elders and local officials," was able to diffuse ethnic violence that had gone unchecked by the state during Kyrgyzstan's deadly 2010 ethnic riots. The absence of effective state institutions enables self-centered and shortsighted decisions: a foreign company's pollution of local lands and waters, a husband's irresponsible spending of family resources, and ethnicity-based destruction of property. Local actors, however, drawing on shared norms, can mobilize to create formal and informal institutions that effectively mitigate economic choices that may be detrimental. Although rule of law in Central Asia may be weak, Central Asians are not prisoners to a Hobbesian world of unbridled self-interest. Collective action is possible and, indeed, frequent, and, as a result, everyday life for many Central Asians is orderly, even in the absence of an orderly state.

107 Kievskaiya Street

A different kind of individual agency can be seen in how Natalia and Victor Lozitskiy fought off the attempted expropriation of their office building, 107 Kievskaiya, in central Bishkek. The Lozitskiys, in contrast to Imankodjoeva and her Karek organization, do not have an extensive circle of neighbors and friends to mobilize in defense of their property. What the Lozitskiys do have—and what Natalia Lozitskaya in particular has—is a deep under-standing of Kyrgyz economic regulations and how individuals, often with the shadowy backing of state elites, manipulate these regulations and the court system in an effort to steal assets. Lozitskaya and her husband are ethnic Ukrainians who moved to Kyrgyzstan in their youth. Now nearing retirement, Lozitskaya has had an extensive career serving as an advisor to various Kyrgyz government economic agencies. She worked closely with the (1990–2005) Akaev and the (2011–17) Atambaev governments. She did not find work with the 2005–2010 Bakiev government, and it was during this period that she and Victor became the targets of an attempted property grab.

I did not know the Lozitskiys when I first visited the building at 107 Kievskaiya (figure 23-1). I was there in 1998 to buy a topographic map in advance of a summer trek in Ala Archa National Park. I made several more visits to the building over the next two decades. In addition to the Cartograph-ic Institute, 107 Kievskaiya is home to international organizations as well as DHL shipping. The building is a five-story gray concrete block from the Brezhnev period that looks every year its age. Architecturally unremarkable, the building's location is nevertheless highly desirable. In the center of the city, 107 Kievskaiya is a short walk to government offices and Bishkek's financial, commercial, and cultural centers. The location is also set back fifteen meters from the road, a welcome feature in increasingly traffic-clogged Bishkek.

A colleague with an office at 107 Kievskaiya introduced me to the Lozits-kiys in the summer of 2015. Natalia is an accounting specialist and, through-out the 1991–2005 Akaev presidency, served as an advisor in Kyrgyzstan's Accounts Chamber. Natalia's husband, Victor, is a businessman engaged in trade and real estate. In 1995, Victor used profits from his beverages company to purchase 107 Kievskaiya, along with a nearby dilapidated property. The previous owners were heavily in debt and were keen to unload 107, which, at the time, was a poorly run and money-losing dormitory. The Lozitskiys sold the second property at a loss and, having exhausted their reserves, struggled to raise capital to renovate 107 Kievskaiya. In 1996, the Lozitskiys entered into a contract with the Arlington, Virginia–based development nonprofit, Counterpart International. Counterpart agreed to pay $6,000 in advance rent and the Lozitskiys agreed to use this advance to renovate the fifth floor of 107 Kievskaiya, the soon-to-be home of Counterpart's Bishkek office. With access to a dependable rent stream, the Lozitskiys renovated the remaining floors of 107 and soon attracted several more tenants.

There are multiple pathways to wealth in Central Asia. Like the Lozits-kiys, one can start small—like Victor with his Bishkek beverages compa-ny—and leverage assets to purchase and gradually improve and expand wealth. An alternative pathway is *reiderstvo*, or asset-grabbing, and this is the route that Dinara Kalkanova, the Lozitskiys's neighbor, attempted in her bid to gain control of 107 Kievskaiya. Reiderstvo is sometimes achieved through force. Armed men may storm a director's office and demand he sign over control of a property or business. But asset-grabbing can also be

23-1 The 107 Kievskaiya Street building, Bishkek, 2021. Photograph by Shairbek Dzhuraev.

pursued through the courts, and this was Kalkanova's preferred strategy in her protracted attempt to win 107 Kievskaiaya from the Lozitskiys.

The Lozitskiys and Kalkanova, in addition to being neighbors, discussed economic matters from time to time. In the mid-1990s, Kalkanova worked with the Kyrgyz trade mission to India, facilitating the travel of Indian and Kyrgyz entrepreneurs as well as shipping Indian goods to Kyrgyzstan on the frequently half-empty flights between the two countries. Kalkanova, knowing her neighbor's expertise in government finance, asked Lozitskaya for advice on the Indian ventures. Lozitskaya recalls: "She was the Kyrgyz sales representative in India. I was then the head of the customs committee. I advised her on how to transport goods, how to clear customs. I helped her. Victor helped her. We were friends; we believed she was a good person."

The Lozitskiys hired Kalkanova to help manage 107 Kievskaiya. Kalkanova, according to the Lozitskiys, played a minor role in the business until the early 2000s. In 2002, Lozitskaya shared with Kalkanova that 107 Kievskaiya was, for the first time, in the black. The revenue from tenant rents were finally sufficient for paying off the debts the Lozitskiys had incurred to finance the building's renovation. At this point, Kalkanova took a sudden interest in the property—not as a partner but, rather, as a plaintiff. She claimed, as she explains in a 2008 letter to the editor in the daily *Slovo Kyrgyzstana*, that the Lozitskiys were guilty of "misappropriating someone else's property by fraud and forgery of documents."

More specifically, Kalkanova claimed that Lozitskaya abused her position as advisor to the chairman of the Kyrgyz Parliament's Accounts Chamber to pressure officials in the Bishkek City Office of Property Registration to unlawfully reregister 107 Kievskaiya in her husband's name. Kalkanova explains, "The text of the February 1, 1996 re-registration indicates one company's name but the seal on the re-registration is from a completely different firm. The Lozitksiys misappropriated someone else's property by fraud and forgery of documents." Kalkanova filed her claim with multiple government bodies. Her charges led to visits from the Kyrgyz financial police and, ultimately, to a criminal case in the Pervomaisky District Court in early 2005. In March 2005, Kyrgyzstan underwent a putsch that led to President Akaev's removal and the ascent of Kurmanbek Bakiev—Akaev's erstwhile prime minister—as Kyrgyzstan's new president. With the arrival of the Bakiev government, the Lozitskiys's legal challenges began to seesaw through the Bishkek city, regional, and even the country Supreme Court. The Lozitskiys took their case public, commissioning in 2008 two articles in *Slovo Kyrgyzstana*. Kalkanova replied in kind, also presenting her case in *Slovo*. The back-and-forth was nasty. Kalkanova accused the Lozitskiys of threatening to harm her and her family. And the Lozitskiys explained in their *Slovo Kyrgyzstana* article how Kalkanova had swindled others, including former foreign minister of the Kyrgyz Soviet Republic Jamal Tashibekova. Tashibekova contracted Kalkanova to renovate a basement floor office suite. This contract, the Lozitskiy article explains, allowed "the goat into the garden." Rather than renovate the suite, Kalkanova rented out the offices and used her forged rental agreement to lay an ownership claim to the basement suite. Kalkanova's claim, upheld by the Bishkek City Court, was ultimately overturned by the Kyrgyz Supreme Court.

In the spring of 2010, the Lozitskiy-Kalkanova case was once again before the Kyrgyz Supreme Court. The Lozitskiys were not optimistic. By this time, they had received unwanted and threatening visits from individuals closely linked to Zhanysh Bakiev, the president's brother and former head of the Kyrgyz State Security Service. The Lozitskiys were convinced that Kalkanova was not working alone, that she had the backing of the Bakiev family. The Supreme Court, moreover, had seen significant turnover among its judges, and the Lozitskiys did not believe that the new court would rule in their favor.

Just as the court was taking up the case, however, mass street protests combined with a putsch led by Bakiev's estranged 2005 coconspirators led to yet another leadership change in Kyrgyzstan. The Bakievs fled Bishkek, first to the south of the country and, eventually, abroad. The Kyrgyz Supreme Court dismissed the Lozitskiy-Kalkanova case. And Kalkanova disappeared.

Natalia now advises the new Kyrgyz government on tax law. Victor is once again a successful businessman. I bumped into Victor in June 2018, on my way to an interview that happened to be in 107 Kievskaiya. Most days he still works from his small office on the fifth floor. He spends his weekends resting on Lake Issyk Kul. He and Natalia are building a house on the lake's north shore. Although Bishkek politics remain unsettled, the Lozitskiys are guardedly optimistic that the reiderstvo attempts they endured under the Bakiev regime will not return. They hope to soon retire to their house on the lake.

Bekabad Cement

While the Lozitskiy's court travails have come to a close, a much larger property rights dispute between Kazakh investors and the Uzbek government had just entered the stage of active litigation. In early April 2014, I received an inquiry from the Jones Day law firm asking if I might provide testimony for a client—Vladislav Kim—they were representing in a case before the World Bank's International Centre for the Settlement of Investment Disputes (ICSID). Lawyers at Jones Day had read my writing on Uzbekistan and invited me to provide a short brief on the nature of Uzbek autocratic rule. In March 2017, the ICSID issued a "Decision on Jurisdiction" that rejected the Uzbek government's claim that the World Bank body is not the appropriate venue for resolving the investment dispute. In December 2020, the Uzbek government agreed to return 51 percent of shares in the disputed asset, Bekabad Cement, to Kim and his co-investors, a move resulting in the discontinuance of the ICSID proceedings. The Vladislav Kim case provides a rare window into both how assets are privatized and, in many cases, later reappropriated by state elites in countries like post-Soviet Uzbekistan.

A central challenge that bedevils transition economies is how to transform state-owned property into private property. Most Soviet-bloc states pursued what, on the surface, appeared to be similar privatization strategies. Citizens were issued privatization vouchers and were free to invest these vouchers in state assets, in everything ranging from the corner grocery to massive state-owned enterprises. Privatization in practice, however, varied dramatically from country to country. Most critically, voucher privatization varied in its (1) ability to accurately establish fair-market valuation of the assets being privatized and (2) its ability to equitably distribute assets among populations within post-Soviet countries. In some countries, most notably in the Czech Republic, multiple transparent auctions did, to a large degree, achieve fair-market valuation and equitable distribution of state-held assets. The Czech government, for example, published bulletins that detailed multiple parameters of assets slated for privatization—revenue, number of employees, debts—and then the government held several rounds of auctions so that investor enthusiasm levels in one auction could inform asset valuation in the next round of auctions. Thus, if in the first round of auctions investor demand excited share supply for any given asset, the government would suspend the auction, raise the price for shares being offered, and then hold a second auction. Conversely, if share supply exceeded demand, the government would lower asset share prices in the next round of auctions.

Central Asian privatization neither included the transparency safeguards of Czech voucher privatization nor was prioritized in the immediate years of post-Soviet Central Asian independence. In the Czech Republic, the privatization process began in early 1992 and was complete by the end of 1993. In Kazakhstan, the leader in economic reform in Central Asia, the process of privatizing state-owned enterprises took half a decade. Kyrgyzstan, while it was quick to privatize small and medium-sized enterprises, has seen the privatization of larger-scale assets extend well into the 2010s. At times, Kyrgyz privatization has come nearly to a full stop. The Asian Development Bank notes, for example, that "between 2000 and 2008 only two privatization transactions of at least $1.0 million were concluded, totaling $2.5 million."

Privatization of large-scale assets in Uzbekistan has proven even slower. The Uzbek government began privatizing state assets in December 1998. At the time, Abdulla Abdukadyrov, the deputy head of the State Privatization Committee, articulated the Uzbek government's high hopes, predicting the state would sell 269 assets by the end of 2001. The Uzbek government struggled, however, to find buyers, particularly for large assets. In part, this struggle is the result of differing policy choices. While managers and individual investors in Uzbekistan—similar to the Lozitskiys in Kyrgyzstan—have been able to privatize real estate and small businesses, Uzbekistan has pursued a different path for the privatization of large-scale enterprises. In contrast to Kazakhstan, the leader in large-scale enterprise privatization in Central Asia, Uzbekistan has not embarked on voucher privatization. Instead, the Uzbek government has created investment funds in which individuals can invest. Public enthusiasm for these funds has been limited, and, moreover, these funds are structured such that the Uzbek government maintains majority control over large enterprise shares. This partial privatization scheme, World Bank economists Asad Alam and Arup Banerji conclude in a 2000 working paper, has "allowed the old, less innovative managers to effectively retain control without accountability to the diverse shareholders."

Partial privatization has led to poor economic performance. Beginning in the 2000s, in an effort to reverse this poor performance, Uzbekistan began actively courting foreign investors. A combination of tight currency controls as well as international financial institutions' unfavorable assessments of these currency controls, however, discouraged international investment in Uzbekistan. Noting the adverse effects of these "multiple exchange rate practices," the International Monetary Fund (IMF) in 2001 urged the Karimov government to rethink its stance toward the international economy: "the Uzbek authorities should reduce, if not eliminate, the above mentioned explicit and implicit distortions as soon and as simultaneously as possible."

Despite this nudge from the IMF, the absence of free currency convertibility in Uzbekistan remained a deterrent to foreign investment. The Karimov government sought to attract outside buyers by extending bespoke incentives such as tax holidays and duty-free exemptions for capital imports. For foreign investors, there is, however, a downside to these case-by-case incentives. As the US State Department's 2013 report on the Uzbekistan investment climate notes, "Requirements for obtaining these benefits are ambiguous, the processes and procedures are cumbersome, and the regulatory environment is capricious." Indeed, it is this capricious and ambiguous nature of the regulatory environment that the Karimov government used in its final years to separate foreign investors from their Uzbek assets.

Promises the Karimov government made to foreign investors at the point of an asset's original sale were systematically broken. These broken promises often come as a surprise to investors. Indeed, the first-time investors typically learned of changed terms of engagement was when the

Karimov government's surprise state inspections uncovered tax, customs, and currency exchange "violations." State prosecutors would then submit these to courts and judges as justification for the state's appropriation of foreign investments.

The Karimov government would refrain, however, from exercising this lever immediately. As the Bekabad and Kuvasay Cement examples illustrate, foreign investors were given time to build newly acquired assets into viable, well-performing enterprises. This time maximized revenues to the Karimov regime: the government enriched itself from the sale of underperforming assets to foreigners, the Karimov government then benefited when foreigners transformed these assets into viable companies, and in a few years' time, the government enriched itself yet again when pliant domestic courts deemed these much-improved companies to be in violation of Uzbek law and, as such, targets in need of nationalization.

The Bekabad Cement litigation at the ICSID illustrates this established pattern of privatization to foreign investors and subsequent state reappropriation of privatized assets. In January 2006, Kazakh businessman Vladislav Kim, along with several other Kazakh investors, paid two Cypriot companies, Raycross Limited and Raybird Limited, $33.98 million for the purchase of the Bekabad Cement and Kuvasay Cement companies. Kim and his colleagues (hereafter Kim) also paid a Mr. Bizakov $3 million for "introducing them to the opportunity." Kim was given the impression, presumably through Mr. Bizakov, that their investment would be safe because "they were dealing with Ms. Karimova," the Uzbek president's daughter.

Over the next four years, Kim invested $127 million to modernize the two cement factories. In early 2010, however, the Uzbek government began investigations into alleged financial and criminal crimes at Bekabad Cement. A government court declared Bekabad Cement company, along with four of its managers, "guilty of criminal charges" and ruled "that a 51% shareholding in BC was to be given over to the Uzbek Government." The Uzbek government initiated similar proceedings against Kuvasay Cement. Here, too, the Uzbek courts ruled in favor of the government and Kim "lost a significant proportion of the shareholding in KC."

President Karimov died in September 2016. And although the new government of President Shavkat Mirziyoyev acknowledged the dubious dealings of the Karimov family—Gulnara Karimova was sentenced in March 2020 to thirteen years of house arrest for tax evasion, money laundering, and extortion—the Uzbek state fought litigation that would see Bekabad Cement returned to the Kazakh investors. Indeed, the Uzbek government argued that the ICSID case should be dismissed because Kim paid Karimova and her fixer, Mr. Bizakov, bribes in order to secure the Bekabad and Kuvasay Cement purchases. The ICSID tribunal rejected this argument in a March 2017 ruling and the Uzbek government, in December 2020, eventually relented and returned majority ownership of Bekabad Cement to Vladislav Kim and his Kazakh co-investors.

Property in Central Asia

For Central Asians and, more broadly, for all of us who think about private property, our analytical point of departure is often the state. We reason that if property rights are to emerge and endure, they will do so through the initiatives of state actors and through the protections of state institutions. And if property protections are absent, they are absent because "the state" failed to act or intentionally undermined rule of law. Indeed, this is the analytical approach of the academic literature I reference in this chapter's state predation discussion.

My chapter does not contest this academic literature. The causal mechanisms that scholars like Hellman, Solnick, and Kotkin cite are present in post-Soviet Central Asia. Rather, what my chapter demonstrates is this academic literature may be incomplete; it tells only part of the post-Soviet property rights story. An exclusively state-centric focus overlooks the role local actors and local agency play in effecting economic and political change.

Central Asians know, through lived experience, that the state alone is not decisive in the establishment of property rights. The Barksoon villagers, not the state, fought for the protection of their lands and local tourism. Natalia and Victor Lozitskiy fought the state in order to defend their property at 107 Kievskaia. And Vladislav Kim and his coinvestors have moved beyond the state, to the international legal system, to retain control of their Uzbek cement factories.

A new wave of scholarship is now documenting this lived, actor rather than state impetus toward private property. Regine Spector, in her study of the Central Asian bazaar, illustrates "how people on the ground confront and wrestle with problems they face, and create their own stable spaces and meaningful work environments." William Campbell Rowe documents how Tajik families use "kitchen gardens" to mitigate the food scarcity that has come with the Tajik state's increasing emphasis on cotton production. And Emil Nasritdinov demonstrates how members of the growing Tablighi movement reassert ownership over religion through "spiritual nomadism" so as to "build new ethical, philosophical, and religious foundations" in spaces the watchful Central Asian state has historically controlled.

Local actor redress of government predation takes time and is not always successful. Nearly a decade passed before Imankodjoeva and her Karek NGO achieved some degree of compensation for Barksoon's lost crops and tourist revenues following the 1998 Kumtor cyanide spill. The Lozitskiys faced multiple setbacks in their efforts to hold their office building at 107 Kievskaiya and, ultimately, it was contingency, a putsch that overthrew the Bakiev government, that saved the Lozitskiys from what otherwise would have been a negative ruling in the Kyrgyz courts. As for Vladislav Kim and his Kazakh colleagues, here we see a decisive victory following protracted litigation at the World Bank's ICSID. The Uzbek government has returned majority ownership of Bekabad Cement to the factory's Kazakh investors. Investing in Central Asia remains a tricky business. Increasingly, though, local actors at all levels of the economy are finding ways to carve out protections amid widespread state failure.

24

Labor

Russell Zanca

Labor in contemporary Central Asia incorporates a broad range of human activities that we commonly think of as the work that people do. This includes the work needed to earn a living, build and accumulate material resources and wealth, and help plan for the future, and also the work we do to maintain our households and the people living within them—physically and psychologically. Anthropologists have long studied and analyzed the kinds of work and laboring activities people undertake to better understand how they constitute the economic and political systems that are the bases of societies.

More than a century ago, it was still more or less possible to write about the *mechanical* and *organic* societies conceived by early social theorists like Émile Durkheim. By mechanical societies, Durkheim meant that the smallest-scale societies—small groups of hunting and gathering families, who labored with interchangeable roles—were limited in degree of specialization and range. By contrast, Durkheim conceived of organic societies as more complex entities requiring mutual dependence and degrees of specialization. His model here included agrarian and industrialized societies wherein people do all sorts of work and cannot produce or manufacture all of the things they need for life on their own. By the 1920s, there remained, arguably, not more than a handful of mechanical societies, scattered in southern Africa, the rainforests of the Americas, Arctic regions, Southeast Asian rainforests, and interior Australia. Conversely, organic societies functioned as complex entities much like the organismic systems of animals. Simply, organic societies feature countless moving parts along with specialized functions to keep the organism alive and thriving. Organic societies, then, featured the types and range of laboring activities that one commonly finds in the Western

24-1   A local Itchan Kala resident constructing his brick home by hand in Khiva, Uzbekistan, 2019. Photograph by Kasia Ploskonka.

world and certainly date back as far as the founding of the first state-level societies of five to six thousand years ago.

I bring up Durkheim here merely to remind readers about how social science writing originally tried to draw definitive distinctions among human societies about the types of society that had formed based on factors such as size, scale, activities, structure, and so forth. Furthermore, when students are introduced to Central Asia, we often stress the history and antiquity of the past several millennia that have been characterized as societies of the steppe and those of the sown—pastoral nomadic peoples and agrarian peoples. While this is not an inaccurate distinction, it certainly does a disservice in terms of pointing out the varieties of work and types of economy ongoing in Central Asia.

While a rural Turkmen or Kyrgyz person today may be more resourceful or skillful than you or I in baking his own bread, milking his own animals, building his own home (figure 24-1), fixing his own electrical wiring, and so on, he is also as dependent as we are on having someone make his clothes, his shoes, his toothbrush, and his television, among other things. Therefore, even in rural or remote areas of Central Asia today, there are no households or communities, effectively, that are self-sufficient and can get on without mass-produced goods—from processed foods to all kinds of other household items. No doubt Durkheim himself would recognize that there are barely any societies on earth living outside of or independent of the greater market forces and nearly all of globalization's encroaching aspects.

Love of Labor

The word *mekhnatkash* often rolled off the tongues of rural people when I began researching rural life and collective farm living in Uzbekistan in the

24-2   Many, such as this former electrician, turned to garden farming after the end of the Soviet Union in order to make ends meet, Kyrgyzstan, 2012. Photograph by David W. Montgomery.

early 1990s. Much later, when I sat down to the intellectual joys and hardships of making sense of my experiences and depicting reality as I thought Central Asians understood it—ethnography sensu stricto—I realized that it was not so easy to translate the term, though I thought I understood it perfectly well in local terms. I wavered between "labor-loving" and "hardworking." Mekhnatkash seemed to require some English compound form beyond industrious, diligent, or energetic. In the end of course, translation is also a bleeding; it is just never quite right. Still, mekhnatkash is the word or active process uppermost in my mind when I think of areas, such as the Ferghana Valley and much of the rest of farming lands in Central Asia (even if there are variations of the term in languages different from Uzbek), and their idealized values of hard work. Furthermore, because my formative experiences as a fieldworking anthropologist coincided with a period of socioeconomic upheaval in Central Asia—the first decade or so of Soviet disintegration cum national independence—being mekhnatkash seemed to be required of any and every able-bodied person, if a good quality of life was to be made. If nothing else, it meant do whatever is necessary to earn money and disabuse yourself of the idea that you could only work in the job or profession you had trained for or were educated in (figure 24-2). The latter represented the Soviet mentality, and the former the new way, the way of national development with independence.

Generally, the early 1990s coincided with a period marked by excitement, upheaval, and disruption. Naturally, these factors were in play in consideration of people's attitudes toward work, their jobs, and whether it was going to be possible to continue to go to work in ways that people had been accustomed to for generations. More important, for those people—from collective farm cotton pickers to urban schoolteachers and factory accountants—the main question they had to ask themselves was whether the jobs they had had would pay them so that they could maintain a lifestyle that they had gotten used to for at least a couple of decades during the late Soviet period. Because the answer was no, the concept of mekhnatkash rose to the fore, as it basically explains that one has to do whatever is necessary to survive and make an income to support oneself and one's loved ones. The hardships of the new dispensation (labeled officially as "Independence") brought on a prolonged period of region-wide resourcefulness.

This chapter about labor focuses on the contemporary period, the first thirty years since the countries of Central Asia became independent. While I discuss types of work that are historically rooted and that people have engaged in for centuries, the focus is on types of labor people do today. My focus tends toward the rural areas of Central Asia, where I have spent most of my time, though I also worked in urban settings. Naturally, the kinds of work people do in the region's cities parallel the kinds of work that practically are universal for city life anywhere today—including car washers, physicists, restaurateurs, cell phone salespeople, plumbers, cab drivers, hairdressers, lawyers, bank tellers, and supermarket cashiers, to name but a few kinds of nearly infinite sorts of city work. While this, naturally, is a contrast to rural work in its largely agricultural and pastoralist forms, it is important to realize that rural areas also feature bakers, welders, retail shop owners, bookkeepers, and technicians, only on a much smaller scale.

History and Labor

Historically or traditionally, scholars who write about Central Asia discuss labor from a perspective that anthropologists might recognize as cultural ecology—that is, how people wrested a living and interacted with their local environments. Therefore, Central Asians of desert, steppe, and mountainous environments practiced a variety of pastoralism—maintaining a variety of herds of sheep, goats, horses, cattle, and camels—and those who inhabited fertile valleys or oases practiced agriculture, raising everything from fruits and vegetables to seed oil crops, wheat, rice, barley, sorghum, and, much more recently, cotton on a large scale. It has also been in the agricultural areas that mulberry trees were cultivated to feed billions of worms to make silk (figure 24-3a, b). Whereas most Karakalpaks, Kazakhs, Kyrgyz, and Turkmen are associated with several forms of pastoralism, and Tajiks and Uzbeks with agriculture, it is important to recognize that one mode of production (pastoralist or agrarian in this case) does not break down ethnically along strict lines. Thus, there have always been Uzbek herders or pastoralists, just as there have been Turkmen, Kazakh, and Kyrgyz farmers on the historical territories of these present national groups.

In the past, anthropologists were wont to associate non-western peoples'

24-3a, b   Workers at a silk factory in Margilan, Uzbekistan, 2005. Photograph by David W. Montgomery.

labor not just with what one might call their economic way of life but also with their material culture—their tools, clothing, everyday products, housewares, and so forth. The knowledge or skills of work that we might associate with craftsmanship, trades, commerce, the arts, and technology often garnered little attention in our field's studies. Anthropologists have the capacity to contribute a lot about discussions of work and labor in any society because their fieldwork studies remain grounded in the day-to-day observations and encounters both in what people say they do as well as what they actually do. This is the perspective we bring, of taking part in people's lives as they live them, our particular "being there" perspective.

Through the middle of the twentieth century, anthropologists routinely referred to a dichotomy of complex and small-scale societies. Complex societies generally represented the history of state-level societies, and then, the industrialized world millennia later. Small-scale societies meant the opposite, mainly hunting and gathering horticultural, and some pastoralist societies. Anthropologists saw these small-scale societies as the primitive, mostly non-western world, and for some it represented a bygone western past. While this reading made for many binaries of the human cultural condition, it had the unintended effects of being ahistorical, judgmental, and, frankly, misinformed about greater connections and similarities among the so-called advanced and primitive societies. For obvious reasons, we have moved past such distinctions, and we recognize that all peoples on earth can be grouped under the state level of human political organization today. And if it was once possible (inaccuracies notwithstanding) to describe some relatively isolated peoples in Central Asia (e.g., Karakalpaks near the Aral Sea or Pamiris of Tajikistan's mountainous areas) as being products of primitive, small-scale societies, today all Central Asians have been incorporated by larger, industrialized nation-states. While we can argue that this process occurred rapidly, it transpired through distinct colonial, Soviet, and independence phases from roughly the 1780s, nearly two-and-a-half centuries of incorporation. To be sure, many thousands of Central Asians of Kazakhstan, Kyrgyzstan, Tajikistan, Turkmenistan, and Uzbekistan still live in rather remote districts and settlements, continuing to herd livestock and raise crops, but their lives and their social networks are bound up with complex societies and their myriad types of labor in ways increasingly akin to people in North America and Europe. Moreover, there is little doubt that such processes of greater industrial and global labor expansion increased markedly during the past quarter century. Curiously, this expansion does not necessarily reflect only changes that have taken place within the countries of Central Asia so much as it does the movement of Central Asians outside of the region as labor migrants.

Central Asia's peoples have made up complex societies for millennia, including ancient and medieval centers of civilization and trade, such as Bactria, Bukhara, Ershi, Khorezm, Khotan, Maracanda, Margiana, Merv, Osh, Parthia, and Turkestan. Among the numerous crafts and professions characterizing Central Asian labor historically, one has to include brick making, silk and wool weaving, silver and gold jewelry and gold threading, extensive overland trading networks, leatherworking, viticulture, baking, woodworking, porcelain, pottery, brass and iron tools and housewares, steel cutlery, textile designs of flax, cotton, and linen, paper making, and so forth. Such a heritage of manufacture and long-distance trade that involved centers in today's China, Iran, India, and Russia, among others, continued through the medieval period, enduring Arab, Mongolian, and other conquests and disruptions all the way through the mid-eighteenth century's Russian colonial expansion that culminated in the full incorporation of Kazakh lands and southern Central Asia by the 1880s. Nevertheless, the establishment of the Soviet Union (1917) and near total Soviet rule throughout Central Asia by the late 1920s has most to do with the shaping of the region's contemporary labor forces.

Soviet Rule in Central Asia

Scholars today expend considerable energy arguing the merits and demerits of Soviet power and its roughly seventy years of rule in Central Asia. Some rail against its newfangled colonialism, Russocentrism, and even outright racism, while others argue that even with its despotism and oppression it brought substantial material and intellectual benefits to the region's peoples. Whatever position one asserts, the Soviet system clearly aimed to modernize and alter the region's economies in ways designed to benefit its colossal national system. In practical terms, this meant that the Soviet system of education and training in schooling and throughout government-controlled institutions, from the civil service to agricultural technology, showed remarkable uniformity in all areas of the vast country. And despite the obvious differentiation and neglect in development that separated, say, northern Kazakhstan, eastern Uzbekistan, and Turkmenistan, in all cases the Soviet government aimed to provide basic education and full employment for all citizens.

While the Soviet educational system itself fostered a basic high-status and low-status division wherein Russian-language schools provided greater lifelong opportunities for pupils and the native-language (e.g., Kazakh or Turkmen) schools did not, schools factored as the gateway to professions and careers once children finished at ages sixteen to seventeen. In rural areas, one important qualification must be considered: not all parents allowed their children to finish their basic schooling, with girls bearing this unfairness disproportionately. Therefore, many girls of rural areas stopped attending school after finishing relatively few grades. Unfortunately, there are no accurate statistics about this because it was more or less forbidden to acknowledge it, and official Soviet statistics did not take into account children who basically were forced to drop out by parents and guardians. This phenomenon of limited schooling in rural areas is a testament to the limits of what scholars from previous generations referred to as totalitarianism, or the totalitarian

Soviet regime, because the state and its local representatives simply could not prevent parents from withdrawing their children from mandatory education.

To a certain extent, the limited schooling reflected older patrilineal and local religious values concerning discrimination toward girls and women, and in other ways limited schooling reflected the necessity for maximizing rural labor in fields and around households, especially for larger peasant families. Either way, it helps to explain why Soviet Central Asian populations remained overwhelmingly rural and nonprofessional or unskilled (beyond the countless tasks and forms of great practical know-how) outside of work associated with farming, herding, and maintaining households. Even at the end of Soviet power—1991—most Central Asian people lived in rural villages and settlements, conservatively estimated at more than 60 percent. In addition to earning government salaries on collectivized and state-owned ranches, pastures, and farms, enterprising rural people could earn additional monies by marketing some of the products they raised and cultivated legally and illegally, including fruits and vegetables, honey, dairy, meat, hides, grains, cotton, raw silk, and even cannabis and opium. Throughout the Soviet period, there were years when the state had stricter and looser attitudes toward at least semi-independent rural merchandising and trading.

Rural people who did not receive formalized training in school, including a variety of what we would recognize as shop classes or home economics classes, or who did not continue on after graduation at technical colleges, teachers colleges, health and medical institutes, and universities, also supplemented official salaries through specialized skills that may have been part of ancestral or more recent legacies. These specialized skills include carpentry, home building, textile production—weaving, seamstering, and so on—milling, baking, dancing, musicianship, cobbling, tool making and tool repair, midwifery, religious instruction, cookery, tree grafting, driving and delivering, and dairying, among others.

Returning to Soviet education, its connection to labor in modern times is crucial. Despite shortcomings indicated previously, Central Asia's peoples largely were literate and received training in all manner of careers and professions for which they found jobs after people finished their education. In urban areas through the 1980s, this meant that if you trained as a traffic control officer, structural engineer, dental assistant, circus performer, neurologist, pianist, railways conductor, accountant, bus driver, jet pilot, hotelier, kindergarten teacher, cement mixer, open air market inspector, retail sales distributor, or cell biologist, chances were good to excellent that you would find permanent employment in these or related fields. The Soviet system prided itself on literacy and full employment.

Notwithstanding what all of this may have meant in macroeconomic terms, let alone what ordinary people may have understood of the relative health and wellness of the Soviet economy, this near-guarantee of getting educated and getting trained for particular jobs and professions was part of what we might call the pact or social contract that the Soviet system fulfilled for its citizens' labors. Thus, people became used to it and expected this system to last well into the future.

Turning back to the rural areas of Central Asia, secondary and tertiary educational institutions tailored training to the constant improvement and expansion of herding and agricultural economies. And after the Second World War, increasingly rural communities were patterned almost on industrial models, including housing and rational planning for nearly all modern/"civilized" human needs. Overall, the new attitude stipulated that rural and urban perspectives on the world should not be disconnected. In addition to training people to run organs of local government (e.g., administration, accountancy, bookkeeping, law enforcement) and to be highly skilled in herd and farm management production (as agronomists, farm machinery experts, telephone line workers, electricians, irrigation managers, hydraulic engineers, machinists, veterinarians, truck and tractor drivers, cross breeders, etc.), people also were educated to fulfill non-region-specific roles. People learned to be shop owners, librarians, theater directors, food service cooks and workers, projectionists, barbers, teachers, dentists, opticians, exterminators, mechanics, and electronics repairmen. While the Soviet system did not forbid rural-urban mobility or migration, it did restrict it via a system of residence identity permits, and it tried to discourage the notion that rural life should or could be stigmatized as backward. The general idea was that people should lead meaningful and fulfilling lives as they built socialism, whether in town or country, and that the labor performed would be adequately compensated. That, in any case, was the ideal.

Women and Work in Soviet Terms

Indeed, during the 1960s throughout Central Asia's hinterlands, in rural state farm and collective farm settlements or villages (practically, there was no other kind of rural living), scholars wrote about not the equivalence or equity per se of country to town life, but they asserted that the villages were becoming more and more *cultured* in ways similar to Soviet urban life. Naturally, one would have been hard pressed to convince city dwellers that this was the case, but rural people often will tell visitors that there was much to connect them to the wider or greater worlds on kolkhozes and sovkhozes in addition to electricity, telephone lines, railway tracks, and roadways. Everything from mixed gender dance parties with Beatles music to gyms, libraries, music lessons, imported foods and clothing, and the emphasis on getting rural people to travel for shopping and vacations to their own republic's cities or even to Russia and beyond had much to do with bringing the wider Soviet world (even the outside world) to Central Asia's villages. And all of this had a significant impact in terms of how people began to consider their future possibilities for jobs, careers, and professions that greatly expanded what we commonly, though not always specifically, define as a formerly "traditional" way of life. From the 1930s on, especially after the Second World War (post-1945), more and more Central Asians worked outside of agriculture, pastoralism, and the myriad crafts and trades long associated with cities. With the rapid expansion of education and training for girls and women, the gender dynamic witnessed a sea change in women doing all manner of work, especially outside their homes and immediate environs.

While scholars overall do not deny that many benefits accrued to Central Asian women during the twentieth century under Soviet rule, one also needs to balance what are statistically and even ethnographically positive developments with their downsides. Simply, many Central Asian women after the Soviet disintegration asserted that education, work, and careers did not indicate greater gender equity in the home or even in the workplace itself. Westerners would refer to sexist practices and attitudes to characterize what Central Asian and other Soviet women referred to as labor's double burden. It meant—and still means—that in many locales and within many families women who worked outside the home, whether in blue-collar or professional jobs, still were excepted to maintain the everyday running of family households, including most, if not all, of the mundane chores associated with housewifery. In my own research in farming villages in a part of Uzbekistan's Ferghana Valley (a valley also partitioned into Tajikistan and Kyrgyzstan) in the 1990s, I discussed education and work with approximately a dozen middle-aged women, and nearly all spoke indirectly or directly about the double burden, though only one woman ever joked that she did not appreciate her education and the ability to do something other than cotton field labor. Historian Marianne Kamp, who conducted extensive historical research—also in Uzbekistan—provides a sober, statistical summary of Uzbek women's gains and shortcomings as a burgeoning part of the rural and urban labor forces from the 1930s to the 1960s. In the end, a mixture of Soviet modernization drives—despite the very uneven development concerns in rural areas—spurred the diversification of Central Asian labor forces. Mass literacy through formal education proved a linchpin from the mid-1930s on to this effect.

The Independence Period

While many similarities of culture in the broadest sense link the Central Asian peoples of the former Soviet Union, along with neighboring and coethnic populations in countries such as Afghanistan, China, and Iran, it is also important to know that the five newly independent countries that emerged after 1991 also are considerably different in terms of living standards and varying economies. (Indeed, it is reasonable to question the essence of *Central Asia* insofar as we scholars axiomatically or conveniently use it as a natural category for this region.) The tensions between what countries have in common and what makes them distinct are products of the Soviet systems legacy of integration alongside thirty years of independence wherein each country followed slightly different paths. For example, Kazakhstan is the most industrialized and today enjoys the region's highest standard of living, whereas Turkmenistan (a mostly isolated and desertified country) is the least industrialized. Mountainous Tajikistan had the highest population growth rates in the former Soviet Union, and populous Uzbekistan (approximately thirty million) perhaps had the best-educated population. The mainly pastoralist and mountainous Kyrgyzstan emerged from the Soviet experience with perhaps the most open political system but today is among the poorest and most corrupt of those five republics. In addition to these phenomenal examples of relative strength and weakness, all of the countries are characterized by diverse regions and populations, which also have been sources of tension and strife, including interethnic resentments and outbreaks of violence in Tajikistan and Kyrgyzstan. These issues stem from perceptions that Sunni Kyrgyz and Shiia Badakhshanis relate differently to the Tajik state, and that urban and farming Uzbek populations of Kyrgyzstan's south live better than the majority of Kyrgyz. Similar issues exist in Uzbekistan, though on the whole the interethnic antagonisms and regional variations are no more natural and permanent than the particular conjunctions of events that can set off tripwires owing to political exploitation of various socioeconomic issues.

Despite warnings from a range of scholars, intelligence analysts, and journalists about chaos and nationalistic enmities at the time the USSR was breaking apart, Central Asia did not go to war with itself in ways that had been predicted. Essentially, there have been no serious clashes between Muslims and non-Muslims, and ethnic minority populations of the countries have not been set upon for the most part. Of course, this is not to say that violence or war will not break out. After all, from 1992 to 1997 a most unpredicted civil war erupted and was sustained in Tajikistan for a welter of reasons, owing variously to hatred of a wealthier region (Khojent) where political power was concentrated on the denial of political rights to religious movements and regional perceptions of mistreatment and poor allocation of resources and funding (in Gharm and Kulob). Still, given the years of socioeconomic stagnation, the sharing of borders with lawless and warring regions of Afghanistan, increased poverty, pockets of Islamic extremism, growing class differences, and state authoritarianism—to mention a few negative developments—the potential for organized and sustained violence within and across national borders remains and most likely will for years to come. Such precariousness and instability make it daunting for people to pursue normal, routinized work, whether in agriculture, construction, manufacturing, or retail business, mainly because there is so little of any of these sectors operating in senses both popular and efficient. It makes for high unemployment, few legitimate sources of sufficient income, and, more or less, forces many young and able-bodied people to move out of the region altogether.

Authoritarianism, Upheaval, and Opportunities for Work and Employment

But how does this turmoil, with several variables of complex, oft-internal wedge issues, affect the labor prospects for tens of millions of Central Asians (upward of fifty million able-bodied people)? At a glance, it would appear to be only detrimental, but disorder and hardships in any one region create opportunities as well, just as powers or forces emerge that previously were unanticipated. What I mean here is that the war of nearly two decades in Afghanistan has created opportunities for Central Asians involved in agriculture, electricity, and all types of machine building and mechanized transportation, owed in part to satisfy Afghanistan's needs. Furthermore, China's rise and role as a major trading partner, customer, and developer of Central Asia's goods, services, and economic needs were not so obvious in the mid-1990s. This leads to a provocative point: were it not for the extant political leadership, despite all of the examples of individual states' shortcomings and troubling policies, civil strife and nationalist conflicts might be far more advanced and devastating than what we now see. The Central Asian countries have not spiraled out of control, and this has not been the result of sheer luck.

Central Asia's political leaders have worked at maintaining secure borders, admittedly to the detriment of free trade, the free flow of people themselves, and perhaps also of job opportunities for those seeking work across borders, which have provided the security necessary to maintain their states' integrity. While there is no question that the Central Asian countries have not enjoyed close relations among neighbors since their inception in 1991, these relationships, again, have maintained peace for the most part. One important reason for the maintenance of this peace is the fact that even the most dictatorial leaders (e.g., Turkmenistan's Berdimuhamedow and Tajikistan's Rahmon) and ardent nationalists (e.g., Kazakhstan's Nazarbayev) have not seriously spoken in favor of altering borders or depriving minority ethnic groups of basic rights in the various countries. And no leaders have called for the expulsion of, or attacks upon, minority groups within their respective countries. While this may be part of the Soviet legacy, it is also testament to the seriousness with which these leaders have sought to keep such chaos and its long-term consequences from their nation-building courses.

Repressive measures toward political dissent and freedom of expression (including lengthy prison sentences and even cruel and unusual punishment of various people of the political opposition in a variety of the new Central Asian states) have marred the reputation of these leaders, hence countries. Moreover, vis-à-vis the West, these repressive measures have made pariahs out of ex-leaders, such as Islam Karimov of Uzbekistan. On top of political repression, corruption and lack of transparency have characterized nearly all levels of state administration, from the bureaucratic workings of ministries to ordinary encounters with border guards at a variety of checkpoints both internal and international. And it is these practices and legacies that may be doing the most damage in terms of a more accessible and steadier growth and development of economies that emerged from the socialist orbit. While there are always people who benefit within and outside of elite circles in political regimes where corruption flourishes, such systems rarely create the conditions that enable the masses of society to participate in growth and improving living standards. These factors have adversely affected labor prospects throughout the region.

Still, to return to the theme from two paragraphs above, responsible national politics have maintained basic peace among Central Asian neighbors. As bad as individual countries' economies have been, they have not been devastated by war, conflict, and mass terror (the exception being Tajikistan from 1992 to 1997). Thus, these states have not failed and may now be in process of strengthening interstate relations and their respective domestic economies. Although relations to Europe and North America have not proven to be pivotal to growth so far, the Central Asian states have worked to balance relations with the powerful regional neighbors of Russia and China. In the near future, it is highly likely that maintaining stable and cooperative relations to these great powers of Central Asia's north and east will have an enormous impact on the relative development of peace and prosperity for all five countries. In part, Central Asians will reconcile themselves to living and working abroad in these neighboring giants. Furthermore, in Russia's case, negative population growth (overall decline of the Russian population) has, in an economic sense, created an ideal condition for the influx of Central Asians as workers despite all of the undocumented perils and racism associated with this growing workforce in Russia. On the other hand, if Central Asian countries benefit from large-scale investments by China and Russia, then it is possible that new labor markets will intensify or emerge to enable more robust Central Asian economies. Some of these could be based on industries such as transportation, petroleum refining, construction materials manufacturing, cotton, meat, and wool production, as well as a variety of niche food markets (figure 24-4)—everything from legumes and fruits to cheeses and nuts.

Central Eurasia's Geopolitics and Development Paths

After 2000, the stakes for each of the five countries became greater and more perilous with regard to their separate abilities to negotiate trade, travel, investment projects, supply lines, infrastructural development, international borders, and the rights of one another's citizens to work in the respective countries of Central Eurasia—including Russia and China. The bottom line is that the Central Asian countries have become more and more dependent on Russia and China for stabilizing and growing their labor sectors as well as for helping to generate growth and development. This appears very likely to be the case for years to come. For years, for example, scholars and analysts reasoned that Turkic Muslims of western China (of Xinjiang province) would press for a kind of political unification with coethnic and culturally similar Central Asian peoples to Xinjiang's west, including the predominant Uyghur population as well as Kazakhs and Uzbeks (in Xinjiang). Not only has this failed to materialize, but the influences, connections, and movements among Central Asians of the former USSR and the Central Asians

24-4   Produce sellers in the local market in Bukhara, Uzbekistan, 2018. Photograph by Kasia Ploskonka.

of China probably experience greater restrictions than during the height of tense relations between the USSR and China (from the early 1960s to the mid-1980s). Simply, the Chinese leadership made it clear from the early 1990s that they would brook no efforts on the part of the newly independent countries to agitate among the long-restive Turkic Muslim peoples of Xinjiang. The respective leaders of the independent countries understand that they deal with China not from a position of strength but from one of weakness. And as leaders raised and steeled in the Soviet system, they understood realpolitik vis-à-vis China well. They have emphasized good relations with China in hopes of China investing in their countries, which will strengthen nationalist goals, thereby elevating them in the minds of their own constituents.

What all this means is that Central Asian leaders probably never fantasized about a confederation of Turkic or Central Asian peoples as some scholars and other intellectuals have. The imagined cultural or religio-cultural conglomerate (e.g., Turkestan) gave way to nation-state imperatives from the inception of Soviet republican sovereignty (Uzbekistan, Tajikistan, etc.). At the end of the twentieth century, this ideal of the independent nation-states proved far more compelling and far more practical in the known political repertoire of the transitioning Soviet apparatchiks and Republican Party bosses (erstwhile Soviet leaders of the Kazakh Socialist Republic, Turkmen Socialist Republic, etc.). After all, this is the paradigm that we have become accustomed to for more than two hundred years. Shared culture, religion, and language do not equate to a willingness to share political power.

Misunderstandings and the Soviet Legacy's Endurance

Westerners often were convinced that Soviet power had been an unmitigated disaster in Central Asians' eyes, and that Russian chauvinism and violent oppression formed the great bête noire of Central Asian existence. In the end, such myopia was belied by ethnographic research on the part of Westerners themselves. Everything that was the Soviet system made Central Asia what it is, given all of the pitfalls and achievements that this implies. However, this was the system that three full generations of people knew. The impact of this legacy remains profound for today's approximately 65 million people in these five countries. And the impact on national economies and labor forces endures. Despite all of the ugliness of authoritarianism, corruption, and gross human rights violations characterizing some of Central Asia's leaders and political systems, republican borders are maintained, interethnic conflicts and violence have been minimized, and the three decades of not-always-neighborly relations within the region are beginning to give way to improvements. One of the biggest questions to be answered concerns how wider regional relations among the new countries and Russia and China will enhance or damage the chances for across-the-board improvements in development, living standards, and the overall quality of life in this region.

Because of factors including continued state control over key sectors of economic domains and enterprises—from lands growing agricultural commodities such as cotton and companies manufacturing airplanes—onerous business income taxes, little development of credit networks for small-scale farmers and entrepreneurs, and general labor gluts owing to relatively large and young populations, millions of Central Asians have taken to seasonal and more permanent work abroad (figure 24-5). The story of Central Asian labor migration is a process that began in earnest nearly twenty-five years ago. It involves millions of people representing both sexes, varying age groups, and all manner of professional and nonprofessional groups of workers, but in the main most labor migrants are young and unskilled workers who remit so much of their wages home that an economy such as Tajikistan's has been nearly half dependent on Tajiks working in Russia for the entire gross domestic product (GDP). For Kyrgyzstan and Uzbekistan migrant remittances in the past few years have accounted for as much as 30 percent and 25 percent of GDP, officially. Given that unofficial or informal work and economy constitute much of these countries' overall wealth, the use of percentages about GDP must be taken with a grain (or two) of salt.

Because Tajikistan, Uzbekistan, and Kyrgyzstan have relatively high percentages of rural habitation and poverty, they have provided the bulk of Russia's Central Asian migrants. Tajikistan, again, is not only an overwhelmingly rural country, but approximately 65 percent of its workforce is in agriculture. One does not need to be an economist to know that in this day and age, countries with such percentages of the population involved in agriculture almost invariably have high rates of poverty.

24-5 Tajik migrant road workers in eastern Siberia, Russia, 2003. Photograph by David W. Montgomery.

Labor in Central Asia

The recent history of labor migration may represent the greatest impact of globalization on Central Asians since Soviet disintegration. Despite the serious rise and incidence of racism, xenophobia, human trafficking, forced labor, and illegal exploitation throughout Russia, vis-à-vis migrants, Central Asians have been deterred mainly by economic downturns alone, not the corruption and dangers they face. Part of this stems from the fact that Russia is a laboring, economic lifeline for Central Asia, and part of it also has to do with the fact that Russia, adjoining Kazakhstan, forms part of the contiguous geography that is Central Eurasia. Simply, Central Asians are used to navigating Russia, and they are more familiar with Russia than any other foreign country, including neighbors such as China, Afghanistan, and Iran. This is a product of history that stretches back more than two hundred years. Cultural values and behaviors are shared between Russians and all other formerly Soviet peoples, and this is why we should expect the relationships among all of these nations to be robust well into the future. Lastly, this in part accounts for why so many outsiders misunderstood the breakup of the USSR, reasoning that Central Asians in particular would want to break completely from Russia. The outsiders misunderstood history and culture, to say nothing of all of the interpersonal interaction among Russians, non–Central Asians, and Central Asians within the territory of the former Soviet Union for several generations.

China's success in Central Asia may be rapid, and they may help with far-reaching economic transformations in a relatively short period of time. More and more, Central Asians may find gainful employment because of

Chinese capital. However, China and the Chinese have a long row to hoe before they become well liked and respected by Central Asians. The prejudices and resentments Central Asians harbor for the Chinese mainly have to do with modern historical unfamiliarity and stereotypes about everything from Chinese rapaciousness to personal hygiene and frightening cuisine. They are the products of ignorance in the strictest sense. Millions of Central Asians also remain skeptical about Chinese development in the sense that they think it mainly benefits elites, or China itself.

To return to my point of departure, Central Asian people see themselves as industrious (mekhnatkash) and business focused. And although the first two decades of independence coincided with authoritarian states that tried to tightly control popular economic activities, especially major commodities industries, such as cotton and natural gas, indications are that most Central Asian governments are beginning to loosen—if ever so slightly—their grips on economic control. Turkmenistan remains the exception. In order for the Central Asian countries to continue to build prosperous societies, they have to check wide-scale corruption, ease the restrictions on cross-border travel among the contiguous countries of the region, relieve citizens of onerous tax burdens, extend credit to small business owners and farmers, invest in agricultural technology and education, negotiate with Russia over fairer and safer terms for migrant work and settlement in Russia, and encourage the independent development of technological solutions to a wide range of environmental and consumer issues that will involve more of the population. Naturally, it is easy to make suggestions and far harder to do away with entrenched interests and established patterns of corruption, nepotism, and so on. Perhaps few single issues will be as important to the region's sustained growth of wealth-generating labor than cooperative international relations and the full safeguarding of the rights of minorities within each country. The more that Central Asians are able to move back and forth across borders and international boundaries relatively unimpeded, and without the onerous imposition of duties for passage and levies on trade goods, the more people will be able to participate in a globalizing economy that at least allows people to make perhaps livable incomes for themselves as they remunerate earnings to immediate and extended family members in Central Asia who themselves have few options for earning adequately. Until this point, poor international relations and relative isolation have ruined labor markets and the chance for prosperity in countries such as Kyrgyzstan, Tajikistan, Uzbekistan, and Turkmenistan.

CASE VI-A

Language as the Wealth of the Turkmen Nation

Victoria Clement

Dil baýlygy—il baýlygy
The richness of language is the wealth of the nation

—Slogan of the International University for the Humanities and Development, Ashgabat, Turkmenistan

Proverbs (*nakyllar*) emphasize that in Turkmen culture, languages are thought of as a means for enriching a person's life. In addition to being abstract instruments of communication and knowledge, languages are also a concrete means of improving oneself materially. In Turkmenistan, as in much of the world, languages are a resource that can help a person to advance socially or economically.

I came to see the power language and literacy imparts to people while living in Turkmenistan in the late 1990s to early 2000s. During those years, the country was transitioning from the Cyrillic script to a Latin-based one. Simultaneously, there was an intense campaign promoting the Turkmen language. Knowledge of the new alphabet and its accompanying language, Turkmen, were crucial factors in accumulating cultural capital in the newly independent state. This meant that to get by in Turkmen society, maintain a job, or enroll in a university, one needed to be competent in this language and its new script.

There is a long history of language policy in Turkmenistan, influenced by both economic and political conditions. Turkmen value languages generally, but it is their own Turkmen language that has been at the center of so much of their modern history.

Dil bilen dana, dil bilmeýän diwana (He who has language is wise; he who does not know language is a fool)

In the late nineteenth century, when the Russian empire moved into Turkmen lands, Russian was the language of standing and status. Turkmen individuals—mostly khans and their sons—who knew or learned Russian were able to act as intermediaries between the empire and the Turkmen tribes. These intercessors held a degree of influence that only language offered. They cashed in on their ability to speak Russian, becoming important translators and, later, officials.

After the Russian Revolution in 1917, and throughout the Soviet period, Turkmen was the language used at home and among friends, while Russian was the lingua franca of the Soviet Union; Russian was used in higher education, law, medicine, technology, science, and politics. Russian also functioned as the role of interethnic communication (*iazyk mezhnatsional'nogo obshcheniia*) between the peoples of the fifteen Soviet republics. If a Russian or an Armenian, for example, came to Turkmenistan for military service or work—as many did after the devastating earthquake of 1948—they would use Russian to communicate. Russian was dominant in official spheres. A Turkmen needed to learn Russian to obtain an elevated position in society or to hold a job in white-collar sectors.

After the fall of the Soviet Union in 1991, conditions changed, and value was reallocated to the Turkmen language through a variety of policies and transitioning attitudes. In the making of independent Turkmenistan, the Turkmen language regained its prestige and soon became the main cultural resource in the new country. Cultural policy was more than a question of how people would read or which alphabet they would use; it determined who rose or fell in society. For example, as the state moved away from Soviet symbols with the fall of the Soviet Union, President Saparmurat Niyazov (Turkmen: Nyýazow) (1991–2006) passed a 1993 law changing the alphabet to a Latin-based script. Discarding the Cyrillic script was an act of shedding the Soviet past in favor of a future that was focused on Turkmen culture and new symbols of independence, like the New Turkmen National Alphabet (*Täze Türkmen Milli Elipbiýi*). After this shift, when Cyrillic was no longer valued in the same way, Russian-only speakers were at a socioeconomic disadvantage. President Niyazov's language policies disrupted the country's workforce by enacting regulations that augmented Turkmen speakers' socioeconomic power, giving them a real advantage in the workplace. These policies undermined the place of Russian-only speakers by dispossessing them of their ability to work because state jobs required employees to speak Turkmen and to write in the new alphabet. As a result, throughout the country there was a surge in the informal economy, where Russian could still be used; Russian was employed, for example, in waitressing, shuttle trade, and privately employed taxis.

In addition to cultural reform, in the post-Soviet period, a general overhaul of various labor sectors resulted in a reduction of jobs, which fell along ethnolinguistic lines. Former elites and many professionals were removed from their jobs for lack of knowledge of Turkmen. President Niyazov had politicized the language question by declaring in 2000 that he wanted to see "the complete and universal introduction" of the national language in public life. He underscored his seriousness in national broadcasts in which he criticized officials who spoke Russian better than they did the national tongue. He even fired his foreign minister specifically for the latter's weak knowledge of Turkmen.

In the fall of 2001, Niyazov announced that each state sector would be responsible for ensuring their employees' proficiency in Turkmen. The medical institute, the law school, universities, and government offices slowly began to transition to Turkmen as the language of official communication. The Language Institute at Magtumguly University worked to codify or formally establish Turkmen equivalents for Russian-language terms, one field at a time: medical, military, education, and so on. Implementation of this policy was not only about abstract linguistic or cultural power but also redefining access to economic power by denying work to non-Turkmen speakers. Government ministries offered their workers night classes in Turkmen and schoolteachers underwent language exams.

VI-A-1   An elementary school teacher in the Ashgabat suburb of Köshi, Turkmenistan, 2007. Photograph by Victoria Clement.

Yet, over the next few years, many of those who were illiterate in Turkmen lost their jobs. The loss of teachers was substantial. Between 1999 and 2002, the state dismissed twelve thousand teachers, largely representative of non-Turkmen ethnic groups such as Russians, Armenians, and Uzbeks, from their positions. The official reason for this loss of work was budgetary concerns, but many in Turkmenistan believed that the real reason was the shift in language policy.

Dil—akylyň açary (Language is the key to intellect)

Russian was never eliminated from Turkmen society, but it did lose its status as the premier language. The 1993 "three language policy" (üç dil syýasaty), which established Turkmen, Russian, and English as the languages of Turkmenistan, demonstrated the order of importance each language held in Turkmenistan. Niyazov, who instituted this policy, asserted that knowledge of English would aid Turkmenistan in catching up to global standards. He even explained that one underlying reason for the country's transition in the 1990s from the Cyrillic alphabet to a Latin-based one was that, "as usage of the Cyrillic alphabet had made it easier for Turkmen to learn Russian, so would a Latin script assist them in learning English, the international language of technology." With the rise of the internet and computer technologies and the prevalence of English language globally, English continues to grow in importance in Turkmenistan.

Official Turkmen publications note, "Ongoing reform in education is designed to become one of the fundamental programs of the state's comprehensive development, to ensure a solid humanitarian and personal basis for further progressive development." Today, one way that adults and youth alike are pursuing language study is through private institutes or education centers. Even though the state maintains a great deal of control over many aspects of society, the growing number of private schools and centers allows for a new form of entrepreneurship and encourages limited forms of personal growth. In allowing these centers and schools to develop, the Turkmen government is placing some of the responsibility for self-improvement on the individual citizen.

For more than twenty years, the newspaper *Turkmen dili* (Turkmen language) has published articles about language policy and language history and offered readers examples of linguistic variants so they could develop their literacy skills in Turkmen. More recently, there have also been articles in this newspaper discussing the role of foreign languages and the importance of these in raising a young generation that is "learned, well brought up, and patriotic" (*bilimli, terbiýeli, watansöýüji*). This importance underscores calls by current president Gurbanguly Berdimuhamedow (Russian: Berdimuhamedov) (2007–present) for greater numbers of "highly trained specialists," who he hopes to see employed at private companies and state organizations. The president has emphasized that "language training is the most important advantage for young specialists, it enriches a person, opening up great opportunities." The state has also noted that certain sectors of the economy need workers for whom foreign language training would be useful: financial and banking systems, international investment projects, transportation and communications systems. Moreover, there is a need for "general economic development, which requires innovation." Official sources make clear that President Berdimuhamedow sees a relationship between economic policy and educational reforms in his administration.

One official source tells us, "Of no less importance was the activation of international contacts in education, for the intellectual diplomacy is a connecting link between cultures, educational and scientific systems of different states and nations, a firm human 'bridge' in the present and future of bilateral and multilateral relations." To this end, students, especially those who study abroad—in Russia, Belarus, Turkey, Romania, Malaysia, and China, for example—are expected to become "bridges" as they grow into specialists in information technology, electronics, agriculture, metallurgy, construction, tourism, economics and management, ecology, and oil and gas. The president has commented on this expectation, writing: "Knowledge of foreign languages and computer technologies by our specialists is, to a great extent, an advantageous factor in establishing scientific contacts."

The stress on foreign language study intensified in 2017, in part due to the Fifth Annual Asian Indoor and Martial Arts Games, which were held in Ashgabat September 17–27. During that ten-day period, visitors from around the world came into the capital city, where the government displayed traditional Turkmen hospitality by welcoming guests in their native languages or an international language. As a result, there was an increase of language study that enhanced the "three-language policy." This surge in language studies was not due solely to the Asian Games, but the Games deepened the concentration on foreign languages seen in recent years.

Dili süýjiniň dosty köp (The person whose tongue is sweet has many friends)

President Berdimuhamedow has continued the three-language policy and enhanced it through support for other foreign languages such as Mandarin. One of the manifestations of the continued importance of languages as a resource in Turkmen society is the role of private education centers (*okuw merkezi*), where students pay for classes in languages and computer literacy. In a country with an estimated 40–60 percent unemployment and where the average monthly state salary is around $500, people are paying nearly $200 per twelve-week class to study foreign languages. They are studying not only English and Russian but also German, French, Mandarin, and Japanese. This is a significant investment of financial resources and time, demonstrating that the values found in ancient Turkmen proverbs persist today.

There are long-standing foreign language centers at the Institute of Language and Literature, named for Magtumguly, as well as at the World Languages Institute, named for Azady, but they are located in the capital, Ashgabat, which not everyone can access. In 2014, the Turkmen government established the International University for the Humanities and Development (Halkara Ynsanperwer Ylymlary we Ösüş Uniwersiteti), also in Ashgabat, where English is the language of instruction and there are ties to several foreign institutions such as Wright State University. Additionally, there are extensive efforts made by foreign missions to promote language learning, such as the US Embassy's American Corners and until 2011 the Peace Corps, which serve provincial centers, but which do not quench the thirst for learning English. None of these are enough to meet the popular demands for courses in languages and computers and, except for the US efforts, do not directly serve the provinces. Due to this need, provincial educational centers like Zehinli Nesil and Bagtaýýar Merkezi have prospered, offering courses in languages, computer skills, mathematics, and accounting. Other centers offer courses in chemistry, biology,

and physics, or business etiquette. These schools or centers, which are scattered around the country, represent local entrepreneurship. That is, they are licensed by the state but are privately owned by Turkmen citizens. The purpose of the institutions is to educate. They do not have an underlying ideological or religious focus as did, for example, the Islamist Turkish (Gülen) schools that operated in Turkmenistan from 1993 to 2011.

The school Hukuk Biznes we Tehnologiýalar Mekdebi (School of Business, Law and Technology) advertises refresher courses for those who are already employed, underscoring in its ads that it will aid students in finding employment. This educational center, in operation since October 25, 2011, employs twenty teachers and has more than four hundred students. Training is conducted in Turkmen, Russian, and English, in the mornings, afternoons, and evenings, respectively. At the end of the course, certificates are issued. Such certificates are used by recipients to enhance their qualifications on the job market but do not replace traditional diplomas. There is little chance that these private educational centers will ever replace conventional universities, which in Turkmenistan are all state run.

To advance their methods of teaching English, the privately owned school Päk Nesil has partnered with Oxford University Press, while the school Dalçyn has become affiliated with Cambridge University Press, which opened a bookstore on the premises of Dalçyn. This bookstore, along with a café and resource center where students can find movies, literature, and textbooks, allows for language immersion. These educational centers and language institutes are making significant contributions to Turkmen society as they help individuals gain the skills necessary to participate in the marketplace. Certificates from one of the

VI-A-2   Schoolchildren mark a national holiday in Ashgabat, Turkmenistan, 2019. Photograph by Victoria Clement.

centers shows not only that an individual has studied a language or a skill but that the individual is hard-working and disciplined, qualities that would make a candidate stand out as they apply for jobs.

Dil görki söz, ýüz görki göz (As eyes beautify a face, a word beautifies a language)

History demonstrates that all languages, not just Turkmen, are valued in Turkmenistan. Russian, English, and, more recently, Mandarin have played especially important roles in Turkmen society. Shifts in political circumstances changed the emphasis placed on each of these languages, but the idea that it is important to study languages persists in Turkmen culture, in part because language proficiency corresponds to opportunity and mobility. There remains a strong nationalist narrative in Turkmenistan in which the Turkmen language endures. However, there is at the same time a pragmatic "openness" to other languages. This is reflected in state policy as well as the labor market. Prospects are open to people who are multilingual. Citizens are attending private schools and centers, paying out of their own pockets and taking classes in their spare time because they see foreign languages as resources; languages not only develop the mind but also allow access to work, study, and international experiences. While the presidents of independent Turkmenistan have promoted foreign language study, the country's population is pursuing language study even beyond what the government mandates by enrolling in courses at private education centers.

Family as a Risk Management Institution in Changing Work Contexts

Sophie Roche

Young people growing up during the Soviet period were integrated into an educational system that would gradually accord each youth a place in society and a job through which to participate in it. Komsomol was the last step for youth between fourteen and twenty-eight years after *oktyabryat* (seven to ten years) and *pioner* (ten to fourteen years). Between 1924 and 1926, Komsomol grew sixfold, and there were four times more Komsomol than party members. It reached the scale of mass movement in the 1950s with 65 percent of eligible age groups attaining membership. Already by 1930, the word unemployment had been eliminated from the Soviet vocabulary and the right to work established as doctrine. The development of labor force participation was highly gendered and accompanied by political discourses on women in society. A survey done in 1986 showed Tajikistan standing apart from other Soviet republics with a relatively high percentage of people engaged in the informal economy, particularly in household economy, with the number of women rising from 20 percent in 1975 to 25 percent in 1985 and exceeding one-third in rural areas. This not only refers to women—who after marriage often dropped out of the labor market—but equally to the informal economy in which rural communities were involved. The bazaar developed out of this informal economy characterized by trading networks and entrepreneurs embedded in political and religious groups. With independence in 1991, work biographies changed and new opportunities arose, including labor migration. As such, and in response to local pressures, masses of Central Asians began to leave for Russia, engage in religious education by traveling abroad, and develop private businesses.

In short, migration has become the main experience shaping households, country economies, and educational considerations. It is also a context of struggle and hardship to which individuals and communities must react. In this chapter, I look at the family as the main institution of risk management in times of crises, showing how families consider work contexts, political conditions, and social security not as problems that individuals need to solve by themselves but as family matters. Particular attention is paid to siblingship and the ability of the family to place siblings in different sectors in order to increase resilience during economic collapse and political changes.

From a Soviet Life Course to Family Risk Management

The Soviet life course was ideologically paved even if not all young people followed it. A person would move from oktyabryat to pioner to Komsomol before finally reaching party membership. The result of such a structured organization was the development of a standard life course similar throughout the USSR. Thus, from Russia to Tajikistan, we find a similarly early age at first marriage and first child, with differentiation only in the higher order of children. Since collectivization the northern tier of the USSR experienced a sharp drop in fertility within one generation, whereas in the southern tier fertility rose constantly until the 1980s. While marriage remained the key access to society, to an apartment, to gain respect and rights, youths were accorded a particular place as the builders of communism and the future of the Soviet state. Komsomol activists were employed to build water canal systems, dams, housing, agriculture, and shock construction sites and hence participated in Soviet modernization programs. Schoolchildren were socialized into collective work through cotton-picking work as part of official curricula. Whereas the Soviet regime established structures in order to control socialization of youth, the family remained a key institution shaping careers of its members.

Having mapped ways of socialization into a Soviet political society, we should not think of the latter as a static period that dissolved with the collapse of the Soviet Union. Instead, what matters are the modes of adapting to a post-Soviet economy. The family plays a key role in this process of adaptation of the workforce as well as in meeting the tremendous changes in the conditions of work opportunities and resources. Since independence, many political organizations, such as the Komsomol, simply ceased to exist, while alternative structures introduced by the Tajik ruling party—for instance, *akhtaron* (starts), *varisoni somini* (adherents of Somoni), and *somoniyon* (membership in the People's Democratic Party of Tajikistan)—never developed the same dynamic as their Soviet forerunner. Alongside this, a smooth transition was no longer expected between school education, marriage, and work. Massive school dropout and search for job opportunities beyond the village and country marked the 1990s. The civil war in Tajikistan militarized a generation of youth that struggled to return to a normal life after the war. For many young people, there is no logical continuity between education, the job market, and a decent family life. States have become unable to provide appropriate employment for their well-educated youth. And, like elsewhere in the Global South, Central Asian societies struggle with a youth bulge that the economy is unable to absorb.

Against this background, the work context that young people found in the 1990s and 2000s was marked by a highly competitive economic field, political corruption, devaluation of educational attainment, a skill gap and exploitation of resources benefiting a small group of elites. While a few youth made use of their education on the job market or establish a business, those who failed were still taken care of by their families. The mismatch between educational attainments and the labor market (skill gap) has been one of the major reasons for the Arab Spring revolts, and this problem also affects the Central Asian countries. In this highly insecure political and economic field, the family—thought of as social unit of individuals who feel socially, economically, and emotionally bound and actively live and reproduce family relations—has gained a key position. Siblings grow up attentive to take care of one another, aware that it has been reliance within the family that helped Tajiks adapt to the changing political and economic contexts.

Siblings play a crucial role in the risk management strategies of Tajik families; parents (and grandparents) retreat from work as soon as their children are old enough to take over responsibilities. Risk management among siblings is understood as encouraging or discouraging, of supporting certain ambitions or forbidding them and establishing a social unity through individual diversification. This behavior is learned during childhood and youth. Siblings compete for positions and only over time begin to see themselves as interdependent. As sisters depend on their brothers until they have sons of age to care for them, they may choose to care for one brother whom they deem capable of finding a good job more than for the others. Brothers in return have a word on the education of their sisters and whether they can work or not as long as they live at the parental home.

Brothers distribute their income in a way that promotes their own family along with their brothers and, if unmarried or divorced, their sisters. Women, in their role as wives, daughters, and sisters, are central to the family economy and contribute to the risk management strategy in important ways, such as tending animals in the summer pasture, working low-paid factory jobs, or otherwise entering the job market. Whereas married women generally hand over their income to their husbands, divorced or unmarried daughters have greater freedom in how they contribute their money—often either managing an independent life or caring for children.

Below, I offer three vignettes of how Tajik families have adapted to the chang-

ing economic and political conditions by managing their family members strategically. While the vignettes cover a range of Tajik experiences—a business family, an agricultural family, and an urban family—they are neither exhaustive nor representative. Rather, they illustrate the scope of possibilities, opportunities, and strategies that families use to reduce the risk and insecurity experienced since the 1990s.

Mirzokhoja's Family, Farming in Jirgatol

Whereas in the early 1990s many rural families left the collective farm before claiming their share, some decided to develop their agricultural business. The limited amount of arable land made it a competitive good. Whereas in the south agriculture continues to be dominated by cotton plantation, in the mountainous areas potatoes turned into the new "gold" of farmers.

Mirzokhoja (born in 1949), Mirzokarim (born in 1965), and Mirzovali (born in 1972) are three brothers living in the remote mountains of Tajikistan with one sister married and living in the southern plains of the country. The father entrusted Mirzokhoja, as the eldest son, to make major decisions such as deciding the level of education for his siblings to pursue. According to Mirzokhoja, his father—a rich farmer and religious leader until the Bolshevik persecuted them as kulak in the 1930s—felt unable to decide about educational matters. In the new political and social environment, the father tried to remain invisible and promote his children to follow the opportunities that the new system offered. Mirzokhoja studied in Dushanbe and upon his return took over an administrative job.

His younger brother, Mirzokarim, went for higher education and came back with a "red diploma" (diploma with distinction), but Mirzokhoja decided Mirzokarim could not pursue further studies (kandidat nauk), as he was needed in the village. Unable to pursue an academic career, Mirzokarim became a teacher in the local school and engaged in farming after the Soviet Union collapsed. Similarly, the eldest sister was married off before she could go for higher education (that the regime had offered her). The youngest brother, Mirzovali, did not pursue higher education because of the civil war. He did complete professional training in 2006 to become a teacher, but the job is poorly paid.

With one brother in agriculture, one in the state sector, and one in Russia (Mirzovali), the Soviet-educated brothers diversified their paths and reacted to the changing working conditions in newly independent Tajikistan. Later, all three brothers combined farming and teaching, and Mirzokhoja also became the leader for international development organizations (UNDP and German Agro Action). Whereas in the first decade of 2000 farming appeared to be a lucrative income, import and fluctuating prices have turned farming into a high-risk activity.

Mirzokhoja had children from two wives. His second wife's eldest son hardly attended school due to the civil war but took over the responsibility of the farmland for his father. The second son was sent for higher education and the youngest was sent to Russia when the job market worsened. The eldest daughter was married fast, the second daughter was sent for higher education, and the two other daughters were kept at home.

This family history shows the transformation of an agricultural family into a multisited family. Throughout the year I lived with this family, I observed constant fighting among siblings in regard to work. All children avoided agricultural work, which they considered low in status, and instead dreamed of a white-collar job that would bring enough income to live a comfortable life. Changing work contexts do not only require changing skills but also constant interaction between family members, evaluation of new job opportunities, and the management of family labor. Families in Tajikistan work to reduce the risk that changing contexts bring by allowing some members to explore new careers, such as educational or labor migration, and keeping others engaged in the subsistence economy.

The Rahmonov Family, Russian Migration

The Rahmonov family lives in a village in the Rasht Valley. During the Soviet period, the father worked as a teacher in the local school. His income was sufficient to feed the family, since in the family compound they grew vegetables, had fruit trees, and held a couple of cows and sheep for their own consumption. The father has five sons who needed to be cared for and eventually married off. When the Soviet Union collapsed, he was not payed for months, and the civil war made the job as a teacher dangerous. In his village, teachers became the primary target of *mujaheds* (opposition fighters during the civil war) who considered teachers collaborators of the state. Another job option did not exist in the village, so the father dropped his job as a teacher and left for Russia to find work. During the war, the eldest son was taken to fight with the mujaheds, but his mother did not want to lose her son in combat, so a few days after his departure, she went to the mountains and brought him back. He was immediately sent to Russia to join his father and dropped out of school.

Over the course of a decade, the

father returned to visit his family on occasion. After the 1997 peace agreement, schools reopened, yet salaries were too low to live on. In Russia he had found work on Moscow's Cherkiz bazaar. He worked first as a porter and later as a trader. His oldest son (born in 1981) joined him in Moscow. Together, they earned enough money to feed the family and allow the next brother (born in 1983) to pursue higher education to Dushanbe. The brother became a doctor, but instead of learning, he had bought most exams and remained unable to practice his profession. While in this case, the expectation that investing in higher education would secure the family with a well-educated doctor did not work out, other families successfully financed a "doctor" for the family.

The third son tended the family garden and the animals, and ran the shop that the father had opened in their native village with the savings from Russia. Until 2009, this family ran the only shop in the village and thus were considered wealthy. When the father left Russia in the early 2000s, the oldest son took over the business and financed his and his brothers' marriages and bought a family car. The fourth brother (born in 1988) was a roamer and escaped any work at home. He was sent to Russia in the hope that he would mature there. However, in Russia he became a burden, so his brother sent him back home. He married anyway and continued to live on the family budget. The youngest brother (born in 1991) showed interest in Islam from childhood onward and became the religious specialist of the family. For some youth, religion is not simply a belief but also thought of as a profession. Unfortunately for most, religious education yields limited employment opportunities. Being responsible and intelligent, he was sent to join his brother in Russia, although

he would have preferred to study. The family considered education a waste of money, as the brother who had become a doctor remained unemployed.

The eldest brother has a messy way of running his business (sending money whenever the family back in Tajikistan asks), keeping track solely of the debts spiraling beyond his control. To date, he has not been able to leave his trade, caught between family and debts. His younger brother spent most of his time studying Arabic and Islam using his mobile phone, transforming into an online Islamic scholar—though with poor business results. Finally, he accepted a position that paid a fixed salary of 40,000 rubles per month (around US$650).

This family managed their sons rather successfully, increasing the wealth of all members (the family is considered one of the richest in the village). They invested in sons with different careers in order to be able to generate income through different sources. This was a reaction to the political and economic insecurity that the collapsing Soviet Union and the civil war had caused.

Several children, and especially sons, reduce the risks of political instability, social insecurity, ecological unpredictability, and individual caprices. Despite the position of international organizations that large families tend to be poor, Tajik family practices rest on large families and a strategic management of children to reduce risk of failure of individual family members. This is how families react to an insecure political context, a poor labor market, and volatile ecological conditions. This of course does not mean that all large families are successful, as other factors, such as health conditions, access to land, and a lack of curiosity to try out new livelihoods, may negatively impact families.

Abduzamat's Family, Urban Khujand

The arrival of the Bolsheviks and industrialization of what is today northern Tajikistan changed the context of work for the population. In order to keep pace with the textile and mining industry, the city of Khujand received migrants from all over the Soviet Union. Within a few years local artisan workshops were closed and the workers employed in the factories outside town. With the creation of these factories, the whole livelihood of the town changed. If before the Soviet period, Islam had provided the rhythm of work and life, the new industry required another pace of life rhythm that sirens would set, since watches were not popular. Work shifts and the new order of time impacted family life and school attendance. Poor laborers and artisans welcomed this transformation; for the religious and political elite, many whom were landowners, the changes were less favorable, as they were persecuted by the new regime.

Abduzamat (born in 1904) and his brother were wood-carvers from an artisan family of Khujand. Woodcarving was a highly developed profession, as decorated wooden pillars in houses and mosques attest. Yet with the arrival of the Bolsheviks and Russians, the wood-carver profession disappeared and Abduzamat's family was completely transformed through this regime change. One of his younger sons was taken to the new capital, Dushanbe, to work for the military. He married a Russian woman but later divorced her. The eldest son found a position within the city's collective farm (kolkhoz) just outside town, which saved the family from starvation during the famine when shops inside town were nonexistent. The next two sons earned their living as shoemakers, having adapted to the new opportunities available.

The artisan family became a labor force for the new state, integrating into the new system while abandoning the previous system of family artisan workshops common in Khujand. The brothers continued to cooperate and help another to accumulate wealth and prestige.

The youngest of Abduzamat's sons had five sons and one daughter (born between 1934 and 1954). These sons were recruited into the Soviet job market after basic school education. In the mid-1950s, Abdukarim (born in 1940) began working at a garage where his elder brother worked. Two more brothers joined them, while one brother entered the factory that produced spare parts for cars. Abdukarim became a leader at the garage, a job that he used to recruit family members. He considered his job to be of high status not only because he had a regular, good salary but also because communism accorded workers to be the pillar of society. He had three daughters and no sons, but he expected that the Soviet Union would last and the state would care for his family, a task previously assigned to brothers.

In this town, the Soviet Union made it possible for each brother to generate enough income for himself. While care and family dependency remained important—especially among the elite families—the new work context affected family relations. In Khujand, worker families complained of extended family solidarity falling apart.

The collapse of the Soviet period has allowed pre-Soviet caste-like structures (tabaqa) to reemerge as a way to claim economic niches. Tura (former religious and political leaders) today invest in the education of the young generation, whereas the former artisan families, like Abduzamat's, see their sons becoming "businessmen." Trade turned into the main economic activity for many people in Khujand in the 1990s—the Panshambe bazaar in the center of town, for example, is growing rapidly, with around-the-clock activity—and since has developed into an important sector throughout Central Asia. The factories that once employed the majority of workers were taken over by foreign investors who pay so poorly that only women and elderly people remain.

Family as a Risk Management Strategy

The decision to migrate, work in agriculture, engage in business, or pursue higher education is not just linked to individual choice. Instead, families decide based on individual skills, family needs, and the social, political, and economic context. Crises, regime change, and wars in Tajikistan have been overcome through family risk management strategies. Rural families increase security by placing children in different employment sectors—one in migration, one in secular education, one in religious education, one taking over the family farm, and so forth. Whereas many families follow this strategy consciously and systematically, others fail to do so or are unsuccessful for a number of reasons, such as lack of intellectual capacity, health, opportunity, and so forth.

Along with changing work context, the value of work shifts, and with it the prestige linked to work. The Soviet Union devalued agricultural work for the sake of industrial work. The position of teacher, a highly valued job during the Soviet period, lost prestige since independence because of the low payment and lack of job opportunities for graduate students. Business has become a flexible opportunity within the informal sector, with the many risks that this includes (no legal frame, no social security, no pension). The work migrants do in Russia is of little prestige, whether in the bazaar or in social services, but it has the capacity to be converted into high prestige in Tajikistan.

While the three vignettes foregrounded male siblings in family risk management, sisters are as important as brothers and may take over financial responsibilities or act within the family or in any other role. More than gender, however, unity through diversity is at the core of this strategy. Risk management through siblings helps families recover from civil war tragedies, react to economic crises in Tajikistan and Russia, and survive ecological crises in the mountains. Families do so by adapting to emerging economic opportunities, changing land rights, and pluralizing professional jobs.

CASE VI-C

Domestic and Foreign Policies in the Context of Eurasian Integration

Olivier Ferrando

Over the first thirty years following the collapse of the Soviet Union, relations between Russia and the five Central Asian states have fluctuated. The establishment of a Customs Union between Russia, Belarus, and Kazakhstan in 2010, followed by the creation in 2014 of the Eurasian Economic Union (EAEU) between the three founding states, quickly joined by Armenia and Kyrgyzstan, show the increasing willingness of Russia and its partners to strengthen regional cooperation. However, Russia's intervention in Ukraine in 2014 through the de facto annexation of Crimea and support for rebel fighters in Eastern Ukraine disrupted the regional strategic agenda. Meanwhile, China has increased its influence in the region through the implementation of its Belt and Road Initiative, involving infrastructure development and large-scale investments in Central Asia. As such, this case explores both domestic and foreign policies in light of the process of Eurasian integration and the consequences of the ongoing Ukrainian crisis.

A Regional Integration Project with Obstacles

Russia seems to remain the most prominent external power in Central Asia in terms of its high-level political relationships and its security cooperation in the region. Indeed, besides the recent creation of the EAEU, the Collective Security Treaty Organization (CSTO) has dealt with regional security issues between Russia, Belarus, Kazakhstan, Kyrgyzstan, Tajikistan, and Armenia since 1994. But Russia is no longer the number one trading partner of Central Asia countries. It was overtaken by China in 2010, when China's role and significance as an economic actor started growing steadily and relentlessly throughout the region and the world more broadly. As Figure VI-C-1 shows, in 2017 China was the number one trading partner of Kyrgyzstan (20.1 percent of total trade versus 16.4 percent with Russia), Uzbekistan (20.2 percent versus 17.5 percent), and, most dramatically, Turkmenistan (55.2 percent versus 3.7 percent).

Despite the creation of a single economic space guaranteeing the free movement of goods, capital, services, and people, Russia has also not managed to maintain its leading trade position with Central Asia, in particular with Kazakhstan and Kyrgyzstan, both members of the EAEU. This can be explained by a combination of factors that have chal-

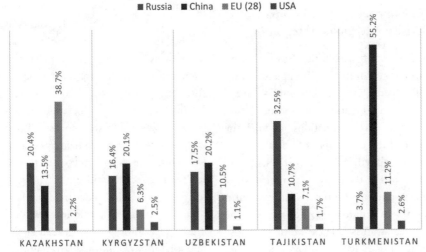

VI-C-1   Top trading partners, total trade (2017).

lenged Russia's economy, including: a failure to diversify the country's economy and reduce dependence on commodity exports, the effect of the dramatic fall in oil prices, and the impact of Western sanctions. As a result, in 2014 the value of the Russian ruble depreciated by more than 45 percent against the US dollar, with subsequent economic impacts rippling through Central Asia and the EAEU.

Russia's economic downturn particularly impacted Tajikistan, the region's poorest country, dependent on Russia as a major source of investment and labor market. If Tajikistan was famous for its world record of remittance inflows to gross domestic product in 2008 (49.3 percent), the transfers of money remarkably dropped to 26.9 percent in 2016. The weakening of the ruble also put pressure on local currencies across the region, spurring inflation. Central banks in Kyrgyzstan and Tajikistan dipped into limited reserves to ease their currencies' slides. But they could not prevent from following the ruble downward, and the costs of imported essentials rose, providing a strong reminder of their dependence on Russia. Even more radically, in response

to the weakening of the Russian ruble, the National Bank of Kazakhstan chose to devalue its national currency against the US dollar by 19 percent in February 2014 and again by 33 percent in August 2015, with the objective to make the tenge a floating currency henceforth determined solely by the market.

Just before Russia's economic slowdown, Moscow committed in early 2014 to allocate up to $1.2 billion to enable quicker integration of Kyrgyzstan into the EAEU through the creation of a Russian-Kyrgyz Development Fund (RKDF) meant to promote the modernization of Kyrgyzstan's economy and the upgrading of its border facilities: a $500 million grant from Russia's federal budget, a $500 million credit, and a further $200 million credit. This was an obvious financial incentive to attract Kyrgyzstan into the EAEU. And Bishkek did join the regional organization on August 6, 2015. However, as of October 2018, Russia had disbursed only $200 million in grants to build the necessary infrastructure in Kyrgyzstan and $226 million in credits to launch the RKDF—all told, only a third of its promised financial commitment.

The Impact of the Ukrainian Crisis on Regional Integration

On March 10, 2015, the British Foreign Secretary Philip Hammond stated that "President Putin's actions [in Ukraine] [. . .] fundamentally undermine the security of sovereign nations" and thereby echoed the concerns of Russia's neighbors. Indeed, while gaining strategic positions in the Black Sea and boosting his popularity at home, Vladimir Putin could "alienate the other part of the Russian traditional near-abroad," whose perception of Russia will now be marked by a certain anxiety and cautiousness.

To assess the impact of the Ukrainian crisis on Central Asia, we should remember that the first negative effect of the crisis is the mere fact that Ukraine, who was meant to be a founding member state of the EAEU, has not taken part in the regionalization process. Given its size and economic power, Ukraine would have balanced the Russian leadership and given a clear legitimacy to the integrative project. Without the participation of Ukraine and following the Russian annexation of Crimea, the EAEU is widely perceived as an instrument to consolidate Russia's influence on its near-abroad. In line with this geopolitical logic, three out of the five Central Asian states could feel particularly vulnerable due to the presence of the Russian army on their territory: the largest Russian military facilities abroad are the 201st Motor Rifle Division deployed in Tajikistan (about 7,500 people); the Kant military airbase near Bishkek, which has been rented from Kyrgyzstan until 2027; and the Baikonur space center in Kazakhstan, which is under lease until at least 2050.

A second negative effect of the Ukrainian crisis is the refusal of Kazakhstan to go beyond a mere economic integration. In the rounds of negotiations prior to the signature of the Treaty on the Eurasian Economic Union, Kazakhstan blocked the inclusion of any political aspects, which were supported by Russia. Even relatively harmless and symbolic, institutions typically existing in most international organizations (like an interparliamentary assembly) were not established within the treaty due to a firm position of Kazakhstan. In its Foreign Policy Concept for 2014–2020, Kazakhstan's Ministry for Foreign Affairs underlined the fact that "Eurasian economic integration" must be based on principles such as the "inviolability of political sovereignty" and "mutual benefit." Even in economic terms, trades within the EAEU represent a limited 8.6 percent of the overall trade. The European Union is the leading economic partner to both Russia (42.2 percent of total trade) and Kazakhstan (38.7 percent); Russia is the second ranking trading partner with Kazakhstan (20.4 percent) (see figure VI-C-1).

And relations with the European Union show a lack of consistency in the EAEU practices. The European Union declined to recognize the EAEU as a legitimate partner until Russia meets its commitments under the Minsk agreement to help end the conflict in eastern Ukraine. Besides, the Western sanctions imposed on Russia after Crimea's annexation significantly impacted the economic situation of Russia's partners and the cohesion among EAEU member states, thereby further straining relations between Russia and Kazakhstan. Russian countersanctions on Western products and the reintroduction of border controls created some tension within the organization since these have been unilateral actions of Russia using nontariff measures (e.g., health regulations) to introduce these sanctions. Kazakhstan and other members of the EAEU refused to support these measures, partly to avoid the escalation of the conflict and partly for economic reasons. The food sanctions against the European Union resulted in one of the most serious conflicts within the Eurasian Economic Union, leading to the rise of smuggling food between Europe and Russia through other EAEU member states.

Furthermore, the economic slowdown in Russia has increased the likelihood of protectionist measures both in Russia and in Kazakhstan. Food products were at the center of a trade conflict between the two countries, both refusing to sell the other's products citing health issues, though Kazakhstan was actually trying to avoid the market being overtaken by cheaper Russian products due to the ruble's deflation.

The Kazakh Response to the Ukrainian Crisis

The crisis in Ukraine brought attention to separatist and ethnic issues in Kazakhstan, a topic that was very important after independence when, according to Edward Schatz, most "Western analysts understood Kazakhstan's cultural mix as an ethnic tinderbox." Russia's actions in Crimea prompted others to ask if their country could be threatened by this aggressive turn in Russian foreign policy, justified by the necessity and the duty to protect ethnic Russians from a violent and illegitimate power. In Kazakhstan, Crimea's annexation changed perceptions that tended to look at Russia as a reliable and predictable partner and revived fears of separatism. Northern Kazakhstan, where the ethnic Russian population is concentrated, has long been seen as a potential target of President Putin. Indeed, if ethnic Russians represent a minority of 23.7 percent of the population at the national level, the share is more than 40 percent in four out of the six regions bordering Russia, including 50.4 percent in North-Kazakhstan region.

The probability of a Crimea-like scenario in Kazakhstan, however, is very low and fears are largely unjustified, on the following grounds: (1) northern Kazakhstan does not have the same symbolical and strategic importance for Russia/Russians as does Crimea; (2) Kazakhstan and Russia have enjoyed a close relationship and President Nazarbayev has tried—despite Kazakhization of the country—to promote ethnic harmony; (3) there is no organized Russian national groups that could facilitate such a process; and (4) from a geopolitical perspective, Kazakhstan does not maintain the same relationships with Western organizations as does Ukraine (e.g., after the Euromaidan uprising, Ukraine signed an Association Agreement with the European Union and made joining NATO a priority).

Despite such a Crimea-like scenario in Kazakhstan being unlikely, what actually matters are the concrete policy consequences in Kazakhstan, based on how the decision-making elite both perceived and apprehended the events in Ukraine. Internal instability was the first prism through which the crisis in Ukraine was assessed, leading to various changes in domestic policies by the government. In 2014, two amendments were introduced in Kazakhstan's Criminal Code: the first increased the sanctions for separatism, while the second introduced sanctions for spreading rumors and false information. Kazakh authorities became much more sensitive to what could be perceived as "separatism promotion." For instance, a young ethnic Russian blogger was arrested and sentenced to five years in jail for polling residents of a small city in the region of East-Kazakhstan about the Ukrainian crisis.

In September 2017, Kazakhstan adopted a new military strategy. Even though it makes no direct reference to the events in Eastern Ukraine, it expresses concern over "the possible deployment of hybrid methods and [. . .] the threat of incitement and escalation of armed conflict on the Republic of Kazakhstan's border space." Another sign of concern might be the appointment of Imangali Tasmagambetov as Minister of Defense in October 2014. Tasmagambetov is a leading political figure in Kazakhstan, who served as mayor of Almaty and Astana (now Nur-Sultan), prime minister, and ambassador of Kazakhstan in Russia. Entrusting him with the strategic task of reforming Kazakhstan's armed forces in 2014 illustrates Kazakhstan's goal to better cope with growing security challenges in an increasingly volatile regional environment. The military policy should not be entirely assessed through a lens of "Russian aggression," however, as Russia remains a crucial partner in the strategy. For instance, one of the objectives of Kazakhstan is to deploy a "cyber-security shield" by 2022, and, within this framework, Kazakh and Russian firms are working closely to monitor and respond to cyberattacks.

If Kazakhstan's domestic policies have been quite strict and reflect a certain sense of urgency in regard to the Ukrainian crisis, Kazakhstan's foreign policy has arguably been more cautious. The reaction to the events in Crimea was twofold and, therefore, ambiguous. The official statements, including Nazarbayev's speeches, always insisted on the necessity to respect international law, and thus territorial integrity and sovereignty of other states, and called for a peaceful and political solution. Kazakhstan even offered its services as a mediator in the conflict. However, when looking at the official communiqué following the referendum in Crimea, the discourse is different. Considering the "free expression of the will of the population [of the Au-

tonomous Republic]," Kazakhstan seems to acknowledge the right for Russia to protect its nationals (and national interests) in Ukraine. This statement angered the Ukrainian government, and, in its clarification, Kazakh officials said that it did not recognize the referendum or the annexation, merely the fact that it was probable that a majority of Crimeans had reasons to favor joining Russia.

One may have the impression that Kazakhstan was trying to appear as neutral as possible without condemning the Russian ally. This foreign policy was labeled as "politics of positive neutrality," with cautious support given to Moscow while maintaining relations with Ukraine. Kazakhstan has avoided taking a position on the situation in Eastern Ukraine or in recognizing the new status of Crimea. During the vote of the Resolution 68/262 titled "Territorial Integrity of Ukraine" at the United Nations General Assembly on March 27, 2014, Kazakhstan and Uzbekistan abstained (while Russia, Belarus, and Armenia voted against). Interestingly, Tajikistan, Turkmenistan, and Kyrgyzstan did not show up at the session.

The Ukrainian crisis has marked a sharp turning point in Central Asian perception of the EAEU. After the initial shock of the annexation of Crimea, Central Asian states have gradually come to the conclusion that they should continue dealing with Moscow. Still none are prepared to be totally controlled by Russia, while all of them seek to balance Russia's influence by dealing with the West and China. Beijing has clearly taken advantage of this multivectoral act to promote itself as a less interfering partner and a more reliable investor in the region. It is these types of great power dynamics, however, that influence domestic politics and concerns about integration.

DISCUSSION QUESTIONS

PART VI: CONTEXTS OF WORK

21. Resources

1.   What is gained and lost in viewing the world as a set of "resources"?

2.   What are local concepts of the right use of resources, particularly in transboundary areas? How are lines drawn between "local" and "foreign" users in the exploitation of resources?

22. Economics

3.   What are the socioeconomic costs of the neoliberal growth model in Central Asia?

4.   How viable are alternative economic projects in the context of global neoliberal capitalism?

23. Property

5.   We think of states, particularly autocratic states, as being all powerful. As this chapter illustrates, states indeed have immense power. Individuals, though, are not powerless, even when confronted with autocratic rule. How do Central Asians protect their property in a legal environment where property rights are far from guaranteed?

6.   Central Asia illustrates an uncomfortable truth about wealth: while wealth can be acquired through hard work, often it is an individual's proximity to power that determines one's economic fortunes. In what ways do government connections help wealth accumulation in Central Asia? In your own society? And should property rights today be extended to people who, in the past, secured wealth through privileged access to corrupt governments?

24. Labor

7.   Although Central Asia accurately may be characterized as featuring much linguistic and cultural unity, why do Central Asians seem to favor their current independent state's model rather than seeking a kind of united federation that might span international borders?

8.   Why did labor migration become such a vital issue and fact of life for Central Asians after independence, and why will it more than likely continue?

Case VI-A: Language as the Wealth of the Turkmen Nation

9.   Why did the Turkmen, who speak a Turkic language, use the Russian language as a lingua franca in the years before independence? Why did English become so important to Turkmen after 1991?

10. Why would a country change its alphabet, as Turkmenistan did multiple times?

Case VI-B: Family as a Risk Management Institution in Changing Work Contexts

11. Political transformations, civil wars, and crises affect generations and the relationships among them. What kind of risk management do families implement to make sure that their members manage radical changes successfully and that young people integrate into new systems?

12. Economic opportunities, politics, and education affect the path of youth. How have changing work contexts, labor markets, political regimes, crises, and disasters affected young people?

Case VI-C: Domestic and Foreign Policies in the Context of Eurasian Integration

13. Is the Eurasian Economic Union (EAEU) spreading wealth and stability in Eurasia?

14. How do Western states and organizations (e.g., the US, EU, NATO, OSCE) foster regional cooperation in Central Asia?

FURTHER READING

21. Resources

Asian Development Bank. *Asian Water Development Outlook 2016: Strengthening Water Security in Asia and the Pacific.* Manila: Asian Development Bank, 2016.

Baialieva, Gulzat, Jeanne Féaux de la Croix, and Aibek Samakov. *Naryn-Syr Darya: Three River Stories.* http://en.syr-darya.org.

Çalişkan, Koray. *Market Threads: How Cotton Farmers and Traders Create a Global Commodity.* Princeton, NJ: Princeton University Press, 2010.

D'Souza, Rohan. "Filling Multipurpose Reservoir with Politics: Displacing the Modern Large Dam in India." In *Large Dams in Asia: Contested Environments between Technological Hydroscapes and Social Resistance*, edited by Marcus Nüsser, 61–74. Heidelberg: Springer, 2013.

Ferry, Elizabeth E., and Mandana E. Limbert, eds. *Timely Assets: The Politics of Resources and their Temporalities.* Santa Fe, NM: School for Advanced Research Press, 2008.

Gullette, David, and Jeanne Féaux de la Croix, eds. *Everyday Energy Politics in Central Asia and the Caucasus: Citizens' Needs, Entitlements and Struggles for Access.* London: Routledge, 2016.

International Crisis Group. *Water Pressures in Central Asia.* Report 233, Europe and Central Asia. September 11, 2014. https://www.crisisgroup.org/europe-central-asia/central-asia/233-water-pressures-central-asia.

McNeish, John-Andrew, and Owen Logan, eds. *Flammable Societies: Studies on the Socio-economics of Oil and Gas.* London: Pluto, 2012.

Sehring, Jenniver, and Alfred Diebold. *From the Glaciers to the Aral Sea: Water Unites.* Berlin: Trescher, 2012.

Øverland, Indra, Heidi Kjaernet, and Andrea Kendall-Taylor, eds. *Caspian Energy Politics: Azerbaijan, Kazakhstan and Turkmenistan.* London: Routledge, 2010.

Wooden, Amanda E. "Images of Harm, Imagining Justice: Gold Mining Contestation in Kyrgyzstan." In *ExtrACTION: Impacts, Engagements, and Alternative Futures*, edited by Kirk Jalbert, Anna Willow, David Casagrande, and Stephanie Paladino, 169–83. London: Routledge, 2017.

Yalcin, Resul, and Peter Mollinga. "Water Users Associations in Uzbekistan: The Introduction of a New Institutional Arrangement for Local Water Management." In *When Policy Meets Reality: Political Dynamics and the Practice of Integration in Water Resources Management Reform*, edited by Peter Mollinga, Anjali Bhat, and V. S. Saravanan, 97–126. Berlin: LIT, 2010.

22. Economics

Aliev, Timur M. "Kazakhstan: Resource Curse or Dutch Disease?" *Problems of Economic Transition* 57, no. 10 (2016): 1–28.

Appel, Hilary, and Mitchell A. Orenstein. *From Triumph to Crisis: Neoliberal Economic Reform in Postcommunist Countries*. Cambridge: Cambridge University Press, 2018.

Jäger, Philipp Frank. "Flows of Oil, Flows of People: Resource-Extraction Industry, Labour Market and Migration in Western Kazakhstan." *Central Asian Survey* 33, no. 4 (2014): 500–516.

Laruelle, Marlène, ed. *China's Belt and Road Initiative and Its Impact in Central Asia*. Washington, DC: George Washington University, Central Asia Program, 2018.

McMann, Kelly M. *Corruption as a Last Resort: Adapting to the Market in Central Asia*. Ithaca, NY: Cornell University Press, 2014.

Myant, Martin, and Jan Drahokoupil. *Transition Economies: Political Economy in Russia, Eastern Europe, and Central Asia*. Hoboken, NJ: Wiley-Blackwell, 2011.

Pomfret, Richard. *The Central Asian Economies in the Twenty-First Century: Paving a New Silk Road*. Princeton, NJ: Princeton University Press, 2019.

Sanghera, Balihar. "The Moral Economy of Post-Socialist Capitalism: Professionals, Rentiers and Fraud." In *Neoliberalism and the Moral Economy of Fraud*, edited by David Whyte and Jörg Wiegratz, 57–71. London: Routledge, 2016.

Sanghera, Balihar, and Elmira Satybaldieva. "Moral Sentiments and Economic Practices in Kyrgyzstan: The Internal Embeddedness of a Moral Economy." *Cambridge Journal of Economics* 33, no. 5 (2009): 921–35.

Sanghera, Balihar, and Elmira Satybaldieva. "The Other Road to Serfdom: The Rise of the Rentier Class in Post-Soviet Economies." *Social Science Information* 59, no. 3 (2020): 505–36.

Sanghera, Balihar, and Elmira Satybaldieva. "Selling Debt: Interrogating the Moral Claims of Financial Elites in Central Asia." *Capital and Class* (2020). https://doi.org/10.1177/0309816820943174.

Sanghera, Balihar, and Elmira Satybaldieva, *Rentier Capitalism and Its Discontents: Power, Morality and Resistance in Central Asia*. London: Palgrave Macmillan, 2021.

Sayer, Andrew. *Why We Can't Afford the Rich*. Bristol: Policy Press, 2015.

Yessenova, Saulesh. "Borrowed Places: Eviction Wars and Property Rights Formalization in Kazakhstan." In *Economic Action in Theory and Practice: Anthropological Investigations*, edited by Donald C. Wood, 11–45. Bingley, UK: Emerald, 2010.

Yessenova, Saulesh. "The Tengiz Oil Enclave: Labor, Business, and the State." *Political and Legal Anthropology Review* 35, no. 1 (2012): 94–114.

Yilamu, Wumaier. *Neoliberalism and Post-Soviet Transition: Kazakhstan and Uzbekistan*. London: Palgrave Macmillan, 2018.

23. Property

Hellman, Joel S. "Winners Take All: The Politics of Partial Reform in Postcommunist Transitions." *World Politics* 50, no. 2 (1998): 203–34.

Kotkin, Stephen. "Stealing the State." *New Republic*, April 1998.

Nasritdinov, Emil. "Spiritual Nomadism and Central Asian Tablighi Travelers." *Ab Imperio* 2012, no. 2 (2012): 145–67.

Rowe, William Campbell. "'Kitchen Gardens' in Tajikistan: The Economic and Cultural Importance of Small-Scale Private Property in a Post-Soviet Society." *Human Ecology* 37, no. 6 (2009): 691.

Solnick, Steven Lee. *Stealing the State: Control and Collapse in Soviet Institutions*. Cambridge, MA: Harvard University Press, 1998.

Spector, Regine A. *Order at the Bazaar: Power and Trade in Central Asia*. Ithaca, NY: Cornell University Press, 2017.

Volkov, Vadim. *Violent Entrepreneurs: The Use of Force in the Making of Russian Capitalism*. Ithaca, NY: Cornell University Press, 2002.

24. Labor

Hirsch, Francine. *Empire of Nations: Ethnographic Knowledge and the Making of the Soviet Union*. Ithaca, NY: Cornell University Press, 2005.

Keller, Shoshana. *Russia and Central Asia: Coexistence, Conquest, Convergence*. Toronto: University of Toronto Press, 2020.

Megoran, Nick. *Nationalism in Central Asia: A Biography of the Uzbekistan-Kyrgyzstan Boundary*. Pittsburgh: University of Pittsburgh Press, 2017.

Mostowlansky, Till. *Azan on the Moon: Entangling Modernity along Tajikistan's Pamir Highway*. Pittsburgh: University of Pittsburgh Press, 2017.

Reeves, Madeleine. *Border Work: Spatial Lives of the State in Rural Central Asia*. Ithaca, NY: Cornell University Press, 2014.

Case VI-A: Language as the Wealth of the Turkmen Nation

Clement, Victoria. *Learning to Become Turkmen: Literacy, Language, and Power, 1914–2014*. Pittsburgh: University of Pittsburgh Press, 2018.

Landau, Jacob M., and Barbara Kellner-Heinkele. *Language Politics in Contemporary Central Asia: National and Ethnic Identity and the Soviet Legacy*. London: I. B. Tauris, 2012.

Case VI-B: Family as a Risk Management Institution in Changing Work Contexts

Adirim, Itzchok. "A Note on the Current Level, Pattern and Trends of Unemployment in the USSR." *Soviet Studies* 41, no. 3 (1989): 449–61.

Alimova, Dilarom, and Nodira Azimova. "Women's Position in Uzbekistan before and after Independence." In *Gender and Identity Construction: Women in Central Asia, the Caucasus and Turkey*, edited by Feride Acar and Ayşe Günes-Ayata, 293–304. Leiden: Brill, 2000.

Fuller, Graham E. *The Youth Factor: The New Demographics of the Middle East and the Implications for U.S. Policy*. Analysis Paper 3. Washington, DC: Brookings Institution, 2003.

Goody, Jack. *Domestic Groups*. Reading, MA: Addison-Wesley, 1972.

Juricic, Andrew. "The Faithful Assistant: The Komsomol in the Soviet Military and Economy, 1918–1932." PhD diss., University of Alberta, 1995.

Joseph, Suad. "Brother/Sister Relationships: Connectivity, Love, and Power in the Reproduction of Patriarchy in Lebanon." *American Ethnologist* 21, no. 1 (1994): 50–73.

Keller, Shoshana. "Trapped between State and Society: Women's Liberation and Islam in Soviet Uzbekistan, 1926–1941." *Journal of Women's History* 10, no. 1 (1998): 20–44.

Kuniansky, Anna Shapiro. "Fertility and Labor Force in USSR: Theories and Models." PhD diss., University of Houston, 1981.

Mulderig, M. Chloe. *An Uncertain Future: Youth Frustration and the Arab Spring.* Pardee Papers 16, Boston University, 2013. https://www.bu.edu/anthrop/files/2013/04/Pardee-Paper-16.pdf.

Pilkington, Hilary. *Russia's Youth and its Culture: A Nation's Constructors and Constructed.* London: Routledge, 1994.

Roche, Sophie. *Domesticating Youth: Youth Bulges and Their Socio-political Implications in Tajikistan.* New York: Berghahn Books, 2014.

Roche, Sophie, ed. *The Family in Central Asia: New Research Perspectives.* Berlin: Klaus Schwarz, 2017.

Schmoller, Jesko. *Achieving a Career, Becoming a Master: Aspirations in the Lives of Young Uzbek Men.* Berlin: Klaus Schwarz, 2012.

Yurchak, Alexei. *Everything Was Forever, Until It Was No More.* Princeton, NJ: Princeton University Press, 2006.

Case VI-C: Domestic and Foreign Policies in the Context of Eurasian Integration

Allison, Roy. "Protective Integration and Security Policy Coordination: Comparing the SCO and CSTO." *Chinese Journal of International Politics* 11, no. 3 (2018): 297–338.

Gould-Davies, Nigel. "The Politics of Eurasianism: Identity, Popular Culture and Russia's Foreign Policy." *International Affairs* 95, no. 5 (2019): 1186–87.

Lewis, David. *Strategic Culture and Russia's "Pivot to the East": Russia, China and "Greater Eurasia."* Security Insights No. 34. Garmisch-Partenkirchen: George C. Marshall European Center for Security Studies, July 2019.

Obydenkova, Anastassia, and Alexander Libman. *Autocratic and Democratic External Influences in Post-Soviet Eurasia.* London: Ashgate, 2015.

Oliphant, Craig. *Russia's Changing Role in Central Asia: The Post-Ukraine Context, and Implications.* FPC Briefing. London: Foreign Policy Centre, 2015.

Popescu, Nicu, ed. *Eurasian Union: The Real, the Imaginary and the Likely.* Brussels: European Union Institute for Security Studies, 2014.

PART VII

CONTEXTS OF VISION

States, and groups more broadly, face a challenge in articulating a vision that organizes a population. Without an organizing narrative, social ordering and collective action struggle with legitimacy. In this section we turn to ways in which these visions are advanced and altered—and the messiness that sometimes follows. Visions of society are dynamic, and in looking at thematic approaches and cases that complicate the picture, we see the various ways in which "visions" are advanced.

Svetlana Kulikova looks at the role of media in informing and shaping ideas about society. She shows how the Soviet development of media influenced the current media landscape, where newspapers remain significant but are paired with other emerging forms of media. In looking at markers of press freedom and sustainability, she shows aspects of media control, which is largely a higher-level effort to control narratives supportive of state (or elite) prioritized agendas.

Laura Adams focuses on the development of national identity as a macro-level approach to groups coalescing around ethnic heritage and traditions. What we quickly see, however, is that frames such as "ethnic" are not always obvious. Balancing that which is national and that which is universal—that which is particular and that which is generalizable—is constructed around conflicting discourses over what counts as belonging. And it is common that efforts to construct national identity are criticized by those left out or by those with competing visions of how people should be grouped.

All visions take place within a particular environment, with national identity often being tied to land. In her chapter on environment Amanda Wooden shows the political and social contexts in which people experience place and the natural world. She shows how ecological and topological variations impact the region and how the experience of climate change and extractive industries leads to protest, adaptation, and securitizing language about the environment, specifically around who controls and should have voice over it.

The question of voice comes through in Noor Borbieva's chapter on development, where we see the impact of concepts of modernity on development and on what counts as progress. While the tsarist focus was on making the region profitable, the independent states experienced structural adjustments to the market economy that shaped how society collectively engaged with the world. Development activities (which carry their own agendas and visions) advanced by Western international structures tried to support democratization and civil society, and this became a place for different visions to play out about what society should be.

The cases in this section approach the question of vision by situating the state in relation to efforts to control and shape the population. Edward Lemon looks at Tajik efforts to govern and manage extremism, countering extremism through state repression and efforts to create loyalty to the state. Jennifer Murtazashvili looks at the role of customary governance in Afghanistan, Uzbekistan, and Tajikistan and how customary organizations offer legitimacy, enhance state capacity, and are often quite effective in governing. And Aksana Ismailbekova looks at informal politics and lineage organizations in Kyrgyzstan to show the role that kinship—another way of envisioning the group—continues to play in politics.

25

Media

Svetlana Kulikova

No contemporary nation can exist without media and communication systems that serve as information bloodlines in increasingly knowledge-driven societies. Media systems are necessary to connect modern governments to their people because of a country's geographic span, difficult terrain, size of population, complex industrial and agricultural infrastructure, and rapidly advancing technology. Media are instrumental in creating shared meaning and in imagining what the leaders envision the nation to be and want to achieve for its citizens. Media have become such important players in developing, fostering, and maintaining our culture that most of the time we take them for granted, especially with the pervasiveness of Internet technologies and social media. Modern media and communication devices create the feeling that the whole world is literally at our fingertips. As twenty-first-century citizens of a globalized world, we expect information to be easily accessible and responsive to our needs. The familiar phrase "Just Google it!" is an indication of how much information humanity has developed and accumulated collectively and how easily it can be accessed today through multiple devices at our disposal.

Despite the general global tendency to expand the accessibility and improve the quality of information, however, not all citizens of the world have equal access to—or the opportunity or ability to use—information. Central Asia presents a microcosm of the variety of media systems existing in today's world, from the tightly controlled media environment in totalitarian Turkmenistan, which is almost entirely sealed off from outside influences, to the economically thriving but politically restricted media in Kazakhstan and the independent but economically struggling media in Kyrgyzstan. How did this variety come to be and where is it going? In this chapter we address these questions by outlining key historical developments and current trends that are shaping the media landscape in Central Asia.

Media in Soviet Central Asia

To understand the current media landscape in Central Asia, we need to look back at the region's Soviet past, as it still lingers over media systems and practices and explains at least some of the commonalities in how the national power elites in the now independent republics use and control the media toward their goals. The Soviet government always used media for propaganda purposes. The founder of the Soviet state, Vladimir Lenin, believed that the dissemination of information and investment in education would create a new type of a human being—a supranational Russian-speaking Soviet person—who would build a communist society at home and abroad. To create such a person, the government promoted Russian as a lingua franca for all ethnic groups, encouraged the settlement of Russians in non-Russian peripheries, forced the Russification of the names of people and places, and used other measures to create a shared culture, such as promoting the vision of the Soviet Union as *druzhba narodov* (friendship of the nations)—that is, a happy friendly community of the equally important ethnic groups comprising it.

In the early years of the Soviet state, the national elites in the new republics pushed back by advocating the preservation of ethnic identity in the form of language and culture. This resulted in the Soviet policy of *korenizatsiia* (indigenization), which tried to reconcile the philosophical, political, and cultural differences between the central government and the peripheral republics. As a part of this effort, in the 1920–1930s the Soviet government rapidly developed the system of local, regional, republic-wide, and union-wide newspapers that became not only the vehicles of state propaganda but also instruments for increasing literacy and for developing a sense of shared community.

Systems theory, one of the few Western approaches favored by Soviet scientists and politicians, is helpful in explaining why this was deemed important. The flow of information from the center to the farthest, or most peripheral, parts of the vast country occupying one-sixth of the planet's land mass was vital for cohesiveness and consistency of public life. It also served as a form of feedback from the peripheries to the center that was necessary for corrective management. In this historical context, the word "peripheral" literally meant "remote" and had no denigrating meaning that may be associated with it today. On the contrary, in public discourse it was often used as a benevolent moniker, showing that the center in Moscow cared for and promoted development of all of the system parts equally (see figure 25-1 for a summary of this development for the Soviet newspapers).

In Central Asia, the Soviet government was publishing newspapers in both Russian and the language of the titular ethnic group, and in most republics, also the language of the largest non-Russian ethnic minority group,

Figure 25-1   **Soviet Newspapers in Central Asia**

Newpaper's Title in USSR	Language	Start Year	1975 Print Run	Current 2019 Name, Year Changed	2019 Print Run
Kazakhstan					
Socialistik Kazakhstan (Socialist Kazakhstan)	Kazakh	1919	150,000	*Yegemen Qazakstan* (Sovereign Kazakhstan), 1991	185,000
Kazakhstanskaya Pravda (Kazakhstan's truth)	Russian	1920	170,000	No change	100,000
Dustlik Bairogy (Friendship banner)	Uzbek	1991	N/A	*Janubiy Qozogiston* (Southern Kazakhstan), 1998	14,000
Kyrgyzstan					
Soviet Kyrgyzstan	Kyrgyz	1924	120,000	*Kyrgyz Tuusu* (Kyrgyz word), 1991	20,000
Soviet Kyrgyzstan	Russian	1925	132,000	*Slovo Kyrgyzstana* (Kyrgyzstan's word), 1991	6,000
Lenin Yuli (Lenin's way)	Uzbek	1932	45,000	*Ush Sadosi* (Echo of Osh), 1991	2,000–4,000
Tajikistan					
Soviet Tajikistan	Tajik	1925	160,000	*Jumkhuriyat* (Republic), 1991	24,000
Kommunist Tajikistana (Tajikistan's communist)	Russian	1925	60,000	*Narodnaya Gazeta* (People's paper), 1991	10,000
Soviet Tajikistan	Uzbek	1924	35,000	*Khalq Ovozi* (People's voice), 1991	7,000
Turkmenistan					
Soviet Turkmenistan	Turkmen	1920	140,000	*Turkmenistan*, 1992	23,000
Turkmenskaya Iskra (Turkmen spark)	Russian	1924	60,000	*Neutral Turkmenistan*, 1995	50,000
Uzbekistan					
Soviet Uzbekistan	Uzbek	1918	683,000	*O'zbekiston Ovozi* (Voice of Uzbekistan)	17,600
Pravda Vostoka (Truth of the Orient)	Russian	1917	250,000	No change	30,000
Soviet Uzbekistan	Tajik	1924	35,000	*Ovozi Tojik* (Voice of the Tajik), 1992	18,000

Sources: *Bolshaya Sovetskaya Entsiklopedia* [Great Soviet encyclopedia], 3rd ed., 1969–1978, https://www.booksite .ru/fulltext/1/001/008/107/009.htm; BBC country profiles http://news.bbc.co.uk/2/hi/country_profiles/.

such as Tajiks in Uzbekistan or Uzbeks in Tajikistan and Kyrgyzstan. It is worth noting that Kazakhstan received official permission from Moscow to start an Uzbek-language newspaper for its sizable Uzbek community around Chimkent (Shymkent after 1993) in southern Kazakhstan only in April 1991, several months before the Soviet Union collapsed. Most of these papers started in 1924–1925, when the larger Turkestan Autonomous Soviet Socialist Republic (ASSR) was broken up into various elements: the Turkmen Soviet Socialist Republic (SSR), Uzbek SSR, Tajik ASSR, and Kara-Kyrgyz and Karakalpak Autonomous Oblasts of Russia. Soviet Central Asia assumed its modern boundaries by 1936 when the Kirghiz ASSR was further delimited into a Kazakh ASSR, the Kazakh and Kara-Kyrgyz ASSRs were elevated to the status of Union republics, and Karakalpak Oblast was merged with the Uzbek SSR. It is also worth noting that the oldest newspaper in the region, *Pravda Vostoka* (Truth of the Orient), was established in April 1917 by imperial Russia under the name of *Nasha Gazeta* (Our newspaper) and was given its current name in 1924, perhaps reflecting a still lingering Soviet-Russian Orientalist view of Central Asia as the far outpost of the Russian empire (albeit not the farthest, which would be the Far East).

All these republic-level newspapers were official vehicles for disseminating information and propaganda for the republics' Communist Party Central Committees. Just like their Russian-language counterparts, the major all-Union newspapers such as *Pravda, Izvestiya,* and *Komsomolskaya Pravda,* they published important state documents, including new legislation and policies, and disseminated the national news at the republic's level. They did not completely duplicate the content of the national papers but, rather, covered local news in politics, culture, sports, and other stories of interest for their readers.

Currently, these newspapers are still the official media of the respective governments and serve as newspapers of record for enacted legislation and official policies. Today they are usually subsidized by the national and regional governments, although many of them are struggling to survive because of budget cuts. Similar to commercial newspapers, they increasingly rely on advertising and subscription fees. There have been drastic reductions in current print runs compared to 1975 for all newspapers except for *Yegemen Qazakstan,* which is purposefully heavily subsidized by the Kazakh government not only for prestige but also with the intent of disseminating consistent government policies and ideology (see figure 25-1). For other newspapers, the cuts are explained not only by weaker government support but also by the global trend of shrinking newspaper audiences driven by the expansion of Internet-based media, which has shifted media consumption toward digital platforms. The Russian-language newspapers in Central Asia are also losing their print run because of the shrinking population of their target audience and the elevation of the native languages.

Radio was the second media technology that the new Soviet government developed aggressively and rapidly at about the same time as newspapers. Before the Bolshevik Revolution, radio was a bulky nascent technology used by the naval empires for ship-to-shore communication and for communication between the troops on the First World War front lines. Lenin recognized the power of radio as a relatively inexpensive, accessible, and powerful content-carrier for the young Soviet state, and he personally supervised its development. The first radio station started to broadcast in Moscow in late November 1917, less than one month after the Bolshevik Revolution. Its first content was Lenin's passionate speeches outlining his vision of the new Soviet state. Compare this to the start of commercial radio in the United States. On Election Day, November 2, 1920, Westinghouse sponsored the broadcast of election results by KDKA station in Pittsburgh that had been created by Dr. Frank Conrad, an amateur radio operator who liked to share his favorite music and sports scores using a ham device he had assembled in his garage. In the Soviet Union, as a result of Lenin's government directives, by the end of the 1930s even the most remote areas of the country were connected into a single all-Union radio system. During the Second World War, radio played a critical role in informing the citizens about what was going on in the Nazi-occupied territories and on the front lines as well as in mobilizing support for the war effort.

After the war ended, the state used newspapers and radio to mobilize and accelerate the reconstruction effort. The war and reconstruction delayed the implementation of television in the Soviet Union, which Soviet scientists had been developing since 1930s, parallel to television in the United States and Germany. In the United States, television became available in the mid-1940s, immediately after the end of the Second World War. In the Soviet Union, television became available in the late 1950s, and black-and-white TV sets were found in a majority of Soviet homes by the early 1970s. Color TV technology reached a tipping point in the early 1980s. Broadcast television peaked during the last years of the Soviet Union, today known as a period of general stagnation. By 1985, when Gorbachev came to power and started perestroika and glasnost, television had achieved 90 percent penetration rate in Soviet households, and radio boasted nearly universal coverage with 99.9 percent penetration rate.

Radio and television played key roles in communicating a coherent and consistent vision of statehood across the huge Soviet territory. When the Cold War started after the "hot" Second World War of 1939–1945, it brought in fierce ideological and economic competition for global influence between the Soviet Union and the United States. The Cold War created a bipolar world with a new information war front, both at home and abroad, and intensified the importance of propaganda as the electronic media could reach all areas of the country quickly and effectively. Domestic Soviet propaganda was universal, giving consumers little choice in terms of content diversity. There were two national radio stations, *Tsentralnoye Radio* (Central Radio) and *Radio Mayak* (Radio Lighthouse), both broadcasting up to twenty-three hours a day. They were supplemented with one or two republic-level news and educational stations, broadcasting in each Soviet republic in the language of the titular ethnic group. In compact regions with sizable ethnic minorities within the republics, there was limited programming in the languages of those minorities—for example, Uzbek-language programming in the Tajik SSR and Kyrgyz SSR or Tajik-language programming in Kyrgyzstan and Uzbekistan. In the Jambul Oblast of Kazakhstan and Talas Oblast of Kyrgyzstan, a one-hour weekly program in German was broadcasting on the oblast radio frequency for the German minority (Volga Deutsch) who had been resettled there from the Volga region at the onset of Second World War.

The audiences also had only a few options on television. At the peak of the Soviet Union, the national, all-Union Central Television channel (Russia's Channel One today, which still broadcasts to Central Asia) was broadcasting on average thirteen hours a day. It was the official government voice, covering news and providing educational and entertainment content, including from about sixty to ninety minutes of children's programming per day. In different parts of Russia and the European Soviet Republics, there were three additional channels, broadcasting news, entertainment, education, music, sports, and other types of programming. In Central Asia, another centralized channel titled Orbita (The orbit), today's Russia on Channel 2, was repackaging old and new content from the Central TV, broadcasting on average over twelve and a half hours a day. In addition, each Soviet republic had its own television channel in the language of the titular ethnic group, broadcasting on average six or seven hours a day, and in many regions, there was regional programming on local channels of three or four hours a day. Local television had limited capacity in producing original content, although each republic encouraged development of its own movie industry, which was feeding content to television. Specifically, Kyrgyz and Kazakh cinema held a notable place in Soviet moviemaking, with its own distinct style and approach to acting and film production.

Most of the media content in the Soviet Union glorified the history and traditions of the young country, the heroism of the Soviet people during the Second World War and postwar reconstruction, and commitment to the goal of achieving the communist society. The programming celebrated thirtieth, fortieth, fiftieth, and subsequent anniversaries of the Great October Socialist (Bolshevik) Revolution and Victory in the Second World War. The various channels broadcast theater plays, classical music, and ballet performances and created displays of patriotism even out of sporting events. As Sergei Lapin, director of the Central Committee on Radio and TV Broadcasting in 1970–1985 described the programming his agency was responsible for:

> Television and radio programs reflect the atmosphere of unbreakable moral and political unity of our society, solidarity of the [Communist] party and people with Lenin's CPSU Central Committee, the atmosphere of work dedication and creative spark, optimism and confidence of the Soviet people in a better tomorrow. Together with other media of mass information and propaganda, TV and radio ensure openness and transparency, as well as effectiveness of the all-Union socialist competition to increase the output and quality of production, and to fulfill the five-year economic plans.

In general, the Soviet government was always open about the use of media for propaganda and mobilization ("agitation" in Russian) purposes. It was also so obvious for the citizens that, by the mid-1980s, they were quite weary, skeptical, and even cynical about the government. Smuggling Western clothes and music albums and underground printing of domestic dissidents' and banned foreign literature works (*Samizdat*) were proliferating. People found ways of catching the waves of the Voice of America and Radio Free Europe. In their kitchens Soviet citizens were making jokes about the moving target of achieving the communist society in a single country after the goal of a global proletariat revolution was abandoned. First the Party promised that communism would have been built by 1960, then by 1970, and finally—by 1980. When 1980 with its spectacularly lavish Moscow Olympics (boycotted by most Western countries) both came and went, even the most zealous ideologues understood that the Soviet Union could not last much longer in its current form, especially after three deaths in three years of aged and sickly Communist Party leaders (Brezhnev, Chernenko, and Andropov), whose funerals were broadcast live to the entire world. This is why when the much younger Michael Gorbachev came to power in 1985 and promised reforms, the citizenry sighed with relief and renewed hope in government and the future.

Gorbachev's policies of perestroika and glasnost initiated a time of unprecedented openness and transparency for the country in general and the media in particular. The market reforms allowed for commercialization and independent ownership of media, and new newspapers, magazines, radio, and TV channels started to spring up around the country. Cable TV appeared, initially as closed-circuit pirate networks connecting several apartment blocks in urban areas, generally run by the most entrepreneurial residents of each neighborhood who broadcast pirated Western movies and music videos from their apartments. These ventures later expanded, consolidated, and grew into networks of channels that provided cable TV content similar to today's cable providers.

Glasnost freed the media to expose abuses of power and corruption, to criticize bad government policies, and publicize recently unearthed historical materials about past Soviet practices of repression and mass killings that had until then been kept secret. This short period of a little over five years—from 1985 when Gorbachev started the reforms, to 1991, when the Soviet Union collapsed after a failed coup against him—was unprecedented in terms of the degree of freedom and independence from the government enjoyed by the press. This era reshaped Soviet media and created an environment poised for future media democratic development. Unfortunately, those anticipated democratic developments of the media did not occur in all fifteen of the newly independent states.

Media in Post-Soviet Central Asia

After the Soviet Union collapsed, all five Central Asian republics declared themselves to be constitutional presidential republics. All of them have articles in their constitutions guaranteeing freedom of thought, speech, and expression for citizens, if not freedom of the press explicitly. At least based on the legal framework, all these countries should have a free press. In reality, however, the situation with media freedom in the region is far from democratic.

A comparative overview of media in Central Asia by types (see figure 25-2) shows that Kazakhstan leads the region in terms of the number of media outlets relative to its population size, but most media are controlled by the ruling elite, either directly through state ownership or through inclusion in

Figure 25-2   Media in Central Asia by Country, 2018

	Kazakhstan	Kyrgyzstan	Tajikistan	Turkmenistan	Uzbekistan
Print media					
Newspapers	1,156	159	367	28 (all print	1,015 (all
Magazines	1,169		239	media)	print media)
Broadcast					
Radio stations	61	26	34	1	35
TV stations	108	25	30	7	65
Cable operators	108	6	7	1	1
News agencies	41	11	11	1	4
Population, millions	17.9	6.1	8.9	5.3	32.6

Source: Compiled from 2018 IREX Media Sustainability Index and BBC country profiles.

the media conglomerates controlled by Nazarbayev's loyalists. Kyrgyzstan's media market is the most diverse in terms of state and private ownership and is comparable to Tajikistan's in terms of ratio to the population size. Uzbekistan has a relatively developed print media sector, but its broadcast media (i.e., traditional over-the-air radio and TV), the only cable operator (i.e., provider of access to cable TV and Internet), and three of the four news agencies (i.e., organizations collecting national and local news for media outlets) are all controlled by the state. Turkmenistan has the least developed media in terms of both the number of media outlets and owners, as all media except for three newspapers are state controlled.

International Assessments of Press Freedom in Central Asia

According to the theory of democratic transitions first proposed by Juan Linz, the media system in any country exists in a symbiotic relationship with its political, social, and economic system. On the spectrum of regime types, fully consolidated democracies with free and open markets will have the most effective and thriving independent media systems, and fully consolidated autocracies with strictly regulated internal markets or planned economies tend to use various mechanisms and practices to keep media systems under tight control. In between, there are semi-consolidated and hybrid regimes that implement various types of media controls depending on which direction the regime is moving to consolidate: toward a democracy or toward an autocracy. Since media are knowledge systems that deliver information to the populace, every authoritarian regime tries to control its media systems so that they consistently deliver the uniform government message to the citizens. This characteristic of authoritarian regimes—tendency to control the media—is a long-term trend in Central Asia.

Freedom House, a US-based nonprofit that evaluates the state of overall freedom in all countries of the world, has been ranking Central Asian republics separately since 1991 (see figure 25-3). Freedom House uses a composite

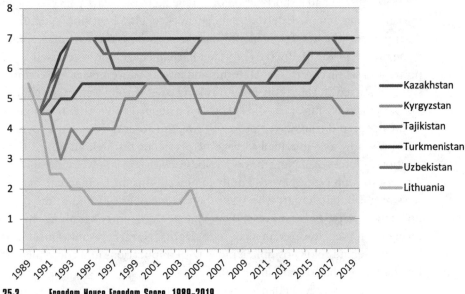

25-3   Freedom House Freedom Score, 1989–2019.

score of two dimensions to evaluate freedom. The first concerns political rights, which include political pluralism and participation, as in citizens' ability to run for office and be elected; the diversity of competing political parties; a regular, open, and transparent electoral process; and the accountable and transparent functioning of the government. The second concerns civil liberties, which include freedom of expression and belief, associational and organizational rights, rule of law, personal autonomy, and individual rights. The score ranges from 1 to 7, where the "free" category, the lower zone of the graph, refers to the countries with a score of between 1.0 and 2.5; "partly free" refers to the countries receiving a score of between 3.0 and 5.0; and "not free" refers to the countries with a score of between 5.5 to 7.0. All countries started out at the same rating of "Not Free" in 1989–1991, when they were republics in the Soviet Union, with a score of between 4.5 and 5.5. Lithuania is shown on the graph as a benchmark of comparison as it was a part of the Soviet Union and is now a member of the European Union. Its trajectory illustrates the ideal democratic transition from a hybrid regime to a fully consolidated democracy.

As the ratings for the five Central Asian republics show, only Kyrgyzstan became freer in the early 1990s, during President Askar Akaev's first term. However, Kyrgyzstan remains—at the time of writing—only "Partly Free," because of Akaev's overt attempts to stay in power, which resulted in his ouster in 2005; the violent revolution in 2010 that displaced Akaev's successor, Kurmanbek Bakiev, and that led to ethnic violence between Uzbeks and Kyrgyz in the south; and later semi-successful parliamentary and judicial reforms. October 2020 mass protests after the rigged parliamentary elections resulted in another government shake-up and the coronavirus pandemic ravaging the country (at the time of writing) keeps Kyrgyzstan volatile.

Kazakhstan had a short period of balancing in the "Partly Free" zone in the early 1990s, immediately after independence. However, since Nursultan Nazarbayev—the first president of Kazakhstan, who was given an exception to be president for life by the country's Parliament in 2007—consolidated power and set up controls on all forms and levels of government, the country steadily stayed in the "Not Free" ranking area through 2017. In March 2019, the seventy-nine-year-old Nazarbayev stepped down after thirty years as president and transferred power to Kassym-Jomart Tokayev, a loyalist interim who was confirmed to become president through an out-of-turn election in June 2019. Nazarbayev's critics saw this as a power move and an attempt to keep Nazarbayev's family in power—his media magnate daughter Dariga, in particular, who was a Senate member elevated to the chair position in 2019. These moves did not change the country's rankings by the Freedom House. However, in May 2020, Dariga Nazarbayeva was dismissed from her Senate chair position, a move with implications and consequences for the family that remain uncertain.

Tajikistan's independence was marred by the civil war with Islamic groups in the early 1990s. As one of the poorest and least developed republics of the Soviet Union, the country took a long time to recover from the war. In 1994, once President Emomali Rahmon resumed office (he was ousted during the war in 1992), he also gradually consolidated power and turned Tajikistan into a fully consolidated autocracy. In 2017 the president's thirty-year-old son, Rustam Emomali, was appointed the mayor of Tajikistan's capital, Dushanbe, and his daughter, Ozoda Rahmon, was appointed the president's chief of staff, which signaled that the presidential family was grooming the children to take over the reins from the sixty-six-year-old leader.

Power in Turkmenistan did not leave the hands of the first president, Saparmurat Niyazov, until he died in December 2006. Niyazov was the former chairman of Turkmenistan's Communist Party Central Committee and the self-proclaimed father of all Turkmens (Turkmenbashi) who prided himself for keeping his country truly independent and neutral—that is, out of all alliances and supranational structures. He canonized his own biography *Rukhnama* to be the main book for the country and in 1999 was appointed president for life by the Parliament. His successor, former deputy prime minister Gurbanguly Berdimuhamedow, never changed the country's authoritarian system and maintained tight control over all aspects of the country's life, albeit with less eccentricity and petty tyranny than his predecessor was notorious for in the outside world.

Uzbekistan followed a similar pattern. Like his Turkmen counterpart, President Islam Karimov came out of the Communist Party nomenclature, became the first president in 1991, and through extension and change of term limits was reelected president three times until he died in 2016. As one of the most closed authoritarian societies in the world, Uzbekistan stayed in the "Not Free" zone until recently, when the new president, Shavkat Mirziyoyev, started to loosen some of the controls. He released long-term political prisoners, reestablished visa-free travel between Kyrgyzstan and Uzbekistan, and opened the country up for easier travel for foreign tourists.

In summary, the general sociopolitical environment in all five republics of Central Asia remains authoritarian. In fact, with the alarming tendency of the global right-wing populist movements to reemerge and rebound even in established Western democracies, Freedom House titled its 2018 report on freedom in the world "Democracy in Crisis" and pointed out that "some doors closed while others opened" in Central Asia:

> Observers have long speculated about the problems and opportunities posed by presidential succession in Central Asia, where a number of entrenched rulers have held office for decades. In Uzbekistan, speculation turned into cautious optimism in 2017, as the country's new administration—formed following the 2016 death of longtime president Islam Karimov—took steps toward reform. Among other moves, the government ended forced labor in the annual cotton harvest for some segments of the population, and announced plans to lift the draconian exit-visa regime and make the national currency fully convertible. The new administration has also granted more breathing room to civil society; some local groups reported a decrease in state harassment, and a Human Rights Watch delegation was allowed to enter Uzbekistan for the first time since 2010.
>
> In other parts of the [Eurasian] region, however, governments sought to stave off change. In Armenia and Kyrgyzstan, heavily flawed voting highlighted the continuing erosion of democratic norms surrounding elections. The dominant parties in both countries relied on harassment of the opposition, voter intimidation, and misuse of administrative resources to maintain a grip on power.

The "Freedom of the World" report for 2019, titled "A Leaderless Struggle for Democracy," points out an even more pessimistic tendency of fourteen consecutive years of democracy decline and highlights developments in Central Asia as significant for the entire Eurasian region: "Parliamentary elections in . . . Uzbekistan also shut out any genuine opposition, leaving legislatures entirely in the hands of pro-government groups. Longtime president Nursultan Nazarbayev transferred power to a hand-picked successor, Kassym-Jomart Tokayev, through a rigged election in Kazakhstan, and the authorities used arrests and beatings to break up mass protests against the move." The tendency for consolidation of authoritarian regimes in Central Asia continues to threaten overall democratic developments and the status of freedom in the region.

In addition to the "Freedom in the World" report, Freedom House evaluated freedom of the press in a separate, dedicated report. In 2018 the organization stopped producing individual country rankings on freedom of the press, renamed the report "Freedom and the Media," and consolidated it to highlight only the general global and regional tendencies. The most recent detailed report with country rankings, published in 2017, is titled "Press Freedom's Dark Horizon" and covers 2016, so the plot area in the figure (see figure 25-4) ranges in time from 1993 to 2016. No scores are available for Central Asia before 1993.

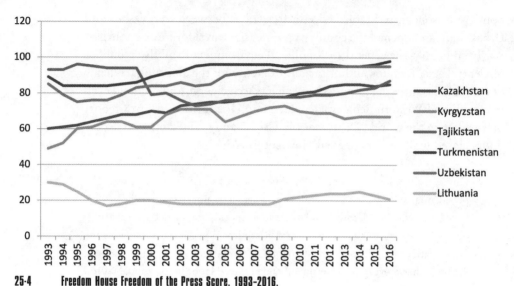

25-4   Freedom House Freedom of the Press Score, 1993-2016.

In 1992, the first full year of independence after the Soviet Union's collapse, all Central Asian countries were designated as "not free," except for Kazakhstan whose freedom of the press was categorized as "partly free." Three components make up the score: (1) legal environment, which refers to laws and regulations providing and enforcing freedom of press and their actual application; (2) political environment, which means the degree of political influence in media content; and (3) economic environment, which refers to structure, transparency, and the concentration of media ownership, the costs of operating media and distributing the content, the role of advertisers and other economic players in media content, the impact of corruption and bribery, and the overall economic health and sustainability of media. The score in three categories ranges from 1 to 30 (free), from 30 to 60 (partly free), and from 60 to 100 (not free).

Lithuania is used for comparison as a country with a free press. Since the media systems are largely a reflection of broader sociopolitical trends in the society, the historical tendency for freedom of the press is similar to the overall freedom score in the region: Kyrgyzstan is ranked as "partly free" or "not free," while the remaining four countries are consistently evaluated as "not free." The 2019 report points out an even deeper downward spiral with media freedom in the region and the world.

The International Research and Exchanges Board (IREX) is another source of expert evaluation of media in transitional regimes. Since 2001 IREX has published an annual media sustainability index (see figure 25-5). The index uses five dimensions to evaluate media sustainability: (1) free speech laws and legal protections of media and journalists; (2) the professionalization of journalism through education, upholding of ethical standards, and skills development; (3) the plurality of news sources; (4) media business management, such as effective operation with the goal of achieving sustainability, if not profitability; and (5) supporting institutions such as NGOs, professional associations and societies, and donors. The scores are

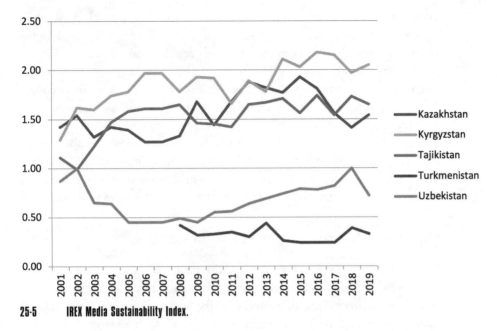

25-5 **IREX Media Sustainability Index.**

divided into four categories: unsustainable, anti–free press (0–1); unsustainable mixed system (1–2); near sustainability (2–3); and sustainable (3–4).

Only Kyrgyzstan achieved near sustainability on the lower end of the scale in 2014, and the trajectory of its movement up and down shows a need to make its media system truly sustainable. Kazakhstan and Tajikistan show similar patterns of moving up and down in the unsustainable mixed area, and the significant downtick in 2017 alarmed all media experts who were watching the general tendency of eroding democratic norms and consolidating authoritarian regimes all over the world. However, both countries showed some improvement in 2019. Uzbekistan is moving into the unsustainable mixed area, which is a result of a gradual and tentative post-Karimov opening up of the country. Turkmenistan—which until Niyazov's death was so closed to the outside world that foreign organizations such as IREX were unable to send in their experts or recruit local experts for the evaluation—consistently stays in the unsustainable, anti–free press area and is unlikely to move out of it under President Berdimuhamedow.

Other international organizations that monitor press freedom and media systems in the world—such as Reporters Without Borders, the Committee to Protect Journalists, Human Rights Watch, the International Center for Journalists, and the Organization for Security and Co-operation in Europe (OSCE) among others—note the same tendencies for Central Asian republics' erosion of democratic norms of press freedom and diversity of independent media. The difference between these organizations' evaluations and the Freedom House/IREX evaluations is that they take a less academic and methodology-driven approach. They are more professionally focused within their specializations and interests, akin to chroniclers or recorders of the most significant events. Some critics point out that all these organizations are evaluating the developments in local cultures from the ethnocentric Western perspective of an ideal media system in a democratic society or based on the ideological affinity between the ranking organization and the evaluating experts. However, Freedom House and IREX regularly reexamine their methodology in order to address the criticism, and they include independent experts from the local cultures in their methodology design process. They also recruit local experts for the actual evaluation and report drafting as sources of expertise and report writers. In any case, even considering the criticism, these rankings provide the best available systematic and consistent view on how individual countries are faring in terms of democratic and press freedom developments compared to other countries and regions of the world.

Direct and Indirect Forms of Media Control

International observers who monitor the media situation in Central Asia point out that the authoritarian rulers of the region rely on and practice both direct and indirect forms of control over the media in their countries. Direct controls include a restrictive legal environment, such as laws that curtail free speech and allow for imprisonment, censorship, and the intimidation of journalists and editors, as well as outright ownership and state affiliation of media outlets. Indirect forms of control include ownership through loyal third persons or family members of the ruling elites, self-censorship by journalists (the practice whereby journalists do not need to be censored or directly told what to write or not to write but restrict and censor themselves based on the knowledge of the policies, preferences, and directives of their editors and owners), and financial controls such as subsidies and advertising streams.

In all five countries, the governments have successfully used their anticorruption, antiterrorism, state secrets, hate crimes, propaganda, and defamation laws to imprison, sue into bankruptcy, or threaten and intimidate media owners, editors, and journalists. One example is the May 2018 detention of Radio Free Europe/Radio Liberty journalist Soltan Achilova in Turkmenistan for photographing Victory Day celebrations, in violation of the state secrets law. Another example comes from Kazakhstan, where in September 2017 an Almaty court convicted Zhanbolat Mamay, editor of the independent *Sayasy Kalam: Tribuna* newspaper, on politically motivated money-laundering charges. In July 2018 a Tajikistan court handed a twelve-year prison sentence to Khayrullo Mirsaidov, an investigative journalist reporting on local authorities' corruption, on trumped-up embezzlement and false reporting charges. In Kyrgyzstan, in June 2017 a Bishkek court slapped an unthinkably large fine of $260,000 on the Internet portal Zanoza.kg in a defamation suit on behalf of the outgoing President Almazbek Atambaev. His successor, President Sooronbay Jeenbekov, "won" the defamation suit in February 2018 against 24.kg news agency.

In Uzbekistan, which had the worst record in Central Asia in terms of human rights violations against journalists, the trend seems to be reversing after Karimov's death. In February 2017 Uzbekistan's leadership released long-imprisoned journalist Muhammad Bekjanov, who had spent eighteen years in prison on trumped-up connections with the 1999 bombings in Tashkent and an assassination attempt on President Karimov. In February 2018 Yusuf Ruzimuradov, Bekjanov's colleague at the *Erk* (Freedom) newspaper who had spent nineteen years in prison on the same charges, was released as well. Overall, in 2016–2018, the new Uzbekistan government continued to release dozens of journalists and public activists imprisoned by the Karimov regime and changed the leadership at the national security agency, which for decades had been issuing false charges and condoning imprisonment, harsh interrogation, and torture for journalists and political dissidents to get confessions and prison terms. International experts are cautiously optimistic that these changes will result in a better legal and operational environment for journalists and citizen activists.

As for ownership patterns, in four of the five Central Asian republics most of the strategic media—that is, as major newspapers, TV channels, and radio stations with a broad reach at all levels from national to local—belong to either the state or the ruling families directly. In Turkmenistan and Uzbekistan, most media have been state controlled since independence. There are hardly any private media, and those that arc in private hands avoid covering politics. Media may mildly—or, using the authoritarian term, "constructively," meaning without challenging the fundamentals of the system or the top government—criticize local governments, uncover corruption at local levels if it does not go all the way to the top, and provide superficial non-obliging suggestions and recommendations for governments to function better. Journalists and editors seem to subscribe to the ruling government ideology and practice self-censorship, whereby they know exactly what can be covered and who is untouchable, especially the president and his kinship. Although there is little hope that the situation in Turkmenistan will change anytime soon under President Berdimuhamedow, international observers point out that in Uzbekistan in the years after Karimov's death there has been some loosening of tight controls over the media and more private media are springing up, often with the help of the Public Fund for Support and Development of Non-State Media.

In Kazakhstan and Tajikistan, media are more diverse in terms of ownership: there are state, private, and independent media, as well as grassroots media run by nascent NGOs. However, on closer examination, the private and independent media that have viable commercial potential and influence are in the hands of the ruling families through ownership by loyalists. *FerganaNews.com* reported that Kazakhstan's largest media empire, which includes the former state news agency and broadcast network Khabar, was controlled by Dariga Nazarbayeva, the first president's eldest daughter. The same source states that ruling elites control other major media holdings as well, such as those belonging to the loyalist media magnate Arman Baitasov, Timur Kulibaev (husband of Dinara Kulibaeva, former president Nazarbayev's middle daughter), former prime minister Karim Masimov, and loyalist billionaire Bulat Utemuratov. In Tajikistan, the pattern is similar: President

Rahmon, his elder son, Rustam, and their loyalists control most of the country's media, with the only difference being the scale and profitability. Media holdings are smaller and make less money in Tajikistan than in Kazakhstan, the largest and arguably richest Central Asian country.

Concentration of ownership in the hands of the ruling elite plagued media in Kyrgyzstan as well, where Presidents Akaev and Bakiev gave their children control of the most significant media in the country. After the 2010 revolution and transformation of the country into a parliamentary republic, Bakiev's media assets were broken up and sold. Now they are controlled by various competing groups representing diverse political factions, which ensures diversity of the media. This, however, does not preclude concentration of these media in other powerful hands, as demonstrated by the example of the former prime minister, presidential candidate, and current fugitive Omurbek Babanov, who was charged with corruption and incitement of ethnic hatred during the 2017 presidential election and who reportedly used to control a sizable media holding with major newspapers and regional broadcast channels.

In addition to the challenges described above, the media in the two poorest countries of the region—Kyrgyzstan and Tajikistan—have to cope with a lack of resources. Many media in these countries, particularly in rural areas, are struggling to survive as their real-world customer and subscription base is shrinking, while government subsidies provided by the Soviet regime to rural and minority media are dwindling and other sources of revenue such as advertising and donor support are insignificant or nonexistent. During election seasons, governments can use this vulnerability as a form of control because they can offer subsidies and advertising revenue in exchange for the outlet's endorsement of particular candidates. These trends present a test of the sustainability of traditional media since younger generations of media users increasingly look online for their sources of information and entertainment.

Internet and Online Media in Central Asia

The global Internet boom of the early 2000s brought in enthusiasm about the role that Internet-based media could play in democratization. Many scholars believed that, as the most open, unregulated, and free system of communication, the Internet would facilitate democratic developments in transitional and hybrid regimes and open up authoritarian government systems. However, today we are seeing how China controls not only access to the Internet but also the web content within its national boundaries, and many other authoritarian regimes are following its example. In 2020 the world witnessed the continued power of "fake news," which refers to the weaponization of social media to spread misinformation and disinformation in ways that poison electoral and political discourse even in established democracies. Media-monitoring organizations are increasingly concerned about diminishing freedom on the Internet and overall media freedoms in the world. In an unprecedented move, Freedom House downgraded the

Figure 25-6

Internet Penetration in Central Asia

	Population (2018 est.)	Internet Users (Year 2000)	Internet Users June 30, 2018	Penetration (% Population)	Facebook Users December 31, 2017
Kazakhstan	18,403,860	70,000	14,063,513	76.40	2,500,000
Kyrgyzstan	6,132,932	51,600	2,493,400	40.70	650,000
Tajikistan	9,107,211	2,000	3,013,256	33.10	170,000
Turkmenistan	5,851,466	2,000	1,049,915	17.90	20,000
Uzbekistan	32,364,996	7,500	15,453,227	47.70	800,000

Source: Internet World Statistics, Asia, https://www.internetworldstats.com/stats3.htm.

United States from the score of 1–2 on political rights in 2018 and expressed concerns over President Donald Trump's overuse of the term "fake news" in relation to legitimate and verified news stories and his labeling media and journalists critical of him as "enemies of the people."

Central Asia developed its Internet infrastructure late in comparison with Russia and other former Soviet republics. By 2000 a total number of users in each country was in the thousands (see figure 25-6). Despite aggressive goals set by the countries' governments, by 2018 only one country (Kazakhstan) achieved a penetration rate equivalent to the lower range of developed countries such as Portugal or Poland, while the other four countries do not have even half of their populations using the Internet.

Since the Internet usage data in figure 25-6 are self-reported by the national telecommunication agencies, it is possible they are not accurate. However, even with that caution, the data show that Uzbekistan made significant gains in providing access for its citizens in the years after Karimov's death, while Kyrgyzstan's slowdown in Internet usage growth, compared to Kazakhstan, may be explained by the mountainous terrain. This is a challenge for Tajikistan as well. In all countries of the region, the state-controlled national telecommunication agencies are the leading providers of Internet, and in Turkmenistan and Uzbekistan they are the exclusive providers. Private ISPs exist in Kyrgyzstan, Kazakhstan, and Tajikistan, but they still rely on the national telecommunication networks as the actual infrastructure, which gives the governments in these countries unprecedented and exclusive control of access to the Internet and web resources. Kyrgyzstan's Internet faces an additional challenge as it still uses Kazakhstan's satellites and broadband infrastructure. A project on the crowdfunding platform Patreon that is raising funds for Kyrgyzstan's first satellite, being built by young women engineers, may diminish the country's dependency on its neighbor's infrastructure.

Kazakhstan, Kyrgyzstan, Uzbekistan, and to a limited extent Tajikistan are improving their Internet infrastructures, with many urban regions equipped with 4G, LTE, and 5G technologies that provide broadband and high-speed Wi-Fi connectivity. Kyrgyzstan is also becoming a regional and global leader in IT software development, thanks to low labor costs and high levels of specialized computer engineering education. Under the current

25-7 Reading the newspaper the morning after the First Kyrgyz Revolution, Bishkek, 2005. Photograph by David W. Montgomery.

leadership of Turkmenistan's President Berdimuhamedow, the country's Internet infrastructure will likely remain under strict government control and available only to the citizens who are perceived to be loyal to the regime.

IREX and Freedom House reports indicate that patterns in the infrastructure and usage of the Internet in Central Asia are similar to those in developed countries—for example, urban areas have faster networks than rural or sparsely populated areas; usage cost is affordable for most citizens; most Internet users are young and technologically savvy, and they access the Internet from both desktop and mobile devices; and mobile phone connections are starting to overtake landline connections. The Internet is slowly redefining the media, forcing media professionals and owners to adjust to the digital age in terms of both content and delivery. Most Internet users are online for entertainment, social networking, nonpolitical news, and even shopping, as more businesses sell their products online.

International reports point out that the Internet has also been used for political purposes, such as informing and mobilizing citizens. For example, both the 2005 and 2010 Kyrgyzstan's revolutions were covered by Diesel.kg, an indigenous independent Internet forum where Bishkek residents posted and shared verified facts and witness accounts of what was going on in the city, exposed hoaxes and rumors, shared videos from the cameras monitoring public squares and spaces, and mobilized people's brigades to prevent looting and hooliganism in the absence of police. Many politicians, government officers, and media in Kyrgyzstan used the Diesel forum as a source of trustworthy information during those extraordinary events (see figure 25-7). In contrast, when Facebook was being used in Kazakhstan for the same purposes during the December 2011 Zhanaozen oil workers' strike, in which at least fourteen people were killed by the police, Nazarbayev's government closed access to Facebook in the country. That move also inadvertently closed Facebook access for users in Kyrgyzstan, because of the country's ISPs' use of Kazakhstan's satellites. In another instance, during the summer 2010 violent ethnic clashes between Uzbeks and Kyrgyz in southern Kyrgyzstan, the governments of both countries banned or restricted their citizens from accessing the other country's traditional and Internet-based media in order to control messaging about the events. Overall, these developments paint a bleak picture of authoritarian rulers controlling the information their citizens receive through the media with every technique and method at their disposal.

Trends and Future Challenges

The alarming developments in media described above do not go unnoticed. In his November 8 opening remarks at the 2018 conference on Central Asian Media in Astana, OSCE representative on freedom of the media Harlem Désir pointed out some troubling recent trends in the region, where governments use threats of terrorism and ethnic violence, as well as fake news and biases in coverage, as pretexts for introducing more restrictive laws on freedom of the media. He called on the governments to improve the legal, economic, and operational environment of the media, emphasizing that:

> A diverse and strong media landscape contributes to more democratic societies and more efficient governments in many ways. The quality of governance improves, when leaders are held to account. Public spending improves, when transparency will be asked by the media. Transparency and media freedom contribute to the fight against corruption. Media are the first to detect new and difficult issues in society, and they give the floor to individuals and groups with diverse interests and concerns. Free media also offer the space to debate different possible solutions to issues faced by the society. And in front of new risks like terrorism, there is no strong and resilient society without free and independent media.

Désir pointed out that the largest challenge for Central Asia lies in the area of providing a legal environment for a thriving independent media, ensuring the diversity of media in terms of ownership, as well as a plurality of voices and languages; media and journalists' continuous professionalization and improving ethical standards of practice; and support of media from various organizations, donors, and sponsors. Thus, in addition to global trends that all media face such as the digitalization and commercialization of media products, the rise of global infotainment, fake news, and outright disinformation that blight the public discourse everywhere, media in Central Asia face both formidable challenges and exciting opportunities to reinvent themselves going forward.

26

National Identity

Laura L. Adams

Nur-Sultan (formerly Astana), the capital of Kazakhstan, has a shopping mall that is built to look like a tent. Its name is Khan Shatyr, which means "tent of the Khan" (figure 26-1). Khan Shatyr has stores such as Levi's and Adidas, a large and diverse food court, and an indoor beach that has an entrance fee of between ten and fifteen thousand tenge, almost 10 percent of the average monthly wage in Kazakhstan. Khan Shatyr is a symbol of a national identity that roots itself both in an idea of its noble nomadic past and in a prosperous, urban, and globalist present. Inside Khan Shatyr, you hear a lot of Russian spoken, even by ethnic Kazakhs, which also tells you something about Kazakhstan's relationship to its Soviet past. Khan Shatyr, like many aesthetic expressions of national identity, both invokes ideas about the past and translates them into something new.

National identity in Central Asia is not just about ethnic heritage and traditions; it is expressed through layers of sometimes conflicting discourses and is vibrant with tensions between official identity projects and alternatives to those official identities. I will illustrate these dynamics by portraying national identity in post-Soviet Central Asia as three concentric circles, each of which defines a somewhat different dimension of the nation: an inner ethnic core, a middle circle that refers to supra-ethnic identities, and a large outer circle that brings in universal themes. In many cases, I illustrate this model of national identity by describing both state-sponsored cultural projects and ethnographic research that illuminates the lived experience of national identities. I will also contrast how Central Asians talk about their own national identities with analytical perspectives about identity coming from my own US context. This juxtaposition gives a sense of how many

26-1   Khan Shatyr Entertainment Center as seen through the archway of a government building, Nur-Sultan, Kazakhstan, 2016. Photograph by Laura L. Adams.

Central Asians see themselves while acknowledging how a social scientist's critical and analytical perspective on these issues may be very different.

Ethnic Identity as Inherent or Constructed

Ethnicity is based on a sense of belonging to a particular group that shares characteristics such as language, a common homeland, genetic heritage, cuisine, family patterns, and so on. People in Central Asia often use a metaphor to explain attitudes and behavior that they think of as ethnic: "It's in our blood." Ethnicity is one of those ideas that seems obviously true since one can find evidence of it all around. But there are various ways ethnicity can be understood, ranging from what seems to be common sense to the performative. My common sense is not about blood, it is about genetics, and it tells me that I am Scottish because my ancestors were Scottish, and therefore it makes sense for me to exhibit behaviors I associate with being Scottish, such as being frugal and wearing a tartan every now and then. In the common sense of blood or genetics called essentialism, these characteristics are part of an ethnicity that is internal to me and I am simply expressing them. In contrast, the performative approach to identity argues that there is no "there" internally, no ethnic essence to be expressed; there are only repeated behaviors and persistent ideas about reality. Those of us with a strong sense of ethnic identity believe these behaviors and ideas are genetic or "in our blood" because we come to identify with our own enactment of this identity, which is shaped from birth by those around us. Somewhere in between these views, the constructivist approach shows us that ethnic identity, like other terms we use to describe groups of humans, tends (1) to draw somewhat arbitrary boundaries between groups; (2) to mask the fact that diversity within the group is almost always greater than the distance between groups; and (3) to have a sporadic, relational, and dynamic character.

As a social scientist I have come to reject my commonsense ideas about ethnicity. I do not believe that genes I inherited from ancestors in Scotland five generations ago have a strong effect on my behavior and preferences. And though I find the Central Asian metaphor of ethnic characteristics being "in their blood" both poetic and evocative, it is not an adequate explanation for ethnic identity. The analytical perspective I privilege here is that (1) identities are not given or unchanging but have to be activated and then repeatedly performed in order to be meaningful to individuals or to be mobilized through group action and (2) our identities become more important to us when we are interacting with someone with a different identity, and that is why boundaries of identity are more important than essences of identity. The question to ask about a particular ethnicity is not "What is it?" but "How does it work?" However, we need to understand Central Asian ethnicity both in its vernacular terms (ethnic identity is invoked in everyday life and has a meaning to those who invoke it) and as a process of construction and contestation by individuals and institutions. For the purposes of this chapter, I focus on the latter and recommend the numerous ethnographic accounts in this book to give an understanding of the former.

The idea of national identity that I explore here goes beyond ethnicity and involves the way that various Soviet and contemporary political projects and institutions have built on ethnic identity. The ethnic core of the Soviet concept of national identity (*natsional'nost'*) has always been in tension with other identities that people today do not think of as "ethnic" but, rather, that played a significant role in the socioeconomic life of people such as region, tribe, or extended clan. The dynamic relational nature of identity means that

LAURA L. ADAMS

it always contains elements of comparison and sometimes of contestation. So, for example, in Kyrgyzstan people who identify as ethnically Kyrgyz talk about the differences between northerners and southerners; in Turkmenistan comparisons are made between the Tekke and Yomud tribes; and Uzbeks and Tajiks dispute to whom the culture of Bukhara "belongs." This dynamism is not an indication of instability or the potential for conflict but, rather, is a feature of most ethnic identities most of the time.

This dynamic view of ethnic identity was not the approach taken by most historians and ethnologists in the Soviet Union, who wanted to define and fix the content of ethnic identities in an orderly scientific way. This was important because of the political decision to build the individual Soviet Socialist Republics (SSRs) around *natsional'nost'*, a national identity based on an ethnic core. Nation-building on the basis of a core ethnic group came to be seen by the Bolsheviks as a valuable tool in the administration and inculcation of Soviet power. Soviet scholars, especially ethnographers, were employed in drawing the borders as well as in institutionalizing the national identity of the new Soviet republics. Porous boundaries that permitted trade, migration, and alliance-building were turned into borders with administrative consequences in the 1920s and 1930s. These borders and national institutions did not simply delimit one territory from another; they served as the foundation for attempting to delimit one ethnic group from another, with varying results. Prior to the Soviet era, Central Asian collective identities corresponded to religion, geography, or kinship rather than to ethnicity. The unintended consequence of building so many institutions around nationality was to strengthen the significance of ethnicity (especially language and cultural characteristics) throughout the USSR.

But Soviet national identity was not just about that ethnic core; it also relied on universal ideas of Marxism and modernity. Part of the universalism of Central Asian national identity is grounded in a colonial hierarchy that placed different aspects of culture on a scale from "backward" to "progressive." Local Central Asian customs were often seen as backward, and the customs of urban socialist Russia were seen as progressive. Thus "backward" aspects of Central Asian societies were often replaced with "progressive" Russian standards, especially in the realm of material culture: Russian-style houses, clothing, and food, for example, were held to be self-evidently healthier and more rational than their Central Asian analogues. The "internationalization of national cultures," as the Soviet slogan went, was seen as a means of development by enriching national culture through the adoption of new forms and genres of culture. According to the point of view prevalent in the Brezhnev era, the Russian presence in Central Asia was beneficial in that it acquainted the urban population with classics of Russian literature, achievements in science, technology, painting, theater, and music. Other progressive social changes were less concrete but nonetheless brought the "Asian nationalities" closer to Europeans in terms of their cultural habits: rising levels of education, printing books in native languages, the opening of museums and libraries, participation in clubs, and the creation of ethnic music and dance groups.

Another aspect of the Soviet approach to national identity is rooted in an essentialist framework related to the genetic view. Soviet scholars used a method called ethnogenesis to trace the origins of ethnic groups back to some definitive point in time when, for example, Tajiks became Tajiks and Kazakhs became Kazakhs. European and local scholars alike wanted to tell a coherent historical story about the evolution of each of the Soviet nationalities and to have a clear picture of the culture and language of each group. Scholars sometimes generated controversy by seeming to lay claim to the heritage of other nationalities and retroactively making past inhabitants of the territory into today's Kyrgyz, Turkmen, or Uzbeks.

Let us look at the example of the creation of Uzbek natsional'nost' and the internationalization of Uzbek national culture. Following the Soviet principle that in order to develop socially and economically every nation must have a territory and its own set of national institutions, borders of the Uzbek SSR were negotiated, ethnographers defined various practices and customs as Uzbek, linguists determined which dialect would serve as the official national language, and administrators carried out policies such as ethnic quotas in higher education that gave a new significance to having Uzbek nationality in your official documents. Over time, this process "consolidated" local variations of group identities into a single Uzbek nationality. Other kinds of identities such as Sart (urban-dwelling), Muslim, Chaghatai (a language/lineage), Xoja (a lineage), and Turk faded but did not disappear, in the wake of the top-down and rapid development of an Uzbek national language, literature, and culture. Significantly, this process was not just driven by ideologues or scholars from Moscow but, in the first decade of Soviet power, by the pre-Soviet Muslim intelligentsia who pursued nationhood as a path to modernity. The consolidation of Uzbek national identity by these reformers rejected existing solidarities and created a new divide between the Uzbek and Tajik nationalities in the sedentary populations of the south. Similar processes took place in the Soviet-era histories of Kyrgyzstan and Turkmenistan.

But we also need to pay attention to contestation at the boundaries of this new Uzbek identity. In many parts of southern Uzbekistan, the population is bilingual in Uzbek and Tajik, and although ethnicity is important (for example, interethnic marriage, even between Uzbeks and Tajiks, is not common), the actual substance of these ethnic differences is very vaguely defined in everyday understandings. It is mainly on the official level (government institutions, mass media, academia) that clear ethnic boundaries are drawn, and it is also on the official level that some of the sharpest disagreements about heritage and belonging take place.

Starting with the national delimitation of the Central Asian republics that drew new borders in the 1920s, many Central Asians found that their homeland ended up in "someone else's" territory or that they were part of a new nation that had been relegated to a residual category in the Soviet nationalities

26-2   The Mausoleum of Ismail Samani in Bukhara, Uzbekistan, 2011. Photograph by Laura L. Adams.

schema and administrative structure. By drawing the border in such a way that the urban Turkic-Persian hybrid cities of Samarqand and Bukhara were both included in Uzbekistan, Soviet-era decision makers gave the Uzbeks the right, as it were, to a rich and glorious heritage, artificially cutting off today's Tajiks from a legacy that was also theirs. Uzbekistan has claimed legacies such as Samarqand's Timurid architectural monuments and has retroactively categorized Amir Temur himself as the "grandfather" of the Uzbek nation. Uzbekistan's claims have been contested openly by post-Soviet Tajik intellectuals, but the government of Tajikistan has opted instead to focus its national heritage campaigns around the ninth- and tenth-century Samanids, the first native (Iranian) Muslim dynasty to rule the region from Balkh and Herat in modern Afghanistan to Ferghana and Chach in Uzbekistan. Unfortunately for Tajik nation builders, one of the only remaining architectural monuments from this era, the mausoleum of Ismail Samani, is located in Bukhara in Uzbekistan (figure 26-2). Thus, the divisions caused by borders drawn in the 1920s and 1930s continue to trouble today's leaders who seek to unite heritage, territory, and people within a single nation-state.

National Identity beyond Ethnicity

Russian speakers in Central Asia have a saying: *vostok—delo tonkoe* (literally, "the East is a delicate matter"), which is invoked to explain particular customs across Central Asia and indeed, Asia more broadly (including Russia). Here I focus on the ways in which Central Asian national identities are related to pre-Soviet and contemporary supranational identities. These relationships make specific claims to Asian, Eastern, or Muslim values and heritage shared by the neighboring peoples of Central Asia. It sounds strange to Westerners accustomed to cultural relativism and political correctness to hear Central Asian intellectuals talk about "Eastern people" and their own "Oriental cultures," happily explaining stereotypes that might sound offensive coming from anyone else. Going beyond the stereotypes, though, these ideas about Asian and Muslim culture are an important dimension to how Central Asians see themselves and others who are similar to them, such as other Persian and Turkic peoples. The "Oriental" aspect of national identity in Central Asia often refers not to the geography of Asia as much as to shared aspects of material and cultural heritage. This framing excludes many other Asian and Muslim groups outside of Central Asia; it also excludes local citizens of Russian, European, and Korean descent (of whom there are many, especially in Kazakhstan and Kyrgyzstan).

Another dimension of this transnational aspect of national identity can be found in visions of geopolitics. Leaders of Kazakhstan and Uzbekistan have stated that Asian models of economic development—such as Singapore and Malaysia—are more appropriate for them than "Western" liberal models, because as "Eastern peoples," they want economic dynamism that is guided by a strong leader. However, those same leaders do not feel any particular sense of kinship with, say, Cambodians and other non-Muslim peoples of Asia whom they consider to be less developed than they are. There have been attempts at the elite level to build regional organizations to promote security and economic cooperation on the basis of a Eurasian or South/Central Asian common interest, but they have not yet had large-scale effect.

Transnational ideas about being Muslim, nomadic, Tengrist, Eurasian, and part of the Silk Road have more cultural power today than these geopolitical visions. The Muslim identity is often a uniting factor when it is invoked in reference to other Central Asians ("we are all Muslims"). Most Central Asians identify as Muslim, though for many Central Asians their approach to Islam is not necessarily orthodox but more a way of living and relating to others. Central Asians perceive their Muslim identity as something they share (and share with others around the world). However, the shared Muslim identity with others outside of Central Asia is a fraught topic, since the Central Asian governments tend to make distinctions between "our kind of Islam" and "alien forms of Islam." Beyond the boundaries of Central Asia, Muslim identity has come to be associated with danger by many Central Asians, and attempts at cooperation with the Middle East have foundered on fears of radical ideas making their way into Central Asia. For what are often very similar reasons, Turkic and Persian ethnic groups in neighboring China and Afghanistan are kept at arm's length, even though they are certainly seen as fellow Muslims and some are even seen as ethnic kin by Uzbeks, Kazakhs, and others.

Muslim identity both complements and conflicts with national identity in Central Asia. Although most of the states of Central Asia subsume Islamic heritage in favor of national heritage, official state ideologies also selectively incorporate Islamic elements as long as they are perceived as authentic (local to the territory of the nation-state) and nonthreatening (depoliticized). Sufism and the practice of visiting the shrines of saints in Uzbekistan, for example, is a popular practice that local people view as good Muslim piety but that has also been brought into state discourse as a local and therefore authentic expression of religious identity. In contrast, various campaigns took place in Tajikistan between 2015 and 2017 to prohibit "alien Islamic garments," ban Arabic names in favor of Persian names, and forcibly shave men's beards, all in the name of promoting Tajik national (and only incidentally Muslim) forms of cultural expression.

Another identity that crosses borders is the nomadic identity, which has official sanction in Kazakhstan and Kyrgyzstan. In contrast, "sedentary" identity in places like Tajikistan and Uzbekistan is more implicit and is associated with historical urban centers. During the Soviet period, this distinction between nomadic and sedentary identities was discussed by Marxist historians, who posited stages of historical development where nomadism is a more primitive economic form than the urban merchant culture of southern Central Asia. In Bolshevik Central Asia, this nomad/sedentary distinction was used by intellectuals in Turkestan and Bukhara to differentiate their nation from the Kazakhs' and to put Uzbeks in a more elevated place in the Soviet hierarchy of nations. But as scholars such as Diana Kudaibergenova show, nomadic identity is a fruitful area of exploration and critique for contemporary artists in Kazakhstan. The "Punk Shamanism" movement she studies draws on exactly those aspects of Kazakh culture (nomadism, shamanism, the steppe) that were denigrated by Soviet cultural hierarchies and questions the ideologies and power structures that attempted to erase these things from the cultural memory of Kazakhstan.

Today, nomadic identity plays a big role in Kazakhstan, Kyrgyzstan, and Turkmenistan, though there are many minorities and members of other ethnic groups (including some Uzbeks and Tajiks) who also identify with a

26-3   A woman practicing a ritual at a sacred site in Kyrgyzstan. Photograph courtesy of Aigine Cultural Research Center.

nomadic past. Prominent among the symbols of this identity are horses, yurts, traditional foods, crafts, musical instruments, and spiritual elements involving sacred sites in nature and shamanism (figure 26-3). The nomadic identity shows up in a number of interesting ways in popular culture including the Kazakh blockbuster film *Nomad: The Warrior*; Kyrgyzstan's World Nomad Games; the Spirit of Tengri Contemporary Ethnic Music Festival in Almaty; and Kazakh music videos where traditional nomadic images combine with music that is in recognizably international pop, rock, and dance styles.

The Spirit of Tengri festival also invokes a slightly different version of the theme of nomadic identity, one that emphasizes an ethnic heritage that is not exclusively Kazakh, combining ideas about Turkic, nomadic, and animistic/shamanistic traditions with a modern sensibility of musical style. Tengrism as a philosophical movement views the identity of various Russian and Central Asian Turkic groups through a pre-Soviet, pre-Islamic lens, when the Turkic peoples were defined by their relationship to nature as symbolized by their worship of the sky (Tengri). Tengrism is another example of how nomadic identity is often framed as a postcolonial critique of Soviet-era ideas about national identity. It is also an indigenous critique of secular and globalized ideas about culture and tradition and a secular critique of the connection between national identity and Islam. Advocates of Tengrist perspectives on national identity tend to incorporate a history-oriented national identity and a critique of Islam that frames it as an external force that is not compatible with fundamental aspects of Kazakh or Kyrgyz ethnicity.

An example of this nature-oriented moral perspective on national identity comes from the work of Aigine Cultural Research Center, which is part of a global fourth-world-peoples movement seeking to revive indigenous knowledge and spirituality. Aigine sponsors educational programs and research on topics such as sacred sites and traditional knowledge, the variations of the epic *Manas* as recited by contemporary Manaschi, and Kyrgyz musical heritage. Aigine staff also organize activities that take on a more mass scale, such as the one-thousand-strong *komuz* (stringed instrument) ensembles who perform for official occasions of national importance, such as the 2016 World Nomad Games and celebrations of the writer Chingiz Aitmatov.

The Eurasian/Silk Road identity is the third main supranational identity that is officially invoked and unofficially contested. The Eurasian/Silk Road aspect of national identities in Central Asia blends a geopolitical and economic vision of the nation in relation to other countries. The Eurasian version of this is more closely related to Russian political-historical thought, and elites in countries such as Kazakhstan and Kyrgyzstan (with a higher proportion of Russian speakers in their population) are interested in what it would mean to be part of a shared sociopolitical space with Russia again, with common Eurasian values, networks, and a vision of the future. Kazakhstan's positioning of itself as between Europe and Asia emphasizes the country's geopolitical importance and economic status, while at the same time evoking a more "traditional" Eastern value system involving communal, rather than individual, values and a respect for authority.

The Silk Road version of this identity is a more common trope in Uzbekistan, Tajikistan, and Turkmenistan than is the Eurasianist one. In Uzbekistan, the metaphor of the Great Silk Road links memories of a glorious past to ambitions for the future by portraying Uzbekistan as a crossroads of civilizations and an important nexus of history but also a nexus for current diplomatic and economic relationships with other countries. Along with these more official discourses, Kudaibergenova's research shows that there is also a postcolonial critique among independent artists in Kazakhstan who employ the Silk Road metaphor as a critique of how political elites mark the boundaries of the nation and of the claims that state-authorized art makes on heritage and place.

The Tension between Nationalism and Universalism

The outermost circle of Central Asian national identity is civic, a view of the nation as universalist, modern, and multiethnic. This view is firmly grounded in Soviet ideology and institutions that emphasized internationalism (the Soviet people saw themselves as part of a universal working class) and multiethnic statehood (expressed in the idea of *druzhba narodov*, friendship and cooperation of the peoples of the Soviet Union). This view is also deeply connected to globalization, international law, universal human rights, and the geopolitical landscape of the years since the breakup of the Soviet Union. These modern, universalist, multiethnic aspects of national identity come into tension both with a colonial and Soviet past, in which Russian language and culture were seen as superior to the other Soviet languages and cultures, and with the current realities of borders, interethnic violence, and the rise of populism and xenophobia. The latter phenomena I characterize as nationalism, where national identity is used not just to reinforce the boundary around the group but to attack those perceived as outside that boundary.

Initially after the collapse of the Soviet Union, there was a strong continuing emphasis in official ideology on civic-national identity as the post-Soviet manifestation of friendship of the peoples. The degree to which a state pursued policies that were demonstrably civic (versus ethnic) was largely related to demographics. In Uzbekistan, for example, Uzbeks comprised a much larger proportion of the population than Kazakhs in Kazakhstan and Kyrgyz in Kyrgyzstan. This meant that the ethnic component of national identity played a strong role in Uzbekistan, though not one that completely overwhelmed the civic component. The Central Asian states generally adopted fairly open citizenship and language laws during the 1990s. After decades of pressure to speak Russian, the titular language was now each country's state language, though in Kazakhstan and Kyrgyzstan the Russian language retained an official status. In countries such as Kazakhstan, having a "Russian-speaking" identity as a Kazakh is something that signals one's generation (older Central Asians are more likely to speak Russian) as well as a cultural orientation. Central Asian governments explicitly promoted the use of the titular language by all citizens, though these efforts were often largely symbolic and increases in local language use happened more gradually and organically. The post-Soviet backlash against the discourse of Russian cultural superiority has been subtle and wrapped up in complex intra-elite political negotiations, especially in Kazakhstan. Backlash mainly took the form of "the renewal of national culture": culture production that was coded by elites and read by the public as an answer to assumptions of Russian superiority.

Because of these cultural campaigns and the growing influence of non-Russians in key sectors in government, there was a widespread perception of ethnic discrimination in jobs and education that favored the titular nationality. Fears of violence and loss of educational and employment opportunities prompted a large proportion of the Russian-speaking population to leave Central Asia in the 1990s. During the 2000s all of the countries but Kazakhstan became much more focused on ethnic identity and less concerned with projecting an image as a modern civic nation. Indeed, Turkmenistan never really tried to seem like a civic nation. In contrast, Kazakhstan in the 1990s and 2000s took steps to maintain more of a civic nationhood. Ethnicity was a salient, though not decisive, factor in the political and economic life of Kazakhstan. The political elite sidelined Kazakh nationalists, patronage networks crossed ethnic lines, and minorities were given symbolic participation in the state through the Assembly of People of Kazakhstan.

The desire to have a good reputation internationally also plays a factor in the balance between ethnic and supranational identities. The international brand of these countries has tended to emphasize the centrality of Central Asia to international trade networks, as in marketing slogans such as "the Heart of Eurasia" (Kazakhstan), "a Crossroads of Civilizations" (Uzbekistan), and all manner of Silk Road–related allusions. This geopolitical positioning is pursued with particular zeal by Kazakhstan. International law, multilateral treaties, human rights norms, economic compacts, security alliances, and global culture have all played a role in balancing the financial and cultural interests of a multinational elite and a Soviet cultural legacy of tolerance, on one side, against the narrow agenda of ethnic nationalists on the other.

However, Kyrgyzstan provides examples of how demographic and socioeconomic tensions can override a generally tolerant and cosmopolitan national identity. Kyrgyzstan, like its neighbors, came out of the Soviet experience with a rather internationalist identity that contained both civic and ethnic components. Early post-Soviet official discourse emphasized continuity with the Soviet past in a time of great upheaval and tried to frame President Askar Akaev's government as one that had the interests of both Kyrgyz and non-Kyrgyz citizens at heart. As time went on, this dual identity was used in different ways in response to the changing political contexts the country found itself in. But although Kyrgyzstan has remained the most democratic of the Central Asian countries, its civic national identity has come under threat in ways that are different from those in Uzbekistan and Kazakhstan, which have different ethnic and political dynamics.

Although, as Erica Marat shows, moderates have continued to advocate in favor of a broader civic identity, Kyrgyz nationalism has definitely gained a more dangerous reputation than its peers, and the relative strength of civil society in Kyrgyzstan means that people can be mobilized for liberal or illiberal causes. President Akaev's civic/ethnic national identity evolved to emphasize its ethnic component under President Kurmanbek Bakiev, resulting in tension between Kyrgyzstan's ethnic Kyrgyz and Uzbek citizens, the latter of whom were increasingly portrayed in public discourse as a threat to the nation's sovereignty, as David Gulette and John Heathershaw argue. This tension during the Bakiev era was particularly sharp in the south, for a number of reasons: there were structural inequalities dating back to the Soviet era, which led to ethnic conflict in 1990; the population of ethnic Uzbeks was much higher in the south; state-sponsored conspiracy theories circulated about Uzbeks making a grab for political power; and fears about sovereignty were amplified by uncertainty over state borders. These tensions culminated in the interethnic riots that took place in southern Kyrgyzstan during June 2010, which took the lives of several hundred people.

As in other parts of the world, nationalism in Central Asia has increasingly taken on an illiberal populist slant that attacks the expansion of human, civic, and political rights as a threat to national sovereignty. The nationalist defense of "traditional gender norms" has been especially vigorous in Kyrgyzstan with legislative as well as physical attacks on Kyrgyzstan's feminist and LGBTQ communities. Nationalist groups and individual Kyrgyz men have violently policed appropriate behavior and dress for Kyrgyz women both at home and abroad in the name of national identity and honor, in some cases with the blessing of the state security services. In Kyrgyzstan and other parts of Central Asia, gender, class, and ethnicity entwined in a battle to reinterpret national identity in the context of a modern global marketplace. As Mohira Suyarkolova shows in her analysis of gender and nationalism in Kyrgyzstan, proper or authentic Kyrgyz femininity or masculinity is often performed and policed through clothing: a man's white hat (*ak kalpak*) and a woman's hijab are sites of a broad and deep debate over ethnic, religious, and gender identity in Kyrgyzstan.

The Future of the State as Arbiter of National Identity

The Central Asian states have largely tried to continue the Soviet practice of defining national identity from the top down. However, different groups have resisted these official interpretations through academic discourse, citizen debates on social media, artistic movements, and populist movements that attempt to get a more culturally conservative vision of ethnic identity into the public sphere. As Kudaibergenova shows, artists in Kazakhstan have taken to criticizing not just the content of the official national identity but also the state's continuing attempts to monopolize it. In Tajikistan, the Islamic Revival Party was repressed not just because it was a threat in the electoral arena but also because it challenged the state's monopoly on defining religious culture. In most of Central Asia, the state attempts to silence or marginalize these alternative discourses, sometimes because of their content but more often because the independent production even of "mainstream" culture and ideas is a potential threat to an authoritarian state.

Central Asian governments and elites feel that if they control the content of national culture and continue to propagate a tolerant and cosmopolitan worldview, they will avoid destabilization and conflict. However, Central Asian leaders are going to have to grapple with the idea that social conflict is inevitable and therefore it should be managed rather than suppressed. Their aspirations to market economies and more democratic practices are in conflict with the state's monopolization of power. Commitments to regional and global identities are in conflict with a commitment to the idea of a stable and unchanging ethnic core identity. Barring a wave of ethnic or religious violence, the real threat to the authoritarian status quo may come from social groups questioning the state monopoly on how national culture is defined, whether from a globalist, nationalist, or spiritual direction.

LAURA L. ADAMS

27

Environment

Amanda E. Wooden

Osh—the second-largest city in Kyrgyzstan, forty kilometers from the Uzbekistan border—lies along the Ak-Buura (White Camel) River Valley. The Ak-Buura River and Solomon's Mountain shape the neighborhoods in this dense and famously green city and are sources of pride for residents. The Ak-Buura River is a crucial heat reliever in the summer; it is a place for children to swim and play, a spot where families picnic listening to the rapids, and a green space for a relaxing evening walk. The Alai Mountain glacial waters that form the Ak-Buura are stored upstream from Osh in the Soviet-era Papan Reservoir. Downstream from the reservoir in Osh, the river becomes an urbanized waterway, its channelized banks dividing the city.

In 2006 I lived in the home of a Kyrgyz woman right on the banks of the Ak-Buura in Osh. We reveled in its nightly sounds. The river noisily warned us of impending storms coming off the mountains and possible sewage overflow; it told us to turn off our taps before the city authorities did. The Ak-Buura shaped life in this city at the center of the Ferghana Valley, a region that depends on mountain-sourced water for its thriving agriculture. Despite this dependency, its cultural meanings, and the obvious reverence for the river, waste was scattered down the embankment along the river's edge near our house, and elsewhere. The interface of valued waterways and urban solid waste is an obvious contradiction in this beautiful city, as in many of the world's urban areas.

One evening, walking home along the Ak-Buura, I observed my neighbor dumping trash into the river. After a few more such instances, I began asking my housemate, my neighbors, and other residents: "Why do people do this? Why fill the river with trash?" One neighbor answered: "The city services no longer come to pick up the waste. They force me to choose between trash sitting in our *dvor* (courtyard in Russian, *koroo* in Kyrgyz) to attract dogs and rats where my children play, or throwing it in the river and hoping it washes downstream. I do not want to throw it in the river; I know it is not good. What I am to do? This is the choice I have. This is the choice officials give us." Over years of studying environmental politics in Kyrgyzstan, I often heard people express extreme frustration of forced choices between bad options, in urban waste decisions, gold-mining communities, waterway sharing, pastures and forests use.

When working with Osh city, oblast (province), and national ministerial officials on an OSCE (Organization for Security and Co-operation in Europe) waste reduction and recycling project, I heard repeatedly the common tropes that elites and those with power tend to use about society and environmental issues. Officials commented that people throw trash in the river because they are ignorant or they do not care about waste and pollution. They concluded that solving the city waste issue is just a matter of education and information. Some of these stereotypes and scapegoating fit into growing nationalistic conversations or narratives distributing blame to the poor and middle class for issues that governments tend not to solve without pressure being put on them to do so. Related governmental and elite narratives I heard remove people's agency, undermine the legitimacy of their concerns, or the "authenticity" of protests in order to diminish their power. These dismissive narratives include commentary about outsiders funding protesters or about people only organizing when manipulated. International analysts and short-term development workers, with little experience of living with industrial pollution or the waste from everyday product consumption, easily pick up these discourses. These simplifications match up with dominant modern—both Western and Soviet—views of a stark separation between humans and nature, as well as racist ideologies, or colonial, capitalist perspectives about poverty and "good governance." National economic elites and Western visitors, steeped in capitalism, consume the most material goods and energy, at the same time tending to devalue environmental concerns and to assume that selfish economic motives alone drive people.

As one can see, I too did not fully understand peoples' varying motivations and the complicated meanings that places have for them until I learned to appreciate better their experiences and values. When consumption processes separate us from production and waste disposal, we too easily attribute the causes of pollution or overconsumption to individual human behaviors and "failings," rather than to the systems that shape and constrain the way people live and the choices they must make. We repeat tropes about those historically blamed for society's ills: the poor, the minoritized or racialized groups, women, and the formally unschooled. However, in Osh, I observed behaviors and heard explanations that offered a conflicting narrative. Environmental issues are part of social and political narratives, closely intermingled with economics and political power, shaped by dominant ideologies.

Popular news coverage of environmental issues typically does not report on these tensions. Environmental analyses often focus on scientific or economic explanations, highlighting outcomes without searching for a deeper social contextualization of these issues. Rarely do we appreciate the challenges of contesting environmental damage and its accompanying public health problems, but such is the everyday struggle, the "slow violence" experienced by the poor, the realm of grassroots environmentalist efforts.

As in the Soviet period, those Central Asian environmental organizations that do not directly challenge the state or the elites or that do not focus their work on sources of systemic problems tend to be considered "safe" and are allowed to function in some of Central Asia's more authoritarian places and receive the most positive news portrayals and international funding where greater opportunities for expression exist. However, community members are organizing against polluters, generating creative communitarian solutions to environmental issues, and using off-line social networks to pressure for change in many places hidden from news coverage and in ways critical of dominant institutions. Social media and independent investigative journalist outlets created new ways of sharing the stories of grassroots environmental efforts. There are also times and places where mobilization is exceedingly difficult because apathy, indifference, and resignation reign in the face of seemingly intractable predicaments, feelings of disempowerment, and failed resistance efforts.

Just as the ways in which people respond to environmental topics are pluralistic and complex, so too nature is heterogenous, complicated, and social. Our assumptions about what we consider social (thus, human) and what we consider natural (nonhuman or "wild") are socially and ideologically formed. These two seemingly separate realms are actually linked, overlapping, and inseparable, a concept reflected in various Central Asian cultural practices.

Often, we can better grapple with these complications by paying attention to the meanings that people express about places that are important to them. To understand a fuller range of what is environmental to various people in Central Asia requires us to challenge our anthropocentric views of "nature" as a space separate from humans or simply a resource for human use, to view beyond human boundaries. The "environment" is not an easily defined set of issues; it certainly concerns ecosystem functioning but also involves complicated cultural and political entanglements.

Grappling with what the "environment" means in context in Central Asia requires recognizing global connections, understanding how these transformations are experienced, and considering the power of ideology in shaping how people relate to the ecosystems in which they live. "Nature" is social as well as material; it is both places and living beings we can identify and an abstract idea of what we imagine as other than us. We reveal these human imaginations, what popular and dominant narratives hide, by looking beyond individual behavioral explanations, evaluating causes rather than just outcomes, and paying attention to human communities' complicated daily relationships with other living beings and landscapes in flux. This critical, system-focused, and historical lens—in conversation with decolonial approaches—enables us to identify longer-lasting and more just solutions to the all-encompassing environmental issues we face in Central Asia and beyond.

Geographic and Socioenvironmental Conditions

As Maya Peterson writes, "Central Asian landscapes today—including the Aral Sea region—reflect not just human attempts to control nature, but the legacies of a colonial experiment." One way to think about "the environment" is as a landscape, a term that encapsulates both ecosystems—the webs of life in which multiple species interact across particular spaces that in tandem enable them to function—and the human social systems and relationships developing within and across these ecosystems. The connections that humans and other beings have to these systems and spaces give them meaning beyond just where we live and work and make them places of both practical and emotional importance.

Today, Central Asia is an ecologically and topographically varied, glacier-dependent, mostly arid and semi-arid, landlocked region. Its ecosystems include deserts, semi-arid shrub and grasslands called "steppe," riverine valleys and wetlands, conifer forests, alpine meadows, tundra, and mountain ranges such as the Pamir and Tien Shan. Glacial meltwater and snowmelt combine with groundwater sources and precipitation to form large rivers that flow downstream into endorheic (terminal) alpine or desert lakes. The Amu Darya (Amudaryo) and Syr Darya (Sirdaryo) are the largest rivers, and notable large saline and alpine lakes include the Aral, Balkhash, Caspian (Hazar deňizi, Kaspiy teñizi), and Issyk Kul. Parts of Central Asia are densely (human) populated, especially along river lowlands, such as the Ferghana Valley. In contrast with these urbanized areas are the high steppe of Kazakhstan, high mountain reaches of Afghanistan, Kyrgyzstan, and Tajikistan, and deserts across China, Kazakhstan, Turkmenistan, and Uzbekistan (such as Kyzylkum, Karakum, Muyunkum, and Taklamakan in the Tarim/Altishahr Basin). Some particularly human-impacted life-diverse areas in Central Asia are the Aral Sea basin wetlands, Caspian coasts, tugay riverine woodlands, montane ecosystems, and unique nut-fruit forests.

Caspian oil extraction began in the nineteenth-century Russian colonization period, driven by global industrialization and demand for oil, and Central Asia–wide industrialization in a variety of spheres developed in earnest during the Soviet era. Much of the region boasted strategic mining facilities and was used to diverse ends, ranging from the production of metals, fabrics, and agricultural products (especially wheat, rice, and cotton) to the development of military weapons, launching space vehicles, and training astronauts. Like many countries pursuing industry-led modernization, limited environmental regulations and inadequate oversight in the USSR created a myriad of difficulties, including a legacy of polluted sites from uranium and other heavy mining and production, fossil fuel extraction, and weapons testing. A Soviet-era example of industrialized pollution is poorly stored obsolete pesticides (e.g., DDT or Aldrin), which are persistent organic pollutants (POPs). In locations such as Suzak, in Jalalabad Oblast (province), Kyrgyzstan, these POPs are leaching into drinking water supplies and creating a serious health hazard for many living organisms.

In the thirty years since Soviet dissolution, Central Asia has become a fossil fuel and minerals dominated regional economy. Kazakhstan is now the world leader in uranium production, with fifty uranium mines and five of the world's top ten producing mines, such as Tortkuduk and Moinkum near Shymkent. Uzbekistan is the fifth-largest producer of uranium, and Kyrgyzstan processes uranium ore and (until a recent national controversy, see below) had uranium mines in development. The oil and gas industry likewise have continued to grow since the Soviet era. Turkmenistan is the world's fourth-largest gas producer, and Kazakhstan is the sixteenth-largest oil producer. Together Kazakhstan, Turkmenistan, and Uzbekistan produce about 10 percent of the world's total oil. As a result, in the Caspian Basin water pollution from oil and gas extraction, processing, and transportation is severe.

In heavily industrialized areas, where residents have limited or no access to environmental impact studies, an atmosphere of fear or frustration about suspected health problems may persist. When I lived in southern Kyrgyzstan, some people expressed apprehension about what was happening to the cross-border water supply from several industrial facilities, including one of the last remaining mercury-processing facilities in the world, located in Aidarken (Khaidarkan). Mercury is notorious for long-term health damage potential and this aging Soviet facility sits close to an interstate water canal near the Sokh enclave in the Ferghana Valley. International organizations such as the Global Environmental Fund have pressed for closing and remediating this site; however, this is controversial locally for workers, simultaneously the most exposed and most economically reliant. Poor governmental choices about governing industrial activity—such as improper permitting, limited impact analysis or regulation, lack of transparency in contracting, unresponsive regulatory actions to damages, and worker safety and health issues—contribute to tension between residents and the state. It is worthwhile considering where industrialization creates community conflicts, where people may not be able to voice such frustrations, or alternatively where people have creatively dealt with these difficulties. Often these different reactions and outcomes exist in the same locales, with residents voicing and actualizing different experiences and subjectivities. For example, as Philipp Frank Jäger observes, "while most Europeans are aware of oil as consumers, for citizens in western Kazakhstan processes around oil touch many levels of their everyday lives."

Outside of extractive industries, animal husbandry and irrigated agriculture are the most important economic sectors in much of Central Asia, as the majority of the region's population remains rural and as economic

27-1   New building construction and a canal in Bishkek, with the Kyrgyz Ala-Too range visible to the south, Kyrgyzstan, 2019. Photograph by Amanda Wooden.

insecurity in many places has reinforced livestock as a material form of capital. An important social rubbing point is between these rural economies and expanding industrial activities such as mining. Because of recent labor migration and the rapid urbanization of cities such as Dushanbe, Ashgabat, Almaty, and Bishkek, both urban and rural areas have undergone considerable transformation, shaping pastoral lifestyles both socially and materially. Compounded by the wave of new construction, the usual old city challenges abound: overburdened transport infrastructure, old water pipes and canals, coal-fired power plants, improper sewage treatment for increased populations, and inadequate trash collection (figure 27-1). Additionally, *novostroiki* (new settlements) often have limited or no municipal services. In Bishkek, much grumbling surrounds the construction of suspiciously permitted *elitni dom* (expensive high-rise buildings that tower over the city), sometimes boasting an "ecologically clean location" and enabling money laundering through apartment purchases.

Places such as Osh, Tashkent, Bishkek, and Dushanbe were renowned in the Soviet era for their green spaces, traditional markets, and Soviet modernist architecture, and a small-town feeling, which some lament are rapidly lost in the capitalist era. A concern across several cities in Central Asia is the mass destruction of green spaces and tree cutting, razing of historic buildings, and subsequent dissolution of older neighborhood social structures such as the mahalla to make space for municipal "modernization" and "urban renewal" projects. Ubiquitous plastics and other types of growing solid waste also result from new consumerist lifestyle practices.

Increasing car ownership and traffic are hallmarks of suburbanizing cities, together with continued coal-based heating and energy production that contribute to increased air pollution, demonstrating the individualization of comfort and class distinctions. As municipalities and national governments around the world shift from greenhouse-gas-emitting energy sources in the face of climate change reality, this Central Asian urbanization and peoples' responses to this process all become part of global discussions.

Climate Change in a Glacier-Dependent Region

Climate change is one of the most important issues that face Central Asia; residents are starting to become aware of the significant implications for the energy sector and the regions' waterways. Climatologists and hydrologists identify Central Asia as one of the world regions most sensitive to global climate change, because of its aridity, hydrological systems, and particularly fragile vegetation in some places. The region currently has a glacio-nival (glacier-dependent) hydrological regime. Central Asia's glaciers have recorded (on average) steady declines over the last fifty years, varying by glacier location and size. The smaller lower-elevation glaciers, closest to populated areas, are receding the fastest. For example, as Annina Sorg and others report, the likely earlier loss of glaciers in the northern Tien Shan, compared with other ranges in the region, highlight the particular vulnerability of the Chong Kemin glaciers, which provide approximately 40 percent of water for the important agricultural region of Chuy province, Kyrgyzstan. People living in rural areas in view of and directly dependent on low-lying glaciers in Kyrgyzstan are now discussing how they will cope with these changes both practically and emotionally.

Glacial decline has sped up since the 1970s, and as Daniel Farinotti and others found, "at this pace, half of the total glacier ice volume estimated to be present in the Tien Shan today (roughly 900Gt) would be lost by the 2050s." The result will be greater variation in regional water supply levels between seasons and between years. These projected decreases in Tien Shan Mountain glacier surface areas and volume mean that the region will shift to a precipitation dependent (pluvio-nival) hydrological regime within the twenty-first century. The ramifications for agriculture and residents' agrarian lifestyles will be significant but will also be regionally varied because of shifting precipitation patterns and possible climate change amplifications.

Increased aridity from higher rates of evapotranspiration will alter soil moisture levels and will change vegetation. Regionally, precipitation is predicted to increase in the winter and decrease in the summer. Glacial runoff will increase significantly before mid-century, contributing to flooding, which is already an annual concern along the Syr Darya in Kazakhstan. Sorg and her coauthors predict these increased flows will turn at the tipping point (peak water), after which "decreasing melt water amounts from strongly reduced glacier volume and area" are expected. Central Asia will most likely reach peak water between 2020 and mid-century. "Even in the most glacier-friendly scenario, glaciers will lose up to two thirds (~60 percent) of their 1955 extent by the end of the 21st century."

Permafrost is a major amplification factor (or feedback loop) for climate change, because permafrost serves as a carbon sink (sequester) until it warms, when decomposing microbes release methane into the atmosphere, contributing more to climate change. Permafrost also is a crucial but hidden part of regional water storage and supply and is thus important for ecosystem health and food production. In Central Asia, reduction in the permafrost with increased temperatures will have consequences that few scientists are currently evaluating, a glaring hole in our understanding.

Research by climatology and hydrology scholars such as Sorg on Central Asian glacier loss points to "the need for immediate planning of mitigation measures in the agricultural and energy sectors to assure long-term water security in the densely populated forelands of the Tien Shan" such as Bishkek. There is a more immediate climate-induced hazard of breach potential for moraine-dammed glacial lakes in these mountain ranges (such as Lake Petrov in Kyrgyzstan, sitting just above the tailings pond for the Kumtor mine) and a number of naturally dammed lakes in the Pamir Mountains of Tajikistan (such as Sarez).

Other than the hazard of severe weather events, residents predominantly talk about the slow but noticeable processes of change: seasonal shifts, visible glacier loss and darkening, increased sedimentation in rivers impacting irrigation, frequency of dry spells, reduced insect and bird populations, and extreme heat and cold events. Climate change impacts are already happening in Central Asia, and people who are experiencing them know it. Using the vocabulary of global climate change is relatively new in Kyrgyzstan, even as the awareness of these locally noticeable changes is not. A national public opinion survey that I conducted in 2009, participant observation, and nearly two hundred interviews nationwide over the last decade, all showed a limited voiced concern with global climate change as such, which is especially understandable in a country that contributes so little to the process at that scale. By 2015 people were regularly talking about weather changes, glacier losses, and environmental futures. In 2019 these became common topics in everyday life in Kyrgyzstan, and people are discussing the climate in increasingly worried tones.

It is important to note that global fossil fuel emissions impact the shrinkage of Central Asia's glaciers, and the whole region's water future is dependent on whether major greenhouse-gas-producing countries drastically and rapidly reduce their emissions. Recognizing this harsh reality of climate change requires us also to grapple with the role of Central Asia in global economies of oil, gas, and coal, especially as those sectors will change with the probable shift away from fossil fuels. The twenty-first century will be tumultuous for hydrocarbon economies and extractive industries in Central Asia. What will happen to the Central Asian economies as renewables and non-fossil-fuel conventional energy sources replace oil and gas globally? Seeking to address climate change will create opportunities for healthier fuel use in the region and possibly better energy sector jobs in less dangerous conditions. However, some seemingly sound solutions could also create new environmental problems and force social transitions, in turn amplifying the impacts of climate change on livelihoods. For example, extractive industries are a big part of some local economies, and rapid decarbonization and changes in global demand for some minerals—via fossil fuel divestment, shuttering coal plants, and electrification—will soon have labor consequences in Central Asia.

In addition to grappling with the rate of glacier loss, analysts and policy makers need to pay more attention to the impact of the changing climate on the region's population, in order to provide proper guidance about new infrastructure, the requisite cessation of fossil fuel extraction, and conventional energy dependency. Food security is always a paramount issue for people in Central Asia, especially during financially difficult times and droughts, because agriculture is a key component of household and national income for much of the region. For example, people protested about food in Kazakhstan in 2007 during the world food price spike, and again in 2013. Support for sustainable and resilient food systems needs to be front and center in addressing the region's social and economic dilemmas.

For household energy security in this coming regional transformation, governments and development organizations should work now to shift investment away from the hydrocarbon industry and into renewable energy at multiple scales—and not just for commercial interests. At the household level, in parts of Kyrgyzstan and Tajikistan chronic electricity outages at times led to small-scale solar power use, especially for those living off the grid. Community-level investments—instead of individual purchases or donor contributions at the household level—with collective maintenance and medium-scale grid development may be a more socially just and sustainable approach. Wind and solar power development at a larger scale began in 2014–2015 in the Yereymentau and Zhambyl regions of Kazakhstan (figure 27-2). However, as corporate renewable energies expand in Central Asia, the social disruption from shifting energy prices is also possible—for example, if policy makers introduce new tariff systems to make renewable energy prices more competitive with coal and oil, a common market-tool recommendation. As Tobias Kraudzun learned, for the poor in Tajikistan, coal prices are already beyond reach even without these kinds of pricing manipulations.

The more mountainous upstream countries in the region with limited conventional energy sources—Afghanistan, Kyrgyzstan, and Tajikistan—face a complex mix of climate change, poverty, relatively limited energy infrastructure, and reliance on fossil fuel imports. Thus, policy makers seek to expand coal mining, such as at Kara Keche in Kyrgyzstan. This outdated planning derives from continued reliance on coal for heating and electricity production, a desire for national sources (after shipments of imported coal from Kazakhstan purportedly were radioactive), difficulty in finding investors for costly large dam construction, and politicians' fear about public reprisals for increased electricity tariffs.

27-2   Korday wind farm in Jambyl Province, south-eastern Kazakhstan, 2018. Photograph by Amanda Wooden.

In light of these energy source, employment, and pricing difficulties, up-stream governments may seek to revive plans for large-scale hydropower for more sustainable investments (entailing serious implications for displaced populations and ecosystems at a time of ecological stress), as water storage for the high-flow years and a conventional non-fossil-fuel energy prove less reliable over the long term. Contrary to most mainstream counting of hydropower as a "green" energy, large dam construction is arguably a net greenhouse gas emitter. Embodied carbon from building materials such as cement (necessary for dam construction) and construction energy consumption are among the major sectoral global greenhouse gas sources. Dam-altered ecosystems contribute to methane at levels that exceed reservoir carbon sink potential. Increased sedimentation at times of high flows shortens the life of dams, while these structures have limited usefulness for energy production as those flows decline in the post-peak-water era. Planning to both mitigate and adapt to climate change must be with full understanding of these interconnected issues.

It is worth noting that climate change—although significant and an overarching predicament—is not the only serious environmental concern to consider for the region. Climate change also interacts with and amplifies other human alterations of ecosystems. For example, many oak trees in the region are visibly diseased, a common topic of conversation raised by friends while strolling in Bishkek. Introduced insects bringing fungus to these trees have been able to spread because of reduced bird populations and possible increased vulnerability of the trees with air pollution and temperature changes. Temperature changes and shifting disease vectors will alter where trees will be able to live, which species survive in which locations, in turn altering urban livability for humans. Increased evapotranspiration at higher temperatures will combine with waterways already under pressure such as groundwater overdraft in the Aral Sea basin, and surface-water depletion from irrigation along waterways crossing the Kazakhstan-China border such as the Ile River and its tributaries, the Zhetysu (seven rivers), to create difficulties for people relying on irrigated agriculture for their main source of income. These key environmental problems also interact in human understanding and imagination. Public awareness about other forms of ecological harm contributes to acceptance of climate change seriousness. Global warming became "visible" politically and nationally in Kyrgyzstan in large part because of the damage caused by mining to glaciers at Kumtor.

Critical Approaches to Extractive Industries

Extraction became an important industry in the region during the Soviet era. Today mining, particularly for gold, is the major export income earner for Kyrgyzstan. Kazakhstan leads the world in uranium mining and processing. The oil and gas industries constitute an economic centerpiece of the economies of Turkmenistan, Azerbaijan, northern Caucasus, Kazakhstan, and Uzbekistan. Coal remains a key source of heating and electricity for much of the region. The environmental impact of extraction, or "underground political ecologies," in the region is understudied, especially in Turkmenistan and Uzbekistan—in part because these are often politically unsafe topics. Extractive industries driven by global demand for mineral resources and fossil fuels, both directly and indirectly, drive or contribute to global climate change, which in turn alters Central Asia's regional water regime (hydrological system). This water regime shift will significantly affect Central Asian lifestyles and livelihoods. The transportation of various minerals other than fossil fuels and the embedded carbon in their production processes are additional contributors to greenhouse gas emissions. Thus, if efforts to address climate change are taken seriously, the impact of the global mining industry operating in Central Asia, driven by materials consumption elsewhere, must be fully appreciated.

The Kumtor mine in Kyrgyzstan is a prime example of how economics is environmental, how extraction can contribute to and interact with climate change to create harm, and how people do challenge even the most economically valuable industries. This gold mine (run by a Canadian company) is located in a glacial zone at four thousand meters in the Ak Shirak Range of the Tien Shan Mountains. The largest gold producer in Kyrgyzstan, Kumtor is the only open-pit mine in the world actively removing glaciers to extract gold (figure 27-3). Centerra Gold's Kumtor Operating Company created a tailing pond between Lake Petrov and the Kumtor River, a tributary of the Naryn River. The unlined tailing pit holds more than thirty-four million cubic meters of wastewater and tailings from the cyanide leachate and other chemicals used to process gold at Kumtor. This waste lake relies on underlying permafrost for continuous, permanent, impermeable containment. Thawing of the permafrost—which is happening worldwide with climate change—underneath this extensive tailing pit at the headwaters to the Naryn

27-3 View of the Kumtor open-pit gold mine above 4,000 meters elevation in the Ak Shirak Range, Kyrgyzstan, 2013. Photograph by Amanda Wooden.

River is a risk for the watershed. There is also the potential of breach and glacial lake outburst flooding at Lake Petrov above the tailing pond.

This mine remains a source of controversy, dividing the population about whether income from Kumtor and the jobs connected to it are worth the damage to glaciers. The destruction of the glaciers resonates socially. As the impacts of mining on glaciers in the Ak Shirak Range became widely known, public opinion about and social mobilization against Kumtor grew more critical and expanded from just the nearby communities to become a national consideration. People in Kyrgyzstan now are talking about what shrinking glaciers mean for their future and are debating exactly whose mountain, glacier, and gold it is. In 2014, the Jorgorku Kenesh (Kyrgyzstan's parliament) passed a national law on glaciers, which would have forced the closure of Kumtor's open-pit mine, but then-president Almaz Atambaev did not sign it into law. In 2017 Atambaev's administration asked the Jorgorku Kenesh to make changes to the national water code, which created an explicit exception for Kumtor to continue damaging the Ak Shirak glaciers, angering activists and residents. President Sadyr Japarov and his Mekenchil (patriotic) party allies came to power after the contested 2020 elections, having previously challenged the Kyrgyz government agreements with Centerra Gold. In May 2021, responding to popular sentiment, Japarov announced a temporary emergency government takeover of the Kumtor mine. International arbitration with Centerra and a government investigation of former officials for corruption in contract negotiations began shortly thereafter. From mine inception and permitting, and despite national controversy, the regulatory process failed to more than legalize environmental damage. This case highlights the great difficulty experienced by people who live in the mine's vicinity in making a choice between seeking protection of an ecosystem where you live and where you make your livelihood and a job that is only possible with some extent of destruction of that ecosystem—this is not a choice that residents typically request. In some Central Asian mining communities, as elsewhere in the world, residents talk about the injustice of such forced choices.

Uzbekistan's Muruntau mine is an example of an important facility that surely has had environmental impact but about which there is limited public information. Muruntau is the largest open-pit gold mine in Central Asia and one of the largest and deepest open-pit mines in the world. As Uzbekistan continues to open politically, the environmental and health impact of sites such as Muruntau may become public. Although we cannot assume that the only part of this story is harm, and labor perspectives can be quite different, environmentalists and nearby residents may voice their concerns or we may learn of resistance that people have engaged in quietly. Even known and accessible mines such as the Kara-Keche coal mine in Naryn Oblast in Kyrgyzstan have untold environmental impacts, witness the visible signs of acid mine drainage, which causes severe water and soil contamination.

Uzbekistan's new openness—much as in Afghanistan—is already part of a minerals rush, a process in which a number of international mining and fossil fuel firms compete with one another for exploration and development licenses. Despite international media coverage uncritically lauding this economic liberalization process as wholly positive, a more careful awareness would provide perspective on the ways in which rapid privatization and the quick expansion of the extractive industry into Uzbekistan and Afghanistan cause social and environmental disruption. The unfolding of such disruption occurs over time, so appreciating the potential impact of change requires consideration of social effects beyond economics over larger (time) scales.

Mining metals for renewable energy technologies or uranium for nuclear power could boom with the shift in global energy demands. Lithium mining, needed for the increasing demand for electric car batteries, has already begun in several Central Asian communities. The region does need more sustainable and self-sufficient energy sources, and solar power plants are in development—for example, in Uzbekistan. However, extraction oriented toward raw materials export, even if for renewable energy use elsewhere, is still potentially damaging to Central Asia. Globally, as in Central Asia, some of the same fossil fuel companies are now pursuing the development of renewables without bearing responsibility for the costs of their climate and other ecological damages. Alternatively, a shift to renewable energies, especially if at least in some instances it is decentralized and community-based, could provide a counterbalance to large-scale commercial ventures, with new forms of education and employment likely emerging.

Whether uranium will be part of the energy supply transformation is still a globally debated question. If nuclear energy becomes a large part of the climate-era generation of fuels, what are the implications for residents in already heavily uranium-mined areas of Kazakhstan or Uzbekistan? International press often cover radioactivity in Central Asia as just a matter of Cold War legacy and Soviet failures. Yet there is physical, psychological, and political fallout continuing today from the legacy of radioactive waste and weapons testing in the region. For example, Kathleen Purvis-Roberts, Cynthia Werner, and Irene Frank found that in Kazakhstan the contemporary political context both shapes and reimagines people's memories of what the Soviet state did to them. Uranium mining and processing sites along with weapons testing zones continue to represent ongoing exposures and require renewed scientific attention and sociological study. Legacy sites in several countries such as Min-Kush or Mailuu-Suu, Kyrgyzstan, could be impacted by climate driven landslides and flooding as the region moves toward peak water. Emerging new or recultivated uranium mines and processing facilities, particularly in Kazakhstan, are difficult to study in this "neoliberal authoritarian" context. People have adapted and responded to the nuclear power and weapons industries in the past, such as thirty years ago in the Nevada-Semipalatinsk Anti-Nuclear Movement in Kazakhstan. With greater information about such legacies (the histories of both harm and resistance), the public may be able to influence better contemporary choices about nuclear power and a fuller consideration of economic development alternatives. As recent events in Kyrgyzstan show, residents are often not supportive of uranium mining when they find out about it before development. In 2019, for example, after learning that Canadian Azarga's subsidiary company UrAsia was developing a uranium mine in development near Kyzyl-Olmpo village, residents of Ton Rayon of Issyk Kul region of Kyrgyzstan led a national movement demanding a ban on licensing uranium extraction. More than thirty-two thousand people signed a petition to this effect. This mass action and overwhelming popular opinion against uranium mining—noticeable all-over social media, in press coverage, and during daily conversations—led to the Zhorgoku Kenesh (parliament) passing a law that banned uranium and thorium mining or imports.

Evaluating pollution legacies is also important for health care considerations, particularly for workers. Central Asian studies of labor and mining and urban political ecologies provide insight into the complications involving newly capitalistic communities and provide useful comparisons with de-industrial contexts elsewhere, such as in steel cities of the midwestern United States or postcommunist eastern Europe. These comparative lessons help us make sense of development orthodoxies such as neoliberal antiregulatory policy recommendations. They highlight what happens to industrial waste when the manufacturing sector collapses and the state does not regulate properly, and they provide insight into the emerging environmental problems involved with expanded mining, such as habitat destruction, runoff, and chemical use and disposal.

Environmentalists often utilize conceptualizations of justice to grapple with these legacies and current dominant perspectives, providing guidance for better policies. Residents challenge extractive industries in Kyrgyzstan, oil workers go on strike in Kazakhstan for safer conditions and better pay, and doctors in Uzbekistan try to call attention to the health impacts of the Aral Sea shrinkage. Scholarly environmental justice ideas emerged out of community activism in the United States about environmental maldistribution, where pollution problems are concentrated in poor and racialized communities, and where these communities on average have the least access to green space or clean water. Hallmarks of many community-based environmental mobilizations in Central Asia are the anger and frustration at the unfairness marked by a lack of transparency in decision making, with the realization as to who bears the costs and who gains the profits from privatization and industrialization and how polluting industries are legalized but protests criminalized. These reactions intermingle with frustration at postindustrial urban decline and changes in pastoral livelihoods. It is often these kinds of intense and emotional social movements that come as a surprise to elites who are accustomed to having access to and can afford a better quality of life or can leave when the government does not provide. At these moments of seemingly eruptive public dissent (which are, in reality, slow-to-boil reactions), news coverage tends to suggest that these protest reactions are dangerous. The "danger" is not attributed to the polluters who endanger people's lives and livelihoods giving rise to these frustrated reactions but, rather, to the political and economic instability "caused" by the protests. In a corporatized context, the state does not hold the polluter responsible; it holds to account those who are resisting corporatization.

Beyond Danger and Securitization Discourses about Environmental Harm

During my time in Osh in 2006, a colleague told me of his family's plan to migrate to Russia. He asked me for help to locate a place that would make sense for the climate changes of the next fifty years. "I know you study this stuff. Can you look at some maps and show me some of the good places to be?" Migration is a central component of twenty-first-century environmental changes. In ways both similar to and interacting with how the state holds protesters responsible for damage that begins with industrialization, anti-immigration narratives in Europe, Russia, and the United States as well as in Kazakhstan, Kyrgyzstan, Tajikistan, and Uzbekistan are danger discourses distracting attention and responsibility from root causes such as climatic changes. Jäger's research reveals how the water-supply problems in the northern Aral region drive some people to resettle in oil boomtowns such as Aktobe, where migrants (and especially women migrants) struggle to find affordable housing and jobs. Given the changing water future for Central Asia and for regions to its south, environmental migration requires new attention. We can look at securitization narratives concerning energy and the Aral Sea issue to grapple with what alternative ways of considering harm might be available.

Much reporting and scholarship about Central Eurasian energy and electricity generation—as well as about water—is state-centric, often uses danger discourses, and focuses on international affairs, national elite politics, and conflict. This work typically does not deal with citizens' everyday experiences and needs. Likewise, by "securitizing" water scarcity and climate change, the environment becomes something to control or to battle, which distracts us from the problem causes. This securitizing approach utilizes a twentieth-century modernist understanding of nature as the enemy; it discursively moves us away from identifying the human causes and addressing them and moves us toward controlling the outcomes, often via technological means that can create new environmental and related social difficulties. Since defeating the "enemy" becomes important "at all costs," we skip both causal factors and real problem solving, and we discount social costs.

The Aral Sea exemplifies the need for both natural-scientific and social-humanistic understandings as well as evaluations of people's everyday experiences within historical context. The Aral Sea, once the fourth-largest lake in the world, has shrunk by approximately 90 percent since the 1960s, largely because of water diversions for irrigated agriculture. It was largely the Cold War Soviet goals for cotton independence that drove this desiccation process. However, as Peterson's research demonstrates, the Soviet irrigation dreams for transforming Central Asia's deserts and modernizing societies began in Imperial Russia and continue in the post-Soviet era, a view of controlling nature and colonizing people shared across political ideologies. The Aral Sea as one whole ecosystem no longer exists, despite some claims about "saving" the lake. The dramatic changes in this ecosystem slowly alter meso-climates and temperature and impact agricultural production regionally. By 2014 the eastern portion of what was once the Aral ceased to exist as a lake (figure 27-4). A new desert has formed in the former lake basin called the Aralkum. The environmental, health, and economic ramifications of the massive change in the Aral Sea ecosystem include a shortened growing season, desertification, dust storms, soil and water salinization, water logging, species loss, and a myriad of health problems among residents such as skin disorders and esophageal cancer. Restoration efforts now focus on the Small Aral (in Kazakhstan) and the former deltas of the Amu Darya and Syr Darya. The most important impacts on area residents are the continuing challenges of access to freshwater, soil quality loss, and reductions in the length of the growing season. A long growing season is crucial for community-scale food production as well as for the lucrative state-controlled cotton sector. The Aral Sea crisis has also figured into regional narratives about the water-energy nexus, causing Uzbekistan and Kazakhstan to criticize Kyrgyzstan's and Tajikistan's upstream hydroelectricity development plans.

We see, however, an optimistic change in a small portion of the former Aral, due to the World Bank-funded construction of the Kokaral (green island) dam in the Northern Aral Sea, also known as the Small Aral Sea (comprising only 9 percent of the former total surface area of the whole lake). While recognizing what became possible for some local residents in the partial recovery of fishing in this northernmost part of the former Aral Sea basin in Kazakhstan, it becomes clear that, even with this dam, the Small Aral will never fully recover. Despite this, the World Bank and the Kazakh government see this as a success. Yet, as Kristopher White explains, the choice to dam this small part means a

27-4   Locals visiting the remains of abandoned ships at the former Muynak Sea Port, which now lies 150 kilometers from the water and has become a memorial for environmental damage in northern Karakalpakstan, Uzbekistan, 2019. Photograph by Kasia Ploskonka.

faster process of desiccation in the larger ecosystem. This dam effectively led to the division of the lake into separate bodies; it is not the Aral Sea anymore but, rather, several smaller water bodies, with the southern parts shrinking faster because of this dam. William Wheeler also upends the crisis and disaster narratives of the Aral, discussing the political work this narrative does in giving "hope of a utopian transformation." He unsettles the environmental disaster narrative with careful ethnography in the northern Aral Sea region to see how this discourse actually functioned politically to mobilize a response—albeit a partial one that had ramifications for the survival of the ecosystem as a whole. Although residents in the Aral Sea region "are aware of environmental problems, especially dust and salt in the air, many actively contest the disaster narrative, describing how TV crews film only the poorest, oldest inhabitants, then wait a few days for a dust storm, to portray the situation as catastrophic!" That is, the decline of the Aral Sea was complicated for residents; it is not "lost" and it is not "saved." People fundamentally changed the Aral, it is no longer the Aral, and through this process people are shaping new social and cultural lives.

It is interesting to consider this historical example, of how people changed their lives in reaction to the Aral Sea's ecosystem alteration, in evaluating climate change realities and futures. It is difficult for anyone writing about environmental topics to avoid "crisis and harm speak" given the challenging, pressing, and existential damage and violence considered in these topics. However, environmental topics are stories beyond victimization. There are ways of revealing what it is like to live with impairment without sensationalizing it, of giving space to the voices of those (humans and nonhumans) who experience this harm on a daily basis and are forced to adapt to it, of listening to their strengths and valuing their responses. As Macarena Gómez-Barris reminds us, "If we only track the purview of power's destruction and death force, we are forever analytically imprisoned to reproducing a totalizing viewpoint that ignores life that is unbridled and finds forms of resisting and living alternatively." In exploring the great difficulties that people experience, we see creative resilience and at times beauty in how people and other living creatures adapt and resist these damaging environmental changes.

Already Adapting and Everyday Resistance

The vignette at the beginning of the chapter demonstrates one response to the unpleasant visual, health, and odor problems of consumer lifestyles and municipal services inadequacy-driven urban waste. Some residents in Osh alternatively challenged this situation with advocacy or by publicly criticizing municipal authorities; residents regularly sought improved sanitation services by sending letters to and complaining in person at the mayor's office. Environmental street protests (*meetingi*) are unsurprising to those living in a place impacted by pollution, waste, or scarcity. Most of the time, protests are neither sudden nor unexpected. They both build on frustrations and grievances that have developed over time and interact with other political concerns such as corruption or regulatory capture. Organizing people on a large scale is difficult, as the default responses of adaptation and acquiescence are easier routes. Resistances are also micro level and typically not demonstrated as street actions. The daily slow-boiling dynamics of environmental disputes become noticeable through engaged observation and listening to those impacted. Examples of scholarship using these practices include critical assessments of the international development sector and the state, ethnographies that focus on people's material lived experiences at the micro level in irrigation networks and mining communities, and participatory research approaches with people living and working in forestry and pastures.

Residents in Kyrgyzstan and Tajikistan, for example, register and verbalize the severity of glacier decline, even if not everyone understands the causes. This has become a significant worry for some, as droughts and electricity shortages have highlighted what a reduced water future might look like. A drought in 2008–2009 contributed to street protests and the government overthrow in Kyrgyzstan in 2010, a process I refer to as a "hydroelectric revolution." However, well before these events, signs of stress among residents were noticeable. In 2009, when I visited my former housemate in Osh, she was using an all-in-one small solar-powered electrification system with a radio, a phone charger, and a few lightbulbs all connected. We sat drinking tea while she and visiting family members criticized the authorities and discussed corruption in the energy sector. In 2009–2010 the Kyrgyz government partially privatized the water sector and introduced rate increases for electricity, water, and heating that helped trigger protests against the government. This rate increase was widely unpopular in light of the daily electricity shortage experienced by most residents of Kyrgyzstan in 2008–2009. The Kyrgyz government blamed the electricity shortage on the previous years' drought and reservoir water levels that were lower than necessary to generate hydroelectric power. However, the Kyrgyz authorities had mismanaged the water reserves, including selling electricity to neighboring countries. When the government announced rate increases in winter 2009, protests began in the cities that were the hardest hit by electricity shortages, Naryn and Talas. Government forces cracked down on protesters on April 7, 2010; citizens and opposition politicians responded by storming the White House and running President Kurmanbek Bakiev out of power.

Electricity availability, aging coal-fired power plants, rolling blackouts, and winter vulnerability for the urban and rural poor all continue to upset people about the basic needs their government fails to provide in both Tajikistan and Kyrgyzstan. Likewise, the costs of natural gas and of energy in general remain an acute budgetary problem for these two countries. There remains a tension in electricity and water tariffs policies between a need to recoup costs, public expectations of government, and public vulnerability to even slight rate increases. Kyrgyzstan and Tajikistan need alternative energy systems, energy decentralization, and upgraded urban and rural electric systems and power grids. They also require an upgraded water-supply infrastructure (storage, irrigation canals, drinking-water filtration, sewerage), as do their downstream neighbors Kazakhstan, Turkmenistan, and Uzbekistan, who are even more dependent on the regional water systems. The water privatization schemes often recommended by Western development organizations are politically difficult and socially unacceptable to many Kyrgyzstanis, where people view water as a public good (Soviet, Islamic, and pre-Islamic cultural influences shape this view). Alongside any cultural meanings of water, for many Kyrgyzstanis increased water costs would be financially unfeasible. Thus, policy makers must find alternative means to address these basic needs, especially considering what climate change brings to the region.

During Kyrgyzstan's events from January to April 2010, public outrage was a predictable outcome of the corrupt practices—including those around access to electricity, water, and food—that are experienced on a daily basis. David Gullette and Jeanne Féaux de la Croix suggest the various ways people in Central Asia experience energy in their daily lives "might articulate conceptions of 'moral economy.'" The Soviet modernization goals of electrification did not reach the eastern Pamirs, and the struggle for energy sources remains, particularly in the winter, and it is worse today without state supplementation. Kraudzun explains how residents in Tajikistan's Gorno-Badakhshan region face the challenge of choosing between using dwarf shrub (primarily *teresken*) for heating, which requires costly gasoline to collect, or using expensive coal, or keeping the dwarf shrubs for their foraging livestock. This unattractive choice leads people to criticize government officials who seek to maintain a ban on teresken removal, demanding that the state provide them coal.

Chronic absence of electricity is a symbolic physical reminder of Hazara historical social exclusion in Afghanistan, according to Melissa Kerr Chiovenda. Electricity shortages fuel Hazara perceptions of marginality and disenfranchisement and form the centerpiece of Hazara civil rights protests for a more just society. Discussions among Hazara people about what kind of energy development to pursue responds to goals for large-scale development and what Chiovenda calls an "illuminated" future of educational and industrial development. Electricity is a physical reminder of possibilities long denied them by the Afghan state. Similar to these explorations of energy lives, other important topics and studies of everyday socioecological experiences in the region engage with the cultural life of nature, labor issues in mining, community-based and participatory approaches to forestry and agropastoralism, and political ecology of development, gendered relations, and science.

One argument made by Alexander Cooley and John Heathershaw is that the post-Soviet "neoliberal authoritarianisms" of several Central Asian states—to varying extents and changing over time—are responsible for this mix of social predicaments. Current environmental difficulties result from both legacy challenges and the particular ways in which market economies emerged in the region, along with shifting cultures of consumption and conflicting ideas about success and "progress." Although new forms of environmentalism were able to emerge in this neoliberalized context, these activism opportunities are limited where and when authoritarian controls are tighter. Additionally, urban environmental organizations in the post-Soviet space may have a tendency to replicate some limitations of mainstream Western environmentalisms.

Since the 1980s global neoliberal shift, many national and international environmental organizations in the West responded to anti-environmental corporate pressure by mainstreaming. They softened critical standpoints and "professionalized," focusing their work on lobbying, fund-raising, and public relations campaigns and centering much of their work on market approaches and individual responsibility narratives. The replication of these limitations by some professionalized Central Asian environmental NGOs occurs in part because they often must rely on Western development organizations for funding and are required to follow their donor's organizational goals, prescription guidelines, and programmatic language. Development organizations in turn tend to be state-centric and rely on the host governments' approval for continuation of their work. One common critique of mainstream environmental organizations in Central Asia is that they focus primarily on organizing workshops and conferences rather than publicly challenging government inaction or substantively addressing critical issues at stake. Some of the imported mainstream environmental ideas that rub against various collectivist social norms in Central Asia include market-based sustainability programs requiring internalizing costs through privatization (e.g., of electricity, water delivery, trash collection) or conservation measures without adequate attention to social needs. Development organizations working on rural environmental issues face criticism for importing mismatching Western approaches or models used in other regions and inadequately understanding or incorporating place-specific local knowledge of ecosystems developed and adapted over generations.

In juxtaposition, people in Central Asia are organizing at the grassroots level to resist some of these industrialization processes and to protect green spaces and important cultural sites. They are creating new forms of exchange outside of markets, critical artistic expression about environmental topics, and alternative ways of seeing the natural world and living as part of it. Thus, neoliberalism also gives rise to creative and radical resistance, sometimes as a rejection of capitalist and Western forms of environmentalism and at other times in creative adoption and hybridization of these practices. One example of creative community work on the urban waste matter was by Kyrgyz artist Aida Sulova, who created the anti–plastic bag campaign Zhil Bil Paket ("Once Upon a Plastic Bag") and garbage bin street art. In Kazakhstan, the artist Pasha Cas is renowned for his jarring installations that draw attention to a range of socioenvironmental matters—such as the murals he painted in the steel mine city Temirtau (*Dancing!*), the Semipalatinsk nuclear weapon testing ground (*This Is Silence*), Pavlodar (*A Mutant Fish*), and Almaty (*Reflection*).

Residents of Almaty and Bishkek regularly discuss their sadness and anger about trees being cut for construction and about their air pollution worries. Residents have voiced these frustrations at public meetings and on social media. Both climate- and pollution-driven tree losses and official or state-condoned mass tree removals have spurred a revival of interest in botanical gardens, living walls, and greenery. The overall loss of greenspace has motivated people to block bulldozers in Kyrgyzstan and to pressure their city governments to cease cutting down trees and privatizing greenspace. In 2011 in Kazakhstan, a residents' movement formed to demand the cessation of ski resort development plans on Kok Zhailau Mountain in Ile Alatau National Park near Almaty. More than 33,500 people signed a petition organized by the "Save Kok-Zhailau" initiative group, and more than 17,500 signed an open letter, "In Defense of Kok-Zhailau." In response to this multi-year public outcry, in April 2019 the Almaty akim (mayor) announced a pause on the project until city administrators could further study the impact and location, and in October of that year, President Kassym-Jomart Tokayev banned construction at Kok Zhailau. In Kazakhstan, BozjyranySaqtaiyk (Save Bozzhyr) movement activists were arrested in July 2021 while protesting hotel construction at the iconic Bozzhyr Tract in Mangystau region, and in September 2021, "SOS Taldykol" activists used their bodies to challenge construction and development at a system of reservoirs on the outskirts of the capital Nur-Sultan. Thus, the visible vegetative changes already afoot and the pace of urban alterations have reinvigorated and reinvented domestic environmentalisms in some Central Asian places, with creative communitarian solutions, artistic protest expressions, and political involvement as key characteristics.

Some community organizations are pursuing neoliberal environmentalism, such as how to shop "greener," while others are tapping into ideas about nature that draw on a mix of pre-Soviet, Islamic, or pre-Islamic, non-Western cultural practices, including ideas about the inseparability between humans and other beings and the soulfulness of life forms. These indigenous and hybrid cultural influences can enable different ways of thinking about the future and draw on valuable community-centered cultural understandings that have long histories in Central Asia. Despite the development sector and elite stereotypes of rural residents creating harm and lacking environmental awareness, people have and share a variety of non-Western dynamic ecosystem-based knowledges about how to live sustainably with other forms of life. Soviet authorities replaced some of this knowledge with Western natural science understandings, and people adapted some of these "indigenous environmental knowledges" into hybrid forms during those years. Residents pass down these place-specific hybridized understandings within their families and share them in informal collective aid networks that circumvent state or corporate control.

Central Asian elites tend to adopt capitalistic lifestyles into their environmental attitudes and activism. In contemporary Central Asian social life and online debates, people engage in more critical evaluation of donor work and urban upper middle-class forms of environmentalism that make sustainability about consumerism. Central Asian residents, activists, and scholars increasingly grapple with corporate social responsibility and the so-called social contract (also known as the social license to operate or extract), questions of legality and resources, anticolonial and decolonial approaches to sustainability, and gender studies of ecology and development. These critical approaches more carefully dissect capitalism and traditionalism than other standpoints.

Place-based knowledge, sacred ecologies, and moral geographies in Kazakhstan and Kyrgyzstan demonstrate what "socio-nature" is and how people cling to places that are important to them and make meaning of their environment during seeming crisis moments. Eva-Marie Dubuisson and Anna Genina's work taps into ideas of mobility in relation to Kazakh ancestral worldviews rooted in a sense of place, connecting relationships with and within nature to identifying the mismatch of state boundaries with mobile pasture practices. Elsewhere, Dubuisson reveals ancestral worldviews in Kazakhstan via sacred geographies and social commentaries such as aitys performances (dueling poets). In this worldview, ancestors collapse the distance between natural and lived worlds, between times and across spaces, and protect not only the living but also the land, including from developers (Soviet and contemporary). Jeanne Féaux de la Croix explores various histories and contemporary cultural aspects of three kinds of iconic places that generate reverence in Toktogul Valley, Kyrgyzstan—pastures, mazars (sacred sites), and dams. She writes about the systems of value, meanings of a good life, and the ways in which people respond emotionally to these special places in times of turmoil. She challenges the kinds of environmental understandings that form the basis of so many development interventions, including identifying the textures of "resilient social fabric" in Kyrgyzstan. Jake Fleming demonstrates how trees impact local resource politics in an ethnographic study of grafting in southern Kyrgyzstan's walnut-fruit forests. The relationships between forest residents, village grafters, and the trees with whom they partner, all strengthen public forested spaces, create less hierarchy, and allow residents to engage in collective aid, production outside of market spaces and corporate plantations, and "everyday forms of resistance" against state power. In my own research on how glaciers have begun to play a political role in Kyrgyzstani conversations about climate change and mining, I note seemingly new prominent and revived discussions of these geological bodies as alive, in motion, emotional, and connected to Kyrgyz traditions and myths, as well as to emerging and nontraditional ideas about the future.

Socio-Natures in Central Asia

Current environmental conundrums of global climate change, Central Asian hydrological regime shifts, and massive biodiversity loss are on a scale that humans have not previously experienced; this will be central to twenty-first-century economic, social, political, and cultural life. Hydrocarbon energy economies such as Turkmenistan's will significantly transform this century, increasing temperatures and shifting precipitation patterns will alter agronomy, permafrost melting will become a climate change feedback loop, the majority of the region's glaciers will melt, biomes will be altered, and species—including humans—will adapt, move, or go extinct as their habitats change.

Appreciating the intersection of the environment with the social world allows us to see everyday realities in Central Asia and imagine possible public responses to the needs of this new era. When we grapple with how people experience nature and the cultural elements present in environmental understandings and meanings, we are better able to realize that "the environment" is actually us. It is inseparable from economics, and environmental issues are political. There is concern and resistance not only in protest movements but also in everyday and micro rebellions. It is necessary to improve our ability to notice different peoples' shifting understandings of the world, its ecosystems, and their places within those systems. We may hear the ways in which people are changing their own lives, and how other-than-human species are not in climate denial but are already shifting so as to survive, and what these adaptations mean for human-nature relationships. This fuller understanding is ethically and practically important. Conventional ways of viewing the environment—derived from colonial and modernization worldviews such as the irrigation dreams that transformed the Aral Sea or the neoliberal extractivism that damaged Ak Shirak's glaciers—also will not provide a full enough picture to make appropriate decisions and to design effective policies fundamentally important for surviving and thriving in the new ecosystems of Central Asia. When we move beyond speaking about environmental issues in solely crisis terms, or merely as an instrument for human needs and understand how the environment is experienced in dynamic local contexts, we may be able to engage in comprehensive problem solving to sustain life rather than reactionary policy making to uphold the status quo that created this situation. We must engage in better listening and find new ways to respond effectively to the processes of environmental change, transformation, adaption, and resistance that are undoubtedly to come.

28

Development

Noor O'Neill Borbieva

"Development," as I use the word in this chapter, refers to a project, directed and funded by outside actors, to reform a society in an ideal image. This understanding of the term was articulated by President Harry Truman in his inaugural speech of 1949. In that speech he promised to make scientific and technological knowledge available to underdeveloped states in the hopes of jump-starting their economies and bringing prosperity to a greater portion of the globe, making "the benefits of our scientific advances and industrial progress available for the improvement and growth of underdeveloped areas." His words marked a shift in the understanding of development; formerly understood as something that just happens, it was now understood as something one agent does to another.

Throughout the twentieth century, and even into the twenty-first, that "something" that one agent does to another is bring about "modernization," a term that means different things in different contexts. In the development sector the vision of modernization most commonly promoted is that of W. W. Rostow, as articulated in his celebrated 1959 article on the stages of economic development, where Rostow defined modernization as a universal process of change. It includes industrialization, growing technological capacity, rising GDP, expanding infrastructure, and political and economic stability. The development projects I discuss here reflect this vision: they bring money, technology, and technical knowledge into Central Asia in the hopes of promoting prosperity and freedom.

From Russian Colonialism to Independence

It would be a grave oversight to talk about development in Central Asia without acknowledging the impact of Russian and Soviet efforts. When Russian armies arrived in Central Asia in the late 1800s, the region's agricultural production supported limited specialization and stratification in cities. Nomadic tribal confederations, also stratified, occupied the surrounding nonarable regions (deserts, mountain ranges), practicing animal husbandry and trading with the sedentary communities.

The Russian empire was eager to profit from control of Central Asia. It invested in infrastructure, including repairing irrigation systems that had been in disrepair since the Mongol invasions and building roads and a railway. The Russians also expanded the production of cash crops such as cotton. The Soviet regime was even more aggressive, forcibly integrating the region into a unionwide command economy. Nomadic populations were made sedentary, the land and property of the wealthy were seized by the state, and farming and animal husbandry were organized in large collective enterprises. The regime invested heavily in infrastructure, expanding cities and building schools, roads, dams, and factories. It intensified resource extraction and expanded cash crop production. The regime altered Central Asian cultural institutions as well; it dismantled religious institutions, prohibited long-standing practices that were considered exploitative (child marriage, polygamy, etc.), and created an exacting system of ethnic categories that still shapes life in the region.

Although the Soviet command economy was imperfect, characterized by an overinvestment in heavy industry and resource extraction, markets in which supply and demand were rarely in sync, and areas of environmental devastation, the Soviet regime was responsible for some improvements in the level of human development in the region. The regime gave citizens basic economic rights and protections including free education and health care along with guaranteed employment and housing. Living standards were relatively low, but the costs of essential goods and services were within the reach of most families. High levels of social spending in Central Asia were possible thanks to the Soviet Union's redistribution networks, which moved wealth from more productive regions to less productive regions. These patterns of wealth redistribution increased social mobility. At independence, according to the UN Human Development Index, the Central Asian republics had achieved a medium level of development. The republics scored highly on many health indicators. A particular success of the regime was increased literacy. In 1917 the literacy rate in the region was around 5 percent (and substantially lower among women and nonurban populations). At independence, it was nearly universal. Another success was increased gender equity; Soviet policies on gender and investments in education afforded women greater personal freedom and more professional opportunities.

After independence in 1991, the five republics of Central Asia suffered a rapid decline in economic and human potential. The productive capacity of the region fell with the breakdown of unionwide trade and production networks. Factories were privatized and many were ultimately dismantled, their valuable machinery and metals sold abroad. Unemployment and poverty rates rose. The loss of subsidies from Moscow meant state coffers had less money for social welfare programs. The region experienced a period of hyperinflation from 1991 until about 1995. The salaries of professionals working in the public sector—teachers, doctors, factory managers—became nearly worthless, if they were paid at all. Often, professionals had to accept other forms of payment, such as flour. Many professionals left their jobs to join the informal economy, working as taxi drivers, shuttle traders, or bazaar retailers. Life expectancy and other health indicators worsened.

Development Aid in Independent Central Asia

When the five republics became independent, global superpowers and international financial institutions (IFIs) immediately offered aid in the form of loans and grants, and many of the republics remain dependent on aid today. Aid comes from multilateral donors (donors that distribute aid from many contributing nations), such as the European Union, the World Bank, the International Monetary Fund, and the Asian Development Bank, as well as bilateral donors (donors that distribute aid from one contributing nation), such as Russia or the United States. The goals of this aid are varied and include economic and political development, national security, and humanitarian assistance.

In the early years after independence, much economic aid was provided on condition that recipient states transition command economies to capitalist economies that were also integrated into world markets. This transition could be achieved through "structural adjustment" reforms that included privatizing government assets, adopting convertible currencies, and liberalizing trade. Republics that agreed to these reforms were eligible to receive grants and loans from IFIs. Structural adjustment reforms did not affect all the Central Asian republics equally. Republics with alternative sources of income preferred to limit reforms, while poorer republics, desperate for money to help them rebuild their economies, implemented the reforms fully in order to secure lucrative loans and grants.

Although IFIs were optimistic that structural adjustment reforms would lead to economic growth, in reality the results were mixed. There were clearly long-term benefits to establishing market-based institutions, but critics point out that structural adjustment dismantled the Soviet welfare system and social safety net when citizens needed them most. They say that structural adjustment reduced public and social services and expenditures on health and education as proportions of GDP and that this meant the (avoidable) loss of a significant amount of the human capital developed thanks to Soviet investments in health and education. Critics point out that structural adjustment reinforced existing inequalities, because elites were well positioned to benefit from privatization. They note that the loans themselves increased borrowers' external debt burdens without securing anticipated levels of growth. Finally, they object to the neoliberal ideology that informed structural adjustment, with its moralizing discourses that blamed the failure of economic reforms on the "culture" of local populations while ignoring the political, structural, and social issues (corruption, authoritarianism, imperialism, etc.) that also hindered development.

Beyond these loans tied to structural adjustment, the Central Asian republics have received aid from all the global superpowers. These states recognize the strategic importance of the region's location and its potential as a source of natural resources, especially energy resources. Russia and China do not disclose aid figures, so the exact amount and nature of their aid to Central Asia is difficult to determine, but it is clearly sizable. China has invested in high-profile infrastructure projects such as road, railway, and pipeline construction as well as resource extraction. Russia's aid goals are diverse, so its aid to the former Soviet republics likely goes toward a variety of development goals and arrives as both loans and grant.

The United States is one of the most generous donors to the Central Asian republics. Very soon after independence it began sending aid to the region in the form of support for democratization and civil society, education, security, and economic development. It also provided humanitarian aid where needed. After 9/11 the United States increased its involvement in the region, stepping up aid to democratization projects and local security forces and opening military bases in Kyrgyzstan and Uzbekistan (both have since closed). Today, the United States provides aid to the region under the following broad rubrics: economic development, health, democracy/human rights/governance, education/social services, and peace/security. The five republics receive varying amounts of US aid. Kyrgyzstan, Tajikistan, and Uzbekistan receive the most aid (between ten and twenty million dollars a year in recent years), and this aid is divided among the rubrics listed above. Kazakhstan receives much less aid from the United States, and that aid is designated for peace/security only. Turkmenistan has received almost no aid from the United States in recent years.

Minor players in the region include Turkey, Iran, the Arab states, India, Pakistan, and Japan. Turkey hoped to forge links based on cultural and linguistic similarities, but many of Central Asia's leaders were turned off by the paternalistic tone of Turkish outreach. Turkey's most recognizable contribution is in the education sector, and it is not a project funded by the Turkish government but, rather, by an organization with ties to the Turkish spiritual leader Fethullah Gülen. This group, which is sometimes called the Nurcu movement because of its dedication to the teachings of the twentieth-century Kurdish mystic Said Nursi (1877–1960), opened a network of schools across the region, and the schools quickly gained a reputation for excellence. Although the schools were not overtly religious, some Central Asian leaders grew wary of the group's religious connections, and the schools were closed down in Tajikistan, Turkmenistan, and Uzbekistan. The schools remain open in Kazakhstan and Kyrgyzstan. Arab states are often mentioned in connection with the funding of Islamic infrastructure. Arab donors have tried to keep a low profile, but the Islamic resurgence they have promoted since independence is one of the most visible changes in the region.

Diverse Paths at Independence

At independence the five formerly Soviet republics in Central Asia—long members of a vast union that fostered open travel and trade and in which republic borders were all but nonexistent—were suddenly five separate states with different leaders and diverging interests. Even as they established separate currencies, exacting visa regimes, and prohibitive trade restrictions, the five republics also took very different economic, political, and social paths. Although development aid comes into the region from many places and for many reasons, I focus below on two particularly high-profile aid projects: structural adjustment (meant to shift command economies to market economies) and democratization.

Structural Adjustment and Economic Development

Kazakhstan under President Nursultan Nazarbayev favored a steady but controlled integration into world markets. The republic implemented some structural adjustment reforms, notably privatization, price deregulation, and trade liberalization, but it was able to keep these processes on its own terms thanks to its vast oil and gas reserves and high oil prices. Since independence, the republic has enjoyed stable growth. It has the highest per capita GDP in the region, attracts a robust amount of foreign direct investment (FDI), and has achieved international prominence by joining and even chairing the Organization for Security and Co-operation in Europe. The republic's prosperity has made it a preferred destination for labor migrants from other republics in the region, and it reportedly has become an aid donor in its own right. Its challenges include an undiversified economy, economic inequality, and authoritarianism.

Although the Turkmen SSR was one of the poorest republics in the Soviet Union, it possessed considerable oil and gas reserves. Because of this mineral wealth, independent Turkmenistan did not feel compelled to implement structural adjustment. Instead, the regime of President Saparmurat Niyazov implemented only modest free market reforms, leaving many resources under state control. The government also invested in infrastructure, including upgrading roads and building pipelines. Observers were hopeful that Turkmenistan would benefit by selling its oil and gas on world markets. Unfortunately, feuds with Russia and the lack of convenient pipelines limited the republic's ability to profit from its mineral wealth. Additionally, the republic's narcissistic and capricious ruler scared away FDI. Observers hoped to see some political liberalization after Niyazov's death in 2006, but his successor, Gurbanguly Berdimuhamedow, has retained Niyazov's authoritarian leadership style.

Uzbekistan boasts the largest population in the region and considerable agricultural capacity. At independence Uzbekistan implemented some free market reforms, including limited privatization, price deregulation, and trade liberalization. The government retained control of the financial sector, maintaining a positive trade balance and regulating banking and FDI. Today, the republic remains dependent on cotton production, paying low prices to citizen growers and selling the cotton at high prices on the world market. Wealth from the agricultural sector allowed the authoritarian regime of President Islam Karimov to promote a policy of *mustaqillik* or "self-reliance," which is to say Uzbekistan has resisted becoming dependent on international development assistance.

The two poorest republics, Kyrgyzstan and Tajikistan, both agreed to extensive structural adjustment. A beneficiary of subsidies from Moscow during the Soviet era and possessing only modest stores of mineral wealth, Kyrgyzstan agreed to an extreme form of structural adjustment known as "shock therapy" in return for millions of dollars in grants and loans. In the immediate wake of these reforms and loans, Kyrgyzstan's economy contracted. Tajikistan also agreed to extensive structural adjustment reforms, but whatever hopes international observers held for Tajikistan's smooth transition to a free-market economy were dampened when a civil war broke out in 1992. The international community was called upon to help negotiate a peace treaty. The treaty, signed in 1997, affirmed the legitimacy of President Emomali Rahmon's regime in return for promises (mostly unrealized) of political reform. Today, Tajikistan remains the poorest republic in the region. As of 2010 its main sources of revenue were the drug trade (as much as 40 percent of GDP), international aid, and remittances from citizens who worked abroad.

Democratization

In addition to promoting economic development in the formerly Soviet republics, the international community, especially the United States, has invested heavily in the promotion of democracy. In 1992 the US Congress passed the Freedom Support Act, which allocated money to support democratization and free market reforms in the former Soviet republics. One focus of this aid was "civil society," a term that refers to the non-state sector of human activity in which citizens freely associate, define their interests, and engage in activism. Civil society is the space in which citizens freely associate, define their interests, and engage in voluntary altruistic activism. The development community viewed a vibrant civil society as the means by which formerly Soviet citizens could secure power and prevent the rise of authoritarian regimes.

When the Central Asian republics became independent, international

28-1a, b   NGO workers (*top*) and an NGO training (*bottom*) in Tajikistan, 2008. Photograph by David W. Montgomery.

donors interested in building civil society began to fund small nongovernmental organizations (NGOs). NGO activity grew at an astonishing rate during the 1990s and into the 2000s. According to Jeanne Féaux de la Croix, Central Asian NGO workers experienced that era as a time of "grant rain," when the international community poured money into the civil society sector almost more quickly than the organizations could absorb it. Efforts to expand the sector became known as "capacity building," which is less about helping individual NGOs meet their communities' needs than about building the size and sustainability of the entire sector. On the ground, this meant encouraging existing NGOs to identify and train potential leaders and engage in outreach and education (figure 28-1a). The most common NGO-led activity of this era was the *trening* (training). At trainings, seasoned NGO leaders met with interested citizens and taught them how to identify local problems, find potential local and international donors, and write competitive grant proposals defining solutions (figure 28-1b). This focus on capacity building fostered a circularity that troubled observers; projects that had the best chance of being funded tended to be those that proposed more trainings on leadership and grant writing, and at those trainings participants were taught how to write grant proposals for more trainings.

Like nonprofit organizations in the United States, NGOs in the former Soviet Union promoted a variety of causes and filled numerous civic functions. NGOs administered microloan programs, promoted entrepreneurship, supported tourism, engaged in conflict prevention and mediation, promoted ethnic and religious tolerance, combated human trafficking, resettled refugees, cared for the poor and elderly, prevented the spread of disease, and advocated for sexual minorities. In taking on these responsibilities, they met social welfare needs that had once been the purview of the socialist state and that the governments of the independent republics, because of structural adjustment reforms, no longer had the capacity to address.

Although international funding for civil society remains robust, the project has many critics. One criticism of civil society promotion in the former Soviet Union is that the international community's determination to create new NGOs overlooked an existing cohort of experienced and deserving organizations, founded during perestroika. In the 1980s Mikhail Gorbachev had appealed to citizens to organize at the community level, and the result was a lively independent sector. In those late Soviet years, citizens had free time and living costs were low, so the sector thrived. After the economic struggles of independence set in, however, citizens could no longer devote time to volunteer work. Meanwhile, the international community preferred to identify, vet, and train its own leaders and fund them to create new organizations rather than support existing organizations. By 2000, few NGOs founded before independence still existed.

Critics also question whether the new "independent" sector is really very independent. NGOs' reliance on international funding means their activism tends to reflect external donors' agendas more than local needs and sensibilities. Evidence that this can cause disagreement comes from studies of HIV/AIDS prevention initiatives, as documented by ethnographers Laëtitia Atlani-Duault, Svetlana Ancker, and Bernd Rechel. Rates of infection in the region are low but rising, and the Central Asian republics have limited resources to devote to the problem. Many have requested aid from the international community. Initially, programs run by the Central Asian republics themselves called for the mandatory testing of at-risk individuals. International donors, however, were unwilling to fund projects that included mandatory testing because of concerns about anonymity. In such circumstances, where the international and local communities disagreed about the proper response to a problem, the international community's response was usually adopted because of its greater financial power. The result, however, was that many projects (and the NGOs that oversaw them) did not earn the support of the communities in which they were active.

Similar tensions are evident in the field of conflict prevention. In the late 1990s and early 2000s international donors funded a cohort of NGOs involved in preventing conflict, but when Madeleine Reeves studied the issue in the early 2000s, she discovered that these projects often failed because they were based on a misunderstanding of the causes of conflict. Although donors were concerned about ethnic and national conflict, data from Reeves's informants suggest that most conflict in border regions was caused by resource shortages and the travel and trade restrictions that resulted from increasingly militarized borders—militarization that was being funded by the same international community in the form of aid for peace/security. Another limitation on NGOs' responsiveness to local concerns is the fickle nature of international funding. Donors' interests change quickly in response to international political currents. If one year the international community is concerned about humanitarian crises, the next year it might be more interested in human trafficking or Islamic extremism. These shifts encourage donors to favor short-term projects that promise quick outcomes instead of investing in long-term solutions that address the concerns of local communities. Furthermore, donors must be able to demonstrate to their constituents that they are distributing money effectively. This means they prefer to fund projects whose impacts will be quickly visible and easily quantifiable.

Many critics note that the NGO sector is widely perceived as a conduit for interference by external powers. Donor organizations rarely hide the self-serving nature of their aims. US government agencies have never been shy in connecting US aid to US national interests. USAID acknowledges that US foreign assistance has two purposes: promoting US strategic interests and providing assistance to needy communities while improving lives in the developing world. The Freedom Support Act explicitly connects economic growth in the former Soviet Union to potential financial gain by the United States. Furthermore, available research suggests that a large percentage of development money stays in the developed world in the form of salaries and contracts.

A related concern is that the NGO sector is just as elitist as political networks. Although many NGO leaders come from rural and underrepresented areas, and although many are motivated by a sincere desire to help their communities, the longer they spend working in the sector the more their priorities adjust to match those of the international community. The most successful leaders settle in urban centers, learn foreign languages, travel internationally, and earn relatively high salaries. They are viewed as an elite, perhaps different from but no less out of touch than the governing elite. Furthermore, because salaries in the sector are so high, competition for jobs is intense. Observers and NGO workers both complain that, when hiring, NGO leaders rely on their personal and professional networks rather than on merit-based competitions. This concern calls attention to a related concern raised by critics: civil society is supposed to comprise volunteer organizations, which is to say, organizations that bring people together beyond family or professional commitments to address shared concerns. In Central Asia, however, NGOs are staffed by full-time paid workers, and the sector offers lucrative careers to the region's most skilled and educated professionals, which is to say, the sector is highly professionalized.

Finally, critics point to the failure of civil society activism to change attitudes about democracy. In Kyrgyzstan, initial reporting on the 2005 Tulip Revolution credited civil society activism with overthrowing the unpopular and corrupt regime of Askar Akaev. Later scholarship corrected this view, however, revealing that NGO networks likely played a smaller role than the elite networks. In Kazakhstan, a long-standing network of well-funded prodemocracy NGOs has failed to persuade the public to put pressure on the government to reform. Recent public attitude surveys suggest that Kazakhstani citizens prefer authoritarianism, if it ensures stability and prosperity, to the NGOs' democratic ideals. According to these surveys, many citizens view foreign-funded prodemocracy groups as being out of touch with their needs and values.

Development in Perspective

Many mainstream economists are optimistic about development aid, arguing that aid encourages modernization and that modernization improves health and well-being across the globe. These enthusiasts argue it is imperative that wealthy nations and individuals give aid generously. The UN perspective maintains that every wealthy nation should dedicate a minimum of 0.7 percent of its GDP to foreign aid.

Critics note, however, that since 1950, the wealthy states of the world have spent over two trillion dollars on aid to poor states with very little to show for it. Economist Angus Deaton has argued that development aid may actually hinder economic growth. Statistics for Africa show that growth decreases as aid increases, whereas the opposite is true of India and China, which received relatively little aid but have achieved the highest rates of growth in recent years. Deaton believes aid depresses development because it distorts the relationship between states and their citizens. In a functioning polity, the need to raise funds through taxation forces a regime to listen to its citizens. A high level of aid, not unlike the presence of valuable natural resources, undermines this delicate relationship. Without the need or the ability to tax, a regime will not be incentivized to prioritize citizens' demands or create effective institutions. Daron Acemoglu and James Robinson argue, similarly, that development aid strengthens what they call "extractive" institutions (institutions that take wealth from citizens and funnel it to elites), leaving economies unable to grow. According to their analyses, where extractive institutions dominate, elites are able to steal incoming foreign aid and use it to reinforce their power.

Recent research suggests that capital in the form of private investment and remittances serves poor countries better than foreign aid (see figure 28-2 for basic economic indicators for the five republics). What economic growth we are

Figure 28-2: Basic Economic Indicators for Central Asian Republics.

	Kazakhstan	Kyrgyzstan	Tajikistan	Turkmenistan	Uzbekistan
Total size (rank)	2.72 M km² (1)	199,950 km² (4)	144,100 km² (5)	488,100 km² (2)	447,400 km² (3)
2020 Population (rank)	19.09M (2)	5.96M (4)	8.87M (3)	5.53M (5)	30.56 (1)
2020 Population growth rate	0.89%	0.96%	1.52%	1.06%	0.88%
2020 Net migration per 1,000	0.4	−5	−1.1	−1.7	−1.9
2017 Maternal mortality rate per 100K births	10	60	17	7	29
2020 Infant mortality rate per 1,000 live births	17.9	23.3	28.8	30.8	16.3
2020 Life expectancy at birth	M: 66.8 F: 76.8	M: 67.7 F: 76.2	M: 65.9 F: 72.3	M: 68.2 F: 74.5	M: 71.7 F: 78
2020 Fertility (children/ woman)	2.16	2.54	2.51	2.04	1.74
2020 Urban population	57.7%	36.9%	27.5%	52.5%	50.4%
Year: GDP PPP in 2017 dollars	2017: $478.6B 2016: $460.3B 2015: $455.3B	2017: $23.15B 2016: $22.14B 2015: $21.22B	2017: $28.43B 2016: $26.55B 2015: $24.83B	2017: $103.7B 2016: $97.41B 2015: $91.72B	2017: $223B 2016: $211.8B 2015: $196.5B
Year: GDP real growth rate	2017: 4% 2016: 1.1% 2015: 1.2%	2017: 4.6% 2016: 4.3% 2015: 3.9%	2017: 7.1% 2016: 6.9% 2015: 6%	2017: 6.5% 2016: 6.2% 2015: 6.5%	2017: 5.3% 2016: 7.8% 2015: 7.9%
GDP per capita, PPP in 2017 dollars (rank)	2017: $26,300 2016: $25,700 2015: $25,800 (1)	2017: $3,700 2016: $3,600 2015: $3,500 (4)	2017: $3,200 2016: $3,000 2015: $2,900 (5)	$2017: $18,200 2016: $17,300 2015: $16,500 (2)	2017: $6,900 2016: $6,700 2015: $6,300 (3)
2017 GDP composition by sector	Agriculture: 4.7% Industry: 34.1% Service: 61.2%	Agriculture: 14.6% Industry: 31.2% Service: 54.2%	Agriculture: 28.6% Industry: 25.5% Service: 45.9%	Agriculture: 7.5% Industry: 44.9% Service: 47.7%	Agriculture: 17.9% Industry: 33.7% Service: 48.5%
Population below poverty line (year)	2.6% (2016)	32.1% (2015)	31.5% (2016)	0.2% (2012)	14% (2016)
GINI index (higher=unequal)	26.3 (2013)	33.4 (2007)	32.6 (2006)	40.8 (1998)	36.8 (2003)
Inflation (consumer prices)	2017: 7.4% 2016: 14.6%	2017: 3.2% 2016: 0.4%	2017: 7.3% 2016: 5.9%	2017: 8% 2016: 3.6%	2017: 12.5% 2016: 8%
2017 Debt (external)	$167.5B	$8.16B	$5.75B	$539.4M	$16.9B
Literacy rate (year)	99.8 (2015)	99.6 (2018)	99.8 (2015)	99.7 (2015)	100 (2016)

Source: CIA World Factbook, https://www.cia.gov/library/publications/the-world-factbook/.

seeing in Central Asia today is likely more closely related to the high flow of remittances than to aid handouts. According to World Bank figures, the value of remittances has been over $1.0 billion a year to Tajikistan since 2006 (the 2020 total was $2.2 billion), to Uzbekistan since at least 2010 (the earliest year for which figures are available; the 2020 total was $7.0 billion), and to Kyrgyzstan since 2008 (the 2020 total was $2.2 billion). Foreign aid to these republics is much less in comparison. Kyrgyzstan and Tajikistan receive the highest amount of aid per capita (2019 figures provided by the Organization for Economic Co-operation and Development indicate total Official Development Assistance to Kazakhstan as $55.0 million, to Kyrgyzstan as $449.0 million, to Tajikistan as $367.0 million, to Turkmenistan as $25.0 million, and to Uzbekistan as $1.2 billion). FDI also remains limited, in part because of existing regimes' reputations for corruption and unfair business practices. Kazakhstan and Turkmenistan receive the highest levels of FDI, mostly in the natural resources sector, but if regimes could reduce corruption, these figures might improve.

Ultimately, the promise of prosperity in Central Asia rests not only on foreign cash flows into the region but also on citizens' ability to trade and establish business partnerships with each other. One unfortunate result of independence was that the region broke into five republics, and each one has distanced itself from its neighbors. Today, citizens of the five republics look at each other across militarized borders; travel and exchange are limited by complicated visa regimes and expensive trade restrictions. In order for the region to prosper, the five republics and their neighbors must commit to an ethos of mutual prosperity through open trade and increased cooperation. Absent such an ethos, the region's prosperity will remain uncertain.

CASE VII-A

Governing Extremism through Communities in Tajikistan

Edward Lemon

Protests erupted across Tajikistan in late September 2016. Rather than being directed at the government, they targeted opposition groups, the Islamic Revival Party (IRPT) and Group 24, and their "foreign sympathizers." A silent protest by opposition members at the Organization for Security and Co-operation in Europe's Human Dimension Implementation Meeting in Warsaw triggered the counter protests in Tajikistan. Students in Dushanbe burned a flag with a photo of the IRPT leader Muhiddin Kabiri's face on it (figure VII-A-1).

State media highlighted the national scale of the protests, which took place in town centers and university campuses across the country. Villagers in Bohtar marched through the streets with signs declaring "No to the Enemies of the Tajik People!" In a statement, teachers in the southern district of Panj affirmed: "We will never allow traitors [*hononi*] to live among us. We condemn them." A student from the Tajik Technical University told state media agency Khovar: "Young people are trying to keep the peace, stability and independence [of our country], and mobilize [*sarcham'ona*] people to work in this direction. We will not allow any foreign power [*nerui horiji*] to undermine the independence of our state." These protests, which took on the appearance of

being initiated and led by the community and which targeted groups the government has labeled "extremist," point to an important, if understudied, aspect of counter extremism in Central Asia: the involvement of citizens. Much of the literature on extremism in Central Asia has focused on the process by which individuals are radicalized, the threat posed by Islamic extremism and the (in)effectiveness of government responses. A great deal of ink, for example, has been spilled on the nineteen hundred Tajik citizens who have joined the Islamic State. Yet they make up an estimated 0.02 percent of Tajikistan's population. What about the remaining 99.98 percent of the Tajik population? How are they represented and shaped by state-led counter extremism? In this chapter I reverse the dominant approach to studying extremism and terrorism in Central Asia. Instead of looking at how the government frames those few citizens who do join "extremist" groups, I examine the other subjects of this discourse, the vast majority of citizens who do not join "extremist" groups. I look at how the government promotes resilience and loyalty rather than how it disciplines deviant behavior and disloyalty.

Put differently, much of the analysis on counter extremism has focused on what Michel Foucault calls sovereign

VII-A-1   Young people burn images of opposition leaders in Dushanbe, September 2016. Photograph courtesy of Radio Ozodi.

power and disciplinary power. Sovereign power limits, bans, and prevents certain behaviors, in this case actions by those identified as "extremists," claiming a monopoly on violence. It is a destructive form of power. Disciplinary power is based on the socially constructed division between normal and abnormal. Those who are abnormal—the homosexual, the vagrant, the extremist—are subject to disciplinary measures requiring them to conform. But here I highlight how counter extremism also involves the third type of power identified by Foucault: biopower. Where disciplinary power regulates the potentially "bad" practices of citizens, biopower promotes certain "good" ways of living to replace these practices. Biopower is "part of a new type of governing for which life is a reservoir that must be tapped into rather than subjected to legal or disciplinary structures." It is a form of power that focuses on administering, developing, fostering, and securing life. Biopower is not purely enforced from the top down. Instead, it is a "pastoral" form of power. Elites promote certain forms of life, but it is up to the subjects themselves to adopt practices that conform with this vision.

Countering extremism, then, is not merely about the destructive acts of banning groups, arresting their followers, and regulating religion with the aim of securing the region's secular authoritarian regimes. Rather, it constitutes a productive set of policies that attempt to mold citizens to adopt a secular understanding of Islam, instill in them an appreciation of the "harmonious" and "peaceful" status quo, and encourage them to mobilize to defend the state against threats. Ultimately, the government is seeking to counter extremism through the communities themselves, creating subjects who monitor themselves and others for the signs of antigovernment "extremism."

Through the example of the September 2016 protests in Tajikistan, which targeted exiled opposition activists from the IRPT and Group 24 along with their families who remained in Tajikistan, I touch upon the themes of media, nationalism, and development. Counter extremism involves the use of the state media to offer guidelines for how citizens should behave in order to contribute to the state's vision for the development of the "democratic" secular state. As the student from the Tajik Technical University demonstrates, discourses on extremism are interlinked with narratives on the nation; they set the anti-Tajik, "foreign," violent, extremist Other in opposition to the patriotic, loyal, peaceful, Tajik Self. Counter extremism narratives contain the government's vision on how politics should be—peaceful, harmonious, stable.

Hegemonic Protests in Tajikistan

Inheriting an understanding of the relationship between religion and security from the Soviet Union, the government of Tajikistan has created a dichotomy between "good," state-controlled, safe, moderate Islam and "bad," unofficial, dangerous, extremist Islam. Although Islam has been framed by the regime as a key component of national identity, the Tajik state also promotes and builds a secular (*dunyavi*) national culture, training young people in the "spirit of patriotism [*rirhiyai vatandirsti*]."

In an article entitled "Social Consciousness and Societal Security [*amniyati jam'iyati*]," the head of the State Security Committee Saymumin Yatimov presents education as a battle between foreign and national influences. Yatimov argues that a "secure public consciousness [*amniyati shuuri muqarrari*], is the most important component for public safety [*amniyati jam'iyati*]." Rather than securing matters purely through repressive means, the government is attempting to instill values in its citizens that will inhibit their critical thinking and make them less likely to resist the regime. State institutions play a central role in this, but citizens themselves also share responsibility. Officials repeatedly call on citizens to monitor other community members and to consciously work on themselves. President Emomali Rahmon argues that the responsibility for countering extremism does not lie solely with the government but lies with communities too: "Indeed,

it is important that our compatriots [*hamvatononi*], and in particular teenagers and young people [*javonon*], especially in the context of the modern world's most sensitive dangers [*nooromu hassosi*], learn to separate truth [*haqro*] from falsehood. They must always be vigilant [*zirak boshand*], take the right path in life [*rohi durusti zindagiro*], to study science and try to educate themselves, and to refrain from any harmful [*ziyonovar*] acts." Responsible and loyal citizens need to be vigilant (*zirak*) to what is going on around them and resilient to extremist messaging. As the prosecutor general from Rudaki district states, "it is every citizen's patriotic duty [*fardi vatandirsti*] to guide the young people toward a democratic society [*demokrativu huquqbunyod hidoyat*], so that they contribute to the stability of their national state." The Tajik state is not a panopticon; it relies on horizontal surveillance among citizens.

The September 2016 protests highlight some of these dynamics. The protests targeted two opposition groups, both of which the government has labeled extremist. Group 24 was classified by the government as an extremist organization in October 2014 following calls for protests in Dushanbe. Following a long process of marginalization, the IRPT (part of the civil war–era opposition that was allocated 30 percent of government posts in the 1997 peace accord) was outlawed in August 2015 and was then declared a terrorist organization after being accused of plotting a coup in September 2015. The state media portrayed the popular response to the September 2016 opposition protests as evidence that this effort to shape public consciousness was working. Protestors reaffirmed the hegemonic narrative, declaring their allegiance to the Tajik state and accusing the opposition of spreading lies and being supported by foreigners. Not only did they publicly conform with the government's message, they accepted responsibility for countering extremism. In a joint statement students at the Tajik National University stated that "strenuous efforts should be made to instill the values of 'nation' [*vatan*], 'people' [*millat*], and 'reconciliation' [*vahdat*] in every citizen." And as a teacher stated in an opinion piece published in the state newspaper *Jumhuriyat*, this is not only the responsibility of the government: "every citizen [*shahrvan*] is responsible for protecting [*hifzi*] national values and contributing to the strengthening of national unity."

Although the state media gave the impression that the September 2016 protests were community led, the group behind many of the actions, Avangard (founded in 2015), has close links to the Ministry of Internal Affairs. Avangard's stated goal—to "prevent the creation of an alien culture, recruitment of young people to different groups of extremists, and to promote increasing respect for the national values of the Tajik people"—reflects the government's own narrative on extremism. In the summer of 2015 the ministry paid for the movement's leaders to travel to Russia and establish links with the migrant community there. Members of the group meet frequently with officials and have been given electronic tablets as a reward for their work. Avangard's position as officially nongovernmental, yet unofficially governmental, points to the blurred boundary between state and civil society in Tajikistan. Counter extremism in Tajikistan forms an important component of authoritarian governance; it is interlinked with relations of power. Through its efforts against "extremists," the regime attempts to secure itself.

Relations of Power and Community Counter Extremism

To understand what this mobilization of the Tajik population to counter extremism means for our understanding of governance in Central Asia, I draw on the thinking of French thinker Michel Foucault. Power lies at the center of Foucault's approach. For Foucault, power "is never localized here or there, never in anybody's hands, never appropriated as a commodity or piece of wealth. Power is employed and exercised through a net-like organization." Rather than being something that actors possess and wield, according to Foucault, power is a relation between agents. Power, therefore, is de-centered and polyvalent rather than hierarchical. Power is not always destructive; it can be productive too. Foucault was concerned with uncovering how practices of power produce political subjects. In his essay "The Subject and Power," Foucault wrote that his objective in his later work was to examine the ways in which human beings turn themselves into subjects.

Through state counter extremism efforts, Tajiks are constituted as political subjects. Although such measures directly target the small minority of opposition activists who have been labeled "extremists," the main audience of counter extremism is made up of members of the population who are not political extremists. The regime attempts to mobilize these people based on the belief that "as patriotic young people [*javononu*], [they] must fight the false interests [*gumrohu manfiathoi*] that oppose [*ziddi*] the Republic of Tajikistan." Government-led counter extremism in Tajikistan involves the cultivation of political subjects who simultaneously remain resilient to the messages of opposition "extremists" and mobilize to actively support the government. The ideal subjects are not totally docile; they are able to separate truth (what the government says) from falsehood (what the opposition says). Political engagement is only permissible insofar as it is directed at supporting the regime.

Interesting parallels exist with Soviet attempts to mold political subjects. As Oleg Kharkhordin concludes, the ultimate achievement of Soviet individualization was the creation of a subject who constantly readjusts his- or herself by staging mini-trials about their deeds. Ideal Tajik subjects will uphold national values, condemning those who do not. During the Soviet Union, newspapers were filled with stories claimed to be written by citizens extolling the benefits of life in the USSR and denouncing religious individuals. After the 1990 riots in Dushanbe, the pages of Soviet newspapers were filled with the "positive" stories of ordinary citizens going on with their lives, with headlines such as "We Will Live! [*Budem Zhit'*]," and "No to Extremism! [*Ekstremizmu Nyet!*]." These articles called on people to remain "united" (*edini*) and committed to the principles that organized Soviet life: the *kollektiv* (collective) and *druzhba narodov* (friendship of peoples). Although the language has changed, the form that the discourse has taken in independent Tajikistan bears a striking resemblance to that which came before.

"Securing" the Public

Countering extremism involves state repression, but it also involves the promotion of certain ways of living *appropriately*. Through counter extremism, the government is attempting to create citizens who are loyal, who will monitor one another, and who are unlikely to challenge the regime. Measuring the effectiveness of these measures remains difficult. Are citizens merely performing their loyalty publicly while privately disavowing the regime, or do many citizens genuinely support the regime's counter-extremist policies and participate willingly? Evidence from various studies indicates a mixture of responses from citizens in Tajikistan ranging from support, to acceptance, to resistance. It is clear, however, that the state's attempts to build docile secular subjects can never be fully realized. As Foucault argues, where there is power, there is resistance.

Customary Governance and the State in Central Eurasia

Jennifer Brick Murtazashvili

In this case study we explore the various ways in which governments across Central Eurasia have sought to engage self-governing customary organizations at the community level to build the legitimacy and capacity their states. Specifically, we compare the interaction between state and society across Uzbekistan, Tajikistan, and Afghanistan. These countries are ideal for comparison because they are characterized by similar forms of community-based self-governing organizations whose legitimacy is based in tradition and custom. In all three countries, neighborhoods and the informal rules that organize them interact with the state. These three cases of community-to-state relations inform us about strategies to build government legitimacy, as governments in these three states have pursued distinct strategies toward these self-governing organizations: in Uzbekistan the state has sought to co-opt them; in Tajikistan the state has pursued a policy of benign neglect; and in Afghanistan the government has sought to replace them with alternative bodies. Exploring the different strategies the governments have employed toward these organizations can help explain broader governance outcomes across the three contiguous countries.

Informal Organizations in the Developing World

Central Eurasia is rich in self-governing organizations that provide a wide range of goods and services. Customary governing organizations are a kind of informal organization whose basis of legitimacy is rooted in tradition or custom. These organizations are not static or "frozen in time" but instead evolve to respond to challenges—both internal and external—to the environment in which they operate. In countries around the world, customary governing organizations respond to conflict and violence, but they also adapt to demands of the citizens they serve.

Throughout the developing world there is an increasing realization of the importance of governance that occurs outside of, and often despite, formal channels of the state. In some instances, the persistence and evolution of self-governing organizations is a response to state weakness; in other contexts, self-governance is a purposeful strategy that is undertaken to evade government encroachments. It is valuable to assess the institutional divergence that took place between these three neighbors across time and space. Government policies in these three countries sought to engage customary authority at the community level but with different results.

Customary Governance in Central Eurasia

Local governance across sedentary Central Eurasia revolves around communities. Throughout the three countries discussed here, the most commonly used term to describe these communities is "*mahalla*." This is a term used to describe a neighborhood within a city or a large village with roots in the Persian word *mahalli*, which translates as "neighborhood" or simply "local." Sometimes it is used interchangeably with *gozar*. In rural areas, especially those areas where villages have few households, the term "village" (e.g., *qishloq, deh, qala*) is more important than "neighborhood."

Prior to colonial rule in Central Eurasia, there were similar patterns of village governance across this region. Although governments have interacted with these organizations in distinct ways over the past one hundred and fifty years, these community-based organizations share a set of defining features. First, they are typically called mahallas, with governance centered around communities. Second, communities are typically led by an informal leader or a set of leaders, usually male, described as "white beard(s)." Throughout periods of the past, these "white beards" have either had formal authority bestowed upon them by governments, have interacted closely with government to provide public goods, or have been the target of government repression. In other words, there is no "pure" form of community-based governance in Central Eurasia. These are dynamic organizations with long histories in subverting, cooperating with, or being co-opted by formal states.

Community governance arrangements are defined less by their geographic features than by the rules that govern them. Across all three countries these community-based organizations are characterized by leaders who have been selected by communities to represent community interests to people outside the community—including people from other communities, the government, or even international NGOs. Historically, the term "white beards" was used to signify their esteemed status, but in more contemporary times they are called *rais* or "leader." In Tajikistan and Uzbekistan, the term *rais* is far more common in urban areas, because in those spaces mahalla leaders have taken on official duties associated with the state. This was true during the Soviet period and particularly true of contemporary Uzbekistan (see below). In Afghanistan, the term *malik* or *khan* was once used to signify tribal or clan ruler, but often this term is used interchangeably with "white beard" or elder.

Most communities are governed by a self-governing organization that has a range of responsibilities from resolving disputes and providing community services to organizing, arranging, and supervising local rituals. Some research immediately following the collapse of the Soviet Union argued that such governance was organized on the principle of solidarity groups, but more recent scholarship contests this and argues that it is a place where groups come together to transcend kinship based groups. Over time—especially as governments have engaged with these organizations— these once organic structures have evolved into neighborhood, rather than kinship, associations that transcend ethnicity, religion, or place of origin.

Their role has become much more pronounced in recent years as the scope of the state has contracted across this environment. Although Afghanistan and the countries in the former Soviet Union have been characterized by substantial political change and even conflict, community governance structures across Central Asia have often provided a bulwark of stability in a dynamic political, economic, and social environment. They provide a source of convening power that is unparalleled among any public organization in the region.

Two of the three countries considered here—Afghanistan and Tajikistan—witnessed extraordinary political violence over the past several decades. The Tajik civil war from 1992 to 1997 resulted in the deaths of upward of fifty thousand civilians and spurred vast internal migration and upheaval. In Afghanistan, the Saur revolution in 1978 followed by the Soviet invasion in 1979 sparked decades of conflict and left millions dead or displaced. In both countries, community-level institutions have responded to changing political environments, often by becoming more representative of local interests. As communities have organized to respond to changing circumstances, so too have the governments, which increasingly view self-organized structures as opportunities of as well as threats to state consolidation and centralized versions of political order.

In the Soviet successor states of Uzbekistan and Tajikistan, shortly after gaining independence, governments showed renewed interests in these organizations as vehicles to promote the legitimacy of their newly formed governments. In Afghanistan governments began exploring new ways to promote community engagement after the fall of the Taliban government in 2001. Although government interventions in Afghanistan began almost a decade after those in Uzbekistan and Tajikistan, we can observe rationales for different strategies.

Customary Authority in Historical Perspective

Over the past century and a half, governments and imperial powers in Central Eurasia sought to manipulate community governance to build stronger states. In Afghanistan various monarchs sought to interfere in community life and either control or even extinguish community self-governing mechanisms. Abdur Rahman Khan, during his bloody reign from 1880 to 1901, sought to eliminate customary leaders in an effort to consolidate central control and eliminate potential rivals for power. In the 1970s Daud Khan sought to co-opt local leaders by putting them on the government payroll and formalizing their authority. The Saur revolution in 1978, which led to the ascension of the People's Democratic Party of Afghanistan, and the subsequent Soviet invasion in 1979 led to decades of civil strife. Customary leaders were killed in large numbers—by either the Soviet Army, the Afghan secret police, or by mujahideen groups who saw these local leaders as a threat to their legitimacy.

During the Soviet period, the mahalla remained the center of community life in both urban and rural areas. Soviet ethnographer Sergey Poliakov noted that communities rather than the Communist Party were the primary source of local power throughout Central Asia. In his account of rural life he argued that customary authority and the traditional roles these bodies played were modified but not eliminated during Soviet rule. These customary bodies provided local public goods and services (such as dispute resolution) and influenced the selection of members of local soviets (councils). These local organizations also regulated informal economies through their ability to raise funds for local religious organizations and events.

Uzbekistan

After the collapse of the Soviet Union, the government of Uzbekistan under the leadership of Islam Karimov embarked on a state-building project that was a continuation of Soviet authoritarian policies, but which replaced the ruling Communist ideology with an authoritarian ideology justified in terms of local culture and practices. The government formalized mahallas as units of local governments so as to provide legitimacy for authoritarian practices. At the same time, it tried to use these organizations as a way to target social assistance.

Policies toward local self-governance resembled internal colonization, with the state seeking to assert direct control of communal and political life at every level. In the years after independence, the Karimov government formulated a law on subnational governance that placed mahallas firmly under government control. Rather than operating as independent, self-governing organizations sitting ambiguously between the community and the state, mahallas became instruments of the government. As formal units of government, mahallas were given a range of obligations they had to fulfill. Specifically, under a 1999 law, mahallas were required to select a leader (rais) to lead a mahalla committee. Mahallas were also to select an individual to serve as a *posbon* (literally, "defender of the people"). The posbon serves as a local informant who works closely with the Ministry of Interior and local security agencies to gather surveillance on citizens within the community. Rather than representing citizen interests to the state, the rais, the mahalla committee, and the posbon are all employees of the state.

In addition to surveillance, mahallas have taken on substantial administrative roles. Mahallas are now demarcated and serve as election precincts. A 1994 law on social welfare began to task mahallas with distributing public assistance to families. Mahalla committee members became responsible for targeting welfare assistance to the neediest families in their communities. Rather than establish a set formula for assistance, the law gave committee officials substantial leeway in determining beneficiaries through a decentralized and flexible system of targeting. Although analysis of such programs has been limited because of the inability to conduct research in Uzbekistan, household survey data indicate that the flexible scheme seems to have been effective in reaching the poorest. On the other hand, the program targets those of Central Asian ethnicities far better than it does minority groups. Decentralized decision making over government resources in an authoritarian environment has also led to some suspicion that targeted welfare assistance has led to corruption among mahalla committee members.

Although mahalla committees have become agents of the government, mahallas as social organizations continue to play an important role. Despite formalization, informal mahalla leaders continue to be selected by communities who elect mahalla leaders (Uzbek *oqsoqols*, white beards), who work together with mullahs to officiate rituals and resolve disputes. Conversely, formal mahalla committee members can play important roles in the spiritual and communal lives of citizens by organizing funerals, pilgrimages, and other life-cycle rituals.

Tajikistan

Community self-governance in Tajikistan was disrupted and transformed by a devastating civil war that left tens of thousands dead and resulted in large-scale internal migration. In the first few years after the conclusion of the war in 1997, the government in Dushanbe had a relatively laissez-faire attitude toward customary authority and self-governance. Unlike Uzbekistan, where the government actively sought to control and manipulate mahallas, the Emomali Rahmon government largely left these organizations to their own devices.

Initially, the government of Tajikistan sent strong signals that it wanted to devolve some decision making over local governing arrangements to the local level. It embarked on an ambitious local government reform that effectively dismantled Soviet-era village committees and created larger consolidated units at the subdistrict level. This appeared to be a recognition by Tajik government authorities that they could not afford the massive scope of the state they had inherited. The government adopted a new law on local governance that created a new administrative unit, the *jamoat*. This is a subunit of district government (effectively a fourth tier of government). The government did not replace village committees but instead left communities to govern themselves. Unlike Uzbekistan, which formalized mahallas, the move to create jamoats as an aggregation of villages seemed to be a move toward allowing more community autonomy. In 2008, however, the government adopted a law that gave the government some discretion to regulate "public self-initiative" bodies including mahallas. Although the government has the right to register mahallas, this has not been done in practice.

Associational life at the community level has been a bright spot in an otherwise authoritarian landscape. The government has become authoritarian in recent years, suppressing dissent at every level. Despite this, mahallas remain an important source of self-governance.

According to a 2013 survey across rural Tajikistan, most citizens believed that mahallas were accountable to citizens more than all other local governing institutions. When asked whether mahalla committees work for the community or for the state, 75 percent of respondents said they work for the community, 17 percent said they work for the community and the state, while just 5 percent said they work solely on behalf of the state. Finally, more than three-fourths of respondents indicated that someone on the mahalla committee had provided guidance to people in the community during the past year.

Mahalla governance has been able to coexist with an authoritarian state. These survey data indicate that, for many public goods and services, individuals turn to mahallas more than they turn to the state. Just as in Uzbekistan, an informal mahalla exists alongside formal mahalla committee structures. According to this 2013 survey, 40 percent of respondents said customary leaders are often involved in dispute resolution and other matters at the community level.

Migration has had an important role on gender dynamics within mahalla life in Tajikistan. Because millions of Tajik men migrate to Russia and other Central Asian republics for work, women appear to be taking on important leadership roles that were once reserved for men within mahallas. For example, in the same survey, nearly two-thirds of respondents indicated that there are women members on the mahalla committee. Women are also leading mahalla committees in large numbers in the absence of men.

Afghanistan

Despite violent upheaval, community-based customary authority remains a vibrant source of self-governance in Afghanistan. After 2001 the newly established Government of the Islamic Republic of Afghanistan began to consider how to deal with customary authority. Government officials and international patrons supporting the state-building effort after 2001 made two contradictory assumptions about customary authority, both of which shaped future policy. Some assumed it had withered away during previous decades of conflict. This meant that there was a complete social vacuum in Afghan villages. Another perspective maintained by some government officials and many Western donors was that this authority remained and served as an obstacle to democracy and local development. As a result, with billions of dollars in assistance from the World Bank and other donors, the Afghan government tried to create new community development councils. The Afghan Ministry of Rural Rehabilitation and Development, which implemented these new councils, reported that these new councils were a new form of government that would serve "as a viable alternative to the traditional local governance structure[s]" and a "vehicle to re-build the social fabric and relationships at the grassroots level."

Just as in the former Soviet republics of Tajikistan and Uzbekistan, self-governance remains most salient at the community level. And just as in Uzbekistan and Tajikistan, a large village can consist of several mahallas with a distinct set of decision makers (also known as "white beards"). Despite efforts to formalize these bodies during the Soviet period, these organizations in Tajikistan have embarked upon a unique path.

Both public opinion and ethnographic work collected over the past fifteen years in Afghanistan demonstrate the resilience of customary governing organizations in both urban and rural areas. Although central government authorities in Kabul actively sought to replace customary authority, customary organizations and leaders have remained steadfast. According to most public opinion surveys, customary authorities remain among the most trusted public organizations in the country. In 2017 customary councils had the highest level of support of any public organization, except for religious leaders. With 66 percent of the population stating they have some or a lot of confidence in these organizations, they are far more trusted than government ministers (36 percent) or domestic (48 percent) or international NGOs (42 percent). Similarly, 82 percent of respondents in this survey said customary councils are fair and to be trusted. When individuals reported having a dispute, 67 percent took their dispute to customary community leaders.

•

Governments in Central Eurasia have employed customary authority in different ways that have promoted distinct visions of local development and, to some extent, a new nationalism. In Uzbekistan the government sought to formalize mahallas so as to promote a cohesive national identity as well as to promote local control over communities. Strong-handed policies that formalized customary organizations undermined their legitimacy. The government of Tajikistan realized its fiscal limits and took a hands-off approach to customary authority, at least in the first twenty years after independence. It allowed local organizations to flourish but did not seek direct control over their activities. The laissez-faire approach witnessed in Tajikistan until recently may have been a more fruitful approach to maintaining citizen voice, but under the growing authoritarianism such freedom was fleeting.

JENNIFER BRICK MURTAZASHVILI

In Afghanistan, Western-oriented government officials sought to weaken the role played by customary authority in order to promote a new, uniform social order based on a centralized state. Efforts to replace customary organizations with state-backed solutions in Afghanistan have proved a costly failure. Despite efforts to ignore, replace, or work around customary authority in the region, their role has never been as important as it is today.

CASE VII-C

Lineage Associations and Informal Politics in Mapping Kyrgyz Leadership

Aksana Ismailbekova

Kyrgyzstan is a kinship rich society. In this patrilineal society a Kyrgyz man's identification is relational, meaning that he cannot be identified as Kyrgyz without being linked to other male relatives such as fathers, grandfathers, and forefathers. More specifically, the Kyrgyz view their lineage identity or ancestral belonging as a given or natural part of identity, thus it cannot be changed, removed, or left out of any matter. Exclusion of any kind from such lineages equates with an existential threat to being a man, of not being identified as Kyrgyz any more, and being marginalized from the extended networks of kinsmen. Such exclusion also equates with the betrayal of one's family, children, and community.

In Kyrgyz genealogy there are forty lineages that unite all Kyrgyz people as a nation. Kyrgyz people believe that they stem from lineages that were headed by the respected elders of lineage groups (*aksakal*). During the Soviet times such lineages were banned, being considered backward and regressive in public and mass media. Nonetheless, people continued to rely on kinship networks. Although kinship was spoken of as being backward, the underlying reason for its prohibition was that the lineage networks were those most able to push back against the state. Lineage groups or descent groups in Kyrgyzstan were not destroyed or eradicated during the Soviet era; rather, kinship was preserved and incorporated into the Soviet state and economic structures—e.g., collective farms (*kolkhoz*) and state farms (*sovkhoz*) and other institutions—partially because kinship was so embedded in the local culture and mode of life.

In post-Soviet Kyrgyzstan, however, kinship systems have continued to flourish and function because they are compatible with the nation-building project of the state and because the state itself is not strong enough to oppose kinship groups. Consequently, these lineage groups deeply penetrate contemporary Kyrgyz politics, and the increasingly visible and organized forms that lineage seems to be taking in Kyrgyz politics and society in the guise of lineage associations. Relationships of trust are possible in these types of associations in ways that are not found in the state.

These lineage associations not only promote local culture and tradition, they also function as mutual aid societies, providing jobs and support to individuals in need. These associations have become much more than just self-help organizations. They hold their own congresses and sports events; they have their own consulates, their own youth wings and women's divisions, and their own symbols. They even play a critical role in the process of electoral mobilization and penetrate deeply into institutions. In short, they almost function as lobbies or even as quasi-political parties. Close observations of the functioning of lineage associations highlight the dynamic relationship between modernity and traditionalism. One can discover modernity at the level of "modern" associations, formal meetings, registrations, and slogans and yet discover traditionalism at the level of lineages, kin networks, and local cultural values.

There are forty Kyrgyz lineages, and each one has its own unique history, with its own genealogy. The forty lineages are divided into three political factions: left wing (*sol kanat*), right wing (*ong kanat*), and internal wing (*ichkilik*). Each wing has its own consulate (*ordo kengesh*). The lineage associations have forty lineage leaders, each of whom is entitled to be represented at the state, business, and community level. These lineage associations are united under the umbrella of the Kyrgyz People's Unification Associations. Each faction and each lineage association has its own respected leader, with the head of the Kyrgyz People's Unification Association being appointed annually from among the heads of each division. In other words, every year there is a change of leadership by faction. The heads of the factions and representatives of each lineage meet regularly and discuss many questions and issues, such as producing genealogical books, promoting young people's politics, and discussing means of supporting each other in times of need.

To give a sense of how these associations work, I turn to the Sarybagysh lineage, which has a particularly rich history. In 2014, for example, a former head of the State National Security Committee, Keneshbek Duyshebaev, was elected head of the Sarybagysh lineage group. In summer of 2014, an informal gathering (*kurultai*) of the Sarybagysh lineage was held on the shore of Lake Issyk Kul, with the participation of almost 450 people. Delegates from the Sarybagysh lineage included historians, public figures, politicians, businessmen, thirty-nine elders representating the other Kyrgyz thirty-nine lineages, and some members of parliament; all were selected based on their professional qualifications. They met and shared their thoughts on electing Duyshebaev as the leader of the lineage. According to Duyshebaev, together with close colleagues and associates, they established a public association known as Sarybagysh—Tagay bij uulu. The declared agenda of the project was to clarify the history of their own ancestors in genealogy and to educate the younger generation in the basics of kinship values as inherited from their forefathers.

At the end of the meeting, they read the Qur'an in memory of the heroes of their lineage such as Tagay Byi, Manap Byi, and Kalygul. This is a common practice among Kyrgyz when they pray for their ancestors by reciting Qur'an. During the informal gathering, according to Duyshebaev, the meeting was not convened for discussions about the unification of the Sarybagysh lineage; rather, the point of the gathering was simply to get to know each other better. At this kurultai there was no talk of politics. The main discussion concerned the friendship of all Kyrgyz people. At present, the lineage association is involved in a project to publish books about famous people from the Sarybagysh lineage. Members are also actively engaged in efforts to unite lineages and promote peace and cooperation among the lineages.

According to the Sarybagysh lineage association's leader: "It is important to preserve the unique phenomenon of our lineages and genealogies, that have been preserved for centuries. The importance of Kyrgyz kinship is that children should know their seven fathers and the need to transfer the genealogical knowledge to the offspring is great." However, according to some reports, during the kurultai people also discussed preparations for the upcoming (at the time) 2017 presidential election. More precisely, they discussed the possibility of nominating a candidate for the presidential elections from the Sarybagysh lineage—such as Kanat Isaev, who has served as mayor of Tokmok, Chuy Oblast governor, and deputy of two convocations of the Kyrgyz parliament and is seen as an experienced politician whose reputation has been growing among the Kyrgyz people. It is said that a well-known psychic, Melis Karybekov, told people that the next president would be a representative of the Sarybagysh lineage. But just before the presidential elections in October 2017, Isaev was arrested on suspicion of preparing a forcible seizure of power. Following the kurultai meeting, the lineage members did not put Isaev forward as candidate for president, but they declared that if he decided to run for president, then the lineage would support him, just as they had supported then president Almaz Atambaev, who belongs to the Kytai lineage. In spite of the difficulties that former president Kurmanbek Bakiev's behavior caused the lineage associations, it appears that lineage associations are still heavily involved in selecting possible presidential candidates.

The lineage associations are legal entities in Kyrgyzstan. Their main mission is to promote local culture and tradition, thereby contributing to the nation-building project of Kyrgyzstan. However, the lineage associations are engaged in politics, which is not allowed according to law. They get around questions of legality by conducting their politically oriented activities in informal ways.

The duality of lineage associations also consists in the fact that there is still a lingering sense in Kyrgyzstan that open politics by the lineage associations should be taboo since it openly promotes principles of cronyism in society and politics. In other words, the dualism of lineage associations is based on how they support culture and tradition but also advance a political agenda. Nonetheless, this is the reality of the situation because of the linkage of conceptions of genealogies in constructing nationalist symbols and national identity. Indeed, there is an older Soviet-educated generation of people who view these associations in a strongly negative way, even though they themselves function as part of these networks. A group of members of the older generation (above fifty years old)—imbued with strong Soviet propaganda, education, and knowledge—continue to consider lineage association as criminal, savage, and a betrayal of modern society. However, members of this group of Soviet-educated elders are nevertheless part of the large extended networks, and they actively participate in the life-cycle events of their own relatives. They would prefer such networks to be private, domestic, and small. The reality is that the lineage associations are increasingly gaining and striving for open forms within Kyrgyz politics and society, controlling patronage, mobilizing voters, organizing protests, and inhabiting various parts of the state bureaucracy.

Some have called for the associations to come out of the shadows and take on a formal, legal, constitutional role, including even the creation of a national kurultai based on the associations. In contrast, some representatives of NGOs, state authorities, politicians, and local political experts view the lineage associations through a prism of tribalism and backwardness. I argue that the lineage associations function as a kind of constraint and control mechanism on the political sphere, ensuring that no single leader is able to gain sufficient power to become a dictator. At the same time, the associations help contain local corruption. Many members use their lineage associations as a starting point for finding solutions for a number of problems, ranging from finding jobs to getting access to medical treatment and hospitals.

Questions remain as to whether the associations should take on a more open formal role in Kyrgyz politics or should continue as informal entities behind the scenes. Underlying this debate is the question as to whether it would be better for political stability if the lineage associations operated behind the scenes or in a more formal role in the political structure. Either way it seems that lineage associations will not disappear from the political scene. And there would be enormous risks involved in politicalizing lineage by bringing it out of the closet and into the open. Thus, the stability of Kyrgyzstan may in fact depend on the continued functioning of this duality with regard to lineage and the persistence of informal politics. The tension between formal and informal political influence is important yet often overlooked when focusing on state-approved actors.

DISCUSSION QUESTIONS

PART VII: CONTEXTS OF VISION

25. Media

1. In what way does the historical legacy of the Soviet Union still define how the media in Central Asia function and operate? What are some ways to reduce and mitigate those consequences and make the media truly independent?

2. The author lists some direct and indirect forms of media control as practiced in Central Asia. Can you give some examples of those, and perhaps other forms of media control, from your country? What do these examples tell us about the importance that governments assign to media and what are some ways for the media to avoid control? What do you think is the future of media in the region and what are the most important tendencies—digitalization, democratization, diversification of ownership, etc.—that will shape it?

26. National Identity

3. In your country, what are some ways that different aspects of identity such as religion, ethnicity, and gender come up in arguments about how people dress, what music people listen to, or what is good or bad art in your country? Are some of these controversies about having a modern versus a traditional national identity?

4. What do you think Central Asian governments and elites should do about national identity so that it does not become violent nationalism? Pick one government, think about what problems this government is struggling with and what its current approach is, and offer one policy reform or program that you think might help.

27. Environment

5. How do competing interests on the environment play out at local, national, and regional levels? How does this impact our thinking about environmental risks and opportunities?

6. Talk through the various ways in which the environment has been manipulated and the different levels of impact such changes have had on different parts of the population. From a local perspective, are there different ways of thinking about the environment that could improve the relationship people have with it?

28. Development

7.   What evidence do you see that development donors and agencies are interested in changing the cultures (i.e., values, practices) of the societies in which they operate, as opposed to promoting purely material changes? In your view, is it problematic when donors try to change the culture in foreign societies? Why or why not?

8.   What goals, selfish and otherwise, motivate donors to send aid to foreign countries? In your view, what goals are justified in motivating donors and what goals are problematic?

Case VII-A: Governing Extremism through Communities in Tajikistan

9.   What are the similarities and differences between the community-based approaches described in this case and approaches to violent extremism in other parts of the world?

10.   To what extent do government counter extremism policies continue to be shaped by the Soviet past?

Case VII-B: Customary Governance and the State in Central Eurasia

11.   Do you think that customary village governance is compatible with the existence of modern states?

12.   What do you think are some of the drawbacks of local community structures?

Case VII-C: Lineage Associations and Informal Politics in Mapping Kyrgyz Leadership

13.   Kyrgyzstan is not the only society in the region or in the world to consist of myriad lineage groups. Instead of pretending that this facet does not exist, imagine openly recognizing and addressing—even accommodating politically—the functional role of kinship networks in Kyrgyzstan. How should we think about the negative and positive associations of lineage ties?

14.   How do lineage ties and informal politics accommodate to and/or influence local and national challenges? What do we miss by not considering the implications of informal relationships in assessing political structures?

FURTHER READING

25. Media

Eurasianet. https://eurasianet.org/.

Freedman, Eric, and Richard Shafer, eds. *After the Czars and Commissars: Journalism in Authoritarian Post-Soviet Central Asia.* East Lansing: Michigan State University, 2011.

Institute for War and Peace Reporting, Central Asian Bureau for Analytical Reporting (CABAR). https://cabar.asia/en/#.

Institute for War and Peace Reporting. "How Central Asia Gets Its News." October 2, 2019. https://iwpr.net/global-voices/how-central-asia-gets-its-news.

Khalilova, Aziza. "Mass Media of Uzbekistan: Development from the First Years of Independence and Current Condition." *International Journal of African and Asian Studies* 36 (2017): 55–57.

Kulikova, Svetlana. "Not by Ideology Alone: History and Development of Radio in Russia." In *The Palgrave Handbook of Global Radio*, edited by John Allen Hendricks, 244–72. London: Palgrave 2012.

Kurambayev, Bahtiyar, and Eric Freedman. "Ethics and Journalism in Central Asia: A Comparative Study of Kazakhstan, Kyrgyzstan, Tajikistan and Uzbekistan." *Journal of Media Ethics* 35, no. 1 (2020): 31–44.

Rollberg, Peter, and Marlène Laruelle. "The Media Landscape in Central Asia: Introduction to the Special Issue." *Demokratizatsiya: The Journal of Post-Soviet Democratization* 23, no. 3 (2015): 227–32.

26. National Identity

Finke, Peter. *Variations on Uzbek Identity: Strategic Choices, Cognitive Schemas and Political Constraints in Identification Processes.* New York: Berghahn Books, 2014.

Gullette, David, and John Heathershaw. "The Affective Politics of Sovereignty: Reflecting on the 2010 Conflict in Kyrgyzstan." *Nationalities Papers* 43, no. 1 (2015): 122–39.

Kudaibergenova, Diana T. "'My Silk Road to You': Re-imagining Routes, Roads, and Geography in Contemporary Art of 'Central Asia.'" *Journal of Eurasian Studies* 8, no. 1 (2017): 31–43.

Kudaibergenova, Diana T. "Punk Shamanism, Revolt and Break-up of Traditional Linkage: The Waves of Cultural Production in Post-Soviet Kazakhstan." *European Journal of Cultural Studies* 21, no. 4 (2017): 435–51.

Murzakulova, Asel, and John Schoeberlein. "The Invention of Legitimacy: Struggles in Kyrgyzstan to Craft an Effective Nation-State Ideology." In *Symbolism and Power in Central Asia: Politics of the Spectacular*, edited by Sally N. Cummings, 144–63. London: Routledge, 2010.

Marat, Erica. "'We Disputed Every Word': How Kyrgyzstan's Moderates Tame Ethnic Nationalism." *Nations and Nationalism* 22, no. 2 (2016): 305–24.

Rancier, Megan. "'The Spirit of Tengri': Contemporary Ethnic Music Festivals and Cultural Politics in Kazakhstan." In *Kazakhstan in the Making: Legitimacy, Symbols, and Social Changes*, edited by Marlène Laruelle, 229–46. Lanham, MD: Lexington Books, 2016.

Suyarkulova, Mohira. "Fashioning the Nation: Gender and Politics of Dress in Contemporary Kyrgyzstan." *Nationalities Papers* 44, no. 2 (2016): 247–65.

27. Environment

Agyeman, Julian, and Yelena Ogneva-Himmelberger, eds. *Environmental Justice and Sustainability in the Former Soviet Union.* Cambridge, MA: MIT Press, 2009.

Bichsel, Christine. *Conflict Transformation in Central Asia: Irrigation Disputes in the Ferghana Valley.* London: Routledge, 2009.

Brown, Kathryn L. *Plutopia: Nuclear Families, Atomic Cities, and the Great Soviet and American Plutonium Disasters.* New York: Oxford University Press, 2013.

Féaux de la Croix, Jeanne. *Iconic Places in Central Asia: The Moral Geography of Dams, Pastures and Holy Sites.* Bielefeld: Transcript, 2016.

Freedman, Eric, and Mark Neuzil, eds. *Environmental Crises in Central Asia: From Steppes to Seas, from Deserts to Glaciers.* New York: Routledge, 2015.

Humphrey, Caroline, and David Sneath. *The End of Nomadism? Society, State, and the Environment in Inner Asia.* Durham, NC: Duke University Press, 1999.

Kalinovsky, Artemy M. *Laboratory of Socialist Development: Cold War Politics and Decolonization in Soviet Tajikistan.* Ithaca, NY: Cornell University Press, 2018.

Peterson, Maya K. *Pipe Dreams: Water and Empire in Central Asia's Aral Sea Basin.* Cambridge: Cambridge University Press, 2019.

Rumer, Boris. *Soviet Central Asia: 'A Tragic Experiment'.* New York: Routledge Press, 1990.

Wooden, Amanda E. "Another Way of Saying Enough: Environmental Concern and Popular Mobilization in Kyrgyzstan." *Post-Soviet Affairs* 29, no. 4 (2013): 314–53.

28. Development

Acemoglu, Daron, and James A. Robinson. *Why Nations Fail: The Origins of Power, Prosperity, and Poverty.* New York: Crown, 2012.

Allworth, Edward, ed. *Central Asia: One Hundred Thirty Years of Russian Dominance, A Historical Overview.* 3rd ed. Durham, NC: Duke University Press, 1994.

Ancker, Svetlana, and Bernd Rechel. "'Donors Are Not Interested in Reality': The Interplay between International Donors and Local NGOs in Kyrgyzstan's HIV/AIDS Sector." *Central Asian Survey* 34, no. 4 (2015): 516–30.

Atlani-Duault, Laëtitia. *Humanitarian Aid in Post-Soviet Countries: An Anthropological Perspective.* Translated by Andrew Wilson. London: Routledge, 2007.

Babajanian, Babken. "Promoting Empowerment? The World Bank's Village Investment Project in Kyrgyzstan." *Central Asian Survey* 34, no. 4 (2015): 499–515.

Borbieva, Noor O'Neill. *Visions of Development in Central Asia: Revitalizing the Culture Concept.* Lanham, MD: Lexington Books, 2019.

Cieślewska, Anna. *Community, the State and Development Assistance: Transforming the Mahalla in Tajikistan.* Kraków: Księgarnia Akademicka, 2015.

Cooley, Alexander, and John Heathershaw. *Dictators without Borders: Power and Money in Central Asia.* New Haven, CT: Yale University Press, 2017.

Deaton, Angus. *The Great Escape: Health, Wealth, and the Origins of Inequality.* Princeton, NJ: Princeton University Press, 2013.

Féaux de la Croix, Jeanne. "How to Build a Better Future? Kyrgyzstani Development Workers and the 'Knowledge Transfer' Strategy." *Central Asian Survey* 32, no. 4 (2013): 448–61.

Kavalski, Emilian, ed. *Stable Outside, Fragile Inside? Post-Soviet Statehood in Central Asia.* Farnham, Surrey, UK: Ashgate, 2010.

Laruelle, Marlène, and Sébastien Peyrouse. *Globalizing Central Asia: Geopolitics and the Challenges of Economic Development.* London: Routledge, 2015.

Petric, Boris. *Where Are All Our Sheep? Kyrgyzstan, a Global Political Arena.* Translated by Cynthia Schoch. New York: Berghahn Books, 2015.

Radnitz, Scott. *Weapons of the Wealthy: Predatory Regimes and Elite-Led Protests in Central Asia.* Ithaca, NY: Cornell University Press, 2010.

Reeves, Madeleine. *Border Work: Spatial Lives of the State in Rural Central Asia.* Ithaca, NY: Cornell University Press, 2014.

Rist, Gilbert. *The History of Development: From Western Origins to Global Faith.* Translated by Patrick Camiller. 3rd ed. London: Zed Books, 2008.

Rostow, W. W. "The Stages of Economic Growth." *Economic History Review*, n.s., 12, no. 1 (1959): 1–16.

Spector, Regine A. *Order at the Bazaar: Power and Trade in Central Asia*. Ithaca, NY: Cornell University Press, 2017.

Walzer, Michael. "The Idea of Civil Society: A Path to Social Reconstruction." *Dissent* 38 (1991): 293–304.

Yilamu, Wumaier. *Neoliberalism and Post-Soviet Transition: Kazakhstan and Uzbekistan*. Cham, Switzerland: Palgrave Macmillan, 2018.

Case VII-A: Governing Extremism through Communities in Tajikistan

Lemon, Edward, and Hélène Thibault. "Counter-extremism, Power and Authoritarian Governance in Tajikistan." *Central Asian Survey* 37, no. 1 (2018): 137–59.

Montgomery, David W., and John Heathershaw. "Islam, Secularism and Danger: A Reconsideration of the Link between Religiosity, Radicalism and Rebellion in Central Asia." *Religion, State and Society* 44, no. 3 (2016): 192–218.

Rasanayagam, Johan. "Counter-extremism, Secularism and the Category of Religion in the United Kingdom and Uzbekistan: Should We Be Studying Islam at All?" In *Constructing the Uzbek State: Narratives of Post-Soviet Years*, edited by Marlène Laruelle, 151–68. Lanham, MD: Lexington Books, 2017.

Tucker, Noah. "Terrorism without a God: Reconsidering Radicalization and Counter-Radicalization Models in Central Asia." CAP Papers, no. 225. Central Asia Program, Institute for European, Russian, and Eurasian Studies, George Washington University, September 2019.

Case VII-B: Customary Governance and the State in Central Eurasia

Ahmed, Akbar S. *The Thistle and the Drone: How America's War on Terror Became a Global War on Tribal Islam*. Washington, DC: Brookings Institution Press, 2013.

Allan, Nigel J. R. "Defining Place and People in Afghanistan." *Post-Soviet Geography and Economics* 42, no. 8 (2001): 545–60.

Cieslewska, Anna. *Community, the State and Development Assistance Transforming the Mahalla in Tajikistan*. Krakow: Archeobooks, 2015.

Dadabaev, Timur. "Community Life, Memory and a Changing Nature of Mahalla Identity in Uzbekistan." *Journal of Eurasian Studies* 4, no. 2 (2013): 181–96.

Gaston, Erica, Akbar Sarwari, and Arne Strand. "Lessons Learned on Traditional Dispute Resolution in Afghanistan." United States Institute of Peace, Building Peace no. 3, April 2013. https://www.usip.org/sites/default/files/Traditional_Dispute_Resolution_April2013.pdf.

Murtazashvili, Jennifer Brick. *Informal Order and the State in Afghanistan*. New York: Cambridge University Press, 2016.

Nojumi, Neamatollah, Dyan Mazurana, and Elizabeth Stites. *Afghanistan's Systems of Justice: Formal, Traditional, and Customary*. Medford, MA: Tufts University, Feinstein International Famine Center, 2004.

Shahrani, M. Nazif, and Robert L. Canfield, eds. *Revolutions and Rebellions in Afghanistan: Anthropological Perspectives*. Berkeley: University of California Press, 1984.

Urinboyev, Rustamjon, and Måns Svensson. "Corruption, Social Norms and Everyday Life in Uzbekistan." In *Corruption and Norms: Why Informal*

Rules Matter, edited by Ina Kubbe and Annika Engelbert, 187–210. Cham, Switzerland: Springer International, 2018.

Wardak, Ali. "Building a Post-war Justice System in Afghanistan." *Crime, Law and Social Change* 41, no. 4 (2004): 319–41.

Case VII-C: Lineage Associations and Informal Politics in Mapping Kyrgyz Leadership

Gullette, David. *The Genealogical Construction of the Kyrgyz Republic: Kinship, State, and "Tribalism"*. Folkestone, Kent, UK: Global Oriental, 2010.

Ismailbekova, Aksana. *Blood Ties and the Native Son: Poetics of Patronage in Kyrgyzstan*. Bloomington: Indiana University Press, 2017.

Ismailbekova, Aksana. "Mapping Lineage Leadership in Kyrgyzstan: Lineage Associations and Informal Governance." *Zeitschrift für Ethnologie* 143, no. 2 (2018): 195–220.

Jacquesson, Svetlana. "Power Play among the Kyrgyz: State versus Descent." In *Representing Power in Modern Inner Asia: Conventions, Alternatives and Opposition*, edited by Isabelle Charleux, Grégory Delaplace, Roberte Hamayon, and Scott Pearce, 221–44. Bellingham: Western Washington University, Centre for East Asian Studies, 2010.

Light, Nathan. "Genealogy, History, Nation." *Nationalities Papers* 39, no. 1 (2011): 33–53.

Roy, Olivier. *New Central Asia: The Creation of Nations*. New York: New York University Press, 2007.

PART VIII

CONTEXTS OF AESTHETICS

Contexts are taught, learned, and experienced, but it is through translation that they are shared. Most often, we think of translation in terms of language, but words are only part of the effort to convey meaning. Here, we look at aesthetics as a form of translating context. The aesthetic frame gives commentary on history and the human condition, critiquing the structures (and structural constraints) of life and its struggles more broadly. Often, it offers new ways of interpreting and sharing experience, as well as new ways of thinking about where and who we are. The aesthetics of experience are captured in various ways, but here we look at music, art, literature, and film—forms of communication central to the development of social life yet also often part of the backdrop in which earlier parts of this volume play out.

In his chapter, Will Sumits gives us a sense of the ways in which meaning is conveyed through sound. We see a diversity of musical traditions across the region and the emergence of musical geographies, including the classical musical traditions of sedentary urban societies and the epic singing traditions of nomadic societies. We also see how music evolves in response to the social and political environments out of which it is created, giving us an appreciation for the dynamic context from which expression emerges.

Aliya de Tiesenhausen similarly connects creativity to social and political experience, focusing on the context of the globalization of the art scene. Art emerges as one of the earliest expressions of the profound, and from the Bronze Age onward, we see how it plays a role in the production of culture and the facilitation of meaning. And, as Tiesenhausen shows, art is not only a record of aesthetic tastes but also a record of tension, control, and protest.

The same, though in a different form, could be said of literature. Ranging the emotional spectrum, it conveys the most basic of sentiments associated with sociality, from hope to despair, and often shapes how people understand experience. In their chapter, Rebecca Gould and Amier Saidula look at the emergence of literature in form but also, importantly, situate literature of the region more broadly as world literature. In doing this, they highlight the breadth of literature's significance and show how it emerges out of dominant traditions—Turkic, Persian, Arabic—not of nationality. Yet as thematic genres form, we see the beginnings of national identity in

617

literature and within literature; as elsewhere, the categories themselves are contested.

More recent as an aesthetic form, film has been an influential medium in shaping the public imagination. Charting the emergence of Central Asian cinematography from the early 1900s, Michael Rouland shows how film evolved from then to the present. Often with dual purpose, we see how film is used to entertain and convey political messages, to inform and inspire imagination about everyday life, both universal and unique to the nation.

Taken together, aesthetics is central to understanding the creative relationship between context and meaning. In Artemy Kalinovsky's case, we see the lasting effects of the Soviet cultural project played out in Tajikistan. Tanya Merchant explores the dutar as an instrument that evolved into "traditional" and "folk" variants as part of a Soviet agenda, yet in Uzbek ensembles both are found negotiating the sonic space. Georgy Mamedov takes the transforming nature of aesthetics a step further, showing how a radical art project in Kyrgyzstan used science fiction as a medium to imagine societies where gender and sexual discrimination ceased being the dominant experience of many in contemporary society.

A concern of this book has been how contexts are translated to action. Mamedov's case takes us a step in the direction of applying insights of aesthetic context to influencing social change, but this is a theme that underlies all the contributions in this section. Thus, it is important to appreciate the transformative nature of aesthetics on understanding, for it is out of the imaginative space in art that new ways of living evolve.

29

Music

Will Sumits

Men and women begin arriving at a teahouse tucked away on a side street in a central neighborhood of Tashkent. Passing through a small entrance and quaint dining room, they meander through the back door that opens to a large courtyard filled with traditional *tapchan* platforms that serve both as seats and tables. Tonight, one of them will also become an impromptu stage. Although they have arrived empty-handed, most of them share one thing in common; they are musicians. It is the evening of an important national holiday, and a concert of *maqom* music has recently ended at the nearby National Conservatory. Now the musicians, teachers, and some students have gathered for food and conversation, which will inevitably be accompanied by a bit of spontaneous music.

The music here in the teahouse differs greatly from the earlier concert performance. The members of the large orchestra, who were so formal and rigid on stage, have now begun to unwind. Their state-sponsored performance has segued to an unofficial gathering of friends and colleagues, and they are now less bound to their roles as official representatives of the "national" music of Uzbekistan. Here in the teahouse, a solitary musician accompanies himself on a long-necked lute with silk strings called a *dutar*. He is one of the old masters, well respected by all, and as he plays there is not a person who does not stop and listen attentively. The sounds of his fingers against the silk strings resound a crisp yet gentle melody full of subtle vibrato that meanders along descending valleys and ascending peaks until giving way to increasingly rapid tremolos at the culmination of the song.

Earlier in the day, at a local park not far from this teahouse, the holiday festivities had a very different musical performance on display. A young

Kazakh in a shiny neon-blue polyester costume, covered in traditional motifs and embroidered with glittery thread, swings his arm around and around playing an imaginary air *dombra* as he shouts didactic lyrics of traditional songs from his homeland in the steppe to distorted techno beats blasting from an overamplified speaker system. The audience is an intriguing mix of people from different linguistic and cultural backgrounds found throughout Central Asia, and they appear semiattentive and mildly amused in a way that suggests they have previously seen dozens of similar performances.

At first glance, the musical worlds of Central Asia appear to be laden with contradictions: modern versus traditional, cosmopolitan versus nationalist, nomadic versus urban. But seeing the diversity of Central Asian music in terms of diametrically opposed ends of one simple spectrum masks much of the complex layering and musical diversity in the region. Between the antithetical boundaries of these musical worlds is a continuum of variegated musical strata that exist simultaneously in multiple contexts according to different political, social, cultural, and historical spheres that are perpetually interacting with one another.

Although we cannot hope to be exhaustive, we will explore several musical traditions that exemplify the diversity of musical textures that have been cultivated in Central Asia, and that can act as a window into the social, political, and historical circumstances that have helped shape the traditions up to the present day. For our purposes, it will suffice to consider two broad categories of music that seem to be on opposite ends of the musical spectrum in Central Asia: the "classical" maqom traditions of sedentary city dwellers and the epic singing traditions of the historically nomadic peoples of the steppes.

Musical Geographies of Central Asia

In the center of the largest landmass in the world, Central Asia has been a musical crossroads shaped by millennia of cultural interactions occurring in the wake of overland trade, migrations of peoples, and political conquests. Forgetting for a moment the political borders that have been in place for the past century, it may be helpful to view Central Asian musical forms with regard to language families and patterns of settlement. Turan, Sogdiana, and Transoxiana are all names that have been used to designate various regions within Central Asia. Turkestan was a name used by Persian geographers to refer to areas inhabited by Turkic peoples, and because of the ubiquity of Turkic languages and peoples that inhabit Central Asia, this name has often been used in reference to greater Central Asia. Around 90 percent of the inhabitants of Central Asia speak a Turkic language, while much of the remainder speaks forms of Persian. Similar to a language that is found in myriad dialects and accents, music throughout the region is also characterized by highly localized nuances. Aside from the many Turkic and Iranian ethnic subgroups in the region, there are also pockets of Arab, Caucasian, Jewish, Russian, and others that contribute to the culturally pluralistic makeup of Central Asian musical traditions. However, the sharpest stylistic divide in regard to musical forms parallels the differences between nomadic and settled lifestyles that are closely tied to the geography of the Central Asian landscape.

The regions long known as Transoxiana and Ferghana today comprise much of the independent republics of Uzbekistan and Tajikistan. This region between the Amu Darya and Syr Darya Rivers is home to ancient urban centers that have been important staging grounds in the development of the sciences, music, art, calligraphy, architecture, philosophy, and the spirituality of classical and medieval Islamic civilization. These cities served as a crossroads for traders, travelers, and pilgrims, and were home to local sedentary populations. They were centers of learning that yielded many figures notable for their contributions to the history of religion, science, and the arts. Bukhara, Samarkand (Samarqand), Khoqand (Kokand), Khujand, Khiva, and other cities were important political and artistic centers of the Timurid and Samanid empires, and were outposts of earlier Persian and Arabic empires. Since the sixteenth century, these cities were centers in the independent khanates and emirates of Bukhara, Khoqand, and Khiva, before they were eventually absorbed into the Soviet Union at the beginning of the twentieth century. This area of Transoxiana in southern Central Asia is characterized by primarily sedentary patterns of agriculture and urban development, and this has been a strong force guiding the development of the distinct musical aesthetics and traditions found therein.

The arid steppes and pasturelands to the north comprise the modern-day independent republics of Kazakhstan and Kyrgyzstan. There are some mountainous and forested regions along the easterly and southern borders of these countries, but the vast majority of the geography is not suited to agriculture. The populations inhabiting these areas have relied on a traditionally nomadic lifestyle based on pastoralism. The limitations on material culture that result from the strictures of nomadic life have made oral tradition indispensable among pastoralists. Music is the primary vehicle for the transmission of oral tradition. The political history of the past century has brought about a sharp decrease in pastoralism, but the nomadic lifestyle that persisted since time immemorial continues to be strong in the cultural memory of the Kazakh and Kyrgyz populations. Musical and epic traditions that developed out of oral culture continue to retain their place among the most highly valued art forms. Although the populations of modern-day Kazakhstan and Kyrgyzstan are largely sedentary today, the centuries of nomadic lifestyle that shaped their musical traditions are still evident.

As we will see, the differences between the settled lifestyle of urban populations and the itinerant nomadism of pastoral societies in many ways informs the stark contrast between epic oral traditions of the steppe and the classic and folk genres that have been cultivated in urban and rural agricultural societies. These differences notwithstanding, the nomadic and settled societies in Central Asia have much in common. Their close geographic proximity to one another has ensured a certain degree of cultural interaction, and shared linguistic roots have enabled a basic level of communication. While the cultural milieu of urban centers of learning have shaped the musical traditions according to an aesthetic framework that differs considerably from that of the pastoralists in the steppe, they share deep historical and cultural roots that place prime importance on oral tradition and reinforce social and spiritual mores through musical performance. Another commonality is their shared recent history as part of the Soviet Union and subsequent independence. The impact of Soviet ideology and policy on music over the course of the twentieth century is important to consider, as it is the historical prelude to the current state of traditional and modern music in the region.

The cultural pluralism that had long characterized the region in the precolonial era was defined largely through the diversity of clan affiliations, tribal unions, and ethnolinguistic subgroups existing under an overarching umbrella of shared religion and linguistic roots. Although linguistic affinities and tribal affiliations across the region have the potential to be a strong unifier, it was seen as a potential threat to Soviet sovereignty, and policies were put in place to segregate speakers of closely related languages. The political boundaries delineated by Soviet strategists in the early twentieth century were not an accurate reflection of the ethnolinguistic and cultural topography of the region. Fearing the unifying potential of religion and shared cultural traits to undermine the creation of the new proletariat culture of the Soviet state, the cultural strategists of the early Soviet era sought to suppress both clan-based tribal identities and religious identities through the creation of a distinct national consciousness for each of the five newly formed Soviet republics of Central Asia. Music became a powerful medium in actualizing these objectives and was used as a tool in creating national consciousness in all of the Central Asian republics.

As geopolitical borders were opaquely transposed upon the culturally pluralistic societies of Central Asia as part of Soviet nationalizing efforts, much of the tribal affiliation and clan diversity became obscured, paving the way for melting pots of national consciousness. Using nationality as a generic classification in discussions of traditional music can be problematic because it instantly positions the discussion within a political framework that alludes to the long and complex history of Russian colonialism and Soviet nation-building efforts. This is useful when discussing the politics of Soviet cultural policy and its effects on music in the twentieth century but can obfuscate discussions of musical history. Referring instead to precolonial monikers such as Turkestan, Transoxiana, or Sogdiana can often bypass the associations with twentieth-century Soviet history but may present readers with other challenges to properly contextualize the discussion with regard to the history, geography, and music of the region.

Similarly, when discussing the recent musical history of post-Soviet Central Asia, it is important to recognize how post-Soviet nation-building in these countries has perpetuated many of the same policies that were originally put in place to limit each state's autonomy at the beginning of the

Soviet era. Some historians and musicologists have bemoaned the coercive changes implemented under Soviet policy and its post-Soviet legacy. While it is true that Soviet-era policies on music did bring about significant changes in the ways music was performed, as well as its functions in society, these changes did not simply replace earlier models but added yet another layer to the multifaceted world of Central Asian music.

Classic Music Traditions of Sedentary Urban Societies

Maqom is a musical term that is imbued with prestige owing to its associations with the "classic" traditions that were cultivated around the court and at centers of learning and science. For much of the Islamic world, *maqām* refers to a musical mode and is closely associated with an elaborate theoretical system that defines a large corpus of musical modes used in the performance of art music. However, in Central Asia today, maqom refers to a suite form of musical performance that progresses through various rhythmic cycles and musical modes. It is also the name most commonly used to refer to the art music tradition as a whole, including the rhythms and modes that have been incorporated into a vast repertoire of pieces that have accumulated over the past centuries. The musical works that form the core repertoire of today's maqom suite performance traditions have their roots in earlier song forms and are closely tied to the theoretical maqām system of musical modes that was central to the "science of music" for more than a millennium. In Central Asia, the maqom traditions are practiced primarily in the urban centers of Transoxiana and Chinese Turkestan, but it is important to acknowledge the common history and theoretical foundation that they share with diverse maqām traditions scattered across the greater Middle East.

The development of the maqām system of musical modes is well documented in musical treatises and historical sources. The thirteenth through fifteenth centuries produced several brilliant musical theorists who were active at the imperial courts in Baghdad and Herat, and it is from their works that the modal system of maqām gradually expanded and became canonized. Due to the analytical and methodical approach employed by these theorists, they are often referred to in academic literature as the "Systematist school" of music theory. Their efforts resulted in a comprehensive system that classified more than a dozen species of tetrachords and pentachords, and more than one hundred different musical modes. A large corpus of rhythmic cycles and a variety of song forms were also detailed in their works. The music theory of the Systematist school serves as a historical bond that links many different maqām traditions across a wide geography. It is from this common foundation that the myriad maqām performance traditions evolved throughout the greater Middle East and Central Asia.

The Systematist school of theory reached its apex in Central Asia at the end of the fifteenth century. It was at the Timurid court of Husayn Bayqara (ruled 1470–1506) in Herat that the modal music theory of maqām reached its most fully developed form and became the foundation upon which today's maqom traditions developed in Central Asia and throughout the Middle East. Immediately following the end of Timurid rule in Herat, the talented musicians and artists that had congregated there began to disperse to other cities. Some of them returned to Bukhara and Samarkand. The musical treatises that were written in Bukhara during the sixteenth century show a direct link in the transmission of musical knowledge from the musical scholars of Timurid Herat at the end of the fifteenth century to the musicians active in Bukhara during the rule of the Shaybānid dynasty (1500–1598). These sixteenth-century treatises from Bukhara continue to describe the theoretical system of musical modes, but they lacked the mathematical precision that characterized the works of the previous century, instead espousing a simplified system for learning and performing the corpus of musical modes. These treatises described a core group of twelve maqāms, as well as secondary groups of twenty-four *shu'ba* and six *avāz*, both being groups of musical modes that were derived from the central group of twelve maqāms. These groups of musical modes, the twelve maqāms along with the twenty-four *shu'ba* and six *avāz*, became the accepted foundation of musical knowledge that was essential for musicians practicing the urban art music of Central Asia. The musical modes were held in high regard, not only because they represented the pinnacle of the erudite musical "science" of Islamic civilization, but because they possessed the capacity for evoking a wide array of emotional states in the listener. It is their inherent faculty as powerful emotive stimuli that have imbued the musical modes with an ability to express the ineffable.

Despite frequent mention of the established theoretical model of the maqām system in musical literature of the sixteenth and seventeenth centuries, the content of these treatises shows a gradual shift away from theory and an increased emphasis on musical performance. This shift from theory to practice in the musical literature may reflect the efforts of musicians to contribute to the achievements of earlier theorists by applying a systematic approach to the classification and structuring of the performance repertoires. It is from these works that we see the first indications of a tradition based on the performance of compound musical forms, or "suites" of music performed in sequences of different maqām modes. Several late seventeenth-century manuscripts describe a performance tradition based on the performance of four suites of music, called the *chahār shadd*. Each of these modal suites cycle through a long sequence of musical modes. This tradition of modal suite performance paved the way for the maqom traditions that would later appear in nineteenth-century texts. As the repertoire accumulated more and more pieces, and continued to develop specific guidelines for the structure of suite performance, several new suites grew out of the earlier body of four primary suites.

At some point the term *maqom* acquired an extended meaning in Central Asia and began to be used to refer to the suite form. Since the early nineteenth century, and still in modern-day Uzbekistan and Tajikistan, maqom refers to a suite form of music performance and also more generally to

29-1   **Kazakh musician playing dombra, late nineteenth century.**

the body of different musical suites of "classical" art music that forms the core repertoire of several local traditions. In Bukhara, Samarkand, and parts of Tajikistan, the tradition is referred to as *shashmaqom* and consists of six large suites of music. In Khoqand, Tashkent, and the Ferghana Valley, the tradition is referred to as *chormaqom* and consists of four primary suites and a body of other "classic" songs and mini-suites. In Khiva, there is a body of suites specific to the long-necked lute *dutor*, and these are known as the *dutor maqomlari*. In the first half of the nineteenth century, a Khivan court musician traveled to Bukhara and learned the known shashmaqom repertoire and brought it back to Khiva, where it was assimilated into the Khivan tradition and became known as the *alti-yarim* maqom tradition. The shashmaqom of Bukhara, the alti-yarim maqom of Khorezm, and the Ferghana maqom traditions can all be considered as distinct yet interrelated traditions that maintain their own musical identities while remaining a part of the overarching maqom phenomenon as it evolved in Central Asia.

Our understanding of the musical life of urban Central Asia during the pre-Soviet era is based on extant historical accounts, musical treatises, and song-text collections. Owing to the history and prestige that has long been attributed to the maqom traditions, it is often assumed that maqom performance was centered at the kingly and princely courts that were scattered across precolonial Turkestan. This assumption is due to the fact that the notoriety of talented musicians, and indeed of the tradition itself, was bolstered by their presence in the court, thereby imbuing the maqom tradition with an aura of regality. Furthermore, the extant musical literature was often the work of an intellectual elite that had direct or peripheral affiliations with the court. Educated musicians close to the court undoubtedly played an important role in organizing the repertoire into the canons of maqom suites as we know them, but it is very likely that the maqom traditions enjoyed a vibrant life outside of the official court settings as well. We know of many prominent maqom musicians from the nineteenth century, but very few of them are known to have had affiliations with the courts in Bukhara, Khoqand, or Khiva. In other words, the presence of musicians at the court does not preclude the existence of unsung heroes who escaped the annals of history. Even today, talented maqom musicians can be found in many villages and rural locales. Local musical heroes may not achieve the same notoriety as musicians in the capital cities who frequently appear on television and radio broadcasts, but their contributions to the living tradition are significant and can have a long-lasting and far-reaching impact. Today the various local maqom traditions in Central Asia comprise distinct repertoires yet share many characteristics. Most importantly, they share a common musical aesthetic that is informed by many of the same principles that have guided centuries of classical Persian and Turkic poetry in Central Asia, as well as the traditions of Islamic mysticism that have served as an important foundation of the spiritual and moral character of sedentary Central Asian populations. They all utilize many of the same musical instruments as well as common song structures and some rhythmic cycles. There is a large body of shared musical terminology denoting the names of musical modes, maqom suites, and rhythms, as well as theoretical and performance nomenclature. Many of the same melodies can be found, often in slightly divergent forms, shared among these various local maqom traditions.

The similarities in musical performance and aesthetics are a natural result of the geographical proximity of their respective populations, and a long history of interaction that has witnessed shifting empires, migrations, extensive trade both within and beyond the region, and the spread of religion, science, and art according to the historical trends of the time. However, these similarities do not obscure the differences that distinguish local traditions from those of their neighbors, or those of other traditions in the greater Middle East and Central Asia with which they share historical ties. Recognizing the differences between a maqom performance from Ferghana and that of Khiva is likely to be a difficult task for the uninitiated, but these seemingly subtle differences are easily apparent to musicians within the region.

One of the more overt distinguishing characteristics of these local traditions can be seen in the language of the sung poetry. For example, the shashmaqom tradition of Bukhara and Samarkand was historically sung in Persian-Tajik up until the early twentieth century. The extant nineteenth-century compilations of shashmaqom poetic texts, called *bayoz*, consist almost exclusively of Persian poems. Among the poets that were favored for shashmaqom performance were Rumi, Shams Tabrizi, Hilali, Jami, and many others. In the twentieth century, the ideology of Soviet policies on art and music brought about a large-scale nationalization effort whereby the Persian texts of the Bukharan shashmaqom tradition were systematically replaced with those of Turkic Chaghatai poets, such as those of Navai, Fuzuli, Nizami, and others. In this way, the patrimony of the Chaghatai Turkic poets of precolonial Turkestan was celebrated while simultaneously obfuscating the multilingual cosmopolitanism that had long characterized the urban centers of Central Asia. One of the primary aims of these efforts was the creation of a national "Uzbek" identity along with its "national music," which included not only the shashmaqom tradition but also the maqom and folk traditions of Khiva and the Ferghana Valley.

It was not only the language of the music that was affected by these policies, but a concerted effort to modernize the "archaic" aspects of the folk and maqom music in Central Asia was overseen by a team of international musicologists in collaboration with Soviet policy makers. The musicologists, which included Russian and Armenian specialists, conducted extensive studies of the local traditions and began to make changes to the instruments, the music intervals of the scales, the song lyrics, and performance contexts. For example, the fretting system of the traditional long-necked lutes *tanbur* and dutar were altered so that they no longer contained the microtones that were so characteristic of nineteenth-century performance, but instead were arranged according to diatonic and chromatic Western models. Instrument makers were asked to build new instruments that were based on traditional models but in varying sizes to accommodate the bass, tenor, alto, and soprano voices of western-style orchestral arrangements. Poetic texts were scrutinized and secularized, and new songs were composed to celebrate Uzbekistan's newly forged national identity.

Precolonial intellectuals in Central Asia had already begun the search for symbols of a national music identity, but it was the Soviet policy makers who fully developed and implemented concepts of cultural and musical "heritage" in the Central Asian states from the beginning of the Soviet era. Constructed notions of heritage served multiple purposes, the most important of which aimed to reconcile the traditional Islamic culture of the region with the creation of a proletarian class of the Socialist society. The ideas of "heritage," aside from their sociopolitical functions, were also instrumental in the efforts to collect, standardize, and canonize the musical "heritage" of the past. In effect, what had been a living tradition up until the dawn of the Soviet era began to be officially viewed as "heritage" from the past.

The subtle perceived difference between what constituted the "old" heritage of the past versus the "new" musical practices led some leading Uzbek musicians and musicologists to preserve the traditional repertoires in carefully edited collections of musical notations of both the classic maqom music and folk repertoires. These efforts may have immortalized the musical repertoires by preserving them for posterity, but in being preserved as the officially recognized versions they also became frozen in time. Some scholars have touted the adverse effects of Soviet cultural policy's constructed "national musical heritage" by suggesting that such preservation efforts have somehow extracted all of the lifeblood of the living tradition in ways that preclude innovation and new traditional compositions. Such conjectures are not unwarranted, but it should be remembered that the public performances of "national" music, both during the Soviet era as well as in present-day Central Asia, are exactly what they purport to be. The officially sponsored

Кокандъ. Сартянки-музыканты, пѣвицы.

29-2   Uzbek women playing dutar in the city of Khoqand, late nineteenth century.

"national" music is only one face of a tradition that extends far below the surface of these public performances and includes many other layers of living musical tradition that are far less vulnerable to the precepts of official policy.

In some cases, these other layers of the maqom and folk traditions become more apparent the further one strays from state political and cultural institutions such as the National Conservatory or Ministry of Culture. In villages and other rural locales, local musicians are further from the contemporary state sponsorship of music, but they are also further from the constraints of nationalist ideologies that continue to linger in the state apparatus of many post-Soviet countries of Central Asia. Paradoxically, it is often the Soviet-era "Houses of Culture" found in small towns all throughout the region that continue to serve as a meeting point for local musicians, and here the living tradition is often much more apparent, especially outside of official working hours. At gatherings of friends, it is not uncommon for a musician to sing one of his own compositions with a carefree abandon that is wholly inconsistent with the politically conditioned aesthetics of state-sponsored performances.

Epic Singing Traditions of Nomadic Societies

Moving north from the old cities and agrarian rural societies of Central Asia, we come across the vastly different landscape and cultural domain of the arid steppes, deserts, and mountains of Kyrgyzstan and Kazakhstan. As with the other Central Asian republics, the political borders do not always accurately reflect the shifting cultural boundaries of the historically nomadic groups that inhabit the region. The social structures and lifestyle of nomadic cultures have shaped their cultural expression, and the resulting musical aesthetics are considerably different from those of sedentary city-dwellers farther south. Widespread urbanization since the onset of the Soviet era has brought an end to much of the pastoral nomadism that had prevailed for centuries prior, but despite a newfound sedentary lifestyle, the aspects of musical tradition that are closely linked with a nomadic lifestyle have remained at the core of musical performance in modern-day Kazakhstan and Kyrgyzstan.

The cultural expression of the historically nomadic cultures of Central Asia, as with many nomadic cultures elsewhere in the world, is rooted in the oral tradition. The dichotomy between written and oral tradition is closely tied to differences in patterns of settlement and land usage. Oral tradition is present to varying degrees in all culture, but it is indispensable to nomadic cultures whose lifestyle offers less recourse to written texts, books, and libraries. Cultural histories, spiritual doctrines, moral teachings, folktales, mythologies, and eulogies are kept alive in the cultural memory through oral tradition, and in Central Asia this is most often accomplished through song. The many genres of song forms include ritual songs, lyrical songs, improvised poetic traditions, sung poetic competitions, and epic songs. Many of the genres of short song are also part of the repertoires of the epic singer, and are often included within the performance of epic song.

Central Asia is a land of epics. Epic song is an important form in both sedentary urban culture and nomadic societies, but the songs differ in that the epic forms of urban milieus are primarily lyric epics and are loosely tied to literary works, while historically nomadic peoples have preserved their epics orally. The nomadic epic singing traditions integrate cultural histories with tales of the heroic deeds of important historical and legendary figures, simultaneously conveying important moral lessons. As such, the epics themselves are repositories of cultural knowledge and history and can be considered as an intangible unwritten cultural encyclopedia preserved in the minds of the bards who transmit them. The bards are living guardians of cultural history and traditional wisdom whose role as carriers and transmitters of tradition has earned them a highly respected place in society. In addition to providing entertainment, they are also seen as teachers, spiritual guides, and pillars of cultural wisdom.

In the past, a bard was called an *irchi* (Kyrgyz) or a *zhyrau* (Kazakh), terms that loosely reflect the bard's roles as musician, oral poet, and epic singer. These terms are still used today, but since the late nineteenth century several other terms have been adopted that distinguish between the different roles fulfilled by the bard. The terms *jomokchu*, *tokmo aqin*, *jamakchi*, or *zhirshi* have gained usage to refer variously to epic singers and oral poet-musicians, although the different terms convey slight distinctions between their respective performance domains and repertoires. Similarly, Soviet pedagogy led local and Russian scholars to classify the various subgenres of musical performance and oral traditions in Kazakhstan and Kyrgyzstan. In the past, the epic had been a broadly defined genre that encompassed many of these subgenres, but the past century has witnessed a gradual stratification in both their classification and in the distinctions between the types of bards who perform them.

The intermingling of legend, history, tradition, and storytelling in the performance of epic song serves to transmit cultural knowledge and entertain at the same time. The distinction between *logos* and *mythos* was of concern in ancient Greek epistemology, and history and mythology have long been considered antithetical modes of explaining the past in academic scholarship. However, among traditionally nomadic societies, the boundaries of history and mythology are much more fluid. Without regular recourse to books, libraries, and paper, the peoples of the steppes of Central Asia are lacking a written history. For this reason, the retelling of history has fallen on bards who are less likely to be concerned with an accurate retelling of a factual history than with presenting a narrative that encapsulates important cultural ideas through a quasi-historical account of important events from the distant past. Recounting the heroic deeds of historical personages is done in much the same way as with legendary figures, and so the distinction between fact and fiction often becomes blurred in the oral histories of nomadic cultures.

For example, the well-known epic tale *Ker-Ogly* is considered to be one of the early Turkic epics and can be found in many versions from Turkey to western China. In Kazakhstan, the tale spans a timeline that stretches back into mythological time but also narrates historical events and battles from the sixteenth and seventeenth centuries. The miraculous birth of the hero Ker-Oglu is recounted in detail, and his deeds imbue him with both supernatural abilities and an infallible moral integrity. Also present in the Kazakh version are genealogical aspects linking Ker-Oglu with the Teke Jaumit tribal lineage, a lineage that also links most Kazakhs to one of the strongest of the twenty-four tribes of the Oghuz federation of Turkic tribes that was formed in the eighth century. The story of Ker-Ogly emphasizes bravery, heroism, loyalty, and justice through the mytho-historical narrative of a legendary hero and role model integral to the history of the Kazakh people. The epic reinforces the cultural and historical identity of the people and simultaneously bolsters social mores, all while providing a didactic form of entertainment rooted in oral tradition.

In much of Central Asia, epics are sung to musical accompaniment performed on a variety of plucked lutes. In Kazakhstan, epic singers accompany themselves on a two-stringed, long-necked lute called dombra (Kazakh *dombyra*), while Kyrgyz bards play a fretless plucked lute with three strings called *komuz*. Another distinguishing feature of epic performance is the use of a guttural singing style. There are a few exceptions, the most notable being that of the Kyrgyz epic tale *Manas*. The Manas epic is unique in that it has traditionally been recited without musical accompaniment and is not performed in a guttural recitative style. The performer of the Manas epic, known as a *manaschi*, does not consider their performance to be singing but rather as recitation. The recitation is accompanied by hand gestures and body movements that help to emphasize certain parts of the story and may serve as a type of mnemonic device to aid the reciter in his memory of the epic. The Manas epic is one of the longest epics of Central Asia. An extensive version of the entire Manas epic, according to the recitation of a well-known manaschi named Sayakbay Karala, was transcribed by Soviet researchers over the course of a decade beginning in 1936, and their edition of the epic consisted of more than five hundred thousand lines. These lines are not memorized word for word of course, and the detail with which the epic is told depends largely on the individual bard's familiarity with various parts of the story. The recitation of the epic involves a great deal of extemporization, and this improvisatory aspect of the epic recitation is an aspect of oral tradition that is highly valued among traditionally nomadic cultures of Central Asia.

The art of improvised speech and song permeates much of the performing arts in Kazakhstan and Kyrgyzstan, and is so prevalent that even normal day-to-day speech and brief exchanges or greetings are often infused with shades of rhythm and spontaneous musicality. Several musical genres are based solely on improvised poetry and song. One of these genres is a form of improvised poetry competition that is found among both Kazakhs and Kyrgyz. The *aitys* (Kazakh) or *aytish* (Kyrgyz) is a public competition between two bards who exchange verses on a particular topic or theme in an attempt to outwit the other through their extemporized rhetoric. These competitions are the domain of a type of bard called *aqin*s (Kyrgyz; *aqyn* Kazakh), who specialize in improvised poetry, composition, and didactic poetic songs. There are several different types of aytish competitions that follow different guidelines as to the content of the exchanges.

For example, the *tabishmak aytish* is a type of riddle competition in which the first aqin will present a riddle through questions sung in verse. It is then the duty of the second aqin to respond to these questions by providing clever answers that often highlight traditional wisdom in a comical manner. The aytish is a true battle of wit, and other types include competitions based on themes of eloquence, wisdom, storytelling, or even insults. Perhaps the most difficult type of aytish that is practiced by professional aqins is the *alim sabak aytish*. It consists of brief exchanges that must continue to follow the alliteration and rhyme scheme initiated by the aqin who begins the aytish. It becomes increasingly more difficult as the competition goes on, as the exchanges become more and more brief, eventually working their way down to single-line exchanges and finally to half-line exchanges, where the second aqin must seamlessly complete the phrases begun by the first aqin. This type of aytish exemplifies the importance placed on both quick-wittedness and eloquence, and it is only natural that these qualities would be cherished in cultures that are based almost exclusively in the oral tradition.

Another genre of song that is performed by aqins and falls under the umbrella of the epic traditions is a poetic and song form called *terme*. This genre is often referred to as "wisdom songs." These brief songs are didactic in nature and emphasize the essential qualities and character traits that are most cherished in Kazakh and Kyrgyz society. Honor, justice, honesty, bravery, loyalty, respect, and patience are only a few of the qualities that may be conveyed through the didactic messages of terme songs. These songs contain moral advice that is most often expressed through themes that revolve around the everyday human experience, such as the different stages of life, interpersonal and familial relations, social status, and tragedies. In this way, terme songs provide advice about what qualities and actions will be most beneficial in dealing with a broad array of common experiences. As with other genres of sung oral poetry, the terme is highly dependent on the performer's improvisatory abilities. Each singer will impart their own style as they craft the melody, adjoining themes that may include proverbs, references to historical role models, and Islamic dictums.

Although Islam was slower to take root in the traditionally nomadic societies of Central Asia, it has had an enduring influence on the spiritual and musical life of the region. Islam became firmly established in the eighteenth and nineteenth centuries primarily through the proselytization efforts of Sufi dervishes, whose teachings were largely aligned with the preexisting moral and social codes adhered to by nomadic societies. In many regards, Islam was adopted by pastoralist communities in a way that allowed for the integration of the spiritual animism that had guided their expressive culture since long before the arrival of Islam. The primacy of the written word in Islam, revolving around the Qur'an, slowly brought about an increase in literacy among nomadic pastoralists. Likewise, the establishment of Islamic institutions such as *madrasa*s and the revered tombs of Sufi saints began to serve as nexuses of sedentary communities centered around Islamic learning and practice. It is in this milieu that a tradition of written poetry began to be cultivated by the *jazgich aqins* in the late eighteenth and nineteenth centuries, and that would continue during the Soviet era. The mass sedentarization of pastoral communities did not begin in earnest until the beginning of the twentieth century. Sedentary lifestyles brought about changes in the cultural ethos of the previously nomadic society, but these changes have occurred very gradually while the underlying sentiments of expressive culture have largely preserved the aesthetic values engendered by their pre-Soviet nomadic lifestyles and worldviews.

It is difficult to gauge how the long-term effects of sedentary lifestyle will effect change in the musical traditions of historically nomadic cultures of Kazakhstan, Kyrgyzstan, and other parts of Central Asia. Many of today's musicians in Kazakhstan and Kyrgyzstan are using performance and education methodologies that incorporate traditional approaches mixed with contemporary Western pedagogies. Since gaining their independence, there have been efforts in the new Republics to revive pre-Soviet pedagogies for teaching music, but even these projects have been realized in ways that behoove sedentary city dwellers. Intimately familiar with both traditional methods of oral transmission, and with the highly systematized pedagogy implemented under Soviet rule, today's music educators have managed to integrate beneficial aspects of multiple systems into a new curriculum that reflects their current social context as modern urban sedentary members of a historically nomadic society.

A good example of this synthesis of systems can be seen in Bishkek at the Centre Ustat-Shakirt, a music school that aims to revive traditional teaching styles according to master-apprentice methods of musical transmission. Here, it is not unusual to find a full ensemble of students playing *temir komuz* (jaw harps), reading notated scores of traditional *kui* melodies arranged in five-part harmony for five jaw harp players. On the surface, it may seem contradictory that performance and education methods so closely tied to Soviet and Western models would continue to be practiced in an independent school that claims to "revive" the precolonial music learning methodologies of oral transmission from master to apprentice. But for the music teachers at the school, there is no inherent contradiction. As traditional musicians, they know the importance of oral tradition, and as music pedagogues educated in the Soviet era, they have also witnessed both positive and negative aspects of Soviet cultural education policies. In their eyes, the use of written notations and musical literature does not undermine the orality of their traditionally nomadic culture but instead serves to make them more versatile musicians in the cosmopolitan urban environment in which they live.

Music in Central Asia

In exploring some of the musical traditions of Central Asia, we have touched on various aspects of a multilayered musical world in order to see how patterns of settlement, religion, and politics have helped shape the aesthetic ethos of music performance, music education, and the transmission of musical traditions. The classic maqom traditions of sedentary populations of Transoxiana were cultivated in the urban environments that served as the municipal centers of learning and political rule. Here they had been historically rooted in a long-standing tradition of spiritual poetry and musical literature that produced a highly systematized scientific theory of music at an early date. Tied to this unified theory, a variety of different performance traditions developed across the greater Middle East. In Central Asia, local maqom traditions grew into vast repertoires of "classic" music that integrated melodies in many different musical modes and rhythmic cycles, and drew upon centuries of spiritual poetry written in Persian and Turkic languages. The poetic and theoretical components are tied to written literature, but the music itself was transmitted aurally for generations, changing and evolving over time. And while its associations with the elite and ruling classes have instilled this tradition with a prestige that has ensured it with an important place in the musical history of the region, it is worth noting that this erudite tradition of urban modal music is firmly built on the rich folk traditions that have been the musical lifeblood among the rural agrarian peoples throughout Transoxiana and the Ferghana Valley.

In contrast, the music of the traditionally nomadic peoples of the steppe is largely lacking a history of its own despite the fact that it is through music and song that the pastoralists of Central Asia have preserved their own history. The various genres of epic song recount oral histories of the clans and tribal unions that comprise the modern-day Kazakhs, Kyrgyz, and other nomadic peoples. At the same time, the epic traditions join historical narrative with legend, myth, and spiritual beliefs that reflect both Islamic and animistic cosmologies. They preserve the ethos of traditionally nomadic worldviews through didactic wisdom songs and highlight the immensely valued skill of extemporized orality and quick-witted speech through improvised song competitions.

Musical change that has occurred as a result of the ever-evolving social and political environments during the twentieth century reflects music's reflexivity and inherent ability to adapt along with a culture's constructed identities, which are continually being reinvented, both autonomously and subjectively, in multiple domains. For this reason, the cultures of Central Asia maintain multiple musical identities that coexist on multitiered levels simultaneously. Official state-sponsored "traditional" music performances can differ considerably from unofficial public performances, and the music played at private events or informal gatherings may be guided by yet a different set of aesthetic guidelines.

In this brief chapter, we have had to limit our consideration to select traditions and some of their most representative genres, but the musical diversity of Central Asia extends to include a much wider variety of musical geographies and styles than can be mentioned here. The palette of musical timbres that resound throughout Central Asia is a testament to the cultural, linguistic, and religious pluralism that has been nourished by a long history of intercultural exchange, innovation, and creative invention.

30

Art

Aliya de Tiesenhausen

This chapter looks at Central Asian art and culture in the context of the gradual globalization of the art scene. On the one hand, the view of Central Asian culture in the West is defined by exhibitions and the tourist industry, which encourage an image of the region steeped in traditions coming from the Middle Ages. On the other hand, the current situation in Central Asia is reflected in the creation of art that presents an image of a region in the middle of an identity crisis—between post-Soviet, postcolonial, and postnomadic. The roots of contemporary art lay in historical contexts that include the coexistence of nomadic and sedentary lifestyles, the rise of Islam, Russian colonialism, the establishment of Soviet control and values, and independence—all seen and presented from varying points of view using contemporary media.

Throughout the region, we can see the role art plays in the facilitation of meaning and the production of culture. Visual art in particular employs the wide use of metaphor and allusion to create and develop ideas and encourage thought beyond existing philosophical or textual constructs. When used by official outlets—when art is closely linked to the state or other power structures—the result is a form of propaganda that supports and encourages official doctrines, even if those doctrines lay outside observable reality. On the other hand, when used covertly by the art community, it can offer a window to alternative modes of thinking that challenge existing societal stereotypes or channel political protest. Art is therefore both a record of aesthetic tastes of the period in which it was created and of social norms and alternatives that existed at the same time.

We see this dual nature of art as recorder of the past and commentator on the present across various periods, from the pre-Soviet cultural context to the development of professional arts during the early Soviet period and Eastern Avant-Garde; within the rise of Socialist Realism, with its prescribed norms of both subject matter and technique; the relaxation of state-imposed artistic constraint following the death of Joseph Stalin; and the period of perestroika and the road toward the dissolution of the USSR. The art scene since the early 1990s saw notable shifts in subject matter and techniques, including increased exhibition opportunities in the early 2000s and, more recently, greater interest shown by the art world in art from the region itself. In the second decade of the twenty-first century, various developments have affected Central Asian art—including both new private and governmental support of the arts—suggesting future projects, as well as the ways they may affect art and culture in the region, being part of a dialogue about art's reception abroad.

Central Asian visual culture, for example, has been receiving wider international attention since the mid-2000s. Exhibitions around the world have covered the period of around three thousand years ago up to the present day. In 2005, the Royal Academy of Arts in London staged the exhibition *Turks: A Journey of a Thousand Years, 600–1600*, which included sections on both Chinese Central Asia and the Timurid and Turkmen dynasties. That same year, the first Central Asian Pavilion was part of the Venice Biennale—one of the most significant arenas for international contemporary art. It included works of artists who since the collapse of the Soviet Union have experimented with new forms of media, including video, photography, installation, and performance art. At the end of 2017, the British Museum opened a highly acclaimed exhibition, *Scythians: Warriors of Ancient Siberia*. This was the first time the British public had an opportunity to get acquainted with Scythian culture, which dates back to 900–200 BCE. Across Central Asia, Scythians are well known and seen as glorious ancestors, preceding the Huns, the Turks, the Persians, and the Mongols.

These three exhibitions give us just a hint at what Central Asian art and culture are. Major museums around the world hold fragments of this region's history, such as colorful silk ikats and tiles at the Victoria and Albert Museum in London, or fifteenth-century manuscripts at the Metropolitan Museum of Art in New York. Judging from both the museum collections and most exhibitions, Central Asian culture dwells primarily in the middle ages. This is further epitomized by the architectural and archaeological monuments of Samarkand (Samarqand), Bukhara, and Khiva in Uzbekistan, Turkestan in Kazakhstan, and Merv and Konye-Urgench in Turkmenistan—all recognized as UNESCO heritage sites. While that period may be considered by some as the golden age for the region, there are several other diverse eras worth noting. They lay on the extremes in terms of historical time. One is the period of petroglyphs, which as Renato Sala and Jean-Marc Deom note, "South Kazakhstan hosts one of the biggest concentrations of petroglyphs on earth. Figures executed during a period between 3000BC and 1000AD, are counted by millions and many of them are endowed with very high historical significance and aesthetic beauty." On another side lays the transformation of the art scene—during the Soviet Union and the explosion of creativity that followed its dissolution in 1991.

Historical Note on Visual Culture

From the Stone and Bronze Ages up until today, visual imagery acts as a record of its time. While for the earlier period it acted as the main source of lasting information, it continues to provide us with knowledge not only about human existence but also about the transformations of the environment—from the disappearance of species to changing climates. Architectural heritage of the Middle Ages recounts the political and religious structures of society. Glorification of some became the norm. However, as Central Asian architecture demonstrates, it was not only grandeur that was in vogue but also an almost transcendent nature desired by those in power and communicated through the combination of color, light, and ornament—inspiring awe and admiration rather than fear.

The significance of Islam meant that visual arts were mostly constricted to abstract compositions, so as to avoid creating human likenesses. This was one of the reasons for the advancement of the use of ornament in textiles and applied arts, which became the main sources of visual décor in dwellings and costume. Intricate carpets in rich tones of deep crimson, delicate fabrics with geometric patterns known as ikat, stark combinations of dark and light in both feltwork and ceramics (symbolizing duality in life), and silver jewelry (at times elaborate, at other times simple) all are well-known examples of Central Asian design and craft. Beyond their visual impact, Central Asian craft often carried significant meanings understood in society. While a carpet or textile could signify larger, more philosophical takes on life, jewelry could give off direct and unambiguous information about the wearer's status in society and position in a family.

Central Asia in the Russian Eye

The widespread use of ornament in Central Asia has attracted the attention of artists—mostly coming from Russia—since the region became part of the Russian empire in the eighteenth century. Central Asia, along with the Caucasus, became Russia's "East" or Russia's internal "Other." The Russian Revolution in 1917 brought with it great change in political, social, and artistic life. The avant-garde and its experiments not only influenced the Central Asian art scene, but the artists themselves borrowed certain visual language that allowed for flatness, abstraction, and the free use of colors.

The most prominent and well-known Russian Orientalist painter was Vasily Vereshchagin. He worked in the late nineteenth century and witnessed the Russian military campaign in Central Asia firsthand. His work does not fit easily with European orientalism of the same period. While there are some examples of eroticized native traditions, a large number of his works are devoted to documenting architectural monuments in great detail and observation of traditional dress—no odalisque in sight (European, both British and to a greater extent French, tradition of Orientalism relied heavily on the use of the subject of Oriental harem as a space for the accepted depiction of the female nude). His depictions of military campaign were deemed deeply problematic, because he showed war for what it is—death on all sides—bringing both sides of the campaign on equal footing. Thus, these works, prohibited from being shown in Russia at the time, were an unacceptable vision for any empire whose colonizing efforts were often presented as a mission of progress and enlightenment.

While Vereshchagin faithfully depicted Central Asian ornament as seen in architecture and dress, the generation of artists following after him utilized an eastern aesthetic—known for its purity of color, flatness of surface, and geometric design—as inspiration for their own styles. Eastern influence on the Russian avant-garde in general was well documented by the exhibition *The Russian Avant-garde, Siberia and the East* at Palazzo Strozzi in Florence in 2013–2014 and the accompanying catalogue. In her essay "Beyond Orientalism," Jane A. Sharp points out that "by turning to the southern (and eastern) periphery of the empire, Russian avant-gardists of the period of the 1910s and 1920s were able to resolve their problematical relationship with the West." If Russia was Europe's East, Central Asia became the East of the East.

The interest and involvement of Russian artists in Central Asia lead to the creation of what has since become known as "Turkestan Avant-garde." This movement, or rather combination of movements, was united by a mixture of geographical location and desire to find an alternative to several things at once, including traditional and classical arts, Russian realism and European orientalism, and later Socialist Realism. What was particularly significant, was that both Russian and Central Asian artists, male and female, became involved in this outburst of creativity. Some of the most prominent figures were Alexander Volkov, Ural Tansykbayev, Nadejda Kashina, Elena Korovai, Alexander Nikolaev (Usto-Mumin), and Viktor Ufimtsev, to name but a few.

Soviet Transformations of Artistic Space

From the 1930s onward, the Soviet state exercised very tight control over the art sphere. On the one hand, this meant that officially employed artists were well-respected individuals; they were allocated studios, given materials, and ordered commissions for major exhibitions and inclusion in museum collections. On the other hand, to be an official artist meant that one had to follow a strict set of rules relating to the subject matter of works, how this subject was addressed, and the techniques and styles used to depict it. A variety of styles and movements that characterized the early part of the twentieth century were replaced by the insistence of the state on Socialist Realism. This was a doctrine based on the use of "realism" as a form together with the use of traditional fine art media of painting and sculpture, to most significantly portray the desired realities—such as progress, optimism, and success—of Soviet social and economic life. Artists who did not conform lost privileges and sometimes even their freedom. However, even within these tight constraints, there were artists who managed to express certain levels of (subversive) artistic creativity. The works of earlier generations (or earlier works of artists who continued to work, adapting their style to new realities) were also endangered, as they were criticized for their lack of ideology and "formalism" in their use of nonrealist styles. As discussed below, in the example of the Nukus Museum of Art, some exposed themselves to great risk in order to save works of artistic merit that fell out of favor with authorities, showing both the hegemonic reach of the state and the commitment of some to preserve the earlier examples of artistic visions.

Alexander Volkov is widely considered to have been "a charismatic mentor to an entire generation of painters." He was one of the founders of the Uzbekistan School of Art and is known as the Master of *The Pomegranate Teahouse*. It is his most celebrated work, painted in 1924 and considered to be a masterpiece of both Turkestan and Russian avant-garde; it belongs to the Tretyakov Gallery, the main museum of Russian art in Moscow (figure 30–1). While born in Ferghana (in 1886 in Khoqand Khanate; contemporary Uzbekistan), Volkov was ethnically Russian and educated in Russia, yet his work and legacy are a combination of Western and Eastern influences and subject matters: from church frescoes to Russian symbolism; from Cubism to Mexican murals; from colorful geometric motifs on traditional Uzbek textiles to the white fluffiness of cotton; from the dark rich heat of teahouses in his oil paintings to the light and breezy hustle-and-bustle of Central Asian everyday life in his watercolors; from abstract *Mosaic. Flowers* (1914, figure 30–2) to (almost) Socialist Realist workers (figure 30–3).

Volkov's professional life spanned the period that included the Russian Revolution, the Stalinist purges, and the Second World War. While great changes swept across all sectors of social and private lives, transformation in the art sphere revealed the changing nature of state involvement and attitudes toward visual culture. As can be seen using Volkov's example, the early part of the twentieth century was filled with experimentation, the adoption of various existing styles (e.g., Cubism) and the creation of some new ones (e.g., Suprematism) in Russia, and the variety that the Turkestan avant-garde brought with itself. The latter distanced itself from Russian and European realism and embraced a combination of influences from Persian miniatures and Russian icons in the works of Alexander Nikolaev (Usto-Mumin), to impressionism and postimpressionism, including Fauvism, in the works of Ural Tansykbayev and others. By the 1930s, all styles were deemed inappropriate except Socialist Realism, which was supposed to represent the great progress and joy of Soviet life. Artists reacted to these changes differently.

Volkov covered the subjects of communal labor, in particular cotton harvesting, in the early 1930s. These paintings, however, continued to exhibit a dark Cubist aesthetic, together with a certain monumentality similar to that of Diego Rivera. Figures in these works seem squashed to fit into the picture frame. Facial expressions are uncertain and tired. All these

30-1   Alexander Volkov, *Pomegranate Teahouse*, 1924. Oil on canvas, 105 × 116 cm, State Tretyakov Gallery. Photo courtesy Andrei Volkov.

30-2   Alexander Volkov, *Mosaic, Flowers*, 1914. Oil on canvas, 15.5 × 49 cm, Private Collection. Photo courtesy Andrei Volkov.

characteristics differentiated Volkov's works from typically Socialist Realist works depicting labor as a joyous effort with resulting success. Volkov suffered for his "formalism," as it was described then, and was left out of exhibitions and publications for a number of years—a heavy price to pay in an art world where only commissions were issued by the state.

30-3   Alexander Volkov, *Cotton Harvest*, 1931. Oil on Canvas, 125 × 139.5 cm, State Tretyakov Gallery. Photo courtesy Andrei Volkov.

Ural Tansykbayev followed a slightly different road. His early works exhibited an interest in shape and color as well as Central Asian landscape. It seems a mixture of Fauvism and Russian avant-garde served as his main influence. However, once the new rules came into force, he revisited his early realist education. His later landscapes are sweeping images of endless hills and fields, with happy people, electricity, and sunshine. This transformation was illustrative of the pressure that the artists felt to radically change their styles and conform to the directives. In *The Desert of Forbidden Art*, a film about the State Art Museum of the Republic of Karakalpakstan, named after I. V. Savitsky (also known as the Nukus Museum of Art), the narrator describes that Tansykbayev was on the road to see his early works when he died. It is suggested that it was too difficult for the artist to see the betrayal of his own values—in the museum he would have found the works from the earlier period, when artists were free to experiment with both subject matter and technique. In later periods (after the 1930s), Tasnykbayev, in order to retain his position as an artist and get commissions and materials to work, needed to adopt a prescribed style of Socialist Realism. The majority of artists in that period had to adopt Socialist Realism, but some—such as Alexander Volkov—did so to a lesser extent, while Tansykbayev had a complete change of method, style, and subject matter, which is evident through a comparison of his works.

The museum where some of Tansykbayev's earliest works are stored is located in Nukus, Karakalpakstan, Uzbekistan. It is a remote city south of the drying Aral Sea. The museum is a work of art in itself. In the 1960s, Igor Savitsky, an artist traveling from Russia with an ethnographic exhibition, managed to remain in the region, establish a museum, and amass two collections of traditional applied arts and of Russian and Turkestan avant-garde. Savitsky, by all accounts, was a master convincer, as he managed to get works from artists and their families and also to get the go-ahead and the finances from the regional officials to both acquire works and create a museum. The avant-garde works he was collecting were not accepted by major museums in Soviet centers (e.g., Moscow and Leningrad in Russia, or Tashkent in Uzbekistan). By creating this collection, Savitsky managed to both save works that might have otherwise disappeared and bring them together.

In 1998, an exhibition—*Les Survivants des Sables Rouges*—containing works from Nukus was staged in France at the Conseil Regional de Basse-Normandie. This was the only exhibition of the museum's collection outside the former Soviet Union. In fact, the first exhibition in Moscow took place only in 2017. However, the attention to the museum collection has been increasing ever since the dissolution of the Soviet Union. Probably the largest collection of Russian avant-garde works outside Russia, it is also a depository of the early works of Central Asian artists such as Tansykbayev—a time capsule of the early twentieth-century history of Central Asian art.

The years between the 1930s and 1950s were characterized by the overarching dominance of Socialist Realism. However, it was also the time when younger native Central Asian artists received training in professional arts such as painting and sculpture both in Central Asia and, increasingly, in Russia. This training resulted in the creation of national schools of painting. The attention of artists when they returned to their republics was devoted to a new and changing reality, including education and literacy, emancipation and changing family structures, and new methods in agriculture and industry. Some of the greatest artists of the period in Kazakhstan, for example, were Kanafia Telzhanov, Kamil Shayakhmetov, and Moldakhmed Kenbayev. Women artists, such as Aisha Galimbayeva and Gulfairus Ismailova, even though a minority, occupied a significant position in the creation of national schools.

The Road Toward Collapse and Independence

During the next decade came a whole new generation of artists known collectively as the "artists of the sixties." Spanning both the 1960s and the 1970s, they represent the period after the death of Stalin and a certain political and social thaw. Their interests shifted both in terms of painterly style and subject matter. There was a return to the use of flat surfaces of paint and cubist elements; however, mostly the images remained realist and descriptive. The subjects also remained within the contemporary situation but lost the gilding of success, progress, or joy. One of the masterpieces associated with the period is the work by Salikhiddin Aitbaev, titled *Happiness* (1966), which depicts a couple illustrated in traditional roles of "defender man" and "delicate woman"—yet both monumental. Their facial expressions are problematic, though; they seem to look into the distance with a certain sadness and sternness. This combination of visible sadness and textual happiness may have been an early example of the conceptual attitude to art in Central Asian art history. The image was used by Syrlybek Bekbotayev for his *Happiness*, from the series *Modernist Paradigm*, 2017, an installation with parts of the original painting copied onto moving cogs, resembling a large clock and rotating endlessly, never able to display the original picture, just as images rotate in society and as memories in our heads.

In the last decade of the Soviet Union, Central Asian art branched into a mixture of spiritual, surrealist, national, and abstract. Artists were discovering wider possibilities for artistic expression but relied on existing art education. The two-dimensional canvas remained the main base for creation. Disintegration of existing social structures and questioning of governmental bodies led to the first active search for identity, showing an interest in national history and ancient religions and traditions. Once the Soviet Union collapsed in 1991 and the Central Asian republics became independent, the art sphere, just as all other spheres of life, was in complete turmoil and discovered a new freedom, not only from state institutions but also from rules existing within the art establishment.

Painter Abdrashit Sydykhanov's *Dog Eating Its Pups* (1989) is a stark departure from expectations and a very physical depiction of violence, even if not human. Architect Rustam Khalfin took a different course, experimenting with installation art and video. Among his most famous works was a temporary sculpture of a man seemingly built into a building, with various dexterities visible in different rooms. He also, together with Yulia Tikhonova, created a video titled *Northern Barbarians 2*, which shows a naked couple having sex on top of a horse. Khalfin attested that he got the idea from eighteenth-century Chinese chronicles, which described "the northern barbarians" doing everything on horses, including making love. This video as well as works on paper were shown in the artist's solo exhibition *Rustam Khalfin: Seeing through the Artist's Hand* in London in 2007. Khalfin has also explored his own invention—*Pulota*—a concept of emptiness and fullness brought together in the form of a vision through a folded hand. Sydykhanov and Khalfin are considered by many younger artists to be the main mentors and influencers for the future development of the art scene in Kazakhstan.

New Freedoms and New Identities

Starting from the late 1980s, while there have been a large number of artists working in what can be considered conservative forms of art—such as painting and sculpture—a younger generation has embraced video, performance, photography, and installation. A lot of this activity originated in artistic movements such as Green Triangle or Red Tractor, which were created and run by groups of artists who provided space and the opportunity to discuss new discoveries, including in music, and apply it to new forms of art. They were also helped by various noncommercial and nongovernmental organizations. The Soros Center for Contemporary Art, Almaty, directed by Valeria Ibraeva, organized workshops and lectures for artists as well as provided exhibition space.

In Kyrgyzstan, Gulnara Kasmalieva and Muratbek Djumaliev are a wife and husband powerhouse, working as artists, educators, and curators. One of their most famous videos, *Trans Siberian Amazons* (2004), follows a train journey of middle-age women who are small-scale sellers traveling the Trans-Siberian Railway transporting cheap wares and singing outdated pop songs. Such transporters were a fairly widespread phenomenon at the time, which was a result of the collapse of economy following the disintegration of the Soviet Union. The video is stark in its apparent simplicity—a document of a nondescript journey. It is imbued with a sense of hopelessness and repetition. The road is a modern equivalent of the Silk Road, of which Central Asia was a vital part. There is a collision of periods: Soviet (the temporal location of the subjects' youth) and contemporary (the realization of the dreams of the late Soviet generation, which turn out to be less than rosy). When exhibited at the Central Asian Pavilion at the Venice Biennale in 2005, the screens were set into walls of plastic checkered bags closely associated with the semilegal or illegal trade in which many Central Asian migrants are forced to engage. Venice, of course, had its own associations as the original destination point of the Silk Road, and in 2005 it played a role in bringing Central Asian contemporary art's presence into the international art scene.

Kasmalieva also staged performances, one of which involved cutting hair. Long strands of artificial hair were cut together with the artist's real hair in a ritual-like event. It is at once a search for identity and a form of its critique, as the Central Asian states plunged into identity formation, including their search for unique histories and traditions.

In Kazakhstan, artists such as Erbolssyn Meldibekov and Almagul Menlibayeva established themselves as creators of images that play with and challenge stereotypes. Meldibekov's video and photo works of the early 2000s feature Asiatic characters engaging in compositions that suggest violence in its intrinsic, partly metaphoric, but all-penetrating state. *My Brother—My Enemy* (2001) shows two men with partly shaved heads facing each other with guns protruding from their mouths. In *Pastan*, one man constantly verbally abuses the other man and hits him on the cheeks, while the other sits there accepting his fate. The works bring to the fore the opposition of human versus human with its at once inherent senselessness yet primordial nature of survival.

In his later works, Meldibekov addresses the transitory nature of monuments. Even though theoretically transitory and monumental seem like opposite terms, in Meldibekov's works they coincide. With irony, typical for him,

Meldibekov creates *Transformer* (2013), seemingly a construction toy for kids with several sets of instructions, each one leading to a different end result, a different monument. In another work, *Pedestal* (2017) (see figure 30–4a-d), he traces the changing monuments that occupied the same place and reflected societal changes associated with revolutions in neighboring Kyrgyzstan—1917, 1991, 2005, and 2010. Similar transformations have taken place all over Central Asia and the former Soviet Union. On the one hand, they may represent a desire to move away from what is seen as outdated ideologies; on the other, they demonstrate an attempt at erasing history, which whether good, bad, or ugly, nevertheless forms existing society. In the case of Kyrgyzstan, the most prominent monument in Ala-Too Square in the center of Bishkek is dedicated to Manas, a semi-mythological hero from national epic—claiming the site where the statue of Lenin stood between 1984 and 2003, replaced by a statue of *Erkindik* (Freedom), which stood until 2011 when it was supplanted by Manas—which for Meldibekov is a sign of return to archaic values and a betrayal of democratic impulse of the earlier periods. The removal of monuments, documents, or memories takes as its aim the obliteration of history but succeeds only in leaving unresolved national traumas.

Almagul Menlibayeva is one of the first Central Asian artists who attempts in her works to investigate the existing pains, be that nuclear test sites, the ecological disaster of the dying Aral Sea, the position of women in history and in contemporary society, or the lost pre-Soviet and pre-Islamic roots. Her main media are video and photography; recently she also started working with digital image manipulation. Each image she creates is a carefully crafted construction, visually attractive and evocative in questioning expectations. Menlibayeva works on stereotypes and subverts them. In *Aisha Bibi* (2010) (see figure 30–5), there is a combination of the recognizable, the beautiful, and the slightly odd. The title speaks of the person to whom the mausoleum in the background was dedicated. It brings up a significant woman in history, highlights a historic monument of exceptional design complexity, and brings to the fore the complex mix of femininity and masculinity, where a young woman with long braided hair is wearing a frilly dress (often associated with national costume) while also wearing a multitude of typical Central Asian skullcaps usually reserved for men. This juggling of narrative and visual material makes Menlibayeva one of the most successful Central Asian artists on the international art scene.

There are several other women working closely with memory. Like Menlibayeva, they live and work outside of Kazakhstan, which possibly gives them an alternative perspective—in between the outsider and insider. One of them is Asel Kadyrkhanova. She is best known for her installation titled *The Machine* (2013) (see figure 30–6). This installation was created for an exhibition about Stalinist repressions and included a typing machine, red thread, and paper. The machine was one of the first created to type in the Kazakh language using Cyrillic letters, the thread creates a bloodlike web of connections, and papers are copies of original arrest warrants. The artists draws her own thread between the erosion of national language with

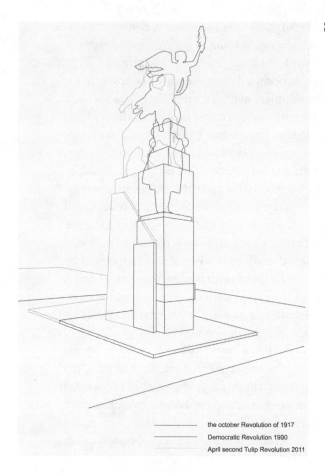

the october Revolution of 1917

Democratic Revolution 1990

April second Tulip Revolution 2011

30-4 (a-d) Erbolssyn Meldibekov, *Pedestal*, 2016–17. Installation, wood, and digital prints. Courtesy of the artist.

30-5   Almagul Menlibayeva, *Aisha Bibi*, 2010. Duratrans lightbox, 91 × 122 cm. Edition of three plus two artist's proofs. Courtesy American-Eurasian Art Advisors LLC. Almagul Menlibayeva ℗ All rights reserved.

its gradual replacement by another one (Kazakh-Russian) and the destruction—moral and physical—of the intellectual elites, both symbolizing the obliteration of Kazakh national consciousness and a loss of memory.

An artist from Uzbekistan, Vyacheslav Akhunov, also delves into the Soviet past. He reinterprets Soviet-era propaganda posters collaging iconic images such as Lenin and Rolex together. He created a small-scale exhibition in a work titled *1m²* (1978–2007), in which he places miniature versions of propaganda images and his reworking of them into a seemingly endless number of open matchboxes standing each matchbox on its side and fitting into the space implied by the title. The artist revels in repetition, so symbolic of the Soviet era desire for conformity. In his work *Total Inventory: Roster of Infinity* (2007), he meticulously writes out consecutive numbers in writing books and on pebbles and street signs carefully documenting the result. A seemingly obsessive artistic gesture, it once again reverts memory to Stalinist Gulags or even Nazi camps with their numbering systems reducing humans to numerals.

Likewise, Askhat Akhmedyarov in Kazakhstan engages the Soviet past while at the same time criticizing the present. His large-scale installation in the shape of a hammer and sickle—the most recognizable part of the coat of arms of the Soviet Union—was made out of reed (see figure 30–7). It was first displayed at an exhibition and later taken to a field and burned. The artist addresses the history of northern Kazakhstan, with its sweeping artificial transformations. One took place in the 1960s with the state program known

30-6   Asel Kadyrkhanova, *The Machine*, 2013–18. Installation, typewriter, red thread, copies of arrest warrants. Collection of the artist and the National Museum of the Republic of Kazakhstan. Photo courtesy Thierry Bal.

30-7   Askhat Akhmedyarov, *If Pain Could Burn*, 2017. Photograph on aluminum, private collection. Courtesy of the artist.

30-8   Saule Suleimenova, *Sunset Street Workers*, 2015. Plastic bags,boards, 140 × 100 cm. Courtesy of the artist.

30-9   Saule Dyussenbina, *Battle Ornament*, from the series *Wallpaper "Kazakh Funny Games,"* 2016. Printed wallpaper. Courtesy the artist.

as the "Virgin Lands Campaign," where large parts of northern Kazakhstan's land were converted into wheat fields. Migration from Russia and other Soviet republics in order to provide an extensive labor force tipped the ethnic balance in the then Kazakh Soviet Socialist Republic, making Kazakhs the minority. Akhmedyarov's work suggests that the move of the capital of Kazakhstan in 1998 was a project of similar importance and scale to the "Virgin Lands Campaign." It also changed ecological and societal structures in the region and the whole country and once again was directed from above. Reed is the most common greenery associated with the marshy lands of northern Kazakhstan, and Akhmedyarov's use of the plant to create a once indestructible symbol of communism is a suggestion that all things come and go.

Saule Suleimenova lives in Almaty, the old or "southern" capital of Kazakhstan. She works mostly within a general format of a canvas-like artwork. However, she plays with the media—for one series using painting on photography, for another using collages made out of old plastic bags in what she calls "cellophane painting." She deals with subjects such as the sale of land into foreign hands—a proposed law to allow it provoked widespread protests; the useless and oppressive bureaucracy; and the layering of national memory. In her *Sunset Street Workers* (2015) (figure 30–8), she accentuates the overbearing hopelessness of menial work by using stark color combinations of overflowing plastic bags, a nod to the environmental degradation and social injustices so widely understood in the global world today.

Saule Dyussenbina's works bring the topical home. She makes wallpapers, plates, and tablecloths with repetitive ornament, cheekily hiding CCTV cameras among the roses, propagandistic symbols of progressive modern Kazakhstan, or mincers producing Central Asian heroes (see figure 30–9). Ironic and direct, her works provoke inquisitive reactions to themes that are rarely raised in public in the region. Some are unique to the country or the area; others—such as the works with CCTV cameras or ram's horns locked in a shape of fashion brand Chanel's emblem—are raising issues of surveillance and consumerism that are internationally relevant.

Art in Central Asia

Central Asian visual arts have a long history stretching from the Bronze Age, via the Scythians, the Turks, and the Persians, toward the domineering Soviets and feisty contemporaries. Throughout the past two centuries, Central Asia has also been extensively depicted by artists both coming from the outside and residing within. In broad terms the art of the region has been heavily characterized by the political context. In Soviet times, art followed the political will of the powerful, while in the post-Soviet period there is wide variety of subtle and direct criticism of both the Soviet and contemporary state structures. The artists then and now deal with myriad issues including societal, cultural, environmental, gender, and more.

Central Asian art as an entity is itself an invented phenomenon. United by geographical and historical links, the grouping has been at the root of the presence of art in general and individual artists from the region on the international art scene. While in this chapter the main countries discussed are Kazakhstan, Kyrgyzstan, and Uzbekistan, the term *Central Asia*, especially in the context of group exhibitions, can include Turkmenistan and Tajikistan, as well as Mongolia, Xinjiang (China), and Afghanistan. At other times, Caucasus and Turkey are added to this grouping. This flexibility of the term also seems to influence the choice of titles for the shows. "Between Heaven and Earth: Contemporary Art from the Centre of Asia" or "East of Nowhere: Contemporary Art from post-Soviet Asia" both imply a certain complexity of the geopolitical and geographic location of the region. The variety of countries that can be included and the choice of wording for exhibition titles together produce an image of Central Asia that seems to denote both an enormous geographical region that includes everything that other major regions do not (Far East, Middle East, Eastern Europe) and an almost mythical and fictional construct that similarly occupies an outsider position, in between known and unknown places.

In 2018, Alex Ulko, an art commentator from Uzbekistan, coined the term *post-Venetian* to characterize the period in Central Asian art that started around 2013. Between 2005 and 2013, Central Asian art presentations in the West centered on the pavilions at the Venice Biennale. All supported by nongovernmental organizations, they brought together artists from the former Soviet republics, where their work was presented and analyzed together. Since 2013, it seems that there is less interest in, or less funding for, regional projects. Individual artists have started moving beyond the geographical framework that constrains them and defines them as "Central Asian artists." There is still a working network of connections, but it exists on artists' terms, rather than as a result of an artificial grouping. Almagul Menlibayeva exhibited in a private Azerbaijan pavilion at the Venice Biennale (commissioned by YARAT, it was an alternative to the official pavilion), while Erbolssyn Meldibekov and Syrlybek Bekbotayev make works that directly reference events or locations in Central Asian states other than their home countries. At the same time, in Kazakhstan, private galleries dedicated to contemporary art have started to appear and stage curated shows of the artists' works—including bringing artists from neighboring countries—such as an exhibition of Gulnara Kasmalieva from Kyrgyzstan at the Aspan gallery in Almaty.

A twofold process is taking place: one is the participation of artists in international art fairs and events and another is a "return" of contemporary art to exhibition spaces at home. All this after a quiet period in the early 2000s, when most contemporary art was destined for abroad. This increase in art's visibility possibly led to the nascent interest in contemporary art from official organizations and institutions. In 2018, Kazakhstan's ministry of culture launched a program titled "Rukhani Zhangyru," part of which is dedicated to organizing exhibitions abroad—London, Berlin, Jersey City (United States), and Suwon (South Korea)—under an umbrella title "Focus Kazakhstan." Uzbekistan has staged its own biennale in the same year. A return to Venice could also be possible for both Uzbekistan and Kazakhstan, though as official national pavilions, not as a regional conglomerate.

Central Asia has gone through significant upheaval throughout the period of independence. The art sphere has been part of these changes, both as a recorder of transformation and as an advocate for change. Today, art continues to be a form of influence used by artists, curators, and organizations to present their point of view. In London, in 2019, the Seventh Annual Doctoral Research Workshop on Central Asia was dedicated to the subject of influence, under the title "Art and Culture—Actors or Representatives?" Bringing together visual art, cinema, literature, performing arts, and music, it staged a discussion on the delicate balance between art as provocateur and art as ambassador. This question is one defining the very active and changing situation in Central Asian art.

31

Literature

Rebecca Ruth Gould and Amier Saidula

To write about Central Asian literatures is to run up against a definitional quandary. Is there a single entity called Central Asia, or does it consist of many disparate yet intersecting cultures? More importantly, *who* has the power to make such determinations? When this question is considered from the vantage point of political science or other contemporary disciplines, the answer is simple: Central Asia is a geopolitical formation consisting of four Turkic-speaking countries (Turkmenistan, Uzbekistan, Kazakhstan, and Kyrgyzstan), along with Persian-speaking Tajikistan. A more capacious definition—such as that adopted here—would also include in this rubric the literature of the Uyghurs, a Turkic people who were the earliest to adapt a sedentary life, and at present mostly reside in the Xinjiang Uyghur Autonomous Region of the People's Republic of China (PRC). The literary culture of the Uyghur has a long history within the Turkic-speaking world; however, its future is clouded with uncertainties, as Uyghur society is experiencing an unprecedented acculturation under the communist Chinese regime.

Before the Nation

The straightforward definition of Central Asia as a geographic entity comprised of five nation-states is rooted in a Soviet mentality that naturalizes state borders, and that makes such divisions coterminous with ethnic, national, and linguistic identity. Prior to the Soviet period, the region was simply referred to as Turkistan in Russian sources. Prior to that, it was called the "region beyond the river [*mā warā' al-nahr*]" in Arabic and Persian sources. Even earlier, before the region's Islamicization, Romans referred to the land beyond the Oxus River (Amu Darya), which currently overlaps with Uzbekistan, Tajikistan, southern Kyrgyzstan, and southwest Kazakhstan, as Transoxiana. Pre-Islamic Persians referred to the region as Turan, and the Achaemenids called this region Sogdiana. Each label indexed a different set of religions and ethnicities, as well as a different relationship to an ever-shifting imperial center.

Because national boundaries are particularly deceptive when applied to the study of culture, and because, in Central Asia as elsewhere in the world, literature transgresses the borders that modern nations use to divide people from each other, our account of Central Asian literature has relied by and large on premodern cultural geographies that transcend modern geopolitical borders. On other occasions, we deploy modern and contemporary terms in critical ways that resist the conventional logic of nation-states. Among these are the view that the literary histories of certain Turkic peoples, such as Uzbeks and Uyghurs, can be fundamentally disentangled. This assumption has too frequently generated differentiating exercises that exhibit what Sigmund Freud once referred to as the "narcissism of small differences."

Examining Central Asian literature as world literature means transgressing the boundaries of Central Asian nation-states, as well as looking beyond the monolingualism that they, like most nation-states, tend to enshrine. Given the recent vintage of many of these states, it also in some cases means rejecting the contemporary frameworks that block or distort our apprehension of premodern texts and contexts. It means attending to Central Asia's outermost peripheries, to the extent that periphery comes to appear as a vibrant crossroads of literary culture. The border zones of particular concern to us here are the Caucasus and the rest of West Asia (including Afghanistan and Iran), China to the west (particularly the Xinjiang Uyghur Autonomous Region), and South Asia (both India and Pakistan) to the south.

As will be seen, the difficulty of defining Central Asia for all times and places has given this region the role of a perpetual border zone that shapes and reshapes the landscape of world literature, particularly in relation to South Asian, Soviet, and West Asian (Arabic and Persian) traditions. Rather than treating the definitional challenge as a problem to be ignored or simplified, we begin with a concept of Central Asia as a region with boundaries that are imprecise and that perpetually fluctuate according to political regime and disciplinary perspective. For premodern authors of the Islamic world, Central Asia was a region that encompassed the Tian Shan and Altay mountains, the Amu Darya and Syr Darya, the Tarim Basin, and that provided a home to a range of Turkic and Persian literary cultures. This understanding, while necessarily imprecise, encompasses the cultural and linguistic diversity of the literatures we have included within the rubric of Central Asian literatures.

Prior to modernity, few writers from what is now Central Asia conceived of themselves, or of the literatures in which they worked, as distinctively Central Asian. Their traditions were Persian, Turkic, and Arabic, but they were not specifically national, let alone ethnic. Further, Turkic, as will be seen later in the chapter, describes not one but many different languages and literatures that are impossible to wholly disentangle from one another. While premodern Central Asian writers may have identified themselves and their literary creations with a specific language and tradition, they did not identify with a specific nation. Central Asian literature's Turkic identity begins in early modernity, with the writings of the Chagatai poet Nava'i (1441–1501), who is claimed as a literary predecessor by many Turkic peoples, including the Uzbeks and Uyghurs. Nava'i's contributions, however, built on earlier cosmopolitan beginnings, most notably New Persian and the literature that emerged following the Arab conquests of Central Asia in the seventh and eighth centuries, its conversion to Islam, and the establishment of Persian- and Turkic-speaking Islamic dynasties. Before turning to the literary revolution unleashed by Nava'i—arguably Central Asia's most famous poet—we first examine the New Persian and early Turkic literary beginnings that pioneered the trajectories of Central Asian literatures' subsequent transregional circulation.

Early Turkic Beginnings

Ancient Chinese sources attest that the Uyghur presence in Xinjiang dates back to their migration to the Turfan region, the oases settlement to the east of Tarim Basin that lies beyond the western end of the Great Wall of China. While Uyghur scholars believe that the modern Uyghur are direct descendants of those early migrants, many European historians disagree, instead considering the Uyghur an amalgamation of various peoples. Today, the Uyghurs are an ethnic and religious minority within the PRC and are mostly concentrated in the Xinjiang Uyghur Autonomous Region of China's northwest.

Archaeological findings in the Xinjiang region suggest that the ancient inhabitants of the Tarim Basin, a vast land surrounded by the Tian Shan mountains to the north, and the Pamir Plateau and Karakorum Range to the west and south, respectively, including the Uyghurs, used twenty-six different alphabets over the course of their two-thousand-year history, including Chinese, old Uyghur, Aramaic, Sogdian, and Tocharian scripts. They all comprise the literary heritage of Central Asia. The ancient Turkic alphabet was among the first alphabets to be used by the Uyghur and other Turkic Khanates. We still know little about the origin of this alphabet and how long it was in use. Undeciphered but similar signs discovered in the ancient ruins in Kazakhstan, Khotan, and Korla regions of Xinjiang suggest that this alphabet may have been in use since the fourth and fifth centuries BCE or even earlier.

The Aramaic-based Old Turkic script was the first alphabet to be used before the Sogdian script-based alphabet was adopted by the Kingdom of Qocho (840–1200). By the tenth century, eastern Turks once again reverted back to the Old Turkic alphabet. The Sogdian-based script was also in use at the time. The Old Uyghur language later evolved into the modern Yugur and was in use until the eighteenth century by the Yugur people of

31-1   Eid Gah mosque in Kashgar, built around 1442, is the largest mosque in Xinjiang, 2006. Photograph by
        Amier Saidula.

Gansu province, who follow Tibetan Buddhism and self-designate as "Yellow Uyghurs" (*Sali weiwu*). *The Book of Redemption* (*Khuasto Anfit*), a fifth-century Manichean religious text discovered in Turfan, was composed in the Old Uyghur alphabet. Subsequently, the Mongol, Khitan, and Manchu alphabets were also based on the Old Uyghur alphabet.

In 934, at the young age of twelve, the future Qarakhanid ruler Sultan Satuq Bughrakhan (d. 955) converted to Islam. As a result of his allegiance to Islam, he obtained a fatwa from his teacher to commit parricide and established himself as the ruler of Kashgar. Islamic learning was prized at the Qarakhanid court, ruled over by Sultan Satuq Bughrakhan. Until 999, when the Persianate Samanid dynasty fell, the Qarakhanids ruled over the western part of Tarim Basin and the northeastern parts of Kazakhstan and Kyrgyzstan. With the demise of the Samanids, most of its domains were annexed by the Qarakhanids and Ghaznavids. The Arabic script gradually replaced all pre-Islamic scripts and became the official alphabet of the Qarakhanid domain. Following the Qarakhanid conversion to Islam, an already Persianized Arabic alphabet became enriched with Turkic sounds that made it compatible with the lexical and phonetical requirements of Turkic languages. Along with New Persian, Qarakhanid Turkic laid the foundations with later Turkic scripts as well as for Central Asia's modern Turkic languages.

Qarakhanid literary history is in many respects the prehistory of the modern Turkic literatures of Central Asia. The tenth-century linguist Mahmud Kashgari and his contemporary Yusup are among the earliest known Turkic Central Asian writers. Both authors are buried in Kashgar, the second largest city in Xinjiang and one of the former capitals of the Qarakhanid empire.

Kashgari composed poetry, later collected into an Arabic *divan*. At the same time, he was a linguist and anthropologist whose major achievement was a Turkish-Arabic dictionary that gathered together words, phrases, proverbs, sayings, poetry, and folk wisdom from across the Turkic world. In addition to languages and dialects, Kashgari writes about life cycle rituals such as childbirth and child naming, folklore, and Turkic cuisines. For instance, when he explains the meaning of the word *Qaghut*, a kind of food prepared from millet, he provides detailed accounts of the ingredients used and how the food is prepared. Fredrick Starr describes Kashgari's reports on cuisine, kinship, and folk medicine as "relentlessly enthusiastic and resolutely non-judgmental."

Promoting Turkic culture was one of Kashgari's main goals. He insisted on the superiority of Turks in his poetry and made his intention of promoting this culture clear. As he wrote in the introduction of the divan: "Turks are the Kings of the age, appointed to rule over mankind . . . [God] strengthens those who [are] affiliated with them and those who work on their behalf." Kashgari also ascertains that the ethnonym Turk was given by God: "Turk is the name of the son of prophet Noah, it was given to him by heaven, and his descendants are all called Turk as well."

Yusup Khass Hajib (1019–1085; hereafter called "Yusup") was born in the Qarakhanid capital of Balasagun, in what is now modern Kyrgyzstan. He was the first author to use eastern Turkic in an extended literary work, *Wisdom of Royal Glory (Kutat-ku Bilik)*, a mirror for princes who taught political wisdom to kings. He emphasized wisdom and courage as the qualities one expected from a good leader and highlighted the importance of law (*qanun*) for long-lasting rule. Among his most memorable verses are:

> When the ruler is ignorant, nothing works well.
> In the hands of ignorant dynasties fall.

> تۆسىل بولسا بەگلەر نئشنى پۆتۆرەمەس ،
> تۆسىل بەگ پۆتۆن بىلگۆ بەگلىك يەمەس

> When the brave lead the spineless,
> even the timid become fearless.

> يۆرەكلىگ يۆرەكسىزگە بولسا باشى ،
> يۆرەكلىك بولۇر تۆترۇ تەگمە كىشى

> Suppression is fire. It burns if you go near it.
> Law is water. When it runs, life thrives around it.

> كۆيەرنۇت تۆرۈر كۆچ ياغۇسا كۆيەر ،
> تۆرۇ سۈر تۆرۈر ناقسا نىمەت ئۆنەر

> If you wish to rule forever
> Pass laws. Defend your land and your people.

> تۆزۈن ئەل يەيمىن تەسە ناي بۆگگۆ ،
> تۆرۇ تۆز يۇرىتغۇ بودۇتۆغ كۆگگۆ

Yusup complained openly about the lack of Turkic-language books. He summed up his work by acknowledging that

REBECCA RUTH GOULD AND AMIER SAIDULA

The Arabs and the Tajiks have books of plenty,
but in our language this is the only one.

ئەرەپچە، تاجىكچە كىتابلار تۆكۈش بىزىن تىلىمىزچە بۇ يۇمغى ئۇقۇش

Then he urges his readers to pray for him when reading this book

Composed these Turkish lyrics for yourself.
When reading, remember praying for me.

بۇ تۆركىچە قوشۇغلار تۆزەتتىم سانا

ئۇقۇردا ئۇنىتما دۇنا قىل مانا

Persian Beginnings

Some medieval chronicles date the first Persian poet to the extemporaneous declaration of Mohammad Vasif under the Saffarids (861–1003). Others (e.g., that of the thirteenth-century critic Muhammad 'Awfi) look deeper into the past and identify the beginnings of Persian poetry with the Sasanian ruler Bahram Gur (406–436 CE), whose empire included parts of Central Asia. Such accounts highlight the pre-Islamic origins of Persian and thereby add luster and longevity to Persian and Central Asian literary history.

Although Persian existed as a written medium prior to the Arab invasion, the subsequent adaption of New Persian to the Arabic script helped to give the language (and the script) universal currency across the eastern Islamic world, particularly in Turkic domains. New letters were incorporated by adding dots (such as پ) and lines (such as گ), and Persian became heavily inflected by the Arabic lexicon. These transformations in turn paved the way for Turkic languages to be written in the Arabic script, as Uyghur (alone among contemporary Central Asian languages) is today.

The earliest extant records of New Persian as a literary language date back to the Tahirid and the Saffarid dynasties, which ruled over parts of what are now Iran and Iraq in a context of 'Abbasid imperial hegemony. Although Arabic was the predominant language of learning across Central Asia at this time, the Taharids and Saffarids in particular were eager to promote the emergent New Persian literary culture. It was under the Samanids (r. 819–999) of Central Asia, which at its peak included Khorasan (modern Afghanistan and a large part of northwest Iran) and Transoxiana (Tajikistan, Uzbekistan, southern part of Kyrgyzstan and Kazakhstan), however, that New Persian poetry flourished most. Meanwhile, in Baghdad, the capital of the 'Abbasid empire, even when literary production was dominated by Arabic, poets of Persian and Sogdian origin (including Abu Nuwas, Bashar ibn Burd, Ziad 'Ajam, and Ishaq ibn Hassan Kharimi Sughdi) led the way in innovating new genres and new literary styles.

The Samanid poet Rudaki (858–941), who according to many of his biographers was blind, is among the most outstanding inaugural voices of

New Persian poetry. Rudaki's poignant lyrics repeatedly lament the loss of the beloved as in the following verse:

> To God I'll complain bitterly about the loss of the beloved.
> Like a nightingale on the rosebush at dawn.

به حق نالم ز هجر دوست زارا

سحرگاهان چو بر گلبن هزارا

As in many world poetries, the most moving Persian poems begin with loss. Although Rudaki was most prolific as a writer of odes (*qasidas*), Central Asian Persian poets also made significant contributions to the Persian lyric genre (*ghazal*), which was based on the qasida's opening section (*taghaz-zul*). As a lyric genre, the ghazal rewrote the literary geography of Asia, as peoples from a range of Muslim and non-Muslim cultures across West, South, and Central Asia undertook to adapt the genre to their local literary traditions.

In addition to the ghazal and the qasida, Rudaki pioneered in other genres. He is considered to be the first poet to compose *ruba'i*, a genre of rhyming quatrains made famous a century later by Omar Khayyam (1048–1131) of Nishapur, a flourishing city of Khorasan (Iran), near the border with what later became Turkmenistan. Alongside stand-alone lyrics, other genres flourished during this period. Ferdowsi's *Shahnama* (c. 1025) is an epic that revolves around tensions between mythical Turkic and Iranian peoples, and as such explores one of the basic fault lines of Central Asian literary history. In most literary circles and particularly at the court, the qasida, however, remained the dominant genre of literary culture, and the preeminent means available to poets to express their affiliations with kings and to gain access to power.

The qasida was generally a genre reserved for the court and used to appease, celebrate, and placate rulers, until it was transformed by a poet who hailed from the territory of what is now Pakistan, on the southern border of present-day Central Asia: Mas'ud-i Sa'd-i Salman of Lahore (1046–1121). Born two centuries after Rudaki, Mas'ud-i Sa'd took up where his predecessor left off. His poems borrow the form of Rudaki's qasidas while introducing a new theme: the prison poem (*habsiyya*). With this genre, which was expressive of increased tensions between poets and rulers as well as the increased confidence of poets in their art, Mas'ud-i Sa'd inaugurated a Persian literature of incarceration. This literature is without counterpart (although it does have precedents) in Arabic or, indeed, in any world literary tradition. As a consequence, he placed poetry on a new footing within and beyond the courtly domain. He also extended the range of the Persian literary canon. Mas'ud-i Sa'd was imprisoned for a total of eighteen years on the eastern edge of the Ghaznavid empire (975–1186), which encompassed most of present-day Central Asia.

The Emergence of Thematic Genres

The Persian prison poem was from the beginning a genre dense with metaphors and other figures of speech. Building on the experience of incarceration but also reaching well beyond autobiography, it used the insights poets gleaned from imprisonment by their rulers for insubordination to connect poets across Central Asia, South Asia, and the Caucasus. The second pioneer of this genre, after Mas'ud-i Sa'd, was Khaqani of Shirvan (1120–1199). Khaqani passed most of his life in the Caucasus, aside from his two pilgrimages to Mecca. Although he himself did not travel further eastward, his verses migrated widely across South and Central Asia. Equally, Khaqani's literary education was shaped by the poets and scholars of Central Asia. One of Khaqani's closest friends, the rhetorician Rashid al-Din Watwat (d. 1182), was on close terms with the famed Quranic exegete al-Zamakhshari of Khwarazmia (d. 1144), a region of western Central Asia, bordering the Aral Sea.

For the next several centuries, and well into the twentieth century, South Asian poets from Ghalib (1797–1869) to Faiz Ahmed Faiz (1911–1984) regularly quoted Mas'ud-i Sa'd in their verse whenever they wanted to evoke the experience of political persecution and to associate their voices with a longer history of incarceration. By deftly deploying such citational lineages, they created a name for themselves in a transregional pantheon of literary luminaries that spanned West, South, and Central Asia. Even when later Indo-Persian poets appeared to operate primarily within an Indo-Persian tradition, they inevitably invoked a broader Central Asian literary tradition that reached from Bukhara and Samarqand, to Kashgar and Yarkand, to Herat and Ghazni, to Nishapur and Tus, to Shirvan and Ganja. As poets skillfully deployed the literary techniques encoded within the prison poem, a poetic genre conceived on the eastern edge of the Ghaznavid empire spread across the Persianate world, including Central Asia, and altered relations between aesthetics and politics for poets, readers, and kings.

Adaptations and Translations

The links between West, Central, and South Asia that are reflected in the circulation of the prison poem can be seen in other genres as well. Perhaps the most striking example of Persian literature's transregional circulation is the *masnavi*, a narrative poem genre consisting of rhymed couplets. Although early Persian poets such as Fakhr al-Din Gorgani of Khorasan (fl. 1055) produced masnavi narratives, the master of the genre, Nizami (1141–1209) of Ganja (the second largest city in the present-day post-Soviet state of Azerbaijan), is regarded as the true pioneer of this genre, for Central Asia and beyond. Nizami's masnavis were foundational, not just to Persian literary history but also to the literatures of neighboring regions, including Turkic and Urdu literary traditions.

After his death, Nizami's masnavis were collected into a five-part composition, called alternately *khamsa* (the Persian pronunciation of the Arabic term for "five") or *panj ganj* ("five treasures" in Persian). The five poems in Nizami's khamsa consist of a didactic poem, generally considered to be the earliest text in the set, titled *Treasury of Secrets* (*Makhzan al-Asrar*, c. 1163), the love stories of *Layla and Majnun* (1192) and *Khusrow and Shirin* (c. 1177–80), and epic romances telling the lives of Alexander the Great (*Iskandarnameh*, c. 1194) and Bahram Gur (*Haft Paykar*, 1197). Even as its components shifted across centuries and with every individual poet, the five-part form that was first attached to Nizami's name and literary legacy subsequently came to be regarded as the dominant paradigm within which the major poets of Central Asia framed their life's work.

The masnavis of Nizami circulated widely, as did the imitations Nizami's text inspired, first by poets across the eastern Islamic world working in Persian (Amir Khusrow of Delhi and Jami of Herat) and subsequently in Turkic languages, such as Chagatai, Ottoman, and Uyghur. The khamsa form also inspired literary production in Georgian, both through the mediation of Turkic Central Asian literary traditions and directly through Persian. Georgian poets who imitated Persian masnavis did so on the basis of the masnavis of Central Asian poets Jami and Nawa'i as much as on the basis of Nizami's originals, composed in the more proximate Caucasus. The proliferation of many different versions of the same story troubles the distinction foundational to modern understandings of translation between translation and adaptation. More often than not, the new version of a masnavi was in the same language as the original, and versions in new languages drew on textual precedents beyond the source text.

Particularly ambitious poets, most notably Jami, supplemented Nizami's khamsa with additional masnavis of their own, thereby presenting an alternative standard for Persian literary production. For example, Jami's *Seven Thrones* (*Haft Awrang*, 1468–85) was a septet that replaced Nizami's five-part khamsa as the gold standard for literary excellence. By adding two more narratives to the canonical five-part form, Jami made his ambition to be the greatest Persian poet of the early modern world visible to the world. While Jami's septet mirrors Nizami's quintet in that it includes *Leyla and Majnun* and the narrative of Alexander the Great, it lacks Nizami's other three narratives. In their place, Jami adds two more narrative romances cast as love stories: *Yusuf and Zuleyka* and *Salman and Absal*. He also adds three more didactic poems: *Chain of Gold* (*Selselat al-dhahab*), *Rosary of the Pious* (*Sabhat al-abrar*), and *Gift of the Free* (*Tohfat al-ahrar*). The overall effect of these changes is to tilt the balance of Jami's literary oeuvre toward Sufi themes, in keeping with his reputation as a Naqshbandi, one of the major branches of Sufism. Although the Sufi element was already present in Nizami's poetry, it becomes more prominent in Jami, who carried literary allegory to a new level.

Most significant for understanding Central Asian literature as world literature are the many adaptations that both Nizami and Jami inspired in

REBECCA RUTH GOULD AND AMIER SAIDULA

Chagatai and other Turkic languages. Before entering into this terrain, it is necessary to further explore the Turkic languages of Central Asia, and to better understand the foundation on which Nawa'i built when he inaugurated Central Asian literature as a distinctive literary culture that, beyond simply offering variations on New Persian, pioneered its own vernacular aesthetic.

Nawa'i was not the first innovator within Turkic literatures, but for the eastern Turkic Central Asian world, his work marks the moment when it became evident that literary excellence could be attained in languages other than Persian. Nawa'i's innovations in Chagatai contributed greatly to the decline of Persian as the sole prestige language of Central Asia. While Nawa'i's works have linguistic precedents in the lexicon of al-Kashgari and the political treatise of Yusup, unlike these authors, Nawa'i succeeded in using the Persianate tradition to pioneer a new vernacular literary idiom, not just for his own milieu but for posterity. A pivotal chapter in Central Asian literary history therefore belongs to the complex—and contested—story of Chagatai, a language claimed by many eastern Turks today as the earliest form of their literary language. The contestation over the origins and ownership of Chagatai attests to its formative role in shaping eastern Turkic literature.

Turkic Early Modernities

Central Asian Turkic languages can be divided into three groups: Oghuz (a group that includes Turkman, Azeri, and the Turkish spoken in Turkey), Qipchaq, and Chagatai. The last one—also referred to as eastern Turkic or western Uyghur—enjoyed the greatest prestige within Central Asia, even to the extent that it shaped later literary production in Turkmen, a language (of present-day Turkmenistan) belonging to the Oghuz Turkic language group. Magtumguly (1724–ca. 1807), the first major Turkmen poet, began his literary career by writing poems in Chagatai, before switching to Turkmen. Until the emergence of modern Uzbek, Kazakh, Kyrgyz, and Uyghur in the nineteenth and twentieth centuries, Chagatai was the dominant literary language of Turkic Central Asia. Chagatai can be further divided into Early Chagatai (thirteenth to fourteenth centuries) and Classical Chagatai (fifteenth to nineteenth centuries), with a final division corresponding (roughly) to modern Uzbek. The erosion of Chagatai as a literary language is closely connected with the impact of Soviet linguistic policies across the Central Asian republics, extending even to Xinjiang.

It was only in the early modern period that Central Asian writers came to think of themselves as authors working on regional themes, and in local idioms, and that they began to consider themselves representatives, not only of specific languages and traditions but of specific *peoples*, and eventually, specific *nations*. This transformation is reflected in the rapid ascendancy of Chagatai, a language first cultivated under the Timurids (1370–1507). While borrowing much of its lexicon from the Persian literary language, Chagatai is Turkic in its grammar. Its closest literary precedent can be considered

Qarakhnid Turkic, the language of Yusup and Kashgari. Among its most famous authors is Babur (1483–1530), the first Mughal ruler of India, whose autobiography, the *Baburnama* (1529), is among the most important examples of this genre. While Chagatai was, like New Persian, an ornate language far removed from local speech patterns, it was also different from New Persian for the Turkic-speaking population in that it connected to a language in wide use in daily contexts while also reviving long-standing indigenous Turkic literary traditions.

Chagatai first developed under Mongol rule, in which context it functioned as one among many literary languages of the Mongol dynasties that ruled over western Central Asia, Khorasan, and parts of India. Although it was officially renamed Old Uzbek following the establishment of the Soviet Republic of Uzbekistan in 1924, Chagatai is by no means a direct predecessor of spoken Uzbek. Uyghur scholars consider Chagatai to be a predecessor of modern Uyghur and argue that it was based on a Uyghur Turkic dialect. These scholars argue that Chagatai combines the Khaqaniya language, the court language of Qarakhanids, and the Qocho Uyghur language of Turfan, along with loan words from Arabic and Persian. Modern Turkic nations therefore have sharply conflicting narratives concerning the origins and identity of Chagatai.

Lexical influences from Persian and Arabic distanced Chagatai from the earlier Turkic idioms of Yusup and Kashgari. These lexical layers also expanded the content and repertoire of Chagatai Uyghur. Stylistic and linguistic expression in particular was strongly influenced by Persian and Arabic literary traditions, and most authors who composed in Chagatai were also well versed in these languages. While Kashgari tried to persuade his ruler and patron, the Abbasid caliph al-Muqtadi, it was time to study the Turkic language and engage with Turkic culture, it was not until Nawa'i that a literary Turkic language was able to compete with Persian and Arabic in terms of nuance and expressive range.

At the same time, the distinctiveness of Chagatai as a Turkic literary language gave rise to new tensions. Partly in response to the influx of Persian lexical elements into Chagatai, Nawa'i composed a manifesto in 1499, shortly before his death, called "The Judgment of Two Languages" (*Muhakamat al-Lughatayn*). As the title suggests, this work considered the respective merits of Chagatai (a language he simply referred to as Turki) in relation to Persian, which was in many Central Asian literary circles the prestige language for literary culture. The treatise was composed under the influence of his patron, Sultan Husayn Bayqara (1469–1506). Nawa'i's modern editor Ruqayyah Nuri claims that the author was motivated by "love for his native language and the desire to honor and glorify it, as well as to prove its equivalence with other languages, with the exception of Arabic, the language of religion."

After assaying the unique capacities of Turki as a literary medium compared to Persian, Nawa'i criticizes his fellow Turki poets for relying too heavily on Persian. "Turki poets and writers should have used their own tongue and not resorted to others," he writes. "If they were capable of composing in both tongues, they should have composed most in their own tongue and only rarely in another." Nawa'i assumes the impossibility of the coexistence of multiple languages within the same text, and within a single literary culture. This attitude was to become increasingly characteristic of linguistic modernity, across Turkic Central Asia and beyond, partly due to the increasing normalization of the nation-state paradigm. Nawa'i's treatise is one of the earliest and most outspoken manifestos in favor of monoglossia over heteroglossia.

Prose adaptations of Nawa'i's poems flourished after his death. Centuries later, two authors from the region of Yarkand on the rim of the Tarim Basin in what is now northwest China rendered Nawa'i's *Khamsa* into Uyghur prose within two decades of each other. Prose versions based on Nawa'i's *Layli and Majnun* and *Farhad and Shirin* (and notably not the Persian versions of Nizami or Jami) were produced by Omar Baqi in 1792. Mullah Sidiq Yarkandi produced a prose version of part of Nawa'i's khamsa (called *Nasriyi khamsa navo'i* in Uyghur) in 1813. This collection included four of Nawa'i's masnavis: the two romances *Farhad and Shirin* and *Layli and Majnun*, along with *The Seven Spheres* (*Sabi'i Sayyare*) and *The Wall of Alexander* (*Saddi Iskandar*). In keeping with tradition, it is referred to as a khamsa ("five"), even though it has only four parts. Mullah Tursun and Mullah Tukhti Quma'i from Hami in eastern Xinjiang also produced their own versions of Nawa'i's khamsa. For these early modern Turkic writers, Nawa'i appears to have entirely eclipsed both Nizami and Jami in terms of literary influence. In fact, many important manuscript copies of Nawa'i works now preserved in the National Library of Uzbekistan were done by scribes bearing the sobriquet al-Kashgari, which is suggestive of a Uyghur origin. Through such substitutions, led by Uyghur writers, literary Persian progressively receded from the literary landscape of early modern Central Asia.

Beginnings of National Identity

While Rudaki, Kashgari, Mas'ud-i Sa'd, Yusup, Jami, and Nawa'i loom large in Central Asian literary history, they cannot be claimed by any specific ethnolinguistic tradition. Even if we divide these authors into Persian versus Turkic (with all the internal variation these terms imply), it will be necessary to acknowledge that, with the arguable exception of Nawa'i, who dedicated himself to the eradication of Persian elements from literary Chagatai (even as he continued to compose poetry in Persian alongside Turki), these authors did not indulge in ethnic dichotomies themselves. Only in the late nineteenth century did Central Asian literatures acquire recognizably national forms as Uzbek, Kazakh, Kyrgyz, Tajik, Turkmen, and Uyghur. From the cosmopolitan point of view of medieval and early modern Central Asian literatures, the modern tendency to divide literatures according to ethnicity and national identity can seem artificial and contrived. At the same time, ethnic and national divisions testify to the new literary identities, and the new relationships to language, that were reverberating across the colonial and postcolonial world during the nineteenth century.

In Kazakh, writers such as Abai Qunanbaiuly (1845–1904) collected Kazakh folklore and produced *The Book of Words* (*Qara sözderi*), a philosophical treatise, partly in verse, that criticizes Russian colonial policies and promotes education and literacy. Abai's ethnographic orientation is paralleled in Uyghur by the large number of regional histories composed in that language during the early twentieth century, most notably Sayrami's *History of Peace* (*Tarikhi Aminiya*, 1903) and *History of Hamid* (*Tarikhi Hamidi*, 1911). As a sign that ethnic consciousness had not yet entirely pervaded Central Asian literature, even Sayrami did not use the term *Uyghur* in reference to his land or people.

With the arrival of Jadidism, a social reform movement that focused on modernizing the methods of instruction and on incorporating ideas from European learning, and the spread of Pan-Turkic ideas across the Turkic world, from Tatarstan to Istanbul, Central Asian literatures broke even more decisively with the classical educational system that encouraged rote learning and imitation of past conventions. The content of their writings, as much as their writing styles, began to reflect the influence of new political ideologies. A nationalistic (and no longer merely ethnic) tone became even more evident in the works of Uyghur, Uzbek, Kazakh, Turkmen, and Tajik writers following the October revolution of 1917. The Tajik writer Sadriddin 'Ayni (1878–1954) is an outstanding example of a writer who transitioned from the tsarist to the Soviet period with relative ease while also maintaining links with the classical Persian tradition. His autobiography (1949–54) circulated widely throughout the Soviet period, in Russian as well as Tajik.

Modern ideas such as freedom, justice, democracy, and progress came to drive literary production in Central Asian literatures under the influence of the Jadids. The Tajik writer Ahmad-i Donish (1827–1897) is often regarded as a predecessor of the Jadids, who died before the movement took off. An entire generation of Jadid writers died in the fateful Stalinist purges of 1938: multilingual Uzbek intellectual Abdulrauf Fitrat (1886–1938), Abdullah Qadiri (1894–1938), Abdul Hamid Suleyman (1893–1938, whose pen name was Cholpan), and Fayzulla Khojaev (1986–1938). Prior to their untimely deaths, these writers of Uzbek origin attained renown across Turkic and Persianate Central Asia.

The literary and social movement that the Jadids spearheaded across Central Asia also inspired a return to the classical past, particularly to long-forgotten Turkic texts. In 1911, Nazar Khwaja (1887–1951) from Gulja (in the Kazakh Autonomous Prefecture) carefully studied Yusup's *Wisdom of Royal Glory* and published the first major scholarly research on this text in *Shura* (Soviet), a journal printed in Tataristan. In the early 1950s, Muhammad Payzi (1909–1967) translated a major thirteenth-century Arabic-language compendium on the rhetorical sciences: Sakkaki's *Key to the Sciences* (*Miftah al-'ulum*), thereby extending a commentarial tradition that was already well established in Arabic, and that included original works in their own right, such as Taftazani's *Mutawwal* (1390). In 1955, Payzi and his brother Ahmad Zihayi translated Kashgari's *Compendium of Turkic Languages* into modern Uyghur, thereby completing the movement from an ancient cosmopolitan literary tradition that spanned Turkic Central Asia into a more local tradition addressed primarily to Uyghurs.

In the early decades of the twentieth century, inspired by the Jadid movement, the Uyghur intelligentsia initiated a new indigenous literary awakening, known as *Aqartish* (literally "whitening"), that promoted Uyghur identity. From the late nineteenth century and until the mid-twentieth century, this movement produced many celebrated literary works. Abdu Khaliq Uyghur, Nazar Khuja Uyghur Balisi, Lutpulla Mutellip, and many other poets wrote about the Uyghur people's self-awakening. Abdu Qadir Damollah, Memet Eli Tukhtaji, Abdu Rahim Nizari, and others promoted modern education in their writings, organized literary societies, established modern schools, and published journals and newspapers in the new literary languages to propagate for their common cause: awakening and fortifying a new national identity.

The later 1950s marked a watershed moment in Soviet Central Asian literature, during which writers began to examine social problems more personally and controversially than they had been able to do since the 1920s. Another shift that took place during the middle of the twentieth century was an increase in Central Asian writers who turned to Russian as their primary medium of literary production. Among this group, the best known is the Kyrgyz Chingiz Aitmatov (1928–2008), who also served as the Soviet Union's and subsequently as Kyrgyzstan's ambassador to the European Union, NATO, and UNESCO. From Aitmatov's point of view, Russian was as much a language of Central Asia as was the various Turkic languages and Persian.

The last decades of the twentieth century witnessed the flourishing of local Central Asian literatures, sometimes in the medium of Russian. The Russophone Kazakh writer Olzhas Suleimanov composed his landmark work of experimental fiction *Az i Ya* (1975). Meanwhile, Uyghur literature flourished within the PRC. Along with Mandarin, Uyghur became the language of education and government in Xinjiang. The 1980s and 1990s saw an unprecedented amount of original work written in contemporary Uyghur. This short-lived achievement, which ended with the close of the last century, has produced a significant body of historical novels, translations, editions, and reprints of older texts. Fiction writing in particular flourished. In Uyghur alone, Zurdun Sabir, Teypjan Eliyop, Ehtam Umar, Abdu Shukur Memet Imin, Turghun Almas, Abdurehim Otkur, Yasinjan Sadiq Choghlan, and Jalalidin Bahram transformed the landscape of contemporary Uyghur literature.

Uzbek literature had a range of literary luminaries during the twentieth century, including the aforementioned Jadid figures. Cholpon is best known as a poet, but he is also the author of an important novel, *Night* (1934). The multilingual reformer Abdulrauf Fitrat wrote in Persian and Chagatai. Ghafur Ghulom, translator of (among other writers) Shakespeare and Sa'di into

Uzbek, and the short story writer Abdulla Qahhor, who translated Pushkin and Tolstoy into Uzbek, enriched modern Uzbek literature and increased its global horizons. Perhaps the most internationally prominent and influential contemporary Central Asian writer is Hamid Ismailov (b. 1954), an Uzbek writer originally from Kyrgyzstan and former head of the BBC's Central Asian service who resides in London. Ismailov has authored many novels in both Uzbek and Russian, and his works are regularly translated into English.

Of particular relevance to the study of Central Asian literature is Ismailov's first Uzbek-language novel to be published in English, *The Devil's Dance* (2016, trans. 2017). This novel tells the story of the Jadid Uzbek writer Abdulla Qadiri, who, along with the other major writers of his generation, was arrested and executed at the height of Stalin's purges, in the same year as Fitrat and Cholpon. The title of *The Devil's Dance* is taken from a short story composed by Qadiri. Ismailov uses this title for his novel in an effort to evoke Stalin's purges and in an allusion to the era of the Uzbek Khanate (142–1501). Narrated from Qadiri's prison cell, Ismailov's novel also, in metafictional *Don Quixote* fashion, presents the text of another novel, which Qodiriy had planned to write about the nineteenth-century Uzbek poet-queen Oyxon, but that he was unable to complete before his execution. Ismailov's novel-within-a-novel is among the most experimental of recent Central Asian fictions. Like Suleimanov's *Az i Ya*, it is both a commentary on the past and an intervention into the present. While Ismailov's fiction is informed by his direct (and ongoing) experience of persecution by the Uzbek state, Uyghur writers today are disproportionately targeted for persecution within the PRC.

Scripts and Nations

All Central Asian scripts have undergone radical changes during the twentieth and twenty-first century. While Tajik and Kyrgyz continue to be written in Cyrillic, Turkmen adopted a Latin script immediately following the breakup of the Soviet Union in 1991, following a decree by then President Saparmurat Niyazov. Uzbek adopted the Latin script in 1992, but the change was implemented more gradually through schools. In 2017, a decree issued by the president of Kazakhstan, Nursultan Nazarbayev, declared that the Kazakh language would transition completely from Cyrillic to a Latin script by 2025. Meanwhile, there is significant political mobilization for returning to the Arabic script within Tajikistan. Commentators have speculated that, given Tajikistan's unique status as the only Central Asian state that uses a variant of Persian as its official language, "the country's linguistic loneliness" may have partly motivated the debate (along with perhaps also the influence of Iran) within Tajikistan around the adoption of the New Persian script. By contrast, most debates around script reform within Turkic Central Asia pertain to Latinate scripts, which are increasingly relevant to Central Asians' social and economic futures.

Among contemporary Central Asian languages, only Uyghur is currently written in the Arabic script. The dependence of other Central Asian languages on Cyrillic and Latinate scripts shapes Central Asians' access to their cultural heritage and their ability to read New Persian, Chagatai, and Arabic texts as they were originally written, and in manuscript form. Like all other Central Asian languages, Uyghur witnessed many changes during the twentieth century within China and Soviet Central Asia. The Soviet Union initially replaced Central Asian languages' Arabic script with Latin alphabets, and then gradually introduced the Cyrillic script from the late 1920s onward.

When the relationship between these two socialist allies became tense during the late 1950s, China replaced the Cyrillic with a Latin alphabet known as New Uyghur Script (*Uyghur Yengi Yeziqi*), which soon became the official alphabet and was used for almost a decade. In 1982, the New Uyghur Script was abolished, and the Arabic alphabet, known as Old Uyghur Script (*Uyghur Kona Yeziqi*), was reinstated in a modified form. Officially, this was done by the PRC in response to Uyghurs' demand for a restoration of their old alphabet, but some believe that the actual goal was to create a barrier between the Uyghur and other Central Asian Turks, and to curb the spread of pan-Turkism that could potentially unite the Uyghurs to their Uzbek, Kazakh, Kyrgyz, and Turkmen counterparts across the Chinese border. Due to the increasing importance of the Latin script for technological literacy across Central Asia and the PRC, the Uyghur intelligentsia have in recent years advocated for reintroducing the Latin alphabet. Uyghur scholars in Xinjiang petitioned the provincial government to reintroduce the Latin alphabet, a step that the provincial government officially took in 2008.

Beyond Bordered Identities

This brief discussion of Central Asian literature as world literature has shown that the very categories "Central Asia" and "literature" have been, and must be, continuously contested. Continuously subjected to the competing claims of imperial and ethnic identities, and notwithstanding centuries of pan-Turkic ideology, Central Asian literatures have rarely been conceptualized as a unity. And yet, the multilingual cultures and traditions they represent have always existed in close relationship to one another, to the extent that distinguishing among them has not always been possible. We have not sought here to impose a false coherence onto a region that has been home to Islam, Christianity, Manicheanism, Buddhism, Zoroastrianism, and state-mandated atheism, as well as countless Turkic and Persian idioms and scripts.

Rather than arguing for Central Asian literature as a singular tradition, we have aimed to suggest here the diversity of the region's literary history alongside some common themes. Among these are: the persistence of the past within the present, the close (and ever-evolving) link between language and identity, the political power of transregional solidarity, and the capacity of cosmopolitan languages such as Persian and Chagatai to forge links across cultures and geographies. In more recent times, a common theme is the propensity for transnational pan-Turkic ideology, also grounded in the perception of a shared language, to be treated as a threat by the contemporary security state (both Soviet Russia and Maoist China) and persecuted accordingly.

"Central Asian literature" is a contradictory rubric. Always subject to perpetual revision, this label should not be allowed to reference any single fixed geography. Whatever definition is proposed will be contested by Uzbeks, Uyghurs, Tajiks, Kazakhs, Kyrgyz, Turkmen, and Russians, and rightly so. Just as "Central Asian literature" is ill-suited to capture its own internally diverse geographies, Central Asia is a contradictory rubric when used as a framework for discussing the past because it is a construct rooted in modernity. None of the medieval or early modern authors discussed in these pages described themselves as Central Asian, let alone as Uyghur, Kazakh, Kyrgyz, or Uzbek. These labels were fixed at a much later date; they belong to the era of the nation-state that was inaugurated within Central Asia with the Russian conquest (1839–1895) and that became further entrenched under Soviet rule.

Now, in the aftermath of the Soviet experiment, another challenge looms: How will Central Asians define themselves and their literatures in centuries to come? How will they construct their literary identities? Will Uzbeks conceptualize their literature as constitutively different from Uyghurs, and Kazakhs from Kyrgyz, notwithstanding their shared history and kindred cultures and languages? To the extent that literature is able to resist the ethno-nationalizing trends of contemporary nation-states, and to counter modern nationalisms with older cosmopolitanisms, it will have revealed its capacity for bringing about political change in the present. This capacity of literature has long been familiar to Central Asian poets and their audiences. It was recognized at the turn of the first millennium by the New Persian Central Asian literary critic Nizami 'Aruzi (fl. 1110–1161), who described poetry as an art that, in stirring up the "irascible and concupiscent faculties," causes "great affairs in the order of the world [nezam-i 'alam]." Given that 'Aruzi's insight into poetry as a political force has persisted throughout Central Asian literary history, giving rise to new genres, new political formations, and new ways of being, poetic insight—and aesthetic experience generally—may yet help to shape politics and culture amid the rampant crackdowns on dissent and freedom of speech within post-Soviet states, as well as within the PRC.

REBECCA RUTH GOULD AND AMIER SAIDULA

32

Film

Michael Rouland

Film is the communion of minds and peoples.

—KHODJAKULI NARLIEV

Walking down what is surely the longest red carpet in the world at the Eurasia International Film Festival, behind Jeremy Irons no less, one is struck by the opulence and aspiration of it all. Since 1998, the Kazakh government has sought to place itself, and Central Asia as a whole, at the center of something bigger—at the center of Europe and Asia—by using film as a vehicle to demonstrate their arrival. The Kazakh film industry has embraced a parade of Hollywood and global movie stars and filmmakers, such as Steven Seagal, Mohsen Makhmalbaf, Kim Ki-duk, Gérard Depardieu, Richard Dreyfuss, Sigourney Weaver, Emir Kusturica, and Catherine Deneuve, as guests in their annual film festival to affirm this vision and promote Kazakhstan as a desirable place to make films. For the past decade, film director Timur Bekmambetov has also emerged as a global ambassador of film from the region. Yet, despite this glitzy facade, the past and present of Central Asian film is rich and complicated. As other chapters in this book reveal, Central Asia is a beautiful, diverse, and complex place. And that translates well into film. The contradistinctions of local and global, innovation and stagnation, music and eerie silence, hot deserts and frozen mountain peaks, tight urban quarters and open steppe blend together in a poetic tapestry that has inspired generations of Central Asian filmmakers.

The transformative power of the cinema to inform, inspire, and uplift has been a key part of Central Asian culture for more than a century. Overtaking music and literature as the dominant artistic forms of the region in the mid-Soviet era, Central Asian film has proven innovative, resilient, and globally significant since the 1960s. Countless heroes and antiheroes have danced and drifted across the Central Asian film screens and have marked the remarkable transformation of the region. Early Soviet films made the Russian revolution accessible to viewers; later films entrenched civic and national pride; and the last Soviet films in the region challenged, confounded, and entreated viewers. More recent films—those of the first three decades of independence—brought new opportunities and challenges as the world rediscovered Central Asia as a global crossroads.

Filmic Origins

The advent of Central Asian cinematography began when Uzbek photographer Hudaibergen Divanov returned from a Khivan diplomatic mission to St. Petersburg in 1907 with a Pathé camera. Soon, Divanov produced the first Uzbek documentary, featuring the khan of Khiva riding in a phaeton in 1910. Subsequently, he memorialized the people and space during this formative era in films such as *Architectural Monuments of Our Land* (1913) and *The Sites of Turkestan* (1916). His photographic style was unobtrusive and architectural, choosing long shots capturing the realism of everyday life rather than the photographic and ethnographic portraits of his contemporaries.

While little is known from this early period in Central Asian film, it is clear that the region was not left out of film's international artistic movement. In the 1920s, a true transformation took place, however, when cinematic transformation coincided with a new era in state-building and state control. Central Asia, like the rest of the Soviet Union, witnessed a social and political revolution where film played an instrumental part in inculcating and educating the masses with images of modernity. Soviet officials deployed agitation-propaganda trains and "red caravans" to communicate new lessons of history, politics, and hygiene, and to explore the immense physical and cultural geography of the Soviet Union. Film proved to be an especially important propaganda vehicle for the Soviets. As Vladimir Lenin observed in 1922, "For us the most important of all the arts is the cinema." Understanding its particular significance for Central Asia, he would later add: "We need to pay special attention to organize movie theatres in the villages and in the East, where it will seem new and where it will be particularly successful."

From an institutional perspective, film theaters and studios began to take root across the region. In March 1923, the Turkestan State Committee for Cinematography began to screen early Soviet silent classics delivered from Moscow: Yakov Protazanov's *Father Sergius* (1918), Ivan Perestiani's *Arsen Dzhordzhiashvili* (1921) and *Little Red Devils* (1923), and Lev Kuleshov's *Extraordinary Adventures of Mr. West in the Land of the Bolsheviks* (1924). The same committee soon set up documentary film production facilities in Alma-Ata, Poltoratsk-Ashgabat, and Tashkent. And Moscow officials assigned two major film studios the responsibility to help the region—North-West Cinema (*Sevzapkino*) in Leningrad and Proletarian Cinema (*Proletkino*) in Moscow. The first three Central Asian film studios appeared in quick succession. First, Bukharan officials established a short-lived joint venture with

MICHAEL ROULAND

North-West Cinema in the Bukharan-Russian Cinematographic Company (*Bukharo-russkoe kinotovarishchestvo*) in April 1924. Then, Uzbek officials converted a Tashkent mosque in Tashkent into the "Star of the East" (*Shark Yulduzi*) film studio in July 1925. Finally, two Russian cameramen from North-West Cinema founded the Ashkhabad Film Studio (*Ashgabat kinofabrika*) to produce local documentaries and propaganda films.

Central Asian films of the 1920s captured the confusing intersections of a world turned upside down. This was depicted in the deliberate juxtaposition of Soviet and Russian modernity with Central Asian backwardness, but its messages were often contradictory. Sometimes officials would enhance and castigate local exoticisms for the wide audience of Soviet viewers, as in *The Minaret of Death* (1925), *The Leper* (1928), and *The Last Bey* (1930). Other times Central Asian films served to celebrate socialist values in Central Asian viewers, as in *The Muslim Woman* (1925), *The Veil* (1927), and *The Second Wife* (1927). These early tensions between Russian modernity and Central Asian backwardness, exoticism and education, center and periphery remained throughout the Soviet era.

The predominant images of early Central Asian films were distinctly political in nature and depicted the unveiling of women, massive irrigation projects, construction of schools and hospitals, and expansion of the Bolshevik party system. At the same time, a new genre of Central Asian adventure films began to appear as well. Bringing together exotic landscapes of the region and swashbuckling tales of revolutionary heroes, popular films, such as *Jackals of Ravat* (1927), *Behind the Vaults of the Mosque* (1928), and *The Covered Wagon* (1928), demonstrated that socialist ideology could coexist with entertainment. Arguably, the most important Soviet film shot in the region was Viktor Turin's *Turksib* (1929), based on the construction of the Turkestan-Siberian Railway across Kazakhstan. The first intertitles read, "Turkestan—in Central Asia—a land of burning heat." The film would depict the munificent exchange of Russian technology and grain for the cotton of Central Asia, "Free the land for cotton. Cotton for all Russia." Like similar films, Mikhail Kalatozov's *Salt for Svanetia* (1929) and Dziga Vertov's *Three Songs for Lenin* (1934), *Turksib* reflected images of the "Soviet East" as abundant but backward places in need of Russian modernization and industrialization.

The Birth of National Cinemas

In the early years, Soviet Central Asian film was not organized or understood as distinct national cinemas but rather pan–Central Asian film movements. Moreover, the industry was driven by directors and producers from Leningrad and Moscow who used Central Asia as a large outdoor backdrop for messages approved by the party elite. In the 1930s, this all began to change as the first generation of Central Asian directors took the reins and local perspectives provided a new window into the Soviet experience. Nabi Ganiev's *The Rise* (1931), a key early film that reflected this shift in perspective, was shot entirely in Uzbekistan by an Uzbek director. The film depicts the struggle of Komsomol activists to modernize a local cotton factory. Ganiev's next two films, *Ramazan* (1933) and *Dzhigit* (1935), detailed local struggles—religious and armed, respectively—with anti-Soviet forces in the region. Suleiman Khodjaev's feature film *Before Dawn* (1933) sought to reinforce national mythmaking and nationalism in the creation of Soviet Uzbekistan. Tajik and Uzbek film director Kamal Yarmatov's early films, such as *Far Away at the Border* (1931), *Right of Honor* (1932), *Emigrant* (1934), and *Friends Meet Anew* (1939), brought the travails of pan-Islamism, transborder populations, and early Bolshevism to the screen.

Despite these early advances by native Central Asian film directors, directors from Moscow and Leningrad brought the predominance of local films to the screen and built the foundation of cinema in the region. Yuli Raizman's *The Earth Thirsts* (1930), Alexander Ledashchev's *I'll Be Back* (1935), and Yevgeni Ivanov-Barkov's *Dursun* (1940) were instrumental in Turkmenistan. Uzbek cinema had many vibrant founders and influences in Kazimir Gertel's *Jackals of Ravat* (1927), Mikhail Averbakh's *The Veil* (1928), Oleg Frelikh's *The Leper* (1928) and *The Daughter of a Saint* (1931), Alexander Usoltsev-Garf's *The Oath* (1937), Arnold Kordium's *Azamat* (1939), and Mikhail Yegorov and Boris Kazachkov's *Asal* (1940). Liudmila Pechorina's *When Emirs Die* (1932) and Mikhail Verner's *Living God* (1934) took on distinctly Tajik topics. In Kazakhstan, we observe the roles of Mikhail Karostin's *The Freeze* (1931) and *Accursed Trails* (1935) and Moisei Levin's *Amangeldy* (1938) and *Raihan* (1940) to set the foundation for the film industry there. And while the combination of foreign directors, Russian chauvinism, and socialist realism may have stymied local cultural creativity, early Central Asian cinema distinctly shows through these limitations in form and content.

The true birth of national cinemas in Central Asia was not led by design, however; it was forged from the exigencies of war. During the major evacuations in the Second World War, writers, artists, and filmmakers descended on Central Asia to preserve the Soviet film industry. In particular, the three major Soviet film studios, Leningrad Film Studio, Moscow Film Studio, and the All-Ukrainian Photo Cinema Administration in Kiev, all relocated their facilities and personnel in 1942 to Almaty, Kazakhstan, and created the Central United Film Studio. The most famous Soviet directors, Sergei Eisenstein, Vsevolod Pudovkin, Grigori Alexandrov, Sergei Yutkevich, and the Vasiliyev "brothers," all moved to Central Asia to create and produce the most important wartime films for the Soviet Union.

The development of the nascent Central Asian film industry and its native directors was effectively put on hold during this time. In particular, Kamal Yarmatov and Nabi Ganiev, who were the most important Central Asian directors of the time, became assistants to Russian directors and their talents were largely ignored. There were a few notable exceptions that articulated the early culmination of national film movements. In Kazakhstan, Adolf Minkin and Semen Timoshenko's *To the Sounds of the Dombyra*

(1943) served as a musical documentary with the most important Kazakh musicians of the era, while Yefim Aron and Grigori Roshal embraced a national mythmaking in *Songs of Abai* (1945). In Uzbekistan, famed Russian director Yakov Protazanov contributed his last film on an Uzbek theme, *Nasreddin in Bukhara* (1943), and Nabi Ganiev depicted the fifteenth-century legend *Tahir and Zuhra* (1945) by comparing this early Turkic struggle with the Nazi invasions. In Turkmenistan, Mered Atakhanov directed *The Magic Crystal* (1945) with fragments from the seminal national operas *Abadan* and *Zohre and Tahir.*

After the war, the Soviet Union produced few films, and Central Asia was not spared. Yet the films that were made proved to be important in the film history of Central Asia and balanced old and new myths. Kamal Yarmatov described his film *Alisher Navoi* (1947) as his "crowning film," and Soviet critics applauded his balance of Uzbek history and modernism. Nabi Ganiev's *Daughter of Fergana* (1948), a contemporary drama about the life of a young woman who picks cotton, does not entirely abandon local customs to embrace Soviet collectivization. There were additional signs that Central Asian cinema was preparing for a significant transformation. Khodjakuli Narliev later recalled: "In the 1950s, we had a very strong student movement. The Ministry of Culture sent, literally, train cars full of students to Moscow schools every year. When these students came back, a growth spurt occurred in all the industries." A new generation of filmmakers would soon set Central Asian cinema on an innovative and transformative path that gained worldwide recognition.

Landscape and Poetry in Central Asian Film

By the mid-1950s, it was already clear that something new was happening in Central Asian film. In Kazakhstan, Shaken Aimanov began to experiment with filmic form and theatrical content in his *Poem about Love* (1954), adapted from the opera *Kozy Korpesh and Baian-Sulu*. Aimanov's later film *Our Dear Doctor* (1957) received popular acclaim by combining everyday life experiences with musical comedy. In Tajikistan, Bension Kimyagarov brought sophisticated and nuanced perspectives in *Dokhunda* (1956) and *The Fate of the Poet* (1959) to challenging Tajik historical topics. And *Son, It's Time to Get Married* (1959) by Tahir Sabirov was a timeless, popular comedy set on enduring generational conflicts. Uzbekistan had the region's most active studio in the 1950s. *Downfall of the Emirate* (1955) by Vladimir Basov and Latif Faiziev, *Avicenna* (1956) by Kamal Yarmatov, and Yuldash Agzamov's *Furkat* (1959) tackled historical lessons without submitting to socialist propaganda. Yuldash Agzamov's *I Am Delighted by You* (1958) and Shukhrat Abbasov's *The Whole Neighborhood is Talking about It* (1960) were comedies that tackled the dynamics of rural and urban life, and they were both considered among the most important Uzbek films of all time. The growing popularity of film as an artistic genre in Central Asia combined

32-1   Gena Tkachenko (Vanya) and Abil Azizov (Sarsanbai) in *You Are Not an Orphan* (Uzbekfilm, 1962).

with the creation of films moving away from binary stereotypes. They were also genuinely interesting to watch.

The early 1960s was a bellwether for a new Central Asia, and it was captured on film. First, a new generation of Central Asian filmmakers arrived on the scene to reinvigorate the film industry. Second, these directors proved versatile enough to satisfy both the growing domestic demand for national cinema and the competing ideological demands of Moscow. Third, they tended to reach across national boundaries and blur distinctions between the burgeoning national film studios. And finally, they produced a plethora of films from Central Asia that crossed into many genres and subjects: light comedies, coming-of-age narratives, contemporary dramas, historical adventures and folk heroes, and a new kind of "poetic cinema." Imbued with commercial and artistic successes, this was Central Asia's Golden Age of cinema, and it lasted well into the 1970s.

The continued focus on early Soviet revolutionary heroism remained, but the heroes became more complex and the socialist ideological lessons became less clear. Melis Ubukeev's *White Mountains* (1964), Bension Kimyagarov's *Hasan Arbakesh* (1965), Bolotbek Shamshiev's *Gunshot at the Mountain Pass* (1968), Shukhrat Abbasov's *You Are Not an Orphan* (1962) and *Tashkent—City of Bread* (1968), Shaken Aimanov's *End of the Ataman* (1970), and Kamal Yarmatov's trilogy of the revolution—*Storm over Asia* (1965), *Horsemen of the Revolution* (1969), and *Death of the Black Consul* (1970)—rendered clashes

MICHAEL ROULAND

32-2   Director Tolomush Okeev and cinematographer Kadyrzhan Kydyraliev. Photo taken during the filming of *Sky of Our Childhood* (Kyrgyzfilm, 1967) by Vladimir Lazarev.

of civilizations, traditional alongside glimpses of the bright Soviet future. Men were not the only Central Asian heroes of historical drama. Notably, Tolomush Okeev's *Worship the Fire* (1972), Mazhit Begalin's *Song about Manshuk* (1970), as well as Khodjakuli Narliev's *Daughter-in-Law* (1972) and *When a Woman Saddles a Horse* (1974) all brought images of heroic and resilient women to the screen. These historical characters and clichés proved popular with domestic audiences, while Central Asian filmmakers often viewed them as penance in order to create their more meaningful aesthetically driven films.

For Soviet and international audiences, the new "poetic cinema" coming from Central Asia proved a revelation. Bulat Mansurov's *The Contest* (1963) was the first film to announce a poetic trend from the region by combining musical and philosophical parables with experimental camerawork and cadence. Although the film was distinctly Turkmen in form, it quickly fomented an aesthetic revolution across all of Central Asian cinema that drew upon Italian Neorealism and the French New Wave. Three important films from across the region simultaneously reflected this transformation. Elyor Ishmukhamedov's *Tenderness* (1966) evoked a completely different aesthetic, staged with teenagers in contemporary Tashkent, with a similar cinematic realism that captured the contours of life without much dialogue. Tolomush Okeev's *Sky of Our Childhood* (1966) was an autobiographical film and memorial to fading nomadic traditions that captured the harshness and beauty of nomadic life for newly urbanized audiences that were losing contact with that world. Shaken Aimanov's *Land of the Fathers* (1966) rendered a powerful and emotional story of a grandfather and grandson as they travel to Russia and, in accordance with Kazakh traditions, seek to reclaim the body of their lost son and father who died during the war. These directors embraced a poetic style that experimented with time, space, color, shadow, and sparse dialogue while capturing the unique beauty and aesthetics of the Central Asian landscape.

In the 1970s, Central Asian literature and epics returned again to the screen, reaching further into the past. Bension Kimyagarov directed a trilogy of films based on the Persian poet Ferdowsi's eleventh-century *Shahnameh*, *The Legend of Rostam* (1970), *Rostam and Suhrab* (1971), and *The Legend of Siyavush* (1976), and thereby avoided Soviet ideology and the Russian "friendship of the peoples." Shukhrat Abbasov offered a biopic about the Persian scholar and scientist in *Abu Raihan Biruni* (1974). Popular recent literature was brought to film as well. Mukhtar Auezov's novel *Kokserek* was translated to film by Tolomush Okeev in *The Fierce One* (1973). And Chinghiz Aitmatov provided a steady stream of literary inspirations for Central Asian cinema in Okeev's *The Red Apple* (1975) as well as in Bolotbek Shamshiev's *The White Ship* (1975) and *The Early Cranes* (1979).

The popular Soviet Russian film, Vladimir Motyl's *White Sun of the Desert* (1969), depicting the humor and travails of a civil war hero in Turkmenistan, instigated a new genre of Soviet "Easterns" that was quickly embraced by Central Asian film studios. Ali Khamraev became the master of the genre in a quick succession of films: *Extraordinary Commissar* (1970), *The Seventh Bullet* (1972), and *Without Fear* (1972). In a twist on similar films from the 1920s, Khamraev brought a Central Asian hero to the center of the story while positively affirming a requisite partnership with Russians and revealing a more complex social reality on the ground. Davlat Khudonazarov's *First Spring of Youth* (1979) revisited the revolutionary era and offered an important counterpoint to the genre with a poetic film that challenged assumptions about the emancipation of Central Asian women.

From an institutional perspective, Central Asian cinema gained the backing of Soviet authorities and became a focal point in Soviet relations with the Third World. From 1968 until 1988, the biennial Tashkent Festival of Asian, African, and Latin American Cinema brought together film directors and producers from around the world to showcase their work in Tashkent, Uzbekistan. At its height in the 1970s, the festival became the most important venue in the world to observe non-Western films and reflected the Soviet Union's political aspiration to compete with Hollywood and Bollywood for dominance in the global film industry.

The Kazakh New Wave and National Independence

Leonid Brezhnev's economic stagnation again afforded few films across the Soviet Union, but a new generation of young Central Asian filmmakers

32-3   Viktor Tsoi (Moro) in *The Needle* (Kazakhfilm, 1988).

soon returned from Moscow in the late 1980s and provoked yet another revolution in the region's film form and content. Their deep disillusionment and skepticism of Soviet society resulted in bleak films dripping with irony. At the center of this change is a group of Kazakh students—Amanzhol Aituarov, Ardak Amirkulov, Serik Aprymov, Amir Karakulov, Rashid Nugmanov, Darezhan Omirbaev, and Talgat Temenov—who studied together under Sergei Soloviev at the All-Union State Institute of Cinematography. Their workshop made the film *Wild Pigeon* (1985), which won a special jury prize at the Venice Film Festival in 1986, and they had a distinct influence on Soloviev's own award-winning film *Assa* (1987), which brought Soviet rock music to millions of viewers for the first time. At the Moscow International Film festival in 1989, organizers used the term *New Wave* as a label for the recent Kazakh films in competition. As film critic and festival director Forrest S. Ciesol observed at the time: "It is unlikely, however, that even the most forward-looking among us would have predicted that the next wave would be from Soviet Kazakhstan."

Rashid Nugmanov's *The Needle* (1988) created a new hero with real-life legend and Soviet rock star Viktor Tsoi on location in Kazakhstan. Layering genres and media to critique the dissonance of Soviet urban life and to reveal its profound social and ecological breakdown, Nugmanov rendered a distinctly late Soviet film with a Central Asian perspective on the need for change. Similarly, Serik Aprymov's *The Last Stop* (1989) brings the emptiness of Kazakh rural life to the screen, replete with poverty, drunkenness, and a suicide, while our protagonist feels he must escape to the city. Abai Karpykov's *Little Fish in Love* (1989) reveals the city, full of hope, hoping to overcome the Kazakh divide between rural and urban lives. Karpykov's view is more hopeful than the deep pessimism of Nugmanov and Aprymov. Ardak Amirkulov's *The Fall of Otrar* (1990) offered an early historical epic of pan-Turkic unity before Genghis Khan overruns the region. Amir Karakulov's *Homewrecker* (1991) is a psychological drama set on a deadly love triangle.

The sentiment of the Kazakh New Wave, like film movements in the past, quickly spread across Central Asia. Djanik Faiziev's *Who Is This?* (1989) explored the corruption of sending schoolchildren to the countryside to pick cotton in order to bolster production, revealing a rural life of ecological contamination, social disorder, and local despondence. But the film was swiftly banned in Uzbekistan. Bakhtiyar Khudoinazarov's *Little Bro* (1991) depicted two brothers traveling by train across Tajikistan to meet their father. Their journey revealed the dark reality of a place at the precipice of civil war with barren landscapes, rampant poverty, and regional divisions. Importantly, this young generation of filmmakers did not maintain a monopoly on pessimistic films or visual experimentation at the time. Khodjakuli Narliev, the leading filmmaker in Turkmenistan for a generation, brought a biting allegory for the loss of Central Asian identity to the screen in *Mankurt* (1990), based on Aitmatov's popular novel *The Day Lasts More Than a Hundred Years*.

Darezhan Omirbaev's *Kairat* (1991) represents the culmination of the Kazakh film movement through his nuanced portrayal of the growing divisions and inequities between rural and urban life. Recalling the poetic cinema of the 1960s, Omirbaev also draws upon the visual metaphors, fragmentation, and long takes of the French New Wave to reveal a tragic world of loneliness at the end of the Soviet era. Omirbaev's work marks an important shift from the films of the late Soviet era to the global art house cinema of the 1990s. The collapse of the Soviet Union and subsequent independence of the five Central Asian republics had decidedly diverse impacts on each of the former Soviet republics, and noticeably their national cinemas began to develop differently as well. The 1990s were a decade of political and cultural consolidation, while each respective Central Asian government offered economic austerity and little investment in cultural enterprises. As a result, Central Asian filmmakers set their own paths in the world.

In many ways, Kazakh cinema fared the best during this difficult time. The recently acclaimed directors of the Kazakh New Wave secured foreign funding to make films largely for the international film festival circuits, while domestic audiences rarely observed this world-renowned auteur cinema. In *Cardiogram* (1995) and *Killer* (1998), Darezhan Omirbaev completed a trilogy based on the central character from *Kairat* and extended his story of the loneliness and dislocation of Kazakhs caught between poor villages and changing cities in a world spinning out of control. Serik Aprymov also completed a trilogy out of his masterpiece, returning to his native village for *Aksuat* (1998) and *Three Brothers* (2000) to continue his generational discussion on Kazakh village life. Alongside international ventures, the Kazakh Film Studio produced two films designed to celebrate national heroes in Ardak Amirkulov's *Abai* (1995) and Kanymbek Kasymbekov's *Zhambyl* (1996), but they failed to reach popular audiences.

A similar pattern emerged in Kyrgyzstan and in Tajikistan, where film directors sought foreign funding as domestic audiences disappeared. Aktan

MICHAEL ROULAND

Arym Kubat (earlier known as Aktan Abdykalykov) created his own trilogy of coming-of-age films in *The Swing* (1993), *Beshkempir: The Adopted Son* (1998), and *The Chimp* (2001), which brought critical and international success to Kyrgyz cinema. In Tajikistan, Mairam Yusupova's *The Time of Yellow Grass* (1991) offered a final view of the Tajik countryside before the devastation of civil war with the eye of a documentary filmmaker. Djamshed Usmonov's *The Flight of the Bee* (1998), codirected with Byung-hun Min, offered a view of the new Tajikistan and village life through the lens of the postsocialist marketplace. Bakhtiyar Khudoinazarov's *Luna Papa* (1999) offers one of the most important films of the fin de siècle era with a post-modern and postapocalyptic view of contemporary Tajik life. Khudoinazarov assembled an international cast and crew from seven countries to compliment his parodic blending of traditional, Soviet, and post-Soviet values in the film. Ultimately, the Tajik film enterprise was untenable, and Yusupova emigrated to Russia, Usmonov emigrated to France, and Khudoinazarov emigrated to Germany. The cinema in Turkmenistan faced an even more dire circumstance when Saparmurat Niyazov shut down the national film studio in 1998 and the founders of Turkmen cinema—Khodjakuli Narliev, Maya-Gozel Aime-dova, Bulat Mansurov, and Usman Saparov—all left for Russia.

Uzbekistan was a lone place of optimism in Central Asian cinema during the 1990s, as the Uzbek government continued to provide financial support and protect the domestic film industry. Notably, Yusuf Azimov's *Before Dawn* (1994) offers a sensitive portrayal of the collapse of collective farms in the late 1970s as Soviet power eroded, corruption grew, but hard work remained a virtue. Yusup Razykov, filmmaker and head of the Uzbek Film Studio from 1999 to 2004, provided a hard look at the Soviet past in *Orator* (1998) through a satire on the contradictions between Islamic rites and Bolshevik empowerment of women.

At the end of the 1990s, Uzbekistan alone produced films for its own market. Certainly, Kazakh and Kyrgyz directors were feted with numerous awards at international film festivals, but local audiences were unaware of their award-winning films. Tajik and Turkmen films were virtually nonex-istent. Cinema in Central Asia reflected the effects of political uncertainty and economic collapse while the availability of bootleg Hollywood and Russian movies further challenged the domestic marketplace for films. New investment in film production and technology, however, changed the situa-tion in some republics. For the first time in the history of cinema in Central Asia, the paths and influences of the national cinemas drastically diverged, with Tajik directors looking to Iran, Uzbek directors looking to India, and Kazakh directors looking to Russia.

Return of National Film Studios and the State

For the first two decades of the 2000s, film in Central Asia remained frag-mented and ill-supported by local audiences and state organs alike. While there have been glimmers of hope and promise for a bright future, the region has struggled to sustain the excellent quality of films produced in the Soviet era. Kyrgyzfilm Studio fully funded very few films in this era, including Adil Chekilov's *Cloud* (2004), Nurlan Abdykadyrov's *Petrarch's Readings* (2007), and Temir Birnazarov's *Unknown Route* (2008); although entertaining, none of them were particularly remarkable artistically. Rather, it was internationally acclaimed directors Marat Sarulu, Ernest Abdyjaparov, and Aktan Arym Kubat who quickly returned Kyrgyz cinema to international recognition by cobbling together public and private funds through their local production studios, Oy Art and Aytysh Film.

Marat Sarulu's *My Brother, Silk Road* (2001), *Song from the Southern Seas* (2009), and *Slow Sea, Fast River* (2013) reveal the contours of human emotions, the search for community, and reconciliation amid the rootlessness of village life. His film, *The Move* (2014), is a three-hour-long epic that explores historical memory as Kyrgyz families move toward the future. Ernest Abdyjaparov's *Village Authorities* (2004) and *Pure Coolness* (2007) are poignant, witty, and entertaining contemporary dramas about everyday life, while his more recent *Taxi and Telephone* (2014), a Kyrgyz-German coproduction, looks back on Bishkek in the 1960s.

Aktan Arym Kubat continued to burnish his reputation by producing high-quality films (and even star in his own films) in *Light Thief* (2010) and *Centaur* (2017) about idealism in a corrupt world. Meanwhile, his son, Mirlan Abdykalykov, transitioned from being the star and assistant of Aktan Arym Kubat's early films to directing his own important films in *Heavenly Nomadic* (2015) and *Running to the Sky* (2019). Other standout films during this period that explore the beautiful, complex, and humorous intersections of Kyrgyz pastoral traditions and modernity include: Gaziz Nasyrov and Talgat Asyrankulov's *Paradise Birds* (2006), Marat Alykulov's *Adep Akhlak* (2008), Nurbek Egen's *The Empty Home* (2012), Taalaibek Kulmendeev's *Munabia* (2017), Aibek Daiyrbekov's *The Song of the Tree* (2018), and Zaheed Mawani's *Harvest Moon* (2018).

In 2004, the Tajik government recommitted to promoting the local film industry, while the first Didor International Film Festival took place in Dushanbe, providing additional institutional support for a new generation of Tajik filmmakers. With the support of acclaimed Iranian director Mohsen Makhmalbaf, who directed two films himself in Tajikistan—*The Silence* (1998) and *Sex and Philosophy* (2005)—and briefly lived there in exile, Tajik film slowly embarked on a new era. Early digital video efforts, *Statue of Love* (2003) by Umedsho Mirzoshirinov and *Wanderer* (2005) by Gulandom Muhabbatova and Daler Rahmatov, garnered some domestic success while being panned by international critics. The real breakthrough arrived with Nosir Saidov's *True Noon* (2009), the first Tajik film in production after eighteen years of independence, which depicts the absurdities of village life while navigating the arbitrary decisions of the state. Saidov's second film *Teacher* (2014) explores the last days of an old teacher and his teacher son in a village torn between the Soviet past and Islamic future. Sharofat Arabova's first film, *Tasfiya* (2014), renders a parable set in pastoral Tajikistan on migrant actors and ensconced in color, light, and metanarratives. Daler Rakhmatov's *Air Safar* (2015) is a popular comedy centered on the mistaken identities of a Tajik farmer and a French traveler who appears in the Tajik mountainside. Umedsho Mirzoshirinov's *The Breakthrough* (2016) portrayed a version of Romeo and Juliet, narrated by a Pamiri woman who travels to Russia. Finally, Muhiddin Muzaffar's *Narrow* (2018) provides a critical examination of the power of tradition in Panjakent, northern Tajikistan.

Since independence and the closure of Turkmenfilm Studio in 1998, filmmakers in Turkmenistan have struggled to rekindle a native film industry. The studio reopened in 2007 with a new name, Oghuz Khan, as a gesture to the legendary khan of the Turkic peoples. The following year, three video feature films appeared with transparent political messages: Oraz Orazov's *Melody of the Soul* (2008), Basim Agaev's *It's Called Life* (2008), and Durdy Niyazov's *Repentance* (2008). This early promise evaporated; although a recent film in Batyr Batyrov's *Way to Perfection* (2019), depicting Turkmen youth interest in martial arts, may indicate another nascent film movement afoot.

The new century in Uzbekistan brought several independent studios into competition with the primacy of Uzbekfilm Studio, and Uzbek films proliferated as a result. Zulfikar Musakov's *Boys in the Sky* (2002) and *Boys in the Sky 2* (2004) were blockbusters, exploring the humor and antics of four young men from Tashkent. The Uzbek government sought to build on this enthusiasm in March 2004 and declared a more active role by the state. Choosing quantity over quality, Gulnara Abikeyeva observed that "Uzbek cinema is going the Bollywood way." As director of Uzbekfilm from 1998 to 2004, Yusup Razykov dominated the Uzbek artistic landscape in the new millennium with *A Dance for Men* (2002), *Comrade Boykenzhaev* (2002), *The Healer* (2003), and *The Shepherd* (2005). These introspective films represented a kind of interlude between the Soviet filmmaking of the past and the Uzbek commercial cinema of the future.

In contrast to films destined for international festivals, popular Uzbek films created a simple recipe for success in a domestic "film boom" by highlighting the ruptures between the rich and poor, the city and village, evident in Said Mukhtorov's *Marjona* (2004), Rustam Sagdiev's *The Unexpected Bride* (2006), Ayub Shahobiddinov's *The Other* (2008), Jahongir Poziljonov's *Rich Guy* (2008), and Bahrom Yaqubov's *Super Bride* (2008). Uzbek audiences loved these films despite their lack of critical acclaim or international interest.

A new generation of Uzbek directors has sought to bridge this gap between popular and artistic cinema. Yalkin Tuychiev's films, such as *The Teenager* (2005), *P.S.* (2010), *Afgon* (2012), and *House for the Mermaids* (2017), address common themes of spirituality, intergenerational discord, memory, and loneliness. Ayub Shahobiddinov's *Parizod* (2012) tells the story of a young woman with mystical powers who changes the lives of those around her. Saodat Ismailov's *40 Days of Silence* (2014) similarly explores the lives of four women brought together by a vow of silence in a story of motherhood, tradition, and freedom in modern society.

The political transformation that has followed the death of longtime Uzbek president Islam Karimov in 2016 can be seen in Jakhongir Akhmedov's *Islomkhodja* (2018), a fascinating historical drama exploring the mysterious death of Islomkhodja at the turn of the twentieth century and subtlety suggesting a historiographical revisiting of the Soviet and Karimov eras. The Uzbek action thriller *Scorpion* (2018) by Muhlisa Azizova portends a broader global engagement in Uzbek cinema. Umid Khamdamov's *Hot Bread* (2018) recently became Uzbekistan's first entry in the international feature film category for the Academy Awards and follows a pattern of intergenerational tension as a young woman feels the pull of city life.

Of all the new Central Asian states, Kazakh film has consistently demonstrated a balance between artistic success and financial support, whether in auteur cinema or state-supported blockbuster films. On one side, the traditional masters of Kazakh cinema have continued to make auteur films with modest international support: Amir Karakulov's *Don't Cry* (2002), a study of the bonds of women of different ages; Serik Aprymov's *The Hunter* (2004), a mystical exploration of Kazakh values; Darezhan Omirbaev's *Shuga* (2007), a modern take on Leo Tolstoy's *Anna Karenina*, and *Student* (2012), based on Fyodor Dostoevsky's *Crime and Punishment*; Rustem Abdrashev's *Patchwork Quilt* (2007), a wry and jaunty commentary on the postsocialist transition of village life; and Ardak Amirkulov's *Goodbye, Gulsary* (2008), an emotional account of challenging Soviet officialdom in defense of a prized horse. In the 2000s, a number of Russo-Kazakh coproductions emerged in Kazakhstan—namely, Gulshat Omarova's *Schizo* (2004) and *Native Dancer* (2008), Sergei Bodrov's *Mongol* (2007), Sergei Dvortsovoi's *Tulpan* (2008), and Rustem Abdrashev's *Gift to Stalin* (2008), but this moment seems to have passed quickly.

Ermek Amanshaev, head of Kazakhfilm from 2008 to 2019, sought to promote a closer relationship with the government, to bolster a domestic market, to foster a new generation of filmmakers, and to illustrate a view of history that reinforces state politics and soft-power messaging. A pivotal example is the big-budget international project *The Nomad* (2005), directed by Sergei Bodrov, Ivan Passer, and Talgat Temenov. This film brings a pivotal moment in Kazakh history to the screen with a Hollywood cast for the first time, but the film was panned for its heavy-handed nationalism and contrived action sequences. Satybaldy Narymbetov's *Mustafa Shokai* (2008) is another government effort to rewrite Kazakh history, resulting in a confusing revisionist heroism for a divisive and irredeemable historical figure. Slambek Taukel's *Makhambet* (2008) similarly rewrites Khan Zhangir and the poet Makhambet as distinctly Kazakh while erasing their broader historical significance for the

Central Asian region. Ermek Tursunov's *Kelin* (2009) offers a virtually silent, pre-Islamic, and ahistorical film designed to capture the exotic imagination of foreign audiences, and apparently this worked, since it made the short list of Academy Award nominations for Best Foreign Film in 2010.

Other notable and positive historical and national themes are explored in Slambek Taukel's *Promised Land* (2011), about the Stalinist era deportation of multiple ethnic groups to Kazakhstan and the multicultural Kazakh harmony that greets them. Ermek Tursunov's *Old Man* (2012), a stunning, timeless epic set on the Kazakh steppe, is loosely based on Ernest Hemingway's *Old Man and the Sea*. Tursunov's *The Stranger* (2015) revisits the Stalinist 1930s with a more ominous view of Russians. Satybaldy Narymbetov's *Amanat* (2016) examines the dual struggles of Kenesary Kasymov and the historian Ermukhan Bekmakhanov, who would write about the Kazakh national hero and his liberation movement.

With a massive budget of $7 million for a Central Asian film, Akan Sataev's *Myn Bala* (2011) depicts an army of teenagers achieving victory in battle in 1729 against marauding Mongolian Dzungars. Satayev observed that the film's patriotic message is aimed especially at young people, "so they know the price our ancestors paid for our freedom, for our independence, and so they appreciate it." The film was specifically timed for release during the celebrations of twenty years of independence. At the same time, Rustem Abdrashov's *The Sky of My Childhood* (2011) offers a flattering but thoughtful portrait of the early life of President Nursultan Nazarbayev that attempts to capture life in Soviet Kazakhstan during the 1940s and 1950s. More recently, Rustem Abdrashev set out to make a ten-part historical epic, titled Kazakh Khanate, that explains the creation of the first Kazakh state in 1465 amid the collapse of the Golden Horde. *Diamond Sword* (2016) and *The Golden Throne* (2019) are the first two installments of the series, advertised abroad as a Kazakh "Game of Thrones." Producer Arman Asenov observed, "Remember when [Russian President Vladimir] Putin declared that Kazakhstan was a country that had no history? It probably strongly spurred us on."

A key part of the Kazakh government's investment in film has been the staging of the Eurasia International Film Festivals first in 1998 and continuously since 2005. Recalling the Tashkent Festival of Asian, African, and Latin American Cinema from the Soviet era, this annual event usually held in Almaty, Kazakhstan, is the major film festival in Central Asia and links the Kazakh film industry to the world. Kazakh-born producer and director Timur Bekmambetov encapsulates this new linkage. Gaining prominence through his Russian blockbusters *Night Watch* (2004) and *Day Watch* (2006), he moved to Hollywood in 2005 to write, produce, and direct a multitude of films while maintaining his ties to the Russian and Kazakh film industries.

In an entirely different direction, a group of young Kazakh filmmakers, forming the movement Partisan Cinema in 2014, declared in an internet manifesto their intention to confront the fact that "cinema and society have separated and no longer cross each other's paths" and to adopt new principles guided by a modest budget, social realism, and rejection of bourgeois forms of cinema. Zhasulan Poshanov's *Toll Bar* (2015), a film based on a true story about a conflict between a security guard at a club and a wealthy client, was the first example in this new style. With intensity and high frequency, Adilkhan Erzhanov's *Night God* (2018), *The Gentle Indifference of the World* (2018), *A Dark-Dark Man* (2019), and *Atbai's Fight* (2019) soon followed in passionate explorations of everyday corruption.

Advancing Kazakh commercial cinema for more than a decade, Akan Sataev has proven to be one of the most prolific and versatile Kazakh film directors. He has made crime dramas and action films in *Racketeer* (2007), *Strayed* (2009), *The Liquidator* (2011), *Racketeer 2* (2015), *Hacker* (2016—his first English-language feature film), and *Districts* (2016). He also made a wartime drama in *The Road to Mother* (2016), a psychological thriller in *Alone* (2017), a realistic urban drama in *Businessmen* (2018), and an allegory in *The Leader's Way* (2018), about the move of Kazakhstan's capital to Astana (renamed Nur-Sultan in 2019). His historical dramas *Myn Bala* (2011), on the heroism of children, and *Tomiris* (2019), about the heroism and leadership of women, have elevated the genre in form and content for the region.

In the past few years, Kazakh films continue to succeed domestically and internationally while dealing with complex, nonbinary concerns. Sergei Dvortsevoy's *Ayka* (2018) depicts a Kyrgyz labor migrant who abandons her newborn and avoids loan sharks in Moscow. Sharipa Urazbayeva's *Mariam* (2019) bends the limits between documentary and fiction in a real-life story of the titular character playing herself in a fight for survival when her husband disappears in a remote village on the steppe. *The Horse Thieves* (2019) by Yerlan Nurmukhambetov and Lisa Takeba (2019), a Kazakh-Japanese coproduction, offers a kind of new age western on the Kazakh steppe. Most recently, Ermek Tursunov's *Guardian of the Light* (2020) tells the story of a soldier who returns from the Second World War with a film projector and shares his love for cinema across the remote villages of the Kazakh Steppe. This film image of memory and longing recalls the origins of Central Asian film in the hands of Hudaibergen Divanov at the turn of the twentieth century.

The Transformative Nature of Central Asian Film

Looking back at Central Asian film history, we observe in extraordinary detail how well film has captured the diverse geographic and cultural tapestry of Central Asia. Film provides a valuable, durable, and direct lens into the experiences of everyday life, real or imagined. Film offers perspective and shapes the imagination of locals and outsiders alike. As the nations and peoples of Central Asia forged new identities in the twentieth century, film has proven to be a crucial venue to explore politics, social undercurrents, and history. And, for outside viewers, film renders an intimate portrait of this geographic center of the Eurasian landmass. At the same time, Central Asia film as a whole has been remarkably good, artistically significant, and aesthetically pioneering. Although copies of the films can be hard to find, even in the region, Central Asian film is entertaining, enriching, and exciting. Many Central Asian actors, directors, screenwriters, and cinematographers have been recognized as global masters of the genre at festivals in Cannes, Venice, Berlin, and Moscow.

Central Asian film builds on a strong Soviet film foundation, derived as part of a fascinating filmic experiment at the All-Union State Institute of Cinematography in Moscow. The transformative ideas of Sergei Eisenstein and Dziga Vertov brought the revolution and socialism to Soviet cinema while exploring the competing demands of mass entertainment, political consciousness, and artistic creativity. Successive generations of students studied the optimistic comedies and musicals of the 1930s, the patriotic films of the 1940s, the subtle nuance and grief of the 1950s, the poetic radicalism of the 1960s, the melodramas of the 1970s, and the angst of the 1980s. Importantly, students there could also learn from films by John Ford, Alfred Hitchcock, Billy Wilder, Akira Kurosawa, Ingmar Bergman, Federico Fellini, Satyajit Ray, Stanley Kubrick, François Truffaut, and Martin Scorsese that were not available to the Soviet public due to their ideological content. Blending socially significant film and artistic excellence resulted in a profound education for Central Asian filmmakers that remains influential into the 2020s.

While the draw of Moscow may be diminished in the 2020s, Central Asian filmmakers have maintained important ties to Russia while positioning Central Asia as a crossroads of global cinema, free from Moscow's dominance. After several decades of transition from a state-funded film industry, Central Asian film is on the verge of another breakthrough that benefits from both state and private funding as well as the intellectual, financial, and artistic openness unprecedented in the region's history. We can be sure that the films will continue to capture the beauty and complexity of Central Asia's rich architectural heritage; combinations of nomadic, Islamic, Turkic, Persian, Russian, and Soviet legacies; epic landscapes and natural beauty; rural and urban dichotomies; and the dynamic tension between past and future.

CASE VIII-A

Soviet Cultural Construction and Its Afterlives

Artemy M. Kalinovsky

In April 2017, a group of Tajik policemen went to the Lahuti Theater in Dushanbe to see a performance of *Charhi Gardon* by the playwright Nur Tabarov. Apparently moved by the performance, the minister of the interior issued an order to his subordinates to attend the theater at least once a month. As the ministry's press secretary explained, "attending theatrical productions will raise the spiritual and moral level of the brave guardians of order, as well as help them ease the fatigue of a long work day." The order was surprising, not least because law enforcement does not generally have a reputation for patronizing the arts. Nevertheless, the incident reveals the surprising endurance of Soviet approaches to cultural production, or rather, the way that elements of the Soviet cultural project have survived, sometimes shorn of their original context, decades after the collapse of the USSR.

In what follows, I explore the history of the Soviet cultural project in Central Asia, focusing on Tajikistan. I argue, first, that both cultural production and *culturedness* were adapted in local contexts by intellectuals and artists who were not necessarily the most enthusiastic supporters of the Soviet Union,

but who were nevertheless committed to the possibilities offered by the state to develop and transmit their cultural ideals. Second, that the Soviet Union made possible both the nationalization of cultural production and ideals, which also meant their democratization. Culture and culturedness now belonged to the entire nation (itself a product of Soviet policy), not just a small cosmopolitan elite. Finally, to a more limited extent, this cultural project contained an element of internationalism, making it possible to share certain cultural codes with others across the USSR and beyond.

The Soviet Cultural Project

In the book *Persianate Selves: Memories of Place and Origin before Nationalism*, Mana Kia argues that in post-Qajar Iran, Persianate culture, under European influence, had been nationalized and acquired a xenophobic component. Kia's work seeks to recover the more cosmopolitan culture and *adab* (most simply translated as "etiquette," but more on this later) that stretched geographically from South Asia to the Middle East. But there is another way of looking at the relationship between adab (or other forms of culturedness) and nationalism: the modern nation-state took cosmopolitan notions of culturedness and, while drawing a set of boundaries around the community that could participate in this form of culture, simultaneously democratized it in a radical way, bringing the whole citizenry of the new imagined community into a shared cultural world. Rather than sidelining the cultural elites, this process gave them a new importance, since they were now responsible not just for the cultivation for and transmission of adab among a relatively select group, but for its diffusion into the population at large. They had at their disposal the educational and cultural institutions of the modern nation-state: schools, universities, newspapers, publishing houses, and theaters.

At first glance, the Soviet Union would seem to fit this pattern poorly. After all, the Bolsheviks claimed to be making a radical break with the pre-revolutionary past; cultural forms and forms of behavior associated with old elites would seem to be anathema to the Bolshevik's project. Yet, as Michael David-Fox has pointed out, the precise nature of the Bolshevik's cultural program was a matter of continuous debate both before and after the revolution, a "two-way street between Communists' attempt to remake others and their ongoing quest to transform themselves." The Soviet Union invested in and promoted various forms of high culture, as well as the cultural elevation of workers and peasants. It also espoused a commitment to anti-imperialism abroad and tried to offer a model at home through what Terry Martin aptly termed the "Affirmative-Action Empire." These two priorities sat together uneasily. The Bolshevik's notion of culture emerged from debates about Russia's place in Europe, and Soviet conceptions of high culture inevitably drew upon European debates.

The idea of *kul'turnost'* emerged in the late nineteenth century among a Russian intellectual elite concerned about the country's cultural development relative to Western Europe and the education of the masses. In the Soviet period, it was carried over into various campaigns and educational programs. As Vadim Volkov has argued, it reflected a "complex of practices aimed at transforming external and internal features of the individual which emerged following the urbanization of the late 1920s and 1930s." In one sense, Soviet kul'turnost' was about turning peasants into good urban citizens. It included modes of dress, behavior in public transportation, the use of free time (theaters and museums were cultured; drinking and brawling were not), and cleanliness in the home. As Catriona Kelly and Vladimir Volkov point out, kul'turnost' was not unique to the Soviet Union; many norms on behavior could have been found in many premodern etiquette books, while the ideas of how to fit an individual in society would have been similar across the industrialized world.

But the Soviet state was unique in a number of ways. The Bolsheviks had rejected bourgeois culture even as they came to appropriate many of its trappings. And the Soviet Union combined a universalist ideology with proclaimed support for, even celebration of, cultural difference. Applying notions of kul'turnost' to the Muslim periphery of the former tsarist empire thus created a whole new set of problems. The elitism of one group of Russians proscribing modes of behavior for another now took a distinctly colonial tone. As Adeeb Khalid notes, "The difference between indigenous elites' view of overcoming backwardness and the Europeans' was nevertheless fundamental. It was a question of politics: who would set the agenda, who would implement it, on whose terms, and for whose good. For Central Asians, the goal of social transformation was to put Central Asians into the modern world, and the nation occupied center stage. For the vast majority of Europeans, the uplift of the natives was a task for the Europeans, to be accomplished on their terms and in the interests of the Soviet state as a whole."

Still, the commitment to anti-colonialism created room for local intellectuals to adapt, resist, and negotiate this cultural project. Sometimes, local elites translated or adapted *kul'turnost'* in ways that accorded with their own goals; at other times, it was the different understanding of cultured behavior that seemed to bring the limits of the Soviet project into sharp relief.

It may seem strange to speak of Soviet kul'turnost' alongside a concept like adab. After all, adab is not simply about correct knowledge and proper behavior for a good Muslim but also the internalization of rules and beliefs associated with the faith. In the words of Ira Lapidus, adab is the "foundation of the soul or personality of the human being as a whole. In this larger, and religious, sense, *adab* is part of a system of Muslim ideas, part of an interrelated set of concepts that constitutes the basic vocabulary of Islamic belief and makes up a Muslim anthropology of man." But besides adab in this general sense, there were also the proper modes of behavior for different professions or classes—for the aristocracy, or for members of the *ulema*, for example. Once we begin to abstract notions of adab as a set of governing norms and forms of cultural capital, its similarities to other forms of culturedness no longer seem so strange. As Adeeb Khalid puts it (drawing on Bordieu), "In nineteenth-century Central Asia, proper *adab* marked the boundaries of civility and status and was a crucial element in cultural capital recognized in urban

society." The main site of transmission was the school, or *maktab*. Moreover, in the nineteenth-century, notions of adab began to undergo a transformation among self-styled modernizing elites. The community was increasingly viewed in national, rather than strictly religious, terms. According to Anke von Kugelgen, the Jadid reformers of the late nineteenth and early twentieth centuries "addressed the human as such; the Jadid teachings are intended to form a good child, mother and father, worker or citizen, on behalf of the respective nation or union." Moral education became a "subject of its own."

The 1917 revolutions, and the incorporation of Central Asia into the USSR, did not lead to an easy fusion between Russian notions of culturedness and Jadid notions of adab. On the contrary, while some of the Jadids may have accepted Soviet power as a tool that could further their own reformist tools, their relationship with the new Soviet state was usually problematic at best. Yet, like the prerevolutionary intelligentsia in Russia, they were involved in the project long enough—as teachers, writers, scholars, and administrators—that they left a clear mark on how later generations of the elite saw themselves and their role in society, the kinds of qualities they valued in a person, and the political forms of cultural production they valued.

While there was no attempt to codify a new adab among the secularized urban intelligentsia of the Central Asian republics, there was certainly a set of characteristics that marked out the "boundaries of civility" and provided the "cultural capital" for those born into the group and those who aspired to be a part of it. Soviet-Russian notions of kul'turnost' no doubt had their impact on this new form of adab, but even more important, the Soviet state's commitment to culture and culturedness translated into investments in educational institutions and cultural production, which became a vehicle for transmitting these new values and the desired sites of employment for members of this group. This rather extensive list actually comes down to three key characteristics. This first is knowledge—the pursuit of it, the possession of it, and the commitment to pass it on. The second is a combination of generosity, kindness, and humility. Typically, these qualities are highlighted in someone who was obviously an important person yet did not behave in a haughty way. The third was commitment to the national language and to national culture more broadly.

Just like their counterparts in Russia, the prerevolutionary intellectuals who helped codify the new adab were repressed and physically eliminated in two waves: first in the early 1930s and then in the terror of 1936–1939. A few, including the Jadid writer Sadriddin Ayni, survived. In the postwar period, as institutions of higher learning were rapidly expanded across the region, their ideas found a broader audience. Educators such as the philosopher Mohammad Osimov (Osimi) built on their institutional position as professors and administrators and the cultural capital that came from their association with figures like Ayni to reach a new generation of students, many of them children of the working class and peasantry.

High Culture

Cultural production was a marginal concern for Bolsheviks before 1917; the articulation of a vision for cultural production relegated primarily to collectives like the *Vpered*, a group of artists and intellectuals such as Petr Bogdanov and Anatolii Lunacharsky. After 1917, however, the Bolsheviks came to embrace theater and different literary forms for their potential to enlighten the masses.

And though the Vpered's group influence continued to be felt in organizations such as the proletkult,' over the course of the 1920s, cultural production was gradually brought under the oversight, if not the control, of the party. In the 1930s, cultural production was brought firmly within the party's ideological sphere with the articulation of "socialist realism" as a guiding principle. Simultaneously, however, the state greatly expanded its patronage of the arts, including classical forms neglected in the 1920s, such as opera.

The Jadid reformers in Central Asia had similarly turned to theater as a tool of enlightenment in the decades before the First World War. In a sense, their participation in the Soviet project was based on the premise that they could continue their enlightenment work with the financial support and infrastructure of the Soviet state. By the early 1930s, their vision no longer suited Soviet authorities, and the theatrical, musical, and literary projects they were involved in were taken over by a new generation, more loyal to the Soviet cause. Yet this did not mean that Moscow simply dictated the terms of forms of the new high culture.

The Soviet idea of development was revolutionary—defined by a break with the past—but also teleological. Literary culture was higher than oral culture, and polyphony was not just more advanced than unisonal music—the latter only survived in primitive conditions caused by political oppression. These were not firm beliefs, and the emphasis on the development of "high" culture, even at its height, in the 1930s, sat uneasily with a veneration of everything "folk," while the need to define a sharp break with the past often gave way to a veneration of "classical" cultural production, major literary and artistic figures, and even forms. This confusion helped limit the dominance of any one cultural idea and

VIII-A-1   The National Opera Theater in Dushanbe undergoing renovations, 2008. Photograph by David W. Montgomery.

created the space where the definition of Soviet Central Asian culture could be contested and negotiated.

Opera provides a kind of limit case for this trend. Unlike the other forms of cultural production promoted by the Soviets, opera had virtually no local precedent, nor a local elite interested in the creation of opera as a project. Moreover, the introduction of opera seems to be the clearest case of imposing European cultural forms into the former colonies of the Russian empire. For the Soviets, the creation of "national" operas was a crucial part of the nation-building project; an opera house and a "national" repertoire was as much an attribute of a (Soviet) nation as borders, a parliament, or a language. Over the course of the 1930s, opera buildings were constructed in every Soviet republic; composers were sent from Moscow and Leningrad to work with local musicians and ethnomusicologists to create new operas rooted in local musical traditions.

Creating a truly "national" theater meant not only assembling a Tajik cast and artistic staff but creating productions that were actually Tajik—in the Tajik language and rooted in Tajik musical and storytelling traditions. In fact, the theater's creators and promoters were pursuing two potentially contradictory objectives: to find a genuinely local cultural tradition but to then "elevate" it by employing European standards of stagecraft, acting, set design, and dramaturgy. In the process of creating "national" theater, literature, and other art forms, we see Stalin's famous formula, "national in form, socialist in content," turned on its head. The content is in fact both national and socialist, but the form is decidedly European. Getting Tajik writers, even those who had signed up to the Soviet project and were members of the writer's union to work in these forms proved challenging—the Tajik literati preferred poetry and were slow to adopt these new forms.

Yet the writers who were most enthusiastic about the Soviet projects and supported the adoption of new forms also proved staunch defenders of what they saw as their classical inheritance. Mirzo Turson-zade, Abdulqasem Lahuti, and others may have been enthusiastic about adopting new forms, but they

ARTEMY M. KALINOVSKY

also stood their ground to see that those forms were used to preserve and spread what they saw as their cultural heritage. They criticized the composers working in the musical theater and the opera for focusing only on "folk" elements. "The problem is that the classical [heritage] of Tajikistan is completely forgotten," Lahuti complained in 1939. "It is not right that everything is being built entirely on folklore. The inheritance of world culture needs to be used, and we need to pay attention to classical compositions." This applied both to themes and to music. Tursun-zade similarly called it a travesty that party officials had labeled Shah-Maqam "music composed for the emir" and refused to support musicians who could play it. "They do not understand that this music comes from the people." Their views won the day, and writers and composers began turning to classical themes and motifs in their works. In the 1950s, Tajik composers began to question the emphasis on polyphonic music, as well as the presumption that the only "professional" musicians and composers were those who had studied at a conservatory and knew musical notation.

Opera never achieved a mass following in Tajikistan, or even much support among the elite. But the opera theater did not stand alone. Rather, it was a symbolic centerpiece of all of the investment that went into cultural construction in the republic. In the 1950s, composers and other cultural figures fought for the creation of a conservatory, which they eventually got. Meanwhile, educators and local party activists from across the republic petitioned for music schools, theaters, and resources to put together local choirs and mount amateur productions. To create an opera theater, one needed to train musicians, singers, and composers, and to find potential professionals one needed music schools and amateur productions. These

institutions became sites of transmission for "traditional" as much as modern music. Theatrical forms other than opera found a more enthusiastic audience. The Lahuti theater, which performed drama in translation as well as original Tajik pieces, was much more popular with audiences than opera. In the postwar decades, Tajik artists and directors opened new theaters, including one for children; the actor Mahmud Vahidov became hugely popular for his solo performances of Shakespearean monologues, Russian classics, and Persian poems.

Higher Education and Adab

While opera failed to find much support among Tajik elites, many of them embraced the larger cultural project, including theater and literary culture, wholeheartedly. The expansion of higher education in the decades after 1945 changed the dynamics of transmission. Adab was not just something transmitted from mentor to student, although those kinds of relationships remained important. Now adab could be mass produced, so to speak. The universities and technical institutes set up in the late 1940s and 1950s were dominated by descendants of the old elites. In Tajikistan, these were primarily Samarkandi and Bukhari (like Ayni, who served as the first president of the Academy of Sciences of Tajikistan when it was founded in 1954) and, increasingly, Khujandis.

The Polytechnic Institute in Dushanbe, founded in 1956, was led by Osimi, a physicist, philosopher, and veteran of the Second World War who had helped defend Leningrad. He encouraged the institute to develop a lively cultural life, including amateur theater, sports, and literary events. Osimi also personally took groups of students to the theater. Later, when some of these students became teachers, they continued these practices. Academic and semiacademic clubs (*kruzhki*) were equally important, and literary evenings were a big part of social life both at the state university and especially at the Polytechnic Institute. These evenings helped familiarize participants with classical and modern works in Tajik, as well as foreign poetry and literature being published in Russian and Tajik for the first time. It was also where many students discovered the key Russian poets of the thaw, including Yevgeny Yevtushenko and Andrei Voznesensky, as well as more controversial poets who were coming back into vogue, such as Marina Tsvetaeva and Sergey Yesenin. Such events helped socialize students into the social life of the intellectual class and encouraged their self-identification as cultural leaders connected to other Soviet elites but with their own local mission.

In the sphere of higher education, in other words, Russian kul'turnost' and adab most obviously become enmeshed. First, the growing popularity of some Russian writers among the younger intelligentsia suggested a shared cultural world. Second, both the cultural *forms* and the forms of transmission were shared. One might see different plays and read different novels, but one learned to prize the theater and literature. The new institutions of higher education, and the funding and facilities that came along with them, provided the Central Asian elite with resources to spread their vision of culturedness to a younger generation.

Finally, while the revolution cut off Central Asians from the Persianate "cosmopolis" that encompassed elites from South Asia to the Middle East, the post-1953 engagement with the postcolonial world created new connections that made it possible for Central Asian intellectuals to think of themselves as part of a cultural sphere that extended far beyond Soviet borders. Central Asian

performers, writers, and intellectuals went abroad as cultural ambassadors, and were encouraged to establish and maintain ties with counterparts abroad, especially those who were somewhat sympathetic to the Soviet Union. Soviet Central Asian intellectuals connected with their counterparts in countries like India, Pakistan, Afghanistan, Iran, and Iraq on the basis of a shared literary heritage as well as on their ambition to draw on that heritage while modernizing cultural forms. Versatile performers like Vahidov were in demand as far away as Iraq (where the actor sadly passed away while on tour in 1977). Professors from the university bragged that their students not only knew the Persian classics, but that more people were learning the Arabic alphabet than ever before. For those who spent extended periods abroad, adab in the broader sense made it possible to establish deeper connections with local intellectuals and cultural figures. The literary historian Hudoinazar Asozoda, who worked as a translator in Afghanistan, drew upon his literary education and on his knowledge of etiquette to establish close friendships with Afghanistani figures, visiting their homes and inviting them over for *palov* (pilaf), and spending the evenings discussing literature and reciting poetry from memory.

But going abroad also meant facing questions about cultural autonomy in the USSR and the authenticity of one's own cultural development. Asozoda recalled being told by a leftist intellectual named Tohiri Badahshi that "you are not independent Tajiks, without Moscow's permission you cannot do anything. Soviet Tajiks have no real political power; Moscow gives orders and you just follow." Writing some three decades later, Asozoda admitted that he learned much from Badahshi and others in Afghanistan, and that "their beliefs were not without influence on my worldview."

Limits of Democratization and of National Identity

Like all nationalizing projects, Soviet national culture created exclusions as well as inclusions. In Tajikistan, the professional cultural elite, initially dominated by families from Bukhara and Samarkand (Samarqand), eventually became the province of those from Khujand, in the north of the republic. As Volkov noted, the Soviet concept of kul'turnost' was in part a project of turning peasants into civilized urbanites, and this was just as true in Central Asia as it was in Russia. But not everyone could adapt to this new cosmopolitan requirement with equal ease. Young men and women from the provinces found that their regional accents in Tajik, and their relatively poor knowledge of Russian, made acclimation in the more cosmopolitan environment of the capital city more difficult. Finding a place among the republic's intellectuals meant not just acquiring knowledge but adopting modes of dress, and manners of socializing and of conversation; it meant adopting the more formal literary language that intellectuals like Ayni had worked to codify. Moreover, as this cultural elite grew, its newest members found it increasingly difficult to find a place in the professional literary and cultural world—a problem that, in the Soviet context, carried with it consequences for housing, and thus for inclusion in urban life more generally.

These tensions burst open at the end of the Soviet era, as perestroika made it possible to voice discontent with the system. Some cultural figures lamented the lack of opportunity aspiring young artists and literati found in the system; others offered an even more fundamental critique of the Soviet cultural project, and especially the role of Russian language and culture in the life of the republic. Yet figures like the poet Loiq Sherali, who lamented the loss of Tajik among the republic's elite, greatly overstated their case. In fact, only 30 percent of Tajiks spoke Russian, and fewer still spoke it as their primary language. What bothered cultural figures like Sherali was that neither the republic's peasantry nor its political and technical elite could read, speak, and write the literary form of Tajik cultivated by the cultural elite over the course of the twentieth century. Even as the call for "reviving" Tajik served to promote national mobilization, it also laid the groundwork for a future division between the educated elite and the rest of the citizenry.

Perhaps the greatest frustrations came from the young people who had moved to the city or had grown up in it but were not of it. The 1960s and 1970s saw a wave of resettlement from the countryside to cities across the USSR; many of the new arrivals settled in new suburbs at or beyond the city limits. To some of the city's more established residents, these newcomers were uncouth, speaking funny provincial accents, and more likely to spend their time drinking and brawling than enjoying cultured activities. Along with Central Asian traders, foreign students, and other "out of towners," they formed a peripheral class that "real" urbanites look at with suspicion. Urbanization was much less dramatic in Central Asian cities, but it produced some of the same tensions, as new arrivals felt alienated from the often Russophone residents of major cities like Dushanbe and Tashkent, on the one hand, and from the "national" elites who had dominated the city's educational and cultural institutions for generations, on the other.

Those tensions outlived the collapse of the Soviet Union and the civil war that engulfed Tajikistan in 1992. Many Tajik intellectuals hoped that independence would bring a flowering or renaissance of Tajik culture, as well as a consolidation of their national project. What has happened instead is more complicated. The economic collapse of the post-Soviet era deprived cultural and educational institutions of state support; civil war violence drove many into emigration and proved deadly for some who remained (Osimi was killed in 1996). Since the late 1990s, older elites have been displaced from their places in universities and cultural institutions by individuals more closely associated with the new regime.

Despite all of the criticism directed at the Soviet cultural and political project in the late 1980s, the independence period has not seen a wholesale rejection of the Soviet legacy. Adab has been nationalized even further, becoming more closely identified with the nation and losing the connections to a more cosmopolitan or internationalist culture promoted during the Soviet era. But the Soviet cultural project survives in ghostly and seemingly anachronistic ways, such as when a government minister orders police officers to go to the theater as a way to make them better people. The opera has lived on, too, sometimes relatively well funded, as in Kazakhstan, periodically forbidden (in Turkmenistan from 2001 to 2009), and sometimes with help from foreign donors, as in Tajikistan. Indeed, in 2013 the theater released an illustrated volume commemorating its history, referring to the opera theater as a "Temple of Art."

CASE VIII-B

Sound, Aesthetics, and Instrumental Variance in Dutar Ensembles in Tashkent

Tanya Merchant

When I arrived in Tashkent, Uzbekistan, in the summer of 2002, I connected with two master teachers of the *dutar* (two-stringed lute): Ruzibi Hodjayeva (Roza opa) and Malikakhon Ziyaeva (Malika opa). With their help and guidance, I found myself in several settings where the dutar played an important role in shaping the sonic landscape. One that I did not expect was the variety of dutar ensembles. In this chapter, I focus on the first dutar ensemble I observed and rehearsed with—a typical student ensemble run by Roza opa—and explore the two versions of the dutar that appeared in that ensemble as it sought to prepare young musicians for public performances.

These two versions of the dutar stem from different historical periods. Instrument makers created them with different sonic and ideological goals in mind, and performers continue to use them for differing (though often overlapping) goals. The "traditional" dutar underwent some innovations over the centuries, but instrument makers and dutar performers consciously maintain sonic continuity with its historical construction and function. The "reconstructed" dutar—also called the "folk" dutar or "modernized"

dutar—originated in the 1930s and underwent significant changes in construction and sound in order to meet the needs of Soviet concert halls and their ensembles. This redesigning and reconstructing of folk instruments was a vital part of the larger Soviet project of "uplifting" folk music, therein placing the reconstructed dutar within a program of nation building. Both versions of the dutar appear in various contexts in independent Uzbekistan, one of which is the dutar ensemble.

The dutar is common throughout Central Asia, including two versions of the instrument in Uzbekistan (as well as a different one in the territory of Karakalpakstan). There also are manifestations of the dutar in Tajikistan, Turkmenistan, Afghanistan, and the Xinjiang region of China. The instrument's name means "two strings," and it usually maintains that format, except in Afghanistan, where innovations have led to three-, five-, and fourteen-stringed dutars. The dutar I learned in Tashkent is a form of the instrument common in Uzbekistan and Tajikistan, which have similar instrumentaria and some shared musical repertoires.

The version of the instrument that musicians in Tashkent call "traditional" is made of apricot or mulberry wood and has a long neck with tied frets that are usually made of nylon string—an innovation of the historical gut frets that is not seen as disrupting its traditional sound or form. It has two silk strings that are plucked and strummed by hand and tuned via tension tuning. Soviet acoustician Ashot Petrossiants created the other version of the dutar common in Tashkent when he opened an instrument laboratory in the Tashkent Conservatory in 1936 to redesign Central Asian instruments for use in Soviet concert halls and large ensembles. The reconstructed dutar has nylon strings; fixed, equal-tempered metal frets; and metal machine tuning pegs to adjust the pitch of each string. The timbre and volume of the two types of dutar differ significantly. Silk strings create a softer volume and more diffuse timbre, while nylon is louder with a more direct timbre that Petrossiants designed to carry through a large concert hall. The difference in tuning provided by the two fret systems—tied nylon frets with different-sized gaps between various intervals and glued-in metal frets spaced to create equal-tempered intervals—is perceptible to practitioners, though often dismissed as insignificant and imperceptible to the general public.

Each version of the dutar is taught in a different department of the Uzbek State Conservatory of Music, and each department focuses on different repertoires, though there is significant overlap. In the Traditional Music Department (An'anaviy Fakulteti), the primary focus is on Central Asian *maqom* repertoires: music rooted in major court cities like Bukhara, Samarqand, and Khiva, which traces back at least to the nineteenth century and as far back as the fifteenth century. The *Shashmaqom*—"Six Maqoms"—of Bukhara is the most famous maqom repertoire that originated within the borders of present-day Uzbekistan. Many other repertoires also deemed traditional or classical are taught in this department, as well as newly composed works that are written in the traditional style. The teaching style common in this department focuses on learning pieces by ear, though fluency in playing from written music is also highly valued.

The reconstructed dutar is taught in the Arranged Folk Music Department (Halq Chol'gu Fakulteti: lit., People's Performance Department). This department's focus is on all manner of composed works: compositions by Uzbek composers, folk melodies arranged for reconstructed instruments (either solo, in small ensembles, or in folk orchestras), and European classical compositions arranged for reconstructed instruments. Written music is much more common as a pedagogical tool in this department, though teaching and learning by ear is still commonplace.

These separate departments came about at different points in the twentieth century. The Arranged Folk Music Department opened in 1951 and the Traditional Music Department opened in 1970. Many dutarists play music of both categories at some point in their career. Most music schools (magnet schools for music) and after-school programs use reconstructed dutars and other reconstructed instruments, since they are more affordable, more common, and are available in smaller sizes thought to be more appropriate for young students. (These smaller sizes are the result of Petrossiants's creation of consorts for the instruments that he reconstructed with soprano, alto, tenor, and bass versions [similar to the violin family].) There is some understandable competition and tension between musicians in each style, since most musicians are deeply invested in their chosen style of music and are often put in competition with other musicians for resources (funding, prizes, publicity, employment, etc.). Despite this, there is also much friendship and collaboration among dutarists in Tashkent, who all seek ways to further develop and disseminate their music.

Both styles of music, both conservatory departments, both versions of the dutar, and dutarists of all ages have the dutar ensemble in common. These ensembles exist throughout Uzbekistan, in Tashkent as well as in cities and villages throughout the country. The most famous is the State Dutar Ensemble, which was founded after the Second World War and was long associated with the Uzbek State Radio and Television Station (but is now separate from that institution). That dutar ensemble includes young women who perform the dutar and sing (and occasionally accompany themselves on frame drum). This is considered a traditional ensemble, though performing publicly in concert was not thought to be appropriate for women before the women's liberation movement in 1920s Soviet Uzbekistan. Instead, the traditionality of this ensemble is rooted in the silk-stringed, nonequal-tempered version of the instrument the women played and the repertoire performed that focused on music often called classical (*mumtoz*), in the sense that it predates the twentieth century. This dutar ensemble created a standard version for dutar ensembles in music schools, conservatories, and elsewhere—largely populated by women providing concert performances of the national repertoire.

The dutar is associated with femininity because of its silk strings and softer timbre, as well as its status as the only nonpercussion instrument that Uzbek women historically played. This association, however, does not feminize the men and boys who play it (and have

throughout history). This is a common phenomenon throughout many cultures in which men can play instruments associated with women and femininity with no consequence to their masculinity. In my experience in Tashkent, dutar ensembles were more often mixed gendered than the public image of women's dutar ensemble would lead one to believe, because they often grew out of a dutar instructor's studio that usually features men and women.

Rehearsing with a Girls Dutar Ensemble

The first dutar ensemble I encountered in Tashkent rehearsed in the Uzbek State Conservatory. Roza opa directed the ensemble and continued leading rehearsals with the girls dutar ensemble that she ran for a local music school straight through the summer holidays. She explained this as her response to the students' enthusiasm and desire to continue playing together, even during vacation periods. Thus, I found myself in a studio in the nearly empty Uzbek State Conservatory of Music on many sweltering afternoons in July and August of 2002. Roza opa and four to ten school-age girls would gather in her studio and rehearse arranged folk melodies, songs, and compositions on their dutars. They played the dutar together and occasionally some of them would sing or accompany the group on the frame drum (*doyra*). As they played through their repertoire, Roza opa would stop them occasionally and demonstrate the proper strumming patterns or a slower version of a particularly challenging passage. She would emphasize the importance of having all members of the group strumming in the same way, with the same fingers in the same direction, so that the visual and kinesthetic unison of a group of girls all moving in the same way together highlighted the sonic unison that

VIII-B-1   Ensemble Nozanin, founded in 2015 by director Ruzibi Hodjayeva. Performers include her current conservatory students and alumni, 2019. Photograph courtesy of Ruzibi Hodjayeva.

they strove to play. This means that both bodies and sound were intended to be collective yet singular, even though this abstract ideal was not always achieved by the students (or indeed, by any group). Still, students and teacher worked tirelessly in that stuffy studio, week in and week out, to learn repertoire, memorize it, and prepare for performances that would demonstrate their accomplishments and provide musical satisfaction for themselves and their audience.

For a single-instrument ensemble, the instruments the girls played had surprising diversity. Some were silk-stringed traditional dutars and some were reconstructed with nylon strings. Some were handed down from relatives, some were new, some were expensive professional instruments, but most were student instruments that required perseverance to tune and repair. The instruments produced diverse timbres and volume levels, as well as slight variations in pitch depending on whether the instrument used traditional tuning or equal temperament.

Nonetheless, in Roza opa's ensemble, these two types of dutar sounded together, largely uncommented on: nylon and silk vibrating in rhythmic unison and as near to unison pitch as any group of instrumentalists can play when some have equal-tempered frets and others do not. Outside of rehearsal, she would often comment about how both styles of dutar—and dutar performance—were more similar than different; that the public does not recognize the difference; and that performers of each style had much to learn from one another. "It is necessary not to separate [the two styles of dutar]. Traditional performance and [arranged] folk style should not be separated from one another. Traditional performing style is necessary. [Arranged] folk style is also needed."

This ensemble's repertoire often came from written scores, especially melodies from Roza opa's book of dutar pieces *Dutorim Sozim Manim* (My dutar, my instrument). The piece the ensemble rehearsed most in the summer of 2002 was Roza opa's arrangement of "Ayvon" (Patio) by Tuxtasin Jalilov. This is a song sung from the perspective of a protagonist who has fallen in love with a neighbor and sings of passion and devotion, despite the neighbor passing by without noticing. The tune has a large vocal range of over an octave and features a few large jumps in pitch for dramatic effect. Roza opa would coach the girls to sing and play simultaneously and work with them to phrase those jumps carefully so that they did not increase volume abruptly as their voice jumped to a higher register. She encouraged them to breathe in sync with the phrasing of the lyrics and made sure that they did not neglect their dutar technique while singing. She had her students memorize both the song and the dutar arrangements and did not refer them to the written notation. Roza opa's teaching emphasized the importance of these unison gestures, and she worked enthusiastically to guide her students in that direction. Although she would occasionally consult the written arrangement and share it with me, she taught the members of her ensemble by ear, teaching each new piece to the ensemble phrase by phrase, then having the ensemble play it back for her, at which point she would correct mistakes and give students advice about how to hold their bodies, improve their strumming technique, increase nuance in dynamics and phrasing, and enhance the tone of their playing by pressing strings more firmly or closer to the frets. When the ensemble was ready to perform Ayvon (or any similar piece), they would sit in semicircular fashion, smiling and manifesting musical arrangements with collective synchronicity.

●

After performing together in a student ensemble such as Roza opa's for years, young women would face several choices about how (or if) to continue their musical development. Some would progress to dutar study in one of the institutions known as *kollej* or *uchilishche* (specialist school—a magnet school equivalent to the final two years of high school) and eventually in either the Traditional Music Department or the Arranged Folk Music Department of the Uzbek State Conservatory of Music. After graduation, they could find themselves in one of the prominent dutar ensembles (e.g., Ensemble Nozanin pictured in figure VIII-B-1, directed by Roza opa, including current conservatory students and alumni), in folk orchestras, maqom ensembles, or as teachers in after-school programs, music schools, kollejs, or the conservatory. Regardless of their eventual educational and career outcomes, Roza opa and teachers like her guide young women from a variety of backgrounds and economic situations, playing a variety of dutars through a pedagogy that emphasizes the value of musical practice connected to femininity, tradition, innovation, and national pride. Young women's dutar ensembles continue to create a unique sonic space for the negotiation of those values through musical performance.

CASE VIII-C

Translating Art into Politics through Central Asian Feminist and Queer Fantasy

Georgy Mamedov

To Make Art Politically

At the end of "The Work of Art in the Epoch of Its Mechanical Reproduction," Walter Benjamin makes a clear distinction between Fascism and Communism: Fascism turns politics into art, and Communism responds by turning art into politics. But how does art become politics? This question acquired new relevance for many artists and cultural workers worldwide in the wake of the 2008–2009 financial crisis and the political upheaval that followed, including the Arab Spring and Occupy movement. The April Revolution of 2010 in Kyrgyzstan, interethnic conflict in the south of the country the same year, and the bloody suppression of the workers in the Kazakh city of Zhanaozen in December 2011 were the local context in which we, a group of contemporary artists and curators from three different Central Asian countries, addressed the same question to ourselves. In March 2012, Oksana Shatalova, a curator and artist from Kazakhstan; Asel Akmatova, a gallerist and art manager from Bishkek; and I joined forces to launch a new cultural institution—the School of Theory and Activism-Bishkek (STAB).

We saw STAB as a "radical insti-tution" by which we meant that in our practice we sought to paradoxically blend a neutral openness of a public cultural space—library, lectures, and film screenings—and an unapologetic militantism of a leftist art collective. In the six years that followed, STAB became a regional hub for exploring a variety of answers to the question of how to make art politically. Our first intention was to create a meeting point for art and politics. We wanted to in-stigate dialogue, collaboration, and, as a result, *solidarity* between artists and activists. We organized workshops and educational events for artists and activists; produced visual and publicity materials for political campaigns by unions, leftist groups, and LGBT and feminist organizations; and explored various genres of politically engaged art. Later, we moved away from this rather mechanically combined approach to art and politics and tried to identify more nuanced and specific ways of making art politically. At some point, we were convinced that how art becomes politics is a question about transformation and the operationalization of imagination.

We started our journey in this di-rection with an archaeology—in the

Foucauldian sense—of radical imagination, focusing on futuristic and utopian aspects of the Soviet project in Central Asia. Part of that archaeological endeavor was reading and discussing Soviet science fiction at reading groups, film screenings, and lectures. However, the most notable of those archaeological studies was the project "Bishkek: Chronicles of Radical Imagination," which resulted in the book *Bishkek Utopian*, tracking the traces of the Soviet concrete utopia in the urban space of Bishkek. We labeled these studies "future-in-the-past" and saw them as necessary prerequisites before moving into fantasizing the proper "future-in-the-future"—that is, of proposing a utopia of our own.

In 2017, on the occasion of the centennial anniversary of the October Revolution, we thought we were equipped enough with the knowledge of the past to dare to fantasize about the future. We invited political and social activists to contribute to the collection of feminist and queer science fiction, *Utterly Other* (*Sovsem Drugie*), that we imagined as a radical and innovative way of politicizing art and, more specifically, imagination.

Science Fiction as Activism

Utterly Other includes fifteen stories authored by feminist, LGBT, and other social activists from Kyrgyzstan, Kazakhstan, Russia, and the United States. At first glance, what makes *Utterly Other* an up-front political publication is the fact that it was written by activists, most of whom had never written literature before. While the use of science fiction as a medium for initiating change may seem somewhat incongruent with the more conventional forms of politicized aesthetics, such as media campaign, political cartoons, posters, and so forth, it also leads people to question what is activist in fantasizing about the future, and are there not more pressing issues that activists should attend to than indulging in utopian dreams?

These are fair questions. Social activism oftentimes operates in the mode of urgency; we mobilize against injustice, violence, or threats to our lives and freedom. However, what underlines urgency and mobilization in activism is an ultimate desire to radically transform existing social relations. Simply put, activists are driven by a desire to make the world a better place. But what does this "better" mean? How do we imagine transformed social relations? These are questions science fiction can answer, as it supplies us with images of alternative social realities that can provide inspiration for political action.

When we think of radical imagination, we tend to focus on its utopian dimension. In the case of *Utterly Other*, inspiration for this radical utopianism came from the Soviet tradition of science fiction that we previously thoroughly studied. Despite all the shortcomings of Soviet socialism, for Soviet science fiction authors such as Ivan Yefremov, Arkady and Boris Strugatsky, and Genrich Altov (Altshuller), to name the few with whom our collection is in some sort of dialogue, the future was a viable political category. Soviet science fiction authors, and we can probably claim regular citizens as well, engaged in fantasizing about the future as a way to imagine how the socialist system could be improved and advanced. We live in a completely different reality, that of late capitalism, in which imagination faces fierce political resistance. Mark Fisher described this resistance as "capitalist realism": "the widespread sense that not only capitalism is the only viable political and economic system, but also that it is now impossible even to imagine a coherent alternative to it." In these circumstances, we cannot expect even the most radical fantasy to simply describe the future only in positive terms. It will by default involve a negative, or let us say critical, element. As Ursula K. Le Guin once said, "We live in capitalism. Its power seems inescapable. So did the divine right of kings. Any human power can be resisted and changed by human beings. Resistance and change often begin in art, and very often in our art, the art of words."

Utterly Other was our intentional response to the political homophobia that has been on the rise in Kyrgyzstan since 2014, when the Kyrgyz parliament initiated the bill against the so-called gay propaganda. While the Kyrgyz deputies had been "selflessly" defending the country against "major" national security threats—namely, imaginary gay pride parades and same-sex marriages—in the call for contributions to the *Utterly Other* we invited feminist and queer activists to come up with their visions of a "better world," one that would be free of alienated labor, exploitation, racism, sexism, and homophobia but also leave behind nations, states, marriages, and even genders, thus potentially presenting the reader with the world in which all the hegemonic forces of contemporary social structures are removed.

However, as noted previously, the political meaning of activist fantasy is not only in its utopian imagination. It also contains a sufficient critical element. Fantasizing the future may shed critical light on the present, and in discussing science fiction as a form of activism I want to focus on this critical aspect of radical imagination that happened to be the most striking in *Utterly Other*.

Ideological Fantasy and "Nation above Rights"

In discussing activist science fiction as political fantasy, we see that it radically confronts what Slavoj Žižek defined as *ideological fantasy*: a vision of a society that is not antagonistic, "a society in which the relation between its parts is organic, complementary." Ideological fantasy strives to eliminate any contradictions and differences within the complex social fabric by presenting society as "an organic Whole, a social Body in which the different classes are like extremities, members each contributing to the Whole according to their function."

Political fantasy, thus, is a form of radical critique that challenges ideology not only on its discursive level but aims at deconstruction of the very fantastic foundation of ideology—that is, the organic metaphor of a society. However, political fantasy does not just perform a critical function toward the ideology; it also offers an alternative. For Žižek, as a Lacanian, fantasy supports reality; it is the glue that sticks together always fragmented social experience. Therefore, the ultimate political goal is not to discard fantasy from social reality but to be aware of its presence and to be able to choose the fantasy that would enable us to assemble a different vision of society. This can only be done with the means of a radical imagination, and, thus, science fiction—as a vehicle of radical imagination—plays a crucial political role.

Let me first describe how political homophobia that has been part of the Kyrgyz political discourse since 2014 is informed by the ideological fantasy of a society as an organic whole. Throughout the 1990s and early 2000s, Western media and political scientists described Kyrgyzstan as "the Switzerland of Central Asia," highlighting the country's mountainous terrain and economic liberalization carried out in the context of relative political democratization. Indeed, radical economic liberalization was, at least partially, conditioned by political liberalization. Massive economic losses experienced by the working and middle classes were measured against few gains of rights and freedoms.

As noted earlier, 2014 was a turning point in the country's flirtation with economic and political liberalism. In 2014, the Kyrgyz parliament initiated a bill against what got characterized as "gay propaganda." The Kyrgyz version of the bill was almost identical to the infamous Russian law passed in 2013.

Despite Kyrgyzstan being one of the post-Soviet republics most loyal to Vladimir Putin's Russia, the copy-pasted bill was suspended between the second and third hearings in parliament. However, the appearance of this discriminatory bill in the Kyrgyz public discourse triggered heated parliamentary and media debate on "traditions versus rights" in which homosexuality epitomized Western moral degradation and against which the strict observance of prudent national traditions was the only remedy. This debate, on its own turn, triggered an unprecedented wave of violence against LGBT people. In 2015–2016, rightwing nationalists systematically attacked LGBT-friendly events and offices of LGBT organizations. In 2017, the Kyrgyz regime found a concessional way to pacify the right-wing nationalists who were dissatisfied that the "gay propaganda" legislation was not adopted. The new version of the constitution, voted in referendum, included the redefinition of marriage as a voluntary union between a man and a woman. The previous version did not specify genders of those entering the union, which was presented as a loophole for legalizing same-sex marriages in Kyrgyzstan.

Since 2014, the political polarization of Kyrgyz society has intensified and at times developed into open confrontation. In December 2019, a group of women and men in traditional Kyrgyz costumes moved for four hours around Bishkek in a bus decorated with the slogan "Nation Above Rights." At one of the stops along the "Famous Route"—this is how the organizers described their action—the minister of culture and tourism joined the group to express his support of its cause. "Famous Route" was a performative response to the international feminist exhibition "Feminnale"—which presented the works of fifty-six international artists and was an homage to seventeen female labor migrants who died in a warehouse fire in Moscow in 2016—at the National Museum of Fine Arts. One of the organizers of the "Famous Route" told the press that the main message of their action was that "other nations must get used to respecting our culture." What sparked such a reaction from the right-wing nationalists who self-define as "national patriots" was a nude performance at the opening of the show. As a result of the public scandal caused by that performance, six other exhibits were removed from the display by decree of the minister of culture, who also fired the director of the museum.

A few months later, on March 8, 2020, a group of masked men wearing Ak-kalpaks (traditional Kyrgyz hats) attacked a Women's Day rally before it even started. Police present at the scene did not intervene. Several dozen participants in the peaceful march were detained and kept in the police precinct for three hours. None of the perpetrators were identified. The violent attack, however, found broad ideological support among Kyrgyz politicians, including sitting Members of Parliament, one of whom claimed that "there are limits to democracy. We have our own culture, our traditions. If they do not correspond to them, it is not right." Verbal and physical attacks on those who "do not correspond" is presented as righteous and justified by the vision of the nation as an organic and pure unity. Another deputy was even more straightforward in this respect in her comments about the purpose of the "gay-propaganda" legislation: "It [homosexuality] is not ours, and if it is not ours, society must alienate it from itself, in order to become clean, pure and good."

Liberal discourse often confronts these kinds of statements by appealing to their factual incorrectness. Gays and lesbians are not really different from the rest of the population: they want to love and be loved, just like anyone else; they are not evil or filthy; and if more people personally knew a queer or two, they would not see them as perverts. This line of argument remains within the charted space of ideological fantasy. Its message is simple: do not exclude them from the whole; assimilate.

The problem with this line of argument is that it does not acknowledge the fantastic foundation of ideological discourse. Ideological fantasy is not an extrapolation of reality (e.g., if you *knew* them, you would not hate them); it is the reality that is an extrapolation of fantasy. In other words, it does not matter if gays and lesbians are not at all as they are pictured in the conservative imagination; the way they are perceived is not determined by reality but is purely fantastic. The function of the fantasy is to compensate for the impossibility of ideological promise. Society does not exist as an organic whole in any possible reality. Society, as Marxism teaches us, is based on the fundamental conflict of interests between those who own the means of production and those who have no other choice but to sell their labor. Differences, not similarities, form the social fabric.

Totalitarian ideology is aware of this conflict and the impossibility of societal unity. Thus, the figure of the Other—the pervert, the intruder, the filthy—is absolutely necessary to compensate for that impossibility. Our society *will* become clean, pure and good, *only when* we exclude the elements that do not belong. Ideological fantasy is structural, which means that who exactly performs the role of the alien is historically changeable. Žižek develops his notion of ideological fantasy on the example of anti-Semitism in Nazi Germany. The Jew was an alien impeding the final purification and unification of the German nation. Today, in many postsocialist countries including Kyrgyzstan, it is the Gay. In other places and instances, it may be the Muslim, the Refugee, the Foreign Agent, the Fifth Column, and so on.

The liberal logic that appeals to reality may succeed in integrating an alien or two into the society through assimilation, thus only opening a slot for another pariah. Therefore, emancipatory politics must focus not only on debating the facts but on a radical confrontation with the fundamental fantasy that stitches those facts together. And the way to challenge hegemonic fantasy is to fantasize differently. In other words, translating art into politics means replacing ideological fantasy with political fantasy.

Utterly Other, Political Fantasy against Ideological Fantasy

The striking revelation that a reader of *Utterly Other* may experience comes from a dramatic vision of society that falls apart. Many stories in the book depict the future in which society as an organic unity no longer exists. Let me retell the three stories from the book that express this in the most vivid and dramatic way.

In Syinat Sultanalieva's "Element 174," people inhabit new planets in the solar system. The main character, a masculine-acting clandestine lesbian and daughter of the powerful clan leader on Earth, visits the planet Umai as an ambassador. Umai is the home planet for the descendants of women who were expelled from Earth many generations ago. They were supposed to die out on the planet not fit for human life, but instead of terraforming Umai, they adapted themselves to the new environment and built a queer feminist world on the planet, which later becomes Earth's major geopolitical challenger in the solar system.

A similar motif of survival on an-

VIII-C-2 Syinat Sultanalieva reads her story at the *Utterly Other* book launch in STAB. March 2018, Bishkek. Photo credit: STAB.

other planet, despite the odds, is central to another story, "Hollow," by Mia Mingus. Hollow is the planet-camp for disabled from Earth who have been sent there regularly as babies. Since the planet is so remote and deprived of any technological devices to escape from it, the inmates were left there without a watch. They turn their confinement into a new living environment, clumsy and imperfect but inclusive and sensitive to all their needs and abilities.

In "Another Dimension," Oksana Shatalova does not send her characters to other planets. They all live on Earth, but in two totally separated dimensions. Her story features the world of highly advanced technological development in which people with opposed value systems once decided to simply stop seeing each other. Started as an application of social media algorithms discarding undesirable content from one's feed, the separation grew in scale and ended up as two worlds on one planet, Heaven and Hell. Heaven is a patriarchal paradise in which men are called masters and women constantly take care of children. They do not even have to give birth to them, as Heaven's government is so generous that it supplies every household with mechanical babies to nurture. What is going on in Hell is not quite clear, but obviously nothing good, something that from Heaven's point of view is continuous perversion and moral degradation. Shatalova's largely dystopian narrative still contains a glimmer of hope, as it tells the story of a young woman who manages to escape from Heaven to Hell and comes back to rescue her sister from the real hell of Heaven.

In all three stories, it is not just that we do not see the unity in society; it is that the radical split, the refuge, appears the only way to survive. An alternative reality—queer, inclusive, and environmentally harmonious—is possible only as the result of radical separation and cutting all ties with oppressors. The resource for dialogue or even mere cohabitation within a radically fractured society seems to be totally exhausted.

Does this imply helpless surrender and defeat of progressive forces against the conservative tendency? Instead of straightforwardly jumping to such pessimistic conclusions, I would propose to look at these narratives of unbridgeable separation more closely and treat them not as signs of giving up but as examples of a critical account of contemporary Kyrgyz reality. One can even say prognostic, if juxtaposed with the facts of utter ideological confrontation of the recent years outlined previously. I suggest that this prognostic effect is not random but is a function of science fiction as a genre, if we are to approach it politically.

Political Fantasy as Critical Utopia

To elaborate on this point, we can look more closely at the poetics of science fiction as a vehicle of political fantasy with the help of Darko Suvin, a literary scholar and theorist of utopia. According to Suvin, the political meaning of science fiction as a specific literary genre is not so much in imagining the future for the sake of the future as it is in providing an alternative account of the present reality. He described the heuristic effect of science fiction for understanding political reality as "cognitive estrangement." Borrowing the term *estrangement* from Russian Formalists (*ostranenie*) and Bertolt Brecht (*Verfremdung*), Suvin elaborates it specifically for science fiction. If in realist literature *estrangement* (commonly, but not accurately, translated into English as "alienation") works to defamiliarize the familiar, in science fiction it works in reverse, by presenting the unfamiliar as if it was familiar. However, the achieved effect is similar. If estrangement in realist art makes us aware of the things that we take for granted, in science fiction we become aware of the aspects of our reality that we cannot fully grasp or describe in more conventional languages of political or nonfictional writing. Imagination as the main artistic device in science fiction becomes "a means to understanding the tendencies latent in reality."

Science fiction is thus the mirror of ideological reality. If ideological discourse hides its fantastic foundation, science fiction brings the fantasy to the forefront, enabling us to see the facts not as they appear, held together by invisible glue, but as they are and as they could be. In fictional worlds, characters easily transcend space and time. This is that exact unfamiliar that science fiction routinizes. Interplanetary travels and interspecies small talk serve as a setting in which all-too-earthly and human dramas unfold. However, this fantastic setting is crucial, as it crystalizes all our familiar tensions and conflicts to a degree that can give us a new perspective on them.

This perspective can be simultaneously critical and utopian. The *Utterly Other* narratives of radical separation may sound disturbingly dystopian, as behind their exaggerated and alarmist account of reality we see not only facts but also fears and tears of those "who do not correspond" and must be "alienated." The tricky thing about ideological fantasy is that it does actually inform and guide real-life actions, from mobbing feminist marches to sending people to concentration camps. However, these stories are not merely dystopian but also critically utopian. Critical utopia is not idealistic; it does not offer a blueprint of the future, but through exaggerated critique of the present reality it offers a glimpse into the potentially alternative future.

What is this glimpse in the case of *Utterly Other*? This glimpse is precisely expressed in the title of the book. The alternative to the violent ideology of xenophobia and exclusion for the sake of the desired but impossible unity is not in assimilation of differences but rather in their flourishing. In each story, refuge leads to the preservation and celebration of the utter otherness. Separation is indeed a dystopian scenario, but it does not have to be the only one. An alternative that we can gather from the activist imagination is in replacing the ideological fantasy of organic unity with the political fantasy of solidarity. The solidarity that, at its best, is that "the free development of each is the condition for the free development of all."

DISCUSSION QUESTIONS

Part VIII: Contexts of Aesthetics

29. Music

1. What differing social and cultural circumstances among the nomadic and settled peoples of Central Asia have contributed to shaping their distinct musical traditions?

2. How have political upheaval, nationalism, and cultural policies had a direct impact on the development of musical traditions in Central Asia during the twentieth century? Based on the recent history of Central Asia during the twenty-first century, what changes and musical developments do you foresee in Central Asian musical cultures in the decades to come?

30. Art

3. Does art play a decolonial mission in Central Asia, or can it only be a reflection of contemporary social relations?

4. Does the geopolitical grouping of art benefit or detract from the analysis of Central Asia and its art? Would more state involvement with contemporary art impact its critical status?

31. Literature

5. What were the major genres of Central Asian literature, and how have these genres changed over time?

6. What is the role of Persian and Turkic literatures within Central Asian literary culture, and how do these literary traditions relate to and diverge from each other?

32. Film

7. How did the Soviet experience impact the development of Central Asian film?

8. How do recent Central Asian films explore nationality, politics, and identity on-screen?

Case VIII-A: Soviet Cultural Construction and Its Afterlives

9. To what extent can we speak of a Soviet *adab*?

10. To what extent can the connections established between Soviet Central Asian intellectuals and their counterparts abroad be understood as a new "cosmopolis?"

Case VIII-B: Sound, Aesthetics, and Instrumental Variance in Dutar Ensembles in Tashkent

11. Discuss the origins and musical contexts of the two different versions of the dutar in Tashkent. Then consider how other instruments are created with different models and versions, such as acoustic versus electric guitars, wooden versus plastic recorders, bluegrass versus Renaissance mandolins, or another set of instrument versions with which you are familiar. Compare the differences in one of those pairs of instrument models and their resulting sounds, aesthetics, and contexts.

12. How does music connect different time periods—past, present, and future— and shape both performers' and audiences' understanding of the context in which they live?

Case VIII-C: Translating Art into Politics through Central Asian Feminist and Queer Fantasy

13. Why is it important to make art politically? Is it necessary for artists to be politically engaged?

14. Should political and social activists use art and imagination in their struggles? Can science fiction really contribute to societal changes? Could you bring examples of creative activism similar to *Utterly Other* from other geographical or social contexts?

FURTHER READING

29. Music

Harris, Rachel. *The Making of a Musical Canon in Chinese Central Asia: The Uyghur Twelve Muqam*. Aldershot: Ashgate, 2008.

Levin, Theodore. *The Hundred Thousand Fools of God: Musical Travels in Central Asia (and Queens, New York)*. Bloomington: Indiana University Press, 1996.

Levin, Theodore, Saida Daukeyeva, and Elmira Köchümkulova, eds. *The Music of Central Asia*. Bloomington: Indiana University Press, 2016.

Levin, Theodore, and Valentina Süzükei. *Where Rivers and Mountains Sing: Sound, Music, and Nomadism in Tuva and Beyond*. Bloomington: Indiana University Press, 2006.

Merchant, Tanya. *Women Musicians of Uzbekistan: From Courtyard to Conservatory*. Urbana: University of Illinois Press, 2015.

Slobin, Mark. *Kirgiz Instrumental Music*. New York: Society for Asian Music, 1969.

Sipos, János. *Kazakh Folksongs: From the Two Ends of the Steppe*. Budapest: Akadémiai Kiadó, 2001.

Sultanova, Razia. *From Shamanism to Sufism: Women, Islam, and Culture in Central Asia*. London: I. B. Taurus, 2011.

30. Art

Abykayeva-Tiesenhausen, Aliya. *Central Asia in Art: From Soviet Orientalism to the New Republics.* London: I. B. Tauris, 2016.

Ibraeva, Valeria. "100 Years of Solitude: Cultural Decolonization and its Artistic Forms." Institute of Contemporary Art Zagreb, 2020. http://www.institute.hr/wp-content/uploads/2020/05/Valeria-Ibraeva_100-Years_Kazakhstan.pdf.

Kudaibergenova, Diana. "Contemporary Art in Central Asia as an Alternative Forum for Discussions." Voices on Central Asia, June 25, 2018. https://voicesoncentralasia.org/contemporary-art-in-central-asia-as-an-alternative-space-for-discussions/.

Sorokina, Yuliya. "From Evolution to Growth: Central Asian Video Art, 1995–2015." *Studies in Russian and Soviet Cinema* 10, no. 3 (2016): 238–60.

Tlostanova, Madina. *What Does It Mean to Be Post-Soviet? Decolonial Art from the Ruins of the Soviet Empire.* Durham, NC: Duke University Press, 2018.

31. Literature

'Arudi, Nizami-i. *Chahar Maqaleh of Nizami-i-Arudi of Samarqand.* Translated by Edward G. Browne. London: Luzac, 1921.

Aini, Sadriddin. *The Sands of Oxus: Boyhood Reminiscences of Sadriddin Aini.* Translated by John R. Perry and Rachel Lehr. Costa Mesa, CA: Mazda, 1998.

Allworth, Edward A. *Evading Reality: The Devices of 'Abdalrauf Fitrat, Modern Central Asian Reformist.* Leiden: Brill, 2002.

Cho'lpon, Abdulhamid Sulaymon o'g'li. *Night and Day.* Translated and edited by Christopher Fort. Boston: Academic Studies, 2019.

Czaplicka, Marie Antoinette. *The Turks of Central Asia in History and at the Present Day: An Ethnological Inquiry into the Pan-Turanian Problem, and Bibliographical Material Relating to the Early Turks and the Present Turks of Central Asia.* Oxford: Clarendon, 1918.

Gould, Rebecca Ruth. *The Persian Prison Poem: Sovereignty and the Political Imagination.* Edinburgh: Edinburgh University Press, 2021.

Hajib, Yusuf Khass. *Wisdom of Royal Glory (Kutadgu Bilik): A Turko-Islamic Mirror for Princes.* Translated and edited by Robert Dankoff. Chicago: University of Chicago Press, 1983.

Halman, Talat S. *Contemporary Turkish Literature: Fiction and Poetry.* Rutherford, NJ: Fairleigh Dickinson University Press, 1980.

Halman, Talat S. *A Millennium of Turkish Literature: A Concise History*, edited by Jayne L. Warner. 1st ed. Ankara: Republic of Turkey Ministry of Culture and Tourism, 2008, Rev. ed. Syracuse, NY: Syracuse University Press, 2011.

Ismailov, Hamid. *The Devils' Dance.* Translated by Donald Rayfield and John Farndon. London: Tilted Axis, 2018.

Nawā'ī, Mīr 'Alī Shīr. *Judgment of Two Languages; Muhakamat al-Lughatayn*, translated by Robert Devereux. Leiden: Brill, 1966.

Sharma, Sunil. *Persian Poetry at the Indian Frontier: Mas'ûd Sa'd Salmân of Lahore.* Delhi: Permanent Black, 2001.

Starr, Frederick S. *Lost Enlightenment: Central Asia's Golden Age from the Arab Conquest to Tamerlane.* Princeton, NJ: Princeton University Press, 2014.

Tabatabai, Sassan. *Father of Persian Verse: Rudaki and His Poetry.* Amsterdam: Amsterdam University Press, 2011.

Wells, Charles. *The Literature of the Turks: A Turkish Chrestomathy.* London: Bernard Quaritch, 1891.

32. Film

Abikeyeva, Gulnara. *The Heart of the World: Films from Central Asia*. Almaty: Kompleks, 2003.

Cummings, Sally N. "Soviet Rule, Nation and Film: The Kyrgyz 'Wonder Years.'" *Nations and Nationalism* 15, no. 4 (2009): 636–57.

Djagalov, Rossen, and Masha Salazkina. "Tashkent '68: A Cinematic Contact Zone." *Slavic Review* 75, no. 2 (2016): 279–98.

Dönmez-Colin, Gönül. *Cinemas of the Other: A Personal Journey with Film-Makers from the Middle East and Central Asia*. Bristol: Intellect, 2012.

Dönmez-Colin, Gönül. *Women, Islam, and Cinema*. London: Reaktion Books, 2004.

Drieu, Cloé. *Cinema, Nation, and Empire in Uzbekistan, 1919–1937*. Bloomington: Indiana University Press, 2019.

Isaacs, Rico. *Film and Identity in Kazakhstan: Soviet and Post-Soviet Culture in Central Asia*. London: I. B. Tauris, 2018.

Ji-Seok, Kim, Gulnara Abikeyeva, Gulbara Tolomushova, and Sadullo Rahimov, eds. *The Unknown New Wave of Central Asian Cinema*. Seoul: Pon Puksuu, 2013.

Jones, Kent. "Lone Wolves at the Door of History." *Film Comment* 39, no. 3 (2003): 54–57.

KinoKultura (online journal). http://www.kinokultura.com/.

Pruner, Ludmila Z. "The New Wave in Kazakh Cinema." *Slavic Review* 51, no. 4 (1992): 791–801.

Rouland, Michael, Gulnara Abikeyeva, and Birgit Beumers, eds. *Cinema in Central Asia: Rewriting Cultural Histories*. London: I. B. Tauris, 2013.

Case VIII-A: Soviet Cultural Construction and Its Afterlives

Clark, Katerina. *Moscow, The Fourth Rome: Stalinism, Cosmopolitanism, and the Evolution of Soviet Culture, 1931–1941*. Cambridge, MA: Harvard University Press, 2011.

David-Fox, Michael. *Crossing Borders: Modernity, Ideology, and Culture in Russia and the Soviet Union*. Pittsburgh: University of Pittsburgh Press, 2015.

David-Fox, Michael. "What Is Cultural Revolution?" *Russian Review* 58, no. 2 (1999): 181–201.

Djagalov, Rossen. *From Internationalism to Postcolonialism: Literature and Cinema between the Second and the Third Worlds*. Montreal: McGill-Queen's University Press, 2020.

Kalinovsky, Artemy M. *Laboratory of Socialist Development: Cold War Politics and Decolonization in Soviet Tajikistan*. Ithaca, NY: Cornell University Press, 2018.

Khalid, Adeeb. *Making Uzbekistan: Nation, Empire, and Revolution in the Early USSR*. Ithaca, NY: Cornell University Press, 2015.

Kia, Mana. *Persianate Selves: Memories of Place and Origin before Nationalism*. Stanford, CA: Stanford University Press, 2020.

Kirasirova, Masha. "'Sons of Muslims' in Moscow: Soviet Central Asian Mediators to the Foreign East, 1955–1962." *Ab Imperio* 2011, no. 4 (2011): 106–32.

Levin, Theodore Craig. *The Hundred Thousand Fools of God: Musical Travels in Central Asia (and Queens, New York)*. Bloomington: Indiana University Press, 1999.

Pickett, James. *Polymaths of Islam: Power and Networks of Knowledge in Central Asia*. Ithaca, NY: Cornell University Press, 2020.

Roberts, Flora J. "Old Elites under Communism: Soviet Rule in Leninobod." PhD diss., University of Chicago, 2016.

Case VIII-B: Sound, Aesthetics, and Instrumental Variance in Dutar Ensembles in Tashkent

Djumaev, Alexander. "Power Structures, Culture Policy, and Traditional Music in Soviet Central Asia." *Yearbook for Traditional Music* 25 (1993): 43–50.

Merchant, Tanya. *Women Musicians of Uzbekistan: From Courtyard to Conservatory.* Urbana: University of Illinois Press, 2015.

Sultanova, Razia. *From Shamanism to Sufism: Women, Islam and Culture in Central Asia,* London: I. B. Tauris, 2011.

Case VIII-C: Translating Art into Politics through Central Asian Feminist and Queer Fantasy

Bagdasarova, Nina. "Securing an LGBT Identity in Kyrgyzstan. Case Studies from Bishkek and Osh." *International Quarterly for Asian Studies* 49, no. 1–2 (2018): 17–40.

Bagdasarova, Nina. "The Space–Time Continuum of the 'Dangerous' Body: Lesbian, Gay, Bisexual and Transgender Securityscapes in Kyrgyzstan in Surviving Everyday Life." In *The Securityscapes of Threatened People in Kyrgyzstan*, edited by Marc von Boemcken, Nina Bagdasarova, Aksana Ismailbekova and Conrad J. Schetter, 179–202. Bristol: Bristol University Press, 2020.

Graeber, David. *Direct Action: An Ethnography.* Edinburgh: AK Press, 2009

Hatherley, Owen. "'Where Our Tomorrow Is Already Yesterday': Bishkek." In *The Adventures of Owen Hatherley in the Post-Soviet Space.* London: Repeater Books, 2018.

Suyarkulova, Mohira. "'Nobody Is Going to Want Her Like This': Disability, Sexuality, and Un/happiness in Kyrgyzstan." *Kohl: A Journal for Body and Gender Research.* 6 (Fall 2020): 187–200.

von Boemcken, Marc, Hafiz Boboyorov, and Nina Bagdasarova. "Living Dangerously: Securityscapes of Lyuli and LGBT People in Urban Spaces of Kyrgyzstan." *Central Asian Survey* 37, no. 1 (2018): 68–84.

Translating Contexts into Policy

*David M. Abramson, Laura L. Adams,
and David W. Montgomery*

The goal of this book has been to provide information about Central Asia in a way that lays a foundation for a more holistic engagement with the region, one that appreciates the varied contexts in which people live. By presenting information through a variety of contextual lenses, the authors have shared ways of understanding Central Asia that help guide readers away from viewing Central Asia through a single, fixed (or stereotyping) lens. This ability to think through contexts, not just information, becomes especially important when we compare the book's purpose of providing knowledge *for* something, as opposed to simply knowledge *of* something. Much of academic writing and the university itself is concerned with knowledge *of* the world: information that gives new and different insights as to how one might more appropriately or more accurately see an issue. In contrast, some readers of this book will use it as background knowledge for further, nonacademic engagement with the region; their need is knowledge *for* a particular purpose.

Below we offer some thoughts on how to apply information about contexts. Drawing on our collective experience both in academia and in US governmental and nongovernmental organizations focused on policy making, diplomacy, or development, we share a necessarily partial perspective on how to apply this book to work in the world outside of the university. For us, diplomacy and development policy are a generalized framework for guiding the allocation of resources, determining the prioritization of problems to be addressed, and implementing action toward prioritized ends in the context of international relations. The point is that context adds nuance to the application of knowledge in a way that reduces overreliance on stereotypes and historical tropes in diagnosing and remedying foreign policy problems. In thinking

715

through how to use the book in a policy context, we offer a way to broadly consider how to take knowledge out of the classroom and into the world.

Those concerned with the policy relevance of the numerous studies in this volume, however, might observe that very few of the chapters match up topically with issues of obvious concern to policy makers focused on Central Asia, including those spelled out by US government agencies as diplomatic priorities. There are few chapters on typical "policy" topics, such as terrorism, judicial and police reform, corruption, forced labor, trafficking in persons, women's rights, drug trafficking, conflict resolution, foreign relations with neighboring states, military training, press freedom, and so on. There are only a few exceptions, such as Ferrando's chapter on integration and the Eurasian Economic Union, Wooden's discussion of environmental issues, Borbieva's chapter on development, and Kulikova's chapter on media. This is not an oversight on the part of the editor but is intentional; this volume is about the multiple contexts that can usefully inform policy decisions on many of these topics.

While it would be helpful to be handed a single guide to policy basics in the region—everything one needs to know before starting a new posting at Embassy-Bishkek or as director of the Office of Central Eurasian Affairs— one can usually find such resources in the files of a well-organized predecessor or as otherwise conveyed through institutional memory. The various topics offered here, precisely because they are contextualizing, have a much longer shelf life. This is because the very structures, institutions, norms, modes of interaction, values, moral principles, and the ways of translating and expressing them are what define Central Asia as a region, its constituent countries, and subnational groupings. And yet, despite these aspects of culture that are both consistent and observable, even the way Central Asians invoke, deploy, manipulate, question, subvert, and feel constrained by them are patterned. In other words, behaviors are not determined by sets of unchanging rules and norms. Rather, the challenge is to translate these contextualizing patterns of behavior into policy.

Constraints of Policy Contexts

We acknowledge the constraints that policy makers and implementers are under when applying this book's contextualizing approach to their work. For readers coming from an academic background, it can be difficult to understand why policy makers and development practitioners boil down the complexity of the world into frameworks, three-point strategies, logic models, theories of change, and so on. As practitioners ourselves, we appreciate that the object of analysis in policy work is defined by the national interest of the country sponsoring the policy, leading to discrepancies between local and international definitions of problems and their solutions. But the biggest challenge of making use of contexts is the tension between the time needed to better understand a problem and the need to enact solutions as soon as possible. Decisions will be made, whether they are informed by

DAVID M. ABRAMSON, LAURA L. ADAMS, AND DAVID W. MONTGOMERY

reliable information or not, so a policy analyst needs to be prepared to apply different contextual lenses in order to quickly make sound and timely recommendations concerning a particular situation.

Other tensions that good contextual knowledge can mitigate include the tendency to essentialize, idealize, or overgeneralize. A policy maker, in part because of time pressure, is tempted to reduce the essence of a topic to single-factor explanations in the absence of contradictory or complicating information. It is easy to make what we already know the essence of what needs to be known and to see everything else through that single focus: for example, Uzbeks have a good market economy because they have traditionally been merchants. But as Adams points out in her chapter, as soon as we think we know something about national identity, we should dig deeper. A knowledge of contexts can help us do that. Essentializing can also take the form of seeing a traditional social organization like clan or regional identity as defining a problem or determining an outcome, rather than seeing it as a factor that structures how problems are seen and what actions are perceived as possible.

Similarly, perhaps we idealize the spirit of Kyrgyz democracy or Afghan institutions of local self-governance and therefore fail to see their effects on women and marginalized groups. This can also show up as a tendency to uncritically accept arguments from local interlocutors about what is "traditional" and therefore undesirable or impossible to change. Overgeneralization happens when we see the similarities between two contexts and, confident of our understanding of one context, project it as a model onto the other. This can happen when, for example, US Foreign Service officers who have served in Afghanistan or Eastern Europe come to Central Asia and see the similarities but lack the knowledge of the local context to understand that what appears similar on the surface may actually endure thanks to very different institutions, norms, and practices—as Mostowlansky's and Murtazashvili's cases in this book remind us.

Translating Contexts for Policy

Policy by definition identifies a problem in need of change. For example, a lack of democracy, economic and political overdependence on other countries, Russian influence and Soviet legacies, violent extremism, and so on are descriptions of political conditions US policy makers see as problems in need of change. Central Asian governments might agree with the United States on a given problem, but not necessarily on how to address it. However, it is the goal of US foreign policy to provide resources to encourage the change that the United States would like to see. Policies toward Central Asia—like policies anywhere—are designed to address what is understood to be in the "national interest," whether tied to security, economic, or ideological issues. However, identifying "problems" that need fixing, or at least nudging in a particular direction in line with US interests, tends to bring us to define those problems in a way that freezes them somewhat in space and time.

One example is the focus on the theological or ideological context of radicalization when displacement and ineffective state governance may be more explanatory of its origins and impetus (see Epkenhans, Lemon, Montgomery, Heathershaw, Satybaldieva and Sanghera, Reeves, and Aitieva). A good translation of context into policy, then, keeps analysis of these problems dynamic. This helps to challenge the policy imagination and ensure that policies designed to further another country's national interests are compatible with and, at the very least, do not inadvertently undermine the interests shared by Central Asian governments, societies, or special interest groups.

In order to translate contexts into policy, it is useful to distinguish text from context. If text is the message—the primary narrative, or generally what is communicated directly—then context is the accompanying information (the "with text") that justifies, explains, or even challenges what is communicated. Translating context into policy, then, can occur in multiple ways. This volume offers text and context but in doing so seeks to explain and challenge or question existing narratives or characterizations of Central Asia that have emerged through particular historical and political lenses (e.g., the post–Cold War global order, postcolonialism, the Global War on Terror, and so on). There is less of an emphasis on justifying existing framings because effective scholarship generally seeks to raise questions and offers new and original ideas, rather than merely supporting what we believe we already understand. This applies equally to studies of policy making, which frequently question how policies are justified and reinforced.

The historical context chapters in this volume explain how Central Asia's long history of being situated on the margins of or borders between territorial empires has bequeathed it (in the eyes of Westerners) a narrative legacy of seeming isolation, as a backwater that consequently has been poorly studied and (mis)understood. The chapters that contextualize Central Asia as a geographical region (Diener and Megoran) challenge these assumptions by demonstrating Central Asians' roles as global actors—labor migrants (Laruelle), adherents to and promoters of transnationally shared ideologies (communism [Igmen], nationalism [Adams]) and religion (mostly Islam [Khalid, Montgomery, Schatz, Louw]); and elites investing and off-shoring capital in banks, businesses, and real estate (Cooley). If we view these problems through a particular lens of Central Asia's marginalization and Cold War era theories, we might miss the contextual factors that have already led these countries down a different path. Central Asian elites are enmeshed in global financial networks through money laundering and deposits in safe bank accounts abroad; Central Asian labor migrants have become a major force in local economies and they have, by the millions, beaten paths to Russia and beyond for work and sent back remittances to support their families at home (Laruelle, Reeves, Aitieva, Roche); Central Asian Muslims hoping to deepen their faith in Islam have already made transnational ties to the erstwhile largely inaccessible world of Islam beyond socialism's borders (Epkenhans, Schwab); and thousands of activists, revolutionaries, devout

DAVID M. ABRAMSON, LAURA L. ADAMS, AND DAVID W. MONTGOMERY

believers in Islam, the misguided, and socially or financially disenfranchised individuals have fought on behalf of various militant groups in war zones far from their home countries. Knowing about these global movements and connections can help those crafting US policies—from democracy to counterterrorism and from economic development to anti-corruption—assess when to strike productive compromises between US interests and those of counterpart Central Asian governments, on the one hand, and when to abort a particular project, on the other.

We also can see the problem of overgeneralization when the United States applies a programmatic solution developed in one environment to the Central Asian context. For example, collaborative counterterrorism programs that seek to work with a specific government to prevent its country from "exporting" militants abroad fall short when that country exports mass numbers of labor migrants to a third country, Russia, where only there do they join militant networks that facilitate onward movement to conflict zones, such as Iraq and Syria—and only in relatively small numbers. Reeves's research on labor migration and Aitieva's on existing in the diaspora—alongside Satybaldieva and Sanghera's on economics and Heathershaw's on politics—provide critical context of the third-country environment leading recruitment to militancy, a process that is often beyond the control of sending countries like Tajikistan and Kyrgyzstan. Moreover, chapters capturing how Central Asians envision their individual and collective futures, including the openings and constraints for pursuing moral and material lives (Louw, Schatz, Schwab), provide contexts for better understanding how, when, and why Western and Central Asian approaches to, and definitions of, threats to "national security" are generally at such variance with one another (Lemon).

Another aspect of translating context into policy has to do with Central Asians' values, knowledge, and life priorities. These are and always will be different from those expressed and reflected in those of other governments. So, introducing context to policy narratives will at the very least provide policymakers with guidance for assessing how certain policies will play in the region generally or in specific countries. These could include identifying the priorities of specific Central Asian stakeholders, assessing how governments are likely to view and debate a given policy, and anticipating how a government will respond.

From Policy to Programs

The implementation of the United States' and other countries' foreign policy in Central Asia involves diplomats and bureaucrats of governmental and intergovernmental agencies who manage complex procurements and grant programs. It also involves a wide range of regional and international nongovernmental or for-profit development, humanitarian, and religious organizations who carry out the bulk of the programmatic work in cooperation with Central Asian governmental and nongovernmental organizations. Just as contextualized knowledge can be used to craft better policies in Central Asia, better solutions can be implemented when a deeper understanding of context helps to mitigate the temptation to essentialize or overgeneralize problems in need of solutions. Looking at the interconnection of chapters in the book's thematic groupings, such as "Contexts of Structure," is an excellent place for development practitioners to begin.

Further, chapters throughout this book demonstrate that implementers of development programs need a contextualized understanding of local communities in order to solve difficult problems. In Central Asia and elsewhere, top-down, policy-driven solutions to complex development problems often exacerbate deficiencies in local governance and generate other unintended negative consequences. These unintended consequences can be mitigated when community participation is combined with corporate/government accountability initiatives. Community-based approaches are also generally more effective at addressing complex problems of health, income, environment, governance, and justice. For development practitioners—whether in government agencies, donor organizations, or working on implementing programs on the ground—the chapters in this book provide ways of seeing development problems differently and may offer ways to work with communities to achieve more positive, people-driven solutions to these problems.

While the economic and environmental problems of Central Asia are well known to development practitioners working there, some of the chapters in this book highlight areas of resilience and capacity in Central Asian societies that can be complemented by development programs aimed at solving some of these problems. Economic and environmental issues have often intersected with civic mobilization in Central Asia, so practitioners should not assume the absence of existing civic infrastructure, critical discourse, and expert local knowledge to build on. Wooden's chapter shows the ways that communities, primarily in Kyrgyzstan and Kazakhstan, have mobilized around environmental and economic issues as local problems, but which also affect national level politics. These community members may be the most knowledgeable sources of policy solutions to balance local economic and environmental priorities.

Another area of economic resilience in Central Asia comes from fluid family structures and migration strategies. As the chapter by Aitieva shows, one of the great strengths of Central Asian communities is the density and crosscutting nature of network ties. Family, clan, village, district, and school ties enmesh most Central Asians in a safety net that stretches thousands of miles into Russia (see also the chapters by Roche, Schatz, Ismailbekova, and Werner). Fluid family structures allow the household economy to be buoyed by multiple members whose contributions shift seasonally and in accordance with life cycle stages. Locality-based networks protect labor migrants in Russia from having to take the worst jobs and endure abusive working conditions and dangerous living situations. Lifelong ties to classmates provide employment networks and mutual aid in the form of loans and material

DAVID M. ABRAMSON, LAURA L. ADAMS, AND DAVID W. MONTGOMERY

support, and to the extent that schools are ethnically integrated, these school ties are a strength that mitigates ethnic or kin-based factionalization.

Development programs in Central Asia since the early Soviet era have taken the oppression of women and girls as an object of their analysis. What is newer to the development lens in the twenty-first century is (1) an understanding of the role that masculinity plays in social change, (2) a human rights lens that looks at the diversity of sexual orientation and gender identity in Central Asia, and (3) a more complex understanding of how gender intersects with numerous other identities (socioeconomic status, religion, age) in ways that affect the problems that development practitioners want to solve (see Peshkova's chapter on this).

Gender roles are dynamic and contested in Central Asia today, and even when people talk about "traditional" women's roles, they are to some degree putting their own contemporary spin on what they imagine or want these roles to be. Similarly, family roles and responsibilities tied to gender and age are important but very fluid and complex, as McBrien shows in her chapter. Development practitioners can never assume that they fully understand gender in the context they are engaging with, and gender equity and social inclusion programs that look at not only individuals but also household structures and neighborhood norms—and further take an iterative approach to gender analysis—will be more effective and inclusive.

Another area of intensive foreign assistance programming over the past twenty years has been the prevention of violent extremism (PVE). PVE programs developed in a context where both the Anglo-American and Soviet perspectives see religion as a private and stigmatized practice. As a result, PVE programs have framed all sorts of religious behavior in Central Asia as suspicious and potentially violent. As Montgomery, Schwab, Louw, Schatz, and Lemon show in their chapters, the meaning of private religious practice in the region is varied, but when it strays out of the boundaries of individual or family behavior, or takes on a moral critique that implicates public actors, the reaction of state actors is often severe, ranging from public ridicule to imprisonment on exaggerated charges of extremism.

Central Asian secular governments and publics tend to have an aversion to anything other than cultural expressions of Islam (i.e., to perspectives that seek to reform politics or even broader social behavior independently of government-backed initiatives), in part because of Soviet anti-religious legacies (see Khalid's chapter). So when an incident of violent religious extremism takes place, as elsewhere in the world, it creates an aura of suspicion around not just others with "extreme" religious views but with any devout religious practice. Furthermore, as Lemon's and Epkenhans' chapters show, governments use these incidents as ways to shape citizens' values, promote a more secular understanding of Islam, and foster popular support for the state by changing community-level behavior.

Foreign donors have collaborated with Central Asian governments in various ways to prevent violent extremism in Central Asia, often blurring the distinction between how religion is viewed in Afghanistan/Pakistan versus in Central Asia. This exemplifies how a policy based on national interest and the foreign assistance used to address it define a social problem in Central Asia without an adequate understanding of the diagnosis. PVE programs in Central Asia, as elsewhere, need to be based on careful analysis, not just of demographic and geographic hot spots and associated ideological and socioeconomic dynamics but also of the ways that state actors in Central Asia tend to use such interventions to reinforce their power, stigmatize religious belief and behavior, and eliminate political rivals.

A Conclusion in Context

In the 1930s, neuropsychologist Alexander Luria visited the Ferghana Valley to look at the impact of the Soviet Revolution on the indigenous populations. He was interested in how people attribute and infer meaning, especially how the way people live shapes their cognitive structures. Within the Soviet context, his was a mission both of science but also of application, for what was learned would come to shape the educational categories Soviet citizens would learn. An example from his research, however, gives a sense of how external biases frame both the problem and the solution.

> Subject: Mirzanb, age thirty-three, uneducated; works in a village; has been in Fergana once, never in any other city. Is shown drawings of: *glass-saucepan-spectacles-bottle*.

> "I don't know which of the things doesn't fit here. Maybe it's the bottle? You can drink tea out of the glass—that's useful. The spectacles are also useful. But there's vodka in the bottle—that's bad."

> *Uses principle of "utility" to classify objects.*

> Could you say that the spectacles don't belong in this group?
> "No, spectacles are also a useful thing."
> Subject is given a complete examination of how three of the objects refer to the category of "cooking vessels."
> So wouldn't it be right to say the spectacles don't fit in this group?
> "No, I think the bottle doesn't belong here. It's harmful!"
> But you can use one word—vessels—for these three, right?
> "I think there's vodka in the bottle, that's why I didn't take it. . . . Still, if you want me to. . . . But, you know, the fourth thing [spectacles] is also useful."

> *Disregards generic term.*

> "If you're cooking something you have to see what you're doing, and if a person's eyes are bothering him, he's got to wear a pair of glasses."

DAVID M. ABRAMSON, LAURA L. ADAMS, AND DAVID W. MONTGOMERY

But you can't call spectacles a vessel, can you?

"If you're cooking something on fire, you've got to use the eyeglasses or you just won't be able to cook."

The lesson of Luria's insights is significant. One can assume he went in with the best of intentions of understanding the difference between traditional and less educated populations as part of the Soviet agenda of educating the masses, and the interview above points precisely to differing perspectives on context. From the Western perspective, how locals categorized certainly seemed foreign, but their reasoning was not flawed. This is not a relativist argument but, rather, a claim that in order to understand Central Asia, we need to appreciate a context other than our own. And the broader discussion around application is relevant here.

At its face, this book covers a lot of topics. But its very composition makes an argument about what it is we need to know to appreciate the context in which people make sense of their worlds. Much of our analytical world—academically, professionally, socially—has become specialized. If we look at politics, we often only look at politics and the intrigues of the elites making decisions in those spaces. But the context in which those decisions are made are diverse, including the latent and manifest influencers of social life—such as, but not only, historical contexts, educational contexts, economics, aesthetic expression, and social relations. And we can play this out differently for any event.

Not everything, of course, is weighed equally in all situations. This we almost instinctively know, for there is an active process in which we socially navigate the world that is rooted in experience; experience and the particularity of interests—biases, prejudices, aspirations, goals—lead us to prioritize some aspects of social life more than others. But we also must be cautious that we do not assume certainty without some appreciation of histories and the way the other understands then. This involves a level of intellectual humility: listening for various sounds, watching the backdrop in which events unfold, and allowing other categories of ordering to hold as much explanatory weight as our own. As such, this book aims to be a resource for thinking through the region and for allowing contexts to guide understanding.

ABOUT THE CONTRIBUTORS

Aigoul Abdoubaetova is the head of the Research and Training Unit at the OSCE Academy, Bishkek, Kyrgyzstan. Her publications have appeared in *Central Asian Affairs*.

David M. Abramson is a Russian foreign policy analyst at the US Department of State. He has contributed chapters to edited volumes including *Islam, Society, and Politics in Central Asia* and *Anthropologists in the SecurityScape: Ethics, Practice, and Professional Identity*.

Laura L. Adams works at Freedom House in Washington, DC, and previously worked at the US Agency for International Development and the Davis Center for Russian and Eurasian Studies at Harvard University. She is the author of *The Spectacular State: Culture and National Identity in Uzbekistan*.

Medina Aitieva is an independent researcher. Her dissertation was titled *Reconstituting Transnational Families: An Ethnography of Family Practices between Kyrgyzstan and Russia*.

Judith Beyer is a professor of social and political anthropology at the University of Konstanz. Her books include *The Force of Custom: Law and the Ordering of Everyday Life in Kyrgyzstan*, *Practices of Traditionalization in Central Asia*, and *Ethnographies of the State in Central Asia: Performing Politics*.

Noor O'Neill Borbieva is a professor of anthropology at Purdue University, Fort Wayne. She is the author of *Visions of Development in Central Asia: Revitalizing the Culture Concept*.

David Brophy is a senior lecturer in modern Chinese history at the University of Sydney. His books include *Uyghur Nation: Reform and Revolution on the Russia-China Frontier*, *In Remembrance of the Saints: The Rise and Fall of an Inner Asian Sufi Dynasty*, and *China Panic: Australia's Alternative to Paranoia and Pandering*.

Victoria Clement is founder of the consulting firm Central Asian Insights, the course coordinator for Central Asia at the Foreign Service Institute with McColm and Company, and an international affairs analyst at the National Guard Bureau with ITA International. She is the author of *Learning to Become Turkmen: Literacy, Language, and Power, 1914–2014*.

Alexander Cooley is the Claire Tow Professor of political science at Barnard College and director of Columbia University's Harriman Institute for the Study of Russia, Eurasia and Eastern Europe. His books include *Great Games, Local Rules: The New Great Power Contest in Central Asia*, *Dictators without Borders: Power and Money in Central Asia*, *Exit from Hegemony: The Unraveling of the American Global Order*, and *Logics of Hierarchy: The Organization of Empires, States, and Military Occupations*.

Aliya de Tiesenhausen is an independent scholar of Soviet and post-Soviet Central Asian art. She cocurated *Focus Kazakhstan: Post-Nomadic Mind* and is the author of *Central Asia in Art: From Soviet Orientalism to the New Republics*.

Alexander C. Diener is a professor of geography at the University of Kansas. His books include *One Homeland or Two? The Nationalization and Transnationalization of Mongolia's Kazakhs*, *Borders: A Very Short Introduction*, and *The City as Power: Urban Space, Place, and National Identity*.

Eva-Marie Dubuisson is an assistant professor in the Department of Languages, Linguistics, and Literatures in the School of Sciences and Humanities at Nazarbayev University in Kazakhstan. She is the author of *Living Language in Kazakhstan: The Dialogic Emergence of an Ancestral Worldview*.

Tim Epkenhans is professor of Islamic Studies at the University of Freiburg (Germany). He is the author of *The Origins of the Civil War in Tajikistan: Nationalism, Islamism, and Violent Conflict in Post-Soviet Space*.

Jeanne Féaux de la Croix leads research on environmental issues in Central Asia in the Department of Social and Cultural Anthropology at Tübingen University. Her books include *Iconic Places in Central Asia: The Moral Geography of Pastures, Dams and Holy Sites*, *Everyday Energy Politics in Central Asia and the Caucasus: Citizens' Needs, Entitlements and Struggles for Access*, and *Central Asian Worlds*.

Olivier Ferrando is assistant professor at Lyon Catholic University and the former regional director of the French Institute of Central Asian Studies (IFEAC) in Bishkek, Kyrgyzstan. He is the editor of *1989, année de mobilisations politiques en Asie centrale* (*1989, A Year of Political Mobilisations in Central Asia*).

Benjamin Gatling is associate professor and director of the Folklore Studies Program at George Mason University. He is the author of *Expressions of Sufi Culture in Tajikistan*.

Emmanuel Giraudet is a cartographer and research associate at the French National Center for Scientific Research (CNRS) and a member of the Center for Iranian Studies (CeRMI) in Paris. He is one of the leaders of the digital atlas of the Caucasus and Western and Central Asia, *CartOrient*.

David Gullette is an independent researcher. His books include *The Genealogical Construction of the Kyrgyz Republic: Kinship, State and "Tribalism"* and *Everyday Energy Politics in Central Asia and the Caucasus: Citizens' Needs, Entitlements and Struggles for Access*.

Rebecca Ruth Gould is a professor of Islamic world and comparative literature at the University of Birmingham. Her books include *Writers and Rebels: The Literature of Insurgency in the Caucasus*, *The Routledge Handbook of Translation and Activism*, and *The Persian Prison Poem: Sovereignty and the Political Imagination*.

John Heathershaw is a professor of international relations at the University of Exeter. His books include *Dictators without Borders: Power and Money in Central Asia*, *Paradox of Power: The Logics of State Weakness in Eurasia*, and *Post-conflict Tajikistan: The Politics of Peacebuilding and the Emergence of Legitimate Order*.

Ali İğmen is a professor of Central Asian History and director of the Oral History Program at California State University, Long Beach. He is the author of *Speaking Soviet with an Accent: Culture and Power in Kyrgyzstan*.

Gulnora Iskandarova has worked in education for many years, focusing on differentiated instruction strategies and student learning. She completed a graduate degree in teaching at the American University of Central Asia.

Aksana Ismailbekova is a research fellow at Leibniz-Zentrum Moderner Orient. She is the author of *Blood Ties and the Native Son: Poetics of Patronage in Kyrgyzstan*.

Artemy M. Kalinovsky is a professor of Russian, Soviet, and post-Soviet studies at Temple University. He is the author of *Laboratory of Socialist Development: Cold War Politics and Decolonization in Soviet Tajikistan* and *A Long Goodbye: The Soviet Withdrawal from Afghanistan*.

Marianne Kamp is an associate professor of Central Eurasian Studies at Indiana University. Her books include *The New Woman in Uzbekistan: Islam, Modernity, and Unveiling under Communism* and *Muslim Women of the Ferghana Valley: A 19th-Century Ethnography from Central Asia*.

Botakoz Kassymbekova is a postdoctoral research fellow at the Liverpool John Moores University. She is the author of *Despite Cultures: Early Soviet Rule in Tajikistan*.

Adeeb Khalid is the Jane and Raphael Bernstein Professor of Asian studies and history at Carleton College. His books include *Central Asia: A New History from the Imperial Conquests to the Present*, *Making Uzbekistan: Nation, Empire, and Revolution in the Early USSR*, *Islam after Communism: Religion and Politics in Central Asia*, and *The Politics of Muslim Cultural Reform: Jadidism in Central Asia*.

Natalie Koch is an associate professor in the Department of Geography at Syracuse University's Maxwell School of Citizenship and Public Affairs. Her books include *The Geopolitics of Spectacle: Space, Synecdoche, and the New Capitals of Asia* and *Critical Geographies of Sport: Space, Power, and Sport in Global Perspective*.

Svetlana Kulikova (Lana V. Kulik) is an assistant professor in the Department of Media, Communication, and Public Relations at Thiel College. She has contributed chapters to edited volumes including *After the Czars and Commissars: The Press in Post-Soviet Authoritarian Central Asia* and *The Handbook of Global Radio*.

Marlène Laruelle is a research professor of international affairs in the Elliott School of International Affairs at George Washington University; director of the Institute for European, Russian and Eurasian Studies and the Central Asia Program; and codirector of PONARS (Program on New Approaches to Research and Security in Eurasia). Her books include *Globalizing Central Asia: Geopolitics and the Challenges of Economic Development*, *The 'Chinese Question' in Central Asia: Domestic Order, Social Changes, and the Chinese Factor*, and *Central Peripheries: Nationhood in Central Asia*.

Edward Lemon is a research assistant professor at the Bush School of Government and Public Service (Texas A&M University) in Washington, DC. He is the editor of *Critical Approaches to Security in Central Asia*.

Scott C. Levi is a professor of Central Asian history at The Ohio State University. His books include *The Rise and Fall of Khoqand, 1709–1876: Central Asia in the Global Age* and *The Bukharan Crisis: A Connected History of 18th-Century Central Asia*.

David G. Lewis is an associate professor in international relations at the University of Exeter. His books include *Russia's New Authoritarianism: Putin and the Politics of Order*, *The Temptations of Tyranny in Central Asia*, and *Interrogating Illiberal Peace in Eurasia*.

Morgan Y. Liu is an associate professor of anthropology in the Department of Near Eastern Languages and Cultures at The Ohio State University. He is the author of *Under Solomon's Throne: Uzbek Visions of Renewal in Osh*.

Maria Louw is an associate professor in the Department of Anthropology at Aarhus University. She is the author of *Everyday Islam in Post-Soviet Central Asia*.

Georgy Mamedov is a lecturer in the Television, Cinema and Media Arts Department at the American University of Central Asia, Bishkek, Kyrgyzstan, and chair of the board of the LGBT organization Labrys Kyrgyzstan. His books include *Kniga o schastie dlia molodyh (i ne ochen) LGBT (i ne tolko) ludei*, *Sovsem Drugie: Sbornik feministskoi and kvir-fantastiki*, *Kvir-kommunizm eto etika*, *Ponyatiya o sovetskom v Tsentralnoi Azii*, and *Bishkek Utopicheskii*.

Julie McBrien is an associate professor of anthropology and codirector of the Amsterdam Research Centre for Gender and Sexuality, both at the University of Amsterdam. She is the author of *From Belonging to Belief: Modern Secularisms and the Construction of Religion in Kyrgyzstan*.

Eric McGlinchey is an associate professor of politics at George Mason University's Schar School of Policy and Government. He is the author of *Chaos, Violence, Dynasty: Politics and Islam in Central Asia*.

Nick Megoran is a professor of political geography at Newcastle University. His books include *Nationalism in Central Asia: A Biography of the Uzbekistan-Kyrgyzstan Boundary*, *Central Asia in International Relations: The Legacies of Halford Mackinder*, and *Interrogating Illiberal Peace in Eurasia: Critical Perspectives on Peace and Conflict*.

Tanya Merchant is an associate professor in the Music Department at the University of California, Santa Cruz. She is the author of *Women Musicians of Uzbekistan: From Courtyard to Conservatory*.

Martha C. Merrill is an associate professor of higher education administration at Kent State University. She has published articles on education in Central Asia in *Asian Education and Development Studies*, *Central Asian Survey*, *Central Eurasian Studies Review*, *European Education*, *Higher Education in Russia and Beyond*, and *International Higher Education*.

David W. Montgomery is a research professor in the Department of Government and Politics and the Center for International Development and Conflict Management at the University of Maryland, and director of program development for CEDAR—Communities Engaging with Difference and Religion. His books include *Practicing Islam:*

Knowledge, Experience, and Social Navigation in Kyrgyzstan, Living with Difference: How to Build Community in a Divided World, and *Everyday Life in the Balkans.*

Alexander Morrison is fellow and tutor in history at New College, Oxford. His books include *Russian Rule in Samarkand 1868–1910: A Comparison with British India* and *The Russian Conquest of Central Asia: A Study in Imperial Expansion, 1814–1914.*

Till Mostowlansky is a research fellow in anthropology at the Graduate Institute, Geneva. He is the author of *Azan on the Moon: Entangling Modernity along Tajikistan's Pamir Highway.*

Jennifer Brick Murtazashvili is director of the Center for Governance and Markets and an associate professor of international affairs at the University of Pittsburgh. Her books include *Informal Order and the State in Afghanistan* and *Land, the State, and War: Property Institutions and Political Order in Afghanistan.*

Emil Nasritdinov is an associate professor in the Department of Anthropology at the American University of Central Asia, Bishkek, Kyrgyzstan. His publications have appeared in *Central Asian Survey, Central Asian Affairs, Ab Imperio,* and *Transnational Social Review.*

Mathijs Pelkmans is a professor of anthropology at the London School of Economics and Political Science. His books include *Fragile Conviction: Changing Ideological Landscapes in Urban Kyrgyzstan, Defending the Border: Identity, Religion, and Modernity in the Republic of Georgia,* and *Ethnographies of Doubt: Faith and Uncertainty in Contemporary Societies.*

Svetlana Peshkova is an associate professor of anthropology at the University of New Hampshire. She is the author of *Women, Islam, and Identity: Public Life in Private Spaces in Uzbekistan.*

Sebastien Peyrouse is a research professor in the Central Asia Program at the Institute for European, Russian and Eurasian Studies at George Washington University. His books include *Turkmenistan: Strategies of Power, Dilemmas of Development, The Chinese Question in Central Asia: Domestic Order, Social Change, and the Chinese Factor,* and *Globalizing Central Asia: Geopolitics and the Challenges of Economic Development.*

Johan Rasanayagam is a senior lecturer in social anthropology at the University of Aberdeen. His books include *Islam in Post-Soviet Uzbekistan: The Morality of Experience* and *Ethnographies of the State in Central Asia: Performing Politics.*

Madeleine Reeves is a professor of social anthropology at the University of Manchester. Her books include *Border Work: Spatial Lives of the State in Rural Central Asia, Ethnographies of the State in Central Asia: Performing Politics, Affective States: Entanglements, Suspensions, Suspicions,* and *The Everyday Lives of Sovereignty: Political Imagination beyond the State.*

Sophie Roche is an associate professor at the Ruprecht Karls University of Heidelberg. Her books include *Domesticating Youth: The Youth Bulge and Its Socio-political Implications in Tajikistan* and *The Faceless Terrorist: A Study of Critical Events in Tajikistan.*

Michael Rouland is director of research for the Russian Strategic Initiative at the US Department of Defense and an adjunct professor of Russian studies at Georgetown University. He is coeditor of *Cinema in Central Asia: Rewriting Cultural Histories*.

Amier Saidula is a senior research associate with the Institute of Ismaili Studies, London. He has contributed chapters to edited volumes including *The Modern History of the Ismailis: Continuity and Change in a Muslim Community*, *People of the Prophet's House*, and *Identity, History and Trans-Nationality in Central Asia: The Mountain Communities of Pamir*.

Balihar Sanghera is a senior lecturer in sociology at University of Kent's School of Social Policy, Sociology and Social Research. His books include *Rentier Capitalism and Its Discontents: Power, Morality and Resistance in Central Asia* and *Theorising Social Change in Post-Soviet Countries: Critical Approaches*.

Elmira Satybaldieva is a scholar in Eurasian politics and development based at the Conflict Analysis Research Centre, University of Kent. She is the coauthor of *Rentier Capitalism and Its Discontents: Power, Morality and Resistance in Central Asia*.

Edward Schatz is a professor of political science at the University of Toronto. His books include *Slow Anti-Americanism: Social Movements and Symbolic Politics in Central Asia*, *Paradox of Power: The Logics of State Weakness in Eurasia*, *Political Ethnography: What Immersion Contributes to the Study of Power*, and *Modern Clan Politics: The Power of "Blood" in Kazakhstan and Beyond*.

Wendell Schwab works in the Bellisario College of Communications at the Pennsylvania State University. His publications have appeared in *Central Asian Affairs*, *Central Asian Survey*, and *Contemporary Islam*.

Will Sumits is a research associate at the Orient-Institut Istanbul and has been a lecturer in ethnomusicology at the University of Central Asia, Dushanbe, and at the Advanced Music Research Center (MİAM) of Istanbul Technical University. His research on the history of Central Asian musical traditions has been published in several books and international journals.

Julien Thorez is a geographer and associate research professor at the French National Center for Scientific Research (CNRS) and a member of the Center for Iranian Studies (CeRMI) in Paris. His publications focus on contemporary Central Asia (borders, transport, migrations, urban transformations), and he is the editor in chief of *CartOrient*, a scientific website for diffusing cartographical studies on the Caucasus and Western and Central Asia.

Tommaso Trevisani is an associate professor in the Department of Asian, African and Mediterranean Studies at the University of Naples L'Orientale. He is the author of *Land and Power in Khorezm: Farmers, Communities, and the State in Uzbekistan's Decollectivisation*.

Cynthia Werner is a professor of anthropology and the director of ADVANCE within the Office of the Dean of Faculties at Texas A&M University. Her publications have appeared in *Central Asian Survey*, *American Anthropologist*, *Journal of Royal Anthropological Institute*, *Europe-Asia Studies*, and *Human Organization*.

Jennifer S. Wistrand is an assistant teaching professor at Miami University and has worked as a consultant to the World Bank and a policy advisor for the US Department of State.

Amanda Wooden is an associate professor of environmental studies and sciences at Bucknell University. Her publications have appeared in *Central Asian Survey*, *Post-Soviet Affairs*, *Political Geography*, and *PS: Political Science and Politics*.

Russell Zanca is a professor of anthropology at Northeastern Illinois University and an associate at the University of Chicago's Center for Eurasian, East European and Russian Studies. His books include *Life in a Muslim Uzbek Village: Cotton Farming after Communism* and *Everyday Life in Central Asia Past and Present*.

INDEX

polygamy, 131, 289, 294–95, 325, 331, 334, 583

privatization, 143, 187, 387, 452, 454, 459–60, 463, 465, 480–82, 571, 573, 577–78, 585–87

Programme for International Student Assessment (PISA) 418

proletarian, 130, 320, 532, 622, 627

propiska, 197, 221, 232, 240, 241, 243, 467

Putin, Vladimir, 5, 9, 216, 232, 235, 251, 255, 516–17, 685, 705

Qaralaev, Sayaqbay, 55

qazi (*kazi*, Islamic judge), 109–10, 403

Qing, 92–96, 103, 158–62

Qongrat tribe, 93, 98–99

Rahmon, Emomali, 57, 62–63, 70, 73, 140, 153–55, 157, 385, 465, 495, 536, 542, 587, 596, 603

raja (payments among kin), 242, 249

Rashidov, Sharof R. 133, 135

Rasulov, Akbar, 393–94, 399, 404

Rasulov, Jabbor, 135

reiderstvo (asset-grabbing), 477–79

remittances, 6, 13, 155, 192–93, 214, 229, 235, 237, 249–50, 255, 295, 307, 319, 467, 498, 515, 587, 591, 593, 718

resettlement, 112, 113, 185, 695

ritual, 77, 132, 135, 166, 182, 184–85, 291–94, 312, 314, 315, 321, 324, 345, 362, 367, 370, 375, 398, 420, 422–24, 429, 600, 602, 629, 644, 658

Rudaki: district, 596; poet, 52–54, 659–60, 665

Ruziev, Kobil 413

Ryskulov, Turar, 125

SADUM (Spiritual Administration of the Muslims of Central Asia and Kazakhstan), 71–73, 132, 163–67, 367–68, 373

Safavid, 40, 88–89

Sakha, Republic of, 213, 234, 236, 239–40, 245–47, 250–52, 254

Samanids, 53, 54, 621, 657, 659

Samarkand (Samarqand), 86–90, 97, 100, 105, 108, 111–15, 117, 122, 344–45, 365, 551, 621, 624, 625, 626, 636, 661, 695, 698

Second World War (Great Patriotic War): experience of, 21, 26, 68, 69; media, 531–32; post-war development, 5, 128, 458, 492–93; post-war reforms, 492; relocation, 126, 129, 134, 431, 674; religious restrictions, 132, 163, 367; stories, 56; veteran of, 693

sedentary population, 23–24, 26, 365, 550, 621, 633

Seifullin, Saken, 125

seminomadic, 116, 132, 330, 331, 365

Semirechie, 104, 108, 111–13, 116

separatism, 7, 383, 517

Shahnameh, 59, 678

Shanghai Cooperation Organization (SCO), 7–8, 10, 11, 50

sharia (Islamic law), 109, 165, 331, 374, 376, 396–97, 403

Shia. *See* Islam

shopping mall, 200, 207–10, 546

Siberia, 37–38, 78, 96, 111, 126, 159, 164, 230

Silk Road, 7, 12–13, 22, 27, 39–42, 44, 85, 90, 162, 257, 467, 552, 555, 557, 644, 682

Skobelev, Gen. Mikhail Dmitrievich (1843 – 1882), 43, 96, 105

social contract, 157, 218, 491

social media: communication medium, 57, 250, 307, 548, 579; journalism and, 423, 430, 527, 561, 572; misinformation, 542, 707; restrictions of, 18; violence, 250

Socialist Realism, 130, 636, 638–42, 674, 691

Solomon's Mountain, 62, 372, 559

Spiritual Administration of the